1 MONTH OF FREE READING

at

www.ForgottenBooks.com

By purchasing this book you are eligible for one month membership to ForgottenBooks.com, giving you unlimited access to our entire collection of over 1,000,000 titles via our web site and mobile apps.

To claim your free month visit:
www.forgottenbooks.com/free1055995

* Offer is valid for 45 days from date of purchase. Terms and conditions apply.

ISBN 978-0-331-76038-5
PIBN 11055995

This book is a reproduction of an important historical work. Forgotten Books uses
state-of-the-art technology to digitally reconstruct the work, preserving the original format
whilst repairing imperfections present in the aged copy. In rare cases, an imperfection in
the original, such as a blemish or missing page, may be replicated in our edition. We do,
however, repair the vast majority of imperfections successfully; any imperfections that
remain are intentionally left to preserve the state of such historical works.

Forgotten Books is a registered trademark of FB &c Ltd.
Copyright © 2018 FB &c Ltd.
FB &c Ltd, Dalton House, 60 Windsor Avenue, London, SW19 2RR.
Company number 08720141. Registered in England and Wales.

For support please visit www.forgottenbooks.com

ANNUAL REPORTS

OF THE

WAR DEPARTMENT

FOR THE

FISCAL YEAR ENDED JUNE 30, 1901.

REPORT OF THE
CHIEF OF ENGINEERS.
PART 1.

WASHINGTON:
GOVERNMENT PRINTING OFFICE.
1901.

ANNUAL REPORT

OF THE

CHIEF OF ENGINEERS,

UNITED STATES ARMY.

1901.

ENG 1901——1

134845

REPORT
OF
THE CHIEF OF ENGINEERS,
UNITED STATES ARMY.

OFFICE OF THE CHIEF OF ENGINEERS,
UNITED STATES ARMY,
Washington, October 1, 1901.

SIR: I have the honor to present for your information the following report upon the duties and operations of the Engineer Department for the fiscal year ending June 30, 1901:

OFFICERS OF THE CORPS OF ENGINEERS.

The number of officers holding commissions in the Corps of Engineers, United States Army, at the end of the fiscal year was 131.

Since the last annual report the Corps of Engineers has lost five of its officers—Brig. Gen. John M. Wilson, who was retired from active service April 30, 1901, at his own request, under the provisions of the act of Congress approved June 30, 1882; Brig. Gen. Henry M. Robert, who was retired from active service May 2, 1901, by operation of law, under the provisions of the act of Congress approved June 30, 1882; Brig. Gen. John W. Barlow, who was retired from active service May 3, 1901, at his own request, under the provisions of the act of Congress approved June 30, 1882; First Lieut. Louis C. Wolf, who was retired from active service June 29, 1901, on account of disability incident thereto, under the provisions of section 1251, Revised Statutes, and Second Lieut. Walter H. Lee, who was killed June 10, 1901, by insurgents near Lipa, Luzon, Philippine Islands.

There were added to the Corps of Engineers, by promotion of graduates of the Military Academy, ten second lieutenants on March 5, 1901, to rank from February 2, 1901.

By the act of February 2, 1901, "To increase the efficiency of the permanent military establishment of the United States" the Corps of Engineers now consists of 160 officers and three battalions of four companies of enlisted men each. The authorized enlisted strength of each company on a peace footing is 100 men, and on a war footing is 164.

The increase in the number of engineer officers and troops was necessary to meet the requirements of the military service in the new possessions of the United States, and the necessity of keeping up the increasing number of public works assigned to the Corps of Engineers by law.

At the close of the fiscal year 32 officers of the Corps of Engineers and eight companies of the engineer battalions were on duty in or en route to the Philippines, China, Cuba, Porto Rico, and Alaska. The duties of the engineer officers and troops in the island possessions have consisted of reconnaissances, map making, repairing and construction of roads, railroads, bridges, and ferries, sanitary and municipal engineering, all of which duties have been creditably performed.

By the act of February 2, 1901, the increase in the number of officers in the corps was limited to the junior grades and thereby destroyed the then existing ratio of field officers to subalterns. This ratio was such that a reasonable rate of promotion was assured the junior officers of the corps and made it an incentive to the graduates of the Military Academy to enter the corps whenever so recommended. Now the chance of promotion is greatly decreased, and the indications as shown by the comparatively few officers of the Army applying for transfer to the corps under the provisions of the law are that it will be difficult to attract the honor graduates to the corps in the future. To remedy this unintentional injustice to the corps it is urgently recommended that such an increase be made in the number of field officers of the corps as will reestablish the ratio prevailing before the passage of the said act.

On the 30th of June, 1901, the officers were distributed as follows:

Commanding the Corps of Engineers and Engineer Department, and Light-House Board	1
Office of the Chief of Engineers and Light-House Board	1
Office of the Chief of Engineers	3
Division Engineer and Isthmian Canal Commission	1
Division Engineer and Board of Engineers	1
Division Engineer and California Débris Commission	1
Division Engineer, Board of Engineers, and river and harbor works	1
River and harbor works	14
Division Engineer, Mississippi River Commission, Missouri River Commission, and light-house district	1
Fortifications and river and harbor works	24
Light-House Establishment	4
Board of Engineers, fortifications, and river and harbor works	1
Washington Aqueduct	2
Military attaché to United States legations	1
Fortifications, river and harbor works, and California Débris Commission	1
River and harbor works and light-house districts	6
Mississippi River Commission, Missouri River Commission, and light-house district	1
Fortifications and light-house district	1
Division of the Philippines	15
Missouri River Commission, fortifications, and river and harbor works	1
Post of Fort Totten, United States Engineer School, and Third Battalion of Engineers	12
Mississippi River Commission	3
Public buildings and grounds, District of Columbia	1
Board for improvement of harbor at Island of Guam	1
Department of Cuba	2
Engineer Commissioner, District of Columbia	1
River and harbor works, Yellowstone National Park, and Fort Washakie military road	1
United States Military Academy	3
Assistants to Engineer Commissioner, District of Columbia	2
Mississippi River Commission and light-house district	1
En route to the Philippines with the Second Battalion of Engineers	14
Department of the East	1
Board of Engineers	1
California Débris Commission	1
Building for Government Printing Office	1
Changing station	2
Leave of absence	3
Total	131

THE BOARD OF ENGINEERS.

The regulations for the government of the Corps of Engineers provide for a Board of Engineers, consisting of not less than three officers, to be designated by the Chief of Engineers with the sanction of the Secretary of War. This Board acts in an advisory capacity to the Chief of Engineers upon important questions of engineering. One of the principal duties of the Board is to plan or revise, under direction of the Chief of Engineers, projects of permanent fortifications for the defense of the United States.

Owing to the intimate relations existing between the Corps of Engineers and the Artillery Corps regarding defense, it was deemed expedient during the year to add an artillery officer to the Board for service whenever matters concerning the preparation of plans of defense in all its branches were under consideration.

The composition of this Board and its operations during the past fiscal year are given in its report.

(See Appendix No. 1.)

BOARD ON TORPEDO SYSTEM.

The Board for the consideration of the existing torpedo system has continued the study of this system, especially in the light of reports submitted by officers of the Corps of Engineers in charge of submarine-mine defenses during the Spanish-American war.

Changes in minor details only have so far been proposed.

To this Board have been referred for examination and report descriptions submitted to this office of inventions connected with submarine-mine defenses.

The composition of this Board and its operations during the past fiscal year are given in its report.

(See Appendix No. 2.)

FORTIFICATIONS.

The scheme of national defense upon which work has now been in progress since 1888 is based upon the recommendations of the Board on Fortifications and other Defenses, popularly known as the Endicott Board, outlined in its report dated January 16, 1886. This Board indicated the localities where defenses were most urgently needed, the character and general extent of the defenses, and the estimated cost, and recommended for first consideration the names of 27 principal ports, arranged in the order of their importance. At the time of its report the coasts of the United States were undefended, except by obsolete ordnance mounted in old-style masonry forts entirely incapable of coping with ships protected by armor and armed with powerful breech-loading cannon, such as had been uniformly adopted for the fleets of the world. Moreover, the manufacture of modern seacoast guns and carriages in the United States had not yet been entered upon or designs therefor perfected.

The first fortification appropriation act designed to carry out the recommendations of the Endicott Board was approved September 22, 1888. This act created the Board of Ordnance and Fortification and made appropriations for commencing the manufacture of modern seacoast ordnance, but made no provision for the construction of any batteries. The first appropriation for the construction of gun and mortar batteries was contained in the act of August 18, 1890, since which time appropriations of varying amounts have been made regularly each year for carrying forward the adopted scheme of coast defense—for the manufacture of ordnance, for the construction of batteries, and for the necessary torpedo defenses.

The defensive details for each locality have been carefully elaborated from time to time by The Board of Engineers in projects which have received the formal approval of the Secretary of War prior to the actual beginning of any work. Up to the present time projects for permanent seacoast defenses have been adopted for 31 localities in the United States, as follows:

1. Penobscot River, Maine.
2. Kennebec River, Maine.
3. Portland, Me.
4. Portsmouth, N. H.
5. Boston, Mass.
6. New Bedford, Mass.
7. Narragansett Bay, Rhode Island.
8. Eastern entrance to Long Island Sound.
9. New York, N. Y.
10. Philadelphia, Pa.
11. Baltimore, Md.
12. Washington, D. C.
13. Hampton Roads, Virginia.
14. Entrance to Chesapeake Bay at Cape Henry.
15. Wilmington, N. C.
16. Charleston, S. C.
17. Port Royal, S. C.
18. Savannah, Ga.
19. St. Johns River, Florida.
20. Key West, Fla.
21. Tampa Bay, Florida.
22. Pensacola, Fla.
23. Mobile, Ala.
24. New Orleans, La.
25. Sabine Pass, Tex.
26. Galveston, Tex.
27. San Diego, Cal.
28. San Francisco, Cal.
29. Mouth of Columbia River, Oregon and Washington.
30. Puget Sound, Washington.
31. Lake Champlain.

The detailed project for the defense of the entrance to Chesapeake Bay at Cape Henry, Virginia, was approved by the Secretary of War during the fiscal year. The defense of several additional localities in the United States is also under consideration, for which no formal projects have yet been prepared or approved by the Secretary of War.

Considerable study has also been given to the subject of seacoast defenses for Porto Rico and the Hawaiian Islands, and, in view of the importance of these island possessions, active measures for their defense should no longer be delayed. A detailed project for the defense of San Juan, Porto Rico, at a total estimated cost of $1,800,000, has already been prepared, and preliminary projects for Pearl Harbor and Honolulu, Hawaii Ter., are also available. The work of construction can be commenced whenever Congress appropriates the necessary funds.

Of the existing projects for the United States, as enumerated above, many have from time to time been revised to keep pace with the changes in ordnance and in ships' armament and construction. Nearly fifteen years have elapsed since the adopted scheme of coast defense was formulated by the Endicott Board. At that time the rapid-fire gun was in its infancy and ships were characterized by their extremely heavy armament and great thickness of armor. With the rapid development of the rapid-fire gun and the increase in the resisting powers of armor by means of the Harvey and Krupp processes, there has followed a material change in ship construction, necessitating corresponding changes in the details of coast defenses. In accordance with the recommendations of the Endicott Board, the earlier detailed projects contemplated mounting a considerable number of the heaviest guns at the more important harbors in armored works. The tendency toward a reduction in calibers of heavy guns, coupled with the adoption of a disappearing carriage for the 12-inch gun, has, up to the present time, rendered armored defenses unnecessary, and the United States has thus far not embarked upon the construction of armored casemates and turrets, to which many European governments stand committed for their land defenses. Although rapid-fire guns were proposed in the earlier projects, no definite numbers or calibers were assigned until 1896, since which time nearly all of the earlier projects have been subjected to one or more revisions, resulting in the incorporation of a definite programme as to the rapid-fire armament, a reduction in the number and caliber of the heavy guns, a reduction in the number of mortars, and the general elimination of armored defenses. These revisions have resulted in marked economies without any sacrifice to the defensive requirements, and they will be continued as changes in ordnance and ships or other causes may render desirable.

While the inauguration of the modern system of seacoast defenses for the United States dates from the year 1890, when the first appropriation for constructing gun and mortar batteries was made, it was not until the year 1896 that Congress began to make appropriations commensurate with the magnitude of the undertaking. Stimulated by the larger appropriations of more recent years and the war with Spain, the seacoast defenses of the United States are to-day, eleven years after the actual commencement of work, about 50 per cent completed. Twenty-five of the principal harbors of the United States have now a sufficient number of heavy guns and mortars mounted to permit of an effective defense against naval attack. During the past fiscal year considerable progress has been made toward the installation of an adequate rapid-fire armament, which is now a matter of first importance.

Gun and mortar batteries.—Existing approved projects for seacoast defenses contemplate the mounting of about 464 heavy guns of 8, 10, 12, and 16-inch caliber, of about 1,041 rapid-fire guns from 6-pounder to 6-inch caliber, and of about 704 mortars, at an approximate total cost for the engineering work now estimated at $50,000,000.

The act of March 1, 1901, contained no provision for the construction of mortar batteries. While the numbers of mortars in the earlier projects have been reduced greatly, it is believed that there are still a number of points at which new batteries should be constructed. During the summer of 1901 a series of tests of the actual results of firing the mortars at Fort Preble, Portland Harbor, Maine, were to be conducted. When the new information is available further recommendations will be made.

The several appropriations made by Congress for the construction of gun and mortar batteries since the inauguration of the present system of coast defense have been as follows:

Act of—		Act of—	
August 18, 1890	$1,221,000.00	May 7, 1898	$3,000,000.00
February 24, 1891	750,000.00	July 7, 1898	2,562,000.00
July 23, 1892	500,000.00	March 3, 1899	1,000,000.00
February 18, 1893	50,000.00	May 25, 1900	2,000,000.00
August 1, 1894	500,000.00	March 1, 1901	1,615,000.00
March 2, 1895	500,000.00		
June 6, 1896	2,400,000.00	Total	23,757,009.02
March 3, 1897	3,841,333.00		
Allotments from the appropriation for "National Defense," act of March 9, 1898	3,817,676.02		

The foregoing does not include $306,506.71 allotted and expended from the appropriation for "National Defense" for the construction, during the war with Spain, of a number of emergency sand batteries on the Atlantic and Gulf coasts, and which have since been abandoned, they not forming any part of the approved scheme of permanent defenses and having been armed chiefly with old-type obsolete ordnance, nor an appropriation of $992,000 for reconstruction and repair of the fortifications to protect the harbor of Galveston, Tex., as this simply replaces in good order the works injured in the hurricane of September 8, 1900, which wrecked Galveston.

The total number of seacoast guns and carriages for which the Chief of Ordnance reports his Department has made provision, and the corresponding permanent emplacements for which the Engineer Department has made provision with the funds appropriated for construction of gun and mortar batteries, including allotments from the appropriation for "National Defense," are shown in the following table:

Type of gun or carriage.	Total carriages provided.	Total emplacements provided.
12-inch mortar carriages, model 1896	a 306	296
12-inch mortar carriages, model 1891	b 85	80
12-inch disappearing carriages, L. F., model 1901	9	9
12-inch disappearing carriages, L. F., model 1897	35	35
12-inch disappearing carriages, L. F., model 1896	27	27
10-inch disappearing carriages, A. R. F., model 1896	3	3
10-inch disappearing carriages, L. F., model 1901	5	5
10-inch disappearing carriages, L. F., model 1896	74	74
10-inch disappearing carriages, L. F., model 1894	35	35
8-inch disappearing carriages, L. F., model 1896	38	40
8-inch disappearing carriages, L. F., model 1894	26	26
12-inch gun-lift carriages, altered to barbettes	3	3
12-inch gun-lift carriages, model 1891	2	2
12-inch barbette carriages, model 1892	c 28	27
10-inch barbette carriages, model 1893	d 11	9
15-inch smoothbore carriages altered for 8-inch rifles	21	e 21
8-inch barbette carriages, model 1892	f 9	g 9
6-inch disappearing carriages, model 1898	29	29
6-inch rapid-fire pedestal mounts, U. S. Ordnance Department	46	46
15-pounder rapid-fire carriages	142	142
6-pounder rapid-fire field carriages and rampart mounts	70	(h)
6-inch rapid-fire (Vickers Son & Maxim), pedestal mounts	8	8
5-inch balanced-pillar mounts, model 1896	82	82
5-inch rapid-fire (navy pattern, Brown wire gun)		21
4.7 inch rapid-fire (Armstrong pattern), pedestal mounts	34	34
4.7 inch rapid-fire (Schneider pattern), pedestal mount	1	i 1
4-inch Driggs-Schroeder rapid-fire	4	4

a The number of carriages of this type provided for exceeds by 10 the number which the Chief of Engineers has notified the Chief of Ordnance are required for the emplacements he has provided.
b One in use at West Point.
c One in use at Sandy Hook Proving Ground.
d One at Buffalo Exposition and one at Sandy Hook Proving Ground.
e Temporary. Armament removed from 15.
f One at West Point and one at Sandy Hook Proving Ground.
g Five temporary. Armament removed from 3.
h Movable mounts.
i Temporary.

The foregoing table shows that up to the present time provision has been made for emplacing 325 heavy guns, 387 rapid-fire guns, and 376 12-inch mortars.

During the fiscal year just closed operations were carried on with unexpended balances of the appropriations carried by the regular fortification appropriation acts approved May 7, 1898, March 3, 1899, and May 25, 1900, and the deficiency act approved July 7, 1898. The number of emplacements of each kind provided for under each of the foregoing acts is exhibited in previous annual reports. Under the fortification act of March 1, 1901, it is proposed to provide emplacements for the following number of guns:

12-inch.	10-inch.	6-inch rapid-fire.	15-pounder.
10	5	26	23

The total number of emplacements of every kind provided for by all appropriations to date is as follows:

12-inch.	10-inch.	8-inch.	Rapid-fire.	12-inch mortars.
103	126	96	387	376

In this total are included seventy 6-pounder rapid-fire guns on movable mounts not requiring permanent emplacements, temporary emplacements for twenty-one 8-inch B. L. rifles on modified 15-inch carriages, one temporary emplacement for 4.7-inch rapid-fire gun, and five temporary emplacements for 8-inch guns on barbette carriages. The foregoing temporary emplacements were built during the war with Spain from the "National Defense" funds. The 8-inch guns will be transferred from time to time to permanent emplacements as these are completed, and a number of them have already been so transferred. While it is proposed eventually to disarm these temporary emplacements, they can again be used in case of emergency, and have for this reason been included in the foregoing enumerations.

The deficiency act of July 7, 1898, provided funds for mounting 25 each of 5-inch and 6-inch Brown segmental wire-wound rapid-fire guns on navy-pattern mounts. Although considerable delay was experienced in securing the necessary data from the Chief of Ordnance, 21 emplacements for the 5-inch guns are now completed. No emplacements for the 6-inch guns have been built. Neither wire-wound guns nor mounts can be supplied by the Ordnance Department, as the contractors have failed and Congress did not reappropriate the funds to be applied to making other types of 5-inch and 6-inch rapid-fire guns.

The status of emplacements for which funds have been provided by Congress is as follows at the close of the fiscal year:

	12-inch.	10-inch.	8-inch.	Rapid-fire.	12-inch mortars.
Guns mounted	72	112	a 86	88	263
Ready for armament	14	1	6	b 202	65
Under construction	17	13	4	97	48
Total	103	126	96	387	376

a Seventeen of these, which had been mounted temporarily, have since been dismounted.
b Including seventy 6-pounders not requiring permanent emplacements.

At the close of the previous fiscal year there were reported mounted:

12-inch.	10-inch.	8-inch.	Rapid-fire.	12-inch mortars.
57	105	75	53	240

A comparison of the last two tables shows an addition to the completed seacoast armament of fifteen 12-inch guns, seven 10-inch guns, eleven 8-inch guns, thirty-five rapid-fire guns, and twenty three mortars.

Reference was made in previous annual reports to the completion of all contract works authorized under act of June 6, 1896, except the contract of the Venable Construction Company, of Atlanta, Ga., for the construction of a gun battery and a mortar battery at Key West, Fla. Although the contractors did more or less work during the fiscal year ending June 30, 1900, except during the period of a yellow-fever outbreak, the results accomplished were incommensurate with the magnitude of the work, and shortly after the close of the fiscal year, after the date of completion had been extended nine times, the contractors abandoned work. The work was readvertised, and contract let on December 24, 1900, to L. L. Leach & Son, of Chicago, Ill. They have done nothing beyond getting the plant ready for work.

For continuing the work of construction of gun and mortar batteries in accordance with approved projects an estimate of $4,000,000 is submitted.

Dynamite batteries.—The act of May 25, 1900, appropriated the sum of $180,000 for pneumatic dynamite batteries. This appropriation was based upon estimates for the construction of magazines and protecting parapets for the existing dynamite battery at Sandy Hook and for those under construction by contract with the Ordnance Department at Fishers Island, New York, and Port Royal, S. C. The contracts with the Ordnance Department under which the several dynamite batteries in the United States were constructed did not provide for the erection of any protecting parapets or of any magazines for the safe storage of the ammunition, and the object of the appropriation was to supply these omissions, without which the batteries could not be served in an engagement. Work upon the battery at Sandy Hook has been completed. That at Fishers Island has been begun. At Port Royal the Ordnance Department contractors for the gun were not ready, by the close of the fiscal year, to have work on the parapet begun.

On June 5, 1901, the Board of Ordnance and Fortification reported on this type of battery as follows: "It is the unanimous opinion of the Board that the pneumatic dynamite gun batteries have become obsolete by more recent developments in the means of defense, and the Board does not consider these batteries at the present time of sufficient utility to warrant further expenditures in their construction or the extensive repair of those already installed." Since the close of the fiscal year the Secretary of War has directed the discontinuance of work on the dynamite batteries at Fishers Island and Port Royal.

Range and position finders.—During the fiscal year operations were continued in the installation of range and position finders as required by the approved plans of fire control prepared by an artillery board. The act of May 25, 1900, appropriated $150,000, and the act of March 1, 1901, appropriated $150,000 more, for this purpose. It was proposed to construct about 25 additional range-finder stations, for which plans and estimates had been ordered before the beginning of the fiscal year 1901, which would have provided about 55 main stations for use out of a total projected number of 175 required for batteries completed and building. Many details of the fire-control system do not yet appear to have been definitely settled by the artillery, especially the use of depression position finders upon artificial elevations on low sites, as contemplated by the present approved plans of fire control. Objection has been made by experts to the use of high towers on low sites, an objection which is shared in by the Engineer Department. After a number of these towers had been built, patterned after the experimental tower at Sandy Hook, which was adopted by a mixed board of artillery, ordnance, and engineer officers, objection was made to the size of the observation room. Work on new towers was at once stopped, till an expression of the exact views of the artillery could be obtained. At the close of the fiscal year no definite statement had been made, and work was, in consequence, suspended. To enable the Engineer Department to continue its share of the work of installing range and position finders an estimate of $150,000 is submitted. As soon as the size of room is settled, this sum will be needed.

Preservation and repair of fortifications.—Operations under this appropriation have been limited during the fiscal year mainly to the preservation of the engineer material in the new batteries, to the application of remedial measures for improving the conditions of the magazines of the earlier works as regards dampness, and to the care and preservation of the torpedo material stored at each harbor. The mechanical and electrical appliances in the modern batteries demand unremitting attention to prevent deterioration and damage under the destructive influences of the moist sea air, and the limited annual appropriations for preservation and repair of fortifications barely suffice to meet the numerous needs of the ever-increasing number of batteries. The new works already constructed represent an expenditure of approximately $23,000,000 for the engineering work alone, for which an annual appropriation of $100,000, less than one-half of 1 per cent of the cost of the work, has been made for preservation and repair. An estimate of $300,000 is submitted, to provide for works of preservation and repair during the ensuing year, as it has not been possible to do all necessary work the past season under the usual appropriation of $100,000.

Supplies for seacoast defenses.—The acts of May 25, 1900, and March 1, 1901, each appropriated the sum of $25,000 for tools and electrical and engine supplies for use of the troops for maintaining and operating light and power plants in gun and mortar batteries. This is designed to enable the Engineer Department to meet the requirements of paragraph 382, Army Regulations, prescribing the articles required by the coast artillery for the service of the batteries which are to be supplied by the Engineer Department. Requisitions are made directly upon the Chief of Engineers, and authorized articles are purchased and issued by the district engineer officers with as little delay as possible. This system has proved satisfactory. An estimate of $25,000 is submitted for the same purpose for the next fiscal year.

Sea walls and embankments.—The act of May 25, 1900, appropriated $50,000 for the general construction of sea walls and embankments, and $150,000 specifically for a sea wall and filling in at Fort Caswell, N. C. The former appropriation has been applied to the construction of sea walls at Fort Schuyler, N. Y., Fort Monroe, Va., Fort Smallwood, Md., and Gardiners Point, N. Y., at all of which points protective works were urgently required for the preservation of defensive works against encroachment by the sea. The works were completed during the year. The appropriation of $150,000 for a sea wall and filling in at Fort Caswell, N. C., was based upon a special estimate to Congress as a result of an extraordinary storm tide on September 30, 1899, which broke over the reservation and did serious damage to the buildings and batteries. At the close of the fiscal year the concrete wall was complete, and a contract for fill behind the wall had been let.

The act of March 1, 1901, appropriated $100,000 for the general construction of sea walls and embankments. This appropriation is being applied to the construction of sea walls at fortifications for the defense of the eastern entrance to Long Island Sound, New York Harbor, Narragansett Bay, Baltimore, Md., Hampton Roads, Virginia, and New Orleans, La.

Based upon reports of district engineer officers showing the necessity for their construction, an estimate of $150,000 is submitted for the construction of sea walls and embankments at a number of localities.

Sites.—During the past year negotiations have been continued under acts prior to that of March 1, 1901, for the acquisition of sites at Boston Harbor (two sites), Narragansett Bay (three sites), New York Harbor (extension of Fort Newton, three tracts), Port Royal, S. C., San Francisco Harbor, San Diego Harbor, St. Johns River, Florida, Fort St. Philip, La., and Cape Henry, Virginia. With few exceptions, these sites must, from various causes, be acquired by condemnation proceedings, which are slow and tedious. The acquisition of one site at Narragansett Bay, two tracts at Fort Newton, one site at San Francisco, and the remainder of the site required at Port Royal, S. C., was completed during the fiscal year. All the remaining tracts above named are still under negotiation and in various stages of progress.

A number of sites still remain to be acquired to carry out the approved projects of seacoast defenses, and an estimate of $2,000,000 is submitted to continue the work. The most important of the sites still to be acquired are one in Boston Harbor, the property of the city, and one at the southern entrance to New York Harbor, rendered necessary by the proposed new deep-water entrance now under construction.

Submarine mines.—All torpedo material necessary to enable a quick and effective defense to be made is now in store at each harbor for which torpedo defenses are at present projected. With few exceptions, all harbors are now equipped with torpedo storehouses, cable tanks, and mining casemates, kept in good condition by thorough and detailed semiannual inspections. Torpedo experiments, with a view to improvements in the adopted system, have been carried on at the United States Engineer School and elsewhere, and such experiments, as well as inventions or ideas submitted by individuals, are considered by a Board of Engineer officers known as the Board on the Torpedo System.

Mining casemates and additional storage facilities are still required at several localities. For these purposes, and for the continuation of torpedo experiments, an estimate of $100,000 is submitted.

By the Army reorganization act of February 2, 1901, the carrying out of the torpedo defense of the seacoast was devolved upon the artillery troops. By the end of the fiscal year the material had been reported ready for transfer at the following points:

Portsmouth, N. H.	Charleston, S. C.
New Bedford, Mass.	Port Royal, S. C.
Narragansett Bay.	Savannah, Ga.
Eastern entrance to Long Island Sound.	Key West, Fla.
New York Harbor, eastern and southern entrances.	Tampa, Fla.
	Pensacola, Fla.
Philadelphia, Pa.	Mobile, Ala.
Baltimore, Md.	New Orleans, La.
Washington, D. C.	San Diego, Cal.
Hampton Roads, Virginia.	San Francisco, Cal.
Wilmington, N. C.	Columbia River.

Actual transfers had been made as follows:

Eastern entrance to Long Island Sound.	Pensacola, Fla.
Southern entrance to New York Harbor.	Mobile, Ala.
Baltimore, Md.	San Diego, Cal.
Charleston, S. C.	Columbia River.
Savannah, Ga.	

Searchlights and electrical connections.—The fortification appropriation act of March 1, 1901, appropriated $150,000 for the purchase and installation of searchlights for the defenses of New York Harbor. Under this appropriation work is well advanced.

The construction of the national seacoast defenses has now reached a point where most of the heavy guns are in position, a considerable portion of the light rapid-fire emplacements and some of the rapid-fire guns are completed, and it is becoming important to inaugurate the systematic installation of searchlight apparatus for night defenses. Experience in New York Harbor and elsewhere has shown that economy in installation and the keeping of the electric plants in good order in time of peace are promoted by habitually using the fortification plants for post illumination also. Efficiency and economy demand that the mains and conduits for both defensive and post lighting should be planned and supplied by the same department. For this reason, and with the concurrence of the Quartermaster-General, an estimate for the post mains and conduits is included in the estimate of the Chief of Engineers. The Quartermaster's Department will submit estimates for the wiring inside of the post buildings, for house fixtures and lamps, and for the outdoor lamps. As the proper coordination of the operations of two separate departments, as well as the comfort of the troops, is involved in the systematic installation of these plants, and as the security of the several harbors against night attack depends on prompt and effective work, the appropriation of the total sum estimated, $500,000 for installation of searchlights and $500,000 for the installation of post mains and conduits, is urgently recommended. These sums will, it is estimated, fully equip four more of the most important harbors with complete searchlight systems, and will connect these searchlight plants and a number of already existing fortification electric plants with the electric lamps in the barracks and quarters already furnished by the Quartermaster's Department.

The following brief summaries of the detailed reports of district officers give a concise statement of the work at each locality during the fiscal year:

Defensive works on coast of Maine.—Officer in charge, Maj. Solomon W. Roessler, Corps of Engineers; assistants, Lieut. Thomas H. Jackson, Corps of Engineers, to September 20, 1900, and Lieut. Charles W. Kutz, Corps of Engineers, since August 31, 1900; Division Engineers, Col. George L. Gillespie, Corps of Engineers (now brigadier-general, Chief of Engineers, United States Army), to April 30, 1901, and Col. Charles R. Suter, Corps of Engineers, since May 9, 1901.

Bar Harbor, Maine.—Two 8-inch converted rifles and two 10-inch smoothbore guns were mounted on temporary wooden platforms in 1898. No repairs have been made during the year.

The two 10-inch guns have been condemned and sold as obsolete. The two 8-inch converted rifles are to be removed to the nearest military reservation, and the remaining ordnance stores are to be sent to Watertown Arsenal.

Penobscot River, Maine.—A few minor repairs have been made. Some accumulated débris has been removed, and three old dilapidated buildings have been sold and removed.

Under an allotment from the appropriation for "Torpedoes for Harbor Defense," a brick storehouse, 56 feet by 27 feet, with traveling crane, for storage of submarine-mining material, has been constructed during the year.

Submarine-mining material was overhauled and cleaned.

Kennebec River, Maine.—Repairs were made to the emergency concrete emplacement that was built in 1898 for one 8-inch B. L. rifle, mounted on 15-inch smoothbore carriage.

Submarine-mining material was overhauled and cleaned.

Portland Harbor, Maine.—During the fiscal year work in constructing new fortifications was in progress at four different sites, on three 12-inch batteries, one 10-inch battery, three 8-inch batteries, two 6-inch batteries, three 15-pounder batteries, two mortar batteries, two mining casemates, and six range-finder stations. Repairs were made on two additional 10-inch batteries that had been transferred to the artillery.

Two of the 8-inch batteries, one of the 12-inch batteries, and one mortar battery were practically completed and transferred to the artillery.

One of the range-finder stations and one 15-pounder battery were also completed.

Of the remaining 12-inch batteries, one is two-thirds completed with one gun mounted, and on the other work has recently been started and is well under way. It is expected that both will be completed during the present season.

The 10-inch battery is nearly completed, lacking only part of the sand fill and a small concrete traverse the construction of which is deferred pending the starting of work on an adjacent battery. Guns are mounted.

The third 8-inch battery is nearly completed, lacking only the loam cover for the sand parapet and some excavation in the roadway in rear. All carriages are assembled and one gun mounted. The battery will be completed ready for transfer during the present season.

Of the 6-inch batteries, one is 75 per cent completed and will be finished in the near future. On the other, field work is not yet started.

Of the 15-pounder batteries, the excavation is completed and in one of them the gun platforms are built and floors laid. Both will be completed during the present season.

The unfinished mortar battery is 80 per cent completed. All carriages are assembled. Mortars have not yet been received. The battery will be ready for transfer at the close of the present season.

On the mortar battery now in the hands of the artillery work is in progress looking to the correction of certain defects, leakage, improper floor drainage, and condensation of moisture on walls.

Work on the mining casemates and on five range-finder stations has only recently been started.

Submarine-mine material was overhauled and cleaned.

No work was done during the fiscal year on the older type fortifications in this harbor, except such small repairs as have been necessary from time to time.

(See Appendix 3 A.)

FORTIFICATIONS.   15

Defenses of Portsmouth, N. H.—Officers in charge, Maj. Walter L. Fisk, Corps of Engineers, until December 15, 1900, and Capt. Harry Taylor, Corps of Engineers, since that date; Division Engineers, Col. George L. Gillespie, Corps of Engineers (now brigadier-general, Chief of Engineers, United States Army), until April 30, 1901, and Col. Charles R. Suter, Corps of Engineers, since May 9, 1901.

At the beginning of the fiscal year a battery of two 8-inch B. L. rifles on disappearing carriages had been completed, with the exception of the electric-lighting plant, and turned over to the troops, together with a mining casemate which was constructed in connection with the battery. A cable tank had also been built.

The earth and rock excavation for a battery of three 10-inch B. L. rifles on disappearing carriages had been completed and about one-third of the concrete had been put in.

During the fiscal year this battery was practically completed, only minor details and the work of cleaning up the site and mounting the guns remaining to be done at the close of the year.

The following new work was ordered during the year: Emplacements for two 5-inch rapid-fire wire-wound guns on pedestal mounts, and for two 12-inch B. L. rifles on disappearing carriages. A substantial wharf, for use in connection with the construction of these emplacements, has been built. Owing to the failure of the contractors for furnishing the 5-inch guns to fulfill their contract, the construction of the 5-inch emplacements was indefinitely postponed and the funds withdrawn for use elsewhere.

Plans and estimates for the construction of the 12-inch emplacements were submitted by the local officer.

The construction of a torpedo storehouse was also authorized and the building practically completed.

Minor repairs have been made from time to time as needed on batteries and buildings, and the torpedo material has been cared for.

(See Appendix 3 B.)

Defenses of Boston, Mass.—Officer in charge, Col. Charles R. Suter, Corps of Engineers, until May 31, 1901, after which date in the charge of Capt. Harry Taylor, Corps of Engineers, to whom the works were transferred through Lieut. Col. William S. Stanton, Corps of Engineers; assistant, Lieut. Robert R. Raymond, Corps of Engineers; Division Engineer, Col. Charles R. Suter, Corps of Engineers, since May 31, 1901.

The defenses include three works of old type, one of which is used for a depot for torpedo material.

At the beginning of the fiscal year emplacements were completed for sixteen 12-inch mortars, three 12-inch rifles on disappearing carriages, ten 10-inch rifles on disappearing carriages, two 4.7-inch rapid-fire guns on naval mounts, two 4-inch rapid-fire guns on pedestal mounts, and three 15-pounder rapid-fire guns on balanced-pillar mounts; and all of the guns were mounted and ready for service.

Emplacements for two 12-inch rifles on barbette carriages and two 5-inch rapid-fire guns on balanced-pillar mounts were complete, with carriages mounted ready to receive guns.

Emplacements for two 12-inch rifles on disappearing carriages and two 15-pounder rapid-fire guns on balanced-pillar mounts were complete and ready for armament, which had not been received.

Two range-finder towers and two electric-light plants were also completed ready for use.

Work was in progress upon one underground-conduit system, five range-finder towers, two emplacements for 15-pounder rapid-fire guns on balanced-pillar mounts, and three emplacements for 6-inch rifles on disappearing carriages.

During the fiscal year these works were completed, and two 12-inch rifles on disappearing carriages, three disappearing carriages for 6-inch rifles, and two 15-pounder rapid-fire guns on balanced-pillar mounts were mounted and made ready for service. The following new works were begun: Construction of seven emplacements for 15-pounder rapid-fire guns on balanced-pillar mounts, four emplacements for 6-inch rapid-fire guns on pedestal mounts, three emplacements for 10-inch rifles on disappearing carriages, two storehouses, and a steam lighter. Extensive alterations were begun at one mortar battery.

Of these works, two emplacements for 15-pounder rapid-fire guns were completed, one similar emplacement was completed except earthwork and details, four similar emplacements were well advanced, two emplacements for 6-inch rapid-fire guns were ready for concrete work; on three emplacements for 10-inch rifles excavation was begun and plant partially installed, one storehouse was completed and one begun, repairs at mortar battery were well advanced, and plans and specifications for lighter were completed.

The submarine-mining material on hand was sorted and all obsolete and unserviceable material shipped, or prepared for shipment, to the Engineer Depot.

An extension to the cable storage tank was nearly completed.

Negotiations for the acquisition of additional sites required for the projected defenses were continued throughout the year, a considerable number of titles were examined, and fifty-one lots were paid for.

Minor works of preservation and repair were in progress at the different posts and batteries in the harbor.

(See Appendix 3 C.)

Defenses of southeast coast of Massachusetts and Rhode Island, at New Bedford, Mass., and Newport, R. I.—Officers in charge, Maj. Daniel W. Lockwood, Corps of Engineers, until July 25, 1900; Lieut. Robert P. Johnston, Corps of Engineers, from July 25, 1900, to August 31, 1900, and Maj. George W. Goethals, Corps of Engineers, since August 31, 1900; assistant, Lieut. Robert P. Johnston, Corps of Engineers, until July 25, 1900, and since August 31, 1900; Division Engineer, Col. George L. Gillespie, Corps of Engineers (now brigadier-general, Chief of Engineers, United States Army), until April 30, 1901, and Col. Charles R. Suter, Corps of Engineers, since May 9, 1901.

The defenses include two permanent masonry works of old type, one of which is used in part by the garrison. During the year minor repairs were made to one of the old works.

At the beginning of the fiscal year the following batteries for high-power guns were practically completed: Two emplacements for 8-inch guns on disappearing carriages, one mortar battery of sixteen 12-inch mortars, one battery of two 10-inch guns on disappearing carriages, one battery of two 4.7-inch rapid-fire guns, one battery of two 12-inch guns on nondisappearing carriages, two batteries of two 15-pounder rapid-fire guns each, one battery of three 10-inch guns on disappearing carriages, and one emplacement for 6-inch rapid-fire gun. In addition to the foregoing, two concrete cable tanks for the storage of torpedo material and one brick storehouse for the storage of mining material have been constructed, and an electric-light plant for furnishing light and power was installed in one of the batteries. All the submarine-mining material on hand was cared for during the year.

During the fiscal year the most important operations were as follows: Two battery commanders' stations were completed, one battery of two 5-inch rapid-fire guns was completed with base rings set ready to mount the guns; one mortar battery for eight 12-inch mortars was completed, base rings and carriages assembled and mounted ready for the mortars; a mining casemate was very nearly completed; one cable tank was built, and two brick storehouses for the storage of mining material were practically completed. Funds were allotted for the construction of two emplacements for 10-inch guns on disappearing carriages, and of two emplacements for 15-pounder rapid-fire guns, but active operations could not be commenced, due to litigation over certain negative easements, which the court has not yet acted on. On May 28, 1901, however, authority was given to begin work on these as well as on emplacements for two 6-inch rapid-fire guns. At the close of the fiscal year two batteries of two 15-pounder rapid-fire guns each were practically completed, work having been begun in November, 1900.

A temporary wharf is being replaced by a permanent stone structure.

Negotiations were entered into for acquiring 25 acres of land as a site for fortification works, and decree of condemnation was entered. Payment, however, has not yet been made.

Funds were allotted for installing electric-light plants, and contracts have been made or awarded for the necessary material.

(See Appendix 3 D.)

Defenses of eastern entrance to Long Island Sound and coast of Connecticut.—Officer in charge, Maj. Smith S. Leach, Corps of Engineers; assistant, Lieut. Edward H. Schulz, Corps of Engineers; Division Engineer, Col. George L. Gillespie, Corps of Engineers (now brigadier-general, Chief of Engineers, United States Army), to April 30, 1901, and Col. Charles R. Suter, Corps of Engineers, since May 9, 1901.

The defenses of New London consist of two works of the old type, containing no modern armament, one of which is an open barbette work on the east side of the river, in charge of an ordnance sergeant; the other work is a masonry construction on the west side of the river. The latter work has been garrisoned during the year.

The defenses of the eastern entrance of Long Island Sound are the following:

Two 12-inch B. L. rifles on disappearing carriages, model 1897. This battery was built by contract entered into December 11, 1896, and included the construction of a wharf. The battery was completed and transferred to the artillery on May 12, 1900. Armament is mounted and electric plant installed.

Two 10-inch B. L. rifles on disappearing carriages, model 1896. This battery was built under "National Defense" appropriation, and was begun in March, 1898. It was completed and transferred to the artillery on May 12, 1900. Armament is mounted and electric plant installed.

Two 6-inch rapid-fire guns on pedestal mounts. Allotment for this work was made June 26, 1901. The work will be prosecuted during the coming year.

ENG 1901——2

Range-finder station for 12-inch battery: The allotment for this work is $7,000. Field work began in April, 1901. The station is the typical low site, instrument axis 60 feet above mean low water. At the close of the fiscal year the station is practically complete, except minor details of painting and finishing.

Construction of sea wall: This wall is a random rubble revetment for the protection of the southern shore of the reservation. Work was begun in April, 1901. The exposed bank is subject to disintegration by frost action. The work is about one-quarter completed as to length and about half as to volume.

Two 10-inch B. L. rifles on disappearing carriages, model 1896, and a mining casemate: This work was done under contract entered into August 11, 1897, and included a crib wharf. The battery, with battery commander's station, was completed and transferred to the artillery March 31, 1900. The armament is mounted and electric plant installed. The mining casemate is complete but not equipped, and was transferred to the artillery on April 30, 1901.

Eight 12-inch B. L. steel mortars: Work on this battery was begun about July 1, 1898. At the beginning of the fiscal year the battery was complete, except consolidation of slopes, concreting terreplein, and installing electric plant. The battery was completed in the late fall of 1900. The battery commander's station pertaining to this battery is also complete. The armament is on hand, two carriages and mortars in the right pit are mounted, the remaining base rings are set, and carriages and mortars are on hand. During the year the electric-light plant has been installed, tested, and accepted. The battery, together with the range-finder station, was transferred to the artillery on March 4, 1901.

Two 6-inch rapid-fire guns on disappearing mounts: Work was begun in the early part of 1899. At the beginning of the fiscal year the battery was complete, except consolidation of slopes and electric lighting. The battery was finally completed in the fall of 1900. Carriages are on hand, not mounted; the guns have not yet been received. Electric plant has been installed, tested, and accepted. From an allotment of $2,000 the rear traverse of this battery was adapted for use as a power room, and a casemated shelter was constructed on the left flank of the battery for a 30-inch projector. A track for drill purposes has also been built. The battery, with searchlight, was transferred to the artillery on March 4, 1901.

One 4.7-inch rapid-fire Armstrong gun: This emplacement was built under "National Defense" appropriation, and was completed in 1899. The armament is mounted and electric light installed. The emplacement was transferred to the artillery March 31, 1900.

One 5-inch rapid-fire wire-wound gun: This emplacement was begun in the fall of 1899, and was nine-tenths complete at the beginning of the fiscal year. It was completed in the fall of 1900, except armament, which has not yet been received. Electric lighting is installed. The emplacement was transferred to the artillery on March 4, 1901.

Two 8-inch B. L. rifles on disappearing carriages, model 1896, and two 5-inch rapid-fire guns on balanced-pillar mounts: Work was begun the latter part of 1898. At the beginning of the fiscal year both batteries were practically completed. In the 8-inch battery two carriages and one gun are now mounted; the remaining gun is on hand, but not yet mounted. Electric lighting is installed. The 5-inch rapid-fire emplacements were finished and the carriages mounted; the guns have not yet been received. Electric lighting is installed. These batteries were transferred to the artillery on February 18, 1901.

Two 5-inch rapid-fire wire-wound guns: This battery was begun in the fall of 1899. At the beginning of the fiscal year it was complete, except sodding slopes and electric wiring. The armament has not yet been received. The battery was complete and transferred to the artillery on February 18, 1901.

Bank revetment: On May 1 an allotment of $2,600 was made for a bank revetment of piles and sheet piling. This revetment is to be in front of the temporary barracks, and is intended to prevent the erosion of the bank and also raise the general level of the shore line. At the end of the fiscal year proposals had been called for and received, and award will be made and the work executed this summer.

Two 8-inch B. L. rifles on 15-inch smoothbore carriages, converted: At the beginning of the fiscal year the battery was ready for armament. Guns are on hand; the converted carriages are on hand, but not mounted. Electric light is installed. No garrison is present.

Two 5-inch rapid-fire wire-wound guns: These emplacements, with connecting parades, are built in rear of two 8-inch emplacements. A sea wall has been built for the protection of the site, which is very contracted and not over 5 feet above low water. The battery was completed in the spring of 1900. Armament has not been received. No garrison is present.

Two 12-inch B. L. rifles on disappearing carriages, model 1897; two 10-inch B. L. rifles on disappearing carriages, model 1896; and three 6-inch rapid-fire guns on disappearing mounts: Work was begun in December, 1898. At the beginning of the fiscal year the 10-inch emplacements were completed, except ammunition hoists and electric lighting. Concrete work on the 12-inch emplacements was nearing completion. The armament was all on hand; the 10-inch guns were mounted. During the year the 12-inch guns have been mounted and the work completed, except final test of the electric plant. At the beginning of the fiscal year one of the 6-inch emplacements was finished to loading platform and the other two well under way. The 6-inch emplacements are now finished, carriages are on hand and mounted, guns have not yet been received, and electric plant is being tested. The above batteries were transferred to the artillery on March 7, 1901.

Eight 12-inch B. L. steel mortars: Allotment for this work was made July 7, 1900. During the fiscal year excavation has been made and the center traverse practically completed.

Protection of dynamite battery: On August 1, 1900, an allotment for this work was made. During the year material has been purchased and delivered. Actual work is deferred until test of the gun has been completed.

Preservation and repair of fortifications: An electrician has been on duty during the year, looking after the several electric plants. Repairs have been made to the several fortifications during the year.

Submarine-mining material: This material has been inspected and overhauled and was transferred to the artillery May 20, 1901.

(See Appendix 3 E.)

Defenses of New York Harbor.—Officer in charge of artillery defense and of torpedo defense of southern entrance to harbor: Maj. William

L. Marshall, Corps of Engineers; assistants, Lieut. James A. Woodruff, Corps of Engineers, until September 19, 1900, and Lieut. James F. McIndoe, Corps of Engineers, until March 9, 1901. Officers in charge of torpedo defense of eastern entrance to harbor: Maj. John G. D. Knight, Corps of Engineers, until April 29, 1901, and since that date Maj. William M. Black, Corps of Engineers. Division Engineers, Col. George L. Gillespie, Corps of Engineers (now brigadier-general, Chief of Engineers, United States Army), until April 30, 1901, and Col. Charles R. Suter, Corps of Engineers, since May 9, 1901.

Eastern entrance to harbor.—At the beginning of the fiscal year emplacements had been completed and turned over to the artillery for the following guns and mortars: Two 8-inch, four 10-inch, and one 12-inch gun on disappearing carriages, and sixteen 12-inch B. L. mortars.

The following emplacements, then under way and nearly completed, have since been completed and turned over to the artillery: For eight 12-inch B. L. mortars, altered for new type azimuth circles, three 12-inch guns on disappearing carriages, six 5-inch rapid-fire guns (two not yet provided with carriages), and four 15-pounder rapid-fire guns.

Electric-lighting plants have been built for all the batteries, range-finder stations have been built, and an electric tide indicator has been installed.

Under recent allotment work has been started upon two emplacements for 6-inch rapid-fire guns.

Thirteen hundred and forty-three linear feet of sea wall have been built, and further construction is in progress.

All materials needed for the torpedo defense of the eastern entrance are on hand and in good condition. A storeroom has been provided for the reception of materials pertaining to this defense. A report was made and forwarded as to the submarine-mine work proposed for this defense, accompanied by a tracing and a list of materials. The mine defense of this locality remained in charge of the engineer officer during the year, in accordance with letter from the Adjutant-General, United States Army, of May 7, 1901.

Southern entrance to harbor.—At the beginning of the fiscal year emplacements had been completed and turned over to the artillery for the following guns and mortars, all of which have been mounted, viz: Sixteen 12-inch B. L. mortars; two 12-inch guns on lifts; two 12-inch guns en barbette; six 12-inch guns; sixteen 10-inch guns, and five 8-inch guns, all on disappearing carriages; two 8-inch B. L. rifles on modified 15-inch gun carriages; two 6-inch rapid-fire guns on pedestal mounts; one 5-inch and four 4.7-inch rapid-fire guns; one pneumatic gun battery for three dynamite guns with temporary magazines; and the following in temporary emplacements: One 5-inch siege rifle, one 7-inch siege howitzer, and one 4.7-inch rapid-fire gun. The following structures were completed and turned over to the artillery: Three mining casemates, seven cable tanks, and two storage buildings for submarine-mining materials.

The following emplacements, under construction at the beginning of the fiscal year, have since been completed and turned over to the artillery, viz: For eight 12-inch B. L. mortars two 12-inch guns; and two 6-inch guns on disappearing carriages. Two emplacements for 12-inch guns and two for 15-pounder rapid-fire guns have been completed.

In addition, there are six emplacements for 15-pounder rapid-fire guns completed. These emplacements have not been turned over to the artillery, owing to the fact that the base castings have not been received and set.

During the fiscal year the following additional work has been done: Two 12-inch gun emplacements begun and about half completed; two 6-inch emplacements nearly completed; six emplacements for 6-inch rapid-fire guns on pedestal mounts just begun. One range-finder tower has been built and a second nearly completed. Permanent magazines and parapet have been built for the pneumatic dynamite-gun battery. Two central electric-power stations have been begun.

Under recent allotments extensions of two sea walls have been begun.

A project for enlargement of Governors Island, New York, has been adopted and work is about to begin.

(See Appendix 3 F.)

Defenses of the Delaware River.—Officer in charge, Lieut. Col. Charles W. Raymond, Corps of Engineers; assistants, Capt. Spencer Cosby, Corps of Engineers, and Lieut. James B. Cavanaugh, Corps of Engineers, to July 13, 1900.

The defenses include two masonry works of old type, one of which is in charge of an ordnance sergeant. No new work is contemplated at this site. Modern batteries have been erected at the other site and are being cared for by a small detachment of troops. Modern works of defense are also located at two other points on the river, which are garrisoned.

At the beginning of the fiscal year the following batteries of modern type had been completed and turned over to the artillery: One battery for three 12-inch and three 10-inch guns on disappearing carriages; one battery for two 4.72-inch rapid-fire guns on pedestal mounts; one battery for sixteen 12-inch B. L. mortars; one battery for two 8-inch guns on disappearing carriages, and two 12-inch guns on nondisappearing carriages.

One battery for two 5-inch rapid-fire guns on balanced-pillar mounts was completed, ready for the guns and carriages, in 1897, but was not turned over to the artillery until December, 1900.

The following works were completed and turned over to the artillery during the fiscal year: One battery for three 12-inch guns on disappearing carriages; two batteries, each of two 5-inch rapid-fire guns on pedestal mounts; two batteries, each for two 15-pounder rapid-fire guns on balanced-pillar mounts.

At the close of the year work was in progress on the following emplacements: Two emplacements for 15-pounder rapid-fire guns on balanced-pillar mounts and two emplacements for 15-pounder rapid-fire guns on casemate mounts.

The battery, completed during the year, for three 12-inch disappearing guns, with two 15-pounder emplacements on each flank, is built on a heavy pile-and-concrete foundation, necessitated by the treacherous nature of the soil. The cost of the battery complete, including electric, ventilating, and water-supply systems, was $350,500. One of the 15-pounder batteries cost $4.000 and the other $3,800. No appreciable settlement or cracks have occurred in any part of the three batteries.

No guns or carriages have yet been received for either of the batteries for 5-inch rapid-fire guns completed and turned over to the artillery during the year. Owing to their locations, these emplacements contain larger amounts of concrete and sand than are called for in the typical designs. One battery cost $17,500 and the other $16,800.

Work was started during the year, and is still in progress, upon the conversion of two old magazines into casemates for 15-pounder rapid-fire guns and upon the construction on a pile foundation of two 15-pounder emplacements. Both works will be finished during the coming year.

Two steel instrument towers, for battery commanders' stations, are in course of erection. The work has been seriously retarded by delays in the delivery of materials and by extensive alterations necessitated by the poor fitting of many of the parts. Two stations for Rafferty range finders have been built.

All the torpedo material was examined, put in good condition, and listed for transfer to the artillery. A steel lining is being placed in the cable tank.

During the year, under various allotments from appropriations for "Preservation and Repair of Fortifications," electric-lighting plants were operated and cared for, repairs were made to battery slopes, lead flashing was placed over joints in the platforms to prevent leakage, ironwork was painted, the entrance walls of one battery were torn down and rebuilt, the ground near another battery was cleared and graded, repairs were made to river banks and wharves, and other works of maintenance and repair were carried on.

Under allotments from the appropriation for "Supplies for Seacoast Defenses," electric night lights were placed around the platforms of six emplacements, and materials of many kinds required by the artillery were supplied.

(See Appendix 3 G.)

Defenses of Baltimore, Md.—Officer in charge, Lieut. Col. Oswald H. Ernst, Corps of Engineers; assistant, Lieut. Charles W. Kutz, Corps of Engineers, until August 30, 1900.

There are five forts in the system—four of the modern and one of the old type.

At the beginning of the fiscal year there were already constructed at one site a battery containing one 12-inch and three 8-inch B. L. rifles on disappearing carriages, together with two 4.7-inch rapid-fire guns. A flanking battery for two 15-pounder rapid-fire guns was also constructed, but was without its armament. This was mounted during the present fiscal year.

At another locality a battery for two 12-inch B. L. rifles on non-disappearing carriages was complete with its armament at the beginning of the fiscal year, and two emplacements for 5-inch rapid-fire guns and two for 15-pounder rapid-fire guns had been constructed. The operations of the present fiscal year were mounting the guns in the 15-pounder emplacements, mounting one carriage in the 5-inch emplacement, and setting the base of the other.

At a third reservation there were already constructed one battery containing eight 12-inch B. L. mortars, one battery containing two 12-inch B. L. rifles on disappearing carriages, two emplacements for 5-inch rapid-fire guns with carriages mounted, two emplacements for 6-inch B. L. rifles with disappearing carriages mounted, and two emplacements for 15-pounder rapid-fire guns. The operations of the fiscal year have consisted in adding two emplacements for 15-pounder rapid-fire guns.

At a fourth site two emplacements for 6-inch B. L. rifles were already constructed and the disappearing carriages mounted at the beginning of the fiscal year.

The operations of the fiscal year also consisted, at one site, in the partial construction of a mining casemate, beginning the modification of the coal receptacle for the power plant, putting in a surface drainage system, and reenforcing the rubble sea wall with a concrete backing; at another site, continuing the work of remodeling a masonry fortification; at a third locality, commencing the damp-proofing of the rooms and galleries of a mortar battery, setting the bases for two range finders, putting a concrete backing to a rubble sea wall, and partially filling an embankment; protecting a fourth reservation by the construction of a concrete sea wall; repairing and keeping in good condition all the batteries, the power plants, and submarine-mining material, and furnishing electrical supplies for all the electric installations.

(See Appendix 3 H.)

Defenses of Washington, D. C.—Officer in charge, Lieut. Col. Charles J. Allen, Corps of Engineers.

At the close of the fiscal year 1901 there were completed emplacements for six 10-inch guns, for three 8-inch guns, and for two 4-inch rapid-fire guns. In addition there were under construction emplacements for eight 12-inch mortars, for two 6-inch guns on disappearing carriages, for two 5-inch guns on balanced-pillar mounts, and for five 15-pounder rapid-fire guns on balanced-pillar mounts. It is expected that all of these will be completed during the first half of the coming fiscal year, provided the necessary armament is received. The mortar battery is now ready for its armament, as is the 6-inch battery.

Of the four battery commanders' stations, pertaining to the approved system of fire control, two are completed and two are practically completed, a very small amount of work only remaining to be done to them.

An electric light and power outfit for the 8-inch battery is under construction; public advertisement has been issued inviting proposals for an electric-light plant for the mortar battery; and an electric-light plant for the 6-inch battery has been authorized. Completion of these plants during the next fiscal year is expected.

Necessary repairs were made to the batteries and buildings.

A few repairs to wharf and roadway were authorized late in the year.

(See Appendix 3 I.)

Defenses of Hampton Roads, Virginia.—Officer in charge, Maj. James B. Quinn, Corps of Engineers; Division Engineer, Col. Peter C. Hains, Corps of Engineers.

Two old-style works are in existence at this locality: One, built of earth and masonry, is located on the north side of the channel, and is garrisoned; the other, built entirely of masonry, is located on the opposite side of the channel. The latter is not garrisoned, has no armament, and is in an uncompleted state, work on it having been discontinued owing to settlement of the foundation.

The garrisoned fort at the close of the fiscal year is armed with three

8-inch, eight 10-inch, and two 12-inch high-power guns, sixteen 12-inch mortars, and four 4.72-inch rapid-fire guns. Emplacements for one additional 12-inch and four 15-pounder rapid-fire guns were ready for the armament, and two more 8-inch guns could be mounted on platforms which have been constructed, but not at present occupied. Besides the modern armament enumerated above, quite a large number of old-style pieces still remain.

For the submarine-mine defense, two mining casemates and galleries and a cable storage tank have been built. The fire commander's station and the battery commander's station at the mortar battery have been constructed.

During the fiscal year 1901 a 12-inch battery of two guns was authorized. The site has been graded for the foundation and some of the sheet piling required at outer edge of foundation to prevent wash of sand from underneath by high tides has been driven. Other operations have been confined to finishing, as far as possible, batteries uncompleted at the close of the previous fiscal year, to constructing the battery commander's station at the mortar battery, to constructing a portion of the structures designed for the electric plants for lighting the mortar battery and the batteries to be supplied with current from the electric plant at one of the 10-inch batteries, and to repairing and preserving the various batteries and appliances.

Plans are under way for emplacements for two batteries of two 6-inch rapid-fire guns each. A battery consisting of four 15-pounder rapid-fire guns was also under consideration at the close of the fiscal year.

The armament of this locality was increased by two 12-inch guns, which were mounted during the fiscal year.

(See Appendix 3 J.)

Defenses of the coast of North Carolina.—Officer in charge, Capt. Eugene W. Van C. Lucas, Corps of Engineers; Division Engineer, Col. Peter C. Hains, Corps of Engineers.

The defenses include the old style Fort Macon, the reservation at Southport, and the modern batteries at the mouth of Cape Fear River.

At the beginning of the fiscal year, one battery of four 8-inch B. L. rifles, one battery of two 12-inch B. L. rifles and one 4.7-inch rapid-fire gun, and one central lighting and power plant had been completed and turned over to the garrison; two emplacements for 5-inch rapid-fire guns had been completed and were awaiting armament, and a battery for eight 12-inch mortars and carriages had been completed and the mortars mounted but not yet turned over. The torpedo equipment, including storehouse and cable tank, was complete and ready for service.

The mortar battery has not yet been transferred to the garrison because settlement has been detected, and it is thought best to await the completion of the sea wall and fill, involving possibly further settlement of this battery, so that mortars may be releveled where necessary before transfer is made.

The submarine-mining outfit is complete in all respects, and its transfer to the garrison awaits only the arrival of the responsible officer.

During the year the battery for four 8-inch B. L. rifles has been provided with communicating galleries on the platform level.

One 5-inch rapid-fire emplacement has been provided with a carriage, which has been mounted, the emplacement now being ready for transfer to the garrison.

A concrete sea wall 6,612 feet in length has been built, inclosing the exposed sides of the post, and a contract has been made to fill in all low places to the level of 12 feet above mean low water, which is above the highest recorded storm tide. The fill will probably be completed in February next.

Emplacements for two 15-pounder rapid-fire guns and a fire commander's station have been started and will be completed during the next fiscal year.

With allotments from the appropriation for "Preservation and Repair of Fortifications," three guns in the 8-inch battery have been releveled, safety stops have been provided for the ammunition lifts of the 12-inch battery, and considerable minor repair and improvement work has been done.

(See Appendix 3 K.)

Defenses of the coast of South Carolina.—Officer in charge, Capt. James C. Sanford, Corps of Engineers; assistant, Lieut. Edwin R. Stuart, Corps of Engineers, since February 22, 1901; Division Engineer, Col. Peter C. Hains, Corps of Engineers.

Charleston Harbor.—At the close of the fiscal year 1900 the defenses comprised the following works:

Mortar battery, emplacements for sixteen 12-inch mortars. This battery is completed and the mortars are mounted.

Ten-inch battery, emplacements for four 10-inch rifles on disappearing carriages. This battery is completed and the guns are mounted.

Six-inch rapid-fire battery. This battery consists of one emplacement for 6-inch rapid-fire gun on disappearing carriage and one emplacement for 6-inch rapid-fire gun on nondisappearing carriage. The emplacements are completed and the carriage of the former and the gun and carriage of the latter are mounted.

Two emplacements for 4.7-inch rapid-fire guns are completed and the guns are mounted.

Three emplacements for 15-pounder rapid-fire guns on balanced-pillar mounts are completed.

Twelve-inch battery. Emplacements for one 12-inch B. L. rifle on disappearing carriage and for one 12-inch B. L. rifle on barbette carriage are completed and guns are mounted.

During the fiscal year 1901 the guns and carriages for the 15-pounder rapid-fire battery were received and the guns mounted. Galleries supported by brackets were built connecting the gun platforms at the 10-inch battery. Minor repairs were made at all the batteries.

The torpedo material was cared for and transferred to the artillery. Bids were opened for the construction of a torpedo storehouse, but at the close of the year the contract had not been submitted for approval.

Port Royal Sound, South Carolina.—At the close of the fiscal year 1900 the defenses comprised the following works:

Ten-inch battery, emplacements for three 10-inch rifles on disappearing carriages. The battery was completed and guns mounted.

Emplacements for two 4.7-inch rapid-fire guns were completed and guns mounted.

Temporary emplacements for two 8-inch rifles on 15-inch smoothbore carriages were completed and guns mounted.

During the fiscal year 1901 lots 58 and 59 were paid for and an order given by the court vesting the title to them in the United States.

The torpedo material was cared for and prepared for transfer to the artillery.

No work on the parapet for the dynamite gun was done, due to delay in the completion of the work under the Ordnance Department.

The two 8-inch B. L. rifles were removed from the mounts in the temporary emplacements and the work abandoned.

Minor repairs were made at the batteries, and the property was cared for.

(See Appendix 3 L.)

Defenses of the coast of Georgia and of Cumberland Sound, Georgia and Florida.—Officer in charge, Capt. Cassius E. Gillette, Corps of Engineers; Division Engineer, Col. Peter C. Hains, Corps of Engineers.

These defenses include three masonry works of old type.

During the fiscal year the battery of two 4.7-inch rapid-fire guns has been transferred to the artillery.

No work was done on the two batteries for 15-pounder rapid-fire guns. The guns and their mounts have not yet been furnished by the Ordnance Department.

Allotments aggregating $4,800 were made for supplying an electric plant for and otherwise completing the mortar battery.

Bracketed galleries to connect certain adjacent gun emplacements were installed.

Under allotments from the appropriation for "Preservation and Repair of Fortifications" considerable work to check the drifting and moving of sand was done, and numerous minor repairs were made.

On July 13, 1900, an allotment of $9,000 was made for the construction of a mining casemate. The casemate was completed, thoroughly equipped, and transferred to the artillery, together with all of the torpedo material on hand.

A second mining casemate was fitted up complete and everything put in good condition ready to operate.

No requisitions for supplies were received from post commanders under the appropriation for "Supplies for Seacoast Defenses."

(See Appendix 3 M.)

Defenses of east coast of Florida and of Key West, Fla.—Officers in charge, Capt. Thomas H. Rees, Corps of Engineers, until September 24, 1900, and since March 27, 1901, and Capt. Charles H. McKinstry, Corps of Engineers, from September 24, 1900, to March 27, 1901; assistants, Lieut. Edward M. Markham, Corps of Engineers, until September 11, 1900, and Lieut. Edmund M. Rhett, Corps of Engineers, since September 17, 1900; Division Engineer, Col. Peter C. Hains, Corps of Engineers.

The defenses include two masonry works of old type. One of them, Fort Marion, was built by the Spaniards in the eighteenth century, and is of little value for defensive purposes. It is, however, an interesting historical relic and should be preserved.

The other work has been dismantled of its old armament and a portion of it has been torn down.

Near the mouth of the St. Johns River, where the temporary batteries were built during the war with Spain, the engineer property and torpedo material were cared for during the year with funds provided from the appropriation for "Preservation and Repair of Fortifications."

At the close of the fiscal year proceedings were in progress for the acquisition of 117.7 acres of land, upon which it is proposed to erect permanent batteries.

At Key West emplacements for four 10-inch and two 8-inch guns on disappearing carriages and for eight 12-inch mortars were completed. The original contractors abandoned the work, and a contract for the completion was awarded in December, 1900. At the close of the fiscal year very little work had been executed under the new agreement.

Road covering for roadway to connect two adjacent batteries: Very little work was accomplished pending the completion of the roadway.

Emplacements for five 15-pounder rapid-fire guns were completed and turned over to the artillery command.

One emplacement for 15-pounder rapid-fire gun was in process of construction June 30, 1901.

The contract for a battery commander's station expired by limitation June 28, 1901. No work had been done.

Minor repairs have been made and the torpedo material has been cared for under allotments from the appropriation for "Preservation and Repair of Fortifications."

Supplies for the artillery have been purchased upon approved requisitions, with funds from the appropriation for "Supplies for Seacoast Defenses."

(See Appendix 8 N.)

Defenses of Tampa Bay, Florida.—Officer in charge, Capt. Thomas H. Rees, Corps of Engineers; assistant, Lieut. Edmund M. Rhett, Corps of Engineers, since March 27, 1901; Division Engineer, Col. Peter C. Hains, Corps of Engineers.

At one locality emplacements for three 15-pounder rapid-fire guns were commenced and completed during the fiscal year, and on June 30, 1901, preparations were in progress for constructing an additional emplacement.

Other work done has consisted of caring for the mining material stored at this point, and of miscellaneous minor work connected with the preservation and repair of the completed fortifications.

At another locality operations were begun for building emplacements for two 15-pounder rapid-fire guns, and on June 30, 1901, this work was in progress.

Other work done has consisted of clearing the site of the mortar battery, including the repair of certain buildings and the destruction of others, and of miscellaneous minor work connected with the preservation and repair of the completed fortifications.

(See Appendix 8 O.)

Defenses of Pensacola, Fla.—Officers in charge: Capt. Clement A. F. Flagler, Corps of Engineers, until September 26, 1900, and Capt. William V. Judson, Corps of Engineers, since that date. Assistants: Lieut. Lewis H. Rand, Corps of Engineers, until July 3, 1900, and Lieut. Gustave R. Lukesh, Corps of Engineers, from September 16, 1900, to March 14, 1901; Division Engineer, Col. Peter C. Hains, Corps of Engineers.

A battery, mounting four 10-inch guns on disappearing carriages, was completed in 1897-98. The dynamo room pertaining to this battery has been remodeled and extended during the year. Interplatform communications are being provided of concrete and steel. This battery is in good condition except as follows: Magazines Nos. 3 and 4 and storerooms of Emplacement No. 4 are very damp; shell room No. 4 is damp; dynamo room is rather damp. An allotment has been received for remedying these faults, through the use of detached lead ceilings and brick walls, raised floors, doors, etc.

A battery, mounting two 12-inch guns on disappearing carriages, was completed in 1898–99. Emplacement No. 2 is in good condition. The magazine, shell room, etc., of Emplacement No. 1 have been very damp. Magazine No. 1 has been improved through the use of detached lead ceiling and brick walls, the hanging of doors, and the raising of the floor. An experiment is in progress to determine the practicability of artificially drying the magazine. The other defective chambers are being improved in similar manner.

A battery, mounting eight 12-inch mortars, was completed in 1898–99. Materials and plant pertaining to construction work have been removed and stored. This battery is in fair condition except as to the main gallery, the dynamo room, and the floors of guardrooms and firing chamber, which are damp. An allotment has been received for raising the floors of the guardrooms and firing room. Recently trifling leaks have developed in both powder magazines.

A battery, mounting two 8-inch guns on disappearing carriages, was completed in 1898–99. This battery is in good condition. Interplatform communications are being provided of concrete and steel. Doors are being hung at the entrances to magazines and shell rooms.

A battery, mounting two 4.7-inch rapid-fire guns, was completed in 1898–99. This battery is in good condition.

A battery, mounting four 15-pounder rapid-fire guns on balanced-pillar mounts, was completed and transferred to the artillery on April 30, 1901, the guns and carriages being transported to site by the Engineer Department and mounted by the artillery. The foot of the slope of this battery has been protected from wash by the waters of the lagoon by means of a concrete sea wall.

The defenses include two masonry works of old type, upon which minor repairs have been made during the year.

Minor repairs to plant and to all of the batteries were made, and a boathouse was begun for the naphtha launch belonging to the plant.

The torpedo plant and material received most careful attention and overhauling, and were transferred to the artillery in excellent condition on May 27, 1901.

A searchlight has been installed and connected electrically with the 8-inch battery.

Proposals have been solicited for wiring for exterior lighting.

From time to time electrical supplies were furnished on approved requisitions submitted by the acting engineer officer.

(See Appendix 3 P.)

Defenses of Mobile and of Mississippi Sound.—Officer in charge, Maj. William T. Rossell, Corps of Engineers; assistant, Lieut. Meriwether L. Walker, Corps of Engineers, from January 26 to April 6, 1901; Division Engineer, Col. Peter C. Hains, Corps of Engineers.

These defenses consist of three works of the older type, two of which are in charge of ordnance sergeants, and of modern works:

FORTIFICATIONS.

Site No. 1.—Contains the following batteries:

A battery of two 12-inch B. L. rifles mounted on disappearing carriages.

A battery of eight 12-inch B. L. steel mortars.

A battery of four 8-inch B. L. steel rifles mounted on disappearing carriages.

A battery of two 4.7-inch Armstrong rapid-fire guns on pedestal mountings.

A battery of two 15-pounder rapid-fire guns on balanced-pillar mountings.

Site No. 2.—Contains the following batteries:

A battery of two 8-inch B. L. rifles mounted on modified 15-inch Rodman carriages.

A battery of two 6-inch rapid-fire guns mounted on disappearing carriages.

A battery of two 15-pounder rapid-fire guns on balanced-pillar mountings.

At the beginning of the fiscal year all the batteries at Site No. 1 had been completed and turned over to the artillery, with the exception of the mortar battery. At Site No. 2 only the 8-inch battery had been turned over to the artillery.

At the beginning of the fiscal year work on the mortar battery was finished with the exception of a small amount of concrete, completion of sand parapet, and a few minor details. During the fiscal year all needed sand was filled in parapet; the parapet was then covered with clay and sodded with Bermuda grass; observation stations with stairways leading to them constructed, completing concrete work of battery; installation of electric plant finished, including all minor details; all ironwork repainted; wire fence built around battery, with stiles conveniently placed; plank walks built in rear of battery and assembled parts of mortar carriages cleaned. The battery was finally turned over to the artillery on May 20, 1901.

Concrete work on the 6-inch battery was complete at the beginning of the fiscal year, except building stairways and walk in rear of battery, and the greater part of concrete framing had been removed. During the fiscal year the stairways and walk were built and remaining concrete framing removed, all sand filled in parapet and parapet graded and sodded, ammunition cranes and trolley system installed, and electric plant also installed. Other minor details of battery were completed and the emplacements turned over to the artillery May 20, 1901. An allotment was made by the Chief of Engineers for mounting carriages on these emplacements and this work will be done during the early part of the next fiscal year.

Work on the 15-pounder emplacements at Site No. 2 was all performed during the fiscal year, including connection with the 6-inch battery electric plant from which electric power for this battery will be supplied. This battery was turned over to the artillery on May 20, 1901.

With funds allotted from appropriation for "Sea Walls and Embankments," 556 linear feet of shore protection and 83 feet of riprap ending was constructed at Site No. 1 and proposals invited and received and contract prepared for the building of about 200 linear feet of shore protection to the westward of sea wall heretofore constructed at Site No. 2.

The various defensive works were repaired and preserved, as occasion required, with funds from appropriation for "Preservation and Repair of Fortifications." The submarine-mining material was regularly inspected and kept in serviceable condition, and all of it finally turned over to the artillery on June 15, 1901.

(See Appendix 3 Q.)

Defenses of New Orleans, La., and of Sabine Pass, Tex.—Officers in charge, Lieut. Col. Henry M. Adams, Corps of Engineers, until June 8, 1901, and Lieut. Edward M. Adams, Corps of Engineers, in temporary charge since that date; assistant, Lieut. Edward M. Adams, Corps of Engineers, from September 17, 1900, to June 8, 1901; Division Engineer, Col. Henry M. Robert, Corps of Engineers (now brigadier-general, Chief of Engineers, United States Army, retired), until April 30, 1901.

New Orleans, La.—The defenses of New Orleans include several masonry works of old type and the following modern emplacements:

One battery of two 10-inch B. L. rifles, disappearing carriages.
Two batteries of two 8-inch B. L. rifles each, disappearing carriages.
One battery of two 4.7-inch rapid-fire guns, pedestal mounts.
Two batteries of two 15-pounder rapid-fire guns each, pillar mounts.

Emplacements for two additional 15-pounder rapid-fire guns are practically completed, but guns not mounted.

During the past fiscal year emplacements for four 15-pounder rapid-fire guns were completed and turned over to the care of the artillery. The construction of two additional emplacements for 15-pounder rapid-fire guns was commenced and carried as far toward completion as possible to do in advance of the receipt of the guns and carriages.

Plans and estimates for four emplacements for 6-inch rapid-fire guns were prepared and funds allotted. Work on the construction of two of these emplacements was commenced toward the end of the year.

Efforts were made to purchase additional land for sites, but the owner could not offer a valid title, and the land is to be acquired by condemnation.

Funds were allotted for the repair and raising of a levee, and preparations for commencing the work, when stage of water permits, were made.

Iron hand rails were placed upon platforms of the base-end stations of the range and position finders.

The location of electric-light wires and poles was changed, owing to the construction of new buildings. Electrical supplies were purchased and issued to the artillery.

The superior slopes of the 10-inch and 8-inch emplacements were repaired and additional drains were provided. Minor repairs were made as far as permitted by funds available. Parts of the machinery and ironwork were painted.

The torpedo material was overhauled, inspected, and cared for. Civilian watchmen were employed to care for it.

Sabine Pass, Tex.—No work was done at this locality. The temporary works built during the war with Spain had been abandoned during the previous year. The torpedo property was cared for until in June, 1901, when it was transferred to Galveston Harbor.

(See Appendix 3 R.)

Defenses of Galveston, Tex.—Officer in charge, Capt. Charles S. Riché, Corps of Engineers; assistant, Lieut. Meriwether L. Walker,

FORTIFICATIONS. 31

Corps of Engineers, since April 7, 1901; Division Engineers, Col. Henry M. Robert, Corps of Engineers (now brigadier-general, Chief of Engineers, United States Army, retired), until April 30, 1901, and Col. Amos Stickney, Corps of Engineers, since May 9, 1901.

It was hoped that the 12-inch mortar battery No. 2 and the 15-pounder rapid-fire battery No. 2 would be completed and the mortars and guns mounted during the fiscal year, but the disastrous hurricane of September 8, 1900, was so destructive that no further extensive operations upon the fortification work were attempted during the year.

The batteries and property which at the beginning of the present fiscal year had been reported as complete, and had been transferred to the artillery for their care and use, were, on September 17, 1900, in accordance with telegraphic instructions of the Secretary of War, dated September 16, 1900, retransferred by the artillery to the charge of the Engineer Department.

The condition of these batteries was as follows:

Emplacements for two 10-inch guns, battery No. 1: This battery was practically a total wreck. The central portion was level. Both gun platforms were down and guns were leaning.

Emplacements for two 10-inch guns, battery No. 2: All sheet piling and riprap revetment, sand protection, and sand from under the battery were washed away. The concrete portion of battery was standing on piling, with water underneath. The guns were standing.

Emplacements for eight 12-inch mortars, battery No. 1: This battery was practically a total wreck. The magazines were falling in and the sand protection was nearly all washed away. The mortars were standing.

Emplacements for two 8-inch guns: All sheet piling and riprap revetment, sand protection, and sand from under the battery were washed away. All the concrete portion of battery except the east gun platform, which has cracked off, was standing on piling, with water underneath. The east gun was leaning. The west gun was standing.

Emplacements for two 4.7-inch rapid-fire guns: All sheet piling and riprap revetment, sand protection, and sand from under the battery were washed away. The concrete portion of the battery was standing on piling, with water underneath. The guns were standing.

Emplacements for two 15-pounder rapid-fire guns, battery No. 1: All sheet piling and riprap revetment, sand protection, and sand from under the battery were washed away. The concrete portion of the battery was standing on piling, with water underneath.

Emplacements for three 15-pounder rapid-fire guns: All sheet piling and riprap revetment, sand protection, and sand from under the battery were washed away. The concrete portion of the battery was standing on piling, with water underneath.

The electric light and power plants at 10-inch gun battery No. 1 and at 12-inch mortar battery No. 1 were practically ruined by water. The oil engines can be repaired.

The condition of the uncompleted batteries not transferred to the artillery, after the hurricane, was as follows:

Emplacements for eight 12-inch mortars, battery No. 2: All sheet piling and riprap revetment, sand protection, and sand from under the battery were washed away. The concrete portion of the battery was standing on piling, with water underneath. The mortars and carriages were on hand, not mounted, and were buried in sand.

Emplacements for two 15-pounder rapid-fire guns, battery No. 2:

All sheet piling and riprap revetment, sand protection, and sand from under the battery were washed away. The concrete portion of the battery was standing on piling, with water underneath. Two guns were on hand, not mounted, and were buried in the sand.

The mining casemate is a total loss. The torpedo storehouse was swept away, also the cable tank house. Nearly all the torpedo property was lost; many of the mines have been re-covered. The cable tank was not damaged and the cable stored in it was not lost. The system of tracks for handling torpedo property was practically destroyed.

As soon as possible after the hurricane forces were put to work clearing away wreckage, recovering property, and cleaning and oiling guns, carriages, and equipment.

With funds supplied by the Ordnance Department, all the ordnance on hand has been cared for and preserved from deterioration.

The batteries left standing on piling have been protected from the action of the teredo by pumping sand underneath them, and at the close of the fiscal year all batteries are safe from this danger.

A report of a Board of Engineers as to the damages to fortifications in Galveston Harbor, and estimates for reconstructing and repairing same is printed in the report for 1901 for the Galveston district.

By act of Congress approved March 1, 1901, the sum of $992,000 was appropriated for the reconstruction and repair of fortifications, Galveston, Tex. At the close of the fiscal year plans and specifications had been prepared and forwarded for approval, and the overhauling and repairing of plant and construction of field offices was underway.

(See Appendix 3 S.)

Defenses of lake ports.—Officers in charge of defenses of the Detroit River: Lieut. Col. Garret J. Lydecker, Corps of Engineers, until January 3, 1901, and Maj. Walter L. Fisk, Corps of Engineers, since that date; Division Engineers, Col. John W. Barlow, Corps of Engineers (now brigadier-general, Chief of Engineers, United States Army, retired), from January 3 to May 1, 1901, and Col. Samuel M. Mansfield, Corps of Engineers, since May 9, 1901. Officers in charge of defenses of Lake Champlain: Col. John W. Barlow, Corps of Engineers (now brigadier-general, Chief of Engineers, United States Army, retired), until May 1, 1901, and Capt. Harry Taylor, Corps of Engineers, since that date; assistant, Lieut. Robert R. Raymond, Corps of Engineers, since May 31, 1901; Division Engineer, Col. Charles R. Suter, Corps of Engineers, since May 9, 1901. Officers in charge of defenses of other lake ports in New York: Capt. Graham D. Fitch, Corps of Engineers, until April 24, 1901, and Maj. Thomas W. Symons, Corps of Engineers, since that date; Division Engineers, Col. George L. Gillespie, Corps of Engineers (now brigadier-general, Chief of Engineers, United States Army), until April 30, 1901, and Col. Charles R. Suter, Corps of Engineers, since May 9, 1901.

These consist of four works of older type—two of which are garrisoned, one is in the charge of an ordnance sergeant, and one is in the charge of an ordnance sergeant with a fort keeper employed to care for public property stored there.

Operations during the year consisted of repair to shore protection at one fort and of repairs to fences at another.

(See Appendix 3 T.)

FORTIFICATIONS. 33

Defenses of San Diego, Cal.—Officer in charge, Capt. James J. Meyler, Corps of Engineers; Division Engineers, Col. Samuel M. Mansfield, Corps of Engineers, to November 23, 1900, and Col. Jared A. Smith, Corps of Engineers, since December 15, 1900.

At the beginning of the fiscal year, the modern fortification works consisted of—

Emplacements for four 10-inch B. L. guns on disappearing carriages, completed and armed.

Emplacements for two 15-pounder rapid-firing guns on balanced-pillar mounts, completed except the gun platforms and one blast surface.

Emplacements for two 5-inch rapid-fire guns on balanced-pillar mounts, completed except the gun platforms and a few minor details.

Battery commander's station, in progress of construction.

Mining casemate, cable tank, and torpedo storehouse, completed and torpedo material stored in same.

During the fiscal year the roadway and terreplein in rear of the 10-inch battery were regraded and the cement shed and construction plant were removed from the parade. At the 15-pounder battery one apron was built and the gun platforms partially completed. The gun carriages for the 5-inch battery were received, the gun platforms were completed, and the carriages were mounted by the artillery. This battery was turned over to the artillery on November 17, 1900. The battery commander's station was completed and turned over to the artillery on the same day. Under date of November 9, 1900, an allotment was made for the construction of two emplacements for 15-pounder rapid-fire guns, but the work of construction of this battery was delayed to enable the Department to acquire additional land. On July 27, 1900, an allotment was made for the construction of three datum points for range finders. These datum points have been completed. Regular inspections were made of the torpedo material and the same kept in order. The mining casemate, cable tank, and torpedo storehouse and all torpedo material were turned over to the care of the artillery on May 31, 1901.

With funds allotted from appropriation for "Preservation and Repair of Fortifications," minor repairs and changes were made in the 10-inch battery, and leaks were stopped and dampness corrected in rooms and passages of same.

A survey was made of the northerly end of the military reservation, preparatory to turning a portion of the land over to the Navy Department for use as a coaling station, a small area being reserved for the use of the War Department. A survey was also made of the additional land required.

(See Appendix 3 U.)

Defenses of San Francisco, Cal.—Officer in charge, Lieut. Col. Charles E. L. B. Davis, Corps of Engineers; assistant, Lieut. George B. Pillsbury, Corps of Engineers, from August 1, 1900, to June 22, 1901; Division Engineers, Col. Samuel M. Mansfield, Corps of Engineers, to November 23, 1900, and Col. Jared A. Smith, Corps of Engineers, from December 15, 1900, to May 3, 1901. Officer in charge of torpedo defenses, Lieut. Col. William H. Heuer, Corps of Engineers.

The old defenses included two masonry works and a number of

earthen barbette batteries of old type at various points in the harbor, while eleven platforms have been built for 8-inch converted rifles.

At the close of the last fiscal year the modern defenses consisted of a pneumatic dynamite battery of three 15-inch guns, thirty-two 12-inch mortars mounted in two batteries, a battery of sixteen 12-inch mortars, practically completed, eleven 12-inch emplacements, completed and all guns mounted; two 12-inch gun emplacements, completed with guns and carriages ready for mounting; two 12-inch gun emplacements, under construction and almost completed; five emplacements for 10-inch guns, completed and all of the guns mounted; six emplacements for 8-inch guns, completed and all of the guns mounted; two emplacements for 8-inch guns, almost completed; two emplacements for 6-inch rapid-fire guns on disappearing carriages, completed and the carriages mounted, guns not received; five emplacements for 5-inch rapid-fire guns on pillar mounts, carried as far as could be before mounts are received; four emplacements for 5-inch Brown segmental wire-wound guns, completed except setting base rings, which had not been received; and five range-finder stations, type A, completed.

During the year the work of construction was as follows:

A battery for sixteen 12-inch mortars was entirely completed, four carriages mounted, and two additional carriages ready for mounting; preliminary arrangements for commencing work on a battery for eight 12-inch mortars were being made; two 12-inch guns and carriages were mounted; two emplacements for 12-inch guns were entirely completed, except setting base rings, which were not received; base rings were set in two emplacements for 8-inch guns; an ammunition hoist was installed, a tool room built, and gun and carriage mounted in one of these 8-inch emplacements; five emplacements for 5-inch rapid-fire guns on pillar mounts were completed and the carriages were being mounted; work was commenced on two emplacements for 15-pounder guns and on changing azimuth circles of a mortar battery with mortars of model 1891; two shelters and power houses for 30-inch searchlights were completed; a wharf and tramway were built and work started on several new engineer buildings; a considerable amount of alteration work was done on electric-lighting plants and a new steamer was in course of construction under contract, and land was purchased and paid for for a new site for fortifications.

At the torpdo station the keeper, with such assistance as was necessary, kept the station in good order and made minor repairs during the year.

The roof of the torpedo shed, which was damaged by a windstorm, was repaired, and the keeper's dwelling, which was injured by a landslide, was removed to a more secure location and put in repair.

Much torpedo material was received from the depot and all the obsolete material was either shipped to the depot or condemned and sold.

The buildings are in good condition.

(See Appendix 3 V.)

Defenses of the mouth of the Columbia River.—Officer in charge, Capt. William W. Harts, Corps of Engineers, to August 18, 1900, and Capt. William C. Langfitt, Corps of Engineers, since that date; Division Engineer, Col. Samuel M. Mansfield, Corps of Engineers, to November 23, 1900, and Col. Jared A. Smith, Corps of Engineers, since December 15, 1900.

With the new works are included two works of the old type, with two serviceable 15-inch smoothbore guns (one unmounted) and two serviceable 8-inch converted rifles mounted on front-pintle carriages.

At the close of the fiscal year there had been completed six emplacements for 10-inch rifles on disappearing carriages, three emplacements for 8-inch rifles on disappearing carriages (one experimental carriage not then received), one mortar battery of eight 12-inch rifled mortars on spring-return carriages, four emplacements for 6-inch B. L. rifles on disappearing carriages, and four emplacements for 15-pounder rapid-fire guns on balanced-pillar mounts. There had been also been constructed two electric-light stations, two mining casemates, one torpedo storehouse, two cable tanks, and a wooden platform for 15-inch smoothbore gun. All of the completed emplacements had been turned over to the artillery, and the condition of ordnance was as follows: Five 10-inch guns, mounted, one gun on hand, carriage not received; eight 12-inch mortars, mounted; two 8-inch guns, mounted, one gun on hand, carriage not received; four 6-inch carriages, mounted, guns not received.

During the fiscal year two additional emplacements for 15-pounder rapid-fire guns on balanced-pillar mounts were completed, and these, as well as the two electric-light stations, two mining casemates, one torpedo storehouse, and two cable tanks, including all submarine-mining material, were transferred to the artillery.

Plans and estimates have been approved and allotment was made on June 8, 1901, for the construction of two emplacements for 6-inch rapid-fire guns on Ordnance Department pedestal mounts, the previous allotment having been withdrawn. Assembling the material and preparations for beginning this work are in progress. One serviceable 15-inch smoothbore gun was dismounted to allow of this emplacement being constructed.

Changes in the drainage and water-supply systems affecting the 10-inch and 6-inch batteries were authorized and completed, and storage battery moved from emplacement No. 3 to No. 5 of the 10-inch battery. Details in connection with change of wiring and completion of the electric lighting of the emplacements were attended to, and mixer building, trestles, tracks, etc., removed and grounds cleared of all débris.

For the completed emplacements of modern type the ordnance is now all mounted except four 6-inch rifles, not yet received, and four 15-pounders, guns and mounts not yet received.

(See Appendix 3 W.)

Defenses of Puget Sound, Washington.—Officers in charge, Capt. Harry Taylor, Corps of Engineers, until November 30, 1900, and Maj. John Millis, Corps of Engineers, since that date; assistant, Lieut. Meriwether L. Walker, Corps of Engineers, till January 19, 1901; Division Engineers, Col. Samuel M. Mansfield, Corps of Engineers, until November 30, 1900, and Col. Jared A. Smith, Corps of Engineers, since December 15, 1900.

At the close of the last fiscal year emplacements for nine 10-inch guns and four 12-inch guns on nondisappearing carriages, and for four 10-inch guns on disappearing carriages, and two mortar batteries for sixteen 12-inch mortars each, had been practically completed. Emplacements for four 5-inch rapid-fire guns on balanced pillar mounts had been completed as far as practicable before the receipt of the mounts, emplacements for two 5-inch rapid-fire guns had been partly completed, and emplacements for three 8-inch guns on disappearing carriages had been commenced.

Plans and estimates had been prepared for three emplacements for 10-inch guns on disappearing carriages, for a mortar battery for sixteen 12-inch mortars, for emplacements for two 6-inch rapid-fire guns, and for emplacements for two 5-inch rapid-fire guns and for two 15-pounder rapid-fire guns. These plans and estimates had been in part approved.

A storehouse for torpedo material had been partly constructed, and a temporary storage basin for cable had been built.

There had been mounted complete three 10-inch and two 12-inch guns on nondisappearing carriages, four 10-inch guns on disappearing carriages, and sixteen 12-inch mortars. Carriages for four 10-inch guns and one 12-inch gun, nondisappearing, and for ten 12-inch mortars had also been mounted.

One 10-inch gun, sixteen 12-inch mortars, and two mortar carriages had been received, but were not mounted.

During the year construction work on gun and mortar emplacements was as follows:

Emplacements for three 10-inch guns on disappearing carriages, commenced; for three 8-inch guns on disappearing carriages, nearly finished; for two 5-inch rapid-fire guns on balanced-pillar mounts, practically finished; for two 5-inch guns, mounts not determined, partly built (complete battery to be for three guns); for two 15-pounder rapid-fire guns, partly built; for two 15-pounder rapid-fire guns, commenced; and for four 15-pounder rapid-fire guns, commenced. A battery for eight 12-inch mortars was commenced.

There were mounted complete one 12-inch gun and six 10-inch guns on nondisappearing carriages, and sixteen 12-inch mortars. The cylinders for six 5-inch rapid-fire guns were set, and the top carriages of three of them placed, the latter being partly done by the artillery troops. One 12-inch gun, three 8-inch guns, and eight mortar carriages not mounted were on hand at the close of the year.

A considerable amount of finishing work about the several completed batteries was done, consisting of grading and trimming slopes, laying drains, and road construction.

Contract has been made for two fire commanders' stations and one battery commander's station, and plans have been prepared for one fire commander's station and one battery commander's station in addition.

The torpedo storehouse was practically completed except heating and lighting plant, and the material was stored in it.

(See Appendix 3 X.)

Defenses of San Juan, P. R.—Officers in charge, Capt. William V. Judson, Corps of Engineers, until August 6, 1900, and Capt. Clement A. F. Flagler, Corps of Engineers, since October 19, 1900.

Plans and estimates were prepared for the conversion of a semaphore tower on El Moro into a practice station for a type-A range finder.

Some repairs were made on the masonry work of El Moro.

(See Appendix 3 Y.)

EQUIPMENT OF ENGINEER TROOPS AND CIVILIAN ASSISTANTS TO ENGINEER OFFICERS.

By act of Congress approved May 26, 1900, the sum of $25,000 was appropriated for the equipment of engineer troops in the field, for the procurement of ponton trains, intrenching tools, instruments, drawing materials, etc., and the sum of $25,000 for civilian assistants to engineer officers serving on the staffs of division, corps, and department commanders, to enable them to secure the employment of surveyors, draftsmen, photographers, and clerks. Both appropriations are limited to the fiscal year 1901. Of the appropriation for equipment of engineer troops there was allotted $24,943.88, leaving a balance of $56.12, which will revert to the Treasury. Of the appropriation for civilian assistants to engineer officers there was allotted $15,862.50, leaving a balance of $9,137.50, which will revert to the Treasury.

With the funds appropriated for the purposes above stated engineering supplies have been furnished, mainly through the Engineer Depot at Willets Point, N. Y., for the various military departments in the United States, the Philippines, and Porto Rico, and the several engineer officers of important military commands and departments have been supplied with the necessary civilian assistants.

For the fiscal year ending June 30, 1902, there was appropriated by the army appropriation act of March 2, 1901, $20,000 for equipment of engineer troops and $25,000 for civilian assistants to engineer officers, and the sum of $25,000 each for engineer equipment of troops and for civilian assistants to engineer officers is estimated as required for the next fiscal year. The title "Engineer Equipment of Troops" is now adopted in the estimates in lieu of "Equipment of Engineer Troops" for the former item of appropriation, for the reason that it has been found necessary to provide engineer equipment to troops of the Army other than the battalions of engineers.

For details of expenditures under these appropriations see Appendixes No. 3 Y, 5, and 6.

ESTIMATES OF APPROPRIATIONS REQUIRED FOR 1902–1903.

Fortifications.

For gun and mortar batteries:		
For construction of gun batteries	$4,000,000	
For installation of range and position finders	150,000	
		$4,150,000
For sites for fortifications and seacoast defenses		2,000,000
For searchlights for harbor defenses:		
For purchase and installation of searchlights	500,000	
For installation of post mains and conduits	500,000	
		1,000,000
For protection, preservation, and repair of fortifications		300,000
For preparation of plans for fortifications		5,000
For supplies for seacoast defenses		25,000
For sea walls and embankments		150,000
For filling in Fort Delaware Reservation		120,000

For torpedoes for harbor defense:
  For the purchase of submarine mines and necessary appliances to operate them; for closing the channels leading to our principal seaports including our island possessions; for needful casemates, cable galleries, etc., to render it possible to operate submarine mines, and for continuing torpedo experiments $100,000
  For tugboat, to transfer to the artillery 25,000
                                                                        ————— $125,000

    Total 7,875,000

For engineer equipment of troops.. 25,000
For civilian assistants to engineer officers 25,000

POST OF FORT TOTTEN, N. Y.

This post was under the command of Maj. John G. D. Knight, Corps of Engineers, until April 29, 1901, when he was relieved by Maj. William M. Black, Corps of Engineers.

During the year $7,202.45 were allotted for the repair of buildings, roads, and walks; $34,258 for a new artillery barracks; $6,909 for a new ordnance storehouse, and $775 for a boathouse. All of the new buildings were completed and occupied.

The older buildings on the post were built from time to time as funds became available, and the greater part of them are now practically unserviceable. To provide for the garrison required under the new conditions, viz, the engineer band, 3 companies of engineer troops, and 2 companies of artillery, and the extra officers under instruction at the Engineer School, with a total of 30 officers, there should be provided 9 sets of married officers quarters, one building for 8 unmarried officers, 1 administration and school building, 1 band barracks, 1 artillery barracks, and 1 addition to the quartermaster and commissary storehouse, and 5 buildings should be moved and refitted. The total estimated cost of the work is $163,000.

The post offers advantages for the Engineer School which are not found at any other military reservation. It should be enlarged, and for reason of sanitation and to gain some of the needed land, the marsh on its western and southern boundaries should be reclaimed and filled.

The total estimated cost of the land required and of filling and reclaiming 14 acres of marsh land is $114,000. It is believed that the importance of the post and school fully warrant the expenditures recommended.

UNITED STATES ENGINEER SCHOOL.

The engineer officer in command of the post of Fort Totten is the commandant of the school. The captains commanding the engineer companies on duty at the post are the instructors. The object of the school is to supplement the theoretical and primary course of engineering instruction given at the United States Military Academy, by theoretical and practical work, and by examination of works of engineering which are being carried on in the vicinity. The course is intended primarily for officers assigned to the Corps of Engineers, and secondarily for officers of other branches of the service who may desire to obtain a knowledge of special branches of the course. The usefulness of the school could be further extended by admitting officers of the National Guard for special instruction.

The regular work of the school was interrupted during the latter part of the fiscal year by the necessity for organizing and training the additional companies of engineer troops authorized by the act for the reorganization of the Army.

The work of compiling a field manual adapted to the requirements of our military system was begun, Chapters I, II, and III have been compiled, and are now under revision. Chapter IV has been commenced.

ENGINEER TROOPS.

Until March 2 the engineer troops of the garrison consisted of Companies C and D. Companies A, B, and E of the Battalion of Engineers were on duty in the Philippines. A detachment of 50 men from Companies C and D was stationed at West Point after the departure of Company E from that station July 24, en route for China. While en route the destination of Company E was changed to the Philippines. The duties of the engineer troops in the Philippines was most varied in character and is reported elsewhere. A detachment of 1 officer and 20 enlisted men from Companies A and B accompanied the Pekin relief expedition, and performed varied service in addition to taking an active part on the firing line in the attacks on Tientsin and Pekin.

The duties of the companies in the United States are detailed in the report of the commanding officer.

In the reorganization prescribed in accordance with the act approved February 2, 1901, the First Battalion of Engineers was formed in the Philippines from the companies serving there, and the new companies were designated A, B, C, and D. The Second Battalion was formed from Companies C and D at Fort Totten, and the new companies designated E, F, G, and H. The companies of the Third Battalion were formed as follows: I, K, and L from a detachment of 45 men from former Companies C and D (of whom 11 were absent on detached service and furlough), after the departure of the Second Battalion for the Philippines June 17, and M from the detachment at West Point. At the end of the fiscal year the nucleus of the companies serving at Fort Totten was organized provisionally as Company I, to be divided as soon as the number of men available should be sufficient to provide an organization for the three companies. Before its departure the Second Battalion was instructed as fully as possible in its duties as engineer soldiers.

Under the organization of the Army the Engineer Battalions must be prepared to perform any or all classes of engineering work. Experience has shown that full measure of efficient engineer service can not be rendered at all times so long as the engineer troops under the present organization are habitually dismounted. In campaigns conducted by cavalry or mounted infantry, to which engineers are and should be attached, it would appear that the best interests of the service would be met if one company of each of the battalions of engineers be mounted and provided with the necessary pack animals for carrying equipment, etc. By such an organization it will always be possible to have a large detachment of engineer troops in the immediate advance, ready and prepared to do any kind of expert service required to facilitate the operations of troops, whether it be the demolition of obstacles, the repair of roads, the construction of bridges, or the collection of information with field sketches.

The facilities for instruction at Fort Totten are sufficient (providing additional area be obtained), with the exception of instruction in railroad construction and operation. For this a plant is required, the estimated cost of which is $10,000. The necessity for such instruction is evident, and the appropriation is recommended.

ENGINEER DEPOT.

The general property in the Engineer Depot has been cared for.

Materials, tools, etc., needed for current repairs and instruction of engineer troops; instruments for issue to officers engaged on public works and surveys, and professional works for library of Engineer School, have been purchased during the year at a total expense of $9,985.59.

Additions have been made to the ponton and bridge equipage by the purchase of materials needed, and three divisions of each advance guard and reserve ponton trains have been completed.

Work was undertaken in May to overhaul, assort, and repair the old ponton wagons, of which there have been about 659 in store since the close of the civil war. At the close of the fiscal year, 99 of these wagons were completed by hired labor and are now serviceable for use in the field. This work will be continued, and it is hoped that a large number of these old wagons will be made entirely serviceable.

A number of engineering models have been sent from the Engineer Museum to the Pan-American Exposition.

A new Engineering Field Manual was under preparation and the chapter on surveys and reconnaissance is practically completed.

Numerous purchases and issues have been made of intrenching tools, materials, instruments, and drawing materials for use of engineer troops serving in our island possessions. The cost of the materials so purchased amounted to $10,999.17.

The Second Battalion of Engineers was fitted out for service in the Philippines with astronomical and surveying instruments, reconnaissance and drafting materials, field photographic outfit, blacksmiths', carpenters', plumbers', and intrenching tools and materials, and a library of technical books.

Supplies for the four companies of the Third Battalion, recently organized, have been procured with the limited funds available at the close of the fiscal year.

Purchases to the amount of $87,982.70, from Philippine funds, have been made, consisting of materials for road construction, such as road rollers, road plows, carts, wagons, pile drivers, scows, and miscellaneous tools and hardware.

Purchases of submarine mining materials to supply deficiencies at various localities have been made, and the issues made during the year amounted to over 1,000,000 pounds.

Torpedo manuals of the several editions have been called in with a view to their transfer to the Artillery Corps.

STATEMENT OF FUNDS.

Congress has appropriated as follows:

I. For Engineer Depot at Willets Point, N. Y., for fiscal year ending June 30, 1899:
July 1, 1900, balance unexpended.................................. $1,350.00
June 30, 1901, expended during fiscal year....................... 1,350.00

II. For Engineer Depot at Willets Point, N. Y., for fiscal year ending June 30, 1900:
July 1, 1900, balance unexpended.................................. 753.09
August 6, 1900, turned into the Treasury............... $333.17
June 30, 1901, expended during fiscal year............ 419.92
                           753.09

III. For Engineer Depot at Willets Point, N. Y., for fiscal year ending June 30, 1901... 10,000.00
June 30, 1901, expended during fiscal year............. $8,373.41
June 30, 1901, amount pledged......................... 1,612.18
June 30, 1901, to be turned into the Treasury.......... 14.41
                          10,000.00

IV. Torpedoes for Harbor Defense:
 1. Act March 3, 1899, for "Torpedo Experiments"—
  July 1, 1900, balance unexpended............................. 2,715.76
  July 1, 1901, balance available............................... 1,808.72

 2. Act March 3, 1899, for "Purchase of Designated Classes of Torpedo Material"—
  July 1, 1900, balance unexpended 22,522.45
  June 30, 1901, expended during fiscal year 22,522.45

 3. Act May 25, 1900, for "Purchase of Submarine Mining Materials," etc.—
  July 13, 1900, amount allotted 16,500.00
  July 1, 1901, balance available............................... 2,922.28

 4. Act March 1, 1901, for "Purchase of Submarine Mining Materials," etc.—
  April 19, 1901, amount allotted 17,000.00
  July 1, 1901, balance available............................... 16,300.00

V. Equipment of Engineer Troops, 1900:
 1. For "Instruments," etc.—
  July 1, 1900, balance unexpended 811.70
  June 30, 1901, expended during fiscal year........... $782.10
  June 30, 1901, withdrawn during fiscal year.......... 29.60
                          811.70

 2. For "Fitting out Ponton Trains"—
  July 1, 1900, balance unexpended 906.91
  June 30, 1901, expended during fiscal year........... $904.09
  June 30, 1901, withdrawn during fiscal year.......... 2.82
                          906.91

Fiscal year, 1901—
 3. For "Instruments, Intrenching Tools," etc.:
  June 30, 1901, total of allotments received during fiscal year... 11,000.00
  July 1, 1901, balance available............................... .83

 4. For "Completing Ponton Trains:"
  June 30, 1901, total of allotments received during fiscal year... 8,250.00
  July 1, 1901, balance available............................... 6.46

VI. "Preservation and Repair of Fortifications:"
Act March 3, 1899, for "Purchase of Hygrometers and Thermometers"—
July 1, 1900, balance unexpended $424.16
June 30, 1901, amount expended and withdrawn during fiscal
year... 424.16

VII. Appropriation "Philippine Commission." Act One. Public Civil Funds, United States Military Government of the Philippines:
For "Materials for Road Construction in the Philippines"—
November 17, 1900, amount assigned 100,000.00
June 30, 1901, expended during fiscal year.... $87,982.70
June 17, 1901, transferred to disbursing agent
Philippine revenues, Washington, D. C..... 12,017.30
————— 100,000.00

NEW APPROPRIATIONS.

I. For Engineer Depot at Willets Point, N. Y., for fiscal year ending
June 30, 1902 .... $22,000.00
II. For Equipment of Engineer Troops, for fiscal year ending June 30, 1902. 9,000.00

ESTIMATES OF APPROPRIATIONS REQUIRED FOR 1902–1903.

The reservation at Willets Point, N. Y., having been found to be of insufficient extent to accommodate all the military interests centered there, has been transferred to the artillery since the close of the fiscal year 1901, and the engineer troops and school will be moved to Washington Barracks, D. C., within a few weeks, under orders of the Secretary of War, issued September 3, 1901. The Engineer Depot, or parts thereof, will also be moved from Willets Point to another post, or to other posts, before the next appropriation therefor becomes available.

UNITED STATES ENGINEER DEPOT.

For incidental expenses of the depot, including fuel, lights, chemicals, stationery, hardware, machinery, pay of civilian clerks, mechanics, and laborers, extra-duty pay to soldiers necessarily employed for periods not less than ten days as artificers on work in addition to and not strictly in the line of their military duties, such as carpenters, blacksmiths, draftsmen, printers, lithographers, photographers, engine drivers, telegraph operators, teamsters, wheelwrights, masons, machinists, painters, overseers, laborers; repairs of, and for materials to repair, public buildings, machinery, and unforeseen expenses................................. $10,000.00
For purchase and repair of instruments, to be issued to officers of the Corps of Engineers and to officers detailed and on duty as acting engineer officers, for use on public works and surveys.. 3,000.00
————— $13,000.00

UNITED STATES ENGINEER SCHOOL.

For equipment and maintenance of the United States Engineer School at Washington Barracks, D. C., including purchase of instruments, implements, and materials for use of the school and for instruction of engineer troops in their special duties as sappers and miners; for land and submarine mines, pontoniers, torpedo drill, and signaling; for purchase and binding of professional works of recent date treating of military and civil engineering and kindred scientific subjects, for the library of the United States Engineer School; for incidental expenses of the school, including fuel, lights, chemicals, stationery, hardware, machinery, and boats; for pay of civilian clerks, mechanics, and laborers; for extra-duty pay to soldiers necessarily employed for periods not less than ten days as artificers on work in addition to and not strictly in the line of their military duties, such as carpenters, blacksmiths, draftsmen, printers, lithographers, engine drivers, telegraph operators, teamsters, wheelwrights, masons, machinists, painters, overseers, laborers; repairs of, and for materials to repair, public buildings, machinery, and unforeseen expenses, and for travel expenses of officers on journeys approved by the Chief of Engineers and made for the purpose of instruction: *Provided*, That the traveling expenses herein provided for shall be in lieu of mileage and other allowances $40,000.00

To provide means for the theoretical and practical instruction at the United States Engineer School, by the purchase of text-books, books of reference, scientific and professional papers, and for other absolutely necessary expenses 5,000.00

$45,000.00

(See Appendix No. 5.)

OPERATIONS OF THE ENGINEER DEPARTMENT IN THE PHILIPPINES.

Officers in charge of the engineer department, Division of the Philippines: Maj. John Biddle, Corps of Engineers, to April 28, 1901; since that date, Maj. Clinton B. Sears, Corps of Engineers.

Officers on duty as assistants to the division engineer: First Lieut. Frederick W. Altstaetter, Corps of Engineers, to January 22, 1901; Capt. C. F. O'Keefe, Thirty-sixth Infantry, United States Volunteers, all year; First Lieut. Alvin R. Baskette, Thirty-seventh Infantry, United States Volunteers (now first lieutenant, Third Infantry, United States Army), since January 9, 1901; Second Lieut. George E. Stewart, Nineteenth United States Infantry (now first lieutenant, Fifteenth Infantry), since July 20, 1900.

Engineer officer, Department of Northern Luzon; Capt. George A. Zinn, Corps of Engineers, since September 6, 1900. Engineer officer, Department of Southern Luzon: First Lieut. John C. Oakes, Corps of Engineers, to May 28, 1901; First Lieut. Sherwood A. Cheney, Corps of Engineers, since that date.

I. FIRST BATTALION OF ENGINEERS.

This battalion was organized in Manila from the old Companies A, B, and E under authority of General Orders, No. 22, current series, Adjutant-General's Office. Maj. Clinton B. Sears, Corps of Engineers, was assigned to command by General Orders, No. 79, current series, Division of the Philippines. The designation of Company E was changed to Company C and a new Company D was organized by transferring men from the other three companies. The present strength of the battalion is 12 officers and 396 enlisted men.

The duties of the battalion during the year have been principally road reconnaissances and the construction and repair of roads, bridges, and ferries.

Lieut. Frederick W. Altstaetter, Corps of Engineers, was captured by the insurgents on August 1, 1900, and released on November 23, 1900.

On June 10, 1901, Lieut. Walter H. Lee, Corps of Engineers, was killed during an attack on the insurgent intrenchments near Lipa.

II. OFFICE WORK AND SUPPLY DEPARTMENT.

The office work has been the usual routine. The supply department has purchased (both in the United States and in the Philippines) large quantities of tools, lumber, and other materials for the construction of roads, bridges, and ferries.

III. MAP WORK.

The compilation of maps and reconnaissances has been continued throughout the year. Over 8,800 maps (chiefly blue prints) have been distributed throughout the division.

Instruments of various kinds have been issued to officers in the division for use in obtaining data for the compilation of maps.

IV. ROADS AND BRIDGES.

This work has been carried on under an appropriation from the island funds. Examinations of the roads and estimates for their repair were made by officers of the First Battalion of Engineers. The actual work was carried on under direction of officers of the Corps of Engineers so far as possible, but it was found necessary to obtain the services of officers of other branches of the service on account of the large amount of work to be done.

The Quartermaster's Department supplied transportation to the extent of 587 mules and 148 wagons.

About 700 miles of road in the island of Luzon have been repaired more or less completely or rebuilt entirely.

V. EXPENDITURES.

(a) Funds allotted by the Chief of Engineers:

"Civilian Assistants to Engineer Officers, 1901:"
Received		$7,000.00
Expenditures	$4,774.57	
Turned into subtreasury at San Francisco	2,225.43	
		7,000.00

"Equipment of Engineer Troops, 1901:"
Received		$3,000.00
Expenditures	$586.94	
Turned in to subtreasury at San Francisco	2,413.06	
		3,000.00

(b) Public civil funds:

Allotments from appropriation for construction of highways and bridges:
Amount received		$780,500.00
Expenditures:		
For tools, supplies, office expenses	$196,961.85	
For construction	549,985.72	
Balance on hand	33,552.43	
		780,500.00

VI. GENERAL REMARKS.

The military operations in the division for the year have been on a small scale and the services of engineer troops in the field have not been required. The road and bridge work, however, has been extensive and important. The lack of a sufficient number of engineer officers and troops has been a serious handicap in the prosecution of this work.

(See Appendix No. 6.)

SERVICE OF OFFICERS OF THE CORPS OF ENGINEERS IN THE FIELD, WITH TROOPS, AND AS OFFICERS OF UNITED STATES VOLUNTEERS, SINCE APRIL, 1898.

BRIG. GEN. GEORGE L. GILLESPIE.

May 26 to June 7, 1898.—Member of Board of officers to examine applicants for commissions in the First Regiment, United States Volunteer Engineers.

May 27, 1898.—Appointed brigadier-general, United States Volunteers.

June 3, 1898.—Assigned to First Army Corps, Chickamauga Park, Ga.

June 28, 1898.—Assigned to the command of the Department of the East, to relieve Brig. Gen. Royal T. Frank.

June 30, 1898.—Assumed command of the Department of the East.

October 4, 1898.—Relinquished command of the Department of the East.

October 31, 1898.—Honorably discharged from the Volunteer Army of the United States.

COL. PETER C. HAINS.

May 27, 1898.—Appointed brigadier-general of volunteers.

June 3, 1898.—Directed to report to Major-General Brooke, at Chickamauga Park, for assignment to duty with the troops in the camp which had been established there.

June 19, 1898.—Reported to General Brooke at Camp Thomas for duty and was assigned to the command of the Third Division of the First Army Corps.

June 29, 1898.—Was assigned to the command of the Second Brigade of the First Division of the First Army Corps, consisting of the Fourth Ohio, Fourth Pennsylvania, and Third Illinois Volunteer Infantry.

Remained in Camp Thomas getting the brigade into shape for operations in foreign parts until July 22, when the brigade departed for Porto Rico via Newport News. Arrived at the latter place Sunday, July 24, and embarked for Porto Rico on the 29th, the United States auxiliary cruiser *St. Paul* carrying the Fourth Ohio as well as brigade headquarters.

August 1, 1898.—The *St. Paul* arrived at Guanica, P. R., anchoring off the harbor. Was informed that the steamer *St. Louis*, with Major-General Brooke and staff on board and the Third Illinois Volunteer Infantry, had gone to Ponce. Left Guanica about 2 p. m. and arrived at Ponce about 5.30 p. m., August 1.

August 2, 1898.—The brigade left Ponce and proceeded to Arroyo, where it arrived about 10.30 a. m. During the two days following the landing of the brigade was effected by means of lighters.

August 5, 1898.—By direction of General Brooke, commanding the First Army Corps, left Arroyo at 7 a. m. with the Fourth Ohio Volunteers, Colonel Coit commanding, and 2 Sims-Dudley dynamite guns, to seize and hold the town of Guayama, about 5 miles to the westward. It was reported that the town was occupied by about 300 Spaniards. After a slight skirmish, in which 4 men were wounded, the town was captured. There is a good macadamized road leading from Guayama to San Juan. Preparations were made to advance on this road simultaneously with a column from Ponce composed of troops under command of Maj. Gen. J. H. Wilson. August 8, 1898, a reconnaissance was made by 2 companies of the Fourth Ohio on the main road to San Juan, which brought on an action at Las Palmas, in which 3 men were wounded.

By direction of Major-General Brooke the brigade remained in Guayama until the 13th, on which day an advance was made up the main road by a part of the brigade, while General Hains took 11 companies of the Fourth Ohio by a circuitous route to the left, with a view to reaching the flank and rear of the Spanish force, located on a high ridge about 5 miles beyond Guayama. The remainder of the brigade, together with several batteries of artillery and two or three troops of cavalry, was to proceed up the main road toward Cayey. The troops, after a hard march in a tropical sun, were recalled by the announcement that hostilities had been ordered to cease pending negotiations for peace. The command therefore returned to Guayama. Remained in camp at this place until August 25, when he received orders to return to the United States and resume his duties as member of the Nicaragua Canal Commission. Arrived in New York on September 6, on the transport *Chester*, which also conveyed the Fourth Pennsylvania Volunteer Infantry, one of the regiments of his brigade, en route to be mustered out of service.

September 14, 1898.—Took station at Baltimore, and resumed his duties as division engineer.

November 30, 1898.—Honorably discharged from the volunteer service.

LIEUT. COL. OSWALD H. ERNST.

May 27, 1898.—Appointed brigadier-general of volunteers.

June 3, 1898.—Ordered to Chickamauga Park.

June 13, 1898.—Arrived at Chickamauga Park and was assigned to the command of the First Brigade, First Division, First Army Corps. The division was commanded by Maj. Gen. J. H. Wilson, and the corps by Maj. Gen. John R. Brooke. The troops composing the brigade were the Third Wisconsin, the Fifth Illinois, and the First Kentucky, volunteer infantry regiments. In command of the brigade until October 17, 1898.

July 6, 1898.—Left Chickamauga by rail, the Fifth Illinois and the First Kentucky regiments having been replaced by the Second Wisconsin and the Sixteenth Pennsylvania regiments. After two weeks' detention in Charleston, S. C., Brigadier-General Ernst sailed July 21 with a portion of the brigade, the remainder sailing the next day.

July 26, 1898.—Reached Guanica, P. R. General Miles ordered the brigade to Ponce.

July 27, 1898.—Arrived at Ponce, P. R., disembarked, and went into camp.

The next few days were devoted to unloading the stores, wagons, and animals. Small expeditions were sent out to break up hostile rendezvous and capture arms in the vicinity. Particular care was given to instruction in outpost duty. The command was here supplied with the Krag-Jörgensen musket in place of the Springfield, with which it had previously been armed. A battalion of the Sixteenth Pennsylvania was pushed out to Juana Diaz, a town 8 miles from Ponce on the main military road to San Juan, and was supported by the remainder of the regiment encamped about midway between Ponce and Juana Diaz. The country beyond was carefully reconnoitered.

August 6, 1898.—The brigade moved forward on the San Juan road, the division commander being present and directing its movements. Attached to it were Battery B, Fourth Artillery, and Battery F, Third Artillery; also Troop C, Volunteer Cavalry, of Brooklyn, N. Y.

August 8, 1898.—The enemy was encountered in some force at Coamo, his strength being reported as about 400 well-seasoned Spanish troops in intrenchments. It was determined to attempt the capture of the entire force. The Sixteenth Pennsylvania was sent by a night march over a mountain trail to occupy the road in the rear of Coamo. Starting at 5 p. m. August 8, it was expected to be in position by 7 a. m. August 9, at which hour the main attack in front would begin. Promptly at the hour fixed on the morning of the 9th the main attack in front was opened by the artillery firing upon a blockhouse which obstructed the advance and which was destroyed after a feeble resistance. The Second and Third Wisconsin had been deployed and pushed forward into the town without meeting further opposition except that caused by the destruction of bridges and the natural difficulties of the ground, the enemy having determined to withdraw. In his attempt to do this he encountered the Sixteenth Pennsylvania and suffered severely. His loss in killed was 9, including the commanding officer. His wounded, many of whom he carried away, were supposed to number about 40. One hundred and sixty-seven prisoners were captured. The retreating enemy was pursued by Troop C. About 5 miles beyond Coamo, however, the pursuit was checked by artillery fire from the main Spanish position in front of Aibonito. Our loss in the affair of Coamo was 6 men wounded. With a different method of attack it might easily have exceeded that of the enemy. General Ernst was recommended by the division commander, General Wilson, and by the commander of the expedition, General Miles, for promotion to the grade of major-general of volunteers "for gallant and meritorious conduct in the engagement at Coamo, P. R., August 9, 1898."

The enemy's position in front of Aibonito was found to be one of the strongest military positions in the world. The force occupying it was reported to be 1,800 infantry and a battery of modern field guns, all well intrenched. A front attack being inexpedient, the approaches by either flank were carefully reconnoitered, Colonel Biddle and Lieutenant Pierce again taking the most active part in that work.

August 13, 1898.—The camps had been struck and the brigade was about to start on its flank march, the advance guard being in column on the road when orders were received to suspend operations, a peace protocol having been signed. It had been the intention to leave the artillery, the cavalry, and one battalion of infantry at Coamo, and to take all of the remaining infantry who were able to undergo a severe march, with such baggage and supplies as could be carried on 200 pack mules, and by mountain trails to move to the main road in rear of Aibonito, repeating on a larger scale the maneuver at Coamo.

Upon the suspension of operations the brigade settled down in its camp at Coamo, where it remained until the 1st of October. In the latter part of August the Second Wisconsin and Troop C were detached and sent back to the United States.

A battalion of the First Volunteer Engineers under Major Sewell joined the command temporarily, and was employed in repairing the bridges destroyed by the Spaniards in their retreat. During this period Colonel Ernst's attention was given to the preservation of peace between the inhabitants of the country, among whom party feeling had become much embittered.

About the end of September, arrangements for the evacuation of the island by the Spanish troops having been completed, Colonel Ernst occupied Aibonito and Cayey, each with one company of the Third Wisconsin, and sent detachments to the neighboring towns, his troops entering each town simultaneously with the departure of the Spaniards.

About the 1st of October the brigade was ordered to proceed, by easy marches, to San Juan. It began the movement, and had got as far as Cayey when it was met with orders to return to Ponce to take transports to the United States.

October 9, 1898.—He sailed for New York with the Sixteenth Pennsylvania in the transport *Minnewaska*, leaving the Third Wisconsin and the two batteries in camp at Ponce awaiting transportation. Upon arrival in New York orders were found for the Sixteenth Pennsylvania to proceed home to be mustered out, and railway trains in readiness for their transportation. The Third Wisconsin followed soon afterwards, and was disposed of in a similar manner.

October 17 to December 26, 1898.—On waiting orders at Washington, D. C.

December 20, 1898.—Order issued directing him to report for assignment to duty as inspector-general of Cuba, on the staff of Maj. Gen. John R. Brooke, military governor.

January 1, 1899.—Arrived at Habana, Cuba.

January 2, 1899.—Assigned as Inspector-General of the Division of Cuba. His duties were of varied character, such as the payment of the Cuban army, and the controversy between the Marinao Railway and the Seventh Army Corps. Inspections of importance were upon occasion especially assigned to him. Remained at Habana until May 6, 1899.

June 12, 1899.—Honorably discharged from the Volunteer Army.

For his conduct in the Porto Rican campaign he was recommended for promotion by Maj. Gen. J. H. Wilson, commanding his division.

In a letter of Lieut. Gen. Nelson A. Miles, commanding the United States Army, to the honorable Secretary of War, July 7, 1900, he says:

I desire to place on record my opinion of the professional qualities of Col. Oswald H. Ernst, Corps of Engineers. During the Spanish-American war Colonel Ernst was brigadier-general of volunteers, commanding First Brigade, First Division, First Army Corps. He had his troops under excellent discipline, and his brigade, which was a part of the expeditionary force to Porto Rico July 28, 1898, was conspicuous in the affairs at Coamo, P. R., August 9, and continued to press the enemy at Aibonito until operations were suspended on August 13.

For his successful conduct of operations at Coamo he was mentioned in dispatches and recommended for promotion. He displayed in this engagement, and in the subsequent dispositions to turn the almost impregnable Spanish position at Aibonito—where the main force of the enemy held one of the strongest positions in the world—the highest tactical and strategical qualities of an accomplished general. His marked skill in the disposition of troops, his fertility of resource, and the power of command exhibited by him during the short term of hostilities, were of the first order; and I consider it a duty and a privilege to respectfully submit for consideration and record this judgment of a conspicuously efficient officer.

LIEUT. COL. WILLIAM LUDLOW.

April 18, 1898.—Appointed engineer officer on the staff of the Major General Commanding the Army.

May 4, 1898.—Appointed brigadier-general, United States Volunteers.

May 5, 1898.—Announced as chief engineer officer temporarily of the United States forces at Tampa, Fla., under the command of Brigadier-General Shafter.

Organized the engineer equipment, Fifth Army Corps, before the Santiago expedition left Tampa, June 14, 1898, and accompanied the expedition as an officer of General Miles's staff and "chief engineer of the army in the field."

June 14, 1898.—Sailed from Fort Tampa, Fla., on the transport *Segurança.*

June 22, 1898.—Landed at Daiquiri, Cuba; directed the landing of pontons loaded with tools.

June 23, 1898.—Was directed by General Shafter to proceed with the transport *Alamo* to Aserraderos and supervise the embarkation of General Garcia's army. A trestle was constructed out from the shore, 180 feet long, by the Engineer Battalion. The Cubans embarked on transports June 25, 1898, and were landed at Siboney June 26, 1898.

June 28, 1898.—Assigned to the command of the First Brigade, Second Division, Fifth Army Corps, and reported to General Lawton.

June 29, 1898.—Assumed command of brigade.

On the 30th, in connection with the division commander, General Lawton, and General Chaffee, commanding the Third Brigade, made an extended reconnaissance to the front and right, covering the ground from El Poso to Marianajay, the Ducrot House, and the country to the eastward of Caney, after which the plans of operations for the next day were determined.

July 1, 1898.—Occupied in fighting the battle of Caney. His brigade was to occupy the road leading westward from Caney toward Santiago and cut off the retreat of the garrison should it attempt to escape.

The artillery opened about 6.30 a. m. His brigade was moved rapidly toward Caney, and, arriving about 1,000 or 1,200 yards therefrom, was greeted by a sharp Mauser fire that swept the roads and cut leaves from the trees. The brigade was immediately deployed. The brigade moved steadily forward under a scorching fire that produced many casualties, although every endeavor was made to take advantage of cover, trees, hedges, grass, bushes, and the like. The enemy had made elaborate preparations, and the blockhouses, numerous intrenchments, and rifle pits, almost invisible, and multiplied loopholes in the houses gave them many points of vantage, in addition to which they had studied the range and the shooting was accurate and incessant. The dash and intrepidity of the men, however, could not be restrained, although they were constantly cautioned not to expose themselves, to aim deliberately, and not to fire unless at a definite object. They were also instructed to ignore the blockhouses as a waste of ammunition, and try to kill the men in the rifle pits or when exposed outside of them. For about three hours the firing from both brigades and from the garrison was very heavy, and the list of casualties shows how severe the work was. From 12 to 1 there was a lull, when the action again became violent, and at 3 p. m. the Third

Brigade (Chaffee) captured the stone fort with a rush, and hoisted the American flag. The garrison, however, held on until about 4.30 p. m., when the volley firing of a portion of General Ludlow's brigade into a sunken intrenchment in their front, which had done great execution among the American troops and had evidently been occupied by the best part of the garrison, compelled its evacuation. Among the captives was General Vara del Rey. As soon as the American dead and wounded and those of the enemy could receive due attention it was proposed to put the command in camp after a day of extraordinary exertion, but orders were received to take the road at once to the Ducrot House, thence toward Santiago. The brigade lay part of the night on the road west of the Ducrot House, without rations, and then was marched by a narrow, dark trail toward Marianajay, en route to El Poso and Santiago.

July 2 to 10, 1898.—The brigade held right of line and intrenched successively four brigade positions for investment of Santiago. On the night of July 5, 1898, made a reconnaissance toward the city and personally established an advanced trench commanding points at which the Spaniards were constructing fieldworks. Made daily reconnaissances to extend the line of the flanking movement. On July 11 held extreme position near head of bay.

August 5, 1898.—Relieved from duty at headquarters of the army at Ponce, P. R.

August 13, 1898.—Sailed from Santiago for Montauk Point, L. I., on transport *Mobile;* arrived there August 18.

September 7, 1898.—Commissioned major-general of volunteers.

September 7, 1898.—Appointed member of Board of officers to make regulations for the government of troops on transports. The Board made its report on October 26, 1898.

October 13, 1898.—Assigned to the command of the Second Division, First Army Corps, Columbus, Ga. In command until December 13, 1898.

December 13, 1898.—By direction of the President, was appointed military governor of Habana.

December 21, 1898.—Arrived at Habana, Cuba, and assumed the duties as military governor of the city of Habana.

December 30, 1898.—Assigned to the command of the Department of Habana, Cuba. His report dated August 1, 1899, is printed in the Annual Report of the Major-General Commanding the Army, 1899, part 1, page 214 et seq., and his report dated June 1, 1900, is printed in the Annual Report of the Major-General Commanding the Army, 1900, part 2, page 7 et seq.

Honorably discharged from the Volunteer Army of the United States to take effect April 13, 1899, to enable him to accept commission as general officer of volunteers under act of March 2, 1899.

Appointed by the President brigadier-general of volunteers under act approved March 2, 1899, with rank from April 13, 1899.

January 21, 1900.—Volunteer commission vacated.

Appointed by the President brigadier-general, United States Army, to take effect January 21, 1900.

LIEUT. COL. WILLIAM R. LIVERMORE.

April 23, 1898.—Favorably recommended by the Chief of Engineers for appointment as brigadier-general of volunteers.

May 9, 1898.—Appointed chief engineer, with rank of lieutenant-colonel, United States Volunteers.

June 3, 1898, to March 10, 1899.—Assigned as chief engineer, Seventh Army Corps. Laid out encampments for about 50,000 men with great success, and rendered assistance to officers of other departments in the construction and arrangement of buildings, etc.

October 4, 1898, until November 11, 1898.—Appointed member of commission of officers for locating camps, etc., in Cuba, on which duty visited Cuba October 9 to November 12, 1898.

December 13, 1898.—Arrived at Habana with Seventh Army Corps.

January 24 to March 10, 1899.—Assigned as engineer officer, Department of the province of Habana.

March 10, 1899.—Detailed as military attaché to the United States legations at Copenhagen, Denmark, and Stockholm, Sweden; stationed at Copenhagen, Denmark, since April 28, 1899, collecting information and report upon military subjects—seacoast defenses of Norway; field artillery in Sweden; new inventions of small arms; competitive trial of rapid-fire field artillery; maneuvers in Denmark—and visiting arsenals, engineer establishments, factories, shops, exhibits in Scandinavia, Germany, and at Paris.

May 12, 1899.—Honorably discharged from the Volunteer Army.

MAJ. CLINTON B. SEARS.

February 9, 1901.—Appointed a member of Board on improvement of harbor of Guam, vice Biddle, and on completion of that duty was ordered to proceed to Manila.

February 20, 1901.—Relieved from duty at Duluth, Minn.

March 15, 1901.—Sailed from San Francisco on transport *Indiana*.

April 15, 1901.—Arrived at Manila.

April 16, 1901.—Reported for duty to the commanding general, Division of the Philippines.

April 22, 1901.—Assigned to duty as engineer officer, Division of the Philippines.

April 25, 1901.—Relieved from duty as member of Board on improvement of the harbor of Guam.

April 26, 1901.—Charged with the organization and command of the First Battalion of Engineers.

April 27, 1901.—Relieved Capt. John Biddle as engineer officer, Division of the Philippines.

The duties of this office include a general supervision of all civil and military engineering works carried on in the Philippine Islands under direction of the military governor. The civil works include at present the improvement of the harbor of Manila and of the Pasig River and the construction of military roads and bridges in the islands, as far as available funds will permit, under allotments made by the civil commission and approved by the military governor.

In the works of construction and repair of roads and bridges the three companies of engineer troops, namely, A, B, and E, are employed under various lieutenants of engineers now on duty in the islands, the companies being broken up into small squads and scattered throughout the island of Luzon.

The work has been pushed forward with as great diligence as the conditions would permit, the various roads being constructed under the immediate direction of the officers of engineers or under quartermasters or line officers detailed for the purpose. Great difficulty has been encountered in getting labor, material, and plant. Notwithstanding these difficulties, however, a great deal of good work has been done.

June 7 to June 30, 1901.—Accompanied Major-General Chaffee, U. S. A., on a tour of inspection from Manila to Cotabato, island of Mindanao, and return, visiting the most important intermediate posts on the coasts, going and returning. Some twenty-five places were officially visited, and upon twenty-two of these written reports were submitted to Major-General Chaffee immediately upon return to the transport. These reports in each instance described the harbor and its essential points as to depths, area, outlines, anchorage, and safe weathering facilities, the general nature of the terrain for 5 miles or more about the post, the character and conditions of the roads, bridges, and trails leading out from the place, the character of the surrounding country as to affording facilities for the operations of artillery; upon itineraries and reconnaissance maps made at the place under direction of the commanding officer; as to minerals, such as the precious metals, coal, oil, etc., reported as existing in the neighborhood, and any other matters of commercial interest which fell under his observation.

MAJ. WILLIAM M. BLACK.

May 9, 1898.—Appointed chief engineer, with the rank of lieutenant-colonel, United Stated Volunteers.

May 25 to June 8, 1898.—Assigned as chief engineer, Third Army Corps, under Major-General Wade, Camp G. H. Thomas, Chickamauga Park. Principal duties, the instruction of volunteer troops in reconnaissance.

June 10, 1898.—Transferred as chief engineer, Fifth Army Corps.

June 11, to December 2, 1898.—On special duty under the Major-General Commanding the Army, and disbursing officer of the appropriation for expeditionary force to Cuba.

Until July 11, 1898.—On duty at Tampa, Fla. Organized a Provisional Battalion of Engineers and trained them in their duties as pontoniers. Bought and shipped engineering material for the expeditionary force to Porto Rico.

July 12, 1898.—Left Tampa on the steamer *Lampasas* with the provisional battalion, the materials for the engineer train, and the ponton train, under orders to join the commanding general at Santiago, Cuba.

July 19, 1898.—Arrived at Guantanamo, and the battalion built a ponton pier for landing the stock from the transports. On the 21st this pier was dismantled, and the materials reshipped.

July 25, 1898.—Commanded the first landing party from the army at Guanica, which captured that place.

July 29, 1898.—Arrived at Port Ponce, and on duty in Porto Rico until September 8, in charge of various engineering works in connection with the armies in the field; unloading transports, boat service, gathering materials for a pier, buoying the harbor, care of the engineer depot, forwarding tools and materials to the troops at the front, road construction, etc.

September 19, 1898—Reported for duty at Headquarters of the Army. Engaged in settling the accounts of the expeditionary force to Cuba.
December 3, 1898.—Relieved from duty on the staff of the Major-General Commanding the Army and reported for duty to the Chief of Engineers.
December 19, 1898.—On temporary duty in the Office of the Chief of Engineers.
December 19, 1898.—Ordered to Habana for duty on the staff of Major-General Ludlow, United States Volunteers.
January 2, 1899.—Reported for duty to the commanding general, Department of Habana, and was placed in charge of all engineering work in the city and harbor of Habana. The organization of the engineer department for the city of Habana was immediately begun. This department as organized was modeled on the organization and duties of the office of the Engineer Commissioner of the District of Columbia, excepting that it included the street cleaning and removal and disposal of refuse. The relative duties of the engineer and sanitary departments of Habana were practically the same as those of the engineer department and health office of the city of Washington.

The first work necessary was the cleaning of the streets of their accumulation of garbage, and the cleaning, disinfecting, and repairing of all public buildings and fortifications as a necessary preliminary to their occupancy by United States troops. Work was begun at once upon the preparation of an accurate map of Habana and its surroundings, showing the sites of all permanent and temporary defenses, and supplemented by detailed plans of all defenses and photographic views of the defenses and of the country commanded. The existing maps available (more than 40 in all) were found to be inaccurate and the work had to be done de novo.

January 24, 1899.—Engineer officer, Department of Habana.
June 13, 1899.—Honorably discharged from the Volunteer Army.
June 13, 1899, to May 1, 1900.—Engineer officer of Habana.
December 29, 1899, to November 15, 1900.—Chief engineer, Division of Habana.
November 15, 1900, to April 23, 1901.—Engineer officer, Department of Cuba.

As chief engineer of Division (afterwards Department) of Cuba was charged with the supervision of the work of the engineer department, city of Habana; also works of the port of Habana and survey of fortifications around Habana and of the Department of Habana, with preparation of plans and sections of fortifications and photographs of surroundings, and until January 23, 1901 (when this work was transferred to the engineer department of the city of Habana), with the repair and renovation of state buildings.

Preparation of a complete map of the island of Cuba.

Disbursing officer of the appropriation for the expeditionary force to Cuba.

Supervision of the work of the acting engineer officers of the department.

The most noteworthy works which have been carried out under his supervision have been as follows:

Organization of an efficient department of municipal public works, Habana.

Preparation of regulations for organizing and operating a department of public works for the island of Cuba.

Cleaning the streets and public buildings and fortifications of Habana.

Preparation of a project, with complete plans and specifications, for sewering and paving the city of Habana; the erection of an electrozone plant; the erection of a garbage crematory; the erection of an electric-light plant at the Quartel de la Fuerza; the erection of military stables; the erection of stables for municipal plant; the erection of a passenger landing; the erection of a new pumping station to supply water to the higher portions of the city; constructing an emigrant detention station at Trisconia; converting Quartermaster Storehouse No. 6 into a modern chemical and bacteriological laboratory for medical college, University of Habana; placing the swine slaughter house in a sanitary condition; installing modern sanitary appliances and also a steam laundry and kitchen in the carcel (prison); renovation and repair of the Beneficencia Orphan Asylum and installing steam laundry and kitchen therein; renovation and repair of Mercedes Hospital, installing electric-light plant and system of ventilators therein, and erecting an operating room with all the latest sanitary conveniences; constructing modern court rooms at the Audiencia, Vivac, and Dragones Barracks; the extension of the water system to the various hospitals, to Regla, Luyano, and across the harbor to Casa Blanca, Morro, and Cabanas; dredging in the harbor of Habana and at the mouth of Matadero Creek; constructing Luz wharf; general care and repair of wharf; removing wreck of the *Atocha* from harbor; making current observations near the mouth of Habana Harbor and installing and observing three self-registering tide gauges; repairing and repaving streets; cleaning and sprinkling streets and collection and disposal of garbage; care and preservation of parks and opening new parks; renewing and repairing old water mains and laying new mains; cleaning, repairing, and disinfecting sewers; extending the sewers under Machina wharf and at the foot of Tacon street; providing for the collection and disposal of night soil; preparing projects for the repair and renovation of San Lazaro Hospital, for converting San Ambrosio Hospital into a modern prison; for converting Cabana into a penitentiary, for repairing and renovating Tacon market; for a modern abattoir, and for water works at Santiago; making studies and recommendations for the Habana Electric Railway and supervising installation; inspecting and reporting on various public works throughout the island, carried on under the direction of the acting engineer, officers, and department of public works; making plans and specifications for schoolhouse at Santiago; inspecting and reporting on the Trisconia Railroad, on project for dredging Cardenas Harbor, on project for dredging Santiago Harbor, on project for dredging at Isabela de Sagua, on public works at Cienfuegos, Santiago, Mantanzas, and Guantanamo; reports on military zones and reservations, on water supply and sewer system for Santiago, on projects for various roads throughout the island, and report on various concessions in Habana; assisting in preparing a charter for the city of Habana; drafting a code of laws and regulations for municipal contracts.

June 13, 1899.—Honorably discharged from the Volunteer Army.

Commended for the handling of his troops at Guanica by Commander Richard Wainwright, United States Navy, in letter dated September 28, 1898.

Commended by the Major-General Commanding the Army in report of November 5, 1898, for services in Porto Rico.

SERVICE OF OFFICERS IN THE FIELD, WITH TROOPS, ETC. 55

Commended by Brigadier-General Ludlow for services in Habana in his reports for the year ending June 30, 1899, and for the period ending May 1, 1900.

Commended by Major-General Wood, United States Volunteers, in report dated June 30, 1900, for work as chief engineer, Division of Cuba.

Commended by General Wood at the time of his relief from duty in Cuba.

June 6, 1901.—Letter of the Chief of Engineers to the Secretary of War recommends that—

Maj. William M. Black, Corps of Engineers (formerly chief engineer of the Third Army Corps, with the rank of lieutenant-colonel, United States Volunteers), be brevetted lieutenant-colonel, United States Army, and colonel United States Army, for gallant and distinguished services at Guanica, Porto Rico, July 25, 1898, and that he be appointed brigadier-general of volunteers for faithful and efficient services as chief engineer of the Department of Cuba January 2, 1899, to April 23, 1901, especially for his professional skill in modifying and improving the sanitary condition of Habana.

MAJ. GEORGE M'C. DERBY.

May 9, 1898.—Appointed chief engineer with the rank of lieutenant-colonel, United State Volunteers.

June 3, 1898.—Transferred to Major Willard his duties and left New Orleans.

June 5, 1898.—Arrived at Tampa, Fla., and reported to Major-General Shafter, United States Volunteers.

June 5 to October 13, 1898.—Chief engineer, Fifth Army Corps.

June 6, 1898.—Embarked on transport *Segurança*.

June 14, 1898.—Fleet of transports sailed for Santiago.

June 20, 1898.—The fleet arrived off Santiago Harbor.

June 22, 1898.—Landed at Daiquiri. In charge of detail making reconnaissances of roads.

June 27, 1898.—In charge of repairs of the roads between Siboney and the front.

By direction of the commanding general, inspected and selected routes and positions and kept him informed as to the location of troops and their operations at the extreme front.

June 30 and July 1, 1898.—Made valuable observations with a war balloon with reference to the roads leading to Santiago; directed construction of trenches.

On duty in Cuba and Montauk Point, N. Y., until September 6, 1898.

October 13, 1898.—Relieved from duty with the Fifth Army Corps.

October 13, 1898.—Detailed as chief engineer, Second Army Corps.

November 6, 1898.—Reported to commanding general, Second Army Corps, at Camp Meade, Pa., and assigned to duty as chief engineer, November 7, 1898; accompanied headquarters to Augusta, Ga., arriving there November 19. While with Second Army Corps was engaged in topographical work, in instructing volunteer engineer troops in reconnaissance work, field engineering, and target practice, and made a survey and detailed maps of Camp Meade.

March 18, 1899.—Relieved from duty with Second Army Corps.

March 20, 1899.—Left Augusta, Ga.

May 12, 1899.—Honorably discharged from the volunteer service.

Major-General Shafter, in a report dated September 13, 1898, recommended that Lieutenant-Colonel Derby be brevetted colonel for gallantry in the face of the enemy on the 1st and 2d of July, 1898, and that he is brevetted brigadier-general for faithful and meritorious service in ascending, under a hot fire, in a war balloon on July 1, and thereby gaining valuable information.

Commended by Major-General Shafter in report dated November 21, 1898, for valuable services rendered during the campaign before Santiago de Cuba.

Commended by Brigadier-General Kent in report dated July 7, 1898, for services in discovering roads by observations from a war balloon.

Commended by Major-General Young in report dated May 7, 1899, for prompt, faithful, and efficient services while under his command.

June 6, 1901.—In a letter to the Secretary of War the Chief of Engineers, United States Army, recommended that—

Maj. George McC. Derby, Corps of Engineers (formerly chief engineer of the Fifth Army Corps with the rank of lieutenant-colonel, United States Volunteers), be brevetted lieutenant-colonel, United States Army, and colonel, United States Army, for gallantry in the face of the enemy on the 1st and 2d of July, 1898, and that he be appointed brigadier-general of volunteers for faithful and meritorious services in ascending, under a hot fire, in a war balloon, July 1, and thereby gaining valuable information.

MAJ. JAMES L. LUSK.

April 30, 1898.—Left West Point, N. Y., in command of Company E, Battalion of Engineers.

May 1, 1898.—Sailed from New York City on the transport *Alamo*.

May 5, 1898.—Arrived at Key West, Fla., and received orders to proceed to Port Tampa, Fla. Mutiny of firemen suppressed without bloodshed.

May 7, 1898.—Arrived at Port Tampa, Fla., on the *Alamo;* disembarked and established camp for the company. Regular drills were commenced and materials landed. Whole engineer outfit on *Alamo* restowed and methodically arranged for use during a disembarkation.

May 9, 1898.—Appointed lieutenant-colonel and chief engineer, United States Volunteers.

May 15, 1898.—Company C, Battalion of Engineers, arrived at Tampa by rail.

May 15 to 25, 1898.—Commanding Battalion of Engineers, Fifth Army Corps, Tampa, Fla.

May 26, 1898.—Relieved from duty with Fifth Army Corps, Tampa, Fla.

May 27, 1898.—Reported for duty to Maj. Gen. W. M. Graham, United States Volunteers, commanding Second Army Corps, Camp Russell A. Alger, Falls Church, Va.

May 27 to September 18, 1898.—Chief engineer, Second Army Corps.

May 27, 1898, until August 16, 1898.—On duty at Camp Alger.

He found the water supply meager and much of it from doubtful sources, but, by sinking an artesian well for each regiment, by about June 25 the water famine was ended.

Under instructions of June 5, 1898, member of board of officers which reported unfavorably upon site south of Alexandria, Va., proposed as a site for encamping the Second Corps.

Under orders of July 28, 1898, with the inspector-general of the corps, selected site for a bivouac for the corps while on a proposed practice march to and from Washington, D. C.

Under orders of August 2, 1898, with the inspector-general of the corps, examined several sites for an encampment for the Second Corps in the general direction of Manassas, Va. After much labor a site near Thoroughfare Gap was recommended, and was occupied for a time by the Second Division.

Mapped route for proposed march of the corps from Camp Alger and Thoroughfare Gap to Middletown, Pa.

August 17, 1898, until September 18, 1898.—On duty at Camp George Gordon Meade, Middletown, Pa. Laid out camp, water mains, selected regimental camping grounds, etc.

At both camps did much work in building and repairing bridges and culverts, improving roads, surveying and mapping, and printing maps, and instructing officers of volunteers in road sketching and road reconnaissance.

In his report of September 15, 1898, to the Adjutant-General, United States Army, Maj. Gen. W. M. Graham, United States Volunteers, states:

In addition to the supply of good and sufficient water, the Engineer Department had a great deal of work to do in repairing roads and bridges, making maps, surveying and locating camps, which were all successfully accomplished under the able and efficient officer at the head of the department. Great credit is due Colonel Lusk for the manner in which camps were laid out. His efforts were most indefatigable and the work performed by him was of a most arduous and exacting nature.

September 18, 1898.—Reported to Chief of Engineers, United States Army, and assigned to duty as his assistant.

December 7, 1898.—Honorably discharged from the Volunteer Army.

MAJ. GEORGE W. GOETHALS.

May 9, 1898.—Appointed chief engineer with the rank of lieutenant-colonel.

May 30, 1898.—Assigned to duty as chief engineer, First Army Corps, with headquarters at Chickamauga Park.

While at Chickamauga Park was engaged in mapping the park to show the sites occupied by the various regiments, brigades, divisions, corps, etc., and in making survey, with plans and estimates, for increasing water supply, and in the instruction of volunteer officers and troops in reconnaissances and outpost duty.

June 14, 1898.—Appointed lieutenant-colonel First United States Volunteer Engineers, but declined.

July 23, 1898.—General Brooke, with his staff and headquarters, left Chickamauga National Park; arrived at Newport News on the 25th, and embarked on the steamer *St. Louis* on the 28th.

While en route to Porto Rico, was required to collect from a number of Porto Rican scouts who were taking passage to join General Miles all the information concerning the island, roads, etc., needed by the commanding general for intelligent operations.

July 31, 1898.—Arrived at Guanica, P. R.

August 2, 1898.—Disembarked at Arroyo, P. R., and was assigned to command the outpost duty for the first forty-eight hours and was then charged with the construction of a wharf to facilitate the landing of supplies, which could not be readily done on the beach on account of the surf. In this latter work was assisted by Maj. Spencer Cosby, U. S. V. (first lieutenant, Corps of Engineers, U. S. A.). Also in making reconnaissances within the lines of outposts occupied by the United States, and after the signing of the protocol, in clearing obstructions along the road from Arroyo to Caya and constructing two temporary bridges, which had been made necessary by the demolitions of the Spaniards. In this work was assisted by Maj. Spencer Cosby, U. S. V., and Capt. S. B. Williamson, of the Third Volunteer Engineers.

Assigned as chief engineer on the staff of Major-General Brooke, commanding the Department of Porto Rico, October 1, 1898; accompanied Major-General Brooke (who had been detailed as a member of the evacuation commission) to San Juan, where he performed the various duties assigned to him, particularly that of inspecting the fortifications there and reporting thereon to the commission.

Relieved from duty in the Department of Porto Rico October 20, 1898.

Honorably discharged from the Volunteer Army, to take effect December 31, 1898.

MAJ. JOHN BIDDLE.

May 9, 1898.—Appointed chief engineer, with the rank of lieutenant-colonel, United States Volunteers.

June 1, 1898.—Transferred to Maj. Dan C. Kingman works in his charge and left Nashville, Tenn.

June 2, 1898.—Arrived at Chickamauga Park, Ga., and reported to Major-General Brooke, United States Volunteers.

June 2 to October 7, 1898.—Assigned as chief engineer, Sixth Army Corps, acting chief engineer, First Division, First Army Corps. Engaged in locating camps, drainage, water supply, target practice, instructing volunteer officers, etc.

July 20, 1898.—Sailed from Charleston, S. C.

July 27, 1898.—Arrived at Guanica, P. R., but disembarked at Ponce next day. After landing in Porto Rico was engaged in reconnoitering the enemy's positions, exploring, and mapping the country.

August 9, 1898.—Participated in the capture of Coamo, P. R., under Brig. Gen. O. H. Ernst, United States Volunteers. The Sixteenth Pennsylvania, Colonel Hulings commanding, led by Lieutenant-Colonel Biddle, having made a turning movement through the mountains, striking the Aibonito road half mile beyond town, captured entire garrison, amounting to 150 men.

August 21, 1898.—Was designated with two other officers by Maj. Gen. James H. Wilson, United States Volunteers, to proceed to Washington, D. C., taking with them the royal ensign of Spain, captured by the troops at Coamo on August 9, for the purpose of presenting same to the President at the Executive Mansion. The flag seems to be the only one taken in actual battle in the conquest of this island.

October 3 to October 27, 1898.—On temporary duty at Headquarters of the Army.

October 13, 1898.—Detailed as chief engineer, Second Army Corps.

November 6, 1898.—Reported for duty at Camp Meade.

November 7, 1898.—Assigned as chief engineer, Second Army Corps.

November 17, 1898.—Departed for Augusta, Ga., arriving there November 19, 1898.

November 21, 1898.—Relieved Captain Burr as acting chief engineer, Second Army Corps.

Organized the engineer battalion, Second Army Corps.

December 1, 1898.—Left Macon, Ga., to proceed to Cuba to create camps for troops of the First Army Corps.

December 5, 1898.—Arrived in Trinidad, Cuba, with the Fourth Tennessee Volunteers, and assisted in placing them in camp at that point and at Sancti Spiritus, making examination of the country from Trinidad to Sancti Spiritus.

December 21, 1898.—Arrived at Matanzas.

A battalion of Third United States Volunteer Engineers was on duty at Matanzas from December 22, 1898, to April 15, 1899, and was placed directly under his orders.

On the arrival of this battalion, which until the late afternoon of January 1, 1899, were the only troops at this point, there were 15,000 to 20,000 Spanish soldiers in the city, assembled from different towns in the province.

The camp established was within the city limits, but the landing of the engineer battalion had to be made on the San Juan River and all property carried out in wagons to the camps, which was quietly and promptly done. Before the arrival of the troops, January 1, the battalion had built a dock at the camp for unloading.

On this battalion devolved the honor of receiving the city and province of Matanzas from the Spanish authorities. This ceremony took place with all military ceremonies at noon at Fort San Severino and the city hall. For several days and nights the battalion acted as provost guard and, with the cooperation of the Spanish and Cuban officials, maintained perfect order and quiet in the city.

January 20, 1899.—Reported to Gen. J. H. Wilson upon the destitution among the inhabitants of Matanzas province.

January 24, 1899.—Engineer officer, Department of Matanzas, Cuba.

April 17 to September 19, 1899.—Engineer officer, Department of Matanzas and Santa Clara.

May 12, 1899.—Honorably discharged from the Volunteer Army.

April 29 to May 6 and May 11 to May 24, 1899.—Accompanied Gen. J. H. Wilson in inspections of the province of Santa Clara.

Made plans and estimates for cleaning and repairing streets, emptying cesspools, and for the thorough sanitation of cities and towns, for surveys of harbors, and for construction and repair of roads in the province, and for water supply for Cienfuegos, defenses of Matanzas.

September 19, 1899.—Left Matanzas for New York City.

October 26, 1899.—Sailed from San Francisco.

November 25, 1899.—Arrived at Manila; announced as engineer officer, Department of the Pacific and the Eighth Army Corps.

March 29, 1900.—The Department of the Pacific having been discontinued, announced as engineer officer, Division of the Philippines, and retained charge of this duty until April 27, 1901, when relieved by Maj. Clinton B. Sears.

The character of this work has been both military and civil on account of the nature of the government in these islands. The military work has consisted in the preparation and issue of a large number of maps and blue prints, and, in connection with the officers and men of the engineer companies, in repairing roads in this division under an appropriation of $1,000,000 gold, by the Philippine Commission, Act No. 1. This latter was the main work of the office after July, 1900. A large amount of material for road purposes was ordered from the United

States. There has been considerable delay in receiving this property, due to various reasons, so that even to-day the whole amount has not been received. The material sent has been excellent throughout, and has generally been received in good shape.

The work has been performed by assigning the officers and men of the engineer companies to different sections of road. From its nature the work has been temporary, as it has been done to meet a military emergency; and sufficient funds to build a really first-class highway have not been allotted for any one portion of road. Moreover, the adverse conditions prevailing and difficulties of obtaining material, labor, and plant have limited the amount of work accomplished. At the same time a great deal of work has been done, and as good work as could be done under the circumstances. The organization of the officers and troops for this purpose has been as follows:

The main work being in the island of Luzon, all the engineer officers have been on duty in that island. Capt. George A. Zinn has been engineer officer of the Department of Northern Luzon, and Lieut. J. C. Oakes, engineer officer, Department of Southern Luzon. Companies A and E have been attached to the northern department, with three officers in each company, and Company B to southern Luzon, with three officers in that company, Lieutenant Oakes being in command of the company. These different officers and troops have been under Captain Biddle's command only in the sense that he has been in charge of all work being done by them. They being, however, line troops, and he being in a staff position, direct orders have been given only through the military authorities. The system, however, has worked very well; and to all these officers is due great credit for the good work they have done and for the earnestness and enthusiasm with which they have carried on work under generally disadvantageous circumstances.

On several military expeditions officers and men of the engineer troops have accompanied them as photographers. Since, however, the 1st of July, 1900, there have been no expeditions of sufficient magnitude to warrant sending engineer troops with them, excepting in very small numbers, and the troops have all been busily engaged in their other work. A photographic establishment was kept up under charge of Capt. C. F. O'Keefe, Thirty-sixth Infantry, U. S. V., until his departure for China, in July, 1900, and since then under the charge of Corpl. T. Bourke, Company B, Battalion of Engineers, and Private J. W. Myers, Company B, Battalion of Engineers.

In the line of civil engineering the principal work undertaken has been that of preparing plans and specifications for the improvement of the harbor of Manila, under the supervisory charge of Maj. William E. Craighill, Fortieth Infantry, U. S. V. (captain, Corps of Engineers, U. S. A.).

Several other works of minor importance have been carried on in connection with preparing reports of harbors, etc.

Lieut. Lytle Brown, Corps of Engineers, U. S. A., city engineer of the city of Manila, has in his charge a number of important works, principally a large bridge across the Pasig River, and the Manila waterworks. His work has been entirely satisfactory, but the only control exercised over it by this office has been a very general one.

July 10, 1900.—Directed to submit detailed plans and descriptions of the present defenses of such portions of the Philippine Islands as are under the control of the United States.

SERVICE OF OFFICERS IN THE FIELD, WITH TROOPS, ETC. 61

August 7, 1900, to July 25, 1901.—Member of Board (two naval officers and one engineer officer), under the direction of the Secretary of the Navy, to make a survey, plans, and estimates for the improvement of a harbor at the island of Guam. Attended a meeting of the Board at Guam November 23, to December 26, 1900.

April 28, 1901.—Relieved from duty in the Philippines.

June 26, 1901.—Arrived at San Francisco.

Maj. Gen. James H. Wilson, U. S. V., in a report dated August 23, 1898, highly commended Colonel Biddle for his great activity, endurance, and courage, and recommended that he be brevetted major, United States Army, and colonel of volunteers, for distinguished gallantry under fire at the affair at Coamo, August 9, 1898.

Commended by Brig. Gen. O. H. Ernst, U. S. V., commanding First Brigade, First Division, First Army Corps, for daring and skillful reconnoitering in the movement on Coamo.

Commended by Colonel Hulings of the Sixteenth Pennsylvania Volunteers for valuable services in movement before Coamo.

Commended by Maj. Gen. James H. Wilson, United States Volunteers, in report dated August 1, 1899, for valuable and efficient services in the Department of Matanzas and Santa Clara, Cuba.

Commended by Brig. Gen. James H. Wilson, United States Volunteers, in report dated July 22, 1900, for his enterprise, courage, skill, and ambition.

June 6, 1901.—In a letter to the Secretary of War the Chief of Engineers, U. S. A., recommended:

That Maj. John Biddle, Corps of Engineers (formerly chief engineer of the Sixth Army Corps, with the rank of lieutenant-colonel, United States Volunteers), be brevetted lieutenant-colonel, United States Army, and colonel, United States Army, for distinguished gallantry under fire at the affair at Coamo, August 9, 1898, and that he be appointed brigadier-general of volunteers for daring and skillful reconnoitering in the movement on Coamo, resulting in notable captures, including a royal ensign of Spain, which he was afterwards delegated to bring to the United States and present to the President.

MAJ. HARRY F. HODGES.

June 10, 1898.—Appointed lieutenant-colonel of the First Regiment, United States Volunteer Engineers, commanded by Col. Eugene Griffin.

The regiment was recruited in the Eastern States by its own officers, who, under Colonel Griffin's orders, had established recruiting stations in all the principal cities, the headquarters of this service being under the colonel's immediate charge in New York City. The organization of the regiment was effected at the New York State camp at Peekskill, the use of the grounds, tents, and buildings having been tendered by the State authorities. On June 20, 1898, Lieutenant-Colonel Hodges accompanied the first squad of recruits to the camp, and remained there until the regiment left on August 5; until July 1, 1898, was in command of the camp. As fast as recruits arrived and a provisional selection of noncommissioned officers could be made, the companies were mustered into the service by Lieut. W. M. Cruikshank, First Artillery, mustering officer. The first company was mustered in on June 25, 1898, and the last July 16, 1898.

While the regiment was organizing, a list of the equipment considered necessary was prepared. The list was submitted to the Chief of Engineers, and every article asked for was furnished without delay, the purchases being made through Maj. J. G. D. Knight, Corps of Engineers, in command of the depot at Willets Point.

After a few weeks' drill the regiment broke camp on August 5, 1898, and proceeded by water to New York Harbor, where it boarded the transport *Chester*, lying off Bedloes Island.

August 10, 1898.—The transport sailed for Porto Rico, reaching the Playa de Ponce on August 15. On the 16th and 17th the regiment disembarked and made a temporary camp between the Playa and Ponce, moving again on the 19th, when a more suitable location became available, and making its permanent camp after a second move on September 1.

August 25, 1898.—A reconnaissance was made by a party under command of Lieutenant-Colonel Hodges along the San Juan road from Ponce to the Spanish outposts at Aibonito, a short distance beyond the town of Coamo, to ascertain the damage which had been done to certain bridges injured by the Spaniards during their retreat.

September 1, 1898.—The headquarters of the regiment, with the band and five companies—E, F, G, I, and K—made its permanent camp on a hill a short distance west of Ponce, where it remained until the departure from the island. On September 9 Colonel Griffin, who had been ill in hospital for some time, sailed for the United States.

September 3 until November 13, 1898.—The regiment was under command of Lieutenant-Colonel Hodges.

November 17, 1898.—The portions of the regiment which had been camped near Coamo and Ponce embarked on the transport *Minnewaska* for the return voyage to the United States. The First Battalion made the march from its camp to Ponce, a distance of more than 20 miles, with seven fords, in a little less than seven hours, only one or two men falling out by the way. The march was made at night, and the men were thus saved the discomfort and danger attendant upon severe exertion under the tropical sun. The part of the Third Battalion which had been retained at Guanica, embarked by lighters when the transport reached that harbor. General Henry, the district commander, and Colonel (afterwards General) Castleman, the post commander, expressed in the orders relieving the regiment a sense of the useful service rendered by it while on the island.

January 21, 1899.—Appointed colonel of the regiment, vice Colonel Griffin, who resigned his regimental commission and was shortly afterwards appointed brigadier-general.

January 25, 1899.—Honorably mustered out of the volunteer service.

January 25 to February 12, 1899.—On duty in the office of the chief mustering officer of the State of New York.

February 12 to April 25.—On special duty, under the orders of the Chief of Engineers, making an inspection of coast defenses on the island of Porto Rico, of which inspection a report was made to the Department under date of April 13, 1899.

May 19, 1901.—Left Cincinnati, Ohio.

May 23, 1901.—Arrived at Habana and reported to General Wood.

May 25, 1901.—Assigned to duty as chief engineer of the Department of Cuba and charged with supervision of the work of the engineer department, city of Habana, with preparation of a map of the island of Cuba; with harbor works of the port of Habana, and with surveys near the city of Habana.

As chief engineer, exercises supervision over—

Works near Santiago de Cuba, comprising water supply of Santiago and Guantanamo; works of harbor improvement, sewerage and paving at Santiago, construction of road Santiago to San Luis, and repair of roads near Santiago.

Works near Holguin, comprising municipal works at Holguin and Gibara; water supply for Holguin; relocation of road with construction of twenty bridges and crossings between Banes and Bijaru; telephone line, Holguin to Barajagua; bridges at Santa Maria and Las Tunas, and road improvement, Tunas to Monati.

Works in Puerto Principe, comprising water supply of city of Puerto Principe, including boring certain artesian wells; making map of city of Puerto Principe and repair of the streets.

Work near Matanzas, comprising municipal works, city of Matanzas; construction of a deep-water pier, harbor of Matanzas; extension of sea wall up San Juan River.

Work in San Luis, comprising municipal works, San Luis.

Works near Cienfuegos, comprising municipal works; preparation of project for water supply.

Works in province of Habana, comprising municipal works, Marianao and Quemados; road work, Columbia Barracks to Vedado.

As chief engineer, is charged with inspection of works of internal improvement in provinces of Pinar del Rio, Habana, Matanzas, and Santa Clara, executed by the civil department of public works.

CAPT. EDWARD BURR.

May 30, 1898.—Relieved from duty in temporary charge of Washington aqueduct.

June 2, 1898.—Assumed command at Port Tampa, Fla., of Company E, Battalion of Engineers, and, as senior officer present, assumed command of the Battalion of Engineers attached to the Fifth Army Corps, composed of Companies C and E, Battalion of Engineers.

June 6, 1898.—Battalion embarked on steamer *Alamo* for transportation with expedition to operate against Santiago de Cuba.

June 7, 1898.—Appointed lieutenant-colonel Second United States Volunteer Engineers.

June 13, 1898.—Ordered to take station at Chicago, Ill., as lieutenant-colonel Second Regiment, United States Volunteer Engineers, order being revoked before received.

June 14, 1898.—Sailed with his command from Port Tampa, Fla., with expedition against Santiago de Cuba.

June 22, 1898.—Landed a detachment of the battalion about 4.30 p. m. to make repairs to a small pier at Daiquiri, Cuba; that was the only place used for the landing of the expedition on that day. Earlier in the day (about 12 m.) three pontons with bridge material and intrenching tools had been sent inshore for possible use in connection with the debarkation of the army, but no use was made of them. After landing this material, the repair of the pier by covering it with rough flooring of planks where it was only a railroad trestle or was in bad repair, was begun about dark, when troops ceased coming ashore, and continued until midnight. This work was resumed at dawn on the 23d and completed before debarkation of troops recommenced, the two detachments going on board the transports at 8 a. m., with the exception of an officer (Lieutenant Ferguson), 3 noncommissioned officers, and 12 privates, left to guard the property on shore, including the pontons, which had been beached. The officers ashore on this duty were Captain Burr and Lieutenants Rees and Ferguson.

About noon on June 23 the command on the steamer *Alamo* proceeded to Aserraderos, about 20 miles west of Santiago, to assist in the embarkation of General Garcia's Cuban army, stated to number about 4,000 men. Arriving about 5 p. m., the landing at Aserraderos was examined, and on the 24th a light pier 128 feet long was built by the command to reach a depth of water of 4 feet. On the 25th the Cubans to the number of about 3,000 were embarked, and during the night the transports returned to Daiquiri. On the 26th orders were received from the commanding general to place the command in camp at Siboney and to build at that point a pier for unloading supplies, there being no landing facilities other than a narrow beach. Began debarking engineer material and baggage, completing this work on June 27 and putting command in camp at 6 p. m. On the 27th a small pier was built out to 5 feet of water for the use of small boats. The construction of a pier to 9 feet depth of water was commenced on the 28th and continued to include the 1st of July, between which dates the following work was also done, viz: Repaired railroad over creek at Siboney; built bridge over same creek, one-half mile west on the Santiago road, the material being carried out by the men in the entire absence of any transportation; repaired water-pipe line supplying Siboney; repaired road from Siboney west toward Santiago. During this period the operation of the ore railroad from the mines northeast of Siboney to Santiago was placed under his charge so far as it was under control of our forces. This road was repaired where necessary, as were also two locomotives, and was operated in handling supplies and in transporting the Thirty-third Michigan Volunteers to Aguadores and back on July 1 in connection with the operations of that date.

June 26, 1898.—Directed to assume command of the battalion of engineers serving with the Fifth Army Corps. Landed command at Siboney, Cuba.

Late on the afternoon of July 1 orders were received for the command to be at general headquarters at or before daylight on the 2d, and the command marched out at 9.30 p. m., arriving at headquarters at 12.30 a. m.

July 2, 1898.—Ordered to continue in command of engineer troops on duty with United States forces in Cuba and to report in person accordingly to Maj. Gen. William R. Shafter, U. S. V.

July 2, 1898.—The command was ordered forward to repair the road at and near the crossing of the San Juan River, but as it was entirely without transportation, only the usual infantry equipment of tools was available, together with a few axes, picks, and shovels picked up at headquarters. No satisfactory results were accomplished by the day's work, which was underspent fire from the front, by which one man was slightly wounded; pickets were thrown out on both flanks as a protection against guerrilla fire, which had been troublesome.

July 3, 1898.—The command was ordered to repair the road about 4 miles in rear of headquarters and was moved into camp at Sevilla, tools being brought up from Siboney by one wagon which had been secured. This work continued until the 5th, when the command returned to Siboney under orders to complete the pier previously begun.

July 6, 1898.—Work was resumed on pier at Siboney and completed on July 12. This pier consisted of a pier head 20 feet square, built of 12 by 12 inch timbers and ballasted with scrap iron, both of which were obtained from the railroad yards at Siboney. The depth at the pier head was about 9 feet. The shore connection was built upon similar smaller cribs and the railroad tracks were laid to the outer end of the pier. Much delay and difficulty was experienced in this work by reason of insufficient tools and the continuous swell on the beach, both of which made the work slow and at times dangerous. While the noncommissioned officers of the command were in general of excellent quality and well trained in many ways, they lacked experience as foremen of squads for heavy timber work and for rough road repairs, both of which items should become a part of the regular training of engineer troops.

From July 6 to July 22, 1898.—The command had charge of the operation of the ore railroad referred to above for the local transportation of supplies and for the transfer of yellow fever patients to the isolation hospital camp, about 2 miles northeast; also of the local water supply. Until July 16 much work was done for the repair of the road eastward of Siboney toward Daiquiri and westward toward Santiago, after which date the base of the army was transferred to Santiago.

July 16, 1898.—Made examination of the railroad bridge across the San Juan River at Aguadores. Its repair was commenced July 17 and completed July 19 by Captain Rees. This bridge was a high steel trestle across the lower end of the deep gorge of the San Juan River. The two west spans had been thrown down by the destruction of the west trestle, bent by the Spaniards by means of dynamite. These two spans were replaced by three timber spans, built of heavy timber brought by train from Siboney. The repairs included about 60 feet of trestle, with an extreme height of about 25 or 30 feet.

After completing the above work the railroad was repaired and operated through from the mines to the ore pier at La Cruz, one mile south of Santiago, and the command was transferred by rail on July 22, with all its equipment, to La Cruz, where it remained until July 27, awaiting wagon transportation for its baggage and tools. July 27 the command was transferred by wagon and rail to a camp near the Purgatoria Bridge at Cuevitas, on the railroad from Santiago to San Luis in the interior, leaving part of its equipment and a small guard at the Santa Cruz ore pier. From this camp assistance was to be given the railroad officials in repairing first the Boniata Bridge (2 miles north) and subsequently the Purgatoria Bridge, both of which bridges (trestles) had been partially burned by the Cubans during the campaign. Work was commenced on the Boniata bridge on July 29 and was in progress when the command was turned over to Lieutenant Reese, July 31, 1898.

July 31, 1898.—Released command of the Battalion of Engineers of the Fifth Army Corps.

August 1, 1898.—Sailed from Santiago de Cuba to join Second Regiment, United States Volunteer Engineers.

August 20, 1898.—Joined Second Regiment, United States Volunteer Engineers, at Camp Wikoff, Montauk, Long Island, having been authorized to delay ten days in so doing.

The work of the Second Regiment, United States Volunteer Engineers, at Camp Wikoff, at Montauk, Long Island, comprised the laying out, pitching, and striking of camps for other troops, the erection, and subsequently the operation, of the camp water supply, including wells, pipe lines, pumps, and filter, much work in connection with the general hospital, road repairs, the erection and starting of the Signal Corps electric lighting plant.

The main water supply was under Captain Burr's immediate charge and included the supervision of driven wells by contract, the laying of several miles of pipe (in part by civilian labor) from 6 inches to 1 inch, reaching all the camps; the erection of tanks, the installation and operation of pumps, and a filter, all for a supply of 500,000 gallons a day. This water supply proved to be excellent and efficient, except for occasional stoppages in some camps, but its quality for a camp to be occupied for a length of time could be assured only by efficient filtration.

October 5, 1898.—Proceeded to Camp George C. Meade, near Middletown, Pa., to command 2 companies of regiment attached to Second Army Corps.

October 6, 1898.—Assigned as acting chief engineer, Second Army Corps.

The engineer work at Camp Meade had been nearly completed under Lieut. Col. James L. Lusk, chief engineer, and Capt. A. H. Weber, Second Volunteer Engineers, acting chief engineer, Second Army Corps, when Captain Burr relieved the latter on October 6, 1898. It consisted mainly in the supervision of the camp water supply (constructed under contract) and its operation, the laying out of regimental camps, and making topographical surveys of the camp and vicinity. Subsequent to October 6, 1898, he continued this work as acting chief engineer, Second Army Corps, until about October 30, 1898. On the latter date he proceeded to Augusta, Ga., with two companies of his regiment attached to this corps and was engaged upon preparing corps headquarters, in erecting storehouses, and in caring for certain matters pertaining to the water supply of the camp at that place. The corps having been scattered into several camps and the Augusta camp being occupied by only one division, it was laid out by the chief engineer of that division, acting under the direct orders of the corps commander.

November 21, 1898.—Relieved from duty as acting chief engineer, Second Army Corps.

May 16, 1899.—Mustered out as lieutenant-colonel, Second Regiment, United States Volunteer Engineers.

CAPT. GRAHAM D. FITCH.

May 14, 1898.—Left Willets Point, N. Y., in command of Company C, Battalion of Engineers, by rail for Port Tampa, Fla.

June 20, 1898.—Appointed engineer officer with the rank of major, United States Volunteers.

May 15 to June 6, 1898.—At Port Tampa, Fla.

June 6, 1898.—Embarked on transport *Alamo* and sailed with fleet June 14, 1898.

June 20, 1898.—Arrived off Santiago Harbor, Cuba.

June 22 to June 27, 1898.—At Siboney, Cuba.

After the rest of the army had disembarked at Daiquiri, the Battalion of Engineers on the transport *Alamo* was taken to Aserraderos. There a bridge was built for embarking General Garcia's Cuban army. Returning, he landed at Siboney, where he first engaged with the rest of the battalion in constructing a pier for landing supplies, but very soon was directed by General Shafter's chief engineer, Lieut. Col. G. McC. Derby, to investigate the possibility of repairing the local railway equipment and operating the road. The Spaniards had hurriedly inflicted all possible damage on the machine shop and all of the locomotives, but Captain Fitch, with the assistance of a few skilled engineer soldiers, succeeded in putting two locomotives in working condition. The railroad was thereafter constantly used, and he remained in charge of it until the Battalion of Engineers was ordered to the front.

June 29, 1898.—In company with General Bates and two of his staff, made reconnaissance with locomotive and flat car, manned by a small guard of engineer soldiers, to within a mile of Aguadores Bridge. Then, leaving the train in charge of the enlisted men, he advanced on foot to within a few feet of the east end of Aguadores Bridge, at the other end of which the Spaniards were intrenched. He then returned to Siboney.

Late in the afternoon of June 30 he received a written communication from General Duffield, stating that "General Shafter directs me to have you give me at 3.30 a. m. to-morrow enough cars to move the Thirty-third Michigan Regiment—about 900 men." After working with his railroad detachment all night he reported on time, and by 9 a. m., after making two trips (owing to insufficient number of cars), had transported the Thirty-third Michigan Regiment to Aguadores. Was present during the attack, and then transported the troops back to Siboney. At about 8 p. m. that day (July 1) the Battalion of Engineers started for the front, reaching General Shafter's camp about 1 a. m. Next morning they proceeded on to the San Juan River ford, and were engaged during the remainder of the day in repairing it, being under fire, though not in view of the enemy. Thereafter his duties consisted mainly in railroad repairing.

July 29, 1898.—Relieved of command of Company C, Battalion of Engineers.

July 29 to August 9, 1898.—Division engineer, Second Division, Fifth Army Corps.

August 10, 1898.—Temporarily commanding Battalion of Engineers, Fifth Army Corps.

December 31, 1898.—Honorably discharged from the Volunteer Army.

CAPT. GEORGE A. ZINN.

July 6, 1900.—Transferred to Captain Sibert duties at Louisville, Ky., and left Louisville July 8, 1900.

July 12, 1900.—Arrived at San Francisco and reported at headquarters Department of California.

July 13, 1900.—Directed to take station in San Francisco until the arrival of Company E, Battalion of Engineers, and then to assume command of that company.

July 29, 1900.—Joined Company E, Battalion of Engineers, and assumed command.

August 1, 1900.—Sailed from San Francisco on transport *Meade*.

September 3, 1900.—Arrived at Manila Bay.

September 6, 1900.—Disembarked and proceeded to Caloocan.

September 6, 1900.—Relieved from command of Company E, Battalion of Engineers, and assigned as engineer officer, Department of Northern Luzon, with station in Manila. As engineer officer of the department Captain Zinn has had charge of extensive repairs to roads and bridges in the department, and has had a number of officers and detachments of engineer soldiers working under his supervision at many widely scattered localities.

CAPT. WILLIAM C. LANGFITT.

May 24, 1898.—Ordered to be relieved from duty of inspecting the submarine-mine defenses of the northeast coast of the United States and command of Company B, Battalion of Engineers, and transferred to command of Company A, Battalion of Engineers, and ordered to join the Philippine expeditionary forces.

May 24, 1898.—Returned to Willets Point, N. Y.

May 26, 1898.—Left Willets Point, N. Y., to join Company A, which had preceded him.

June 1, 1898.—Reported to the commanding general of the expeditionary forces and assumed command of Company A. The company was attached to the expeditionary forces.

June 7, 1898.—Appointed major, Second United States Volunteer Engineers.

June 13, 1898.—Was ordered to organize Third Battalion, Second Regiment, United States Volunteer Engineers, at San Francisco, and to comply with this order was relieved from command of Company A June 20, 1898, and from duty with the expeditionary forces June 24, 1898.

The Third Battalion of the Second United States Volunteer Engineers was organized and went into camp at the Presidio, San Francisco. It was equipped, drilled, and prepared for service as rapidly as possible.

July 6, 1898.—Was directed to report in person to Maj. Gen. Wesley Merritt, commanding the expedition to the Philippine Islands, to continue on duty with the expedition in command of the engineer troops. General Merriam, commanding the Department of California and expeditionary forces at San Francisco, decided that the above order meant that the battalion should be attached to the expeditionary forces and sent to the Philippines as soon as equipment completed and transportation available. Order to this effect was issued July 20, 1898, and he reported to the commanding officer of the expeditionary forces.

July 22, 1898.—Was ordered to report with the four companies composing the battalion to commanding general, Department of California, to accompany first detachment of troops to Honolulu, at which point it was to take temporary station.

July 29, 1898.—Sailed on transport *St. Paul* for Honolulu with Col. T. H. Barber, First New York Volunteer Infantry, to aid in selection and preparation of camp site for that regiment and the battalion.

August 6, 1898.—Arrived at Honolulu, Hawaii. In charge of engineering work, construction of temporary barracks for garrison at Honolulu, including water supply and sewerage. The organization followed, arriving August 14 and August 17, and all were established by the 20th in camp, prepared under Captain Langfitt's direction.

November 15, 1898.—Appointed member of Board of officers for selection of site for hospital at Honolulu.

December 7, 1898.—The First New York Volunteer Infantry having been ordered to San Francisco for muster out, assumed command of all United States forces in the Hawaiian Islands, remaining in command until April 20, 1899, when he was relieved by Maj. S. M. Mills, Sixth Artillery.

December 9, 1898.—Appointed mustering officer at Honolulu.

March 23, 1899.—Appointed member of Board of officers for the purpose of determining and recommending harbor lines to be established in the harbor of Honolulu, H. I.

April 20, 1899.—Left Honolulu on board the steamship *Australia* with the battalion.

May 16, 1899.—Honorably mustered out as major, Second United States Volunteer Engineers.

August 25, 1899.—Arrived at San Francisco and went into camp at the Presidio.

The following is a brief record of work performed by the battalion under Captain Langfitt's command:

The usual drills were had when possible to include battalion movements. Special instructions were given in sanitation, and as a result the health of the battalion was markedly good, in spite of the epidemic of typhoid fever which prevailed among the First New York Volunteer Infantry while at Honolulu; most, if not all, of the few cases occurring in the battalion being among men detailed as nurses for fever patients of other organizations in the hospital.

At San Francisco during organization, at Honolulu, and again at San Francisco while being mustered out, the battalion made an excellent impression by its good behavior and clean and orderly camp. The officers and men, as a rule, were willing, obedient, and anxious to carry out all orders. Under Captain Langfitt's direction the battalion built a temporary post at Honolulu, and laid out water supply and sewerage. The buildings consisted of 1 headquarters, 1 guardhouse, 4 barracks, 4 bath houses, 1 hospital, 1 quartermaster and commissary building, 2 stables, and other outbuildings. These are still in use and give satisfaction. Local circumstances forced their erection on the site selected, but it is nevertheless a fairly good one. Set of plans was forwarded to Office of Chief of Engineers. After approval of plans each company, under its company officers, built one barrack. The general buildings were constructed by detail of men under supervision of the adjutant and quartermaster.

In addition to the above work, Captain Langfitt personally inspected many sites and was member of Board to select permanent site for post at Honolulu, of Board to select site for pavilion hospital, of Board to report on harbor lines for Honolulu Harbor, and reported on defenses of Honolulu and Pearl harbors.

November 19, 1898.—Maj. Gen. H. C. Merriam, commanding Department of California, in his indorsement on monthly sanitary report of Asst. Surg. E. J. Barrett, Second United States Volunteer Engineers, dated Camp McKinley, H. I., November 1, 1898, says:

> This excellent and comprehensive report affords one more proof of excellent management of the battalion of the Second Regiment, United States Volunteer Engineers, under command of Maj. W. C. Langfitt. It is my understanding that this battalion is by this date housed in temporary buildings and on a new site near their former camp.

Capt. Sedgwick Pratt, Third Artillery, chief mustering officer, remarks on the discharge of Maj. W. C. Langfitt, Second Regiment, United States Volunteer Engineers:

> Graduated United States Military Academy, June, 1883. Service honest and faithful; character excellent. The discipline, bearing, the good conduct of the battalion commanded by him, and its esprit de corps bear testimony to his ability as a commander of troops.

Maj. Edward Field, acting inspector-general, Department of California, in a report to the Inspector-General, U. S. A., of an inspection of the post of Honolulu, H. I., made November 21 to December 2, 1898, states:

> The commanding officer, Major Langfitt, is captain in the Engineer Corps, U. S. A., and a man of the highest executive ability.
> The engineers are valuable anywhere from their exceptional officers and special qualifications. They would make excellent garrison soldiers, for they are regulars in all the essential points, and in the field for the purpose for which they were organized they would be invaluable.

CAPT. HIRAM M. CHITTENDEN.

May 9, 1898.—Appointed chief engineer, with the rank of lieutenant-colonel.

May 30, 1898.—Detached; assigned as chief engineer, Fourth Army Corps; Mobile, June 6, 1898, to June 8; Tampa, June 8 to August 11, 1898; Huntsville, August 13 to February 14, 1899.

About two months of this service was at Tampa, the principal point of embarkation of troops for the front, and there were no operations of consequence in the line of his duties at that point.

His principal work there was as disbursing officer in paying for the considerable quantities of engineering material purchased for the equipment of the various expeditions.

Was sent to Fernandina, Fla., and there laid out an encampment and arranged for the water supply for the troops at that point.

The rest of his service was at Huntsville, Ala. At that point he had charge of practically all the work of locating, laying out, and supplying with water the encampment for about 14,000 troops in about forty different camps. The principal work involved in this duty was that pertaining to the water supply, which was all obtained from the large spring in the center of the town. The distribution of this supply involved the laying of about 120,000 feet of pipe of different sizes.

The maintenance of roads was another important part of the work, owing to the considerable amount of work made necessary by the excessive traffic and the heavy and unusual rains.

The entire encampment was mapped in a most thorough manner by Capt. A. O. Powell, Second Regiment, United States Volunteer Engineers.

The road work was, for a part of the time, under the care of Lieuts. C. I. Jackson and O. S. Durfree, and the care of the water supply was for a short time in the charge of Capt. Fremont Hill, all of the Second Regiment, United States Volunteer Engineers.

In connection with the provisions of a water supply for the encampment Captain Chittenden personally conducted an extensive improvement of the city waterworks of Huntsville. This improvement, so far as his own work was concerned, related mainly to the proper walling in of the spring and the construction of a suitable canal to carry off the surplus water. The work involved an expenditure of about $10,000 and belonged exclusively to civil engineering.

Of the officers who served under his immediate direction he especially commends Maj. Edward L. Pinckard and Capt. A. O. Powell, of the Second Regiment, United States Volunteer Engineers.

The two companies forming part of the Second Battalion of the Second Regiment, United States Volunteer Engineers, were of great service to the encampment, and the work required of them was at all times willingly and efficiently done.

February 25, 1899.—Honorably discharged from the Volunteer Army.

CAPT. DAVID D. GAILLARD.

April 28, 1898.—Assigned to duty as engineer officer on the staff of Gen. James F. Wade, U. S. A., and served in this capacity from May 3 to June 11, 1898, in camp at Tampa, Fla., and Chickamauga Park, Ga.; at the latter place from May 26 to June 11, 1898, as acting engineer officer of the Third Army Corps, his duty consisting principally in instructing volunteer officers in foot reconnaissances and construction of hasty intrenchments.

June 7, 1898.—Appointed colonel of the Third Regiment, United States Volunteer Engineers. From that date until July 20, 1898, organizing regiment at Washington, D. C.

July 22 to September 20, 1898.—In camp with regiment at Jefferson Barracks, Mo., organizing, equipping, and drilling regiment.

September 21 to November 11, 1898.—In camp with regiment near Lexington, Ky., as part of the First Army Corps, instructing regiment in drills, target practice, and practice marches. While in camp at this place six companies of the regiment, companies G, H, I, K, L, and M (450 officers and men), under command of Maj. Willoughby Walke, United States Volunteers (captain of artillery, U. S. A.), made on October 29 what is believed to be the longest single day's march of the Spanish-American war—27 miles. About one-half of the men were in heavy marching order. Camp was reached at 8.15 p. m. Thirty men fell out or straggled en route, and but five were footsore when inspected the following morning. To Major Walke is due the credit for the excellent previous training which led to this result.

November 13 to December 16, 1898.—The regiment was camped at Macon, Ga., and formed a part of the First Division of the First Army Corps. At midnight, November 19, 1898, under verbal orders of Maj. Gen. Jas. H. Wilson, United States Volunteers, proceeded with the entire regiment to the camp of the Sixth Virginia Volunteer Infantry (Colored) 2 miles distant, which regiment was reported to be in a mutinous condition; secured their arms, placed a guard around their camp, and brought all of these arms back to the guard tents of the Third U. S. Volunteer Engineers. The entire operation was carried out without bloodshed, and without alarming the citizens of Macon.

December 16, 1898.—The Third Battalion, under command of Lieut. Col. Edgar Jadwin, United States Volunteers (first lieutenant of engineers), left Macon for Matanzas, Cuba.

February 1, 1899.—Headquarters and the Second Battalion left Macon for Cienfuegos, Cuba.

February 14, 1899.—The First Battalion left for Pinar del Rio, Cuba.

While at Macon the regiment, besides the usual infantry drills, received instruction in scouting, reconnoitering, and outpost duty, and especially in engineering drills, such as hasty intrenchments, the construction of blockhouses, single-lock, trestle, and crib bridges, fascine, gabion, and hurdle work, single towers and road improvement.

The Third Battalion, under command of Lieut. Col. Edgar Jadwin, disembarked at Matanzas, Cuba, December 23, 1898, and had the honor of raising the American flag over the city of Matanzas January 1, 1899, the day marking the end of Spanish sovereignty in Cuba. The battalion was commanded by Lieut. Col. Jadwin until illness required his return to the United States. The command then devolved upon Capt. C. W. Sturtevant, until the arrival of Maj. Willoughby Walke on March 15, 1899. The work done by this battalion in the province of Matanzas, Cuba, was as follows: The construction of a dock 80 feet by 95 feet, with approaches, the piles for the dock being driven to a penetration of 8. feet by means of a hand pile driver; locating, laying out, and preparing camp sites in the vicinity of Matanzas for the Second United States Cavalry, the One hundred and sixtieth Indiana, Third Kentucky, Twelfth New York, and Eighth Massachusetts regiments, infantry, and also brigade headquarters; building a target range for the Second United States Cavalry, and another for the use of the infantry; repairing of Fort San Severino for occupancy by Tenth United States Infantry; laying about 3,500 feet of 4-inch water main, constructing two tanks and the necessary water troughs along the Paseo; constructing road to earthen batteries at the mouth of Matanzas Bay; transporting from earthen batteries to Fort San Severino all heavy ordnances, cartridges, shot, and shell; superintending the unloading of all Government transports from December 13, 1898, to April 14, 1899; surveying, sketching, and preparing plans of all barracks, forts, and hospitals in the city of Matanzas and its vicinity; constructing sinks, garbage sheds, etc., for brigade camp; making house to house sanitary inspection of the city of Matanzas; locating cesspools, water-closets, sources of water supply, etc.; cleaning streets, caring for sewers and drains, and supervising other matters pertaining to the sanitary condition of the city of Matanzas; inspection and report upon all the railroads of the province; construction of a Government dock 175 feet by 80 feet; reconnaissance in detail of the entire province of Matanzas by various members of the regiment.

On January 2, 1899, the following letter commanding the conduct of the officers and men of the Third Battalion was received by Colonel Jadwin:

MATANZAS, CUBA, *January 2, 1899.*

To Lieut. Col. EDGAR JADWIN,
Commanding Third Battalion, Third United States Volunteer Engineers.

SIR: The commanding general of the Spanish forces at Matanzas has requested me to express, on the part of the lieutenant-general commanding the Spanish forces in Cuba, and on the part of the officers under his command at Matanzas, their thanks and appreciation for the consideration and soldierly conduct shown them by the officers and men under your orders on the occasion of taking possession of this city by the United States forces on January 1, 1899.

I desire also to state that the conduct of the battalion since its arrival here, and under somewhat difficult conditions, has been, in my opinion, exemplary, and worthy of the reputation for discipline and efficiency already attained by the Third United States Volunteer Engineers.

Very respectfully,

JOHN BIDDLE,
Lieutenant-Colonel, Chief of Engineers, First Army Corps.

The regimental headquarters and the Second Battalion arrived in Cienfuegos, Cuba, just as the last of the Spanish troops were sailing from the island, and reported to Maj. Gen. J. C. Bates, United States Volunteers, military governor of the province of Santa Clara.

February 10 to April 10, 1889.—Chief engineer of the Department of Santa Clara, but directed to retain command of his regiment.

The work done by the Second Battalion in the province of Santa Clara was as follows: A report, accompanied by maps and photographs, upon all the forts, batteries, and permanent defenses of the province; street cleaning, sanitary inspection, and street improvement; survey of the city by Lieut. Lee Shaffer, bench marks being left on every block and elevation being recorded at every street intersection; an inspection and report upon the water supply of Cienfuegos, Cuba; boring of an artesian well; reconnaissance of the Matagua and Hanabanilla falls, in the mountains to the eastward, as possible sources of water supply; reconnaissances by various members of the regiment of about 800 miles of roads in the province, of which about 443 miles only were platted, owing to the lack of time; a reconnaissance map in detail of the region about Cienfuegos, within the line of defenses which incloses the "cultivated zone," 40 square miles in all; an inspection and report upon all railroads of the province of Santa Clara; reports by various officers upon the necessary improvements to barracks in the province; a hydrographic survey of a portion of the harbor of Cienfuegos. Maj. J. L. Van Ornum, United States Volunteers, most efficiently commanded this battalion during its entire service in Cuba.

The First Battalion arrived in Pinar del Rio February 22, 1899, under command of Capt. F. L. Averill, Maj. Stephen M. Foote, the regular commander of this battalion, having been left sick in the United States. The work done by this battalion in the province of Pinar del Rio was as follows: The cuartel was cleaned and repaired; a contour map for the location of barracks in the city of Pinar del Rio was prepared, and preliminary lines for the necessary water supply and sewerage laid out; about 92 miles of road reconnaissance was made and platted; signal stations over a considerable area in the vicinity of the city of Pinar del Rio were erected, to be used in triangulation, but the battalion was ordered back to the United States when a base had been measured and only a few angles taken.

Early in April all of the battalions received orders to prepare to return to the United States for muster out.

The Second Battalion sailed from Cienfuegos April 13, and the First and Third battalions from Habana April 15. Both transports arrived at the mouth of Savannah River at the same time, and the entire regiment was reunited and sent into quarantine at Dawfuskie Island, South Carolina (Major Foote resuming command of the First Battalion at this time), where it remained from April 18 to 23, 1899, and was then ordered into camp at Fort McPherson, Ga., to be mustered out of the service. The regiment remained in camp at Fort McPherson from April 24 to May 17, 1899, being mustered out of the service on the latter date.

May 17, 1899.—Honorably mustered out as colonel, Third United States Volunteer Engineers.

CAPT. WILLIAM L. SIBERT.

July 5, 1899.—Left Willets Point in command of Company B, Battalion of Engineers, en route to Manila, P. I.
August 10, 1899.—Arrived at Manila Bay.
August 13, 1899.—Disembarked.
August 17, 1899.—Company B, with all officers present, reported at San Fernando for duty under Major-General MacArthur, commanding First Division, Eigth Army Corps.
August 17, 1899.—Marched with detachment of 44 men to Angeles, reaching there at 6.30 a. m. the 18th, for the purpose of rescuing two engines wrecked by the insurgents on the bridge about 1 mile north of Angeles. This bridge was beyond the line of outposts. One engine was placed on the track on the 18th and one on the 19th. The engineer troops were attacked both days, but were under the protection of the Twelfth Infantry. The engineer detachment joined the firing line during both affairs.

Capt. Millard F. Waltz, commanding Second Battalion, Twelfth Infantry, in a report dated September 1, 1899, said:

During this engagement Captain Sibert asked if he might deploy his engineers on the firing line, and, as the men had never been under fire and were eager to embrace the opportunity, permission was given, and they promptly dropped tools and used their rifles. They comported themselves very well.

Company B, Battalion of Engineers, remained on duty with the Second Division until September 30. A detachment of 16 men from Company A, Battalion of Engineers, joined Company B for duty August 22. The command did outpost, patrol, and escort duty.

On September 14 Captain Sibert assumed the duties of chief engineer, Department of the Pacific and Eighth Army Corps, to date from September 2, 1899.

On September 15 Captain Sibert was assigned, in addition to his other duties, to the command of the Battalion of Engineers, Eighth Army Corps, consisting of Companies A and B.

Assembled material for ponton trains, bridge construction, and railroad repairs, and prepared maps for use of Major-General Lawton, Major-General MacArthur, and Brigadier-General Wheaton prior to their movements in Northern Luzon in October, 1899.

October 7 to October 14, 1899.—As chief engineer, accompanied General Schwan's expeditionary brigade against the insurgents in the vicinity of Imus.

October 10, 1899.—With Geary's battalion of the Thirteenth Infantry, and a piece of artillery as escort, made a reconnaissance from San Francisco de Malabon toward Buena Vista, when an action with insurgents ensued.

The engineer company received the following special mention in Gen. Theodore Schwan's official report on this campaign:

The engineer company, acting mostly under the personal supervision of the chief engineer, Captain Sibert, but under the immediate command of Lieutenant Stickle, an energetic and capable young officer, has already been mentioned for its prompt construction of an efficient ferry across the Tibagan River. The service thereafter rendered by this company was constant and invaluable. In fact, but for its work numerous obstacles of various kinds would have indefinitely delayed or barred the passage of artillery and train. While approaching San Francisco de Malabon, where the enemy was supposed to be in force and expected to give battle, the company asked for and was assigned a place in the firing line. Captain Sibert, not only in his capacity as engineer, but also on the firing line, notably on the afternoon of October 10, on the Buena Vista road, contributed in a marked degree by his efforts to the success of operations.

This engineer company referred to above, or parts of it, was under fire at Cavite, Viejo, Putol, Rosario, and near San Francisco de Malabon.

November 14 to December 17, 1899.—In charge of repairs to bridges and damages by washouts on line of Manila and Dagupan Railroad and rolling stock, for which work he was commended by Generals Schwan, MacArthur, and Otis.

December 19 to December 30, 1899.—Detailed as member of Board of officers to consider question relating to traffic on the Manila and Dagupan Railroad while under military control.

November 25, 1899.—Relieved from duty as engineer officer, Department of the Pacific, by Capt. John Biddle.

January 2 to February 5, 1900.—Commanding engineer detachment forming part of General Schwan's expeditionary brigade in its campaign through Cavite, Laguna, Batangas, and Tabayas provinces, Southern Luzon. The detachment, or parts of it, took part in engagements near Muntinglupa, Binan, Silan, Magallanes, and at San Diego.

Highly commended in letter of General Schwan, March 16, 1900, and in special report of General Bates.

In his official report, February 8, 1900, General Schwan says:

Capt. William L. Sibert, Corps of Engineers, the senior engineer officer with the command, was utilized principally in making investigations concerning lines of communication and supply and roads over which movements of troops could be made. I can not commend too highly the work of this officer; his constancy, his tact, his professional skill, are worthy of special recognition.

In a letter of General Schwan to the Adjutant-General U. S. A., February 11, 1900, he says:

I know of no individual officer who contributed more to the success of the movement than did Captain William L. Sibert, Corps of Engineers. Not only as an engineer officer, in the surmounting, removal, and avoidance of road obstacles, were his services brought into requisition. His good work extended to and had the effect of facilitating and expediting every operation that was undertaken in the course of the campaign To me he proved, as he did on former expedition, a safe and most valuable prop. I can not sufficiently emphasize my appreciation of the services of this accomplished, discreet, and withal modest officer.

Though my acquaintance with the officers of the Army is quite extensive, I know of none who possesses the qualities requisite in the command of a volunteer regiment in a higher degree than Captain Sibert, or who, by reason of his past service, better merits the appointment of colonel of volunteers. It is hoped that the War Department may see its way clear in the future to recognize in some marked way the excellent work he has rendered in the field and with troops.

February 10, 1900.—Was directed to take charge of and operate the Manila and Dagupan Railway, furnishing such transportation service as army needs required, and to open up the same to public traffic. Captain Sibert was addressed while performing this temporary duty as chief engineer and general manager of the railway. The operating force for the railroad under the new conditions was organized, rates established, tickets and all necessary blanks printed. On February 20 public traffic was inaugurated. The road was thus operated until April 20.

March 10, 1900.—Senior member of a Board to inventory and transfer the Manila and Dagupan Railroad and its appurtenances to the owners of the road, and to report upon the condition of the road and roadbed when captured from the insurgents, and its condition when transferred and the cost of labor and material expended thereon by the military authorities. This duty was completed and the railroad transferred to its owners April 20, 1900.

May 5, 1900.—Sailed on the transport *Meade* for the United States.
May 31, 1900.—Arrived in San Francisco.
June 6, 1901.—In a letter to the Secretary of War the Chief of Engineers, United States Army, recommended:

That Capt. William L. Sibert, Corps of Engineers, chief engineer of the expeditionary troops under the command of Brigadier-General Schwan, United States Volunteers, to Northern Luzon, October 7-14, 1899, be brevetted major, United States Army, and lieutenant-colonel, United States Army, for distinguished services as engineer and on the firing line, October 10, 1899, on the Buena Vista road, where he contributed in a marked degree to the success of the operations of that day, and that he be appointed brigadier-general of volunteers for "soldierly conduct and excellent service throughout the campaign" in northern and southern Luzon.

CAPT. JOSEPH E. KUHN.

May 31, 1898.—Appointed major and chief engineer, United States Volunteers.
April 12, 1899.—Honorably discharged from the volunteer service.

CAPT. WILLIAM E. CRAIGHILL.

July 16, 1898.—Appointed major and chief engineer, United States Volunteers. Declined, August 1, 1898.
August 17, 1899.—Appointed major, Fortieth Infantry, United States Volunteers.
September 23, 1899.—Joined the regiment.
Assigned to command of the Second Battalion by verbal order of the regimental commander. With the regiment, commanding battalion at Fort Riley, Kans., while en route to and at the Presidio, San Francisco, Cal.; en route to Philippine Islands; at Camp Alva, on the north line of defenses of Manila, and in camp on the Luneta, city of Manila. En route to Philippine Islands commanded on the transport *Indiana*, with Companies E, F, G, H, I, K of the regiment and detachment of recruits and casuals. At Camp Alva, in command of the guard of the pumping station.
October 30, 1899.—Left Fort Riley.
November 6, 1899.—Arrived Presidio.
November 23, 1899.—Sailed from San Francisco.
December 27, 1899.—Arrived Manila, P. I.
December 29, 1899.—Disembarked and marched to Camp Alva, defenses of Manila.
January 27, 1900.—Marched to camp on Luneta, in Manila.
February 4, 1900.—Embarked on transport *Francisco Reyes*, with battalion, the colonel commanding, for Legaspi, Albay province, southern Luzon.
February 6, 1900.—Arrived Legaspi.
February 7, 1900.—Disembarked and marched about 4 miles to Daraga.
February 7 to March 18, 1900.—Commanding post of Daraga, Companies F and H.
February 8, 1900.—Commanding reconnaissance about 1 mile in front of Daraga, with Company F, Fortieth Infantry, and two com-

panies of Forty-seventh Infantry, engaged with Philippine insurgents. Drove the enemy from their trenches about half a mile; destroyed their barracks and captured one small brass cannon.

February 14, 1900.—Engaged at Malabog with Companies E, F, and H.

February 22 to February 23, 1900.—In column composed of Companies E, F, G, and K, and three companies of Forty-seventh Infantry, under command of Colonel Howe, of Forty-seventh Infantry, marched from Daraga to Guinabatan, about 20 miles and return, February 22 and 23, 1900. Engaged at Malabog February 22, and, commanding the advance guard, engaged with the enemy's rear from Malabog to Kamalig, about 11 miles, and at Kamalig on same date. Drove the enemy out of Kamalig and occupied the town. Four companies engaged from 9 o'clock a. m. until about 3 p. m.

February 23, 1900.—Engaged at Guinabatan, and took part in occupation of that town. Returned to station at Daraga same day.

March 14, 1900.—In column commanded by Colonel Howe, Forty-seventh Infantry, seven companies and one piece of artillery, marched to Ligao, 32 miles, commanding Companies E, F, G, and H.

March 14, 1900.—Engaged near Malabog, at Camalig, and at Guinabatan. Took part in occupation of Ligao.

March 14, 1900.—Commanding reconnaissance, five companies, (E, F, G, and H of Fortieth and one company of Forty-seventh Infantry), with one piece of artillery, marched to Oas, Libon, and Polangui, and returned same day to Ligao, about 22 miles.

March 17, 1900.—Returned to station at Daraga. Engaged en route at and near Kamalig.

March 18, 1900.—Relieved at Daraga, concentrated the battalion at Legaspi, and embarked on transport *Francisco Reyes* to join the regiment in the expedition to northern Mindanao under command of Major-General Bates. Participated in occupation of Surigao and Cagayan, island of Mindanao, on March 27 and 29, and with battalion occupied Yligan without opposition on March 31, 1900. In command of post of Yligan from this date until August 13, 1900, when relieved by S. O., No. 95, Headquarters Division of the Philippines, dated July 23, 1900, and directed to proceed to Taku, China, reporting to Major-General Chaffee for duty.

August 27, 1900.—Left Manila on transport *Sumner.*

September 6, 1900.—Arrived at Taku, China.

September 22, 1900.—Assigned to duty on Major-General Chaffee's staff.

October 5 and October 7, 1900.—Assigned to duty as member of the department of military intelligence to observe the French and Russian forces.

October 22, 1900.—Appointed a member of the Board of officers convened to consider the subject of brevets and medals of honor in connection with the services performed by the China relief expedition.

November 2, 1900.—Active operations having ceased, relieved at own request, November 2, 1900, and ordered to return to Manila.

December 9, 1900.—Arrived in Manila.

December 11, 1900.—Ordered to rejoin regiment.

December 20, 1900.—Rejoined at Cagayan de Misamis, headquarters of the regiment, commanding companies F and H at that post until relieved by S. O., No. 15, Headquarters Department of Mindanao and

Jolo, Cagayan, January 25, 1901, and ordered to report to adjutant-general, Division of the Philippines for special duty.

February 4, 1901.—Arrived in Manila.

February 11, 1901.—Assigned with station in Manila to supervisory control of the harbor improvements authorized by the act for improving the port of Manila, passed by the United States Philippine Commission October 15, 1900.

June 24, 1901.—Mustered out as major of Fortieth United States Volunteer Infantry.

CAPT. CHARLES S. RICHÉ.

May 20, 1898.—Appointed colonel First United States Volunteer Infantry.

June 4 to October 28, 1898.—Commanding First United States Volunteer Infantry.

July 22, 1898.—Regiment left Galveston.

July 23, 1898.—Arrived at Gouldsboro, La.

July 27, 1898, to August 18, 1898.—In camp at fair grounds, New Orleans, La.

August 18, 1898.—Left New Orleans, La.

August 19, 1898.—Arrived at Camp Hawley, Galveston, Tex.

September 20, 1898.—Assistant mustering officer for the State of Texas, with station at Galveston.

October 28, 1898.—Mustered out of service as colonel First United States Volunteer Infantry.

CAPT. THOMAS H. REES.

May 14, 1898.—Left Willets Point, N. Y., by rail for Port Tampa, Fla., on duty with Company C, Battalion of Engineers.

May 15, 1898.—Arrived at Port Tampa, Fla. Companies C and E were organized as the engineer battalion of the Fifth Army Corps, and he was appointed adjutant, but continued to perform company duty with Company C and had charge of battalion infantry drills and company engineering drills while in camp at Port Tampa.

June 6, 1898.—Embarked on transport *Alamo*.

June 14, 1898.—Sailed with fleet; destination unknown.

June 20, 1898.—Arrived off Morro Castle, mouth of Santiago Harbor.

June 22, 1898.—Disembarked at Daiquiri; was in charge of pontons carrying intrenching tools to shore.

Proceeded to Aserraderos to assist in preparing for embarkation of General Garcia's Cuban army of 3,000 men.

June 26, 1898.—Returned to Siboney, Cuba; constructed small crib work pier for boat landing.

June 27 and 28, 1898.—In charge of unloading engineer material from transport at Siboney.

June 29, 1898.—Assigned in charge of construction of railroad pier at Siboney. This work was interrupted by a march to the front and work on stream crossings and roads, but was finally completed on July 12. A crib work pier 130 feet long, to a depth of 10 feet of water, was constructed and railroad track extended to its end.

July 13 to 16, 1898.—In charge of detachments working on roads.

July 17 to 19, 1898.—In charge of construction of railroad trestle to replace portion of Aguadores bridge destroyed by Spanish troops.

July 20, 1898.—Repaired a washout in the railroad where the embankment had been destroyed by waves.

July 22, 1898.—Moved camp with all engineer material and stores to La Cruz, 1 mile from Santiago. Thence moved to Cuabitas and was placed in charge of rebuilding railroad trestles over Purgatoria Creek and Virgin Creek. These trestles had been burned by the Cuban forces under General Garcia.

August 1, 1898.—Assigned by orders to command of Engineer Battalion, Fifth Army Corps, and remained in command until its return to former stations in the United States.

August 23, 1898.—The battalion embarked on transport *Minnewaska* and reached camp Wikoff September 1, 1898.

September 4, 1898.—Battalion organization ceased and Company C returned to its former station at Willets Point, and Company E to its former station at West Point.

Commends most highly the zeal, good judgment, and untiring energy displayed by Lieut. H. B. Ferguson, in execution of the work in the Santiago campaign.

From that time until January 9, 1900, served as commanding officer of Company C, Battalion of Engineers, and as instructor of military engineering at the United States Engineer School.

March 14 to July 24, 1899.—Was ordered to proceed with Company C, Battalion of Engineers, to Camp Meade, Pa., and to reestablish that camp for the volunteer regiments returning from Cuba for muster out. Was assigned to command of the camp and the returning regiments were carried as "casually at post." This duty continued till July 24, when he was ordered to return with the company to Willets Point.

The officers under his immediate command at Camp Meade were Lieuts. E. R. Stuart and G. M. Hoffman, Corps of Engineers. Their assistance in laying out the camp, pitching and flooring the tents for five regiments, draining the ground, and building roads, etc., was most valuable and all their work was most efficiently accomplished.

December 5, 1898.—Lieut. Col. George McC. Derby, U. S. V., invited attention to the excellent service rendered by Captain Rees during the Cuban campaign, and recommended his promotion in the volunteer service.

December 9, 1898.—The Chief of Engineers, U. S. A., recommended to the Secretary of War that he be brevetted major for valuable and efficient services at Santiago, Cuba.

CAPT. CHARLES L. POTTER.

May 11, 1898.—Relieved from duty at Portland, Oreg.

May 13, 1898.—Arrived at San Francisco and reported to the adjutant-general, Department of California.

May 20, 1898.—Reported to General Otis and assigned same date as engineer officer of expeditionary force.

May 30, 1898.—Reported to General Merritt and assigned as engineer officer of Department of Pacific.

June 22, 1898.—Appointed lieutenant-colonel and chief engineer, United States Volunteers.

June 23, 1898.—Designated as chief engineer of Eighth Army Corps. Outfitted the command and purchased material in San Francisco for an engineer depot at Manila. Loaded material on steamer *Morgan City*, which sailed June 27.

June 29, 1898.—Sailed with General Merritt and staff on steamer *Newport*.

July 25, 1898.—Arrived at Cavite.

July 28, 1898.—Was directed to report to General Greene in Camp Dewey to make a reconnaissance of the front of the Spanish lines; made reconnaissance with Lieutenant Connor.

August 13, 1898.—Accompanied General Merritt and personal staff during the capture and occupation of Manila.

August 15, 1898.—President of board to count Spanish public funds.

September 1, 1898.—Assigned as chief engineer of Department of the Pacific and Eighth Army Corps.

October 10, 1898.—Appointed auditor of public accounts, which position was held until September 20, 1899.

December 24, 1898.—Was sent by special steamer to take messages from General Otis to General Rios, at Iloilo.

December 28, 1898.—Was sent to Iloilo by General Otis with dispatches to General Miller.

January 4, 11, and 24, 1899.—Was sent to Iloilo with similar dispatches.

February 8, 1899.—Was sent to Iloilo with instructions to General Miller to occupy the town. Was present at the capture of Iloilo and Jaro.

February 26, 1899.—Was sent to accompany a battalion of infantry to Cebu and carry out certain instructions from General Otis.

April 5, 1899.—Was appointed president of a board to proceed to Malolos and receive, inventory, and receipt for, bring to Manila, and turn over to the treasurer of public funds, money, and property of the insurgent government, captured by the United States troops at that place.

June 21, 1899.—Was sent by General Otis to Iloilo and Jolo to make a report on the situation at these two points.

August 19, 1899.—Was appointed on a board to examine into the wreck of the transport *Hooker* and fix the responsibility for the same.

September 2, 1899.—Honorably discharged as lieutenant-colonel, chief engineer, United States Volunteers.

September 13, 1899.—Was relieved from duty as chief engineer as of September 2, 1899, by Capt. W. L. Sibert, Corps of Engineers.

September 20, 1899.—Relieved from duty as auditor of public accounts, Philippine Islands.

October 17, 1899.—Sailed for the United States.

December 10, 1899.—Arrived at San Francisco.

The above list contains all special work, and is in addition to regular work of supplying troops with tools and material, constructing and repairing roads, bridges, and ferries, and making reconnaissances, surveys, and maps, all of which was under the general and a portion under the personal direction of the chief engineer.

SERVICES PERFORMED BY ENGINEER TROOPS.

Upon the first organization of the expeditionary forces the engineer officer telegraphed for a proper quota of regular and volunteer engineers.

Company A, Battalion of Engineers, 3 officers and 60 men, **arrived in San Francisco early in June, 1898.**

One officer was relieved and 1 reported, and the company recruited to 120 men before sailing.

A detachment of 20 men sailed under Lieutenant Connor on the first expedition, May 25, and the remainder of the company under Lieutenant Echols with Lieutenant Kerr sailed with General MacArthur on June 27, 1898.

The detachment with the first expedition was in Camp Dewey employed in reconnaissances and road and bridge work.

The whole company, in two detachments, accompanied the brigade commanders in the capture of Manila.

Lieutenant Echols being sick and finally relieved, and Lieutenant Connor being detached, Lieutenant W. G. Haan, Third United States Artillery, was put in command of Company A, Battalion of Engineers, September 7, 1898, and remained in command until relieved by Lieutenant Wooten, March 3, 1899.

The company was engaged in detachments in reconnaissances, in building and repairing roads, bridges, and ferries, in clearing obstructions from the river, and general work of engineer troops.

The company acted as infantry on February 5, in the first day's fight with insurgents, when its services and that of its commanding officer were commended by Col. James F. Smith, commanding First California Volunteers.

The company again made a reconnaissance on February 15, 1899, and was engaged an hour and a half with a force of insurgents. Special mention was made of Private John Varney on this reconnaissance.

The company was used as infantry to hold the southern line during General Schwan's campaign in Cavite province, in October, 1899.

During a great portion of the time covered by this report, officers were so scarce as to necessitate the direct supervision of important works by sergeants of the company. Those performing the most important duties were Sergeants Kennedy, Fisher, and Freeman, but it is not intended by mentioning these to detract from the importance of work performed by other noncommissioned officers and privates.

CAPT. FRANCIS R. SHUNK.

January 13, 1899.—Left West Point, N. Y.
March 11, 1899.—Arrived at Manila.
March 13, 1899.—Took command of Company A, Battalion of Engineers, and continued in this command until December 27, 1899, when he was relieved by Second Lieut. William P. Wooten. During this time the headquarters of the company was at Malate, in the suburbs of Manila. Parties of from 5 to 20 men were constantly engaged in building and repairing roads, bridges, and ferries, and removing obstructions from waterways in the vicinity of Manila; the field of these operations extending from Malabon on the north to Imus on the south. This work was done under his personal supervision, and was collectively of importance.

On March 23, 1899, two detachments were, by order of the chief engineer (Lieut Col. Potter, U. S. V.), sent to join General MacArthur and General Wheaton, respectively, and Captain Shunk requested and obtained permission to accompany one of these parties for a short time, and remained with General MacArthur until the capture of Malolos, returning on April 2. During this time the detachment did very hard work; built 3 bridges and 2 ferries, and constructed approaches for wagons to a ford and a railroad bridge.

April 25, 1899.—In charge of the buildings and property pertaining to the civil departments of public works, harbor improvements, department of mountains, department of mines, and department of agriculture.

Late in September, 1899.—The company was ordered out, in an emergency, for outpost duty, and spent two days at Culiculi.

Early in October, 1899.—The company was again ordered out as infantry to protect Paranaque, and stayed for two days.

October 7 to 14, 1899.—They were directed to report to General Schwan at Bacoor. Here a ferry was built across the Imus River. During its construction Captain Shunk was taken sick and obliged to return to Malate. Lieutenant Stickle took command of the company, and remained with General Schwan during his expedition into Cavite province.

October 8, 1899.—He was taken ill and compelled to return to Manila in command of that portion of his company in the city. Was in charge of repairs to roads and bridges outside of the city limits in the vicinity of Manila until he returned to the United States.

December 29, 1899.—Left Manila on transport *City of Peking.*
January 24, 1900.—Arrived at San Francisco.
March 25, 1900.—Reported at Fort Totten for duty.

CAPT. EUGENE W. VAN C. LUCAS.

May 31, 1898.—Appointed division engineer officer with the rank of major, United States Volunteers.

July 7, 1898.—Relieved from duty at Willets Point.

July 9, 1898.—Reported for duty at Headquarters, Fourth Army Corps, Tampa, Fla., and assigned as chief engineer, Second Division, Fourth Army Corps, until August 11, 1898. Had charge of drill work and assisted in straightening out accounts and records of equipment purchased. At Fernandina he assisted in laying out the camp for troops moving from Tampa.

November 25, 1898, to January 1, 1899.—Chief engineer, Third Division, Second Army Corps, in camp at Athens, Ga.

January 1 to March 1, 1899.—Chief engineer, Second Division, Second Army Corps, in camp at Greenville, S. C. Organized a division engineer's office, having attached to it on special duty several young officers of volunteers, who were systematically trained in reconnaissance work, foot and mounted, with satisfactory results for the time employed. Without previous training they were able after six weeks' work to do ordinary road reconnaissance work in advance of a moving column, with rapidity and accuracy, and also cover any given territory in the same way.

Was unable to do much effective work as division engineer until January 1, 1899, owing to lack of equipment. His conclusion on this point is that the engineer equipment of a corps, division, brigade, or regiment, etc., should be decided on and listed, so that upon assignment to duty an officer may make requisition for the proper equipment, which should be kept in store at the Engineer Depot, ready for such requisition.

January 14 to February 4, 1899.—Acting chief quartermaster, Second Division, Second Army Corps.

February 24, 1899.—Relieved from duty with Second Army Corps.

March 21, 1899.—Honorably discharged from the Volunteer Army.

CAPT. HENRY JERVEY.

March 8, 1901.—Joined Second Battalion of Engineers. Commanding Company E and battalion.

June 17, 1901.—Left Willets Point, New York, commanding Second Battalion of Engineers, Companies E, F, G, and H.

June 23, 1901.—Arrived at San Francisco.

June 25, 1901.—Sailed from San Francisco on the transport *Hancock* en route to Manila.

CAPT. WILLIAM V. JUDSON.

August 23, 1899.—Relieved from duty in New York City and sailed for Porto Rico.

August 26, 1899.—Arrived at San Juan, P. R., and was assigned to duty as engineer officer, Department of Porto Rico, and president of the board of public works.

As engineer officer of the department, was charged with the usual issues of engineer instruments and material to line officers; with the preparation of a map of Porto Rico; with the expenditure upon road work, largely to relieve distress incident to the hurricane of August, 8, 1899, of $200,000 from the emergency fund, War Department, and of $750,000 from the appropriation "Refunding Customs Revenue to Porto Rico;" with various investigations and reports relating to applications for franchises, referred to him by the department commander; with the preparation of certain maps and reports relating to public lands; and with the supervision of construction of a large wharf at San Juan, P. R., under authority of the Secretary of War; recommended harbor lines for San Juan Harbor; submitted project for submarine-mine defense of San Juan Harbor.

As president of the board of public works, of which there was but one other member during a large part of the time, he acted as executive officer, and was charged with the following: The organization of a force for the work to be undertaken; the construction and repair of roads and the building of bridges, including surveys for new roads and the preparation of typical plans and specifications for roads and their appurtenances; the construction and repair of public buildings, under which head many schoolhouses, jails, wharf buildings, etc., were planned or built, and many public buildings were renovated, repaired, and fitted with modern plumbing; the maintenance and construction of light-houses, under which head two important light stations were built and put in operation, one upon Vieques Island and one upon Mona Island; and harbor works, under which head little was done save to construct or repair a sea wall about 800 feet long at San Juan to afford a landing for small craft, the construction and equipment of a machine shop at San Juan, and the maintenance of an antiquated dredging plant at the latter harbor.

He was the only engineer officer in Porto Rico, and there were no engineer troops there.

His principal work was with roads, and he secured some very efficient civilian assistants. They endured many hardships, including sickness for most of them and death for a few, and under the strain put upon them by the necessity of working as many laborers as possible to relieve distress, they did most excellent work.

April 30, 1900.—Relinquished office of president of board of public works.

May 1, 1900.—As assistant to the engineer, Third light-house district, assumed local charge of light-house engineer work in Porto Rico.

July 5, 1900.—Charged with the removal of wrecked steamer *Cristóbal Colón* in the eastern entrance to the harbor of San Juan, P. R.

August 6, 1900.—Left Porto Rico on leave of absence.

September 27, 1900.—Transferred his duties in Porto Rico to Captain Flagler and took station at Montgomery, Ala.

CAPT. E. EVELETH WINSLOW.

April 30, 1898.—Left West Point, N. Y., with Company E, Battalion of Engineers, for duty in the field.

May 1, 1898.—Sailed from New York City on the transport *Alamo*.

May 6, 1898.—Arrived at Key West, Fla., and having received orders for Port Tampa, Fla., arrived at that place May 7, 1898.

May 7 to June 6, 1898.—In camp at Port Tampa. Company landed materials, performed the usual camp duties, and company was instructed in infantry and engineer drill.

May 25, 1898.—The United States forces at Tampa were organized into the Fifth Army Corps, and Company E and Company C (the latter company arrived May 16, 1898) became the Engineer Battalion of that corps.

June 6 to 14, 1898.—On board the *Alamo* at Tampa.

June 14, 1898.—The *Alamo* sailed with the fleet of transports.

June 20, 1898.—The fleet arrived off Santiago Harbor.

June 22, 1898.—Tools and materials were landed at Daiquiri, and the pier was repaired.

June 23, 1898.—Pier was built at Aserraderos for the embarkation of the Cuban army under General García. On June 24 the Cubans were embarked, and on June 26 they were landed at Siboney.

A temporary landing pier was built. In the meanwhile the landing of tools and supplies was begun, all being carried in pontons from the vessels to the beach. The next day this work was continued and by noon all the company equipage, baggage, and rations, all intrenching and pioneer tools had been put ashore. All the bridge material except that used in landing was left on the *Alamo*. In the afternoon the company landed in pontons and went into camp for the night near the locomotive roundhouse.

June 28.—The camp was moved to a better site, an engineer depot was established in a storehouse near the beach and on the railroad, and the tools and materials were moved into it. Work was begun on a large and more permanent landing pier, and a road and railroad bridge over the creek were repaired.

The road to the front was under repair for a distance of nearly 2 miles by a detail under Lieutenant Winslow, a bridge 60 feet long being built over the creek.

July 1, 1898.—Telephone orders were received from corps headquarters directing that the battalion proceed at once to the front and be there by daybreak. Accordingly camp was at once broken, and all equipage and rations except those to be taken on the persons of the men were stored at the engineer depot, where they were left under a small guard. After everything had been put away the battalion, at about 9.30 p. m., began its night march, and arrived about 1.30 a. m. at corps headquarters near Sevilla. Here a halt was made, the men getting such rest as they could without even putting up shelter tents. The next morning, after collecting such tools as could be obtained, the march was continued to the creek crossing at the foot of the San Juan hill. Here a halt was made, and work was at once begun on this crossing, sloping the banks, digging out mud, and replacing it by gravel, covering bad places with brush, etc., the work not being completed till late in the afternoon. All this work was carried on under the constant though irregular fire of bullets aimed by the Spaniards at our troops on the hill in front. Lieutenant Winslow was in charge of detail of skirmishers sent out to protect the engineers working on the ford from Spanish sharpshooters concealed in the palm trees.

Upon the completion of this work at the ford the battalion was formed and marched back to corps headquarters and camped there for the night. About 10 o'clock the camp was aroused by the firing during the Spanish sortie, and in obedience to orders from General Shafter the battalion was formed and remained under arms awaiting orders until the cessation of the firing at the front, when it was allowed to turn in again. The next morning, July 3, the battalion remained awaiting orders till about 10 a. m., when, the orders being received, it broke camp and marched back to a point about halfway between Siboney and corps headquarters, near the battlefield of Guasimas. Here it went into camp, and the next morning resumed work on the roads, which had become almost impassable.

July 6 to 20, 1898.—Lieutenant Winslow was in charge of road work in vicinity of Siboney.

July 22 to 27, 1898.—In camp at La Cruz. Lieutenant Winslow was in charge of repairs to the road leading to Santiago and a portion of Calle de la Christina, Santiago.

July 27 to August 22, 1898.—The battalion was in camp at Purgatoria bridge; repaired Boniata and Purgatoria bridges.

August 22, 1898.—Camp broken.

August 23, 1898.—Sailed from Santiago on the transport *Minnewaska* and landed at Montauk Point, Long Island, August 30, 1898.

September 1–3, 1898.—At Camp Wikoff.

September 4, 1898.—Arrived at West Point, N. Y., with and in command of Company C, Battalion of Engineers. In command until November 15, 1898.

CAPT. CLEMENT A. F. FLAGLER.

May 17, 1898.—Appointed engineer officer with the rank of major, United States Volunteers.

May 21, 1898.—Relieved from duty at Willets Point.

May 25, 1898.—Reported to Maj. Gen. James H. Wilson, commanding Sixth Army Corps, at Camp Thomas, Ga. Assigned as chief instructor of volunteer staff officers. In the selection of camps, and outfitting and preparing transports, he performed valuable services.

May 25, 1898, to September 10, 1898.—Engineer officer, First Division, First Army Corps.

July 20, 1898.—Sailed from Charleston, S. C., with the Porto Rican expedition as engineer officer on the staff of Maj. Gen. J. H. Wilson, then commanding the First Division, First Army Corps.

July 27, 1898.—Arrived at harbor of Guanica, but did not disembark until the following morning at Ponce Playa. No resistance was experienced, and immediately after landing he accompanied Lieut. Col. John Biddle, United States Volunteers, to Ponce. Took possession of the barracks and engineer office, and brought troops at once from the Playa to guard them. He then assisted Lieutenant Haim, of the marines, in releasing political prisoners from the jail at Ponce.

Having been detailed as picket officer of the division he at once began posting pickets to the north and east of the town, and finished this work at 2 a. m. on the 29th. Next day he completed the work by posting outposts to the west on the Yauco and Adjuntas roads. From that day until the expedition left Ponce he visited each outpost daily; the cordon extending gradually until it required about 35 miles' riding. During this period made reconnaissance, examined spies, and assisted Colonel Biddle in the preparation of maps.

August 5, 1898.—While reconnoitering the enemy's position east of Coamo River, in company with Captain Latrobe, of General Wilson's staff, with an orderly, an interpreter, and two native guides, was fired upon from an outlying house and one of the horses was killed.

August 7, 1898.—The expedition left Ponce and camped on the Descalabrado River until the engagement at Coamo on the 9th. Spent the time reconnoitering and posting outposts.

August 9, 1898.—At the engagement at Coamo was directed by General Wilson to take Troop C, of the New York Cavalry, attack and capture a Spanish outpost at Banos de Coamo, and then reach Coamo as soon as possible and follow the Spaniards if in retreat. The banos had been deserted before he reached it, and hastening to Coamo he found the action there over, and hurried on up the military road after the retreating Spaniards. Passed two partially demolished bridges, one almost entirely so, and about 5 miles from Coamo was stopped by artillery fire from the enemy's battery on Mount Asomante. That afternoon and next morning repaired the bridge so as to be practicable for artillery. Established an outpost there which was not changed until the promulgation of the peace protocol. Numerous shots were exchanged at long range from time to time between this outpost and the enemy, but the range was about 1,800 yards and no harm was done.

August 12, 1898.—During the bombardment of Asomante was sent by General Wilson with a cavalry detail to a peak a mile on the enemy's left rear, from which to signal movements in the lines. After the bombardment reconnoitered up the Cuyon Valley to the Salinas trail, at a point a few miles southeast of Aibonita, with a view to using this route for a flanking movement, but found it almost impracticable for any large body of troops.

After the signing of the protocol, acted as summary court for division headquarters. Also spent four days pursuing alleged bandits with a cavalry detail in the vicinity of Bermejalas, and made a route sketch of the trails connecting Coamo, Barros, and Barranquitas.

September 2, 1898.—Sailed for New York in command of the transport *Mississippi*, arriving there September 10.

December 31, 1898.—Honorably discharged from the Volunteer Army.
September 26, 1900.—Transferred the duties in his charge to Capt. William V. Judson, and relieved the latter of charge of the removal of the wrecked steamer *Cristóbal Colón* in entrance to San Juan Harbor, Porto Rico. This wreck was removed May 27, 1901, under contract, the work being done by means of a diver and the explosion of charges of dynamite.
October 19, 1900.—Reported to the commanding general, Department of Porto Rico, and assigned as engineer officer, Department of Porto Rico.

On duty under the Treasury Department as assistant to the light-house engineer of the Third light-house district, and placed by him in immediate charge of the subdistrict of Porto Rico, comprising 15 light-houses. Work on these houses since his assumption of the duty has comprised only repairs, painting, drainage, etc.

The principal work under his charge has been the construction of public roads in the island of Porto Rico, under appropriations from the "Emergency Fund, War Department (Act of March 3, 1899)," and "Refunding Customs Revenue collected from Porto Rico for the relief of its government and people." A synopsis of this work from the time of its inception before his duty in the island began, is as follows:

In laying out a scheme for a new road construction in Porto Rico the distribution of work and money had to be governed by the following existing conditions, viz, the roads already built, the physical character of the country, and the necessity for distributing the work over the entire island so as to relieve the distress.

Up to the time of the American occupation the existing roads constructed previously consisted of about 158 miles, distributed as follows:

	Miles.
San Juan to Ponce Playa	82.46
Catano to Toa Alta	14.88
Anasco to Penzuelo Bridge through Mayaguez	14.26
Cayey to Guayama	15.74
Ponce toward Adjuntas	9.30
Rio Piedras to Rio Grande	16.12
Utuado toward Arecibo	3.10
San Sebastian toward Moca	1.86
Total	157.72

The island of Porto Rico with an area of about 3,600 square miles has a coast line, not measuring sinuosities, of about 270 miles. Along this coast line are scattered the more important ports of San Juan, Arecibo, Aguadilla, Mayaguez, Ponce, Arroyo, Humacao, and Fajardo, and the lesser ports of the class of Guanica, Nagaubo, etc.

There is a coastal plain averaging not more than a few miles in width running practically around the entire island. The interior of the island is composed of round, very irregular hills or mountains averaging in height, say, from 1,500 to 3,800 feet. Besides the main east and west range there are mountains that do not exist in ranges, but lie in very confused groupings between the rivers in a way that greatly increases the difficulties of location and construction of roads or railroads. The sugar lands lie in the coastal plain and the tobacco and coffee lands in the interior high lands or mountains.

In distributing this work over the island it was decided to adopt the policy of building roads from the interior, or coffee and tobacco lands, to the nearest port, with the exception of one main road which was projected running entirely across the island from Arecibo to Ponce. In this way the distribution of road work seemed to be scattered best over the island, affording a means of livelihood to the laboring classes and also opening up the inner portions, which at present have both to take in and out all their products and necessaries of life by pack mules over trails that are more or less dangerous, and frequently impassable for days during the rainy season.

The allotments that have been made to carry on road work in Porto Rico under the War Department have been as follows:

"Emergency Fund, War Department;" allotment made October 25, 1899.	$200,000
"Refunding Customs Revenue, etc.;" allotment made March 20, 1900	610,000
"Refunding Customs Revenue, etc.;" allotment made April 9, 1900	50,000
"Refunding Customs Revenue, etc.;" allotment made June 19, 1900......	90,000
Total..	950,000

The first allotment of $200,000 from the "Emergency Fund, War Department," was expended with the exception of about $1,500 by July 31, 1900.

Of the $750,000 allotted from the "Refunding Customs Revenue" appropriation, all but $84,720.34 has been expended or earned by contractors up to March 1, 1901, and the balance will be worked out probably by June 30, 1901.

The roads to which these allotments have been applied are as follows:

1. From Arecibo to Ponce.—This road will be about 50 miles long. About 12 miles were built before annexation, and 10.6 are under construction by the insular government.

2. Aguadilla to Moca.—The distance is about 4.2 miles. The work was done by day labor, and the purchase of materials in open market, at a total cost of $11,123.84.

3. Moca to San Sebastian.—This section, in connection with the last mentioned, will make an excellent road from Aguadilla to San Sebastian, 14.4 miles in length, of which about 3½ miles were built by the Spaniards.

4. Guayama to Arroyo.—About 4 miles in length. The cost was $25,091.85.

5. Toa Alta to Carozal.—About 3 miles in length, at a cost of $27,577.05.

6. Caguas to Humacao Playa.—This road will connect the main highway between San Juan and Ponce with the east coast of Humacao Playa, the cost of the first section being $110,000, while that of the second will be about $135,000.

7. Camerio toward Bayamon.—The appropriation made was $60,000, and the work was completed, the amount being sufficient to construct about 4 miles of road.

8. Mayaguez to Las Marias.—The distance is approximately 18 miles, but much of the old road is in a fair condition and only about 4 miles of entirely new road will be built and about 6 miles of old road constructed; $100,000 was allotted to this work.

In addition to the several roads mentioned it became necessary to afford employment to the destitute near the towns of Ponce, Lares, and San Sebastian, and it was decided, as a means of employment, to have a large quantity of stone broken, which would provide suitable work to the unskilled, and also to the women and children. The stone was conveniently placed for future road work, either construction or repairs, and has been turned over to the board of public works of the insular government.

In all, the expenditure for breaking stone, including supervision, was $33,515.29, and 27,581 cubic yards of stone were purchased and broken.

In addition to road work, other duties pertaining to the Department of Porto Rico were the issuance of instruments for reconnaissance on practice, marches of troops and the examination of route sketches prepared. Considerable work was also done in the investigation of War Department titles to lands, surveys of reservations, etc.

November 17, 1900.—Appointed recorder of Board of officers to make examination and report to the Secretary of War respecting public lands owned by the United States in Porto Rico required for the use of the military and naval establishments. Report of the Board was submitted December 15, 1900.

November 19, 1900.—Placed in charge of the preservation and repair of the defenses of San Juan. Detailed estimate of these repairs for the fiscal year ending June 30, 1902, has been prepared and submitted.

In a report dated August 23, 1898, Maj. Gen. James H. Wilson, U. S. V., says:

Maj. Clement A. P. Flagler, United States Volunteer Engineers, captain, United States Corps of Engineers, joined me at Camp Thomas on the 25th day of May, 1898, and was at once assigned to duty as chief instructor of volunteer staff officers, in which capacity, as well as in the selection of camps and in the performance of various other duties connected with outfitting and preparing transports for the proper transportation of troops, he rendered most valuable services. After disembarkation at Ponce, he displayed great activity and intelligence in reconnoitering the enemy's positions and exploring the country, and especially in placing our advance guards and pickets. He is an officer of rare enterprise, ability, and courage, and I recommend that he be brevetted major in the United States Army for gallant and meritorious service in the Porto Rican campaign.

Also, Maj. Clement A. F. Flagler, United States Volunteers, of my staff, has, at his own request, been ordered to Washington to report to you for duty.

It gives me pleasure to say that Major Flagler has rendered very efficient service indeed with me, not only in the routine duties of an engineer officer, but he has also displayed the greatest gallantry in the presence of the enemy. I do not know how a young officer could have higher talents or greater qualifications than he has for the military service. I commend him to your most favorable consideration.

It seems to me quite as praiseworthy in him to desire to return to regular duty with the engineers as it was to obtain service in the field against the public enemy. I hope you will be able to give him a district of engineering work, for I am sure he will discharge whatever duty you intrust to him with marked ability and fidelity.

June 6, 1901.—In a letter to the Secretary of War the Chief of Engineers, United States Army, recommended that—

Capt. Clement A. F. Flagler, Corps of Engineers (formerly engineer officer, First Division, First Army Corps, with the rank of major, United States Volunteers), be brevetted major and lieutenant-colonel, United States Army, for gallant and distinguished services in the affair at Coamo, August 9, 1898.

CAPT. WILLIAM W. HARTS.

July 13, 1898.—Appointed engineer officer of volunteers, with the rank of major.

November 30, 1898.—Honorably discharged from the Volunteer Army.

March 31, 1901.—Joined Company H, Second Battalion of Engineers.

June 17, 1901.—Left Willets Point.

June 23, 1901.—Arrived at San Francisco.
June 25, 1901.—Sailed from San Francisco on transport *Hancock*, en route to Manila.

CAPT. ROBERT M'GREGOR.

March 16, 1901.—Joined Company F, Second Battalion of Engineers, commanding company.
June 17, 1901.—Left Willets Point, N. Y.
June 23, 1901.—Arrived at San Francisco.
June 25, 1901.—Sailed from San Francisco on the transport *Hancock*, en route to Manila.

CAPT. EDGAR JADWIN.

June 9, 1898.—Appointed member of Board of officers to ascertain suitable camp ground for forces in the field; report of the Board was submitted June 15, 1898.
June 20, 1898.—Appointed major, Third Regiment, United States Volunteer Engineers.
June 27, 1898.—Appointed member of Board of officers to meet at Galveston, Tex., to examine applicants for commissions in the Third United States Volunteer Engineers. The Board met at Galveston July 5–6.
July 8, 1898.—Returned to Washington and remained there till July 11.
July 11–August 11, 1898.—On recruiting duty in Texas, Arkansas, and New Mexico.
August 11 to December 15, 1898.—Served with regiment at Jefferson Barracks, Mo., Lexington, Ky., and Macon, Ga.
August 11 to September 15, 1898.—Commanded First Battalion, Third United States Volunteer Engineers.
September 15, 1898, to May 17, 1899.—Lieutenant-colonel Third United States Volunteer Engineers.
December 15, 1898.—Left Macon, Ga., in command of the Third Battalion, Third United States Volunteer Engineers, and detachment of the hospital and signal corps.
December 22, 1898, to February 28, 1899.—Commanded detached battalion of regiment at Matanzas, Cuba.
December 23, 1898.—Disembarked at Matanzas, Cuba.

On arrival of this battalion, which until the late afternoon of January 1, 1899, were the only troops on duty at this point, there were 15,000 to 20,000 Spanish soldiers in the city assembled from different towns in the province.

The camp established was in the city limits, but the landing of the Engineer Battalion had to be made on the San Juan River and all property carried out on wagons to the camp, which was quietly and promptly done. Before the arrival of the troops, January 1, the battalion had built a dock at the camp for unloading.

On this battalion, January 1, 1899, devolved the honor of receiving the city and province of Matanzas from the Spanish authorities. This ceremony took place, with all military ceremonies, at noon, at Fort San Severino and the city hall. For several days and nights the battalion acted as provost guard, and, with the cooperation of the Spanish and Cuban officials, maintained perfect order and quiet in the city.

The work performed by this battalion was, in addition to the regular drills, parades, etc.: Building pile and stone wharf near camps;

building pile wharf at custom-house dock; laying out and preparation of camp sites and target ranges for all troops; repair and building of roads leading to and around camp; laying of water pipe to camps; construction of troughs; general control and supervision of water supply for troops (this necessitated considerable labor and constant care); survey of forts and batteries; bringing in of guns and carriages from outlying batteries; superintendence of cleaning and sanitation and surveying of the city of Matanzas; making plats and estimates of all public buildings in the province; investigation of water supplies; copying and distributing of maps; reconnaissance with troops and singly, covering the greater part of the province.

February 28 to March 11, 1899.—On hospital ship *Missouri.*
March 11, 1899.—Arrived at Savannah.
May 17, 1899.—Mustered out of the volunteer service.
January 2, 1899.—The following letter, commending the conduct of the officers and men of the Third Battalion, was received by Colonel Jadwin:

MATANZAS, CUBA, *January 2, 1899.*
To Lieut. Col. EDGAR JADWIN,
Commanding Third Battalion, Third United States Volunteer Engineers.

SIR: The commanding general of the Spanish forces at Matanzas has requested me to express, on the part of the lieutenant-general commanding the Spanish forces in Cuba, and on the part of the officers under his command at Matanzas, their thanks and appreciation for the consideration and soldierly conduct shown them by the officers and men under your orders, on the occasion of taking possession of this city by the United States forces on January 1, 1899.

I desire also to state that the conduct of the battalion, since its arrival here, and under somewhat difficult conditions, has been, in my opinion, exemplary and worthy of the reputation for discipline and efficiency already attained by the Third United States Volunteer Engineers.

Very respectfully,
(Signed) JOHN BIDDLE,
Lieutenant-Colonel, Chief Engineers, First Army Corps.

CAPT. SPENCER COSBY.

June 13, 1898.—Appointed engineer officer, with the rank of major, United States Volunteers.
July 23, 1898.—Relieved from duty under immediate orders of Lieutenant-Colonel Raymond.
July 25, 1898.—Arrived at Newport News, Va., and reported to Major-General Brooke.
July 26, 1898.—Assigned temporarily to duty with Headquarters First Army Corps, as division engineer.
July 28, 1898.—Sailed for Porto Rico.
July 31, 1898.—Arrived at Ponce.
August 2, 1898.—Landed at Arroyo.

During operations in Porto Rico he served continuously on staff of Major-General Brooke.

October 10, 1898.—Relieved from staff duty to enable him to comply with paragraph 28, Special Orders, No. 215, Headquarters of the Army, Adjutant-General's Office, September 12, 1898, ordering him back to Philadelphia. Directed by the Secretary of War, in accordance with request of General Brooke, to remain in Porto Rico until his services could be spared.

During the period of his service with General Brooke he was given but little independent work to perform; most of the engineering work on which he was engaged was done in conjunction with and under the orders of Lieut. Col. G. W. Goethals, United States Volunteers, Chief Engineer, First Army Corps. The principal works of this kind were the building of a landing pier for troops and supplies at Arroyo, road reconnaissances in the vicinity of Guayama, and repairing bridges destroyed by the Spaniards on the military road beyond Guayama. On August 13, 1898, General Brooke ordered a general advance of his force in two columns from Guayama toward the interior; Captain Cosby was directed to act as engineer officer of the column commanded by Brigadier-General Hains, United States Volunteers, which was to turn the intrenched position of the Spaniards on the heights north of Guayama while the main column attacked them in the front. This movement was stopped while being executed, by receipt of news of the suspension of hostilities due to signing of the protocol. He submitted a reconnaissance sketch of the route pursued by General Hains.

From Guayama, where United States forces remained for three weeks after the signing of protocol, he accompanied General Brooke to Rio Piedras, a suburb of San Juan, and remained in camp there until relieved. Shortly before the Spaniards turned the city over to the Americans he made a careful inspection of the fortifications, in company with Lieutenant-Colonel Goethals and a major of engineers of the Spanish army.

Under date of November 16, 1898, he submitted to the chief of engineers a report of his services as above, and accompanied it with a series of notes describing the fortifications, etc., of San Juan, and also a translation of a descriptive memoir. prepared by a Spanish engineer officer, of a project for the erection of a howitzer battery at San Juan.

December 31, 1898.—Honorably discharged from the Volunteer Army.

CAPT. JOHN S. SEWELL.

May 31, 1898.—Appointed major, First United States Volunteer Engineers.

June 13, 1898.—Appointed recruiting officer, First United States Volunteer Engineers at Boston, Mass.

July 10, 1898.—Commanding First Battalion, First United States Volunteer Engineers, and recruited enough men for two companies at Boston, Mass., in which work he was assisted by Capt. Azel Ames.

August 5, 1898.—Left Camp Townsend, Peekskill, N. Y., with regiment.

August 6, 1898.—Sailed from New York City on the transport *Chester*.

August 15, 1898.—Arrived at Ponce, P. R., and went into camp.

August 27, 1889.—Appointed a member of a military commission for the trial of natives accused of burning the village of E Coto.

September 3, 1898.—Before the commission finished its sittings, the first battalion of the regiment was ordered to move to Coamo, twenty miles east of Ponce, and go into camp.

During its stay at Coamo, September 3 to November 5, 1898, under his direction the battalion rebuilt two brick arch bridges which had been blown up, repaired another which had a large hole blown through the crown, repaired the abutments of a steel-girder bridge which had been prepared for destruction, also many retaining walls, and the road itself at points where either time or the retreating Spaniards had made such work necessary; also built floors and frames for the hospital tents of a large field hospital at Coamo. After the departure of

General Ernst's brigade from Coamo, was charged with the maintenance of order in the Coamo district until the First Regiment, United States Volunteer Engineers, was ordered home.

November 18, 1898.—Sailed from Ponce, P. R., on transport *Minnewaska*.

November 24, 1898.—Arrived at New York City.

January 21, 189'. Commissioned lieutenant-colonel, First United States Volunteer Engineers.

January 24, 1899.—Honorably discharged from the Volunteer Army.

March 6, 1899.—Commended by the Chief of Engineers.

April 17, 1899.—Commended by Col. Eugene Griffin, First United States Volunteer Engineers, and brigadier-general, U. S. V.

LIEUT. CHARLES P. ECHOLS.

May 4, 1898.—Temporarily relieved from duty at the Military Academy and reported to the commanding general, Department of the East, for duty as engineer officer on his staff.

May 23, 1898.—Relieved and reported to commanding officer, Willets Point, for duty with Company A, Battalion of Engineers.

May 24, 1898.—Left Willets Point with Company A, Battalion of Engineers, en route to the Philippines.

May 29, 1898.—Reported at San Francisco with Company A, Battalion of Engineers.

June 11, 1898.—Designated as recruiting officer for Company A, Battalion of Engineers.

June 20, 1898.—In command of Company A, Battalion of Engineers.

June 27, 1898.—Sailed with General MacArthur's command on the transport *Indiana*.

July 31, 1898.—Arrived in Manila; landed at Cavite August 2.

August 13, 1898.—Accompanied General MacArthur's command with detachment of engineers in capture of Manila. Made survey and map of battlefield of Manila. Was engaged with a detachment of engineers in raising steamer in the Pasig River, fired and sunk during the capture of Manila.

September 5, 1898.—Relieved from further duty at United States Military Academy, West Point, N. Y.

November 11, 1898.—Relieved from duty in the Department of Pacific and ordered home on account of his appointment as associate professor of mathematics, October 7, 1898.

January 26, 1899.—Resigned commission of first lieutenant, Corps of Engineers.

CAPT. JAY J. MORROW.

September 15, 1898.—Commissioned major, Third United States Volunteer Engineers.

Honorably discharged on tender of resignation, to take effect October 6, 1898.

March 19, 1901.—Joined Company G, Second Battalion of Engineers, commanding company.

June 17, 1901.—Left Willets Point.

June 23, 1901.—Arrived at San Francisco.

June 25, 1901.—Sailed from San Francisco on the transport *Hancock* en route to Manila.

CAPT. JAMES B. CAVANAUGH.

July 14, 1900.—Reported to the Superintendent U. S. Military Academy for duty with Company E, Battalion of Engineers.
July 24, 1900.—Left West Point with company.
July 29, 1900.—Arrived at San Francisco, Cal.
August 1, 1900.—Sailed on transport *Meade.*
September 4, 1900.—Arrived at Manila.
September 6 to October 1, 1900.—In command of Company E, Battalion of Engineers, with headquarters at Coloocan. Repaired roads and buildings damaged by a typhoon.
October 1, 1900, to July 19, 1901.—In command of Company A, Battalion of Engineers, with headquarters first at Bayombong, and subsequently at Dagupan, P. I.

Between October 15 and December 1, 1900, he personally examined and made estimates for the repair of the roads and bridges between Dagupan and San Quintin, Lingayan and San Isidro, Salasa and Sual.

With the allotment of $70,000 and part of a subsequent one of $10,000 the Dagupan-San Quintin road has been made easily passable from Dagupan to Asingan, and from Tayug to San Quintin, and for most of the distance where the road was impassable last rainy season it is now in excellent condition. Due to insufficient funds, the allotment being less than one-third the original estimate, the stretch of 5 miles from Asingan to Tayug and most of that part of the road which was already passable during the rainy season were not touched.

On the Salasa-Sual road all the necessary bridges were replaced and all repairs to roadbed made that were necessary to make it easily passable during the rainy season.

The allotment for the Camiling-Bayombong road was relatively so small that it was merely a question of expending the available funds to the best advantage. The impassable parts of the road have been repaired, necessary bridges and culverts put in, a flying ferry, with overhead steel cable 1¼-inch diameter and 575-foot span, put in at Oaoa across the Agno River, and a similar ferry is being put in at Camiling across the Camiling River. These ferries are identical in form and have sufficient capacity to carry a loaded escort wagon with 4-mule team. This work has greatly improved the condition of the road and made it passable except during the brief periods of highest water, when the whole country is flooded. The total work done upon these roads includes the construction of 136 bridges and culverts with spans varying from 4 to 280 feet, repairing and metaling over 20 miles of roadbed, and the construction and installation of two substantial ferries. The Salasa-Sual road was completed on July 15. The work upon the Camiling-Bayombong road, which consists of a small amount of metaling and the completion of the Camiling ferry, September 1. Work upon the Dagupan-San Quintin road, which is consigned to minor repairs and maintenance, and for which the supplemental allotment of $10,000, Mexican currency, was made, can be carried on indefinitely and will be continued for the present to keep the engineer transportation employed.

In addition to these three roads, other less important pieces of work have been accomplished. Under an allotment of $2,500, Mexican currency, a substantial pile bridge, 16 feet wide and 120 feet long, built of native hard wood, was put in at Binmaley, province of Pangasinan.

Under an allotment of $500, Mexican currency, and an authority to use material on hand for the purpose, a ferry was built for crossing the Cayanga River at San Fabian, P. I., and a second one for use on the Calmay River at Dagupan, P. I. The first of these is now in operation as an ordinary rope ferry, and the second will be similarly installed as soon as the native bridge now in use goes out with high water, as usual.

In the execution of the work outlined herein the assistance rendered by the enlisted men of Company A has been invaluable.

LIEUT. ROBERT P. JOHNSTON.

June 7, 1898.—Appointed captain, Second Regiment United States Volunteer Engineers.
May 16, 1899.—Mustered out.

LIEUT. WILLIAM J. BARDEN.

October 20, 1899.—Relieved from duty at New London, Conn.
October 21, 1899.—Reported to the commanding general, Department of the East, and ordered to join his station at Matanzas.
October 28, 1899.—Reported for duty to the commanding general, Department of Matanzas and Santa Clara.
October 31, 1899, to July 23, 1900.—Assigned as chief engineer officer of the department.

The purely military work under his charge was carried on under allotments from the Chief of Engineers, and was chiefly confined to office work and the preparation of maps, blue prints, and photographs, and the distribution of these and of engineering and reconnaissance instruments and supplies received from the engineer depot at Willets Point to the post commanders throughout the department.

His civil duties consisted in examinations and reports upon various matters and the following construction work, carried on with insular funds: Repair of streets, street cleaning and sanitation, and construction of fire department building, Matanzas; constructing Trinidad-Casilda road; Tillet's farm drainage ditch, Cienfuegos; sanitation and building two bridges, San Jose de los Ramos; extension of water-supply system, Bolondron; construction of temporary water-supply system, Trinidad, and the survey of Matanzas Harbor.

On July 24, 1900, reported for duty to the division commander of Cuba, at Habana, and was assigned to duty as chief engineer of the city of Habana. The chief works under his charge in that capacity are as follows: Repair and maintenance of streets and roads, including construction and repair of macadam, granite-block, and vitrified-brick pavements; survey for establishment of street grades; street cleaning; collection and disposal of refuse by removal to sea and cremation; care and preservation of parks; care and improvement of city water supply; maintenance and repair of old sewerage system and preparation of plans and specifications for a new system; collection and disposal of night soil; care and operation of electrozone plant, and the repair and renovation of municipal buildings. The average monthly expenditures for the work of the city engineer department since July, 1900, have been $129,711.33. Since January 23, 1901, the work of preparation of plans, renovation, repair, and construction of state buildings, previously under the charge of the chief engineer, Department of Cuba, has been under his charge.

April 23 to May 25, 1901.—Acting chief engineer, Department of Cuba, and in charge of harbor improvements, works of the port, and survey of fortifications.

Commended by Gen. J. H. Wilson in his report of July 22, 1900, for his services in the Department of Matanzas and Santa Clara.

LIEUT. HARRY BURGESS.

July 13, 1900.—Reported to the commanding general, Department of California, for assignment to duty in the Philippines.

July 13, 1900.—Ordered to take station in San Francisco, Cal., until the arrival of Company E, Battalion of Engineers, and to then join that company for duty.

July 29, 1900.—Joined Company E, Battalion of Engineers.

August 1, 1900.—Sailed from San Francisco on transport *Meade*.

September 4, 1900.—Arrived at Manila.

September 6 to September 30, 1900.—On duty with Company E, Battalion of Engineers.

October 1, 1900.—In command of Company E, Battalion of Engineers. Had charge of and directed repairs to roads and bridges from Manila to Coloocan, from Coloocan to Malabon and Novaliches, from Malolos to Baliuag, from San Fernando to San Isidro, from San Isidro to Gapan, and from Balanga to Dinalupijan, and of the building and repairing of ferries at Quingua and Arayat.

The local road work has consisted in ditching, shaping, grading, raising in places, partially graveling and rolling, and in building bridges and culverts. October 25 to November 16, 1900, with a mounted detail from the company, inspected roads and bridges in central Luzon; 170 miles of roads were inspected and reported upon. December 17 to December 24, 1900, with a detail from the company, inspected and reported upon 90 miles of roads.

May 30, 1901.—Adjutant First Battalion of Engineers.

June 13, 1901.—Recruiting officer and on temporary duty as quartermaster and commissary, and in temporary command of Company D, First Battalion of Engineers.

LIEUT. GEORGE M. HOFFMAN.

May 14, 1898.—Left Willets Point, N. Y., for Port Tampa, Fla., by rail, with Company C, Battalion of Engineers.

May 15, 1898.—Arrived at Port Tampa, Fla.

May 17, 1898.—Appointed acting commissary and acting quartermaster of the Field Battalion of Engineers, Fifth Army Corps, consisting of Companies E and C of the Battalion of Engineers.

In camp at Port Tampa, Fla., until June 6, 1898, when he embarked on the transport *Alamo*.

June 6-14, 1898.—On board the *Alamo*.

June 14, 1898.—The *Alamo* sailed with the fleet for Cuba.

June 20, 1898.—Arrived off Santiago Harbor.

June 22, 1898.—Disembarked at Daiquiri, Cuba. Relieved from duty with the field battalion on the landing of the Fifth Army Corps at Daiquiri, Cuba, and detailed under the immediate orders of Lieutenant-Colonel Derby, U. S. V. (captain, Corps of Engineers), chief engineer Fifth Army Corps, for reconnaissance duty in command of a detachment of Company E. The duties of this detachment were to keep up with the advance of our column toward Santiago as near as consistent with making a map of the road and surrounding country along the line of march, and to turn in at headquarters every night, if practicable, a map of the route passed over, with report on information collected.

In this and subsequent work outside our lines toward Santiago and along the trenches the enlisted men did good service.

July 1, 1898.—In charge of a field office established at headquarters for consolidating and blue-printing maps, and to which all officers on reconnaissance work were ordered to report.

July 2, 1898.—The engineer officers on reconnaissance work, at their own request, were permitted to rejoin the battalion with their parties, and with it worked all day, under fire, repairing Aquadores ford.

July 3 to August 23, 1898.—Reconnaissance and map work was continued at Santiago, and work on maps and reports continued at Montauk Point, N. Y., until September 20.

September 20, 1898, to March 15, 1899.—On duty with Battalion of Engineers and at Engineer School.

March 15 to July 21, 1899.—At Camp Meade, Pa., on duty with Company C, Battalion of Engineers, preparing camp for volunteers returning from Cuba.

The officers engaged on reconnaissance work in Cuba were Lieutenants Batson, Corday, Guy Smith, of the cavalry; Lieut. A. White, of the infantry, and Lieutenants Cheney and Hoffman, of the Corps of Engineers. All maps were consolidated at the field office and blue prints were issued from time to time—generally after important additions—to the division commanders and other officers of the Army and of the Navy. The first blue prints were sent out July 3.

Finished maps and complete reports were forwarded to the Chief of Engineers, upon completion, at Montauk Point, N. Y.

December 5, 1898.—Lieut. Col. George McC. Derby, United States Volunteers, invited attention to the excellent service rendered during the Cuban campaign by Lieutenant Hoffman, and recommended his promotion in the volunteer service.

December 9, 1898.—The Chief of Engineers, United States Army, recommended to the Secretary of War that he be brevetted first lieutenant for valuable and efficient services at Santiago, Cuba.

LIEUT. WILLIAM D. CONNOR.

May 24, 1898.—Left Willets Point, N. Y., with Company A, Battalion of Engineers.

May 29, 1898.—Arrived at San Francisco.

June 15, 1898.—Left Camp Merritt, Cal., and sailed from San Francisco on transport *China* with detachment of 20 men from Company A, Battalion of Engineers, in the second Philippine expedition. Had charge of signaling and signal instruction until the signal officer and men detailed for that duty learned and became proficient in the code and the sending and receiving of messages.

July 15, 1898.—Arrived at Manila Bay and disembarked at Cavite July 17.

July 19 to July 21, 1898.—Made reconnaissances of the south lines of the Spanish lines around Manila.

July 21 to July 25, 1898.—Together with Major Bell (now brigadier-general) made a reconnaissance of the lines around the city beginning at the north side, at Malabon, and connecting on the south with the reconnaissance that he had previously made. The notes of both were turned in by Major Bell to Adjutant-General Babcock for General Merritt's information.

July 28, 1898.—Went to Camp Dewey; was engaged on road repair near camp, bridge repair at Paranaque, reconnaissance and mapping of the territory near our lines until the taking of Manila.

August 13, 1898.—Accompanied General Greene in the capture of Manila.

In the taking of the city Company A was assigned a dangerous line of march, i. e., up the well-known Calle Real and the other platoon on the Cingalon road. All the men behaved well under fire.

Made personal examination of bridge across the river near the fort which had been damaged by a shell, and repaired the same while under fire, tore down Spanish breastworks where they crossed the road, and put the road in condition so that the Hotchkiss battery could pass.

August 15 to August 23, 1898—Was engaged, together with Lieutenant Moffet, U. S. N., in blowing up the obstructions in the mouth of the river Pasig.

Commends Corporal Fischer for valuable services in the preparation of maps while in Camp Dewey and Sergeant John Kennedy while in Camp Dewey and in the taking of Manila.

August 23, 1898.—In charge of public waterworks and water supply of the city of Manila. His work in connection with the water supply was that which would naturally devolve upon a superintendent and manager of a water supply for a city of about 350,000 inhabitants. The conditions of a state of insurrection made the work more onerous and difficult than it otherwise would have been.

He found the pumps in a very bad condition, as they were very old, and the pistons were badly worn all around from continuous use for twenty years, and the entire plant, never too well kept in repair, had been utterly neglected for over two months.

On the 24th enough of the employees had been persuaded to return to the station and commence work, and the engines were started that day. There has been a constant supply of water since then, except for the thirty-six hours before the waterworks were retaken after the outbreak of the insurgents on February 4, 1899.

The pumping station is $8\frac{1}{4}$ miles outside the walled city, and the deposito (reservoir) is $4\frac{1}{2}$ miles from the same point. Both of these places were in the insurgents' territory until February 6, and this made the work very troublesome and difficult. Sometimes it was impossible to go out to the works at all on account of the hostility of the natives, and once they marched Lieutenant Connor back to the American lines in front of about 15 rifles.

Work on the erection of the new engines was pushed as rapidly as possible, and on October 16 one engine was started, and the other one shortly afterwards. During this work there occurred two floods unprecedented for years, and the river rose vertically 35 feet, flooding the engine rooms and stopping the engines.

Suddenly putting about 23,000 men in barracks in the city necessitated putting in new water service in the new barracks and in the camps occupied by our soldiers. A large force of workmen have been constantly employed to expedite this work as much as possible.

When the insurrection broke out, on February 4, the pumps were not working, and all hands were engaged in cleaning out the filter galleries. Work ceased at once and all the natives fled to the mountains. However, before they left they dismantled the engines by taking off and disposing of the low-pressure cylinders (all four), and doing the same to the high-pressure valves and the covers of the valve boxes. These parts were found upon systematic search buried in the coal shed, with several tons of coal piled upon the spot.

The parts had been found about 3 o'clock p. m. of the 7th, and he had one pump running the next morning at 10, and the second one running in the afternoon. From this time until March 1 the engines were run by soldiers, who did excellent work. A new set of native employees was gotten together, and but little trouble has been encountered since then in keeping all places full.

On night of February 4, 1899.—Acting aid-de-camp to Brig. Gen. Irving Hale, who states that he rendered arduous and efficient service, being frequently under fire.

On night of February 5, 1899.—Acting aid-de-camp to Brig. Gen. Samuel Ovenshine, who states that Lieutenant Connor's services were most acceptable and valuable, and that he did gallant duty under fire during insurgent attack on Manila.

On night of February 8, 1899.—Acting aid-de-camp to Brig. Gen. Irving Hale.

About March 4 to March 14, 1899.—Acting aid-de-camp to Brig. Gen. Loyd Wheaton in the Pasig River campaign, and again in the Malolos campaign, March 25 to April 1, 1899.

April 26, 1899.—Assigned as city engineer under the provost-marshal-general of Manila.

May 29 to June 4, 1899.—Acting aid-de-camp to Brig. Gen. Robert Hall.

June 9, 1899.—Assigned as chief engineer of the city and suburbs of Manila.

As city engineer the first great work was to repair the bridges and public works of the city. They had been neglected for nearly four years and were in a corresponding state of decay.

Recognizing the importance of a clean food supply, he took up the question of city markets, and when he left he had the largest city market tripled in size and replaced with a new steel and concrete market, then nearly completed. The second largest was under contract, and he had obtained orders to submit plans and estimates for three more smaller markets to complete the replacement of the old by the new class of markets. The money granted for the two markets under construction was $570,000, Mexican money, and a similar amount was necessary for the other three.

A map of the city was nearly completed, showing all corners as they were when the Americans entered the city. All city bridges were repaired and practically rebuilt in many cases. The Bridge of Spain was being widened, and plans and specifications were given out for bids on a new bridge across the Pasig under an allotment of $198,000, Mexican money, made for that purpose.

Two garbage incinerators were built.

May —, 1900.—Was sent to Jolo, Jolo, P. I., to report on a new water supply and the sanitary condition of the source of supply for that port, and also to report upon the advisability of fortifying that port.

June 30, 1900.—Relieved from duty in the Division of the Philippines.

July 15, 1900.—Left Manila.

July 21 to August 7, 1900.—Delayed in Japan by authority.

August 29, 1900.—Arrived at San Francisco, Cal., on transport *Thomas.*

December 27, 1898.—Brig. Gen. R. P. Hughes, United States Volunteers, provost-marshal-general, Manila, invited attention to Lieutenant Connor, saying that—

> He has been serving in this office constantly since the occupation of the city. He took hold of the waterworks and succeeded in getting a reasonable supply of water distributed through the city system in fifteen days. He has greatly improved the supply since and no failures have occurred. In addition to this he has been constantly engaged in other matters pertaining to his branch of the service and his work has always given entire satisfaction.
>
> Inasmuch as the department commander has asked for additional engineers of the rank authorized for divisions, etc., I wish simply to bring the case of Lieutenant Connor before you as a young officer of industry, energy, and ability, who has gone through all the operations of the army corps out here and is certainly worthy of any special promotion that the situation might authorize granting him.

June 14, 1899.—Col. E. B. Williston, Sixth United States Artillery, provost-marshal-general, Manila, requested that—

> First Lieut. William D. Connor, United States Army, be not detailed on any duty which will relieve him from his present position at this place. Lieutenant Connor's duties here are strictly in the line of his profession, and I do not think that he can be better engaged in any other position in the service.
>
> He has charge of the engineering work in the city of Manila and its suburbs, and if detailed elsewhere at this time, it will cause a great detriment to the work already begun. Other duties, equally if not more important will be added, which require the services of a competent engineer, and preferably one who has had experience in this city.

And July 1, 1900, Col. E. B. Williston again commended Lieutenant Connor, saying that he—

> Has been in charge of the department of water supply since August 24, 1898, and of the department of public works since June 10, 1899. Both of these departments belong to this office, and Lieutenant Connor's services have been rendered under my personal observation. In both departments he has performed varied and important duties to the entire satisfaction of all concerned, and has gained the merited reputation of being an able engineer, and an efficient, energetic, and capable officer.

A personal letter from Judge Taft, president of the Philippine Commission, to the Secretary of War, contains the following:

> I think that we shall request you to assign Lieutenant Connor, engineer, to assist us in our work when we get to it in improving Manila. He goes home for a rest but he is anxious to return. He is a gifted engineer and is intensely interested in working out the sewer, the canal, and the water problems of Manila.

LIEUT. JOHN C. OAKES.

July 5, 1899.—Left Willets Point, N. Y., with Company B, Battalion of Engineers, for San Francisco, for duty in the Philippines.

July 13, 1899.—Sailed with Company B for Manila, P. I.

August 10, 1899.—Arrived at Manila.

August 13, 1899.—Disembarked.
August 17, 1899.—Reported to General MacArthur at San Fernando.
August 17 to October 1, 1899.—The company performed infantry duty with the Second Division, Eighth Army Corps, guarding bull trains, guarding railroad, making reconnaissances, and doing guard duty.
September 15, 1899.—Assigned to command of Company B, First Battalion of Engineers.
September 27, 1899.—Assigned to First Division, Eighth Army Corps.
October 2, 1899.—Proceeded with the company to Manila, leaving 40 men at San Fernando, to accompany General Lawton's division from San Fernando to the east and north.
October 4, 1899.—Reported to General Lawton and on the same date was announced as engineer officer of the First Division, Eighth Army Corps.
October 9, 1899.—Moved with headquarters of Company B and 40 men, with General Young's brigade of the First Division, Eighth Army Corps, and had charge of all operations of engineering nature during General Lawton's campaign to the north. On October 29, the detachment of 40 men was increased to 76 men.
October 10 to October 26, 1899.—Made practicable the road from San Fernando to San Isidro.
October 26 to December 1, 1899.—Accompanied General Lawton's command from San Isidro to near San. Jacinto; built bridges across the Tombo and Toboatin rivers, across small streams near Cabanatuan and near Aliaga, at Binalonan and at San Jacinto. This detachment commenced its return trip to San Isidro December 3, 1899, making some road repair as it marched. From San Isidro it marched to San Miguel, making the road practicable for a column of troops. It then marched to Malolos, and returned to Manila December 16, 1899.
During the two months and several days the detachment was in the field it worked over 100 miles of road, and made it passable during a season when many heavy rains occurred; put in ferries at Arayat, San Isidro, Cabanatuan, Toboatin, and Talavera Creek; replaced several of these when destroyed by typhoons, built or rebuilt 40 bridges of all sizes, estimated total length of 1,100 feet, and assisted in getting the provision trains over crossings, notably at the Toboatin River and at Cabanatuan.
December 22, 1899.—Left with 71 men for San Isidro and Cabanatuan to replace bridges and ferries destroyed by floods. Returned to Manila January 1, 1900.
January 6, 1900.—Left Manila with Lieuts. S. A. Cheney, Engineers, and Horton W. Stickle, Engineers, and 48 enlisted men, to report to Brig. Gen. Loyd Wheaton, U. S. V., at Bacoor.
This detachment served under General Wheaton's orders until February 9, 1900, repairing roads and bridges for General Wheaton's advance south, and later in putting roads and bridges in good repair for the supply of his troops.
April 7, 1900.—Assigned as chief engineer officer, Department of Southern Luzon.
Since February 9, 1900, the headquarters of Company B has been in Manila, and the members of the company have been utilized to furnish foreman in charge of laborers at work on roads and bridges; to build

bridges in emergencies when destroyed by flood or other causes; to make maps of territory occupied.

April 7, 1900.—Orders were published changing the First Division, Eighth Army Corps, to the Department of Southern Luzon, and announcing him as chief engineer of the department, in addition to his duties as company commander.

Under his supervision and the operation of Company B, Battalion of Engineers, bridges have been constructed at Paranaque, Imus. Cainta, and San Cristobal River; the Pasig and Bacoor ferries installed; roads built and repaired from Pasig to Antipolo, San Pedro Macati to Santa Ana, Pasay Cavalry Barracks to Pasay, Calamba to Cabuyas, Calamba to Balayan, Naic to Indan, Bacoor to Silang, and in the Exposition Grounds at Manila.

May 22, 1901.—Relieved from duty in the Philippines.
May 28, 1901.—Left Manila.
June 26, 1901.—Arrived at San Francisco.

LIEUT. SHERWOOD A. CHENEY.

May 14, 1898.—Left Willets Point, N. Y., for Port Tampa, Fla., by rail, with Company C, Battalion of Engineers.
May 15, 1898.—Arrived at Port Tampa, Fla. In camp until June 6, 1898, when embarked on transport *Alamo.*
June 7-14, 1898.—On board *Alamo.*
June 14, 1898.—The *Alamo* sailed with the fleet for Cuba.
June 20, 1898.—Arrived off Santiago Harbor.
June 22, 1898.—Landed at Daiquiri, Cuba. Detached from Company C, Battalion of Engineers, for reconnaissance duty with Lieutenant-Colonel Derby; started out after the advanced guard mapping the roads and country and continued work during the campaign. After the surrender made a regular survey of the fortifications.
July 7, 1898.—Assigned temporarily to duty under Lieut. Col. G. McC. Derby, U. S. V., chief engineer of General Shafter's staff.
August 18, 1898.—Arrived at Camp Montauk, Long Island, N. Y.
September 4, 1898.—Arrived at Willets Point.
September 26, 1899.—Left Willets Point, N. Y.
October 1, 1899.—Reported to commanding general, Department of California.
October 5, 1899.—Sailed from San Francisco.
November 2, 1899.—Arrived at Manila and reported to the commanding general, Department of the Pacific.
November 3, 1899.—Assigned to duty with Company A, Battalion of Engineers.
November 6, 1899.—Accompanied General Wheaton's expeditionary brigade to San Fabian, Pangasinan, in command of a detachment of two officers and 30 men. The detachment was occupied one week in unloading the supplies of the expedition, and thereafter until January 1, 1900, in repairing roads and bridges from San Fabian to Dagupan, Santo Tomas to San Jacinto, and from Dagupan to Humingan.
December 23, 1899.—Relieved from duty with Company A, Battalion of Engineers, and ordered to report to the chief engineer, Department of the Philippines and Eighth Army Corps, as assistant. Reported January 3, 1900; remained on that duty until July 17, 1900.

During this period was temporarily attached to Company B, Battalion of Engineers, to accompany General Wheaton's column into Cavite province in January, 1900, where he was engaged in making maps and repairs to roads and bridges. Also accompanied Gen. J. M. Bell's expeditionary brigade to the Camarines in February, 1900, being temporarily assigned as engineer officer on the staff of Maj.-Gen. J. C. Bates, U. S. V. Made sketches of the road from landing on San Miguel Bay to Nueva Caceres and from Nueva Caceres to Iriga. In March and April, 1900, made an estimate for the repair of the road from Salasa, Pangasinan, to Subig, Zambales, via Bolinao, with road sketch. Made examination and reported upon existing fortifications of Manila City and harbor in June, 1900.

July 17, 1900.—Temporarily attached to the Department of Southern Luzon, and assigned to duty with Company B, Battalion of Engineers. Made three inspections of the roads of supply in Cavite province.

Permanently relieved from duty as assistant to the chief enginner on September 3, and assigned to duty with Company B. Made examination and estimate for the repair of roads from Calamba to Batangas, Batangas to Nasugbu, in September and October, 1900.

November 15, 1900.—Placed in charge of work of repairing roads and bridges from Calamba to Balayan, via Batangas.

Extract from report of William H. Bisbee, colonel Thirteenth Infantry, commanding:

The conduct of Lieut. S. A. Cheney, Engineers, U. S. A., in voluntarily assisting Lieutenant Pierce on the left of his company, where the fire was most severe and where both casualties in Company K occurred, is worthy of special mention.

LIEUT. FREDERICK W. ALTSTAETTER.

May 16, 1900.—Sailed from San Francisco on the transport *Logan*.

June 14, 1900.—Arrived at Manila and reported to the commanding general, Division of the Philippines; was immediately assigned to duty in the office of the chief engineer of the division as his assistant.

July 26, 1900.—Left Manila to make examination of the roads and trails leading from Manila to San Isidro via Norzagaray and San Miguel.

August 1, 1900.—While in command of a detachment of 14 privates was captured by insurgents after an engagement on the road between San Miguel and San Isidro, lasting about three hours. About 350 insurgents were in the engagement. Was kept captive on Mount Corona until November 20, when his release was effected by exchange.

January 15, 1901.—Relieved from duty with the chief engineer, Division of the Philippines, and assigned to duty with Company E, Battalion of Engineers.

January 21 to January 28, 1901.—On duty with Company E, Battalion of Engineers, at company headquarters at Coloocan.

January 29, 1901.—In charge of road work at Arayat and vicinity on the San Fernando-Cabiao via Arayat. The work consists in building timber bridges and culverts, raising and grading the road and covering it with gravel or stone. In some places entirely new road is built, involving a considerable amount of cleaning of bamboo, brush, and trees.

LIEUT. HARLEY B. FERGUSON.

April 29, 1898.—Assigned to duty with Company E, Battalion of Engineers, West Point, N. Y.

April 30, 1898.—Left West Point with company for service in the field (Cuba).

May 1, 1898.—Sailed from New York City on the transport *Alamo*.

May 5, 1898.—Arrived at Key West, Fla., and having received orders for Port Tampa, Fla., arrived at that place May 7, 1898.

May 7 to June 6, 1898.—In camp at Port Tampa. Company landed materials, performed the usual camp duties, and was instructed in infantry and engineer drill.

May 25, 1898.—The United States forces at Tampa were organized into the Fifth Army Corps, and Company E and Company C (the latter company arrived May 16, 1898), Battalion of Engineers, became the engineer battalion of that corps.

June 6 to 14, 1898.—On board the *Alamo* at Tampa.

June 14, 1898.—The *Alamo* sailed with the fleet of transports.

June 20, 1898.—The fleet arrived off Santiago Harbor.

June 22 to 26, 1898.—Landed at Daiquiri in command of a detail; a large quantity of intrenching tools and materials were landed and a temporary depot established for distribution of the tools to troops; repaired the pier.

June 27, 1898.—Rejoined the battalion at Siboney, Cuba, with the pontons and tools not yet issued, having made the dangerous passage 6 miles along a rocky shore in a heavy sea in open and heavily loaded pontons.

June 28, 1898.—The camp was removed to a better site, an engineer depot was established in a storehouse near the beach on the railroad, and the tools and materials moved into it. Work was begun on a large and more permanent landing pier and a road and a railroad bridge over the creek were repaired.

July 1, 1898.—Was present at the demonstration at Aguadores made by the brigade under General Duffield.

Telephone orders were received from corps headquarters directing that the battalion proceed at once to the front and be there at daybreak. Accordingly, camp was at once broken and all equipage and rations except those to be taken on the persons of the men were stored at the engineer depot, where they were left under a small guard. After everything had been put away, the battalion, at about 9.30 p. m., began its night march, and arrived about 1.30 a. m. at corps headquarters near Sevilla. Here a halt was made, the men getting such rest as they could without even putting up shelter tents. The next morning after collecting such tools as could be obtained the march was continued to the creek crossing at the foot of the San Juan hill. Here a halt was made and work was at once begun on this crossing, sloping the banks, digging out mud and replacing it by gravel, covering bad places with brush, etc., the work not being completed till late in the afternoon. All this work was carried on under a constant though irregular fire of bullets aimed by the Spaniards at our troops on the hill in front.

Upon the completion of this work at the ford the battalion was formed and marched back to corps headquarters and camped there for the night. About 10 o'clock the camp was aroused by the firing during the Spanish sortie, and in obedience to orders from General Shafter the battalion was formed and remained under arms awaiting orders until the cessation of the firing at the front, when it was allowed to turn in again. The next morning, July 8, the battalion remained awaiting orders till about 10 a. m., when, in compliance with orders received, it broke camp and marched back to a point about halfway between Siboney and corps headquarters near the battlefield of Guasimas. Here it went into camp, and next morning resumed work on the roads, which had become almost impassable.

July 5, 1898.—Appointed second lieutenant, Corps of Engineers.
July 6–20, 1898.—Engaged at work on roads near Santiago and Siboney.
July 7 to September 3, 1898.—Temporarily commanding Company C, Battalion of Engineers, Fifth Army Corps.
July 22–27, 1898.—The battalion was in camp at La Cruz.
July 27 to August 22, 1898.—The battalion was in camp at Purgatoria Bridge.
August 22, 1898.—Camp was broken.
August 23, 1898.—Sailed from Santiago on transport *Minnewaska* and landed at Montauk Point, Long Island, August 30, 1898.
September 1–3, 1898.—At Camp Wikoff.
September 4, 1898.—Arrived at West Point with Company E.
December 10, 1898.—Relieved from duty with Company E and assigned to duty at Willets Point, U. S. Engineer School, and Company B, December 11, 1898.
July 5, 1899.—Left Willets Point with Company C, Battalion of Engineers, for duty in the Philippines.
July 13, 1899.—Sailed from San Francisco.
August 10, 1899.—Arrived at Manila.
August 17, 1899.—Reported at San Fernando for duty under Major-General MacArthur, commanding First Division, Eighth Army Corps.
September 27, 1899.—Commanded a detachment of engineers at the capture of Porac, having accompanied the artillery so as to insure a roadway on which it could reach the places indicated. The detachment took part in the engagement as artillery support.
September 27, 1899.—Assigned to the repair of the Manila and Dagupan road under the direction of the Chief Engineer Officer, which work had previously been done by the Quartermaster's Department, United States Army. As soon as any part of the railroad became a line of transportation it was turned over to the Quartermaster's Department. Built and repaired track, bridges, locomotives, and cars frequently under the fire of the insurgents; collected materials.
November 8, 1899.—Commanded an engineer detachment accompanying the advance of the army to Malabacat, and did all the engineer work necessary for movement of troops.
November 11, 1899.—Reported to Colonel Smith, Seventeenth United States Infantry, and accompanied this column in the movements to Capas via Conception, this being part of a movement to capture Bambam.

Extract from report of J. H. Smith, colonel, Seventh Infantry, November 5 to November 30, 1899.

Second Lieut. H. B. Ferguson, Corps of Engineers, United States Army, was with me from November 11 until we reached Tarlac. He had an extremely difficult task to perform in overcoming one of the worst pieces of road I ever took a command over, and he displayed wonderful energy, and, with Lieutenant Wooten, maintained the standard of their corps.

Extract from report of Allston Hamilton, first lieutenant, First Artillery, commanding platoon Light Battery E, First Artillery.

The road would have been impassable for guns or escort wagons in many places but for the skill and energy of the engineer detachment under Lieutenant Ferguson, aided by the willing efforts of the battalion of the Seventeenth Infantry under Captain Roach. My horses were exhausted and I feared for results.

January 2 to February 5, 1900.—Accompanied engineer detachment forming part of General Schwan's expeditionary brigade in its campaign through Cavite, Laguna, Batanga, and Tabayas provinces, southern Luzon.

General Schwan, in his official report of February 8, 1900, says:

Lieut. H. B. Ferguson, Corps of Engineers, who accompanied Major Nolan's cavalry into Silan, did some bold reconnaissance work in locating a more practicable route for the train. With a detachment of 4 cavalrymen he traversed 5 miles of unknown country, with a fleeing enemy in front, capturing one machine gun, which he disabled.

February 14, 1900.—Commanded detachment accompanying expedition into the Camerines provinces under the command of Brig. Gen. James M. Bell, United States Volunteers. Engaged on road and bridge work about Caceres.

June 17, 1900.—Detached from Company B.

June 26, 1900.—Went aboard the transport *Logan*, commanding a detachment from Company B, Battalion of Engineers. Leaving Manila the next day, he reached Nagasaki on July 2 and arrived off Taku, China, July 6. Three men were on board the transport *Port Albert*, which carried the transportation, lumber, and engineer property, and arrived off Taku July 12.

July 7, 1900.—Accompanied Colonel Liscum, commanding United States forces, when he went ashore to arrange for landing. Found excellent wharves, and that lighters drawing 8 feet could cross the bar at high tide, and if not too long could proceed to Tientsin. The railroad was at that time repaired for about 17 miles out of Tongku. Returned that night.

July 8 and 9, 1900.—In company with Capt. C. F. O'Keefe, Thirty-sixth Infantry, United States Volunteers, took notes and photographs at the Taku forts, returning to the ship on the 10th. Captain O'Keefe, on special duty as photographer in the engineer office at Manila, was sent with the expedition with equipment from that office.

July 11, 1900.—Captain O'Keefe went ashore with a battalion of the Ninth Infantry. Sergeant Hurtt and 3 privates also went ashore equipped for sketching work.

July 12, 1900.—The *Port Albert* arrived, and the transportation, lumber, and engineer property were landed July 12–15, 1900. Assistance was obtained from Admiral Remey, U. S. N.

July 15, 1900.—Went by train to the destroyed bridge, 8 miles from Tientsin, and from there to Tientsin by wagon road.

Mr. C. D. Tenny, president of the Tientsin University, gave the use of his drawing-room and dark room in the university building; also a copy of the Mollendorf maps, and procured 2 Chinese draftsmen to copy and translate the Japanese and Chinese maps obtained. These draftsmen were employed from July 17 to August 3. During this time 2 members of the detachment were on duty as draftsmen and 1

1 was making blue prints, 2 were sketching in the vicinity of the engagement of July 13 and in the city of Tientsin, the remainder were preparing boats and material for the advance, using lumber brought on the *Port Albert*. Five boats were prepared and loaded with balk and chess to make rafts of 6 bays each 16 feet long. The engineer property, including extra rope, 175 shovels, and 75 picks, was loaded on these boats. Two hundred boards (2 inches by 12 inches by 12 feet) were given to the British engineer officer with the understanding that our boats combined would make a bridge for both forces.

August 2, 1900.—In General Orders, No. 2, Headquarters China Relief Expedition, was designated chief engineer officer, on the staff of the commanding general.

About 1,500 small intrenching shovels were hauled from the Chinese arsenal, and, with the approval of the commanding general, 800 were issued to the troops (about one to every third man). A lookout ladder 18 feet long, with a hinged stiff-leg support, was made for the use of the artillery, and was of some service at Yangtsun, August 6. For the advance 2 wagons were assigned to the engineer detachment, one being loaded with uprights, balk, and chess, prepared to make a bridge 30 feet long and up to 20 feet high. The information received was that no timber whatever fit to use for bridges was to be found between Teintsin and Pekin; this was not true and the lumber carried was left at Yangtsun by the direction of the commanding general. The other wagon carried the tools and rations of the detachment.

Two men were left at Tientsin sick, 2 with 20 coolies brought the boats up the river, the remainder marched with the relief column on August 4, reaching Pekin on August 14. Sergeant Carroll and 12 men with 20 coolies were with the wagons. Sergeant Hurtt and Corporal Dolan, with 1 assistant each, were sketching.

The work on the road consisted of cutting down the ridges and filling in the gullies where the old embanked roads were worn and washed out, and in making ramps where it was necessary to pass to or from the old road. The bridge of boats at Pehtsang was repaired by putting in two new stringers and covering a portion of the roadway with millet laid crosswise and then with about 4 inches of earth.

August 14, 1900.—Material had been found and instructions were given to make two 30-foot ladders, and to prepare several 60-foot lengths of rope for possible use in scaling the wall in the attack of the 15th, to be planned after reconnaissances on the 14th. The two advance companies of this reconnaissance had begun scaling the wall when ordered to retire, and the orders were changed. The batter of the wall is formed by drawing in the successive layers of brick, leaving steps of about 1¼ inches. With this and the additional footing where bricks had fallen out the men were able to climb up in the corner formed by a bastion and the wall. With a detail of 6 men from the infantry, extemporized scaling ladders were completed in time to be used by about one-fourth of the two companies.

August 15, 1900.—Two ladders borrowed from the British were lashed together and raised against the Tuan gate tower (second gate south of the Forbidden City), but as the attack there ceased, the principal use of this ladder was by a man who carried up the colors.

August 27 and 28, 1900.—Sergeant Hurtt and 8 men were repairing the road between Tung Chow and Pekin.

September 16, 1900.—Lieutenant Ferguson reported to Brig. Gen. J. H. Wilson, U. S. V., to accompany the expedition to the supposed Boxers' headquarters at the temples at Ba Da Tsun, 15 miles northwest of Pekin. The United States force consisted of 800 men and 2 guns. The British commander, with 1 battery and about 800 men, placed himself under General Wilson's orders. Ba Da Tsun was reached about 9.30 a. m. on the 17th, and from there, by General Wilson's direction, Lieutenant Ferguson accompanied a reconnaissance of 3 troops of British Bengal Lancers, 1 company of Sikhs, and a detachment of sappers and miners, about 8 miles farther west, where they disabled the machinery in an arsenal near San Chia Tien. The United States troops returned to Pekin on the 18th.

September 24, 1900.—The road between Pekin and Tung Chow was examined, and from September 26 to October 3, 1900, it was repaired by a detail of 9 engineer soldiers, in charge of 100 coolies, guarded by 30 marines. A new road was made along the bank of the old sunken road for 3 miles west from the stone bridge across the canal, and for short distances at other places; the old road was corduroyed and drained in various places, and 2 small bridges were made near Tung Chow. During part of the month (about 20 days) 3 men were in charge of 15 coolies digging a drain, about one-half mile long and 1 foot deep, in front of the temple of agriculture, and 2 carpenters with 2 helpers were employed putting windows and partitions in the buildings used for headquarter offices and for quarters for staff officers.

From November 8 to 15, 1900.—With 10 engineer soldiers and escort of 10 cavalrymen a direct mail route from Pekin to Hohsiwu was located and marked with 175 signboards.

December 28, 1900.—With a detail of 8 men he reported to Col. T. J. Wint, Sixth Cavalry, for duty with his command of one company of infantry, part of a squadron of cavalry (150 men), and two guns ordered to Hohsien Ho, by way of Matow, and return by Tung Chow. The command crossed the Peiho on ice at Matow on December 29. The river is about 90 yards wide here. The ice was about 5¼ inches thick. The teams were taken out and crossed on a path made by throwing straw and earth on the ice. The wagons and guns were pulled over with ropes reaching across the river. The command reached the Peiho opposite Tung Chow at 2 p. m., December 31. The Peiho and the Shoho join about 1 mile below Tung Chow. The ice was melting below the junction and on the Peiho. Fifteen men from the cavalry were detailed to assist the engineer detail, and a bridge of boats was built 90 feet long in prolongation of a sort of embanked pier reaching about halfway across the Peiho; 7 boats were used, 4 being found at the site and 3 brought from about 300 yards below. The bridge was crossed the next morning and the Shoho was crossed on the ice, the guns and wagons being pulled across with ropes. The command reached Pekin 2 p. m., January 2, 1901.

January 2, 28, and 29, 1901.—Attended the meeting of the military commission appointed to consider the defense of the legation quarter.

From February 27 to March 18, 1901.—Captain O'Keefe and Lieutenant Ferguson were carrying out instructions to investigate the possibility of selecting a summer camp between Tongku and Shanhaikwan. After looking over the country, especially in the vicinity of the Peitaiho (20 miles west from Shanhaikwan), a site 1 mile square was marked out between the railroad and the bay just east of Peitaiho.

April 9, 1901.—Visited the forts at Tientsin.

Has made plans of the United States legation district, Pekin, and of the portions of the city under American control; also sketches of the roads in the immediate vicinity of the city, and from Pekin to Tung Chow, to Matow, to Hohsiwu, and to the Great Wall at Nankow Pass.

May 22, 1901.—Left Pekin, China.

About May 25, 1901.—Sailed from Taku with detachment, on the *Sumner*, en route to Manila.

Rejoined company in Manila June 5, 1901.

LIEUT. WILLIAM P. WOOTEN.

December 22, 1898.—Relieved from duty at Willets Point, N. Y.

February 27, 1899.—Joined Company A, Battalion of Engineers, at Manila.

March 5 to 11, 1899.—In command of Company A.

March 23, 1899.—Two detachments were, by order of the Chief Engineer (Lieutenant-Colonel Potter, U. S. V.), sent to join General MacArthur and General Wheaton, respectively. Lieutenant Wooten accompanied General Wheaton's brigade at the capture of Malolos, and remained with General MacArthur until December 29.

August 9, 1899.—Took part in the advance on Calulut.

September 27 to 28, 1899.—Commanded a detachment of engineers at the capture of Porac, having accompanied the artillery so as to insure a roadway on which it could reach the places designated. The detachment took part in the engagement as artillery support.

November 5 to December 17, 1899.—Engaged on repairs to the Manila and Dagupan Railroad.

December 27, 1899.—Relieved Capt. F. R. Shunk of command of Company A, Battalion of Engineers.

January 2 to February 10, 1900.—Accompanied engineer detachments forming part of General Schwan's expeditionary brigade in its campaign through Cavite, Laguna, Batangas, and Tabayas provinces, southern Luzon. His services were commended in General Schwan's official report of February 8, 1900, and in his letter of March 16, 1900, to Captain Sibert.

March 10, 1900.—Detailed as a member of a board to inventory and transfer the Manila and Dagupan Railroad and its appurtenances to the owners of the road, and to report upon the condition of the road and roadbed when captured from the insurgents, and its condition when transferred and the cost of labor and material expended thereon by the military authorities. This duty was completed and the railroad transferred to its owners April 20, 1900.

April 7, 1900.—Assigned as chief engineer officer, Department of Northern Luzon.

May 31, 1900.—Arrived at San Francisco on transport *Meade*.

August 4, 1900.—Relieved from further duty in the Division of the Philippines.

August 15, 1899.—Commended by Maj. J. S. Mallory, inspector-general, Second Division, Eighth Army Corps, for skill and ingenuity in improvising materials for building and repairing bridges, and also for good work with his detachment in repairing roads and making reconnaissance.

Extract from report of J. H. Smith, colonel Seventh Infantry, November 5 to 30, 1899:

Second Lieut. W. P. Wooten, Corps of Engineers, U. S. A., was with me at Magalang until we reached Tarlac, and his engineers were very efficient in clearing the route of march of obstacles, and proved to be a very efficient officer.

LIEUT. LYTLE BROWN.

May 13, 1898.—Assigned to duty with Company E, Battalion of Engineers.
May 14, 1898.—Left Willets Point for duty with the company.
May 19, 1898.—Joined company in camp at Port Tampa, Fla.
June 6 to 14, 1898.—On board transport *Alamo*.
June 14, 1898.—The *Alamo* sailed with the fleet of transports.
June 20, 1898.—The fleet arrived off Santiago Harbor, and on June 22, 1898, tools and materials were landed at Daiquiri and the pier was repaired.
June 23, 1898.—A pier was built at Aserraderos for the embarkation of the Cuban army under General Garcia. On June 24, 1898, the Cubans were embarked, and on June 26 were landed at Siboney, where a temporary landing pier was built. In the meanwhile the landing of tools and supplies was begun, all being carried in pontons from the vessels to the beach. The next day this work was continued and by noon all the company equipage, baggage and rations, all intrenching and pioneer tools had been put ashore. In the afternoon the company landed in pontons and went into camp for the night near the locomotive roundhouse.
June 28.—Camp was moved to a better site, an engineer depot was established in a storehouse near the beach and on the railroad, and the tools and materials moved into it. Work was begun on a large and more permanent landing pier, and a road and railroad bridge over the creek were repaired.
He repaired the pipe line supplying water to Siboney.
July 1, 1898.—Telephone orders were received from corps headquarters directing that the battalion proceed at once to the front and be there by daybreak. Accordingly the camp was at once broken and all equipage and rations except those to be taken on the persons of the men were stored at the engineer depot, where they were left under a small guard. After everything had been put away the battalion, at about 9.30 p. m., began its night march, and arrived about 1.30 a. m. at corps headquarters, near Sevilla. Here a halt was made, the men getting such rest as they could without even putting up shelter tents. The next morning, after collecting such tools as could be obtained, the march was continued to the creek crossing at the foot of the San Juan hill. Here a halt was made and work was at once begun on this crossing, sloping the banks, digging out mud and replacing it by gravel, covering bad places with brush, etc., the work not being completed till late in the afternoon. All this work was carried on under a constant though irregular fire of bullets aimed by the Spaniards at our troops on the hill in front.
Lieutenant Brown was in charge of a detail of skirmishers sent out to protect the engineers working on the ford from Spanish sharpshooters concealed in the palm trees.
Upon the completion of this work at the ford, the battalion was

formed and marched back to corps headquarters and camped there for the night.

About 10 o'clock the camp was aroused by the firing during the Spanish sortie, and in obedience to orders from General Shafter the battalion was formed, and remained under arms awaiting orders until the cessation of the firing at the front, when it was allowed to turn in again. The next morning, July 3, the battalion remained awaiting orders till about 10 a. m., when, orders being received, it broke camp and marched back to a point about half way between Siboney and corps headquarters, near the battlefield of Guasimas. Here it went into camp, and next morning resumed work on the roads, which had become almost impassable.

July 3 to July 27, 1898.—Detached from Company E, under orders of Lieutenant-Colonel Derby, chief engineer, Fifth Army Corps, in charge of road work done by details from various infantry regiments.

July 27 to August 22, 1898.—The battalion was in camp at Purgatoria Bridge; repaired Boniata and Purgatoria bridges.

August 22, 1898.—Camp broken.

August 23, 1898.—Sailed from Santiago on transport *Minnewaska* and landed at Montauk Point, Long Island, August 30, 1898.

September 1 to 3, 1898.—At Camp Wikoff.

September 4, 1898.—Arrived at West Point, N. Y.

June 26, 1900.—Relieved from duty at Willets Point, N. Y.

July 11, 1900.—Reported to commanding general, Department of California.

July 17, 1900.—Sailed from San Francisco on transport *Sumner.*

August 21, 1900.—Arrived at Manila and reported to commanding general, Department of the Philippines.

August 23, 1900.—Reported for duty to the chief engineer of the division and detailed for temporary duty in his office.

September 5, 1900.—In temporary charge of the office of the chief engineer of Manila, under the direct orders of the provost-marshal-general.

December 8, 1900.—Detailed as city engineer of Manila and has charge of the department of public works and water supply of Manila. The duty of this office is entirely civil in character.

It consists of the maintenance and operation of the system of water supply; the completion of a large steel market building, known as the Divisoria Market; the completion of the widening of the Bridge of Spain over the Pasig River; the construction of a stone quay for a market on the Pasig River front; the construction of a steel market on the Pasig River front, known as the Quinta Market; the construction of a heavy steel highway bridge across the river Pasig; the completion of a projected survey of the city of Manila and the making of a map of the city; a preliminary estimate for a sewerage system for the city; the construction of a sea wall along the bay front at the south end of the Luneta driveway; the protection of the Malecon driveway on the bay front by a riprap fill; the estimate and design, specifications, etc., for a new steel market in the Old Walled City; and the preparation of numerous small estimates, maps, and drawings, together with various small pieces of work incident to the general decay and dilapidation to be found in a town of the character of Manila. The supervision of all buildings in the city, the preparation and enforcement of a system of building regulations, and the issue of building permits.

The water-supply system is composed of a pumping station on the San Mateo River, about 7 miles from the city, there being four pumps of a combined capacity of 40,000 cubic meters per twenty-four hours, a conduit to the distributing reservoir 3 miles from the city, a 26-inch main iron pipe line into the city, and the system of city distribution. The water is sold through the meter system in houses, and is gratis at a number of public hydrants throughout the city. The water rents are paid at the office of the department of public works and water supply. The present water supply is fast becoming inadequate, and a stadia survey was made along the San Mateo Valley to the mountains, and the stream was gauged to determine the feasibility of getting a supply of pure water by gravity flow.

There is no sewerage system in Manila at present, and the difficulty in devising one at reasonable cost is magnified by the low level site, it being on an average of 2¼ meters above mean low tide. An efficient system on the pumping or air-lift plan would cost about three and a half million dollars, United States currency. The greatest discouragement to spending money for a sewer system for this city is that so large a per cent of the population is too poor to make the proper sanitary house connections with the sewers, should such exist.

LIEUT. ROBERT D. KERR.

June 13, 1898.—Relieved from duty at Willets Point, N. Y.
June 18, 1898.—Reported at San Francisco and assigned to Company A, Battalion of Engineers.
June 27, 1898.—Sailed with company with General MacArthur's command.
July 21, 1898.—Died at sea of spinal meningitis.

LIEUT. EARL I. BROWN.

March 8, 1901.—Joined Company F, Second Battalion of Engineers.
June 17, 1901.—Left Willets Point, N. Y.
June 23, 1901.—Arrived at San Francisco, Cal.
June 25, 1901.—Sailed from San Francisco on transport *Hancock* en route to Manila. In charge of mess on the transport.

LIEUT. AMOS A. FRIES.

March 8, 1901.—Joined Company G, Second Battalion of Engineers.
June 17, 1901.—Left Willets Point, N. Y.
June 23, 1901.—Arrived at San Francisco.
June 25, 1901.—Sailed from San Francisco on the transport *Hancock* en route to Manila. Assigned as police officer on the transport.

LIEUT. JAMES A. WOODRUFF.

March 8, 1901.—Joined Second Battalion of Engineers as battalion adjutant.
June 17, 1901.—Left Willets Point.
June 23, 1901.—Arrived at San Francisco, Cal.
June 25, 1901.—Sailed from San Francisco on the transport *Hancock* en route to Manila.

LIEUT. WILLIAM KELLY.

July 14, 1900.—Reported to the commanding general. Department of California.
July 17, 1900.—Sailed from San Francisco, Cal., on transport *Sumner*.
August 21, 1900.—Arrived at Manila, P. I., and reported to the commanding general, Division of the Philippines.
August 23, 1900.—Reported for duty to the chief engineer of the division.
September 3, 1900.—Assigned to duty with Company B, Battalion of Engineers.

Made estimates for building road from the landing of Laguna de Bay to Binan, Laguna Province; for repairing road and bridges from Legaspi, Albay Province, to Nueva Caceres, Province of Camarines Sur, and from Nueva Caceres to Pasacas, Province of Camarines Sur; for the repair of road and bridges from Santa Cruz to Majayjay, Laguna Province; and for building a wharf at Batangas, Province of Batangas.

In command of a detachment of 11 men of Company B, Battalion of Engineers, building a road from Naic to Indan, Cavite Province.

Since March 1, 1901.—Has been in command of a detachment of 20 men from Company B, Battalion of Engineers, building roads and bridges in the province of Camarines Sur.

Up to the present time about 20 bridges, ranging in length from 15 feet to 90 feet, have been built. Nine miles of the subgrade for the road has been completed, and $3\frac{1}{4}$ miles of macadamizing done.

LIEUT. HORTON W. STICKLE.

April 24, 1899.—Reported at Manila and assigned to Company A, Battalion of Engineers. Engaged in building and repairing roads, bridges, and ferries.

October 7 to October 14, 1899.—Accompanied engineer detachment with Brigadier-General Schwan's expeditionary brigade to Imus; in command of the detachment after October 8, except in the advance on San Francisco de Malabon, when with 27 men he accompanied a flanking column under Major Bubb.

The engineer company received the following special mention in Gen. Theodore Schwan's official report on this campaign:

> The engineer company, acting mostly under the personal supervision of the chief engineer, Captain Sibert, but under the immediate command of Lieutenant Stickle, an energetic and capable young officer, has already been mentioned for its prompt construction of an efficient ferry across the Tibagan River. The service thereafter rendered by this company was constant and invaluable. In fact, but for its work numerous obstacles of various kinds would have indefinitely delayed or barred the passage of artillery and train. While approaching San Francisco de Malabon, where the enemy was supposed to be in force and expected to give battle, the company asked for and was assigned a place in the firing line. Captain Sibert, not only in his capacity as engineer, but also on the firing line, notably on the afternoon of October 10, on the Buena Vista road, contributed in a marked degree by his efforts to the success of operations.

This engineer company referred to above, or parts of it, was under fire at Cavite, Viejo, Putol, Rosario, and near San Francisco de Malabon.

November 5 to November 12, 1899.—Accompanied engineer detachment with Brigadier-General Wheaton's command in its campaign in the vicinity of San Fabian; was under fire while making reconnaissances.

Extract from report of Capt. Godfrey H. Fowler, Thirty-third Infantry, United States Volunteers:

> The greatest credit and praise is due to Lieutenant Stickle, Corps of Engineers, for his bravery and coolness manifested in action, and to him is due the greatest credit for the successful handling of the men with him.

December, 1899.—In command of engineer detachment with Second Division.

January 6, 1900.—Accompanied a detachment under General Wheaton's orders until February 9, 1900, repairing roads and bridges for General Wheaton's advance south, and later in putting roads and bridges in good repair for the supply of his troops.

March 8, 1901.—Assigned to duty with Company C, Battalion of Engineers. Did excellent service in charge of detachments engaged on bridges, roads, and ferries.

April 3, 1901.—Ordered to be relieved from duty in the Philippine Islands and to report to the engineer school and commanding officer, Third Battalion of Engineers.

May 10, 1901.—Relieved from duty in the Philippine Islands.

June 5, 1901.—Sailed from Manila on transport *Kilpatrick*.

June 27, 1901.—Arrived at San Francisco en route to Fort Totten.

LIEUT. LEWIS H. RAND.

July 3, 1900.—Relieved from duty under orders of Captain Flagler at Montgomery, Ala.

July 11, 1900.—Arrived in San Francisco, Cal., and reported to the commanding general, Department of California.

July 17, 1900.—Sailed from San Francisco on transport *Sumner*.

August 21, 1900.—Arrived at Manila, P. I., and reported to the commanding general, Division of the Philippines, and the chief engineer of the division.

September 1, 1900.—Assigned to duty with Company A, Battalion of Engineers.

December 4, 1900.—Was given detachment of 25 enlisted men and sent to the province of Zambales in charge of the work on roads in northern part. Detachment from time to time decreased, but his present duty still the same. No work completed, as repairs were to be, by order, simply local and temporary; no work of any special magnitude or importance, and difficulties entirely due to lack of communication and proper labor.

LIEUT. EDWARD M. MARKHAM.

March 8, 1901.—Joined Second Battalion of Engineers as battalion quartermaster and commissary.

June 17, 1901.—Left Willets Point.

June 23, 1901.—Arrived at San Francisco.

June 25, 1901.—Sailed from San Francisco on transport *Hancock* en route to Manila.

SERVICE OF OFFICERS IN THE FIELD, WITH TROOPS, ETC. 115

LIEUT. GEORGE B. PILLSBURY.

January 23, 1901.—Joined Company E, Second Battalion of Engineers, at San Francisco.
June 25, 1901.—Sailed from San Francisco on transport *Hancock* en route to Manila.

LIEUT. GUSTAVE R. LUKESH.

March 16, 1901.—Joined Company H, Second Battalion of Engineers.
March 16–31, 1901.—Commanding the company.
June 17, 1901.—Left Willets Point.
June 23, 1901.—Arrived at San Francisco.
June 25, 1901.—Sailed from San Francisco on transport *Hancock* en route to Manila.

LIEUT. JOHN R. SLATTERY.

July 14, 1900.—Reported to Superintendent of the Military Academy for duty with Company E, Battalion of Engineers.
July 24, 1900.—Left West Point, N. Y.
July 29, 1900.—Arrived at San Francisco.
August 1, 1900.—Sailed from San Francisco on transport *Meade*.
September 4, 1900.—Arrived at Manila.
September 6 to December 7, 1900.—On duty with Company E, Battalion of Engineers, at company headquarters.
December 8, 1900, to February 21, 1901.—In charge of road work near Vigan.
March 25 to April 18, 1901.—In charge of road and bridge work near Orani.
April 23 to April 30, 1901.—In charge of road and bridge work near Quingua.
May 1 to June 30, 1901.—In charge of repairing roads and bridges, Zambales province.

LIEUT. EDWARD N. JOHNSTON.

March 10, 1901.—Joined Company E, Second Battalion of Engineers.
June 10, 1901.—Left Willets Point, N. Y.
June 19, 1901.—Rejoined company at Decatur, Ill.
June 23, 1901.—Arrived at San Francisco.
June 25, 1901.—Sailed from San Francisco on transport *Hancock* en route to Manila.

LIEUT. CLARENCE O. SHERRILL.

March 25, 1901.—Sailed from San Francisco on transport *Hancock*.
April 19, 1901.—Arrived at Manila.
April 19 to April 26, 1901.—On duty in the office of the chief engineer, Division of the Philippines.
April 27, 1901.—On duty with Company A, First Battalion of Engineers, at Dagupan.
May 6, 1901.—In charge of construction of roads and bridges on the Bayombong-Camiling road, under the orders of Captain Cavanaugh.

May 18, 1901.—Relieved Lieut. Horton W. Stickle of his duties in connection with the repair of the roads and bridges in the vicinity of Humingan, province of Pangasinan, P. I. The roads extend from Bautista to San Quintin and from Humingan to Cabanatuan. On account of the near approach of the rainy season, the work has been confined largely to finishing parts of the road work already under construction.

LIEUT. ERNEST D. PEEK.

March 10, 1901.—Joined Company G, Second Battalion of Engineers.
June 13, 1901.—Left Willets Point, N. Y.
June 19, 1901.—Rejoined company at Decatur, Ill.
June 25, 1901.—Sailed from San Francisco on transport *Hancock* en route to Manila.

LIEUT. WALTER H. LEE.

April 19, 1901.—Arrived at Manila Bay on transport *Hancock*.
April 20, 1901.—Reported for duty.
April 24, 1901.—Assigned to duty with Company B, Battalion of Engineers, and joined company April 26, 1901, First Battalion of Engineers; was on duty at company headquarters for about ten days, and on duty with road work at Naic and repair of roads and bridges between Balangan and Lipa, and opening of drainage system of Balangan.
June 1, 1901.—In local charge of road work in vicinity of Balayan, Taal, and Batangas, in southern Luzon.

On the evening of June 9, 1901, Lieutenant Lee joined as a volunteer a small force of the Twenty-first Infantry, under command of Capt. William H. Wilhelm, in an expedition against a force of the insurgents under Malvar, intrenched near Lipa. At daylight on the morning of the 10th the insurgent position was attacked, during which attack every American officer, as well as several enlisted men, were killed or wounded.

Lieutenant Lee was first struck in the hand, but refused to have his wound dressed, and continued on the firing line. In a few minutes he was hit again in the abdomen and died in about half an hour.

LIEUT. GEORGE R. SPALDING.

March 18, 1901.—Sailed from San Francisco on transport *Meade*.
April 18, 1901.—Arrived at Manila.
April 20, 1901.—Reported to the commanding officer Company C, First Battalion of Engineers, at Coloocan.
April 29, 1901.—Supervising construction of ferry at Quingua and in charge of bridges and repairs to the Malolos-Baliuag road.
May 30, 1901.—Commanding Company C, First Battalion of Engineers, and took charge of the Manila-Malabon road.
June 29, 1901.—Relieved Capt. F. G. Russell, Thirty-fourth Infantry, United States Volunteers, of charge of the Baliuag-Capan and Bustos-Norzagaray roads.

RIVER AND HARBOR IMPROVEMENTS.

LIEUT. ELLIOTT J. DENT.

March 12, 1901.—Joined Company H, Second Battalion of Engineers.
March 14-16, 1901.—Commanding company.
June 17, 1901.—Left Willets Point.
June 23, 1901.—Arrived at San Francisco.
June 25, 1901.—Sailed from San Francisco on transport *Hancock* en route to Manila.

LIEUT. WILLIAM G. CAPLES.

March 15, 1901.—Sailed from San Francisco on transport *Indiana*.
April 15, 1901.—Arrived at Manila.
April 16, 1901.—Reported to adjutant-general, Division of the Philippines.
April 25, 1901.—Assigned to temporary duty with Company B, Battalion of Engineers, and immediately reported to commanding officer of that organization.
April 18 to May 18, 1901.—Stationed at Imus, Cavite Province, in charge of work on roads and bridges, in the vicinity of Imus and Bacoor.
May 20, 1901.—Assisting Lieutenant Cheney on road work between Calamba and Batangas.
May 26, 1901.—Relieved Lieutenant Cheney of charge of the work between Calamba and Tananan. Making plans and estimates for system of waterworks for Los Banos. Installed reservoir for water supply for hospital at Calamba. Inspected bridge between Tiana and Candeleria, Luzon.

LIEUT. ARTHUR WILLIAMS.

March 10, 1901.—Joined Company F, Second Battalion of Engineers.
June 17, 1901.—Left Willets Point.
June 23, 1901.—Arrived at San Francisco.
June 24, 1901.—Sailed from San Francisco on transport *Hancock* en route to Manila.

RIVER AND HARBOR IMPROVEMENTS.

Appropriations.—The funds with which the works for the improvement of rivers and harbors were prosecuted during the last fiscal year were derived from the appropriations made by the deficiency act, approved January 5, 1899; the sundry civil act, approved March 3, 1899; the river and harbor act, approved March 3, 1899; the sundry civil acts, approved June 6, 1900, and March 3, 1901, and from such balances of former appropriations as were available.

The following works are provided for by permanent appropriations: Removing sunken vessels; operating and care of dredge boats on Upper Mississippi River; removing obstructions in Mississippi River; gauging waters of Lower Mississippi River and its tributaries; examinations and surveys at South Pass, Mississippi River (to January 28, 1901); maintenance of South Pass Channel, Mississippi River (since January 28, 1901); operating snag boats on Ohio River; operating and care of canals, etc.

118   REPORT OF THE CHIEF OF ENGINEERS, U. S. ARMY.

Status of works.—Statements derived from the reports of the officers in charge of the various works, and given herewith, set forth the condition of each improvement and the extent of the work performed during the last fiscal year.

Expenditures.—The total amount actually expended in connection with the improvement of rivers and harbors during the fiscal year ending June 30, 1901, is as follows:

Rivers and harbors (general, including examinations, surveys, and contingencies)	$14,981,000.90
Removing sunken vessels	51,609.97
Operating snag and dredge boats on Upper Mississippi River	25,000.00
Removing obstructions in Mississippi River	86,710.05
Gauging waters of Lower Mississippi River and its tributaries	5,265.96
Examinations and surveys at South Pass, Mississippi River (to January 28, 1901)	6,637.63
Maintenance of South Pass channel, Mississippi River (since January 28, 1901)	29,974.87
Operating snag boats on Ohio River	41,118.69
Operating and care of canals, etc	849,689.03
Prevention of deposits in New York Harbor	76,139.62
California Débris Commission	6,959.89
Total	16,160,106.61

This amount does not include the following:

1. Payments to the James B. Eads estate for "maintaining jetties and other works at South Pass, Mississippi River" (including $500,000 withheld from the original appropriation to insure maintenance of channel for a period of twenty years	$602,083.33
2. Expenditures under Mississippi River Commission	2,422,693.34
3. Expenditures under Missouri River Commission (including Osage and Gasconade rivers)	432,518.54
4. Disbursements under direction of the Secretary of War on account of "surveys and examinations of waterways between the Great Lakes and the Atlantic Ocean"	3,825.80

Estimates.—The following estimates are submitted by the Chief of Engineers for the fiscal year ending June 30, 1903:

Under continuing contracts	$6,489,377.50
Rivers and harbors (general)	19,813,100.00
Examinations, surveys, and contingencies	300,000.00
Under California Débris Commission	15,000.00
Prevention of deposits in New York Harbor	70,260.00
Enlargement of Governors Island, New York	500,000.00

Estimates are submitted by the Mississippi River Commission and Missouri River Commission as follows:

Mississippi River Commission	$3,695,000.00
Missouri River Commission	1,065,200.00

Establishment of harbor lines.—Under authority given to the Secretary of War in section 11 of the river and harbor act approved March 3, 1899, harbor lines have been established during the past fiscal year at the following localities, details of which will be found in the reports of the local officers:

Lubec Harbor, Maine; Penobscot River, at Bangor, Me.; Portland Harbor, Maine; Port Chester Harbor and Byram River, New York; Bronx River, New York; Hudson River, at Troy, N. Y.; Hudson River, from Pleasant Valley Landing to Bloomers, N. J.; Hudson River, in vicinity of Guttenberg, N. J.; Newark Bay, New Jersey; Arthur Kill, at mouth of Rahway River, New Jersey; Shrewsbury River, at Seabright, N. J.; New York Harbor, at College Point, N. Y.; Annapolis Harbor, Maryland; Pamlico River, at Washington, N. C.; Cape Fear River, at Southport, N. C.; Savannah River, at Savannah, Ga.; Hillsboro River, at Tampa, Fla.; Pensacola Harbor, Florida; Ohio River, at Allegheny City, Pa.; Erie Basin and Black Rock Harbor, Buffalo, N. Y.; San Francisco Harbor, California; Coos Bay, Oregon.

Highway bridge over Potomac River, at Washington, D. C.—Section 12 of an act of Congress approved February 12, 1901, provides—

That the Secretary of War be, and he is hereby, authorized to enter into a contract with the Baltimore and Potomac Railroad Company or any other party to construct within two years after the passage of this Act, at a point not less than five hundred feet above the site of the present Long Bridge, a new and substantial bridge for highway travel, of iron or steel, resting upon masonry piers and provided with suitable approaches, and with a sufficient draw, all in accordance with plans and specifications to be approved by the Secretary of War; and there is hereby appropriated (one-half out of the revenues of the District of Columbia and one-half out of any money in the Treasury not otherwise appropriated) the sum of five hundred and sixty-eight thousand dollars, or so much thereof as may be necessary, to be paid from time to time, as the construction of the said bridge progresses, by the Secretary of War, under such regulations as he shall prescribe.

* * * * * * *

By authority of the Secretary of War, a Board of Engineers has been constituted to select a site and to formulate plans, specifications, and estimates for the bridge. The subject is now under consideration by the Board, whose report is expected at an early date.

Chicago Drainage Canal.—In April, 1899, the trustees of the Sanitary District of Chicago requested a permit from the Secretary of War to connect the drainage canal with the West Fork of the South Branch of the Chicago River. On May 8, 1899, the Secretary of War granted a conditional permit to the Sanitary District of Chicago to connect its artificial channel with the Chicago River and cause the waters of said river to flow into the canal.

In accordance with the permission granted, the sanitary trustees made a connection between the drainage canal and the West Fork of the Chicago River. It appearing that the discharge from the river into the drainage canal caused a current under the existing condition of the river which endangered navigation, an order was issued by the Secretary of War, April 9, 1901, reducing the maximum discharge to 200,000 cubic feet per minute. This order was subsequently modified by the Secretary so as to permit an increase of the flow to 300,000 cubic feet per minute between the hours of 4 p. m. and 12 midnight, daily.

The trustees of the Sanitary District are undertaking the enlargement of the waterway of the Chicago River, with a view of providing for the full discharge required by State law without causing such current as will injure the interests of navigation.

Engineer divisions.—The engineering works in the charge of this office are arranged in five divisions, and officers of the Corps of Engineers were assigned as division engineers to overlook these works, as follows:

West of the Rocky Mountains: Pacific Division, Col. S. M. Mansfield to November 23, 1900, and Col. Jared A. Smith since December 15, 1900. East of the Rocky Mountains: Northeast Division, Col. G. L. Gillespie (now brigadier-general, Chief of Engineers, United States Army) to May 3, 1901, and Col. Charles R. Suter since May 9, 1901; Southeast Division, Col. Peter C. Hains; Southwest Division, Col.

Henry M. Robert (now brigadier-general, Chief of Engineers, United States Army, retired) to May 2, 1901, and Col. Amos Stickney since May 9, 1901; Northwest Division, Col. J. W. Barlow (now brigadier-general, Chief of Engineers, United States Army, retired) to May 3, 1901, and Col. S. M. Mansfield since May 9, 1901.

ATLANTIC COAST AND GULF OF MEXICO.

IMPROVEMENT OF RIVERS AND HARBORS IN MAINE EAST OF AND INCLUDING PORTLAND HARBOR.

This district was in the charge of Maj. S. W. Roessler, Corps of Engineers, having under his immediate orders Lieut. Thomas H. Jackson, Corps of Engineers, to September 20, 1900, and Lieut. Charles W. Kutz, Corps of Engineers, since August 31, 1900. Division Engineer, Col. G. L. Gillespie, Corps of Engineers (now brigadier-general, Chief of Engineers, United States Army), to May 3, 1901, and Col. Charles R. Suter, Corps of Engineers, since May 9, 1901.

1. *St. Croix River, Maine.*—In 1855 and 1857 three piers were built in this river at the Ledge, 3¼ miles below Calais, under the supervision of the Light-House Establishment, with funds appropriated for light-house purposes. In 1881 the piers were repaired under the supervision of the War Department with funds provided by the river and harbor act of March 3, 1881. The purpose for which these structures were built was partly to serve as a beacon marking the Ledge, but mainly to serve as a breakwater to ward off boats from the Ledge. It has been submitted by the Light-House Board, through the Treasury Department, that the work pertains especially to the river improvement, and should be supervised and maintained by the War Department in connection with the improvement of said river. The piers are in need of repair, but it does not appear permissible for the War Department to relieve the Treasury Department of the supervision of the work and adopt it as an authorized river and harbor work without further authority from Congress, and even should such supervision be assumed no funds are now available which could be applied to the work. It is estimated by the engineer of the First light-house district that the sum of $150 is needed for immediate work, but to thoroughly repair the piers a much larger sum would probably be required. An estimate of cost for needed repairs will be prepared when an opportunity is offered to secure the necessary information.

2. *Lubec Channel, Maine.*—This channel lies between the eastern extremity of the State of Maine and Campobello Island, Dominion of Canada.

Originally the channel was but 5 feet in depth at mean low tide and but 2 feet at low water of spring tides. A project was adopted in 1879 which, as subsequently modified, provided for a channel 275 feet wide, increasing to 300 feet in the bends, and 12 feet deep at mean low tide. This project was completed in 1890, practically as proposed, at a cost of $168,954.68. In 1894 a new project was adopted which provided for widening the existing channel to a least width of 500 feet, with a depth of 12 feet at mean low tide. The work covered by the new project has been estimated to cost $150,000.

The expenditures to June 30, 1900, amounted to $240,046.79—$168,954.68 on the old project and $71,092.11 on the new. At that date the channel dredged under the project of 1879 had been widened about 170 feet at the entrance and about 190 feet at the turn just above Cranberry Point. The most difficult and expensive part of the work (that in the Narrows) was completed.

Dredging under contract with Augustus R. Wright, which was commenced June 22, 1900, was completed October 19, following, 86,959 cubic yards of material having been removed during the fiscal year, and a total of 96,114 cubic yards under the contract. The widening of the channel on the westerly side was thereby completed and a strip about 2.500 feet long, varying in width from 35 to 67 feet, was dredged on the easterly side in the bend opposite Lubec Narrows light and below. This leaves a strip about 3,900 feet long, having a general width of about 130 feet, to be dredged from the middle and lower part of the entrance channel, on its easterly side, to complete its enlargement as projected.

This channel is an international passage and the benefits resulting from the improvement are almost entirely general. As the tidal currents are very strong and dense fogs prevail a large part of the time, the widening of the channel decreases the chances of stranding and collision.

It was discovered during the progress of dredging that considerable shoaling had taken place in the part of the channel dredged under previous contracts, especially along the easterly side opposite and below Lubec Narrows light.

The commerce is reported as follows:

	Tons.		Tons.
1896	52,300	1899	126,700
1897	53,400	1900	76,800
1898	87,000		

July 1, 1900, balance unexpended	$25,953.21
June 30, 1901, amount expended during fiscal year	25,314.03
July 1, 1901, balance unexpended	639.18

Amount (estimated) required for completion of existing project	53,000.00
Amount that can be profitably expended in fiscal year ending June 30, 1903, in addition to the balance unexpended July 1, 1901 Submitted in compliance with requirements of sundry civil act of June 4, 1897.	53,000.00

(See Appendix A 1.)

3. Narraguagus River, Maine.—The obstruction to navigation consisted in a bar at the mouth of the river, over which there was a navigable depth of less than 6 feet at mean low tide.

The approved project, adopted in 1886, is to dredge a channel not less than 200 feet wide, having a depth of 11 feet at mean low tide up to Long Point and a depth of 9 feet thence to the "Deep Hole," about 1½ miles below the bridge at Millbridge; estimated cost, $50,000.

The expenditures to June 30, 1900, amounted to $71,435.96, of which $49,435.96 was for improvement below Millbridge. Previous to June 30, 1899, the channel had been dredged to the full width of 200 feet up to the old steamboat wharf, with turning basins about 300 feet in width each in front of both the old and the new steamboat wharves.

A survey was made in November, 1899, which showed that considerable filling had taken place, especially in the turning basin at the new steamboat wharf and in the channel immediately below. A contract was made to redredge this turning basin and part of the channel to 11 feet at mean low tide. Work was begun May 31 and completed June 16, 1900, 30,000 cubic yards of material (mostly sawdust and mud) being removed at a cost of 15 cents per cubic yard.

The passing in and out of the steamboat which lands at the new steamboat wharf, four times weekly during a period of eight months each year, aids greatly in retarding the refilling of the dredged channel, but it has been reported that fresh deposits from the almost inexhaustible supply of sawdust on the flats farther up have already greatly shoaled the area dredged in 1900.

The commerce for the last eight years is given as follows:

	Tons.		Tons.
1893	60,875	1897	41,500
1894	95,600	1898	26,147
1895	54,750	1899	23,545
1896	16,175	1900	35,825

July 1, 1900, balance unexpended $564.04
June 30, 1901, amount expended during fiscal year 147.85

July 1, 1901, balance unexpended 416.19

(See Appendix A 2.)

4. Breakwater from Mount Desert to Porcupine Island, Bar Harbor, Maine.—The anchorage in front of the town of Bar Harbor, as well as the wharves at which steamers land, is exposed to storms and seas from southerly directions, at times rendering the anchorage insecure and the landing of passengers and freight at the wharves difficult. The original project was to construct a riprap breakwater on a direct line from Porcupine Island to Dry Ledge, and thence to within a short distance of Mount Desert Island.

In December, 1890, and January, 1893, by authority of the Secretary of War, the project was amended, and now provides for a breakwater on the direct line first proposed, but somewhat shorter, terminating at a distance of about 600 feet from the low-water line on Mount Desert Island, the top of the breakwater to be 20 feet wide at level of mean high tide, and the side slopes to be 1 on 1. The estimated cost of the present project is $420,200.

The expenditures to June 30, 1900, were $174,994.77, at which date the breakwater had been completed for a distance of 700 feet west of Dry Ledge. The total projected length of that portion west of the ledge is 1,440 feet.

Under contract with William S. White the work of depositing stone on and in continuation of the breakwater, which was begun April 28, was completed September 21, 1900. During the fiscal year 9,393 tons of stone was furnished and placed in the work, and a total of 23,291 tons under the entire contract. Most of the stone has been used in raising to full height and section the part of the old work which had settled or been lowered by the action of the waves. The length of the breakwater as built west of Dry Ledge is about 731 feet, leaving 709 feet yet to be built.

The breakwater will require more or less extensive repairs until the side slopes have assumed an angle of rest against wave action.

The benefits to navigation are general in providing a harbor of refuge, and local in making it possible for boats to land at the wharves at all times in safety. The only convenient method of transportation to and from Bar Harbor is by boat.

It has been impracticable to obtain commercial statistics for 1900, but for 1898 it was reported as 22,175 tons, and for 1899 as 24,393 tons.

July 1, 1900, balance unexpended	$15,005.23
June 30, 1901, amount expended during fiscal year	14,713.95
July 1, 1901, balance unexpended	291.28
Amount (estimated) required for completion of existing project	230,200.00
Amount that can be profitably expended in fiscal year ending June 30, 1903, in addition to the balance unexpended July 1, 1901	25,000.00

Submitted in compliance with requirements of sundry civil act of June 4, 1897.

(See Appendix A 3.)

5. *Harbor at Sullivan Falls, Maine.*—Sullivan River has a length of about 6 miles, and is the outlet of a large bay. About midway of its length a point of land projects to such extent as to reduce the width to about one-fourth that immediately above and below, and at this place the slope and velocity are such that the locality is termed Sullivan Falls. The bottom is ledge, the higher portions forming dangerous obstructions to navigation. Hatchers Rock, about midway of the narrow channel at the falls, had originally only about 6 inches of water over it at mean low tide.

Under a project completed in 1875, the sum of $35,000 was expended in removing three old piers, in excavating the obstructing ledges at the falls to a depth of 7 feet at mean low tide, and in placing spindles on two rocks near the mouth of the river. This work was of material benefit to navigation.

Under the act of 1890, an examination was made of Sullivan Falls, and an new project, estimated to cost $35,000, for removing Hatchers Rock and two other points of ledge to a depth of 10 feet at mean low tide was submitted. The first appropriation for work under this last project was by act of June 3, 1896.

The expenditures under the existing project to June 30, 1900, were $9,535.81, and the operations consisted in removing the entire area of Hatchers Rock, and a part of the outer end of ledge C, to a depth of 10 feet at mean low tide.

The improvement not only increases the navigable depth, but also, by removing the cause of eddies and cross currents, has added to the length of time at each high and low tide during which vessels may pass through the rapids with safety.

Vessels can not use the channel at low stages except when the tide is slack. This occurs after the tide has flowed about 2 feet at which time vessels drawing 11 feet can pass through safely.

The improvement may be regarded as permanent.

The commerce for 1896 is given as 51,290 tons; for 1897, as 50,790 tons; for 1898, as 41,700 tons; for 1899, as 42,125 tons, and for 1900, as 35,926 tons.

July 1, 1900, balance unexpended	$464.69
July 1, 1901, balance unexpended	464.69
Amount (estimated) required for completion of existing project	25,000.00
Amount that can be profitably expended in fiscal year ending June 30, 1903, in addition to the balance unexpended July 1, 1901	15,000.00

Submitted in compliance with requirements of sundry civil act of June 4, 1897.

(See Appendix A 4.)

6. *Union River, Maine.*—Originally the channel of Union River was much obstructed, and in the upper part almost closed, at low tide. Under a project completed in 1873 the sum of $30,000 was expended in removing a large quantity of mill waste, ledge, and bowlders, giving a depth of 3 to 4 feet at mean low tide up to the head of navigation at Ellsworth.

A survey of Union River and Bay was made under the act of 1888, and a project was submitted for obtaining a channel through the bar at the mouth of the river by the construction of a jetty, and for a depth of 6 feet at mean low tide in the upper part of the river by dredging. The first appropriation since this survey was by the act of June 3, 1896, which appropriated $15,000 for improving Union River by dredging.

With this appropriation a channel was dredged to the depth of 6 feet at mean low tide to a point about 3,000 feet from its lower end, working upstream; but a section of about 1,000 feet, where harder material was encountered, was not down to grade; also a single cut, 3 feet deep at mean low tide, was dredged from this point up to the wharves at Ellsworth, with a view to affording a measure of immediate relief to commerce.

By the act of March 3, 1899, the sum of $15,000 was appropriated, and the improvement placed under the continuous-contract system.

A survey was made in May, 1899, and report with maps and estimates submitted June 16, 1899. (See Annual Report of the Chief of Engineers for 1899, p. 1026 et seq.)

The estimate then submitted was to obtain, entirely by dredging and ledge excavation, a channel 6 feet deep at mean low tide, with widths, in straight sections, varying from 200 feet to 100 feet, from the mouth of the river to the wharves at Ellsworth, at a cost of $130,000. This estimate for expenditure of funds for completion of the improvement was approved by the Secretary of War June 28, 1899, and is regarded as the existing project.

A contract for completion of the entire work was made with Augustus R. Wright October 16, 1899. The total expenditures to June 30, 1900, were $45,712.06. At that date 10,938 cubic yards of material, almost entirely slabs, edgings, and sawdust, had been removed from a section of channel 90 feet wide, about 900 feet long, and about 4 feet deep, beginning a short distance above the Narrows and working upstream.

Dredging under the existing project was continued until November 15, 1900, when work was suspended for the season. Work was resumed under this contract in the latter part of May, 1901.

By this dredging a channel at the mouth of the river had been made to a depth of 6 feet, with a width of 200 feet for a distance of 600 feet and a width of 120 feet for a farther distance of 3,200 feet. At the lower end of the Narrows a channel had been obtained through hardpan and bowlders and ledge 100 feet wide, 6 feet deep at mean low tide, and about 400 feet long. At the upper end of the Narrows the channel had been dredged to a width of 150 feet for a distance of about 1,000 feet. Full depth has not, however, been obtained throughout this section, the mill waste and loose gravel only having been removed.

At the time of the resumption of work in May, 1901, the entire proposed channel was again carefully sounded and it was found that fresh deposits, brought down during the last freshets, had completely obliterated the channel dredged below the wharves at Ellsworth last season and had made the navigable channel more crooked and its condition worse than before the improvement was commenced. As a result of these new deposits boats drawing not more than the flow of the tide are the only ones that can reach the wharves at Ellsworth.

The soundings made show that to obtain the proposed width and depth of channel between the Narrows and the head of navigation, where the fresh accretions are greatest, will require the removal of 8,000 cubic yards more of slabs and edgings than when the work was begun in May, 1900; or, including the work done in the season of 1900, would indicate a total fill in the channel from 1899 to 1901 of 41,000 cubic yards in situ. There has been no appreciable filling in the Narrows and immediately below. At the mouth of the river, however, the deposit of sawdust on the bar has so largely increased the amount of excavation that after ten days' work it was found necessary to reduce the width of the channel to be dredged from 200 feet to 120 feet.

It was stated in the last annual report that "the improvement can not be regarded as permanent, as the masses of slabs and edgings and sawdust now within the banks of the river will gradually work into the channel and necessitate redredging. At the mills on the river above the head of navigation all the short sawdust and a part of the other waste materials go into the stream."

The shoaling since last season is, however, believed to be exceptional, as the freshet during the spring of 1901 was the highest known for years and brought down vast quantities of refuse material from the banks above ordinary freshet height, but the most disastrous circumstance was the giving way of the dam at the head of tide water, thereby turning loose the accumulations of years of deposits of sawmill waste and silt in the pool above the dam into the river below, the slabs and sticks refilling the channel above the Narrows and a large part of the sawdust being carried farther down and deposited on the bar at the mouth of the river.

The commerce for 1896 is given as 54,000 tons; for 1897, as 57,685 tons; for 1898, as 50,462 tons; for 1899, as 49,800 tons; and for 1900, as 42,580 tons.

July 1, 1900, balance unexpended	$129,287.94
June 30, 1901, amount expended during fiscal year	13,055.11
July 1, 1901, balance unexpended	116,232.83
July 1, 1901, outstanding liabilities	1,609.22
July 1, 1901, balance available	114,623.61
July 1, 1901, amount covered by uncompleted contracts	108,686.24

(See Appendix A 5.)

7. *Bagaduce River, Maine.*—This is a small stream that empties into Penobscot Bay at Castine, Me. The upper part of the river divides into two branches, one called Northern Bay and the other South Bay. Northern Bay near South Penobscot is a shoal sheet of water of about 700 acres area, the bottom of which for the greater part is bare at low tide. There was a narrow channel from Bridges Point to Bowden's wharf which had a depth of less than 2 feet and was obstructed by ledges and bowlders near Winslows Island. The South Bay is obstructed by ledges at Johnsons Narrows. A project for the improvement of the Northern Bay was adopted in 1890 which has for its object the securing of a channel 100 feet wide and 6 feet deep at mean low tide from Bridges

Point to Bowden's wharf, at an estimated cost of $45,000. It is also intended to remove a small quantity of rock obstructing the channel at Johnsons Narrows, at an estimated cost of $1,875.

The expenditures to June 30, 1900, were $21,919.63. At that date the channel had been dredged its entire length for a width of 40 feet, but the full projected depth had not been obtained throughout. At Winslows Island, about midway of the channel, and where it was shoalest, a depth of about 2 feet at mean low tide had been secured by the removal of bowlders.

The removal of rocks and bowlders from the 40-foot wide channel opposite Winslows Island, which was commenced June 15, 1900, was completed as far as practicable August 11 following, 418 tons being removed during the fiscal year and a total of 501 tons under the contract. An open-market arrangement was then made to continue the removal of bowlders over the entire width of the 100-foot channel. This work was completed September 15, at which time 976 tons additional had been removed, making a total of 1,477 tons removed.

Navigation has not been appreciably benefited by the improvement and probably will not be until the projected channel is fully completed. The small vessels carrying brick and merchandise prefer to go in or out across the flats to the north of Winslows Island, where only vessels drawing not more than 8 feet can pass at high tide, rather than to take the chances of running on the rocks by way of the narrow channel to the southward of the island, where there is a depth of 10 or 12 feet at high tide.

The improvement when completed will be fairly permanent except that a gradual washing into the dredged channel of soft mud from the flats on either side will cause some shoaling.

The commerce for the last eight years is given as follows:

	Tons.		Tons.
1893	49,300	1897	86,600
1894	67,850	1898	79,965
1895	85,900	1899	89,500
1896	78,050	1900	86,000

Probably the greater part of this pertains to Castine, at the mouth of the river.

July 1, 1900, balance unexpended	$3,080.37
June 30, 1901, amount expended during fiscal year	2,732.56
July 1, 1901, balance unexpended	347.81
Amount (estimated) required for completion of existing project	21,875.00
Amount that can be profitably expended in fiscal year ending June 30, 1903, in addition to the balance unexpended July 1, 1901	3,000.00
Submitted in compliance with requirements of sundry civil act of June 4, 1897.	

(See Appendix A 6.)

8. *Penobscot River, Maine.*—The improvement of the Penobscot River was first undertaken in 1870, the project being for a channel not less than 150 feet in width, 12 feet deep at low tide as far up as Bangor. This plan was subsequently modified. The existing project for the general improvement of the river may be stated as follows:

To secure a channel depth of 11 feet at extreme low tide for a width of 360 feet in Bangor Harbor; to widen, straighten, and deepen the channel near Crosbys Narrows and Stern's mill to a depth of 12 feet at extreme low tide, and to secure a channel depth of 22 feet at mean low tide between Bucksport and Winterport, the estimated cost of the entire work being $440,000.

The expenditures under the various projects, to June 30, 1900, amounted to $339,934.13, and the objects of the general project have been virtually accomplished.

The available depths are as follows: Bangor Harbor, 14 feet at mean low tide, or 11 feet at extreme low tide; at Stern's mill and Crosbys Narrows, 15 feet at mean low tide, or 12 feet at extreme low tide. The shoal at High Head above Bucksport was dredged to a depth of 22 feet, in accordance with the project, but afterwards shoaled up to a certain extent and subsequently deepened again by the natural scour of the river. Examination made since the dredging was done shows that the depths on the bar vary, and that no material benefit has been obtained by dredging.

In view of the shifting character of this bar, the utter failure to obtain a permanent improvement by dredging, and the fact that it is not in any way a dangerous obstruction to navigation, no further work is recommended upon it at this time.

By act of March 3, 1899, Congress appropriated $28,000 for completing an improvement of the Penobscot River at Bangor, in accordance with project submitted May 3, 1897, which contemplates dredging at the mouth of the Kenduskeag Stream and through both draws of the railroad bridge, and within the basin between the latter bridge and the Post-Office Bridge, so as to obtain a uniform depth of 1 foot above level of extreme low water to within 30 feet of the wharves. The same project also provides for deepening the harbor of Bangor in front of the Boston and Bangor Steamboat wharf by the excavation of ledge to a depth of 11 feet at extreme low tide.

During the fiscal year just ended, 27,428 cubic yards of material was dredged and 15 cubic yards of ledge excavated from the Kenduskeag River, completing this part of the project, with the exception of a small number of bowlders, which will be removed after completion of the rock excavation in front of the Boston and Bangor Steamboat wharf. The progress at this latter place has been retarded considerably by unavoidable circumstances and the time of completion of this contract has been twice extended, first to July 1, 1901, and, owing to the exceptionally high and long-continued spring freshets, and a slight increase of the number of cubic yards of ledge to be excavated, again to October 1, 1901.

About 65 per cent of the ledge excavation has been completed.

The condition of the river in the vicinity of Stern's mill, below Bangor, has not perceptibly changed since the completion of improvements made in 1892; the river has deepened in many places, and for purposes of general navigation the river channel is adequate.

The commerce of the river for the last eight years is given as follows:

	Tons.		Tons.
1893	565,887	1897	790,698
1894	750,313	1898	639,671
1895	617,859	1899	658,632
1896	715,911	1900	917,835

July 1, 1900, balance unexpended $36,365.87
June 30, 1901, amount expended during fiscal year 16,918.37

July 1, 1901, balance unexpended 19,447.50
July 1, 1901, outstanding liabilities 1,701.19

July 1, 1901, balance available 17,746.31

July 1, 1901, amount covered by uncompleted contracts 8,736.92

(See Appendix A 7.)

9. *Rockland Harbor, Maine.*—The first improvement at this point was made to render it a safe harbor of refuge for coastwise shipping during easterly storms.

The original project provided for two breakwaters, and was adopted in 1881.

In 1886 the project was amended so as to raise the height of the breakwater under construction to the level of mean high tide, and in 1890 the project was again modified so as to provide for a further extension southward of the breakwater at Jamesons Point and eliminate from the project the construction of the second breakwater.

By the act of June 3, 1896, Congress adopted a project for dredging the inner harbor in the vicinity of the wharves to depths ranging from 4 feet to 13 feet at mean low tide, and for the removal of two dangerous groups of ledge occupying central positions in the harbor. The estimated cost of this improvement was $402,000.

By the same act Congress combined the latter project with the project for the breakwater as one, and authorized the work to be placed under the continuous-contract system, the combined estimated cost for the two being $1,036,000.

The total expenditures to June 30, 1900, for improvement of this harbor, were $633,031.02. At that date the breakwater had been built its entire contemplated length (about 4,140 feet out from the low-water line), with the top 20 feet wide and about to the plane of mean high tide, except that for a length of about 430 feet at the shore end it had been built to the height of about half tide only.

The total amount dredged to June 30, 1900, was 322,840 cubic yards, place measurement, and 12,702 cubic yards, place measurement, had been removed from the south ledges, and 1,900 cubic yards from Jameson Point Ledge.

An old wreck in the northern part of the harbor (the one referred to in the act of 1896) was removed.

Work of raising the shore end of the breakwater to full section and building a stone cap the entire length, has been carried on throughout the past year, except for a suspension of a couple of months during the severest part of the winter. The inner part has been raised to full height and section, about 2,785 feet of stone cap built out from the shore end, and 209 feet in from the outer end, leaving about 1,351 feet to complete the contract. The cap at the outer end was made 39 feet wide, to form a site for a permanent light and keeper's dwelling.

Dredging under contract with Moore & Wright was completed May 24, 1901; 165,087 cubic yards, place measurement, was removed during the fiscal year, and a total of 487,567 cubic yards under the contract.

Under contract with Dunbar & Sullivan the removal of the south ledges (D and E) has been completed to a depth of 22 feet at mean low tide, and the Jameson Point ledges A and C have been removed to the required depth of 14 feet, with ledge B of same group nearly two-thirds removed to 14 feet. A total of 26,560 cubic yards of ledge has been removed, leaving about 3,613 cubic yards to complete the original contract.

The benefits resulting from these improvements are considerable. The construction of the breakwater will afford a safe and extensive anchorage and harbor of refuge, the excavation of ledges will increase the available anchorage area and remove dangerous obstructions to boats in motion, and the dredging will afford access by vessels of greater draft to the wharves when built out to the harbor line.

No additional funds are asked for, as it is believed that the funds already provided will, at existing contract prices, be sufficient to complete the improvement.

The commerce of Rockland Harbor for the last eight years is given as follows:

	Tons.		Tons.
1893	538,506	1897	594,992
1894	509,853	1898	579,300
1895	615,830	1899	755,649
1896	580,295	1900	553,000

July 1, 1900, balance unexpended	$292,468.98
June 30, 1901, amount expended during fiscal year	129,864.39
July 1, 1901, balance unexpended	162,604.59
July 1, 1901, outstanding liabilities	30,511.04
July 1, 1901, balance available	132,093.55
July 1, 1901, amount covered by uncompleted contracts	54,633.08

(See Appendix A 8.)

10. *Carvers Harbor, Vinalhaven, Me.*—The anchorage at this harbor was limited, and the harbor shoal, there being less than 8 feet at mean low tide over the most of it.

The approved project is to dredge the inner harbor to a depth of 16 feet at mean low tide over an area about 23 acres in extent, and at an estimated cost of $64,000. The survey and estimate were made in accordance with the provisions of river and harbor act of 1894.

The expenditures to June 30, 1900, were $24,211.14. At that date about 14 acres of the proposed area of 23 acres to be dredged for the harbor of refuge had been completed, and about 50 per cent of the total estimated amount of material had been removed therefrom.

Ledge was uncovered about 3 feet above the required depth near the upper end and on both sides of the dredged area, and a rock with its top only 7½ feet below mean low tide was discovered near the upper corner of the steamboat wharf.

It is proposed to make an examination to ascertain more definitely the character of the material remaining to be removed and the extent of the underlying ledge.

The improvement, it is believed, will be fairly permanent, and will be of benefit to navigation in affording a harbor of refuge and increased facilities for reaching the wharves.

The commerce for 1896 is given as 63,078 tons, for 1897 as 63,074 tons, for 1898 as 60,000 tons, for 1899 as 63,390 tons, and for 1900 as 64,500 tons.

130 REPORT OF THE CHIEF OF ENGINEERS, U. S. ARMY.

July 1, 1900, balance unexpended $788.86
July 1, 1901, balance unexpended 788.86

Amount (estimated) required for completion of existing project 39,000.00
Amount that can be profitably expended in fiscal year ending June 30, 1903, in addition to the balance unexpended July 1, 1901 .... 39,000.00
Submitted in compliance with requirements of sundry civil act of June 4, 1897.

(See Appendix A 9.)

11. Georges River, Maine.—This river is a tidal estuary, and the head of navigation is Thomaston, Me. The navigable depth is full 3½ fathoms to a point about 1 mile from Thomaston, but from this point to the head of navigation the channel before improvement, as it wound through the flats, was narrow, with a sharp bend at one point and with a least depth of about 11 feet at mean low tide.

By act of June 3, 1896, Congress adopted a project for dredging the channel to 16 feet at mean low tide, and to a width of 160 feet as far up as the bend, to 220 feet in the bend, and to widths of 125 and 90 feet in front of the town.

The expenditures to June 30, 1900, were $19,787.38. At that date the channel had been dredged to the full projected width and depth for a distance of about 3,600 feet upstream from the 16-foot contour.

There remains to be dredged a strip of channel about 90 feet wide and 900 feet long, requiring the removal of about 16,000 cubic yards of material, scow measurement, to complete the entire project.

Material brought down by the river during freshets will doubtless cause shoaling in the channel, but the process will be slow, and a depth sufficient to accommodate the traffic will probably be maintained for a number of years.

The depth of the dredged channel is such that the vessels using it could be towed out at any stage of tide, but as the business does not seem to warrant the maintenance of a tugboat, they have to wait until near high water and a favorable wind in order to go out or in under sail with safety.

The commerce for the last five years is given as follows: For 1896 as 45,375 tons; for 1897 as 64,250 tons; for 1898 as 59,000 tons; for 1899 as 60,000 tons, and for 1900 as 29,225 tons.

July 1, 1900, balance unexpended $212.62
July 1, 1901, balance unexpended 212.62

Amount (estimated) required for completion of existing project 6,000.00
Amount that can be profitably expended in fiscal year ending June 30, 1903, in addition to the balance unexpended July 1, 1901 .... 6,000.00
Submitted in compliance with requirements of sundry civil act of June 4, 1897.

(See Appendix A 10.)

12. Kennebec River, Maine.—Before the improvements were commenced the main channel of the river between the foot of Swan Island and Gardiner was obstructed by shoals near Beef Rock, with only 10 feet of water at mean low tide; by dangerous sunken ledges in Lovejoy Narrows; by a shoal below South Gardiner with only 8 feet on it at mean low tide, and by a ledge at Nehumkeg Island. The steamboat channel to the west of Swan Island (at Hatchs Rock) was obstructed by a shoal over which there was only 7½ feet of water, and the channel between Gardiner and Augusta, a distance of 6¼ miles, was obstructed by shoals which gave a navigable depth of only 3½ feet of water in low summer tide.

Appropriations were made at various times between 1827 and 1852 for improving the river, and a project was adopted in 1866 for removing rocks and straightening and deepening the upper part of the river.

In 1868 the project was amended so as to give a wider channel, and in 1871 the project was extended. It was again extended in 1872 to include the removal of ledges in Lovejoy Narrows. This project was modified in 1873, and as modified was completed in 1877.

In 1881 a project was adopted for the improvement of the channel west of Swan Island and near the north end of it, and was completed in 1883.

The river and harbor act of 1886 provided for a new survey of the river from Bath to Augusta. This survey was made in 1887, and a project submitted for a further improvement of the river.

In August, 1892, the project was revised and a general project for the improvement adopted, as follows: For a channel depth of 13 feet up as far as Sands Island; 12 feet thence to Hinckley Shoal, and 10 feet thence to Augusta; a steamboat channel 9 feet deep west of Swan Island, and the removal of old bridge piers at Hallowell, all the above depths being referred to mean low tide. The estimated cost of this revised project, which was approved August 19, 1892, was $388,500.

The total expenditures for the river up to June 30, 1900, amounted to $472,660.79, with which the work under the existing project had been completed, with exception of the repair of Beef Rock jetty and possibly some dredging at that locality.

The dredged channel, especially between Gardiner and Augusta, has been found to fill more or less rapidly, probably with material brought down during heavy spring freshets. The parts of the improvement consisting of the removal of ledge are, of course, permanent. Vessels drawing 14 to 16 feet can get up as far as Gardiner at high tide, but only 11 or 12 feet can be carried to Augusta.

No further appropriation is now asked for, as, unless new conditions develop, the funds already appropriated are sufficient for completion of the existing project.

The commerce of the river is given as follows:

	Tons.		Tons.
1892	1,263,145	1897	665,991
1893	970,938	1898	1,211,808
1894	1,207,965	1899	714,199
1895	1,162,972	1900	716,930

July 1, 1900, balance unexpended	$27,689.21
June 30, 1901, amount expended during fiscal year	54.56
July 1, 1901, balance unexpended	27,634.65

(See Appendix A 11.)

13. *Portland Harbor, Maine.*—The entrance to the main part of the harbor of Portland, or the anchorage, has always been good, but before improvement the approach to the inner harbor was obstructed by a shoal known as the Middle Ground over which the depth was only from 8 to 10 feet at mean low tide, while between it and Stamford ledge the greatest available depth was only 16 feet. The best part of the wharf front was exposed to swell from the main entrance, which sometimes made it dangerous for vessels to lie at the docks, and along this front the depth was in some places as shallow as 4 feet.

The first work of improvement undertaken by the Government was the construction of the breakwater. This was begun as early as 1836. It was completed in 1874.

The work of deepening the harbor was begun under the act of Congress of 1868, the plan of improvement being to excavate a channel 300 feet wide and 20 feet deep at mean low tide through the southern slope of the Middle Ground and to remove the bar off the Grand Trunk Railroad wharves to the same depth.

The project was modified in 1870 so as to provide for a channel 400 feet wide, and again in 1871 so as to provide for a channel 500 feet wide. In 1872 further modifications were made by including in the project the dredging of Back Cove and the dredging of the inner harbor up to the harbor commissioner's lines to a depth of 16 feet at mean low tide. The project, modified as above described, excepting some dredging in the inner harbor, was completed by 1876.

Between 1881 and 1885 the Middle Ground was removed to a depth of 21 feet at mean low tide.

A further deepening of a portion of the harbor to 29 feet at mean low tide was next begun under the project of 1886. To this was subsequently added, in 1890, a small amount of dredging in the upper part of the harbor.

In 1894 the project was extended to cover the widening of the upper part of the 29-foot area and the dredging of a channel 25 feet deep to connect the deep water in the lower part of the harbor with deep water in the upper part. This work was completed in 1894.

By the act of June 3, 1896, Congress adopted a project for dredging to 30 feet at mean low tide over the greater part of the harbor at an estimated cost of $770,000, and included in the project the further improvement of Back Cove at a combined estimate of $946,250. The same act appropriated $20,000 for beginning work and authorized the making of a contract for its completion.

After twice advertising, a contract for the entire work was entered into with George M. Valentine & Co., of New York.

Dredging was begun July 2, 1897, and by the terms of contract was to be completed November 20, 1898. Progress from the first was slow and plant inadequate and the contract was extended, under promise of better progress, to November 30, 1899. The firm failed financially April 19, 1899, lost their dredge by seizure for debt, and never afterwards resumed work.

After the retirement of George M. Valentine & Co., Mr. A. R. Wright was employed, under an open-market arrangement, to continue the dredging during the unexpired portion of said company's contract. This period having expired, the unfinished work was advertised. Bids therefor were opened March 27, 1900, and all rejected as too high. The work was again advertised, bids opened June 30, 1900, and the work awarded to the Morris & Cumings Dredging Company of New York.

The work of the fiscal year by this company consisted in the removal of 821,900 cubic yards of material, situ measurement, being the equivalent of 1,031,476 cubic yards, scow measurement. The progress made has not averaged 120,000 cubic yards per month as required by the contract, but it is confidently believed that the work will be completed within the time specified, viz, twenty-one months from date of beginning. One million six hundred and eighty-three thousand six hundred and one cubic yards, situ, are yet to be dredged.

The maximum draft that can be carried to the wharves in Back Cove is about 11 feet, and to the wharves in the lower part of Portland Harbor about 29 feet, at mean low water. The work remaining to be done consists in extending the 30-foot dredging to the lines limiting the project.

The movements of the ocean steamers have been very much facilitated so far, and the arrivals and departures of these large steamers now are independent of the stages of the tide.

The total amount expended on Portland Harbor, including Back Cove, up to June 30, 1900, is $903,209.64.

The commerce of Portland Harbor for the past eight years is given as follows:

	Tons.		Tons.
1893	1,432,805	1897	1,326,844
1894	1,214,887	1898	1,334,752
1895	1,339,064	1899	1,620,284
1896	1,357,575	1900	2,261,008

July 1, 1900, balance unexpended	$359,517.41
Amount appropriated by sundry civil act approved March 3, 1901	21,000.00
	380,517.41
June 30, 1901, amount expended during fiscal year	96,964.84
July 1, 1901, balance unexpended	283,552.57
July 1, 1901, outstanding liabilities	10,825.88
July 1, 1901, balance available	272,726.69
July 1, 1901, amount covered by uncompleted contracts	254,218.78

(See Appendix A 12.)

EXAMINATION AND SURVEY MADE IN COMPLIANCE WITH EMERGENCY RIVER AND HARBOR ACT APPROVED JUNE 6, 1900.

The preliminary examination and survey of *Portland Harbor, Maine, with a view to removing so much of Witch Rock as endangers navigation* were made by Major Roessler and reports thereon dated October 18 and November 17, 1900, respectively, were submitted through the division engineer. A plan for improvement at an estimated cost of $500,000 is presented. The reports were transmitted to Congress and printed in House Doc. No. 85, Fifty-sixth Congress, second session. (See also Appendix A 13.)

IMPROVEMENT OF RIVERS AND HARBORS IN MAINE SOUTH OF PORTLAND HARBOR, IN VERMONT AND NEW HAMPSHIRE, AND IN MASSACHUSETTS NORTH OF LYNN HARBOR; NARROWS OF LAKE CHAMPLAIN, NEW YORK AND VERMONT.

This district was in the charge of Maj. Walter L. Fisk, Corps of Engineers, to December 15, 1900, and of Capt. Harry Taylor, Corps of Engineers, since that date. Division Engineer, Col. G. L. Gillespie, Corps of Engineers (now brigadier-general, Chief of Engineers, United States Army), to May 3, 1901, and Col. Chas. R. Suter, Corps of Engineers, since May 9, 1901.

1. Saco River, Maine.—The first work done on the Saco River was in 1827, when an appropriation was made for the erection of piers, placing beacons or buoys, and removing obstructions. Prior to this the depth of water on the bar was only about 2 feet at mean low tide, while much of the river was deeper. The entrance was also dangerous in rough weather, and the numerous projecting rocks and ledges in the river proper, in connection with the swift currents, made its navigation dangerous.

In 1866 a plan was proposed for the improvement of the mouth of the river and a project was adopted in 1867. The project was for the construction of a breakwater, the removal of sunken rocks, and the rebuilding of some of the most important piers, against which vessels might drift without damage. This project was completed in 1878 at a cost of $169,275.

A resurvey of the breakwater was made in 1883 and a new plan submitted for raising and repairing it and extending it out to Sharps Ledge.

The river and harbor act of 1884 directed a survey to be made of the river. This was done in 1885, and a plan submitted for the improvement of the river proper from its mouth to the head of navigation. In 1890 the two projects were combined so that the one now in process of execution is for improving the Saco River, including the breakwater and jetty.

The total expenditures on both river and breakwater up to June 30, 1900, amounted to $338,597.42, and resulted in removing dangerous ledges, in constructing piers to prevent vessels from being swept on the rocks, in constructing a breakwater on the north side of the entrance, and a jetty on the south side of the entrance to contract the channel way with a view to obtaining a greater depth over the bar, also in deepening the channels in the upper portion of the river by dredging, and the construction of contraction works.

An examination made last year showed that about 3½ feet at mean low water is the maximum draft that can be carried over the bar just outside the breakwater and jetty.

In order to maintain the desired depth the breakwater on the north side should be extended to Sharps Ledge, as contemplated by the plan of improvement submitted in 1883, so as to stop the influx of sand from that side. Some uncertainty exists whether Congress has adopted the plan of extending the breakwater to Sharps Ledge. The probable cost of such extension and some minor repairs is estimated by the officer in local charge to be $200,000. Possibly the full extension may not be required to secure and maintain the projected depth.

During June and July, 1900, the south jetty was repaired in several low places and a beacon was built at its outer end.

The commerce of the last eight years is given as follows:

	Tons.		Tons.
1893	59,765	1897	42,214
1894	47,350	1898	44,508
1895	62,125	1899	46,597
1896	46,956	1900	50,354

July 1, 1900, balance unexpended	$8,177.58
June 30, 1901, amount expended during fiscal year	2,935.95
July 1, 1901, balance unexpended	5,241.63

{ Amount that can be profitably expended in fiscal year ending June 30, 1903, in addition to the balance unexpended July 1, 1901 .... 40,000.00
Submitted in compliance with requirements of sundry civil act of June 4, 1897. }

(See Appendix B 1.)

RIVER AND HARBOR IMPROVEMENTS. 135

2. Cape Porpoise Harbor, Maine.—The harbor at Cape Porpoise is situated about midway between Portland, Me., and Portsmouth, N. H. Originally the harbor had a depth of about 13 feet at mean low tide, but for a small area only, and the entrance was obstructed by a bar on which there was only about 10 feet of water at mean low tide. The anchorage was too small to accommodate the small vessels seeking that place for refuge, without regard to the commerce of the place.

By act of March 3, 1899, Congress adopted a project for securing a channel of entrance 200 feet wide and 16 feet deep at mean low tide and a channel and anchorage within the harbor about 3,000 feet long, 600 feet wide, and 15 feet deep at mean low tide, at an estimated cost of $125,000. By this act the improvement was placed under the continuous-contract system and $70,000 appropriated toward the work. The project is described in the Annual Report of the Chief of Engineers for 1899 page 1050.

The total expenditures on this work to June 30, 1900, were $505.46.

Contract for the entire work at 9.2 cents per cubic yard was entered into and operations thereunder were commenced early in June, 1900, and completed in December of the same year. The harbor is now dredged to full projected dimensions, except a small area in the northern part of the harbor where a quantity of ledge was found. The contract for the removal of this ledge, estimated to contain about 370 cubic yards, has already been let, and the harbor will probably be completed as projected by September 30, 1901. The maximum draft that can be carried in the harbor outside of the ledge mentioned is 15 feet at mean low water.

It has been impracticable to obtain detailed commercial statistics since 1898, when an aggregate of 20,350 tons of coal and fish was reported.

July 1, 1900, balance unexpended	$79,494.54
June 30, 1901, amount expended during fiscal year	66,654.00
July 1, 1901, balance unexpended	12,840.54
July 1, 1901, amount covered by uncompleted contracts	4,218.00

(See Appendix B 2.)

3. Cocheco River, New Hampshire.—Before the improvement was begun the river from Dover to the Lower Narrows was much obstructed by bowlders, ledges, and shoals, the depth being in some places as little as 6 inches at mean low tide. The tide rises and falls about 7 feet.

A project for improvement was adopted in 1871, which provided for a channel 40 feet wide and 4 feet deep from the Lower Narrows up to Collin's wharf. The estimated cost was $45,000. Subsequently more accurate and extended surveys having shown the practicability and importance of extending the improvements up to the head of navigation, the project was extended and the estimate increased to $85,000. This project was completed in 1879. The improvements had opened up a large commerce, employing large vessels where formerly only flatboats had been used, in consequence of which the project was still further extended by providing for a "cut-off" through Alleys Point, widening to 60 feet and deepening to 5 feet the existing channels through Trickeys and Clements Point shoals, and blasting and removing other obstructions. The extended project was completed in 1888.

In 1889 a new survey was made, under the river and harbor act of 1888, and a new project was submitted for obtaining a depth of 7 feet, increased to 7¼ feet in rock, with a width of 50 feet in rock and 60 to 75 feet where the material is less expensive to remove. This project was adopted in 1890 and is estimated to cost $175,000.

The total expenditures for this river up to June 30, 1900, amounted to $253,924.48. These expenditures, under former projects, resulted in giving a channel through the rocky bed of the river 5 feet deep and 40 feet wide in the narrowest parts, where the depth before was only from 6 inches to 2 feet. Under the last project the upper end of the channel at Dover had been deepened to 7 feet at mean low tide for a length of 1,200 feet down river, with a width varying from 100 to 140 feet; from this point the channel is now 50 to 75 feet wide, 7 feet deep at mean low water (and 7¼ feet in rock) for a farther distance of 2,800 feet, making a total length of channel at the upper end of 4,000 feet completed to full proposed dimensions except over a small portion in the lower part, where, owing to ledge, the required depth was not made.

The available depth is but 5 feet at mean low tide.

The commerce for the last eight years is given as follows:

	Tons.		Tons.
1893	66,933	1897	([1])
1894	68,415	1898	131,005
1895	83,151	1899	144,040
1896	59,755	1900	155,180

July 1, 1900, balance unexpended	$6,075.52
June 30, 1901, amount expended during fiscal year	.31
July 1, 1901, balance unexpended	6,075.21
Amount (estimated) required for completion of existing project	85,000.00
Amount that can be profitably expended in fiscal year ending June 30, 1903, in addition to the balance unexpended July 1, 1901	30,000.00

Submitted in compliance with requirements of sundry civil act of June 4, 1897.

(See Appendix B 3.)

4. Exeter River, New Hampshire.—A survey of this river was made in 1874, from its mouth in Great Bay up to the wharves at Exeter, a distance of 8.3 miles, and a project was submitted to obtain a towing channel with a minimum width of 40 feet and a minimum depth from the mouth to Oxbow (5.6 miles) of 12 feet at high tide, and from Oxbow up to Exeter of 10 feet, and to remove the bowlders all the way up between the 10-foot contours down to a depth of 10 feet below high tide, at an estimated cost of $34,000. This improvement was completed in 1882 at a cost of $35,000.

Under the requirements of the river and harbor act of June 3, 1896, a new survey was made from the mouth of the river to the upper bridge at Exeter, N. H., and a report (printed in Annual Report of the Chief of Engineers for 1897, p. 818) submitted, containing a project for a towing channel 40 feet wide, 12 feet deep at mean high tide up to Oxbow, and 11 feet deep at mean high tide thence up to Exeter, the estimate of cost being $12,000. By the act of March 3, 1899, this project was adopted, and the entire amount of the estimate appropriated.

Soon after operations had commenced under this appropriation it

---

[1] No statement could be obtained.

was found that considerable filling in had taken place since the last survey, in 1896, and that the amount of the original estmate of $12,000 would be insufficient to complete the work. An additional estimate is submitted.

The total expenditures to June 30, 1900, were $36,248.79. At that date the channel proposed by the new project had been completed 40 feet wide and 11 feet deep at mean high water from Exeter down river for a distance of 800 feet.

During the fiscal year 1901 this improved channel was extended down as far as Swamscot Bar, opposite Newfields. The available depth up to the wharves at Exeter does not exceed 4 feet at mean low tide, or about 10 feet at mean high tide.

The commerce involved in this improvement consists principally of coal for local consumption, a total of about 10,000 tons being reported annually.

July 1, 1900, balance unexpended................................... $10,751.21
June 30, 1901, amount expended during fiscal year..... .... 10,654.24

July 1, 1901, balance unexpended................................... 96.97

{ Amount (estimated) required for completion of existing project........ 7,000.00
Amount that can be profitably expended in fiscal year ending June 30, 1903, in addition to the balance unexpended July 1, 1901............ 7,000.00
Submitted in compliance with requirements of sundry civil act of June 4, 1897.

(See Appendix B 4.)

5. Harbor of refuge at Little Harbor, New Hampshire.—A survey was made of Little Harbor in 1882, and a plan of improvement proposed for the opening of an entrance channel with a depth of 9 feet at low tide and a width of 100 feet, together with a basin 300 by 700 feet, which was to be protected by a rubblestone breakwater. The estimated cost was $33,000. This project was approved in 1886 and its execution entered upon. In 1887 the project was enlarged to provide for the construction of two breakwaters—one on the north, the other on the south side of the entrance to the harbor—and the dredging of an anchorage about 49 acres in extent in the protected area to a depth of 12 feet at mean low tide. The estimated cost of the enlarged project was $235,000, and the act of 1888 made an appropriation for the work on the enlarged plan.

In October, 1894, after the breakwaters had been completed and a part of the dredging accomplished, the project was amended by reducing the area of the anchorage to be dredged to about 40 acres instead of 49. At the same time the project was revised, and the cost of the entire work placed at $145,000.

Before the improvement the depth in the harbor was only about 6 feet at low tide, and the anchorage was small and exposed.

The expenditures up to June 30, 1900, amounted to $120,634.43. At that date both breakwaters had been completed and the anchorage had been dredged to a width of about 550 feet—9 feet deep at mean low tide for about 115 feet and 12 feet deep for the remaining width.

Operations were continued during the past fiscal year under the appropriation of $12,000 made by the act of March 3, 1899, and on June 30, 1901, the anchorage area had been widened about 75 feet more to the full depth—12 feet.

The available depth is 12 feet at mean low tide over the greater part of the anchorage and the entrance and 9 feet over the remainder of the anchorage.

There is no regular commerce, but during the calendar year 1900 the number of vessels seeking shelter was 180, besides many small fishing boats.

July 1, 1900, balance unexpended	$11,365.57
June 30, 1901, amount expended during fiscal year	11,069.75
July 1, 1901, balance unexpended	295.82

Amount (estimated) required for completion of existing project	13,000.00
Amount that can be profitably expended in fiscal year ending June 30, 1903, in addition to the balance unexpended July 1, 1901	13,000.00
Submitted in compliance with requirements of sundry civil act of June 4, 1897.	

(See Appendix B 5.)

6. Newburyport Harbor, Massachusetts.—Newburyport, Mass., is situated about 2½ miles from the Atlantic Ocean, on the south bank of the Merrimac River. The mouth of the river is obstructed by a sandy bar, over which originally but 7 feet draft at low water could be carried in a narrow, shifting channel.

The object of the improvement is to create through the outer bar a channel 1,000 feet wide and at least 17 feet deep at mean low water, so that vessels may cross the bar and find a harbor at any stage of the tide with as great draft as can reach Newburyport by the river at high tide.

The project submitted September 16, 1880, proposed two converging rubblestone jetties, their outer ends 1,000 feet apart and to be extended parallel to the axis of the channel, if necessary, and the protection of the beach in their vicinity, at a cost, as estimated in 1881, of $365,000. The direction of jetties and shore protection were modified in 1883, and in 1882 the partial closing of Plum Island Basin with a timber dike about 800 feet long and 5½ feet above mean low water was added to the project, increasing the cost to $375,000, as estimated in 1884.

In 1884 a modification of project provided for extension of both jetties parallel to the axis of the channel for a distance of 610 feet, and in 1886 the length of extension was increased to 1,000 feet, increasing the cost of work, as estimated in 1897, $224,547.49. (Annual Report of the Chief of Engineers for 1897, p. 825.)

Both jetties are 15 feet wide on top, which is in a plane 12 feet above mean low water, and have slopes of 1 on 2 on the sea side and 1 on 1 on the shore side.

A map showing the location of the jetties is published in the Annual Report of the Chief of Engineers for 1885.

The total amount appropriated for this work to date is $338,500, $3,000 of which to be expended in the discretion of the Secretary of War in removing North Rock from the harbor.

The total expenditures to June 30, 1900, were $328,779.08. At that date the north jetty was completed for a total length of 2,705 feet and the south jetty for 2,050 feet. The Plum Island dike is 817 feet long, 5½ feet high above mean low water, except near the center, where a weir 150 feet long and 2 feet above mean low water was left temporarily. The sand catch in rear of the south jetty is in two branches, one 480 feet long and one 572 feet long.

No work having been in progress during the fiscal year 1901, the condition of this improvement remained the same as on June 30, 1900.

Such further appropriations as are provided will be expended in the extension of the north and south jetties and in the completion of the dike.

A survey made during June, 1901, shows that there has been some improvement in the depth on the bar, the controlling depth in 1901 being 12.6 feet at mean low water as against 11 feet at mean low water in 1899 when the last previous survey was made. The channel had moved slightly to the north of its 1899 position but retained about the same width as it had at that time.

The commerce of this port last year was reported as 180,600 tons; this year, 128,440.

July 1, 1900, balance unexpended	$9,720.92
June 30, 1901, amount expended during fiscal year	6,261.21
July 1, 1901, balance unexpended	3,459.71
July 1, 1901, outstanding liabilities	13.47
July 1, 1901, balance available	3,446.24

{ Amount (estimated) required for completion of existing project 264,047.49
Amount that can be profitably expended in fiscal year ending June 30, 1903, in addition to the balance available July 1, 1901 .... 75,000.00
Submitted in compliance with requirements of sundry civil act of June 4, 1897.

(See Appendix B 6.)

7. *Merrimac River, Massachusetts.*—The mouth of the Merrimac River is 15 miles northwest from Cape Ann, Massachusetts. Tidewater extends up it a distance of 21¼ miles, or to the foot of the Upper Falls, 1¼ miles above Haverhill, Mass.

Seven incorporated cities and the largest mills in New England are directly interested in this improvement.

Before improvement the channel was narrow and crooked and much obstructed by ledges, bowlders, and shoals. At mean low water vessels drawing not to exceed 7 feet could enter the river and proceed to South Amesbury, 9 miles from the mouth.

The mean rise and fall of the tide at the mouth is 7.7 feet; at Haverhill bridge, 4.6 feet at low-water stage of the river.

Since 1828 the channel of the river has been improved under a succession of projects, the principal one (dated 1870 and modified in 1874) providing for a channel with the following depths at ordinary high-water stages of the river: From the mouth to Deer Island bridge, 5 miles, 16½ feet; thence to Haverhill bridge, 12½ miles, 12 feet; thence to the foot of Mitchells Falls, Hazeltine Rapids, 1½ miles, 10 feet; thence through Mitchells Falls to the head of the Upper Falls, 2½ miles, not less than 4½ feet when the mill water at Lawrence is running. On June 30, 1894, the improvement of the river in accordance with these projects had been completed. Since that date the river has apparently shoaled to some extent in places.

The river and harbor act of June 3, 1896, appropriated $5,000 for the removal of "certain rocks below Rock Bridge," and in 1896–97 the channel at that point was cleared of obstructing bowlders, a total of about 1,060 cubic yards being removed.

The present approved project submitted May 5, 1897, provides for a channel 7 feet deep at mean low water and 150 feet wide (ordinary low-water stage of the river) from Newburyport to Haverhill at an estimated cost of $171,442.70. This project is published in the Annual Report of the Chief of Engineers for 1897, page 865.

The river and harbor act of March 3, 1899, appropriated $40,000 for the improvement of the river under the new project, and in the same year a contract was entered into for dredging the river from Haverhill down as far as available funds would permit, but, owing to the failure of the contractor to begin the work, the contract was annulled in 1900 and the work readvertised. During the past fiscal year a new contract for the work was let under the readvertisement, and up to the close of the year a total of 4,792 cubic yards had been dredged.

The amount expended on the work up to the close of the fiscal year ending June 30, 1900, was $247,285.11.

The commerce involved in this improvement consists of supplies of coal, lumber, etc., for the cities and towns along its banks, the amount of coal reported in 1899 being 52,000 tons, and in 1900 60,000 tons.

July 1, 1900, balance unexpended	$40,081.61
June 30, 1901, amount expended during fiscal year	1,511.03
July 1, 1901, balance unexpended	38,570.58
July 1, 1901, outstanding liabilities	2,412.67
July 1, 1901, balance available	36,157.91
July 1, 1901, amount covered by uncompleted contracts	33,627.96
Amount (estimated) required for completion of existing project	131,442.70
Amount that can be profitably expended in fiscal year ending June 30, 1903, in addition to the balance available July 1, 1901	37,500.00

Submitted in compliance with requirements of sundry civil act of June 4, 1897.

(See Appendix B 7.)

8. *Powow River, Massachusetts.*—Powow River is a tributary of the Merrimac River, which it enters from the north about 3¼ miles above Newburyport. From its mouth tide water extends 9,600 feet in a narrow, crooked channel, not navigable at low water. The mean rise and fall of tide is 6.7 feet.

The project proposed for its improvement is to dredge a channel 9,600 feet long, 60 feet wide, and 12 feet deep at mean high water, estimated in 1897 to cost $100,000. (Annual Report Chief of Engineers, 1897, p. 829.) The object of the improvement is to secure a navigable low-water channel to the wharves at Amesbury.

The expenditures to June 30, 1900, were $46,544.24. At that date the projected 9,600-foot channel was 12 feet deep at mean high water, 45 feet wide for 6,050 feet from its upper end, and at least 30 feet wide for the remaining distance down river. In addition to the above, the channel had been dredged 45 feet wide and 12 feet deep at mean high water for a distance of 318 feet above the upper limit of the 9,600-foot channel. During the past fiscal year the 45-foot width of channel has been extended down river a distance 2,900 feet. At the date of this report the channel is 45 feet wide throughout, except for a distance of 650 feet at the lower end, where it is 30 feet wide.

July 1, 1900, balance unexpended....................................... $4,455.76
June 30, 1901, amount expended during fiscal year..................... 4,396.48

July 1, 1901, balance unexpended....................................... 59.28

Amount (estimated) required for completion of existing project....... 49,000.00
Amount that can be profitably expended in fiscal year ending June 30, 1903, in addition to the balance unexpended July 1, 1901............ 36,000.00
Submitted in compliance with requirements of sundry civil act of June 4, 1897.

(See Appendix D 8.)

9. Essex River, Massachusetts.—Essex River winds between marshy banks for 3¼ miles from the head of navigation at the village of Essex to its mouth, which forms a harbor of refuge for light-draft vessels about 3 miles to the southeastward of the entrance to Ipswich River, Massachusetts. It was originally navigable at high water to the wharves in the town of Essex, a distance of 6 miles, but no navigable low-water channel existed for 12,000 feet below the town wharves. The mean rise and fall of the tide is 8.8 feet.

The project for its improvement was submitted May 15, 1891. It proposed to widen and deepen the upper 12,000 feet of the natural channel of the river, so that 4 feet at mean low water could be carried to the head of navigation, just below the railroad bridge, in a channel 60 feet wide at an estimated cost of $25,000.

On March 23, 1899, this project was so modified as to limit the improvement to that section of the channel below the drawbridge, for the reason that the draw had been closed and the section of channel between that bridge and the railroad bridge was no longer used.

The expenditures to June 30, 1900, were $14,763.78. At that date the channel had been dredged to its full projected depth, 60 feet wide for 4,000 feet below the drawbridge, and at least 25 feet wide for the remaining distance below that bridge.

During the past fiscal year the improvement of this river has been completed in accordance with the above project, the channel now being 60 feet wide and at least 4 feet deep at mean low water from the mouth up to the highway bridge at Essex.

July 1, 1900, balance unexpended....................................... $10,236.22
June 30, 1901, amount expended during fiscal year..................... 6,535.43

July 1, 1901, balance unexpended....................................... 3,700.79

(See Appendix B 9.)

10. Harbor of refuge, Sandy Bay, Cape Ann, Massachusetts.—Sandy Bay is situated at the northeastern extremity of Cape Ann, Massachusetts. It is about 2¼ miles by 2 miles in area, and is fully protected on the west and south by high hills, but fronts the northeast, and is open to the full effects of easterly and northeasterly gales. The great seas of the ocean are broken, however, in a degree by the sunken rocky ledges called Averys Ledge, the Dry and Little Salvages, the Flat Ground, and Abners Ledge, which are directly at the mouth of the bay. Inside these entrance ledges the bay is entirely unobstructed and has an average depth of 50 feet at mean low water. The shore lines of Sandy Bay form a little less than a right angle, and their directions are nearly north and south and east and west. The rocky island of Straitsmouth forms the eastern extremity of one shore line and the steep headland of Andrews Point the northern end of the other.

The proposed improvement contemplates the construction of a national harbor of refuge of the first class. The anchorage covered by the breakwater will contain 1,377 acres, in which the depth exceeds 24 feet at mean low water.

The estimated cost of the improvement is $5,000,000. The original project of 1884 proposed a continuous breakwater 9,000 feet long, divided into two branches. One branch starts at Averys Ledge and runs in a direction a little west of north to Abners Ledge, a distance of 3,600 feet; the other extends 5,420 feet from Abners Ledge in a northwesterly direction, and terminates at the 84-foot contour off Andrews Point.

The axis of the proposed breakwater is approximately at the inner edge of the ledges at the entrance of the bay and about 1 mile inside the Salvages and Flat Ground, which receive the first shock of easterly storm waves.

The southern entrance to the proposed harbor lies between Straitsmouth Island and Averys Ledge, and is to be 1,800 feet wide and at least 30 feet deep. The northern entrance, near Andrews Point, is 2,700 feet wide and 80 feet deep. They are so located with reference to each other that vessels can enter and leave the harbor with any wind.

The substructure in the original project was to consist of a mound of rubblestone to a grade of 22 feet below mean low water, 40 feet wide on top, to be surmounted by a masonry wall.

On March 2, 1892, the project was modified in accordance with a report of a Board of Engineers. The project as modified proposes to construct the entire breakwater of rubblestone, with the following section: On the sea side, from the bottom to 15 feet below mean low water, a slope of 1 on 1½; thence to mean low water, 1 on 3; thence to 18 feet above mean low water, 1 on 1; the width on the crest, 20 feet, and the rear slope, 1 on 0.73, to mean low water; thence to the bottom, 1 on 1; the portion below low water to be built of stone of less than 4 tons weight, the upper portion of stone averaging 6 tons weight.

A plan of the bay, showing the proposed breakwater, was published in the Annual Report of the Chief of Engineers for 1892, page 564.

The report of the Board of Engineers, which the Secretary of War was required to appoint by the act of March 3, 1899, to examine and report upon the project for this work, was published in House Doc. No. 453, Fifty-sixth Congress, first session, and may also be found on page 1184 of the Annual Report of the Chief of Engineers for 1900.

The total expenditures to June 30, 1900, were $928,934.84. At that date 1,202,347 tons of rubblestone had been placed in the breakwater, and its condition was as follows:

Continuing successively from the initial point of the southern arm of the breakwater on Averys Ledge, for a distance of about 240 feet nothing had been done, then about 250 feet was built up to 3 feet below mean low water, about 2,550 feet more to mean low water, and the remainder of the distance to the angle at Abners Ledge, about 500 feet, completed to mean high water. Beginning at this point the western arm was completed for a distance of 2,100 feet to 22 feet below mean low water, 40 feet wide on top.

During the past fiscal year 107,868 tons of rubblestone has been deposited in the substructure of the breakwater, completing the substructure of the southern arm to mean low water except for a distance of 70 feet, over which nothing has been done. A small section of the superstructure of the western arm was also raised to mean low water.

The prospective benefits to commerce and navigation by the construction of this harbor of refuge are increased safety to life and property and a consequent reduction in freight and insurance.

July 1, 1900, balance unexpended	$221,065.16
June 30, 1901, amount expended during fiscal year	62,859.82
July 1, 1901, balance unexpended	158,205.34
July 1, 1901, outstanding liabilities	21,324.89
July 1, 1901, balance available	136,880.45
July 1, 1901, amount covered by uncompleted contracts	121,400.00
Amount (estimated) required for completion of existing project	3,850,000.00
Amount that can be profitably expended in fiscal year ending June 30, 1903, in addition to the balance available July 1, 1901	350,000.00
Submitted in compliance with requirements of sundry civil act of June 4, 1897.	

(See Appendix B 10.)

11. Harbor at Gloucester, Mass.—Gloucester Harbor, an important center for the fishing fleet of New England, is about 20 miles north of Boston. Its inner harbor was originally obstructed by sunken rocks and shoals, and the approaches to the wharves were shallow, varying from 1 to 12 feet. The outer harbor was open to all southerly gales.

The project of 1871 proposed the removal of certain bowlders from the inner harbor and the construction of a breakwater from Eastern Point over Dog Bar to Round Rock Shoal.

The project of 1884 provided for two breakwaters at the entrance of Gloucester Harbor, one to cost $752,000, on essentially the same site as that proposed in 1871, and a supplementary one, through Normans Woe Rock, to cost $607,000.

In the annual report for this harbor for 1887 a general project for its improvement was submitted, based on the survey provided for by the act approved August 5, 1886. This project proposed to remove from the inner harbor 101½ cubic yards of rock known to exist, and to dredge 216,000 cubic yards, scow measurement, at an estimated cost of $65,000, and to construct the breakwater recommended in the project of 1884 that extends from Eastern Point to Round Rock Shoal, at an estimated cost of $752,000.

On May 5, 1897, a project was submitted for the removal of a pinnacle rock in the outer harbor to a least depth of 16 feet below mean low water, and rocks off the ferry landing at Rocky Neck to a level of the surrounding bottom, the work having been authorized by the river and harbor act of June 3, 1896.

On December 18, 1897, a revised project for the construction of the breakwater was submitted. This project proposed to build the substructure of the breakwater of rubblestone up to mean low water and 31 feet wide at that grade, to be surmounted by a superstructure formed of two dry walls of heavy split stone laid with the greatest dimension at right angles to the axis of the breakwater, the interior space to be filled with rubblestone and to be capped by heavy stone, forming a top

144 REPORT OF THE CHIEF OF ENGINEERS, U. S. ARMY.

course 10 feet in width. The project was estimated to cost $698,083.43, and was approved January 4, 1898.

The total expenditures to June 30, 1900, were $169,374.73, and the condition of the improvement at that date was as follows:

Clam Rock had been reduced from 1 foot to 9¼ feet at mean low water; Pinnacle Rock from 8¼ to 16¼ feet, mean low water; rock off Pew's wharf from 2 to 5 feet, mean low water; rocks off J. Friend's wharf from 13 to 17 feet, mean low water. All of the above rocks were reduced to the level of the surrounding bottom. Babsons Ledge had been reduced from 11 to 14 feet, mean low water. A pinnacle rock in the outer harbor had also been removed to a depth of 16 feet below mean low water, and rocks off the ferry landing at Rocky Neck had been reduced to the level of the surrounding bottom.

All the proposed dredging and rock removal had been done, the cost being about $15,000 more than the original estimate ($65,000), and the construction of the breakwater from Eastern Point to Round Rock Shoal was in progress; 106,686 tons of rubblestone had been deposited in the breakwater, completing about 1,650 feet of the substructure to the cross section proposed in the modified project of 1898, and the superstructure had been commenced.

The movement of the vessels in the inner harbor had been greatly facilitated, but no benefit had been derived from work on the breakwater, as no sheltered anchorage had been obtained.

During the past fiscal year operations were continued on the superstructure and about 284 linear feet completed, beginning at Eastern Point.

The work in its present stage has greatly benefited the fishing industry, and its completion will furnish much needed sheltered anchorage in this important harbor.

A line of passenger and freight steamers is operated continuously throughout the year, and other commerce exists in the form of imports of salt, coal, lumber, etc. The estimated value of this commerce is $5,000,000 annually.

The following gross tonnage of shipments and receipts is reported for the past four years:

	Tons.		Tons.
1897	82,600	1899	287,922
1898	86,050	1900	267,475

July 1, 1900, balance unexpended $24,625.27
June 30, 1901, amount expended during fiscal year 21,497.07

July 1, 1901, balance unexpended 3,128.20

Amount (estimated) required for completion of existing project 584,083.43
Amount that can be profitably expended in fiscal year ending June 30, 1903, in addition to the balance unexpended July 1, 1901 .... 150,000.00
Submitted in compliance with requirements of sundry civil act of June 4, 1897.

(See Appendix B 11.)

12. Harbor at Manchester, Mass.—Manchester Harbor is situated about 5¼ miles northeast from the entrance of Salem Harbor, Massachusetts. The channel was 100 feet wide and 6¼ feet deep at mean low water up to Proctors Point. It then shoaled rapidly to a depth of 1¼ feet at The Narrows, 1,400 feet from Proctors Point, and for a farther distance of 2,500 feet to the town wharves no low-water channel existed.

The original project, that of 1887, proposed to dredge a channel 60 feet wide, 4,000 feet long, and 4 feet deep at mean low water from Proctors Point to the town wharves, at an estimated cost of $14,300. This project was completed in April, 1894, giving a channel of full projected width and depth, with an additional width of 80 feet opposite the town wharf.

A chart of the harbor was published in the Annual Report of the Chief of Engineers for 1888, page 466.

The present approved project of improvement was adopted March 3, 1899, and was printed in the annual report for 1897, page 869. It proposes to dredge the natural channel to a least width of 75 feet, and two turning basins, one just below the railroad bridge and one at the town landing, all 6 feet deep at mean low water, at an estimated cost of $25,000.

The expenditures to June 30, 1900, were $19,047.78. At that date the project of 1887 had been completed, and under the project adopted in 1899 the channel had been completed from the 6-foot contour in the bay up to a point northwest of Proctors Point, a distance of 3,200 feet, except over two small ledges which project into the channel about 20 feet on the eastern side, about west of Proctors Point.

No operations have been in progress during the past fiscal year.

The available depth at mean low water that can be carried up to the town wharves is 4 feet.

The commerce involved in this improvement consists of supplies of coal, lumber, etc., for local consumption, about 10,000 tons being reported received in 1899. The improvement in its present condition has greatly facilitated the approach of vessels to the town wharves.

July 1, 1900, balance unexpended	$252.22
July 1, 1901, balance unexpended	252.22

Amount (estimated) required for completion of existing project	20,000.00
Amount that can be profitably expended in fiscal year ending June 30, 1903, in addition to the balance unexpended July 1, 1901	5,000.00
Submitted in compliance with requirements of sundry civil act of June 4, 1897.	

(See Appendix B 12.)

13. Repair of sea wall at Marblehead, Mass.—Marblehead, Mass., is about 12 miles north of Boston, Mass. A part of the town is situated on Marblehead Neck, a peninsula lying east of the mainland and connected therewith by an isthmus about 2,000 feet long and a least width of 105 feet between high-water lines, which forms the southern bound of Marblehead Harbor.

This isthmus is traversed by a highway which is protected for about 1,900 feet of its length by a sea wall of light construction, reported to have been built by the United States Government in the early part of the present century.

A survey of the isthmus was made in September, 1896, and a report and plan of this survey were submitted to the Department on February 4, 1897, and were published in House Doc. No. 289, Fifty-fourth Congress, second session; also, in the Annual Report of the Chief of Engineers for 1897, page 870.

The river and harbor act of March 3, 1899, appropriated $1,000 for the repair of the sea wall at Marblehead, made necessary by the great storm of November, 1898.

An examination of the sea wall was made in November, 1899, at a cost of $8.33. The wall seems to have served its purpose since its construction without sustaining any damage worth mentioning, and there is apparently no need of any repairs now.

July 1, 1900, balance unexpended	$991.67
July 1, 1901, balance unexpended	991.67

(See Appendix B 13.)

14. Channel between North and South Hero islands, Lake Champlain, Vermont.—[This work was in the charge of Col. J. W. Barlow, Corps of Engineers (now brigadier-general, Chief of Engineers, United States Army, retired), until April 30, 1901.] In its original condition this channel was obstructed at its west entrance by a bar through which the channel was but 40 feet wide and 7 feet deep and at its east entrance by a bar through which the channel was 100 feet wide and 8 feet deep.

The only appropriation for this work, $10,000, was made by the river and harbor act of August 11, 1888, which adopted a project to dredge the channel at the two entrances to a width of 150 feet and depth of 10 feet. This appropriation was expended in the following year and the channel reported as completed.

In 1897 it was reported that there was a good channel at the east entrance of the depth and width prescribed in the project, but at the west entrance there was a troublesome bowlder in mid-channel and the channel was 1 to 2 feet shallower in the middle, 2 to 4 feet shallower at its edges, and 25 feet narrower than the project prescribed.

With the appropriation asked for the fiscal year ending June 30, 1903, it is proposed to complete the existing project by widening and deepening the channel to the limits authorized and also remove the bowlder at the west entrance. This work will require the removal of about 4,000 cubic yards of bowlders, etc., at an estimated cost of $1 per cubic yard, the balance to be applied to engineering expenses.

Amount (estimated) required for completion of existing project	$4,300.00
Amount that can be profitably expended in fiscal year ending June 30, 1903	4,300.00

Submitted in compliance with requirements of sundry civil act of June 4, 1897.

15. Harbor at Burlington, Vt.—[This work was in the charge of Col. J. W. Barlow, Corps of Engineers (now brigadier-general, Chief of Engineers, United States Army, retired), until April 30, 1901.] This harbor is situated on the eastern shore of Lake Champlain. In its natural condition ample depth of water existed along its docks and wharves, which were, however, unprotected from the severe storms crossing the lake. The greatest exposure is from the prevalent northwesterly gales, which have a sweep of 15 miles obliquely across the lake.

The original project for improvement, adopted in 1836, provided for the forming of an artificial harbor in front of the city by constructing a breakwater parallel with the shore, and about 1,000 feet distant from the docks and wharves. Work commenced in 1836 and continued at intervals until 1857, when 1,069 linear feet of breakwater had been completed.

In 1867 a Board of Engineers, convened to consider the location and construction of breakwater, recommended that the one previously constructed be extended northward 1,500 feet. Of this extension 831 linear feet was built, and, in addition, 617 linear feet was added at the south end, making its total length 2,517 feet at the close of the fiscal year 1874.

In June, 1874, a plan was adopted for an extension northward of the breakwater for a farther distance of 2,000 feet, the cost being estimated at $340,000. (See Annual Report of the Chief of Engineers for 1874, p. 275.)

In 1884 extensive repairs were begun to the portion of the breakwater built between 1836 and 1857. By June 30, 1886, 3,560 linear feet of breakwater had been completed.

On September 28, 1886, a project was approved extending the breakwater 500 feet northerly and 1,000 feet southerly, keeping the line generally at a distance of from 800 to 1,000 feet from the line of the wharves, at an estimated cost of $150,000, and on August 24, 1894, the project was again amended so as to provide for replacing 3,800 linear feet of the decayed and dilapidated wooden superstructure of the breakwater with one of stone or concrete, at an estimated cost of $173,750.

Further description and history of the work may be found in the Annual Report of the Chief of Engineers for 1897, Part IV, page 3296.

The total expenditures to June 30, 1900, were $595,555.88. At the time of the adoption of the project of 1886 a breakwater 3,560 feet long had been built. From 1886 to June 30, 1900, 1,294 linear feet of wooden superstructure on old sections of the breakwater had been replaced by one of stone, and 600 linear feet of new breakwater, varying in width from 24 to 36 feet, had been built, making the present total length of the breakwater 4,160 linear feet. This structure affords protection to nearly all the docks and wharves along the harbor front.

During the past fiscal year a section of 140 feet of the old timber and stone superstructure was removed and replaced with one of concrete, and a small section of the stone parapet which was seriously damaged by storms in the fall of 1900 was repaired.

The condition of this breakwater was the subject of a special report, dated December 20, 1900, by Col. J. W. Barlow, the officer then in charge, which report was printed in Senate Doc. No. 105, Fifty-sixth Congress, second session, and is herewith as Appendix B 19.

The maximum draft that could be carried to the docks and wharves on June 30, 1901, was 11 feet at mean low water.

The principal items of commerce at this port are coal, lumber, stone, and general merchandise. The tonnage for 1897 was 109,180; for 1898, 116,527; for 1899, 87,630; and for 1900, 131,136.

July 1, 1900, balance unexpended	$15,005.19
Amount allotted from appropriation contained in emergency river and harbor act approved June 6, 1900	5,000.00
	20,005.19
June 30, 1901, amount expended during fiscal year	6,517.49
July 1, 1901, balance unexpended	13,487.70
July 1, 1901, amount covered by uncompleted contracts	8,552.00
Amount (estimated) required for completion of existing project	219,605.00
Amount that can be profitably expended in fiscal year ending June 30, 1903, in addition to the balance unexpended July 1, 1901	40,000.00
Submitted in compliance with requirements of sundry civil act of June 4, 1897.	

(See A ndix B 14.

16. Otter Creek, Vermont.—[This work was in the charge of Col. J. W. Barlow, Corps of Engineers (now brigadier-general, Chief of Engineers, United States Army, retired), until April 30, 1901.] This creek flows into Lake Champlain from its eastern shore. In its natural condition the channel was narrow and tortuous in places, and the available depth from Vergennes to the mouth—a distance of 8 miles—was less than 6 feet.

The original project, adopted in 1872, proposed the formation of a channel 100 feet wide and 8 feet deep from Lake Champlain to Vergennes, and also of a basin at this latter point, at an estimated cost of $58,146. (See Annual Report of the Chief of Engineers for 1872, p. 273.)

In 1882 the project was modified to provide for the removal of rock at the steamboat landing near Vergennes, which increased the cost to $73,748.40. (See Annual Report of the Chief of Engineers for 1882, p. 711.)

In addition an annual expenditure estimated at $1,000 will be required for maintenance after completion of the work.

A detailed statement of the work done prior to June 30, 1897, may be found in the Annual Report of the Chief of Engineers for 1897, page 3299.

The amount expended to June 30, 1900, was $62,500. The condition of the channel at that date was such as to allow boats drawing 8 feet of water to navigate between Lake Champlain and Vergennes during the entire season.

No work was done during the last fiscal year.

The maximum draft that could be carried to Vergennes on June 30, 1901, was 8 feet at mean low water.

The commerce of this creek consists of coal, lumber, iron, kaolin, and general merchandise, and amounted in 1896 to 9,052 tons, in 1897 to 7,680 tons, in 1899 to 7,200 tons, and in 1900 to 8,090 tons.

Amount (estimated) required for completion of existing project....... $11,248.00
Amount that can be profitably expended in fiscal year ending June 30, 1903.   3,000.00
Submitted in compliance with requirements of sundry civil act of June 4, 1897.

(See Appendix B 15.)

17. Narrows of Lake Champlain, New York and Vermont.—[This work was in the charge of Col. J. W. Barlow, Corps of Engineers (now brigadier-general, Chief of Engineers, United States Army, retired), until April 30, 1901.] In its original condition the 15 miles of this waterway, extending from the northern terminus of Champlain Canal, at Whitehall, northerly to Bensons Landing, Vt., had a very narrow and tortuous channel, not more than 9½ to 10 feet deep on the shoals at low water.

The original project, adopted in 1886, was to obtain a channel having a least width of 150 feet and depth of 12 feet at low water from the northern terminus of the Champlain Canal, at Whitehall, N. Y., to deep water in Lake Champlain below Bensons Landing, Vt., a distance of 15 miles, at an estimated cost of $80,000. (See Annual Report of the Chief of Engineers for 1885, pp. 2312–2314.)

Work under this project was completed in September, 1889, at a little more than half its estimated cost, owing to the low prices paid for dredging.

In 1890 a supplemental project was prepared for widening and straightening the middle reaches of the channel, at an estimated cost of $21,000. (See Annual Report of the Chief of Engineers for 1890, p. 2884.) This project was adopted in 1892 and work completed under it in August, 1896.

In 1896 a project was prepared for restoring, widening, and deepening the channel, at an estimated cost of $22,500, the annual maintenance, after completion, being placed at $2,500. (See Annual Report of the Chief of Engineers for 1897, pp. 3302–3303.) This project was adopted in 1899.

The expenditures to June 30, 1900, were $68,425.91. Before the commencement of work under the project of 1899 the channel, which had previously been dredged to 12 feet, had shoaled in places, restricting the draft that vessels could carry through it to not exceeding 10 feet.

On June 30, 1900, shoal places in Kenyons Bay, opposite Pulpit Point and near the south end of the Narrows, had been redredged to a depth of 12 feet. This work increased the available depth for navigation from 10 to 12 feet. Booms had also been placed at and opposite Puts Rock in order to prevent vessels from colliding with the rocky bluffs at these points.

Under an allotment of $1,500 from the emergency river and harbor act of June 6, 1900, a shoal which had formed in Whitehall Harbor was removed in September, 1900, restoring the area dredged to its former depth, 12 feet.

The appropriation asked for fiscal year ending June 30, 1903, is to be applied to dredging about 90,000 cubic yards of material and in constructing and placing about 1,030 linear feet of fender timbers, thereby completing the work.

The maximum draft that could be carried on June 30, 1901, was 12 feet at mean low water.

The tonnage passing through the Narrows consists of timber, pulp wood, salt, sugar, coal, stone, lime, clay, iron, and general merchandise, and amounted in 1897 to 579,873 tons, in 1898 to 498,731 tons, in 1899 to 848,457 tons, and in 1900 to 714,741 tons.

July 1, 1900, balance unexpended	$74.09
Amount allotted from appropriation contained in emergency river and harbor act approved June 6, 1900	1,500.00
	1,574.09
June 30, 1901, amount expended during fiscal year	1,574.09

Amount (estimated) required for completion of existing project	17,500.00
Amount that can be profitably expended in fiscal year ending June 30, 1903	17,500.00
Submitted in compliance with requirements of sundry civil act of June 4, 1897.	

(See Appendix B 16.)

EXAMINATIONS AND SURVEYS MADE IN COMPLIANCE WITH EMERGENCY RIVER AND HARBOR ACT APPROVED JUNE 6, 1900.

The preliminary examinations and surveys of the following localities were made by the local officers and reports thereon submitted through the division engineer:

1. Preliminary examination and survey of Hendersons Point, Portsmouth Harbor, New Hampshire, with a view to removing a portion of said point for the purpose of improving navigation to the navy-yard.— Maj. W. L. Fisk, Corps of Engineers, submitted report on prelimi

150 REPORT OF THE CHIEF OF ENGINEERS, U. S. ARMY.

nary examination August 27, 1900, and report on survey was submitted by his successor, Capt. Harry Taylor, Corps of Engineers, December 21, 1900. Captain Taylor presents a plan for improvement estimated to cost $800,000 if funds are made available for carrying on the work continuously; the cost of the work is estimated at $1,180,000 if work be not prosecuted under a single contract. The reports were transmitted to Congress and printed in House Doc. No. 263, Fifty-sixth Congress, second session. (See also Appendix B 17.)

2. *Preliminary examination and survey of Beverly Harbor, Massachusetts, with a view to the straightening, widening, deepening, and otherwise improving the entrance to the harbor and the approaches to the wharves and docks therein.*—Major Fisk submitted reports on preliminary examination and survey dated August 13, 1900, and November 20, 1900, respectively. He presents a plan for improvement at an estimated cost of $10,000. The reports were transmitted to Congress and printed in House Doc. No. 129, Fifty-sixth Congress, second session. (See also Appendix B 18.)

REPORT ON CONDITION OF BREAKWATER AT BURLINGTON, VT., MADE IN COMPLIANCE WITH CONCURRENT RESOLUTION OF CONGRESS.

Colonel Barlow submitted report dated December 20, 1900, with estimate of cost of repair and completion of the breakwater. The report was transmitted to Congress and printed in Senate Doc. No. 105, Fifty-sixth Congress, second session. (See also Appendix B 19.)

IMPROVEMENT OF RIVERS AND HARBORS IN EASTERN MASSACHUSETTS SOUTH OF AND INCLUDING LYNN HARBOR.

This district was in the charge of Col. Charles R. Suter, Corps of Engineers, to May 31, 1901, having under his immediate orders Lieut. Robert R. Raymond, Corps of Engineers, and of Lieut. Col. W. S. Stanton, Corps of Engineers, since that date.

1. *Harbor at Lynn, Mass.*—An area of shoals extends from the wharves at Lynn 2¼ miles southerly to the sea. It is protected from the sea by the peninsula of Lynn Beach and Nahant.

Before improvement three narrow and crooked channels, in which the depth was but 6 feet at mean low water, extended from the wharves to the sea.

The existing project (report of Board of Engineers, April 10, 1884) is to form a channel 200 feet wide and 10 feet deep at mean low water, from a point near the White Rocks to deep water opposite Little Nahant, and from deep water opposite Sand Point to Lynn harbor line, the upper part of the channel to be maintained by occasional dredging, the lower part by a training wall joining the land at Little Nahant; revised in 1888 to extend the inner channel 400 feet inside the harbor line and to make at its inner end an anchorage basin 500 feet by 300 feet and 10 feet deep at mean low water, at an estimated cost for the revised project of $182,000.

The amount expended to June 30, 1900, was $121,475.64.

The project was completed prior to the beginning of the fiscal year ending June 30, 1901, with the exception of the training wall, the necessity for which was not apparent July 1, 1900 (Annual Report of the Chief of Engineers for 1900, p. 1190).

On June 30, 1901, the maximum draft that could be carried at mean low water over the shoalest part of the improvement was 10 feet.

July 1, 1900, balance unexpended	$7,024.36
June 30, 1901, amount expended during fiscal year	149.10
July 1, 1901, balance unexpended	6,875.26

(See Appendix C 1.)

2. Mystic and Malden rivers, Massachusetts.—The Mystic flows into Boston Harbor and the Malden into the Mystic 3 miles above its mouth.

Before improvement they had no low-water channel.

The existing project, approved by the act of July 13, 1892, is to make the channel in the Mystic, 4¼ miles to the head of navigation in Medford, 100 feet wide and 6 feet deep at mean low water to the first turn above Denning's wharf, thence 4 feet deep at mean low water, the width gradually contracting to 50 feet at the upper end; and to make the channel in the Malden 100 feet wide and 12 feet deep at mean high water to the first bridge, and thence 75 feet wide to the second bridge; at an estimated cost for the Mystic of $25,000 and for the Malden of $37,000; total, $62,000.

The amount expended to June 30, 1900, was for the Mystic $14,986.69 and for the Malden $25,980.25, amounting for both to $40,966.94. Of that amount $993.86 was for maintenance of the channel in the Malden.

The amount expended during the fiscal year ending June 30, 1901, was applied to maintenance of the channel in the Malden.

On June 30, 1901, the maximum draft that could be carried over the shoalest part of the improvement was: in the Mystic 6 feet at mean low water to the first turn above Denning's wharf in Somerville, and 4 feet at mean low water for 4,000 feet above that turn, being 6,440 feet below Medford; and in the Malden 12 feet at mean high water to the first bridge in the city of Malden.

A plan of Mystic River was published in the Annual Report of the Chief of Engineers for 1891, page 674. No plan of Malden River has been published.

Commercial statistics are included in the statement for Boston Harbor, Massachusetts.

July 1, 1900, balance unexpended	$4,033.06
Amount allotted from appropriation contained in emergency river and harbor act approved June 6, 1900	5,000.00
	9,033.06
June 30, 1901, amount expended during fiscal year	6,461.06
July 1, 1901, balance unexpended	2,572.00
Amount (estimated) required for completion of existing project	27,000.00
Amount that can be profitably expended in fiscal year ending June 30, 1903, for works of improvement and for maintenance, in addition to the balance unexpended July 1, 1901	20,000.00
Submitted in compliance with requirements of sundry civil act of June 4, 1897, and of section 7 of the river and harbor act of 1899.	

(See Appendix C 2.)

152   REPORT OF THE CHIEF OF ENGINEERS, U. S. ARMY.

3. Mystic River below the mouth of Island End River, Massachusetts.—Before improvement by the United States the river had been improved so that a maximum draft of 15 feet could be carried at mean low water in a channel of barely practicable width up to Island End River, 2,700 feet above Chelsea drawbridge.

The existing project, approved by the act of March 3, 1899, is to dredge a channel 25 feet deep at mean low water and 300 feet wide from the mouth of the river to a point 3,500 feet above Chelsea bridge, extending 800 feet above Island End River, at a cost, estimated in August, 1899, of $267,547.50.

The amount expended to June 30, 1900, was $23,748.19, all for improvement.

With the amount expended during the fiscal year ending June 30, 1901, a channel of the depth authorized by the project with a least width of 100 feet was obtained up to the mouth of Island End River.

On June 30, 1901, the maximum draft that could be carried over the shoalest part of the improvement was 25 feet at mean low water.

For a description of this part of Mystic River see report for 1900, page 1192.

Commercial statistics are included in the statement for Boston Harbor, Massachusetts.

July 1, 1900, balance unexpended $26,251.81
June 30, 1901, amount expended during fiscal year 23,764.93

July 1, 1901, balance unexpended 2,486.88

{ Amount (estimated) required for completion of existing project 217,547.50
  Amount that can be profitably expended in fiscal year ending June 30,
    1903, in addition to the balance unexpended July 1, 1901 .... 150,000.00
  Submitted in compliance with requirements of sundry civil act of June
    4, 1897.

(See Appendix C 3.)

4. Harbor at Boston, Mass.—The Main Ship Channel.—In its original condition this channel from its entrance (between Point Allerton and Boston light) was ample in depth and capacity in Nantasket Roads and President Roads for the largest vessels, but from Nantasket Roads to President Roads and from President Roads to Boston it was narrow and shoal, having a least width of 100 feet and a least depth of 16 feet at mean low water.

The existing project, approved by the act of July 13, 1892, is to widen the channel to 1,000 feet and to deepen it to 27 feet at mean low water at an estimated cost of $1,250,000.

The amount expended to June 30, 1900, was $825,258.18, all upon improvement.

With the amount expended during the fiscal year ending June 30, 1901, the channel 27 feet deep between President Roads and Boston was increased in width 500 feet, to the full width of 1,000 feet, excepting for a length of 3,400 feet at the "Upper Middle," where its width is still only 500 feet, but at the "Lower Middle" several groups of ledges restrict the available width of the channel to 600 feet.

On June 30, 1901, the maximum draft that could be carried over the shoalest part of the improvement was 26 feet at mean low water.

Broad Sound Channel.—In its original condition (at the adoption of the present project) this channel from President Roads to the sea was

200 feet wide at the shoalest place with a depth of 29 feet at mean low water.

The existing project, approved by the act of March 3, 1899, is to widen the channel to 1,200 feet, and to deepen it to 30 feet at mean low water, at an authorized cost of $455,000.

The amount expended to June 30, 1900, was $213.27, all upon improvement.

With the amount expended during the fiscal year ending June 30, 1901, a channel, 30 feet deep at mean low water and at least 250 feet wide, was dredged from President Roads to the sea.

On June 30, 1901, the maximum draft that could be carried over the shoalest part of the improvement at mean low water was 30 feet.

Sea walls.—In the original condition of the harbor its protecting headlands and the shores of the islands in the vicinity of the channel were without protection from the sea which was encroaching upon them and carrying their débris into the harbor and its channels.

Between 1828 and 1889, 3.75 miles (20,215 feet) of sea walls was built on the most exposed headlands and islands.

Since 1899 the amounts applied to them have been exclusively for maintenance. About 1865 to 1871 the sea walls on Deer Island were extensively rebuilt.

The sea walls have been constructed and maintained in part by specific appropriations for that purpose, and in part by allotments from the appropriations for "Improving Harbor at Boston, Mass." The amounts applied to sea walls and to the improvement of the channel without specific appropriation for that purpose are accounted for in the money statement under "general improvement."

With the amount expended during the fiscal year ending June 30, 1901, minor repairs were made to the sea walls on Rainsford and Castle islands, and the rebuilding of the sea walls on Deer Island, quite extensive demolished by the storms of 1898–99, was commenced at the Middle Head.

Tributary channels.—(a) *Charles River.*—Its original condition and the results accomplished are stated in annual report for 1898, page 868.

The existing project, approved June 14, 1880, is to widen and deepen the natural channel so that it shall be from its mouth to Western Avenue Bridge 7 feet deep and 200 feet wide; thence to Market Street Bridge 6 feet deep and 80 feet wide; thence to the dam at the head of tide water 60 feet wide and 2 feet deep; all depths at mean low water, at an estimated cost of $125,000.

The amount expended to June 30, 1900, was $57,500. No work was done on this improvement during the fiscal year.

(b) *Fort Point Channel.*—Its original condition and the results accomplished are stated in the annual report for 1898, page 868.

The existing project, approved August 5, 1886, is to excavate a channel 175 feet wide and 23 feet deep at mean low water from the entrance to near Federal Street Bridge, at an estimated cost of $78,750.

The amount expended to June 30, 1900, was $18,027. No work was done on this improvement during the fiscal year.

(c) *Chelsea Creek.*—Its original condition and the results accomplished are stated in the annual reports for 1898 and 1900, pages 869 and 1199, respectively.

The existing project, approved June 3, 1896, is to dredge the natural channel to a least width of 150 feet and 18 feet deep at mean low water to the head of navigation, at an estimated cost of $65,000.

The amount expended to June 30, 1900, was $7,015.80. No work was done on this improvement during the fiscal year.

Survey of Boston Harbor.—The emergency river and harbor act of June 6, 1900, directed that a survey of Boston Harbor be made with a view to its further improvement. This survey was made during the summer and fall of 1900, and the report of the survey and a project of improvement was submitted on November 28, 1900. (House Doc. No. 119, Fifty-sixth Congress, second session, and Appendix C 14 of this report.)

The cost of the survey was $17,500, which sum was allotted for the work from the balance available from appropriations for general improvement of Boston Harbor.

The amount of customs revenue collected during the year ending June 30, 1900, was $18,871,849.99, and during the year ending June 30, 1901, $20,123,155.62. The gross tonnage of the port aggregates about 20,770,023 tons annually.

PROJECT FOR GENERAL IMPROVEMENT.

July 1, 1900, balance unexpended	[1]$103,812.16
June 30, 1901, amount expended during fiscal year	24,291.03
July 1, 1901, balance unexpended	79,521.13
July 1, 1901, outstanding liabilities	1,776.95
July 1, 1901, balance available	77,744.18
Amount (estimated) required for completion of existing project	160,500.00
Amount that can be profitably expended in fiscal year ending June 30, 1903, for works of improvement and for maintenance, in addition to the balance available July 1, 1901	163,000.00

Submitted in compliance with requirements of sundry civil act of June 4, 1897, and of section 7 of the river and harbor act of 1899.

PROJECT OF 1892.

July 1, 1900, balance unexpended	[2]$504,542.17
June 30, 1901, amount expended during fiscal year	148,486.77
July 1, 1901, balance unexpended	356,055.40
July 1, 1901, outstanding liabilities	50,231.93
July 1, 1901, balance available	305,823.47
July 1, 1901, amount covered by uncompleted contracts	71,637.94

PROJECT FOR BROAD SOUND CHANNEL.

July 1, 1900, balance unexpended	$321,786.73
Amount appropriated by sundry civil act approved March 3, 1901	133,000.00
	454,786.73
June 30, 1901, amount expended during fiscal year	49,161.70
July 1, 1901, balance unexpended	405,625.03
July 1, 1901, outstanding liabilities	27,570.21
July 1, 1901, balance available	378,054.82
July 1, 1901, amount covered by uncompleted contracts	220,503.50

(See Appendix C 4.)

5. *Town River, Massachusetts.*—This is a small tidal tributary to Weymouth River flowing into Boston Harbor. Before improvement it had a narrow, crooked channel with a least depth of 1½ feet at mean low water.

---

[1] Erroneously reported in annual report for 1900 as $98,812.16.
[2] Erroneously reported in annual report for 1900 as $509,542.17.

The existing project, approved by the act of June 3, 1896, is to dredge a channel 4 feet deep at mean low water, 100 feet wide, and 4,500 feet long to the head of navigation, at a cost estimated August 7, 1896, at $25,000.

The amount expended to June 30, 1900, was $17,723.45, all for improvement.

The amount expended during the fiscal year ending June 30, 1901, was applied to an examination of the condition of the channel.

On June 30, 1901, the maximum draft that could be carried over the shoalest part of the improvement at mean low water was 2.5 feet.

The commerce interested in the improvement of this river is local and approximates $200,000, annual value.

July 1, 1900, balance unexpended	$276.55
June 30, 1901, amount expended during fiscal year	8.06
July 1, 1901, balance unexpended	268.49

{ Amount (estimated) required for completion of existing project 7,000.00
Amount that can be profitably expended in fiscal year ending June 30, 1903, for works of improvement and for maintenance, in addition to the balance unexpended July 1, 1901 .... 12,000.00
Submitted in compliance with requirements of sundry civil act of June 4, 1897, and of section 7 of the river and harbor act of 1899.

(See Appendix C 5.)

6. *Weymouth River, Massachusetts.*—Before improvement Weymouth (Fore) River was navigable at low water 4 miles for vessels drawing 18 feet, and the least low-water depth 3 miles farther was 3 feet; in Weymouth (Back) River 6 feet at mean low water could be carried 7,000 feet to the wharf of the Bradley Fertilizer Company.

The existing project, approved by the act of September 19, 1890, and extended by the act of August 18, 1894, is to obtain in Weymouth (Fore) River a navigable channel 6 feet deep at mean low water for a distance of 7,000 feet, 100 feet wide to near Weymouth Landing, 80 feet wide thence to Braintree bridge, and 50 feet wide above that point; and in Weymouth (Back) River to obtain a channel 12 feet deep at mean low water, and 200 feet wide through the outer bar and to the wharf of the Bradley Fertilizer Company, a distance of 7,000 feet, at an estimated cost for the Fore River of $40,000 and for the Back River of $22,000, a total of $62,000.

The amount expended to June 30, 1900, was for the Fore River $37,323.01 and for the Back River $11,753.59, a total of $49,076.60, all upon improvement.

No work was done during the fiscal year ending June 30, 1901.

The maximum draft that can be carried over the shoalest part of this improvement is 5 feet in the Fore River and 12 feet in the Back River.

The local commerce interested in the improvement of these rivers approximates $750,000, annual value.

July 1, 1900, balance unexpended	$923.40
July 1, 1901, balance unexpended	923.40

{ Amount (estimated) required for completion of existing project 12,000.00
Amount that can be profitably expended in fiscal year ending June 30, 1903, for works of improvement and for maintenance, in addition to the balance unexpended July 1, 1901 .... 12,000.00
Submitted in compliance with requirements of sundry civil act of June 4, 1897, and of section 7 of the river and harbor act of 1899.

(See Appendix C 6.)

7. *Harbor at Scituate, Massachusetts.*—Before improvement the depth on the bar was about 2½ feet at mean low water (the mean range of tides being 9.8 feet); the entrance was obstructed by many sunken bowlders; of the low-water area of about 57 acres, 6 acres had a depth of at least 3 feet at mean low water and there was little protection against the sea.

The existing project, approved by the act of June 14, 1880, is to build, of rubblestone, a north breakwater 800 feet, and a south breakwater 730 feet long, to dredge an anchorage basin of 30 acres and an entrance channel 2,700 feet long and 300 feet wide, with depths at mean low water of 15 feet at the entrance, 12 to 15 feet between the breakwaters, 12 feet immediately back of the south breakwater, 10 feet in the anchorage basin, and 3 feet in the channel to the wharves, at an estimated cost of $100,000 for the breakwaters and $190,000 for the dredging, a total of $290,000.

The amount expended to June 30, 1900, was $101,362.83. The amount expended for maintenance can not be ascertained.

The amount expended during the fiscal year ending June 30, 1901, has been applied to maintenance by redredging and has increased the width of the channel to the wharves to 75 feet (from 50 feet), with a depth of 3 feet at mean low water.

On June 30, 1901, the maximum draft that could be carried over the shoalest part of the improvement at mean low water was 7 feet over the bar into the basin and 3 feet in the channel, 75 feet wide, to the wharves.

For a plan of the improvement see Annual Report of the Chief of Engineers for 1881, page 522, and for work accomplished report for 1900, page 1206.

The commerce of the port consists of supplies of coal, lumber, etc., for local consumption, and approximates an annual value of $85,000.

July 1, 1900, balance unexpended	$2,137.17
June 30, 1901, amount expended during fiscal year	244.43
July 1, 1901, balance unexpended	1,892.74
July 1, 1901, outstanding liabilities	594.12
July 1, 1901, balance available	1,298.62

Amount (estimated) required for completion of existing project 186,500.00
Amount that can be profitably expended in fiscal year ending June 30, 1903, in addition to the balance available July 1, 1901 .... 15,000.00
Submitted in compliance with requirements of sundry civil act of June 4, 1897.

(See Appendix C 7.)

8. *Harbor at Duxbury, Mass.*—Before improvement there was no low-water channel to the wharf.

The existing project, approved by the Secretary of War August 12, 1899, is to dredge a channel 60 feet wide and 6 feet deep at mean low water, through the flats up to the wharf, widening to 100 feet at the curve, at an estimated cost of $17,820.

The amount expended to June 30, 1900, was $11,903.74, all upon improvement.

There have been no funds for work during the fiscal year ending June 30, 1901.

The maximum draft at mean low water that could be carried over the shoalest part of the improvement, June 30, 1901, was 6 feet with a least width of 40 feet, an increase due to the improvement of 7 feet in depth at the wharf.

For history of project see Annual Report of the Chief of Engineers for 1900, page 1209.

The commerce of this port aggregates about $12,500 annual value, and is of a local character.

July 1, 1900, balance unexpended	$96.26
July 1, 1901, balance unexpended	96.26

Amount (estimated) required for completion of existing project	5,820.00
Amount that can be profitably expended in fiscal year ending June 30, 1903, in addition to the balance unexpended July 1, 1901	5,800.00
Submitted in compliance with requirements of sundry civil act of June 4, 1897.	

(See Appendix C 8.)

9. *Harbor at Plymouth, Mass.*—Before improvement a depth of only about 6 inches of water could be carried to the wharves at low tide.

The existing project, approved by the act of March 3, 1899, is to restore, at an estimated cost of $95,700, the works constructed under former projects (and destroyed by the storms of 1898-99) for the preservation of Long Beach, upon which depends the preservation of the basin along the wharves and of the channel to it, both dredged under the completed project of 1884-85.

The amount expended to June 30, 1900, was $196,476.72, of which $60,727.52 was applied to maintenance.

With the amount expended during the fiscal year ending June 30, 1901, 3,391.5 linear feet of dike of riprap was built on Long Beach.

On June 30, 1901, the maximum draft that could be carrried over the shoalest part of the improvement at mean low water—in the channel to the wharves and in the basin along them, dredged under the completed project of 1884-85—was 9 feet in the channel and 9 feet in the basin.

Chart of harbor, showing location of works, is in Annual Report of the Chief of Engineers for 1888, page 460.

The commerce of the harbor consists of supplies of coal, lumber, etc., for local consumption, and approximates an annual value of $220,000.

July 1, 1900, balance unexpended	$71,290.18
June 30, 1901, amount expended during fiscal year	20,136.62
July 1, 1901, balance unexpended	51,153.56
July 1, 1901, outstanding liabilities	4,446.35
July 1, 1901, balance available	46,707.21
July 1, 1901, amount covered by uncompleted contracts	39,283.65

Amount (estimated) required for completion of existing project	20,700.00
Amount that can be profitably expended in fiscal year ending June 30, 1903, in addition to the balance available July 1, 1901	20,700.00
Submitted in compliance with requirements of sundry civil act of June 4, 1897.	

(See Appendix C 9.)

10. *Harbor at Provincetown, Mass.*—This is an important harbor of refuge in the bight at the extremity of Cape Cod.

In its original condition the width and depth of its entrance and the depth of its anchorage were ample for the largest vessels, but actual or threatened inroads by the sea across the low and narrow part of the cape east of the town and at intervals along about 1¼ miles of the narrow beach southwest of the town were a serious menace to the harbor.

Since 1826 dikes and works for beach protection have been constructed in both localities, and have been maintained and extended as conditions required.

Little or no expenditure has been required in the latter years east of the town, but the slender beach southwest of the harbor requires constant care, and has required an average expenditure of about $1,500 annually. A contingent fund of a few thousand dollars should always be available to provide against damage liable in storms of severity, especially if occurring in conjunction with extreme tides.

The amount expended to June 30, 1900, was $154,102.90, of which the part applied to maintenance can not be stated.

With the amount expended during the fiscal year ending June 30, 1901, minor repairs were made to the works for the protection of the beach southwest of the town.

The maximum draft that can be carried to the anchorage is ample for the largest vessels.

A description and plan of works are in the annual reports of the Chief of Engineers for 1876, 1879, and 1886, pages 181, 273, and 574, respectively.

The estimated value of vessels which enter the harbor annually (principally for shelter) is $40,000,000.

July 1, 1900, balance unexpended.. $11,815.54
June 30, 1901, amount expended during fiscal year.................... 1,783.67

July 1, 1901, balance unexpended.. 10,031.87

{ Amount that can be profitably expended in fiscal year ending June 30, 1903, for maintenance of improvement, in addition to the balance unexpended July 1, 1901... 1,500.00
Submitted in compliance with requirements of sundry civil act of June 4, 1897, and of section 7 of the river and harbor act of 1899.

(See Appendix C 10.)

11. Harbor at Chatham, Mass.—Before improvement the entrance was obstructed by three bars, on which the greatest depth at mean low water was 4 feet.

The existing project, approved by the act of September 19, 1890, is to dredge a channel 6 feet deep at mean low water, 200 feet wide through the outer bar, 150 feet wide through the middle bar, and 100 feet wide through the inner bar, at an estimated cost (approved by the act of March 3, 1899) of $13,732.79.

The amount expended to June 30, 1900, was $5,484.90, all upon improvement.

The amount expended during the fiscal year ending June 30, 1901, was in connection with advertising for proposals and entering into a contract for completion of the project.

On June 30, 1901, the maximum draft at mean low water that could be carried over the shoalest part of the improvement was 4 feet.

A description of the harbor is given in the Anual Report of the Chief of Engineers for 1900, page 92.

The commerce involved in the improvement is local in character, and of an approximate annual value of $200,000.

July 1, 1900, balance unexpended	$8,247.89
June 30, 1901, amount expended during fiscal year	68.03
July 1, 1901, balance unexpended	8,179.86
July 1, 1901, outstanding liabilities	6.67
July 1, 1901, balance available	8,173.19
July 1, 1901, amount covered by uncompleted contracts	7,200.00

(See Appendix C 11.)

12. Removing sunken vessels or craft obstructing or endangering navigation.—Under provisions of sections 19 and 20 of the river and harbor act of March 3, 1899, an allotment of $50 was made May 18, 1901, from the indefinite appropriation made by that act, to investigate the location and extent of wreckage complained of as obstructing navigation in Nauset Harbor, Massachusetts.

At the date of this report the necessary information pertaining to this wreckage is being secured.

(See Appendix C 12.)

EXAMINATIONS AND SURVEYS MADE IN COMPLIANCE WITH EMERGENCY RIVER AND HARBOR ACT OF JUNE 6, 1900.

The preliminary examinations and surveys of the following localities were made by the local officer and reports thereon submitted:

1. Preliminary examination and survey of Lynn Harbor, Massachusetts, with a view of securing a channel 200 feet wide and 15 feet deep at mean low water, including the basin extending beyond the inner ship channel and the removal of a small point on the eastern bank of the channel near to said basin.—Col. Chas. R. Suter, Corps of Engineers, submitted reports on preliminary examination and survey dated June 16, 1900, and November 25, 1900, respectively. The estimated cost of the improvement proposed by him is $162,936.84. The reports were transmitted to Congress and printed in House Doc. No. 78, Fifty-sixth Congress, second session. (See also Appendix C 13.)

2. Preliminary examination and survey of Boston Harbor, Massachusetts, with a view to providing channels 2,000 feet wide, or such width as may be necessary, and 35 feet deep from the navy-yard at Charlestown and the Chelsea bridge and Charles River bridge to President Roads, and from President Roads through Broad Sound Channel to the ocean.—Reports were submitted by Colonel Suter on preliminary examination and survey of Boston Harbor, dated June 16, 1900, and November 28, 1900, respectively. The estimates presented by Colonel Suter are as follows:

Upper harbor channel	$7,404,875.50
Broad Sound Channel	3,207,834.96
Total	10,612,710.46

The reports were transmitted to Congress and printed in House Doc. No. 119, Fifty-sixth Congress, second session. (See also Appendix C 14.)

IMPROVEMENT OF RIVERS AND HARBORS IN SOUTHEASTERN MASSACHUSETTS AND IN RHODE ISLAND.

This district was in the charge of Maj. D. W. Lockwood, Corps of Engineers, to July 25, 1900, having under his immediate orders Lieut. R. P. Johnston, Corps of Engineers, in the temporary charge of Lieutenant Johnson from July 25, 1900, to August 31, 1900, and in the charge of Maj. Geo. W. Goethals, Corps of Engineers, since August 31, 1900, with Lieutenant Johnston under his immediate orders. Division Engineer, Col. G. L. Gillespie, Corps of Engineers, (now brigadier-general, Chief of Engineers, United States Army), to May 3, 1901, and Col. Chas. R. Suter, Corps of Engineers, since May 9, 1901.

1. Harbor of refuge at Hyannis, Mass.—This harbor before improvement was an open roadstead exposed to southerly storms. In the years 1827–1838 a breakwater 1,170 feet long was constructed of riprap granite, covering an anchorage of about 175 acres, the entrance to which has a depth of about 15.5 feet. Between the years 1852 and 1882 extensive repairs were made, increasing the width of the base of the breakwater and the size of the stone forming its sides and top.

The existing project approved in 1884 provides for dredging to 15.5 feet depth at low water about 36 acres area north of the existing breakwater, so as to increase the deep-water anchorage by that amount, all at a total cost estimated at that time at $54,743.20.

At the adoption of the existing project the 15.5-foot depth anchorage covered only about 47 acres, and the 36 additional acres to be dredged carried a depth of from 7 to 15.5 feet of water at low water.

The sum of $167,183.44 had been expended at this harbor up to June 30, 1900, of which $123,350.62 had been applied to construction and repairs to the breakwater, and $43,832.82 to dredging and making a survey. Of the 36 acres 26.6 had been deepened to 15.5 feet, and two 25-foot-wide cuts, 13 feet deep at mean low water, had been made in the channel leading to the wharf of the New York, New Haven and Hartford Railroad Company. The survey, report on which was printed in House Doc. No. 79, Fifty-sixth Congress, first session, also at page 1284, Annual Report of the Chief of Engineers for 1900, developed the fact that to complete the existing project would require the expenditure of $32,500, making its total cost $76,312.14.

No work was done during the past fiscal year.

The principal value of this harbor to commerce is as a harbor of refuge for coasters and fishing vessels. The actual commerce of the place consists of general agricultural products, coal, and fish, aggregating 29,000 tons. The increase of anchorage area will afford refuge for more and larger boats.

The unexpended balance, with such funds as may be appropriated by Congress, will be applied to carrying out the present project.

July 1, 1900, balance unexpended	$1,931.06
June 30, 1901, amount expended during fiscal year	69.06
July 1, 1901, balance unexpended	1,862.00
Amount (estimated) required for completion of existing project	32,500.00
Amount that can be profitably expended in fiscal year ending June 30, 1903, in addition to the balance unexpended July 1, 1901. Submitted in compliance with requirement of sundry civil act of June 4, 1897.	32,500.00

(See Appendix D 1.)

2. *Harbor of refuge at Nantucket, Mass.*—This harbor is the only one between the harbors of Marthas Vineyard (Vineyard Haven and Edgartown) and Provincetown, a distance of 100 miles, except the small harbor of Hyannis, on the north side of Nantucket Sound. It has a considerable area, with a depth of water in excess of 12 feet, and the object of improvement is to make it a harbor of refuge for vessels plying between ports north and south of Cape Cod.

The existing project of 1880, as modified in 1885, provides for the construction of two jetties as training walls, one on each side of the harbor entrance, planned so as to allow the tidal currents to assist in scouring out and maintaining a good channel, and for the completion of the work by dredging where necessary to obtain a depth of from 12 to 15 feet at low water in this channel; all at a total cost estimated at $375,000, of which $220,000 was appropriated prior to 1896.

At the adoption of the present project no jetties existed and the channel entrance was barred by a shoal of 1.5 miles in width, on which there was only 6 feet depth of water at low tide, the channel being crooked and subject to changes in location.

During an unusually severe storm in December, 1896, a breach was made through the Haulover Beach between the ocean and the head of the harbor. The breach still remains open, but it does not appear to have affected the depth of water in the entrance to the harbor.

The sum of $304,878.42 had been expended on this work up to June 30, 1900, of which $45,734.75 had been expended in ineffectual dredging between 1829 and 1844, and the balance, $259,143.67, in jetty construction and repair, by which the west jetty had been built to 4,955 feet length, of which 3,955 feet was to full height, then 400 feet to half-tide level, and the outer 600 feet to full height. The east jetty had been built to 834 feet length with full height, then the foundation laid for a length of 191 feet, then came a gap of 160 feet, beyond which 3,655 feet length had been raised to half-tide level, 1,300 feet of which has settled and been considerably washed down, the total length from shore end to outer end being now 4,840 feet. Mounds of heavy stone had been built near the present ends of the jetties to protect lantern staffs, and at intervals of 200 feet along the portions submerged at high water smaller mounds had been built extending above high water. Eight feet of water at mean low tide can be carried into the harbor.

A large portion of the 3,955 feet of the west jetty built prior to 1884 has been damaged somewhat by storms and ice, and, having no core of small stone, allows considerable sand to pass through it. This should be repaired so as to be as sand-tight as possible and raised to its original height. There was expended in 1894 $7,210 in repairs to the jetty. It is estimated that $30,000 more will be required to complete the repairs, in addition to the estimated cost of the project.

No works of improvement were in progress during the past fiscal year.

Further work will consist in raising the incomplete portions of both jetties and extending the same.

The entire commerce of Nantucket Island is carried on at this harbor, amounting in 1900 to about 24,400 tons. The effect of this work will be to afford a place of refuge easy of access and secure from storms for coasters and fishing vessels.

162   REPORT OF THE CHIEF OF ENGINEERS, U. S. ARMY.

July 1, 1900, balance unexpended.. $856.33
June 30, 1901, amount expended during fiscal year..................... 856.33

Amount (estimated) required for completion of existing project........ 115,000.00
Amount that can be profitably expended in fiscal year ending June 30, 1903, for works of improvement and for maintenance................ 115,000.00
Submitted in compliance with requirements of sundry civil act of June 4, 1897, and of section 7 of the river and harbor act of 1899.

(See Appendix D 2.)

3. Harbor at Vineyard Haven, Mass.—Vineyard Haven is a deep indentation in the northern shore of the island of Marthas Vineyard, on the southern side of Vineyard Sound. The existing project of 1887, as modified in 1889, provides for the protection of the "Chops" (or headlands) from erosion and the intervening harbor from being filled by the eroded material, the whole to be done by means of stone sea walls and jetties to be built along the beach in front of the bluffs at both headlands. The total cost was estimated in 1889 at $60,000, the whole of which has been appropriated.

At the adoption of the present project the headlands were gradually wearing away and the adjacent parts of the harbor were shoaling. No protection works were in existence.

The sum of $54,304.26 had been expended on this work up to June 30, 1900, by which there had been built a riprap sea wall of 1,210 feet length and a jetty of 50 feet length and six small spurs extending back from the sea wall to the foot of the bluff at the East Chop, and at the West Chop a riprap sea wall of 880 feet length, three jetties of 150, 135, and 280 feet length, a wharf, and a short breakwater of 60 feet length, and 2,400 feet length of riprap wall along the low-water line, and 13 short jetties running from the sea wall to the foot of the bluff, in front of the bluff on the east side of the West Chop. The works so far constructed appear to have afforded the needed protection.

During the past fiscal year no work of improvement was in progress. An examination of the harbor, "with a view to its further protection and improvement as a harbor of refuge by a breakwater or otherwise," was made in September, 1899, and report thereon transmitted to Congress and printed in House Doc. No. 66, Fifty-sixth Congress, first session; it was also printed at page 1289, Annual Report of the Chief of Engineers for 1900.

The unexpended balance will be applied to repairing existing works.

The commerce of the harbor in 1900 amounted to about 124,000 tons. The benefit to commerce of this work is the preservation of the anchorage area and harbor generally from shoaling.

July 1, 1900, balance unexpended.. $5,695.74
June 30, 1901, amount expended during fiscal year..................... 663.09

July 1, 1901, balance unexpended.. 5,032.65

(See Appendix D 3.)

4. Woods Hole Channel, Massachusetts.—Woods Hole is a waterway or strait connecting Buzzards Bay and Vineyard Sound and lying near the southwestern part of Cape Cod, Massachusetts. The name is also applied to the village and harbor in the near vicinity.

Before improvement the entrance to Little Harbor was obstructed by a bar with but 7.5 feet on it at mean low tide. Great Harbor has ample depth. In the strait the channels were crooked and obstructed by bowlders, and the velocity of the currents at certain stages of the tide was from 5 to 7 miles per hour. The site of the wharves and basins of the United States Fish Commission and Revenue-Marine Service was a submerged point of land extending from the shore of the harbor.

The project of 1879 provided for making a channel through the bar at the entrance to Little Harbor and widening and deepening the channel through the strait. The project of 1883, extended in 1884 and 1886, provided for the construction of retaining walls on shore, a stone pier, and a wooden wharf, mainly for the use of the United States Fish Commission and incidentally for the use of the other branches of the public service, all of which work had been completed prior to 1889. The existing project, that of 1895, provides for deepening the channel through the strait to 13 feet at mean low water and widening the same to 300 feet, estimated to cost $396,000.

The total amount expended on this work up to June 30, 1900, was $153,581.98, with which the entrance to Little Harbor had been dredged to 10 feet depth, and a direct channel to 9 feet depth had been dredged through the strait where none previously existed; the retaining walls, stone pier, and wooden wharves had also all been built and repaired.

Of the above amount $39,998.26 was expended on the existing project, resulting in the removal of all obstructing shoals to a depth of 13 feet at mean low water in the southern half of the channel between its eastern end and the southern branch, known as "Broadway," the greater portion of the shoal at the junction of the two branches, and a shoal in mid-channel just west of this junction.

There is now a fairly good channel of one-half the projected width—150 feet—and 13 feet depth through the strait, but a few small shoal spots west of the junction need to be removed to complete the southern half of the channel.

No work of improvement was in progress during the fiscal year.

Further work will consist in extending the 13-foot depth of channel to the northward until the full width is secured.

The commerce of Woods Hole was about 19,000 tons for 1900, no account being kept of vessels passing through the strait. The deepening of this channel will result in more vessels using it than formerly.

July 1, 1900, balance unexpended	$17.94
June 30, 1901, amount expended during fiscal year	17.94

Amount (estimated) required for completion of existing project	356,000.00
Amount that can be profitably expended in fiscal year ending June 30, 1903	70,000.00
Submitted in compliance with requirements of sundry civil act of June 4, 1897.	

(See Appendix D 4.)

5. *New Bedford Harbor, Massachusetts.*—New Bedford Harbor is an estuary of Buzzards Bay, and is the port of the cities of New Bedford and Fairhaven.

Before improvement the channel had a depth of 12.5 feet at mean low water. The projects of 1874 and 1877 provided for a channel 300 feet wide and 15 feet deep at mean low water from the deep water just above Palmers Island to the wharves of New Bedford. This work was completed in 1877 at a cost of $20,000.

The project of 1887 provided for a channel 200 feet wide and 18 feet deep from Buzzards Bay to New Bedford, at an estimated cost of $35,000, and has been completed.

The existing projects are those of 1895, providing for dredging an anchorage area one-half mile long, 600 feet wide, and 18 feet deep at mean low tide, on the north side of the channel leading from Fairhaven to New Bedford, at an estimated cost of $57,689.33, and of 1899, providing for a channel 250 feet wide and 18 feet deep at mean low water, from the anchorage basin through the new drawbridge between Fish and Popes islands to the deep water above, at an estimated cost of $34,000.

At the adoption of the existing projects the anchorage area was from 12 to 18 feet deep and the least depth in the channel between Fish and Popes islands was about 7.3 feet.

The sum of $126,693.41 had been expended in this harbor up to June 30, 1900, by which a channel 200 feet wide and 18 feet deep at mean low water had been secured from the deep water of Buzzards Bay to New Bedford, the 18-foot channel 250 feet wide leading from the anchorage basin through the new drawbridge connecting Fish and Popes islands had been completed, and 18.4 acres of the anchorage basin had been dredged.

Eighteen feet of water at mean low tide can now be carried from the main channel through the new drawbridge, but owing to the very soft nature of the material through which the channel was dredged the full width of 18 feet depth has not been maintained. In order that the projected width may be secured, it is estimated that an expenditure of $10,000 would be required for redredging the western portion of the channel.

A report of a survey for the further improvement of this harbor was submitted under date of November 17, 1899, and printed as House Doc. No. 169, Fifty-sixth Congress, first session, and at page 1295, Annual Report of the Chief of Engineers for 1900.

No works of improvement have been in progress during the past fiscal year.

The work required to complete the existing project is the completion of the anchorage area and redredging portions of the channel through the drawbridge.

The tonnage of this harbor amounted to about 652,000 tons. The effect of the deep water on commerce is the use of deeper draft vessels than formerly, larger cargoes, and a consequent reduction in water freight charges.

July 1, 1900, balance unexpended	$6.96
June 30, 1901, amount expended during fiscal year	6.96

Amount (estimated) required for completion of existing project	37,689.33
Amount that can be profitably expended in fiscal year ending June 30, 1903.	37,700.00
Submitted in compliance with requirements of sundry civil act of June 4, 1897.	

(See Appendix D 5.)

6. *Taunton River, Massachusetts.*—This river rises in Norfolk County, Mass., and empties into Mount Hope Bay at Fall River. The object of the improvement is to deepen and widen the channel leading to the city of Taunton, at the head of navigation, so that vessels of 11 feet draft can reach the city at high water.

In its original condition the channel was narrow and obstructed by bowlders, and from Berkley bridge to Taunton the depth was in places not more than 5 feet at mean high water. A vessel of 30 tons burden was as large as could go up to Taunton.

From 1870 to 1879, $63,000 was appropriated to secure 9 feet depth at high water. This work was completed in 1879.

The approved project of 1880 provided for the widening and deepening of the river so as to secure a channel of at least 12 feet depth at high water, with 100 feet width from its mouth up to Berkley bridge (above Dighton); thence 12 feet depth with 80 feet width (100 feet width at bends) up to Briggs Shoal; thence 11 feet depth with 80 feet width up to the shipyard; thence 11 feet depth with 60 feet width up to Weir bridge, Taunton; all at a total cost estimated in 1893 at $125,000, all of which has been appropriated.

The sum of $187,999.81 had been expended on this work up to June 30, 1900, by which expenditure all projected work had been practically completed, but the channel had filled up at a few points and needed redredging. About $19,000 of the above amount has been expended in the maintenance of the channel. Vessels of 11 feet draft can reach Taunton at high water, but at some points the 11-foot channel is very narrow. It is estimated that $5,000 every four years will be required to maintain the channel.

The tonnage of 1900 was about 577,000 tons, showing a decrease from previous years.

July 1, 1900, balance unexpended	$0.19
June 30, 1901, amount expended during fiscal year	.19

Amount that can be profitably expended in fiscal year ending June 30, 1903, for maintenance of improvement........................... 5,000.00
Submitted in compliance with requirements of sundry civil act of June 4, 1897, and of section 7 of the river and harbor act of 1899.

(See Appendix D 6.)

7. *Sakonnet River, Rhode Island.*—Sakonnet River is an arm of the sea between the island of Rhode Island and the mainland, extending from the ocean to Mount Hope Bay around the head of Rhode Island. It is at present obstructed at its upper end by two causeways extending across it. These causeways have draw openings, which are of insufficient width and depth for the needs of commerce, and besides offer such obstruction to the ebb and flow of the tides that the currents through them make the passage dangerous even to boats of such dimensions as could pass through them under ordinary circumstances.

The present approved project provides for increasing the width and depth of the draw opening in the Stone Bridge, owned by the State of Rhode Island, so as to provide an opening 100 feet wide and 25 feet deep at mean low water, estimated to cost $40,000.

No work has been done and no funds expended, owing to the fact that the State assembly's permission to the United States to widen and deepen the draw opening in its bridge is conditioned in such a way as to make it inoperative until the railroad company shall have widened and deepened the draw opening in its bridge, and to the further fact that the proposed work involves the total destruction of the present bridge and existing highway, while no provision is made for rebuilding the bridge or restoring the highway. Until the State of Rhode Island grants the Federal Government the unconditional right to proceed with the work authorized by Congress, and provides either for the restoration or discontinuance of the bridge and highway, the Secretary of War can not proceed with the work. The authorities of the State have been repeatedly advised of the existing complications, and of the importance of having the legislature take the proper action to remove them.

The New York, New Haven and Hartford Railroad Company was notified by the Secretary of War to construct a suitable draw in its bridge by May 1, 1899. The time for completing the new draw in the railroad bridge was subsequently extended to May 1, 1900, and later to May 1, 1901, at which date the new bridge and its approaches had been completed and was in use by the company.

The dredging in the draw passage was completed on May 4, 1901.

The general assembly of the State adjourned without enacting such legislation as was desired by the War Department to enable it to commence this work.

The tonnage of the river for the year 1900 amounted to about 15,000 tons.

July 1, 1900, balance unexpended.. $40,000.00
July 1, 1901, balance unexpended.. 40,000.00

(See Appendix D 7.)

8. *Sakonnet Point, Rhode Island.*—Sakonnet Point is a rocky headland, on the eastern side of the mouth of Sakonnet River, and lies about 6 miles east of Newport.

Sakonnet Point, in connection with Churchs Cove, just north of it, forms an anchorage protected from the southeast to northeast, but exposed to storms from the south to the northwest.

About the year 1827 a breakwater about 200 feet long was built, but it has washed down to a considerable extent.

The present project, that of 1897, approved by the river and harbor act of March 3, 1899, provides for prolonging this old breakwater out to a rock just north of it and raising the whole to a height of 8 feet above mean low water, at an estimated cost of $25,000, which has been appropriated.

At the beginning of the last fiscal year the breakwater was nearly completed. During the fiscal year the work was completed and a survey was made of certain rocks in the harbor and a report thereon with an estimate of the cost of their removal was submitted November 19, 1900. This report was printed as House Doc. No. 99, Fifty-sixth Congress, second session, and is herewith as Appendix D 19.

The work done affords good shelter to the landing in Churchs Cove.

The commerce of this place is as stated under the Sakonnet River.

July 1, 1900, balance unexpended $10,278.79
June 30, 1901, amount expended during fiscal year 10,278.79

(See Appendix D 8.)

9. *Pawtucket River, Rhode Island.*—This river, otherwise called Seekonk River, is the upper portion of the Providence River, and extends from Pawtucket to Providence. Before improvement the channel in the river had a ruling depth of about 5 feet at mean low water.

Between 1867 and 1873, $52,000 was appropriated to dredge the channel to 7 feet depth. This work was finished in 1876.

The approved project of 1883 provides for the deepending of the river so as to secure a channel of at least 12 feet depth at low water, with 100 feet width from its mouth, at Providence, up to opposite Grant & Co.'s wharf at Pawtucket, and thence 12 feet depth with 40 feet width through a stone ledge for a short distance farther to Pawtucket bridge; all at a total cost estimated in 1883 at $382,500, of which $205,000 was appropriated prior to 1895.

The river and harbor act of March 3, 1899, provided for straightening that portion of the channel between Ten-mile River and Bucklins Island; and the available balance, together with the further funds provided by Congress, will be applied to this work and to deepening the channel at points where it has shoaled.

At the adoption of the existing project the channel was narrow and only about 5 feet deep.

The sum of $282,171.96 had been expended on this work up to June 30, 1900, by which a channel had been secured 100 feet in width and 12 feet in depth from the mouth of the river, near Providence, up to the lower wharves of the city of Pawtucket; thence a channel of 40 feet width and 12 feet depth had been completed through the ledge rock to the head of navigation.

At the beginning of the fiscal year about one-half the work of straightening the channel between Ten-mile River and Bucklins Island had also been done. The contract for this work was completed October 15, 1900, leaving about 400 feet in length of the channel incomplete. A 12-foot channel is however available by the original route.

The report of a survey with a view to the further improvement of the river was submitted under date of November 25, 1899, and printed in House Doc. No. 113, Fifty-sixth Congress, first session, also at page 1304, Annual Report of the Chief of Engineers for 1900.

The effect of the improvement is to cause the use of vessels of deeper draft than formerly, larger cargoes, and cheaper rates. The completed portion of the channel has already been a great benefit to the commerce of the river, which in 1900 amounted to a tonnage of about 216,060.

The work yet to be done is to straighten and deepen the channel in its lower portions.

July 1, 1900, balance unexpended	$25,347.63
June 30, 1901, amount expended during fiscal year	25,347.63
Amount (estimated) required for completion of existing project	28,580.35
Amount that can be profitably expended in fiscal year ending June 30, 1903	28,500.00
Submitted in compliance with requirements of sundry civil act of June 4, 1897.	

(See Appendix D 9.)

10. Providence River and Narragansett Bay, Rhode Island.—The object of this improvement is to furnish a wide and deep channel for foreign and coastwise commerce from the ocean to Providence.

Before the improvement of the river was commenced in 1853 many shoals obstructed navigation and at one point in the channel, a place called "The Crook," the available low water was but 4.5 feet. Between 1852 and 1873, $59,000 was appropriated to secure first 9 and then 12 feet depth of channel. This work was finished in 1873.

The approved project of 1878, as modified in 1882, provides for deepening the river and deepening and widening its anchorage basins, so as to secure a channel of at least 25 feet depth at low water with 300 feet width from the deep water of Narragansett Bay up to Providence,

168   REPORT OF THE CHIEF OF ENGINEERS, U. S. ARMY.

R. I., and so as to secure anchorage basins of 20 feet depth with 600 feet width, 18 feet depth with 725 feet width, 12 feet depth with 940 feet width, and 6 feet depth with 1,060 feet width from Fox Point to Field Point; all at a total cost estimated in 1882 at $675,000. This project was completed in 1895.

The river and harbor act of June 3, 1896, provided for securing a ship channel 400 feet in width and of a depth of 25 feet at mean low water from Sassafras Point, in Providence Harbor, through Providence River and Narragansett Bay by the most direct route practicable to the ocean, by way of the "Western Passage," so called, at an estimated cost of $732,820.

This project, under which work is now in progress, was put under the continuing-contract system.

The sum of $893,023.79 had been expended on this work up to June 30, 1900, by which Bulkhead Rock had been removed and the channel 300 feet wide and 25 feet deep had been secured to the city of Providence and an anchorage area 1,060 feet wide, with depths varying from 6 to 20 feet, had been dredged, but both the channel and the anchorage area now need some redredging. The new channel 400 feet wide and 25 feet deep had been completed from Sassafras Point down to Conimicut light-house and about one-fourth of the remaining portion had been done.

During the fiscal year the contract for the lower portion of this work was annulled, to take effect January 1, 1901, and a new contract was entered into, the work commencing under the new contract April 1, 1901.

A report of a survey of Providence Harbor with a view to its further improvement was submitted under date of November 11, 1899, and printed in House Doc. No. 108, Fifty-sixth Congress, first session, and at page 1308, Annual Report of Chief of Engineers for 1900.

The available unexpended balance will be applied to continuing the dredging in the new ship channel.

The improvement has been of great benefit to commerce, which in 1900 amounted to about 2,763,500 tons.

July 1, 1900, balance unexpended	$138,108.60
Amount appropriated by sundry civil act approved March 3, 1901	59,000.00
	197,108.60
June 30, 1901, amount expended during fiscal year	17,122.48
July 1, 1901, balance unexpended	179,986.12
July 1, 1901, outstanding liabilities	17,972.26
July 1, 1901, balance available	162,013.86
July 1, 1901, amount covered by uncompleted contracts	222,337.57
Amount (estimated) required for completion of existing project	84,560.00
Amount that can be profitably expended in fiscal year ending June 30, 1903, in addition to the balance available July 1, 1901	84,560.00

Submitted in compliance with requirements of sundry civil act of June 4, 1897.

(See Appendix D 10.)

11. *Removal of Green Jacket Shoal, Providence, R. I.*—This shoal is in that part of Providence River which constitutes the harbor of Providence. It lies off the wharves on the south front of the city and occupies a part of the harbor that is required for anchorage purposes,

covering an area of about 18 acres between the 15-foot curves and about 30 acres in all.

The approved project of 1885 provides for the removal to 25 feet depth at low water of a middle-ground shoal of about 30 acres area in Providence River opposite the city, the portion to be removed to be at least 200 feet distant from the harbor lines of the city, all at a total cost estimated in 1885 at $112,346.

At the adoption of the present project the shoal in many places carried only 1 foot of water and was a very troublesome obstruction.

The sum of $103,917.74 had been expended on this work up to June 30, 1900, by which 23.8 acres out of the original 30 of this shoal had been dredged to 25 feet depth, and a 16-foot depth had been secured over the central and largest portion of the shoal in addition to a 20-foot depth in the main channel, making an important addition to the anchorage facilities of Providence Harbor.

The report of a survey with a view to the further improvement of this locality was submitted November 11, 1899, and printed in House Doc. No. 108, Fifty-sixth Congress, first session, and at page 1308, Annual Report of Chief of Engineers for 1900.

No work was in progress during the year, as no funds were appropriated by the river and harbor act of 1899.

The removal of this shoal will enable vessels to anchor outside of the channel, and thus remove an obstruction to vessels going to or from the Providence wharves.

Further funds will be applied to extending the area of 25 feet depth.

July 1, 1900, balance unexpended	$332.26
June 30, 1901, amount expended during fiscal year	117.84
July 1, 1901, balance unexpended	214.42

Amount (estimated) required for completion of existing project	8,096.00
Amount that can be profitably expended in fiscal year ending June 30, 1903, in addition to the balance unexpended July 1, 1901	8,000.00
Submitted in compliance with requirements of sundry civil act of June 4, 1897.	

(See Appendix D 11.)

12. *Fall River Harbor, Massachusetts.*—Fall River Harbor lies at the mouth of Taunton River, in the northeastern angle of Mount Hope Bay, which empties into the ocean through Narragansett Bay and Sakonnet River. It forms the port of entry of the city of Fall River, the largest cotton manufacturing city in the United States.

Before improvement the reëntrant in the wharf line north of the Old Colony Steamboat Company's wharf was limited to about 6 feet depth of water, and a considerable area of the harbor, especially in front of the upper wharves, carried much less depth of water than existed in its approaches.

The project of 1874 provided for deepening an area in front of the wharves immediatly north of the Old Colony Steamboat Company's wharf 160 feet wide to 12 feet, and an additional width of 100 feet to 11 feet at mean low tide. This improvement was completed in 1878, with an expenditure of $30,000.

The existing project, approved by the river and harbor act of March 3, 1899, provides for a channel 300 feet wide and 25 feet deep at mean low tide along the city front between the Old Colony wharf and deep water at the upper end of the city front, at an estimated cost of $58,060.47.

At the adoption of the present project the proposed new channel had a minimum depth of about 14 feet.

The sum of $49,997.40 had been expended on this work up to June 30, 1900, by which the project of 1874, and the lower reach of the channel of the existing project, embracing nearly one-half of the proposed work, had been completed.

A harbor line for this harbor was approved by the Secretary of War January 12, 1900. Its location has been marked with granite bounds. For description of harbor line, etc., see page 1311 in Annual Report of the Chief of Engineers for 1900.

No work was done during the past fiscal year.

The work required to complete the existing project is dredging the upper portion of the new channel.

The commerce of the port in 1900 amounted to about 3,500,000 tons, and the proposed improvement will give increased facilities for deeper draft vessels.

July 1, 1900, balance unexpended	$2.60
June 30, 1901, amount expended during fiscal year	2.60

Amount (estimated) required for completion of existing project	38,060.47
Amount that can be profitably expended in fiscal year ending June 30, 1903.	38,000.00
Submitted in compliance with requirements of sundry civil act of June 4, 1897.	

(See Appendix D 12.)

13. Newport Harbor, Rhode Island.—This harbor is at the main entrance to Narragansett Bay, and all the year it serves as an easily accessible harbor of refuge to foreign and coastwise commerce.

Before improvement the capacity of the inner harbor was limited by shoals, and it was not adequate to the number and size of the vessels seeking it for refuge. The southern or main entrance was obstructed by a bar which stretched out from Goat Island, and the northern entrance by a sharp rocky spit near Rose Island, and the general business wharves of the city could not be reached at low tide by vessels drawing more than 8 feet.

Between 1873 and 1875, $28,500 was appropriated to secure 12 feet depth in the harbor. This work was completed in 1876.

The approved project of 1880, as modified in 1882, 1883, 1884, 1890, and 1895, provides for the widening and deepening of the channel from Narragansett Bay into Newport, so as to secure 15 feet depth at low water, with at least 750 feet width; for the extension of the 13-foot depth and 10-foot depth anchorage basins; and for dredging a channel 10 feet deep along the State harbor line southward to opposite the gas company's wharf; for the partial cutting off of the shoal spit at the southern end of Goat Island, and for the construction of jetties on the western shore of Goat Island so as to protect the end of this island from erosion and to prevent the drift of sand, etc., around the island into the adjacent parts of the channel and harbor; and for the removal of Spindle Rock, a sharp rocky spit near Rose Island; all at a total cost estimated in 1895 at $206,200.

At the adoption of the existing project this harbor was limited to 12 feet depth at low water, and its anchorage area was too small for the craft seeking harborage at this place during the summer and all the year during storms.

The sum of $105,318.63 had been expended on this work up to June

30, 1900, by which the 15-foot channels and 13-foot and 10-foot anchorage basins and the 10-foot channel had been completed, the shoal spit at the southern end of Goat Island had been cut off, and one jetty 133 feet long had been built westward from Goat Island.

There is now a 15-foot channel through the inner harbor, and all other features of the project have been completed excepting the removal of a few shoal spots of hardpan and bowlders still remaining in the 13-foot anchorage basin.

No work has been done during the past fiscal year.

The work required to complete the existing project is the clearing up of certain shoal places in the harbor proper.

As the improvement of this harbor has progressed there has been a large increase in the size and number of vessels using the harbor. The commerce for 1900 shows a tonnage of about 498,000 tons, principally fish, coal, and general merchandise.

July 1, 1900, balance unexpended	$189.89
June 30, 1901, amount expended during fiscal year	189.89

Amount (estimated) required for completion of existing project	39,200.00
Amount that can be profitably expended in fiscal year ending June 30, 1903.	39,000.00
Submitted in compliance with requirements of sundry civil act of June 4, 1897.	

(See Appendix D 13.)

14. Harbor of refuge at Point Judith, Rhode Island.—Point Judith is the southeastern extremity of South Kingston, R. I., and marks the southwestern entrance to Narragansett Bay. A long ledge, known as Squid Ledge, extends for nearly a mile in a south by easterly direction, about 1.5 miles west of the point.

The existing project of 1889 provides for the construction at this point of a national harbor of refuge nearly a mile square by means of stone breakwaters built partly on Squid Ledge and planned so as to give protection against easterly, southerly, and westerly storms, the mainland itself forming a protection on the north, all at a total cost estimated in 1889 at $1,250,000, all of which has been appropriated.

By the act of July 13, 1892, authority was given to the Secretary of War to make contracts for the completion of the project on the basis of the above estimated total cost, the work to be paid for as appropriations should from time to time be made by law.

At the adoption of the project this point was a specially dangerous place for boats and tows to pass during storms and even ordinarily bad weather.

The sum of $1,243,626.95 had been expended on this work up to June 30, 1900, by which the breakwater had been built to a total length of 6,970 feet, with a height of 10 feet above mean low water. It incloses an area of about 1 square mile with 12 feet of water, and about 0.92 of a mile with 18 feet of water, more than two-thirds of which is over 25 feet deep. Three beacon lights had been established and maintained on the breakwater.

During the past fiscal year no operations were in progress, but three small lights were maintained.

The limit of cost of this improvement, as fixed by law, was based on an estimate prepared in 1889 from the best information then available. Experience and additional information gained since that time show that to secure all the beneficial results designed to be accomplished by the breakwater and to properly strengthen and extend it further appropriations are necessary.

The total amount of the original estimated cost having been appropriated. an estimate of $444,310.98 is submitted as the additional sum that will be required to strengthen the breakwater and make the necessary additions to it, as recommended by a Board of Engineers in report of October 23, 1896. (See Annual Report of the Chief of Engineers for 1897, p. 920.)

It is proposed to apply the balance available to maintenance of lights and repair of the breakwater.

Further work is dependent upon additional appropriations. Four hundred and thirteen vessels of all classes sought refuge in the protected harbor during the year ending December 31, 1900.

July 1, 1900, balance unexpended	$6,411.66
June 30, 1901, amount expended during fiscal year	1,523.73
July 1, 1901, balance unexpended	4,887.93
July 1, 1901, outstanding liabilities	125.00
July 1, 1901, balance available	4,762.93

{ Amount (estimated) required for completion of existing project....... 444,310.98
Amount that can be profitably expended in fiscal year ending June 30, 1903, in addition to the balance available July 1, 1901............... 300,000.00
Submitted in compliance with requirements of sundry civil act of June 4, 1897.

(See Appendix D 14.)

15. Entrance to Point Judith Pond, Rhode Island.—Point Judith Pond is a shallow-draft salt pond, lying in rear of the sandy beach of the Rhode Island shore, just west of Point Judith.

The improvement desired at this place by the people of the neighborhood is the reopening of an old entrance long ago closed by the ocean storms.

The present entrance to this pond is very shallow (less than 3 feet), crooked, and variable in location, and lies about a mile west of the former entrance.

There is at present no approved project for the improvement of this pond entrance.

Up to June 30, 1900, $518.38 had been expended in surveys.

July 1, 1900, balance unexpended	$9,481.62
July 1, 1901, balance unexpended	9,481.62

(See Appendix D 15.)

16. Harbor of refuge at Block Island, Rhode Island.—This island is about 14 miles east of the eastern end of Long Island, and about 10 miles distant from the nearest point of the mainland.

The object of the improvement is to furnish a harbor of refuge for medium draft vessels engaged in foreign and coastwise commerce.

Before construction of the present harbor, Block Island had no harbor which afforded protection for decked vessels.

Between 1870 and 1876, $285,000 was appropriated for a breakwater for a harbor for medium draft vessels, this work being completed in 1878. Between 1880 and 1882, $25,000 was appropriated for dredging an inner basin and the protection of the shore next the breakwater, this work being completed in 1884. In 1884, $15,000 was appropriated for additions to the old breakwater, this money being so spent and work completed in 1884-85.

The project of 1884, as modified in 1888, provided for the construction of a harbor of refuge on the eastern side of the island, consisting of an enlarged inner harbor (or basin), 800 feet square, for small vessels and an exterior harbor for larger ones, at a total cost estimated in 1888 at $75,000. This project was practically completed in 1893.

The existing project, that of 1895, based on the report of the survey ordered in the river and harbor act of August 18, 1894 (see House Doc. No. 83, Fifty-fourth Congress, first session, and page 674, Annual Report of the Chief of Engineers for 1896), provides for raising the entire breakwater to proper height and stopping sand leaks between certain points and dredging the main inner harbor to a depth of 10 feet, at an estimated cost of $83,985.

At the adoption of the present project this harbor was neither large enough nor well enough protected for the proper harborage of the craft seeking refuge at this place during storms and bad weather.

The sum of $412,576.11 had been expended on this work up to June 30, 1900. Under the project of 1888 the gap in the old breakwater had been filled up so as to make the breakwater of 1,900 feet total length; the sea walls of the inner harbor had been completed except as to stone fender piers at the entrance; wooden fender piers had been built for present uses; the worst rocks and bowlders had been removed from the new inner harbor; the shoal west of the breakwater had been dredged to a depth of 9 feet from the steamboat wharf to within 100 feet of the north wall, and the entrance to the inner harbor, which had shoaled up from the drift of sand through the main breakwater, had been partially dredged to a depth of 12 feet and redredged to 10 feet depth several times. The north wall of the enlarged inner harbor had been strengthened and repaired. About $14,000 of the above amount had been expended in maintaining the channel at the entrance to the inner harbor and repairing and strengthening the harbor walls.

No work was in progress during the past fiscal year.

It is estimated that $2,500 will be required each year, until the main breakwater is made sand tight, to dredge the entrance to the inner harbor. The cost of necessary repairs to the main breakwater is included in the estimate for the existing project.

Additional funds, if provided, will be applied to repairing the main breakwater, making it sand tight in certain parts, and to dredging the inner harbor.

In 1900 the commerce amounted to about 63,281 tons, an increase over previous years.

July 1, 1900, balance unexpended	$3,923.89
June 30, 1901, amount expended during fiscal year	2,654.97
July 1, 1901, balance unexpended	1,268.92
July 1, 1901, outstanding liabilities	30.00
July 1, 1901, balance available	1,238.92
Amount (estimated) required for completion of existing project	78,985.00
Amount that can be profitably expended in fiscal year ending June 30, 1903, in addition to the balance available July 1, 1901	10,000.00

Submitted in compliance with requirements of sundry civil act of June 4, 1897.

(See Appendix D 16.)

17. *Great Salt Pond, Block Island, Rhode Island.*—The Great Salt Pond is located about the center of Block Island and contains an anchorage area of 150 acres for vessels drawing 18 feet and over. The work of converting the pond into a harbor of refuge by making a channel through the beach on the west, connecting it with deep water in the ocean, was started by the State of Rhode Island and the town of New Shoreham.

The channel, under the approved project of 1895, is to be 600 feet wide and to have a central depth of 25 feet for a width of 150 feet, sloping gradually to 12 feet in a width of 504 feet, the channel seaward to be protected on the south by a jetty extending to the 18-foot contour and on the north by a jetty about 500 feet long.

At the time work commenced under the General Government a channel of varying width and depth had been dredged with the money appropriated by the State and town, which would permit of 12-foot draft being carried in, although there were two 9-foot spots left in mid-channel. The south jetty had been built out 837 feet and a north jetty 250 feet long had also been built, but at a distance of 720 feet from the south jetty instead of 600 feet, as called for in the adopted project.

Up to June 30, 1900, $51,112.01 of the Congressional appropriations had been expended. The south jetty had been extended out to the 18-foot contour and at that date was undergoing repairs. The work of dredging an 18-foot channel 300 feet wide was in progress and a width of 175 feet had been completed. Under date of June 15, 1900, a modified project was approved, extending the south jetty 350 feet, building a north jetty 600 feet from it and about 1,200 feet long, and providing for a revetment of the banks where the channel passes through the beach, at a cost of $215,000 in addition to what has already been appropriated.

During the past fiscal year the 18-foot channel 300 feet wide was completed and one cut about 30 feet wide and 25 feet deep was made through the center.

About $2,500 has been expended in repairing the south jetty, and it is estimated that $5,000 in addition to this will be required for further repairs to the jetty. The funds for this are on hand.

There is at present a channel of 300 feet width and 18 feet depth at low water.

There remains to complete the existing project the construction of jetties as planned and dredging to secure the width and depths projected.

July 1, 1900, balance unexpended	$38,887.99
June 30, 1901, amount expended during fiscal year	33,634.75
July 1, 1901, balance unexpended	5,253.24
Amount (estimated) required for completion of existing project	215,000.00
Amount that can be profitably expended in fiscal year ending June 30, 1903, in addition to the balance unexpended July 1, 1901	10,000.00

Submitted in compliance with requirements of sundry civil act of June 4, 1897.

(See Appendix D 17.)

18. *Removing sunken vessels or craft obstructing or endangering navigation.*—Schooners *Laura Robinson*, *David Siner*, and *Electa Bailey*, and steamer *Ardanhu.*—The *Laura Robinson* was sunk in June, 1900, in 40 feet depth of water, in main channel, between the Shovelful and

Pollock Rip light-ships. The *David Siner* sank during December, 1900, in 4 fathoms of water at a point about 1¾ miles W.S.W. from Pollock Rip light-ship. The *Electa Bailey* stranded on Hardings Beach, Chatham Mass. The British steamer *Ardanhu* was sunk by collision in Vineyard Sound, near Robinsons Hole, January 23, 1900.

The wrecks, excepting the *Electa Bailey*, were completely destroyed during the year, at a cost to the United States of $5,522.66.

(See Appendix D 18.)

EXAMINATIONS AND SURVEYS MADE IN COMPLIANCE WITH EMERGENCY RIVER AND HARBOR ACT APPROVED JUNE 6, 1900.

Preliminary examinations and surveys of the following localities were made by the local officers, and reports thereon submitted through the division engineer:

1. Preliminary examination and survey of Sakonnet River, Rhode Island, to ascertain the advisability and cost of removing rocks which are an obstruction to navigation.—Report dated July 11, 1900, on preliminary examination, was submitted by Maj. D. W. Lockwood, Corps of Engineers, and report dated November 19, 1900, on survey, by Maj. George W. Goethals, Corps of Engineers. Major Goethals presented a plan for improvement at an estimated cost of $10,000. The reports were transmitted to Congress and printed in House Doc. No. 99, Fifty-sixth Congress, second session. (See also Appendix D 19.)

2. Preliminary examination of Pawtucket River, Rhode Island, with a view to securing a channel 200 feet wide and 18 feet deep from the mouth of the river at Providence to the lower wharves in the city of Pawtucket.—Major Lockwood submitted report July 5, 1900. The improvement of this locality in the manner indicated is not deemed advisable. The report was transmitted to Congress and printed in House Doc. No. 89, Fifty-sixth Congress, second session. (See also Appendix D 20.)

3. Preliminary examination and survey of Ohio Reef (Ledge) located in the east passage of Narragansett Bay, Rhode Island, with a view to determining the advisability of its removal.—Report on preliminary examination, dated July 5, 1900, was submitted by Major Lockwood, and report on survey, dated December 8, 1900, by Major Goethals. A plan for improvement at an estimated cost of $307,200 is presented. The reports were transmitted to Congress and printed in House Doc. No. 217, Fifty-sixth Congress, second session. (See also Appendix D 21.)

IMPROVEMENT OF RIVERS AND HARBORS IN CONNECTICUT, AND OF PAWCATUCK RIVER, RHODE ISLAND AND CONNECTICUT.

This district was in the charge of Maj. Smith S. Leach, Corps of Engineers, having under his immediate orders Lieut. Edward H. Schulz, Corps of Engineers. Division Engineer, Col. G. L. Gillespie, Corps of Engineers (now brigadier-general, Chief of Engineers, United States Army), to May 3, 1901, and Col. Chas. R. Suter, Corps of Engineers, since May 9, 1901.

1. Pawcatuck River, Rhode Island and Connecticut.—The navigable part of the Pawcatuck River extends 5 miles from the town of Westerly, R. I., to its outlet in Little Narragansett Bay; thence the navigable channel extends through Little Narragansett Bay 2½ miles to Stonington outer harbor, which forms the approach to the bay and river. Little Narragansett Bay is about 1¼ miles wide and 2¼ miles long, and is separated from the ocean by a sand beach. Its outlet into Stonington Harbor is about three-fifths of a mile wide. Pawcatuck River has a width of about one-third of a mile at its mouth, and diminishes to 200 feet at Westerly; its average width is 1,000 feet.

Before improvement the channel of the river was crooked and obstructed by numerous shoals, on some of which there was but 1½ feet at mean low water, and 4½ feet was the greatest depth that could be carried across the shoals of the bay. The mean tidal oscillation is 2.6 feet at the mouth of the river and 2.3 feet at Westerly. (For maps see Annual Report of the Chief of Engineers for 1879, p. 314; for 1885, p. 624, and House Doc. No. 62, Fifty-fourth Congress, first session.)

The present approved project, that of 1895, based on the report of the survey ordered in the river and harbor act of August 18, 1894, provides for a channel of 10 feet depth at mean low water from Stonington to Westerly, with a width of 200 feet from Stonington, Conn., to Avondale, R. I., a distance of about 4 miles; a width of 100 feet from Avondale to the lower wharves of Westerly, a distance of about 3 miles, and a width of 40 feet between the upper and lower wharves at Westerly, a distance of about one-half mile, at a total estimated cost of $200,361.60.

The sum of $163,905.85 had been expended up to June 30, 1900, by which the 8-foot channel had been completed under previous projects from Stonington to Westerly, and under the new 10-foot project the 40-foot channel opposite the wharves at Westerly and 1,800 linear feet of the 100-foot channel below the wharves had been completed to the projected depth of 10 feet by the removal of ledge rock and bowlders and by dredging.

Owing to lack of funds nothing in furtherance of the project was done during the fiscal year. The estimate submitted for fiscal year ending June 30, 1903, contemplates extending the channel downstream.

No work having been done at the lower end under the new project, 7 feet at mean low water was the maximum draft that could be carried from Stonington to Westerly at the close of work, and it is believed that the channel across Little Narragansett Bay has shoaled in places to a depth of 6½ feet since that time.

The effects of the improvement are the use of a larger class of vessels than formerly, larger cargoes, and cheaper freights on them.

Table of comparative statistics.

Date.	Vessels of all kinds, each arrival and departure together being counted as one.			Freight tonnage.		
	No.	Draft.	Tonnage.	Received and shipped.	Compared with preceding report.	
					Increase.	Decrease.
		Feet.		*Tons.*	*Tons.*	*Tons.*
1890	1,235	2 to 8	3 to 300	28,667		
1893	2,045	5 to 10	3 to 300	35,968	7,301	
1894	1,774	5 to 10	3 to 300	52,805	16,837	
1895	1,824	2 to 10	3 to 800	43,671		9,134
1896	5,009	2 to 10	3 to 800	39,086		4,585
1897	5,008	2 to 10	3 to 800	46,024	6,938	
1898	4,469	2 to 8	3 to 200	131,602	85,578	
1899	4,405	2 to 8	3 to 200	66,742		64,860
1900	4,290	2 to 8	3 to 200	57,530		9,212

The reported value of this commerce for 1900 was $344,813.

RIVER AND HARBOR IMPROVEMENTS. 177

July 1, 1900, balance unexpended	·$94.16
June 30, 1901, amount expended during fiscal year	1.38
July 1, 1901, balance unexpended	92.78

Amount (estimated) required for completion of existing project	170,361.60
Amount that can be profitably expended in fiscal year ending June 30, 1903, in addition to the balance unexpended July 1, 1901	9,000.00
Submitted in compliance with requirements of sundry civil act of June 4, 1897.	

(See Appendix E 1.)

2. Harbor of refuge at Stonington, Conn.—Stonington Harbor lies on the north side of the eastern entrance from the ocean into Long Island Sound, and its breakwaters are for the purpose of making a harbor of refuge for vessels entering and leaving this entrance. Stonington Harbor originally was an open bay, unprotected from southerly storms and obstructed by a shoal having a low-water depth of about 6 feet at the shoalest part. The mean tidal oscillation is 2.7 feet. (For maps see Annual Report of the Chief of Engineers for 1882, p. 598, p. 632 of 1884, p. 848 of 1893, and for further information p. 585 of 1881.)

The approved project of 1880 provides for the construction of an eastern breakwater as a protection to the outer harbor, this breakwater, about half a mile long, to extend from the vicinity of Bartletts Reef to the vicinity of the middle ground shoal, or until it gives sufficient protection to the harbor against southerly winds, all at a total cost (estimated in 1884) of from $143,000 to $191,000, according to length. This did not include the cost of a light-house foundation on the western end of the structure. The positions of the ends of this breakwater have not been definitely determined.

At the adoption of the present project, that of 1880, the outer harbor had no eastern breakwater.

To June 30, 1900, $148,283.99 had been expended on the present project, with its subsequent additions, completing 2,900 linear feet of the eastern breakwater, at a cost of $143,011.85, and under an addition to the project in 1884 a cut across Noyes Shoal, 160 feet wide and 17 feet deep at mean low water, had cost $4,187.22, and under an addition to the project in 1896 a dike or water break around Stonington Point had cost $3,352.77. The sum of $184,408.83 had been expended on previous projects, including the western breakwater and dredging at the entrance of the harbor, making the aggregate expended to that date under projects for Stonington Harbor $336,395.09. The deepening of the harbor has brought about a large increase in commerce, and the construction of breakwaters affords a harbor of refuge for vessels of all kinds in the inner and outer harbors, which is extensively used as such. The maximum draft that could be carried to the docks at time of last survey, in 1895, was the project depth of 12 feet at mean low water, and as far as known that depth still exists.

During the fiscal year a light was maintained on the unfinished breakwater. Nothing in furtherance of the project was done.

The breakwater is built to a point satisfying the conditions laid down in the original project drawn by the Board of Engineers in 1880, and the project is therefore completed. Arrangements have been made for the transfer of the lighting to the Light-House Board.

Table of comparative statistics.

Date.	Vessels of all kinds, each arrival and departure together being counted as one.			Freight tonnage.		
	No.	Draft.	Tonnage.	Received and shipped.	Compared with preceding report.	
					Increase.	Decrease.
		Feet.		*Tons.*	*Tons.*	*Tons.*
1891	6,300	2½ to 12	4 to 1,500	274,014		
1892	4,018	3 to 12	30 to 1,500	300,000	25,986	
1893	3,201	3 to 12	30 to 1,500	305,750	5,750	
1894	3,201	3 to 12	30 to 1,500	299,870		5,880
1895	3,950	3 to 12	20 to 1,500	322,814	22,944	
1896	4,265	2½ to 12	7 to 1,500	349,650	26,836	
1898	3,465	2½ to 12	25 to 1,500	345,500		4,150
1899	3,465	2½ to 12	25 to 1,500	489,000	143,500	

The estimated value of this commerce for 1899 is $84,984,125.

July 1, 1900, balance unexpended $573.79
June 30, 1901, amount expended during fiscal year 573.79

(See Appendix E 2.)

3. Mystic River, Connecticut.—This project was reported completed last year.

During the fiscal year the small balance remaining was applied to completing the pro rata of office and general expenses allotted to the work at the beginning of the year.

July 1, 1900, balance unexpended $246.85
June 30, 1901, amount expended during fiscal year 246.85

(See Appendix E 3.)

4. Thames River, Connecticut.—This river is a tidal stream formed by the confluence of two small streams at Norwich, Conn., which is the head of navigation, and extends thence to Long Island Sound, a distance of 15 miles. For 11 miles above its mouth the river has a natural channel of 13 to 80 feet depth, but for the upper 4 miles the available depth was originally but 6 feet at mean low water. The tidal oscillation is 3.1 feet at Norwich and 2.5 feet at the mouth. The lower stretch of the river forms the harbor of New London.

Shaws Cove, New London Harbor, is a cove on the west side of Thames River, about 2 miles above its mouth, and constitutes the southern water front of the business portion of the city of New London. It is separated from the river by the embankment and trestle of the New York, New Haven and Hartford Railroad, having a draw of 55 feet width. The natural depth in Shaws Cove was from 2½ to 8 feet at mean low water in a narrow and crooked channel bordered by flats. The latest published maps of the river will be found in the Annual Report of the Chief of Engineers for 1894, page 628, and of Shaws Cove, 1893, page 904. Harbor lines were established in Shaws Cove in 1893, and along the New London water front in 1899.

Under an appropriation made in 1836 a project was adopted for making a channel 14 feet deep at high water (11 feet at low water), by dredging and by building dikes, at an estimated cost of $72,650. Work was stopped in 1839 by exhaustion of appropriations before the project was completed.

The present project, adopted in 1866 and modified in 1876–82–88–92, consists in making and maintaining by dredging and a system of training walls a channel 200 feet wide from New London to Norwich, to be 16 feet deep at mean low water to Allyn Point, and thence to Norwich to be 14 feet deep, together with dredging in Shaws Cove, New London, to make a channel 100 feet wide and 12 feet deep, and an anchorage basin of the same depth and of about 7½ acres area. The estimated cost from the beginning is $457,600. The estimated cost of maintenance is, approximately, $8,000 per year.

Up to June 30, 1900, $402,505.57 had been expended under the present project. Three of the five proposed training walls had been completed and the fourth nearly so. The proposed river channel was completed to Allyn Point; thence to Norwich it had been made the full depth of 14 feet, with widths from 175 to 100 feet, and the larger part of the middle ground at Norwich had been removed. The 12-foot channel in Shaws Cove had been completed, and the anchorage basin had been nearly finished.

During the fiscal year ending June 30, 1901, the balance of funds available was applied to the project by the completion of the work left unfinished by the contractor. The work was done by the United States on open-market basis at prices which protect the Government from loss.

Further appropriations will be applied to maintenance and improvement by restoring project dimensions where impaired and to widening channels which have not yet been opened to full width.

Commerce at Norwich and Allyn Point consists mainly of coal, lumber, and other building materials, iron, and miscellaneous goods. The work done has reduced the cost of transportation by enabling freight to be brought in vessels of 14-feet draft instead of 8 feet. The river commerce of the present day could not have been carried without the increased depth.

Commerce in Shaws Cove consists mainly of lumber and coal. Fishing steamers and pleasure boats use the cove for wintering and for fitting out in the spring. The work done has added materially to the convenience of this navigation and has increased its amount.

Table of comparative statistics.

| Date. | Vessels of all kinds, each arrival and departure together being counted as one. ||| Freight tonnage. |||
| | No. | Draft. | Tonnage. | Received and shipped. | Compared with preceding report. ||
					Increase.	Decrease.
		Feet.		Tons.	Tons.	Tons.
1890	810	4 to 16	100 to 1,500	467,144		
1891	219	4 to 16	100 to 1,500	609,568	142,424	
1893	1,906	4 to 16	100 to 1,600	546,900		62,668
1894	1,217	4 to 16	100 to 1,600			
1896	1,844	5 to 19	100 to 1,900	424,945		121,955
1897	1,762	5 to 19	100 to 1,900	374,724		50,221
1898	2,431	5 to 19	100 to 1,900	459,588	84,864	
1899 a	1,655	5 to 21½	100 to 2,150	1,209,123		
1900	1,969	5 to 21½	100 to 2,150	1,224,490	15,367	

a This report includes all the commerce at and above New London except summer excursion steamers. No comparison between this and the previous reports is possible.

The reported value of this commerce for 1900 was $62,612,320.

July 1, 1900, balance unexpended	$5,994.43
June 30, 1901, amount expended during fiscal year	5,691.19
July 1, 1901, balance unexpended	303.24
Amount (estimated) required for completion of existing project	49,100.00
Amount that can be profitably expended in fiscal year ending June 30, 1903, for works of improvement and for maintenance, in addition to the balance unexpended July 1, 1901	15,000.00

Submitted in compliance with requirements of sundry civil act of June 4, 1897, and of section 7 of the river and harbor act of 1899.

(See Appendix E 4.)

5. *Connecticut River below Hartford, Conn.*—Before the beginning of improvements by the United States the available depth over Saybrook Bar, at the mouth of the river, was 7 feet at mean low water; thence to Hartford the available depth over the shoalest of the river bars was about 5 feet at low water, being generally at its minimum after the spring freshets, and increasing as the period of summer low water continued.

In 1873 a project was adopted for improving the channel at Saybrook Bar, at the mouth of the river, by dredging and by building three jetties at an estimated cost of $336,610. Two of the proposed jetties were completed in 1881, and the third was found to be unnecessary.

The present project, adopted in 1870, modified in 1887, provides for a channel from Long Island Sound to Hartford, Conn., to be 400 feet wide and 12 feet deep at mean low water across Saybrook Bar, and thence to Hartford to be 100 feet wide (or as nearly that as practicable) and 9 feet deep at extreme low water, or about 10 feet at ordinary summer low tide, the channels to be maintained by annual dredging in the river and by enlarging the Saybrook jetties and the Harford dike at an estimated cost—

For annual dredging $10,000
For permanent work, which includes the dredging at Saybrook Bar (estimated in 1889) 130,000

The maintenance of navigable channels by annual dredging has been held paramount in the project, and is the only work of improvement done upon this river since 1887, the available funds at no time having been sufficient for enlarging the dike or Saybrook jetties or for additional dredging at Saybrook Bar. The jetties and the channel between them are constantly deteriorating, and are now in a condition demanding attention.

The total amount expended by the United States for this improvement from 1836 to June 30, 1900, was $487,064.44.

On July 1, 1900, annual dredging was in progress to remove the shoals which had formed during the freshets of the preceding spring. Work ceased August 27, 1900, at which time a depth of 9 feet at extreme low water had been secured on all the bars. The annual dredging for the present season was begun as private work June 3, 1901, and is in progress at the close of the fiscal year. The annual dredging will usually be between May 20 and August 15.

Sketches of the Connecticut River from Hartford to Rocky Hill and of Saybrook Bar were printed in the Annual Report of the Chief of Engineers for 1885, page 636. The river from the Sound to Hartford is shown on Coast Survey charts 253, 254, 255, and 256.

Commerce consists mainly of coal, stone (shipped from Portland and vicinity), building materials, and miscellaneous freight.

The work done and being done has reduced freights on these articles materially, and without the improvements there could be little commerce on the river.

Any appropriation in excess of the estimated cost of annual dredging ($10,000) will be applied to repairs of the Saybrook jetties and the Hartford dike.

Table of comparative statistics.

Date.	Vessels of all kinds, each arrival and departure together being counted as one.			Freight tonnage.		
	No.	Draft.	Tonnage.	Received and shipped.	Compared with preceding report.	
					Increase.	Decrease.
		Feet.		*Tons.*	*Tons.*	*Tons.*
1890	......	7 to 12	100 to 600	1,095,000	......	......
1893	1,200	7 to 12	100 to 1,000	650,000	......	445,000
1894	1,180	7 to 12	100 to 1,000	560,000	......	90,000
1895	1,300	7 to 12	100 to 1,600	712,000	152,000	......
1896	1,300	6 to 12	100 to 1,600	772,000	60,000	......
1897	1,350	6 to 12	100 to 1,600	648,000	......	124,000
1898	1,350	6 to 12	100 to 1,600	665,000	17,000	......
1899	1,400	6 to 12	100 to 1,600	700,000	35,000	......
1900	1,400	6 to 12	100 to 1,600	700,000	......	......

The reported value of this commerce for 1900 was $47,000,000.
No new line of transportation was established during the year.

July 1, 1900, balance unexpended	$9,105.56
June 30, 1901, amount expended during fiscal year	8,779.16
July 1, 1901, balance unexpended	326.40
Amount (estimated) required for completion of existing project	110,000.00
Amount that can be profitably expended in fiscal year ending June 30, 1903, for works of improvement and for maintenance, in addition to the balance unexpended July 1, 1901	30,000.00
Submitted in compliance with requirements of sundry civil act of June 4, 1897, and of section 7 of the river and harbor act of 1899.	

(See Appendix E 5.)

6. *Harbor of refuge at Duck Island Harbor, Connecticut.*—Duck Island Harbor is a bay on the north shore of Long Island Sound. It is about 7 miles west of the mouth of the Connecticut River and midway between the harbors of New Haven and New London. The mean tidal oscillation is 3.8 feet.

The project for this improvement, adopted by the river and harbor act of 1890, provides for the construction of three riprap breakwaters of 3,000, 1,750, and 1,130 feet length, respectively, inclosing and sheltering an area of about 115 acres, with two ample entrances. The adopted grade is 6 feet above high water, with crown of 10 feet and slopes of 2 on 3 outside and 1 on 1 inside. The estimated aggregate cost is $463,540. For map see Annual Report of the Chief of Engineers for 1887, page 644.

To June 30, 1900, $113,906.40 had been expended, and 2,770 linear feet of the west breakwater had been built, extending westwardly from Duck Island to a low-water depth of 17 feet. No work in furtherance of the project was done during the past year from lack of funds. The breakwater was slightly damaged at its west end by the storm of December 4, 1900, and repairs were made at a cost of $202 under the allotment of $300 from the appropriation for emergencies in rivers and harbors in the act of June 6, 1900.

Future appropriations will be applied to the construction of the breakwater eastward from Duck Island.

The commerce to be benefited by this improvement is the passing commerce of Long Island Sound, which may find it convenient or necessary to seek shelter behind the breakwater during storms. Its value can not be estimated with any accuracy.

GENERAL IMPROVEMENT.

July 1, 1900, balance unexpended	$93.60
July 1, 1901, balance unexpended	93.60

⎧ Amount (estimated) required for completion of existing project	349,540.00
⎨ Amount that can be profitably expended in fiscal year ending June 30, 1903, in addition to the balance unexpended July 1, 1901	15,000.00
⎩ Submitted in compliance with requirements of sundry civil act of June 4, 1897.	

MAINTENANCE.

Amount allotted from appropriation contained in emergency river and harbor act approved June 6, 1900	$300.00
June 30, 1901, amount expended during fiscal year	202.00
April 22, 1901, amount deposited to credit of the Treasurer of the United States	98.00

(See Appendix E 6.)

7. *New Haven Harbor, Connecticut.*—New Haven Harbor is a bay in the north shore of Long Island Sound, extending about 4 miles inland and from 1 to 2 miles wide. The Mill and Quinnipiac rivers empty into the head of the harbor from the northeast. They are navigable for about 1 and 3 miles, respectively, above their mouths. The mean range of tides is 6.1 feet.

For maps see Annual Report of the Chief of Engineers for 1889, page 678; page 702 of report for 1896; and House Doc. No. 82, Fifty-fifth Congress, first session.

Harbor lines for New Haven Harbor were established by the Secretary of War November 17, 1894, and were slightly modified and amended by him March 2, 1895, May 20, 1895, and May 5, 1900.

The project, as adopted by Congress, provides for a main channel 20 feet deep at mean low water, 400 feet wide over the outer bar, and 300 feet thence to Tomlinson's bridge, with three anchorage basins of 20, 16, and 12 feet depth, respectively, at mean low water, to accommodate different classes of shipping.

At the beginning of the past fiscal year a continuing contract was in force for the completion of the project at 6 cents per cubic yard. The year's work was devoted to widening the main channel above Fort Hale Bar and to developing the 20-foot and 12-foot anchorage basins. During the year 653,766 yards was removed, making a total of 1,128,070 yards removed under this contract, which is about 34 per cent of the total estimated yardage. The net results of the past two years' work are a channel 20 or more feet deep extending from Long Island Sound to Tomlinson's bridge, 200 feet wide up to the 20-foot anchorage basin, where the width, including a partial development of this basin, becomes 600 feet; 120 feet wide thence alongside the 16-foot anchorage basin, where present depths outside the dredged channel are 16 to 18 feet; and 215 feet wide thence in front of the docks to the bridge, with an increase to about 400 feet in width at the bend opposite Long Wharf; in addition to which the 12-foot anchorage has been dredged over about one-third its area.

The total amount expended to June 30, 1900, was $350,033.51, of which $325,695.34 was expended on prior projects and $24,338.17 on the present one. It is proposed to apply future appropriations to completion of the project by widening the channel and basins already begun.

On June 30, 1901, a maximum draft of 20 feet at mean low water could be carried from Long Island Sound to Tomlinson's bridge, which is the upper limit of the approved project.

The commerce of New Haven consists mainly of coal, iron, lumber, and miscellaneous freights. The increased depth resulting from the improvement has facilitated the transportation of these freights and lessened the delay for tides. A large part of the present commerce could not have been carried on without the improved channel.

Table of comparative statistics.

Date.	Vessels of all kinds, each arrival and departure together being counted as one.			Freight tonnage.		
	No.	Draft.	Tonnage.	Received and shipped.	Compared with preceding report.	
					Increase.	Decrease.
		Feet.		*Tons.*	*Tons.*	*Tons.*
1880	18,845	6	100 1,000	2,205		
1890	18,025	6	100 1,200	2,980	774,587	
1892	29,093	6	100 1,800	3,143	162,600	
1894	29,860	6	100 2,500	3,184,313	41,000	
1895	31,400	6	100 2,600	3,295,800	111,900	
1896	28,650	6	100 2,600	3,052,000		243,900
1899	28,693	6 to 18	100 to 2,000	3,440,700	388,700	
1900	28,693	6 to 28	100 to 2,000	3,472,200	31,500	

The reported value of this commerce for 1900 was $261,643,550.
No new line of transportation was established during the year.

July 1, 1900, balance unexpended	$75,966.49
Amount appropriated by sundry civil act approved March 3, 1901	50,000.00
	125,966.49
June 30, 1901, amount expended during fiscal year	43,709.29
July 1, 1901, balance unexpended	82,257.20
July 1, 1901, outstanding liabilities	9,971.20
July 1, 1901, balance available	72,286.00
July 1, 1901, amount covered by uncompleted contracts	129,535.80
Amount (estimated) required for completion of existing project	66,656.80
Amount that can be profitably expended in fiscal year ending June 30, 1903, in addition to the balance available July 1, 1901	67,000.00

Submitted in compliance with requirements of sundry civil act of June 4, 1897.

(See Appendix E 7.)

8. *Breakwaters at New Haven, Conn.*—The project for this work, adopted in 1879 and modified in 1890, consists of making a harbor of refuge at the entrance to New Haven Harbor by constructing four breakwaters: one extending from Southwest Ledge to Quixes Ledge; one 5,000 feet long, extending from a point 1,000 feet north, 54 degrees east, from Luddington Rock southwesterly across the rock; one about 4,200 feet long, extending northwesterly from a point 6,000 feet south, 54 degrees west, from Luddington Rock; and one about 1,200 feet long, extending southwesterly from Morgan Point on the east side of the harbor entrance. The estimated cost of the whole work from the beginning, in 1879, was $2,151,134.

The anchorage outside of the bar which will be sheltered by this breakwater exceeds 2,000 acres, and has depths of 9 to 26 feet at mean low water.

A sketch of New Haven Harbor, showing the location of the breakwaters as contemplated under the existing project, was printed in the Annual Report of the Chief of Engineers for 1889, page 678, and the last printed sketch may be found in annual report for 1896, page 702.

Up to June 30, 1900, the breakwater from Southwest Ledge to Quixes Ledge had been completed, the Luddington Rock breakwater had been made 4,500 feet long, and 1,490 feet of the west breakwater had been built. The total expenditure to this date had been $833,499.14. The balance available, with future appropriations, will be applied to extension of the west breakwater at its western extremity and in repair of any settlement which may have occurred in the part last built.

A light was maintained on the west breakwater.

The commerce benefited by this work is the passing commerce of Long Island Sound. During 1895, 151,356 vessels were observed passing the breakwaters, and 3,925 vessels were observed at anchor in the mouth of the harbor, where they were partly under their shelter.

No estimate of the value of this commerce can be made.

July 1, 1900, balance unexpended	$1,500.86
June 30, 1901, amount expended during fiscal year	240.00
July 1, 1901, balance unexpended	1,260.86
Amount (estimated) required for completion of existing project	1,316,134.00
Amount that can be profitably expended in fiscal year ending June 30, 1903, in addition to the balance unexpended July 1, 1901	50,000.00

Submitted in compliance with requirements of sundry civil act of June 4, 1897.

(See Appendix E 8.)

9. *Housatonic River, Connecticut.*—The Housatonic is a long, shallow river running southward through Massachusetts and Connecticut, emptying into Long Island Sound just east of Stratford Point, about 15 miles southwest from New Haven. At Derby, 13 miles above its mouth, it receives the discharge of the Naugatuck, a small, rapid river. This point, which has been regarded as the head of navigation, is nearly at the head of tide water. About a mile above there is a dam across the Housatonic River furnishing large water power. For at least 5 miles below Derby the water is always fresh.

The original depth on the worst bars in the river (six in number) was from 3.5 to 4.5 feet at mean low water; there was also a bar across the river's mouth with about 4 feet low-water depth. The mean rise of tide at Derby is 4.2 feet; at the mouth of the river it is about 6.2 feet.

In 1887 the estimates of cost were revised and the project modified, reducing the width of channel in the river to 100 feet and proposing a riprap breakwater to be built to half tide for the first 3,250 feet from shore, and thence for about 2,500 feet farther to be built to 6 feet above high water, at an estimated cost of $202,000. The reasons for this were presented in Senate Ex. Doc. No. 103, Fiftieth Congress, first session, and in the Annual Report of the Chief of Engineers for 1888, page 554. This modification of the project was adopted under the river and harbor act of 1888. In 1893 the project was further modified to provide for building a small dike below Stratford to reduce the amount of dredging required.

RIVER AND HARBOR IMPROVEMENTS.

The present project for improvement, adopted in 1871, with modifications in 1887 and 1893, consists in making and maintaining a channel 7 feet deep at mean low water from Long Island Sound to the head of navigation, about 13 miles, to be 100 feet wide in the river and 200 feet wide over the bar at the mouth, by dredging, removing Drews Rock, building a jetty at Sow and Pigs Reef and a small dike at the bend below Stratford, and protecting the channel at the mouth of the river by a breakwater about 5,750 feet long. The estimated cost, from the beginning in 1871, is $275,500.

A survey called for in the river and harbor act of June 3, 1896, was made, and a report and revised project submitted March 16, 1897. The report is published in House Doc. No. 16, Fifty-fifth Congress, first session, and in the Annual Report of the Chief of Engineers for 1897, page 979.

For maps of the whole navigable part of the river, see Annual Report of the Chief of Engineers for 1882, page 616, and House Doc. No. 16, Fifty-fifth Congress, first session; and of the mouth, Annual Report of the Chief of Engineers for 1886, page 642, and 1887, page 608.

July 1, 1900, the project had been completed, except a part of the Stratford dike and the dredging for maintenance.

During the fiscal year ending June 30, 1901, a contract made prior to its beginning was executed, and the various shoal crossings were restored to substantially the projected dimensions by dredging. Near the upper end the depths prevailing were so near those required that work was not considered necessary.

The balance in hand is held until increased by future appropriations to a sufficient sum to build the Stratford dike.

Additional appropriations will be applied to the construction of the dike near Stratford and in dredging to restore projected dimensions.

The commerce consists mainly of coal, iron, building materials, oysters, raw materials for manufacturers, and miscellaneous freight.

The work done and being done has enabled vessels to enter the lower river in safety, instead of waiting for high tide in an exposed situation outside the mouth of the river, and a large part of the commerce could not have been carried on without the improved channel.

Table of comparative statistics.

Date.	Vessels of all kinds, each arrival and departure together being counted as one.			Freight tonnage.		
	No.	Draft.	Tonnage.	Received and shipped.	Compared with preceding report.	
					Increase.	Decrease.
		Feet.		*Tons.*	*Tons.*	*Tons.*
1890 a	15,124	1 to 8	1 to 300	138,800		
1892 a	12,215	1 to 8	1 to 400	202,325	63,525	
1893 a	12,381	1 to 8	1 to 450	159,830		42,495
1895	1,260	2 to 8	3 to 450	79,647		80,183
1897	1,383	2 to 8	3 to 450	83,200	3,553	
1898 b	650	2 to 8	3 to 450	77,000		6,200
1899 b		2 to 8	3 to 450	64,712		12,288
1900	2,243	2 to 8¼	3 to 450	249,185	c 165,985	

a Includes oyster industry at mouth of river.
b Traffic to Derby and Shelton only.
c Compared with report for 1897.

The reported value of this commerce for 1900 was $1,553,020.

July 1, 1900, balance unexpended $15,911.33
June 30, 1901, amount expended during fiscal year 6,668.32

July 1, 1901, balance unexpended 9,243.01

Amount (estimated) required for completion of existing project 47,000.00
Amount that can be profitably expended in fiscal year ending June 30, 1903, for works of improvement and for maintenance, in addition to the balance unexpended July 1, 1901................................... 20,000.00
Submitted in compliance with requirements of sundry civil act of June 4, 1897, and of section 7 of the river and harbor act of 1899.

(See Appendix E 9.)

10. Bridgeport Harbor, Connecticut.—This harbor extends nearly 3 miles inland from the north shore of Long Island Sound, its width of about a mile at the mouth decreasing to 200 feet between the opposite wharves at its upper end. The channel in every part of the harbor is comparatively narrow, and is crossed by four drawbridges. Before the first work was done by the United States the depth over the bars near the harbor's mouth was 5 feet at low water, and above the bridges from 2 to 5 feet. The mean rise of tide is 6½ feet.

In 1836 Congress appropriated $10,000 for improving this harbor, and again a like amount in 1852. These sums were expended in dredging near the mouth of the harbor, making channels 60 to 100 feet wide and 8 feet deep or more at low tide. The depths made did not prove permanent. Under acts of Congress of June 23, 1866, and July 11, 1870, surveys or examinations of the harbor were made, and the report upon the latter examination proposed a plan for improvement by dredging a channel 100 feet wide and 12 feet deep at extreme low water, and protecting the outer channels by a breakwater extending about 3,000 feet from Long Beach, on the east side of the harbor entrance, all at an estimated cost of $124,000. This project was adopted in 1871, when an appropriation was made for beginning work upon it.

In 1875 the dimensions of the proposed channel were modified to make it 12 feet deep at mean low water and from 200 to 300 feet wide up to the lower or Stratford Avenue Bridge. This was accomplished in 1882, and then the project was again modified to include widening the channel between the inner beacon and the Naugatuck dock, a distance of 3,800 feet, to prevent overcrowding the main channel by vessels entering for shelter, at an estimated cost of $60,000. This work has been nearly completed.

In compliance with the terms of the river and harbor acts of 1878 and 1888, the project was extended to include a channel 100 feet wide and 9 feet deep to the head of navigation at Berkshire Mills, and again, under the terms of the river and harbor act of 1890, to include a breakwater from The Tongue to the innner beacon. The river and harbor act of 1894 also authorized the expenditure of the appropriation made for deepening the channel at the outer bar, and the project was extended to provide for 15 feet depth at that point.

Under the authority of the river and harbor act of 1894, a survey of the harbor was made and the report printed in the Annual Report of the Chief of Engineers for 1896, pages 803–805, and also in House Doc. No. 61, Fifty-fourth Congress, first session, submitted estimates for extending the 15-foot channel to the lower bridge, making it 300 feet wide up to the inner beacon and 200 feet wide above that beacon, which, with the unfinished work of the then existing project, was estimated to cost $90,000.

The river and harbor act of June 3, 1896, appropriated $28,000 for continuing the improvement in accordance with the modified project, $10,000 of which "shall be expended upon Yellow Mill Pond for constructing a channel 12 feet deep and 200 feet wide from the main channel to the causeway, conditioned upon the construction by the city of Bridgeport of a drawbridge at the causeway upon plans approved by the Secretary of War."

In the act of March 3, 1899, Congress adopted a further modified project for Bridgeport Harbor, embracing the channels previously known as Bridgeport Harbor, Johnsons Creek, and Black Rock Harbor, all of which are avenues of Bridgeport commerce.

The project provides for—

First. The main channel 18 feet deep at mean low water, 300 feet wide from the outer bar to the inner beacon, thence 200 feet wide to the lower or Stratford Avenue Bridge.

Second. Anchorage for deep draft, 18 feet at mean low water, 500 feet wide, and 2,000 feet long adjacent to the main channel on the west and immediately above the inner beacon; for light draft, 12 feet deep at mean low water, 500 feet wide, and 1,500 feet long adjacent to the main channel on the west between the 18-foot anchorage and Naugatuck wharf, and of the same depth at mean low water adjacent to the main channel on the east between the steel works point and the lower bridge extending to the harbor line.

Third. Pequonnock River channel from the lower bridge to the head of navigation, about 1 mile, 12 feet deep at mean low water and 100 feet wide.

Fourth. Yellow Mill channel, from the main channel to the head of Yellow Mill Cove, about 1 mile, 12 feet deep at mean low water and 100 feet wide.

Fifth. Johnsons River channel, from the main channel to the head of navigation, about three-fourths of a mile, 9 feet deep at mean low water and 100 feet wide.

Sixth. Black Rock channel, from the head of Black Rock Harbor to the junction of Cedar and Burr creeks, thence up each of these creeks to the head of navigation, with lengths, respectively, of 1¼ miles and one-half mile, 9 feet deep at mean low water and 100 feet wide.

Seventh. The repair and maintenance of the outer and inner breakwaters of the main channel and the one connecting Fayerweather Island with the mainland as now built, and the construction and maintenance of shore protection on Fayerweather Island to check the shifting of the beach.

An appropriation of $50,000 was made in the act cited and a continuing contract authorized.

Harbor lines for this harbor were established by the Secretary of War July 1, 1893, and modified September 19, 1898.

The last sketch of Bridgeport Harbor in the Annual Report of the Chief of Engineers was printed in the report for 1893, page 940, and a complete map was published in House Doc. No. 61, Fifty-fourth Congress, first session.

The amount expended to June 30, 1900, was $297,848.50, and at that date the channel, 12 feet deep at mean low water at the entrance, was 200 feet wide for a length of about 1,300 feet, thence to the inner beacon, 3,100 feet, the 12-foot channel was about 300 feet wide, and thence to Naugatuck dock, 3,800 feet, it was 770 feet wide. From that dock to the lower or Stratford Avenue Bridge, 2,000 feet, it had shoaled so that the depth was from 10 to 11 feet. Within the limits of the 12-foot channel a part of the 15-foot channel had been dredged, which extends from the entrance to the inner beacon, a distance of 1 mile, and is 220 feet in width. Above the lower bridge the channel, dredged 9 feet deep and 60 to 100 feet wide, was still nearly of that depth and width.

A channel 12 feet deep at mean low water and 100 feet wide had been dredged from the main channel to Yellow Mill Bridge.

The breakwater at Long Beach, built in 1871-1873, had settled somewhat and, while still adequate for the protection of the channels contemplated by the earlier projects, required some repairs and extension to secure the desired protection for the broader and deeper channels of the modified project.

The breakwater from The Tongue to the inner beacon had been built to its full projected length with reduced cross section. It required some enlargement to make it permanent.

At the beginning of the fiscal year a continuing contract was in force for completing the project at 5 cents per cubic yard for dredging and $2 per ton for riprap, provided the work was executed in accordance with certain limitations as to rate of progress.

Work under this contract was begun July 9, 1900, and during the fiscal year ending June 30, 1901, there had been dredged 458,241 yards and there had been delivered and placed 8,781 tons of stone.

The dredging was done mostly in the main channel to obtain 18 feet at mean low water below the lower bridge, and in the Pequonnock River channel to obtain 12 feet at mean low water above the bridge. The 12-foot anchorage at the lower bridge was completed, and the Johnsons River channel extended about 700 feet above Pleasure Island wharf. The stonework was applied to repairing the east breakwater and extending it 380 feet and to constructing four jetties on the west shore of Fayerweather Island. The maximum draft of water that can be carried through the improved channels is about 13 feet to the lower bridge and 12 feet thence to within about 500 feet of the upper end.

The commerce of this harbor consists of coal, iron, building materials, and general merchandise. The improvement already made has made it possible to use larger vessels, without which the present commerce of the harbor could not be carried on.

Table of comparative statistics.

Date.	Vessels of all kinds, each arrival and departure together being counted as one.			Freight tonnage.		
	No.	Draft.	Tonnage.	Received and shipped.	Compared with preceding report.	
					Increase.	Decrease.
		Feet.		*Tons.*	*Tons.*	*Tons.*
1890	24,273	6 to 18	100 to 1,000	1,314,157	a 297,000	....
1892	24,223	6 to 18	100 to 1,000	1,324,190	10,033	....
1894	18,572	6 to 18	50 to 1,250	968,659	....	355,531
1895	19,223	6 to 18	50 to 1,250	1,045,769	77,110	....
1896	18,723	6 to 18	50 to 1,250	1,030,451	....	15,318
1897	18,564	12 to 18	100 to 1,250	1,081,973	51,522	....
1898	18,770	12 to 18	100 to 1,250	1,196,563	114,590	....
1899	15,991	12 to 18	100 to 1,250	1,014,564	....	181,999
1900	17,462	12 to 18	100 to 1,250	1,163,960	149,396	....

a Over 1889.

The reported value of this commerce for 1900 was $17,310,430.

July 1, 1900, balance unexpended $100,151.50
Amount appropriated by sundry civil act approved March 3, 1901 .... 50,000.00

150,151.50
June 30, 1901, amount expended during fiscal year 36,300.87

July 1, 1901, balance unexpended....................................... 113,850.63
July 1, 1901, outstanding liabilities..................................... 3,754.59

July 1, 1901, balance available 110,096.04

July 1, 1901, amount covered by uncompleted contracts................. 104,090.25

(See Appendix E 10.)

11. *Saugatuck River and Westport Harbor, Connecticut.*—Saugatuck River is a tidal stream, the navigable part of it extending inland about 4½ miles by course of channel from Long Island Sound to Westport, Conn. It has a natural depth of 5 feet at mean low water, in a rather narrow, crooked channel up to the railroad bridge at Saugatuck, about 3 miles from the Sound; thence the depth, before improvement, decreased gradually until at Westport it was less than 1 foot. The channel was somewhat obstructed by rocks in its upper part.

For nearly 2 miles below Westport the stream is from 200 to 1,200 feet wide; below this it expands into a rather broad inner bay, with a narrow channel following the west, south, and east shores, and then turning abruptly to the southeast and passing to the Sound between Cedar Point on the north and Cockenoes Island on the south. On the south side of the inner bay lies Great Marsh, which is connected with Cockenoes Island by a broad sand flat, nearly bare at low tide; and east of the island a reef of bowlders extends eastward 1½ miles, so that the only entrance to the harbor at low tide is to the eastward of this reef.

The navigable part of the river is crossed by three bridges, all having draws of sufficient size for the commerce of the stream.

The mean rise of tide is about 7 feet.

Improvements of this locality have been made by the United States under the several titles of Saugatuck Harbor, Cedar Point, Westport Harbor, and Saugatuck River.

In 1826 Congress appropriated $400 for a survey of the river and harbor of Saugatuck. In the report of the survey a project was submitted for deepening the channel near Westport, removing two rocks in the river, building a breakwater on Cedar Point, and cutting a canal through Great Marsh, at a total estimated cost of $6,128.65. The project was completed nearly as designed in 1840. The breakwater at Cedar Point was made about 390 feet long, the top being 4 feet above high water and 10 feet wide, and the canal was excavated 1,350 feet long, 44 feet wide at the bottom, and 4 feet deep, and part of the east side was protected by a dry wall. The amount appropriated for and expended upon this project was $14,044.

Appropriations made in 1867 and 1870, $2,500 each, were applied to surveys and to repairing and extending the breakwater at Cedar Point.

Under the river and harbor act of 1882 a survey of the river was made, but no project for improvement was adopted.

A preliminary examination of Saugatuck River was ordered by the river and harbor act of 1890. A project was adopted under the appropriation made in 1892 for beginning work, and it consisted in making a channel 4 feet deep at mean low water and 60 feet wide up to the village of Westport, at an estimated cost of $10,000. This work was completed in 1896.

The river and harbor act of 1894 ordered a survey of Westport Harbor, which was made. The report of this survey is printed in the Annual Report of the Chief of Engineers for 1896, page 806. It is also printed with map in House Doc. No. 67, Fifty-fourth Congress, first session. It proposed a further improvement to provide for repairing the Cedar Point breakwater, removing a ledge opposite Stony Point, or dredging around it, and removing bowlders from the channel, at a total estimated cost of $8,000. Under the terms of the river and harbor act of 1896, appropriating $3,000 for improving Westport Harbor, Connecticut, the project of 1892 was extended to include this work, and the estimated cost was in consequence increased to $18,000.

A sketch of this river and harbor is printed in the Annual Report of the Chief of Engineers for 1894, page 670.

The total amount expended on this improvement up to the close of the fiscal year ending June 30, 1900, was $31,906.10, at which date the 4-foot channel had been completed to Westport, the head of navigation, with width generally of 60 feet.

The Cedar Point breakwater, repaired and extended in 1897, was in good condition. No work was done during the past fiscal year, from lack of sufficient funds.

Additional appropriations will be applied to further removal of bowlders from the channel and restoration of channel dimensions where necessary.

The commerce consists of coal, manufactured goods, farm produce, and miscellaneous articles. The improvements made have rendered navigation of the river practicable at less than full high water.

Table of comparative statistics.

Date.	Vessels of all kinds, each arrival and departure together being counted as one.			Freight tonnage.	
	No.	Draft.	Tonnage.	Received and shipped.	Compared with preceding report.
					Increase. / Decrease.
		Feet.		Tons.	Tons. / Tons.
1893	322	6 to 11	100 to 300	44,400	
1894	320	6 to 8	100 to 250	59,700	15,300
1895		6 to 10½	100 to 300	28,940	80,760
1896	345	4 to 10½	50 to 300	33,507	4,567
1898	106	4 to 10½	50 to 300	22,550	10,957
1899	109	4 to 10½	50 to 300	20,500	2,050
1900	107	4 to 10½	50 to 300	18,700	1,800

The reported value of this commerce for 1900 was $76,900.
No new lines of transportation have been established during the year.

July 1, 1900, balance unexpended	$557.90
June 30, 1901, amount expended during fiscal year	11.20
July 1, 1901, balance unexpended	526.70

Amount (estimated) required for completion of existing project 5,000.00
Amount that can be profitably expended in fiscal year ending June 30, 1903, in addition to the balance unexpended July 1, 1901 .... 3,000.00
Submitted in compliance with requirements of sundry civil act of June 4, 1897.

(See Appendix E 11.)

12. Norwalk Harbor, Connecticut.—Norwalk Harbor or River is a tidal estuary, with a narrow channel extending about 3 miles north from Long Island Sound to the town of Norwalk. Above Norwalk the river is a small fresh-water stream. South Norwalk is on the west bank of the river 1¼ miles below Norwalk. At this point the river is crossed by two drawbridges, the lower one a highway bridge and the other (450 feet above) the bridge of the New York, New Haven and Hartford Railroad. The mean tidal range is 7.12 feet.

In 1867 a company was incorporated under the laws of the State of Connecticut for the improvement of the river. Little work was done, and when the improvement was begun by the United States the low-water depth to South Norwalk was 5 feet and to Norwalk but 1 foot.

By act of March 2, 1829, Congress appropriated $80 for making a survey of the harbor of Norwalk, Conn., with a view to its improvement. The survey was made, and estimates were submitted for making a channel either 10 or 12 feet deep at ordinary high tide, but no money was appropriated for the improvement.

The river and harbor act of 1871 ordered another survey, which was made in that year. The report, printed in Senate Ex. Doc. No. 23, Forty-second Congress, second session, and also in the Annual Report of the Chief of Engineers for 1872, page 900, proposed dredging a channel 6 feet deep and 100 feet wide from Long Island Sound to Norwalk, at an estimated cost of $34,000. This project was adopted under the river and harbor act of 1872. In 1880 the project was modified so as to increase the depth below South Norwalk to 8 feet at mean low water, and the estimate of cost was increased to $84,000, to include this modification and the dredging which had already been done for maintenance of channels. This project was considered completed in 1892.

Under the terms of the river and harbor act of 1894, appropriating $15,000 for continuing this improvement, a project was adopted for dredging and removing the shoal called Ferrys Point, on the west side of the channel, between the railroad docks and Jenning's wharf, making 6 feet depth at mean low water and, if funds should permit, for widening the bend at Keysers Island, near the harbor entrance, making a depth of 9 feet at mean low water, at a total estimated cost of $15,000.

A survey of Norwalk Harbor, ordered by the river and harbor act of 1894, was made, and the report, printed in House Doc. No. 50, Fifty-fourth Congress, first session, also in the Annual Report of the Chief of Engineers for 1896, page 813, contained estimates for an extension of the improvement to provide for a channel 10 feet deep and 150 feet wide to South Norwalk, and for widening two bends at the harbor entrance, at a cost of $62,000. This project was adopted by the river and harbor act of 1896, which appropriated money for beginning work under it, and the project of 1894, thus modified, consists in removing the shoal at Ferrys Point to a depth of 6 feet at mean low water, in making a channel to South Norwalk 150 feet wide and 10 feet deep at mean low water, and in widening the two bends at the harbor entrance at an estimated cost from the beginning, in 1894, of $77,000.

The maintenance of this channel, and of the existing channel above South Norwalk, is estimated to cost about $2,000 per year.

A sketch of Norwalk Harbor, Connecticut, was printed in the Annual

192 REPORT OF THE CHIEF OF ENGINEERS, U. S. ARMY.

Report of the Chief of Engineers for 1885, page 656, and a complete map of the harbor was published in House Doc. No. 50, Fifty-fourth Congress, first session.

The amount expended on this improvement to the close of the fiscal year ending June 30, 1900, was $109,830.25, and on that date a practicable channel 8 feet deep at mean low water extended from Long Island Sound to the railroad bridge at South Norwalk, and a channel 6 feet deep at mean low water from the railroad bridge to the docks at Norwalk. The present project depth of 10 feet at mean low water is not available, because work under this project has covered a part of the channel only.

No examination has been made since the close of work in August, 1899, and, no reports to the contrary having been received, it is believed that the depths of 8 feet below, and 6 feet above, the railroad bridge at South Norwalk are still unimpaired.

Future appropriations will be expended in developing the channels of South Norwalk Harbor and for maintenance.

The commerce of this harbor consists mainly of coal, lumber, oysters, and miscellaneous freights. The increased depth resulting from the improvements has been of benefit to all classes of vessels, and to much of the present commerce is absolutely indispensable.

Table of comparative statistics.

Date.	Vessels of all kinds, each arrival and departure together being counted as one.			Freight tonnage.		
	No.	Draft.	Tonnage.	Received and shipped.	Compared with preceding report.	
					Increase.	Decrease.
		Feet.		*Tons.*	*Tons.*	*Tons.*
1886	2,870	9 to 10	....	438,600	....	....
1890	1,520	7 to 12	100 to 500	312,500	....	126,100
1891	2,126	7 to 12	100 to 500	368,500	56,000	....
1894	....	....	....	136,800	....	231,700
1895	861	4 to 18	50 to 600	201,095	64,295	....
1896 a	993	4 to 14	50 to 600	146,045	....	55,050
1899	1,019	4 to 14	50 to 600	164,755	18,710	....
1900	1,031	4 to 14	50 to 600	172,275	7,520	....

a Does not include trips made by 43 oyster steamers, with total tonnage of 2,505 gross tons.

The reported value of this commerce for 1900 was $6,686,475.
No new lines of transportation have been established during the year.

July 1, 1900, balance unexpended	$169.75
June 30, 1901, amount expended during fiscal year	5.50
July 1, 1901, balance unexpended	164.25
Amount (estimated) required for completion of existing project	50,000.00
Amount that can be profitably expended in fiscal year ending June 30, 1903, for works of improvement and for maintenance, in addition to the balance unexpended July 1, 1901	15,000.00

Submitted in compliance with requirements of sundry civil act of June 4, 1897, and of section 7 of the river and harbor act of 1899.

(See Appendix E 12.)

13. *Five-mile River Harbor, Connecticut.*—This harbor is an inlet on the north shore of Long Island Sound, about 2 miles west of the mouth of Norwalk Harbor, Connecticut. It is about 1 mile long and from 300 to 800 feet wide. About three-fourths of a mile above its mouth it runs bare at low tide. At the mouth the natural low-water

depth was 3 feet, increasing to 9 feet at a point 750 feet out into the Sound. The mean rise of the tide is about 7 feet.

Since 1848, Five-mile River has been largely engaged in oyster growing, and in this business now employs about 140 vessels, which, without the improvement, could only enter or leave the harbor at high tide. Consequently, during their busy season they would be obliged to lie up for the night at other and less convenient harbors.

By act of Congress approved August 5, 1886, a survey or examination of this harbor was ordered, which was reported on under date of December 7, 1886 (printed in the Annual Report of the Chief of Engineers for 1887, p. 639).

In this report a project for improvement was proposed which consisted in-dredging a channel 8 feet deep at mean low water, and 100 feet wide, to extend up the harbor and to be about 6,000 feet long. The project was adopted in 1888, when work under it was ordered by appropriation of $5,000, made by act of Congress of August 11, 1888.

Harbor lines were established for this harbor by the Secretary of War, January 26, 1892.

A sketch of Five-mile River Harbor was printed in the Annual Report of the Chief of Engineers for 1894, page 676.

At the completion of work under the last contract in June, 1899, the projected width of 100 feet and depth of 8 feet had been secured for a distance of about 1,900 feet up the harbor from the Sound, and 60 feet width and 8 feet depth above this for a distance of about 2,600 feet, and so far as known these dimensions remain practically unimpaired. Further dredging is necessary to complete the projected work.

The total amount expended on this improvement to June 30, 1900, was $22,441.59.

The commerce of the harbor consists mainly of coal and shellfish. The increased depth has rendered possible the general use of the harbor by boats engaged in this business.

Table of comparative statistics.

Date.	Vessels of all kinds, each arrival and departure together being counted as one.			Freight tonnage.		
	No.	Draft.	Tonnage.	Received and shipped.	Compared with preceding report.	
					Increase.	Decrease.
		Feet.		Tons.	Tons.	Tons.
1889		2 to 7½	5 to 150			
1891		1½ to 8	2 to 175	10,000		
1892		1½ to 8	2 to 100			
1894	789			11,298	1,298	
1895	789			11,298		
1897 a	8,506	3 to 8	40 to 104	17,160	5,862	
1900 a	10,514	3 to 8	40 to 104	32,600	15,440	

a Includes trips made by 40 small oyster boats.

The reported value of this commerce for 1900 was $436,200.

July 1, 1900, balance unexpended $58.41
July 1, 1901, balance unexpended 58.41

Amount (estimated) required for completion of existing project 22,500.00
Amount that can be profitably expended in fiscal year ending June 30, 1903, in addition to the balance unexpended July 1, 1901............. 5,000.00
Submitted in compliance with requirements of sundry civil act of June 4, 1897.

(See Appendix E 13.)

14. *Stamford Harbor, Connecticut.*—This harbor is on the north shore of Long Island Sound, about 6 miles east of the New York State line. It consists of a bay about a mile long and a mile broad, from the head of which two channels extend up nearly a mile toward the middle of the city. The West Branch, known as Mill River, is a small stream, dammed at Oliver Street Bridge, the head of the harbor. The original low-water depth for a mile below the bridge was from 1 to 3 feet in a crooked channel, and the 7-foot curve in the bay was about 7,500 feet below the bridge. All the wharves are in the upper half of this distance. The East Branch was originally a crooked stream running through salt marshes; it was straightened and deepened by private enterprise and was known as the "Canal." Though nominally under control of the corporation which deepened it, the East Branch has been for a long time practically, and recently has been formally, opened to public use. In 1892 it had an available depth of 6¼ feet at mean low water, with width of about 60 feet nearly to its head, which is about 1¼ miles above its junction with the West Branch.

The mean rise of tide is 7.4 feet.

A survey of Stamford Harbor, ordered by act of Congress of March 2, 1829, was made, and with the report estimates were submitted for dredging channels either 10 or 12 feet deep at mean high water. No work was done under this plan.

The river and harbor act of 1882 authorized a survey of the harbor, which was made the following year. The report proposed improvement by dredging a channel through the West Branch 80 feet wide and 5 feet deep at mean low water, at an estimated cost of $20,000. The project was adopted under the river and harbor act of 1886, which made appropriation for beginning the work, and in December, 1891, after $20,000 had been appropriated and expended, the project was reported completed. The channel of the West Branch had been made 5 feet deep to the head of the harbor, with 80 feet width, except in the upper 1,000 feet, where the width was from 50 to 70 feet.

The river and harbor act of 1890 ordered a survey of Stamford Harbor. The report upon the survey presented a plan for further improving the West Branch at an estimated cost of $95,000. Under the terms of the river and harbor act of 1892 this project was modified to include an improvement of the East Branch and was adopted as modified. The present approved project therefore consists in dredging in the West Branch to make a channel 150 feet wide and 7 feet deep at mean low water, with a basin between the harbor lines at the head of the harbor, and in the East Branch to make a channel 9 feet deep at mean low water, to be 100 feet wide for 8,535 feet, and thence to the head of the harbor, about 1,200 feet, to be 50 feet wide. The estimated cost from the beginning in 1892 is $123,500.

Harbor lines were established in the West Branch by the Secretary of War February 28, 1890, and in the East Branch December 13, 1899.

A sketch of the harbor was printed in the Annual Report of the Chief of Engineers for 1893, page 956.

The amount expended to the end of the fiscal year ending June 30, 1900, was $59,751.48, at which date the West Branch channel was completed to the harbor lines at the head. The East Branch had a channel 9 feet deep at mean low water, from 60 to 80 feet wide up to the steamboat dock, about 8,000 feet, and thence for 1,200 feet from 40 to 60 feet wide.

No work was done during the last fiscal year. The project was modified in connection with the establishment of harbor lines in the East Branch, so as to give increased width near the upper end. The estimate was not increased.

The commerce of this harbor consists mainly of coal, building materials, and unclassified freights. The improvements made have rendered access to the wharves much easier for the class of vessels used in this traffic.

Table of comparative statistics.

Date.	Vessels of all kinds, each arrival and departure together being counted as one.			Freight tonnage.		
	No.	Draft.	Tonnage.	Received and shipped.	Compared with preceding report.	
					Increase.	Decrease.
		Feet.		Tons.	Tons.	Tons.
1890	700	5 to 12	10 to 375	50,000	a 3,890	
1892	2,188	5 to 12½		154,607	104,607	
1893	2,364	5 to 13	40 to 612	233,339	78,732	
1894	2,075	5 to 15	40 to 542	199,964		33,375
1895	2,019	5 to 15	40 to 550	220,506	20,542	
1896	2,210	5 to 15	20 to 550	373,758	153,252	
1898	2,017	5 to 15	20 to 550	252,183		121,571
1899	2,034	5 to 15	20 to 550	257,687	5,504	
1900	2,041	5 to 15	20 to 550	266,878	9,191	

a Over 1889.

The reported value of this commerce for 1900 was $6,185,000.

July 1, 1900, balance unexpended	$1,248.52
June 30, 1901, amount expended during fiscal year	14.19
July 1, 1901, balance unexpended	1,234.33
July 1, 1901, outstanding liabilities	3.00
July 1, 1901, balance available	1,231.33
Amount (estimated) required for completion of existing project	82,500.00
Amount that can be profitably expended in fiscal year ending June 30, 1903, in addition to the balance available July 1, 1901	15,000.00

Submitted in compliance with requirements of sundry civil act of June 4, 1897.

(See Appendix E 14.)

15. Harbor at Coscob and Mianus River, Connecticut.—This harbor is a tidal inlet extending about 2 miles northwardly from Long Island Sound to the village of Mianus, at a point 4 miles east of the New York State line. It has a high-water width of from 800 to 2,000 feet, but the low-water channel is narrow and bounded by mud flats. At low tide there was in 1892, before the improvement of the harbor was begun, a natural depth of 7 feet or more, with width of about 200 feet for the first half mile, the depth above gradually decreasing to almost zero at the head of the harbor. About three-quarters of a mile below Mianus the stream is crossed by a drawbridge of the New York, New Haven and Hartford Railroad. The commerce of the harbor is practically confined to the supplies of the communities along its shores. At Coscob, above the railroad bridge, is a shipyard, where a considerable number of small boats are repaired and some built. At Riverside, below the bridge, are the houses and docks of the Riverside Yacht Club.

The mean rise of tide is about 7¼ feet.

Under authority of the river and harbor act of 1890, a survey of the harbor was made. The report on the survey, printed in the Annual Report of the Chief of Engineers for 1891, page 855, contains a plan and estimate for improvement by dredging to make a channel 6 feet deep at mean low water, with 150 feet width below the railroad bridge and 100 feet width above the bridge to Mianus, at an estimated cost of $36,000. This project was adopted under the river and harbor act of 1892, which made an appropriation for beginning work.

By act of August 18, 1894, Congress made appropriation for continuing the improvement, "including a survey of the lower part of the harbor, with a view of making a turning basin therein." The report upon this survey, printed in the Annual Report of the Chief of Engineers for 1895, page 881, presented plans for a turning basin just inside the harbor entrance, to be 7 feet deep at mean low water and 300 feet wide, to be made by widening the channel on the west side for a length of 2,000 feet, measured along the channel, and 1,500 feet at the west side of the basin. The estimated cost was $18,000.

This modification of the project was adopted under the terms of the river and harbor act of 1896, and the present project for this improvement consists in dredging to make a channel 6 feet deep at mean low water, to be 150 feet wide up to the railroad bridge, and thence to Mianus to be 100 feet wide, with a turning basin on the west side of the channel near the harbor entrance, 7 feet deep at mean low water, 300 feet wide, and extending 2,000 feet along the channel, at a total estimated cost of $54,000.

A sketch of Coscob Harbor and Mianus River was printed in the Annual Report of the Chief of Engineers for 1893, page 958, and one of the lower part of this harbor in the report for 1895, page 882.

The amount expended on this improvement to June 30, 1900, is $18,829.69, and to the same date the channel had been dredged 150 feet wide and 6 feet deep up to the railroad bridge, and of the same depth 100 feet wide for 1,600 feet above the bridge. One-half of the turning basin, 7 feet deep at mean low water, was also dredged.

At the close of the last dredging the depth in turning basin was 7 feet and in channel 6 feet, and no impairment of same has been reported since that time.

The commerce of this harbor is mainly coal, lumber, and miscellaneous products. The benefit to commerce consists only in a broader and deeper channel in the lower part of the harbor, the increased depth being not yet extended to the upper landings.

Table of comparative statistics.

Date.	Vessels of all kinds, each arrival and departure together being counted as one.			Freight tonnage.		
	No.	Draft.	Tonnage.	Received and shipped.	Compared with preceding report.	
					Increase.	Decrease.
		Feet.		*Tons.*	*Tons.*	*Tons.*
1890	3,732	2 to 9	3 to 80	46,900		
1894 a	342	4 to 8	25 to 100	51,600	4,700	
1897 a	424	4 to 8	25 to 100	61,500	9,900	
1898 b	36	4 to 8	25 to 100	25,000		36,500
1899	92	4 to 8	25 to 100	9,360		15,640
1900	99	4 to 8	25 to 100	9,900	540	

a The trips of 83 yachts which belong to the Riverside Yacht Club and anchor in this harbor are not included in the number of vessels given.
b Barges only; daily steam packet withdrawn.

The reported value of this commerce for 1900 was $153,000.

July 1, 1900, balance unexpended ... $170.31
July 1, 1901, balance unexpended ... 170.31

{ Amount (estimated) required for completion of existing project ... 35,000.00
Amount that can be profitably expended in fiscal year ending June 30, 1903, in addition to the balance unexpended July 1, 1901 ... 5,000.00
Submitted in compliance with requirements of sundry civil act of June 4, 1897. }

(See Appendix E 15.)

16. Greenwich Harbor, Connecticut.—Greenwich Harbor is a shallow bay about 2 miles east from the New York State line and extending nearly a mile northward from Long Island Sound. Before improvement the upper part of the harbor ran bare at ordinary low water, and vessels landing at any of the docks, except those in the outer harbor, could enter only at full tide and with draft of not over 6 feet.

The mean rise of tide is about 7¼ feet.

A preliminary examination of this harbor was made in compliance with the river and harbor act of 1894, and the report is printed in House Ex. Doc. No. 25, Fifty-third Congress, third session, and in the Annual Report of the Chief of Engineers for 1895, page 860. The improvement recommended was adopted under the river and harbor act of 1896, which appropriated money to begin the work.

A channel 90 feet wide is to be made from the mouth of the harbor to a causeway at its head, a distance of about a mile, to be 9 feet deep at mean low water to the lower docks and 6 feet deep above. The upper end is slightly enlarged to form a turning basin. The estimated cost was $20,000. Harbor lines were established in 1895.

Up to June 30, 1900, a channel 6 feet deep at mean low water and 45 feet wide was dredged from the 6-foot curve opposite the lower dock to the upper dock, near the upper end of the proposed channel, a distance of half a mile. The amount expended to that date was $5,121.85.

At the close of the work on January 15, 1898, the low-water depth over the improvement was 6 feet, and it is believed that that depth still exists. Owing to lack of funds no work was done during the past fiscal year.

Future appropriations will be applied to dredging the 9-foot channel from the outer harbor to the steamboat dock, and in prolongation of the 6-foot channel near the head of the harbor.

The commerce of Greenwich Harbor consists of coal, building materials, stone, and general merchandise. The improvement is designed to facilitate the transportation of this freight, which previous to the commencement of work could only be done at high water.

Table of comparative statistics.

Date.	Vessels of all kinds, each arrival and departure together being counted as one.			Freight tonnage.		
	No.	Draft.	Tonnage.	Received and shipped.	Compared with preceding report.	
					Increase.	Decrease.
		Feet.		Tons.	Tons.	Tons.
1894		3 to 7	40 to 300	110,000		
1897		3 to 14	40 to 750	198,500	88,500	

The reported value of this commerce for 1897 was $5,432,500. The statistics for 1897 were the last received.

July 1, 1900, balance unexpended $878.15
June 30, 1901, amount expended during fiscal year 26.60

July 1, 1901, balance unexpended 851.55

{ Amount (estimated) required for completion of existing project 14,000.00
Amount that can be profitably expended in fiscal year ending June 30,
1903, in addition to the balance unexpended July 1, 1901 .... 14,000.00
Submitted in compliance with requirements of sundry civil act of June
4, 1897.

(See Appendix E 16.)

EXAMINATION AND SURVEY MADE IN COMPLIANCE WITH EMERGENCY RIVER AND HARBOR ACT APPROVED JUNE 6, 1900.

Major Leach submitted reports on preliminary examination and survey of *Branford Harbor, Connecticut*, dated September 12 and November 2, 1900, respectively, through the division engineer. The plan presented contemplates improvement at an estimated cost of $5,000 and $250 per annum for maintenance. The reports were transmitted to Congress and printed in House Doc. No. 100, Fifth-sixth Congress, second session. (See also Appendix E 17.)

IMPROVEMENT OF RIVERS AND HARBORS IN NEW YORK ON LONG ISLAND SOUND AND ON THE SOUTHERN SHORE OF LONG ISLAND, OF HUDSON RIVER AND HARBORS THEREON, OF HARLEM AND EAST RIVERS, NEW YORK, AND OF RIVERS AND HARBORS IN NORTHEASTERN NEW JERSEY.

This district was in the charge of Col. S. M. Mansfield, Corps of Engineers, since May 3, 1901.

1. Port Chester Harbor, New York.—[This work was in the charge of Maj. E. H. Ruffner, Corps of Engineers, to April 20, 1901, and of Col. J. W. Barlow, Corps of Engineers (now brigadier-general, Chief of Engineers, United States Army, retired), from April 20 to May 3, 1901.] This harbor, situated at the boundary between the States of New York and Connecticut, consists of the tidal part of Byram River and of a bay at its mouth opening into Long Island Sound.

The depth in the river before improvement was 1 foot, and Salt Rock in the river and Sunken Rock in the bay were considered to be dangerous obstructions. Range of tide, 7.4 feet.

The existing project, approved March 3, 1899, provides for a channel 12 feet deep and 70 feet wide from deep water in the bay up to the town dock, and thence 9 feet deep and 60 feet wide to the steamboat dock, the work to be done by dredging and rock removal. Estimated cost, $25,000.

For details of previous project see Annual Report of the Chief of Engineers for 1899, page 1208.

Up to June 30, 1900, $7,353.08 had been expended on present project and $52,000 on previous project.

The expenditures during the year were for dredging and rock removal, and resulted in the completion of the projected channel as to depth and width except at and opposite the southerly point of Fox Island, where the width is only about 60 feet.

The maximum draft that could be carried June 30, 1901, at mean low water over the shoalest part of the channel was 12 feet up to town dock, and thence 9 feet to the steamboat dock.

The commerce of this harbor, consisting mainly of coal, building materials, manufactured goods, and farm produce, amounted to 140,000 tons in 1898, to 169,500 tons in 1899, and to 181,000 tons in 1900.

July 1, 1900, balance unexpended	$17,646.92
June 30, 1901, amount expended during fiscal year	15,506.63
July 1, 1901, balance unexpended	2,140.29
Amount that can be profitably expended in fiscal year ending June 30, 1903, for maintenance of improvement, in addition to the balance unexpended July 1, 1901. Submitted in compliance with requirements of sundry civil act of June 4, 1897, and of section 7 of the river and harbor act of 1899.	5,000.00

(See Appendix F 1.)

2. Mamaroneck Harbor, New York.—[This work was in the charge of Maj. E. H. Ruffner, Corps of Engineers, to April 20, 1901, and of Col. J. W. Barlow, Corps of Engineers (now brigadier-general, Chief of Engineers, United States Army, retired), from April 20 to May 3, 1901.] This harbor, situated on the north shore of Long Island Sound, consists of a narrow inlet opening into a shallow, broad bay.

Before improvement the channel to the old steamboat wharf, half a mile up the inlet, had a depth of 5 feet, mean low water, gradually decreasing to 1 foot at the upper wharves. Various rocks at or near the mouth of the inlet obstructed navigation. Range of tides is 8 feet.

The present project for improvement, approved August 2, 1882, and modified April 27, 1899, provides for the removal of Round Rock to 4 feet depth and Bush Rock and Inner Steamboat Rock to 7 feet depth, and in making a channel 7 feet deep and 100 feet wide from the harbor entrance to the upper wharves. Estimated cost, $43,000.

Up to June 30, 1900, $31,911.80 had been expended in carrying out the work.

No work was done during the past fiscal year, sufficient funds not being available.

The condition of the improvement remains about the same as stated in Annual Report of the Chief of Engineers for 1900, page 1382.

The maximum draft that could be carried June 30, 1901, over the shoalest part of the channel at mean low water was 7 feet.

The commerce of the harbor, consisting mainly of coal and building materials, amounted in 1896 to 29,095 tons, in 1897 to 51,673 tons, and in 1900 to 64,685 tons.

July 1, 1900, balance unexpended	$88.20
July 1, 1901, balance unexpended	88.20
Amount (estimated) required for completion of existing project	11,000.00
Amount that can be profitably expended in fiscal year ending June 30, 1903, in addition to the balance unexpended July 1, 1901. Submitted in compliance with requirements of sundry civil act of June 4, 1897.	11,000.00

(See Appendix F 2.)

3. Larchmont Harbor, New York.—[This work was in the charge of Maj. E. H. Ruffner, Corps of Engineers, to April 20, 1901, and of Col. J. W. Barlow, Corps of Engineers (now brigadier-general, Chief of Engineers, United States Army, retired), from April 20 to May 3, 1901.] This harbor or bay, situated on the northwest shore of Long

Island Sound, 4 miles distant from the New York City limits, is about half a mile wide and five-eighths of a mile long. It is exposed to easterly and southerly storms. Two submerged rocks (Umbrella Rock and Huron Rock) obstruct the entrance, which has a depth of 18 feet, gradually diminishing toward the head of the bay. Range of tide is 7.4 feet.

The present project, approved March 3, 1899, provides for building a breakwater extending southwardly 1,440 feet from the 6-foot curve off Long Beach Point, and for the removal of Huron Rock to a depth of 14 feet at mean low water. Estimated cost, $108,000.

For details of previous project see Annual Report of the Chief of Engineers for 1900, page 1384.

Up to June 30, 1900, $314.65 had been expended on present project and $5,000 on previous project.

The expenditure during the past fiscal year was applied to constructing the breakwater intended to protect vessels using the harbor from easterly and southerly winds, of which about nine-tenths was completed.

The maximum draft that could be carried June 30, 1901, over the shoalest part of the entrance channel at mean low water was 18 feet.

The commerce of the harbor is not large. It is mainly used by the Larchmont Yacht Club, and also by coasting and fishing vessels for night anchorage and as a harbor of refuge.

July 1, 1900, balance unexpended	$49,685.35
June 30, 1901, amount expended during fiscal year	36,412.28
July 1, 1901, balance unexpended	13,273.07
July 1, 1901, outstanding liabilities	4,763.47
July 1, 1901, balance available	8,509.60
July 1, 1901, amount covered by uncompleted contract	7,568.64
Amount (estimated) required for completion of existing project	58,000.00
Amount that can be profitably expended in fiscal year ending June 30, 1903, for works of improvement and for maintenance, in addition to the balance available July 1, 1901	25,000.00

Submitted in compliance with requirements of sundry civil act of June 4, 1897, and of section 7 of the river and harbor act of 1899.

(See Appendix F 3.)

4. East Chester Creek, New York.—[This work was in the charge of Maj. E. H. Ruffner, Corps of Engineers, to April 20, 1901, and of Col. J. W. Barlow, Corps of Engineers (now brigadier-general, Chief of Engineers, United States Army, retired), from April 20 to May 3, 1901.] Before improvement this small tidal stream, emptying into Pelham Bay, was navigable at high tide for vessels drawing 7 feet as far as Lockwoods, a distance of 2¼ miles. The range of tide is 7.1 feet.

The project for improvement, approved March 3, 1873, provided for a channel 100 feet wide and 9 feet deep, mean high water, from deep water in Pelham Bay to a point 3,000 feet above Lockwoods. Estimated cost, $136,500, subsequently reduced to $124,000.

Up to June 30, 1900, $90,802.47 had been expended on the work, of which amount $810.16 was for maintenance.

No work was done during the past fiscal year, sufficient funds not being available.

The condition of the improvement, which is considered to be completed, remains about the same as described in report of Chief of Engineers for 1900, page 1388.

The maximum draft that could be carried June 30, 1901, over the shoalest part of the channel at mean low water was 2 feet.

The commerce, consisting mainly of coal, building material, stone, and miscellaneous freight, amounted to 94,928 tons in 1896, to 286,428 tons in 1899, and to 300,475 tons in 1900.

July 1, 1900, balance unexpended	$197.53
July 1, 1901, balance unexpended	197.53
Amount that can be profitably expended in fiscal year ending June 30, 1903, for maintenance of improvement, in addition to the balance unexpended July 1, 1901. Submitted in compliance with requirements of sundry civil act of June 4, 1897, and of section 7 of the river and harbor act of 1899.	5,000.00

(See Appendix F 4.)

5. *Bronx River, New York.*—[This work was in the charge of Maj. E. H. Ruffner, Corps of Engineers, to April 20, 1901, and of Col. J. W. Barlow, Corps of Engineers (now brigadier-general, Chief of Engineers, United States Army, retired), from April 20 to May 3, 1901.] The navigable part of this small stream, which empties into East River north of Hunts Point, extends from the mouth to West Farms, a distance of 3 miles. At the latter place it is crossed by a dam.

The natural depth was 4 feet, mean low water, at the mouth, decreasing to less than 1 foot at the head of navigation, where the range of tide is about 6 feet.

The project for improvement, approved June 3, 1896, provides for making a channel 4 feet deep and 100 feet wide at and near the mouth, thence decreasing in width to 50 feet at the head of navigation, the work to be done by dredging and rock removal. Estimated cost, $85,985.

Up to June 30, 1900, $14,111.42 had been expended upon the improvement.

The expenditure during the fiscal year was applied to removing 2,630 cubic yards of rock from different ledges between Dongan street and the Northern Union Gas Works, and also from a place near the head of navigation at West Farms, New York City, thereby deepening the channel besides widening and straightening it.

The maximum draft that could be carried over the shoalest part of the channel at mean low water up to Stephens dock was 3 feet; above that point 1 foot.

The commerce of this river, consisting mainly of coal, lumber, building materials, cotton goods, drugs for dyeing purposes, and ice, amounted to 139,310 tons in 1897; to 171,300 tons in 1899, and to 166,500 tons in 1900.

July 1, 1900, balance unexpended	$15,888.58
June 30, 1901, amount expended during fiscal year	12,068.66
July 1, 1901, balance unexpended	3,819.92
Amount (estimated) required for completion of existing project	55,985.00
Amount that can be profitably expended in fiscal year ending June 30, 1903, in addition to the balance unexpended July 1, 1901. Submitted in compliance with requirements of sundry civil act of June 4, 1897.	20,000.00

(See Appendix F 5.)

6. *Mattituck Harbor, New York.*—[This work was in the charge of Maj. E. H. Ruffner, Corps of Engineers, to April 20, 1901, and of

Col. J. W. Barlow, Corps of Engineers (now brigadier-general, Chief of Engineers, United States Army, retired), from April 20 to May 3, 1901.] This harbor is a tidal inlet extending in a southerly direction from Long Island Sound to the village of Mattituck, Long Island, a distance of about 2 miles.

One mile above the mouth a tide milldam with gates has been built across the stream. The depth at the entrance, which is obstructed by a shifting sand bar, is from 1 to 2 feet, thence up to the milldam from 2 to 7 feet at low tide, and above the latter the depth is 6 feet at high tide. The range of tide outside the entrance is 4.8, and below the milldam but 2.2 feet.

The project, approved June 3, 1896, provides for a channel 7 feet deep, mean low water, from the entrance to the dam, and 7 feet deep, mean high water, above the dam to the village, the width to be 80 feet except at the mouth, where it is increased to 100 feet; the entrance channel to be protected by parallel jetties. Estimated cost, $83,000.

No money had been expended on this improvement up to June 30, 1900.

The expenditure during the year was applied to the construction of about 680 feet of the west jetty. This jetty, which is nearly completed, will serve to some extent to fix the entrance channel, but navigation will not be materially benefited until both jetties have been completed, and the entrance channel deepened by dredging.

The maximum draft that could be carried June 30, 1901, over the shoalest part of the channel at mean low water was 1 foot.

The greater part of the local freight is shipped and received by rail, as under the present condition the harbor can be navigated only by boats of very light draft.

July 1, 1900, balance unexpended	$15,000.00
June 30, 1901, amount expended during fiscal year	10,129.08
July 1, 1901, balance unexpended	4,870.92
July 1, 1901, outstanding liabilities	4,140.87
July 1, 1901, balance available	730.05
July 1, 1901, amount covered by uncompleted contract	421.89
Amount (estimated) required for completion of existing project	68,000.00
Amount that can be profitably expended in fiscal year ending June 30, 1903, in addition to the balance available July 1, 1901	18,000.00

Submitted in compliance with requirements of sundry civil act of June 4, 1897.

(See Appendix F 6.)

7. *Port Jefferson Harbor, New York.*—[This work was in the charge of Maj. E. H. Ruffner, Corps of Engineers, to April 20, 1901, and of Col. J. W. Barlow, Corps of Engineers (now brigadier-general, Chief of Engineers, United States Army, retired), from April 20 to May 3, 1901.] This harbor, situated on the north shore of Long Island, is a large and deep inland bay, connected with Long Island Sound by a narrow entrance or inlet.

Before improvement the channel depth outside the entrance was but 4 feet, mean low water, whereas the depth in the harbor was 12 feet and more at low tide up to within 300 feet of the wharves of Port Jefferson village.

Range of tide at entrance, 7 feet; at village wharves, 6.2 feet.

The existing project for improvement, approved September 19, 1890, as modified August 18, 1894, provides for dredging a channel through the harbor entrance 12 feet deep and 200 feet wide, to be protected by extending and enlarging the previously built jetties. Estimated cost, $145,000.

For detailed description of previous project see Annual Report of the Chief of Engineers for 1897, page 1097.

The expenditure on the present project up to June 30, 1900, amounted to $53,104.25, and on previous project to $79,000.

The expenditure during the fiscal year was for riprap stone used in enlarging the jetties, and has therefore resulted in no increase in width or depth of the channel.

The maximum draft that could be carried June 30, 1901, over the shoalest place in the channel, was 12 feet at mean low water.

The commerce of this harbor consists mainly of coal, building materials, farm produce, shellfish, and general merchandise, amounting in 1898 to 24,940 tons, in 1899 to 42,130 tons, and in 1900 to 40,380 tons.

July 1, 1900, balance unexpended	$4,395.75
June 30, 1901, amount expended during fiscal year	4,008.43
July 1, 1901, balance unexpended	387.32
Amount (estimated) required for completion of existing project	87,500.00
Amount that can be profitably expended in fiscal year ending June 30, 1903, in addition to the balance unexpended July 1, 1901	15,000.00
Submitted in compliance with requirements of sundry civil act of June 4, 1897.	

(See Appendix F 7.)

8. *Huntington Harbor, New York.*—[This work was in the charge of Maj. E. H. Ruffner, Corps of Engineers, to April 20, 1901, and of Col. J. W. Barlow, Corps of Engineers (now brigadier-general, Chief of Engineers, United States Army, retired), from April 20 to May 3, 1901.] This harbor is a narrow tidal estuary extending inland from Huntington Bay, Long Island, in a southerly direction, for a distance of about 2 miles.

Before improvement it had a natural available depth of nearly 8 feet, mean low water, for a stretch of 1¼ miles from the entrance southward, thence gradually decreasing to zero toward the head of the harbor. Mean rise of tide, 7.2 feet.

The present project, approved September 19, 1890, provides for dredging and maintaining a channel 8 feet deep and 100 feet wide up to the upper wharves, to be protected by piling, if necessary. Estimated cost, $32,000.

For details of former project see report of the Chief of Engineers for 1897, page 1101.

Up to June 30, 1900, $29,489.06 had been expended in carrying out and maintaining the present project. In addition, $22,500 had been expended on former project.

No work was in progress during the past fiscal year, no funds being available.

The condition of the improvement remains about the same as described in Annual Report of the Chief of Engineers for 1900, page 1398.

The maximum draft that could be carried June 30, 1901, was 8 feet at mean low water.

The commerce of the harbor, consisting mainly of coal, farm prod-

204   REPORT OF THE CHIEF OF ENGINEERS, U. S. ARMY.

uce, building material, and miscellaneous merchandise, amounted to 23,584 tons in 1897, to 46,500 tons in 1899, and to 45,600 tons in 1900.

July 1, 1900, balance unexpended	$10.94
July 1, 1901, balance unexpended	10.94

{ Amount (estimated) required for completion of existing project 2,500.00
Amount that can be profitably expended in fiscal year ending June 30, 1903, for works of improvement and for maintenance, in addition to the balance unexpended July 1, 1901 .... 2,500.00
Submitted in compliance with requirements of sundry civil act of June 4, 1897, and of section 7 of the river and harbor act of 1899.

(See Appendix F 8.)

9. *Glencove Harbor, New York.*—[This work was in the charge of Maj. E. H. Ruffner, Corps of Engineers, to April 20, 1901, and of Col. J. W. Barlow, Corps of Engineers (now brigadier-general, Chief of Engineers, United States Army, retired), from April 20 to May 3, 1901.] This harbor is a small tidal inlet on the east side of Hempstead Harbor, Long Island. Its channel is about 2 feet deep at mean low water, and a bar at the entrance has a foot less depth. Before the improvement was made vessels waiting for tides to enter the harbor were exposed to storms from the north and northwest. Range of tides, 7.7 feet.

The existing project, approved August 11, 1888, and revised June 22, 1895, provides for the construction of a breakwater in Hempstead Harbor, extending from the northwest corner of Glencove dock west-southwestwardly toward Motts Point, so as to shelter the anchorage outside of Glencove Harbor; this breakwater to have a length of 2,000 feet, and to be built to a height of 3 feet above high water, with a top width of 5 feet. Estimated cost, $135,000.

Up to June 30, 1900, $63,000 had been expended in carrying out the work.

No operations were in progress during the past fiscal year, no funds being available.

The condition of the improvement remains about the same as stated in Annual Report of the Chief of Engineers for 1900, page 1400.

The commerce of the harbor, consisting of coal, grain, building materials, and general merchandise, amounts to about 700,000 tons annually.

{ Amount (estimated) required for completion of existing project $72,000.00
Amount that can be profitably expended in fiscal year ending June 30, 1903.   7,000.00
Submitted in compliance with requirements of sundry civil act of June 4, 1897.

(See Appendix F 9.)

10. *Flushing Bay, New York.*—[This work was in the charge of Maj. E. H. Ruffner, Corps of Engineers, to April 20, 1901, and of Col. J. W. Barlow, Corps of Engineers (now brigadier-general, Chief of Engineers, United States Army, retired), from April 20 to May 3, 1901.] Before improvement the controlling depth in the channel up to Flushing was 3.9 feet, mean low water. Range of tides, 7.1 feet.

The existing project, approved March 3, 1879, and modified September 19, 1888, and June 9, 1891, provides for building a dike 4,663 feet long on the west side of the channel, to protect it from filling, and for making and maintaining a channel 6 feet deep at mean low water up to the lower bridge at Flushing. Estimated cost, $173,500.

Up to June 30, 1900, $122,495.53 had been expended upon this improvement. How much of this amount might properly be considered to have been used for maintenance can not be definitely stated, as it was necessary during the progress of the work to dredge some parts of the channel repeatedly.

No work was in progress during the past fiscal year. The improvement remains in about the same condition as reported on page 1401, Annual Report of the Chief of Engineers for 1900.

The maximum draft that could be carried June 30, 1901, over the shoalest part of the channel at mean low water was 6 feet.

The principal articles of commerce are coal, building and paving materials, dyewoods, logwood extracts, and miscellaneous merchandise, amounting to 163,395 tons in 1897, to 158,755 tons in 1899, and to 177,575 tons in 1900.

July 1, 1900, balance unexpended	$504.47
July 1, 1901, balance unexpended	504.47
Amount (estimated) required for completion of existing project	50,500.00
Amount that can be profitably expended in fiscal year ending June 30, 1903, for works of improvement and for maintenance, in addition to the balance unexpended July 1, 1901	5,000.00

Submitted in compliance with requirements of sundry civil act of June 4, 1897, and of section 7 of the river and harbor act of 1899.

(See Appendix F 10.)

11. *East River, New York.*—[This work was in the charge of Maj. E. H. Ruffner, Corps of Engineers, to April 20, 1901, and of Col. J. W. Barlow, Corps of Engineers (now brigadier-general, Chief of Engineers, United States Army, retired), from April 20 to May 3, 1901.] East River is a tidal strait extending from the Battery, New York Harbor, to Throgs Neck, Long Island Sound, a distance of about 16 miles. Before improvement it was much obstructed by rocks and reefs, especially in the part known as Hell Gate.

The range of tide south of Hell Gate is from 4½ to 5 feet, and east of it from 5 to 7 feet.

The project for this improvement, approved July 25, 1868, as modified in 1874 and again on March 3, 1899, provides for the removal of rocky obstructions in the East River between the Battery and Baretto Point to depths varying from 18 to 26 feet, and for the construction of sea walls and dikes where necessary to guide the tidal currents. Estimated cost, $5,639,120.

For further description of project see Annual Report of the Chief of Engineers for 1897, page 1026.

Up to June 30, 1900, $4,395,903.51 had been expended in carrying out this improvement.

The expenditure during the fiscal year was for removal of rocks and bowlders from the channel between Blackwells Island and the Battery.

At Man-O'-War Rock 8,481 cubic yards of rock was removed, or about three-sevenths of the amount required to afford a depth of 26 feet. Little progress was made on the reef off Twenty-sixth street, less than one-tenth of the proposed rock having been taken out to give a depth of 26 feet. From Battery and Shell reefs 19,743 tons of material was removed, thereby widening the channel off the Battery and South Ferry slip. The water front between East Seventh and East Eighteenth streets was deepened several feet in order to facilitate the dockage of vessels.

The maximum draft that could be carried June 30, 1901, at mean low water, over the shoalest part of the localities under improvement is given in the following table:

Localities.	Least depth June 30, 1901.
Part of Battery Reef	19 to 26
Rocky obstructions off South Ferry slips	19 to 26
Diamond Reef	26
Reef off Diamond Reef	26
Coenties Reef	25.5
Rock off 3d street	15.9
Shell Reef, off 9th street and vicinity	15
Pilgrim Rock, off 19th street	24
Rock off 26th street	16.1
Ferry Reef, off 34th street	24
Charlotte Rock, off 84th street	26.5
Man-o'-War Rock	.8
Middle Reef, including Flood Rock, Gridiron, Hen and Chickens, and Negro Heads	18 to 20
Hallets Point	26
Heel Tap	20.5
Frying Pan	18
Pot Rock	22.8
Way Reef	26
Shell Drake	26
Scaly Rock	26
Negro Point	
Reef off Sunken Meadow	17.8
North Brother Island Reef	26
Reef off Baretto Point	24

The traffic on the East River is of very great extent, and is intimately connected with that of New York Harbor proper; it is impracticable to obtain reliable statistics to show what proportion properly belongs to the East River, especially as the heavy coastwise traffic passing through this waterway is carried on in vessels which do not enter or clear at the custom-house.

July 1, 1900, balance unexpended	$239,375.82
June 30, 1901, amount expended during fiscal year	96,902.83
July 1, 1901, balance unexpended	142,472.99
July 1, 1901, outstanding liabilities	35,503.20
July 1, 1901, balance available	106,969.79
July 1, 1901, amount covered by uncompleted contracts	99,904.13
Amount (estimated) required for completion of existing project	1,003,840.67
Amount that can be profitably expended in fiscal year ending June 30, 1903, in addition to the balance available July 1, 1901	200,000.00
Submitted in compliance with requirements of sundry civil act of June 4, 1897.	

(See Appendix F 11.)

12. *Harlem River, New York.*—[This work was in the charge of Maj. E. H. Ruffner, Corps of Engineers, to April 20, 1901, and of Col. J. W. Barlow, Corps of Engineers (now brigadier-general, Chief of Engineers, United States Army, retired), from April 20 to May 3, 1901.] The Harlem River and Spuyten Duyvil Creek, both included in the improvement, are two waterways which join at Kingsbridge, N. Y., and separate Manhattan Island from the mainland. The narrow channel at their junction was obstructed by a ledge of rocks, awash at low tide.

Before improvement the Harlem River had an available depth of 10 feet from the East River to Morris dock, except at Highbridge, where it was only 6 feet. From Morris dock to Fordham Landing there was a crooked channel 7 feet deep, and above the latter place the river could only be used by the smallest class of vessels.

Spuyten Duyvil Creek, from Kingsbridge to the Hudson, had a depth of 4 feet.

The range of tide in the Harlem River is from 5½ to 6 feet, and in the creek and Hudson River 3.8 feet.

The present project for improvement, approved June 18, 1878, and modified October 7, 1886, provides for a continuous channel, 400 feet wide and 15 feet deep, from the East River to the Hudson River, except just north of Highbridge, where the width was made 375 feet, and in the rock cut through Dyckman meadow, where the width was reduced to 350 feet and the depth increased to 18 feet. Estimated cost, $2,700,000.

For previous project see page 173, Annual Report of the Chief of Engineers for 1874.

Up to June 30, 1900, $1,160,962.69 had been expended under present project and $21,000 under previous project.

The expenditures during the past year were applied to dredging the channel through the draw of the reconstructed railroad bridge near Spuyten Duyvil, New York City, where the channel was given a full depth of 15 feet through the draw openings, and in making a payment of $75,000 to the owners of a parcel of land on the south side of the rock cut, for the purpose of releasing the United States from all obligations to remove a pile of stone excavated from the cut and stored upon the land under a written agreement, which agreement provided that, upon its expiration or termination, the premises must be restored to its original level before being surrendered.

The maximum draft that could be carried June 30, 1901, over the shoalest part at mean low water was 12 feet.

The commerce of this river, which is very large and steadily increasing, consists mainly of general merchandise, grain, flour, feed, lumber, building materials, coal, ice, etc.

It was impracticable to obtain complete returns for the calendar year 1900. The last reliable information received was for the year 1895, when the tonnage amounted to over 7,500,000 tons.

July 1, 1900, balance unexpended	$84,037.31
June 30, 1901, amount expended during fiscal year	80,697.67
July 1, 1901, balance unexpended	3,339.64
July 1, 1901, outstanding liabilities	180.00
July 1, 1901, balance available	3,159.64
Amount (estimated) required for completion of existing project	1,455,000.00
Amount that can be profitably expended in fiscal year ending June 30, 1903, in addition to the balance available July 1, 1901	200,000.00

Submitted in compliance with requirements of sundry civil act of June 4, 1897.

(See Appendix F 12.)

13. Newtown Creek, New York.—[This work was in the charge of Maj. E. H. Ruffner, Corps of Engineers, to April 20, 1901, and of Col. J. W. Barlow, Corps of Engineers (now brigadier-general, Chief of Engineers, United States Army, retired), from April 20 to May 3, 1901.] Newtown Creek is an estuary of the East River, extending inland between Kings and Queens counties, N. Y., for a distance of about 4 miles. Before improvement it had a depth of 12¼ feet at the mouth, decreasing to 4 feet at the head. Range of tides, about 4½ feet.

The present project, approved June 3, 1896, provides for a uniform channel 125 feet wide and 18 feet deep, from the East River to the head of navigation, at Metropolitan avenue. Estimated cost, $450,000.

For previous projects see Annual Report of the Chief of Engineers for 1896, pages 760 and 761.

Up to June 30, 1900, $197,314.89 had been expended in carrying out the present project, and in addition the sum of $197,500 on previous projects.

The project is practically completed, but the channel is subject to shoaling, and will therefore require appropriations for maintenance.

No work was in progress during the past fiscal year, none having been required.

The maximum draft that could be carried June 30, 1901, over the shoalest part at mean low water was 18 feet.

The commerce of the creek is very large, consisting mainly of coal, building materials, petroleum and its products, chemicals, etc. It amounted to 2,740,482 tons in 1896 and to 3,228,544 tons in 1897.

July 1, 1900, balance unexpended	$15,685.61
July 1, 1901, balance unexpended	15,685.61
Amount that can be profitably expended in fiscal year ending June 30, 1903, for maintenance of improvement in addition to the balance unexpended July 1, 1901	7,500.00

Submitted in compliance with requirements of sundry civil act of June 4, 1897, and of section 7 of the river and harbor act of 1899.

(See Appendix F 13.)

14. Wallabout Channel, New York.—[This work was in the charge of Maj. E. H. Ruffner, Corps of Engineers, to April 20, 1901, and of Col. J. W. Barlow, Corps of Engineers (now brigadier-general, Chief of Engineers, United States Army, retired), from April 20 to May 3, 1901.] This channel separates Cob Dock, an island in Wallabout Bay, from Brooklyn, N. Y. It is divided into two parts, called east and west channel, respectively, by a stone causeway which connects the island with the navy-yard. The east channel, the part under consideration, had an original depth of from 15 to 20 feet along the line of deepest water, diminishing to 5 feet along the sides. Mean range of tide is 4.5 feet.

The project, adopted in 1899, consists in making the channel from the East River to the causeway 20 feet deep, with widths ranging from 230 to 350 feet. Estimated cost, $40,000.

This improvement was completed in January, 1900, at a total cost to the United States of $18,173.69. The sum of $21,826.31, being unexpended balance from appropriation, act of March 3, 1899, was returned to the Treasury of the United States.

(See Appendix F 14.)

15. Canarsie Bay, New York.—[This work was in the charge of Maj. E. H. Ruffner, Corps of Engineers, to April 20, 1901, and of Col. J. W. Barlow, Corps of Engineers (now brigadier-general, Chief of Engineers, United States Army, retired), from April 20 to May 3, 1901.] This bay forms the northwest part of Jamaica Bay, at Canarsie Landing. The original depth, from the landing to Big Channel, was

4.2 feet, and to Island Channel 1.3 feet, mean low water. Rise of tide, 4.7 feet.

The project for this improvement, approved June 14, 1880, and subsequently enlarged in 1889 and 1896, provides for the construction of two dikes, and dredging between them, where necessary to secure a channel, 100 to 150 feet wide and 6 feet deep, connecting steamboat dock at Canarsie with Big Channel, Jamaica Bay; also for a channel, 4 feet deep and about 50 feet wide, running in a southwesterly direction from Canarsie Landing to Island Channel, and for a channel, 5 feet deep and 50 feet wide, running in a northeasterly direction to Gophel Channel. Estimated cost, $88,000.

For detailed description of project and modifications, see Annual Report of the Chief of Engineers for 1887, page 1114.

Up to June 30, 1900, $64,475.08 had been expended in carrying out the improvement.

No work was in progress during the past fiscal year.

The maximum draft that could be carried June 30, 1901, over the shoalest part, at mean low water, was 6 feet in the main channel, 2¼ feet in the West Branch, and 3¼ feet in the East Branch.

The commerce of Canarsie Bay, consisting mainly of building materials, fertilizers, fish, and coal, amounted to about 50,000 tons in 1896; since then it has not been practicable to obtain reliable statistics.

July 1, 1900, balance unexpended	$524.92
June 30, 1901, amount expended during fiscal year	2.00
July 1, 1901, balance unexpended	522.92

Amount (estimated) required for completion of existing project	23,000.00
Amount that can be profitably expended in fiscal year ending June 30, 1903, for works of improvement and for maintenance, in addition to the balance unexpended July 1, 1901	10,000.00
Submitted in compliance with requirements of sundry civil act of June 4, 1897, and of section 7 of the river and harbor act of 1899.	

(See Appendix F 15.)

16. Browns Creek, New York.—[This work was in the charge of Maj. E. H. Ruffner, Corps of Engineers, to April 20, 1901, and of Col. J. W. Barlow, Corps of Engineers (now brigadier-general, Chief of Engineers, United States Army, retired), from April 20 to May 3, 1901.] This narrow stream, which empties into Great South Bay, Long Island, near Browns Point, had a natural depth of from 1 to 3 feet at low tide, a bar at the mouth having less than 1 foot.

The project for improvement approved September 19, 1890, provides for a channel 100 feet wide and 4 feet deep, to extend from deep water in the bay up to Sayville highway bridge, and to be protected at the entrance by jetties on both sides. Estimated cost, $46,000.

Up to June 30, 1900, $27,536.55 had been expended upon the improvement, of which amount $25,000 had been used to carry out the project and $2,536.55 for maintenance.

No work was in progress during the past fiscal year.

The maximum draft that could be carried June 30, 1901, over the shoalest part at mean low water was 4 feet.

The condition of the improvement remains about the same as described in the Annual Report of the Chief of Engineers for 1900, page 1417.

The commerce of this creek consists mainly of coal, building materials, fish, and shellfish, amounting in 1898 to 10,700 tons; in 1899 to 11,642 tons, and in 1900 to 12,272 tons.

July 1, 1900, balance unexpended	$463.45
July 1, 1901, balance unexpended	463.45

{ Amount (estimated) required for completion of existing project........ 18,000.00
Amount that can be profitably expended in fiscal year ending June 30, 1903, for works of improvement and for maintenance, in addition to the balance unexpended July 1, 1901 .... 8,000.00
Submitted in compliance with requirements of sundry civil act of June 4, 1897, and of section 7 of the river and harbor act of 1899. }

(See Appendix F 16.)

17. *Patchogue River, New York.*—[This work was in the charge of Maj. E. H. Ruffner, Corps of Engineers, to April 20, 1901, and of Col. J. W. Barlow, Corps of Engineers (now brigadier-general, Chief of Engineers, United States Army, retired), from April 20 to May 3, 1901.] Before improvement this small inlet, extending from Great South Bay, Long Island, to the village of Patchogue, had a natural depth of about 2 feet; rise of tide, 1 foot.

The project for improvement approved September 19, 1890, provided for a channel about 5,000 feet long, 60 feet wide, and 6 feet deep, to be protected at its mouth against westerly storms by a jetty 1,700 feet long. Estimated cost, $40,000.

Up to June 30, 1900, $39,293.15 had been expended in carrying out the improvement, which has been completed.

No work was in progress during the past fiscal year.

The maximum draft that could be carried June 30, 1901, over the shoalest part at mean low water was 4 feet.

The emergency river and harbor act of June 6, 1900, provided for an examination and survey of Fire Island Inlet, in Great South Bay, to Patchogue River, with a view to obtaining a channel not less than 10 feet in depth and 200 feet in width, report upon which was published in House Doc. No. 103, Fifty-sixth Congress, second session, and is herewith as Appendix F 34.

The commerce of this river consists mainly of coal, lumber, fish, and shellfish, and miscellaneous merchandise. It amounted in 1898 to 255,200 tons, in 1899 to 266,800 tons, and in 1900 to 274,100 tons.

July 1, 1900, balance unexpended	$706.85
July 1, 1901, balance unexpended	706.85

{ Amount that can be profitably expended in fiscal year ending June 30, 1903, for maintenance of improvement, in addition to the balance unexpended July 1, 1901............. 4,000.00
Submitted in compliance with requirements of sundry civil act of June 4, 1897, and of section 7 of the river and harbor act of 1899. }

(See Appendix F 17.)

18. *Hudson River, New York.*—[This work was in the charge of Col. J. W. Barlow, Corps of Engineers (now brigadier-general, Chief of Engineers, United States Army, retired), to May 3, 1901.] The section of this river now under improvement is the stretch beginning at the State dam at Troy, and extending downstream to Coxsackie, a distance of 28 miles. In its natural condition the navigable depth of the channel between Troy and Albany was 4 feet, between Albany and New Baltimore 7¼ feet, between New Baltimore and Coxsackie 11 feet, and below Coxsackie 12 feet or more.

The existing project, approved July 13, 1892, amended March 30, 1899, consists in making a 12-foot channel between Coxsackie and the State dam at Troy, the channel to be 400 feet wide between Coxsackie and Broadway, Troy, thence gradually decreasing in width from 400 to 150 feet at Jacob street, Troy, thence 150 feet wide to the State dam.

The work was estimated to cost $4,343,863.

For details of previous projects, see Annual Report of the Chief of Engineers for 1900, pages 171 and 172.

The amount expended on existing project up to the close of the fiscal year ending June 30, 1900, was $2,513,386.65. In addition, $1,667,938. was expended on former projects.

The expenditure during the year was for rebuilding 3,270 linear feet of old dikes; for relaying 595 square yards of paving and the protection of 1,000 linear feet of paved dikes; for refilling with rubblestone of 15,913 linear feet of old timber dikes; for dredging of 394,203 cubic yards of sand, gravel, etc., and for excavation of 13,575 cubic yards of rock.

As a result of work during the past fiscal year, the channel width at Troy has been increased from 20 to 110 feet and the depth between Broadway and the Delaware and Hudson Company's bridge has been increased 6 feet. The dredging done was for the purpose of restoring the channel to the dimensions previously obtained.

Of the amount expended, $111,156.16 was used in continuing work under the project, and $48,393.85 was applied to maintenance.

The maximum draft that could be carried June 30, 1901, at mean low water, as established in 1876, was 10¼ feet from Coxsackie to Albany; 11¼ feet from Albany to Congress Street Bridge, Troy; 12 feet from Congress Street Bridge to Delaware and Hudson Company's bridge at Troy, and 5¼ feet from this latter bridge to the State dam.

The amount of commerce within the limits of the improvements now in progress was 4,045,895 tons in 1898; 5,070,800 tons in 1899, and 4,810,927 tons in 1900, and consisted principally of merchandise, grain, lumber, fuel, building materials, and ice.

In addition to this local commerce, a through commerce of more than 10,000,000 tons is carried annually.

July 1, 1900, balance unexpended	$465,119.91
Amount appropriated by sundry civil act approved March 3, 1901	100,000.00
	565,119.91
June 30, 1901, amount expended during the fiscal year	159,550.01
July 1, 1901, balance unexpended	405,569.90
July 1, 1901, outstanding liabilities	43,911.77
July 1, 1901, balance available	361,658.13
July 1, 1901, amount covered by uncompleted contracts	340,240.58
Amount (estimated) required for completion of existing project	1,265,356.44
Amount that can be profitably expended in fiscal year ending June 30, 1903, for works of improvement and for maintenance, in addition to the balance available July 1, 1901	300,000.00
Submitted in compliance with requirements of sundry civil act of June 4, 1897, and of section 7 of the river and harbor act of 1899.	

(See Appendix F 18.)

19. *Saugerties Harbor, New York.*—[This work was in the charge of Col. J. W. Barlow, Corps of Engineers (now brigadier-general, Chief

of Engineers, United States Army, retired), to May 3, 1901.] This harbor is situated at the mouth of Esopus Creek, which empties into the Hudson River on its west shore, about 100 miles above New York City. The creek is from 180 to 500 feet wide, and is navigable for a distance of about three-quarters of a mile above its mouth.

The natural depth in the creek was 7 feet or more at mean low water; the entrance, however, was obstructed by a broad shoal, on which there was an available depth of only about 3 feet. The mean rise and fall of the tide is about 4 feet.

The project for this improvement, approved July 5, 1884, provided for a permanent channel, 300 feet wide and 8 feet deep at mean low water, by means of the construction of parallel dikes and dredging between them, the cost of the work being placed at $52,000. This project was completed in 1892 at an actual cost of $42,000. Since then $12,850 has been expended in maintenance.

No work was done during the past fiscal year, as none was considered necessary.

The river and harbor act of March 3, 1899, provided for an examination and survey of Saugerties Harbor, "with a view of extending the improvement from the westerly end of the south dike westerly to the 'Point of Rocks,' also with a view to removing the loose rock from the channel and continuing the depth of 12 feet at low water toward the head of the harbor." A report on such survey, with estimate of cost of work proposed, was published in House Doc. No. 107, Fifty-sixth Congress, first session, and is printed in the Annual Report of the Chief of Engineers for 1900, pages 1518 to 1520. The estimates there given include improvement from the Hudson River to the steamboat docks.

Attention is invited to the supplemental estimate of cost for continuing this improvement from the steamboat dock to within 600 feet of the dam at head of harbor, printed on pages 1494 and 1495 of the Annual Report of the Chief of Engineers for 1900.

The estimate, submitted in House Doc. No. 107, Fifty-sixth Congress, first session, for a channel, 12 feet deep and 300 feet wide, from the Hudson River to the steamboat landing at Saugerties, is $44,685. The supplementary estimate, for extending an 8-foot channel above steamboat landing to the rapids below the dam on Esopus Creek, and for dredging along wharf front on west side of creek above steamboat landing, is $80,770, making a total estimate for this improvement of $125,455, and $3,000 per annum for maintenance.

The maximum draft that could be carried on June 30, 1901, was 9 feet at mean low water.

The commerce of this harbor consists mainly of bluestone, coal, building materials, and general merchandise, and amounted to 58,368 tons in 1898, to 50,800 tons in 1899, and to 76,673 tons in 1900.

July 1, 1900, balance unexpended $2,150.00
July 1, 1901, balance unexpended 2,150.00

Amount that can be profitably expended in fiscal year ending June 30, 1903, for maintenance of improvement, in addition to the balance unexpended July 1, 1901... 2,000.00
Submitted in compliance with requirements of sundry civil act of June 4, 1897, and of section 7 of the river and harbor act of 1899.

(See Appendix F 19.)

20. Harbor at Rondout, N. Y.—[This work was in the charge of Col. J. W. Barlow, Corps of Engineers (now brigadier-general, Chief of Engineers, United States Army, retired), to May 3, 1901.] This harbor is situated at the mouth of Rondout Creek, which empties into the Hudson River on its west shore, 90 miles above New York City, and is the eastern terminus of the Delaware and Hudson Canal. The creek is a tidal stream for 3 miles above its mouth, with mean rise and fall of tide of about 4 feet.

In 1871 the available depth of water in the harbor was 7 feet at mean low water, the result of improvements made by private parties.

The project for improvement, approved June 10, 1872, contemplated securing a permanent channel, 14 feet deep at mean low water, by constructing parallel dikes and dredging between them, at an estimated cost of $172,500. This project was completed in 1880, at a total cost of $90,000. Since then $29,000 has been expended in maintenance.

The expenditure during the past year was for maintenance, and was used in repairing the dikes, and has therefore resulted in no increase in depth or width in the channel.

The maximum draft that could be carried on June 30, 1901, was 13 feet at mean low water.

The commerce of this harbor consists mainly of coal, cement, lime, bluestone, ice, and general merchandise, and amounted in 1897 to 2,330,000 tons; in 1899 to 1,885,000 tons; and in 1900 to 1,885,000 tons.

July 1, 1900, balance unexpended	$2,058.64
June 30, 1901, amount expended during fiscal year	2,058.64

Amount that can be profitably expended in fiscal year ending June 30, 1903, for maintenance of improvement.................. 2,500.00

Submitted in compliance with requirements of sundry civil act of June 4, 1897, and of section 7 of the river and harbor act of 1899.

(See Appendix F 20.)

21. Harbor at Peekskill, N. Y.—[This work was in the charge of Col. J. W. Barlow, Corps of Engineers (now brigadier-general, Chief of Engineers, United States Army, retired), to May 3, 1901.] This harbor is a prominent indentation upon the eastern shore of the Hudson River, about 45 miles above New York City. It measures approximately 1 square mile east of the 12-foot contour of the river, and the outlying flats, 3,500 feet wide, have a maximum depth over them of 5 feet at mean low water.

A narrow channel, 6 feet deep at mean low water, followed the shore from north to south past the village docks, which enabled steamboats and small craft to transport by water a portion of the commerce originating at the village.

The project for this improvement, approved June 3, 1896, consisted in dredging a channel 100 feet wide and 10 feet deep, from deep water in the Hudson River, on the north, along the inner side of the harbor to deep water on the south. The estimated cost of the work was $50,000. This project was completed in 1899, at a cost of $19,400.

No work was carried on during the past fiscal year.

The commerce of Peekskill Harbor is increasing so rapidly that channels of the dimensions first decided on are no longer adequate. Navigation interests ask that a channel 200 feet wide and 15 feet deep be made along the wharf front, and that the connections north and south with the Hudson River have the same depth and a width of 150 feet. The present channel can be increased to those dimensions without increasing the estimated cost of the improvement, provided as reasonable a price for dredging be procured in the future as was had at the last letting.

The unappropriated amount of the estimate is $30,000, and can be applied to the proposed extension of the project with the authority of Congress, in which case no appropriation for maintenance will be required at present.

The maximum draft that could be carried to the wharves on June 30, 1901, was 10 feet at mean low water.

The commerce of this harbor consists of general merchandise, building material, iron ore, coal, iron, lumber, and molding sand, and amounted to 734,950 tons in 1898, to 1,092,455 tons in 1899, and to 1,800,750 tons in 1900.

July 1, 1900, balance unexpended	$600.00
July 1, 1901, balance unexpended	600.00
Amount that can be profitably expended in fiscal year ending June 30, 1903, for maintenance of improvement, in addition to the balance unexpended July 1, 1901. Submitted in compliance with requirements of sundry civil act of June 4, 1897, and of section 7 of the river and harbor act of 1899.	3,000.00

(See Appendix F 21.)

22. *Passaic River, New Jersey.*—[This work was in the charge of Col. J. W. Barlow, Corps of Engineers (now brigadier-general, Chief of Engineers, United States Army, retired), to November 30, 1900, of Maj. E. H. Ruffner, Corps of Engineers, from November 30, 1900, to April 20, 1901, and of General Barlow from April 20 to May 3, 1901.] This river is a stream of considerable size, rising among the highlands in the northern part of New Jersey and flowing in a general easterly and southerly course into Newark Bay. It is navigable from its mouth to Passaic, a distance of about 16 miles. In its natural condition the navigable depth to Newark was about 7 feet at mean low water; from Newark to Passaic it was about 3 feet. The rise of the tide at the mouth is 4.7 feet, and at Passaic it is 2.5 feet.

The existing project, approved July 13, 1892, provides for obtaining a channel, 200 feet wide and 10 feet deep, from Newark Bay to Center Street Bridge, Newark, and thence a channel, from 50 to 200 feet wide and from 6 to 7½ feet deep, to the head of navigation at Passaic, by means of dikes and dredging. The estimated cost of the work was placed at $547,697. For details of previous projects see report of the Chief of Engineers for 1900, page 177.

The amount expended on the work up to the close of the fiscal year ending June 30, 1900, was $459,379.53, of which $381,510 was used in carrying out the project and $77,869.53 for maintenance. The latter sum must now be added to the estimate for completion of project.

The expenditure during the past year was for widening and deepening the channel at Belleville and Rutherford Park bars and at Passaic City. The proposed depth of 6 feet was attained at Belleville Bar for widths of 50 to 100 feet, at Rutherford Park Bar for widths of 85 to 100 feet, and above Rutherford Park Bar to Passaic City for narrow widths. Of the amount expended, $8,100 was for continuing work and $870.47 for maintenance.

The river and harbor act of March 3, 1899, provided for an examination and survey of this river, with a view to obtaining a channel 10 feet deep from Montclair Railway Bridge to the Center Street Bridge, Newark, and thence 12 feet deep to Staten Island Sound; also for an examination from Montclair Railway Bridge to the city of Paterson. Reports on these examinations and surveys, with estimates of cost of proposed improvements, were published in House Document No. 401, Fifth-sixth Congress, first session, and are printed in the Annual Report of the Chief of Engineers for 1900, pages 1530 to 1552.

The maximum drafts that could be carried on June 30, 1901, were as follows: 9.5 feet to the Center Street Bridge, Newark; 7 feet to the Erie Railroad Bridge, Newark, and 5.25 feet to Passaic.

The commerce of this river consists mainly of building material, iron ore, fertilizers, coal, and general merchandise, and amounted to 1,509,772 tons in 1898, to 1,962,462 tons in 1899, and to 2,037,363 tons in 1900.

July 1, 1900, balance unexpended	$8,970.47
June 30, 1901, amount expended during fiscal year	8,930.47
July 1, 1901, balance unexpended	40.00
July 1, 1901, outstanding liabilities	40.00

Amount (estimated) required for completion of existing project........ 158,087.00
Amount that can be profitably expended in fiscal year ending June 30, 1903, for works of improvement and for maintenance, in addition to the balance unexpended July 1, 1901 .... 30,000.00
Submitted in compliance with requirements of sundry civil act of June 4, 1897, and of section 7 of the river and harbor act of 1899.

(See Appendix F 22.)

23. Channel between Staten Island and New Jersey.—[This work was in the charge of Col. J. W. Barlow, Corps of Engineers (now brigadier-general, Chief of Engineers, United States Army, retired), to November 30, 1900, of Maj. E. H. Ruffner, Corps of Engineers, from November 30, 1900, to April 20, 1901, and of General Barlow from April 20 to May 3, 1901.] This channel is an inland waterway, about 17 miles long, connecting New York Harbor with Raritan Bay. It consists of the Kill van Kull, connecting the Upper Bay with Newark Bay, and the Arthur Kill, connecting Newark Bay with Raritan Bay.

The natural depth through the channel was 15 feet or more, except for a distance of about 1¾ miles in Newark Bay, where there was a shoal with a crooked channel 9¼ feet deep. The mean rise of tide is about 5 feet.

The existing project, approved June 14, 1880, amended October 20, 1890, consists in dredging a channel, 400 feet wide and 14 feet deep, connecting Arthur Kill and Kill van Kull. The cost of the work was estimated at $210,000. For details of previous projects see report of the Chief of Engineers for 1900, page 178.

The amount expended on this work up to the close of the fiscal year ending June 30, 1900, was $190,456.65, of which $114,598.50 was used in carrying out the project and $75,858.15 for maintenance. The latter sum must now be added to the estimate for completion of project. In addition, $80,500 has been expended on other projects, including $5,000 spent on Lemon Creek.

The expenditure during the past year was for maintenance. Small shoals were removed from around the sharp bend at the Corner Stake light and the old channel was redredged where contraction was most marked. The work resulted in the restoration of the channel to a depth of 14 feet for a width of 350 feet.

The river and harbor act of March 3, 1899, provided for an examination and survey of Arthur Kill, or Staten Island Sound, from Kill van Kull to Raritan Bay, with a view to obtaining a 21-foot channel from New York Bay to Raritan Bay.

The reports upon this examination and survey, giving estimates of cost of proposed improvement, were published in House Doc. No. 393, Fifty-sixth Congress, first session, and are printed in the Annual Report of the Chief of Engineers for 1900, pages 1525 to 1530.

The maximum draft that could be carried June 30, 1901, through the Staten Island channel was 14 feet at mean low water.

The freight carried through this waterway consists of oil, coal, ores, clay products, chemicals, fertilizers, grain, machinery, manufactures, and general merchandise, and amounted in 1898 to 10,184,261 tons, in 1899 to 11,311,991 tons, and in 1900 to 11,047,633 tons.

July 1, 1900, balance unexpended	$20,543.35
June 30, 1901, amount expended during fiscal year	18,524.85
July 1, 1901, balance unexpended	2,018.50
Amount (estimated) required for completion of existing project	93,383.00
Amount that can be profitably expended in fiscal year ending June 30, 1903, for works of improvement and for maintenance, in addition to the balance unexpended July 1, 1901	10,000.00

Submitted in compliance with requirements of sundry civil act of June 4, 1897, and of section 7 of the river and harbor act of 1899.

(See Appendix F 23.)

24. Elizabeth River, New Jersey.—[This work was in the charge of Col. J. W. Barlow, Corps of Engineers (now brigadier-general, Chief of Engineers, United States Army, retired), to November 30, 1900, of Maj. E. H. Ruffner, Corps of Engineers, from November 30, 1900, to April 20, 1901, and of General Barlow from April 20 to May 3, 1901.] This is a small creek in the eastern part of New Jersey, which discharges into the Arthur Kill at Elizabethport. Its width varied from 50 to 90 feet, and it had a high-water depth of 4 feet at the head of navigation at Broad street, Elizabeth, 2.62 miles above its mouth. The mean rise of tide at the mouth was 4.7 feet, and at Bridge street, Elizabeth, 3.4 feet.

The existing project, approved March 3, 1879, consists in dredging a channel 60 feet wide and 7 feet deep at mean high water, at an estimated cost of $43,160.

The amount expended on this work to June 30, 1900, was $43,160, of which $27,000 was used for carrying out the project and $16,160 for maintenance. This latter sum is therefore asked for to complete the project.

No work was done during the past year, owing to lack of funds.

The maximum draft that could be carried to Bridge street, Elizabeth, on June 30, 1901, was 1 foot at mean low water and 4.4 feet at high water.

The commerce of this river consists of coal, building materials, and miscellaneous freights. It amounted to 21,650 tons in 1895, 36,066 tons in 1896, and 28,865 tons in 1897.

{ Amount (estimated) required for completion of existing project $16,160.00
Amount that can be profitably expended in fiscal year ending June 30,
  1903, for works of improvement and for maintenance 5,000.00
Submitted in compliance with requirements of sundry civil act of June
  4, 1897, and of section 7 of the river and harbor act of 1899. }

(See Appendix F 24.)

25. *Raritan River, New Jersey.*—[This work was in the charge of Col. J. W. Barlow, Corps of Engineers (now brigadier-general, Chief of Engineers, United States Army, retired), to November 30, 1900, of Maj. E. H. Ruffner, Corps of Engineers, from November 30, 1900, to April 20, 1901, and of General Barlow from April 20 to May 3, 1901.] This river is a moderate-sized stream flowing through the central part of the State of New Jersey and emptying into Raritan Bay at Perth Amboy. It is navigable to New Brunswick, N. J., a distance of 12 miles, where it is the eastern terminus of the Delaware and Raritan Canal. The mean rise of tide at the mouth is 5.1 feet, and at New Brunswick it is 5.56 feet.

In its natural state the channel to New Brunswick was obstructed by several extensive shoals, on which the depth was from $6\frac{1}{4}$ to $8\frac{1}{4}$ feet at mean low water.

The project for improvement, approved June 18, 1878, provided for a channel 200 feet wide and 10 feet deep, from the mouth to the Delaware and Raritan Canal terminus at New Brunswick, to be obtained by dredging, diking, and rock excavation, the cost being estimated at that time at $2,093,662. Recent and more improved methods for doing such work have made it probable that this estimate will not exceed $1,035,000.

The amount expended up to the close of the fiscal year ending June 30, 1900, was $667,692.32, of which $659,192.32 was used in carrying on the work, and $8,500 for maintaining that already done.

No work was done during the past year.

On June 30, 1901, the maximum draft that could be carried to the head of navigation was limited by gravel shoals below the rock cut to 8 feet at mean low water.

The commerce of this river consists principally of coal, ores, lumber, building materials, and general merchandise, and amounted in 1897 to 1,218,752 tons, in 1898 to 1,255,972 tons, in 1899 to 1,523,391 tons, and in 1900 to 1,476,645 tons.

July 1, 1900, balance unexpended... $3,557.68
June 30, 1901, amount expended during fiscal year 7.68

July 1, 1901, balance unexpended 3,550.00

{ Amount (estimated) required for completion of existing project 363,750.00
Amount that can be profitably expended in fiscal year ending June
  30, 1903, for works of improvement and for maintenance, in addition
  to the balance unexpended July 1, 1901............................... 25,000.00
Submitted in compliance with requirements of sundry civil act of June
  4, 1897, and of section 7 of the river and harbor act of 1899. }

(See Appendix F 25.)

26. *South River, New Jersey.*—[This work was in the charge of Col. J. W. Barlow, Corps of Engineers (now brigadier-general, Chief of Engineers, United States Army, retired), to November 30, 1900, of Maj. E. H. Ruffner, Corps of Engineers, from November 30, 1900, to April 20, 1901, and of General Barlow from April 20 to May 3, 1901.]

This is a small stream in the central part of New Jersey, which discharges into the Raritan River, about 8 miles above its mouth.

A private canal about three-quarters of a mile long had been dredged from near Washington, on the South River, to Sayreville, on the Raritan River, which shortened the sailing course about 2 miles.

The depth in the canal was about 3.5 feet, and in the river about 2.5 feet as far as Old Bridge, at the head of navigation, 6.3 miles above the canal. The mean rise of tide at the canal is 5.34 feet, and at Old Bridge, 4.57 feet.

The present project, approved June 14, 1880, provides for correcting the canal outlet and for obtaining, by dredging and diking, a channel 100 feet wide and 8 feet deep to Washington, 1.5 miles above the mouth; thence 6 feet deep to Bissetts, 3.7 miles above the mouth; thence 4 feet deep to Old Bridge, 6.3 miles above the mouth, at the head of navigation. The cost was estimated at $194,695, but was reduced in 1892 to $176,975. For details of previous project see Annual Report of the Chief of Engineers for 1900, page 181.

The amount expended on the present project up to the close of the fiscal year ending June 30, 1900, was $93,000, of which $78,000 was used for carrying on the work and $15,000 for maintenance. In addition, $20,000 has been expended on former projects.

No work was done during the past year.

The maximum draft that could be carried to South River on June 30, 1901, was 8 feet, and to the railroad bridge above, 5 feet at mean low water.

Large brickyards established along the banks of this river give it a commercial importance out of proportion to its size.

The commerce consists principally of brick, clay, coal, and general merchandise, and amounted in 1897 to 308,563 tons, in 1898 to 274,381 tons, in 1899 to 343,202 tons, and in 1900 to 414,288 tons.

{ Amount (estimated) required for completion of existing project $98,975.00
Amount that can be profitably expended in fiscal year ending June 30, 1903, for works of improvement and for maintenance 15,000.00
Submitted in compliance with requirements of sundry civil act of June 4, 1897, and of section 7 of the river and harbor act of 1899.

(See Appendix F 26.)

27. Raritan Bay, New Jersey.—[This work was in the charge of Col. J. W. Barlow, Corps of Engineers (now brigadier-general, Chief of Engineers United States Army, retired), to November 30, 1900, of Maj. E. H. Ruffner, Corps of Engineers, from November 30, 1900, to April 20, 1901, and of General Barlow from April 20 to May 3, 1901.] This bay is a large body of water lying between the southern end of Staten Island and the New Jersey shore. Its greatest width north and south is about 5 miles, and its greatest length east and west is about 7 miles. The Raritan River empties into it at its west end between Perth Amboy and South Amboy, and the Arthur Kill, or Staten Island Sound, extends northward, connecting it with Newark Bay.

This bay had naturally a fairly straight channel, 11 feet deep, to South Amboy. The line of the deepest water, however, followed the Staten Island shore from Perth Amboy to Seguine Point, where it was separated from deep water in the eastern part of the bay by a shoal 1.5 miles broad, with a minimum depth of 14.5 feet. The mean rise of the tide in the bay is 5 feet.

The existing project, approved March 3, 1881, amended September 19, 1890, and June 3, 1896, consists in dredging channels, 300 feet wide and 21 feet deep, from Seguine Point to deep water in the bay; through two shoals opposite Wards Point, and from South Amboy to deep water near Great Beds light. The estimated cost of the work was $507,875.

The amount expended on the work up to the close of the fiscal year ending June 30, 1900, was $441,314.45, of which $297,314.45 was used in carrying out the project and $144,000 for maintenance. The latter sum must now be added to the estimate for completion of project.

No work was done during the past year.

The maximum draft that could be carried June 30, 1901, through the Wards Point Channel was 19.5 feet, and through the Seguine Point and South Amboy channels 21 feet, all at mean low water.

The commerce of the bay consists mainly of coal, brick, manufactures, and general merchandise, and amounted in 1898 to 5,552,474 tons, in 1899 to 6,507,402 tons, and in 1900 to 6,537,977 tons.

July 1, 1900, balance unexpended	$1,185.55
June 30, 1901, amount expended during fiscal year	255.55
July 1, 1901, balance unexpended	930.00

Amount (estimated) required for completion of existing project....... 209,375.00
Amount that can be profitably expended in fiscal year ending June 30, 1903, for works of improvement and for maintenance, in addition to the balance unexpended July 1, 1901 .... 45,000.00
Submitted in compliance with requirements of sundry civil act of June 4, 1897, and of section 7 of the river and harbor act of 1899.

(See Appendix F 27.)

28. Matawan Creek, New Jersey.—[This work was in the charge of Col. J. W. Barlow, Corps of Engineers (now brigadier-general, Chief of Engineers, United States Army, retired), to November 30, 1900, of Maj. E. H. Ruffner, Corps of Engineers, from November 30, 1900, to April 20, 1901, and of General Barlow, from April 20 to May 3, 1901.] This creek is a small tidal stream in the eastern part of New Jersey, which discharges into Raritan Bay at Keyport Harbor. It is navigable up to the bridge of the New York and Long Branch Railroad, about 1¼ miles above its mouth.

In its natural condition the mouth was obstructed by a mud flat, through which a narrow and crooked 3-foot channel existed. Above this flat there was a 4-foot channel for a mile, and beyond, a narrow 3½-foot channel extending nearly up to the head of navigation, at Matawan. The rise of the tide is 4.9 feet.

The existing project for improving this stream, by dredging a 4-foot channel, 100 feet wide, from the mouth to Winkson Creek, about 1 mile, and thence 75 feet wide to the railroad bridge at Matawan, was approved March 3, 1881. The cost was estimated at $33,120.

The amount expended to June 30, 1900, was $42,120, of which $21,000 was used in carrying out the project and $21,120 for maintenance.

No work was done during the past year owing to the lack of funds.

The maximum draft that could be carried June 30, 1901, was 4 feet at mean low water.

The commerce of this creek consists of brick, fertilizers, farm produce and general merchandise, and amounted to 51,000 tons in 1899.

{Amount (estimated) required for completion of existing project..... $12,120.00
Amount that can be profitably expended in fiscal year ending June 30, 1903, for works of improvement and for maintenance........ 7,000.00
Submitted in compliance with requirements of sundry civil act of June 4, 1897, and of section 7 of the river and harbor act of 1899.

(See Appendix F 28.)

29. Keyport Harbor, New Jersey.—[This work was in the charge of Col. J. W. Barlow, Corps of Engineers (now brigadier-general, Chief of Engineers, United States Army, retired), to November 30, 1900, of Maj. E. H. Ruffner, Corps of Engineers, from November 30, 1900, to April 20, 1901, and of General Barlow from April 20 to May 3, 1901.] This harbor consists of a bay about 1 mile broad on the south shore of Raritan Bay.

There was naturally no distinct channel in the harbor, the available depth to the wharves being less than 4 feet at mean low water. A 6-foot channel had been dredged at private expense before the United States assumed charge of the improvement, but it had shoaled again to 5 feet.

The existing project, approved August 2, 1882, contemplated dredging an 8-foot channel, 200 feet wide, from Raritan Bay to the steamboat dock at Keyport, at an estimated cost of $40,475.

The amount expended to June 30, 1900, was $45,475, of which sum, $30,500 was used in carrying out the project, and $14,975 in maintenance. The sum of $9,975 will be required to complete the project, this being the difference between the estimated cost of the work and the amount expended in carrying it out.

No work was done during the past year, there being no funds available for expenditure.

The maximum draft that could be carried June 30, 1901, to the Keyport wharves was 7 feet at mean low water.

The commerce of this harbor consists mainly of farm products, fertilizers, coal, lumber, fish, shellfish, and miscellaneous freight, and amounted to 105,200 tons in 1896, to 109,200 tons in 1897, and to 67,500 tons in 1899.

{Amount (estimated) required for completion of existing project........ $9,975.00
Amount that can be profitably expended in fiscal year ending June 30, 1903, for works of improvement and for maintenance................ 5,000.00
Submitted in compliance with requirements of sundry civil act of June 4, 1897, and of section 7 of the river and harbor act of 1899.

(See Appendix F 29.)

30. Shoal Harbor and Compton Creek, New Jersey.—[This work was in the charge of Col. J. W. Barlow, Corps of Engineers (now brigadier-general, Chief of Engineers United States Army, retired), to November 30, 1900, of Maj. E. H. Ruffner, Corps of Engineers, from November 30, 1900, to April 20, 1901, and of General Barlow from April 20 to May 3, 1901.] This harbor is on the south shore of Raritan Bay, 5 miles from Sandy Hook; Compton Creek is a narrow stream emptying into it. The natural harbor is inside the mouth of the creek, where the depth is from 3 to 6 feet at mean low tide. The creek is navigable for one-quarter of a mile above its mouth, where it is crossed by a highway bridge without a draw.

The entrance to this harbor was obstructed by a broad flat shoal, on which there was a depth of less than 1 foot at mean low tide, the distance between the deep water in the creek and the 4-foot depth in the bay being about one-half mile. The mean raise of tide is 4.5

The existing project, approved September 19, 1890, proposes a channel 4 feet deep connecting Compton Creek with Raritan Bay, the width to be 150 feet in the bay and 75 feet in and near the mouth of the creek, the channel through Shoal Harbor to be protected by a dike if necessary. The estimated cost of the work was $64,130.

The amount expended to June 30, 1900, was $24,000, of which sum $17,000 was applied to carrying out the project and $7,000 for maintenance. This latter sum must now be added to the estimate for completion of the project.

No work was done during the past year, owing to lack of funds.

The maximum draft that could be carried June 30, 1901, in the channel through Shoal Harbor and Compton Creek was 3 feet at mean low water.

The commerce of this locality, consisting of farm and fish products, fertilizers, and general merchandise, amounted to 184,000 tons in 1897, to 194,500 tons in 1898, to 226,000 tons in 1899, and to 179,500 tons in 1900.

Amount (estimated) required for completion of existing project	$47,130.00
Amount that can be profitably expended in fiscal year ending June 30, 1903, for works of improvement and for maintenance	15,000.00
Submitted in compliance with requirements of sundry civil act of June 4, 1897, and of section 7 of the river and harbor act of 1899.	

(See Appendix F 30.)

31. Shrewsbury River, New Jersey.—[This work was in the charge of Col. J. W. Barlow, Corps of Engineers (now brigadier-general, Chief of Engineers, United States Army, retired), to November 30, 1900, of Maj. E. H. Ruffner, Corps of Engineers, from November 30, 1900, to April 20, 1901, and of General Barlow from April 20 to May 3, 1901.] This river is a large tidal basin in the eastern part of New Jersey, and consists of two bays, each having an area of about 3 square miles, and known as the North Branch, or Navesink River, and the South Branch. A channel, called the main stem, unites the two branches at their eastern ends and extends northwardly to the southeast end of Sandy Hook Bay.

Before any improvement was begun by the United States the available depth to Oceanic, on the North Branch, 5 miles above the mouth, was 3.5 feet; to Branchport, on the South Branch, 9 miles above the mouth, it was 2.5 feet. The mean rise of tide at the outer bar is 5 feet, at Highlands bridge 3 feet, and at Seabright bridge 1.3 feet.

The existing project, adopted March 3, 1879, contemplates making 6-foot channels from 150 to 300 feet wide from the outer bar at the mouth to Red Bank, on the North Branch, and Branchport, on the South Branch. The work was estimated to cost $234,062.

For details of previous projects see Annual Report of the Chief of Engineers for 1900, page 185.

The amount expended on the work up to the close of the fiscal year ending June 30, 1900, was $244,000, of which $168,500 was for carrying out the project and $75,000 for maintenance. The sum of $65,562 will be required to complete the project. In addition, $20,500 was expended on former projects.

The expenditure during the past year was for maintenance, and was applied to restoring the channel in the main stem, east of Island Beach. The width was increased to 40 feet, a gain of 40 feet, and the depth to 6 feet, a gain of 4 feet, for a distance of 1,025 feet.

The maximum draft that could be carried June 30, 1901, in the main stem of the river was 2 feet, in the North Branch 5¼ feet, and in the South Branch 4 feet at mean low water.

Attention is invited to that portion of the report of the district officer which contains a statement as to the urgent necessities of this improvement.

The commerce of this river, consisting mainly of coal, farm produce, fertilizers, and general merchandise, amounted in 1898 to 1,003,000 tons, in 1899 to 906,000 tons, and in 1900 to 804,000 tons. The passenger traffic is important, the number of people carried in 1900 being 327,316.

July 1, 1900, balance unexpended (allotment from appropriation contained in emergency river and harbor act approved June 6, 1900	$10,000.00
June 30, 1901, amount expended during fiscal year	3,281.91
July 1, 1901, balance unexpended	6,718.09
July 1, 1901, outstanding liabilities	3,659.37
July 1, 1901, balance available	3,058.72
July 1, 1901, amount covered by uncompleted contracts	2,706.00
Amount (estimated) required for completion of existing project	65,562.00
Amount that can be profitably expended in fiscal year ending June 30, 1903, for works of improvement and for maintenance, in addition to the balance available July 1, 1901	75,000.00
Submitted in compliance with requirements of sundry civil act of June 4, 1897, and of section 7 of the river and harbor act of 1899.	

(See Appendix F 31.)

32. *Manasquan River, New Jersey.*—[This work was in the charge of Col. J. W. Barlow, Corps of Engineers (now brigadier-general, Chief of Engineers, United States Army, retired), to November 30, 1900, of Maj. E. H. Ruffner, Corps of Engineers, from November 30, 1900, to April 20, 1901, and of General Barlow from April 20 to May 3, 1901.] This is a small stream in the eastern part of New Jersey, which empties into the Atlantic Ocean about 26 miles south of Sandy Hook.

In its natural condition the depth in the river for several miles above its mouth varied from 4 to 6 feet. The outlet, however, was obstructed by a shifting sand bar on which the depth did not exceed 1½ feet. After severe storms this outlet was sometimes entirely closed, remaining so until sufficient fresh water had accumulated in the river above to force an outlet into the ocean. The mean range of tide is 2.4 feet.

The existing project, approved March 3, 1899, contemplates obtaining an outlet 6 feet deep, for the river, and also in deepening the channel just above the mouth to the same depth. The estimated cost of the work is $59,300. For details of previous projects see report of the Chief of Engineers for 1900, page 186.

The amount expended to June 30, 1900, was $40,075, of which sum $39,000 was used for carrying out the project and $1,075 for maintenance. This latter sum must now be added to the estimate for completion.

No work was done during the past year as it was found impossible to do sufficient work with the money available to produce any good results.

The available balance will, therefore, be held until another appropriation shall have been made, with the expectation that better prices will be obtained for a greater amount of work.

The maximum draft that could be carried June 30, 1901, was 2 feet at mean low water.

The commerce amounts practically to nothing. The river is used principally by pleasure craft during the summer season.

July 1, 1900, balance unexpended	$5,925.00
July 1, 1901, balance unexpended	5,925.00
Amount (estimated) required for completion of existing project	14,375.00
Amount that can be profitably expended in fiscal year ending June 30, 1903, in addition to the balance unexpended July 1, 1901	9,000.00
Submitted in compliance with requirements of sundry civil act of June 4, 1897.	

(See Appendix F 32.)

33. Removing sunken vessels or craft obstructing or endangering navigation.—(*a*) The wreck *Richard Hall* sunk in Long Island Sound off Port Chester Harbor, New York, forming an obstruction to navigation.

The removal of the dangerous parts of the wreck to a clear depth of 25 feet below mean low water has been completed.

(*b*) The wreck *Macedonia* sunk in the Atlantic Ocean off Seabright, N. J., forming an obstruction to navigation, especially to coastwise vessels.

The removal of the dangerous parts of the wreck to a clear depth of 30 feet below mean low water was completed June 7, 1901.

(*c*) The wreck *Satanella* sunk in the channel of Raritan Bay, New Jersey, near the Old Orchard Shoal light, forming an obstruction to navigation.

The removal of this wreck was completed September 25, 1900.

(*d*) The wreck *Jemima Leonard* burned and sunk in Communipaw Channel, New Jersey, forming an obstruction to navigation.

The wreck was removed and disposed of during September, 1900.

(*e*) The wreck *Success* sunk in the Shrewsbury River opposite Island Beech, New Jersey, forming an obstruction to navigation.

This wreck was removed and disposed of during September, 1900.

(*f*) The wreck *A. S. Hatch* sunk in the channel between Staten Island and New Jersey, near the Corner Stake light, forming an obstruction to navigation.

The wreck was removed during September, 1900.

(*g*) The wreck *Union* sunk in the channel of the Hudson River off Haverstraw, N. Y., forming an obstruction to navigation.

The wreck was removed and disposed of on April 15, 1901.

(*h*) The wreck of an unknown barge sunk in the East River off Greenpoint, N. Y., forming an obstruction to navigation.

The wreck was removed during April, 1901.

(*i*) The wrecks *B. P. Ransom* and an unknown lighter sunk in New York Harbor in the vicinity of Ellis Island, forming obstructions to navigation.

The removal of these wrecks was completed during June, 1901.

The total amount expended during the year in removal of wrecks was $9,163.63.

(See Appendix F 33.)

EXAMINATION AND SURVEY MADE IN COMPLIANCE WITH EMERGENCY RIVER AND HARBOR ACT APPROVED JUNE 6, 1900.

Reports dated August 20 and November 14, 1900, respectively, upon preliminary examination and survey of *Fire Island Inlet, in Great South Bay, to Patchogue River, New York, with a view to obtaining a channel not less than 10 feet in depth and 200 feet in width at mean low water*, were submitted by Maj. E. H. Ruffner, Corps of Engineers, through the division engineer. He presents a plan for improvement at an estimated cost of $66,000 and $2,000 annually for maintenance. The reports were transmitted to Congress and printed in House Doc. No. 103, Fifth-sixth Congress, second session. (See also Appendix F 34.)

IMPROVEMENT OF NEW YORK HARBOR, OF BAY RIDGE, RED HOOK, AND BUTTERMILK CHANNELS, AND OF GOWANUS CREEK CHANNEL, NEW YORK.

This district was in the charge of Maj. W. L. Marshall, Corps of Engineers, having under his immediate orders Capt. James F. McIndoe, Corps of Engineers, to March 9, 1901, and Lieut. James A. Woodruff, Corps of Engineers, to September 19, 1900; Division Engineer, Col. G. L. Gillespie, Corps of Engineers (now brigadier-general, Chief of Engineers, United States Army), to May 3, 1901, and Col. Chas. R. Suter, Corps of Engineers, since May 9, 1901.

1. *New York Harbor, New York.*—Before the improvement of the main entrance into New York Harbor was undertaken by the United States the least depth in mid-channel on the outer bar was 23.7 feet at mean low water, and about the same across three other shoals between the bar and deep water in the harbor. A large proportion of the commerce of the port, carried in vessels of great draft, could cross these shoals only at or near high water.

The project for the improvement of Gedney Channel was approved by the Secretary of War December, 1884, and extended to cover the whole of the main entrance to the harbor December, 1886. It provided for dredging a channel 1,000 feet wide and 30 feet deep at mean low water from deep water below the Narrows through the Main Ship and Gedney channels to deep water outside the bar. The estimated cost was $1,490,000 for dredging 4,300,000 cubic yards. The actual amount dredged to October, 1891, when the work was approximately completed, was 4,875,079 cubic yards.

Up to June 30, 1900, $1,860,543.27 had been expended. The projected channel had been completed and, since 1891, maintained by removing shoals and by widening.

During the past fiscal year shoals on either side of Main Ship Channel have been removed, widening the channel out to nearly its full width of 1,000 feet, and a large shoal on the north side of Bayside Channel, just beyond the Swash Channel, was deepened. The result has been to restore the projected width at these points, which is necessary when vessels meet and pass.

Dredging was also done to deepen and straighten the channel known as Coney Island Channel, and to deepen the approaches to the Government piers at Fort Hamilton and Fort Hancock, New York Harbor.

The maximum draft that could be carried through the entrance channels into the inner harbor June 30, 1900, was 30 feet at mean low water.

The river and harbor act of 1899 provided for maintaining the existing channels in New York Harbor and also for further improving the harbor by making a deep channel 2,000 feet wide and 40 feet deep at mean low water from the Narrows across the bar and to the open sea by way of Ambrose Channel (formerly known as East Channel). Under authority of this act of Congress a project was adopted and a contract entered into for the excavation estimated as necessary to

RIVER AND HARBOR IMPROVEMENTS. 225

complete the entire work. Of the $1,000,000 appropriated by this act the sum of $649.96 had been expended up to June 30, 1900.

As there was no suitable and sufficient plant for such work in existence in this country, the contract was so drawn as to allow the contractor twelve months in which to build a plant before beginning dredging. Unexpected delays were caused by the condition of the iron market in 1898–99, and the plant was not ready to begin excavation until the spring of 1901. Up to the close of the fiscal year 423,209 cubic yards of sand had been removed from the outer side of the bar at the entrance to Ambrose Channel. The work has not yet reached the crest of the bar, and no increase in the available depth of the channel has resulted; it remains 16 feet at mean low water.

The foreign exports and imports for the port of New York during the year ending December 31, 1900, amounted approximately to 11,000,000 tons, valued at $1,177,463,035, being an increase over the valuation in 1886, before the improvement was begun, of $337,186,346. The entire cost of improvement of New York Harbor up to date is less than two-thirds of 1 per cent of the increase in annual value of foreign commerce of the port since the improvement began and is less than one-sixth of 1 per cent of the value of the present foreign commerce per year.

No statistics are kept of the local and coastwise domestic commerce.

AMBROSE CHANNEL.

July 1, 1900, balance unexpended	$999,350.04
Amount appropriated by sundry civil act approved March 3, 1901	130,000.00
	1,129,350.04
June 30, 1901, amount expended during fiscal year	32,719.25
July 1, 1901, balance unexpended	[1]1,096,630.79
July 1, 1901, outstanding liabilities	39,277.81
July 1, 1901, balance available	[1]1,057,352.98
July 1, 1901, amount covered by uncompleted contracts	3,786,911.19
Amount (estimated) required for completion of existing project	2,870,000.00
Amount that can be profitably expended in fiscal year ending June 30, 1903, in addition to the balance available July 1, 1901	300,000.00
Submitted in compliance with requirements of sundry civil act of June 4, 1897.	

GENERAL IMPROVEMENT.

July 1, 1900, balance unexpended	$62,481.25
June 30, 1901, amount expended during fiscal year	46,652.35
July 1, 1901, balance unexpended	15,828.90
July 1, 1901, outstanding liabilities	1,980.61
July 1, 1901, balance available	13,848.29
Amount that can be profitably expended in fiscal year ending June 30, 1903, for maintenance of improvement, in addition to the balance available July 1, 1901	75,000.00
Submitted in compliance with requirements of sundry civil act of June 4, 1897, and of section 7 of the river and harbor act of 1899.	

(See Appendix G 1.)

---

[1] Includes $800 allotted for expenses of Office Chief of Engineers for the fiscal year ending June 30, 1902.

2. *Channel in Gowanus Bay: Bay Ridge, Red Hook, and Buttermilk channels, in the harbor of New York.*—These channels lie along the east shore of the Upper Bay, New York Harbor, and, in the sequence named, form an eastern channel between the Narrows and the East River, separated from the main channel by a broad shoal off the mouth of Gowanus Bay and by Governors Island. The lower part of this waterway, consisting of Bay Ridge and Red Hook channels, had a natural low-water depth of 7 to 12 feet; Buttermilk Channel had a natural depth of 26 feet in a narrow, crooked channel, with Buttermilk and Red Hook shoals on either side.

Prior to 1896 this improvement was carried on under two separate projects, one for improving Buttermilk Channel, adopted in 1880 and modified subsequently so as to provide for the removal of Buttermilk and Red Hook shoals to 26 feet depth at mean low water, and one for improving Gowanus Bay channels, adopted in 1881 and subsequently modified so as to provide for dredging Bay Ridge Channel 800 feet wide and 26 feet deep, Red Hook Channel 400 feet wide and 26 feet deep, dredging the triangular area between these channels to the same depth, and making Gowanus Creek Channel 250 feet wide and 21 feet deep.

By the terms of the river and harbor act of 1896 these works were consolidated and a small improvement of Gowanus Canal was added, and the project of 1896, so adopted, consisted in dredging channels of 26 feet depth at mean low water, with widths as follows: For Bay Ridge Channel, 800 feet; for the triangular area between Bay Ridge and Red Hook channels, maximum width, 900 feet; for the Red Hook Channel, 400 feet; for Buttermilk Channel at Red Hook Shoal, 1,000 feet, and for dredging Gowanus Canal from Percival street to Hamilton Avenue Bridge to the extent of $5,000; at a total estimated cost of $837,300.

June 30, 1899, the project of 1896 had been completed; the amount expended under it was $625,854.47, which with $42,165.58 outstanding liabilities made the total cost of work done under the project $668,020.05.

The river and harbor act approved March 3, 1899, contained the following provision:

Improving Bay Ridge Channel and Red Hook Channel in the harbor of New York: Continuing improvement, $100,000: *Provided*, That the work shall be begun at the forty-foot curve at the southerly end of Bay Ridge Channel, and be continued through it along the Brooklyn shore to Twenty-eighth street until the said Bay Ridge Channel shall have a uniform depth of forty feet at low water and a width of 1,200 feet; and the improvement of the Red Hook Channel shall be begun on its southerly end and at its junction with the Bay Ridge Channel, and be continued through it to its junction on its northerly end with the Buttermilk Channel until said Red Hook Channel shall have been made to a depth of forty feet at low tide and a width of 1,200 feet: *And provided further*, That contracts may be entered into by the Secretary of War for the completion of said Bay Ridge Channel and Red Hook Channel, to be paid for as appropriations may from time to time be made by law, not exceeding in the aggregate $2,400,000, exclusive of the amount herein and heretofore appropriated.

A contract for excavation of the channels so authorized was entered into July 31, 1900, providing for the removal of about 22,000,000 cubic yards of material, measured in scows, at 10 cents per cubic yard. Excavation was begun March 18, 1901, and up to the close of the fiscal year 284,501 cubic yards had been removed.

The work is not yet far enough advanced to have any useful effect upon the channel.

Up to July 1, 1900, no expenditure had been made from the appropriation for the project of 1899.

The funds remaining from the appropriation of 1898 were applied to removing shoals in Buttermilk Channel and with other allotments from act of June 6, 1900, to making the survey of that channel authorized by act of Congress of June 6, 1900.

The commerce of this part of New York Harbor consists of coal, grain, lumber, iron, and other freight, amounting in 1899 to 19,881,825 tons, valued at $764,708,971. The amount of commerce in transit through these channels can not be estimated.

The improvement already made has resulted in making these channels available for vessels of much greater draft than formerly. The maximum draft which could be carried through these channels June 30, 1901, was 26 feet at mean low water.

BAY RIDGE AND RED HOOK CHANNELS.

July 1, 1900, balance unexpended	$362,000.00
November 26, 1900, received for services of steamer *Manisees*	55.00
Amount appropriated by sundry civil act approved March 3, 1901	140,000.00
	502,055.00
June 30, 1901, amount expended during fiscal year	12,839.90
July 1, 1901, balance unexpended	[1]489,215.10
July 1, 1901, outstanding liabilities	10,779.40
July 1, 1901, balance available	[1]478,435.70
July 1, 1901, amount covered by uncompleted contracts	2,189,675.60
Amount (estimated) required for completion of existing project	1,998,000.00
Amount that can be profitably expended in fiscal year ending June 30, 1903, in addition to the balance available July 1, 1901	200,000.00
Submitted in compliance with requirements of sundry civil act of June 4, 1897.	

BAY RIDGE, RED HOOK, AND BUTTERMILK CHANNELS.

July 1, 1900, balance unexpended	$7,262.46
June 30, 1901, amount expended during fiscal year	7,262.46

(See Appendix G 2.)

3. *Gowanus Creek Channel, New York Harbor.*—That part of Gowanus Creek improved under the title of Gowanus Creek Channel is the part from the foot of Percival street on the east to the junction of Red Hook and Bay Ridge channels on the west.

Before improvement Gowanus Creek Channel had an available low-water depth of about 11 feet.

In 1881 a project for improvement of the several channels in Gowanus Bay was adopted which, as subsequently modified, provided for making a depth of 21 feet at mean low water in the Gowanus Creek Channel, with width extending to the harbor lines on either side. This was accomplished in 1893, under parts of appropriations made for the sev-

---

[1] Includes $400 allotted for expenses of Office Chief of Engineers for the fiscal year ending June 30, 1902.

eral channels, of which it is estimated that about $75,000 was applied to Gowanus Creek Channel.

Under the terms of the river and harbor act of 1896 a project was adopted for making the Gowanus Creek Channel 26 feet deep at mean low water between the foot of Percival street and Red Hook Channel, at a total estimated cost of $70,000.

Up to July 1, 1900, $42,646.90 had been expended under this project; the channel through the creek, from Red Hook Channel up to the foot of Percival street, a distance of 3,000 feet, had been dredged 26 feet deep at mean low water, with width of 250 feet at the outer or west end, and 175 feet at the east end, bringing the deep water up to 15 feet from the pier heads.

During the past fiscal year 1,740 cubic yards was dredged, completing a contract.

The middle of the channel, which was dredged five years ago, has shoaled about 3 feet.

The maximum draft that could be carried through this channel June 30, 1901, was 26 feet at mean low water; it was found on either side of the channel.

The work required to complete the project is mainly in the removal of shoals which have formed in the channel since dredging; estimated cost, $20,000.

The commerce received in Gowanus Creek consists of coal, lumber, building materials, and miscellaneous goods, amounting to about 237,300 tons of freight in 1899, valued at $3,048,390. In addition, 2,041,980 tons of freight passed through Gowanus Creek Channel to and from Gowanus Canal, valued at about $20,000,000, making a total tonnage of 2,279,280 tons. The annual value of this commerce is about three hundred times the total cost of the present project.

The improvement has resulted in admitting to this channel vessels of 15 feet greater draft of water than formerly.

Following is a statement of the tonnage of commerce reported as received and discharged at the docks of Gowanus Creek, New York:

	Tons.		Tons.
1895	366,299	1897	215,352
1896	220,748	1899	237,300

July 1, 1900, balance unexpended	$7,353.10
June 30, 1901, amount expended during fiscal year	7,353.10
Amount (estimated) required for completion of existing project	20,000.00
Amount that can be profitably expended in fiscal year ending June 30, 1903	20,000.00
Submitted incompliance with requirements of sundry civil act of June 4, 1897.	

(See Appendix G 3.)

4. Enlargement of Governors Island, New York Harbor.—The sundry civil act of March 3, 1901, contained an appropriation of $200,000 toward the enlargement of Governors Island, in accordance with the plan reported by a Board composed of Maj. Gen. John R. Brooke, Col. (now Brig. Gen.) George L. Gillespie, and Col. Amos S. Kimball, dated August 17, 1900.

The work of enlargement, including construction of a dock and dredging of a channel at an estimated cost of $215,000, and construction of a bulkhead and filling at an estimated cost of $885,000, has been assigned to this office.

The $200,000 provided for the portion of the work to be carried out under direction of the Chief of Engineers will be applied to the construction of a wharf, the dredging of a channel 26 feet deep, and to bulkhead construction and enlargement.

Amount appropriated by sundry civil act approved March 3, 1901 ......$200,000.00
July 1, 1901, balance unexpended 200,000.00

{ Amount (estimated) required for completion of enlargement (bulkhead and filling)[1] 825,000.00
Amount that can be profitably expended in fiscal year ending June 30, 1903, for construction of bulkhead and filling,[1] in addition to the balance unexpended July 1, 1901... 500,000.00
Submitted in compliance with requirements of sundry civil act of June 4, 1897.

(See Appendix G 4.)

5. *Removing sunken vessels or craft obstructing or endangering navigation.*—(a) A canal boat, name unknown, was found sunk in Buttermilk Channel, New York Harbor, with a least clear depth of 23 feet in a channel over 30 feet deep. The boat had evidently been on the bottom a long time. It was removed bodily in September, 1900, and deposited in private wreckage yard back of the bulkhead line at Weehawken, N. J.

(b) The schooner *Grover Cleveland*, a small vessel with cargo of lumber was wrecked and sunk at the Government pier, Sandy Hook, N. J., November, 1900, while discharging. The wreck was worthless, and was a serious obstruction to safe use of the landing. It was pulled to pieces and the pieces removed and placed above high-water mark at Bayonne, N. J.

The amount expended during the year on removal of wrecks was $720.

(See Appendix G 5.)

EXAMINATION AND SURVEY MADE IN COMPLIANCE WITH EMERGENCY RIVER AND HARBOR ACT APPROVED JUNE 6, 1900.

Reports dated June 25 and November 28, 1900, respectively, on preliminary examination and survey of *Buttermilk Channel, New York Harbor, N. Y., with a view to obtaining a channel 40 feet deep at mean low water and 1,200 feet wide*, were submitted by Major Marshall through the division engineer. He presents a plan for improvement at an estimated cost of $1,900,000. The reports were transmitted to Congress and printed in House Doc. No. 122, Fifty-sixth Congress, second session. (See also Appendix G 6.)

IMPROVEMENT OF DELAWARE RIVER AND BAY AND OF CERTAIN WATERS TRIBUTARY THERETO, NEW JERSEY, PENNSYLVANIA, AND DELAWARE, OF CERTAIN RIVERS AND HARBORS IN SOUTHERN NEW JERSEY AND IN DELAWARE, AND OF INLAND WATERWAY FROM CHINCOTEAGUE BAY TO DELAWARE BAY, VIRGINIA, MARYLAND, AND DELAWARE.

This district was in the charge of Lieut. Col. C. W. Raymond, Corps of Engineers, having under his immediate orders Capt. James B. Cavanaugh, Corps of Engineers, to July 13, 1900, and Capt. Spencer Cosby, Corps of Engineers, the entire year.

---

[1] Construction of storehouses and other necessary buildings not included.

1. *Delaware River, New Jersey and Pennsylvania.*—Trenton, the head of natural navigation on the Delaware River, is about 30 miles above the upper part of the port of Philadelphia. In its original condition this part of the river was obstructed by shoals at the following localities: Between Bordentown and Trenton, a distance of about 5 miles, a narrow and circuitous channel existed which carried from 3 to 6 feet at mean low water. At Kinkora Bar, about 9 miles below Trenton, there was a shoal carrying 7¼ feet, and at Five-mile Bar, at the upper part of Philadelphia, a shoal across the Pennsylvania channel, carrying only 3 to 4 feet at mean low water, there being, however, 13 feet of water past Five-mile Bar in the New Jersey channel passing south of Petty Island.

Below Philadelphia the river in its original condition presented obstructions at Mifflin Bar, which reduced the depth at mean low water to 17 feet; at Schooner Ledge and Cherry Island Flats, to 18 feet; at Bulkhead Shoal and Dan Baker Shoal, to about 20 feet, and at Duck Creek Flats to about 20 feet. In that part of the Delaware River between Trenton, N. J., and Bridesburg, Pa., efforts in the past have been directed toward relieving commerce from the obstructions which exist in the upper 9 miles of the river and deepening the channel across Kinkora Bar.

Previous to 1885 the efforts to improve the river between Philadelphia and the bay were confined to dredging, except at Schooner Ledge, where solid rock was removed under appropriations for special localities, and also under general appropriations for the Delaware River below Bridesburg.

A Board of Engineers, convened by direction of the Secretary of War for the purpose of considering the subject of the permanent improvement of Delaware River and Bay, recommended, under date of January 23, 1885, the formation of a ship channel from a point opposite Philadelphia and about midway between the American Shipbuilding Company's yard and the Gas Trust wharf to deep water in Delaware Bay, having a least width of 600 feet and a depth of 26 feet at mean low water. The formation of such a channel was to be obtained, except at Schooner Ledge, where rock would require to be removed, by regulating the tidal flow by means of dikes with recourse to dredging where necessary as an aid to such contracting and regulating works.

The estimated cost of obtaining a channel of the above dimensions was about $2,425,000, which covered the estimated cost of the permanent improvement of the Delaware River between the upper part of Philadelphia and deep water in the bay. The annual cost of maintenance was estimated at 10 per cent of the original cost for dredging and 1 per cent of the original cost for dikes. This estimate of cost did not include the improvement of Philadelphia Harbor, which was a separate project.

In the river and harbor act approved March 3, 1899, Congress adopted a new project for the improvement of the river, providing for the formation of a channel 600 feet wide and 30 feet deep from Christian street, Philadelphia, to deep water in Delaware Bay, at an estimated cost of $5,810,000. This project superseded the project of 1885, which provided for a depth of 26 feet at mean low water. At the time of the adoption of the new project the 26-foot channel, with widths varying from 200 to 600 feet, had been formed from the upper part of Philadelphia Harbor to the bay, except at the following-named localities: Tinicum Island Shoal, depth from 23.6 feet to 26 feet over a distance of about 4,200 feet; above Schooner Ledge, depth from 24 feet to 26 feet over a distance of about 4,800 feet; from below Marcushook to Bellevue, depth from 23 feet to 26 feet over a distance of about 13,500 feet. These distances are measured on the range lines. The distances measured between the 26-foot curves on the lines of deepest water are much shorter.

At the same time there was between Trenton and Philadelphia a channel 6 feet deep at mean low water through Perriwig Bar, a depth of 7 feet in the eastern channel at Bordentown, a channel 8½ feet deep through Kinkora Bar, and a channel 26 feet deep over the whole width through Five-mile Bar.

The entire amount expended on the improvement of the Delaware River from 1836 to June 30, 1900, under appropriations for special localities and the general river, was $2,986,133.36, of which $124,496.75 was expended on the part of the river between Trenton and Philadelphia.

The total amount expended upon the 26-foot project, from its adoption in 1885 until it was superseded by the 30-foot project in 1899, was $1,598,621.51, of which about $200,000 is estimated to have been applied to maintenance.

During the fiscal year ending June 30, 1900, the sum of $31,408.19 was expended in examinations, surveys, in the removal of rock opposite Petty Island, and in operations at Dan Baker Shoal, for the formation of a 30-foot channel and the construction of a bulkhead for the reception of dredged material.

During the past fiscal year the sum of $176,200.21 was expended in surveys, in continuing the work of rock removal opposite Petty Island, and in continuing operations at Dan Baker Shoal for the formation of a 30-foot channel and the construction of a bulkhead for the reception of dredged material.

The changes during the past fiscal year are summarized as follows:

At rock opposite Petty Island the entire rock area has been blasted and dredged over, present operations consisting in redrilling and redredging over detached areas still above the plane of 26 feet below mean low water.

At Dan Baker Shoal the work of bulkhead construction has resulted in the completion of about 8,140 linear feet of the structure up to the close of the fiscal year, with an additional length of 2,200 feet partly constructed. The work of dredging under the 30-foot project was commenced in August, 1900, and up to June 30, 1901, 1,004,338 cubic yards of material had been removed from the channel on the proposed Finns Point and Reedy Island ranges. This work has resulted in the formation of a channel 30 feet deep at mean low water, about 18,900 feet long and from 50 to 300 feet wide, through a part of Dan Baker Shoal.

The greatest draft of water that could be carried at mean low water on June 30, 1901, over the shoalest part of the river below Philadelphia, was about 21 feet at Cherry Island Flats. At one locality in the flats the least low-water depth is about 19½ feet, but the nature of the bottom is such that vessels pass over it without difficulty.

For 1890 the total foreign freight movement of the Delaware River was estimated at 2,922,994 tons, and the total domestic freight movement at 8,433,276 tons; total, 11,356,270 tons. For 1900 the total foreign freight movement was estimated at 4,830,080 tons, and the total domestic freight movement at 19,359,899 tons; total, 24,189,979 tons. Of the latter quantities it is estimated that 4,828,080 tons of foreign freight and 17,677,616 tons of domestic freight (total, 22,505,696 tons) arrived at and departed from the port of Philadelphia.

COMMERCIAL STATISTICS.

The following statement concerning the foreign commerce of the Delaware River for the years ending December 31, 1899 and 1900, are compiled from the reports of the Board of Trade, the Commercial Exchange, and the Maritime Exchange of the city of Philadelphia:

Articles.	1899.	1900.
IMPORTS.	Tons.	Tons.
Chalk	27,865	12,761
Drugs and chemicals	69,127	92,135
Hemp, jute, flax, and their fabrics	28,978	27,425
Iron ore	421,187	511,958
Sugar	422,828	329,009
Miscellaneous	300,455	343,266
Total	1,270,440	1,316,554
EXPORTS.		
Coal	485,604	794,563
Grain and flour	1,297,527	1,443,508
Petroleum and products	851,145	756,134
Miscellaneous	435,294	519,321
Total	3,069,570	3,513,526

The following statement concerning the domestic and coastwise commerce of the Delaware River for the years ending December 31, 1899 and 1900, has been compiled from returns made by shippers, consignees, and carriers:

Articles.	1899. Tons.	1899. Value.	1900. Tons.	1900. Value.
ARRIVING.				
Chemicals	155,603	$3,150,820	86,166	$1,552,918
Coal	527,909	1,654,189	639,840	2,116,301
Lumber	502,549	9,901,674	678,265	7,555,519
Sand	787,018	542,947	942,440	711,719
Miscellaneous	4,118,300	636,073,098	4,384,814	791,984,153
Total	6,091,379	651,322,728	6,731,525	803,920,605
DEPARTING.				
Chemicals	81,792	2,085,405	76,467	1,782,854
Coal	7,322,026	25,453,530	8,025,877	27,801,651
Fertilizers	211,435	1,856,433	158,010	1,527,521
Iron, manufactured	128,681	5,438,186	106,870	4,829,835
Miscellaneous	3,744,909	510,638,104	4,266,150	576,591,018
Total	11,488,843	545,471,658	12,628,374	612,532,879

SUMMARY.

Delaware River.

	Tons.	Value.
Arriving:		
Foreign	1,316,554	$49,186,877
Domestic	6,731,525	803,920,605
Total	8,048,079	853,107,482
Departing:		
Foreign	3,513,526	81,145,966
Domestic	12,628,374	612,532,879
Total	16,141,900	693,678,845
Total foreign	4,830,080	130,332,843
Total domestic	19,359,899	1,416,453,484
Grand total	24,189,979	1,546,786,327

Freight movement of the port of Philadelphia for the year ending December 31, 1900.

	Tons.	Value.
Arriving:		
Foreign	1,314,554	$49,100,877
Domestic	6,548,155	776,292,912
Total	7,862,709	825,393,789
Departing:		
Foreign	3,513,526	81,145,966
Domestic	11,129,461	520,351,632
Total	14,642,987	601,497,598
Total foreign	4,828,080	130,246,843
Total domestic	17,677,616	1,296,644,544
Grand total	22,505,696	1,426,891,387

July 1, 1900, balance unexpended	$556,366.64
Amount appropriated by sundry civil act approved March 3, 1901	61,500.00
	617,866.64
June 30, 1901, amount expended during fiscal year	176,200.21
July 1, 1901, balance unexpended	441,666.43
July 1, 1901, outstanding liabilities	37,710.20
July 1, 1901, balance available	403,956.23
July 1, 1901, amount covered by uncompleted contracts	126,227.39

{ Amount (estimated) required for completion of existing project 5,310,000.00
Amount that can be profitably expended in fiscal year ending June 30, 1903, for works of improvement and for maintenance, in addition to the balance available July 1, 1901 ..... 650,000.00
Submitted in compliance with requirements of sundry civil act of June 4, 1897, and of section 7 of the river and harbor act of 1899. }

(See Appendix H 1.)

2. Schuylkill River, Pennsylvania.—When the improvement was commenced in 1870 there was a channel of entrance into the mouth of the river with a depth of only 10 feet at mean low water, so that the river was not navigable at high water for vessels of more than 15 or 16 feet draft.

The original project under which work was commenced in 1870 proposed the formation of a channel 100 feet wide, with a depth of 20 feet from the mouth of the river to Gibson Point, about 4 miles, and a depth of 18 feet thence to Chestnut Street Bridge, in Philadelphia, about 3 miles.

In 1875 and 1883 this project was amended so as to increase the low-water channel between the mouth and Girard Point, a distance of about 1 mile, to 400 feet wide and 24 feet deep, and from Girard Point to Gibson Point, about 3 miles, to 250 feet wide and 20 feet deep. In 1892 the project was again modified so as to provide for the construction of dikes to maintain a navigable depth at the mouth. The estimated cost of the entire improvement was $529,959.

During the fiscal year ending June 30, 1897, 62,983 cubic yards of material, scow measurement, was dredged from the bar at the mouth of the river. The average depth of the channel across the bar along the line of deepest water was 27.5 feet at mean low water.

During the fiscal year ending June 30, 1898, the pile dike at the mouth of the river was raised and repaired by spiking on the face wall two courses of 12 by 12 inch pine timber, thus raising its height to about 9.5 feet above low water.

The earthen dike connecting with the pile dike was repaired and reconstructed for a distance of 410 feet.

During the fiscal year ending June 30, 1899, the filling of the pile dike was raised to the level of the face wall by the deposit of coarse gravel and bowlders.

During the fiscal year ending June 30, 1900, no work was done under this project and no liabilities were incurred.

The amount expended on this project to June 30, 1900, was $513,900. This expenditure has resulted in the formation of a channel about 125 feet wide and 24 feet deep at mean low water across the bar at the river's mouth; a channel about 250 feet wide and from 20 to 24 feet deep from inside the bar to Gibson Point, except at Yankee Point, where the width is 300 feet, and between Penrose Ferry Bridge and Yankee Point, where the 20-foot channel has narrowed to from 50 to 200 feet; thence to Walnut Street Bridge, a channel of navigable width and from 14 to 20 feet deep. Of this amount about $40,000 had been expended for the maintenance of the dredged channel.

During the five years between 1895 and 1899 the city of Philadelphia was engaged in improving the channel under authorities granted by the Secretary of War under dates of September 3, 1895, and May 14, 1896. Dredging was commenced on November 13, 1895, and was finished on December 26, 1899, available funds having been exhausted. The total amount of material dredged and placed ashore is 615,377 cubic yards. This work has resulted in increasing the depths in the existing channel between Penrose Ferry Bridge and Fifty-eighth street, near Gibson Point, to 22 feet at mean low water, and above Gibson Point to 20 feet, extending the existing channel to a point about 500 feet above Harrison's wharf, in all a distance of about 4.7 miles.

During the past fiscal year the sum of $11,100 was expended in redredging the channel at the mouth of the river to a depth of 26 feet at mean low water over a width of from 115 to 150 feet. This work completes operations under the existing project.

On June 30, 1901, the maximum draft that could be carried at mean low water over the shoalest part of the improved channel was about 20 feet.

The survey of the river provided for in the river and harbor act of June 3, 1896, with a view to further improvement, was completed in December, 1897, and a project and report thereon, submitted March 10, 1898, was printed in House Doc. No. 346, Fifty-fifth Congress, second session; also in the Annual Report of the Chief of Engineers for 1898, page 1114.

The commercial interests of this river are of great and increasing value and importance. At Girard Point are located large grain elevators and wharves. At Gibson Point and Point Breeze, which are near each other and closely related as to commercial requirements, are the large storage tanks and wharves of the petroleum factories. The interests assembled at these three points cover mainly the commerce of the river, and both the grain and oil trade require deep-draft vessels for the convenient and economical transaction of their business. Channel depths are needed which will permit the passage of vessels drawing 24 feet at all stages of the tide. The total freight movement for the year 1900 is estimated at 2,983,954 tons (a decrease of 499,868 tons from the year 1899), and its value at $35,816,737 (a decrease of $3,806,954 from the year 1899).

COMMERCIAL STATISTICS.

The following statement of the foreign and domestic commerce of the Schuylkill River for the years ending December 31, 1899 and 1900, has been compiled from returns made by shippers, consignees, and carriers:

Articles.	1899. Tons.	1899. Value.	1900. Tons.	1900. Value.
ARRIVING.				
Coal	459,283	$1,599,677	538,506	$2,126,516
Iron ore	127,300	1,018,400	78,759	610,072
Stone, building	17,864	111,914	32,451	312,864
Sand	564,068	298,070	355,656	260,479
Miscellaneous	221,649	3,677,508	256,853	3,628,897
Total	1,390,134	6,705,569	1,262,225	6,938,828
DEPARTING.				
Coal	122,485	384,355	18,580	79,679
Grain	578,500	8,500,000	531,328	7,900,000
Petroleum and products	1,136,616	17,109,652	952,528	18,162,528
Miscellaneous	256,087	6,924,115	219,343	2,735,702
Total	2,093,688	32,918,122	1,721,729	28,877,909

July 1, 1900, balance unexpended $11,100.00
June 30, 1901, amount expended during fiscal year 11,100.00

(See Appendix H 2.)

3. Ice harbor at Marcushook, Pa.—This work in its present plan was commenced in 1866, the object being to provide a harbor in the Delaware River to protect vessels against moving ice.

In 1785 the Commonwealth of Pennsylvania built, for the convenience of commerce, piers at Marcushook extending from the shore line into the river. It is assumed that at some subsequent time these shore piers were turned over to the United States, since in 1829 an appropriation was made of $5,000 for repairing these piers, improving the harbor, and removing obstructions. No further appropriation was made until 1866.

At this latter date a project was adopted for the construction of detached piers in the harbor, consisting of stone superstructures upon crib foundations filled with stone, together with the deepening of the harbor by dredging.

In 1888 an increased depth was proposed for the areas protected by the detached piers outside of the natural shore line of the river.

The amount expended from 1866 to June 30, 1900, was $212,284.28, which was applied to the construction and repair of two landing piers, dredging the protected area to a depth of from 18 to 24 feet at mean low water, the placing and replacing of mooring piles, repairs to piers and mooring piles, and the necessary examinations. Of this amount $4,000 was applied to the maintenance of the improvement.

During the past fiscal year no work was done and no expenditures were incurred.

On June 30, 1901, the areas protected by the detached piers had a mean low-water depth varying from 18 to 27 feet.

This harbor is of great value to vessels during the prevalence of ice in the river. The cost of its maintenance is trifling in comparison with the benefit derived from it.

It is proposed to hold the available balance of $1,715.72 for maintenance and repairs as needed.

July 1, 1900, balance unexpended $1,715.72
July 1, 1901, balance unexpended 1,715.72

(See Appendix H 3.)

4. Construction of iron pier in Delaware Bay near Lewes, Del.—The original project for this work proposed the construction of a landing pier about 1,700 feet in length, extending from the shore south of the breakwater into Delaware Bay to a depth of 22 feet at mean low water, the pier to consist of a substructure of wrought-iron screw piles, surrounded with a timber superstructure. The work was commenced in 1871 and completed, except as to superstructure, in 1880.

The work done to June 30, 1890, resulted in the construction of 1,155 linear feet of pier 21 feet in width and 546 linear feet 42 feet in width, or a total length of 1,701 feet. The depth of water at the outer end of the pierhead was about 21 feet at mean low water.

Since construction the pier has been repaired and cared for by the United States.

The total expenditure to June 30, 1900, was $385,339.40. Of this amount $27,000 has been applied to the maintenance of the improvement.

- The right to use this pier for railway purposes, granted in the act of July 15, 1870, has never been exercised and doubtless never will be, as the pier has not sufficient strength to support the weight of modern freight engines. It is therefore impossible to obtain any assistance from the railroad company in maintaining and repairing the structure.

During the past fiscal year no work has been in progress.

The pier is of great use for the purposes of the engineer, lighthouse, and quarantine services. It is of very great value to vessels frequenting the breakwater harbor in winter when the harbor is packed with floating ice, rendering the anchorage dangerous. At such times vessels eagerly seek its shelter and protection.

It is proposed to hold the available balance of $820.60 for maintenance and repairs as needed.

July 1, 1900, balance unexpended	$820.60
July 1, 1901, balance unexpended	820.60

(See Appendix H 4.)

5. *Delaware Breakwater, Delaware.*—The final report of the local officer upon this work was submitted June 19, 1899, and is printed in the Annual Report of the Chief of Engineers for 1899, page 1346.

The depths in the protected anchorage vary from 11½ to 18 feet at mean low water, and the harbor is available for vessels drawing up to about 16 feet.

The amount expended on this work up to June 30, 1900, was $2,807,297.68. No portion of this amount has been applied to maintenance.

During the past fiscal year the sum of $171.45 was expended in making a survey of the breakwater harbor for the purpose of ascertaining what changes have occurred in the interval of two years since the last survey of June, 1899.

The Maritime Exchange of Philadelphia maintains a station on the breakwater, and through cables between the mainland and its station is in communication with the shipping of the harbor. Its reports state that during the year 1900 2,200 vessels, exclusive of tugs, fishing, and small coasting craft, anchored under the protection of the breakwater.

It is proposed to reserve the available balance of $884.57 for repairs to the breakwater and for surveys and examinations of the work.

July 1, 1900, balance unexpended	$1,056.02
June 30, 1901, amount expended during fiscal year	171.45
July 1, 1901, balance unexpended	884.57

(See Appendix H 5.)

6. *Harbor of refuge, Delaware Bay, Delaware.*—The project for the construction of this harbor, which was adopted, approved, and provided for on the continuous-contract system in the river and harbor act of June 3, 1896, includes the construction of a breakwater on the line of least depth along the eastern branch of the shoal known as the "Shears," and the construction of a row of ice piers across the upper end of the harbor to protect it from ice descending the bay, at a total cost not to exceed $4,665,000.

The act provides that in making the contracts the Secretary of War shall not obligate the Government to pay in any one fiscal year, beginning July 1, 1897, more than 25 per cent of the whole amount authorized to be expended.

No expenditures were made upon this improvement previous to June 30, 1896.

Up to the close of the fiscal year ending June 30, 1900, $1,304,289.53 had been expended in the construction of the breakwater, the amount of stone deposited in the work to that date being 1,095,099 tons. No part of this amount was applied to the maintenance of this work.

During the past fiscal year about 277,517 tons of stone was deposited in the breakwater. On June 30, 1901, the substructure had been brought to a width of 41 feet at mean low water for a distance of 8,035 feet, 4,740 feet of superstructure had been fully constructed to a height of 14 feet above mean low water, and 2,680 feet partly constructed.

238   REPORT OF THE CHIEF OF ENGINEERS, U. S. ARMY.

A project for the construction of the ice piers was submitted on April 5, 1900, and approved April 23, 1900. This work was commenced during the past fiscal year, and up to June 30, 1901, 39,562 tons of stone had been deposited in the ice piers, thereby partly constructing the substructures of all ten of the piers, and partly constructing the superstructures of two of them.

The sundry civil act approved March 3, 1901, appropriated $213,000 for continuing the improvement. The funds on hand are considered sufficient for the completion of the work now projected.

The great value of this harbor to commerce is due to its location. It is about equidistant from New York, Philadelphia, and the capes of Chesapeake Bay (the ocean entrance to the ports of Baltimore, Norfolk, and Newport News), and is therefore an especially convenient point of call for the entire commerce of the North Atlantic coast. It is now largely used by vessels awaiting orders to ports for discharge or loading. During the year ending December 31, 1900, 1,924 vessels (not including small craft) called at this locality.

By the construction of the breakwater the usefulness of this anchorage has been greatly increased, not only as a port of call, but also as a harbor of refuge. Vessels bound from northern to southern, or from southern to northern ports are able to go to sea in doubtful weather with the assurance of finding ample protection at the Delaware capes if overtaken by storm.

July 1, 1900, balance unexpended	$722,044.47
Amount appropriated by sundry civil act approved March 3, 1901	213,000.00
	935,044.47
June 30, 1901, amount expended during fiscal year	496,623.56
July 1, 1901, balance unexpended	438,420.91
July 1, 1901, outstanding liabilities	93,397.88
July 1, 1901, balance available	345,023.03
July 1, 1901, amount covered by uncompleted contracts	345,023.03

(See Appendix H 6.)

7. *Rancocas River, New Jersey.*—In its original condition Rancocas River carried a minimum low-water depth of 4½ feet between the mouth and Centerton, a distance of about 7¼ miles, and from Centerton to Mount Holly, a distance of about 5¼ miles, a ruling depth of about 2½ feet.

The original project of 1881 proposed the formation, by a dike at Coates Bar and dredging elsewhere, of a channel from 150 to 200 feet wide and 6 feet deep at mean low water from the mouth to Centerton, and thence to Mount Holly a channel 5 feet deep.

Operations under this project were carried on from 1881 to 1895. To the close of the fiscal year ending June 30, 1895, operations had been directed to the formation of a low-water channel 100 feet wide and 6 feet deep from the mouth to Centerton, and 50 feet wide and 5 feet deep for a distance of about 1¾ miles above Centerton.

During the fiscal year ending June 30, 1896, no work was done.

The appropriation of $2,000 for this river, made in the act of June 3, 1896, was required by the act to be expended in the improvement of the Lumberton Branch, and during the fiscal year ending June 30, 1897, the Lumberton Branch was surveyed, and a project for its improvement by dredging a channel through the shoals which obstructed navigation was submitted and approved.

During the fiscal year ending June 30, 1898, the project was completed by dredging through the shoals at Pattersons Landing, below Paxsons Landing, and partly through the shoal above Paxsons Landing, the channel having a width of 30 feet and a mean low-water depth of 6 feet.

The river and harbor act of March 3, 1899, appropriated $2,000 for this river, to be expended in the Lumberton Branch.

During the fiscal year ending June 30, 1900, the project for the expenditure of this appropriation, which was approved April 8, 1899, was completed by dredging a channel with depth of from 6 to 7 feet at mean low water, and a width of 30 feet through the shoal below Moores Landing.

Up to June 30, 1900, the total expenditures in connection with this improvement amounted to $41,432.68. No part of this amount was applied to the maintenance of the work.

During the past fiscal year no work was done in connection with this improvement.

The maximum draft of water that could be carried at mean low water on June 30, 1901, over the shoalest part of the locality under improvement was about 4½ feet.

The principal commercial interests are the manufacture of phosphorus and the transportation of sand and gravel.

The total value of the freight movement for 1900 was $2,388,110.

COMMERCIAL STATISTICS.

Arrivals and departures for the years ending December 31, 1899 and 1900.

Articles.	1899. Tons.	1899. Value.	1900. Tons.	1900. Value.
ARRIVALS.				
Coal	38,000	$152,000	6,720	$26,880
Iron, pig	5,000	100,000	3,399	67,980
Manure	63,000	94,500	21,952	34,300
Miscellaneous	25,200	370,350	13,900	971,357
Total	131,200	716,850	45,971	1,100,517
DEPARTURES.				
Produce	3,120	420,000	2,000	280,000
Sand and gravel	246,742	211,153	302,904	270,450
Miscellaneous	6,210	337,500	17,015	737,143
Total	256,072	968,653	321,919	1,287,593

July 1, 1900, balance unexpended $467.23
June 30, 1901, amount expended during fiscal year 67.53

July 1, 1901, balance unexpended .... [1] 399.70

(See Appendix H 7.)

8. *Cooper Creek, New Jersey.*—This creek enters the Delaware River in the city of Camden, just above Cooper Point. It is navigable at mean high water for a distance of 9 miles from its mouth for vessels

---

[1] Balance remaining from appropriation of August 18, 1894, and not available for expenditure under the present project.

drawing 5 feet, and for the first 5 miles for vessels of 11¼ feet draft. The mean range of the tide at the mouth is about 6 feet. For a distance of 1¼ miles from the mouth the width of the stream averages about 80 feet at low water and about 120 feet between the banks, and the channel in its original condition had a depth at mean high water of from 12 to 15 feet, except at one place where the depth was 9¼ feet.

The project for this improvement was adopted in the river and harbor act of June 3, 1896, and is printed in the Annual Report of the Chief of Engineers for 1895, page 1102. It provides for the formation by dredging of a channel 70 feet wide at bottom and 18 feet deep at mean high water from the mouth of the creek to Browning's Chemical Works, and a channel of the same dimensions through the bar just outside the mouth, in all a distance of about 9,000 feet. The estimated cost, including contingencies, is $35,000.

The river and harbor act of June 3, 1896, appropriated $37,000 for completing this improvement, of which $2,500, or so much thereof as might be necessary, was to be expended in rebuilding the dike on the Government reservation in the Delaware River at Woodbury Creek.

During the fiscal year ending June 30, 1897, the sum of $2,500 was expended in rebuilding the dike on the Government reservation at Woodbury Creek.

The amount expended on the project to June 30, 1900, including amount expended for rebuilding dike on Government reservation at Woodbury Creek, was $28,175.15. No part of this amount was applied to the maintenance of the improvement.

The dredging resulted in the formation of a channel extending from the mouth to the Camden Iron Works, 7,500 feet long, 50 to 70 feet wide, except at the bridges, where the widths are 30 feet, and 18 feet deep at mean high water, except on the water pipe belonging to the city of Camden, where the high-water depths are 14 to 15 feet.

During the past fiscal year no work has been in progress.

It is proposed to complete the improvement with funds now available as soon as the city of Camden removes or lowers the water pipe at State Street Bridge. The maximum draft of water that could be carried at mean low water on June 30, 1901, over the shoalest part of the locality under improvement was about 8 to 9 feet, which is the low-water depth on the pipe above mentioned. Elsewhere the low-water draft is from 10 to 12 feet.

There are nine large manufacturing plants on this creek, consisting of 1 woolen mill, 1 nickel works, 4 chemical works, 1 glass works, and 2 iron works. It is claimed that with an improved channel the most economical way of receiving materials and shipping products will be by schooners instead of by rail, as at present.

The value of the total freight movement for 1891 was nearly $3,000,000, and for 1900, $2,733,523.

COMMERCIAL STATISTICS.

Arrivals and departures for the years ending December 31, 1899 and 1900.

Articles.	1899. Tons.	1899. Value.	1900. Tons.	1900. Value.
ARRIVALS.				
Chemicals	10,251	$79,380	9,496	$90,900
Coal	51,776	140,013	53,414	157,427
Fertilizer	6,790	88,330	3,480	44,160
Iron, pig	36,272	544,080	34,200	539,200
Miscellaneous	58,222	378,033	52,276	337,636
Total	163,311	1,229,836	152,868	1,169,323
DEPARTURES.				
Iron, manufactured	13,357	333,925	11,300	395,000
Produce	37,500	720,600	30,000	685,000
Miscellaneous	11,615	357,794	35,970	484,200
Total	62,472	1,412,319	77,270	1,564,200

July 1, 1900, balance unexpended $8,824.85
June 30, 1901, amount expended during fiscal year .... .95

July 1, 1901, balance unexpended 8,823.90
(See Appendix H 8.)

9. *Mantua Creek, New Jersey.*—This creek empties into the Delaware River at a point 3 miles below League Island and opposite Mifflin Bar.

In its original condition it was navigable at high water for a distance of one-half mile above its mouth to the phosphate works of the I. P. Thomas & Sons Company for vessels of 13 feet draft; thence 3¼ miles farther to Paulsboro for vessels drawing 9 feet; thence 3½ miles to Parkers Landing for tugs and barges drawing 6 feet, this being the head of steam navigation; thence 4.1 miles to Mantua, 11¼ miles above the mouth, small boats and barges of 3 to 4 feet draft passed up on the tide. The navigable portion is generally bordered by low ground, protected from overflow by earthen banks. The general course of the stream is tortuous, and its navigation is much obstructed by bars, sharp bends, and in the upper portion by stumps and overhanging trees. The stream, on account of its flat watershed, is subject to only moderate freshets, which seldom exceed 2 to 3 feet above tide water. The range of tide is 6 feet at the mouth, 4.5 feet at Paulsboro, 3.4 feet at Berkley bridge, and 2 feet at Mantua.

The low-water width near the mouth averages 160 feet, decreasing to about 100 feet at Paulsboro. Above Paulsboro the width decreases to 88 feet at Parkers Landing, and near Mantua to 50 feet.

The project for this improvement is contained in a report dated October 22, 1897, which is printed in the Annual Report of the Chief of Engineers for 1898, page 1122.

The improvement proposed is the formation, by dredging, of a channel 100 feet wide at the bottom and 12 feet deep from the 12-foot contour in Delaware River to the phosphate works; thence 80 feet wide at bottom and 8 feet deep to Paulsboro, and thence 60 feet wide at bottom, and 7 feet deep to Parkers Landing; the construction (9,000 feet above Berkley) of a cut-off 350 feet long, 50 feet wide, and 3 feet deep; the removal of overhanging trees above Parkers Landing and the supplementing of the channel across the bar at the mouth by jetties on both sides, aggregating 1,350 feet in length, if found necessary for its maintenance.

Two plans for securing the channel were proposed. The first contemplated the formation of a dredged channel by making cut-offs—six in number—through the low lands wherever practicable, avoiding shoals and sharp bends, subject to the condition that all right-of-way privileges could be secured and riparian rights quieted for a sum not exceeding $11,000. The second provided that in case the rights of way could not be secured and riparian rights quieted for the sum of $11,000, the route of the channel between the phosphate works and Parkers Landing should follow the present course of the stream, widening at the bends.

The improvement by the first plan involved the removal of 411,500 cubic yards of material, place measurement, and its cost was estimated at $145,030; the second plan involved the removal of 405,500 cubic yards of material, and its cost was estimated at $141,400. The former plan was the one desired by the people of Paulsboro, as it would shorten the distance between that place and the mouth of the creek nearly 2 miles.

It was proposed to cast the dredged material on the banks and behind the dikes, or otherwise dispose of it so that it shall not impair navigation.

This project was adopted by Congress in the river and harbor act of March 3, 1899, which appropriated $25,000 for the improvement, subject to the following provision:

Provided, That no part of any money appropriated for this project in excess of eight thousand dollars shall be expended for right of way privileges, easements, or other rights above the phosphate works and below Paulsboro, and no part thereof shall be expended for any such purpose unless all such rights are secured for an amount not in excess of said sum of eight thousand dollars.

Up to the close of the fiscal year ending June 30, 1900, the expenditures in connection with this improvement amounted to $3,000, this being the amount of the appropriation of 1882 under an earlier project. No portion of this amount had been expended for maintenance.

During the past fiscal year the rights of way, easements, and other rights necessary for the formation of the proposed cut-offs between the phosphate works and Paulsboro were procured. After condemnation proceedings held during the fiscal year ending June 30, 1900, the required property along the line of the cut-off through the lands of Mr. Howard W. Miller was deeded to the United States, and the sum of $4,642.35, the award for the property taken, was paid to Mr. Miller and Mr. Samuel E. Moore, mortgagee, on September 19, 1900. On the same date the sum of $3,357.65 was paid to Mr. Matthew Gill, this being the purchase price for the necessary right of way through his property. These two amounts together were within the limit of $8,000, as specified in the river and harbor act of March 3, 1899, and secured all the rights of way necessary for the formation of the proposed cut-off channels between the phosphate works and Paulsboro.

A project for the expenditure of the available balance from the appropriation of March 3, 1899, was approved September 28, 1900. This project provides for the formation of a channel 8 feet deep at mean low water and 80 feet wide at bottom between Paulsboro and the phosphate works, by way of the cut-offs, as far as available funds will permit.

During the past fiscal year work under this project was in progress between December 17, 1900, and April 8, 1901.

By the work done 120,819 cubic yards of material, place measurement, was removed from the channel of the creek, of which 8,133 cubic yards was placed in the meadow banks constructed under the contract, and the remaining 112,686 cubic yards was deposited behind the banks on the meadows adjacent to the cuts, thereby completing all three of the cut-offs between the phosphate works and Paulsboro. The total length of cut-off channel of the projected dimensions formed under the contract, as measured between the original low-water lines, was 2,590 linear feet, and the total length of meadow bank constructed along the line of the cut-off channels was 4,880 feet.

The maximum draft of water that could be carried at mean low water on June 30, 1901, over the shoalest part of the locality under improvement was about 8 feet.

The commerce of this creek consists of miscellaneous articles, such as coal, sand, lumber, merchandise, fertilizers, and produce, and is principally of interstate character. The phosphate works, located just above the mouth of the stream, import fertilizer material, potash, pyrites, nitrate of soda, and sulphuric acid, and export manufactured fertilizers.

The shipment of produce to Philadelphia, Chester, and Wilmington is a large industry.

The improvement will greatly benefit these industries and the local commerce.

The value of the total freight movement for 1900 was $3,296,470, an increase of $742,620 over that of 1899.

It is proposed to apply the sum of $40,000, given as the amount that can be profitably expended in the fiscal year ending June 30, 1903, to the improvement of the channel between the Delaware River and Paulsboro, the amount of work to be done to depend on the prices obtained.

COMMERCIAL STATISTICS.

Arrivals and departures for the years ending December 31, 1899 and 1900.

Articles.	1899. Tons.	1899. Value.	1900. Tons.	1900. Value.
ARRIVALS.				
Chemicals	7,505	$77,400	10,862	$108,670
Fertilizer material	19,500	253,000	22,850	275,400
Manure	33,000	66,000	40,000	60,000
Miscellaneous	26,135	745,400	27,430	1,245,700
Total	86,140	1,141,800	101,142	1,689,770
DEPARTURES.				
Fertilizer (manufactured)	24,350	390,750	29,475	421,300
Truck, produce, and grain	33,000	778,500	35,000	840,000
Miscellaneous	22,160	242,800	23,340	345,400
Total	79,510	1,412,050	87,815	1,606,700

July 1, 1900, balance unexpended $25,000.00
June 30, 1901, amount expended during fiscal year 24,847.73

July 1, 1901, balance unexpended 152.27

Amount (estimated) required for completion of existing project 120,030.00
Amount that can be profitably expended in fiscal year ending June 30, 1903, in addition to the balance unexpended July 1, 1901 .... 40,000.00
Submitted in compliance with requirements of sundry civil act of June 4, 1897.

(See Appendix H 9.)

10. *Alloway Creek, New Jersey.* —In its original condition Alloway Creek was obstructed between its mouth and Quinton, a distance of about 10 miles, by shoal areas in the upper half of the stream, which reduced the low-water depths to from 1.3 to 4 feet.

The original project of 1889 proposed the formation by dredging of a channel 6 feet deep at mean low water and 60 feet wide from Quinton to a point about 1,000 feet above Upper Hancock Bridge; thence a channel of the same depth and 75 feet wide to a locality known as the "Square," where the work is to be supplemented by a dike. At a locality known as the "Canal," in addition to a channel of the last-named dimensions, the width of the stream was to be increased to about 150 feet between its low-water lines. The project was modified on December 10, 1896, so as to provide for a dike formed by a single row of piles above Upper Hancock Bridge. This modification does not increase the original estimated cost of the work, which is $25,000.

At the close of the fiscal year ending June 30, 1900, $18,000 had been expended in dredging below the "Square," at the "Square," at "Smith Reeves," at and near the "Canal," just below Upper Hancock Bridge, from Upper Hancock Bridge to a point about 1,400 feet above it, above and below Robinsons Landing, Upper and Lower Fowsers, Upper and Lower Lamberts, and Quinton, and in dike construction at the "Square" and above Upper Hancock Bridge. Channels from 40 to 75 feet wide and 6 feet deep at mean low water had been dredged at the above-mentioned localities, and dikes 300 and 404 feet in length, respectively, had been constructed at the "Square" and above Upper Hancock Bridge. Of this amount about $1,200 had been expended for the maintenance of dredged channels.

During the past fiscal year no work under this project was in progress.

The maximum draft of water that could be carried at mean low water on June 30, 1901, over the shoalest part of the locality under improvement was about 5 feet.

The commerce of this creek consists of miscellaneous articles, such as coal, sand, lumber, and produce, and is principally of a local character. The value of the total freight movement for 1900 was $1,095,400. The improvement has been of much benefit to navigation at a comparatively small cost. About four-fifths of the projected work has been accomplished.

COMMERCIAL STATISTICS.

Arrivals and departures for the years ending December 31, 1899 and 1900.

Articles.	1899. Tons.	1899. Value.	1900. Tons.	1900. Value.
ARRIVALS.				
Coal	9,500	$22,500	10,500	$31,500
Lumber	8,000	35,000	8,000	37,000
Tin plate	1,800	110,000	2,000	150,000
Miscellaneous	26,600	230,700	26,600	232,400
Total	40,900	398,200	42,100	450,900
DEPARTURES.				
Canned goods	9,000	400,000	9,500	400,000
Glass	2,300	150,000	2,500	180,000
Miscellaneous	5,825	59,200	6,625	64,500
Total	17,125	609,200	18,625	644,500

{Amount (estimated) required for completion of existing project.......... $7,000.00
Amount that can be profitably expended in fiscal year ending June 30, 1903. 7,000.00
Submitted in compliance with requirements of sundry civil act of June 4, 1897.

(See Appendix H 10.)

11. *Goshen Creek, New Jersey.*—In its original condition Goshen Creek carried a low-water depth of from 2 to 4 feet, with a least low-water width of 20 feet and a high-water width of 36 feet from Goshen to a point about 4,000 feet below, and thence to the mouth, a distance of about 2,500 feet, a low-water depth of from 3 to 5 feet, with a least width of 30 feet.

The project for its improvement, adopted in 1891, proposed the deepening and widening by dredging of the 4,000 feet of the creek below Goshen Landing to a low-water depth of 3 feet and a width of 30 feet; the formation of a dredged channel 3 feet deep and about 50 feet wide through the bar at the mouth to the limit of the sand beyond the low-water line, and the protection of the channel by a sheet-pile jetty.

The improvement was commenced during the fiscal year ending June 30, 1893, and to the close of the year the sum of $2,770.16 had been expended in widening and deepening the channel to the proposed dimensions over a distance of about 3,975 feet below Goshen Landing. By this work about one-fourth of the projected improvement had been completed and the navigable conditions had been proportionately improved.

During the fiscal year ending June 30, 1897, the pile dike was constructed to its projected length of 600 feet, and 8,002 cubic yards of material was removed from the channel in the vicinity of the dike.

The original cost of the project made in 1891 was estimated at $12,000, this estimate being based on a single appropriation of that amount by which the improvement could be made in a single season. On account of the small appropriations the execution of the work was carried through an interval of several years, and it was not executed with sufficient rapidity to prevent injurious changes, which considerably increased the cost of the improvement.

During the fiscal year ending June 30, 1898, an estimate for the completion of the project, based on a careful survey of existing conditions, was made. In order to maintain the dredged channel it was found necessary to extend the dike somewhat farther inshore and dredge through the bar at the mouth of the creek, which increased the cost of the project from $12,000, as originally estimated, to $17,000.

The river and harbor act of March 3, 1899, appropriated $8,000 for the completion of this improvement. During the fiscal year ending June 30, 1899, a project for the expenditure of this sum and of a balance remaining from a previous appropriation was submitted and approved. The project provides for dredging a channel with a low-water depth of 3 feet entirely through the mouth of the creek and for repairing and extending the existing dike and constructing a short dike on the upper side of the mouth of the creek. Work under this project was commenced during the fiscal year ending June 30, 1899.

During the fiscal year ending June 30, 1900, under this project the existing dike was repaired and strengthened with brush and stone; two parallel brush and stone dikes, on opposite sides of the creek entrance, with a total length of 680 feet, were constructed; 10,436 cubic yards of material, dipper measurement, was removed from the bar at the mouth of the creek, and one of the brush and stone dikes repaired. By the work done the improvement was completed and no further appropriation is required.

The total amount expended to the close of the fiscal year ending June 30, 1900, was $16,158.10, of which amount it is estimated that about $800 had been expended for maintenance.

During the past fiscal year no work has been done in connection with this improvement. The maximum draft of water that could be carried at mean low water on June 30, 1901, over the shoalest part of the locality under improvement was about 2.5 feet.

It is proposed to hold the available balance, $841.72, for repairs, maintenance, and other contingencies.

The commerce of this creek consists of miscellaneous articles, such as sand, oysters, lime, coal, and lumber, and is principally of a local character. The value of the total freight movement for 1900 was $438,900. The improvement has been of much benefit, at moderate cost.

COMMERCIAL STATISTICS.

Arrivals and departures for the years ending December 31, 1899 and 1900.

Articles.	1899. Tons.	1899. Value.	1900. Tons.	1900. Value.
ARRIVALS.				
Bricks	2,000	$8,000	400	$1,200
Fertilizer	1,200	15,200	500	6,000
Grain	5,500	115,500	2,500	50,000
Miscellaneous	7,200	294,400	4,000	214,800
Total	15,900	433,100	7,400	272,000
DEPARTURES.				
Hay	3,500	24,500	1,800	10,800
Oysters and clams	2,500	100,000	1,250	50,000
Miscellaneous	8,600	81,700	9,200	106,100
Total	14,600	206,200	12,250	166,900

July 1, 1900, balance unexpended $841.90
June 30, 1901, amount expended during fiscal year .... .18

July 1, 1901, balance unexpended 841.72

(See Appendix H 11.)

12. Wilmington Harbor, Delaware.—[This work was in the charge of Gen. William F. Smith, United States agent, major of engineers, United States Army, retired, to May 15, 1901.] Previous to 1836, when the first appropriation for the improvement of the Christiana River was made, the low-water depth at the entrance to this stream was about 8¼ feet. The minimum depth in the channel in the portion of the river below Third Street Bridge, Wilmington, was 8 feet. This depth was increased in 1836 by dredging to 10 feet below low water.

Under a project commenced in 1871 and completed in 1881 a 12-foot channel from 100 to 200 feet wide was made from the mouth to above the city of Wilmington.

In 1881 a project was adopted for a 15-foot low-water channel varying from 150 to 75 feet in width from the mouth of the river to the pulp works, and a channel 12 feet deep at low water and 50 feet wide from the pulp works to the Delaware Railroad Bridge, and for the construction of a jetty on the north side of the mouth of the river. Operations on this project were begun in 1882. The originally estimated cost of work under the project was $175,551, which was increased in 1883 to $191,384, owing to a change in the width of the proposed channel to 150 feet throughout. In 1884 the project was again amended by increasing the height of the jetty 4 feet. Under this project a channel was formed to a depth of 15 feet at mean low water over a width of 150 feet, by dredging and rock removal, from the 15-foot curve of depth outside the bar at the mouth to a point 2,515 feet above Market Street Bridge, 80 feet wide for an additional distance of 820 feet, and 40 feet wide for the remaining distance to the pulp works. This work was completed in 1893.

In 1896 and 1897 the channel was redredged to low-water depth of 13 and 15 feet at localities where it had shoaled, and the channel through the Third Street Bridge was made 200 feet wide to embrace both draw openings.

With the $5,000, appropriated in 1896 for improving the channel between Churchman's bridge and Smalley's bridge, in the upper part of the river, a continuous channel 3 feet deep at mean low water and 25 feet wide was dredged for a distance of 3.35 miles from Churchman's bridge toward the bridge at Christiana village, and a similar channel was formed for a distance of 4,033 feet above that bridge toward Smalley's bridge.

The river and harbor act of June 3, 1896, authorized the making of contracts to complete the "modified project," which was understood to be the project for a 21-foot channel, at a cost not to exceed $225,846, as based on the survey of the river made in accordance with the provisions of the river and harbor act of August 18, 1894. The report on this project is printed in the Annual Report of the Chief of Engineers for 1896, pages 973-994.

As it was doubtful whether the project could be carried out under the conditions of the law authorizing a contract, a Board of Engineer officers was convened by the Chief of Engineers to consider and report upon the plan of improvement. The report of the Board is printed in the Annual Report of the Chief of Engineers for 1897, page 1255.

The Board expressed the opinion that the existing project could not be successfully carried out and recommended a modified project, including the construction of a jetty on the south side of the entrance to the river, the rectification of the channel of the Christiana River at the mouth of the Brandywine, and necessary dredging to give a channel of 21 feet at mean low water from the mouth to the upper line of the pulp works. The estimated cost was $377,542. It was stated that the proposed channel is of greater dimensions than the river can naturally maintain and that annual dredging will be necessary. The United States agent in local charge of this work estimated that certain rock work not included in above estimate would increase the cost of work $99,083, making the total estimate $476,625.

As this estimate exceeded the limiting cost in the authorization given in the act of June 3, 1896, no contract for work on the project could, under the law, be made. But the available funds, $15,000, were applied to dredging, in conformity with a recommendation of this Board.

The sundry civil act approved July 1, 1898, appropriated $205,846 for continuing the improvement of Wilmington Harbor, and the river and harbor act of March 3, 1899, made an appropriation for the same work, as follows:

Improving harbor at Wilmington and Christiana River, Delaware: Continuing improvement, forty-five thousand dollars, of which amount twenty thousand dollars, or so much thereof as may be necessary, shall be used for maintenance, and the Secretary of War may enter into a contract or contracts for such materials and work as may be necessary to complete the project of improvement, in accordance with the project submitted by the Board of Engineers, in its report of October third, eighteen hundred and ninety-six, and including the removal of rock from the channel as recommended in the Annual Report of the Chief of Engineers for eighteen hundred and ninety-seven, to be paid for as appropriations may from time to time be made by law, not to exceed in the aggregate two hundred and five thousand seven hundred and eighty dollars, exclusive of the amount herein and heretofore appropriated, that being the amount reported by the Chief of Engineers as necessary to complete said project.

Under these appropriations the following work had been accomplished up to the close of the fiscal year ending June 30, 1900:

A channel had been dredged to a depth of 18 feet at mean low water over a width of 200 feet, except at the drawbridges mentioned below, from the 18-foot curve of depth in the Delaware River to the upper line of the pulp works, a distance of 21,298 feet, thence gradually diminishing to a depth of 10 feet at the Philadelphia, Wilmington and Baltimore Railroad bridge No. 4. Above the latter bridge a channel 7 feet deep at mean low water and 100 feet wide was dredged for a distance of 11,300 feet.

Through the south draw of the Market Street Bridge the required channel had been dredged, but that through the north draw remained incomplete. At all the bridges the width of the channel in the approaches and through them had been made to conform to the lines of the structures and the width of the draw openings.

At the Third Street Bridge the channel through the left draw was somewhat obstructed by a city water main, which sloped from 0 to 6 feet inshore above the 18-foot depth on the bed of the river.

The ledges of rock at the Third Street Bridge were in process of removal to the 18½-foot plane, and subsequently to the 21½-foot plane, 4,570 cubic yards of rock, place measurement, having been removed from them.

A pile and stone jetty consisting of two wings, and with a length of 560 feet, was constructed at the mouth of the Brandywine.

A pile and stone jetty 1,515 feet long, on the south side of the mouth of the Christiana River, and a cross dike 1,170 feet long, from the inner end of the jetty to the shore at high water, were under construction.

The repair and extension of the jetty on the north side of the mouth of the river and the construction of a terminal crib were in progress.

Operations were also commenced on June 25, 1900, on the contract for dredging a 21-foot channel between the pulp works and the Delaware River.

Up to June 30, 1900, the amount expended on the improvement was $571,818.26, of which $169,623.48 had been expended on the present project. No part of this latter-named sum had been applied directly to maintenance.

During the past fiscal year the following work under the project was accomplished:

The jetty and cross dike on the south side of the mouth and the work on the north jetty and terminal crib above referred to were completed.

A channel 7 feet deep at mean low water and 100 feet wide was continued from a point 11,300 feet above the Philadelphia, Wilmington and Baltimore Railroad bridge No. 4 to Newport, a distance of 14,500 feet, and the work remaining incomplete through the north draw of the Market Street Bridge was finished.

Under the contract for the dredging of a channel 21 feet deep at mean low water the section between the Philadelphia, Wilmington and Baltimore Railroad bridge No. 4 and the pulp works, in which the depth increases from 10 feet at the upper end to 21 feet at the lower end, was dredged to the projected dimensions; a channel 21 feet deep and 200 feet wide was dredged from the pulp works to the mouth of the Brandywine; a channel of the same depth and 250 feet wide was formed from the Brandywine to below Lobdells Canal, and a channel of the same width and depth was dredged from the 21-foot curve in the Delaware River for a distance of 1,800 feet inshore. The total length of continuous channel thus formed from bridge No. 4 to below Lobdells Canal is 19,745 feet, with an additional length of 1,800 feet at the mouth.

Under the contracts and the supplemental contracts for the removal of the rock ledges above and below the Third Street Bridge, and under an additional contract dated October 13, 1900, for the removal of another ledge found projecting into the channel just below the north draw of the Third Street Bridge, the latter ledge was completely removed to the plane of 21½ feet below mean low water, 354 cubic yards of rock, place measurement, having been taken out from the area, while work on the removal of the other ledges was rapidly approaching completion.

The water pipe, which was reported as projecting at one place above the plane of 18 feet below mean low water, was lowered by the city authorities during the past fiscal year so that its top is now 25 feet below mean low water.

The maximum draft that could be carried on June 30, 1901, at mean low water over the shoalest part of the improvement between the mouth of the Christiana River and the pulp works, between which limits a 21-foot channel is in process of formation, was 12 feet, and between bridge No. 4 and Newport, within which limits a 7-foot low-water channel has been dredged, the maximum draft was 7 feet.

An examination of the dredged channel between the pulp works and the mouth of the river, made in June, 1901, shows that the areas dredged have rapidly shoaled. The present channel depths vary from 21 feet at the mouth, where dredging is still in progress, to 12 feet at the pulp works, where dredging was completed a year ago. At the pulp works the depth of the channel before dredging was 15 feet. The rapid shoaling of this channel indicates that a depth of 21 feet at mean low water can not be maintained in the Christiana River at reasonable cost, and therefore no appropriation for the maintenance of the 21-foot channel is recommended. A less depth could probably be maintained at reasonable cost if the city of Wilmington should cease to discharge its sewage into the river. The sum of $50,000 can be expended profitably in removing the most troublesome shoals.

The tonnage and value of the leading articles shipped to and from the port of Wilmington in the year 1900, as reported by the Board of Trade, was 729,578 tons, valued at $29,959,490. The foreign commerce amounted to $5,946,896 additional. About $16,000,000 is invested in manufacturing and mercantile interests.

Commercial statistics of the city of Wilmington for the calendar year 1900.

DOMESTIC COMMERCE.

Articles.	Tons.	Value.
Coal and cord wood	50,925	$135,275
Quarry stone and sand	151,865	266,837
Ice	3,460	6,240
Powder	2,690	36,725
Fertilizers	20,973	181,228
Iron supplies and steel	68,395	1,263,990
Lumber, machinery, and cement	53,520	459,895
General merchandise and miscellaneous	377,750	27,659,300
Total	729,578	29,959,490

FOREIGN COMMERCE.

IMPORTS.		
Phosphate rock	643	$375
Nitrate of soda	6,890	183,978
Lumber, sawed	900	8,375
Total	8,433	192,728
EXPORTS.		
Crude oil	385,745	5,679,735
General merchandise		74,433
Total		5,754,168
Total foreign imports and exports		5,946,896

July 1, 1900, balance unexpended $281,222.52
June 30, 1901, amount expended during fiscal year 216,029.39

July 1, 1901, balance unexpended 65,193.13
July 1, 1901, outstanding liabilities 47,121.29

July 1, 1901, balance available 18,071.84

July 1, 1901, amount covered by uncompleted contracts 10,597.90

Amount that can be profitably expended in fiscal year ending June 30, 1903, for maintenance of improvement, in addition to the balance available July 1, 1901 .... 50,000.00
Submitted in compliance with requirements of sundry civil act of June 4, 1897, and of section 7 of the river and harbor act of 1899.

(See Appendix H 12.)

13. *Appoquinimink River, Delaware.*—[This work was in the charge of Gen. William F. Smith, United States agent, major of engineers, United States Army, retired, to May 15, 1901.] At the time of the adoption of the present project there was a mean low-water depth of 2 feet at the entrance into Delaware Bay, and the shoalest depth inside the river was 4½ feet. The most serious obstructions to the navigation of the river were the many bends in the lower and middle sections.

The approved project is based upon a survey made in 1889, and provides for a channel 8 feet deep at mean low water, having a width of 80 feet from the bridge at Odessa to near Townsend's wharf, a distance of 3¼ miles, and a width of 100 feet from this wharf to the mouth of the river, a distance of 5 miles. The estimated cost of the improvement is $39,963.

In 1891 the channel was dredged to the full width of 80 feet and depth of 8 feet at mean low water for a distance of 1,975 feet in a down-river direction, beginning at the lower end of Watkin's wharf, at Odessa, and early in 1893 a farther distance of 4,487 feet was dredged, Of the latter 595 feet was dredged to the approved width, but on account of the settlement and sliding in of the very soft marsh banks upon which the excavated mud and sand were deposited the full approved width of 80 feet could not be made along the remaining 3,892 feet, and it was therefore made only 50 feet until the banks should become firmer. The entire length dredged was 6,462 feet, of which 2,570 feet is 80 feet wide and 3,892 feet is 50 feet wide. The channel was thereby materially improved as far as the work had progressed, giving great relief to the shipping and increased harbor room at Odessa.

During the years 1898-99 the channel was dredged and shoals removed to a width of 50 feet and a depth of 8 feet at mean low water as follows: At the upper point of and through Quarter Mile Reach; from just below Polk's wharf to above the lower corner of the steamboat wharf at Odessa; in Windmill Reach and Toms Bay Reach; below Windmill Reach and in the reach just above the one leading to New Bridge; the cut-off at No Mans Friend Reach was widened to from 60 to 70 feet through the straight portion of it, and still more at the ends, which were made fan shape; a cut-off 625 feet in length was made through the marsh at Thomas Landing, and another, 960 feet long, including approaches, through the marsh just below. An average width of 45 feet and a low-water depth of 6.8 feet in the upper and 6.5 feet in the lower cut-off were obtained, with a low-water depth of 8 feet over a width of about 30 feet extending through both cut-offs. The aggregate length of dredging done in these operations was about 8,000 feet. At the mouth of the river a cut 30 feet wide and 5 feet deep at mean low water was made for a length of 1,100 feet through the marsh from the 5-foot curve of depth inside the river to the 5-foot curve of depth in the slough outside, through which deep water in the Delaware River is reached just below Blackbird Creek.

In the early part of 1900 the two cut-offs at Thomas Landing were dredged to a width and depth of not less than 80 feet and 8 feet at mean low water, respectively; at the mouth of the river the cut across the marsh was widened to 100 feet, the depth made being not less than 5 feet at mean low water; and at Toms Bay a cut 380 feet long was made through a sharp turn in the river, the width and depth made being not less than 35 feet and 6 feet at mean low water, respectively. The result of these operations is a navigable channel through the cutoffs and across the bar at the mouth.

Up to the close of the fiscal year ending June 30, 1900, the amount expended on this improvement was $24,912.07. No portion of this sum had been expended for maintenance.

During the past fiscal year no work was done in connection with this improvement, as no funds were available for the purpose.

The maximum draft that could be carried June 30, 1901, at mean low water over the shoalest part of the river was 5¼ feet.

The commerce for the calendar year 1900 is reported to have been 27,415 tons, valued at $1,730,650. That reported in 1891, shortly after the improvement of the river was begun, was 19,132 tons, valued at $980,975.

COMMERCIAL STATISTICS FOR CALENDAR YEAR 1900.

Class.	Tons.	Value.
RECEIPTS.		
Coal, fertilizers, flour	9,120	$173,345
Horses, potatoes	1,110	69,500
General merchandise	4,350	652,500
	14,580	895,345
SHIPMENTS.		
Canned goods	1,425	92,625
Fruit, wheat, poultry, sheep	11,085	693,930
General merchandise	325	48,750
	12,835	835,305
Total	27,415	1,730,650

July 1, 1900, balance unexpended	$87.93
July 1, 1901, balance unexpended	87.93

Amount (estimated) required for completion of existing project	14,963.00
Amount that can be profitably expended in fiscal year ending June 30, 1903, for works of improvement and for maintenance, in addition to the balance unexpended July 1, 1901	8,000.00
Submitted in compliance with requirements of sundry civil act of June 4, 1897, and of section 7 of the river and harbor act of 1899.	

(See Appendix H 13.)

14. Smyrna River, Delaware.—[This work was in the charge of Gen. William F. Smith, United States agent, major of engineers, United States Army, retired, to May 15, 1901.] This river, formerly called Duck Creek, had, before improvements were begun in 1879, a minimum depth of 2¼ feet within the river and about 4 feet over the bar at the mouth. Navigation was possible only at high tide, and was carried on by one steamer and seven small schooners.

In 1878 a project was made for the improvement of the whole river, including the channel across the bar at the mouth.

By direction of Congress the improvement of the bar was commenced first, and during the following four years three appropriations, aggregating $10,000, were expended in dredging a channel 100 feet wide and 8 feet deep at mean low water across the obstruction. The dredged channel soon filled up again.

A new project was submitted in 1887 for a 7-foot low-water channel 60 feet wide inside the river and 100 feet at the bar, the channel at the latter point to be protected by a stone jetty. The estimated cost of this project is $90,698.40. The first appropriation under the project, that made in 1888, was for dredging, and the appropriations made since have provided for continuing the improvement and have been applied solely to dredging. The estimated cost of the dredging is $37,365.20, and that for the jetty is $53,333.20.

In 1893 the channel was dredged to the approved dimensions for a length of 4,730 feet in seven different localities between Smyrna Landing and Gravel Reach, about 5 miles below. Dredging had been done within these limits previously, but not to the full dimensions. A cut 50 feet wide and 7 feet deep was also made through a narrow bar about a half mile inside the mouth of the river. In 1896 the channel was dredged at various points between Smyrna Landing and Cave Landing Reach, a distance of 20,400 feet. The turning basin and seven shoals below were dredged to the projected dimensions, and shoals at six other parts of this section were dredged to a depth of 7 feet at mean low water, with widths varying between 40 and 60 feet. In 1897-98 the channel was dredged at various points between Cave Landing and Cherrytree Reach, resulting in a channel of the approved dimensions in that section, with the exception of about 300 feet just below Eagle Nest Landing, where the depth and width were at some places slightly less. In the section above Cave Landing six shoals, to and including a part of Walraven Reach, were dredged to the approved dimensions, except one at Deep Hole, where the width made was only 50 feet; and between December, 1899, and February, 1900, the channel was dredged through shoals at Walravens, Beaver House Reach, Rothwells Landing, and Deep Hole Reach, an aggregate length of 2,565 feet over a continuous stretch of 5,210 feet from Walravens Point upstream, resulting in a channel of the projected dimensions from the upper terminus to the bar at the mouth, with a turning basin at Smyrna Landing. This leaves the shoal at the mouth of the river to be removed to complete the dredging originally contemplated.

Under the provisions of the emergency river and harbor act of June 6, 1900, a preliminary examination and survey were made during the past fiscal year with a view to securing two crosscuts to shorten the distance between the head of navigation on this river and Delaware Bay.

The report on the survey was submitted, under date of November 10, 1900, by General Smith, and recommended the construction of two cut-offs 60 feet wide and 7 feet deep at mean low water—one 2,445 feet long, extending from the turn just below Limekiln wharf to the turn just above Mill Creek; the other, 2,200 feet long, extending from below Rothwells Landing to the turn between Deep Hole and Brick Store Landing. The cost of the work was estimated at $15,000.

The reports of the examination and survey are printed in House Document No. 90, Fifty-sixth Congress, second session, and as Appendix H 23 of this report. The expenditure reported as made during the year was on account of this examination and survey.

The maximum draft that could be carried June 30, 1901, at mean low water over the shoalest part of the river was about 5 feet, and 4 feet across the bar.

The amount expended on the improvement of this river up to June 30, 1900, was $42,540, of which $32,540 had been expended on the present project. No portion of this amount had been applied to maintenance.

No work has been done in connection with this improvement during the past fiscal year, as no funds were available therefor.

The commerce on the river during the past calendar year is reported to have been 348,728 tons, valued at $4,195,275. Before the improvements were begun the tonnage was reported to be 204,706, and the valuation $1,944,000.

COMMERCIAL STATISTICS FOR CALENDAR YEAR 1900.

Class.	Tons.	Value.
RECEIPTS.		
Bone, iron ore, and steel	8,000	$87,900
Canned goods, flour, and mill work	10,528	222,800
Cattle, grain, horses, and sheep	63,705	432,825
General merchandise	10,000	400,000
	92,233	1,143,525
SHIPMENTS.		
Railroad ties and ship timber	80,600	206,000
Canned goods, fertilizers, and terra cotta	133,145	903,500
Fruit, grain, cattle, and poultry	30,750	1,462,250
General merchandise	12,000	480,000
	256,495	3,051,750
Total receipts and shipments	348,728	4,195,275

July 1, 1900, balance unexpended.......................... $460.00
June 30, 1901, amount expended during fiscal year................ 207.54

July 1, 1901, balance unexpended.......................... 252.46

Amount (estimated) required for completion of existing project........ 4,365.00
Amount that can be profitably expended in fiscal year ending June 30, 1903, for works of improvement and for maintenance, in addition to the balance unexpended July 1, 1901 .... 5,300.00
Submitted in compliance with requirements of sundry civil act of June 4, 1897, and of section 7 of the river and harbor act of 1899.

(See Appendix H 14.)

15. *Murderkill River, Delaware.*—[This work was in the charge of Gen. William F. Smith, United States agent, major of engineers, United States Army, retired, to May 15, 1901.] This river is a tidal stream and a tributary of Delaware Bay, and flows through Kent County, Del. Its navigable portion is about 9 miles long. The condition of the river was fair for the greater part of its length, the average width and depth being 90 and 6 feet, respectively. Outside the junction with Delaware Bay, however, there was a serious obstruction—the flats, which are nearly bare at low tide and extend for nearly a mile from the shore. The average rise and fall of the tide at the mouth is 4.6 feet.

In 1881 an examination of this river was made and a project submitted for its improvement. No appropriation was made by Congress, however, as the river was at that time in the hands of an improvement and navigation company chartered by the State. This company had expended about $10,000 in rectifying the many bends of the river by cutting straight canals and in dredging a narrow cut across the flats at the mouth. The latter slowly filled up again.

The project for improvement adopted in 1892 is for a 7-foot low-water channel 80 feet wide from the town of Frederica, at the head of navigation, to the mouth of the river, and 150 feet wide from the mouth across the flats outside to the 7-foot curve of depth in Delaware Bay, the cut at the mouth to be protected by forming an embankment of the dredged material on each side, the estimated cost being $47,550.

In 1893 a channel was dug to a depth of 5 feet below mean low water across the flats from a short distance inside the river to the 5-foot curve of depth in Delaware Bay, and in 1895 a cut-off 975 feet long was made at Lower Landing, about 4 miles from the mouth, and shoals

RIVER AND HARBOR IMPROVEMENTS. 255

were dredged at a sharp turn in the river below Frederica at the head of Long Canal, at Coles Shoal, and just inside the mouth of the river. The width of the cut in every case was 40 feet and the depth 7 feet at mean low water. In the winter of 1896–97 a channel was dredged 60 feet wide and 6 feet deep at mean low water from the 6-foot curve in Delaware Bay to the steamboat wharf inside the river, a distance of 4,700 feet, and shoals just above the steamboat wharf, at Broad Reach and Webbs Landing, aggregating 2,482 feet in length, were dredged to a width of 40 feet and a depth of 6 feet, resulting in an unobstructed low-water channel 6 feet deep from that depth in Delaware Bay to Lindells Shoal, a distance of 16,000 feet.

The amount expended on the project to the close of the fiscal year ending June 30, 1900, was $23,360.78. In addition to this, $1,500 was expended in removing a shoal at the mouth of the St. Jones River, as required by the river and harbor act of August 18, 1894. It is estimated that about $5,000 of the above amount had been applied to maintenance.

For the expenditure of the $5,000 provided by the river and harbor act of March 3, 1899, contract was made, after due advertisement, for dredging at 12 cents per cubic yard, place measurement. Under this contract operations were begun August 17 and completed December 14, 1899. During this period shoals at the steamboat wharf at Frederica and 500 feet below, at Long Reach, Bradleys Canal, Goodwins and Lower Landing, aggregating about 4,000 feet in length, were dredged to a width of 40 feet and a depth of 6 feet at mean low water, and at the mouth the channel was dredged to a width of 60 feet and a depth of 6 feet at mean low water to that depth in Delaware Bay, resulting in a channel 6 feet deep at mean low water from the head of navigation at Frederica to Delaware Bay.

The maximum draft that could be carried June 30, 1901, at mean low water, over the shoalest part of the river, was 4 feet, and over the flats at the mouth, 2 feet.

The commerce of the river, which is quite varied, is reported for the past year as 70,619 tons, valued at $2,234,980. There appears to have been quite an increase since the improvements were begun, and a steamboat line has in consequence been established between Frederica and Philadelphia.

COMMERCIAL STATISTICS FOR CALENDAR YEAR 1900.

Articles.	Tons.	Value.
RECEIPTS.		
Bone, rock, phosphate, ship timber	5,657	$81,630
Lime, fertilizers, dressed lumber	5,820	320,750
Horses, hay	1,022	64,700
General merchandise	900	324,000
	13,399	791,080
SHIPMENTS.		
Cord wood, pine and oak piling	15,020	30,450
Canned goods, barrels, baskets	17,278	648,000
Corn, wheat, fruit, cattle	23,972	575,450
General merchandise	950	190,000
	57,220	1,443,900
Total	70,619	2,234,980

July 1, 1900, balance unexpended $139.22
July 1, 1901, balance unexpended 139.22

Amount (estimated) required for completion of existing project 27,764.00
Amount that can be profitably expended in fiscal year ending June 30, 1903, for works of improvement and for maintenance, in addition to the balance unexpended July 1, 1901 .... 8,000.00
Submitted in compliance with requirements of sundry civil act of June 4, 1897, and of section 7 of the river and harbor act of 1899.

(See Appendix H 15.)

16. St. Jones River, Delaware.—[This work was in the charge of Gen. William S. Smith, United States agent, major of engineers, United States Army, retired, to May 15, 1901.] Before the channel was improved the least practicable low-water depth of water to Lebanon, 12 miles above the mouth, was 4 feet, and thence to Dover, 9 miles farther up the river, only 2½ feet.

The original project, made in 1880, was for a 3-foot low-water channel 100 feet wide across the bar at the mouth, protected by a jetty, at an estimated cost of $35,000. The project was modified in 1884 so as to include the removal of shoals in the river to a depth of 6 feet at mean low water. Improvements were not begun until 1885. The proposed channel within the river was reported as nearly completed at the close of the fiscal year ending June 30, 1888, $25,000 having been expended. A modification of the project for the improvement of the entrance was submitted and approved in March, 1889.

This modified project provided for a cut across the bar at the mouth from the 6-foot depth inside the creek to the corresponding depth outside the bar, the width of the cut to be 100 feet, of which 50 feet in the center was to be dredged to a depth of 6 feet, the remainder to a depth of 3 feet below mean low water. The material was to be deposited on either side of the cut to form training dikes, the outer end of the dikes to be strengthened with pile revetments. It also provided for a new cut-off across a very sinuous bend in the upper river about 1 mile below Lebanon and near Wharton's fishery. During the fiscal year 1890, $14,097.64 was expended on the improvement at the mouth, and there then existed, as reported, a clear and unobstructed 6-foot low-water channel, 40 feet wide within the river and nearly 100 feet wide over the bar at the mouth, from Dover to deep water in Delaware Bay.

In compliance with the river and harbor act of August 18, 1894, which provided that of the $6,500 appropriated for the Murderkill River $1,500 should be applied to the removal of a shoal at the mouth of the St. Jones River, a cut 60 feet wide and 6 feet deep at mean low water was dredged in July, 1895, resulting in the removal of about 10,000 cubic yards of material. Upon the completion of this dredging the steamer plying regularly on the St. Jones River could enter and depart at any stage of the tide.

A preliminary examination and survey of the river "from its mouth to the highest point of feasible navigation" were provided for in the river and harbor act of March 3, 1899, and made in that year. The report thereon, which contains a project for further improvement, is printed in House Document No. 166, Fifty-sixth Congress, first session, and in the Annual Report of the Chief of Engineers for 1900, pages 1662–1665.

This project provides for the formation, by dredging, of a channel, 7 feet deep from the curve of 7-foot depth in Delaware Bay to Lebanon, 12 miles above the mouth, the channel at the mouth to have a width of 100 feet and inside the mouth of 60 feet, widening at the bends and in existing cut-offs. The estimated cost of the work is $47,074.50.

The amount expended on this improvement to June 30, 1900, was $41,500. No portion of this amount had been applied to maintenance.

On June 30, 1900, an allotment of $3,500 was made from the emergency river and harbor act of June 6, 1900, for dredging at the mouth of this stream where the channel had seriously shoaled, and for the expenditure of this allotment an open-market agreement was made for dredging a cut 60 feet wide and 6 feet deep at mean low water from the 6-foot curve of depth in Delaware Bay to the 6-foot curve of depth in the river, at 12 cents per cubic yard, place measurement, with no allowance for overdepth. During the past fiscal year work under this agreement was in progress between July 30 and August 14, 1900, when it was completed. The quantity of material removed was 22,960 cubic yards and consisted of mud and sand, which was thrown over on the south side of the channel about 30 to 40 feet from the cut. The depth made ranged from 6 to 7¼ feet at mean low water. The amount expended was $2,946.73. The remainder of the allotment was redeposited in the Treasury.

The maximum draft that could be carried June 30, 1901, at mean low water over the shoalest part in the river, was 4¼ feet, and the same over the flats at the mouth.

The commerce on the river for the year is reported to have been 69,241 tons, valued at $3,569,829; that reported for 1890, five years after the first improvement was begun, was 40,074 tons, valued at $1,387,285.

COMMERCIAL STATISTICS FOR CALENDAR YEAR 1900.

Articles.	Tons.	Value.
RECEIPTS.		
Rawbone, phosphates	6,088	$70,312
Chemicals, flour, tin plate	9,629	477,145
Garden truck, horses, sheep	1,687	179,787
General merchandise	6,725	1,008,750
	24,129	1,735,994
SHIPMENTS.		
Railroad ties, sturgeon, oysters	1,223	169,710
Canned goods, barrel material	14,324	613,150
Fruit, grain, poultry	27,865	846,975
General merchandise	1,700	204,000
	45,112	1,833,835
Total receipts and shipments	69,241	3,569,829

Amount allotted from appropriation contained in emergency river and harbor act approved June 6, 1900............... $3,500.00
June 30, 1901, amount expended during fiscal year............... 2,946.73

November 27, 1900, amount redeposited to the credit of the appropriation. 553.27

(See Appendix H 16.)

17. *Mispillion River, Delaware.*—[This work was in the charge of Gen. William F. Smith, United States agent, major of engineers, United States Army, retired, to May 15, 1901.] This river is a tidal stream, which enters Delaware Bay about 17 miles northwest of Cape

Henlopen. It is navigable for about 12 miles. The mouth of the river is greatly obstructed by a flat foreshore without a channel. Vessels can enter and depart only at high water, the tidal range being about 4 feet.

The river from Milford to the mouth was improved by the General Government between the years 1879 and 1889, and $17,000 was expended in making a channel 40 feet wide and 6 feet deep at mean low water.

The project for the improvement at the mouth of the river, proposed in a report on a survey made in 1891, provides for a cut across the flats in a southeasterly direction, having a width of 150 feet and a depth of 6 feet at mean low water, beginning opposite the light-house and ending in deep water in the bay, the cut to be protected on the upper or north side by a bank made of the excavated material. The estimated cost is $24,000.

In 1893 operations were begun under the project, and at the close of work in that season a pile dike 500 feet long had been built on the north side of the mouth, along the line of the channel, and a channel 80 feet wide and 5 feet deep at mean low water had been dredged for a length of 570 feet, extending from the 5-foot curve of depth in the Mispillion River to a point opposite and 50 feet west from the outer end of the dike, and in 1895 and 1896 a channel was dredged 75 feet wide and 6 feet deep at mean low water from inside the river just above Sandy Point to opposite the mouth of Cedar Creek, and a crib dike 350 feet in length, flanking the new channel on the west side, was built. The dikes were found necessary during the progress of the dredging, owing to the character of the material dredged, which was mainly treacherous sand.

In 1897 a brush and stone extension to the pile dike was built for a length of 200 feet, and a cut 50 feet wide and 6 feet deep at mean low water was dredged over a length of 450 feet near the end of the crib dike, but was soon obliterated during severe storms. A channel 4 feet deep at mean low water and 40 feet wide was then dredged across the Bulkhead Shoal, about 400 feet beyond the mouth, resulting in a continuous channel 4 feet deep from inside the river across the Bulkhead Shoal, and in 1899 a single pile jetty was built for a length of 141 feet, extending from the inner end of the old pile and brush jetty, northward to the high-water line of the Mispillion River, and a similar jetty was constructed from Green Point, due east, for a length of 206 feet. The latter, which is designed to direct the waters of Cedar Creek into the Mispillion currents, was to extend much farther out, but it was found necessary to reduce its proposed length by about one-half, thus permitting the use of the old channel down the bay shore, as a break through a cut made at the mouth by private parties in 1898, under authority of the War Department, had damaged the channel in the route of the original project to deep water in Delaware Bay.

The amount expended to June 30, 1900, was $40,537.31, of which $23,537.31 had been applied to the present project. No portion of this amount was applied to maintenance.

Under date of November 30, 1900, an allotment of $1,050 was made by the Secretary of War from the emergency river and harbor appropriation of June 6, 1900, to be applied to the work of restoring the channel depths in the Mispillion River. This allotment was applied to the removal of the crib dike which was built at the mouth of the river in 1895, and which had become undermined and unserviceable. A contract for the complete execution of this work for the sum of $876 was entered into with Wilson M. Vinyard, of Milford, Del., under date of February 7, 1901. This contract was approved on March 6, 1901.

During the past fiscal year operations under this contract were in progress between February 25, 1901, and May 6, 1901, at which time work was completed, the progress of the work having been considerably interfered with by stormy weather and accidents to the contractor's plant. The total cost of the work, including inspection and superintendence, was $1,022.32.

Under the provisions of the emergency river and harbor act of June 6, 1900, a preliminary examination and survey of this stream were made during the past fiscal year from the 6-foot curve in Delaware Bay to the head of navigation at Walnut Street Bridge, Milford, a distance of 14.4 miles. The report on the survey was submitted under date of October 18, 1900, by General Smith, and recommended the following improvements, viz: The formation of a channel 6 feet deep at mean low water and 60 feet wide, widening to 75 feet at sharp turns from Milford to the mouth, and thence a channel 4 feet deep at mean low water and 150 feet wide across the flats at the mouth to the 4-foot curve in Delaware Bay, the channel at the mouth to be protected by a jetty on the south side 5,000 feet long.

The report also recommended the removal of the dike at the mouth constructed in 1895. The total cost of the work, including contingencies, was estimated at $87,065. The work of removing the crib dike above referred to was authorized and the allotment for the execution of the work was made subsequent to the submission of the report, and the estimated cost of the improvement is therefore reduced by the cost of that work, viz, $1,022.32. The report on the examination and survey are printed in House Document No. 102, 56th Congress, second session, and also as Appendix H 24 of this report.

The maximum draft that could be carried June 30, 1901, at mean low water over the shoalest part in the river was 3 feet, and across the flats at the mouth 1 foot.

The commerce on the river for the year is reported to have been 104,395 tons, valued at $1,736,138. That reported for 1890, ten years after the first improvement was begun, was 44,315 tons, valued at $916,250.

COMMERCIAL STATISTICS FOR CALENDAR YEAR 1900.

Articles.	Tons.	Value.
RECEIPTS.		
Rawbone, rock, and phosphate	46,075	$606,500
Chemicals, fertilizers, and lumber	1,599	26,275
Hay, fruit, and grain	4,830	80,500
General merchandise	18,000	360,000
Total	70,504	1,073,275
SHIPMENTS.		
Railroad ties, timber, and logs	16,255	62,863
Canned goods and fertilizers	9,550	455,000
Grain and fruit	8,086	145,000
Total	33,891	662,863
Total receipts and shipments	104,395	1,736,138

July 1, 1900, balance unexpended	$962.69
Amount allotted from appropriation contained in emergency river and harbor act approved June 6, 1900	1,050.00
	2,012.69
June 30, 1901, amount expended during fiscal year	1,819.44
July 1, 1901, balance unexpended	193.25
Amount that can be profitably expended in fiscal year ending June 30, 1903, for maintenance of improvement, in addition to the balance unexpended July 1, 1901. Submitted in compliance with requirements of sundry civil act of June 4, 1897, and of section 7 of the river and harbor act of 1899.	3,000.00

(See Appendix H 17.)

18. *Broadkill Creek, Delaware.*—[This work was in the charge of Gen. William F. Smith, United States agent, major of engineers, United States Army, retired, to May 15, 1901.] In its original condition the depth of water in the creek was from 3 to 4 feet over the numerous shoals which impeded navigation. The depth at the entrance was from 1¼ to 2 feet at low water.

The original project for improvement, made in 1871, is for a 6-foot low-water navigation, with a minimum width of 40 feet from the mouth of the creek to Milton, the head of navigation, and for a new entrance, protected by a jetty, at an estimated cost of $80,447. This project was modified in 1881 relative to the entrance, and the estimate reduced to $51,450. The channel within the creek was completed in 1890 in accordance with the project, at an expense of $35,000, which was the total amount expended at the close of the fiscal year ending June 30, 1900. No portion of this amount had been expended for maintenance.

After entering, vessels were no longer detained by the shoals at low tide and could proceed directly to their destination.

By authority of the Secretary of War, dated March 20, 1900, the Lewes River Improvement Company completed, about August 1, 1900, at its own expense, an outlet from Broadkill Creek to Delaware Bay by removing a point of land at the junction of the Broadkill with Lewes River, dredging a channel in Lewes River a distance of 2,066 feet, and making a cut from the end of this dredged channel across the cape sands to the high-water line in Delaware Bay. This work renders further improvement at the mouth of the river unnecessary, and no further appropriations are required at present. The maximum draft that could be carried on June 30, 1901, at mean low water over the shoalest part of the channel in the Broadkill and through Lewes River to the cut referred to was 4 feet, and through the cut to Delaware Bay 5½ feet.

It was not practicable to obtain any commercial statistics relating to this improvement.

(See Appendix H 18.)

19. *Inland waterway from Chincoteague Bay, Virginia, to Delaware Bay, at or near Lewes, Del.*—[This work was in the charge of Gen. William F. Smith, United States agent, major of engineers, United States Army, retired, to May 15, 1901.] The original project, based on a survey made in 1884, provided for a channel 70 feet wide at the bottom and 6 feet deep below mean low water in the Delaware Breakwater Harbor connecting the inland bays between Chincoteague Bay and Delaware Bay, the northern outlet to be at or near Lewes, Del. The length of the proposed waterway is about 75 miles, and the cost was estimated at $350,000. This project was modified in 1892, the width of the proposed channel having been reduced to 20 feet at the bottom.

A cut has been made 4 miles long, 20 feet wide at bottom, and 4 feet deep below the mean level of Assawaman Bay across the neck of land lying between Little Assawaman Bay and Whites Creek, a tributary of Indian River Bay, and three temporary wooden bridges built over it. A cut 20 feet wide and 6 feet deep below datum (mean low water at Delaware Breakwater) has been made from that depth in Rehoboth Bay to a point 1,250 feet south of the Delaware, Maryland and Virginia Railroad crossing at Rehoboth, a distance of 9,000 feet; and another cut, in continuation of this, extending to the railroad reservation, a distance of 1,125 feet, has been made to a depth of 2 feet below mean low-water level; and north of the railroad crossing a cut was made to a point 1,000 feet north of the boundary of the railroad track. Of this latter distance the lower 800 feet was excavated to a depth of $9\frac{1}{4}$ feet and the remaining 200 feet to an average depth of 15 feet above datum, the depth of cutting in the first averaging approximately $17\frac{1}{4}$ feet and in the latter about 8 feet. All slopes of excavations were made 2 to 1 along the lines determined by the final width at the base of the proposed cut and the configuration of the ground. The cut between Assawaman Bay and Whites Creek was made and the three bridges built in 1891. The remainder of the work described was done between 1893 and February, 1896.

The amount expended on the project to June 30, 1900, was $167,255.28, no portion of this amount having been applied to maintenance, and the condition of the work between Ocean View and Rehoboth when last examined, in June, 1901, was as follows: The cut made between Whites Creek and the head of Little Assawaman Bay to a depth of 4 feet had shoaled in the middle portion, the depths there being about $2\frac{1}{4}$ feet. These shoals are formed where the sandy side slopes, bare of all vegetation, fall in considerably during heavy rains. The depths in the cut through low or marshy ground had maintained themselves very well. The cut made to a depth of 6 feet from Rehoboth Bay along Millers Creek toward the high ground back of Rehoboth during the working season of 1894 was in fair condition except for the closing of the entrance to the canal by the formation of a bar in line with the bay shore. The formation of this bar was evidently caused by wave action.

The river and harbor act of June 3, 1896, appropriated $25,000 for continuing this improvement, to be used from Delaware Bay to Indian River, but it was not deemed advisable to do any work on this section until certain questions respecting the right of way could be adjusted. That act also provided for securing the right of way over any railroad or through any railroad or county bridge by condemnation proceedings. Such proceedings were instituted, under authority of the Secretary of War, by the United States attorney for the district of Delaware, for the right of way through the crossing of the Delaware, Maryland and Virginia Railroad Company at Rehoboth, Del., resulting in a voluntary deed, dated January 13, 1899, from the commissioners of Rehoboth to the United States, conveying whatever interest that corporation had in the land at the place named, and in an award made by certain commissioners appointed under and by virtue of an act of the general assembly of the State of Delaware, entitled "An act in relation to the proposed canal intended as a free inland waterway connecting Assawaman Bay with Delaware Bay," passed at Dover April 4, 1884, and the supplements thereto, as stated more fully in the Annual Report of the Chief of Engineers for 1899, page 191. The amount of the award is $37,343.58.

Under date of January 15, 1901, the Chief of Engineers approved a recommendation that the "middle" or Ocean Beach Bridge, crossing the section of the waterway between Assawaman Bay and Indian River Bay, near Ocean View, Del., be repaired by the United States, at a cost not to exceed $250, and that notice be given to the proper officials of the State of Delaware that the United States would not in the future repair the other two bridges crossing the waterway in this vicinity, or be in any way responsible for their maintenance. Notice to this effect was given to the levy court of Sussex County, Del., which has jurisdiction in this matter, under date of January 21, 1901. In accordance with the recommendation, the middle bridge was repaired and placed in good order in the month of March, 1901, at a cost of $227.94.

The three bridges crossing the waterway between Assawaman and Rehoboth bays, a distance of 4.6 miles, were built by the United States in 1891, for temporary use only. Since their construction efforts have been made, without avail, to have the roads crossing two of them closed, one bridge in this short distance being deemed sufficient for the needs of travel.

During the past fiscal year an examination of the waterway between the middle bridge at Ocean View and the Delaware, Maryland and Virginia Railroad bridge at Rehoboth was made, for the purpose of preparing a project for the expenditure of available funds appropriated in the river and harbor act of June 3, 1896. It is proposed to submit this project early in the coming fiscal year.

The maximum draft that could be carried at mean low water on June 30, 1901, over the shoalest part of the locality under improvement, was 2½ feet.

July 1, 1900, balance unexpended	$26,494.72
June 30, 1901, amount expended during fiscal year	449.78
July 1, 1901, balance unexpended	26,044.94
July 1, 1901, outstanding liabilities	12.26
July 1, 1901, balance available	26,032.68
Amount (estimated) required for completion of existing project	156,250.00
Amount that can be profitably expended in fiscal year ending June 30, 1903, for works of improvement and for maintenance, in addition to the balance available July 1, 1901	60,000.00

Submitted in compliance with requirements of sundry civil act of June 4, 1897, and of section 7 of the river and harbor act of 1899.

(See Appendix H 19.)

20. Removing sunken vessels or craft obstructing or endangering navigation.—During the past fiscal year the following wrecks were removed under the provisions of the river and harbor act of March 3, 1899: The canal boat *Frank Dodson*, from the mouth of Chester Creek, Pennsylvania; the schooner *Druzilla B. Lee*, from the channel of Dennis Creek, New Jersey; the canal boat *Daisy*, from the channel of Rancocas River, New Jersey, about one-fourth mile above Bridgeboro; the coal barge *Iron State*, from the channel of the Delaware River off Gloucester, N. J.; two unknown wrecks from the channel of the Delaware River below Riverton, N. J.; parts of the schooner *A. T. Coleman*, from the entrance to Absecon Inlet, New Jersey; one compartment of the hinged canal boat *Edward L. Meyers*, from the channel of the Schuylkill River, Pennsylvania, just below the South

Street Bridge, in the city of Philadelphia; one compartment of the hinged canal boat *Meadowbrook*, from the channel of the Schuylkill River opposite the entrance to the reserve basin of the League Island Navy-Yard; the schooner *I. W. Norris*, from the channel of Cedar Creek, New Jersey; the schooner *Mary Baxter*, from the main ship channel of the Delaware River below Billingsport, N. J.; and the schooner *Samuel Applegate*, from the channel of Appoquinimink River, Delaware, below Odessa Landing.

Allotments were made for the removal of the wrecks of the following vessels: Steam tug *Fleetwing*, from the channel of the Schuylkill River, Pennsylvania; this wreck was removed by the owners under private contract, and the allotment was redeposited to the credit of the appropriation; the dredge *Potomac*, from Delaware Breakwater Harbor, Delaware; this wreck was moved by the owners to a point at which it is not a menace to navigation, and the allotment is held pending the owners' operations toward its complete removal; the canal boat *Zeus*, from the channel of Smyrna River, Delaware, an agreement for the removal of which was entered into under date of November 16, 1900, but the work of removal has not yet been completed; and the steamship *Ranald*, in the Atlantic Ocean off Atlantic City, N. J., for the removal of which a contract has not yet been entered into.

The removal of the wreck of the schooner *Lottie K. Friend* from Delaware Bay, under contract dated February 18, 1897, with Thomas Poynter and Elijah D. Register, of Lewes, Del., in progress during the fiscal year ending June 30, 1897, was not completed, and the annulment of the contract was recommended June 16, 1898, and approved June 18, 1898. This wreck has not yet been removed.

The amount expended during the past fiscal year upon removal of wrecks is $6,591.52.

(See Appendix H 20.)

EXAMINATIONS AND SURVEYS MADE IN COMPLIANCE WITH EMERGENCY RIVER AND HARBOR ACT APPROVED JUNE 6, 1900.

Preliminary examinations and surveys of the following localities were made by the local officer and reports thereon submitted:

1. Preliminary examination and survey of Beach Thoroughfare, New Jersey.—Lieutenant-Colonel Raymond submitted reports dated June 22 and November 2, 1900, respectively. He presents a plan for improvement at an estimated cost of $36,000. The reports were transmitted to Congress and printed in House Doc. No. 94, Fifty-sixth Congress, second session. (See also Appendix H 21.)

2. Preliminary examination of Mahon (Harbor) River, Delaware.— Gen. Wm. F. Smith, United States agent, major of engineers, United States Army, retired, submitted report dated August 1, 1900, through the Division Engineer, Col. Peter C. Hains, Corps of Engineers. In the opinion of these officers the cost of the improvement necessary to preserve the harbor there is not warranted by the benefits to be derived therefrom. The report was transmitted to Congress and printed in House Doc. No. 72, Fifty-sixth Congress, second session. (See also Appendix H 22.)

3. Preliminary examination and survey of Smyrna River, Delaware, with a view to securing two short crosscuts to shorten the distance from head of navigation to Delaware Bay.—Reports dated August 7 and November 10, 1900, respectively, were submitted by General Smith through the division engineer. He presented a plan for improvement at an estimated cost of $15,000. The reports were transmitted to Congress and printed in House Doc. No. 90, Fifty-sixth Congress, second session. (See also Appendix H 23.)

4. *Preliminary examination and survey of Mispillion River, Delaware, from its mouth to the head of navigation.*—Reports dated June 19 and October 18, 1900, respectively, were submitted by General Smith through the division engineer. A plan is presented for improvement at an estimated cost of $87,065. The reports were transmitted to Congress and printed in House Doc. No. 102, Fifty-sixth Congress, second session. (See also Appendix H 24.)

IMPROVEMENT OF RIVERS AND HARBORS IN MARYLAND TRIBUTARY TO CHESAPEAKE BAY, AND OF BROAD CREEK AND NANTICOKE RIVERS, DELAWARE AND MARYLAND.

This district was in the charge of Lieut. Col. O. H. Ernst, Corps of Engineers, having under his immediate orders Lieut. Charles W. Kutz, Corps of Engineers, to August 30, 1900.

1. *Susquehanna River above and below Havre de Grace, Md.*—This work was in the charge of Gen. William F. Smith, United States agent, major of engineers, United States Army, retired, to May 15, 1901. The original governing depth was 5 feet at mean low water. The channel above Havre de Grace was narrow and believed to be one cause of ice gorges. Improvements have been in progress since 1852, but the existing project, to give a channel 15 feet deep at mean low water below Havre de Grace and to remove the shoal opposite Watson Island to a depth of 8 feet at the same stage of the tide, at an estimated cost of $168,000, was adopted August 22, 1882. The amount expended on the work to June 30, 1900, inclusive, was $161,155.95, including $49,729.15 for the Fish Commission. The channel below Havre de Grace was dredged to a depth of 12 feet and the shoal near Watson Island partially removed. No work has been done since 1899 and the channels have shoaled again, but to what extent can not be ascertained until an examination is made. The funds available are limited to expenditure above Havre de Grace, and it is deemed best to hold them until further appropriations are made. It was impracticable to obtain complete commercial statistics of the river, but those of Havre de Grace were reported to be 110,250 tons in 1899.

July 1, 1900, balance unexpended	$9,734.05
July 1, 1901, balance unexpended	9,734.05
Amount (estimated) required for completion of existing project	94,500.00
Amount that can be profitably expended in fiscal year ending June 30, 1903, in addition to the balance unexpended July 1, 1901	12,000.00

Submitted in compliance with requirements of sundry civil act of June 4, 1897.

(See Appendix I 1.)

2. *Patapsco River and channel to Baltimore, Md.*—Prior to 1853, when improvements were commenced, the controlling depth was 17 feet. By successive stages (described on pp. 231-232, Annual Report of the Chief of Engineers for 1900) the facilities for navigation from the Chesapeake Bay to Baltimore were improved by dredging, until, in 1892, there was a ship channel of 27 feet depth at mean low water 600 feet wide at bottom except at the angles, where it was over 1,200 feet. The existing project approved July 10, 1896, is to increase the

depth of that channel to 30 feet at mean low water, and was authorized by the act of June 3, 1896. It was estimated to cost $2,500,000 and $50,000 per annum for maintenance. There was $3,808,011.71 expended on the work to June 30, 1900, inclusive. At the beginning of the fiscal year ending June 30, 1901, there was a depth of 30 feet for a width of from 330 to 480 feet in the Fort McHenry division of the channel; from 275 to 320 in the Brewerton; from 290 to 450 in the Cut-off, and from 330 to 380 in the Craighill, while at the end of the fiscal year those widths have been increased to at least 565 feet in the Fort McHenry; 460 in the Brewerton; 450 in the Cut-off, and 565 in the Craighill; making a maximum draft of 30 feet at mean low water for the latter widths that can now be carried over the shoalest portions of the main ship channel from the Chesapeake Bay to Baltimore Harbor.

The continuing contract now existing will complete the project, and for reasons explained in the report of the officer in charge of the district the balance of the estimate unappropriated will not be required. The funds available will complete the contract.

In response to a concurrent resolution of Congress an estimate of the cost of increasing the depth and width of the main ship channel was submitted, and is printed in Senate Doc. No. 118, Fifty-sixth Congress, second session, and as Appendix I 17 of this report.

The tonnage movement of the port has been as follows:

Fiscal year ending June 30—	Tons.	Fiscal year ending June 30—	Tons.
1889	3,243,017	1896	5,363,894
1890	4,237,361	1897	6,868,120
1891	4,495,469	1898	7,339,405
1892	5,224,042	1899	6,843,620
1893	4,607,176	1900	7,941,580
1894	4,752,946	1901	8,055,017
1895	4,794,964		

The following table will illustrate the statistics of the port during the fiscal year ending June 30, 1901:

Dutiable imports have increased	$293,161.00
Free imports have decreased	$436,669.00
Domestic exports have decreased	$9,270,775.00
Tonnage (foreign) has decreased (tons)	46,872.00
Duties collected have increased	$187,095.40
Duties on merchandise in bond have increased	$39,698.75
Duties on merchandise in bond with and without appraisement have decreased	$4,720.89
July 1, 1900, balance unexpended	$432,666.29
Amount appropriated by sundry civil act approved March 3, 1901	475,352.00
	908,018.29
June 30, 1901, amount expended during fiscal year	341,749.53
July 1, 1901, balance unexpended	566,268.76
July 1, 1901, outstanding liabilities	2,000.00
July 1, 1901, balance available	564,268.76
July 1, 1901, amount covered by uncompleted contracts	564,268.76

(See Appendix I 2.)

3. Channel to Curtis Bay, in Patapsco River, Baltimore Harbor, Maryland.—There was a natural depth of 22 feet at mean low water when the existing project was undertaken in 1893, which is for a channel 27 feet deep at mean low water, with a bottom width of 150 feet, at an estimated cost of $85,000. This project was approved July 13, 1892, and is to be found on page 1249 of the Annual Report of the Chief of Engineers for 1893. Up to June 30, 1900, inclusive, $39,861.93 had been expended in dredging, and resulted in a channel of the prescribed depth for a width of 70 feet, and a depth of 25 feet for the remaining width. Funds being exhausted, there were no operations in the past fiscal year. The maximum draft that could be carried June 30, 1901, at mean low water over the shoalest portion of the channel was 27 feet, but this is inadequate for the necessities of the commerce of the harbor.

In response to a concurrent resolution of Congress an estimate of the cost of widening and deepening the channel was submitted, and is printed in Senate Doc. No. 118, Fifty-sixth Congress, second session, and as Appendix I 17 of this report.

Curtis Bay is in the collection district of Baltimore. Commercial statistics are attached to the report for that harbor.

July 1, 1900, balance unexpended	$138.07
June 30, 1901, amount expended during fiscal year	138.07

Amount (estimated) required for completion of existing project	45,000.00
Amount that can be profitably expended in fiscal year ending June 30, 1903.	45,000.00
Submitted in compliance with requirements of sundry civil act of June 4, 1897.	

(See Appendix I 3.)

4. Harbor of southwest Baltimore (Spring Garden), Md.—No work has ever been done by the General Government, although the city of Baltimore dredged a channel which has a controlling depth of 15 feet at mean low water, and a least width of 100 feet. The existing project, adopted June 3, 1896 (see pp. 1005–1007 of the Annual Report of the Chief of Engineers for 1896), is for a channel 27 feet deep at mean low water, 100 feet wide at bottom, with side slopes of three base to one vertical, from the main ship channel near Fort McHenry to the foot of Eutaw street, with a turning basin 400 feet by 400 feet near the upper end, at an estimated cost of $314,000. The appropriation being too small to accomplish any useful result, there have been no expenditures on the work. The commercial statistics for the port of Baltimore include this harbor.

July 1, 1900, balance unexpended	$5,000.00
July 1, 1901, balance unexpended	5,000.00

Amount (estimated) required for completion of existing project	309,000.00
Amount that can be profitably expended in fiscal year ending June 30, 1903, in addition to the balance unexpended July 1, 1901	60,000.00
Submitted in compliance with requirements of sundry civil act of June 4, 1897.	

(See Appendix I 4.)

5. Queenstown Harbor, Maryland.—[This work was in the charge of Gen. William F. Smith, United States agent, major of engineers, United States Army, retired, to May 15, 1901.] The governing depth in the harbor before 1871 was 6 feet, but since that time, with an expenditure of $18,610.57 in dredging and redredging to June 30, 1900, inclusive, the existing project adopted September 30, 1896 (which is similar to former ones), for a channel 8 feet deep at mean low water and 100 feet wide from the 8-foot curve in the Chester River to the inner harbor, has been completed. No dredging was done in the year ending June 30, 1901. The maximum draft that could be carried over the shoalest part at that date was 8 feet.

The tonnage of the harbor is reported to be as follows:

In 1898	25,845
In 1900	12,373
July 1, 1900, balance unexpended	$389.43
June 30, 1901, amount expended during fiscal year	4.25
July 1, 1901, balance unexpended	385.18

(See Appendix I 5.)

6. Chester River, Maryland, from Crumpton to Jones Landing.—[This work was in the charge of Gen. William F. Smith, United States agent, major of engineers, United States Army, retired, to May 15, 1901.] Before operations were undertaken vessels at low tide drawing 6 feet of water could reach Crumpton, 33 miles above the mouth, at low tide, and from that point to Jones Landing, 6¼ miles, the controlling depth was 3 feet. The existing project, adopted October 21, 1890, is for a channel 6 feet deep at mean low water and 60 feet wide from Crumpton to Jones Landing, at an estimated cost of $12,750; in 1896 increased to $14,250, and still later to $19,562.50. With an expenditure of $13,684.09 to June 30, 1900, inclusive, the projected channel was brought to within less than a half mile of Jones Landing by original dredging and redredging after shoaling. There was no work done in the fiscal year ending June 30, 1901. The dredged portion of the channel has generally been well maintained, but at one place has shoaled to a depth of 3.8 feet. Owing to the fact that a part of the channel has not been improved a draft of only 2 feet can be carried through. No statistics of the commerce of the river are available.

July 1, 1900, balance unexpended	$515.91
June 30, 1901, amount expended during fiscal year	249.12
July 1, 1901, balance unexpended	266.79

Amount (estimated) required for completion of existing project	5,412.50
Amount that can be profitably expended in fiscal year ending June 30, 1903, in addition to the balance unexpended July 1, 1901	5,300.00
Submitted in compliance with requirements of sundry civil act of June 4, 1897.	

(See Appendix I 6.)

7. Choptank River, Maryland.—[This work was in the charge of Gen. William F. Smith, United States agent, major of engineers, United States Army, retired, to May 15, 1901.] The controlling depth prior to 1880 between Denton and Greensboro was 2 feet at mean low water. The existing project, adopted June 14, 1880, is for a channel 75 feet wide and 8 feet deep at mean low water from the 8-foot depth near Denton to the bridge at Greensboro, 8 miles above, at an estimated cost of $79,000. The amount expended on the work to the close of the fiscal year ended June 30, 1900, was $59,205.28, and completed the project except for a 1,600-foot length of channel where there was but 7 feet dredged, and also in places where shoaling is reported. There was no dredging done in the fiscal year ending June 30, 1901. The maximum draft that can now be carried over the shoalest part of the channel is 6 feet.

The tonnage of the river is reported to be as follows:

1890	6,904
1899	21,399
1900	157,094

Five steamers make a daily service to Baltimore, and a large number of sailing vessels also trade on the river.

July 1, 1900, balance unexpended	$794.72
June 30, 1901, amount expended during fiscal year	685.79
July 1, 1901, balance unexpended	108.93

Amount (estimated) required for completion of existing project	19,000.00
Amount that can be profitably expended in fiscal year ending June 30, 1903, for works of improvement and for maintenance, in addition to the balance unexpended July 1, 1901	8,000.00
Submitted in compliance with requirements of sundry civil act of June 4, 1897, and of section 7 of the river and harbor act of 1899.	

(See Appendix I 7.)

8. *La Trappe River, Maryland.*—[This work was in the charge of Gen. William F. Smith, United States agent, major of engineers, United States Army, retired, to May 15, 1901.] This stream, formerly known as Dividing Creek, has a length of about 3 miles, and is a tributary of the Choptank River. The original depth prior to 1893 was 4 feet, but this was afterwards increased to 8 feet by dredging under private subscription. The existing project, adopted August 5, 1892, is for a channel 150 feet wide and 11 feet deep at mean low water across the bar at the mouth, and for a width of 75 feet and a depth of 8 feet inside as far as Trappe Landing, with a turning basin at the latter point, at an estimated cost of $7,250, subsequently increased to $9,750. The amount expended to June 30, 1900, inclusive, was $7,213.87, and resulted in completing the project except for a length of 1,200 feet over the bar where the width is but 100 feet. There has been no dredging done since 1895. On June 30, 1901, the average depths were but little less than those required in the project, but there was one place in the channel where the depth was only 7 feet, and one on the bar where it was only 8.5 feet.

The tonnage of the river is reported to be as follows:

1893	29,094
1899	12,593
1900	8,089

Three steamers and 14 schooners are reported as regularly trading on the river.

July 1, 1900, balance unexpended	$36.13
July 1, 1901, balance unexpended	36.13

Amount (estimated) required for completion of existing project	2,500.00
Amount that can be profitably expended in fiscal year ending June 30, 1903, in addition to the balance unexpended July 1, 1901	1,700.00
Submitted in compliance with requirements of sundry civil act of June 4, 1897.	

(See Appendix I 8.)

9. *Warwick River, Maryland.*—[This work was in the charge of Gen. William F. Smith, United States agent, major of engineers, United States Army, retired, to May 15, 1901.] This stream, formerly known as Secretary Creek, is an estuary 2 miles long of the Choptank River, and had an original depth of 4 feet. Prior to 1892 private parties and the General Government had each expended $6,000 in improving it

to a depth of 9 feet for a narrow channel, but August 4, 1892, the existing project was adopted, which is to provide a channel 100 feet wide and 10 feet deep at mean low water from the 10-foot depth in Choptank River to Secretary Landing, at the head of the river, including a turning basin at the latter point, at an estimated cost of $18,600. There had been expended to June 30, 1900, inclusive, $17,816.56, and this resulted in completing the turning basin and the channel except for a length of 450 feet at Devils Wind Gap, and the restoration of the channel at other points where it had shoaled. There was no dredging done in the fiscal year ending June 30, 1901. The draft that can be carried through to the landing is 8.5 feet.

The tonnage for 1900 is reported as 52,791. Two steamers with a daily service and 100 sailing vessels are reported as trading on the river.

July 1, 1900, balance unexpended	$183.44
June 30, 1901, amount expended during fiscal year	171.05
July 1, 1901, balance unexpended	12.39

Amount (estimated) required for completion of existing project	6,600.00
Amount that can be profitably expended in fiscal year ending June 30, 1903, for works of improvement and for maintenance, in addition to the balance unexpended July 1, 1901	4,000.00
Submitted in compliance with requirements of sundry civil act of June 4, 1897, and of section 7 of the river and harbor act of 1899.	

(See Appendix I 9.)

10. *Nanticoke River, Delaware and Maryland.*—[This work was in the charge of Gen. William F. Smith, United States agent, major of engineers, United States Army, retired, to May 15, 1901.] Before the adoption of the existing project a channel 9 feet deep at mean low water and 100 feet wide had been dredged from the railroad bridge at Seaford to a point 8,000 feet below, at a cost of $5,000. The existing project, adopted September 22, 1896, is for a channel 9 feet deep at mean low water and 100 feet wide, the width to be increased to about 150 feet at sharp turns, the improvement to be extended to within 100 feet of the county bridge, where it is to widen out fan-shape, at an estimated cost of $13,000. The amount expended on the work to the close of the fiscal year ended June 30, 1900, was $8,193.97 (which included an appropriation of $5,000 in the act of August 18, 1894, for Broad Creek River, Delaware), and resulted in completing the project with the exception of a length of 720 feet. This stretch was dredged out and the projected channel completed by July 25, 1900. The maximum draft that could be carried June 30, 1901, at mean low water over the shoalest part of the improvement was reported to be 9 feet.

The tonnage of the river is reported to be as follows:

1898	18,121
1899	17,221
1900	87,467

Fifty-five sailing vessels are reported to be engaged in trading on the river.

July 1, 1900, balance unexpended	$2,806.03
June 30, 1901, amount expended during fiscal year	1,953.17
July 1, 1901, balance unexpended	852.86

(See Appendix I 10.)

11. Broad Creek River, Delaware.—[This work was in the charge of Gen. William F. Smith, United States agent, major of engineers, United States Army, retired, to May 15, 1901.] This is a tributary of the Nanticoke River, and in 1881 the governing depth was 1½ feet. In 1889 a channel 6 feet deep at mean low water and 50 feet wide had been dredged from Bethel to Laurel at a cost of $35,000. The existing project, adopted August 5, 1892, is for a channel 70 feet wide and 8 feet deep at mean low water between Bethel and Laurel, at an estimated cost of $15,000. Fifty-one thousand four hundred and thirty-nine dollars and thirteen cents was expended on the work up to the close of the fiscal year ending June 30, 1900, and resulted in a channel of the projected depth and width except for a short distance at the upper end, where it is reduced to 60 feet to secure some wharves which would be endangered if the full dimensions of the project were dredged. There were no operations in the fiscal year ending June 30, 1901. The maximum draft that can be carried to Laurel is 8 feet, but the width has somewhat diminished during the year.

Statistics of the commerce were not available.

July 1, 1900, balance unexpended	$3,560.87
June 30, 1901, amount expended during fiscal year	3,175.12
July 1, 1901, balance unexpended	385.75

(See Appendix I 11.)

12. Wicomico River, Maryland.—[This work was in the charge of Gen. William F. Smith, United States agent, major of engineers, United States Army, retired, to May 15, 1901.] In 1872 the channel was 8 feet deep at mean low water to within 2 miles of Salisbury, and 18 inches at Salisbury. In 1885 there was a channel to Salisbury with a depth of 7 feet at mean low water and a least width of 75 feet, which had cost the United States $50,000. The existing project was adopted December 29, 1890, and provides for a channel 9 feet deep at mean low water with a width of from 100 to 150 feet, from the like depth near Fruitland wharf to the drawbridge at Salisbury, at an estimated cost of $23,200, subsequently increased to $29,998. Up to June 30, 1900, inclusive, there had been $73,198 expended and the dredging involved in the project was completed. But at that date shoaling had taken place to the extent of about 41,200 cubic yards of material. At the close of the fiscal year ending June 30, 1901, the maximum draft that could be carried through the channel was 8 feet.

The tonnage of the river is reported to be as follows:

In 1891	36,252
In 1899	252,292

Only partial statistics for 1900 have been gathered.

July 1, 1900, balance unexpended	$2.00
July 1, 1901, balance unexpended	2.00
Amount (estimated) required for completion of existing project	6,798.00
Amount that can be profitably expended in fiscal year ending June 30, 1903, for maintenance of improvement, in addition to the balance unexpended July 1, 1901	5,500.00

Submitted in compliance with requirements of sundry civil act of June 4, 1897, and of section 7 of the river and harbor act of 1899.

(See Appendix I 12.)

13. Manokin River, Maryland.—[This work was in the charge of Gen. William F. Smith, United States agent, major of engineers, United States Army, retired, to May 15, 1901.] Before 1891 the governing depth was on the mud flats at the mouth, which was less than 2 feet. The existing project, adopted November 24, 1890, is for a channel 6 feet deep at mean low water and 100 feet wide from Locust Point to Sharps Point across the mud flats, a distance of 2¼ miles, at an estimated cost of $30,000. The amount expended up to the close of the fiscal year ending June 30, 1900, was $22,823.38. With those funds a channel was dredged to the project depth except in one short length, where it was a trifle less, but with a width varying, and in no place greater than 80 feet. That channel shoaled again until the controlling depth was 3 feet. Dredging was in progress between August 2 and 15, 1900, inclusive, across the mud flats, where a full depth was given for a width of 80 feet and a length of 1,270 feet. At the same time soundings were taken over the area formerly dredged, showing a range of depths from 4.5 to 7.3 feet. The maximum draft that could be carried through on June 30, 1901, was 4 feet. No commercial statistics were furnished.

July 1, 1900, balance unexpended	[1] $1,676.62
June 30, 1901, amount expended during fiscal year	1,438.67
July 1, 1901, balance unexpended	237.95
Amount (estimated) required for completion of existing project	7,500.00
Amount that can be profitably expended in fiscal year ending June 30, 1903, for works of improvement and for maintenance, in addition to the balance unexpended July 1, 1901	2,000.00

Submitted in compliance with requirements of sundry civil act of June 4, 1897, and of section 7 of the river and harbor act of 1899.

(See Appendix I 13.)

14. *Pocomoke River, Maryland.*—[This work was in the charge of Gen. William F. Smith, United States agent, major of engineers, United States Army, retired, to May 15, 1901.] From 1879 to 1888 a channel 7 feet deep at mean low water and not less than 80 feet wide had been dredged between Snowhill and Shad Landing, a distance of about 4½ miles, at a cost of $20,500. The existing project, adopted October 1, 1896, is for a channel between the same points 9 feet deep at mean low water and from 100 to 130 feet wide, at an estimated cost of $14,000. Up to the close of the fiscal year ending June 30, 1900, $25,365.69 had been expended, and at that date there was a channel 9 feet deep, with widths from 80 to 130 feet, between Nassawango Creek and the county wharf at Snowhill. In the past fiscal year dredging, under contract, resulted in a channel of the project dimensions from Shad Landing to the lower cut-off. From the lower cut-off to Snowhill, a distance of about 1 mile, the channel required widening to complete the project. On September 21, 1900, the maximum draft that could be carried over the shoalest part of the river under improvement was 9 feet at mean low water, but shoaling has since occurred, so that on June 30, 1901, the maximum draft was only 7.5 feet.

The following is the reported tonnage of the river:

1898	45,742
1899	50,866
1900	183,429

One semiweekly steamer and sailing vessels of an aggregate tonnage of 6,610 trade on the river.

---

[1] The amount expended during the fiscal year 1900 was $3,848.38, and not $3,848.28, as appears in the annual report for that year, leaving balance unexpended July 1, 1900, $1,676.62, instead of $1,676.72.

272   REPORT OF THE CHIEF OF ENGINEERS, U. S. ARMY.

July 1, 1900, balance unexpended $3,134.31
June 30, 1901, amount expended during fiscal year 2,985.23

July 1, 1901, balance unexpended 149.08

Amount (estimated) required for completion of existing project......... 6,000.00
Amount that can be profitably expended in fiscal year ending June 30, 1903,
in addition to the balance unexpended July 1, 1901 .... 5,000.00
Submitted in compliance with requirements of sundry civil act of June
4, 1897.

(See Appendix I 14.)

15. *Removing sunken vessels or craft obstructing or endangering navigation.*—The schooner *Wm. H. Roach* was wrecked in the Manokin River, Maryland, in 1899, where it was an obstruction to navigation, and the award of the contract for its removal was under consideration at the close of the fiscal year 1900. The contract was entered into July 7, 1900, and the wreck removed on the 30th of the same month, at a total cost of $399.45.

The bugeye *Columbia* was wrecked in February, 1900, near Deals Island wharf, Maryland, was abandoned and an obstruction to navigation, and the award of the contract for its removal was under consideration at the close of the fiscal year 1900. The contract was entered into July 7, 1900, and the wreck removed on the 27th and 28th of that month, at a total cost of $399.78.

Sunken logs in Back Creek, Maryland, the western outlet of the Delaware and Chesapeake Canal, were reported to be an obstruction to navigation. An examination made at a cost of $14.77 disclosed the fact that the logs had sunk to a depth of 10 feet below mean low water, with 1¼ feet of mud over them, and were no longer an obstruction. Nothing further was done.

The sloop *Laura Wilhelmina* was wrecked in Cambridge Harbor, Maryland, in August, 1900, and lay in 9 feet of water abandoned and obstructing navigation. The wreck was removed March 4, 1901, at a cost of $84.47.

The schooner *Maggie* was wrecked in 1899 in the mouth of North Point Creek, Patapsco River, Maryland, where it was abandoned and an obstruction to navigation. The wreck was removed July 20, 1900, at a cost of $100.

The schooner-rigged scow *Harry Moore* was wrecked October 15, 1900, in Jackson Creek, a tributary of the Chester River, Maryland, where it was abandoned and an obstruction to navigation. The wreck was removed December 6, 1900, at a cost of $150.

The schooner *Sarah E. Vetra* was wrecked January 15, 1901, as a result of a collision with the National Line steamer *Europe* on the edge of the Fort McHenry channel, Patapsco River, Maryland, where it was abandoned and an obstruction to navigation. The wreck was removed February 2, 1901, at a cost of $250.

The barge *Frank Thompson* sprung a leak and was wrecked November 6, 1900, near the front Craighill Channel light, Chesapeake Bay, Maryland, where it was abandoned and an obstruction to navigation. The wreck was removed March 15, 1901, at a cost of $290.

Schooner *Eldridge*, sloop *Ephriam Lyttee*, sloop *Maggie*, and hull of an old pile driver. These craft were wrecked and sunk in Cambridge Harbor, Maryland, in 1897 and 1898, were abandoned, and are an obstruction to navigation. They are all south of the drawbridge, in from 4½ to 7 feet of water. June 11, 1901, an allotment of $633 was made for their removal, and arrangements for the work were in progress at the close of the fiscal year.

The total amount expended during the fiscal year on removal of wrecks was $1,688.47.

(See Appendix I 15.)

EXAMINATION AND SURVEY MADE IN COMPLIANCE WITH EMERGENCY RIVER AND HARBOR ACT APPROVED JUNE 6, 1900.

Reports dated August 1 and November 9, 1900, respectively, on preliminary examination and survey of *harbor of Havre de Grace, Md., with a view to the removal of rocks near the entrance,* were submitted by Gen. William F. Smith, United States agent, major of engineers, United States Army, retired, through the Division Engineer, Col. Peter C. Hains, Corps of Engineers. He presents a plan for improvement at an estimated cost of $15,000. The reports were transmitted to Congress and printed in House Doc. No. 73, Fifty-sixth Congress, second session. (See also Appendix I 16.)

ESTIMATE MADE IN COMPLIANCE WITH CONCURRENT RESOLUTION OF CONGRESS OF JANUARY 22, 1901.

Lieutenant-Colonel Ernst submitted report, dated January 26, 1901, with *estimate of cost of deepening the channel in Curtis Bay, Baltimore, Md., to 30 feet and of widening the same to 250 feet; also of increasing the depth of the main ship channel of Patapsco River and Baltimore Harbor to 35 feet and the width to 1,000 feet.* The report was transmitted to Congress and printed in Senate Doc. No. 118, Fifty-sixth Congress, second session. (See also Appendix I 17.)

IMPROVEMENT OF POTOMAC RIVER AND ITS TRIBUTARIES; OF JAMES RIVER AND OF HARBOR AT MILFORD HAVEN, VIRGINIA, AND OF CERTAIN RIVERS IN VIRGINIA ON THE WESTERN SHORE OF CHESAPEAKE BAY; PROTECTION OF JAMESTOWN ISLAND, VIRGINIA.

This district was in the charge of Lieut. Col. Chas. J. Allen, Corps of Engineers.

1. *Potomac River at Washington, D. C.*—The Potomac River is navigable for vessels, both steam and sail, from its mouth to Georgetown, D. C., a distance of 113 miles. At Washington it changes its character from a distinctly fluvial to a tidal stream. The tide rises as far up as Little Falls, 3 miles above Georgetown, but the flood current is not perceptible above the latter. The mean range of tides at Washington is 3 feet.

At Little Falls, the actual head of navigation, the width of the river at low tide is 150 feet. The width just above the Aqueduct Bridge, which crosses the river at Georgetown, is about 1,200 feet. Below this bridge, along the water front at Georgetown, the width of the river gradually decreases for a distance of one-half mile to the foot of Thirty-first street, where the width is 730 feet. This part of the river is known as Georgetown Harbor, and its navigation was formerly obstructed by several dangerous rocks, which were removed in 1876 and 1883–1885. The depth obtained over these rocks by the improvement was 20 feet at low tide, which is now the ruling depth in the harbor. Georgetown has a wharf frontage of 4,000 feet, extending from the Aqueduct Bridge to the mouth of Rock Creek. At Easbys Point, 1 mile below the bridge, the river width is 974 feet. Prior to the reclamation of the flats the width of river sharply increased from Easbys Point to about 6,000 feet off the foot of Seventeenth street, about four-fifths of a mile below, and this last-named width substantially continued to Giesboro Point, nearly 4 miles below Easbys. Over a great part of this width there was a large deposit of the sediment carried by the river, resulting in the formation of bars in the channel and of wide flats on the left bank.

There were, in 1792, three channels in this part of the river, but since 1834 there have been but two, viz, the main, formerly called the Georgetown, but now known as the Virginia Channel, and the Washington Channel.

Long Bridge, 1¼ miles below Easbys Point, crosses both channels. The Virginia channel was obstructed by two bars. The upper bar extended from Long Bridge to about one-half mile below Easbys Point. The ruling depth on this bar was 8 feet in 1857, while in 1871 it was 10 feet, in 1873 it was 13½ feet, and in 1881, 15 feet. The improvement was due to frequent dredging, but after every freshet the dredged channel was nearly obliterated. The lower bar, 3,200 feet long, was near Giesboro Point, and in 1874 had a ruling depth of 14 feet, which was increased by dredging in 1874–75 to 16 feet. This was the ruling depth in 1881. Between these two bars the channel had depths of 20 to 80 feet. Below Long Bridge the Washington Channel was shoal; its ruling depth in 1878 was 10 feet for the greater part of the wharf front. Off the foot of N street the depth increased to 12 feet, thence gradually deepened to 22 feet off Greenleaf Point, where the Anacostia River enters the Potomac.

The depth in the Washington Channel had been increased by dredging, so that in 1881 a depth of 16 feet could be found along the greater part of the wharf front.

The flats, which, under the conditions above noted, had, prior to the present project, been in gradual process of formation for a long time, extended from the Washington shore to the edge of the Virginia Channel. Between Easbys Point and the old Seventeenth street wharf a large area, in some places 1,500 feet wide, had been raised by accretions to a height of about a foot above mean low tide. Large quantities of sewage were carried at high tide over these flats and distributed by the flow among the rank growth of sedges and aquatic plants with which the flats were covered. As the tide fell this mass of sewage was left exposed to the rays of the sun. These conditions combined to generate effluvia which rendered the adjacent portions of the city almost uninhabitable, and at the same time were reported as causing malarial and other diseases.

The present, which is the original, project for improvement was adopted by the act of Congress of August 2, 1882. It has for its object the improvement of the navigation of the river by widening and deepening its channels, reclamation of the flats by depositing on them the material dredged from the channels, the freeing of the Washington Channel, so far as it can be done, of sewage, and the establishment of harbor lines beyond which no wharves shall be built. To effect these the project provided for 20 feet depth in the channels at low water, for filling in the flats to a height of 3 feet above the flood plane of 1877, and for a tidal reservoir or basin above Long Bridge, to be provided with inlet and outlet gates of ample dimensions, to work automatically, and so arranged as to admit of the basin being filled from the Virginia Channel on the flood tide and discharged into the Washington Channel on the ebb. An ample system of drainage for the reclaimed area was also contemplated.

A training dike on the Virginia shore, extending downstream from the foot of Analostan Island, was added to the project in 1890.

The project also provided for the rebuilding of Long Bridge at an early period during the progress of the improvement, with wide spans upon piers offering the least possible obstruction to the flow of the water, and the interception of all sewage now discharged into the Washington Channel and its conveyance to the James Creek sewer canal, but neither of these works was included in the estimated cost of the improvement, which was $2,716,365. The estimate, as revised in 1897, is $2,953,020.

The total of appropriations for this work, from August 2, 1882, to March 3, 1899, was $2,359,000.

The amount expended to the close of the fiscal year ending June 30, 1900, was $2,229,103.82.

The expenditure resulted in the dredging of a channel 20 feet deep and 550 feet wide through the bar above Long Bridge and in restoring the standard 20-foot navigation by redredging shoals due to freshets; in increasing the width of the natural channel just below Long Bridge by 50 to 500 feet and in deepening it to 20 feet; in dredging a channel 350 feet wide and 20 feet deep through the bar in the Virginia Channel near Giesboro Point; in dredging the Washington Channel to a width of 400 feet and a depth of 20 feet for a navigation channel, and in dredging between this navigation channel and the wall of the adjacent reclaimed area to a depth of 12 feet; in dredging at the junction of the Washington and Virginia channels; in dredging the tidal reservoir (111 acres) to a depth of about 8 feet; in the construction of the reservoir outlet, and in the construction of 35,289 linear feet of sea wall, of which 4,910 linear feet has been taken down and relaid, and 5,965 linear feet of training dike.

The total number of cubic yards of material dredged from the channels from the commencement of the improvement (1882) to date and deposited on the flats is about 11,174,770 cubic yards.

The area of land reclaimed by these operations is 621.12 acres (or, including reservoirs, 739.42 acres), which by act of March 3, 1897, was declared to be a public park, under the name of Potomac Park.

Under date of August 15, 1900, a contract was made with the Atlantic, Gulf and Pacific Company, of New York, for dredging in the Washington and Virginia channels of the Potomac at Washington, D. C. The contractor's dredge having been lost at sea en route to Washington, an entirely new dredge had to be built for the contract. The dredge was built and in readiness for work early in February, 1901. The necessary dredging in the Washington Channel was completed by April 25, since which time the dredge has been operating in the Virginia Channel above Long Bridge. Vessels drawing 20 feet of water can now proceed to the Washington and Georgetown wharves.

The total amount of material dredged from the channels and deposited upon the flats during the past fiscal year was 281,163 cubic yards.

The maximum draft that could be carried through the Washington Channel on June 30, 1901, at mean low tide, was 20 feet; for the Virginia Channel it was the same.

It is proposed to continue the dredging of the Virginia Channel during the present season to the extent of about 384,000 cubic yards.

The benefits to navigation from the improvements have been marked. Vessels can come to Washington loaded more heavily than was formerly the case. The value of the commerce to be benefited may be judged of by examination of the following table, showing the commerce of the port of Washington, in tons, from 1887 to 1900, inclusive:

	Tons.		Tons.
1887	618,972	1894	644,588
1888	581,575	1895	693,450
1889	488,680	1896	723,657
1890	519,696	1897	593,684
1891	551,219	1898	645,239
1892	766,954	1899	715,549
1893	653,433	1900	661,420

The items of work remaining to be completed are the dredging to full width of the Virginia Channel, the maintenance of both the channels (Washington and Virginia), the raising of the incompletely raised portions of the area to the full height contemplated by the project, the completion of the sea wall of the tidal reservoir, the construction of the reservoir inlet, and completion of the training dike on the right of the Virginia Channel above Long Bridge.

Five hundred linear feet of sea wall will have to be built at the northeast corner of the tidal reservoir in case the bathing beach shall ever be discontinued.

July 1, 1900, balance unexpended $129,896.18
June 30, 1901, amount expended during fiscal year 36,908.01

July 1, 1901, balance unexpended 92,988.17
July 1, 1901, outstanding liabilities 650.00

July 1, 1901, balance available 92,338.17

July 1, 1901, amount covered by uncompleted contracts................. 64,543.00

⎰ Amount (estimated) required for completion of existing project 594,020.00
⎱ Amount that can be profitably expended in fiscal year ending June 30, 1903, for works of improvement and for maintenance, in addition to the balance available July 1, 1901... 200,000.00
Submitted in compliance with requirements of sundry civil act of June 4, 1897, and of section 7 of the river and harbor act of 1899.

(See Appendix J 1.)

2. *Potomac River below Washington, D. C.*—The Potomac River below Washington, D. C., is generally a wide and deep body of water, having the characteristics of a tidal estuary rather than of a fluvial stream.

In 1891 a survey of the obstructions to 24-foot navigation was made and a report rendered which was printed as House Ex. Doc. No. 33, Fifty-second Congress, first session. Form this resport the following brief description of the shoals found is taken:

(a) *Kettle Bottom Shoals.*—The Kettle Bottom Shoals, which are the first obstruction to 24-foot navigation met in ascending the river, commence 37 miles from the mouth and extend from Cob Point to Lower

Cedar Point, a distance of 12 miles. They consist of small shoals, old oyster beds, underlaid with mud, over which are depths of from 10 to 16 feet, scattered over the river in an irregular fashion, making navigation difficult for vessels drawing over 16 feet. There is, however, an old channel near the north bank of the river through which 24 feet can be carried except for a short distance near Swan Point, where there is a small shoal with a ruling depth of 23 feet.

(b) *Maryland Point Shoal.*—The next obstruction is Maryland Point Shoal, near Maryland Point, and 67 miles from the mouth. It is 7,000 feet in length, has a ruling depth of 22 feet, and is composed of soft mud.

(c) *Smiths Point Shoals.*—Near Smiths Point are two shoals. The lower, commencing about one-half mile above Maryland Point Shoal, is about 4,500 feet long, has a ruling depth of about 23 feet, and is composed of soft mud. About one-half mile above Smiths Point the upper shoal commences. It is 4,500 feet long, has a ruling depth of 21 feet, and is composed of soft mud.

(d) *Mattawoman Shoal.*—After passing Upper Smiths Point Shoal no obstruction to 24-foot navigation is found until Mattawoman Shoal is reached, 82 miles above the mouth of the river. This shoal is 15,300 feet long and has a ruling depth of 19.5 feet. The lower part is composed of sand and gravel, underlaid with mud, and the upper part of mud.

A reconnaissance of the several bars made June 28 to July 10, 1899, indicated that no material change in the conditions had occurred since 1891, though the depths over the bars appeared to be somewhat less than those of 1891.

During the progress of dredging operations at Mattawoman Shoal in 1900 what appeared to be partly disintegrated ledge rock in considerable quantities was encountered. This was totally unexpected, the survey of 1891 not having discovered it.

The present, which is also the original, project for this improvement was adopted by act of Congress of March 3, 1899, which act further provided for prosecuting the work under a continuing contract. This project contemplates the improvement of the waterway by dredging channels 24 feet deep and 200 feet wide through all obstructions to 24-foot navigation below Washington, D. C., at an estimated cost of $158,400.

The appropriations for this work from March 3, 1899, to March 3, 1901, aggregate $176,000.

The amount expended to June 30, 1900, was $11,858.72. The work done had resulted in dredging a channel 24 feet deep and 200 feet wide for a length of about 4,000 feet, and of the same depth and 160 feet wide for about 2,500 feet additional at Mattawoman Shoal, which is the shoalest of the obstructions to navigation under improvement.

During the fiscal year ending June 30, 1901, about 452,740 cubic yards of material was dredged, under continuing contract, at Mattawoman Shoal. As a result of these operations a channel 24 feet deep and 200 feet wide has been dredged in this shoal for a total length of about 13,000 feet.

The maximum draft that could be carried over the shoals in the Potomac River below Washington, D. C., on June 30, 1901, at low tide was about 21 feet.

The work required to complete the project is the continuation of dredging and the excavation of rock necessary to secure the required dimensions of channels.

The total tonnage annually passing through these channels is estimated at from 900,000 to 1,000,000 tons. In connection with this reference is made to the commercial statistics in the report upon improvement of the Potomac at Washington, D. C.

For the completion of the work provided for under the present project the appropriation of March 3, 1901, appears sufficient; therefore no further appropriation is here asked. A channel only 200 feet wide is, however, regarded as rather contracted for a river of the width and importance of the Potomac, and especially in view of the location of the Washington Navy-Yard upon its shores.

During the ensuing year so much of the unexpended balance as is required will be applied in completing the channels provided for by the existing project by dredging and rock excavation.

It is hoped that an increase in width of these channels to 400 feet may be soon authorized by Congress.

July 1, 1900, balance unexpended	$66,141.28
Amount appropriated by sundry civil act approved March 3, 1901	98,000.00
	164,141.28
June 30, 1901, amount expended during fiscal year	37,453.73
July 1, 1901, balance unexpended	126,687.55
July 1, 1901, outstanding liabilities	733.00
July 1, 1901, balance available	125,954.55
July 1, 1901, amount covered by uncompleted contracts	26,120.00

(See Appendix J 2.)

3. Occoquan Creek, Virginia.—Occoquan Creek is a tributary of the Potomac River, which it enters about 25 miles below Washington, D. C. The stream is navigable from its mouth, at Sandy Point, to the town of Occoquan, a distance of 4 miles. Navigation was obstructed by four bars, which were improved between 1873 and 1880 by dredging and dike construction so as to secure a navigable depth of about 6 feet at low tide. Four appropriations were made from 1873 to 1878, amounting to $25,000, and in 1880 the improvement was regarded as completed. In compliance with the provisions of the river and harbor act of August 11, 1888, a new survey of the creek was made in 1889. The survey showed that of the channels dredged through Lower Mud, Upper Mud, Sand, and Occoquan bars, all, excepting that dredged through Upper Mud Bar, had filled in from 2 to 3 feet in depth since 1880. The act of September 19, 1890, appropriated $10,000 for improving the creek.

The project adopted December 5, 1890, for the new (present) improvement comprises dredging of channels 6 feet deep and from 100 to 150 feet wide through the four bars, and construction of dikes required to secure the depths obtained by dredging. Estimated cost of the project, $45,000.

The total of appropriations for the improvement from September 19, 1890, to and including that of March 3, 1899 (the last appropriation), was $25,000.

The amount expended to include June 30, 1900, was $24,595.86. It resulted in dredging channels from 100 to 150 feet in width and to a least depth of 6 feet through the four bars, and in the construction of 1,585 linear feet of dike at Occoquan Bar and Sand Bar.

The available funds being practically exhausted, no work of improvement was in progress during the past fiscal year.

The maximum draft that could be carried through the channels on June 30, 1901, at mean low tide was about 6 feet, and the width of the channels between 6-foot contours was 100 feet.

The work remaining to be done to complete the project is extension of the dike at Sand Bar about 800 feet, construction of a dike at Upper Mud, and such dredging as may be necessary to restore the channel dimensions called for by the project. Owing to the action of freshets in the upper part and to the great width of the lower part of the stream, and cross-tidal currents in the latter, it is probable that occasional redredging will be required to maintain the depth, even after the essential features of the project shall be completed. The project is not, therefore, regarded as capable of permanent completion as regards dredging.

The work done under the appropriations for this improvement has been of material benefit to the trade and commerce connected with this locality by increasing the original ruling depth of 3 feet at low tide to 6 feet, thus obviating the delays due to waiting for tides and increasing the available draft of vessels navigating the creek. In this connection attention is invited to the appended comparative table of commercial statistics. The articles carried through the channel are mostly sand (for building), railroad ties, piles and wood, coal, fertilizers, flour and grain, and miscellaneous articles, being small in amount.

Receipts and shipments by water.

	Tons.		Tons.
1891	8,205	1897	15,835
1892	56,705	1898	29,865
1894	8,900	1900	69,400
1895	10,475		
1896	41,670	Total for eight years	241,055

Of the total tonnage 104,600 tons was sand.

July 1, 1900, balance unexpended	$404.14
June 30, 1901, amount expended during fiscal year	19.56
July 1, 1901, balance unexpended	384.58
Amount (estimated) required for completion of existing project	20,000.00
Amount that can be profitably expended in fiscal year ending June 30, 1903, in addition to the balance unexpended July 1, 1901	4,500.00

Submitted in compliance with requirements of sundry civil act of June 4, 1897.

(See Appendix J 3.)

4. Nomini Creek, Virginia.—Nomini Creek enters the Potomac River from the right bank about 82 miles below Washington. In 1872 its navigation was obstructed by a bar of oyster shells and sand at its mouth, over which but 3 feet could be carried at low tide. There was a strong cross current just within the mouth. After passing the bar the stream widens, and 8 feet can be carried for about 3½ miles to Nomini Ferry, while 5 feet can be carried for about 6 miles above the mouth.

The project for improvement, adopted in 1873, provided for dredging a channel through the bar 100 feet wide and 9 feet deep. The width was increased to 150 feet in 1879, in order to meet the increased trade. In 1885 the project was again modified by increasing the proposed width to 200 feet, at a cost of $62,500. In 1888 the estimate was increased to $72,500, the channel having shoaled on account of suspension of work from 1883 to 1889. It was difficult to secure permanent results, the channel being exposed to north and northwest winds and to cross-tidal currents. The deterioration of the channel outside White Point was thought to be largely due to material carried into the channel by the flood and ebb currents of Currioman Bay. In order to maintain the channel, the project was modified in 1890 as follows, and which is the *present project:*

The dredged channel to be 150 feet wide and 9 feet deep; a jetty to be constructed from White Point on the east and one from Cedar Island on the west; dikes to be built inside White Point to check the cross currents. Estimated revised cost, $72,500. Examination made in 1897 showed that the east jetty should be made 400 feet longer and that both jetties should be made higher than originally projected, the increased cost bringing the estimate up to $105,000.

The amount expended to include June 30, 1900, was $62,036.87. It resulted in the dredging of the outer channel to a depth of 9 feet at mean low tide by a width of 140 to 150 feet and the construction of 819 linear feet of east jetty, 130 feet of which had been raised to a height of 4 feet above low water.

During the fiscal year ending June 30, 1901, the remainder of the east jetty was raised to a height of 4 feet and the jetty extended, at the same height, 53 feet, or to a total length of 872 feet.

The maximum draft that could be carried through the channel on June 30, 1901, at mean low tide was about 9 feet.

Total of freight transported through the channels under improvement, 1889–1898, was 196,110 tons. The freight consisted of coal, farm produce, grain, lumber, oysters, railroad ties, general merchandise, and wood. The tonnage, by years, is given below.

The work required for completion of the project is extension of the east jetty 347 feet, beginning and building of the west jetty, and a small amount of redredging of the channel where slight shoaling has occurred.

The sum asked for the fiscal year ending June 30, 1903, will be expended in dredging and jetty construction.

Tonnage, by years.

Year	Tons.	Year	Tons.
1889	13,542	1894	25,100
1890	15,825	1895	16,250
1891	62,300	1896	7,425
1892	21,000	1897	7,370
1893	17,658	1898	9,640

This statement is for sailing vessels only. The steamers carry the great bulk of grain and merchandise.

Repeated efforts were made to obtain commercial statistics for 1899 and 1900, but they could not be procured.

July 1, 1900, balance unexpended	$7,963.13
July 30, 1901, amount expended during fiscal year	4,796.75
July 1, 1901, balance unexpended	3,166.38
Amount (estimated) required for completion of existing project	35,000.00
Amount that can be profitably expended in fiscal year ending June 30, 1903, in addition to the balance unexpended July 1, 1901	6,000.00
Submitted in compliance with requirements of sundry civil act of June 4, 1897.	

(See Appendix J 4.)

5. Lower Machodoc Creek, Virginia.—This creek is a tidal estuary on the right bank of the Potomac River and about 85 miles below Washington, D. C. It has a navigable length of about 4 miles. The width between banks at the mouth is 1 mile and between the 12-foot contours the channel width exceeds 3,000 feet. The lower part of the creek for a distance of 1¼ miles above the mouth is three-fourths of a mile to a mile in width, with a navigable depth of 13 feet, affording a safe harbor during northeast to southeast storms.

At the Narrows, 2 miles above the mouth, the stream suddenly contracts to a width of 650 feet, and the channel is obstructed by a sand bar over which but 4 feet could be carried at low tide. This bar has constituted the principal obstruction to navigation.

After passing Narrows Bar a depth of 10 to 14 feet is found in the channel, gradually shoaling to about 9 feet near Cupelo Point, 3 miles above the mouth, and thence to about 6 feet at Drum Bay, the head of navigation, 4 miles above the mouth.

The present approved project, adopted November 29, 1892, provides for dredging a channel 150 feet wide and 9 feet deep at low tide through the bar at the Narrows. The estimated cost was originally $15,000. This estimate was revised in 1897 and reduced to $11,100.

The total of appropriations to date is $9,000.

The total expenditure to the close of the year ending June 30, 1900, was $8,777.87. It resulted in a dredged channel through Narrows Bar 150 feet wide and 9 feet deep for about 1,150 feet (or about two-thirds of the length of the bar), the remaining third (575 feet) being dredged to a depth of 9 feet for a middle width of 110 feet, with a strip on each side 20 feet in width and 6 feet in depth.

The available funds being practically exhausted, no work of improvement was in progress during the past fiscal year.

The maximum draft that could be carried June 30, 1901, over the shoalest part of the locality under improvement was about 9 feet.

The benefit to navigation and commerce from the work already done has been considerable, as large sailing vessels and regular lines of steamers now enter the creek, which was impossible previous to the improvement.

Repeated efforts have been made to obtain commercial statistics for this work, but without success.

July 1, 1900, balance unexpended	$222.13
July 1, 1901, balance unexpended	222.13
Amount (estimated) required for completion of existing project	2,100.00
Amount that can be profitably expended in fiscal year ending June 30, 1903, in addition to the balance unexpended July 1, 1901	2,100.00
Submitted in compliance with requirements of sundry civil act of June 4, 1897.	

(See Appendix J 5.)

6. *Rappahannock River, Virginia.*—The Rappahannock is navigable from its mouth in Chesapeake Bay to Fredericksburg, Va., 106 miles. The ruling depth at the mouth is 5 fathoms, which depth holds to Jones Point, 28 miles above, while 17 feet can be carried to Tappahannock, 41 miles from the mouth. The width at Port Royal, 77 miles from the mouth, is about 1,500 feet, whence it gradually decreases to 350 feet at Fredericksburg. In 1871, prior to the inception of the improvement, 6 feet could be carried to within a mile of Fredericksburg, and thence 4 feet to the town.

The obstructions to navigation before improvement was undertaken were nine bars between Tappahannock and Fredericksburg, over which the ruling depths were from 4 to 10¼ feet.

The *present approved* project, adopted in 1879, amendatory of the original project of 1871, provides for dredging a channel 100 feet wide and 10 feet deep through the bars between Fredericksburg and Port Royal, and one 200 feet wide and 15 feet deep between Port Royal and Tappahannock. Total estimated cost of the revised project, $881,500.

The appropriations for this improvement from March 3, 1871, to date aggregate $267,500, or an average of less than $9,000 per annum.

The amount expended to June 30, 1900, was $254,539.74. It resulted in improvement of seven bars between Fredericksburg and Port Royal, as follows:

Name of bar.	Miles above mouth of river.	Depth at completion of last work.	Depth at time of last survey.
		Feet.	Feet.
Farleyvale	94	10	9¼
Castle Ferry	98	10	9¼
Spottswood	102	10¼	9
Pratt Reach	103	9	9
Bernard	104	9	9
Pollock	105	10	10
Fredericksburg	106	10	8

The amount expended during the fiscal year ending June 30, 1901, was $7,275.97. It consisted in dredging by contract 19,730 cubic yards of material at Fredericksburg and Pollocks bars, affording 10 feet in depth on them.

The work done to date has resulted in a channel affording generally a maximum draft at mean low tide of 7¼ feet carried to Fredericksburg and 9¼ feet to within 4¼ miles of that place.

The work required to complete the project is continuation of dredging and of dike construction where necessary for maintenance of the channels. Many of the old dikes are much in need of repairs. These dikes not only serve to regulate the width of channel, but also serve to retain dredged material from getting back into the channels.

The value of the improvement may be inferred from an examination of the following table of commercial statistics:

Tonnage for—	Tons.	Tonnage for—	Tons.
1888	83,600	1896	[1]161,196
1890	83,830	1897	[1]158,108
1892	[1]126,333	1898	[1]166,586
1893	[1]141,750	1899	[1]167,862
1894	[1]144,070	1900	[1]190,827
1895	[1]151,466		

[1] Furnished by Mr. William D. Scott, Fredericksburg, Va.

The principal articles of commerce are grain, oysters, fertilizers, cattle, farm produce, and general merchandise.

At Fredericksburg Bar new deposits of sand are formed by each recurring freshet, and the annual reports for a number of years past have referred to the necessity of an annual appropriation of $7,500 for removal of such deposits from this bar alone. Owing to the continued shoaling this past spring, which threatened to shut off steamers from Fredericksburg landing, it was decided to apply a part of the funds which had been reserved from the last appropriation for dike repairs to the relief of navigation by dredging so far as the comparatively small amount would go. Accordingly a contract, after advertisement, was made June 4, 1901, with W. H. French, of Norfolk, Va., for the removal of about 10,500 cubic yards from the Fredericksburg channel. Dredging under this contract will be prosecuted during the coming season.

It is proposed to expend the sum asked for the fiscal year ending June 30, 1903, in dredging the bars, in dike construction and repair, and in maintenance of the dredged channel, the dredging to be at Fredericksburg and Spottswood bars and dike construction and repair mainly at the same bars.

July 1, 1900, balance unexpended	$12,960.26
June 30, 1901, amount expended during fiscal year	7,275.97
July 1, 1901, balance unexpended	5,684.29
July 1, 1901, outstanding liabilities	25.00
July 1, 1901, balance available	5,659.29
July 1, 1901, amount covered by uncompleted contracts	3,360.00
Amount (estimated) required for completion of existing project	114,000.00
Amount that can be profitably expended in fiscal year ending June 30, 1903, for works of improvement and for maintenance, in addition to the balance available July 1, 1901	30,000.00

Submitted in compliance with requirements of sundry civil act of June 4, 1897, and of section 7 of the river and harbor act of 1899.

(See Appendix J 6.)

7. *Urbana Creek, Virginia.*—Urbana Creek enters Rappahannock River from the right bank at a point about 16 miles above its mouth. In 1874 a bar existed outside the mouth, over which but 6¼ feet depth could be carried at low tide. In 1882 a shoal within the creek, having a least depth of 7 feet, and near the town of Urbana, was regarded as obstructing steamboat navigation.

The project for improvement adopted in 1879 comprised excavation of a channel 150 feet wide and 10 feet deep through the outer bar; estimated cost, $20,000. This project was modified in 1883 to include dredging through the inner bar, and in 1888 to include jetties at the mouth to maintain the channel. The revised estimated cost was $34,580.

On account of the exposed position of the channel through the outer bar the work suffered from the action of northwesterly winds, which caused shoaling in the channel and a diminution in its width. In April, 1897, a survey was made to determine the extent of change in the channels, and an estimate rendered in June following of the cost of completing the project by dredging and construction of a jetty to protect the channel dredged through the outer bar. This cost, added to the amounts expended to date, increases the estimated cost of the *present project* to $70,000.

284   REPORT OF THE CHIEF OF ENGINEERS, U. S. ARMY.

The appropriations for this work from March 3, 1879, to March 3, 1899, aggregated $33,500.

The amount expended to include June 30, 1900, was $32,530.58. It resulted in securing a channel 10 feet deep and 150 feet wide through the outer bar and a channel 10 feet deep and 135 feet wide through the inner bar, with a small turning basin 10 feet deep at the steamboat wharf.

A contract was made October 29, 1900, for about $720 worth of dredging at Urbana Creek (the funds being a small balance from appropriations) to be done under the same contract for certain dredging in York, Mattaponi, and Pamunkey rivers and Milford Haven, Va. The contractor has been engaged at other of the localities, and no dredging was done at Urbana Creek during the fiscal year ending June 30, 1901.

The maximum draft that could be carried through the channels on June 30, 1901, at low tide, was about 9.5 feet.

The improvement has been of benefit to commerce and navigation by permitting the entrance of sailing vessels to the creek, and enabling one of the steamers of the Weems Line, Baltimore to Fredericksburg, to enter the creek and land at the wharf.

The value of the commerce and navigation of the stream is indicated by the following table of commercial statistics. The principal articles of commerce are oysters, railroad ties, coal, grain, lumber, wood, farm produce, guano, and general merchandise.

COMMERCIAL STATISTICS.

Calendar year—	Reported by Mr. F. A. Bristow.	Reported by Mr. J. D. Gressitt.
	Tons.	Tons.
1891	19,500	22,100
1892	20,095	17,125
1893	55,885	61,290
1894	82,395	88,305
1895	66,530	92,320
1896	137,485	133,925
1897	153,875	181,500
1900	179,543	179,414

Commercial statistics received for 1898 and 1899 were not in a form to be used.

The sum asked for the fiscal year ending June 30, 1903, will be expended in dredging, chiefly at the inner bar, and in maintenance of the outer channel by jetty work.

July 1, 1900, balance unexpended	$969.32
June 30, 1901, amount expended during fiscal year	191.32
July 1, 1901, balance unexpended	778.00
July 1, 1901, amount covered by uncompleted contracts	720.00
Amount (estimated) required for completion of existing project	36,500.00
Amount that can be profitably expended in fiscal year ending June 30, 1903, in addition to the balance unexpended July 1, 1901	10,000.00
Submitted in compliance with requirements of sundry civil act of June 4, 1897.	

(See Appendix J 7.)

8. *Harbor at Milford Haven, Virginia.*—Milford Haven is a tidal estuary of Chesapeake Bay, situated on its western shore, near Cherry Point, at the mouth of Piankatank River, and about 35 miles north of Old Point Comfort. The haven is about 4 miles long and from one-half

mile to 1 mile wide. Its general direction is northwest and southeast. The depth in the channel ranges from 6¼ to 15 feet, but is generally 7 feet or more. The haven has two entrances, one at the northwest end, at Hills Bay, an arm of the Piankatank River, about 2 miles from Cherry Point, and another at the southeast end, on Chesapeake Bay, about 5 miles below Cherry Point, thus separating from the main shore a considerable body of land known as Gwynns Island. Both entrances are obstructed by bars. The southeast entrance is exposed and, as the bar has a ruling depth of but 5 feet, is but seldom used. The northwest entrance from Piankatank River is the one generally used by vessels and steamers entering the haven, and before improvement the bar obstructing this entrance had a ruling depth of 8 feet.

The original—which is also the present—project for improvement was adopted by act of Congress of March 3, 1899, and proposed the dredging of a channel 10 feet deep, with a minimum width of 200 feet, through this bar, at an estimated cost of $12,500.

By act of Congress approved June 6, 1900, it was provided that "The unexpended balance of the appropriation for the improvement of the harbor at Milford Haven, Virginia, or any part thereof, may, in the discretion of the Secretary of War, be used for the improvement of the bar within said harbor." This inner bar has a ruling depth of about 8 feet, but it was not included by the act of March 3, 1899, in the original survey or project, which provided only for the bar at the "entrance."

The amount expended to include June 30, 1900, was $1,518.21. It resulted in providing a channel 10 feet deep at low tide, with a minimum width of about 50 feet entirely through the outer bar. No work had been done on the inner bar.

During the past fiscal year the outer channel was completed to the full projected dimensions, and a contract was let for dredging the inner bar, under the same contract as for certain dredging to be done in York, Mattaponi, and Pamunkey rivers and Urbana Creek, Virginia. The contractor having been engaged at other of the above localities, no work had yet been done upon the inner bar, but it will be done during the coming fiscal year.

The maximum draft that could be carried through the channels on June 30, 1901, at low tide, was about 10 feet on the outer bar and about 8 feet on the inner bar.

To fully complete the dredging needed at the inner bar will require an additional appropriation of $5,000.

The value of the commerce and navigation at this place may be seen by referring to the commercial statistics. The principal articles of commerce are oysters, farm produce, fish, flour, and general merchandise.

Commercial statistics.

	Tons.
Calendar year, 1900	15,031

July 1, 1900, balance unexpended	$10,981.79
June 30, 1901, amount expended during fiscal year	7,372.79
July 1, 1901, balance unexpended	3,609.00
July 1, 1901, amount covered by uncompleted contracts	1,920.00
Amount (estimated) required for completion of existing project	5,000.00
Amount that can be profitably expended in fiscal year ending June 30, 1903, in addition to the balance unexpended July 1, 1901	5,000.00
Submitted in compliance with requirements of sundry civil act of June 4, 1897.	

Se A endix J 8.)

9. *York River, Virginia.*—York River is 41 miles long and discharges into Chesapeake Bay about 16 miles above Old Point. Entering the river, 24 feet can be carried for 32 miles, or up to Potopotank Bar, 9 miles below Westpoint. In 1880 the ruling depth on this bar was 18.5 feet. Westpoint bar, the next obstruction to navigation, commences about 2 miles below and extends up to Westpoint. Before improvement it had a ruling depth of 15.5 feet.

The original project for improvement, adopted in 1880, proposed dredging channels 22 feet deep and 200 feet wide through the bars. In 1884, on account of growth of trade, the width was increased to 400 feet, and in 1887 the project was further amended to include construction of a dike along the right bank at Westpoint bar to maintain the channel. Total cost of the revised, which is the present, project, $308,800.

The amount expended to June 30, 1900, was $228,173.23. It resulted in a dredged channel 105 feet wide and 22 feet deep at Potopotank, and one 22 feet deep and 160 to 260 feet in width at Westpoint bar. This latter channel narrowed and shoaled and had to be redredged. A training dike 10,142 feet long has been constructed at Westpoint bar, and examinations of the channel made subsequent to its construction show that the channel dimensions obtained by dredging are now being maintained.

Under date of October 29, 1900, a contract was made for dredging in York River, Virginia, to be done under the same contract for certain dredging to be done in Mattaponi and Pamunkey rivers, Milford Haven, and Urbana Creek, Virginia.

During the past fiscal year a portion of the channel near the lower end of the dike, where it had not been dredged since the construction of the dike, was dredged under the above contract to a depth of 20 feet at low tide, and the excavated material deposited behind the dike, thus adding greatly to its stability.

The maximum draft that could be carried through the channels on June 30, 1901, at low tide, was about 20 feet.

The work remaining to be done to complete the project is the dredging necessary to complete a channel 400 feet wide and 22 feet deep and the extension and maintenance of the dike.

A large and important commerce has been benefited by this improvement. Westpoint was for years the cotton-shipping point of the Southern Railway Company. In 1896 this company established a new shipping point near Norfolk, Va., and freight carrying on the York River fell off considerably.

While the amount of river commerce is still below what it was prior to 1896, extensive new industries have been and are being established at Westpoint, and there is a demand for the widening of the channels to their full projected width with a depth of at least 20 feet.

The following table shows the tonnage of the river from 1888 to 1894:

Reported for—	Tons.	Reported for—	Tons.
1888	285,480	1892	345,559
1889	328,353	1893	351,390
1890	418,190	1894	379,808
1891	304,338		

Repeated efforts have been made to procure commercial statistics for years subsequent to 1894, but without success.

July 1, 1900, balance unexpended	$11,576.77
June 30, 1901, amount expended during fiscal year	8,441.98
July 1, 1901, balance unexpended	3,134.79
July 1, 1901, outstanding liabilities	342.79
July 1, 1901, balance available	2,792.00
July 1, 1901, amount covered by uncompleted contracts	2,792.00
Amount (estimated) required for completion of existing project	69,050.00
Amount that can be profitably expended in fiscal year ending June 30, 1903, for works of improvement and for maintenance, in addition to the balance available July 1, 1901	6,500.00

Submitted in compliance with requirements of sundry civil act of June 4, 1897, and of section 7 of the river and harbor act of 1899.

(See Appendix J 9.)

10. *Mattaponi River, Virginia.*—The Mattaponi is navigable for small steamers and vessels from its mouth to Aylett, about 39 miles, and can be made navigable for small barges from Aylett to Monday Bridge, 16 miles. The obstructions to a 5½-foot navigation below Aylett consist of seven bars, upon which the ruling depths at low tide vary from 2.4 to 3.8 feet. Above Aylett there are numerous bars, but no work on them has been proposed. The river was also obstructed by snags, wrecks, and overhanging trees.

The original project for improvement, adopted in 1880, provided for removal of snags, wrecks, and leaning trees below Monday Bridge, and the improvement of the bars below Aylett so as to give a depth of 5½ feet at low tide and a channel width of 40 feet. This project was extended by the terms of the river and harbor act of July 13, 1892, which provided for the removal of snags as far up as Guineas Bridge, near Milford Station, on the Richmond, Fredericksburg and Potomac Railroad. Estimated cost of this, which is the present project, $72,100.

The amount expended to June 30, 1900, was $25,678.68. It resulted in the removal of snags, logs, and overhanging trees from the river between Robinsons bar, 34 miles above the mouth, and Monday Bridge, 21 miles above Robinsons, and in keeping the river below Aylett free from such obstructions, and also in the construction of 2,297 linear feet of dike at Robinsons bar.

Amount expended during the fiscal year ended June 30, 1901, $10.08. No work was done during the past fiscal year.

A contract for dredging was made October 29, 1900, for dredging in Mattaponi River, to be done under the same contract as for certain dredging to be done in York and Pamunkey rivers, Milford Haven, and Urbana Creek, Virginia. The contractor having been engaged at other of the above-named localities no work has been done in Mattaponi River during the fiscal year ending June 30, 1901. The work will, however, be done early in the coming fiscal year.

The work already done upon this river has been of benefit to the existing commerce, the amount of which is shown by the following table. As snags and other obstructions form in greater or less degree after every freshet, much of the work done has had to be gone over again. Before any work for improvement was undertaken the trade was limited.

Tonnage by years.

	Tons.		Tons.
1890	32,650	1894	39,300
1891	52,060	1899	44,700
1892	32,690	1900	42,500
1893	36,420		

Commercial statistics for the years 1895–1898 could not be procured.
The maximum draft that could be carried at mean low water over the shoalest part of the channel June 30, 1901, was 2.5 feet at Walker Bar.

July 1, 1900, balance unexpended	$4,121.32
June 30, 1901, amount expended during fiscal year	10.08
July 1, 1901, balance unexpended	4,111.24
July 1, 1901, amount covered by uncompleted contracts	2,668.00
Amount (estimated) required for completion of existing project	42,300.00
Amount that can be profitably expended in fiscal year ending June 30, 1903, in addition to the balance unexpended July 1, 1901	3,000.00
Submitted in compliance with requirements of sundry civil act of June 4, 1897.	

(See Appendix J 10.)

11. Pamunkey River, Virginia.—The Pamunkey River is navigable from its mouth, at Westpoint, on York River, to Hanovertown, a distance of about 59 miles. Seven feet of depth at low water can be carried to Buckland Bar, 38¼ miles above Westpoint. Above this bar are six bars, extending along the river for about 15¼ miles, the ruling depths on which vary from 5½ to 1½ feet, excepting on the Upper or Indian Table Bar, which is exposed at low tide. Besides these bars are logs, snags, and overhanging trees.

The project for improvement, adopted in 1880 and amended in 1885, contemplated 7-foot navigation to Bassett Ferry, 47 miles from Westpoint; thence 5 feet to Wormley Landing, 54 miles; thence 3 feet to Hanovertown, the 7-foot channel to have a width of 100 feet and the other channels 40 feet. The wrecks, snags, logs, and trees obstructing navigation between Garlick Ferry and Hanovertown were also to be removed. The cost of this amended project, which is the present project, was estimated at $32,500.

The total expenditure to June 30, 1900, was $22,618.43. It resulted in removing several times snags and similar obstructions from about 30 miles of river, in removing parts of seven wrecks, and in partly improving Spring and Skidmore bars, 43 and 47 miles, respectively, from Westpoint.

Under date of October 29, 1900, a contract was made for dredging in Pamunkey River, Virginia, to be done under the same contract as for certain dredging to be done in York and Mattaponi rivers, Milford Haven, and Urbana Creek, Virginia. The contractor has been engaged at other of the above localities and no work was therefore done in Pamunkey River during the fiscal year ending June 30, 1901. The work will be done early in the coming fiscal year.

The maximum drafts that could be carried at mean low water over the shoalest part of the channels June 30, 1901, were as follows: In the 7-foot channel, 5.3 feet; in the 5-foot channel, 3.5 feet; and in the 3-foot channel, 2.2 feet.

The commerce of this river amounted, according to reports received, to 50,420 tons in 1893, and 42,250 tons in 1894, the greater part of the latter being railroad ties and wood. There is scarcely any trade on the 5 miles immediately below Hanovertown. The tonnage of the river for 1899 is stated as about 44,600 tons. Commercial statistics for the years 1895 to 1898 and for 1900 could not be obtained.

The work remaining to be done to complete the existing project consists in dredging, construction of dikes, and removal of snags and logs.

July 1, 1900, balance unexpended	$2,881.57
June 30, 1901, amount expended during fiscal year	6.40
July 1, 1901, balance unexpended	2,875.17
July 1, 1901, amount covered by uncompleted contracts	2,116.00

{ Amount (estimated) required for completion of existing project....... 7,000.00
Amount that can be profitably expended in fiscal year ending June 30, 1903, in addition to the balance unexpended July 1, 1901............ 3,000.00
Submitted in compliance with requirements of sundry civil act of June 4, 1897.

(See Appendix J 11.)

12. James River, Virginia.—Prior to 1870 a small sum had been expended with some advantage to navigation, but the improvement was not regularly undertaken by the United States until that year. The original condition of the river between Richmond and its mouth as to depth, width, and general availability for purposes of navigation before its improvement was begun in 1870, was about as follows:

Between the mouth of the Appomattox and Richmond, then a distance of 35 miles, instead of 30 miles, as at present, the canal at Dutch Gap not being navigable, the ruling depth at mean low tide was 7 feet, that depth obtaining on Rocketts Reef at Richmond and on Richmond Bar, 7 miles below. The channel was close and indirect at some points, and was obstructed in Trents Reach, in the bend just above Dutch Gap, 17½ miles below the city, by a shoal on which only 8 feet could be carried and by obstructions placed during the civil war by the Federal authorities.

The channel was also obstructed by wrecks at Graveyard Reach and Chaffins Bluff, 10 miles and 8 miles, respectively, below Richmond.

The channel at Drewry Bluff and Warwick Bar, situated about 7 and 4½ miles, respectively, below the city was almost impassable on account of obstructions placed during the civil war, consisting at each locality of the remains of a military bridge, lines of stone cribs, and sunken vessels.

The ruling depth in the reach between the mouths of the James and the Appomattox, a distance of 69.4 miles, was 15 feet on Harrisons Bar,[1] about 38 miles below Richmond, and on Goose Hill Flats, 71 miles below.

The original project was to give 18 feet depth at full tide to Rich-

---

[1] The United States Coast and Geodetic Survey chart of 1852 shows a depth of 13¼ feet at Harrisons Bar. The United States engineer chart of 1877, prior to which no work was done at the bar, shows 15 feet.

mond, with a channel width of 180 feet from Harrisons Bar to the city docks, the excavation in rock to be 18½ feet. The average rise of tide is 2½ feet. Work on this project was well advanced when Congress, July 5, 1884, adopted another of 22 feet at mean low tide from Richmond to the sea. The width to be given the channel is 400 feet from the sea to City Point, 300 feet from there to Drewry Bluff, and thence 200 feet to Richmond, estimated to cost $4,500,000. A large part of the excavation has been and will be in solid rock, and the cost is necessarily great. Operations consist in dredging, rock excavation, and the contraction and regulation of the waterway by means of dikes and jetties.

Work has been generally done first on the shoalest places in the river, with a view to obtaining the greatest benefit to commerce in the shortest time.

The amount expended on the improvement, to include June 30, 1900, was $1,812,106.28. It resulted in a channel with a ruling depth of 16½ feet at mean low tide and general width of 90 to 100 feet from Hampton Roads to Richmond, excepting at a point in the channel between Jetties 23 and 25, about 1¼ miles below Richmond, where there was an isolated rock on which the depth, at mean low tide, was 14½ feet.

The amount expended during the fiscal year ending June 30, 1901, was $59,363.97. The results derived from this expenditure are as follows:

Increased channel dimensions on Rocketts Reef between the lower city line of Richmond and Jetty B, a distance of 775 feet, from about 14½ to 16½ feet deep by about 50 feet wide, to 18 feet deep by 100 feet wide; channel enlargement on Goode Rocks section between Jetties 28½ and 32, for a distance of 1,115 feet, and on Richmond Bar, between Jetties 32 and 40, a distance of about 1,700 feet, by widening from 90 to 100 feet to 150 feet and deepening the parts widened to 18 feet below mean low water.

The maximum draft that could be carried on June 30, 1901, at mean low water over the shoalest part of the reach under improvement, viz, in Stearns Dike section, from 1 to 1¼ miles below Richmond, was 16½ feet.

With the small balance of appropriations available it is proposed to enlarge the channel and remove obstructions during the coming fiscal year, so far as the funds will admit of.

The value to commerce of an improvement of this river is shown by the following table of river tonnage between 1890 and 1900:

	Tons.		Tons.
1890	743,122	1896	680,935
1891	739,308	1897	661,909
1892	616,755	1898	472,778
1894	616,269	1899	571,802
1895	602,582	1900	609,411

The amount estimated for the fiscal year ending June 30, 1903, is for widening and deepening the channel immediately below Richmond, mostly by rock excavation; for widening and deepening channels by dredging, principally at Warwick and Harrisons bars, Dancing Point Shoals, Swans Point, and Goose Hill Flats; and for maintenance of dikes and jetties.

July 1, 1900, balance unexpended	$110,393.72
June 30, 1901, amount expended during fiscal year	59,363.97
July 1, 1901, balance unexpended	51,029.75
July 1, 1901, outstanding liabilities	1,197.00
July 1, 1901, balance available	49,832.75
July 1, 1901, amount covered by uncompleted contracts	9,854.00
Amount (estimated) required for completion of existing project	3,317,500.00
Amount that can be profitably expended in fiscal year ending June 30, 1903, in addition to the balance available July 1, 1901 Submitted in compliance with requirements of sundry civil act of June 4, 1897.	250,000.00

(See Appendix J 12.)

13. Protection of Jamestown Island, Virginia.—The river and harbor act of 1894 contained an item of $10,000 for protection of Jamestown Island. The shore had been wearing away for years from action of waves, and the erosion had reached a point where protection was required if the old landmark was to be preserved. The appropriation was applied to construction of a wall faced with granite laid without mortar in front of the threatened portion of the island, to grading and turfing the bank behind the wall, and to construction of several groins in front of it. This work was completed in 1895.

The soil of the island is light and easily moved. The funds did not admit of covering the part requiring protection with the kind of work desirable. Storms, especially those of the winter of 1895 and 1896, greatly damaged the work.

The river and harbor act of June 3, 1896, appropriated $15,000 for this protection.

Examination of the eroded front was made during the winter of 1896 and 1897, and a plan for the application of the appropriation of 1896 was decided upon. No work of construction, however, could be undertaken until satisfactory arrangements should be made whereby working parties could go upon certain land the protection of the front of which would have constituted the principal part of the work. Full understanding in that respect was not finally arrived at until the 10th of June, 1899, at which time the remaining permit needed to enable the United States engineer to enter upon the ground was received. In the fall of 1899 an additional examination, including needed borings, was made at the site of the work with the result of revising the plan of 1897 in accordance with conditions observed in 1899. The plan as revised consists of a revetment of closely laid flagstones or concrete blocks, with backing of macadam placed against the slope of the island bank or embankments where the latter occur, the outer toe of embankments and revetment to be buttressed by a line of piles cut off at low water and united by a string piece to which driven sheet piling is to be spiked, the pile buttress to be protected by stone riprap where found necessary. It is expected to protect about 1,350 linear feet of bank with the present funds.

The work of the past fiscal year on the bank protection began in February under contract and was carried on throughout the rest of the year; it is in an unfinished condition.

The amount expended on this work to include June 30, 1900, was $9,953.02, about 96 per cent of which pertains to the old work of 1895.

The protection of this island can not be said to be necessary to the improvement or conservation of the navigation of James River.

July 1, 1900, balance unexpended	$15,046.98
June 30, 1901, amount expended during fiscal year	581.43
July 1, 1901, balance unexpended	14,465.55
July 1, 1901, outstanding liabilities	185.00
July 1, 1901, balance available	14,280.55
July 1, 1901, amount covered by uncompleted contracts	14,000.00

(See Appendix J 13.)

EXAMINATION MADE IN COMPLIANCE WITH EMERGENCY RIVER AND HARBOR ACT APPROVED JUNE 6, 1900.

Lieutenant-Colonel Allen submitted report dated September 12, 1900, on preliminary examination of *Quantico Creek, Virginia.* It is his opinion, concurred in by the Chief of Engineers, that improvement of the locality by the General Government is not advisable. The report was transmitted to Congress and printed in House Doc. No. 101, Fifty-sixth Congress, second session. (See also Appendix J 14.)

IMPROVEMENT OF NORFOLK HARBOR, VIRGINIA, AND ITS APPROACHES, AND OF RIVERS AND HARBORS IN SOUTHEASTERN VIRGINIA AND NORTHEASTERN NORTH CAROLINA.

This district was in the charge of Maj. James B. Quinn, Corps of Engineers. Division Engineer, Col. Peter C. Hains, Corps of Engineers.

1. Harbor at Norfolk and its approaches, Virginia.—This harbor in its original condition could accommodate vessels of 20 feet draft at mean low water as far as the navy-yard, on the Southern Branch, near Norfolk, and to wharves on the Eastern Branch the draft was limited by shoals to about 15 feet at the same stage of the tide. The rise and fall of tides averages 2.7 feet.

The existing project, approved in 1885 and amended in 1890, calls for a channel 25 feet deep at mean low water to within 75 feet of the established pierhead line from the navy-yard, on the Southern Branch, to Fort Norfolk, and from the Campostella Bridge, on the Eastern Branch of the Elizabeth River, to its junction with the Southern Branch. From Fort Norfolk to deep water in Hampton Roads the channel width required is 500 feet to the depth above mentioned. Under the amendment of 1890 a provision for an anchorage near the mouth of the Western Branch, to have 25 feet depth at mean low water, was added. The total estimated cost of improvement under the project is $1,041,744.56.

To June 30, 1900, $1,340,914.40 had been expended, resulting in the accomplishment of all contemplated work with the exception of the dredging of the section of the Eastern Branch between the Norfolk and Western Railroad and the Campostella bridges, and a small area on the Berkley, side at the mouth of the Southern Branch. Under a separate project, approved July 21, 1898, a channel 450 feet wide and 28 feet deep at mean low water was excavated from the navy-yard to Hampton Roads, and the cost thereof ($359,516.42) has been included in the expenditures reported above.

No active work has been done in the past fiscal year, the expenditures reported being in connection with the preliminary examination and making estimate of cost of attaining depth of 28 feet in front of piers at Pinner Point out to the channel, and for locating and plotting new wharves constructed in the harbor for office records.

A draft of 28 feet can be carried at mean low water to the navy-yard above Norfolk.

July 1, 1900, balance unexpended	$3,601.02
June 30, 1901, amount expended during fiscal year	133.79
July 1, 1901, balance unexpended	3,467.23

Amount (estimated) required for completion of existing project	56,774.56
Amount that can be profitably expended in fiscal year ending June 30, 1903, in addition to the balance unexpended July 1, 1901	35,000.00
Submitted in compliance with requirements of sundry civil act of June 4, 1897.	

(See Appendix K 1.)

2. *Western Branch of Elizabeth River, Virginia.*—This river prior to improvement had a 12-foot mean low-water channel from 50 to 300 feet wide.

The existing project, approved September 2, 1896, is to attain a channel 200 feet wide and 20 feet deep at mean low water, to extend from the 20-foot contour in Norfolk Harbor for a distance of about 1 mile up the river from that point. The estimated cost for such a channel was $45,000.

To June 30, 1900, $44,626.23 had been expended, with the result that the channel as projected had been provided.

No expenditures were made during the past fiscal year. On June 30, 1901, a vessel drawing 20 feet of water could navigate over the extent of the improved channel at mean low tide.

July 1, 1900, balance unexpended	$373.77
July 1, 1901, balance unexpended	373.77

(See Appendix K 2.)

3. *Nansemond River, Virginia.*—In its original condition a 5-foot channel existed, which was, however, obstructed by wrecks and snags. At a cost of $37,000, an 8-foot mean low-water channel was provided between 1873 and 1878, and this depth was available for navigation when the present scheme to secure a depth of 12 feet at mean low water from the mouth to Suffolk, Va., was adopted.

The existing project, approved December 18, 1888, is to secure a channel 12 feet deep at mean low water from Suffolk, Va., to Town Point, 100 feet wide on the bottom from the former place to the Western Branch, and from 200 to 400 feet wide at the bottom thence to Town Point. It also provides for a turning basin 200 feet square a short distance below Suffolk. Estimated cost of work to be done thereunder, $152,500.

The district officer states that ample provision will be made for all present commercial requirements if a channel width of 80 feet be attained, and the division engineer is of the same opinion. This result can be accomplished by the expenditure of the available balance in dredging above the Western Branch and an appropriation of $1,000 for the removal of two shoals below to a depth of $12\frac{1}{2}$ feet at mean low water. Unless otherwise directed by law, the attainment of a channel 80 feet wide will be considered as completing the project.

294 REPORT OF THE CHIEF OF ENGINEERS, U. S. ARMY.

On June 30, 1900, $40,127.04 had been expended in attaining a channel 80 feet wide and 12 feet deep at mean low water from Suffolk to the Western Branch and in dredging the turning basin 300 feet below the place first mentioned.

The expenditures reported for the fiscal year ending June 30, 1901, were made in connection with an inspection of the improvement.

At the close of the fiscal year a vessel drawing 10¼ feet could navigate the river at mean low water.

July 1, 1900, balance unexpended	$9,872.96
June 30, 1901, amount expended during fiscal year	3.02
July 1, 1901, balance unexpended	9,869.94
Amount (estimated) required for completion of existing project	1,000.00
Amount that can be profitably expended in fiscal year ending June 30, 1903, in addition to the balance unexpended July 1, 1901	1,000.00
Submitted in compliance with requirements of sundry civil act of June 4, 1897.	

(See Appendix K 3.)

4. Appomattox River, Virginia.—The channel of this stream prior to improvement was narrow and tortuous. Numerous shoals prevented vessels drawing over 6¼ feet from navigating the river at its mean high-water stage.

Under the existing project, approved in 1893, the attainment of a channel 80 feet wide and 12 feet deep at mean high water is contemplated, at a cost of $473,920, and annually for maintenance, $10,000.

The amount expended to June 30, 1900, was $438,796.69, of which the sum of $14,966.69 was applied to maintaining the channel and repairing regulating works.

A channel 80 feet wide and 12 feet deep at mean high water had been dredged between Petersburg and Point of Rocks. Every occurring freshet causes sand to be deposited in the river bed and limits the draft of vessels which can safely use the river to that of the least depth of water over the shoals thus formed.

The expenditures in the fiscal year ending June 30, 1901, amounted to $11.34, and were made in connection with the preliminary examination of the river under the item in the emergency river and harbor act of June 6, 1900, relating to this stream.

On June 30, 1901, a vessel drawing 6 feet could pass up the river as far as Petersburg, Va., at mean low water.

July 1, 1900, balance unexpended	$33.31
June 30, 1901, amount expended during fiscal year	11.34
July 1, 1901, balance unexpended	21.97
Amount (estimated) required for completion of existing project	48,090.00
Amount that can be profitably expended in fiscal year ending June 30, 1903, for maintenance of improvement, in addition to the balance unexpended July 1, 1901	7,000.00
Submitted in compliance with requirements of sundry civil act of June 4, 1897, and of section 7 of the river and harbor act of 1899.	

(See Appendix K 4.)

5. Harbor at Cape Charles City, Va.—This harbor is situated 12 miles north of Cape Charles, on Chesapeake Bay, and is a basin of about 10 acres area. This artificial harbor, and the approaches by channel to it, originally had a good, navigable, 12-foot mean low-water channel.

The project covering the plan of improvement was approved November 13, 1892, and contemplates dredging to 14 feet in the harbor and 16 feet deep, 100 feet wide, at mean low water, at the entrance to the artificial harbor, through Cherrystone Inlet and over the bar 200 feet wide, with jetties of stone to protect the former channel. The estimated cost of the improvement is $143,340.

On June 30, 1900, $45,402.81 had been expended for the work, which consisted in dredging over about one-half of the area of the harbor to a depth of 14 feet at mean low water, excavating channels of the proper dimensions at the entrance to same, and through Cherrystone Inlet and bar to 16 feet at mean low water, and 750 feet of the north jetty constructed.

The sum of $9,301.45 was expended in the past fiscal year for 170 cubic yards of brush used in the foundation for the south jetty, and for 699 tons of large stone placed for that structure, and 209 tons of the same size of stone in the north jetty. The latter was extended out a distance of 125 feet and the south jetty 244 feet, the outer 12 feet only being about two-thirds finished.

On June 30, 1901, a vessel of about 12 feet draft could navigate the channels at mean low water.

July 1, 1900, balance unexpended	$9,597.19
June 30, 1901, amount expended during fiscal year	9,304.45
July 1, 1901, balance unexpended	292.74

Amount (estimated) required for completion of existing project	87,340.00
Amount that can be profitably expended in fiscal year ending June 30, 1903, in addition to the balance unexpended July 1, 1901	25,000.00
Submitted in compliance with requirements of sundry civil act of June 4, 1897.	

(See Appendix K 5.)

6. *Nandua Creek, Virginia.*—Before improvement, the entrance channel to this creek was indirect, narrow, and sinuous, and could only be navigated at mean low water by vessels of 5 feet draft. Within the mouth the channel was sufficient for all commercial needs.

The existing project, approved May 11, 1899, is to secure a direct channel by dredging a distance of 1,200 feet through the bar at the mouth of the creek over a width of 100 feet to a depth of 8 feet at mean low water, at an estimated cost of $6,000.

To June 30, 1900, $2,336.52 had been expended for improvement. The resulting channel from this expenditure was 1,000 feet long, 50 feet wide, and 8 feet deep at mean low water.

During the fiscal year ending June 30, 1901, the sum of $3,634.80 was expended in widening the channel available at the close of the previous fiscal year. With that amount, the channel then existing was widened 25 feet at the bottom, and extended, with a bottom width of 75 feet, 200 feet farther out into the bay, making the channel provided 1,200 feet long, 75 feet wide at the bottom, and 8 feet deep at mean low water.

The channel provided is reported to have shoaled at the interior end to 4½ feet at mean low water, so that vessels of a greater draft can not navigate it.

July 1, 1900, balance unexpended	$3,663.48
June 30, 1901, amount expended during fiscal year	3,634.80
July 1, 1901, balance unexpended	28.68

(See Appendix K 6.)

7. *Waterway from Norfolk, Va., to the sounds of North Carolina.*—
This waterway is composed of Deep Creek, a branch of the Southern Branch of the Elizabeth River, 5¼ miles above the Norfolk Navy-Yard; the Dismal Swamp Canal, extending from Deep Creek to South Mills; Turners Cut, which is artificial and connects the canal with the Pasquotank River, North Carolina; thence by the latter to Albemarle Sound, which connects with Pamlico Sound through Croatan Sound.

The prevailing channels in Deep Creek, the canal (which is the property of a corporation), and Turners Cut, before improvement, were 2½ feet in depth at mean low water. In the Pasquotank River and Croatan Sound vessels of 8 and 10 feet draft, respectively, could be accommodated.

Under the existing project, approved May 11, 1899, a 10-foot channel is to be provided from the mouth of Deep Creek through to Albemarle Sound, and a bar off Croatan light, in Croatan Sound, removed to a depth of 12 feet at mean low water. The improvement of the canal is not included in this project, the object of which is to attain a channel in the waters connected by the canal equal in depth to that in the latter.

The work to be done is covered by a continuous contract, dated August 1, 1899, with the Virginia Dredging Company.

To June 30, 1900, $22,281.07 had been expended. In Deep Creek a channel from 45 to 90 feet wide and 10 feet in depth had been dredged a distance of 10,400 feet upstream from the mouth, and on Turners Cut 48,843 cubic yards of material had been removed in obtaining a depth of 10 feet at mean low water on several shoals and in widening the mouth of the cut on its eastern side. On the Pasquotank River the first point below the mouth of Turners Cut had been dredged off and a portion of the one opposite Sawyers Ferry cut away.

In the fiscal year ending June 30, 1901, the sum of $93,243.52 was expended.

During the fiscal year at Deep Creek a channel extending downstream from the site of the old dam, a distance 3,100 feet, was excavated to a depth of 10 feet at mean low water over widths varying from 75 to 100 feet, and Turners Cut was widened on the western side by a cut 45 feet wide extending over a distance of 12,450 feet, for 7,500 feet of which a depth of 10 feet was made and for 4,950 feet only 8 feet at mean low water was obtained. The shoal at Shipyard Bar, in the Pasquotank River, and the bar in Croatan Sound were both removed in the past fiscal year. In the former case a channel 100 feet wide, 10 feet deep at mean low water, was dredged over a distance of 3,300 feet, and in the latter the channel obtained was 200 feet wide, 12 feet deep at mean low water, and 1,050 feet long.

Over the shoalest part of the waterway a draft of 9 feet could be carried at mean low water on June 30, 1901.

July 1, 1900, balance unexpended	$202,718.93
Amount appropriated by sundry civil act approved March 3, 1901	29,870.00
	232,588.93
June 30, 1901, amount expended during fiscal year	93,243.52
July 1, 1901, balance unexpended	139,345.41
July 1, 1901, outstanding liabilities	275.00
July 1, 1901, balance available	139,070.41
July 1, 1901, amount covered by uncompleted contracts	124,985.60

(See Appendix K 7.)

8. *Inland water route from Norfolk, Va., to Albemarle Sound, North Carolina, through Currituck Sound.*—This route from Norfolk, Va., to Albemarle Sound, North Carolina, is by way of the Southern Branch of Elizabeth River, Albemarle and Chesapeake Canal, North Landing River, Currituck Sound, Coanjock Bay, North Carolina Cut, and North River. The canal mentioned and the North Carolina Cut are controlled and maintained by a private corporation.

The route originally had a good 5-foot mean low-water channel, which was obstructed by snags, sunken logs, and overhanging trees. Sharp bends added to the other difficulties of navigation.

Separate projects for the above-mentioned natural waters were under execution prior to the act of September 19, 1890, when an appropriation for the different works was made in one item. The existing project, approved September 30, 1890, calls for a channel 80 feet wide and 9 feet deep at mean low water, at an estimated cost of $306,667.08.

Before the works were consolidated in a single project, $240,169.69 had been expended, and since then to June 30, 1900, the sum of $40,165.02 had been expended. With these expenditures a channel 60 to 80 feet wide and 9 feet deep at mean low water has been secured through the several sections comprising the waterway.

The expenditures reported for the fiscal year ending June 30, 1901, were made in payment for lengthening and altering the snag boat *Roanoke* and dredging at North River Bar, North Carolina, on which work was engaged from May 1 to 24 and June 22 to 30, 1901. During these periods an aggregate of 312 cubic yards of sand and clay were removed in dredging to the projected depth over a width of 30 feet for a distance of 343 feet.

The draft of vessels using the route is limited to 8 feet, at mean low water, by the bar at the mouth of North River.

July 1, 1900, balance unexpended	$6,834.98
June 30, 1901, amount expended during fiscal year	1,778.52
July 1, 1901, balance unexpended	5,056.46
July 1, 1901, outstanding liabilities	130.67
July 1, 1901, balance available	4,925.79
Amount (estimated) required for completion of existing project	21,667.08
Amount that can be profitably expended in fiscal year ending June 30, 1903, for works of improvement and for maintenance, in addition to the balance available July 1, 1901	14,000.00

Submitted in compliance with requirements of sundry civil act of June 4, 1897, and of section 7 of the river and harbor act of 1899.

(See Appendix K 8.)

9. *Edenton Bay, North Carolina.*—The navigation of this bay was obstructed by a hard sand shoal having 6½ feet of water over it at mean low water. In 1878 and 1879 the Government dredged a channel 100 feet wide and 9 feet deep at mean low water at an expense of $5,000.

The existing project was approved in 1885, and requires that a channel from 150 to 200 feet wide and 9 feet deep at mean low water shall be secured, and a turning basin covering an area of 12 acres provided. The estimated cost of this work was stated at $18,000.

The expenditures to June 30, 1900, amounted to $11,813.32, a channel from 150 to 200 feet wide with 9 feet depth at mean low water having been attained, and 9¼ acres of the turning basin dredged to a like depth.

The expenditures during the fiscal year ending June 30, 1901, were for examinations made of the bay.

A draft of 9 feet could be carried in the dredged channel at mean low water on June 30, 1901.

July 1, 1900, balance unexpended	$186.68
June 30, 1901, amount expended during fiscal year	8.60
July 1, 1901, balance unexpended	178.08
July 1, 1901, outstanding liabilities	4.90
July 1, 1901, balance available	173.18
Amount (estimated) required for completion of existing project	6,000.00
Amount that can be profitably expended in fiscal year ending June 30, 1903, in addition to the balance available July 1, 1901	6,000.00

Submitted in compliance with requirements of sundry civil act of June 4, 1897.

(See Appendix K 9.)

10. Roanoke River, North Carolina.—In its original condition, a draft of 10 feet could be carried to Indian Highland Bar, 67 miles above the mouth, and thence 2½ feet to Weldon, at ordinary low water. The river, however, was badly obstructed by wrecks, snags, logs, and stumps, and trees overhanging the river interfered seriously with the passage of vessels.

The project approved in 1871 is to provide, at all seasons of the year, a channel with a least width of 50 feet from Hamilton to Weldon, 5 feet deep at mean low water, and to clear the river below the former place for the accommodation of vessels navigating the sounds of North Carolina.

On June 30, 1900, $203,960.04 had been expended in clearing the channel below Hamilton of obstructions and toward securing a 5-foot channel to Weldon, a depth of 4 feet having been attained to within about a mile of the place last named.

The expenditures during the fiscal year ending June 30, 1901, were for lengthening the U. S. snag boat *Roanoke*, belonging to this improvement, and equipping the boat with appliances for dredging, and in removing channel obstructions brought down by freshets and lodged in the river between Plymouth and Palmyra.

A draft of 10 feet could be carried on the river as far as Hamilton, and 4 feet from that point to within a short distance of Weldon, at ordinary low water, on June 30, 1901.

July 1, 1900, balance unexpended	$25,377.96
June 30, 1901, amount expended during fiscal year	9,596.85
July 1, 1901, balance unexpended	15,781.11
July 1, 1901, outstanding liabilities	359.33
July 1, 1901, balance available	15,421.78

(See Appendix K 10.)

11. Removing sunken vessels or craft obstructing or endangering navigation— Wreck of schooner Emblem.—This small two-masted craft, carrying a cargo of oysters, sunk in 72 feet of water off Fort Monroe, Va., and the wreck was removed at a cost of $642.50, after bids were solicited by public notice.

Wreck of dredge.—The wreck of this craft was in about 31 feet of water at mean low tide, 6 miles southwest from Old Plantation lighthouse, Chesapeake Bay, and was removed under contract in June, 1901, at an expense of $1,871.75.

(See Appendix K 11.)

RIVER AND HARBOR IMPROVEMENTS. 299

EXAMINATIONS AND SURVEYS MADE IN COMPLIANCE WITH EMERGENCY RIVER AND HARBOR ACT APPROVED JUNE 6, 1900.

Preliminary examinations and surveys of the following localities were made by the local officer and reports thereon submitted through the division engineer:

1. *Preliminary examination and plan and estimate of cost of improvement of Norfolk Harbor, Virginia, with a view to removing bar and securing depth of 28 feet at a point between the 28-foot channel and the pier of the Southern Railway Company.*—Major Quinn submitted reports, dated August 16 and November 9, 1900, respectively. The estimated cost of the plan proposed is $20,000. The reports were transmitted to Congress and printed in House Doc. No. 74, Fifty-sixth Congress, second session. (See also Appendix K 12.)

2. *Preliminary examination and survey of Appomattox River, Virginia, with a view to the deflection of the river at Petersburg.*—Major Quinn submitted reports, dated August 22 and November 23, 1900, respectively. He presents a plan for improvement at an estimated cost of $266,915, and $6,000 annually for maintenance. In the opinion of the division engineer the necessary work will cost $400,000, and $5,000 annually for maintenance. The reports were transmitted to Congress and printed in House Doc. No. 139, Fifty-sixth Congress, second session. (See also Appendix K 13.)

3. *Preliminary examination and survey of Pagan River from Smithfield, Va., to James River, with a view to securing a channel 80 feet wide and 10 feet deep at mean low tide.*—Major Quinn submitted reports, dated August 23 and November 19, 1900, respectively, with plan for improvement at an estimated cost of $28,870. The reports were transmitted to Congress and printed in House Doc. No. 88, Fifty-sixth Congress, second session. (See also Appendix K 14.)

4. *Preliminary examination and survey of Chesconnessex Creek, Virginia, with a view to dredging the same.*—Major Quinn submitted reports, dated August 8 and November 9, 1900, respectively, with plan for improvement at an estimated cost of $5,204. The reports were transmitted to Congress and printed in House Doc. No. 87, Fifty-sixth Congress, second session. (See also Appendix K 15.)

5. *Preliminary examination and survey of waterway from South Mills, N. C., to Albemarle Sound, North Carolina, via Pasquotank River, with a view of obtaining a navigable depth of 16 feet at mean low water.*—Major Quinn submitted reports, dated August 10 and November 17, 1900, respectively. The estimated cost of this portion of the improvement is $1,935,893.62. The reports were transmitted to Congress and printed in House Doc. No. 202, Fifty-sixth Congress, second session. These reports are printed herewith in Appendix L 17, with others by Capt. E. W. Van C. Lucas, Corps of Engineers, on the remaining portion of a proposed waterway from South Mills to Ocracoke and Beaufort inlets.

IMPROVEMENT OF CERTAIN RIVERS AND HARBORS IN NORTH CAROLINA.

This district was in the charge of Capt. E. W. Van C. Lucas, Corps of Engineers. Division Engineer, Col. Peter C. Hains, Corps of Engineers.

1. *Ocracoke Inlet, North Carolina.*—An unsuccessful attempt was made by the Government to improve this inlet, between 1830 and 1837, at a cost of $133,732.40.

300   REPORT OF THE CHIEF OF ENGINEERS, U. S. ARMY.

When the present improvement began in 1895, the governing low-water depths were 12 feet on outside bar and 6½ feet over inner shoals.

The existing project, of July 9, 1894, was to dredge to 9 feet depth and 300 feet width, 700 feet through Beacon Island Slough and 5,000 feet through Royal Shoal, at an estimated cost of $51,513.39. The project was completed in 1896.

To June 30, 1900, $223,030.87 had been expended, $89,298.47 of which since 1890. Nothing has been spent for maintenance.

During the past year work had been restricted to examinations and surveys. The cost of part of survey for proposed inland waterway, 16 feet deep, connecting Dismal Swamp Canal and Beaufort Inlet, was paid from this appropriation, the work including a survey of ocean bar channel and inner channels to sound at Ocracoke Inlet.

The commerce for the year ending December 31, 1900, amounted to 4,900 tons. For the preceding year only a six months' record could be obtained, and the above figures show a proportionate decrease of about 45 per cent. One transportation line was established during the year.

The channels dredged in 1896 have deteriorated and can be redredged at an estimated cost of $40,000.

July 1, 1900, balance unexpended... $15,701.53
June 30, 1901, amount expended during fiscal year..................... 6,665.66

July 1, 1901, balance unexpended 9,035.87

(See Appendix L 1.)

2. Fishing Creek, North Carolina.—Distances: From mouth to Beach Swamp, 17¼ miles; Coffield's bridge, 21.3 miles; Wilmington and Weldon bridge, 40 miles; Bellamy's mill, 44 miles.

When improvement by the United States began, in 1896, the stream was badly obstructed by masses of fallen timber and was navigable by rafts only for a few miles above the mouth.

The existing project, adopted in 1889 and amended in 1896, is to clear the stream of obstructions to Wilmington and Weldon Railroad bridge, at an estimated cost of $22,750, and to maintain the natural channel.

To June 30, 1900, $20,851.19 had been expended, none of which was for maintenance.

During the year ending June 30, 1901, the project has been completed, but the stream is not navigable above Beach Swamp, on account of its tortuous character and rapid current.

During the calendar year 1900 the commerce of the stream amounted to 4,620 tons, an increase of 618 tons over preceding year. No transportation lines were established during the year.

July 1, 1900, balance unexpended $1,898.81
June 30, 1901, amount expended during fiscal year..................... 1,860.97

July 1, 1901, balance unexpended 37.84

Amount that can be profitably expended in fiscal year ending June 30, 1903, for maintenance of improvement, in addition to the balance unexpended July 1, 1901... 2,000.00
Submitted in compliance with requirements of sundry civil act of June 4, 1897, and of section 7 of the river and harbor act of 1899.

(See Appendix L 2.)

RIVER AND HARBOR IMPROVEMENTS. 301

3. Pamlico and Tar rivers, North Carolina.—(One river, called the Pamlico below and the Tar above Washington.) Distances: From Washington to Greenville, 22 miles; Tarboro, 49 miles; Fishing Creek, 56 miles; Little Falls, 88 miles; Rocky Mount, 89 miles.

When improvement by the United States began, in 1877, the river was obstructed by war blockades, rocks, and fallen timbers, the governing low-water depth being 5 feet to Washington and probably less than 1 foot to Tarboro.

The project of 1875 was to obtain a 9-foot channel to Washington; extended in 1879 to clear a 60-foot channel 3 feet deep to Greenville and 20 inches deep to Tarboro; extended in 1889 to clear natural channel to Little Falls; cost estimated in 1891 at $137,200.

To June 30, 1900, $115,348.77 had been expended, of which $13,364.08 was for maintenance.

During the past year the river had been kept clear and the project depth of 3 feet extended to Greenville, a gain of 1 foot in depth since the preceeding year. The governing low-water depths are 8 feet to Washington, 3 feet to Greenville, and about 15 inches to Tarboro. Work was suspended in March on account of lack of funds, the small remaining balance being reserved for care of plant stored at depot.

During the calendar year 1900 the commerce of the stream amounted to 613,895 tons, an increase of 106,414 tons since the preceding year. No transportation lines were established during the year.

For lack of funds the jetties above Greenville have decayed and the channel deteriorated. Estimated cost of restoring channel, $20,000.

July 1, 1900, balance unexpended	$2,651.23
June 30, 1901, amount expended during fiscal year	2,520.44
July 1, 1901, balance unexpended	130.79

Amount (estimated) required for completion of existing project......... 29,500.00
Amount that can be profitably expended in fiscal year ending June 30, 1903, for works of improvement and for maintenance, in addition to the balance unexpended July 1, 1901 .... 20,000.00
Submitted in compliance with requirements of sundry civil act of June 4, 1897, and of section 7 of the river and harbor act of 1899.

(See Appendix L 3.)

4. Contentnia Creek, North Carolina.—Distances: From mouth to Snowhill, 31¼ miles; Speight's bridge, 50¼ miles; Stantonsburg, 63 miles.

When improvement by the United States began, in 1881, the stream was choked with fallen timber, sand bars, and overhanging growth.

The project of 1881 was to clear out obstructions and obtain a depth of 3 feet to Stantonsburg during nine months annually, at a cost, estimated in 1888, of $77,500; amended in 1894 to include maintenance below Snowhill; amended in 1899 to include maintenance to Stantonsburg.

To June 30, 1900, $70,087.78 had been expended, of which $5,693.22 was for maintenance.

During the past year work has been restricted to keeping the channel clear to Snowhill, to which point the project depth exists. Work was suspended in March on account of lack of funds, the small remaining balance being reserved for care of plant stored at depot.

The commerce for the calendar year 1900 was 13,885 tons, a gain of 7,291 tons over the preceding year. No transportation lines were established during the year.

Deterioration of jetties and training walls to the extent of $500 has occurred.

July 1, 1900, balance unexpended	$912.22
June 30, 1901, amount expended during fiscal year	700.02
July 1, 1901, balance unexpended	212.20
July 1, 1901, outstanding liabilities	48.27
July 1, 1901, balance available	163.93

Amount that can be profitably expended in fiscal year ending June 30, 1903, for maintenance of improvement, in addition to the balance available July 1, 1901 .... 2,500.00
Submitted in compliance with requirements of sundry civil act of June 4, 1897, and of section 7 of the river and harbor act of 1899.

(See Appendix L 4.)

5. Trent River, North Carolina.—Distances from mouth at Newbern: To Polloksville, 18 miles; to Lower Quaker Bridge, 27 miles; to Trenton, 38 miles.

When improvement by the United States began, in 1879, there was a depth of 6 feet to Polloksville, and the stream was fairly clear to Lower Quaker Bridge, above which point it was badly obstructed.

The existing project, adopted in 1896, is to maintain a channel 3 feet deep and 30 feet wide to Trenton.

To June 30, 1900, $67,616.82 had been expended, of which $9,800.74 was for maintenance.

During the past year work under the project included clearing the channel of obstructions and dredging two shoals near Trenton to project depth, through which a gain of 1 foot in depth has been obtained. The project depth and width now exist.

The commerce for the calendar year 1900 was 100.057 tons foreign and coastwise and 30,105 tons internal, the former being a gain of 4,216 tons over preceding year and the latter a loss of 11,071 tons. No transportation lines were established during the year.

July 1, 1900, balance unexpended	$1,383.18
June 30, 1901, amount expended during fiscal year	998.86
July 1, 1901, balance unexpended	384.32
July 1, 1901, outstanding liabilities	14.50
July 1, 1901, balance available	369.82

Amount that can be profitably expended in fiscal year ending June 30, 1903, for maintenance of improvement, in addition to the balance available July 1, 1901 .... 2,000.00
Submitted in compliance with requirements of sundry civil act of June 4, 1897, and of section 7 of the river and harbor act of 1899.

(See Appendix L 5.)

6. Neuse River, North Carolina.—Distances: From Newbern to Contentnia Creek, 32 miles; Kinston, 50 miles; Whitehall, 74 miles; Goldsboro (Wilmington and Weldon Railroad bridge), 94 miles; Smithfield, 150 miles.

When improvement by the United States began, in 1878, the river was obstructed by war blockades and fallen timber, and the governing low-water depths were 8 feet to Newbern, 1¼ feet to Kinston, and 1 foot to Smithfield.

The project of 1878, as extended in 1879 and 1880, is to clear the river of obstructions and obtain 8 feet depth to Newbern and 4 feet depth thence to Kinston, all the year round, and 3 feet depth during 9 months of the year to Smithfield.

To June 30, 1900, $302,937.89 had been expended, of which $6,180.14 was for maintenance.

During the year the stream was kept fairly clear to Goldsboro and dredging was carried on between 24 milepost and Biddles Landing, 27¼ miles above Newbern, to which point the project depth now exists. The governing low-water depths are 8 feet (project) to Newbern, 4 feet (project) thence 27¼ miles farther to Biddles Landing, 2½ feet thence to Contentnia Creek, and about 1 foot thence to Kinston. Work was suspended in March on account of lack of funds, the small remaining balance being reserved for care of plant stored at depot.

The recorded commerce for the calendar year 1900 was 234,112 tons, an apparent decrease of 100,029 tons from the preceding year. One transportation line was established during the year.

Jetties and bank protection between Newbern and Kinston have deteriorated to the extent of $50,000.

July 1, 1900, balance unexpended	$3,562.11
June 30, 1901, amount expended during fiscal year	3,439.85
July 1, 1901, balance unexpended	122.26
July 1, 1901, outstanding liabilities	5.40
July 1, 1901, balance available	116.86

Amount (estimated) required for completion of existing project	77,500.00
Amount that can be profitably expended in fiscal year ending June 30, 1903, for maintenance of improvement, in addition to the balance available July 1, 1901	4,000.00
Submitted in compliance with requirements of sundry civil act of June 4, 1897, and of section 7 of the river and harbor act of 1899.	

(See Appendix L 6.)

7. *Inland waterway between Newbern and Beaufort, N. C.*—(Via Neuse River, Clubfoot Creek, Clubfoot and Harlowe Canal (private), Harlowe Creek, and Newport River.) Distances: Newbern to Clubfoot Creek, 21 miles; thence to Clubfoot and Harlowe Canal, 5 miles; thence to Harlowe Creek, 2¾ miles; thence to Newport River, 3¼ miles; thence to Beaufort, 7 miles.

When improvement by the United States began, in 1885, the governing low-water depth between Neuse and Newport rivers was 1 foot.

The project of 1884 is to obtain a channel 5 feet deep and 30 feet wide, at an estimated cost of $92,000.

To June 30, 1900, $28,227.06 had been expended, none of which was for maintenance.

No work of improvement was done during the year, but a survey had been completed for the purpose of estimating the cost of completing this improvement, which has been suspended since 1890, awaiting the cession or sale of the private canal to the United States. The limiting low-water depth is 1.4 feet in Harlowe Creek, the depth in the canal being somewhat greater.

The commerce for the calendar year 1900 was 40,615 tons, an increase of 4,836 tons over the preceding year. No transportation lines were established during the year.

The channel dredged some years ago in Harlowe Creek has deteriorated, and can be restored at an estimated cost of $10,000.

July 1, 1900, balance unexpended	$6,772.94
June 30, 1901, amount expended during fiscal year	317.54
July 1, 1901, balance unexpended	6,455.40
July 1, 1901, outstanding liabilities	135.18
July 1, 1901, balance available	6,320.22
Amount (estimated) required for completion of existing project	57,000.00

(See Appendix L 7.)

8. *Harbor at Beaufort, N. C.*—When improvement by the United States (begun in 1836) was resumed in 1881 the erosion at throat of inlet was causing serious deterioration of the inside channel and threatening deterioration of the bar channel. The governing low-water depths were 15 feet on the bar and 2 feet to Beaufort. The erosion at Shackleford Point and Fort Macon has been stopped by jetties, and a channel 100 feet wide and 7 feet deep dredged from Bulkhead Channel to Beaufort.

The existing project, adopted in 1896, is to maintain jetties and sand fences at Fort Macon and Shackleford Point.

To June 30, 1900, $153,753.35 had been expended, of which $5,908.03 was for maintenance.

The work of the past year has been on maintenance of sand fences and jetties. In addition a survey of bar and inner channels was made in connection with survey for proposed inland waterway 16 feet deep, connecting Dismal Swamp Canal and Beaufort Inlet. A survey of Bulkhead Shoal was also made and shows a decrease of 1 foot in the governing depth. The governing low-water depths are 11.3 feet on the bar and 3¼ feet to Beaufort. Work was suspended in May and the available balance reserved for care of plant stored at depot.

It has been impossible to obtain an accurate record of the year's commerce, but it is thought to be approximately the same as last year.

The channel dredged through Bulkhead Shoel has deteriorated and can be redredged for $1,500.

July 1, 1900, balance unexpended	$1,246.65
June 30, 1901, amount expended during fiscal year	1,147.42
July 1, 1901, balance unexpended	99.23
July 1, 1901, outstanding liabilities	42.58
July 1, 1901, balance available	56.65
Amount that can be profitably expended in fiscal year ending June 30, 1903, for maintenance of improvement, in addition to the balance available July 1, 1901	1,500.00

Submitted in compliance with requirements of sundry civil act of June 4, 1897, and of section 7 of the river and harbor act of 1899.

(See Appendix L 8.)

9. *Inland waterway between Beaufort Harbor and New River, North Carolina.*—Distances: From Beaufort to Swansboro, 30 miles; to New River, 52 miles, with access at Swansboro to the Atlantic Ocean through Bogue Inlet.

When improvement by the United States began, in 1886, the governing low-water depth was 18 inches to Swansboro and 6 inches thence to New River.

The project of 1885, modified in 1896, is to obtain a channel 3 feet deep and 60 feet wide from Beaufort to Swansboro. No project was adopted for the part beyond Swansboro, pending repeal of act of North Carolina legislature granting to private parties exclusive navigation privileges which have now expired by limitation.

To June 30, 1900, $42,524.33 had been expended on the improvement; nothing for maintenance.

During the past year no work has been done, because of small balance available. The present ruling low-water depth is 2 feet.

It has been impossible to obtain an accurate record of the year's commerce, but it is thought to be approximately the same as last year.

Deterioration of dredged cuts to the estimated extent of $8,000 has occurred.

July 1, 1900, balance unexpended	$975.67
June 30, 1901, amount expended during fiscal year	20.01
July 1, 1901, balance unexpended	955.66
Amount (estimated) required for completion of existing project	6,500.00
Amount that can be profitably expended in fiscal year ending June 30, 1903, for works of improvement and for maintenance, in addition to the balance unexpended July 1, 1901	2,500.00

Submitted in compliance with requirements of sundry civil act of June 4, 1897, and of section 7 of the river and harbor act of 1899.

(See Appendix L 9.)

10. *New River, North Carolina.*—When improvement by the United States began, in 1886, the governing low-water depth was 4 feet, and the channel included two circuitous parts around Wrights Island and Cedar Bush Marsh.

Under the project of 1886 a channel 4 feet deep and 100 feet wide was dredged through Wrights Island Cut and one 4 feet deep and 150 feet wide through Cedar Bush Marsh. The latter deteriorated, was abandoned, and as a substitute the project of June 18, 1894, to obtain 4 feet depth around Cedar Bush Marsh by dredging and training wall, was adopted and successfully carried out. This latter channel has since deteriorated to original condition, through lack of maintenance.

To June 30, 1900, $29,609.13 had been expended, none of which was for maintenance.

Nothing has been done during the year and the conditions are unchanged, the governing low-water depth being 3 feet in a narrow, crooked channel, with very little tidal rise.

The commerce for the calendar year 1900 was 3,248 tons, a decrease of 1,362 tons since the preceding year.

The channel with project depth obtained in 1895 has deteriorated and can be restored for $7,500.

July 1, 1900, balance unexpended	$3,390.87
June 30, 1901, amount expended during fiscal year	19.61
July 1, 1901, balance unexpended	3,371.26
Amount that can be profitably expended in fiscal year ending June 30, 1903, for maintenance of improvement, in addition to the balance unexpended July 1, 1901	3,000.00

Submitted in compliance with requirements of sundry civil act of June 4, 1897, and of section 7 of the river and harbor act of 1899.

(See Appendix L 10.)

306   REPORT OF THE CHIEF OF ENGINEERS, U. S. ARMY.

11. Black River, North Carolina.—Distances: From mouth to Point Caswell, 24 miles; Hawes Narrows, 34 miles; Clear Run, 64 miles; Lisbon, 86 miles.

When improvement by the United States was undertaken, in 1887, the river was cleared fairly to Point Caswell and roughly to Lisbon; the governing low-water depths being 4 feet to Point Caswell, 2¼ feet to Hawes Narrows, and 1½ feet to Lisbon.

The existing project, adopted in 1894 and amended in 1899, is to maintain a clear channel to Clear Run, including diking at narrow portions through swamps.

To June 30, 1900, $17,103.78 had been expended, of which $4,501.98 was for maintenance.

Work for the year has consisted of snagging, etc., to maintain cleared channel. No increase in depth has been obtained. The present governing low-water depths are 5 feet to Point Caswell, 2¼ feet to Hawes Narrows, and 1½ feet to Clear Run. Work was suspended in March because of lack of funds, the small remaining balance being reserved for care of plant stored at depot.

The commerce of the past calendar year was 58,087 tons, an increase of 9,554 tons since preceding year. One transportation line was established.

July 1, 1900, balance unexpended	$1,139.62
June 30, 1901, amount expended during fiscal year	830.35
July 1, 1901, balance unexpended	309.27

Amount that can be profitably expended in fiscal year ending June 30, 1903, for maintenance of improvement, in addition to the balance unexpended July 1, 1901 .... 2,000.00
Submitted in compliance with requirements of sundry civil act of June 4, 1897, and of section 7 of the river and harbor act of 1899.

(See Appendix L 11.)

12. Northeast (Cape Fear) River, North Carolina.—Distances: From mouth to Bannerman's bridge, 48 miles; Hallsville, 88 miles; Kornegay's bridge, 103 miles.

When improvement by the United States was begun, in 1890, the river was badly obstructed by logs, snags, and overhanging trees, and was navigable for small steamers to Bannerman's bridge, the governing low-water depth to that point being 6 feet.

The existing project, of 1889, is to clear the natural channel for small steamers to Hallsville and for pole boats to Kornegay's bridge, at an estimated cost of $30,000.

To June 30, 1900, $16,187.20 had been expended, of which $4,572.52 was for maintenance.

During the past year work has consisted of snagging, etc., to maintain cleared channel. The governing low-water depth is 6 feet to Bannerman's bridge, above which point navigation is practicable, even for pole boats, at freshet stages only. Work was suspended in March because of lack of funds, the small remaining balance being reserved for care of plant stored at depot.

The commerce for the calendar year 1900 amounted to 56,748 tons, an increase of 8,479 tons since the preceding year. No transportation lines were established during the year.

July 1, 1900, balance unexpended $1,056.13
June 30, 1901, amount expended during fiscal year 1,051.45

July 1, 1901, balance unexpended 4.68

Amount that can be profitably expended in fiscal year ending June 30,
  1903, for maintenance of improvement, in addition to the balance
  unexpended July 1, 1901... 2,000.00
Submitted in compliance with requirements of sundry civil act of June
  4, 1897, and of section 7 of the river and harbor act of 1899.

(See Appendix L 12.)

13. Cape Fear River above Wilmington, N. C.—Distances: From Wilmington to Kellys Cove, 47 miles; Elizabethtown, 73 miles; Fayetteville, 115 miles.

When improvement by the United States was begun in 1882 the governing low-water depths were 4 feet to Kellys Cove and 1 foot to Fayetteville, and the river above Kellys Cove was badly obstructed by snags, logs, and trees, but navigable at higher stages.

The project of January 26, 1881, is to clear the river to Fayetteville and to obtain a continuous channel (depth not stated) by jettying and dredging; cost estimated in July, 1893, at $275,000 for a 4-foot depth to Elizabethtown and a 3-foot depth to Fayetteville.

To June 30, 1900, $139,546.35 had been expended, $6,106.39 of which was expended for maintenance.

The past year's work has consisted of the maintenance of existing channel by snagging, etc., and also of an examination and survey to determine the cost of 4-foot, 6-foot, and 8-foot navigation between Wilmington and Fayetteville throughout the year. The governing low-water depths are 4 feet to Kellys Cove, 2¼ feet to Elizabethtown, and 2 feet to Fayetteville. Work was suspended in March because of lack of funds, the small remaining balance being reserved for care of plant stored at depot.

The commerce for the calendar year 1900 amounted to 129,622 tons, an increase of 14,745 tons since the preceding year.

July 1, 1900, balance unexpended $3,117.98
June 30, 1901, amount expended during fiscal year 3,037.93

July 1, 1901, balance unexpended 80.05
July 1, 1901, outstanding liabilities 21.36

July 1, 1901, balance available...................................... 58.69

Amount (estimated) required for completion of existing project........ 132,750.00
Amount that can be profitably expended in fiscal year ending June 30,
  1903, for maintenance of improvement, in addition to the balance
  available July 1, 1901.. 6,000.00
Submitted in compliance with requirements of sundry civil act of June
  4, 1897, and of section 7 of the river and harbor act of 1899.

(See Appendix L 13.)

14. Cape Fear River at and below Wilmington, N. C.—When improvement by the United States began on the river channels in 1829 and on the ocean bar in 1853, the governing low-water depths were 10 feet in the river channels, 7½ feet on the main ocean bar, and 8 feet on the New Inlet ocean bar. Under successive projects, including that of 1881, the governing low-water depth between Wilmington and the ocean was gradually increased to 16 feet.

The existing project, of October 6, 1890, is to obtain a low-water depth of 20 feet and a width of 270 feet from Wilmington to the ocean.

To June 30, 1900, $3,291,691.91 had been expended, of which $18,281.82 was for maintenance.

During the year the 20-foot channel at Logs and Big Island Shoal has been widened to 148 feet, and at Brunswick River Shoal to 185 feet, and the minimum depth at Snows Marsh has been increased to 19 feet. The ocean-bar channel has been maintained at project depth and width by the suction dredge *Cape Fear*, and redredging for maintenance has been done at Lilliput and Old Brunswick Cove shoals. The project depth of 20 feet, with least width of 148 feet, has been obtained through all shoals excepting that at Snows Marsh, where the least depth is 19 feet, with a tidal rise of 4½ feet, a gain of 1 foot during the year. Shoaling has taken place in several cuts, and the present governing low-water depth is 17.7 feet, increased at high water to 21 feet.

The commerce of the stream for the calendar year 1900 amounted to 699,356 tons, an increase of 77,504 tons over the preceding year and of 26,148 tons over any previous year on record. Two transportation lines were established during the year.

Deterioration has occurred as follows:

By shoaling in Alligator Creek, Lilliput, Old Brunswick Cove, Midnight, and Reaves Point shoals, about 600,000 cubic yards; estimated cost of redredging	$60,000
Damage by storm, New Inlet dam; estimated cost of restoration	8,000
Damage by storm, Swash Defense dam; estimated cost of restoration	30,000
Damage by decay, etc., Snows Marsh dike; estimated cost of restoration	30,000
Total deterioration	128,000

July 1, 1900, balance unexpended	$96,279.97
March 22, 1901, received for rent of dredge *Cape Fear*	7,593.57
	103,873.54
June 30, 1901, amount expended during fiscal year	71,796.07
July 1, 1901, balance unexpended	32,077.47
July 1, 1901, outstanding liabilities	2,221.74
July 1, 1901, balance available	29,855.73

{ Amount (estimated) required for completion of existing project......... 885,000.00
Amount that can be profitably expended in fiscal year ending June 30, 1903, for works of improvement and for maintenance, in addition to the balance available July 1, 1901.............................. 200,000.00
Submitted in compliance with requirements of sundry civil act of June 4, 1897, and of section 7 of the river and harbor act of 1899.

(See Appendix L 14.)

15. Town Creek, Brunswick County, N. C.—Distances: From mouth to Russells Landing (upper bridge), 20 miles; Rocks Landing, 23 miles.

A previous effort to improve this stream was made in 1882, but abandoned in 1883 for lack of funds.

When improvement was resumed in 1899 the stream was badly obstructed by logs, snags, and trees, and by shoals at mouth and just below Russells Landing, with about 3 feet low-water depth.

The existing project, of 1899, is to remove obstructions to Rocks Landing and dredge channel 5 feet deep and 40 feet wide to Russells Landing.

RIVER AND HARBOR IMPROVEMENTS. 309

To June 30, 1900, $8,279.86 had been expended, none of which was for maintenance.

During the year the project has been completed, by dredging, snagging, etc., to Russells Landing, and by snagging, etc., to Rocks Landing. The governing low-water depth to Russells Landing is 5 feet, with 40 feet width. Beyond Russells Landing navigation is practicable only during freshet stages and amounts to little or nothing.

The commerce for the calendar year 1900 was 9,146 tons, a decrease of 52,713 tons since the preceding year.[1] No transportation lines were established during the year.

July 1, 1900, balance unexpended	$1,220.14
June 30, 1901, amount expended during fiscal year	1,122.59
July 1, 1901, balance unexpended	97.55
Amount that can be profitably expended in fiscal year ending June 30, 1903, for maintenance of improvement, in addition to the balance unexpended July 1, 1901. Submitted in compliance with requirements of sundry civil act of June 4, 1897, and of section 7 of the river and harbor act of 1899.	1,000.00

(See Appendix L 15.)

16. *Removing sunken vessels or craft obstructing or endangering navigation.*—An allotment was made from this appropriation, in May, for an examination of wreck of schooner *Hooper* in Wysocking Bay, North Carolina, reported as an obstruction to navigation. The examination was made and the wreck found to be out of the track of passing vessels and not likely to become dangerous to navigation.

The total amount expended during the year was $89.94.

(See Appendix L 16.)

EXAMINATIONS AND SURVEYS MADE IN COMPLIANCE WITH EMERGENCY RIVER AND HARBOR ACT APPROVED JUNE 6, 1900.

Preliminary examinations and surveys of the following localities were made by the local officer and reports thereon submitted through the division engineer:

1. *Preliminary examination and survey of waterway from Albemarle Sound, North Carolina, to Beaufort Inlet, via Croatan, Pamlico, and Core sounds, with a view of obtaining a navigable depth of 16 feet at mean low water; of Beaufort and Ocracoke inlets with a view of obtaining navigable depths of 18 feet.*—Captain Lucas submitted reports, dated August 8 and November 22, 1900, respectively. The estimates submitted are as follows:

Improvement of route via Ocracoke Inlet	$1,611,500
Improvement of route via Beaufort Inlet	3,597,000
Annual cost of operation of two dredges, about	50,000

The reports, with others by Maj. James B. Quinn, Corps of Engineers, on the remaining portion of a proposed waterway from South Mills to Ocracoke and Beaufort inlets, were transmitted to Congress and printed in House Doc. No. 202, Fifty-sixth Congress, second session. (See also Appendix L 17.)

2. *Preliminary examination and survey of Scuppernong River, North Carolina, with a view to improving the bar at the mouth, and by dredging a channel 1,200 feet long and 150 feet wide and 9 feet deep at mean low tide.*—Captain Lucas submitted reports, dated August 8 and November 17, 1900, with plan for improvement at an estimated cost

---
[1] The reported commerce of 61,859 tons for 1899 is probably much too large.

of $14,000 if done with Government plant and hired labor, or $30,000 if done by contract. The reports were transmitted to Congress and printed in House Doc. No. 131, Fifty-sixth Congress, second session. (See also Appendix L 18.)

3. Preliminary examination and survey of Trent River, North Carolina, with the view of obtaining a depth of 8 feet at mean low water at the city of Newbern and up to the wharves and freight depots of said city; a channel 50 feet wide and 8 feet deep from Newbern through Foys Flats to Polloksville, and a channel 30 feet wide and 4 feet deep from Polloksville to Trenton.—Captain Lucas submitted reports, dated August 9 and November 17, 1900, respectively, with plan for improvement at an estimated cost of $24,000. The reports were transmitted to Congress and printed in House Doc. No. 121, Fifty-sixth Congress, second session. (See also Appendix L 19.)

4. Preliminary examination and survey of Wilmington Harbor, North Carolina, with a view to providing a sufficient width and depth to permit vessels now using said harbor to turn or swing around therein, and of Cape Fear River with the view of obtaining a navigable channel from Wilmington to Fayetteville of 4, 6, or 8 feet at mean low water.—

The reports, dated August 9 and November 24, 1900, contain estimates of cost for improvement as follows:

Wilmington Harbor (dredging) $291,500
Wilmington Harbor (dredging and mooring dolphins, alternate plan) 30,000
Cape Fear River from Wilmington to Fayetteville (4-foot depth) 1,320,000
Cape Fear River from Wilmington to Fayetteville (8-foot depth) 1,350,000

The reports were transmitted to Congress and printed in House Doc. No. 180, Fifty-sixth Congress, second session. (See also Appendix L 20.)

REPORT MADE IN COMPLIANCE WITH CONCURRENT RESOLUTION OF CONGRESS OF JANUARY 25, 1901.

In compliance with this resolution the Chief of Engineers submitted, under date of January 28, 1901, an estimate of $1,000 as the cost of removing obstructions at the mouth of *Brunswick River, North Carolina*. The report is printed in Senate Doc. No. 130, Fifty-sixth Congress, second session. (See also Appendix L 21.)

IMPROVEMENT OF WACCAMAW RIVER, NORTH CAROLINA AND SOUTH CAROLINA, AND OF CERTAIN RIVERS AND HARBORS IN SOUTH CAROLINA.

This district was in the charge of Capt. J. C. Sanford, Corps of Engineers, with Lieut. Edwin R. Stuart, Corps of Engineers, under his immediate orders since February 22, 1901. Division Engineer, Col. Peter C. Hains, Corps of Engineers.

1. Waccamaw River, North Carolina and South Carolina.—In 1880 this stream was navigable for 12-foot boats at all stages of water from Georgetown, 23 miles, to Bull Creek, and at high water 4 miles farther, to Bucks Lower Mills; thence for 7-foot draft boats, at high water, 22 miles farther, to Conway; thence it possessed an obstructed channel for 3-foot draft boats, at ordinary winter water, 68 miles, to Reeves Ferry; thence an obstructed channel, with 3 feet at high water, for 30 miles, to Lake Waccamaw.

The project of improvement, adopted in 1880, provides for a channel 12 feet deep at all stages of water, with 80 feet bottom width from the mouth of the river to Conway, thence a cleared channel to Lake Waccamaw.

The original estimated cost was $29,370, which was revised in 1885 and increased in the annual report of that year to the present figure, $138,400. In the Annual Report of the Chief of Engineers for 1886, page 170, maintenance is estimated at $4,000 per year after completion of improvement.

The total expenditures to June 30, 1900, were $101,303.75. The river had been cleared of snags to a distance of 128 miles above the mouth, and this portion of the river had been frequently resnagged as appropriations permitted. Some work had been done toward increasing the original depths on 8 shoals below Conway. As nearly as could be determined from the records, about $75,977.81 had been expended in originally snagging the lower 128 miles of the river and in constructing pile and plank dikes at 8 shoals, and about $25,325.94 in subsequent maintenance of the cleared channel. Adding the expenditures for maintenance during the past year, $1,283.89, it appears that the total thus far expended in maintenance has been about $26,609.83, which should properly be added to the amount given in money statement below as estimated amount required to complete the project.

During the past year snagging work has been done between the mouth and a point 122 miles above. The snag boat ran about 350 miles and removed 1,707 obstructions from the river and banks, making the total number of obstructions removed since June 30, 1884, 36,857. The records prior to the latter date are not sufficiently in detail to give exact figures. All the expenditures of the year have been for maintenance. The available depths reported as now existing do not differ greatly from the original depths.

With existing balance it is proposed to care for the snagging plant. Under the estimate submitted in money statement below it is proposed, so far as funds provided will permit, to deepen and widen the channel by dredging to the dimensions contemplated by the project, working from the mouth up, and to keep the river clear of snags and other similar obstructions; also to make a survey of the river to determine its present condition and amount now required to complete the project.

Commercial statistics.

Year.	Total tons.	Value.	Year.	Total tons.	Value.
1887		$2,129,281.75	1895	128,466	$2,063,697.00
1889		2,308,915.00	1896	203,388	2,314,175.00
1890	67,195	2,317,368.50	1897	241,300	2,406,390.00
1891	76,245	2,231,112.00	1898	258,191	2,666,280.00
1892	83,108	2,178,369.00	1899	376,822	3,135,214.00
1893	70,976	2,095,548.00	1900	467,887	3,481,072.00
1894	99,298	2,120,864.00			

July 1, 1900, balance unexpended $1,596.25
June 30, 1901, amount expended during fiscal year 1,283.89

July 1, 1901, balance unexpended 312.36

{ Amount (estimated) required for completion of existing project 35,500.00
Amount that can be profitably expended in fiscal year ending June 30, 1903, for works of improvement and for maintenance, in addition to the balance unexpended July 1, 1901 ..... 9,500.00
Submitted in compliance with requirements of sundry civil act of June 4, 1897, and section 7 of the river and harbor act of 1899.

(See Appendix M 1.)

2. Little Pedee River, South Carolina.—The river in its original condition was much obstructed by snags and overhanging trees and by ten bridges without draws. In places it was divided into several branches, in none of which was there a good channel.

Under the plan of improvement adopted in 1888 it is proposed to snag the river and close unnecessary branches, providing for steamboat navigation up to the mouth of Lumber River, 65 miles, and for pole-boat navigation 48 miles farther, to Little Rock, at an estimated cost of $50,000.

The total expenditures to June 30, 1900, were $21,749.99. No work had been done on the river since June 30, 1898. The river had been well snagged up to the mouth of Lumber River and roughly cleared for pole-boat navigation to Little Rock. No work had been done toward increasing the original depths. As nearly as can be determined from the records, about $19,549.99 had been expended in originally snagging the river as above described and about $2,200 in subsequent maintenance of the cleared channel. The latter sum should properly be added to the amount given in money statement below as estimated amount required to complete the project.

During the past year no work has been done.

With existing balance it is proposed to care for the snagging plant. Under the estimate submitted in money statement below it is proposed, so far as funds provided will permit, to snag the river from the mouth of Lumber River to Little Rock and to close unnecessary branches, as provided in the project, and to keep the river clear of snags below the mouth of Lumber River; also to make a survey of the river to determine its present condition and amount now required to complete the project.

Commercial statistics.

Year.	Total tons.	Value.	Year.	Total tons.	Value.
1891	4,614	$52,760	1896	17,050	$198,500
1892	7,115	92,964	1897	13,162	100,400
1893	6,153	101,535	1898	11,900	105,750
1894	8,375	114,600	1899	16,685	144,787
1895	12,438	117,470	1900	23,780	173,500

July 1, 1900, balance unexpended $250.01
June 30, 1901, amount expended during fiscal year 21.33

July 1, 1901, balance unexpended 228.68

{ Amount (estimated) required for completion of existing project 28,000.00
Amount that can be profitably expended in fiscal year ending June 30, 1903, for works of improvement and for maintenance, in addition to the balance unexpended July 1, 1901 .... 1,000.00
Submitted in compliance with requirements of sundry civil act of June 4, 1897, and of section 7 of the river and harbor act of 1899. }

(See appendix M 2.)

3. *Great Pedee River, South Carolina.*—The river in its original condition was dangerously obstructed by logs everywhere. Boats drawing 9 feet of water were able to reach Smith Mills, 52 miles above the mouth. Those drawing 3½ feet could get 54 miles farther up at low water to Little Bluff or at high water to Cheraw, 172 miles from the mouth.

The project of improvement adopted in 1880 provides for a thoroughly cleared 9-foot navigation to Smith Mills and a 3½-foot navigation to Cheraw at all stages of water.

The original project contained no estimate of cost. From 1880 to 1886, inclusive, $47,000 was appropriated. In the Annual Report of the Chief of Engineers for 1886, page 170, it was estimated that $70,000, in addition to this $47,000, would complete the improvement, and that $5,000 a year would be required for maintenance.

The total expenditures to June 30, 1900, were $108,516.37. The river had been well cleared of snags from the mouth to the Wilmington, Columbia and Augusta Railroad bridge, 103 miles, and less thoroughly snagged between the bridge and Cheraw. No work had been done toward increasing the original depths. As nearly as can be determined by the records, about $78,516.37 had been expended in originally clearing the river of snags, and about $30,000 in subsequent maintenance of the cleared channel. Adding the expenditures for maintenance of the channel and plant during the past year, $1,795.23, it appears that the total thus far expended in maintenance has been about $31,795.23, which should properly be added to the amount given in money statement below as estimated amount required to complete the project.

During the past year 52 of the worst obstructions reported were removed, making the total number of obstructions removed since June 30, 1884, 34,946 (records before that date do not give number removed). The snagging plant was cared for and necessary minor repairs made. A preliminary examination and subsequently a survey were made of that portion of the river between Cheraw and the Wilmington, Columbia and Augusta Railroad bridge, and estimate of cost of improvement submitted (printed in House Ex. Doc. No. 124, Fifty-sixth Congress, second session, and as Appendix M 14 of this report). The cost of this examination and survey, $902.76, was paid from the balance of appropriation for improving the river. The remaining expenditures during the year, $1,795.23, have been for maintenance of the channel and of the snagging plant. With the existing balance it is proposed to care for the plant. Under the estimate submitted in money statement below, it is proposed, so far as funds provided will permit, to deepen and widen the channel in accordance with the project and to keep the river clear of snags.

Commercial statistics.

Year.	Total tons.	Value.	Year.	Total tons.	Value.
1891	62,344	$1,367,330	1896	229,964	$1,325,250
1892	92,471	1,401,038	1897	114,177	1,167,914
1893	94,661	1,166,874	1898	75,280	1,228,885
1894	91,025	1,169,070	1899	134,072	1,692,709
1895	106,115	893,430	1900	154,727	2,645,560

July 1, 1900, balance unexpended	$2,983.63
June 30, 1901, amount expended during fiscal year	2,197.99
July 1, 1901, balance unexpended	785.64
July 1, 1901, outstanding liabilities	103.48
July 1, 1901, balance available	682.16
Amount (estimated) required for completion of existing project	5,500.00
Amount that can be profitably expended in fiscal year ending June 30, 1903, for works of improvement and for maintenance, in addition to the balance available July 1, 1901	8,000.00

Submitted in compliance with requirements of sundry civil act of June 4, 1897, and of section 7 of the river and harbor act of 1899.

(See Appendix M 3.)

4. Georgetown Harbor, South Carolina.—This harbor is that part of the Sampit River immediately within the bar at its mouth, near the head of Winyah Bay.

In 1881 a bar 2,850 feet in length, and with a controlling depth of 9 feet at ordinary low water, existed at the mouth of the Sampit River.

The original project, adopted in 1882, provided for dredging a channel across the bar 200 feet in width at bottom and 12 feet in depth at ordinary low water, at an estimated cost of $14,151.94. The material of the bar having been found much more difficult to dredge than had been expected, the estimate was several times revised, being finally fixed at $44,500. (Annual Report of the Chief of Engineers for 1889, p. 1103.)

The work was completed in 1895, the unexpended balance, $1,519.29, being held to await further developments regarding necessity for its expenditure. The total expenditures to June 30, 1900, were $42,980.71. None of this appears to have been expended for maintenance.

The dredged cut having shoaled and narrowed, it was redredged during the past year so far as funds would permit. There were removed 7,509 cubic yards of mud, 81 stumps, and 8 logs, making the channel across the bar of full depth for a width of about 125 feet. The project being completed and no available balance remaining, no further report will be made.

The commerce of Georgetown Harbor is the same as that reported for Winyah Bay.

July 1, 1900, balance unexpended	$1,519.29
June 30, 1901, amount expended during fiscal year	1,076.26
July 1, 1901, balance unexpended	443.03
July 1, 1901, outstanding liabilities	443.03

(See Appendix M 4.)

5. Winyah Bay, South Carolina.—This large bay is connected with the ocean by a passage between the shores of North and South islands 2½ miles long, 1 mile wide at the bay, ¾ mile wide at the gorge, and 1¼ miles wide at the ocean or southeasterly end of North Island. Through the passage, which trends north-northwest and south-southeast, there was a bold channel 36 feet deep at the bay, retaining a depth of not less than 20 feet until about 3,000 feet southerly from the end of North Island and of not less than 15 feet to a point about 1 mile south of the island, where the channel divided into two. One of these two channels, known as the Main Channel continued 3¼ miles farther, through extensive shoals, to the 18-foot contour in the ocean. This channel was south-southeast and in alignment with the main channel through the straits. The other, known as Bottle Channel, after flowing about 2,500 feet southeasterly, 1,500 feet easterly, and about 3,000 feet northeasterly, reached the 18-foot contour in the ocean at a distance of about 1¼ miles in a direction from the point of separation from the main ship channel almost at right angles with the direction of that channel and of the channel through the passage. At mean low water the depth on the crest of the bar was variable in both channels and about 7 to 9 feet in the Main Channel and 6 to 8 feet in Bottle Channel. The mean range of tide is 3½ feet.

The present project, adopted in 1889, provides for the construction of two jetties, springing, respectively, from North and South islands and converging toward the bar, the jetties to consist of mattress foundation and a superstructure of large riprap stone raised to a height of

6 feet above mean low water, the south jetty to extend due east across the bar and the north jetty to converge toward it, so as to produce the necessary contraction on the bar. The depth to be secured is 15 feet at mean low water. The river and harbor act approved June 3, 1896, authorized the completion of the work under continuing-contract system, at a cost of not exceeding $1,996,250, in addition to the $20,000 appropriated by the act. A total of $1,358,500 has been appropriated by sundry civil acts since that date.

The total expenditures to June 30, 1900, were $1,035,515.22, of which $428,750 was appropriated prior to June 3, 1896. The following work has been done: On the north jetty the mattress had been placed a distance of 7,118 feet from the shore end and the jetty had been built up to low water to a point 5,500 feet from the shore end and to a height of 18 inches above low water to a distance of 5,200 feet from the shore end. In addition a small mound of stone had been built at a point where the jetty changed direction. On the south jetty the mattress had been placed to a point 18,063 feet from the shore end, and the stone superstructure, built with practically no top width, had been carried out to a point 13,868 feet from the shore end. The sea-going suction dredge *Winyah Bay* had been built and had removed 510,194.74 cubic yards of material from the jetty channel. Spur jetties had been built to protect the South Island beach and a mud dike to serve as a root for the south jetty. All jetty work done since June 30, 1896, has been under a continuing contract providing for completing the jetties. The controlling depth June 30, 1900, on the outer bar was 13 feet in a narrow channel. On the inner bar it was 11¼ feet, the channel being of good width.

During the past year work under the contract for jetty construction was continued. On the south jetty the mattress foundation was completed, making the total length 21,051 feet from the shore end. The superstructure was extended 4,635 feet to a point 18,503 feet from the shore end. Some mattresses were sunk along the jetty where a tendency to undermine existed. On the north jetty the superstructure was advanced 1,289 feet due east and the mattress foundation to a point 500 feet in advance of this. The dredge removed 327,390.46 cubic yards of material from between the jetties, and 23,702.63 cubic yards from a shoal within the bay.

With existing balance it is proposed to pay the jetty contractor for the work done during the fiscal year 1902 and reserved percentages, to continue dredging, and to secure the shore end of the south jetty by extending it to a junction with the mud dike and by extending the south end of the latter to higher ground, and to pay cost of superintendence of all the above work. Under the estimate submitted in money statement below, it is proposed to continue dredging, in order to secure as quickly as possible a permanent channel of full depth and width.

Commercial statistics.

Year.	Total tons.	Value.	Year.	Total tons.	Value.
1891	261,370	$8,071,600	1897	149,374	$5,817,950
1892	271,986		1898	125,003	5,587,840
1893	268,640		1899	120,587	6,387,858
1894	293,822		1900	129,689	6,749,433
1896	171,059	6,228,350			

July 1, 1900, balance unexpended	$556,734.78
Amount appropriated by sundry civil act approved March 3, 1901	500,000.00
	1,056,734.78
June 30, 1901, amount expended during fiscal year	304,173.73
July 1, 1901, balance unexpended	752,561.05
July 1, 1901, outstanding liabilities	106,495.38
July 1, 1901, balance available	646,065.67
July 1, 1901, amount covered by uncompleted contracts	489,897.77
Amount (estimated) required for completion of existing project	352,750.00
Amount that can be profitably expended in fiscal year ending June 30, 1903, in addition to the balance available July 1, 1901. Submitted in compliance with requirements of sundry civil act of June 4, 1897.	100,000.00

(See Appendix M 5.)

6. *Santee River, South Carolina.*—This river in its original condition was considerably obstructed at all stages of water by sunken logs and snags. Its bar entrance was narrow, crooked, and shifting, with only about 4 feet of water at low tide, and so situated as to be difficult and expensive to improve.

The present project, adopted in 1889, contemplates providing the river with a good outlet into Winyah Bay by cutting a canal 70 feet wide and 6 feet deep at low water from the Estherville plantation to Minim Creek and for snagging the entire river. The estimated cost is $350,000, not including the amount, $99,750, appropriated prior to September 19, 1890, which amount was expended, mainly under the original project of 1880, in constructing a canal from the river through Mosquito Creek to Winyah Bay.

The total expenditures on the Santee River to June 30, 1900, were $261,007.68, of which $161,257.68 was expended under the present project and $99,750 under the project of 1880. At that date the first cut of the Estherville-Minim Creek Canal had been made entirely through to the Santee River, and this had been widened through a portion of its length. From the Santee River proper 1,025 obstructions had been removed. As nearly as can be determined from the records of the expenditures under the present project, about $250,007.68 had been expended in original work and about $11,000 in maintenance. Adding the expenditures for maintenance during the past year, $1,676.08, it appears that the total thus far expended in maintenance has been about $12,676.08, which is added to the amount given in money statement below as estimated amount required to complete the project.

During the past year there have been removed from the canal 79,443 cubic yards of mud, 257 stumps, and 7 logs, widening and deepening the canal for a length of 1,918 feet, and redredging portions where shoaling had occurred due to caving of banks. Except at the Winyah Bay end of the canal, the width is nowhere less than 50 feet, and the depth at mean low water is not less than 5 feet. At the Winyah Bay end, due to the softness of the mud banks, it has been found impossible to maintain a greater width than 40 feet and a greater depth than 4 feet at mean low water. Revetment will here be required.

The existing balance will be used in care of plant. Under the estimate submitted in money statement below it is proposed, so far as funds provided will permit, to widen and deepen the canal in accordance with the project and to keep the Santee River proper clear of snags.

RIVER AND HARBOR IMPROVEMENTS. 317

Commercial statistics.

Year.	Total tons.	Value.	Year.	Total tons.	Value.
1891	100,255	$2,743,000	1896	134,135	$2,204,600
1892	110,523	2,775,800	1897	134,206	2,159,940
1893	124,182	2,679,600	1898	112,205	2,208,800
1894	115,428	2,875,000	1899	154,327	2,679,100
1895	117,690	2,224,800	1900	179,090	2,622,200

July 1, 1900, balance unexpended $6,742.32
June 30, 1901, amount expended during fiscal year 6,704.32

July 1, 1901, balance unexpended 38.00

{ Amount (estimated) required for completion of existing project 194,676.08
Amount that can be profitably expended in fiscal year ending June 30, 1903, for works of improvement and for maintenance, in addition to the balance unexpended July 1, 1901 .... 38,000.00
Submitted in compliance with requirements of sundry civil act of June 4, 1897, and of section 7 of the river and harbor act of 1899. }

(See Appendix M 6.)

7. *Wateree River, South Carolina.*—In its original condition this stream had a low-water depth of from 3 to 4 feet from its mouth, 67 miles, to Camden. The lower 14 miles was completely blocked at all stages of water by logs, snags, etc., and at moderate stages by the bridges of the South Carolina and the Wilmington, Columbia and Augusta railroads, then without draw spans; thence to Camden navigation was possible, but dangerous except during high water. Its commerce was practically nothing.

The present project of improvement, adopted in 1881, provides for safe and unobstructed 4-foot navigation for steamers from Camden to the mouth, at an estimated cost of $60,000.

The appropriation of September 19, 1890, completed the estimate for the project, but four appropriations have since been made for maintenance. As the work is one of snagging only, and as snags are continually forming, it is practically incapable of completion. Snagging work should be done annually in order to keep the channel open.

The total expenditures to June 30, 1900, were $71,143.42. The river had been kept fairly clear of obstructions from the mouth to Camden. Since June 30, 1884, 24,912 obstructions had been removed, the records prior to that date not giving number removed.

During the past year the only work done has been to care for and maintain the snagging plant.

With the existing balance it is proposed to care for the plant. Under the estimate submitted in money statement below it is proposed, so far as funds provided will permit, to resnag the channel from the mouth to Camden.

Commercial statistics.

Year.	Total tons.	Value.	Year.	Total tons.	Value.
1891	1,005	$51,210	1896	35,002	$233,525
1892	2,244	86,040	1897	43,770	202,800
1893	6,242	117,729	1898	83,568	274,050
1894	18,075	94,334	1899	109,170	272,200
1895	21,697	127,565	1900	93,024	155,000

318   REPORT OF THE CHIEF OF ENGINEERS, U. S. ARMY.

July 1, 1900, balance unexpended	$1,356.58
June 30, 1901, amount expended during fiscal year	724.30
July 1, 1901, balance unexpended	632.28
July 1, 1901, outstanding liabilities	69.66
July 1, 1901, balance available	562.62
Amount that can be profitably expended in fiscal year ending June 30, 1903, for maintenance of improvement, in addition to the balance available July 1, 1901. Submitted in compliance with requirements of sundry civil act of June 4, 1897, and of section 7 of the river and harbor act of 1899.	3,000.00

(See Appendix M 7.)

8. *Congaree River, South Carolina.*—In 1886 this stream in its original condition had a low-water depth of 3 to 4 feet from its mouth to the railroad bridge at Columbia; thence 1 foot low water depth 2 miles farther to its head. The navigation of the lower 47 miles was blocked at all stages of water by the South Carolina Railroad bridge and by sunken logs, snags, and overhanging trees. The navigation of the remaining 2 miles was prevented by swift currents and numerous rock ledges and bowlders. Its commerce was nothing.

The project of improvement, adopted in 1886, proposes to secure a thoroughly cleared 4-foot navigation over the lower 47 miles at all stages of water and a cleared channel 100 feet wide through the ledges and bowlders above, at an estimated cost of $54,500.

The total expenditures to June 30, 1900, were $30,673.82. No work had been done on the river since June 30, 1898. The channel had been thoroughly snagged from the mouth to Granby, 2 miles below Columbia, but no attempt had been made to improve the rapids above Granby. A total of 8,549 obstructions had been removed below Granby. As nearly as can be determined from the records, about $19,523.82 had been expended in originally snagging the river and about $11,150 in subsequent maintenance of the cleared channel. The latter sum should properly be added to the amount given in the money statement below as estimated amount required to complete the project.

During the past year no work has been done.

With existing balance it is proposed to care for the plant. Under the estimate submitted in money statement below it is proposed, so far as funds provided will permit, to deepen and widen the channel to the dimensions contemplated by the approved project, working from the mouth up, and to keep the river clear of snags; also to make a survey of the shoals, in order to determine their present condition, with a view to revision, if found necessary, of the estimate for completion of project.

Commercial statistics.

Year.	Total tons.	Value.	Year.	Total tons.	Value.
1891	2,401	$47,840	1896	18,307	$178,900
1892	3,686	62,025	1897	40,857	110,100
1893	2,781	71,125	1898	81,362	201,700
1894	7,974	40,760	1899	88,696	191,700
1895	8,993	45,700	1900	121,363	197,000

July 1, 1900, balance unexpended $326.18
July 1, 1901, balance unexpended 326.18

⎧ Amount (estimated) required for completion of existing project 23,500.00
⎪ Amount that can be profitably expended in fiscal year ending June 30,
⎨   1903, for works of improvement and for maintenance, in addition to the
⎪   balance unexpended July 1, 1901..................................... 10,000.00
⎪ Submitted in compliance with requirements of sundry civil act of June
⎩   4, 1897, and of section 7 of the river and harbor act of 1899.

(See Appendix M 8.)

9. *Congaree River, South Carolina, from Gervais Street Bridge, Columbia, to Granby.*—For original condition of this portion of the river see report on Congaree River, South Carolina.

Pursuant to House resolution dated December 15, 1893, a project and estimate were submitted January 2, 1894 (printed in House Ex. Doc. No. 66, Fifty-third Congress, second session), for extending steamboat navigation from Granby to Gervais Street Bridge, Columbia, by the construction of lock and movable dam near Granby. This document and a letter concerning it were printed on pages 1182–1189, Annual Report of the Chief of Engineers for 1896.

The river and harbor act approved March 3, 1899, appropriated $50,000 for beginning this work, and authorized continuing contracts to be made for its completion, at a total cost not exceeding $200,000 in addition to the $50,000 appropriated. Two appropriations, aggregating $150,000, have since been made for this work.

The total expenditures to June 30, 1900, were $4,911.70. All land required on both sides of the river had been secured, a careful survey of the site had been made, plans and specifications for the lock and dam abutment, except metal work, had been approved, and work under a contract for the construction of a lock-keeper's house and other buildings, at a cost of $3,985, approved May 16, 1900, was in progress, and two water gauges had been established and were being read.

The construction of the keeper's house and other buildings was completed in September. A contract with the Evansville Contract Company, of Evansville, Ind., for constructing the lock and dam abutment, except metal work, at a total cost, based on estimated quantities, of $77,621, was approved October 20, the contract time for completion being January 30, 1902. Work was begun on November 20, but has been greatly interfered with by a series of freshets in the river. At the close of the year the cofferdam was about five-sixths completed, considerable grading had been done, and nearly all the plant needed for the lock work had been installed. A portion of the lock irons had been purchased. A topographical survey of both banks of the river from the lock site to Gervais Street Bridge had been made, a number of cross sections had been taken at the site, and four discharge measurements made. Proposals had been opened June 29 for steel for lock gates.

With existing balance it is proposed to complete the lock and the dam abutment and to begin the construction of the dam. Under the estimate given in the money statement below it is proposed to complete the project.

There is at present no navigation on this part of the river.

July 1, 1900, balance unexpended	$145,088.30
Amount appropriated by sundry civil act approved March 3, 1901	50,000.00
	195,088.30
June 30, 1901, amount expended during fiscal year	11,345.83
July 1, 1901, balance unexpended	183,742.47
July 1, 1901, outstanding liabilities	665.56
July 1, 1901, balance available	183,076.91
July 1, 1901, amount covered by uncompleted contracts	76,410.87
Amount (estimated) required for completion of existing project	50,000.00
Amount that can be profitably expended in fiscal year ending June 30, 1903, in addition to the balance available July 1, 1901. Submitted in compliance with requirements of sundry civil act of June 4, 1897.	50,000.00

(See Appendix M 9.)

10. *Charleston Harbor, including Mount Pleasant and Sullivan Island shore, South Carolina.*—There were originally four channels across the bar, the deepest having about 12 feet depth at low water. Commerce was then using the Pumpkin Hill Channel, about 3 miles south of the present jetty channel. Where the present jetty channel is situated there was then the Swash Channel, with a best depth of 10½ feet of water, too crooked for safe use. The natural channels were shifting in position and variable in depth.

In 1878 it was proposed to establish and maintain, by means of two jetties and auxiliary dredging, a low-water channel of not less than 21 feet depth across the bar. The Swash Channel was selected for improvement. The estimated cost was $3,000,000.

In 1888 it became necessary to modify the height of the crest line of the jetties and to revise the estimate. This increase in the estimate was largely due to the fact that money had been appropriated so slowly that reasonable contract prices could not be obtained. The annual appropriation up to that time had been only 5½ per cent of the original estimate. In the revised project the jetties were increased in height and length, but no change was made in their position or distance apart. The revised estimates were $4,380,500, if the jetties were brought up to low-water level throughout; and $5,334,500, if brought up 3 feet higher.

The total expenditures to June 30, 1900, were $4,123,489.82. At that date there was a channel having an available depth of 19.9 feet at mean low water from Charleston to the ocean. The jetties, which had been completed in 1897, still stood above the mean high-water level, except where a gap had been left in each near the shore end. The seagoing suction dredge *Charleston* had worked since May 1, 1900, on a new range across the outer bar, and had increased the depth on this line from 15.9 to 19.2 feet at mean low water.

During the past year the *Charleston* has continued dredging, and has removed a total of 287,206 cubic yards of material. Her work has been mainly on the new range across the outer bar, which she has deepened to not less than 24 feet at mean low water. She has also deepened to 24 feet, widened and straightened an existing but unused channel through the shoal near the inner end of the jetty channel (work was begun in the previous year), which channel is now lighted and in regular use; deepened to 24 feet a small shoal in the jetty channel proper, and maintained the old channel across the outer bar.

Readvertisement having been approved, proposals were opened November 27, 1900, for the construction of a new and larger dredge, authorized by the river and harbor act approved March 3, 1899, under an enlarged project, submitted November 18, 1898, for obtaining 26 feet at mean low water (printed in annual report for 1899, p. 1551). A contract with the Petersburg Iron Works Company, of Petersburg, Va., for the construction of this dredge at a cost of $144,300 was approved January 15, 1901, the contract time of completion being November 24, 1901. About 13 per cent of the hull has been completed, but no work has yet been done on the propelling or pumping machinery.

An estimate of $95,000[1] for maintenance of this work and for increasing the entrance depth and width is submitted. Of the amount authorized by the river and harbor act approved July 13, 1892, to be appropriated, there still remains unappropriated $208,000. The project on which the above act was based provides for assisting the action of the jetties by dredging.

Commercial statistics.

Year.	Total tons.	Value.	Year.	Total tons.	Value.
1889	211,203	$16,744,951	1895	140,938	$10,586,326
1890	224,962	16,041,397	1896	158,325	11,785,846
1891	274,149	23,110,664	1897	226,750	12,106,763
1892	169,379	11,829,607	1898	214,180	10,956,250
1893	193,336	11,940,129	1899	174,525	6,385,168
1894	208,169	11,560,872	1900	150,631	11,170,910

The total tons shown for each year is the aggregate tonnage of vessels engaged in foreign commerce as entered and cleared at the Charleston custom-house.

The values are the aggregates of the foreign exports and imports as given by the collector of customs. None of the coastwise commerce of Charleston is shown in this statement.

26-FOOT PROJECT.

July 1, 1900, balance unexpended..$175,000.00
June 30, 1901, amount expended during fiscal year.................... 2,387.14

July 1, 1901, balance unexpended....................................... 172,612.86

July 1, 1901, amount covered by uncompleted contracts 144,300.00

{ Amount (estimated) required for completion of existing project....... 110,000.00
Amount that can be profitably expended in fiscal year ending June 30,
  1903, in addition to the balance unexpended July 1, 1901............ 45,000.00
Submitted in compliance with requirements of sundry civil act of June 4, 1897.

---

[1] This estimate includes coppering the hull of the new dredge after about six months' service and such other work on the two dredges and on their wharf facilities as may be required.

21-FOOT PROJECT.

July 1, 1900, balance unexpended	[1]$49,010.18
June 30, 1901, amount expended during fiscal year	31,865.53
July 1, 1901, balance unexpended	17,144.65
July 1, 1901, outstanding liabilities	2,467.34
July 1, 1901, balance available	14,677.31
Amount (estimated) required for completion of existing project	208,000.00
Amount that can be profitably expended in fiscal year ending June 30, 1903, in addition to the balance available July 1, 1901	50,000.00

Submitted in compliance with requirements of sundry civil act of June 4, 1897.

(See Appendix M 10.)

11. Wappoo Cut, South Carolina.—Wappoo Cut in its original condition was a narrow, crooked tidal stream with not over 2 feet depth in some places. It connects Ashley and Stono rivers.

The existing project, adopted in 1888, provides for straightening, widening, and deepening to secure a fairly direct channel 6 feet deep at mean low water and 60 feet wide. It includes the construction of two training walls at the Stono River entrance, revetting Elliotts Cut, constructing three closing dams, and dredging a cut 200 feet wide and 7 feet deep across the Ashley River bar. The estimated cost of the project was $88,000, including expenditures between 1881 and its date.

The total expenditures to June 30, 1900, were $61,216.09. At that date a channel of the project width and depth had been dug and the banks of Elliotts Cut revetted. Two of the closing dams had been built, and a cut about 200 feet wide and 7 feet deep had been dredged across the Ashley River bar. A 6-foot channel existed through the cut, but it was quite narrow in one place; the cut through the Ashley River bar had narrowed considerably. As nearly as can be determined from the records, about $59,290.66 had been expended in original work and about $1,925.43 in maintenance. Adding the expenditures for maintenance during the past year, $1,084.93, it appears that the total thus far expended in maintenance has been about $3,010.36, which should properly be added to the amount given in money statement below as estimated amount required to complete the project.

During the past year a thorough survey was made of the improved portions of the cut, day marks forming a range for entering the Ashley River mouth of the cut were placed on the marsh, and the portion of the cut proper which had narrowed was redredged to full width.

Under the estimate submitted in money statement below, it is proposed, so far as funds provided will permit, to continue work on the project, to redredge the cut across the Ashley River bar, and to maintain the project width and depth.

Commercial statistics.

Year.	Total tons.	Value.	Year.	Total tons.	Value.
1891	140,000	$1,976,000	1895	250,230	$2,260,100
1892		1,997,500	1896	271,800	2,410,000
1893	142,800	1,865,500	1899	235,830	2,005,695
1894	238,350	1,683,000	1900	158,849	2,531,899

[1] Balance stated in annual report for 1900 as unexpended was too large by $0.53, the amount of Auditor's settlements Nos. 11941 and 11944 aggregating $0.53.

July 1, 1900, balance unexpended... $1,283.91
June 30, 1901, amount expended during fiscal year....................... 1,283.91

{ Amount (estimated) required for completion of existing project......... 25,500.00
Amount that can be profitably expended in fiscal year ending June 30, 1903, for works of improvement and for maintenance................. 8,000.00
Submitted in compliance with requirements of sundry civil act of June 4, 1897, and of section 7 of the river and harbor act of 1899. }

(See Appendix M 11.)

12. *Beaufort River, South Carolina.*—There was originally a thoroughly good 7-foot channel between the town of Beaufort and Coosaw River, except at a point called Brickyard, near the Coosaw mouth. The least depth here was about 4 feet at low water, and the channel, when deep enough, was too narrow.

The plan of improvement adopted in 1890 was to deepen and widen the channel by dredging to give a continuous, sufficiently wide 7-foot channel at low water all the way through. The estimated cost was $25,000. A layer of rock having been encountered at a higher level than was found by the preliminary borings, the work could not be completed for the amount of the original estimate. On April 15, 1893, the estimate was increased to $40,000.

The total expenditures to June 30, 1900, were $30,541.30, none of which appears to have been for maintenance of the dredged cut. A channel 7 feet deep had been secured all the way through, but it was much too narrow at the point where the rock was encountered. An examination and later a survey had been made in connection with illegal dumping of material dredged near the Port Royal Naval Station, and removal by the contractor of material illegally dumped had been begun.

During the past year no work was done toward the completion of the project. Inspection of the removal of illegally dumped material was made from time to time until its completion in December.

With existing balance and further appropriations it is proposed, so far as funds provided will permit, to make a survey of the channel to determine present conditions, and to widen the channel in accordance with the project and to maintain its width and depth. As considerable deterioration has probably occurred, a revision of the estimate for completion may have to be made, based on results of the proposed survey.

Commercial statistics.

Year.	Total tons.	Value.	Year.	Total tons.	Value.
1891	202,235	$1,378,800	1895	174,300	$919,750
1892	250,000	1,505,000	1896	100,287	588,000
1893	215,000	1,181,000	1899	114,400	650,000
1894	193,985	950,000	1900	136,635	686,677

July 1, 1900, balance unexpended $458.76
June 30, 1901, amount expended during fiscal year....................... 47.56

July 1, 1901, balance unexpended 411.20
July 1, 1901, outstanding liabilities...................................... 3.45

July 1, 1901, balance available 407.75

{ Amount (estimated) required for completion of existing project....... 9,000.00
Amount that can be profitably expended in fiscal year ending June 30, 1903, for works of improvement and for maintenance, in addition to the balance available July 1, 1901 .... 8,000.00
Submitted in compliance with requirements of sundry civil act of June 4, 1897, and of section 7 of the river and harbor act of 1899. }

(See Appendix M 12.)

13. Removing sunken vessels or craft obstructing or endangering navigation.—Nothing has been done during the past year. From the allotment of $2,000 made April 26, 1900, for the removal of sunken logs, originally forming parts of rafts, from the "inland passage" between Charleston, S. C., and Beaufort, S. C., there remains a balance of $1,421.05, which it is proposed to apply to the removal of such obstructions of this kind as may be hereafter reported, when their ownership can not be determined, and to securing compliance with the law regarding obstructions.

The total amount expended during the year is $176.72.

(See Appendix M 13.)

EXAMINATIONS AND SURVEYS MADE IN COMPLIANCE WITH EMERGENCY RIVER AND HARBOR ACT APPROVED JUNE 6, 1900.

Preliminary examinations and surveys of the following localities were made by the local officer and reports thereon submitted through the division engineer:

1. Preliminary examination and survey of Great Pedee River, South Carolina, between Cheraw and the Wilmington, Columbia and Augusta Railroad bridge.—Captain Sanford submitted reports, dated September 15 and November 19, 1900, with plan for improvement at an estimated cost of $118,345.37, and $4,000 annually for maintenance after completion. The sum of $2,000 will be required annually for maintenance in addition to the amounts appropriated for improvement. The reports were transmitted to Congress and printed in House Doc. No. 124, Fifty-sixth Congress, second session. (See also Appendix M 14.)

2. Preliminary examination and survey of Ashley River, South Carolina, from Charleston to the head of navigation.—Captain Sanford submitted reports, dated September 10 and November 20, 1900, with plan for improvement at an estimated cost of $264,396.29. The reports were transmitted to Congress and printed in House Doc. No. 115, Fifty-sixth Congress, second session. (See also Appendix M 15.)

IMPROVEMENT OF RIVERS AND HARBORS IN EASTERN GEORGIA; OF INSIDE WATER ROUTE BETWEEN SAVANNAH, GA., AND FERNANDINA, FLA., AND OF CUMBERLAND SOUND, GEORGIA AND FLORIDA.

This district was in the charge of Capt. Cassius E. Gillette, Corps of Engineers. Division Engineer, Col. Peter C. Hains, Corps of Engineers.

1. Savannah Harbor, Georgia.—This covers the estuary of the Savannah River from about 2 miles above the city of Savannah to the ocean bar, about 22 miles below the city. In 1873 the channel was in places not more than 9 feet deep at mean low water.

The original plan of improvement is dated August 28, 1873, and was supplemented March 19, 1879. It contemplated the establishment of a channel from the city to the sea practicable at high tide for vessels drawing 22 feet of water. This project was replaced by an enlarged one (January 16, 1882, Annual Report of the Chief of Engineers for 1882, Appendix J 4), contemplating the same channel depth.

A project, adopted in 1890, providing for a mean high-water depth of 26 feet from the city to the sea, is printed as part of Appendix O, Annual Report of the Chief of Engineers for 1890. The channel depth contemplated by it was reported as having been obtained at the end of the fiscal year of 1896, and since then only repair work and dredging have been carried on in accordance with it.

In compliance with requirements of the river and harbor act of August 18, 1894, a supplemental plan of improvement was submitted December 7, 1894, providing for a detached extension of the Oyster Bed training wall, for the purpose of sheltering the anchorage in Tybee Roads, as well as for protecting the ship channel over the outer part of Tybee Knoll against the destructive action of heavy storms. This project, which is printed as part of Appendix M 1 of the Annual Report of the Chief of Engineers for 1895, was authorized by act of Congress of June 3, 1896, its estimated cost being $992,250. The same act authorized the completion of work for improving the inside route from Savannah, Ga., to Beaufort, S. C., at an additional cost of $106,700, and dredging for maintenance in Savannah Harbor, and the sum of $1,005,000 has been appropriated to complete these works.

For a summary of past work see page 1492 of the Annual Report of the Chief of Engineers for 1891; pages 1213 and 1218–1220 of the report for 1896; page 1495, report for 1897; page 1293, report for 1898; page 1561, report for 1899, and page 1915, report for 1900.

The amount expended under the project of 1890 up to June 30, 1896, was $3,460,049.99, of which $974,504.88 was for dredging and $2,356,720.10 for contraction work. There had been previously expended $1,875,061.59. Between June 30, 1896, and June 30, 1900, $552,734 was expended on present project.

From the time of the reported completion of the project of 1890, in July, 1896, until June 30, 1900, extensive dredging was done, both as maintenance and as part of the modification of the project. Nevertheless, shoaling took place.

During the past fiscal year dredging has been carried on for completing the inside route between Savannah, Ga., and Beaufort, S. C., and for maintaining Savannah Harbor. For the former purpose 99,813.4 cubic yards was removed. For maintenance there was dredged 276,933 cubic yards.

At the close of the past fiscal year the project channel was deficient in width and depth and extensive dredging is urgently needed. A balance of former appropriations of about $425,000 could be used to advantage for such dredging, but it does not appear that the balance can be so used until a change of project is authorized by Congress. Legislation which will authorize the abandonment of the training-wall construction and permit the expenditure of the present balance for dredging to restore channel is recommended.

In 1872 the tonnage of vessels arriving and clearing at Savannah Harbor was somewhat more than 1,000,000; the total value of imports and exports, about $34,000,000. Cotton, lumber, wool, hides, naval stores, and rice were principally dealt in. In 1890 the total tonnage had increased to about 2,000,000 and the value of imports and exports to $152,000,000. Besides the articles named above, fruit, produce, and iron were handled extensively.

For the calendar year 1900 the total tonnage was about 2,804,061, and the value of exports and imports about $57,428,217. During the year a new line of steamers to Philadelphia has been established and the direct line to Boston discontinued.

July 1, 1900, balance unexpended..$547,052.47
June 30, 1901, amount expended during fiscal year..................... 107,343.53

July 1, 1901, balance unexpended 439,708.94
July 1, 1901, outstanding liabilities..................................... 14,300.74

July 1, 1901, balance available 425,408.20

Amount that can be profitably expended in fiscal year ending June 30, 1903, for maintenance of improvement, in addition to the balance available July 1, 1901... 50,000.00
Submitted in compliance with requirements of sundry civil act of June 4, 1897, and of section 7 of the river and harbor act of 1899.

(See Appendix N 1.)

2. Savannah River, Georgia.—In its original condition, for the greater part of the year, the river was navigable for steamboats drawing from 4 to 5 feet of water, but during the low-water season there were various shoals in the upper part of the river with low-water depths of less than 3 feet. The chief obstructions to navigation consisted of sand and gravel bars, overhanging trees, snags, and sunken logs.

The existing plan of improvement, submitted in 1890, provides for the establishment of a navigable steamboat channel, 5 feet deep at ordinary summer low water, between the cities of Augusta and Savannah.

This is to be accomplished by (1) removing sand and gravel bars; (2) regulating portions of the river, revetting caving banks, and closing incipient cut-offs; (3) removing snags and logs from the channel, and overhanging trees from the banks of the stream.

The cost of the improvement as given in the project of 1890 is estimated, in round numbers, at $332,000, provided funds are regularly and adequately supplied, besides $3,000 to $5,000 annually for maintenance.

The entire amount expended on the improvement of the Savannah River between Savannah and Augusta, from its commencement in 1880 to the adoption of the project of 1890, was $93,480.09.

The total amount expended under the project of 1890 to June 30, 1900, was $102,013.83.

Seven training dikes for removing sand bars were constructed during the past fiscal year.

The channel from Savannah to Augusta is in fair condition, some snags requiring removal. The project depth of 5 feet can be carried to about Twiggs Bar, 14 miles below Augusta. Three feet at mean low water is the best available draft to Augusta.

After the close of the civil war and prior to the improvement the commerce of the river was unimportant. Since then it has increased. The exports from the river valley are mainly cotton, naval stores, lumber, and wood, while the imports are fertilizers, camp and mill supplies, cotton ties and bagging, and manufactured articles. Excluding logs, timber, and cord wood, the tonnage for the year 1900 amounted to 45,800 tons, valued at $2,260,000, besides 104,167 bushels of rice, valued at $104,167, received at Savannah in small boats and lighters. There was also rafted down the river during 1900 about 5,000,000 feet B. M. of timber, valued at about $150,000.

July 1, 1900, balance unexpended	$72,006.08
Amount appropriated by sundry civil act approved March 3, 1901	100,000.00
	172,006.08
June 30, 1901, amount expended during fiscal year	25,923.56
July 1, 1901, balance unexpended	146,082.52
July 1, 1901, outstanding liabilities	3,361.29
July 1, 1901, balance available	142,721.23
July 1, 1901, amount covered by uncompleted contracts	101,136.47
Amount (estimated) required for completion of existing project	86,000.00
Amount that can be profitably expended in fiscal year ending June 30, 1903, in addition to the balance available July 1, 1901 Submitted in compliance with requirements of sundry civil act of June 4, 1897.	58,000.00

(See Appendix N 2.)

3. Savannah River above Augusta, Ga.—The Savannah River above the city of Augusta is navigable only by pole boats.

The existing plan of improvement, as outlined in the local engineer's report of January 31, 1890, provides for the establishment between Petersburg and the Locks of a downstream channel 12 to 25 feet in width and navigable during ordinary summer low water (or from nine to ten months of every year) for pole boats drawing 2 feet, and of an upstream channel navigable under the same conditions for pole boats drawing 1.3 feet of water. This is to be obtained by (1) removing logs and overhanging trees; (2) excavating rock, sand, or gravel, and with excavated materials raising crests of ledges; (3) constructing training walls to increase flow of water through sluices. The cost of improvement is estimated at $23,000, provided the money is all made available at once, or at $33,000 if supplied in smaller amounts.

The entire amount expended on the improvement of the Savannah River above Augusta from the commencement in 1880 to June 30, 1900, was $58,395.24.

The total amount expended under the present project up to June 30, 1900, was $19,395.24.

Work during the year consisted in blasting out channels through shoals and removing overhanging trees. Only a small amount of work was done. At the close of the fiscal year the project depth of 2 feet was available with some difficulty.

In 1876-77 about 2,000 tons of freight went upstream from Augusta and about 12,000 bales of cotton came down. In the report of 1888 the down-going freight was estimated at about 5,000 bales of cotton, and in 1900 the total freight carried on the river, excluding timber, amounted to about 3,192 tons, valued at $155,000.

July 1, 1900, balance unexpended	$604.76
June 30, 1901, amount expended during fiscal year	540.31
July 1, 1901, balance unexpended	64.45
Amount (estimated) required for completion of existing project	13,000.00
Amount that can be profitably expended in fiscal year ending June 30, 1903, in addition to the balance unexpended July 1, 1901 Submitted in compliance with requirements of sundry civil act of June 4, 1897.	2,000.00

(See Appendix N 3.)

4. Doboy Bar, Georgia.—In 1888 $5,795.40 was spent in harrowing and water-jet work on this bar without result. In its original condition there was about 12 feet at mean low water in the old channel, which was very crooked, so that the entrance was not much used. The project for its improvement, adopted by act of Congress of March 3, 1899, provides for creating a channel by dredging 24 feet deep at mean high water and 300 feet wide, estimated to cost $70,000. The proposed channel is some distance north of the present channel.

During the year 72,666.7 cubic yards of material was dredged, making a total of 119,869.3 cubic yards removed under the project. The contractor has done no work since December 16, 1900. The work done has produced no increase in the navigable depths.

The amount expended to June 30, 1900, was $5,680.09.

July 1, 1900, balance unexpended	$64,319.91
June 30, 1901, amount expended during fiscal year	13,028.47
July 1, 1901, balance unexpended	51,291.44
July 1, 1901, outstanding liabilities	1,629.18
July 1, 1901, balance available	49,662.26
July 1, 1901, amount covered by uncompleted contracts	33,708.11
Amount that can be profitably expended in fiscal year ending June 30, 1903, for maintenance of improvement, in addition to the balance available July 1, 1901. Submitted in compliance with requirements of sundry civil act of June 4, 1897, and of section 7 of the river and harbor act of 1899.	25,000.00

(See Appendix N 4.)

5. Darien Harbor, Georgia.—In its original condition this harbor was more or less obstructed at seven points by shoals, on which were found minimum mean low-water depths of from 6.4 to 10.6 feet. The reaches between the shoals carried depths nowhere less than 12 feet at mean low water. The mean rise and fall of the tide in the harbor is about 6.5 feet.

Operations for improving this harbor have been carried on in accordance with a project of improvement printed in the Annual Report of the Chief of Engineers for 1885. It contemplates the establishment of a navigable channel 12 feet deep at mean low water between Darien and Doboy. The estimated cost of the improvement is $170,000. No work was done under this project prior to the fiscal year ending June 30, 1891.

The total amount expended under the present project up to June 30, 1900, was $104,033.42. There had been expended under a previous project for dredging $8,000, making a total of $112,033.42.

No work was done during the past fiscal year. The available depth in the harbor is about 12 feet, except the channel to the Lower Ridge Mill, which has badly shoaled and needs deepening.

The incoming and outgoing tonnage for 1878 was estimated at about 200,000, and the value of the exports at between $600,000 and $700,000.

In 1900 the total annual trade, consisting mostly of timber, was estimated at 233,400 tons, valued at $1,374,688.

July 1, 1900, balance unexpended	$966.58
June 30, 1901, amount expended during fiscal year	956.12
July 1, 1901, balance unexpended	10.46
Amount (estimated) required for completion of existing project	65,000.00
Amount that can be profitably expended in fiscal year ending June 30, 1903, for works of improvement and for maintenance, in addition to the balance unexpended July 1, 1901	12,000.00
Submitted in compliance with requirements of sundry civil act of June 4, 1897, and of section 7 of the river and harbor act of 1899.	

(See Appendix N 5.)

RIVER AND HARBOR IMPROVEMENTS. 329

6. *Altamaha River, Georgia.*—The chief obstructions to the navigation of the Altamaha River consist in rock ledges, sand bars, snags, sunken logs, and overhanging trees. The rock ledges were confined to the upper portion of the stream, while the other obstructions were found throughout its entire course. The low-water depth at some points did not exceed 1 foot.

The revised plan of improvement, outlined in the local engineer's report of June 12, 1890, provides for the establishment of a navigable steamboat channel 3 feet deep at ordinary summer low water between the junction of the Oconee and Ocmulgee rivers and the town of Darien.

This is to be accomplished by (1) removing rock shoals and sand bars; (2) building deflecting dikes and closing incipient cut-offs; (3) removing snags and logs from the channel and overhanging trees from the banks of the stream, and (4) revetting caving banks.

The cost of the improvement, as given in the project of 1890, is estimated, in round numbers, at $129,000 (provided funds are regularly and adequately supplied), besides from $3,000 to $5,000 for annual maintenance.

The amount expended under the present project for this river up to June 30, 1900, was $52,981.25. There had been previously expended $69,776.59, making a total of $122,757.84.

At the close of the fiscal year 1901 the river was not in good condition, navigation being materially obstructed at several places. Work is urgently needed at Sisters Bluff, Beards Bluff, Carters Bight, and Cypress Nursery.

The work done during the past fiscal year has probably resulted in a better channel at Coupers Bar, but there has been no low water to determine this.

The commerce of the river before the improvement was begun amounted to about 100,000 tons annually, valued at about $1,000,000. During the year 1900 it is estimated to have amounted to 15,000 tons, valued at about $1,025,000, and 162,000,000 feet B. M. of timber, valued at $1,920,000.

Deterioration has occurred in works of improvement at Marrowbone Bar and Beards Bluff. The cost of restoration is estimated at $5,500.

July 1, 1900, balance unexpended	$3,242.16
Amount allotted from appropriation contained in emergency river and harbor act approved June 6, 1900	9,000.00
	12,242.16
June 30, 1901, amount expended during fiscal year	10,369.09
July 1, 1901, balance unexpended	1,873.07
July 1, 1901, outstanding liabilities	11.25
July 1, 1901, balance available	1,861.82

{ Amount (estimated) required for completion of existing project....... 104,000.00
Amount that can be profitably expended in fiscal year ending June 30, 1903, for works of improvement and for maintenance, in addition to the balance available July 1, 1901 .... 20,000.00
Submitted in compliance with requirements of sundry cival act of June 4, 1897, and of section 7 of the river and harbor act of 1899.

(See Appendix N 6.)

7. *Oconee River, Georgia.*—For the greater part of the year this river is navigable for steamboats drawing from 3 to 4 feet, but during the low-water season there are various shoals with low-water depths of not more than 2 feet. The chief obstructions to navigation consist

of sand bars, rock shoals, snags, sunken logs, and overhanging trees. The present plan of improvement, outlined in the report of February 5, 1890, provides for the establishment of a navigable steamboat channel 3 feet deep at ordinary summer low water from Milledgeville to the river's mouth.

This is to be accomplished by (1) removing rafts, rock shoals, and sand bars; (2) enlarging portions of the river, revetting caving banks, and closing incipent cut-offs; (3) removing snags and logs from the channel and overhanging trees from the banks of the stream.

The cost of the improvement is estimated at $171,000, besides from $1,000 to $5,000 for annual maintenance.

The amount expended under the present project to June 30, 1900, was $77,960.79. There had been previously expended $44,822.18, making a total of $122,782.97.

The work done at Bonny Clabber Cut-off will doubtless deepen the channel at that place. The channel is not in good condition. Numerous snags need removal and there are several bad rock shoals above Dublin.

No reliable statistics of the commerce of the river before the improvement was begun are available. From 1880 to 1885 the information at hand only mentions cotton, guano, rosin, spirits of turpentine, and merchandise. All of these in considerable quantities. In 1900 the amount of freight carried on the river amounted to 6,800 tons, valued at about $524,000. Besides this 86,397,623 feet B. M. of timber, valued at about $1,001,629, was rafted down the river.

July 1, 1900, balance unexpended	$2,217.03
Amount allotted from appropriation contained in emergency river and harbor act approved June 6, 1900	3,100.00
	5,317.03
June 30, 1901, amount expended during fiscal year	4,654.61
July 1, 1901, balance unexpended	662.42
July 1, 1901, outstanding liabilities	339.19
July 1, 1901, balance available	323.23
Amount (estimated) required for completion of existing project	127,900.00
Amount that can be profitably expended in fiscal year ending June 30, 1903, for works of improvement and for maintenance, in addition to the balance available July 1, 1901	25,000.00

Submitted in compliance with requirements of sundry civil act of June 4, 1897, and of section 7 of the river and harbor act of 1899.

(See Appendix N 7.)

8. Ocmulgee River, Georgia.—For the greater part of the year the river is navigable for steamboats drawing from 3 to 4 feet, but during the low-water season there are various shoals with depths of not more than 2 feet. The chief obstructions to navigation consist of rock shoals, sand bars, snags, sunken logs, and overhanging trees.

The present plan of improvement, outlined in the report of February 5, 1890, provides for the establishment of a navigable steamboat channel 3 feet deep at ordinary summer low water from Macon to the river's mouth.

This is to be obtained by (1) removing rock shoals and sand bars; (2) closing incipient cut-offs and revetting caving banks; (3) removing snags and logs from the channel and overhanging trees from the banks of the stream.

The cost of the improvement, as given in the project of 1890, is estimated at $210,000, provided funds are regularly and adequately supplied, besides from $1,000 to $5,000 for annual maintenance.

The amount expended under the present project up to June 30, 1900, was $94,056.49. There had been previously expended $79,390.73, making a total of $173,447.22.

The work done during the fiscal year has resulted in marked improvement. Several of the worst shoals are gone and the navigable depth to Hawkinsville is nearly 3 feet, the projected depth. The heavy rock shoals above Hawkinsville have not yet been removed.

No reliable statistics of the commerce of the river before the improvement was begun are available. It is stated to have consisted in 1889 principally of naval stores, cotton, merchandise, camp supplies, etc., and also of timber rafted down the river. In 1887–88 about 14,300 barrels of turpentine and 50,700 barrels of rosin are stated to have been shipped, while probably $300,000 worth of timber was rafted down the river. In 1900 the tonnage amounted to 24,724 tons, valued at $1,310,000, besides 54,000,000 feet B. M. of timber valued at $598,000.

July 1, 1900, balance unexpended	$41,052.78
Amount appropriated by sundry civil act approved March 3, 1901	40,000.00
	81,052.78
June 30, 1901, amount expended during fiscal year	33,824.71
July 1, 1901, balance unexpended	47,228.07
July 1, 1901, outstanding liabilities	2,655.45
July 1, 1901, balance available	44,572.62
Amount (estimated) required for completion of existing project	56,000.00
Amount that can be profitably expended in fiscal year ending June 30, 1903, in addition to the balance available July 1, 1901	35,000.00
Submitted in compliance with requirements of sundry civil act of June 4, 1897.	

(See Appendix N 8.)

9. *Brunswick Harbor, Georgia.*—Over the shoal in East River in front of the lower edge of the city there was, when the existing project of improvement was adopted, a low-water depth of only 1¼ fathoms. The mean rise and fall of the tide is about 6.6 feet. Operations for the improvement of this harbor have been carried on in accordance with a project of improvement printed as Appendix M 12, Annual Report of the Chief of Engineers for 1886. This project is an enlargement and a modification of a previous one printed as Appendix J 7, Annual Report of the Chief of Engineers for 1880.

The following comprise the main features of the plan of improvement:

(a) A training wall projecting from the most easterly point of Buzzard Island and located approximately parallel to and 1,000 feet or less distant from the opposite shore of East River.

(b) A low dam across Turtle River extending obliquely upstream from the upper end of Buzzard Island to the opposite shore of Blythe Island.

(c) Short spur jetties in the lower part of East River.

(d) Dredging in the vicinity of Turtle River Dam and on the shoal in the lower part of East River.

The training walls and spurs were to be constructed of palmetto cribs loaded with stone, or of successive courses of log and brush mattresses loaded with riprap stone. The works were intended to establish and maintain a 15-foot low-water channel across the shoal in East River. The cost of the original project was estimated at $73,187.50, and as modified at $190,000.

In his report of November 26, 1894, concerning a revision of the project of improving harbor at Brunswick the local engineer stated that—

It will be more economical and advantageous to maintain the desired depth of 15 feet at mean low water by keeping the training wall in good condition and by annual dredging than by constructing a dam across Turtle River and further channel contraction.

He also estimated the cost of maintenance at $15,000 per annum, provided that sum be made available each year.

The river and harbor act of March 3, 1899, provided for a preliminary examination and survey of this harbor with a view to further improvement. This examination has been made and reports of results were submitted to Congress and printed in House Doc. No. 40, Fifty-sixth Congress, first session, and in the Annual Report of the Chief of Engineers for 1900, page 1962.

Up to June 30, 1900, there had been expended under the present project for maintenance $25,568.60; there had been expended previously $200,000, making a total of $225,568.60, including $10,000 spent in 1836 for dredging.

At the end of the fiscal year 1901 item "*a*" of the project had been completed and the lower part of East River had been dredged to 15 feet. Items "*b*" and "*c*" and the dredging in Turtle River have not been done. The channel is not self-maintaining. The available depth is now 15 feet at mean low water.

Before the improvement in 1880 the annual tonnage of the port of Brunswick was about 100,000, consisting chiefly of lumber, naval stores, wood, rice, and sundry provisions, and valued at about $1,700,000.

In 1900 the shipments of lumber and merchandise amounted to 733,999 tons, valued at $24,705,743.

July 1, 1900, balance unexpended	$9,431.40
June 30, 1901, amount expended during fiscal year	9,184.34
July 1, 1901, balance unexpended	247.06
Amount that can be profitably expended in fiscal year ending June 30, 1903, for maintenance of improvement, in addition to the balance unexpended July 1, 1901. Submitted in compliance with requirements of sundry civil act of June 4, 1897, and of section 7 of the river and harbor act of 1899.	10,000.00

(See Appendix N 9.)

10. *Inside water route between Savannah, Ga., and Fernandina, Fla.*—The location of this route is shown by a dotted line on Coast Survey charts Nos. 156 and 157, and a detailed description of it and its original condition is given in the Annual Report of the Chief of Engineers for 1892, pages 1311–1326.

The distance from Savannah to Fernandina by the inside route just described is about 160 miles. Touching at Darien en route increases the distance by about 20 miles, and at Brunswick by about 12 miles.

In its original condition the channel depth was less than 5 feet at mean low water in some places.

The original project of improvement, adopted in 1892, provides for the establishment of a channel 7 feet deep at mean low water between Savannah, Ga., and Fernandina, Fla. This is to be accomplished by the improvement of Romerly Marsh, Mud River, Little Mud River, and Jekyl Creek, by means of dredging and the construction of closure dams and training walls of brush mattresses loaded with riprap stone. The estimated cost of the improvement is $105,000, provided that the entire sum is made at once available. If funds are made available in smaller amounts the cost of the improvement will be increased.

Previous to the adoption of this project work had been done on what is now part of the inside route in opening Parsons Cut through Romerly Marshes.

The total amount expended on the inside route project up to June 30, 1900, was $48,867.41; previous to this, $71,108.77, making a total of $119,973.18.

No work was done during the past fiscal year.

At the end of the fiscal year 1901 the depth of the cut through Romerly Marshes had deteriorated to about 3½ feet, but had increased in width. The channel in Jekyl Creek had deteriorated to 5 feet. The cut through Mud River had not been completed.

The value of the commerce passing through this route was estimated in 1890 at between $200,000 and $400,000 per annum. For 1900 it amounted to about 42,000 tons of freight, valued at $2,500,000, and 190,000,000 feet B. M. of timber, valued at $2,000,000. None of this commerce passed over the whole extent of the route.

July 1, 1900, balance unexpended	$132.59
July 1, 1901, balance unexpended	132.59

{Amount (estimated) required for completion of existing project	56,000.00
Amount that can be profitably expended in fiscal year ending June 30, 1903, in addition to the balance unexpended July 1, 1901	30,000.00
Submitted in compliance with requirements of sundry civil act of June 4, 1897.	

(See Appendix N 10.)

11. *Cumberland Sound, Georgia and Florida.*—The available depth at the entrance in its unimproved condition varied from 11 to 12.5 feet at mean low water. The point of crossing the bar was subject to very great changes, its range in a series of years being as great as 1¼ miles. The mean rise and fall of the tide is 5.9 feet.

The existing project, which was authorized by the river and harbor act of June 3, 1896, provides for the construction of two jetties, crossing the bar about 3,900 feet apart, supplemented by dredging, if necessary, the total cost from that date being estimated at $2,350,000. By the above act the Secretary of War was authorized to contract for the completed work in advance of appropriations. A detailed project for completing the work was submitted by a Board of Engineers August 2, 1900, and was approved by the Secretary of War August 7, 1900.

Up to the close of the fiscal year ending June 30, 1900, not including outstanding liabilities, there had been expended on this work from the beginning of work in 1881 $1,333,665.83.

The little dredging done during the past fiscal year has maintained the existing channel across the line of the south jetty to about its previous depth, there being at the close of the year a navigable depth of 16.8

feet. There has been a marked improvement in the channel between the jetties, the extension of the north jetty nearly across the bar being followed by extensive deepening in the channel which has been making in that location for some years. The controlling depth has only increased about 1.5 feet, there being now 8.3 feet at the shoalest place, but the channel has widened greatly and deepened on the inner slope of the bar an average of 4 or 5 feet.

Before improvement (in 1879) the annual in and out bound tonnage at Fernandina was about 300,000 and the value of imports and exports about $2,500,000, lumber, naval stores, and cotton being the principal articles. In 1900 the total value of imports and exports, coastwise and foreign, was reported by the collector of customs as $14,749,286.

July 1, 1900, balance unexpended	$853,834.17
Amount appropriated by sundry civil act approved March 3, 1901	200,000.00
	1,053,834.17
June 30, 1901, amount expended during fiscal year	220,596.36
July 1, 1901, balance unexpended	833,237.81
July 1, 1901, outstanding liabilities	60,127.08
July 1, 1901, balance available	773,110.73
July 1, 1901, amount covered by uncompleted contracts	849,055.01
Amount (estimated) required for completion of existing project	895,000.00
Amount that can be profitably expended in fiscal year ending June 30, 1903, in addition to the balance available July 1, 1901. Submitted in compliance with requirements of sundry civil act of June 4, 1897.	400,000.00

(See Appendix N 11.)

12. Removing sunken vessels or craft obstructing or endangering navigation.—The wreck of an old lighter in Savannah River was removed by hired labor, at a cost of $79.16. The wreck of the river steamer *W. S. Cook* in Savannah Harbor was removed under informal contract, at a cost of $140. Authority was also given for the removal of the wreck of the river steamer *Pete Craig* from Savannah River. This wreck has not yet been removed.

(See Appendix N 12.)

SURVEY MADE IN COMPLIANCE WITH RIVER AND HARBOR ACT APPROVED MARCH 3, 1899.

Preliminary report on survey of *Brunswick Outer Bar, Georgia,* was submitted by Captain Gillette December 4 and final report December 27, 1900, through the division engineer. Improvement of the locality by dredging is proposed, and an estimate of $200,000 for construction of a dredge and operating same for two years is presented. The reports were transmitted to Congress and printed in House Docs. Nos. 179 and 355, Fifty-sixth Congress, second session. (See also Appendix N 14.)

EXAMINATIONS AND SURVEY MADE IN COMPLIANCE WITH EMERGENCY RIVER AND HARBOR ACT APPROVED JUNE 6, 1900.

Preliminary examinations and survey of the following localities were made by the local officer and reports thereon submitted through the division engineer:

1. Preliminary examination and plan and estimate for improvement of Savannah Harbor, Georgia, with a view to securing a depth of 28 feet at mean high water.—Captain Gillette submitted report, dated September 27, 1900, upon preliminary examination, and a report dated November 21, 1900, was submitted by a Board of Engineers, with plan and estimate for improvement at a cost of $1,567.791. The reports were transmitted to Congress and printed in House Doc. No. 123, Fifty-sixth Congress, second session. (See also Appendix N 15.)

2. Preliminary examination of Skiddaway Narrows, Georgia.—Captain Gillette submitted report dated September 26, 1900. In his opinion, concurred in by the division engineer and by the Chief of Engineers, the improvement of the locality by the General Government is not advisable. The report was transmitted to Congress and printed in House Doc. No. 91, Fifty-sixth Congress, second session. (See also Appendix N 16.)

IMPROVEMENT OF RIVERS AND HARBORS ON THE EASTERN COAST OF FLORIDA, AND OF HARBOR AT KEY WEST, FLA., AND ENTRANCE THERETO.

This district was in the temporary charge of Capt. Thomas H. Rees, Corps of Engineers, to September 24, 1900; in the charge of Capt. C. H. McKinstry, Corps of Engineers, from September 24, 1900, to March 27, 1901, and in the temporary charge of Captain Rees since that date, the officer in charge having under his immediate orders Lieut. Edward M. Markham, Corps of Engineers, to September 11, 1900, and Lieut. Edmund M. Rhett, Corps of Engineers, since September 17, 1900. Division Engineer, Col. Peter C. Hains, Corps of Engineers.

1. St. Johns River, Florida.—Previous to the commencement of improvement the mean low-water channel depth across the bar at the mouth varied from 5 to 7 feet, with a tidal range of 5.22 feet. This bar is formed of sand, and was extremely dangerous, as the channel across it shifted continually north and south through a range of about 1 mile.

The least mean low-water channel depth in the river was about 11.5 feet, all obstructions being sand or mud. The tidal range in the river varies from about 4.5 feet at the mouth to about 1 foot at Jacksonville.

The original plan of improvement contemplated the formation of a continuous channel with a mid depth of not less than 15 feet at mean low water from Jacksonville to the ocean, a distance of about 27.5 miles. The two points where work was required to gain this depth were at the bar at the mouth and in a reach of the river near Dames Point, 12 miles above.

The project of 1896 contemplates the dredging of a channel 300 feet wide and 24 feet deep through all shoals, and the construction of training dikes in the river proper, at an estimated cost of $600,000; also the extension of the north jetty at the mouth of the river 1,500 feet, and the south jetty 500 feet, and raising these jetties throughout their entire length, at an estimated cost of $1,509,750; in all $2,109,750.

The amount expended on this improvement by the United States up to June 30, 1900, was $1,600,472.97, of which $183,472.47 was under the present project.

Work upon the north jetty at the mouth continued during the year. The jetty was raised to a mean height of 7 feet above mean low water between stations 3500 and 8611, and the foundation and hearting were extended to station 12949. No work was done upon the south jetty. Dredging in the river above the mouth with the United States dredge

336   REPORT OF THE CHIEF OF ENGINEERS, U. S. ARMY.

Cape Fear, belonging to the Wilmington (N. C.), district, continued at intervals until January 25. Between September 20 and January 26 the dredge worked upon the bar at the entrance at such times as this could be done with safety. A total of 164,571 cubic yards was removed by the dredge during the year. This work resulted in deepening the shoal places in the channel in the river to from 17 to 18 feet. No permanent increase in depth resulted from the work upon the bar and with this additional experience in view a greater extension of the north jetty is considered necessary to afford protection to dredging operations at this place and to break the force of storm waves.

A survey of the river from the entrance to Dames Point was made April 22 to May 7.

At the time of the survey a least depth of 12¼ feet at mean low water was found upon the bar. This is less than was reported last year, but the shoaling is believed to be only temporary. The increased depth in the river above the mouth as a result of the dredging operations has been maintained, excepting one place in Mile Point Cut, where a shoal has formed having a depth of only 15 feet at mean low water over it. The recent survey developed the existence of a shoal in St. Charles Creek Cut having a depth of 16¼ feet over it at mean low water. No dredging has been done at the latter place since 1893. The mean range of tide varies from 5.22 feet at the bar to 1.8 feet at Dames Point. The maximum draft that can be carried at mean low water over the shoalest part of the channel under improvement, which is at present limited by the shoal condition of the bar, is 12¼ feet.

The officer in charge invites attention to the fact that, in order to complete the improvement within a reasonable time and within the estimated cost, it is necessary that the work be placed under the continuous-contract system or that more adequate appropriations be made. He also recommends the construction of a hydraulic dredge, adapted for use in the river and on the bar, at an estimated cost of $150,000.

The commercial statistics show that the value of the commerce of the port of Jacksonville is now about $22,000,000. As compared with the value placed upon the commerce of this port in 1895, there has been an increase of about 50 per cent, which can be directly attributed to the effect of the works of improvement.

July 1, 1900, balance unexpended	$216,527.03
June 30, 1901, amount expended during fiscal year	150,387.65
July 1, 1901, balance unexpended	66,139.38
July 1, 1901, outstanding liabilities	34,825.98
July 1, 1901, balance available	31,313.40
July 1, 1901, amount covered by uncompleted contracts	24,111.31
Amount (estimated) required for completion of existing project	1,709,750.00
Amount that can be profitably expended in fiscal year ending June 30, 1903, in addition to the balance available July 1, 1901 Submitted in compliance with requirements of sundry civil act of June 4, 1897.	350,000.00

(See Appendix O 1.)

2. St. Johns River at Orange Mills Flats, Florida.—By a resolution passed in May, 1898, Congress requested the Secretary of War to furnish information as to the condition of this locality with reference to navigation for ocean-going craft, and to submit an estimate of the cost of such improvement as might be necessary.

In response to this resolution a report was submitted and is printed on pages 1344 to 1348, Annual Report of the Chief of Engineers for 1898. This report contemplated the formation of a channel 200 feet wide and 13 feet deep at mean low water through the shoals between Jacksonville and Palatka, at an estimated cost of $120,000.

The river and harbor act approved March 3, 1899, adopted this project and appropriated the sum of $40,000 for carrying it into effect.

A survey was made in 1899, embracing the four shoals in the stretch between Jacksonville and Palatka. It was found that the ruling depths on these shoals were: Forresters Point Shoal, 11.6 feet; Orange Mills Flats Shoal, 9.8 feet; Racy Point Shoal, 10.7 feet; and Tocoi Point Shoal, 11.1 feet.

A contract for dredging through Orange Mills Flats was entered into November 14, 1899. Work was commenced under this contract on April 2, 1900, and was completed October 23, 1900. A channel 13,164 feet long and from 120 to 160 feet wide was dredged, connecting the 13-foot contours on each side.

The amount expended on this improvement up to June 30, 1900, was $12,650.25.

While the available channel depth across Orange Mills Flats proper has been increased from 9.8 feet to 13 feet, the available depth is still limited by Racy Point Shoal to 10.7 feet, which was the maximum draft that could be carried at mean low water June 30, 1901.

Commerce has increased 31 per cent by reason of the increased facilities afforded.

July 1, 1900, balance unexpended	$27,349.75
June 30, 1901, amount expended during fiscal year	27,064.22
July 1, 1901, balance unexpended	285.53

{ Amount (estimated) required for completion of existing project 80,000.00
  Amount that can be profitably expended in fiscal year ending June 30, 1903, in addition to the balance unexpended July 1, 1901............ 35,000.00
  Submitted in compliance with requirements of sundry civil act of June 4, 1897.

(See Appendix O 2.)

3. *Volusia Bar, Florida.*—The bar is located at the south end, or head, of Lake George, St. Johns River, about 162 miles from the mouth.

Before any improvement was commenced the channel over the bar was very crooked and had a least depth varying from 3¼ feet to 4¼ feet.

The project of 1879 contemplated the construction of two jetties carried out beyond the bar, with their outer ends from 200 to 250 feet apart.

With the appropriations made since the inception of the project two jetties have been built, starting from opposite sides of the river bank at the south edge of the lake and converging until upon the bar they are 230 feet apart. The east jetty is 3,400 feet long and the west jetty 2,200 feet. They are built to the level of mean low water throughout nearly their entire lengths. Two rows of firmly set piles provided with waling pieces confine boats to a 100-foot channel across the crest of the bar.

There being no funds available no work has been done during the past fiscal year.

The amount expended to June 30, 1900, was $31,000.

The maximum draft that can be carried through the improved channel at low water is 5 feet.

An appropriation of $2,000 is required each year for maintenance. With this sum piling will be renewed and such dredging done as may be necessary for maintaining a low-water depth of 5 feet.

{ Amount that can be profitably expended in fiscal year ending June 30, 1903, for maintenance of improvement.............................. $2,000.00
Submitted in compliance with requirements of sundry civil act of June 4, 1897, and of section 7 of the river and harbor act of 1899. }

(See Appendix O 3.)

4. Oklawaha River, Florida.—The Oklawaha River has its source in Lake Apopka, central Florida, flows slightly west of north for about 104 miles, measured along the axis of the channel, then almost due east for 21 miles farther, when it unites with the St. Johns River. The Oklawaha River is the principal outlet of a number of large lakes, the aggregate area of which is about 175 square miles.

From Lake Griffin down for a distance of about 28 miles the river flows through a wide savanna submerged about 1 foot under water and covered with a dense growth of saw grass. On this reach the river averages from 30 to 40 feet in width and has a least channel depth of about 5 feet; the current is very sluggish. The impediments to navigation on this portion of the river are the numerous bends, the narrow channel, floating islands, and eelgrass. From the savanna to the mouth, a distance of about 58 miles, the banks are covered with a dense growth of cypress and other timber. On this reach the river averages from 60 to 70 feet in width and the least channel depth is 4 feet. The average velocity of the current is considerably greater than on the upper river, being about 1.3 feet per second. The principal obstructions to navigation here 'ɔ snags and overhanging trees.

The project fo the improvement of this river, adopted June 23, 1891, consists in removing snags, overhanging trees, floating islands, and other obstructions of like character, so as to give a fair navigable channel of 4 feet depth from the mouth to Leesburg, at the head of Lake Griffin, a distance of 94 miles. The estimated cost of this work is $26,000.

The amount expended on this work to close of the fiscal year ending June 30, 1900, was $20,000. Of this sum the appropriations made since the act of September 19, 1890, aggregating $10,000, have been for maintenance.

There were no operations during the past year.

With the funds appropriated the stream has been cleared of obstructions for a distance of about 60 miles from its mouth. The mean draft that can be carried at low water is 4 feet.

{ Amount (estimated) required for completion of existing project $15,000.00
Amount that can be profitably expended in fiscal year ending June 30, 1903, for works of improvement and for maintenance 3,000.00
Submitted in compliance with requirements of sundry civil act of June 4, 1897, and of section 7 of the river and harbor act of 1899. }

(See Appendix O 4.)

5. St. Augustine Harbor, Florida.—The approved project, submitted April 26, 1889, and modified February 27, 1893, is to protect the shores on the north and south sides of the entrance from erosion, the work consisting of groins constructed of riprap on brush foundation and capped with concrete.

Work began in 1889. Seven groins in all have been built, three on the north beach and four on Anastasia Island on the south side of the entrance. Their lengths vary from 220 to 549 feet.

The erosion of the north side of the entrance has ceased and the shore has built out to the extremities of the groins. On the south side it has been partially stopped, continuing especially in the vicinity of the innermost groin.

The appropriation made in act of August 18, 1894, has not been expended, as there seemed to be no immediate necessity for further work to protect the beach.

The amount expended up to June 30, 1900, was $64,999.90.

This improvement, being confined to the protection of the outer shore lines of the entrance, has had no effect whatever on the character and amount of commerce, which is practically nothing, as far as water transportation is concerned.

The maximum draft that can be carried over the bar at mean low water varies from 6 to 9 feet.

July 1, 1900, balance unexpended $6,000.10
July 1, 1901, balance unexpended 6,000.10

Amount (estimated) required for completion of existing project 24,000.00

(See Appendix O 5.)

6. Indian River, Florida, between Goat Creek and Jupiter Inlet.—A project adopted May 23, 1894, contemplated making a continuous channel 5 feet deep at low water and at least 75 feet wide in the straight reaches, with as much greater width in the turns as might be required, at an estimated cost of $44,000.

Work under the appropriation of July 13, 1892, was commenced by the U. S. hydraulic dredge *Suwanee*, July 28, 1895, and the channel previously dredged by the Florida Coast Line Canal and Transportation Company was widened at Long Canal, High Bank Canal, Curved Canal, and Conch Bar by dredging a cut 50 feet wide and 6 feet deep along one side.

The amount expended on this part of the river to June 30, 1900, was $15,000.

The maximum draft that can be carried through Indian River is 5 feet at mean low water.

Negro Cut, Indian River Inlet.—The river and harbor act of August 18, 1894, appropriated $5,000 for dredging at this locality. The urgent deficiency act of March 2, 1895, made a further appropriation of $15,000 for the same work.

The present project, approved November 18, 1894, contemplates the formation of a channel 100 feet wide and 6 feet deep from the channel of Indian River through Negro Cut to the bar at Indian River Inlet and the construction of a training wall for its protection, at an estimated cost of $32,775.

The channel dredging called for by the project was completed September 26, 1896.

The river and harbor act of March 3, 1899, authorized the expenditure of the balance available of former appropriations for the construction of the training wall, and also appropriated a further sum of $5,000 for dredging.

The amount expended on improvement at Negro Cut to June 30, 1900, was $19,773.40.

The U. S. dredge *Suwanee* commenced work under the act of March 3, 1899, on June 25, 1901, and to the close of the fiscal year had removed 1,986.9 cubic yards of material.

Jupiter Inlet.—By act of Congress approved February 26, 1896, an appropriation of $500 was made to open this inlet for the passage of boats and small vessels. Work was begun September 5 and was satisfactorily completed September 19, 1896.

The inlet again closed in 1900. Under allotments of $1,000 from the emergency river and harbor appropriation of June 6, 1900, work of reopening the inlet was commenced February 6, but abandoned March 13, owing to the very low stage of the river.

In June, 1901, as a result of very heavy rains, the river rose so much that the citizens of the vicinity, aided by the work already done, were enabled to open the inlet. It is reported that there is now a channel through the inlet 200 feet wide and 8 feet deep.

Transportation on Indian River has been decreased by the extension of the railroad along the west bank to Miami. The line of steamers which formerly ran on the river no longer does so.

INDIAN RIVER BETWEEN GOAT CREEK AND JUPITER INLET.

Amount (estimated) required for completion of existing project	$29,000.00
Amount that can be profitably expended in fiscal year ending June 30, 1903	2,000.00
Submitted in compliance with requirements of sundry civil act of June 4, 1897.	

NEGRO CUT, INDIAN RIVER INLET.

July 1, 1900, balance unexpended	$12,726.60
June 30, 1901, amount expended during fiscal year	1,585.47
July 1, 1901, balance unexpended	11,141.13
July 1, 1901, outstanding liabilities	997.99
July 1, 1901, balance available	10,143.14

JUPITER INLET.

Amount allotted from appropriation contained in emergency river and harbor act approved June 6, 1900	$1,000.00
June 30, 1901, amount expended during fiscal year	969.25
July 1, 1901, balance unexpended	30.75
July 1, 1901, outstanding liabilities	29.01
July 1, 1901, balance available	1.74

(See Appendix O 6.)

7. *Harbor at Key West, Fla., and entrance thereto.*—The work contemplated under this improvement is the deepening of the channel across the northwest bar. Previous to the inception of the project there was a depth of 10.5 feet on the bar at mean low water. The mean range of tide is 2.5 feet.

The existing project was submitted in November, 1889, and provides for the construction of a jetty on the northeast side of the passage, to be supplemented by a jetty on the western side.

It was thought, also, that dredging might be necessary. The depth of water to be obtained is 17 feet at mean lower water.

The amount expended to June 30, 1900, was $352,108.38.
No work was accomplished during the past fiscal year.

The bar had shoaled to a depth of 10 feet, and an allotment of $5,000 was made from the emergency appropriation of June 6, 1900, for restoring the depth of 12.5 feet, but through failure of contractor and excessive bids no work has been accomplished.

This experience emphasizes the necessity for the construction by the United States of a suitable dredge for work of this character at Key West and other harbors of this district, where similar cases of high prices and unsuitable plant have hampered the work done under contract. This same matter is referred to in the report on the improvement of the St. Johns River.

The maximum draft that can be carried across the northwest bar is the same as was reported June 30, 1900, viz, 10 feet at mean low water.

GENERAL IMPROVEMENT.

July 1, 1900, balance unexpended	$391.62
June 30, 1901, amount expended during fiscal year	73.29
July 1, 1901, balance unexpended	318.33

Amount (estimated) required for completion of existing project	200,000.00
Amount that can be profitably expended in fiscal year ending June 30, 1903, in addition to the balance unexpended July 1, 1901	100,000.00
Submitted in compliance with requirements of sundry civil act of June 4, 1897.	

MAINTENANCE.

Amount alloted from appropriation contained in emergency river and harbor act approved June 6, 1900	$5,000.00
June 30, 1901, amount expended during fiscal year	208.63
July 1, 1901, balance unexpended	4,791.37
July 1, 1901, outstanding liabilities	17.15
July 1, 1901, balance available	4,774.22

(See Appendix O 7.)

8. *Removing the water hyacinth from Florida waters.*—Under the provisions of the sundry civil act approved June 4, 1897, a Board of Engineer officers was appointed to investigate the extent of the obstruction of the navigable streams of Florida, Louisiana, and other South Atlantic and Gulf States, by the aquatic plant known as the water hyacinth, and to perform such experimental work as might be deemed necessary to determine a feasible plan or method of checking or removing such obstructions.

The Board recommended the construction of a steamer fitted with crushing machinery, and the use of log booms as adjuncts to the operation of the boat.

The river and harbor act approved March 3, 1899, appropriated $25,000 for the construction of a boat, $1,000 for log booms, and $10,000 for operating expenses.

The construction of the boat was deferred until one intended for a similar purpose in the Louisiana district was tested. The work of the latter boat indicated, in the opinion of the officer in charge of this district, that the crushing process, even under the most favorable conditions, was too slow and expensive to be considered practicable.

A chemical method is recommended for adoption by the officer in charge of the district, and it is proposed to await further action by Congress before the work is proceeded with.

The water hyacinth is reported to be thriving most vigorously, and the removal of the plant from the streams of this district is of the utmost importance to the interests of navigation. The lumber interests are suffering great financial loss. Water communication on many of the tributaries of the St. Johns River has practically been abandoned, and great inconvenience is frequently occasioned in the main river itself by floating masses of the plant. It is, therefore, recommended by the officer in charge that Congress take the necessary action to enable the funds appropriated in act of March 3, 1899, to be expended otherwise than provided therein and that an additional appropriation of $30,000 be made for continuing operations.

The amount expended to June 30, 1900, was $573.23.

July 1, 1900, balance unexpended	$35,426.77
June 30, 1901, amount expended during fiscal year	476.35
July 1, 1901, balance unexpended	34,950.42
Amount that can be profitably expended in fiscal year ending June 30, 1903, in addition to the balance unexpended July 1, 1901. Submitted in compliance with requirements of sundry civil act of June 4, 1897.	30,000.00

(See Appendix O 8.)

9. *Dredge for river and harbor improvements in Florida.*—The river and harbor act approved March 3, 1899, appropriated $35,000 for the construction of a dredge, with snagging outfit, for works on the coast of Florida and tributary waters. Specifications for a suitable boat were prepared and bids for the construction of a boat were opened March 7, 1901. The lowest bid for the boat complete, delivered at Jacksonville, Fla., was $67,100, and all bids were rejected.

There are many improvements in this district for which the appropriations are so small and the work of such a varied and peculiar character that it is impracticable to have them done by contract. Work of this character has heretofore been done by the U. S. dredge and snag boat *Suwanee*, which is so old and so nearly worn-out that it requires special effort to keep her in commission, and a new boat is badly needed.

The plans for the proposed boat have recently been carefully reconsidered with a view of modifying them in order to reduce the cost, but it is the opinion of the officer in charge that the design can not be changed in any essential feature and still provide for a boat capable of satisfactorily performing the duty required of it, and he recommends that an additional appropriation of $35,000 be made for the construction of the boat. No additional work is proposed upon this boat until further action of Congress.

July 1, 1900, balance unexpended	$33,107.52
June 30, 1901, amount expended during fiscal year	1,441.84
July 1, 1901, balance unexpended	31,665.68
Amount (estimated) required for completion of existing project	35,000.00
Amount that can be profitably expended in fiscal year ending June 30, 1903, in addition to the balance unexpended July 1, 1901. Submitted in compliance with requirements of sundry civil act of June 4, 1897.	35,000.00

(See Appendix O 9.)

IMPROVEMENT OF RIVERS AND HARBORS ON THE WESTERN COAST OF FLORIDA, SOUTH OF AND INCLUDING SUWANEE RIVER.

This district was in the charge of Capt. Thomas H. Rees, Corps of Engineers. Division Engineer, Col. Peter C. Hains, Corps of Engineers.

1. Caloosahatchee River, Florida.—An examination of this river, with a view to its improvement, was made in 1879. In 1887 a survey was made from Lake Okechobee to the mouth.

Before improvements commenced upon this river there was a practicable channel 5 feet deep at mean low water from the mouth to 4 miles above Myers. The portion of the river which has the characteristics of an estuary was principally obstructed by oyster beds. Above, as far as Fort Thompson, the ruling depth was 3½ feet on the shoal at Beautiful Island. This portion was obstructed by snags and overhanging trees.

The project adopted in 1882 called for deepening the channel by dredging from the mouth to Fort Myers, so as to give a depth of 7 feet at mean low water for a width of 100 feet. In 1886 and 1888 this project was modified so as to include the improvement of the upper river as far as Fort Thompson by the removal of snags and overhanging trees and by deepening the channel near Beautiful Island to a depth of 4 feet.

The amount expended up to June 30, 1900, was $31,705.90, of which the appropriations since 1890, amounting to $6,000, have been applied to maintenance of improvement.

During the fiscal year ending June 30, 1901, there was expended for the maintenance of this improvement the sum of $1,894.10, with the result that 362 snags and 592 overhanging trees were removed.

The maximum draft that can be carried at mean low water is 7 feet as far as Myers and 4 feet above that place as far as Fort Thompson, which is about 22 miles west of Lake Okechobee.

The water-borne tonnage on this river for the past fiscal year was 22,737 tons, as against 33,101 tons for the previous year.

July 1, 1900, balance unexpended	$1,894.10
June 30, 1901, amount expended during fiscal year	1,894.10

{ Amount that can be profitably expended in fiscal year ending June 30, 1903, for maintenance of improvement................................. 1,000.00
Submitted in compliance with requirements of sundry civil act of June 4, 1897, and of section 7 of the river and harbor act of 1899.

(See Appendix P 1.)

2. Charlotte Harbor and Peace Creek, Florida.—Work upon this improvement was commenced under an appropriation of $35,000 made by the river and harbor act of September 19, 1890, for improving, dredging, and deepening the channel of Charlotte Harbor and Peace Creek to the pier at Punta Gorda.

The survey from Boca Grande to Punta Gorda made under this appropriation disclosed a channel depth of 19 feet at mean low water on the bar, 9 feet on the shoals south of Cape Haze, and 10 feet upon the shoals near the wharf at Punta Gorda. The rise of the tide is approximately 2 feet.

The approved project contemplates the improvement of the channel so as to give a depth of 12 feet at mean low water from the wharves at Punta Gorda to Boca Grande over a width of 200 feet. The estimated cost was $127,500, reduced in 1896 to $100,000.

The amount expended up to June 30, 1900, was $99,934.42.

There have been no expenditures for maintenance. It is estimated that $1,000 per annum will be necessary for this purpose.

No work was done during the fiscal year ending June 30, 1901.

A draft of 12 feet at mean low water can be carried from the city of Punta Gorda to the Gulf of Mexico.

The water-borne tonnage for the past fiscal year was 85,475 tons, as against 102,048 tons for the previous year.

July 1, 1900, balance unexpended	$65.58
June 30, 1901, amount expended during fiscal year	65.58
Amount that can be profitably expended in fiscal year ending June 30, 1903, for maintenance of improvement	1,000.00

Submitted in compliance with requirements of sundry civil act of June 4, 1897, and of section 7 of the river and harbor act of 1899.

(See Appendix P 2.)

3. Sarasota Bay, Florida.—Previous to any attempt at improvement there was a navigable channel with a minimum depth of 5 feet extending throughout the length of Big Sarasota Bay, excepting in two reaches, Palma Sola Pass and Long Bar, which have a total length of 5,400 feet. In these reaches the available depth was 4.3 and 3.5 feet, respectively. The tidal range in the bay is about 1.5 feet.

Between Sarasota and Caseys Pass, at the south end of the bay, the available channel depth was 1.2 feet at mean low water, except through the Mangroves, where it was nothing.

The original project contemplated the formation of a continuous channel 100 feet wide and 5 feet deep at mean low water from Tampa Bay to the town of Sarasota, Fla., a distance of 21¼ miles, the estimated cost being $17,500.

The act of Congress of June 3, 1896, appropriated $2,500 for improving Sarasota Bay from Tampa Bay to Caseys Pass, while previous to that date the improvement was only for Sarasota Bay from Tampa Bay to Sarasota, Fla. The survey of 1889 was made, as directed, from Tampa Bay to Caseys Pass, and an estimate was presented amounting to $37,500 for securing a channel 75 feet wide and 3 feet deep at mean low water through the obstructing shoals below Sarasota. Under the act of June 3, 1896, the latter project is included in the improvement, so that the total estimate of cost for the modified project is now $55,000. The amount expended to June 30, 1900 was $13,206.22.

During the fiscal year ending June 30, 1901, the U. S. dredge *Suwanee* excavated from the proposed channel 35,764.4 cubic yards of sand and made a cut 50 feet wide, 4.5 feet deep at mean low water, and 4,540 feet in length. The deep water in Little Sarasota Bay has not yet been reached. There remain 4,000 feet to be dredged through before this channel will become available. A draft of 5 feet at mean low water can be carried through the cuts in Sarasota Bay.

The commerce in vegetables, fruits, and cattle is growing. All trade is conducted by water transportation, and the improvement of the channels affords a safe route for small vessels in any weather.

July 1, 1900, balance unexpended	$4,293.78
June 30, 1901, amount expended during fiscal year	4,293.78
Amount (estimated) required for completion of existing project	37,500.00
Amount that can be profitably expended in fiscal year ending June 30, 1903, for works of improvement and for maintenance	15,000.00

Submitted in compliance with requirements of sundry civil act of June 4, 1897, and of section 7 of the river and harbor act of 1899.

(See Appendix P 3.)

4. *Manatee River, Florida.*—For 12 miles from its mouth in Tampa Bay this river has the characteristics of an estuary. Previous to improvement in the estuary the general depth of the river varied from 7 to 20 feet. At the mouth there was a long shoal with a depth of 7 feet. Between Palmetto and Braidentown there was another bar covered by from 3 to 5 feet of water.

An examination of the river with a view to its improvement was made in 1881, and a project adopted in 1882 which contemplated forming a channel 100 feet wide and 13 feet deep from Tampa Bay to Shaw and McNeills points.

In 1886 the project was modified so as to provide a channel 100 feet wide and 8 feet deep at mean low water from Tampa Bay to Manatee, Fla.

This channel was completed, and in 1892 the original project was again adopted. The revised estimate for this work is $73,000.

Under the terms of the river and harbor act of June 3, 1896, which provided that $3,000, or so much thereof as necessary, of the funds appropriated for improving this river should be used in improving the cut-off into Terraceia Bay, a project for making a channel through the cut-off 100 feet wide and 6 feet deep was submitted, and approved on June 23, 1897. It was estimated that this channel would cost $20,000. Previous to improvement there was a channel through this cut-off, for rowboats only, of 1 foot at mean low water.

The amount expended to June 30, 1900, was $56,926.78, including $3,000 for the cut-off into Terraceia Bay.

No work was done during the fiscal year ending June 30, 1901.

The present condition of the river is such (June 30, 1901) that a least depth at mean low water of 9 feet can be obtained from Tampa Bay up the river to Braidentown, 8 feet to Ellenton, and 7 feet to Rocky Bluff, which is about 11 miles from the bay.

A draft of 6 feet can be carried through Terraceia Cut-off.

The commerce of the locality consists of agricultural products, fertilizers, lumber, and general merchandise.

The increase in tonnage due to improvement of this stream for several years past is shown by the following statement:

	Tons.		Tons.
1893	6,872	1897	23,800
1894	11,552	1898	24,310
1895	11,718	1899	43,542
1896	21,000	1900	55,162

July 1, 1900, balance unexpended	$73.22
June 30, 1901, amount expended during fiscal year	73.22

Amount (estimated) required for completion of existing project	27,000.00
Amount that can be profitably expended in fiscal year ending June 30, 1903, for works of improvement and for maintenance	5,000.00
Submitted in compliance with requirements of sundry civil act of June 4, 1897, and of section 7 of the river and harbor act of 1899.	

(See Appendix P 4.)

5. *Tampa Bay, Florida.*—Tampa Bay is a large landlocked body of water, on the west coast of Florida, with an average width of from 6 to 7 miles, and a length, exclusive of its two tributary bays, of about 25 miles, in a general northeast and southwest direction. Its two tributary bays are Old Tampa Bay, entering at the northwestern end, and Hillsboro Bay, entering at the northeastern end.

Across the bar at the entrance and up to the point of division the channel has a depth of from 20 to 38 feet at mean low water. Old Tampa Bay is about 15 miles long, with an average width of 6 miles. Its narrowest point is where it joins Tampa Bay, where its width is a little less than 2¼ miles. This bay is generally shallow, but at the southern end has several deep channels. One of these leads along the eastern shore at a distance of about three-fourths mile from the beach and forms the approach to and harbor of Port Tampa. Between deep water in Tampa Bay and the deep channel in Old Tampa Bay are two bars, upon which the depth in 1889 was only 17 feet.

Tampa Bay is the approach to the city of Tampa and to Port Tampa, the former at the head of Hillsboro Bay and the latter on the eastern shore of Old Tampa Bay. Port Tampa is about 9 miles from Tampa, with which it is connected by railway and of which it is the deep-water port.

The present project was inaugurated by Congress under the act of March 3, 1899, in item of appropriation, as follows:

Improving Tampa Bay, Florida: For improvement of Tampa Bay, Florida, from its entrance into the Gulf of Mexico to Port Tampa, seventy-five thousand dollars: *Provided*, That a contract or contracts may be entered into by the Secretary of War for such materials and work as may be necessary toward securing a channel depth of twenty-seven feet from said Gulf of Mexico to Port Tampa, and of a width of five hundred feet across the bar and three hundred feet in the bay, as proposed in the report of November fourteenth, eighteen hundred and ninety-eight, published in House Document Number Fifty-two, Fifty-fifth Congress, third session, to be paid for as appropriations may from time to time be made by law, not to exceed in the aggregate six hundred and seventy-five thousand dollars, exclusive of the amount herein appropriated.

Bids were opened for this work on June 29, 1899. It is proposed under the specifications to secure, first, a 24-foot depth throughout the channel in order to benefit commerce as quickly as possible, and afterwards to increase this depth to 27 feet.

The amount expended under the present project to June 30, 1900, was $33,405.87.

During the fiscal year ending June 30, 1901, work was continued in accordance with the project and under the continuing contract with the Alabama Dredging and Jetty Company. The amount of material dredged from the channel was 268,571.9 cubic yards, and the minimum depth attained in the dredged cuts was 20.4 feet. The maximum draft at mean low water that can be carried over the shoalest part of the channel is 19.9 feet.

COMMERCIAL STATISTICS.

Phosphate rock:	Tons.
1891	15,482
1892	65,406
1893	98,637
1896	197,413
1897	165,606
1898	169,916
1899	201,403
1900	265,294

Total commerce, including phosphate rock:
1896 | 276,638
1898 | 236,156
1899 | 238,305
1900 | 350,761

RIVER AND HARBOR IMPROVEMENTS. 347

July 1, 1900, balance unexpended	$176,594.13
Amount appropriated by sundry civil act approved March 3, 1901	127,000.00
	303,594.13
June 30, 1901, amount expended during fiscal year	42,820.09
July 1, 1901, balance unexpended	260,774.04
July 1, 1901, outstanding liabilities	6,000.00
July 1, 1901, balance available	254,774.04
July 1, 1901, amount covered by uncompleted contracts	452,956.80

Amount (estimated) required for completion of existing project	413,000.00
Amount that can be profitably expended in fiscal year ending June 30, 1903, in addition to the balance available July 1, 1901	75,000.00
Submitted in compliance with requirements of sundry civil act of June 4, 1897.	

(See Appendix P 5.)

6. *Hillsboro Bay, Florida.*—Hillsboro Bay is the northeastern arm of Tampa Bay. It is about 10 miles long in a general north and south direction, and has an average width of about 4½ miles. The city of Tampa is located at the head of this bay at the mouth of the Hillsboro River. It is separated from the 12-foot depth in the bay by a flat about 3 miles wide. Originally there existed through this flat a narrow channel, with an average available depth of about 5 feet, formed by the waters of Hillsboro River.

The present project, inaugurated by Congress under the act of March 3, 1899, contemplates the formation of a channel in Hillsboro River, from a point about 100 feet south of the bridge crossing the river at Lafayette street to the mouth of the river, and from there along the line of shortest distance to the 12-foot contour in Hillsboro Bay; this channel is to be 12 feet deep at mean low water, 200 feet wide in the river, and 150 feet wide in the bay. The estimated cost of the proposed work is $300,000, with $1,000 annually for maintenance.

The act of March 3, 1899, appropriated $125,000 for this improvement.

The amount expended under the existing project to June 30, 1900, was $30,953.62. No expenditures have been made for maintenance. During the fiscal year ending June 30, 1901, the work was continued under the contract in force at the beginning of the year. There were removed from the channel 212,524.9 cubic yards of soft material and 2,989.32 cubic yards of rock. A channel has been formed with a depth of 12 feet and a width of 60 feet in the bay and 80 feet in the river. Vessels drawing 12 feet can now reach the city wharves at mean low water. The available depth at high water is 14 feet and vessels which formerly had to anchor in the bay and lighter their cargoes to the city at great expense can now come to the wharves. The narrowness of the present channel makes its navigation difficult.

The commerce of Hillsboro Bay for the year ending December 31, 1898, amounted to 32,070 tons; for the year ending December 31, 1899, it was 110,240 tons, and during the past year 361,323 tons. Statistics for previous years are not available.

July 1, 1900, balance unexpended $94,046.38
June 30, 1901, amount expended during fiscal year 81,687.86

July 1, 1901, balance unexpended 12,358.52

{ Amount (estimated) required for completion of existing project 175,000.00
Amount that can be profitably expended in fiscal year ending June 30, 1903, in addition to the balance unexpended July 1, 1901 .... 150,000.00
Submitted in compliance with requirements of sundry civil act of June 4, 1897.

(See Appendix P 6.)

7. *Anclote River, Florida.*—This river has a total length of about 20 miles, and is a small stream until it reaches a point about 3 miles from the mouth, where it receives the water flowing from a large spring called Tarpon Springs, situated at the head of Tarpon Bayou, through which it flows into the Anclote River. The thriving town of Tarpon Springs is located about the head of the bayou and between it and the river. The river below Tarpon Springs is badly obstructed by sand shoals and oyster bars, through which the channel pursues a narrow and tortuous way, with a depth varying from 2 to 14 feet at mean low water.

The existing project was adopted by the river and harbor act of March 3, 1899, and contemplates securing a channel 100 feet wide and 6 feet deep at mean low water from Anclote Anchorage to Sponge Harbor, and thence 4 feet deep at mean low water to the county bridge at Tarpon Springs, at an estimated cost of $51,500.

The amount expended to June 30, 1900, was $1,884.37.

During the fiscal year ending June 30, 1901, the work in progress at the beginning of the year was continued till August 18, when funds were exhausted. During this period 11,375.8 cubic yards of material was removed. A cut 50 feet wide and 7 feet deep at mean low water was made through the worst shoals.

The available depth throughout the channel is still limited to about 3 feet at mean low water on shoals that have not yet been dredged. The mean range of tide is 2 feet.

July 1, 1900, balance unexpended $3,115.63
June 30, 1901, amount expended during fiscal year 3,115.63

{ Amount (estimated) required for completion of existing project 46,500.00
Amount that can be profitably expended in fiscal year ending June 30, 1903. 20,000.00
Submitted in compliance with requirements of sundry civil act of June 4, 1897.

(See Appendix P 7.)

8. *Withlacoochee River, Florida.*—The project for the improvement of this river calls for the removal of snags, loose rocks, overhanging trees, and the deepening of some of the prominent shoals and a bar at the mouth, so as to form a channel having an available depth of 2 feet during about half the year from the mouth of the river in the Gulf of Mexico to Pembertons Ferry, a distance of 77 miles. The project was practically completed November 14, 1892.

The amount expended to June 30, 1900, was $23,914.88.

The improvement has not resulted in any marked benefit to commerce because the period during which navigation is open does not correspond with the season when it is necessary to move the horticultural products of the region.

Large deposits of phosphate have been discovered along the river since the original project for improvement was inaugurated, and the sole means of transporting the mining output is by railroad. The cost of this transportation to the nearest seaport amounts to about one-half the value of the phosphate when delivered aboard ship.

A survey of the river was completed in May, 1897, and report thereon, with plans and estimates for a new project, was printed in the Annual Report of the Chief of Engineers for 1898, pages 1363–1369.

No work was done during the fiscal year ending June 30, 1900, and none is contemplated for the next fiscal year.

The maximum draft that can be carried to the head of navigation in the river is 2 feet.

Under plans that received the approval of the Secretary of War April 21, 1894, and subject to inspection by the district engineer officer, the Dunnellon Phosphate Company is engaged in deepening the channel in order that the products of the mines may be lightered to vessels in the outer anchorage.

July 1, 1900, balance unexpended	$785.12
June 30, 1901, amount expended during fiscal year	18.62
July 1, 1901, balance unexpended	766.50

(See Appendix P 8.)

9. *Suwanee River, Florida.*—The project for the improvement of the Suwanee River was adopted in 1879. The reach of the river covered by the project extended from its mouth in the Gulf of Mexico to Ellaville, a distance of 135 miles. At that time the obstructions in this portion of the river consisted of shoals composed of soft, unstratified limestone mixed with flint, extending partly or entirely across the river, in some instances covered with shallow deposits of sand and in others bare; also snags and overhanging trees. The channels across these shoals were often narrow and very crooked. Their depth at mean low water would vary from 15 inches to 3 feet. At places large isolated limestone bowlders in the channel were imminent sources of danger to navigation.

An examination of the river with a view to its improvement was made in 1879. The estimated cost of the work to be done was $55,158.

The proposed improvement consists in deepening the bar at the passes by dredging, the removal of snags and overhanging trees along the river, and deepening and improving the channel at various places by the removal of rocks and snags and construction of wing dams, so as to straighten, widen, and deepen the channel. The depth to be obtained is 5 feet through the bars at the passes for a width of 150 feet and up the river as far as Rollands Bluff (Branford), a distance of 75 miles. From there to Ellaville, a distance of 60 miles, the depth is to be 4 feet and the width 60 feet. The amount expended to June 30, 1900, was $50,958.18.

The work accomplished during the past fiscal year was confined to the shoal which obstructed the entrance to the river.

The U. S. dredge *Suwanee* opened a channel through this shoal about 3,000 feet long, 100 feet wide, and from 5 to 6 feet deep at mean low water. Before this work was done the available depth at the shoalest point was about 3 feet at mean low water.

The maximum draft that can be carried at low water is 5 feet from the Gulf to Branford and 3 feet from there to Hudson, 10 miles below Ellaville.

350 REPORT OF THE CHIEF OF ENGINEERS, U. S. ARMY.

July 1, 1900, balance unexpended	$4,041.82
June 30, 1901, amount expended during fiscal year	3,834.18
July 1, 1901, balance unexpended	207.64
Amount (estimated) required for completion of existing project	10,158.00
Amount that can be profitably expended in fiscal year ending June 30, 1903, in addition to the balance unexpended July 1, 1901. Submitted in compliance with requirements of sundry civil act of June 4, 1897.	5,000.00

(See Appendix P 9.)

EXAMINATION AND SURVEY REQUIRED BY RIVER AND HARBOR ACT APPROVED MARCH 3, 1899.

Captain Rees was charged with the duty of making a preliminary examination and survey of *Kissimmee River, Florida, and connecting lakes and canals flowing into Lake Okechobee, thence down the Caloosahatchee River to the Gulf of Mexico, with a view to improving the navigation of the channels therein*, required by the river and harbor act of March 3, 1899, and, if possible, report thereon will be submitted in time for transmission to Congress at its next session.

IMPROVEMENT OF RIVERS AND HARBORS IN WESTERN GEORGIA AND FLORIDA AND IN EASTERN ALABAMA.

This district was in the charge of Capt. C. A. F. Flagler, Corps of Engineers, to September 19, 1900, and of Capt. W. V. Judson, Corps of Engineers, since that date, the local officer having under his immediate orders Lieut. Lewis H. Rand, Corps of Engineers, to July 3, 1900, and Lieut. Gustave R. Lukesh, Corps of Engineers, from September 16, 1900, to March 14, 1901. Division Engineer, Col. Peter C. Hains, Corps of Engineers.

1. *Carrabelle Bar and Harbor, Florida.*—The town of Carrabelle is situated about 20 miles east of Apalachicola, on Carrabelle River, which empties into St. George Sound. The river forms the inner harbor, and the channel along the water front varies from 9 to 15 feet in depth, with a width of about 100 feet.

A bar 6,000 feet wide between 10-foot contours interposes between the inner harbor above mentioned and Dog Island anchorage, a protected portion of St. George Sound showing 4-fathom depths over a considerable area.

Vessels enter Dog Island anchorage from the Gulf of Mexico via East Pass, which has limiting low-water depths of about 17 feet.

The river and harbor act of June 3, 1896, adopted a project for improvement, and appropriated $10,000 to be used in making a 10-foot channel by dredging from the mouth of Carrabelle River to the channel in the bay (St. George Sound).

No estimate of the cost of this improvement had then been submitted.

The river and harbor act of March 3, 1899, provided for examination of East Pass. Report upon same, with plan and estimate for improvement, is published on pages 2152 et seq., Annual Report of the Chief of Engineers for 1900. This proposed project involves securing a channel across the sea bar, 20¼ feet deep and 150 feet wide, at a cost of $18,950, and closing an opening in Dog Island at a cost of $8,500.

The emergency river and harbor act of June 6, 1900, provided for an examination and survey of Carrabelle Harbor. Report upon same, with map, plan, and estimate, is published in House Doc. No. 227, Fifty-sixth Congress, second session, and is also herewith as Appendix Q 17. This proposed project involves securing a channel 10 feet deep and 100 feet wide from Dog Island anchorage (St. George Sound) to the city of Carrabelle, at a cost of $47,300. This estimate is the only one made from an actual survey, and the project is practically identical with the project already adopted by Congress.

The amount expended up to the close of the fiscal year ending June 30, 1900, was $19,521.28, and the work has been confined to dredging upon the bar at the river mouth.

No work of importance was carried on during the past fiscal year.

The maximum draft that could be carried through the channel at low water June 30, 1901, was 6 feet, although only one lump showed so shoal a depth, there being generally from 7 to 8 feet in the dredged channel.

The commerce of the port of Carrabelle, Fla., consists principally of timber, naval stores, dressed and kiln-dried lumber, shingles, and miscellaneous articles. The value of the lumber and naval-stores business is estimated at $1,828,000.

July 1, 1900, balance unexpended	$478.72
June 30, 1901, amount expended during fiscal year	387.37
July 1, 1901, balance unexpended	91.35
July 1, 1901, outstanding liabilities	55.77
July 1, 1901, balance available	35.58

Amount that can be profitably expended in fiscal year ending June 30, 1903, for maintenance of improvement, in addition to the balance available July 1, 1901... 10,000.00
Submitted in compliance with requirements of sundry civil act of June 4, 1897, and of section 7 of the river and harbor act of 1899.

(See Appendix Q 1.)

2. Apalachicola Bay, Florida.—The town of Apalachicola lies at the mouth of the river of that name, the deep water of which forms its inner harbor. Between the inner harbor and a considerable 3-fathom depth anchorage area in Apalachicola Bay interposes a bar at the river mouth, the average width of which was originally 7,000 feet between 8-foot contours and the minimum depth 3.5 feet.

Across this bar the lumber exported is lightered either to the 3-fathom anchorage area in Apalachicola Bay or through Bulkhead Shoals to the anchorage off Carrabelle, the latter some 20 miles distant. The 3-fathom anchorage area is entered via West Pass, where originally the depth was about 13 feet. The original depth over Bulkhead Shoals was less than 4 feet.

The existing project, except for Bulkhead Shoals, approved by act of March 3, 1899, provides for a channel 18 feet deep at mean low water through the West Pass, along the northern shore of St. George Island, and across the bay to the water front of Apalachicola, estimated to cost $350,000 and $20,000 or $30,000 annually for maintenance of completed work.

The project for improvement of Bulkhead Shoals was adopted in 1891, and involved the dredging of a channel 100 feet wide and 9 feet deep.

The amount expended on this improvement up to the close of the fiscal year ending June 30, 1900, including the cost of channel dug through Bulkhead Shoals, was $173,428.99.

Nothing has been done during the past fiscal year beyond making necessary inspections.

The channel through Bulkhead Shoals remains practically as when dredged in 1892, with a minimum low-water depth of about 8 feet.

The channel over the bar at the river mouth has been gradually shoaling since the last dredging was done in 1897, and is now very troublesome and expensive to the lighterage business crossing it. The maximum depth that can be carried across it at mean low water is but 5 feet.

The channel across the sea bar at West Pass, which was dredged to 17 feet in 1900, shows now a maximum available low-water depth of about 15 feet. The general depths are much greater than this; in fact, the channel has remained practically as dredged last year, except at the extreme outer end of the channel, where a lump has formed with minimum depth stated. Due to the formation of this lump, many vessels loaded Apalachicola lumber at the anchorage near Carrabelle, although some use was made of West Pass.

The commerce of this port consists of timber, cotton, naval stores, staves, a large quantity of dressed and kiln-dried lumber, shingles, laths, and miscellaneous freights. The value of these exports, foreign and domestic, during the past fiscal year was returned at $334,034, and the value of the timber and naval-stores business at Apalachicola is estimated at $1,000,000.

July 1, 1900, balance unexpended	$571.01
June 30, 1901, amount expended during fiscal year	440.69
July 1, 1901, balance unexpended	130.32
July 1, 1901, outstanding liabilities	127.88
July 1, 1901, balance available	2.44

Amount (estimated) required for completion of existing project....... 330,000.00
Amount that can be profitably expended in fiscal year ending June 30, 1903, for works of improvement and for maintenance, in addition to the balance available July 1, 1901 .... 40,000.00
Submitted in compliance with requirements of sundry civil act of June 4, 1897, and of section 7 of the river and harbor act of 1899.

(See Appendix Q 2.)

3. *Apalachicola River, the Cut-off, and Lower Chipola River, Florida.*—The Apalachicola River, from the junction of the Chattahoochee and Flint rivers to the Gulf of Mexico (Apalachicola Bay) has a length of about 137 miles and a low-water slope of about 3 inches to the mile, as indicated by the best data at hand. The width varies from 150 to 300 yards, and the available depth was originally 6 feet at low water, except where obstructed by snags and sunken logs.

The Confederate authorities obstructed the channel at a point about 47 miles above the mouth, causing the river to break through, by a channel known as Moccasin Slough, into the river Styx, the latter a tributary entering the Apalachicola a few miles below the Confederate obstructions. Moccasin Slough was very narrow and tortuous and much obstructed by rafts of logs, etc. The old channel, due to the Confederate obstructions, has gradually filled up.

About 55 miles above the mouth steamboats may leave the river, reentering it about 17 miles farther down, after passing through the Cut-off, Lower Chipola River, and Lee Slough, thus making several important landings.

The original project, approved by the act of June 23, 1874, contemplated securing a channel 100 feet wide and 6 feet deep at low water by the removal of snags and overhanging trees and widening and straightening Moccasin Slough and the Elbows at an estimated cost of $80,333.

Act of September 19, 1890, approved of an addition to the project involving the clearing of a channel 60 feet wide and 5 feet deep through the Cut-off, Lee Slough, and the Chipola River, at a cost of $7,500.

The amount expended on the work to close of fiscal year ending June 30, 1900, was $62,490.23. This expenditure has improved Moccasin Slough sufficiently for present purposes and maintained the river reasonably free of snags, etc.

During the past year the work has been confined to the removal of the annual accumulation of snags, and the river has been maintained in good condition. A dredge is being constructed for use upon the Chattahoochee, Flint, and Apalachicola rivers.

The commerce of this river is so combined with that of the Chattahoochee and Flint rivers that a separation is impossible. The commerce of all these streams amounted to about $2,000,000 in 1898, about $4,000,000 in 1899, about $4,777,000 in 1900, and about $11,000,000 in 1901.

July 1, 1900, balance unexpended	$9.77
Amount allotted from appropriation contained in emergency river and harbor act approved June 6, 1900	1,500.00
	1,509.77
June 30, 1901, amount expended during fiscal year	1,509.77

Amount (estimated) required for completion of existing project	21,000.00
Amount that can be profitably expended in fiscal year ending June 30, 1903, for works of improvement and for maintenance	10,000.00
Submitted in compliance with requirements of sundry civil act of June 4, 1897, and of section 7 of the river and harbor act of 1899.	

(See Appendix Q 3.)

4. Upper Chipola River, Florida, from Marianna to its mouth.—This river flows in a southerly direction through a low, flat, and sparsely settled country, a distance of about 98 miles, from Marianna to the head of the Dead Lakes. It has a general low-water depth of 5 feet and width varying from 60 to 200 feet. It is greatly obstructed by rock shoals, snags, and overhanging trees. Three bridges form obstructions, their headways above low water being 17, 16, and 15 feet, respectively.

At one shoal ("Look and Tremble") there is a fall of 5 feet in 40 over rock bottom. This shoal is about 53 miles above the Dead Lakes. About 25 miles above the Dead Lakes there is, at Sister Islands, a mud bar over which but 2 feet can be carried at low water.

No funds were available for the improvement of this stream until an appropriation of $5,000 was made by act of March 3, 1899, to be expended in accordance with project submitted. The project contemplates clearing out a low-water channel 3 feet deep and 60 feet wide from Marianna to the foot of the Dead Lakes, estimated to cost $41,000, exclusive of necessary plant, which would comprise a snag boat, drilling barge, and dump scow. (See Annual Report of the Chief of Engineers for 1899, p. 1417.)

The amount expended to June 30, 1900, was $4,950.55, which resulted in the removal of snags, logs, etc., from Marianna to Sister Islands.

Nothing was done during the last fiscal year.

The river is still obstructed by shoals at Sister Islands, "Look and Tremble," and at numerous points above, as well as by the bridges mentioned. The channel below Sister Islands is much obstructed by snags, cypress stumps, and logs, and this same condition obtains through the Dead Lakes, which must be traversed by boats for 20 miles on their way to the Apalachicola River via the Cut-off or Lower Chipola River and Lee Slough.

The commerce of this stream consists principally of naval stores, round and square timber, lumber, and other miscellaneous freights, the estimated value of which was on June 30, 1901, $514,000.

Large quantities of pine and cypress timber are rafted down this stream, the value of which is not known.

July 1, 1900, balance unexpended	$49.45
June 30, 1901, amount expended during fiscal year	49.45
Amount (estimated) required for completion of existing project	36,000.00
Amount that can be profitably expended in fiscal year ending June 30, 1903	4,000.00

Submitted in compliance with requirements of sundry civil act of June 4, 1897.

(See Appendix Q 4.)

5. *Flint River, Georgia.*—At low water this river was navigable for boats drawing 3 feet from its mouth to Bainbridge, a distance of 36 miles, but the channel was narrow, crooked, and greatly obstructed by logs, snags, and overhanging trees. Above Bainbridge the channel was so obstructed by rock shoals, loose rock, and bowlders that there was no navigation except on a rise of 4 feet, when steamboats could run to Albany, 105 miles above the mouth. Above Albany to Montezuma, the latter point 182 miles above the mouth, the channel was so obstructed by sand and rock shoals, bowlders, snags, logs, and overhanging trees that the river was not navigable at a low-water stage.

The original project called for a channel 100 feet wide and 3 feet deep at extreme low water from the mouth of the river to Albany, Ga., at an estimated cost of $184,862.

This project was amended in 1870 to give a channel for light-draft steamers at moderate stages of water from Albany to Montezuma by the removal of logs, snags, and overhanging trees, cutting through rock reefs, and deepening sand bars by contraction works, at a cost of $15,000.

The amount expended up to the close of the fiscal year ending June 30, 1900, was $210,129.76. As the result of work done, the river is now navigable throughout the year from Albany down to Newton, 33¼ miles, and from Bainbridge to the mouth, 36 miles, there being a good channel with 3 feet available at low water throughout these sections.

Between Bainbridge and Newton, 35¾ miles, boats do not attempt to run through, except at a 5-foot stage, as the channel is still much obstructed by logs, snags, bowlders, and rock reefs. Considerable work has been done between these points, however, and the same will be available when the improvement of this section has been completed.

Between Albany and Montezuma, 77 miles, no navigation is attemped, as the river is much obstructed in a manner similar to the section last mentioned. This portion of the river has been cleared of snags, etc., in accordance with the project, repeatedly, and it is recommended that for the present no further work be done thereon.

No work was done on this improvement during past fiscal year; a dipper dredge, however, is under construction for use on the Flint, Chattahoochee, and Apalachicola rivers.

The commerce of the lower part of this stream is so combined with that of the Chattahoochee and Apalachicola rivers that it is impossible to give a separate statement in regard to it. The commerce of that part below Albany down as far as the improvement has been carried is estimated to be 29,674 tons, valued at $1,500,000, for the past fiscal year.

July 1, 1900, balance unexpended	$870.24
June 30, 1901, amount expended during fiscal year	299.58
July 1, 1901, balance unexpended	570.66
July 1, 1901, outstanding liabilities	72.61
July 1, 1901, balance available	498.05
Amount (estimated) required for completion of existing project	117,000.00
Amount that can be profitably expended in fiscal year ending June 30, 1903, for works of improvement and for maintenance, in addition to the balance available July 1, 1901	40,000.00

Submitted in compliance with requirements of sundry civil act of June 4, 1897, and of section 7 of the river and harbor act of 1899.

(See Appendix Q 5.)

6. *Chattahoochee River, Georgia and Alabama.*—(a) *Below Columbus.*—Columbus, Ga., lies 223 miles above the junction of this river with the Flint and 360 miles above the mouth of the Apalachicola River, which is formed by the confluence of the Chattahooche and the Flint. Columbus is at the head of navigation and boats have always ascended to this point, but navigation was originally difficult and dangerous by day and impossible by night, owing to the large accumulation of logs, snags, and overhanging trees, and sand, rock, and marl shoals obstructing the channel.

The project for improvement, adopted in 1873, provided for a low-water channel 100 feet wide and 4 feet deep from Columbus, Ga., to Chattahooche, Fla., at the junction of the Flint, which was to be obtained by the removal of logs, snags, and overhanging trees; cutting through the rock and marl shoals, and scouring out sand bars by works of contraction and shore protection. The estimated cost of this work from Chattahoochee, Fla., to Eufaula, Ala., 139 miles, was $145,247. No estimate of cost for that part between Eufaula, Ala., and Columbus, Ga., was made.

The amount expended on this work to the close of the fiscal year ending June 30, 1900, was $323,074.12.

The river was in a fair condition at that date, with an available low-water depth of 3¼ feet below Eufaula, Ala., but between Eufaula and Columbus there was a number of bars and isolated obstructions which caused trouble, particularly at extreme low stages of the river. Navigation above Eufaula was then virtually suspended.

During the past fiscal year snags were removed from the river throughout its length, and work of jetty repair and extension and marl excavation was carried on at a number of the worst places.

Under contract with the M. A. Sweeney Shipyard and Foundry Company, of Jeffersonville, Ind., a dredge boat is being constructed for use upon the Apalachicola, Flint, and Chattahoochee rivers.

The river is constantly receiving an influx of snags from caving banks. These must be removed annually. A large number of sand bars and shoals still need improvement between Columbus, Ga., and Eufaula, Ala., and the wing dams and training walls built in the past require repairs and maintenance.

The maximum draft that can be carried over the shoalest part of the river under improvement is scant 3 feet.

The commerce of this stream is so combined with that of the Flint and Apalachicola rivers that a separation is impossible. It is stated under the report of the Flint River as being 118,765 tons, valued at $11,146,125, in 1901, as against 86,858 tons, valued at $4,777,190, in 1900.

July 1, 1900, balance unexpended	$31,925.88
June 30, 1901, amount expended during fiscal year	13,715.03
July 1, 1901, balance unexpended	18,210.85
July 1, 1901, outstanding liabilities	10,475.35
July 1, 1901, balance available	7,735.50
July 1, 1901, amount covered by uncompleted contracts	10,311.75
Amount that can be profitably expended in fiscal year ending June 30, 1903, for works of improvement and for maintenance, in addition to the balance available July 1, 1901	90,000.00

Submitted in compliance with requirements of sundry civil act of June 4, 1897, and of section 7 of the river and harbor act of 1899.

(b) *Between Westpoint and Franklin.*—This section of the river is 38 miles long, and is divided into a series of pools, varying in length from half a mile to 5 or 6 miles, by rock shoals and rapids, some of which have a fall as great as 8 feet in a mile. The width of the pools varies from 300 to 500 feet, with a depth of not less than 4 feet. The width of the shoals is from 800 to 1,000 feet, with a depth of water of only a few inches. There was therefore no navigable channel.

The river and harbor acts of 1892, 1894, and 1896 each provided that $5,000 of the sum appropriated for the Chattahoochee River, Georgia and Alabama, should be spent on this section, the project adopted being to "remove the lesser rock shoals, sand and gravel bars by excavation and works of contraction; to remove overhanging trees from the banks, and snags, logs, and other obstructions from the channel, and to overcome the more serious obstructions by the construction of locks and dams, to give a minimum depth of 3 feet at low water in the channel between Westpoint and Franklin, a distance of 38 miles."

By act of March 3, 1899, the balance remaining from above appropriations, together with an additional $5,000, was made available for a survey of this section of the river. A preliminary report upon this survey was published in House Doc. No. 111, Fifty-sixth Congress, second session, and is also herewith as Appendix Q 16. The cost of a 4-foot channel, 100 feet wide, was ascertained to be $1,149,914.

No work has been done during the past fiscal year.

The amount expended on this work to June 30, 1900, was $19,708.55, which resulted in obtaining a low-water channel 50 feet wide and 3

feet deep through Roberts, Flat Rock, and Haynes Island shoals, and the making of the survey and estimates mentioned above.
There is no commerce on this part of the river at present.

July 1, 1900, balance unexpended	$291.45
June 30, 1901, amount expended during fiscal year	10.67
July 1, 1901, balance unexpended	280.78
July 1, 1901, outstanding liabilities	117.60
July 1, 1901, balance available	163.18

(See Appendix Q 6.)

7. *Choctawhatchee River, Florida and Alabama.*—The Choctawhatchee River is 162 miles long, from Newton, Ala., to its mouth in Choctawhatchee Bay, an arm of the Gulf of Mexico. Hollis Bridge is 7 miles, Pate Landing 12 miles, Geneva 37 miles, and Caryville 62 miles below Newton.

Originally the channel was much obstructed by snags, logs, sand and gravel bars.

The project for improvement, as amended in 1890, contemplates the creation of a low-water navigable channel throughout, by removing logs, snags, and overhanging trees, by excavating rock and marl shoals, and by contraction works and shore protection.

The amount expended on this river up to the close of the fiscal year ending June 30, 1900, was $149,247.01.

The work done has secured a good navigable channel from Geneva to Caryville, with a low-water depth of 3½ feet. This portion of the river is constantly used by steamboats, which occasionally ascend to Pate Landing, between which point and Geneva a partially improved navigable channel exists.

Below Caryville there is no steamboat navigation at present, but immense quantities of saw logs and hewn timber are floated down. Below Caryville the work of first importance is the deepening of the bar at the mouth of the river (Cypress Top) to 5 feet to enable tugs to handle the timber floated down.

During the fiscal year ending June 30, 1901, the work consisted in the removal of logs, snags, and other obstructions from the channel, and overhanging trees, etc., from the banks between Pate Landing, 12 miles below Newton, Ala., and Caryville, Fla., a distance of 50 miles. On December 10, 1900, the snag boat *Choctawhatchee* was snagged and sunk near Pate Landing. A new hull for this boat has been under construction and is now nearing completion at Pine Barren, Fla.

The commerce of this stream is mainly cotton, miscellaneous stores, saw logs, timber, and lumber, the value of which for the fiscal year ending June 30, 1901, is estimated to be about $1,024,650.

July 1, 1900, balance unexpended	$10,629.61
June 30, 1901, amount expended during fiscal year	8,842.74
July 1, 1901, balance unexpended	1,786.87
July 1, 1901, outstanding liabilities	215.98
July 1, 1901, balance available	1,570.89
Amount that can be profitably expended in fiscal year ending June 30, 1903, for works of improvement and for maintenance, in addition to the balance available July 1, 1901	18,000.00

Submitted in compliance with requirements of sundry civil act of June 4, 1897, and of section 7 of the river and harbor act of 1899.

(See Appendix Q 7.)

8. *Lagrange Bayou, Florida, including Holmes River, Florida, from Vernon to its mouth.*—Holmes River empties into the Choctawhatchee River about 40 miles above the mouth of the latter. It is a wide and deep stream to the town of Vernon, 25 miles above its mouth, but was originally greatly obstructed by sunken logs, fallen timber, and overhanging trees, and was only available for navigation by small sailing craft and barges which occasionally made trips up to Vernon.

The present project for the improvement of the stream provides for making a navigable channel, by removing logs and snags from the channel and overhanging trees from its banks, from its mouth up to the town of Vernon.

The total amount expended on this improvement up to the close of the year ending June 30, 1900, was $7,144.50 (of which $4,983.70 was upon Holmes River and $2,160.80 upon Lagrange Bayou) and resulted in clearing the channel of all obstructions that were then found, making the channel sufficiently available for the small craft that used the stream.

Nothing was done during the past fiscal year.

The commerce of the stream consists of cotton, turpentine, rosin, molasses, honey, and miscellaneous articles, which are carried by water to Pensacola to market.

July 1, 1900, balance unexpended	$2,855.50
June 30, 1901, amount expended during fiscal year	635.30
July 1, 1901, balance unexpended	2,220.20

(See Appendix Q 8.)

9. *Harbor at Pensacola, Fla.*—The available depth across the inner bar at the entrance to this harbor in 1879, previous to any work of improvement, was 19.5 feet, the width of the channel being contracted by the growth of the Middle Ground Shoal to the southward. The harbor entrance and channel way was also obstructed by wrecks, and the western shore line in the vicinity of Fort McRee was cutting away rapidly, and almost the whole of old Fort McRee had been washed away.

The project of 1877 considered only the removal of the wrecks; that of 1878 called for the removal of these wrecks and for making a survey to determine further recommendations for improvement. The project of 1881 provided for dredging a channel 300 feet wide and 24 feet deep at mean low water for the temporary relief of navigation, and also for protecting the shore line near Fort McRee with a view to preventing further injurious changes. Dredging under this project was carried on at various times between 1881 and 1893, and at the close of the dredging operations in August, 1893, the available channel was 225 feet wide, with a depth of 24 feet at mean low water. Two groins, one 360 and the other 220 feet long, were completed in 1890, and still serve the purpose of holding the shore line.

In 1891 a special Board of Engineers presented a project for opening a new channel across the Caucus Shoal, following the direction of the ebb current, by means of two jetties, assisted by dredging if necessary. The estimated cost of this project was $1,830,000. In 1895, upon the report of a special Board of Engineers, no change was made in the project of 1891, but it was recommended that dredging be tried, using one of the hydraulic dredges belonging to the United States, to open up a channel 26 feet deep at mean low water and as wide as practicable on the line of the deepest water across the Caucus Shoal and approximately on the line of the axis of the jettied channel proposed by the Board in 1891. In December, 1895, this channel was opened by the U. S. dredge *Gedney* to a width of 120 feet and depth of 24 feet at mean low water. The channel across Caucus Shoal, now known as Caucus Channel, has a length of about 10,000 feet.

In 1896, the same Board that recommended the first amendment to the project of 1891 submitted a second amendment, to expend all funds available in continuing the work of dredging across the Caucus Shoal, and if funds sufficient were made available by Congress to build a dredge and open the channel across the Caucus Shoal to a width of at least 300 feet and a 30-foot depth at mean low water, with such side slopes as the material would assume. Until a channel be opened by dredging across the Caucus Shoal, as above proposed, the Board recommended that the construction of jetties for its maintenance be not considered.

The river and harbor act of March 3, 1899, extended this project to "securing a channel depth of 30 feet at mean low water from the Gulf of Mexico to the dock line at the east end of the city of Pensacola."

The amount expended up to the close of the fiscal year ending June 30, 1900, was $646,007.96. The work done resulted in the removal of the wrecks obstructing the channel; the construction of two groins near old Fort McRee, which have served the purpose of retaining the shore line and are now in good condition; in dredging a large amount of material from the inner bar, and in opening up an entirely new 30-foot channel across the Caucus Shoal.

On June 30, 1901, the maximum draft which could be carried through the channel at low water was 27.3 feet.

In view of the large amount of dredging required in Pensacola Harbor for securing and maintaining the requisite channel depths it is considered very desirable that a Government dredging plant should be secured.

The commerce of this port is very large. For the fiscal year ending June 30, 1899, the foreign and coastwise exports were reported as $14,936,084; in 1900, as $14,828,580, and in 1901, as $14,710,649.

July 1, 1900, balance unexpended	$73,992.04
June 30, 1901, amount expended during fiscal year	61,419.45
July 1, 1901, balance unexpended	12,572.59
July 1, 1901, outstanding liabilities	524.61
July 1, 1901, balance available	12,047.98

Amount (estimated) required for completion of existing project....... 683,200.00
Amount that can be profitably expended in fiscal year ending June 30, 1903, for works of improvement and for maintenance, in addition to the balance available July 1, 1901 .... 275,000.00
Submitted in compliance with requirements of sundry civil act of June 4, 1897, and of section 7 of the river and harbor act of 1899.

(See Appendix Q 9.)

10. *Blackwater River, Florida and Alabama.*—This is a short tidal stream entering Blackwater Bay, the latter an arm of Pensacola Bay. About 5 miles above the mouth of the river is Milton, Fla., and adjoining Milton is Bagdad, Fla., both towns being important shipping points for lumber designed for export via Pensacola. From 12 miles above Milton to the mouth of the river there was originally a deep channel, nowhere less than 9 feet in depth below Milton except at Hunts Bar, about 1 mile below the town, where the maximum depth

360   REPORT OF THE CHIEF OF ENGINEERS, U. S. ARMY.

was 6 feet. Between the river mouth and 10-foot depths in Pensacola Bay lies a stretch of 10 miles, with depths varying from 7 to 10 feet.

A project was submitted in 1882 (see Annual Report of the Chief of Engineers for that year, p. 1309) which contemplated a 9-foot channel throughout the waterway above described. Act of March 3, 1899, appropriated $5,000 for that part of the waterway within the river proper, in accordance with above-mentioned project.

The amount expended to June 30, 1900, was $4,366.66, and resulted in the removal of Hunts Bar as an obstruction to navigation.

Nothing has been done during the past fiscal year.

The greatest draft that could be carried through the channel June 30, 1901, was about 10 feet, which is more than maximum drafts allowable in the continuation of the waterway below the river mouth.

The commerce of this river is principally lumber and timber, which is carried to Pensacola, Fla., for export. It is quite large, but no information as to its amount has been obtained.

July 1, 1900, balance unexpended	$633.34
June 30, 1901, amount expended during fiscal year	633.34

(See Appendix Q 10.)

11. Escambia and Conecuh rivers, Florida and Alabama.—These two names apply to one and the same river, which flows through a heavily timbered country in southern Alabama and western Florida into Escambia Bay, an arm of Pensacola Bay. Its timber forms a large part of all that is exported from Pensacola. Originally the river was much obstructed by snags and by marl and sand bars, and a bar at the mouth seriously interfered with navigation.

The project is based upon reports of examinations and surveys printed in the Annual Report of the Chief of Engineers for 1879, pages 843-852, and provides for the improvement of the river from its mouth to Indian Creek, Alabama, an estimated distance of 293 miles, by the removal of logs, snags, and overhanging trees, by excavating rock shoals, by works of contraction and shore protection, and by dredging a channel through the bar at the mouth.

The amount expended to June 30, 1900, was $88,993.69, and has maintained the river fairly free from snags, besides opening and reopening the bar at the mouth from time to time.

The work done during past fiscal year has been confined to snagging operations.

The commerce of this stream is mainly timber, lumber, and saw logs. It is reported as being valued at about 60 per cent of the timber export trade of Pensacola.

July 1, 1900, balance unexpended	$506.31
Amount allotted from appropriation contained in emergency river and harbor act approved June 6, 1900	1,500.00
	2,006.31
June 30, 1901, amount expended during fiscal year	1,947.30
July 1, 1901, balance unexpended	59.01
July 1, 1901, outstanding liabilities	4.50
July 1, 1901, balance available	54.51
Amount that can be profitably expended in fiscal year ending June 30, 1903, for maintenance of improvement, in addition to the balance available July 1, 1901	20,000.00

Submitted in compliance with requirements of sundry civil act of June 4, 1897, and of section 7 of the river and harbor act of 1899.

(See Appendix Q 11.)

12. *Alabama River, Alabama.*—This river, from Wetumka (on the Coosa River, which 11 miles below joins the Tallapoosa to form the Alabama proper) to its junction with the Tombigbee, forms a 323-mile link in a waterway 815 miles long, from the Oostenaula and Coosawattee rivers, Georgia, to the Gulf of Mexico. Of this waterway, the whole of the Alabama and over 300 miles besides is now navigable.

This river was originally so obstructed by logs, snags, overhanging trees, and shoals, many with depths of but 2.5 feet, that navigation was practicable at low stages only by day.

The project, as amended in 1891, contemplates a low-water channel 6 feet in depth, to be secured by means of the removal of snags and overhanging trees, contraction works, blasting, dredging, and shore protection.

The estimate submitted in 1891 amounted to $386,251, and was based upon an assumption that $100,000 should be provided annually. Ten thousand dollars annually was the estimate for maintenance, including snagging.

The amount expended to June 30, 1900, was $354,046.02.

The maximum draft that could be carried through the channel at low water June 30, 1901, was 3 feet.

The commerce of this stream is important, consisting principally of cotton, cotton seed, fertilizers, grain, lumber, shingles, naval stores, staves, and a large quantity of miscellaneous freight of all descriptions, estimated for the past fiscal year as 119,634 tons, valued at $8,375,000.

July 1, 1900, balance unexpended	$40,953.98
June 30, 1901, amount expended during fiscal year	13,471.21
July 1, 1901, balance unexpended	27,482.77
July 1, 1901, outstanding liabilities	11,365.72
July 1, 1901, balance available	16,117.05
July 1, 1901, amount covered by uncompleted contracts	10,080.00
Amount (estimated) required for completion of existing project	196,251.00
Amount that can be profitably expended in fiscal year ending June 30, 1903, for works of improvement and for maintenance, in addition to the balance available July 1, 1901	35,000.00

Submitted in compliance with requirements of sundry civil act of June 4, 1897, and of section 7 of the river and harbor act of 1899.

(See Appendix Q 12.)

13. *Coosa River, Georgia and Alabama.*—The Coosa is formed by the Oostenaula and Etowah rivers, which have their sources in northern Georgia. The town of Rome, Ga., is situated at their junction. The Etowah is not navigable. The Oostenaula is formed by the junction of the Coosawattee and Connesauga rivers, 60 miles northwest of Rome. The Oostenaula and its tributary, the Coosawattee, are navigable for light-draft boats the year round from Rome to Carters Landing, a distance of 105 miles. These rivers have been improved by works of contraction and channel excavation.

The Coosa River has always been navigable for light-draft boats from Rome, Ga., to Greensport, Ala., an estimated distance of 162 miles. This part of the river is of such a character as to make its improvement by works of contraction and channel excavation entirely practicable.

From Greensport, Ala., to Wetumka, Ala., a distance of 142 miles,

362   REPORT OF THE CHIEF OF ENGINEERS, U. S. ARMY.

the improvement requires the building of locks and dams in conjunction with works of contraction and channel excavation.

With the Coosa opened to navigation there would be a continuous water route of transportation from Carters Landing on the Coosawattee to Mobile, Ala., a distance estimated at 815 miles. This water route includes the Coosawattee, Oostenaula, Coosa, Alabama, and Mobile rivers.

The Coosa is divided by legislative action into two parts, that lying between Rome and the East Tennessee, Virginia and Georgia Railroad bridge, and that lying between the bridge and Wetumka. The first is 236 miles long; the second is 68 miles.

(a) *Between Rome, Ga., and East Tennessee, Virginia and Georgia Railroad bridge.*—The present project provides for the removal of the lesser rock shoals and sand and gravel bars by excavation and works of contraction, and for the construction of 8 locks and dams to overcome the more serious obstructions. This project was based upon recommendations contained in the reports of the various examinations and surveys printed in the Annual Reports of the Chief of Engineers for 1871, 1872, 1875, 1878, 1881, and 1890.

Locks 1, 2, and 3, commenced prior to 1890, have been long since completed. They are situated, respectively, 0.68 mile, 3.86 miles, and 5.24 miles below Greensport, Ala., and have available lengths of 175 feet and widths of 40 feet.

The modification of the project as the result of the survey of 1889 (reported upon in 1890) contemplates locks below No. 3, 52 feet by 280 feet in the clear, with 6 feet on the miter sills, and intermediate channel improvements to a depth of 4 feet.

Lock No. 4, 25.89 miles below Greensport, of the larger dimensions above mentioned, together with its appurtenances, has been under construction, with desultory appropriation, since 1886. It is still incomplete.

There has been expended to June 30, 1900, $979,793.61, accomplishing the lock construction above mentioned, building the 4 dams, and effecting channel improvements as far down as Lock No. 4, to which point navigation is now carried on, except in lowest stages, interruptions then occurring a short distance above Lock No. 4.

Owing to the small balance available nothing was done during the past fiscal year except maintenance of existing structures and care of the large amount of plant on hand.

On June 30, 1901, the maximum draft that could be carried at low water between Rome, Ga., and Lock No. 4 was 2 feet.

The commerce of this portion of the river is of great importance. It consists principally of cotton, cotton seed, fertilizers, timber, lumber, staves, grain, and miscellaneous articles.

July 1, 1900, balance unexpended	$5,228.79
June 30, 1901, amount expended during fiscal year	3,988.22
July 1, 1901, balance unexpended	1,240.57
July 1, 1901, outstanding liabilities	801.23
July 1, 1901, balance available	439.34
Amount (estimated) required for completion of existing project	1,158,523.00
Amount that can be profitably expended in fiscal year ending June 30, 1903, for works of improvement and for maintenance, in addition to the balance available July 1, 1901	250,000.00

Submitted in compliance with requirements of sundry civil act of June 4, 1897, and of section 7 of the river and harbor act of 1899.

(b) *Between Wetumka and East Tennessee, Virginia and Georgia Railroad bridge.*—On account of the numerous rapids this section has never been navigable.

The project adopted as the result of the survey of 1889 (reported upon in 1890) contemplates slack-water navigation, and involves, besides channel excavation, the construction of 23 locks and dams.

The locks are to be 280 feet by 52 feet in the clear, with 6 feet on the miter sills, and the channel between locks is to have a least depth of 4 feet.

The lowest lock of the series, known as No. 31, has been completed except as to gates, but the dam has not been built.

There is no navigation possible upon this section of the river.

There was expended to June 30, 1900, $380,531.54, which has resulted in the above-described lock, channel excavation between this lock and the next above, and the obtaining of data and the preparation of plans for other locks and dams.

No work was done during the past fiscal year except care and preservation of public property pertaining to the improvement and making necessary repairs to houses and grounds in the vicinity of Lock No. 31.

The condition of this part of the Coosa River is such that the entire section must be improved and connection made above and below before any commerce can be developed.

July 1, 1900, balance unexpended	$29,468.46
June 30, 1901, amount expended during fiscal year	3,229.68
July 1, 1901, balance unexpended	26,238.78
July 1, 1901, outstanding liabilities	224.54
July 1, 1901, balance available	26,014.24
Amount (estimated) required for completion of existing project	4,916,390.00
Amount that can be profitably expended in fiscal year ending June 30, 1903, in addition to the balance available July 1, 1901	15,000.00
Submitted in compliance with requirements of sundry civil act of June 4, 1897.	

(See Appendix Q 13.)

14. Operating and care of canals and other works of navigation on Coosa River, Georgia and Alabama.—The expenses of operating and care of Locks Nos. 1, 2, and 3, and the improved channel as far down as Dam No. 4, during the fiscal year ending June 30, 1901, amounting to $8,510.75, exclusive of outstanding liabilities ($434.57) on June 30, 1901, have been paid from the permanent-indefinite appropriation provided by section 4 of the act of July 5, 1884.

(See Appendix Q 14.)

15. Removing sunken vessels or craft obstructing or endangering navigation.—The local officer has been charged with the duty of removing the wreck of the steamer *Mascot* from the Flint River. High water prevailing since the receipt of the allotment has compelled postponement of this work until the approaching working season.

(See Appendix Q 15.)

SURVEY MADE IN COMPLIANCE WITH RIVER AND HARBOR ACT APPROVED MARCH 3, 1899.

Preliminary report, dated June 5, 1900, on survey of *Chattahoochee River between Westpoint and Franklin, Ga.*, was submitted by

Captain Judson, through the division engineer, with plan for improvement at an estimated cost of $1,149,914. The report was transmitted to Congress and printed in House Doc. No. 111, Fifty-sixth Congress, second session. (See also Appendix Q 16.)

If possible, final report on survey will be submitted in time for transmission to Congress at its next session.

EXAMINATION AND SURVEY MADE IN COMPLIANCE WITH EMERGENCY RIVER AND HARBOR ACT APPROVED JUNE 6, 1900.

Reports upon preliminary examination and survey of *Carrabelle Harbor, Florida*, were submitted through the division engineer by Captain Flagler and Captain Judson under date of July 12 and December 15, 1900, respectively. The plan presented by Captain Judson contemplates improvement at an estimated cost of $47,300. The reports were transmitted to Congress and printed in House Doc. No. 227, Fifty-sixth Congress, second session. (See also Appendix Q 17.)

IMPROVEMENT OF RIVERS AND HARBORS IN WESTERN ALABAMA AND EASTERN MISSISSIPPI, AND OF BOGUE CHITTO, LOUISIANA.

This district was in the charge of Maj. Wm. T. Rossell, Corps of Engineers, having under his immediate orders Lieut. Meriwether L. Walker, Corps of Engineers, from January 26 to April 6, 1901. Division Engineer, Col. Peter C. Hains, Corps of Engineers.

1. *Mobile Harbor, Alabama.*—This channel had originally a depth of 5¼ feet through Choctaw Pass and 8 feet on Dog River bar.

The history of this improvement previous to the adoption of the project of 1899 has been given in previous reports.

There was expended on this work since its inauguration in 1826 to June 30, 1900, $3,736,743.84.

Act of March 3, 1899, appropriated the sum of $100,000, and granted authority to enter into continuous contract or contracts to the amount of $500,000 in addition, with a view of ultimately securing a channel 23 feet deep and 100 feet wide at bottom, with appropriate side slope.

It is understood that Congress by this item of appropriation adopts the project published in House Doc. No. 199, Fifty-fourth Congress, first session, and printed on page 1463 of the Annual Report of the Chief of Engineers for 1896.

Contract was entered into with the National Dredging Company for work under the appropriations of $600,000 above mentioned, and operations were carried on from June 26, 1899, to February 2, 1901, when funds were exhausted.

At the beginning of the fiscal year there was a channel of navigable width, with a depth varying from 19 to 25 feet at mean low water, but available throughout for vessels drawing 22.5 feet on account of softness of the material which had filled in.

During the fiscal year 3,637,739 cubic yards of material was removed, of which 60,994 cubic yards was removed from the river, and the rest from Mobile Bay, making cuts in the river of 40 and 80 feet width and an aggregate length of 8,220 feet, and in the bay cuts of from 40 to 100 feet width and a length of 63,801 feet. Some of the cuts formerly made in Mobile Bay were increased to 150 and 200 feet in width, and there is now available a channel varying in width from 40 to 200 feet, depth 23 feet, from the wharves at Mobile to the Gulf. The channel will have to be widened considerably where now narrow in order to afford the projected 100 feet width at bottom with appropriate side slope, and to this purpose it is proposed to apply "the amount that can be profitably expended in fiscal year ending June 30, 1903."

COMMERCIAL STATISTICS.

[Compiled from the records of the Mobile Cotton Exchange.]

Articles.	1901.	1900.	1899.	1898.
	Tons.	Tons.	Tons.	Tons.
Lumber	170,586	212,696	123,098	76,079
Timber	270,585	190,782	164,232	97,765
Cotton	31,262	51,469	65,647	86,550

July 1, 1900, balance unexpended	$511,886.84
June 30, 1901, amount expended during fiscal year	507,775.50
July 1, 1901, balance unexpended	4,111.34
July 1, 1901, outstanding liabilities	275.40
July 1, 1901, balance available	3,835.94

Amount (estimated) required for completion of existing project 1,040,000.00
Amount that can be profitably expended in fiscal year ending June 30, 1903, for works of improvement and for maintenance, in addition to the balance available July 1, 1901 ..... 350,000.00
Submitted in compliance with requirements of sundry civil act of June 4, 1897, and of section 7 of the river and harbor act of 1899.

(See Appendix R 1.)

2. Black Warrior River, Alabama.—The original condition of this river was such as to be practically closed to navigation on account of shoals at and above Tuscaloosa.

The name "Black Warrior" is given to that portion of the Warrior River above the city of Tuscaloosa, Ala.

The original project for improvement of Black Warrior River was approved in 1887, the object being to obtain a channel 6 feet deep, by means of five locks and dams, from Tuscaloosa to Daniels Creek, 13¼ miles, at an estimated cost of $741,670.

During the fiscal year of 1896 three locks were completed and opened to navigation, giving a total lift of 30.3 feet. All locks of the system are to be 52 feet wide, 322 feet between hollow quoins, and 285 feet available length.

River and harbor act of March 3, 1899, provided for the construction of Lock No. 4 on this river, at a cost not to exceed $190,500, and this full amount has been appropriated for the work. Contract was entered into, and the lock is now well under way of construction.

The total amount expended on the improvement to June 30, 1900, was $613,271.44.

July 1, 1900, balance unexpended	$127,302.56
Amount appropriated by sundry civil act approved March 3, 1901	53,676.00
	180,978.56
June 30, 1901, amount expended during fiscal year	49,338.48
July 1, 1901, balance unexpended	131,640.08
July 1, 1901, outstanding liabilities	13,195.96
July 1, 1901, balance available	118,444.12
July 1, 1901, amount covered by uncompleted contracts	106,890.80

(See Appendix R 2.)

3. Operating and care of locks and dams on Black Warrior River, Alabama.—These locks and dams are near Tuscaloosa, Ala., and are known as Locks Nos. 1, 2, and 3. They were finished and opened to commerce in November, 1895, and on July 1, 1896, their operation and care became a charge under the general law of July 5, 1884.

During the fiscal year these locks have been operated and cared for by two lock hands at each lock under the supervision of a lock master. In addition to their operation, much repair work was done on the locks. The total expense during the year for operating and repair was $8,623.76.

The commerce through the locks during the year ending June 30, 1901, amounted to 4,255 tons coal, 1,718 tons lumber, 1,804 tons stone, 845 tons sand, 12 tons corn, 18 tons oats, 10 tons hay, and 487.75 tons general merchandise.

(See Appendix R 3.)

4. Warrior and Tombigbee rivers, Alabama and Mississippi.—(a) *Warrior River, Alabama.*—In its original condition this river was obstructed to such an extent by snags, logs, overhanging trees, etc., as to make navigation at low water impossible, and dangerous during high water. The minimum depth of channel was 1 foot and the minimum width 60 feet.

The original project for the improvement was to deepen the channel by jetty construction and to remove snags and overhanging trees.

In 1897 an estimate of $1,320,000 was submitted for the construction of 6 locks and dams on the Warrior River, to give a lift of 60.2 feet, thus affording a channel of 6 feet depth all the year round.

River and harbor act of March 3, 1899, provided for building 3 of these 6 locks and dams at a cost not to exceed $660,000. Contract for building the 3 locks was made in February, 1900, but the season was so unfavorable, on account of high water and sickness, as to greatly retard the work. However, cofferdams with earth levees have been built to heights of from 8 to 20 feet around the lock pits, and most of the excavation has been done; much of the material has been prepared and delivered at the lock sites, and things are in readiness to push the work to the utmost during the season of 1901.

Under an allottment of $4,000 from emergency appropriation of June 6, 1900, made July 9, 1900, all the most dangerous and troublesome obstructions were removed from Warrior River channel, but it will require the expenditure of about $15,000 annually to maintain this channel.

The total amount expended on the improvement to June 30, 1900, was $256,376.13.

COMMERCIAL STATISTICS.

Articles.	1901.	1900.	1899.
	Tons.	Tons.	Tons.
Cotton	1,725	2,300	2,500
Grain	5,000	3,500	3,000
Iron	32	30	21
Logs and timber	62,400	74,000	
General merchandise	3,550	3,500	2,400
Total	72,707	83,330	7,921

RIVER AND HARBOR IMPROVEMENTS. 367

July 1, 1900, balance unexpended....................................	[1]$393,623.87
Amount appropriated by sundry civil act approved March 3, 1901....	240,000.00
Amount allotted from appropriation contained in emergency river and harbor act approved June 6, 1900.................................	4,000.00
	637,623.87
June 30, 1901, amount expended during fiscal year........ $160,305.56	
Unexpended balance of allotment from emergency act turned back into Treasury............................. 308.76	
	160,614.32
July 1, 1901, balance unexpended.................................	477,009.55
July 1, 1901, outstanding liabilities................................	28,007.98
July 1, 1901, balance available.....................................	449,001.57
July 1, 1901, amount covered by uncompleted contracts..............	286,165.12
Amount that can be profitably expended in fiscal year ending June 30, 1903, for maintenance of improvement, in addition to the balance available July 1, 1901... Submitted in compliance with requirements of sundry civil act of June 4, 1897, and of section 7 of the river and harbor act of 1899.	20,000.00

(b) *Tombigbee River from its mouth to Demopolis, Ala.*—The original condition of the navigable channel of this portion of the river was such as to admit of steamboat navigation during only about six or eight months of the year, or during high water. The minimum width of the channel was about 100 feet and the minimum depth 2 feet. The project of 1879 was to afford a channel of navigable width and 4 feet deep at ordinary low water from the mouth up to Demopolis, Ala., by removal of snags, logs, and overhanging trees and the improvement of the worst bars.

The present project was adopted in 1890 and slightly modified in 1897, and is to secure a channel 6 feet deep at low water by removal of logs, snags, and trees and the construction of bank revetment and locks and dams, at an estimated cost of $600,000. There are to be three locks, each 52 feet wide, 322 feet long (285 feet available length), and with a total lift of 31 feet.

The total amount expended on this improvement to June 30, 1900, was $377,739.44, of which about $50,000 was for maintenance.

Work during the past fiscal year has been confined to care and preservation of public property with money regularly appropriated for this improvement, and to the removal of the most dangerous obstructions with an allotment of $4,000 made July 9, 1900, from the emergency act of June 6, 1900. There were not sufficient funds available to attempt any further work on lock (No. 1) at McGrews Shoals, which is complete with the exception of about 50 feet of the floor, one-third of filling behind bank wall, and putting in gates and valves. The dam is yet to be constructed, and considerable work should be done to protect banks of river above the lock.

With such funds as may be provided it is proposed to preserve the channel, to complete lock at McGrews Shoals, make survey for sites of the other two locks above on the Tombigbee River, and progress, as far as funds will permit, in the construction of lock next above that one at McGrews Shoals.

---
[1] Erroneously reported as $393,623.67 in annual report for 1900.

COMMERCIAL STATISTICS.

Articles.	1901.	1900.	1899.
	Tons.	Tons.	Tons.
Cotton	12,375	16,500	17,250
Grain	5,000	3,500	8,000
Iron	32	30	21
Logs and timber	92,076	75,920	
General merchandise	35,500	35,000	30,240
Total	144,983	130,950	50,511

July 1, 1900, balance unexpended		$2,260.56
Amount allotted from appropriation contained in emergency river and harbor act approved June 6, 1900		4,000.00
		6,260.56
June 30, 1901, amount expended during fiscal year	$5,683.90	
Unexpended balance of allotment from emergency act turned back into the Treasury	19.19	
		5,703.09
July 1, 1901, balance unexpended		557.47
July 1, 1901, outstanding liabilities		282.35
July 1, 1901, balance available		275.12

{ Amount (estimated) required for completion of existing project....... Indefinite.
Amount that can be profitably expended in fiscal year ending June 30, 1903, for works of improvement and for maintenance, in addition to the balance available July 1, 1901 .... 200,000.00
Submitted in compliance with requirements of sundry civil act of June 4, 1897, and of section 7 of the river and harbor act of 1899.

(c) *Tombigbee River from Demopolis, Ala., to Columbus, Miss.*—The original condition of this section of river was such as to admit of navigation only during high water. The minimum width of the channel was 70 feet and the minimum depth was 2 feet, and it was obstructed by snags, logs, overhanging trees, etc.

Up to 1890 all appropriations were made general for the Tombigbee River, and the project for this section was for a 3-foot channel at mean low water, to be secured by removal of obstructions and overhanging trees. By the river and harbor act of September 19, 1890, Congress adopted a channel depth of 6 feet at low water, from Demopolis to Columbus. To secure such a channel the building of locks and dams is necessary, but no provision has yet been made by Congress for inaugurating such work. The fall in the river from Columbus to Demopolis is 107.8 feet.

The total amount expended on the improvement to June 30, 1900, was $130,606.10. The condition of the river at that date would permit of its navigation by light-draft boats on a slight rise above ordinary low water, though the channel was more or less obstructed by snags and slip-ins.

This part of Tombigbee River was worked over and the accumulation of obstructions removed during the fiscal year. The river can now be navigated on a slight rise above ordinary low water.

RIVER AND HARBOR IMPROVEMENTS. 869

COMMERCIAL STATISTICS.

Articles.	1901.	1900.	1899.
	Tons.	Tons.	Tons.
Cotton	2,000	750	813
Cotton seed	2,000	225	200
General merchandise	1,500	750	600
Total	5,500	1,725	1,613

July 1, 1900, balance unexpended	$29,393.90
June 30, 1901, amount expended during fiscal year	13,286.63
July 1, 1901, balance unexpended	16,107.27
July 1, 1901, outstanding liabilities	285.00
July 1, 1901, balance available	15,822.27
Amount that can be profitably expended in fiscal year ending June 30, 1903, for maintenance of improvement, in addition to the balance available July 1, 1901. Submitted in compliance with requirements of sundry civil act of June 4, 1897, and of section 7 of the river and harbor act of 1899.	15,000.00

(d) *Tombigbee River from Fulton to Columbus, Miss.*—The original condition of this section of river was such that navigation was impossible except during very high water. The minimum width of the channel was 50 feet and the minimum depth 1 foot, and it was much obstructed by logs, snags, and overhanging trees.

The project of 1873 was to obtain a good high-water channel at an estimated cost of $35,000, and was completed in 1882 at a cost of $27,293.65. Work done since has been in preservation.

The first specific appropriation for this portion of the river was made in 1892, and since then $21,516.85 was expended to June 30, 1900, making the total expenditures to that date $48,810.50. Though there were quite a number of obstructions in the river at that time, its condition would permit of the free passage of large rafts of logs and timber during high water.

During the past fiscal year about half of this stretch of river was worked over and obstructions removed therefrom, leaving the river navigable during high water according to the project.

COMMERCIAL STATISTICS.

Articles.	1901.
	Tons.
Pine and cypress timber	19,083
Hard-wood timber	34,592
Total	53,675

July 1, 1900, balance unexpended	$1,483.15
June 30, 1901, amount expended during fiscal year	1,272.27
July 1, 1901, balance unexpended	210.88
July 1, 1901, outstanding liabilities	175.00
July 1, 1901, balance available	35.88
Amount that can be profitably expended in fiscal year ending June 30, 1903, for maintenance of improvement, in addition to the balance available July 1, 1901. Submitted in compliance with requirements of sundry civil act of June 4, 1897, and of section 7 of the river and harbor act of 1899.	3,000.00

ENG 1901——24

(e) *Tombigbee River from Walkers Bridge to Fulton, Miss.*—The original condition of this part of the river was such that navigation for even small rafts was possible only during high water, and then it was troublesome and dangerous.

The project of 1888 was to obtain a good high-water channel by the removal of snags, logs, and overhanging trees at an estimated cost of $11,000, and was completed in 1891 at a cost of $6,517.18. Work done since has been in maintenance.

The total amount expended on the improvement to June 30, 1900, was $13,940.07. The condition of the river at that date was such that large rafts could be brought down on a 3-foot rise above ordinary low water.

During the past fiscal year no work was done on this improvement, and there are at present many obstructions in the channel which should be removed in order to insure its safety for high-water navigation, as it is much used in bringing down rafts of logs and timber.

July 1, 1900, balance unexpended	$59.93
June 30, 1901, amount expended during fiscal year	2.42
July 1, 1901, balance unexpended	57.51
July 1, 1901, outstanding liabilities	25.00
July 1, 1901, balance available	32.51
Amount that can be profitably expended in fiscal year ending June 30, 1903, for maintenance of improvement, in addition to the balance available July 1, 1901. Submitted in compliance with requirements of sundry civil act of June 4, 1897, and of section 7 of the river and harbor act of 1899.	500.00

(See Appendix R 4.)

5. *Noxubee River, Mississippi.*—The original condition of this river was such that navigation was impossible except by small flats during four or five months of the year. The minimum width of the river was 60 feet and the minimum depth of the channel was 1¼ feet.

The original project, adopted in 1880, was to afford a channel for small river steamers during nine months of the year from the mouth to Macon, Miss., at an estimated cost of $65,245.25. The project was completed in 1889 at a cost of $47,527.52, and all work done since has been in preservation of same.

The total amount expended on the improvement to June 30, 1900, was $61,817.62. The river was then navigable for light-draft boats up to Macon, Miss., the head of navigation, on a 6 to 8 foot stage of water. During the past fiscal year no work was done on this improvement, expenditures being in payment for care and preservation of public property.

The wisdom of doing further work on this river is a question upon which the citizens of the locality are not agreed, petitions having been addressed to the Secretary of War both for and against a discontinuance of the improvement and the abandonment of the river as a commercial highway.

July 1, 1900, balance unexpended	$182.38
June 30, 1901, amount expended during fiscal year	182.38
Amount that can be profitably expended in fiscal year ending June 30, 1903, for maintenance of improvement. Submitted in compliance with requirements of sundry civil act of June 4, 1897, and of section 7 of the river and harbor act of 1899.	2,000.00

(See Appendix R 5.)

6. *Pascagoula River above the mouth of Dog River, Mississippi.*—Before this improvement was commenced the channel through the bar at the mouth of the river had a least depth of 3 feet; from the mouth up 10 miles the river was navigable for vessels of 6½ feet draft; thence up to the junction of Leaf and Chickasahay rivers navigation was impossible except during high water. The minimum width of channel was 60 feet and the minimum depth 1 foot, but it was much obstructed by logs and snags.

Under various projects this river was improved by removing obstructions from the junction of the Leaf and Chickasahay rivers, which form the Pascagoula River, down to Mosspoint, a few miles above the mouth; from Mosspoint to the mouth a channel 12 feet deep and 80 feet wide was dredged and a dam built at Lowery Island; from the mouth across the bar to the 12-foot contour line in Mississippi Sound a channel was excavated to a depth of 9 feet and partially completed to a depth of 12 feet.

The river and harbor act of March 3, 1899, made a separate appropriation for improvement of Pascagoula River from the mouth of Dog River to the 12-foot contour line in Mississippi Sound, about 15 miles, no provision being made for snagging, etc., in the river above. Quite a number of obstructions and overhanging trees have accumulated since last work was done, and it is very necessary to the further navigation of the river that these be removed.

The total amount expended on this improvement to June 30, 1900, was $200,500, of which about $21,000 only has been applied to removing obstructions and overhanging trees. No work of this kind has been done since 1897 and there are no funds available for such.

For commercial statistics see "Pascagoula River and Horn Island Harbor, Mississippi."

{ Amount that can be profitably expended in fiscal year ending June 30, 1903, for maintenance of improvement........................... $4,000.00
Submitted in compliance with requirements of sundry civil act of June 4, 1897, and of section 7 of the river and harbor act of 1899.

(See Appendix R 6.)

7. *Pascagoula River and Horn Island Harbor, Mississippi.*—Originally the anchorage at Horn Island Harbor had a depth of about 21 feet except over the shoals known as the "Bulkhead" and the "Neck," where the depth ranged between 17.5 and 19.7 feet. The Pascagoula River from 3 miles above the mouth of Dog River to the 12-foot contour in Mississippi Sound had a depth of 12 feet above Scranton except near Dog Island, near Lowrey Island, and at the mouth of Belle Fontaine Bayou. Below Scranton there was 12 feet depth in places, but only for narrow widths.

The project adopted in 1899 was to afford a 12-foot channel from 3 miles above the mouth of Dog River to the 12-foot contour in Mississippi Sound, 150 feet wide above railroad bridge at Scranton, Miss., and 300 feet wide below said bridge, and to dredge a channel 500 feet wide to a depth of 20 feet over the shoals in Horn Island anchorage.

At the beginning of the present fiscal year the work above the railroad bridge at Scranton, Miss., had been completed, a channel varying from 50 to 200 feet in width, though not continuous, had been dredged for a distance of about 21,000 feet in Pascagoula River below the railroad bridge, and a channel 150 feet wide and 4,000 feet long had been excavated to a depth of 20 feet over the "Bulkhead" in Horn Island Harbor.

During the past fiscal year Pascagoula River channel was completed to the desired width of 300 feet through reaches 1 to 7, 9,600 feet, widening the eighth and last reach to 200 feet throughout its length of 18,400 feet, and leaving but 100 feet width of this last reach to complete the river work; all dredged to a depth of 12 feet. The channel of 150 feet width in Horn Island Harbor was widened to 400 feet throughout its 4,000 feet length.

The total amount expended on this work to June 30, 1900, was $43,764.61.

COMMERCIAL STATISTICS.

[Furnished by the Pascagoula Commercial Club, Scranton, Miss.]

Articles.	1901.		1900.	
	Tons.	Value.	Tons.	Value.
Lumber and timber	409,754	$2,015,000	214,500	$1,608,000
Creosoted lumber, timber, and piles	6,780	120,000	7,500	150,000
Rosin	9,625	165,000	8,750	150,000
Turpentine	4,000	220,000	8,750	225,000
Charcoal	8,000	60,000	10,000	50,000
Fish	150	10,000	150	10,000
Oysters	1,788	30,000	1,688	30,000
Wool	30	9,000	25	10,000
Total	440,127	2,629,000	246,863	2,233,000

July 1, 1900, balance unexpended $273,835.39
June 30, 1901, amount expended during fiscal year 144,942.78

July 1, 1901, balance unexpended 128,892.61
July 1, 1901, outstanding liabilities 25,561.15

July 1, 1901, balance available 103,331.46

July 1, 1901, amount covered by uncompleted contracts 103,331.46

(See Appendix R 7.)

8. *Chickasahay River, Mississippi.*—The original condition of this river was such that only small rafts could be brought down during high water, and it was troublesome and dangerous for them even then. The minimum width of the channel was 50 feet and the minimum depth 6 inches, and it was filled with logs and snags.

The original project—that of 1890—was to obtain a high-water channel from the mouth up to Shubuta, Miss., 130 miles, by removal of obstructions and overhanging trees. The river and harbor act of June 3, 1896, modified the project and limited the improvement to that part of the river from the mouth up to railroad bridge near Bucatunna, Miss., 75 miles.

The total amount expended on this improvement to June 30, 1900, was $19,400.07, of which $7,000.34 was in preservation of improvement, and at that time there was a good high-water channel which could be navigated on a 4-foot rise up to Bucatunna, Miss., as projected. The work of the past year has been limited to the care and preservation of public property, as there were no funds available for work in the river. Naturally quite a number of logs, snags, and other obstructions have accumulated, and it will be necessary to remove these in order to maintain the improvement.

COMMERCIAL STATISTICS.

[Approximate.]

Articles.	1901.	1900.	1899.
	Tons.	Tons.	Tons.
Logs and timber	121,152	100,960	90,960
Rosin	1,104	920	700
Turpentine	360	300	250
General merchandise	60	50	......
Staves	990	900	1,125
Total	123,666	103,130	93,035

July 1, 1900, balance unexpended	$99.93
June 30, 1901, amount expended during fiscal year	50.00
July 1, 1901, balance unexpended	49.93
Amount that can be profitably expended in fiscal year ending June 30, 1903, for maintenance of improvement, in addition to the balance unexpended July 1, 1901. Submitted in compliance with requirements of sundry civil act of June 4, 1897, and of section 7 of the river and harbor act of 1899.	1,500.00

(See Appendix R 8.)

9. *Leaf River, Mississippi.*—Originally it was impracticable to navigate this river on account of the logs, snags, and overhanging trees that obstructed the channel. The minimum width of the river was 100 feet and the minimum depth 2½ feet.

The original project was adopted in 1890, and was to afford a channel for high-water navigation from Bowie Creek to the river's mouth, 75 miles, by removal of obstructions and overhanging trees. This project was completed in 1897. Work done since has been for maintenance.

The total amount expended on the improvement to June 30, 1900, was $16,743.28, of which $5,724.24 was in maintenance. The condition of the river then was such as to permit of its navigation by light-draft boats and rafts of logs and timbers on a slight rise above low water. No work was done in the way of removing obstructions during the past season, as there were not sufficient funds available, and the condition of the improvement at this time is not so good as it might be in consequence.

COMMERCIAL STATISTICS.

[Approximate.]

Articles.	1901.	1900.	1899.
	Tons.	Tons.	Tons.
Logs and timber	85,200	71,000	66,000
Rosin	3,450	2,875	2,835
Turpentine	3,744	3,120	2,025
General merchandise	87	72	......
Total	92,481	77,067	70,860

July 1, 1900, balance unexpended	$756.72
June 30, 1901, amount expended during fiscal year	168.50
July 1, 1901, balance unexpended	588.22
July 1, 1901, outstanding liabilities	50.00
July 1, 1901, balance available	538.22

{ Amount that can be profitably expended in fiscal year ending June 30, 1903, for maintenance of improvement, in addition to the balance available July 1, 1901... 2,000.00
Submitted in compliance with requirements of sundry civil act of June 4, 1897, and of section 7 of the river and harbor act of 1899. }

(See Appendix R 9.)

10. Channel from Gulfport to Ship Island Harbor, Mississippi.—By the river and harbor act approved March 3, 1899, contract was authorized for dredging a channel from Ship Island Harbor to Gulfport, Miss., and an anchorage basin at the end of channel next to the shore, at a cost not to exceed $150,000; and for the maintenance of this channel and basin for a term of five years after its completion for the sum of $10,000 annually.

This work was first advertised in 1899, but no bids for its performance were then received. It was again advertised in January, 1901, one bid being received and accepted from Spencer S. Bullis, of Gulfport, Miss. Contract was entered into with Mr. Bullis, by the terms of which he agreed to dredge a channel 300 feet wide and 19 feet deep at mean low water from the anchorage at Ship Island Harbor to Gulfport, Miss., and an anchorage basin of similar depth and not less than 2,640 feet by 1,320 feet in area at the end of channel next to the shore, for $150,000, work to be completed within two years from date of commencement; and to maintain said channel and basin for the term of five years from the date of its completion for the sum of $10,000 annually, subject to a penalty of $30 per day for each and every day said channel and anchorage basin is not maintained in accordance with the terms of contract. Work was commenced on April 16, 1901, and is in progress at end of fiscal year.

No money has yet been appropriated by Congress to pay for this work.

Under an allotment made April 20, 1901, of $1,000 from the permanent-indefinite appropriation made by section 4 of the river and harbor act of July 5, 1884, this work has been surveyed and laid out, and the dumping of the material, etc., is being supervised by inspectors appointed by this office.

{ Amount that can be profitably expended in fiscal year ending June 30, 1903...$150,000.00
Submitted in compliance with requirements of sundry civil act of June 4, 1897. }

(See Appendix R 10.)

11. Ship Island Pass, Mississippi.—Originally the depth of water over the outer bar at Ship Island Pass was sufficient for vessels drawing 20 to 21 feet. Under an act of Congress approved June 16, 1898, a survey was made to determine a plan and estimate for a channel 26 feet deep through this bar. (See House Doc. No. 120, Fifty-fifth Congress, third session; also Annual Report of the Chief of Engineers for 1899, p. 1787.)

By the river and harbor act of March 3, 1899, an appropriation of $40,000 was made for this improvement. With these funds a channel 26 feet deep was dredged through the bar at Ship Island Pass. A survey of this channel was made in May, 1901, and shows that the channel has shoaled slightly in one place to a depth of 25.6 feet, and has deepened in another. There is an available channel for vessels drawing 26 feet.

The total amount expended on the improvement to June 30, 1900, was $39,397.14.

July 1, 1900, balance unexpended		$602.86
June 30, 1901, amount expended during fiscal year	$286.98	
Amount turned back into the Treasury	304.12	
		591.10
July 1, 1901, balance unexpended		11.76
July 1, 1901, outstanding liabilities		11.76

(See Appendix R 11.)

12. Mouth of Pearl River, Mississippi.—The depth of water over the channel way leading from the mouth of Pearl River to deep water in Mississippi Sound was about 7 feet.

The original project of 1886 was for a channel 100 feet wide and 12 feet deep.

By river and harbor act of March 3, 1899, an appropriation of $18,199.80 was made to dredge a channel 300 feet wide and 9 feet deep. Under this appropriation a contract was entered into and dredging was commenced November 13, 1899, and continued to February 5, 1900, completing the channel to a width of 300 feet with a depth of 9 feet at mean low water, as projected.

A survey was made in May, 1901, by which it was ascertained that with the exception of the lower part of the channel, which has shoaled about two-tenths of a foot, the depth of 9 feet has been maintained.

The amount expended on this improvement to June 30, 1900, was $27,713.08.

For commercial statistics, see "Pearl River below Rockport, Miss."

July 1, 1900, balance unexpended		$486.72
June 30, 1901, amount expended during fiscal year	$140.84	
Amount turned back into the Treasury	345.88	
		486.72

(See Appendix R 12.)

13. Pearl River below Rockport, Miss.—This work was formerly reported on under the title of "Pearl River below Jackson." An act of Congress approved April 21, 1900, authorized the construction of a bridge across Pearl River at Rockport without a draw, thus virtually making Rockport, 246 miles from the mouth of the river and 67 miles below Jackson, the head of navigation for this section of the river. The river and harbor acts of June 3, 1896, and March 3, 1899, limited the improvement to that part of the river between the head of Holmes Bayou and Monticello, Miss. Prior to improvement the condition of this river was such as to permit of no navigation except during high water, and then it was difficult and dangerous.

The first project was adopted in 1880, being for a 5-foot channel at low water, but this depth was found impracticable, and the project was modified in 1885 to provide for a 2-foot channel at low water.

The total amount expended on the improvement to June 30, 1900, was $153,810.44, of which about $50,000 was in preservation. The condition of the river at that date would permit of its navigation from the mouth to Monticello, 211¾ miles by boats of about 3 feet draft, at mean low water. The same conditions now exist, no work except the care of plant having been permissible during the year.

Of recent years the improvement of this part of Pearl River has been limited to the 160 miles between the head of Holmes Bayou and Monticello. The 51 miles of river from the head of Holmes Bayou to the mouth of West Pearl River is much more in need of improvement, especially the channel through Holmes Bayou, which is quite narrow and much obstructed, and this part of the channel must necessarily be used by most of the craft navigating the river above.

COMMERCIAL STATISTICS.

Articles.	1901.	1900.	1899.
	Tons.	Tons.	Tons.
Logs, pine	202,944	28,896	26,074
Timber	24,358		
Lumber	28,563	46,200	28,634
Turpentine, rosin, and general merchandise	2,835	200	
Total	258,700	75,296	54,708

July 1, 1900, balance unexpended	$1,314.56
June 30, 1901, amount expended during fiscal year	665.96
July 1, 1901, balance unexpended	648.60
July 1, 1901, outstanding liabilities	50.00
July 1, 1901, balance available	598.60

Amount (estimated) required for completion of existing project 33,000.00
Amount that can be profitably expended in fiscal year ending June 30, 1903, for works of improvement and for maintenance, in addition to the balance available July 1, 1901 .... 10,000.00
Submitted in compliance with requirements of sundry civil act of June 4, 1897, and of section 7 of the river and harbor act of 1899.

(See Appendix R 13.)

14. Pearl River between Carthage and Jackson, Miss.—The original condition of this part of the river was such as to render navigation impossible except during high water, and even then it was difficult and dangerous. The minimum width of the river was 100 feet, and of the channel 40 feet; the minimum depth was about 1 foot.

The project for this work provides for securing and maintaining a channel 2 feet deep at low water.

The total amount expended on the improvement to June 30, 1900, was $38,392.25, of which $12,377.27 was in maintenance of work, and at that time the 2-foot channel had been maintained in accordance with the project. Some obstructions have accumulated since the last work was done, but the river is still navigable for light-draft boats on a slight rise above mean low water.

No commercial statistics were obtainable.

July 1, 1900, balance unexpended	$157.75
June 30, 1901, amount expended during fiscal year	30.00
July 1, 1901, balance unexpended	127.75

{ Amount that can be profitably expended in fiscal year ending June 30, 1903, for maintenance of improvement, in addition to the balance unexpended July 1, 1901... 1,500.00
Submitted in compliance with requirements of sundry civil act of June 4, 1897, and of section 7 of the river and harbor act of 1899.

(See Appendix R 14.)

15. Pearl River between Edinburg and Carthage, Miss.—The original condition of this portion of the river was such that navigation at low water was impossible and even during high water difficult and dangerous. The minimum width of the channel was 30 feet and the minimum depth of water about 3 inches.

The original project for this work was adopted in 1884, and was to afford a high-water channel from Edinburg to Carthage, about 25 miles, during six or eight months of the year, and to maintain same at an annual cost of $500 by removal of obstructions and overhanging trees.

The total amount expended here to June 30, 1900, was $17,082.09, of which $11,225.01 was in preservation of improvement. The highwater channel had been maintained, though the river was somewhat obstructed by logs, snags, etc., as the funds appropriated in 1899 had not been sufficient to remove all the accumulation of two years. Nothing was done during the past fiscal year, there being no money available for the work.

There is considerable rafting of timber done on this part of Pearl River, but statistics as to quantities, etc., were not obtainable.

July 1, 1900, balance unexpended	$167.91
June 30, 1901, amount expended during fiscal year	167.91

{ Amount that can be profitably expended in fiscal year ending June 30, 1903, for maintenance of improvement............................ 500.00
Submitted in compliance with requirements of sundry civil act of June 4, 1897, and of section 7 of the river and harbor act of 1899.

(See Appendix R 15.)

16. Bogue Chitto, Louisiana.—The original condition of this stream rendered navigation impossible except during very high water, owing to shoals and bars at the mouth and snags, logs, and overhanging trees obstructing the channel above. The minimum width of the channel was 80 feet and the minimum depth 3 feet.

The project adopted in 1890 provided for securing a clear 3-foot channel from the mouth up to Alford's bridge, near Summit, Miss., 190 miles, by closing the west mouth of the river, several run-out bayous, and removing obstructions and overhanging trees, at an estimated cost of $55,000. The improvement has never been carried farther up than Cross River, 80 miles above the mouth, as the funds appropriated have been in small amounts, and part of them had to be applied to maintenance.

The total amount expended on the improvement to June 30, 1900, was $24,505.30, and the condition of the river at that time was such that it could be navigated from the mouth up to Cross River by lightdraft boats, which is about its condition now.

378   REPORT OF THE CHIEF OF ENGINEERS, U. S. ARMY.

COMMERCIAL STATISTICS.

Articles.	1901.	1900.	1899.
	Tons.	Tons.	Tons.
Logs and timber, pine and cypress	17,954	23,000	18,000
Lumber	39,966		
Total	57,920	23,000	18,000

July 1, 1900, balance unexpended $494.70
June 30, 1901, amount expended during fiscal year 494.70

{ Amount (estimated) required for completion of existing project....... 30,000.00
Amount that can be profitably expended in fiscal year ending June 30,
1903, for works of improvement and for maintenance................. 7,500.00
Submitted in compliance with requirements of sundry civil act of June
4, 1897, and of section 7 of the river and harbor act of 1899. }

(See Appendix R 16.)

17. *Removing sunken vessels or craft obstructing or endangering navigation.*—The sunken schooner *Fleet Wing*, being abandoned by its owner, became a dangerous obstruction to the navigation of the Mobile River, Alabama. After advertisement the wreck was entirely removed by George F. Holleman, of Mobile, Ala., under contract dated February 4, 1901, whose bid for the work was $179.50.

(See Appendix R 17.)

EXAMINATIONS AND SURVEYS MADE IN COMPLIANCE WITH EMERGENCY RIVER AND HARBOR ACT APPROVED JUNE 6, 1900.

Preliminary examinations and surveys of the following localities were made by the local engineer, and reports thereon submitted through the division engineer:

1. *Preliminary examination and survey of Mobile Harbor, Alabama, with a view to obtaining channels of a width of 300 feet at the bottom across the bar below Fort Morgan, with appropriate side slopes, and with mean depths of 25 and 30 feet, respectively.*—Major Rossell submitted reports dated June 25 and December 1, 1900, respectively, with estimates as follows:

For a 25-foot channel.. $13,750
For a 30-foot channel.. 91,750

The reports were transmitted to Congress and printed in House Doc. No. 219, Fifty-sixth Congress, second session. (See also Appendix R 18.)

2. *Preliminary examination and survey of Warrior and Tombigbee rivers, Alabama, with a view to the construction of locks and dams Nos. 1, 2, and 3, below Tuscaloosa.*—Major Rossell submitted reports dated June 25 and December 4, 1900, respectively. The estimated cost of the improvement is $760,000. The reports were transmitted to Congress and printed in House Doc. No. 178, Fifty-sixth Congress, second session. (See also Appendix R 19.)

RIVER AND HARBOR IMPROVEMENTS. 379

INSPECTION OF THE IMPROVEMENT OF THE SOUTH PASS OF THE MISSISSIPPI RIVER.

The inspecting officer during the year was Lieut. Col. H. M. Adams, Corps of Engineers.

The act of Congress of March 3, 1875, amended by acts of June 19, 1878, and March 3, 1879, made provision for the construction, by James B. Eads or his representatives, of jetties and other works in South Pass of the Mississippi River, to secure and maintain a channel 26 feet in depth through the pass, and through the jetties at the mouth of the pass a channel "26 feet in depth, not less than 200 feet in width at the bottom, and having through it a central depth of 30 feet without regard to width." An annual payment of $100,000 was provided for the maintenance of such a channel for twenty years after first obtaining it by the works built. The required channels were secured in July, 1879.

The period of twenty years is exclusive of all periods of time during which the required channel was not maintained. This period expired on January 28, 1901, and the contract terminated on that date.

The object of the examination and survey of South Pass was to determine whether the channel was maintained as required by law, and to enable an engineer officer to issue the certificates for the quarterly payments, and "such other information as the Secretary of War may direct." The expenses of this work were provided for by a permanent appropriation made by act of August 11, 1888.

The required channel was maintained by the representatives of James B. Eads during the year throughout South Pass and through the jetties until January 28, 1901, on which date the contract terminated.

On January 29, 1901, the United States took charge of the improvement and its maintenance. (See report herewith on Maintenance of South Pass channel, Mississippi River, p. 385).

(See Appendix S.)

IMPROVEMENT OF RIVERS AND HARBORS IN SOUTHERN LOUISIANA AND EASTERN TEXAS, AND OF HOMOCHITTO RIVER, MISSISSIPPI.

This district was in the charge of Lieut. Col. H. M. Adams, Corps of Engineers, to June 8, 1901, with Lieut. E. M. Adams, Corps of Engineers, under his immediate orders since September 17, 1900, and in the temporary charge of Lieutenant Adams since June 8, 1901. Division Engineer, Col. Henry M. Robert, Corps of Engineers (now brigadier-general, Chief of Engineers, United States Army, retired), to May 2, 1901.

1. *Chefuncte River and Bogue Falia, Louisiana.*—Prior to improvement: *Chefuncte River;* a bar, on which depth of water was 4½ feet, obstructed the mouth of the river; from the mouth up to a point of junction with Bogue Falia, 10 miles above, the river was from 300 to 800 feet wide and 15 feet deep, navigable for steamers and sailing vessels, but obstructed by snags and overhanging trees; above this point, not navigable. *Bogue Falia;* navigable for small steamers from point of junction with Chefuncte up to Grants Landing, 4 miles above, for sailing vessels drawing 5 feet, to Covington 2 miles farther, but obstructed by snags and overhanging trees; beyond Covington, not navigable.

The original project, adopted in 1880, provided for dredging through the bar at the mouth of the Chefuncte River, and for removal of all obstructions between the mouth of the river and Covington, on Bogue Falia; estimated cost, $5,460. This project was modified in 1884 to provide for building a breakwater to protect the channel across the bar; estimated cost, $1,500. The work of maintenance was commenced in 1892 under project approved August 10, 1892.

Under the projects described the work of improvement and maintenance has been carried on since 1880. The breakwater was constructed in 1884.

Amount expended up to June 30, 1900, $10,355.02, of which $3,855.02 was for maintenance. On that date there existed, from Lake Pontchartrain to Covington, a channel sufficient for the commerce of the locality. During the fiscal year ending June 30, 1901, the work was confined to the removal of snags and logs from the existing channel. Sixteen miles was cleared; the improvement is not permanent as obstructions continue to form. The entire distance is open to vessels drawing 5 feet.

Comparative statement of receipts and shipments for ten years.

Year ending May 31—	Tons.	Change in tonnage from previous year.	
		Increase.	Decrease.
1892	50,054	4,533	
1893	30,284		19,770
1894	242,464	212,180	
1895	49,778		192,686
1896	67,680	17,902	
1897	110,034	42,354	
1898	99,505		10,529
1899	97,789		1,716
Calendar year 1899	156,500	58,711	
Calendar year 1900	86,856		69,644

July 1, 1900, balance unexpended	$144.98
June 30, 1901, amount expended during fiscal year	104.25
July 1, 1901, balance unexpended	40.73
Amount that can be profitably expended in fiscal year ending June 30, 1903, for maintenance of improvement, in addition to the balance unexpended July 1, 1901	1,000.00

Submitted in compliance with requirements of sundry civil act of June 4, 1897, and of section 7 of the river and harbor act of 1899.

(See Appendix T 1.)

2. *Tickfaw River and its tributaries, Louisiana.*—Prior to improvement these streams—the Tickfaw, Blood, Natalbany, and Ponchatoula—offered a 9-foot channel, navigable for steamers and schooners for an aggregate length of 38 miles; the channel was obstructed by snags, logs, and overhanging trees.

The original project, adopted in 1881, provided for removal of snags, logs, and similar obstructions so far as appropriations would permit; estimated cost, $10,230. The work of maintenance was commenced in 1892, under project approved August 10, 1892. Under these projects the work has been carried on since 1881. In 1896 it became necessary to remove the water hyacinths from the mouth of the Tickfaw, and in 1899 to clear away bar which had formed in the same locality. About 30 miles of the river and tributaries has been improved.

Amount expended up to June 30, 1900, was $11,914.30, of which $3,914.30 was for maintenance. On that date the streams were in fair condition, except for the hyacinths, which accumulate very rapidly. The Tickfaw had a navigable depth of 6 feet for 30 miles from its mouth; the Natalbany had a depth of 6 feet for 12 miles from its mouth; the Blood and Ponchatoula rivers were used principally for floating logs.

During the fiscal year ending June 30, 1901, no work was done in the improvement of these streams. The improvement is not permanent; snags, logs, and hyacinths continue to accumulate. The channels are available for vessels drawing 6 feet.

Comparative statement of receipts and shipments for nine years.

Year ending May 31—	Tons.	Change in tonnage from previous year.	
		Increase.	Decrease.
1893	13,994	2,587	
1894	40,003	26,009	
1895	23,384		16,619
1896	72,851	49,467	
1897	58,115		14,736
1898	75,579	17,464	
1899	52,961		22,618
Calendar year 1899	79,300	26,339	
Calendar year 1900	55,540		23,760

July 1, 1900, balance unexpended	$85.70
June 30, 1901, amount expended during fiscal year	65.51
July 1, 1901, balance unexpended	20.19

Amount that can be profitably expended in fiscal year ending June 30, 1903, for maintenance of improvement, in addition to the balance unexpended July 1, 1901 .... 1,000.00
Submitted in compliance with requirements of sundry civil act of June 4, 1897, and of section 7 of the river and harbor act of 1899.

(See Appendix T 2.)

3. *Amite River and Bayou Manchac, Louisiana.*—Prior to improvement the Amite River was navigable for small steamers for a distance of 45 miles from its mouth; Bayou Manchac for a distance of about 10 miles. Both streams were obstructed by snags and overhanging trees.

The original project, adopted in 1880, provided for clearing the obstructions from the Amite above Bayou Manchac, so as to obtain a channel 5 feet in depth at low water; estimated cost, $23,760. In 1883 this project was modified so as to extend the work from Bayou Manchac to Lake Maurepas at an additional cost of $8,000. In 1888 Congress added to the project removal of obstructions in Bayou Manchac.

The work of maintenance was commenced in 1892, under project approved August 13, 1892.

Under the projects described the work has been carried on since 1880; Amite River was improved for 42 miles from its mouth and the bar at its mouth removed; Bayou Manchac was improved for a distance of 10 miles from its mouth, and a turning basin made at the upper limit of improvement.

Amount expended up to June 30, 1900, was $33,584.95, of which $8,784.95 was for maintenance. On that date the Amite had a navigable channel 60 feet wide and 5 feet deep for a distance of 42 miles from its mouth; Bayou Manchac was navigable for 10 miles by vessels drawing 5 feet.

During the fiscal year ending June 30, 1901, no work was done toward the improvement of these streams. The improvement is not permanent, as snags accumulate. The channel is available for vessels drawing 5 feet.

Comparative statement of receipts and shipments for ten years.

Year ending May 31—	Tons.	Change in tonnage from previous year.	
		Increase.	Decrease.
1892	18,530	738	
1893	22,099	3,569	
1894	157,902	135,803	
1895	42,983		114,919
1896	55,103	12,120	
1897	49,509		5,594
1898	54,749	5,240	
1899	60,305	5,556	
Calendar year 1899	59,850		455
Calendar year 1900	25,400		34,450

July 1, 1900, balance unexpended	$215.05
June 30, 1901, amount expended during fiscal year	85.18
July 1, 1901, balance unexpended	129.87
Amount that can be profitably expended in fiscal year ending June 30, 1903, for maintenance of improvement, in addition to the balance unexpended July 1, 1901. Submitted in compliance with requirements of sundry civil act of June 4, 1897, and of section 7 of the river and harbor act of 1899.	2,500.00

(See Appendix T 3.)

4. Closing crevasse in Pass a Loutre, Mississippi River.—Pass a Loutre is one of the three outlets of the Mississippi River. The crevasse forms an outlet from Pass a Loutre into an arm of the Gulf known as Garden Island Bay, and was caused by the wearing away of the south bank of that pass at a locality 1¼ miles below Head of Passes.

The ditch where the crevasse first broke was 3 feet wide in 1872, and gradually increased from year to year. In January, 1891, the crevasse began to widen rapidly, but could not be checked on account of high water in the river. In July, 1891, it was 860 feet wide and 25 feet deep. Several attempts were made near this time by the estate of James B. Eads to close the crevasse, but it seemed a hopeless task and was abandoned. On November 18, 1896, the crevasse was 2,230 feet wide, and on February 26, 1897, Congress appropriated $250,000 for the closure.

The project approved July 10, 1897, provided for building a dam 6,650 feet long, in two sections, 1,900 and 4,750 feet long, respectively, forming an angle of 112° at a distance of 3,000 feet below the mouth of the crevasse; the dam to be constructed of Wakefield sheet piling backed with a double row of piles securely braced and bolted to stringers and the sheet piling, using a third row of brace piles where the depth of water exceeded 20 feet.

Under this project a contract for the work was approved December 10, 1897. Work was carried on from December 14, 1897, to January 27, 1898, and from August 5, 1898, to November 13, 1898. On the last-named date the work was considered completed and was accepted. At that time it seemed that the closure would prove a permanent success, notwithstanding the high stage of the river. A severe storm arose that night and on November 14 the dam gave way in two localities and 170 feet of it washed out. From time to time since then the break in the dam has widened, and on June 30, 1901, it was 709 feet, 31 feet being lost within the past year.

On February 17, 1898, Congress allotted $10,000 from this appropriation for the expenses of a survey and report by a Board of Engineer officers upon the practicability of securing a channel of adequate width and of 35 feet depth at mean low water of the Gulf of Mexico throughout Southwest Pass, Mississippi River. The survey was completed in 1898, and report submitted on January 7, 1899. This report is printed in House Doc. No. 142, Fifty-fifth Congress, third session, and in the Annual Report of the Chief of Engineers for 1899, as Appendix U 19.

The amount expended from this appropriation up to June 30, 1900, was $229,991.50, of which $6,723.78 was for the survey of Southwest Pass.

No work toward closing the crevasse was attempted during the past year, the amount available being insufficient for the purpose.

July 1, 1900, balance unexpected	$22,008.50
June 30, 1901, amount expended during fiscal year	3.58
July 1, 1901, balance unexpended	22,004.92

(See Appendix T 4.)

5. Outlet of the Mississippi River.—The river and harbor act of March 3, 1899, appropriated $200,000 for constructing a sill across Pass a Loutre and for constructing and operating two dredges for improving the outlet of the Mississippi River. The act further provided that a continuing contract might be entered into for these improvements, not to exceed $300,000, exclusive of the amount therein appropriated.

The item in the act is as follows:

Improving outlet of the Mississippi River by constructing a sill across Pass a Loutre and by constructing and operating two dredges, two hundred thousand dollars: *Provided,* That a contract or contracts may be entered into by the Secretary of War for such materials and work as may be necessary to carry on such improvements, to be paid for as appropriations may from time to time be made by law, not to exceed in the aggregate three hundred thousand dollars, exclusive of the amount herein appropriated. A board of four engineers shall be appointed by the President, of whom at least two shall be from civil life, who shall prepare and report, as soon as conveniently may be done, a project for securing a navigable channel of suitable width and of thirty-five feet depth at mean low water of the Gulf of Mexico throughout the Southwest Pass of the Mississippi River. Said board of engineers shall submit detailed estimates of the cost of each and every feature of the project, and they shall report especially whether it is necessary to construct inner jetties; and if, in their judgment, inner jetties should be constructed, they shall provide for the location of the same, so as to involve the least cost consistent with the safety and efficiency of the work hereby contemplated. The sum of twenty thousand dollars, or so much thereof as may be necessary, is hereby appropriated to defray the cost of said board and of the preparation of said project.

It not being practicable to construct two hydraulic dredges of sufficient capacity for the desired work within the limit of cost fixed by the above-mentioned law, Congress provided in the emergency river and harbor act of June 6, 1900, as follows:

Outlet of Mississippi River: Section one of the act entitled "An Act making appropriations for the construction, repair, and preservation of certain public works on rivers and harbors, and for other purposes," approved March third, eighteen hundred and ninety-nine, be, and the same is hereby, amended as follows: In the paragraph

384 REPORT OF THE CHIEF OF ENGINEERS, U. S. ARMY.

beginning "Improving outlet of the Mississippi River," strike out the word "two" before the word "dredges" and insert in lieu thereof the words "one or more."

The sundry civil act of June 6, 1900, also contained the following legislation affecting this work, viz:

> The Secretary of War is hereby authorized and empowered, in his discretion, in case any unusual obstruction to navigation in the channel of South Pass, Mississippi River, should occur during the fiscal year nineteen hundred and one, to use any dredges or tug boats of the Mississippi River Commission for the purpose of removing the same. And the sum of twenty-five thousand dollars, or so much thereof as may be necessary, is hereby appropriated, to be expended in the discretion of the Secretary of War in improving or altering such dredge or dredges so as to make the same available for use in said South Pass.

*   *   *   *   *   *   *

> Improving passes of the Mississippi River: For completing improvement by constructing sill across Pass a Loutre and by constructing and operating one or more dredges, three hundred thousand dollars.

On September 23, 1899, the Secretary of War approved a project covering the $200,000 appropriated by the act of March 3, 1899, which provides for the allotment of $50,000 for sill construction and $150,000 for dredges and for the construction of a mattress sill, weighted with stone, across the head of Pass a Loutre.

A project for the expenditure of the appropriation of $300,000, made by the sundry civil act of June 6, 1900, for completing the improvement of the passes of the Mississippi River by constructing a sill across Pass a Loutre, and by constructing and operating one or more dredges, was approved by the Secretary of War July 2, 1900, and provides for an allotment of $125,000 for completion of the sill and $175,000 toward the construction of one dredge.

The sum of $1,153.74 was expended on this work up to June 30, 1900, of which $980.79 was for dredge and $172.95 for sill.

Sill.—Bids for the sill construction were opened on March 7, 1900, and on March 26 the lowest bid, at a total estimated cost of $171,402.65, was accepted. A contract was entered into and the work was commenced July 1, 1900. The work was successfully completed on December 31, 1900, at a total cost of $174,914.06.

Dredge.—Several hydraulic dredges having been provided for by the river and harbor act of March 3, 1899, the whole subject of plans and specifications was placed under the supervision of one officer. Plans and specifications for a seagoing hydraulic dredge, estimated to cost $325,000, have been prepared, and bids have been received. All bids were rejected as being in excess of available funds. The specifications have since been revised and the work has been readvertised.

The Board of Engineers appointed to prepare and report a project for securing a channel of 35 feet depth through Southwest Pass to the Gulf submitted a report thereon January 11, 1900. The report was transmitted to Congress and is printed in House Doc. No. 329, Fifty-sixth Congress, first session, and on pages 2287-2302, annual report for 1900.

July 1, 1900, balance unexpended $498,846.26
June 30, 1901, amount expended during fiscal year 176,930.54

July 1, 1901, balance unexpended 321,915.72
July 1, 1901, outstanding liabilities 353.65

July 1, 1901, balance available 321,562.07

(See Appendix T 5.)

6. *Maintenance of South Pass channel, Mississippi River.*—The act of Congress of March 3, 1875, amended by acts of June 19, 1878, and March 3, 1879, made provision for the construction, by James B. Eads or his representatives, of jetties and other works in South Pass, to secure and maintain a channel 26 feet in depth through the pass, and through the jetties at the mouth of the pass a channel "26 feet in depth, not less than 200 feet in width at the bottom, and having through it a central depth of 30 feet without regard to width." A contract was made for the maintenance of such a channel for a period of twenty years. This contract expired on January 28, 1901, since which date the channel has been maintained under the provisions of the act of June 6, 1900, viz:

In case of the termination of said contract, by virtue of the provisions hereof or by expiration of said contract, the Secretary of War is hereby directed to take charge of said channel, including the jetties, and all auxiliary works connected therewith, and thereafter to maintain with the utmost efficiency said South Pass Channel; and for that purpose he is hereby authorized to draw his warrants from time to time on the Treasurer of the United States, until otherwise provided for by law, for such sums of money as may be necessary, not to exceed in the aggregate for any one year one hundred thousand dollars.

The sundry civil act of June 6, 1900, also contained the following legislation affecting this work, viz:

The Secretary of War is hereby authorized and empowered, in his discretion, in case any unusual obstruction to navigation in the channel of South Pass, Mississippi River, should occur during the fiscal year nineteen hundred and one, to use any dredges or tug boats of the Mississippi River Commission for the purpose of removing the same. And the sum of twenty-five thousand dollars, or so much thereof as may be necessary, is hereby appropriated, to be expended in the discretion of the Secretary of War in improving or altering such dredge or dredges so as to make the same available for use in said South Pass.

The dredge *Beta* was repaired under the direction of the secretary of the Mississippi River Commission and temporarily transferred for this work. She arrived at South Pass January 24, 1901, and began operations February 4, 1901, continuing until June 30, 1901, when she left the pass to be returned to the charge of the Mississippi River Commission. By the use of this plant the channel was maintained with the utmost efficiency during the entire period from January 29 to June 30, 1901, as was determined by frequent surveys and examinations.

The following table gives the depth and width of channel that existed June 30, 1901:

Locality.	Central depth.	Available width of—			Remarks.
		26-foot channel.	28-foot channel.	30-foot channel.	
	Feet.	*Feet.*	*Feet.*	*Feet.*	
Goat Island reach	30.3	243	165	100	9 miles above South Pass light.
Grand Bayou reach	29.2	265	160		5¼ miles above South Pass light.
Upper Base reach	29.4	270	155		1¼ miles above South Pass light.
Port Eads reach	30.9	265	135	86	500 feet above South Pass light to East Point.

The amount expended on this work from January 29 to June 30, 1901, was $42,101.71, including $12,126.84 outstanding liabilities that could not be paid until after June 30. The sum of $1,959.19 was expended from the appropriation made by sundry civil act of June 6,

386   REPORT OF THE CHIEF OF ENGINEERS, U. S. ARMY.

1900, for modifications and repairs to the dredge *Beta* after her arrival at South Pass.

This work should be provided with a suitable dredging plant for which funds are not now available.

For report on inspection of improvement of South Pass up to January 28, 1901, under the Eads contract, see page 379, herewith.

INDEFINITE APPROPRIATION.

Amount appropriated by act of June 6, 1900, for fiscal year 1901	$100,000.00
June 30, 1901, amount expended during fiscal year	$29,974.87
June 30, 1901, outstanding liabilities	12,126.84
June 30, 1901, total cost of operations during fiscal year	42,101.71
June 30, 1901, balance reverting to Treasury	57,898.29

APPROPRIATION FOR ALTERING DREDGES.

April 2, 1901, amount allotted	$7,860.28
June 30, 1901, amount expended since April 2, 1901	1,959.19
June 30, 1901, balance unexpended	5,901.09

(See Appendix T 6.)

7. *Bayou Lafourche, Louisiana.*—Bayou Lafourche is an outlet of the Mississippi River, forming a junction 70 miles above New Orleans. It is about 105 miles long, and flows into the Gulf of Mexico. In its original condition it was obstructed by logs, snags, and overhanging trees. The project of 1879 provided for the removal of such obstructions to improve low-water navigation. Work under this project was carried on until 1885, with appropriations aggregating $30,000.

The project of June 11, 1886, provided for the construction of a lock to connect the bayou with the Mississippi River and for dredging a channel 75 feet wide and 5 feet deep at mean low water of the Gulf, at an estimated cost of $450,000, and $8,000 annually thereafter for maintenance. Work under this project was confined to dredging to maintain low-water navigation, the appropriations at any one time being insufficient to warrant the commencement of the lock, and the exigencies of commerce not permitting a suspension of the dredging.

The project of 1886 was modified on September 23, 1896, and held in abeyance the construction of the lock, restricting operations to dredging to maintain low-water navigation, at an estimated cost of $25,000 per annum.

The project of July 11, 1895, for the expenditure of $40,000 appropriated August 18, 1894, recommended that $30,000 be reserved for the purchase of a dredge whenever it should become advisable to make such purchase.

Dredging operations, under the modified project of 1896, were carried on in 1897 and 1898 from the head of the bayou to about 3 miles below Thibodeaux, improving about 38 miles of channel. This improvement is not permanent, as sand bars form each year after the subsidence of floods in the Mississippi River.

The project of July 11, 1895, so far as the reservation of $30,000 for purchase of a dredge is concerned, was modified on December 7, 1899, to allow the expenditure of $9,000 of this amount in dredging to maintain flatboat navigation during low water. With these funds and the

$7,500 appropriated March 3, 1899, dredging was carried on from August 9, 1899, to January 22, 1900. A number of sand bars and other obstructions were removed, and a depth of 3 feet during low water was secured from the head of the bayou at Donaldsonville to a point 8 miles below.

The amount expended on this work up to June 30, 1900, was $230,591.71.

More obstructions having formed since last dredging was done, the project of July 11, 1895, was further modified on May 11, 1900, to allow the expenditure of funds remaining to the credit of this appropriation in dredging during the low-water season. Dredging was carried on from July 25, 1900, to December 8, 1900. Two wrecks, 71 snags, and 91,683 cubic yards of material were removed over a distance of 5¼ miles, maintaining a channel 60 feet wide and 3 feet deep during low-water season of 1900. Dredging was commenced again on June 25, 1901, to maintain the channel during the low-water season of 1901.

The conditions existing in the bayou at this time are the same that prevailed on June 30, 1900. Steamboats ply the stream for about eight months of each year, but during the remaining months the commerce is carried by flatboats from the Mississippi River. The width of the bayou at low water is about 60 feet; the navigable depth is 18 inches.

Comparative statement of receipts and shipments for ten years.

	Tons.	Value.	Change in tonnage from previous year. Increase.	Decrease.
Year ending May 31—				
1892	171,885	$5,660,662		45,388
1893	212,476	7,422,285	40,591	
1894	273,686	8,842,942	61,210	
1895	263,607	9,224,554		10,079
1896	229,891	5,629,237		33,716
1897	217,292	4,988,875		12,599
1898	269,398	7,367,783	52,106	
1899	206,516	6,553,864		62,882
Calendar year—				
1899	157,258	5,436,250		49,258
1900	210,315	14,936,859	53,057	

July 1, 1900, balance unexpended $21,908.29
June 30, 1901, amount expended during fiscal year 9,707.40

July 1, 1901, balance unexpended 12,200.89
July 1, 1901, outstanding liabilities 372.62

July 1, 1901, balance available 11,828.27

July 1, 1901, amount covered by uncompleted contracts 8,049.37

(See Appendix T 7.)

8. *Bayou Plaquemine, Grand River, and Pigeon Bayous, Louisiana.*—Prior to 1867 the largest steamboats could pass through Bayou Plaquemine into Grand Lake and other connecting water routes, but at that time the police jury of Iberville Parish closed the bayou by means of a dam, shutting out the waters of the Mississippi. Grand River and Pigeon Bayous were obstructed by snags, logs, overhanging trees, and sand bars.

The present project is based upon legislation by Congress, according to project and estimate submitted February 11, 1887, and provides for dredging a channel in Bayou Plaquemine 60 feet wide and 6 feet deep from deep water up to the Plaquemine dike, constructing a lock to connect the bayou with the Mississippi River, securing the mouth of the bayou from further caving, and removing obstructions from Grand River and Pigeon Bayous; total estimated cost, $1,708,250.

The protection of the bank of the Mississippi River at the mouth of the bayou was added to the improvement in 1888, and in act of July 13, 1892, the improvement of Grand River and Pigeon Bayous was also incorporated.

The act of June 3, 1896, authorized continuing contracts to be entered into to complete the project of improvement, not to exceed $1,173,250, exclusive of the amounts therein and previously appropriated.

The project of 1887 was modified on April 10, 1899, to allow for dredging Bayou Plaquemine to a depth of 10 feet and a width of 125 feet.

Dredging was carried on in Bayou Plaquemine in 1890, 1891, 1892, and 1894, resulting in securing a channel 6 feet deep and 60 feet wide from the mouth to the railroad bridge.

An allotment of $75,000 was made from the appropriation of 1888 for securing the bank of the Mississippi River at the head of the bayou. Five submerged spur dikes, placed at intervals of about 900 feet, with intervals protected by revetment, were completed in 1894. These dikes and revetments form a continuous protection 1,400 feet long below the site of the lock and 1,200 feet above, with an interval of 500 feet opposite the lock site, left for excavating the necessary channel to the lock.

In 1893, 1894, and 1897 obstructions were removed from the mouth of Bayou Sorrel and down Grand River through Pigeon Bayou to Grand Lake, a distance of 30 miles. Flat Lake, at the mouth of Grand River, was dredged in 1893 and 1897.

With funds appropriated in 1894 the work of constructing a cofferdam, excavating, and driving a pile foundation for the lock, was carried on from 1895 to 1898 and completed.

In 1891 a project for the construction of a lock was submitted, but the funds available were insufficient to warrant its commencement at that time. The Board of Engineer officers appointed to prepare plans and specifications estimated the cost of the lock at $700,000. Revised plans and specifications for the construction of the lock and approaches were approved October 27, 1897, and December 2, 1897, respectively, and a continuing contract for the work was entered into May 28, 1898, and approved June 17, 1898. The work was commenced in August, 1898. On June 30, 1901 the floor and walls of the lock had been completed; miter sills, inlet pipes, and snubbing hooks had been placed. The excavation for the approaches, the fill behind walls, construction of connection levees, and erection of gates remained to complete the lock.

A contract for the construction of power house and operating machinery for the lock, for $114,000, was entered into November 18, 1899. This work will be commenced when the lock is nearer completion.

Plans for an approach to the lock, to be constructed on the river side at an estimated cost of $114,000, were approved April 20, 1901. The execution of this work will be deferred until the lock is nearer completion.

Work has been carried on since October 29, 1899, under contract dated July 15, 1899, for the rectification of Bayou Plaquemine. About one-third of the work provided for under the contract has been completed to the required depth of 10 feet and width of 125 feet.

Work of dredging and removing obstructions from Grand River was carried on under contract of November 25, 1899, until April 20, 1901. Obstructions were removed from mouth of Bayou Plaquemine to 2 miles below Bayou Pigeon, and at Bay Natchez, a distance of 30 miles. During the past year a survey of Flat Lake and Bay Natchez was made, and a project for dredging a 60-foot channel through them has been adopted.

The sum of $671,244.05 was expended on these improvements up to June 30, 1900.

During high water there is a depth of from 10 to 12 feet in these streams, but during low water there is a depth of only 4 feet in Bay Natchez and 4½ feet in Flat Lake.

Comparative statement of receipts and shipments for ten years.

	Tons.	Change in tonnage from previous year.	
		Increase.	Decrease.
Year ending May 31—			
1892	131,875	1,696	
1893	78,756		58,119
1894	133,752	54,996	
1895	120,542		13,210
1896	92,379		28,163
1897	57,055		35,324
1898	76,626	19,571	
1899	89,301	12,675	
Calendar year—			
1899	111,750	22,449	
1900	88,543		23,207

July 1, 1900, balance unexpended $758,755.95
Amount appropriated by sundry civil act approved March 3, 1901 ...... 210,000.00
                                                                      ──────────
                                                                      968,755.95
June 30, 1901, amount expended during fiscal year 185,478.25

July 1, 1901, balance unexpended 783,277.70
July 1, 1901, outstanding liabilities 34,356.38

July 1, 1901, balance available 748,921.32

July 1, 1901, amount covered by uncompleted contracts................. 455,198.16

(See Appendix T 8.)

9. Bayou Courtableau, Louisiana.—Bayou Courtableau lies within the Atchafalaya Basin, and is tributary to the Atchafalaya River. Prior to improvement the Atchafalaya River had formed a large deposit of sand, known as Little Devil Bar, at the mouth of Bayou Courtableau. It was proposed by the project of 1880 to improve the bayou below Port Barre by closing some of the run-out bayous, in order to confine the water in the Courtableau, and to wash out the bar with the increased current; after this was accomplished, to contruct a timber lock and dam to provide slack-water navigation to Washington,

La., a distance of 28 miles. The estimated cost of the improvement was $40,000. The project was modified in 1883 to provide for the construction of a masonry instead of timber lock, increasing the original estimate to $78,500.

With appropriations aggregating $36,200, work was carried on under this project to 1895. The larger run-out bayous were closed with dams, and the increased current was effective in the partial removal of the bar. The dams were broken from time to time, and the bar at the mouth of the bayou formed again. The dams were repaired in 1891 and subsequent years. The construction of a lock has not been commenced, as it is believed that it will not be of benefit until the bar at the mouth is permanently removed.

During the high water of 1896, a large accumulation of logs formed at the neutralization point of the bayou current and the backwater of the Atchafalaya. The raft rapidly increased in size and density until in 1899 it was about 3 miles long and completely obstructed navigation.

An appropriation of $2,500 was made June 3, 1896, but the amount was insufficient for the removal of the raft, and it was held for increase.

Act of March 3, 1899, appropriated $20,000 for the removal of the raft and preventing its re-formation. The project approved April 7, 1899, provided for removing the log raft to restore navigation, and for construction of a floating boom across the mouth of the bayou to prevent the entrance of drift from the Atchafalaya River.

Under this project the raft was removed, the logs being drifted down the run-out bayous, and a channel from 60 to 110 feet wide was secured. A log boom floating between piles was constructed at the mouth of the bayou.

The sum of $55,828.88 was expended on this improvement up to June 30, 1900.

During the past fiscal year the work has been confined to maintenance of the channel through the log raft. The proposition of John J. Keegan to remove all logs and drift so as to clear the 60-foot channel for $1,800 was accepted on March 8, and the work begun on March 25, 1901. On April 22, 1901, the work was completed and the 60-foot channel secured. The bayou is navigable only during high water.

Comparative statement of receipts and shipments for seven years.

Year ending May 31—	Tons.	Decrease in tonnage from previous year.
1890	35,867	
1891	32,618	3,249
1892	20,041	12,577
1893	14,848	5,193
1894	9,195	5,653
1895	4,095	5,100
1896	1,994	2,101

No commerce since 1896.

July 1, 1900, balance unexpended $2,871.12
June 30, 1901, amount expended during fiscal year 2,738.58

July 1, 1901, balance unexpended 132.54

(See Appendix T 9.)

10. Bayou Teche, Louisiana.—Bayou Teche is an important commercial stream of southern Louisiana, and finds its outlet into the Gulf of Mexico through Atchafalaya River. Prior to improvement it had a depth of 8 feet to St. Martinville, La., but navigation was rendered dangerous by numerous obstructions. Above St. Martinville the bayou was navigable by steamboats during high water. The project of 1870 provided for the removal of obstructions from the head to the mouth of the bayou. Work under this project was carried on from 1870 to 1886, the stream being cleared of logs, snags, wrecks, overhanging trees, and a number of sand bars. The improvement was not permanent, and other obstructions formed.

The project of 1891 provided for the removal of obstructions between St. Martinville, La., and the mouth of the bayou, a distance of about 80 miles. Work under this project has been carried on since 1891, obstructions being removed as appropriations were made. Up to June 30, 1900, $80,545.81 had been spent upon this improvement. On that date the available depth up to St. Martinville was 5 feet. No work has been done during the past fiscal year. The bayou is comparatively free from snags, but has shoaled to such an extent that at points the available depth is only 3 feet.

Comparative statement of receipts and shipments for ten years.

	Tons.	Change in tonnage from previous year.	
		Increase.	Decrease.
Year ending May 31—			
1892	64,866		
1893	115,080	50,214	
1894	383,154	268,074	
1895	279,928		103,226
1896	293,685	13,757	
1897	303,029	9,344	
1898	238,783		64,246
1899	286,091	47,308	
Calendar year—			
1899	272,975		13,116
1900	212,109		60,866

July 1, 1900, balance unexpended $454.19
June 30, 1901, amount expended during fiscal year 292.47

July 1, 1901, balance unexpended 161.72

{ Amount that can be profitably expended in fiscal year ending June 30, 1903, for maintenance of improvement, in addition to the balance unexpended July 1, 1901 .... 7,500.00
Submitted in compliance with requirements of sundry civil act of June 4, 1897, and of section 7 of the river and harbor act of 1899. }

(See Appendix T 10.)

11. Channel, bay, and passes of Bayou Vermilion, Louisiana.—Condition prior to improvement: The upper 12 miles of Bayou Vermilion had a depth of only 2 feet, but below this the depth was not less than 5½ feet through the bayou, bay, and passes, with a width from 100 to 400 feet. The channel was obstructed by snags, logs, and overhanging trees.

The original project of 1892 provided for the removal of these obstructions and the erection of guide piles to mark the channel over the bars in Vermilion Bay; and provided for a depth of 5½ feet of water up to the railroad bridge near Lafayette, La., a distance of 50 miles. Estimated cost, $25,000.

With appropriations aggregating $12,500, the removal of obstructions was carried on in 1892, 1893, and 1895, and the stream placed in navigable condition to Broussard's bridge, a distance of 34 miles from the mouth. The guide piles were driven in Vermilion Bay in 1893.

Act of June 3, 1896, appropriated $1,000 for continuing the improvement, but the amount was insufficient to cover the work required and was held for increase.

The appropriation of 1896 was augmented by one of $2,500, made March 3, 1899. With these funds work was carried on from November 8, 1899, to February 3, 1900, and the stream cleared of obstructions from Abbeville, La., to the railroad bridge.

Amount expended up to June 30, 1900, was $15,992.53. On that date the bayou was navigable to a point 30 miles above the mouth for vessels drawing 5¼ feet; from that point to the railroad bridge it had a navigable depth of 2¼ feet.

During the fiscal year ending June 30, 1901, no work was done toward this improvement. An examination completed January 22, 1901, showed that the guide piles in Vermilion Bay have nearly all disappeared and that, with the exception of shallow water on the bar at the mouth, the channel was ample in width and depth for the commerce of the locality. The channel is available to Abbeville for vessels drawing 5¼ feet.

Comparative statement of receipts and shipments for eight years.

	Tons.	Change in tonnage from previous year.	
		Increase.	Decrease.
Year ending May 31—			
1894	43,882	8,151	....
1895	12,993	....	30,829
1896	13,022	29	....
1897	6,126	....	6,896
1898	8,862	2,736	....
1899	14,969	6,107	....
Calendar year—			
1899	7,650	....	7,319
1900	21,150	13,500	....

July 1, 1900, balance unexpended.. $7.47
June 30, 1901, amount expended during fiscal year.................... 7.47

{ Amount (estimated) required for completion of existing project........ 9,000.00
Amount that can be profitably expended in fiscal year ending June 30, 1903, for works of improvement and for maintenance............... 9,000.00
Submitted in compliance with requirements of sundry civil act of June 4, 1897, and of section 7 of the river and harbor act of 1899.

(See Appendix T 11.)

12. Mermentau River and tributaries, Louisiana.—Prior to improvement these streams afforded depths varying from 7 feet to 30 feet; the channel through Grand Lake was 6 feet in depth; at the mouth of the river the depth was 13 feet. The width varied from 70 feet at Viterboville to 350 feet at Lake Arthur. The channel was crooked and obstructed by snags and logs.

The original project, adopted in 1892, provided for the removal of obstructions in the upper river and for building brush dams to remove the mud flat in the lower river. Estimated cost, $23,615.25.

With an appropriation of $7,500, made in 1892, snagging operations were carried on under contract from December 8, 1892, to March 7, 1893, resulting in the improvement of the channel of Mermentau River for 38 miles from the lower end of Lake Arthur.

In 1894 an appropriation of $5,000 was made for continuing the improvement, and a project was submitted, but as the funds available were insufficient the amount was held for increase before undertaking further work.

A further appropriation of $5,000 having been made on June 3, 1896, a project was approved June 15, 1897, providing for construction of brush dams in Mud Lake (an enlargement of Mermentau River) and for dredging to secure immediate results. Under this project work was carried on from December 24, 1897, to April 14, 1898. An upper dam 2,500 feet long and 5 feet wide and a lower dam 3,000 feet long were constructed. The average depth of the dredged channel was 8 feet and the width 50 feet.

The act of March 3, 1899, appropriated $6,115.25 for completing the improvement. Under project approved July 8, 1899, it was proposed to expend this amount in redredging the channel.

By the dredging operations of 1899 a channel through Mud Lake 6.5 feet deep and 3,877 feet long was secured.

Amount expended up to June 30, 1900, was $22,006.42, of which $5,399.84 was for maintenance. On that date the channel was ample for the commerce of the locality, being navigable at mean low tide by vessels drawing 5 feet.

There were no operations on this improvement during the fiscal year ending June 30, 1901.

Comparative statement of receipts and shipments for nine years.

	Tons.	Change in tonnage from previous year.	
		Increase.	Decrease.
Year ending May 31—			
1893	16,250		
1894	5,437		10,813
1895	15,955	10,518	
1896	16,459	504	
1897	12,210		4,249
1898	18,650	6,440	
1899	22,236	3,586	
Calendar year—			
1899	2,866		19,370
1900	27,034	24,168	

July 1, 1900, balance unexpended $1,608.83
June 30, 1901, amount expended during fiscal year 40.61

July 1, 1901, balance unexpended 1,568.22

{ Amount that can be profitably expended in fiscal year ending June 30, 1903, for maintenance of improvement, in addition to the balance unexpended July 1, 1901... 2,500.00
Submitted in compliance with requirements of sundry civil act of June 4, 1897, and of section 7 of the river and harbor act of 1899. }

(See Appendix T 12.)

13. Mouth and passes of Calcasieu River, Louisiana.—Prior to improvement there was a depth of 6½ feet of water over the outer bar at the entrance to Calcasieu Lake. Calcasieu Lake, which is 15 miles long, had a depth of 6 feet; the depth over the inner bars was 3½ feet, and from the upper bar to Lake Charles, La., there was not less than 8 feet of water.

The original project for improvement, adopted in 1872 and modified in 1881, provided for obtaining a channel of navigable width and depth across the inner bars. A channel 8 feet deep and 70 feet wide, for a distance of 7,500 feet, was dredged through the inner bars in 1874, 1882, and 1883, but in 1885 the channel had shoaled to 3½ feet. In accordance with project approved in 1886, the cut was redredged and a plank revetment on each side of the cut was commenced. The revetment was not finished, and the cut again filled.

An appropriation of $10,000 made in 1888 for the construction of a revetment, and another of $75,000 made in 1890 for constructing jetties, in accordance with projects submitted in 1886, were held for increase. These amounts were supplemented by an appropriation of $100,000, made in 1892.

The project approved August 13, 1892, under which the present work is being conducted, provides for dredging a channel 50 feet wide and 8 feet deep through the inner bars, revetting this channel to prevent the return of the dredged material; to build parallel jetties of brush and stone at the entrance to the outer pass, and to dredge out between these jetties to secure a depth of 12 feet, if necessary. The total estimated cost of these improvements is $600,000.

The revetment was completed August 16, 1893. Dredging at the foot of Calcasieu Lake was carried on in 1894–95 and in 1898. A channel 8 feet deep and 50 feet wide was secured, connecting deep water in Calcasieu Lake and Pass. The construction of the east jetty at the entrance to the pass was carried on in 1894, 1895, and 1896, and of the west jetty in 1897.

During 1900, with an appropriation of $35,000, the foundation of the west jetty was extended 1,000 feet, making a total length of 3,200 feet.

Amount expended up to June 30, 1900, was $435,893.24. On that date there was a depth of 7 feet in the outer and 6½ feet in the inner channels.

During the fiscal year ending June 30, 1901, no work was done upon these improvements. An examination, completed January 17, 1901, showed that the revetment of the channel in Calcasieu Lake was in a dilapidated condition; that the available depth in this channel was 4½ feet, and that portions of the capping of the jetties had been displaced.

It is estimated that $307,681 will be required to repair and complete the jetties; $10,000 for repair of channel revetments, and $10,000 annually to maintain dredged channels.

RIVER AND HARBOR IMPROVEMENTS. 395

Comparative statement of receipts and shipments for nine years.

	Tons.	Change in tonnage from previous year.	
		Increase.	Decrease.
Year ending May 31—			
1893	207,545		16,650
1894	344,973	137,428	
1895	254,394		90,579
1896	202,775		51,619
1897	141,029		61,746
1898	190,017	48,988	
1899	174,651		15,366
Calendar year—			
1899	16,829		157,822
1900	139,580	122,751	

July 1, 1900, balance unexpended.................................... $606.76
June 30, 1901, amount expended during fiscal year................... 60.99

July 1, 1901, balance unexpended.................................... 545.77

{ Amount (estimated) required for completion of existing project....... 307,681.00
Amount that can be profitably expended in fiscal year ending June 30, 1903, for works of improvement and for maintenance, in addition to the balance unexpended July 1, 1901............................... 165,000.00
Submitted in compliance with requirements of sundry civil act of June 4, 1897, and of section 7 of the river and harbor act of 1899.

(See Appendix T 13.)

14. Johnsons Bayou, Louisiana.—This stream flows into Sabine Lake, Texas. A preliminary survey, made in 1897, showed a minimum channel depth in the bayou of 12 feet, but upon the bar at the mouth there was only 2¼ feet of water.

The project approved April 10, 1899, provided for dredging through the bar so as to produce a channel 6 feet in depth and of such width as the appropriation, $2,500, would permit. The dredging was carried on during December, 1899, and the required 6-foot channel, 60 feet wide, was secured.

To June 30, 1900, $2,261.35 had been expended upon the improvement.

No work has been done during the past fiscal year. The stream is navigable for vessels drawing 5 feet.

Comparative statement of receipts and shipments for two years.

Year ending Dec. 31—	Tons.	Increase in tonnage over previous year.
1899	3,163	
1900	3,594	431

July 1, 1900, balance unexpended................................ $238.65
July 1, 1901, balance unexpended................................ 238.65

(See Appendix T 14.)

15. Removing the water hyacinth from Louisiana waters.—Under the provisions of the sundry civil act of June 4, 1897, a Board of Engineer officers was appointed to investigate the extent of obstruction to navigation in the streams of Florida and Louisiana by the water hyacinth, and determine a method of checking or removing the plants. The Board recommended the construction of boats fitted with crushing appliances, and also the use of log booms as adjuncts to the operation of the steamers. The report of the Board was printed in House Doc. No. 51, Fifty-fifth Congress, third session, and also on page 1615, Annual Report of the Chief of Engineers for 1899.

In accordance with the recommendation of the Board, Congress appropriated by the river and harbor act of March 3, 1899, $25,000 for the construction of a boat, $1,000 for log booms, and $10,000 for operating expenses for removing the plants from Louisiana waters.

A steamboat was purchased and fitted with machinery for raising and crushing the plants. This boat was operated on Bayou Plaquemine from July 9, 1900, to June 1, 1901, when funds for operations became exhausted. Approximately 188,800 square yards of plants was removed.

A boom with a gate arranged to allow the hyacinths to float out with the tides and to prevent their return was constructed at the mouth of Bayou Teche, Louisiana, last year. At the present time this boom is out of working order and is not operated.

The total amount expended on this work to June 30, 1900, was $12,645.75. The balance of funds unexpended June 30, 1901, belongs to the appropriation for construction of boat and is not available for operating expenses.

July 1, 1900, balance unexpended	$23,354.25
June 30, 1901, amount expended during fiscal year	15,320.21
July 1, 1901, balance unexpended	8,034.04
July 1, 1901, outstanding liabilities	52.33
July 1, 1901, balance available	7,981.71

Amount that can be profitably expended in fiscal year ending June 30, 1903, in addition to the balance available July 1, 1901 .... 20,000.00
Submitted in compliance with requirements of sundry civil act of June 4, 1897.

(See Appendix T 15.)

16. *Mouths of Sabine and Neches rivers, Texas.*—Both rivers flow into Sabine Lake, Texas. Prior to improvement there was 3½ feet of water on the bar at the mouth of the Sabine River and 3 feet on the bar at the mouth of the Neches. Dredging was carried on at the mouth of the Sabine River in 1880 and 1895, and a channel 60 feet wide and 7 feet deep was secured. At the mouth of the Neches dredging was carried on in 1880, 1889, and 1895, and a channel 50 feet wide, 5 feet deep, and 8,000 feet long was obtained, the funds being exhausted before deep water in Sabine Lake was reached. In 1897 the channel at the mouth of the Sabine River still afforded a depth of 7 feet, while the channel at the mouth of the Neches had shoaled to 4 feet.

The act of March 3, 1899, appropriated $10,000 for improving the mouths of these streams, the appropriation to include the expenses of a reexamination of the proposed channel through Sabine Lake by a Board of Engineer officers.

The Board constituted in compliance with this act submitted on August 11, 1899, a report on the proposed channel through Sabine Lake, and the report is printed in House Doc. No. 100, Fifty-sixth Congress, first session, and on page 2302, annual report for 1900.

The project approved July 14, 1899, provided for dredging from deep water in the Neches River to deep water in Sabine Lake.

Under this project an 8-foot channel, 7,829 feet long, was dredged from the 7-foot contour in Neches River to the 6-foot contour in Sabine Lake. A part of the appropriation was expended in deepening the channel across the bar at the mouth of the Sabine River. On June 30, 1901, the available depth at the mouth of the Sabine River was 6¼ feet; at the mouth of the Neches, 4¼ feet.

Up to June 30, 1900, there had been expended upon this work $9,925.29, of which $171.49 was for reexamination of the proposed channel through Sabine Lake.

During the fiscal year ending June 30, 1901, no work was done upon this improvement.

The amount of commerce for the calendar year 1900 was 36,484 tons.

Comparative statement of receipts and shipments for two years for Neches River, Texas.

Year ending December 31—	Tons.	Decrease in tonnage from previous year.
1899	93,750	
1900	a 4,336	89,414

a Incomplete. Full statement could not be obtained.
See report upon Sabine River, Texas, for statistics.

July 1, 1900, balance unexpended $74.71
July 1, 1901, balance unexpended 74.71

Amount that can be profitably expended in fiscal year ending June 30, 1903, for maintenance of improvement, in addition to the balance unexpended July 1, 1901 .... 4,000.00
Submitted in compliance with requirements of sundry civil act of June 4, 1897, and of section 7 of the river and harbor act of 1899.

(See Appendix T 16.)

17. Sabine River, Texas.—This stream is about 470 miles long, and for a greater part of its length forms the boundary between Texas and Louisiana. It flows into the Gulf of Mexico through Sabine Lake. Prior to improvement there was a depth of 3½ feet of water over the bar at the mouth of the river; from the mouth to Orange, Tex., there was ample depth; above Orange the stream was obstructed by logs and snags.

The original project, adopted in 1871 and modified in 1873, provided for deepening the main outlet of the river at a cost of $18,000.

The project of 1889 provided for the closure of two branches forming Old River, to throw all the water into the "Narrows," and for the removal of obstructions. These projects were completed in December, 1890, and a navigable channel provided for vessels drawing 5 feet for a distance of 30 miles above Orange, Tex.

The project of 1892 provided for removing obstructions between Orange, Tex., and Sudduths Bluff, a distance of 50 miles, at an estimated cost of $10,000. This work was completed in 1895.

On June 30, 1899, the dams built in 1890 were in good condition and fulfilling the requirements for which built. The river from the mouth to Morgans Bluff, a distance of 33 miles, was in fairly good condition, but obstructions had formed between Morgans Bluff and Sudduths Bluff, a distance of 31 miles, since 1895.

With $2,000 appropriated in 1896 and a like amount in 1899, the work of maintenance was carried on between May 17 and June 30, 1900, under project approved July 8, 1899. The river was cleared of obstructions from Morgans Bluff to within 28 miles of Sudduths Bluff. The above improvement was continued until July 13, 1900, when work ceased on account of lack of funds. One-half mile of river was cleared. The stream, where improved, is in fair condition, with the exception of obstructions formed by loose logs and deadheads.

The sum of $49,063.42 was expended on these improvements up to June 30, 1900, of which $363.42 was for maintenance.

Vessels drawing 5 feet can go 64 miles above the mouth of the river, and above Sudduths Bluff, for about 300 miles, vessels of light draft can run during high water.

In connection with this work see preceding report for improving the mouths of the Sabine and Neches rivers, Texas.

Comparative statement of receipts and shipments for nine years.

	Tons.	Change in tonnage from previous year.	
		Increase.	Decrease.
Year ending May 31—			
1893	146,363		
1894	245,657	99,294	
1895	182,738		62,919
1896	271,257	88,519	
1897	245,364		25,893
1898	275,506	30,142	
1899	270,642		4,864
Calendar year—			
1899	407,372	136,730	
1900	a 32,148		375,224

a Incomplete. Full statistics could not be obtained.

July 1, 1900, balance unexpended	$3,636.58
June 30, 1901, amount expended during fiscal year	3,474.91
July 1, 1901, balance unexpended	161.67

(See Appendix T 17.)

18. Harbor at Sabine Pass, Texas.—Sabine Pass, about 7 miles long, is the outlet of Sabine Lake into the Gulf of Mexico. Prior to improvement it had a least depth of 25 feet, except over a bar 200 feet long opposite the town of Sabine Pass, over which there was a depth of 18 feet, and a bar 200 feet long opposite Fort Point, where there was a depth of 17 feet. Beyond the shore line, where the pass enters the Gulf of Mexico, there was a bar 3¼ miles wide between the interior and exterior 18-foot bottom curves, over which there was only a depth of 6 feet at mean low tides. Channels 12 and 15 feet deep were dredged through the outer bar in 1878 and 1880, but the improvement was not permanent and the cuts soon filled.

The project of 1882 proposed to construct parallel jetties of brush and stone, extending from shore across the bar out to deep water in the Gulf, the jetties to be 1,800 feet apart and about 4 miles long; dredging between jetties to be carried on, if necessary, to obtain deep water through the pass into the harbor. The estimated cost of the improvements was $3,177,606.50.

By the river and harbor act of 1896 contracts were authorized to be entered into for the completion of the project of improvement, the cost being limited to $1,050,000.

Act of June 4, 1897, appropriated $100,000 for the purchase of a dredge boat for Sabine Pass, and $30,000 for operating same during the fiscal year 1898, and a project to that effect was approved June 29 1897. There having been delays in the construction of the dredge boat, the project was modified by act of March 17, 1898, making available for immediate use $15,000 of the $30,000 appropriated for dredging. Under this latter act dredging in the channel was done in July, 1898, at a cost of $13,702.97. The remainder of the $30,000 reverted to the Treasury.

Act of March 3, 1899, appropriated $150,000 for straightening, widening, and otherwise improving the main ship channel by removal of oyster reefs and flats and other material between a point 1,000 feet north of the United States life-saving station and a point opposite the United States light-house. A project covering the proposed work was approved by the Secretary of War on March 27, 1899.

The work of jetty building began in 1883, and, with successive appropriations, has been carried on since then.

The project approved December 8, 1896, for the expenditure of the $1,050,000 authorized by act of 1896, provided for the construction of 5,300 linear feet, more or less, of the east jetty, and 6,600 feet, more or less, of the west jetty, at a cost of $985,000, and that $65,000 be expended in the enlargement and maintenance of the dredged channel.

A contract for this work was approved June 22, 1897, and work was commenced on August 10, 1897. On June 30, 1897, the east jetty had a length of 19,500 feet, and the west jetty 14,875 feet. On June 30, 1900, the east jetty had been extended to a length of 25,100 feet, of which 21,540 feet was capped, 960 feet was riprap, and 2,600 feet was foundation only; and the west jetty to 22,000 feet, of which 15,250 feet was capped, 1,800 feet was riprap, and 4,950 feet was foundation only. About 3,000 feet of the previous work was capped in 1897. Dredging in the channel under this contract was carried on in 1897 and 1899, which increased the depth to 25 feet and the width to 100 feet.

A contract for dredging in Sabine Pass channel, within the area prescribed by act of March 3, 1899, was entered into July 27, 1899. Under this contract only 1,414 cubic yards of material had been removed up to June 30, 1900.

A contract for the construction of a hydraulic dredging steamer with two 10-inch pumps was entered into January 19, 1900.

The sum of $3,032,036.99 was expended on these improvements up to June 30, 1900.

During the past fiscal year the contract for jetty work has been completed as provided for by the act of June 3, 1896. This work was finished on August 6, 1900. Owing to unusual and unexpected settlement that has taken place in the jetties and to damage done by hurricane in September, 1900, it is desirable that additional work be done in order that the full benefits of the improvement be obtained. It is estimated by the local officer that $1,116,573 will be required to build up, complete, and repair the jetties in accordance with the original project.

Dredging was done in the channel between the jetties from November 28, 1900, until January 3, 1901, with an allotment of $8,000 made July 19, 1900, from the emergency appropriation of June 6, 1900, for rivers and harbors.

The hydraulic dredging steamer *Sabine*, built under contract of January 19, 1900, with funds provided by act of June 4, 1897, was completed and accepted on January 14, 1901. Dredging between the jetties was carried on with this dredge from February 9 to June 30, 1901, when available funds were practically exhausted. The sum of $30,000 per annum will be required to operate this dredge and maintain the channel between the jetties.

Dredging in the main ship channel opposite Sabine was carried on under contract dated July 27, 1899. A total of 219,273 cubic yards of material was removed during the year. Only about one-seventh of this contract has been completed.

Reports, with estimate, of a preliminary examination of Sabine Pass with a view to widening and straightening the main ship channel, and increasing the depth, from a point 1,000 feet north of the life-saving station to Sabine Lake, were submitted June 28 and July 14, 1900, and were printed as House Doc. No. 70, Fifty-sixth Congress, second session, and are also herewith as Appendix T 20.

A special report on the damage done to the jetties by hurricane of September 8, 1900, was submitted September 25, 1900, and printed as House Doc. No. 152, Fifty-sixth Congress, second session. It is also herewith as Appendix T 21. The estimated cost of repairs is $100,000.

On June 30, 1901, there was a navigable channel of 22 feet at mean low water between the jetties and up to Sabine, excepting at one point where there is a depth of only 21.8 feet.

Comparative statement of receipts and shipments for nine years.

	Tons.	Change in tonnage from previous year. Increase.	Decrease.
Year ending May 31—			
1893	15,050		22,978
1894	40,966	25,916	
1895	47,691	6,725	
1896	48,886	1,195	
1897	87,632	38,746	
1898	238,400	150,768	
1899	326,982	88,582	
Calendar year—			
1899	326,484		488
1900	217,489		109,005

July 1, 1900, balance unexpended..$396,415.98
Amount allotted from appropriation contained in emergency river and harbor act approved June 6, 1900 .... 8,000.00

 404,415.98
June 30, 1901, amount expended during fiscal year...................... 261,115.44

July 1, 1901, balance unexpended... 143,300.54
July 1, 1901, outstanding liabilities..................................... 9,912.26

July 1, 1901, balance available.. 133,388.28

July 1, 1901, amount covered by uncompleted contracts 114,034.74

{ Amount that can be profitably expended in fiscal year ending June 30, 1903, for works of improvement and for maintenance, in addition to the balance available July 1, 1901 .... 300,000.00
Submitted in compliance with requirements of sundry civil act of June 4, 1897, and of section 7 of the river and harbor act of 1899.

(See Appendix T 18.)

19. Homochitto River, Mississippi.—About 8 miles above Fort Adams, Miss., the Homochitto enters the Mississippi River. For the first 3 miles it is called the "Narrows," and for a distance of 12 miles farther it takes the name of "Old River." A preliminary examination in 1896 showed that the Narrows had a depth of 5 feet at low water and a width of 150 feet, except for about 1 mile, where it is very narrow and shoal. This part of the river was obstructed by snags and trees. Old River was about 1,000 feet wide, 2 feet deep over the shoalest places at low water, and is clear of obstructions. Above Old River the Homochitto had a navigable depth of 8 feet and a width of 150 feet for a distance of 45 miles, but was thickly obstructed by snags, logs, and overhanging trees.

The act of March 3, 1899, appropriated $16,000 for removing obstructions between the mouth of the river and the Yazoo and Mississippi Valley Railroad, a distance of about 60 miles, and a project was approved April 18, 1899, covering this work.

Work under this project was commenced November 27, 1899. Obstructions were removed from the Narrows, and the action of natural scour removed most of the bars. Obstructions were also removed from 9 miles of channel above Old River up to June 30, 1900.

Amount expended up to June 30, 1900, was $9,222.86. On that date the channel, for a distance of 18 miles from the mouth, was navigable during high water by vessels drawing 6 feet and during low water by vessels drawing 2 feet.

During the fiscal year ending June 30, 1901, the work of removing snags and similar obstructions was continued until funds were exhausted. The channel has been cleared for 18 miles from the mouth to a width varying from 60 to 200 feet, except in Old River, where the width is 1 mile.

Commercial statistics for the past year could not be obtained; the commerce for the previous year was 3,815 tons.

July 1, 1900, balance unexpended	$6,777.14
June 30, 1901, amount expended during fiscal year	6,192.86
July 1, 1901, balance unexpended	584.28

(See Appendix T 19.)

EXAMINATION AND SURVEY MADE IN COMPLIANCE WITH EMERGENCY RIVER AND HARBOR ACT, APPROVED JUNE 6, 1900.

Reports dated June 28 and July 14, 1900, respectively, upon preliminary examination and plan and estimate for improvement of *Sabine Pass, Tex., with a view to widening and straightening the main ship channel and increasing the depth, if necessary, from 1,000 feet north of the United States life-saving station to Sabine Lake*, were submitted to Lieutenant-Colonel Adams through the division engineer. The estimated cost of the improvement proposed is $25,000. The reports were transmitted to Congress and printed in House Doc. No. 70, Fifty-sixth Congress, second session. (See also Appendix T 20.)

402   REPORT OF THE CHIEF OF ENGINEERS, U. S. ARMY.

REPORT UPON DAMAGE TO GOVERNMENT WORKS AND LOSS OF ENGINEER PROPERTY AT SABINE PASS, TEX., INCURRED DURING THE STORM OF SEPTEMBER, 1900.

Lieutenant-Colonel Adams submitted report dated September 25, 1900. The estimated cost of repairing the damage is $100,000. The value of the property lost is $1,500. The report was transmitted to Congress, and printed in House Doc. No. 152, Fifty-sixth Congress, second session. (See also Appendix T 21.)

IMPROVEMENT OF CERTAIN RIVERS AND HARBORS IN TEXAS.

This district was in the charge of Capt. C. S. Riché, Corps of Engineers, with Lieut. Meriwether L. Walker, Corps of Engineers, under his immediate orders, since April 7, 1901. Division Engineer, Col. Henry M. Robert, Corps of Engineers (now brigadier-general, Chief of Engineers, United States Army, retired), to May 2, 1901, and Col. Amos Stickney, Corps of Engineers, since May 9, 1901.

1. *Galveston Harbor, Texas.*—Galveston Harbor embraces an anchorage area of over 1,960 acres, of which 1,500 acres has a depth of more than 20 feet, and 460 acres has a depth of more than 30 feet. It affords vessels excellent shelter from storms. Waterways connect it with Houston and with Brazos River.

The entrance to this harbor was originally obstructed by two bars, known as the inner and outer. The natural depth on the inner bar was about 9¼ feet, and on the outer bar about 12 feet. These shallow depths prevented all but the lightest-draft vessels from using the harbor, and necessitated the lighterage of cargoes to the larger vessels anchored in the deep water beyond the outer bar.

Prior to 1874 the projects for improving this harbor related to dredging operations on a small scale, and were only expected to afford temporary relief to navigation.

The project for the permanent improvement of this harbor by jetties was adopted in 1874, and modified in 1880 and 1886. It was expected that upon their completion, a least depth of 25 feet would be obtained on the outer bar (see Annual Report of the Chief of Engineers for 1880, p. 1221 et seq.).

The 1886 project provided for a possible depth of 30 feet, by constructing jetties to a height of 5 feet above mean low tide and extending them to the 30-foot contour in the Gulf, and supplementing the action of the tidal scour by dredging. The estimated cost of this revised project was $7,000,000.

The total amount expended under the foregoing plans to June 30, 1900, was $8,385,079.11, with an additional sum of $100,000 subscribed by the city of Galveston in 1883. Of this amount $1,478,000 was expended previous to 1886.

This expenditure resulted in a depth of 26 feet at mean low tide on the outer bar, an increase of 14 feet since work began, and a depth of 26 feet at mean low tide on the inner bar, an increase of 16 feet during the same period. This increased depth of water enabled vessels to load to their full capacity at the Galveston wharves, thereby making the lighterage of cargoes no longer necessary.

At the end of the fiscal year 1900, the completed south jetty extended 35,603 feet. On the same date the completed north jetty extended 25,907 feet.

The expenditure during the fiscal year ending June 30, 1901, was for operating the U. S. dredge *Gen. C. B. Comstock* in maintaining, strengthening, and widening the channel between the jetties, expenses of resurvey and chart of Galveston Bay, and contingent expenses of the work. Also $21,000 was expended in removing the U. S. dredge *Gen. C. B. Comstock* from off Pelican Flats, where she had been stranded by the hurricane of September 8, 1900.

The depth of water on the outer and inner bars remains practically the same as at the end of preceding fiscal year.

Commerce has been greatly benefited by the improvement of this harbor, as shown by the increased size and tonnage of the vessels using the port. The amount of freight handled during the fiscal year was 1,826,826 tons.

The total amount of ocean commerce transported to and from Galveston during the fiscal year was: Cotton and cotton products, 851,357 tons; ore, 795 tons; wool, 12,695 tons; grain, 426,824 tons; sugar, 321 tons; coal, 136,011 tons; flour, 12,885 tons; lumber and timber, 135,082 tons; cement, 22,523 tons; petroleum, crude, 9,900 tons; fuel oil, 13,356 tons; general merchandise, 205,073 tons.

The hurricane of September 8, 1900, damaged the jetties to a considerable extent, and a report of a Board of Engineers showing the effect of this hurricane on the jetties and the main ship channel, with an estimate for repairing same at a cost of $1,500,000, is contained in House Doc. No. 134 Fifty-sixth Congress, second session. The report is printed herewith as Appendix U 16.

It will be necessary, for a time at least, especially since the jetties have been damaged, to maintain a dredge at Galveston to remove any shoaling that may take place in the improved channel, and it is estimated that $50,000 will be required during the next fiscal year for the maintenance and operation of the dredge belonging to this improvement. This is the amount that will be needed each and every year for this purpose.

July 1, 1900, balance unexpended	$143,220.89
Collected from Quartermaster's Department, United States Army	719.83
	143,940.72
June 30, 1901, amount expended during fiscal year	91,507.64
July 1, 1901, balance unexpended	52,433.08
July 1, 1901, outstanding liabilities	3,151.31
July 1, 1901, balance available	49,281.77

{ Amount (estimated) required for completion of necessary repairs.... 1,500,000.00
Amount that can be profitably expended in fiscal year ending June 30, 1903, for maintenance of improvement, in addition to the balance available July 1, 1901........................... 50,000.00
Submitted in compliance with requirements of sundry civil act of June 4, 1897, and of section 7 of the river and harbor act of 1899.

(See Appendix U 1.)

2. Deepening the channel from Galveston Harbor to Texas City, Tex.--This channel is designed to afford a channel 100 feet wide at bottom and 25 feet deep, north of Pelican Island, from Galveston Harbor to Texas City, Tex. The natural depth on the line of the proposed channel is from 4 to 8 feet. During 1895 and 1896 a channel 16 feet deep was dredged by the Texas City Terminal Company. No work having been done since then, it had, at the beginning of present operations shoaled nearly to its natural depth.

During the fiscal year the channel has been dredged to an average depth of 17 feet and 120 feet wide at bottom, for a distance of 14,350 feet. To procure this channel there was removed 815,060 cubic yards of material. Work was delayed on account of the contractor's plant being washed ashore during the hurricane of September 8, 1900.

No commercial statistics for the fiscal year ending June 30, 1901, could be obtained.

July 1, 1900, balance unexpended	$250,000
July 1, 1901, balance unexpended	250,000
July 1, 1901, amount covered by uncompleted contracts	250,000

(See Appendix U 2.)

3. Galveston ship channel and Buffalo Bayou, Texas.—These improvements have heretofore been reported on individually under the headings of "Ship channel in Galveston Bay, Texas," and "Buffalo Bayou, Texas." The river and harbor act of March 3, 1899, combines the work under one item.

The ship channel in Galveston Bay and Buffalo Bayou are two links in the waterway connecting Houston with deep water in Galveston Bay, the other link being the San Jacinto River and the Morgan Canal.

In their natural state these two waterways had a depth of from 4 to 8¼ feet. The project adopted for the improvement provided for a channel 100 feet wide and 12 feet deep. Dredging was carried on for a number of years, furnishing a channel sufficient for the character of vessels heretofore navigating these channels.

In 1892 the Government purchased the Morgan Cut and Canal, 5.43 miles long, from the Buffalo Bayou Ship Channel Company for the sum of $92,316.85.

The approved project for the expenditure of the available funds consists in dredging a channel about 80 feet wide and 17¼ feet deep from deep water in Galveston Harbor, through Galveston Bay and Morgan Cut (Division 1), and constructing pile and brush dike from Morgan Cut to Redfish Bar. The sum of $25,000 is reserved for expenditure for expenses of administration, surveys, and maintenance above Division 1 (through San Jacinto Bay to Houston, Tex.).

The amounts expended on these channels to June 30, 1900, are as follows:

Ship channel in Galveston Bay	$812,065.15
Buffalo Bayou, Texas	210,150.14
Purchase of Morgan Cut and Canal	92,316.85
Total	1,114,523.14

During the past fiscal year active operations were carried on under contract with Charles Clarke & Co., of Galveston, Tex.

The dike piling advanced a distance of 21,000 feet from Morgan Canal.

The brush filling between dike piling advanced a distance of 14,100 feet from Morgan Canal.

The dike and channel are complete a total distance of 11,300 feet from Morgan Canal, with a navigable depth of 17 feet and 70 feet wide at bottom.

The total amount of commerce brought down Buffalo Bayou during the fiscal year amounted to 154,459 tons; of this, 118,738 tons were cotton, 1,927 tons cotton products, 3,008 tons coal, 8,286 tons lumber, 4,000 tons building material, 8,500 tons wood, and 10,000 tons general merchandise.

GALVESTON SHIP CHANNEL AND BUFFALO BAYOU, TEXAS.

July 1, 1900, balance unexpended	$300,000.00
July 1, 1901, balance unexpended	300,000.00
July 1, 1901, outstanding liabilities	708.35
July 1, 1901, balance available	299,291.65
July 1, 1901, amount covered by uncompleted contracts	279,291.65
Amount (estimated) required for completion of existing project	3,700,000.00
Amount that can be profitably expended in fiscal year ending June 30, 1903, in addition to the balance available July 1, 1901. Submitted in compliance with requirements of sundry civil act of June 4, 1897.	300,000.00

SHIP CHANNEL IN GALVESTON BAY.

July 1 1900, balance unexpended	$36,960.70
June 30, 1901, amount expended during fiscal year	36,960.70

BUFFALO BAYOU.

July 1, 1900, balance unexpended	$18,599.86
June 30, 1901, amount expended during fiscal year	12,747.76
July 1, 1901, balance unexpended	5,852.10
July 1, 1901, outstanding liabilities	5,852.10

(See Appendix U 3.)

4. Operating and care of Morgan Canal, Texas.—The expenses of caring for this canal during the fiscal year ending June 30, 1901, amounted to $360, which was paid from the permanent-indefinite appropriation provided by section 4, act of July 5, 1884. A statement contained in the report of the local engineer officer shows the items of expenditure.

The amount of $5,000 allotted July 11, 1901, is to be expended in repairing bulkhead to canal, boundary fence to reservation, and salary of watchman in charge of canal for the fiscal year 1902. No work had been done on repairs to bulkhead and fence to close of fiscal year.

(See Appendix U 4.)

5. Trinity River, Texas.—The improvement of this stream has been limited to that portion lying between the mouth and Liberty at the head of tide water, a distance of 39 miles. The river empties into Galveston Bay through several mouths or passes, opposite each of which a bar existed on which the depth of water did not exceed 3¼ feet at mean low tide.

The project adopted for this improvement on June 18, 1878, consisted in the removal of snags from the river below Liberty and in dredging a channel 80 feet wide by 6 feet deep across the bar at the mouth of the pass then in use by vessels. The estimated cost of the work was $22,581.40. (See Annual Report of the Chief of Engineers for 1873, p. 685 et seq.) On May 4, 1889, an amended project was adopted. It contemplated the erection of two parallel jetties at the mouth known as the Middle Pass, placed about 275 feet apart and extending about 7,750 feet into Galveston Bay; also in closing the other two principal passes by submerged dams, the object being to create and maintain a channel 6 feet deep at mean low tide at the mouth of the river. The revised cost of the improvement was placed at $89,500. (See Annual Report of the Chief of Engineers for 1889, p. 1557 et seq.)

The amount expended on this improvement to the close of the fiscal year ending June 30, 1900, was $77,249.37.

At that date the west jetty had been completed, its length being 7,359 feet, and a channel 100 feet wide by 5 feet deep had been secured at the mouth of the river.

By act of Congress approved March 3, 1899, an appropriation was made for the construction of a dredge boat and snagging outfit in connection with the improvement of Brazos River between Velasco and Richmond, West Galveston Bay channel, Double Bayou, and the mouths of adjacent streams, which, by the law, will be available for use on the Trinity River.

The total amount of freight carried during the fiscal year between Wallisville and the mouth was 16,390 tons, of which 25 tons were cotton, 75 tons cotton seed, 600 tons charcoal, 40 tons stock, 15,000 tons lumber, and 150 tons wood, and 500 tons general merchandise.

July 1, 1900, balance unexpended $6,750.63
July 1, 1901, balance unexpended 6,750.63

(See Appendix U 5.)

6. Channel in West Galveston Bay, Texas.—West Galveston Bay is a body of water covering about 39 square miles, and lies between Galveston Island and the mainland. It extends from Galveston Bay to the west end of Oyster Bay and is connected with the Gulf of Mexico by San Luis Pass, at the western extremity of Galveston Island, and with the Brazos River by the Galveston and Brazos Canal. The natural depth of the bay was from 2½ to 3 feet.

The project for improving the bay was adopted on June 13, 1892, and consisted in widening, deepening, and straightening the channel so as to give a width of 200 feet and a least depth of 3½ feet from Galveston Bay to San Luis Pass and a channel 100 feet wide and 3 feet deep along Christmas Point in Oyster Bay, both channels to be properly defined by beacons. The estimated cost of the improvement was $28,998.80. (See Annual Report of the Chief of Engineers for 1892, p. 1556 et seq.) On July 8, 1896, authority was given to modify the project so as to afford a depth of 5 feet instead of 3½ feet, provided the cost of the work should not be increased.

By act of Congress approved March 3, 1899, an appropriation was made for construction of a dredge boat and snagging outfit in connection with improvement of Brazos River between Velasco and Richmond, West Galveston Bay channel, Double Bayou, and the mouths of adjacent streams, which, by the terms of the law, will be available for use in West Galveston Bay.

The amount expended to June 30, 1900, was $19,775.97.

This expenditure resulted in an unobstructed channel 100 feet wide and from 3 to 3½ feet deep from Galveston Bay to the Galveston and Brazos Canal. Beacons were also erected to define the channel.

No work was done during the past fiscal year.

No commercial statistics for the fiscal year ending June 30, 1901, could be obtained.

July 1, 1900, balance unexpended $5,224.03
July 1, 1901, balance unexpended 5,224.03

(See Appendix U 6)

7. *Mouth of Brazos River, Texas.*—The improvement of the mouth of this stream has heretofore been undertaken by the Brazos River Channel and Dock Company, they having partially constructed a system of parallel jetties.

The river and harbor act approved March 3, 1899, contains the following item:

> Mouth of Brazos River, Texas: For dredging, and such other work as may be deemed most effective in the judgment of the Secretary of War in improving and developing the harbor, eighty-five thousand dollars: *Provided*, That no part of said sum shall be expended until the Brazos River Channel and Dock Company shall file with the Secretary of War a transfer to the United States of the jetties, and auxiliary works; also a release of all rights and privileges conferred upon said company by its charter or by the Act of Congress approved August ninth, eighteen hundred and eighty-eight, to charge or collect tolls for the use and navigation of said river; and the Secretary of War is directed to have an examination made of the mouth of the Brazos and the jetties, and report to Congress the estimated cost of extending the jetties one-half mile, and the estimated depth and width of the channel to be obtained by such extension, and the estimated cost of obtaining twenty feet of water and a channel one hundred and fifty feet wide.

Under date of April 25, 1899, the Brazos River Channel and Dock Company filed with the Secretary of War a transfer to the United States of these jetties and auxiliary works, also a release of all rights and privileges conferred upon the said company by its charter or by the act of Congress aproved August 9, 1888, to charge or collect tolls for the use and navigation of the river.

The proposed work at this locality consists in putting the present jetties at the mouth of the river in a fair condition to resist the effects of storms and to protect a dredge while working between them, also to make a beginning in the construction of spur dikes to narrow the channel between the jetties, and to dredge a channel as far up as the light-house to a depth of 18 feet at mean low tide and 150 feet wide.

The amount expended on this improvement up to June 30, 1900, was $175,964.99.

A contract was entered into on October 19, 1899, for doing the necessary jetty work at the mouth of the river.

Work was carried on during the past fiscal year up to and including September 7, 1900, just prior to the hurricane of September 8, 1900.

The condition of the jetties before and after the hurricane is given in the report of the district officer, Appendix U 7.

The estimate for completion of existing project has been increased by $175,000, the amount estimated by Board of Engineers to be necessary for repair of damages by the hurricane of September 8, 1900. The report of the Board is printed in House Doc. No. 133, Fifty-sixth Congress, second session, and is herewith as Appendix U 17.

No commercial statistics for the fiscal year ending June 30, 1901, could be obtained.

July 1, 1900, balance unexpended $67,785.01
June 30, 1901, amount expended during fiscal year 54,305.74

July 1, 1901, balance unexpended 13,479.27

{ Amount (estimated) required for completion of existing project 325,000.00
Amount that can be profitably expended in fiscal year ending June 30,
 1903, in addition to the balance unexpended July 1, 1901 .... 120,000.00
Submitted in compliance with requirements of sundry civil act of June
 4, 1897.

(See Appendix U 7.)

8. Brazos River between Velasco and Richmond, West Galveston Bay channel, Double Bayou, and the mouths of adjacent streams.—The river and harbor act approved March 3, 1899, provides as follows:

For the improvement of the Brazos River between Velasco and Richmond, West Galveston Bay Channel, Double Bayou, and the mouths of adjacent streams, sixty-five thousand dollars, out of which said sum a suitable dredge and snagging outfit may be provided to carry on said work and to be used on other approved projects on the Texas coast, including streams emptying into the Gulf of Mexico and bays connected therewith.

Heretofore the projects embraced in this improvement have been independent (see improving Brazos River, Texas, between Velasco and Richmond, Annual Report of the Chief of Engineers for 1895, p. 1838 et seq.; improving channel of West Galveston Bay, Annual Report of the Chief of Engineers for 1892, p. 1556 et seq., and improving Double Bayou, Annual Report of the Chief of Engineers for 1898, p. 287 et seq.).

The object of this improvement, in part, is to obtain and maintain a navigable channel depth of from 4 to 6 feet across the bars at the mouths of most of the streams and bayous along the Texas coast by dredging and snagging, the plant to be owned and operated by the United States.

The improvement is intended to develop a light-draft inland navigation tributary to Galveston and other Texas harbors which will afford cheap transportation by light-draft steamers and barges to the fertile coast country of Texas.

During the past fiscal year plans and specifications were prepared and contracts entered into for the various parts of the dredge.

No commercial statistics for the fiscal year ending June 30, 1901, could be obtained.

July 1, 1900, balance unexpended $65,000.00
June 30, 1901, amount expended during fiscal year 1,529.32

July 1, 1901, balance unexpended 63,470.68
July 1, 1901, outstanding liabilities 311.66

July 1, 1901, balance available 63,159.02

July 1, 1901, amount covered by uncompleted contracts.................. 35,771.00

{ Amount that can be profitably expended in fiscal year ending June 30,
 1903, in addition to the balance available July 1, 1901................ 75,000.00
Submitted in compliance with requirements of sundry civil act of June
 4, 1897.

(See Appendix U 8.)

9. *Brazos River, Texas*.—This improvement is at present limited to that portion of the river lying between Richmond and Velasco, a distance of about 89 miles; its low-water level is affected by the Gulf tide as far up as Bolivar Landing, 40 miles above Velasco. The course of the river is tortuous, and the channel was obstructed by shoals and snags.

The project for improvement was adopted June 3, 1896, and consisted in the removal of snags and overhanging trees. It was estimated that $10,000 would put this portion of the river in good navigable condition at ordinary stages, and that an annual expenditure of $2,500 would keep it in this condition (see Annual Report of the Chief of Engineers for 1895, p. 1838 et seq.).

No work has been done under this project.

By act of Congress approved March 3, 1899, an appropriation was made for the construction of a dredge boat and snagging outfit in connection with improvement of Brazos River, West Galveston Bay channel, Double Bayou, and the mouths of the adjacent streams. This plant will be available for use on this river.

Amount expended on this improvement to June 30, 1900, $21.57.

No commercial statistics for the fiscal year ending June 30, 1901, could be obtained.

July 1, 1900, balance unexpended	$4,978.43
June 30, 1901, amount expended during fiscal year	.78
July 1, 1901, balance unexpended	4,977.65

(See Appendix U 9.)

10. *Aransas Pass, Texas*.—Aransas Pass is on the south coast of Texas, 175 miles southwest of Galveston and 125 miles north of the Rio Grande, and is the outlet of Aransas Bay to the Gulf of Mexico. The area of the bay is about 80 square miles. It is connected with Corpus Christi Bay on one side and with the shallow bays of Mosquite, St. Charles, and Copano on the other.

For projects and work done by the United States Government and private corporations at Aransas Pass, see Annual Report of the Chief of Engineers for 1898, page 1527 et seq.

The river and harbor act of March 3, 1899, contains the following item:

> Improving Aransas Pass, Texas: For dredging and other improvement of Aransas Pass Harbor, sixty thousand dollars: *Provided*, That the Secretary of War is hereby authorized to contract for the removal of that portion of the old Government jetty in said harbor from the end nearest the curved jetty constructed by the Aransas Pass Harbor Company to the wreck Mary, in such manner as to in no wise interfere with the curved jetty now located in said harbor: *And provided further*, That said contract shall not be let by the Secretary of War nor said work done until the said Aransas Pass Harbor Company shall have properly released and surrendered all rights and privileges heretofore granted to it in said harbor by Congress, also the jetty constructed in said harbor.

The Aransas Pass Harbor Company, under date of March 27, 1899, released and surrendered all rights and privileges heretofore granted to it in Aransas Pass Harbor by Congress; also the jetties constructed in said harbor.

At the beginning of the fiscal year the approved project for work at this locality was to be confined to constructing two parallel jetties; also in removing a portion of the old Government jetty and in dredging, with a view of obtaining a channel 20 feet deep, with a bottom width of 300 feet.

A contract was in force with Charles Clarke & Co., of Galveston, Tex., for removing the old Government jetty and dredging. No work was done under this contract, and it having been ascertained that the old Government jetty, which it was claimed was acting as an obstruction to scour, was down quite deep and covered with sand and not acting as an obstruction, it was decided to annul the contract without prejudice to the contractor or to the United States, and same was annulled by supplemental articles of agreement.

A new project was submitted and approved for expenditure of the available funds, and is to consist in repairing the curved jetty from inner end of existing structure as far out as available funds (about $75,000) will permit (about 3,000 feet).

Bids for doing the work were advertised for, and at the close of the fiscal year contract is being entered into.

During the year borings were taken over the old Government jetty to ascertain its condition.

The amount expended on this improvement to June 30, 1900, was $544,129.01, exclusive of $9,938.93, subscribed by citizens of Rockport and Corpus Christi.

The amount expended during the fiscal year was for cost of inspection, surveys, and office expenses.

No commercial statistics for the fiscal year ending June 30, 1901, could be obtained.

July 1, 1900, balance unexpended	$97,120.99
June 30, 1901, amount expended during fiscal year	4,565.71
July 1, 1901, balance unexpended	92,555.28
July 1, 1901, outstanding liabilities	314.18
July 1, 1901, balance available	92,241.10
Amount (estimated) required for completion of existing project	1,680,000.00
Amount that can be profitably expended in fiscal year ending June 30, 1903, in addition to the balance available July 1, 1901	350,000.00
Submitted in compliance with requirements of sundry civil act of June 4, 1897.	

(See Appendix U 10).

11. Harbor at Brazos Santiago, Tex.—No work has been done on this improvement since 1884. This work was dropped from the list of improvements in the Galveston district in December, 1895, and the available balance returned to the Treasury.

Owing to the shoaling of the bar, practically cutting off all water communication, authority was secured to use the balance, $57,476, remaining in the Treasury, it being the intention to dredge a channel over the bar to give temporary relief to the locality. Project has been approved with a view to hiring a dredging plant. Bids for hiring a plant were received during the past fiscal year, but were rejected on account of prices being excessive, and as a recent survey showed a navigable depth of 8 feet, which was all that was necessary, no work was attempted during the year. The amount expended during the year was for office expenses, etc., and survey.

No commercial statistics for the fiscal year ending June 30, 1901, could be obtained.

July 1, 1900, balance unexpended $57,144.85
June 30, 1901, amount expended during fiscal year 1,958.01

July 1, 1901, balance unexpended 55,186.84

(See Appendix U 11.)

12. Removing sunken vessels or craft obstructing or endangering navigation.—During the hurricane which visited Galveston September 8, 1900, a great many barges, schooners, etc., and one steam vessel were wrecked and sunk in Galveston Bay and vicinity, and same have become a menace to navigation.

The wrecks to be removed are the steamer *Cumberland*, an iron oil tank, barges *Jules* and *Alice*, and tug *Kate*.

Permission has been granted to remove these wrecks, and an allotment of $2,500 made for expenses of same.

At the close of the fiscal year contract had been entered into for removing the wrecks.

The amount expended during the year was $33.36.

(See Appendix U 12.)

EXAMINATIONS AND SURVEYS MADE IN COMPLIANCE WITH EMERGENCY RIVER AND HARBOR ACT APPROVED JUNE 6, 1900.

Preliminary examinations and surveys of the following localities were made by the local officer and reports thereon submitted through the division engineer:

1. Preliminary examination and survey of Galveston Bay, Texas, with a view to widening, deepening, and extending the present channel from the Gulf of Mexico to a point opposite Fifty-first street, Galveston.—Captain Riché submitted reports dated November 15 and December 21, 1900, with plan for improvement at an estimated cost of $1,585,000. He states that if one contract should be authorized for the entire work the estimate would be reduced to $1,500,000. An estimate of $25,000 is submitted as the amount required annually for maintenance of the improvement after completion. The reports were transmitted to Congress and printed in House Doc. No. 264, Fifty-sixth Congress, second session. (See also Appendix U 13.)

2. Preliminary examination of Trinity River, Texas, between Dallas and Fort Worth.—Captain Riché submitted report dated October 13, 1900. It is his opinion, concurred in by the division engineer and by the Chief of Engineers, that the improvement of the locality by the General Government is not advisable at the present time. The report was transmitted to Congress and printed in House Doc. No. 83, Fifty-sixth Congress, second session. (See also Appendix U 14.)

3. Preliminary examination and survey of Brazos River, Texas, from its mouth to the city of Waco, with a view of procuring navigable depths of 4, 5, and 6 feet.—Captain Riché submitted report on preliminary examination August 29, 1900, and preliminary report on survey December 22, 1900. Final report on survey dated January 30, 1901, was submitted, with alternative plans for improvement estimated to cost—

By locks and dams $5,950,000
    Additional annual expense for maintenance 225,000
By open-channel work and locks and dams, combined 3,725,000
    Additional annual expense for maintenance 145,000

The reports were transmitted to Congress and printed in House Docs. Nos. 283 and 450, Fifty-sixth Congress, second session. (See also Appendix U 15.)

Captain Riché was also charged with the duty of making examination and survey of *Galveston, Tex., inner harbor*, and report thereon will be submitted in time for transmission to Congress at its next session.

REPORT UPON EXAMINATION OF THE EFFECT OF THE STORM OF SEPTEMBER 8, 1900, ON THE JETTIES AND MAIN SHIP CHANNEL AT GALVESTON, TEX.

A Board of Engineers submitted report dated November 23, 1900. The estimated cost of necessary repairs to the jetties is $1,500,000. The report was transmitted to Congress and printed in House Doc. No. 134, Fifty-sixth Congress, second session. (See also Appendix U 16.)

REPORT UPON EXAMINATION OF THE EFFECT OF THE STORM OF SEPTEMBER 8, 1900, ON THE JETTIES IN BRAZOS RIVER.

A Board of Engineers submitted report dated November 23, 1900. The estimated cost of the necessary repairs to the jetties is $175,000. The report was transmitted to Congress and printed in House Doc. No. 133, Fifty-sixth Congress, second session. (See also Appendix U 17.)

WESTERN RIVERS.

IMPROVEMENT OF CERTAIN RIVERS AND WATERWAYS IN LOUISIANA, TEXAS, ARKANSAS. AND MISSISSIPPI TRIBUTARY TO MISSISSIPPI RIVER; WATER GAUGES ON THE MISSISSIPPI RIVER AND ITS PRINCIPAL TRIBUTARIES.

This district was in the charge of Maj. Thomas L. Casey, Corps of Engineers. Division Engineer, Col. Henry M. Robert, Corps of Engineers (now brigadier-general, Chief of Engineers, United States Army, retired), to May 2, 1901, and Col. Amos Stickney, Corps of Engineers, since May 9. 1901.

1. *Red River Louisiana, Arkansas, and Indian Territory.*—The improvement of Red River was begun in 1828, and appropriations aggregating $535,765.50 were made for the purpose between 1828 and 1852, but operations were suspended from 1852 until 1872, during which interval the results of former work were lost.

The improvement was resumed in 1872, at which time the river above Shreveport, La., was closed by the great raft, then 32 miles long and growing as each flood brought additions of drift from above. Below Shreveport the gradual enlargement of Tones Bayou Outlet depleted the main channel and threatened its closure to navigation. The falls at Alexandria, La., were impassable at low stages. Snags, stumps, sunken logs, and leaning timber rendered navigation difficult and dangerous at all stages, and the wrecks of 200 steamboats lay in the channel between the mouth and the head of navigation.

The project adopted in 1872 contemplated removing the raft and closing Tones Bayou. It has been amplified since to include the removal of jams, snags, wrecks, leaning timber, etc.; opening and enlarging the channel through the falls at Alexandria, deepening shoal places, closing outlets, and fixing caving banks; to improve and keep navigation open from the head of Atchafalaya River, Louisiana, to Fulton, Ark., 508.6 miles. The nature of the work requires that it be continued for many years, and no estimate for completion is given on this account. The river and harbor act of March 3, 1899, provided for extending work above Fulton to mouth of Kiamichi River, Indian Territory, previously carried on under separate appropriations.

The river and harbor acts of July 13, 1892, and August 18, 1894, provided that work under the appropriations of these acts for Red River should be carried out in accordance with the plan of Maj. J. H. Willard, Corps of Engineers, the officer then in local charge of the work. Major Willard's plans included the "construction of a substantial system of levees to restrain the greatest floods, either alone or in partnership with the riparian States." The construction of levees was begun by the United States in 1892, in conjunction with the State of Louisiana and local levee districts, in accordance with what was understood to be the will of Congress as expressed by the wording of the item of appropriation.

Since 1892, in conjunction with the State of Louisiana and local levee districts, 139.28 miles of new levees and 93.58 miles of enlargement, containing 8,827,399 cubic yards, were built at a total cost of $1,246,687. The proportion of this levee work constructed by the United States was about 17½ per cent, and its proportion of the total cost was about 19 per cent.

The total amount expended from 1872 to June 30, 1900, for work between the Atchafalaya River, Louisiana, and the Kiamichi River, Indian Territory, was $1,507,174.10, with the following chief results: In the old raft region there flowed in the course marked out for it a broad and deep river, safe for navigation at all but the lowest stages, with a channel constantly scouring, the bottom having lowered as much as 15 feet, and the low-water line having followed it to a certain extent. In addition to opening hundreds of miles of navigable waterway, the removal of the raft drained the fertile valley and reclaimed thousands of acres of productive lands. Tones Bayou Outlet was closed by a heavy earthen dam connecting with the levees above and below it; the main channel of the river below the outlet had widened and scoured until it was capable of carrying the discharge at flood stages, and navigation of the stretch formerly impaired by the outlet was uninterrupted at the lowest stages. The falls at Alexandria had been made passable for steamboats at all stages the year round, an increase of about two months in the period of navigation. Persistent snagging operations, repeated from time to time, kept the river open, prevented formation of raft, reduced the dangers of navigation to a minimum, and enabled steamboats to make regular trips; the river being open from the Atchafalaya River to Fulton to boats of 3-feet draft at very low stages, say barely a foot above zero on the Shreveport gauge. All of the chief outlets along the right bank below the Arkansas line to Tones Bayou, Louisiana, were closed. Operations during the fiscal year ending June 30, 1901, were confined to snagging work for the general improvement of the river.

The commerce of Red River consists of large shipments of cotton, cotton seed and its products, lumber, staves, saw logs, etc., with heavy return freights of general merchandise and plantation supplies, and for the fiscal year 1901 aggregated 155,474 tons, valued at $6,339,000.

The amount of business for the past twelve years, as reported to and compiled for comparison in the report of the district officer, shows great variations from year to year, probably due to crop conditions, periods of very low water, and other causes, ranging in quantity from 66,376 to 228,630 tons per annum, with estimated values of from $3,419,000 to $9,185,000. The average for the twelve years is 108,653 tons, valued at $5,382,000. To this should be added the commerce of Ouachita River, entering Red River at the mouth of Black River, the average of which is 160,553 tons, valued at $6,118,000, making a total of 269,206 tons, valued at $11,500,000.

The estimate of $135,000 presented is for repairs of and additions to plant, surveys, snagging work, and contingencies, but does not include an estimate for levee work.

The officer in local charge submits in his report an additional estimate of $550,000 for the construction of levees. It is respectfully recommended that such an amount as Congress may consider proper for expenditure for levee construction as a part of the improvement of the Red River may be appropriated or allotted separately from the appropriation or allotment for other items of improvement. The construction of levees on the Red River has been heretofore carried on under the assumption that Congress has, by the wording of the item, approved of such work; but it appears proper that, if such work is approved of by Congress as a part of the improvement of Red River, the instructions as to the work should be definite.

Under authority of the Secretary of War dated April 29, 1901, the unexpended balance of $2,760.97 for "construction of levees" was transferred to the allotment for "general improvement," the amount being too small to undertake any levee work.

The recommendation made in the last report that legislative action be taken to transfer the balance of allotment for Little River to the allotment for general improvement is repeated. It is recommended also that similar action be taken for the transfer of the balance for Sulphur River to the allotment for general improvement, further work in that tributary not being required.

July 1, 1900, balance unexpended	$89,825.90
June 30, 1901, amount expended during fiscal year	48,980.31
July 1, 1901, balance unexpended	40,845.59
July 1, 1901, outstanding liabilities	22.68
July 1, 1901, balance available	40,822.91

Amount that can be profitably expended in fiscal year ending June 30, 1903, in addition to the balance available July 1, 1901 .... 135,000.00
Submitted in compliance with requirements of sundry civil act of June 4, 1897.

(See Appendix V 1.)

2. Cypress Bayou, Texas and Louisiana.—The waterway from Jefferson, Tex., to Red River near Shreveport, La., known as Cypress Bayou and the lakes, evidently was an unnavigable stream until the advance of the great Red River raft above Shreveport had caused its bottom lands to fill and become what are now designated as Fairy, Sodo, and Cross lakes. Before a channel was opened through the raft in 1873, there was some navigation to points above that obstruction through lakes and overflowed lands, and at high stages steamboats followed that route to the head of Willow Pass, where boats for Jefferson turned to the west and reached that town by a tolerably direct course up Fairy Lake and Cypress Bayu.

Work on the part of the United States for improving navigation between Shreveport and Jefferson, by the removal of stumps and sunken logs, etc., and by dredging at the narrow passes, was begun under the river and harbor act of June 10, 1872, and a total sum of $133,701.33 has been appropriated for the purpose in the twenty-nine years since operations commenced, in addition to $12,000 for surveys. The removal of the Red River raft, and the subsequent closure of the outlets and construction of levees along the right bank of Red River, caused its bottom to scour and deepen, reduced the water supply of the lakes to their natural drainage, except during extreme floods, and made them drain more rapidly, shortening the period of navigation year by year until 1897, when it ceased altogether.

On account of this condition, Congress called for a survey to ascertain whether navigation could be permanently improved by locks and dams. The report upon this survey was printed in the report of the Chief of Engineers for 1893, pages 2065 to 2082, to which reference is invited. A plan was formulated for the construction of a dam across Sodo Lake just above Albany Flats, and for an inlet from Red River through Cottonwood Bayou, with a lock at the head of that bayou, 29¼ miles above Shreveport. This plan failed to receive the sanction of Congress, however, presumably because of its great cost in comparison with possible commercial benefits that might be derived; but the two succeeding river and harbor acts appropriated a total sum of $15,000 "for dredging and removing obstructions and straightening channel between Jefferson, Tex., and Shreveport, La." The project for expenditure of this money, approved June 14, 1897, contemplated improving the channel from Jefferson to the mouth of Twelve-mile Bayou by the removal of logs and stumps, widening it by dredging, easing the curves, clearing the banks of the bayou of leaning timber, and marking the channel through the lakes. Immediately after approval of this project, a dredge belonging to the plant of the district was towed to Shreveport, where it has been waiting since July 5, 1897, but during the four years since there has been no stage sufficient for it to cross Albany Flats and enter the lakes. During the period of lowest water in 1898 the route was worked over from Jefferson to Shreveport; the stumps, logs, leaning timber, etc., were removed, and the channel through the lakes was marked with signboards.

The total amount expended to June 30, 1900, was $139,080.37. The amount expended during the fiscal year ending June 30, 1901, was for care of the plant waiting at Shreveport.

It appears that navigation between Shreveport and Jefferson can be restored only by a costly system of locks and dams, upon which a large sum might be expended without adequate return of commerce. It is the opinion of the district officer, concurred in by the Chief of Engineers, that the expenditure of the available funds for dredging will afford no relief to navigation.

July 1, 1900, balance unexpended $6,620.96
June 30, 1901, amount expended during fiscal year 885.60

July 1, 1901, balance unexpended 5,735.36

(See Appendix V 2.)

3. *Ouachita and Black rivers, Arkansas and Louisiana.*—The improvement of Ouachita River was commenced in 1871, at which time

navigation was much obstructed by snags, sunken logs, wrecks, leaning and caving trees, etc., and at low stages a greater part of the river was unnavigable, on account of numerous rock, gravel, and sand bars.

A project was entered upon in 1871 for a temporary improvement between Arkadelphia, Ark., and Trinity, La., by the removal of snags, etc., and dredging at the worst bars. In 1872 a project for improvement by locks and dams was entered upon, but it was abandoned in 1874 for various reasons, the chief one being that the locks would be idle at the time required for use until a permanent improvement was obtained at the mouth of Red River. The project approved June 30, 1874, under which work has continued since, contemplated the removal of snags, logs, wrecks, leaning timber, etc., below Camden, Ark., to Trinity, La.; Black River below Trinity, 56 miles long, connecting the Ouachita with Red River, was added by river and harbor act of 1884. The distance from Camden to the mouth of Black River is 350 miles. No estimate of cost is given, as the nature of the work requires that it be continuous.

The total amount expended to June 30, 1900, was $547,378.57, but of that sum $131,295.69 was expended prior to the project of 1874.

To comply with a requirement of the river and harbor act of 1894, a survey was in progress for the purpose of preparing new plans and estimates for an improvement by locks and dams.

During the fiscal year ending June 30, 1901, snagging operations and office and field work of the survey were continued, but all the data required for a comprehensive report upon a project for improvement by locks and dams had not been acquired. A final report probably will be submitted by January 1, 1902.

The commerce of Ouachita River and its tributaries is considerable, consisting of shipments of cotton, cotton seed, lumber, staves, saw logs, and miscellaneous articles, with return freights of general merchandise and plantation supplies, and for the fiscal year 1901 aggregated 215,888 tons, valued at $8,642,000. Most of the cotton is shipped direct to New Orleans, and large quantities of staves are shipped to that city each year for export. The business of the past twelve years as reported to the district officer and compiled for comparison in his report, ranges between 73,679 and 239,197 tons per annum, with values estimated at $3,293,000 to $10,234,250. The average for the twelve years is 160,553 tons, valued at $6,118,000.

Under a readjustment of the allotments in April, 1901, the sum of $14,000 was transferred from the allotment for survey to that for general improvement.

The available funds are to be applied to continuing snagging operations and to completion of the survey. The estimate presented below is for needed repairs in the snag boat *O. G. Wagner* and continuing snagging work, etc., under the project of 1874.

July 1, 1900, balance unexpended	$65,121.43
June 30, 1901, amount expended during fiscal year	33,232.11
July 1, 1901, balance unexpended	31,889.32
July 1, 1901, outstanding liabilities	125.45
July 1, 1901, balance available	31,763.87
Amount that can be profitably expended in fiscal year ending June 30, 1903, in addition to the balance available July 1, 1901	50,000.00

Submitted in compliance with requirements of sundry civil act of June 4, 1897.

(See Appendix V 3.)

4. Bayou Bartholomew, Louisiana and Arkansas.—The States of Louisiana and Arkansas made expenditures at various times for the improvement of this stream, which was navigated to a considerable extent as far back as 1843. In 1880 it was navigable at high stages for light-draft boats for a period of about three months in the year, but an examination made that year showed that passageway for steamboats was much obstructed by snags, sunken logs, wrecks, leaning timber, etc.

In the river and harbor act of 1881 Congress entered upon a project for the removal of these obstructions, to afford safe navigation and extend the period thereof, between the mouth and Baxter, Ark., about 180 miles above. After sixteen years' work, with small and intermittent appropriations, this project was practically completed in 1897 to McComb Landing, Ark., the present head of navigation, about 138 miles above the mouth, at a cost of $45,873.53. This work resulted in safer navigation, increasing the period to about six months of the year, enabling larger boats to make trips in half the time formerly required, and reducing freight rates about 50 per cent. There being no demand for navigation above McComb Landing, subsequent expenditures were for maintenance of the improvement under the project approved March 24, 1899, the sum of $5,339.89 having been applied to that purpose to the close of the fiscal year ending June 30, 1900, making the expenditures to that date aggregate the sum of $51,213.42.

Work was not resumed during the fiscal year ending June 30, 1901, but it is proposed to apply the small balance now available toward maintaining the improvement when a favorable opportunity is afforded for a transfer of plant and organization from other work.

Drift, caving and sliding banks, and the rapid growth of vegetation constantly add new obstructions, which accumulate more rapidly and become more difficult to remove each year. The average annual cost of maintaining unobstructed navigation at stages on which steamboats can run is estimated at $2,500.

The country along Bayou Bartholomew is very productive and well settled, but much of the trade has been diverted to the railroads, the stages of the bayou (formerly the only way of shipment) frequently not being coincident with the needs of transportation. The river trade consists of shipments of cotton, cotton seed, saw logs, staves, and miscellaneous articles, with return freights of general merchandise and plantation supplies, which during the fiscal year 1901 aggregated 15,970 tons, valued at $254,000. In the last twelve years the freights reported annually range between 6,633 and 49,299 tons, with values estimated at $97,000 to $826,000, varying widely according to crop conditions and periods of navigation. The average for the twelve years is 15,720 tons, valued at $373,600.

July 1, 1900, balance unexpended	$786.58
June 30, 1901, amount expended during fiscal year	1.49
July 1, 1901, balance unexpended	785 09

Amount that can be profitably expended in fiscal year ending June 30, 1903, for maintenance of improvement, in addition to the balance unexpended July 1, 1901. Submitted in compliance with requirements of sundry civil act of June 4, 1897, and of section 7 of the river and harbor act of 1899.	5,000.00

(See Appendix V 4.)

5. *Bœuf River, Louisiana.*—The improvement of this stream was undertaken by the State of Louisiana more than sixty years ago, and navigation to Point Jefferson, La., was opened in 1840. When work was commenced by the United States the river was navigable to Point Jefferson at high stages, but passage was difficult and dangerous on account of overhanging timber, and snags and logs in the channel.

The project approved August 19, 1881, contemplated removing these obstructions so as to afford safe navigation at high stages to Wallace Landing, La., 19 miles above Point Jefferson and about 170 miles above the mouth. This project was completed in 1896 at a cost of $40,992.84. The work put the stream in safe navigable condition at stages high enough to permit boats to cross the bars, and enabled steamboats to save thirty-six hours on the trip, but the improvement was not permanent, as new obstructions are added continually.

Under the river and harbor act of 1886 a supplemental project was entered upon for the closure of three outlets near Point Jefferson, to confine the flow to the main channel, and in 1887–88 the outlets were closed by dams as securely as possible, by uniting with the efforts of planters whose lands would be protected from overflow, the proportion of the cost borne by the United States having been $5,441.78. This work gave immediate benefit to navigation, by causing the bars below the outlets to scour, but the dams were destroyed in 1890 during an overflow from the Mississippi River, due to crevasses in the levees near the head of Bœuf River, and sufficient funds for their restoration have not been provided. Soundings made in 1896 showed a very considerable shoaling below the outlets. The estimated cost of closing them substantially is $30,000. Under project approved March 28, 1899, work for the closure of the outlets has been deferred, as it would be unwise to begin operations until ample funds for the purpose are provided, and $2,500 per annum for maintenance of the work performed under the original project was recommended.

The total amount expended to June 30, 1900, was $48,936.91.

As no work for maintenance of the improvement had been performed since December, 1898, an examination of the stream was made in April, 1901, when it was ascertained that the new obstructions, caused by drift, sliding and caving banks, and the rapid growth of timber, were so extensive and numerous that the allotment of $2,500 made in 1899 was not sufficient for their removal. Upon the recommendation of the district officer, concurred in by the Chief of Engineers, the Secretary of War authorized an additional allotment of $2,500, and work for maintenance of the improvement was resumed May 6, 1901, at Point Jefferson, and at the close of the fiscal year ending June 30, 1901, had been carried downstream 65 miles to near Tanglewood, La.

Operations will be continued to the mouth of the river, and upon their completion the organization and equipment will be transferred to the work of improving Tensas River and Bayou Maçon, Louisiana.

The commerce of Bœuf River consists of shipments of cotton, cotton seed, and large quantities of staves sent to New Orleans for export, with return freights of general merchandise and plantation supplies, aggregating in the last fiscal year 7,800 tons, valued at $320,000. The amount of business reported for the past twelve years varies between 2,435 and 11,261 tons per annum, with estimated values ranging from $69,000 to $636,500; the average being 6,935 tons, valued at $299,000.

July 1, 1900, balance unexpended	$12,063.09
June 30, 1901, amount expended during fiscal year	2,214.25
July 1, 1901, balance unexpended	9,848.84
July 1, 1901, outstanding liabilities	541.79
July 1, 1901, balance available	9,307.05

{ Amount (estimated) required for completion of existing project 23,000.00
Amount that can be profitably expended in fiscal year ending June 30, 1903, for works of improvement and for maintenance, in addition to the balance available July 1, 1901 .... 23,000.00
Submitted in compliance with requirements of sundry civil act of June 4, 1897, and of section 7 of the river and harbor act of 1899.

(See Appendix V 5.)

6. *Tensas River and Bayou Maçon, Louisiana.*—These streams were navigable at high stages before their improvement was undertaken by the United States, but passage for steamboats was difficult and dangerous on account of leaning timber and of numerous snags, logs, stumps, etc., in the channel.

The project approved April 1, 1881, contemplated removing the obstructions in Tensas River between its mouth and Dallas, about 134 miles above, to give ease and safety to and extend the period of navigation, at an estimated cost of $23,000. Bayou Maçon, the chief commercial branch of Tensas River, was added under the same head of appropriation by river and harbor act of 1884, and the project, approved July 26, 1884, contemplated the same class of work from the entrance of the bayou into Tensas River to Floyd, about 98 miles above, at an estimated cost of $17,000.

The total amount expended to June 30, 1900, was $35,862.44, of which sum $11,947.02 was applied to work in Tensas River and $23,915.42 to work in Bayou Maçon. With these expenditures Bayou Maçon to Floyd, and Tensas River to Westwood Place, about 75 miles above its mouth, were put in fairly good navigable condition at medium and high stages, and the project for improving Bayou Maçon was practically completed during the fiscal year 1899. Upper Tensas River above Westwood Place was unnavigable, and there had been no demand for its improvement until 1899, when efforts were made to induce resettlement of the deserted plantations along its banks and to secure a continuance of the improvement to Dallas, as contemplated by the project of 1881.

The original plans were for completing work in both streams in one season of low water, at a cost of $40,000, which is the aggregate of all the appropriations made at intervals during the past twenty years. As new obstructions are adding continually, it was impracticable to complete the work in Tensas River as planned, and to maintain what has been accomplished since 1881 will require an annual expenditure of about $2,500 for some years to come.

No work was done during the fiscal year ending June 30, 1901, but it is proposed to transfer the party and outfit now employed in Bœuf River, La., to Bayou Maçon during the period of low water this autumn, and, after the removal of the obstructions added since 1899, to continue operations up Tensas River as far as the available funds will permit.

The commerce of the river and bayou consists chiefly of shipments of cotton, cotton seed, staves, etc., with return freights of plantation supplies and general merchandise. The amount of business, as reported for the past twelve years, ranges from 2,649 to 23,605 tons per annum, with values estimated at $122,500 to $999,500. The average for the twelve years is 14,373 tons, valued at $548,800. The commerce of the fiscal year 1901 aggregated 17,312 tons, valued at $375,000.

July 1, 1900, balance unexpended	$4,137.56
July 1, 1901, balance unexpended	4,137.56

{ Amount that can be profitably expended in fiscal year ending June 30, 1903, for maintenance of improvement, in addition to the balance unexpended July 1, 1901... 2,500.00
Submitted in compliance with requirements of sundry civil act of June 4, 1897, and of section 7 of the river and harbor act of 1899.

(See Appendix V 6.)

7. *Yazoo River, Mississippi.*—Before this work was commenced the period of navigation was limited to high stages on which steamboats could pass the wrecks of gunboats, steamers, and rafts sunk to prevent passage during the war of the rebellion, and the channel, also, was much obstructed by a great number of snags, stumps, tree slides, and sunken logs, and by a heavy growth of leaning timber along the banks.

Under river and harbor act of 1873 nine wrecks were removed by contract in 1873–74, and in 1874 a project was submitted for clearing the river of existing obstructions in a period of four years at a cost of $120,000, with annual appropriations thereafter for maintenance. The funds provided by Congress were not sufficient to carry out that plan, and as floods, sliding and caving banks, and the rapid growth of vegetation along an alluvial stream add new obstructions continually, and render snagging operations necessary from year to year in the interest of safe and uninterrupted navigation, the work has continued under a project for the removal of obstructions so far as funds provided will permit.

The amount expended during the twenty-seven years ending June 30, 1900, was $270,481.53, an average of about $10,000 per year, including the charges for purchase, repairs, and care of plant when not in commission. The results of the work performed, however, were marked. The large number of wrecks that blocked the channel at low stages and limited the period of navigation had been removed so as to present no obstruction, and the repeated work for the removal of snags, logs, leaning timber, etc., opened and maintained steamboat navigation from the mouth to the head of the river the year round, although various reaches were more or less obstructed at the lowest stages.

During the fiscal year ending June 30, 1901, the U. S. snag boat *Columbia* was employed at the low-water period of the autumn of 1900 in removing obstructions from the channel and banks. Operations extended from the mouth to the head, and a greater part of the river was worked over a second time. In addition to snags, logs, leaning trees, etc., part of the wreck of the steamer *Ferd R.* and the shaft from the steamer *Rover* were removed by the *Columbia.*

The commerce of Yazoo River and tributaries, as reported for the past eleven years, ranges between 102,098 and 254,235 tons annually, with values estimated at $2,840,000 to $8,314,000. The average for the eleven years is 189,661 tons, valued at $4,922,600.

The chief shipments are cotton, cotton seed, lumber, staves, etc., with return freights of general merchandise and plantation supplies. As soon as the river reaches a sufficiently low stage for effective work, snagging operations will be resumed and will continue until the available funds are exhausted.

Work in the Yazoo River and its tributaries could be carried on with greatest economy and the best results obtained if the streams were grouped as a system under one general head, and with this view the appended estimate is made. If sufficient plant is acquired and the work thoroughly completed, the subsequent cost of its maintenance should decrease each year.

The recommendations made in the report for 1900, for legislative action to authorize the transfer of the unexpended balances of $2,036.14 allotted for constructing pumping dredge and $5,000 allotted for removing the bar at Yazoo City to the allotment for general improvement of the river, are renewed.

July 1, 1900, balance unexpended	$24,518.47
June 30, 1901, amount expended during fiscal year	7,263.07
July 1, 1901, balance unexpended	17,255.40
July 1, 1901, outstanding liabilities	.24
July 1, 1901, balance available	17,255.16

Amount that can be profitably expended in fiscal year ending June 30, 1903, in addition to the balance available July 1, 1901 .... 90,000.00
Submitted in compliance with requirements of sundry civil act of June 4, 1897.

(See Appendix V 7.)

8. *Mouth of Yazoo River, and harbor at Vicksburg, Miss.*—The shifting bar at the mouth of the Yazoo is the most serious obstruction to the navigation of that river and its tributaries, a system comprising about 800 miles of navigable waterways. At low stages steamboats are prevented from entering or leaving the river without lightering, and it frequently happens that navigation across the bar is closed entirely at the busiest season of the year. In the river and harbor act of 1890 Congress ordered a survey to be made with a view to giving free passage the year round for vessels engaged in navigation of the river. A report upon the survey was submitted in February, 1892, and Congress entered upon the plan for improvement proposed therein with an appropriation for preliminary work in the next river and harbor act.

The project approved October 15, 1894, contemplated making a new mouth or outlet for Yazoo River from its former mouth on Old River, 9.8 miles above the present outlet to the Mississippi, through deep water in Old River, across a neck of low land to Lake Centennial, and around the head of De Soto Island and down Lake Centennial to the Mississippi River, entering it upon the channel side at Kleinston Landing. Lake Centennial is an old bend of the Mississippi River, cut off in 1876 above the present low-water landing at Kleinston, and Vicksburg Harbor is that part of the old channel along the city front and extending down to Kleinston Landing. The original estimate of cost was $1,500,000, which was revised in 1893 and reduced to $1,200,000, upon a basis of completion in three years. The sundry civil act of March 3, 1901, appropriated the balance of the latter estimate to complete the improvement.

The amount expended to June 30, 1900, was $202,405.03. With this expenditure the right of way for the main cut between Old River and Lake Centennial was acquired by purchase; borings were made at intervals to determine the character of the material to be excavated; the entire line from Old River to Kleinston was cleared and grubbed and the débris removed or burned, and 388,215 cubic yards of earth had been excavated along the diversion route, the greater part of the excavation having been performed by scraper work upon the higher ground at both ends of the main cut to enable dredges to work over the elevated portions at high stages.

July 20, 1900, a contract was entered into with the Atlantic, Gulf and Pacific Company for 7,500,000 cubic yards of excavation to complete the improvement, at a price of 12.4 cents per cubic yard. This contract was approved by the Chief of Engineers August 10, 1900, and provided that the work should begin by February 13, 1901, and be completed within thirty months. Operations with a powerful hydraulic dredge commenced November 19, 1900, and a second dredge of the same character was put to work December 17, 1900. These two machines were employed in Vicksburg Harbor until March 19, 1901, and excavated 1,026,743 cubic yards of material, using a large proportion of the spoil in building dikes to impound the water in Lake Centennial and maintain a stage of about 27 feet on the gauge at Kleinston. Upon the first sufficiently high stage both dredges were moved to the main cut, where a large clam-shell dredge, built at Vicksburg by the contractors, was added to the plant. Operations at the main cut were commenced March 25, and at the close of the fiscal year ending June 30, 1901, 845,021 cubic yards of material had been excavated and used in building the dam across the west arm of Lake Centennial, the approach thereto, and in closing the new outlet or West Pass, which opened during the flood of 1900 from the lake to the river. The total quantity of material excavated under this contract during the fiscal year was 1,871,764 cubic yards, showing a very satisfactory rate of progress.

While the margin for contingent expenses, surveys, etc., is small, it is believed that with no unforeseen contingencies the existing contract will complete the approved plan for this work.

The commerce of Yazoo River and tributaries, as reported for the past eleven years, averages 189,661 tons, valued at $4,922,600 per annum. Statistics of the commerce of the mouth of Yazoo River and Vicksburg Harbor have been collected, as far as practicable, for the past six years, and are compiled for comparison in the report of the district officer. The average of the entire commerce reported for the six years is 301,566 tons, valued at $8,000,600 per annum.

July 1, 1900, balance unexpended	$487,594.97
Amount appropriated by sundry civil act approved March 3, 1901	510,000.00
	997,594.97
June 30, 1901, amount expended during fiscal year	220,596.72
July 1, 1901, balance unexpended	776,998.25
July 1, 1901, outstanding liabilities	23,214.78
July 1, 1901, balance available	753,783.47
July 1, 1901, amount covered by uncompleted contracts	735,101.25

(See Appendix V 8.)

9. *Tallahatchie River, Mississippi.*—Before this work was undertaken the river was navigable to Sharkey, about 65 miles above the mouth, for six months of the year, but passage for steamboats was dif-

ficult and dangerous on account of the great number of obstructions in the channel and along the banks. Above Sharkey the growth of leaning timber was so heavy that at places the branches of trees upon opposite banks overlapped, and this condition, together with the numerous snags, logs, and stumps in the channel, rendered that part of the stream nearly impassable at all stages.

Congress entered upon a plan for improvement in 1879, the project contemplating the removal of the wreck of the ocean steamship *Star of the West*, sunk in the channel about 8 miles above the mouth during the war of the rebellion, and of snags, sunken logs, leaning timber, etc., to give ease and safety to navigation from the head of Yazoo River to the mouth of Coldwater River, estimated to be about 100 miles above. It was proposed to do the work then required in two seasons, at a cost of $40,000, but the entire amount appropriated in twenty-two years has been $55,500, of which the river and harbor acts of 1880, 1881, and 1882 required the expenditure of $10,000 above the mouth of the Coldwater to Batesville, in what is known as the Little Tallahatchie River. As new obstructions are brought into the river every year by drift and by sliding and caving banks, as the timber grows rapidly along shore, and as the shifting and scouring of the channel discloses snags and logs embedded in the bottom or lodges them upon bars, a modified project was approved March 21, 1899, in which it was estimated that an expenditure of $10,000 in one working season would be required to put the river in fairly good navigable condition between Yazoo and Coldwater rivers, and that about $2,500 a year will be needed for maintenance for some time to come.

The total amount expended to June 30, 1900, including the $10,000 above mouth of the Coldwater, was $52,700.59, which benefited navigation considerably. The wreck of the steamship *Star of the West* was destroyed, and obstructions were removed from the channel and banks so as to permit steamboats to run to Sharkey the year round, and to Coldwater River at moderately high stages.

During the fiscal year ending June 30, 1901, the U. S. snag boat *Columbia* was employed in removing snags, stumps, logs, leaning trees, etc., from September 10 to 19 and from November 1 to December 5. Operations extended from the head of the Yazoo River to the mouth of Coldwater River, and the small balance available will be used for continuing this work.

The estimate presented below is for completion of the existing project.

The commerce of Tallahatchie River consists chiefly of shipments of cotton, cotton seed, and timber, with return freights of general merchandise and plantation supplies. The totals reported for the past eleven years range between 22,132 and 92,817 tons per annum, with values estimated at $735,000 to $2,428,000, the average for the period being 47,998 tons, valued at $1,448,000.

July 1, 1900, balance unexpended	$2,799.41
June 30, 1901, amount expended during fiscal year	1,768.74
July 1, 1901, balance unexpended	1,030.67
Amount (estimated) required for completion of existing project	10,000.00
Amount that can be profitably expended in fiscal year ending June 30, 1903, in addition to the balance unexpended July 1, 1901	10,000.00

Submitted in compliance with requirements of sundry civil act of June 4, 1897.

(See Appendix V 9.)

10. *Big Sunflower River, Mississippi*.—An examination of this river in 1878 showed that the stream was navigable for very light boats about six months of the year, but that navigation was much obstructed by snags, sunken logs, leaning timber, sand bars, and shoals. Leaning timber impeded navigation at all stages, and the low-water channel at many places was so filled with snags and logs as to give no greater depth than 18 inches, and was so narrow as to afford passage only for the smallest craft.

Congress entered upon a project for the improvement with an appropriation of $20,000 in the river and harbor act of March 3, 1879. The original plan contemplated completion of the work for the removal of obstructions to Clarksdale, about 180 miles above the mouth, and the construction of wing dams to scour a depth of about 40 inches on the bars, in three or four consecutive seasons of low water, at a cost of $66,000. During the first four years $37,000 was appropriated, and fairly good progress was made. Since 1882, however, the appropriations have been small, permitting an average annual expenditure of $2,368, and little has been accomplished beyond maintenance of the early work.

New obstructions are added every year by the rapid growth of vegetation along the banks, and by floods, caving and sliding banks, etc., and, under the project approved March 21, 1899, it is estimated that $20,000 will be required to complete the improvement, and $3,000 annually thereafter for maintenance.

The amount expended to June 30, 1900, was $76,284.92. The work performed enabled boats to run to Woodburn, 77 miles above the mouth, the year round, and at ordinary stages to make the trip in little more than half the time formerly required, but the passage was difficult and dangerous at low stages. Freight rates were said to have been reduced 50 per cent. Faisonia, about 100 miles above the mouth, was considered the head of navigation.

The U. S. snag boat *Columbia* was employed August 17 to 22, 1900, in removing snags brought into the lower part of the river during the preceding high-water period. Nothing further was done during the fiscal year ending June 30, 1901.

The small balance available will be required for care of plant used upon this work. The estimate herewith is for completing work under the existing project.

The commerce of this river consists of shipments of cotton, cotton seed, and miscellaneous articles, with return freights of plantation supplies and general merchandise. The quantities reported annually for the past twelve years vary between 8,931 and 53,222 tons, with values estimated at $251,000 to $1,457,000. The average for the twelve years is 32,443 tons, valued at $989,000.

July 1, 1900, balance unexpended	$715.08
June 30, 1901, amount expended during fiscal year	421.58
July 1, 1901, balance unexpended	293.50
Amount (estimated) required for completion of existing project	20,000.00
Amount that can be profitably expended in fiscal year ending June 30, 1903, in addition to the balance unexpended July 1, 1901 Submitted in compliance with requirements of sundry civil act of June 4, 1897.	20,000.00

(See Appendix V 10.)

11. *Water gauges on the Mississippi River and its principal tributaries.*—This work was in the charge of Major Casey until February 4, 1901, when it was transferred to the secretary of the Mississippi River Commission, by authority of the Secretary of War of January 25, 1901.

Details of the year's work will be found in the report of the Commission.

July 1, 1900, amount allotted for fiscal year ending June 30, 1901	$6,000.00
February 4, 1901, amount expended	3,574.43
February 4, 1901, balance transferred to Capt. Mason M. Patrick, Corps of Engineers, secretary Mississippi River Commission	2,425.57

(See Appendix V 11.)

EXAMINATIONS MADE IN COMPLIANCE WITH EMERGENCY RIVER AND HARBOR ACT APPROVED JUNE 6, 1900.

Preliminary examinations of the following localities were made by the local officer, and reports thereon submitted through the division engineer:

1. *Preliminary examination of Red River in the States of Louisiana, Arkansas, and Texas, and in the Indian Territory, from Shreveport, La., to Denison, Tex.*, etc.—Major Casey submitted report September 20, 1900. In his opinion, concurred in by the division engineer and by the Chief of Engineers, improvement of the locality by the General Government in the manner indicated in the act is not advisable. The report was transmitted to Congress and printed in House Doc. No. 84, Fifty-sixth Congress, second session. (See also Appendix V 12.)

2. *Preliminary examination of the river and harbor in front of Camden, Ark., on the Ouachita River, with a view to improving said harbor and grading and protecting the river bank in front of said city.*—Major Casey submitted report August 7, 1900. In his opinion, concurred in by the division engineer and by the Chief of Engineers, improvement of the locality in the manner indicated in the act is not advisable. The report was transmitted to Congress and printed in House Doc. No. 96, Fifty-sixth Congress, second session. (See also Appendix V 13.)

IMPROVEMENT OF ARKANSAS RIVER, AND OF CERTAIN RIVERS IN ARKANSAS AND MISSOURI.

This district was in the charge of Capt. Robert McGregor, Corps of Engineers, to March 13, 1901; in the temporary charge of Capt. Charles L. Potter, Corps of Engineers, from March 13 to April 27, 1901, and in the charge of Capt. Graham D. Fitch, Corps of Engineers, since April 27, 1901. Division Engineer, Col. Henry M. Robert, Corps of Engineers (now brigadier-general, Chief of Engineers, United States Army, retired), to May 2, 1901, and Col. Amos Stickney, Corps of Engineers, since May 9, 1901.

1. *Removing obstructions in Arkansas River, Arkansas and Kansas.*—Appropriations for operating snag boats on Arkansas River have been made intermittently since 1832. Many of the early appropriations were combined with those of other rivers.

The river was, previous to improvement, seriously obstructed by snags, overhanging timber, reefs, and bars. The banks and bed are very unstable, making frequent contributions of snags and logs, and rendering snagging operations a continuous necessity.

426   REPORT OF THE CHIEF OF ENGINEERS, U. S. ARMY.

The existing project, approved September 9, 1886, is to operate snag boats over the navigated portions of the river.

Up to the close of the fiscal year ending June 30, 1900, there had been expended on this work $874,872.80,[1] of which $745,533.46 was expended under previous projects and $129,339.34[1] was expended on existing project. All expenditures have been for maintenance.

The project does not contemplate a direct increase in depth.

Navigation above Pinebluff was suspended during a portion of the year. The depths in the channel during that time were about 23 inches up to Dardanelle and about 18 inches up to Fort Smith.

The commerce of this stream consists of plantation products and supplies, timber and cooper stuffs, and general merchandise. Tabulation showing yearly tonnage and value is given under the heading "Improving Arkansas River, Arkansas."

July 1, 1900, balance unexpended	$14,410.66
June 30, 1901, amount expended during fiscal year	6,339.07
July 1, 1901, balance unexpended	8,071.59
July 1, 1901, outstanding liabilities	33.55
July 1, 1901, balance available	8,038.04
July 1, 1901, amount covered by uncompleted contracts	6,000.00
Amount that can be profitably expended in fiscal year ending June 30, 1903, for maintenance of improvement, in addition to the balance available July 1, 1901	35,000.00

Submitted in compliance with requirements of sundry civil act of June 4, 1897, and of section 7 of the river and harbor act of 1899.

(See Appendix W 1.)

2. Arkansas River, Arkansas.—The first work on this stream looking toward permanent improvement was at Fort Smith, Ark., in fiscal year 1878. This was followed by other local works until in fiscal year 1888, when the permanent improvement of the river as a whole was undertaken.

In the original condition the channel of the river, in addition to being obstructed by snags, was for nearly all of its length obstructed by shifting sand bars, and in its upper reaches by gravel bars and some rock reefs. The low-water depths varied considerably during the different low-water seasons. In ordinary low waters navigation above Fort Smith was suspended for eight weeks, and for five weeks no boats could pass above Dardanelle. In extreme low waters navigation over the entire river was suspended.

The existing project, adopted by act of August 11, 1888, is to remove rock and gravel reefs by blasting and dredging, to contract the channel by dikes or dams, permeable or solid, of such construction as the local conditions require, and to hold the channel so obtained by revetment where necessary, the project to include the river from Wichita, Kans., to the mouth, a distance of 771 miles.

From the appropriations made for the improvement of this river there had been expended to June 30, 1900, $1,214,887.75. Of this $37,914.20 was expended under allotments to "removing snags, etc.," leaving $1,176,973.55 expended under projects for permanent improvement. Of this latter amount $179,500 was for original construction

---

[1] In addition to this there has been applied to this work $37,914.20, allotted from appropriation for improving Arkansas River, Arkansas.

under special projects, $704,811.93 was for original construction under existing project, and $292,661.62 was for repairs and reconstructions.

The operations during the past fiscal year were confined to repairing the bank revetment at Red Fork, and to care of and repairs to plant. Under the allotment for "removing snags, etc.," the snag boat *Arkansas* was received from the contractor and was operated for thirty-eight days above Little Rock. Contract for repairing the snag boat *C. B. Reese* was made.

During the periods of lowest water the channel depths were about 3 feet to Pinebluff, 23 inches to Little Rock, 20 inches to Dardanelle, 18 inches to Fort Smith, and 12 inches to Fort Gibson.

House Doc. No. 150, Fifty-sixth Congress, second session, gives report of the Board of Engineers appointed to report a plan for the improvement of this river (see Appendix W 10, herewith). The estimated cost of the improvement from its mouth to the mouth of Grand River (461 miles) is $25,263,400. The Board emphasizes the statement that satisfactory results and economy in cost can not be obtained unless funds of sufficient magnitude be provided to keep a working plant in continuous operation. Pending the action of Congress upon this report, the district officer makes no recommendation for future appropriations under this title.

COMMERCIAL STATISTICS, YEAR ENDING MAY 31—

Year.	Value.	Tons.	Year.	Value.	Tons.
1895	$2,380,420	50,498	1899	$2,470,131	68,057
1896	2,408,720	54,261	1900	2,078,940	75,654
1897	1,657,218	66,07	1901	2,623,797	71,998
1898	1,626,756	58,578			

The packet company organized last year for the purpose of operating a boat between Pinebluff and New Orleans has withdrawn from the river. Of the commerce reported, that carried in flatboats or in rafts was 24,100 tons, having an estimated value of $41,700.

July 1, 1900, balance unexpended $38,612.25
Amount allotted from appropriation contained in emergency river and harbor act approved June 6, 1900 .... 10,000.00

48,612.25
June 30, 1901, amount expended during fiscal year .... [1]40,086.25

July 1, 1901, balance unexpended .... [2]8,526.00
July 1, 1901, outstanding liabilities 520.65

July 1, 1901, balance available 8,005.35

July 1, 1901, amount covered by uncompleted contracts................. 3,000.00

(See Appendix W 2.)

3. White River, Arkansas.—The early operations on this stream were confined to the usual snagging operations. Construction of wing dams and works of a similar nature was begun in fiscal year 1879.

In its original condition the river was much choked by drift piles, logs, and snags, and in its upper reaches by bowlders and gravel shoals. At the time of adopting the project for permanent improvement in

---
[1] Removing obstructions, etc., $19,664.35; on project, $10,421.90; Red Fork, $10,000.
[2] $7,421.45 for removing obstructions, etc.; $1,104.55 for project.

1888, the river from Newport to the mouth was reasonably free from snags, and the controlling depth on shoals was said to be about 3 feet at ordinary low water. Above Newport the river was still much obstructed by timber, and from Batesville up there were numerous bad shoals, rendering navigation uncertain.

The existing project, approved October 9, 1888, is to contract the channel, remove rocks and bowlders, and operate snag boats.

Up to June 30, 1900, there had been expended under this appropriation title $370,618.73. Of this amount $4,000 was allotted to Cache River, $11,061.46 was spent on special works at Batesville, and $166,000 was for previous projects, leaving $189,557.27 expended on the existing project. Of this latter amount, approximately $108,815 was for original construction and $80,742.27 for snagging and maintenance.

Little work was done during the past year, a snag boat having been operated for a period of only 16 days. This gave some relief to navigation between Newport and Buffalo Shoals. During the low-water season of the past year 30 inches was reported as the maximum draft that could be taken from Newport to the mouth of the river. Above Newport navigation to Batesville was suspended during the low-water season.

The river is in need of snagging operations throughout, in need of dredging between Jacksonport and Batesville, and extensive repairs to plant are needed.

The balance available at the close of this year will be used in paying for repairs to snag boat *C. B. Reese* and in caring for property until other funds become available.

COMMERCIAL STATISTICS, YEAR ENDING MAY 31—

Year.	Value.	Tons.	Year.	Value.	Tons.
1895	$2,494,377	73,759	1899	$1,619,351	117,891
1896	2,056,991	74,882	1900	2,244,222	134,696
1897	2,435,814	73,962	1901	1,691,085	144,674
1898	1,415,018	102,337			

The old Memphis, Tenn., and Newport, Ark., transportation line which has been dormant for several years began to operate on this stream again in December, 1900.

July 1, 1900, balance unexpended	$14,196.27
June 30, 1901, amount expended during fiscal year	1,978.58
July 1, 1901, balance unexpended	12,217.69
July 1, 1901, outstanding liabilities	266.49
July 1, 1901, balance available	11,951.20
July 1, 1901, amount covered by uncompleted contracts	9,000.00
Amount that can be profitably expended in fiscal year ending June 30, 1903, for maintenance of improvement, in addition to the balance available July 1, 1901	14,500.00

Submitted in compliance with requirements of sundry civil act of June 4, 1897, and of section 7 of the river and harbor act of 1899.

(See Appendix W 3.)

4. Upper White River, Arkansas.—Earlier works on this portion of White River were made under the appropriations for improving White River, Arkansas, and are fully reported upon under that head.

The original condition of the river and previous projects for its improvement are also reported there.

The existing project, based on a report printed in Annual Report of the Chief of Engineers for 1897, page 1992, is to provide slack-water navigation from Batesville, Ark., to Buffalo Shoals, 89 miles, by 10 fixed dams with concrete locks. The locks are to be 175 feet between hollow quoins and 36 feet wide, with a depth of about 4 feet on the lower miter sills. The estimated cost is $1,600,000, based on having funds sufficient to construct one lock and dam complete each working season.

Up to June 30, 1900, there had been expended on this work $22,694.08.

During the year ending June 30, 1901, the work at Lock and Dam No. 1, near Batesville, was carried well forward, and at Lock and Dam No. 2 the abutment was nearly completed, lock house was completed, and work on cofferdam for the lock was well under way.

The balance available July 1, 1901, will be expended at Lock No. 2. In addition to the amount available July 1, 1901, $24,100 will be required to complete main dam, guide cribs, and lock house at Lock No. 1; $107,375 will be required to build dam and guide cribs at Lock No. 2, and $216,000 will be required to complete Lock and Dam No. 3, making a total of $347,475.

COMMERCIAL STATISTICS.

Year ending May 31—	Value.	Tons.
1899	$548,335	9,059
1900	1,260,716	39,253
1901	639,855	28,522

July 1, 1900, balance unexpended	[1]$287,305.92
June 30, 1901, amount expended during fiscal year	[2]192,804.55
July 1, 1901, balance unexpended	[3]94,501.37
July 1, 1901, outstanding liabilities	27,870.06
July 1, 1901, balance available	66,631.31
July 1, 1901, amount covered by uncompleted contracts	7,659.60
Amount (estimated) required for completion of existing project	1,290,000.00
Amount that can be profitably expended in fiscal year ending June 30, 1903, in addition to the balance available July 1, 1901 Submitted in compliance with requirements of sundry civil act of June 4, 1897.	270,000.00

(See Appendix W 4.)

5. *Buffalo Fork of White River, Arkansas.*—The appropriation made by act of March 3, 1899, is the first and only one ever made for this stream.

In its original condition this stream was obstructed by overhanging

---

[1] By correction of error, 99 cents, made in entering settlement by Treasury Department March 1, 1899, with Missouri Pacific Railway Company, for passenger service, claim No. 133110.
[2] Lock and Dam No. 1, $121,975.05; Lock and Dam No. 2, $70,829.50.
[3] $15,330.87 for Lock and Dam No. 1; $79,170.50 for Lock and Dam No. 2.

timber and by bowlders and rocks projecting above the bed of the shoals. The slope is steep and the bends abrupt. The low-water depth on the shoals is about 5 inches. The amount expended on the work up to June 30, 1900, was $3,043.06.

Nothing was done during the past year. The work done the preceding year was of material benefit. It is believed that when the present amount available is expended the demands of commerce will be met. No further appropriations are recommended.

Commercial statistics.—The commerce for Buffalo Fork this year was rafted railway ties. It amounted to 718 tons, valued at $1,940. Last year it was 998 tons of rafted cedar and railway ties, valued at $8,436.

July 1, 1900, balance unexpended	$456.94
June 30, 1901, amount expended during fiscal year	8.50
July 1, 1901, balance unexpended	448.44
July 1, 1901, outstanding liabilities	3.75
July 1, 1901, balance available	444.69

(See Appendix W 5.)

6. *Cache River, Arkansas.*—In its original condition this stream was much obstructed by snags, drift, and overhanging timber. The low-water depth on the controlling shoals was 6 to 8 inches.

The existing project, approved August 11, 1896, is to remove snags and similar obstructions between the mouth and James Ferry, 79 miles.

The amount expended on this stream to June 30, 1900, from direct appropriations was $9,952.85, and from allotments from appropriations for White River, Arkansas, $4,000, making a total of $13,952.85. Of this amount, $9,000 was expended on previous project, leaving $4,952.85 expended on existing project.

Nothing was done on this river during the past year. Operations on it in preceding years are said to have made navigation possible on a stage 3 feet less than that required before the work was done. The Choctaw, Oklahoma and Gulf Railway Company has placed a draw span in its bridge across this river, thus enabling steamboats to proceed from the mouth of the river to the head of navigation. The expenditures the past year were payments of liabilities incurred in previous years and expenses connected with inspection of above-mentioned bridge.

COMMERCIAL STATISTICS, YEAR ENDING MAY 31—

Year.	Value.	Tons.	Year.	Value.	Tons.
1895	$25,494	12,603	1899	$52,936	7,667
1896	62,483	20,748	1900	29,961	11,215
1897	108,460	34,990	1901	27,700	9,174
1898	36,635	10,198			

About 95 per cent of the commerce reported is timber in various forms. About 61 per cent of the commerce reported is rafted.

July 1, 1900, balance unexpended	$47.15
June 30, 1901, amount expended during fiscal year	47.15
Amount that can be profitably expended in fiscal year ending June 30, 1903, for maintenance of improvement. Submitted in compliance with requirements of sundry civil act of June 4, 1897, and of section 7 of the river and harbor act of 1899.	1,000.00

(See Appendix W 6.)

7. *Black River, Arkansas and Missouri.*—In its original condition this river had a controlling depth of 2 to 2¼ feet at low water. The river, especially that portion above the mouth of Current River, was almost impassable at low stages on account of snags, drift, and overhanging timber. Pocahontas was considered the head of navigation, and rafting was impossible above the Arkansas and Missouri State line.

The existing project, approved April 2, 1881, is to remove snags, cut overhanging timber, build wing dams, and close sloughs. The estimate for the cost of the work was, in 1884, modified to $8,000 annually.

The total amount expended on this river to June 30, 1900, was $108,448.56, of which $15,000 was expended under the head of "Improving Black River, Arkansas," and $14,000 was expended under the head of "Improving Black River, Missouri," leaving $79,448.56 expended on the existing project. Of this latter amount something was spent in building dams, but the greater part was for snagging and maintenance of channel.

Little was done during the fiscal year ending June 30, 1901. A hand-propelled snag boat was operated over the river from the mouth of Current River to Corning Mills (61 miles). The work was not of sufficient amount to afford much benefit to navigation interests. The channel depths reported during the low-water season of this year were 30 inches to mouth of Current River, 2 feet to Brookings, and 18 inches from there to Poplarbluff.

This river is in need of much work, and the plant is in need of much repair.

COMMERCIAL STATISTICS, YEAR ENDING MAY 31—

Year.	Value.	Tons.	Year.	Value.	Tons.
1895	$1,085,415	132,433	1899	$529,336	83,404
1896	891,437	111,278	1900	966,961	129,698
1897	1,704,799	111,611	1901	989,635	185,714
1898	788,640	115,612			

Forty per cent of the commerce reported is rafted saw logs, railway ties, and piling.

July 1, 1900, balance unexpended	$2,051.44
June 30, 1901, amount expended during fiscal year	1,787.63
July 1, 1901, balance unexpended	263.81
July 1, 1901, outstanding liabilities	45.00
July 1, 1901, balance available	218.81

Amount that can be profitably expended in fiscal year ending June 30, 1903, for maintenance of improvement, in addition to the balance available July 1, 1901.................................. 21,700.00
Submitted in compliance with requirements of sundry civil act of June 4, 1897, and of section 7 of the river and harbor act of 1899.

(See Appendix W 7.)

8. *Current River, Arkansas and Missouri.*—Although the United States made some improvements to this stream in 1873 and again in 1882 and 1883, regular improvement of it did not begin until the fiscal year ending June 30, 1895.

The original condition of this stream was such that no steamboat navigation above the mouth of Little Black River was attempted except when the river was at high stages. Below Little Black River navigation was suspended when the river was below the medium stage. The natural depths were not available on account of snags and leaning timber.

The existing project, approved September 8, 1894, is to improve the channel to Vanburen, Mo., by usual snagging operations and by contracting the channel at the worst shoals by wing dams. No wing dams have been built.

The amount expended up to June 30, 1900, was $20,597.29, $7,000 of which was expended on previous projects and $13,597.29 of which was expended in snagging operations under the existing project.

During the fiscal year ending June 30, 1901, a snag boat was operated in the river from Johnsons Landing to State Line Shoal (16.5 miles). The work done enabled the raftsmen to double the size of their rafts. The channel depths at ordinary low water were reported as being 3 feet to Pierces Landing, 2 feet to Loggy Bend, 20 inches to State Line Shoal, about 12 inches to Doniphan, and 6 to 10 inches to Tucker Bay.

The snag boats heretofore used on this river are in need of repair, and more work is needed on the river.

COMMERCIAL STATISTICS, YEAR ENDING MAY 31—

Year.	Value.	Tons.	Year.	Value.	Tons.
1895	$362,447	31,205	1899	$239,869	43,050
1896	227,291	29,867	1900	578,834	65,043
1897	581,528	17,078	1901	222,135	59,502
1898	306,216	52,417			

Forty-six thousand seven hundred and seventy tons of the commerce reported was rafted saw logs and ties.

July 1, 1900, balance unexpended $1,402.71
June 30, 1901, amount expended during fiscal year 1,086.80

July 1, 1901, balance unexpended 315.91
July 1, 1901, outstanding liabilities 16.91

July 1, 1901, balance available 299.00

{ Amount that can be profitably expended in fiscal year ending June 30, 1903, for maintenance of improvement, in addition to the balance available July 1, 1901.. 6,900.00
Submitted in compliance with requirements of sundry civil act of June 4, 1897, and of section 7 of the river and harbor act of 1899. }

(See Appendix W 8.)

9. *St. Francis River, Arkansas.*—The improvement of this stream was provided for in the early appropriations for improvement of Western rivers. Except the occasional building of a dam across a slough, snagging operations have been the means relied upon for its improvement.

In its original condition this stream was not navigable at any stage above Lester Landing. Between Lester Landing and Marked Tree navigation was possible at high stages only, and below Marked Tree it was difficult at medium stages. Snags and fallen timber were the principal obstructions.

The existing project, approved October 21, 1884, is to remove drift, logs, and snags from the channel and overhanging timber from the banks from the mouth to Kennett, Mo. (279 miles), and close chutes and sloughs in "The Sunk Lands," so as to make the river navigable at high stages to Kennett, Mo., at medium stages to Marked Tree, and at low stages to a point about 30 miles below Madison, Ark.

The amount expended up to June 30, 1900, was $64,244.13, $15,000 of which was expended on previous projects, leaving $49,244.13 as the amount expended on the existing project. The amount expended on construction of dams has been insignificant.

The condition of the river June 30, 1900, was good for navigation at any navigable stage from the mouth to Madison, fair for navigation at 4-foot stage or over to Marked Tree, and through "The Sunk Lands" a passable high-water channel existed. The operations of the fiscal year ending June 30, 1901, were limited to the river from Marked Tree to Ash Bend, 40 miles. These made a fair low-water channel up to that point. During the low-water season there is no navigation in any portion of the river, there being only 12 to 14 inches in the channel over the shoals.

COMMERCIAL STATISTICS, YEAR ENDING MAY 31—

Year.	Value.	Tons.	Year.	Value.	Tons.
1895	$321,439	38,107	1899	$315,459	27,892
1896	401,457	67,740	1900	194,237	45,065
1897	1,117,891	97,348	1901	269,425	55,510
1898	237,481	23,819			

Saw logs make up about 94.6 per cent of the total tonnage reported, and rafted saw logs make up about 56 per cent of the total tonnage. A new transportation line began operating out of Marked Tree late in the year.

July 1, 1900, balance unexpended	$2,755.87
June 30, 1901, amount expended during fiscal year	2,499.68
July 1, 1901, balance unexpended	256.19
July 1, 1901, outstanding liabilities	50.58
July 1, 1901, balance available	205.61

Amount that can be profitably expended in fiscal year ending June 30, 1903, for maintenance of improvement, in addition to the balance available July 1, 1901 .... 8,000.00
Submitted in compliance with requirements of sundry civil act of June 4, 1897, and of section 7 of the river and harbor act of 1899.

(See Appendix W 9.)

EXAMINATION AND SURVEY MADE IN COMPLIANCE WITH EMERGENCY RIVER AND HARBOR ACT APPROVED MARCH 3, 1899.

A Board of Engineers submitted report November 3, 1900, upon preliminary examination and survey of *Arkansas River, with a view to its permanent improvement.* The Board estimates the cost of improvement at $25,263,400, and states that in addition a snag boat should be provided at a cost of $75,000 and provision made for its maintenance and operation at a cost of $25,000 per year. The report was transmitted to Congress and printed in House Doc. No. 150, Fifty-sixth Congress, second session. (See also Appendix W 10.)

EXAMINATION AND SURVEY OF EAST BANK OF MISSISSIPPI RIVER, FROM HICKMAN, KY., TO SLOUGH LANDING, TENN., MADE IN COMPLIANCE WITH EMERGENCY RIVER AND HARBOR ACT APPROVED JUNE 6, 1900.

Col. G. L. Gillespie, Corps of Engineers, president Mississippi River Commission (now brigadier-general, Chief of Engineers, United States Army), submitted reports of June 24 and November 1, 1900, by Capt. E. Eveleth Winslow, Corps of Engineers, upon preliminary examination and survey of the *east bank of Mississippi River between the highlands, near the city of Hickman, Ky., and Slough Landing, in Lake County, Tenn., with a view to constructing such works as may be required to prevent overflows along said section of the river.* A plan is presented for improvement at an estimated cost of $400,000, the expense to be borne equally by the General Government and by the board of levee commissioners of Lake County, Tenn., and others interested in the project. The reports were transmitted to Congress and printed in House Doc. No. 130, Fifty-sixth Congress, second session. (See also Appendix X.)

REMOVING SNAGS AND WRECKS FROM MISSISSIPPI RIVER; IMPROVEMENT OF MISSISSIPPI RIVER BETWEEN THE OHIO AND MISSOURI RIVERS, OF HARBOR AT ST. LOUIS, MO., AND TO PREVENT THE MISSISSIPPI RIVER FROM BREAKING THROUGH INTO CACHE RIVER AT BEECHRIDGE, ABOVE CAIRO, ILL.

This district was in the charge of Capt. Edward Burr, Corps of Engineers. Division Engineer, Col. Henry M. Robert, Corps of Engineers (now brigadier-general, Chief of Engineers, United States Army, retired), to May 2, 1901, and Col. Amos Stickney, Corps of Engineers, since May 9, 1901.

1. *Removing snags and wrecks from the Mississippi River below the mouth of the Missouri River.*—Before this work was inaugurated, and for many years afterwards, the navigation of the river was very much interfered with by numerous snags, logs, etc., which had lodged in the channel, and to which new additions were made with each rise in the river. A large number of wrecked flatboats, barges, steamboats, and all manner of river craft are found in the navigable channels, and menace life and property.

For the removal of these obstructions appropriations were made as early as 1824. The project adopted consisted of building boats suitable for removing the snags, logs, rack heaps, etc., and operating them whenever the stage of water was favorable and funds were available.

The amount expended upon this work on the reach of the river below the mouth of the Missouri prior to 1879 can not now be definitely ascertained, for the reason that during much of the time appropriations were made at irregular intervals in lump sums, to be applied to several streams as their needs or the terms of the law might require. From March 3, 1879, when the first specific appropriation was made, up to June 30, 1900, there had been expended $1,547,124.54. This expenditure made great improvement in the navigation of the river and lessened the danger to boats. During the fiscal year ending June 30, 1901, the sum of $86,710.05 was expended.

Two steel snag boats were employed in removing the obstructions to navigation between the mouth of the Missouri River and New Orleans, and during the year removed 3,566 snags and 28 drift piles. Nineteen thousand seven hundred and forty-six trees were felled and 19,185 miles was run.

An annual appropriation, not to exceed $100,000, for carrying on this work was made by the act of August 11, 1888. Under this appropriation the two snag boats will patrol the river and remove obstructions where necessary.

For recapitulation of commercial statistics reference should be made to report upon improving Mississippi River between Ohio and Missouri rivers.

Amount drawn under section 7, act of August 11, 1888 .... $86,710.05
June 30, 1901, amount expended during fiscal year 86,710.05

July 1, 1901, amount available for fiscal year 1901-2 .... 100,000.00

(See Appendix Y 1.)

2. Mississippi River between Ohio and Missouri rivers.—The original condition of the navigable channel of this portion of the Mississippi River before the work of improvement was begun was such that the natural depth at low water was in many places from 3½ to 4 feet. The channels were divided by islands, which formed sloughs and secondary channels, through which a great deal of the volume of the flow was diverted, to the detriment of navigation.

The first work for improvement began in 1872, and was continued for a number of years as appropriations were made, the works consisting of dikes and dams of brush and stone, erected with a view to confining the low-water volume to a single channel, and of revetments, to hold and preserve the banks where necessary or advisable to do so.

The present project is a continuation of the plan adopted in 1881. It contemplates confining the flow of the river to a single channel having an approximate width below St. Louis of 2,500 feet, the natural width in many places being from 1 to 1½ miles. This result is to be accomplished by closing sloughs and secondary channels and by building out new banks where the natural width is excessive, using for this purpose permeable dikes or hurdles of piling that collect and hold the solid matter that is carried in suspension or rolled on the bottom by the river. The banks, both old and new, are to be revetted or otherwise protected where necessary to secure permanency. Pending the completion of the permanent improvement, the low-water channel is to be improved each season by the use of dredges and other temporary expedients.

The object of the improvement is to obtain eventually a minimum depth, at standard low water, of 6 feet from the mouth of the Missouri to St. Louis, and of 8 feet from St. Louis to the mouth of the Ohio.

The original estimate of the cost of the improvement, as revised in 1883, is $16,397,500.

The total amount expended to June 30, 1900, was $9,155,433.03, exclusive of $180,000 allotted by acts to projects for improvement between the Illinois and the Missouri rivers, including Alton Harbor.

The amount expended during the fiscal year ending June 30, 1901, includes $42,718.52 expended during the year for dredge plant, portable jetties, and for operating the same. The total amount thus far expended for what is termed temporary channel improvements is $576,208.05, much of which has been for plant that is now on hand and available for future work. The approximate value of this plant is $225,526.27.

The result of the expenditure of this amount has been the partial improvement of the whole reach of the river from St. Louis to Cairo. During the past year there was at all times during open navigation a channel depth of 5 feet or more throughout this reach, and, excepting for a few days, a depth of 6 feet or more. The river reached a low-water stage of 3.4 feet below standard low water.

The work done during the past year in the line of permanent improvement consisted in repairs to existing contraction works and revetments and a further extension of the same in localities where work had been commenced, in addition to new works in localities where no work had heretofore been done.

For the permanent improvement of the river new works were constructed or extended opposite the mouth of the Missouri River, at Osborne Field, Rush Towhead, Penitentiary Point, Ste. Genevieve, Mo., Horse Island (opposite Chester), Liberty, Ill., Devils Island, and Buffalo Island for the protection of caving banks and at Ste. Genevieve, Ill., for the improvement of a shoal crossing.

Repairs were made to existing revetments at Danby Landing, Liberty, Mo., and to Cairo protection, and to existing hurdles at Liberty, Mo.

Dredging for the improvement of the low-water channel was carried on at Sulphur Springs, Crystal City, Stantons Towhead, Winter Harbor in Old River, Manskers, and Bainbridge. Buoys were maintained on all shoal crossings during the low-water season.

With the present appliances and such others as may be developed for the temporary improvement of low-water channels, it is expected that a navigable depth of at least 6 feet will be maintained between St. Louis and Cairo during all low-water stages that the river is open to navigation, and until the projected depth is obtained throughout by the extension and completion of the works for the permanent improvement. There can be no doubt of the ultimate success of this permanent improvement and of its value to the commercial interests involved.

To prevent the suspension of this important work for lack of funds, the river and harbor act of June 3, 1896, made provision for three years' work from July 1, 1897, to be paid for as appropriations should be made by law, at the rate of $673,333.33 annually. The last of these annual appropriations was provided by the act of March 3, 1899, and was practically exhausted by June 30, 1900. By suspending all operations during the last half of the previous fiscal year sufficient funds were reserved for emergencies and for urgent low-water operations during the past season. To the amount thus reserved $100,000 was added by allotment from the act of June 6, 1900, but the total of all available funds, after deducting allotments for specific localities, was sufficient for only three months' work with a limited force after reserving sufficient funds for the care of the large and valuable plant belonging to this work until other appropriations become available. All operations were suspended during the last half of the fiscal year, and there appears no probability of resuming them during the next fiscal year. The total loss of time by reason of the failure of appropriations will therefore be at least two years. The loss to the Government and to the commerce of the Mississippi River by the interruption of work on this important improvement can not be even approximately stated. The care and depreciation of plant will alone cost the Government more than $100,000 for each year's suspension, with absolutely no return. The improvement not only makes no progress, but actually retrogrades, and navigation interests are decreasing from failure to obtain and maintain such channels as are necessary for economical transportation. It seems now certain that the procuring of satisfactory channels at all seasons of open navigation is merely a matter of providing funds in sufficient amounts to do the work economically. The local officer states that $150,000 is required annually for temporary low-water operations alone.

The sundry civil act approved March 3, 1899, requires that from the appropriation made by that act for improving the Mississippi River from the mouth of the Ohio River to the mouth of the Missouri River the sum of $10,000 "shall be expended for the protection of the bank on the Missouri side and to deepen and to straighten the channel at Wittenberg, in Perry County, in the State of Missouri." Captain Burr, the local officer, reports that a careful examination and survey of the locality in which the work is proposed to be done under this allotment of $10,000 have been made and fail to show that any work is necessary for the protection of the bank on the Missouri side or for straightening the channel at any point in the neighborhood of Wittenberg; the Missouri bank requires no attention, and the channel is in a good and satisfactory condition. I recommend, therefore, that the provision requiring the expenditure of funds at this locality be repealed, and that authority be given for use of the amount on the general work for improvement of the Mississippi River between the mouth of the Ohio and the mouth of the Missouri.

Recapitulation of commercial statistics.

	1897.	1898.	1899.	1900.
	Tons.	Tons.	Tons.	Tons.
Receipts and shipments at St. Louis	1,046,035	906,168	669,815	757,590
Transferred by ferries at St. Louis	3,042,674	4,033,871	5,036,730	5,218,967
Shipped from landings between St. Louis and Cairo	69,815	53,785	30,716	52,640
Total	4,158,524	4,993,824	5,737,261	6,029,197

July 1, 1900, balance unexpended	[1]$491,875.11
March 26, 1901, transferred from appropriation for preventing break in Mississippi River at Beechridge, Ill	1,044.56
Redeposited, canceled, and disallowed vouchers:	
July 28, 1900	21.71
August 10, 1900	.84
December 20, 1900	13.00
	492,955.22
June 30, 1901, amount expended during fiscal year	336,841.01
July 1, 1901, balance unexpended	156,114.21
July 1, 1901, outstanding liabilities	4,083.97
July 1, 1901, balance available	[2]152,030.24
July 1, 1901, amount covered by uncompleted contracts	12,249.60
Amount that can be profitably expended in fiscal year ending June 30, 1903, for works of improvement and for maintenance, in addition to the balance available July 1, 1901 Submitted in compliance with requirements of sundry civil act of June 4, 1897, and of section 7 of the river and harbor act of 1899.	673,333.00

(See Appendix Y 2.)

[1] $3.13 less than amount stated in previous annual report.
[2] Distributed under subheadings as follows:

For bank protection at Cairo, Ill., act of July 5, 1884	$2,571.70
For revetting bank opposite mouth of Missouri River, act of March 3, 1899	30,872.84
For from mouth of Ohio River to mouth of Missouri River, act of June 6, 1900	96,336.10
For protection of bank on Missouri side and to deepen and straighten channel at Wittenberg, Mo., act of March 3, 1899	10,000.00
Amount covered by uncompleted contracts	12,249.60
	152,030.24

438   REPORT OF THE CHIEF OF ENGINEERS, U. S. ARMY.

3. Harbor at St. Louis, Mo.—St. Louis Harbor is about 18 miles long, and divided into two nearly equal parts by the Eads Bridge. The upper part, included between the bridge and the northern limits of the city, is about 10 miles in length.

Three miles above the Eads Bridge is the Merchants Bridge. The lower part of the harbor, included between Eads Bridge and the River Des Peres, is 8 miles long. The channel in this part of the harbor has sufficient depth and accessible landings at all points. Good depth exists above the Merchants Bridge.

Congress, by act approved September 19, 1890, appropriated $182,000 for improvement of this harbor.

The navigable reach between the Eads Bridge and Merchants Bridge was at that time obstructed by a number of middle bars. The project adopted for improvement of the harbor under the appropriation of 1890 consisted in a contraction of the waterway between those bridges to a width of about 2,000 feet, in order to concentrate the flow upon the bars, and thus cause scour to the depth desired. The contraction works consisted of a series of hurdles extending out from the Illinois shore, the object of the hurdles being to collect deposits of material brought down during floods, and thus build up a new bank out to the line desired.

This work, which was accomplished by the close of the fiscal year ending June 30, 1892, caused extensive deposits of sediment along the line of hurdles, and has resulted in considerable increase in channel depth, with corresponding benefit to navigation.

Amount expended to July 1, 1900, $150,762.03. There was no expenditure during the past fiscal year.

The full amount of the estimate for the improvement of this part of the harbor has been appropriated. With the unexpended balance it is proposed to replace the ends of the hurdles where damaged by ice and scour and to make them permanent. A project for this expenditure has been approved.

For recapitulation of commercial statistics reference should be made to report upon improvement of Mississippi River between Ohio and Missouri rivers.

July 1, 1900, balance unexpended $31,237.97
July 1, 1901, balance unexpended 31,237.97

(See Appendix Y 3.)

4. To prevent the Mississippi River from breaking through into the Cache River at or near a point known as Beechridge, a few miles above Cairo, Ill.—The sundry civil act approved June 4, 1897, contains an item providing for this work which reads as follows:

For the purpose of preventing the Mississippi River from breaking through into the Cache River at or near a point known as Beach Ridge [Beechridge], a few miles north of Cairo, whereby the National Cemetery at Mound City, at the mouth of the Cache River, and the marine hospital at Cairo would be in imminent danger of destruction, the sum of one hundred thousand dollars, or so much thereof as may be necessary, is hereby appropriated, to be immediately available.

The project for this work not being based upon a survey under the Engineer Department and the extent of the work contemplated not being known, an estimate of its total cost could not be given. From a study of the conditions involved, it would seem that the object of the appropriation could best be carried out by revetting as great a length of the bank of the Mississippi River in the vicinity of Beechridge railroad station as the funds would suffice.

The project for the expenditure of the amount appropriated contemplates commencing at a suitable point on the bank of the river a short distance above the nearest point to Beechridge station, building a short hurdle out into the stream to protect the head of the revetment, and then revetting the banks in the usual manner down as far as the funds will suffice.

Under this project and during the previous fiscal years a hurdle 275 feet long was constructed, and 9,435 linear feet of subaqueous mattress was placed. This mattress is about 130 feet wide, and follows the form of construction used in this section of the Mississippi River, the upper 440 feet being built of brush and the remainder of lumber. The bank above the mattress was revetted with stone to the 33-foot stage, Cairo gauge, from the upper end to a length of 5,000 feet, and to the 25-foot stage for the remaining 4,435 feet.

During the past fiscal year repairs were made where required. The work is in good condition. The amount expended to June 30, 1900, was $92,303.98.

The work is being done by purchase of material in open market and hired labor, using Government plant belonging to the general improvement of the river between the mouth of the Missouri and the mouth of the Ohio River.

The funds available will be sufficient to complete, including work already done, about 10,000 feet of revetment to a height about the 30-foot stage.

In accordance with the requirements of the river and harbor act of March 3, 1899, an examination and survey of the Mississippi River have been made at and near Beechridge "with a view to ascertain whether there is danger of said river breaking through into Cache River, and whether it is desirable to make further specific appropriations to protect the bank of the Mississippi River at said place; and, if so, the cost thereof." A report thereon, with an estimate of cost, was transmitted to Congress and printed in House Doc. No. 90, Fifty-sixth Congress, first session, and in the annual report for 1900, at page 2672.

For recapitulation of commercial statistics reference should be made to report upon improvement of Mississippi River between Ohio and Missouri rivers.

July 1, 1900, balance unexpended	$7,784.97
June 30, 1901, amount expended during fiscal year	1,354.41
July 1, 1901, balance unexpended	6,430.56
July 1, 1901, outstanding liabilities	3.50
July 1, 1901, balance available	6,427.06

(See Appendix Y 4.)

EXAMINATION MADE IN COMPLIANCE WITH EMERGENCY RIVER AND HARBOR ACT APPROVED JUNE 6, 1900.

Report dated August 31, 1900, upon preliminary examination of *Harrisonville Harbor, Illinois, in the Mississippi River, with a view to restoring it*, was submitted by Captain Burr through the division engineer. In his opinion, concurred in by the division engineer and the Chief of Engineers, improvement of the locality by the General Government in the manner indicated by the act is not advisable. The report was transmitted to Congress and printed in House Doc. No. 71, Fifty-sixth Congress, second session. (See also Appendix Y 9.)

440   REPORT OF THE CHIEF OF ENGINEERS, U. S. ARMY.

OPERATING SNAG BOATS AND DREDGE BOATS ON UPPER MISSISSIPPI RIVER; IMPROVEMENT OF MISSISSIPPI RIVER BETWEEN MOUTH OF MISSOURI RIVER AND ST. PAUL, MINN., AND OF LA CROSSE HARBOR, WISCONSIN; OPERATING AND CARE OF GALENA RIVER IMPROVEMENT, ILLINOIS, AND OF ILLINOIS AND MISSISSIPPI CANAL AROUND THE LOWER RAPIDS OF ROCK RIVER, ILLINOIS.

This district was in the charge of Maj. C. McD. Townsend, Corps of Engineers. Division Engineer, Col. J. W. Barlow, Corps of Engineers (now brigadier-general, chief of engineers, United States Army, retired), to May 3, 1901, and Col. S. M. Mansfield, Corps of Engineers, since May 9, 1901.

1. Operating snag boats and dredge boats on Upper Mississippi River.—By the river and harbor act of August 11, 1888, provision was made for operating snag boats and dredge boats on the Upper Mississippi River under a permanent appropriation, the sum so expended not to exceed $25,000 annually.

The snag boat *General Barnard*, over 21 years old, was condemned in September, 1900, and replaced by the *Colonel Mackenzie*, built and outfitted at Jeffersonville, Ind., at a cost of $35,000.

During the past year the *General Barnard* was employed from July 2 to August 9, 1900, and the *Colonel Mackenzie* from April 15 to June 30, 1901, removing snags and similar obstructions and otherwise assisting interests of navigation between Minneapolis and the mouth of Missouri River.

The total amount expended for snag-boat service to June 30, 1900, was $824,584.

The total amount of freight transported on the Upper Mississippi River during the calendar year 1900 was about 2,400,000 tons, and the ton-miles 600,000,000; in 1899, 2,900,000 tons and 641,348,000 ton-miles.

The amount expended during the fiscal year ending June 30, 1901, was $25,000.

(See Appendix Z 1.)

2. Mississippi River between Missouri River and St. Paul, Minn.—Under this head is carried on the improvement of through navigation and also such special harbor or levee work as is provided for by Congress. Systematic work was begun in 1878, and such good results have been secured as to demonstrate that with a continuance of operations under liberal appropriations the low-water channel of the Mississippi River between St. Paul and the Missouri River can be made sufficiently deep, available, and permanent to satisfy the demands of commerce.

The navigation interests are very large and important. The amount of freight carried during season of 1900, including logs and lumber, was approximately 2,400,000 tons, and the ton-miles 600,000,000, this being a decrease from 1899 of 500,000 tons freight and 41,348,000 ton-miles.

The original condition of the channel between the Missouri River and St. Paul was such that in low stages the larger boats were unable to proceed farther up river than La Crosse or Winona, and in many seasons at points much lower down their progress was checked or seriously hindered.

The original project for the improvement, adopted in 1879, and which has not been materially changed, proposed the contraction of the channel or waterway by means of wing and closing dams to such an extent as, by means of the scour thereby caused, to afford a channel of sufficient width and of a depth of 4.5 feet at low water, to be eventually increased to 6 feet by further contraction.

There was expended on the improvement to June 30, 1900, the sum of $9,566,571.72. At that date and for many years previous the condition of the channel was such as to permit the passage of the largest river boats at very low stages through to St. Paul.

During the past year work has been carried on by hired labor and use of Government plant between St. Paul and Dubuque, at Rock Island and Des Moines rapids, and between Hannibal and the Missouri River, and under formal contract between Winona and La Crosse, Lansing and Le Claire, Rock Island and Montrose, Keokuk and Saverton, and Hamburg and the Illinois River. At all localities where work was performed good results were obtained. Under various special allotments made by Congress operations were carried on at La Crosse Harbor, Clinton, Flint Creek to Iowa River levee, Warsaw to Quincy levee, Quincy Bay, and bar at Quincy. There was expended for channel improvement during the year $408,000, and an increased depth was obtained at many localities, never less than 1 foot and generally more. The maximum draft that could be carried June 30, 1901, at mean low water (stage 1.5 feet above extreme low water) was, as nearly as could be ascertained, 4.5 feet.

As regards the Flint Creek to Iowa River levee, for which the original approved estimate was $305,000, there has been appropriated $300,000, so that an additional $5,000 is needed to complete the work.

For Rock Island Harbor the estimate is $25,000, and $10,000 has been appropriated. The balance, $15,000, is needed to complete the improvement.

July 1, 1900, balance unexpended	$641,050.63
June 30, 1901, amount expended during fiscal year	432,062.51
July 1, 1901, balance unexpended	208,988.12
July 1, 1901, outstanding liabilities	11,579.30
July 1, 1901, balance available	197,408.82
July 1, 1901, amount covered by uncompleted contracts	70,964.36
Amount that can be profitably expended in fiscal year ending June 30, 1903, in addition to the balance available July 1, 1901 Submitted in compliance with requirements of sundry civil act of June 4, 1897.	826,667.00

(See Appendix Z 2.)

3. Operating and care of Des Moines Rapids Canal and dry dock.—During the past fiscal year the Des Moines Rapids Canal was open for navigation 233 days, during which time there passed through it 904 steamboats and 373 barges, carrying 31,160 passengers, 27,903 tons of merchandise, and 23,845 bushels of grain. There also passed through the canal 57,087,982 feet B. M. of lumber, 24,329,000 feet of logs, 21,285,025 shingles, and 17,320,126 laths. This shows a small increase over the previous year in freight and passengers, but a considerable falling off in lumber, logs, etc., due to the long prevailing high stage of the river, which permitted boats to go over the rapids.

The draft afforded by the canal is 5 feet at extreme low water, which may be increased to 6 feet at high stages.

The dry dock was in constant use during the whole year.

The cost of operating and care of the canal is provided for by an indefinite appropriation made by act of July 5, 1884.

The amount expended during the year was $48,595.91.

(See Appendix Z 3.)

4. Operating and care of Illinois and Mississippi Canal around the lower rapids of Rock River at Milan, Ill.—[This work was in the charge of Maj. J. H. Willard, Corps of Engineers, to March 30, 1901.] This canal is 4¼ miles in length, surmounting a fall of 18 feet, and was formally opened to navigation April 17, 1895.

During the past fiscal year the canal was open for navigation 239 days, during which time there passed through it boats and barges aggregating 37,460 tons, carrying 6,238 tons of freight, chiefly coal, and 1,470 passengers, showing a decrease of 12,444 tons freight as compared with the previous year, due to the closing of the coal mines.

The draft afforded by the canal is 7 feet, the locks, 3 in number, having a length of 170 feet between miter sills and a width of 35 feet.

The cost of operating and care of the canal is provided for by an indefinite appropriation made by act of July 5, 1884.

The amount expended during the year was $4,806.18.

(See Appendix Z 4.)

5. Operating and care of Galena River improvement, Illinois.—This improvement, consisting of a lock and dam in the Galena River, was purchased by the United States in March, 1894, under provisions of act of Congress of September 19, 1890, at a cost of $100,000.

During the past fiscal year the lock was open for navigation 238 days, in which time there passed through it 623 boats and barges, carrying 2,995 passengers and 807 tons of merchandise. This shows an increase, as compared with the previous year, of 84 boats and barges and 43 tons of freight.

Considerable repairs to the lock were made.

The draft that can be carried at extreme low water is 2 feet, as limited by the depth on the lower miter sill of the lock.

The cost of operating and care of the improvement is provided for under indefinite appropriation made by act of July 5, 1884.

The amount expended during the year was $12,077.01.

(See Appendix Z 5.)

6. La Crosse Harbor, Wisconsin.—The approved project contemplates the construction of a lateral bulkhead, a cross dam, and a certain amount of filling between bulkhead and shore.

The full amount of the estimate has been appropriated, and no further funds are asked for.

During the year the bulkhead and cross dam were completed and the filling was commenced.

July 1, 1900, balance unexpended	$16,184.31
June 30, 1901, amount expended during fiscal year	7,988.25
July 1, 1901, balance unexpended	8,196.06

(See Appendix Z 6.)

CONSTRUCTION OF RESERVOIRS AT HEAD WATERS OF MISSISSIPPI RIVER; IMPROVEMENT OF MISSISSIPPI RIVER FROM ST. PAUL TO MINNEAPOLIS, MINN.; OF RIVERS IN WISCONSIN AND MINNESOTA TRIBUTARY TO MISSISSIPPI RIVER; OF WARROAD RIVER, MINNESOTA, AND OF RED RIVER OF THE NORTH, MINNESOTA AND NORTH DAKOTA; GAUGING MISSISSIPPI RIVER AT ST. PAUL, MINN.

This district was in the charge of Maj. F. V. Abbot, Corps of Engineers, to August 10, 1900, in the charge of Maj. D. W. Lockwood, Corps of Engineers, from August 10, 1900, to May 27, 1901, and in the temporary charge of Capt. H. M. Chittenden, Corps of Engineers, since May 27, 1901. Division Engineer Col. J. W. Barlow, Corps of Engineers (now brigadier-general, Chief of Engineers, United States Army, retired), to May 3, 1901, and Col. S. M. Mansfield, Corps of Engineers, since May 9, 1901.

1. *Mississippi River between St. Paul and Minneapolis, Minn.*—In its natural condition this channel in its upper portions can only be navigated at low water by very small boats, and at higher stages the current is so swift in places as to make all navigation difficult. The improvement of this section of the river by the construction of locks and dams was inaugurated by the river and harbor act of August 18, 1894, which provided for commencing the construction of Lock and Dam No. 2, located near Meekers Island. The river and harbor act approved March 3, 1899, authorized the completion of Lock and Dam No. 2, together with Lock and Dam No. 1, under continuing appropriation at a total cost, for both locks and dams, of $1,166,457.

A Board of Engineers in a report submitted April 22, 1901, proposed certain modifications of plan which, if followed, will increase the cost of Lock and Dam No. 1 from $598,235 to $733,000. The district engineer states that it is probable Lock and Dam No. 1 can be built for $100,000 less than No. 2. On this basis the cost of Locks and Dams Nos. 1 and 2 will be $1,366,000. The difference between the estimates made in 1894 and 1901 is due to the advance in prices of labor and material, estimated at 15 per cent, and in the stronger type of dam now proposed for No. 2. An increase in the limit of cost as now fixed by law which will permit the desired change in plans will be in the interest of the work.

The amount expended to June 30, 1900, was $236,096.67. During the past year the excavation and foundation of Lock No. 2 were completed, except the laying of 50,000 feet B. M. of flooring. Seven-eighths of the concrete walls has been built. The material for lock gates has been purchased and delivered. The erection of the lower gate was commenced in June last. The filling behind land wall has been one-third finished.

Two-thirds of the lands and flowage rights for Lock and Dam No. 1 have been obtained. Test borings in bed of river at site of No. 1 were commenced June, 1901.

No effect on the navigable channel can result until both locks and dams are completed. There are no commercial statistics to report, as steamboats can not navigate this section of the river in its present condition.

July 1, 1900, balance unexpended $299,781.00
Amount appropriated by sundry civil act approved March 3, 1901 ...... 157,000.00

456,781.00
June 30, 1901, amount expended during fiscal year 157,135.06

July 1, 1901, balance unexpended 299,645.94
July 1, 1901, outstanding liabilities 10,544.97

July 1, 1901, balance available 289,100.97

Amount (estimated) required for completion of existing project........[1] 473,579.33
Amount that can be profitably expended in fiscal year ending June 30, 1903, in addition to the balance available July 1, 1901 .... 250,000.00
Submitted in compliance with requirements of sundry civil act of June 4, 1897.

(See Appendix A A 1.)

2. Construction of reservoirs at head waters of Mississippi River.—
The object of these reservoirs is to collect surplus water, principally from precipitation of winter, spring, and early summer, to be systematically released so as to benefit navigation on the Mississippi River below the reservoir dams.

Dams have been constructed as follows: At Lake Winnibigoshish, Leech Lake, Pokegama Falls, Pine River, and Sandy Lake.

The total amount expended to the close of the fiscal year ending June 30, 1900, was $1,013,883.48. These expenditures cover cost of construction of five dams and their operating machinery, of superintendence and contingencies, of certain awards for damages, of repairs and partial renewals; also of operating the dams up to February 1, 1895.

The expenditure has resulted in some benefit during the low-water season to the navigable portions of the Mississippi River from Grand Rapids, Minn., to the confluence of the Mississippi and St. Croix rivers, about 22 miles below St. Paul.

The reasons given in the Annual Report of the Chief of Engineers for 1897, page 1681 et seq., for limiting the system to the reservoirs now actually constructed, have become more forcible as the country has been settled and lands have increased in value. The policy for the future should be to replace the present timber structures, which are annually becoming more and more decayed, by permanent dams of concrete or masonry, to define by proper surveys the areas which the United States actually owns, and to acquire by purchase flowage rights over the large areas which, without any legal right, are now annually overflowed by the filling of the reservoirs, and the estimate presented contemplates such work.

The renewal of the dam at Lake Winnibigoshish has been completed during the past year. It is a concrete and steel structure with earthern embankments. The Leech Lake dam was one-third rebuilt and material for entire structure purchased. It will also be of concrete. The cost of completing the dam is placed at $20,000, and for rebuilding the Pokegama Falls and Pine River dams, $250,000. It will cost $30,000 to complete the Pine River reservoir dikes, and $20,000 to

---

[1] The amount here given is the original estimate of $1,166,457 less the amount already appropriated, Congress not yet having authorized any increase of the estimate. The amount which will be actually required on the basis of the estimate of April 22, 1901, is $683,122.33.

complete the flowage surveys. It is estimated that $75,000 will be required for the title to lands which are now submerged by the operation of the reservoirs without any legal right. The exact sum can not be given till the completion of the surveys shows just the areas needed. The above items, plus $40,000 for contingencies, aggregate $435,000.

This estimate is in excess of that heretofore submitted owing to increase in cost of labor and materials, and cost of additional work, the necessity of which has been developed since former estimates were submitted.

For commerce benefited, reference is made to the commercial statistics of the Lower Mississippi River.

July 1, 1900, balance unexpended $101,616.52
June 30, 1901, amount expended during fiscal year 91,171.33

July 1, 1901, balance unexpended 10,445.19
July 1, 1901, outstanding liabilities 7,622.60

July 1, 1901, balance available 2,822.59

Amount (estimated) required for completion of existing project........ 435,000.00
Amount that can be profitably expended in fiscal year ending June 30, 1903, for renewals, dikes, surveys, and lands, in addition to the balance available July 1, 1901 .... 300,000.00
Submitted in compliance with requirements of sundry civil act of June 4, 1897.

(See Appendix A A 2.)

3. Operating and care of reservoirs at head waters of Mississippi River.—The river and harbor act of August 18, 1894, made applicable to the reservoirs at head waters of Mississippi River, "so far as concerns their care, preservation, and maintenance," the provisions of the general appropriation for "operating and care of canals and other works of navigation, indefinite," contained in section 4 of the river and harbor act of July 5, 1884. The first allotment was made January 25, 1895, and the expenses from February 1, 1895, have been paid from the indefinite appropriation.

During the past fiscal year repairs were made to the wagon road between Lake Winnibigoshish and Leech Lake dams, to the embankment at Lake Winnibigoshish dam, and to the quarters at Pine River and Sandy Lake dams. A pile fence was built below the log sluice at Lake Winnibigoshish dam to protect the bank from scour by an eddy that had formed. A new house for dam tenders at Lake Winnibigoshish reservoir was commenced.

The reservoir system has practically been out of operation for the past two years while the reconstruction of Lake Winnibigoshish and Leech Lake dams has been in progress. The cost of reconstruction is defrayed from the appropriation for construction of reservoirs at head waters of Mississippi River.

Amount expended to June 30, 1900...................................$123,425.37
Amount expended during the past year 16,655.78

(See Appendix A A 3.)

4. Chippewa River, including yellow banks, Wisconsin.—The original low-water depth did not exceed a foot and a half, and the channels were narrow; at the mouth the depth did not exceed a foot. The first examinations and surveys were made in 1874. The project included revetment of caving banks and the construction of spur dams from Eau Claire to the mouth, a distance of 56 miles. The estimated cost was $139,892.50. The estimate has been revised three times. The last (1888) is $272,487.72.

The total expenditures from the beginning, in 1877, to June 30, 1900, aggregate $200,641.10.

On June 30, 1899, the work had resulted in a 3-foot depth at the mouth and improved depths elsewhere. A depth of 3 feet exists wherever the dams are fully completed.

The work of the past year has been repairs.

The river traffic at present is confined to the rafting of manufactured lumber and the running of loose logs. In 1900 the tonnage of rafted lumber was 232,000 tons, and of loose logs 700,000 tons. The traffic has decreased one-half since 1892 and 1893.

The maximum draft that could be carried June 30, 1900, at mean low water over the shoalest part of the river under improvement was 18 inches.

July 1, 1900, balance unexpended	$1,108.90
June 30, 1901, amount expended during fiscal year	1,045.13
July 1, 1901, balance unexpended	63.77
July 1, 1901, outstanding liabilities	18.00
July 1, 1901, balance available	45.77
Amount (estimated) required for completion of existing project	70,737.72

(See Appendix A A 4.)

5. *St. Croix River, Wisconsin and Minnesota.*—Before the improvement was begun the low-water depth in the channel above Lake St. Croix was but 2 feet on many of the bars. In Lake St. Croix and below the channel over the Hudson and Catfish bars was narrow and tortuous.

The project adopted in 1875, and amended as to cost in 1882 and 1889, contemplates removal of snags, bowlders, bars, etc., and the contraction of the low-water channel from Taylors Falls to the head of Lake St. Croix; widening and straightening the channel where it is narrow or tortuous in Lake St. Croix by dredging and contraction works. The improvement of the harbor and water front of Stillwater, Minn., was added by the river and harbor act of June 3, 1896.

The object of the improvement is to furnish an open channel 3 feet deep from Taylors Falls to the confluence with the Mississippi River, 52.3 miles, and better harbor facilities at Stillwater. The last estimate placed the cost at $136,700.

In a report upon a preliminary examination and survey of the river from Taylors Falls to Stillwater, submitted in 1899 and printed in House Doc. No. 104, Fifty-sixth Congress, first session, a project was recommended for the annual expenditure of $1,000 "to keep the river in as good order as is needed for the small steamboat traffic which now exists or is likely to exist in the future."

Amount expended to June 30, 1900, was $131,409.50.

The expenditures during the fiscal year ending June 30, 1901, resulted in increasing the low-water depth near Taylors Falls from 2 feet to 2¼ feet. The maximum draft that could be carried June 30, 1901, at mean low water was 3 feet at and below Stillwater and 2¼ feet above Stillwater.

The tonnage passing over the river is approximately 2,000,000 tons per annum of loose logs, tows of lumber and log rafts. Excursion steamers annually carry about 40,000 persons from Taylors Falls to Stillwater.

July 1, 1900, balance unexpended	$5,090.50
June 30, 1901, amount expended during fiscal year	4,198.73
July 1, 1901, balance unexpended	891.77
July 1, 1901, outstanding liabilities	18.00
July 1, 1901, balance available	873.77

{ Amount that can be profitably expended in fiscal year ending June 30, 1903, for maintenance of improvement, in addition to the balance available July 1, 1901.. 1,000.00
Submitted in compliance with requirements of sundry civil act of June 4, 1897, and of section 7 of the river and harbor act of 1899. }

(See Appendix A A 5.)

6. *Minnesota River, Minnesota.*—The river and harbor act of March 3, 1899, provided $1,000 for removing the bar at the mouth of this river.

Originally there was 1 foot of water on this bar at low water. The project provided for simple dredging. The estimated cost was $500 every year for maintenance.

Amount expended upon all projects to June 30, 1900, was $132,191.33, of which sum $692.08 was expended in 1899-1900 in removing bar at mouth.

No work was done during the past year.

The commerce consists of small pleasure launches and occasional excursion steamers.

July 1, 1900, balance unexpended	$308.67
June 30, 1901, amount expended during fiscal year	2.01
July 1, 1901, balance unexpended	306.66

{ Amount that can be profitably expended in fiscal year ending June 30, 1903, for maintenance of improvement, in addition to the balance unexpended July 1, 1901.. 500.00
Submitted in compliance with requirements of sundry civil act of June 4, 1897, and of section 7 of the river and harbor act of 1899. }

(See Appendix A A 6.)

7. *Red River of the North, Minnesota and North Dakota.*—When the improvement of this river began the navigation of the reach from Breckenridge to Moorhead (97 miles) was difficult at all stages, and impossible at low water. The second reach, from Moorhead to Grand Forks (155 miles), had a ruling depth at low water of 1.5 feet. The third reach, from Grand Forks to the boundary line of the United States (143.5 miles), had a ruling low-water depth of 2 feet. The lowe water navigation of Red Lake River was obstructed by bowlders between Thief River Falls and High Landing, a distance of 35 miles, and by a bad bar at its connection with Red Lake.

The present project is the same as the original (adopted December, 1877), except that an open-channel improvement was substituted in 1886, by act of Congress, for the proposed lock and dam at Goose Rapids, and the improvement of Red Lake River between Thief River Falls and Red Lake was added by the terms of the river and harbor act of Congress of June 3, 1896.

The object of the improvement is to provide an open channel on the Red River of the North from Breckenridge to the northern boundary line, 395.5 miles, as follows:
 1. Breckenridge to Moorhead (97 miles), a channel capable of being navigated during high and medium stages of water.
 2. Moorhead to Grand Forks (155 miles), a channel 50 feet wide and 3 feet deep at low water.
 3. Grand Forks to the northern boundary line (143.5 miles), a channel 60 feet wide and 4 feet deep at low water.

Also to provide a 3-foot open-channel improvement of the Red Lake River and Red Lake from Thief River Falls to and including Red Lake, a total distance of 135 miles.

The original estimated cost was $364,598.17, increased in 1883 to $398,598.17. The estimate was revised in 1887, after Congress had substituted an open-channel improvement for lock and dam at Goose Rapids, and placed at $252,598.37. An increase of the latter estimate was authorized May 8, 1893, to $310,320. Congress, in 1896, added $5,000 to the estimate of cost by attaching the improvement of Red Lake River to the project. In 1899 $4,000 of the $10,000 authorized was allotted to Red Lake River, so that the present estimate of cost is $319,320 for both rivers from the beginning of operations.

The total amount expended to June 30, 1900, including work on Red Lake River, was $292,741.92.

On June 30, 1899, the object had not been attained on the first division of the Red River of the North, which has for some years been closed against all navigation by permanent pile bridges. The Secretary of War has approved leaving these bridges as they stand, as there was no navigation affected thereby. The object was attained on the third division and on all but 13 miles of the second, but annual dredging will be needed to maintain the depth. On Red Lake River work has been confined to removing snags, bowlders, and other similar obstructions. During the past year dredging for maintenance was done on the main river north of Grand Forks, and snags, etc., were removed from the lower 8¼ miles of Red Lake River.

On the Red River of the North the expenditures for the past fiscal year were $7,210.86.

On Red Lake River the expenditures for the last fiscal year were $1,170.21.

Navigation on Red River is confined to comparatively short reaches north and south of Grand Forks, and consists mainly in the transportation of wheat to Grand Forks by 3 steamboats (100, 23, and 12 tons, respectively), and 10 barges. The tonnage during the year 1900 was 20,000.

On Red Lake River 3 steamers of 50 tons each and one of 24 tons were carrying general merchandise and passengers, the total tonnage in 1900 being 288, and 571 passengers. Ninety-three million feet B. M. of logs was run on the river during the year. Five steamboats are run on Red Lake towing logs, the quantity moved being about 60,000,000 feet B. M.

The maximum draft that could be carried June 30, 1900, at mean low water over the shoalest part of the river under improvement was nothing on the first division, 2 feet on the undredged 13 miles of the second division, and 4 feet on the third division of the Red River of the North, and 18 inches on Red Lake River.

RIVER AND HARBOR IMPROVEMENTS. 449

July 1, 1900, balance unexpended	[1]$10,258.08
June 30, 1901, amount expended during fiscal year	8,381.07
July 1, 1901, balance unexpended	1,877.01
July 1, 1901, outstanding liabilities	151.00
July 1, 1901, balance available	1,726.01
Amount (estimated) required for completion of existing project	16,320.00
Amount that can be profitably expended in fiscal year ending June 30, 1903, for maintenance of improvement, in addition to the balance available July 1, 1901	10,000.00

Submitted in compliance with requirements of sundry civil act of June 4, 1897, and of section 7 of the river and harbor act of 1899.

(See Appendix A A 7.)

8. *Bar at mouth of Warroad River, Minnesota.*—The river and harbor act approved March 3, 1899, as amended by the emergency river and harbor act approved June 6, 1900, appropriated $3,000, or so much thereof as may be necessary, for improving the mouth of Warroad River, Minnesota.

No work has been undertaken beyond making surveys. The balance of funds available is held subject to action by Congress upon a preliminary report, plan, and estimate submitted in 1900 and published in House Doc. No. 92, Fifty-sixth Congress, second session, and in Appendix A A 14 of this report. The estimate was $45,000 for a dredging plant and two years' expenses running the dredge. The maximum draft that could be carried June 30, 1901, at mean low water over the shoalest part of the mouth of the river was 4½ feet.

Amount expended to June 30, 1900, was $582.39.

The commerce into the river was 600 tons in 1899. The figures for 1900 could not be obtained.

July 1, 1900, balance unexpended	$2,417.61
June 30, 1901, amount expended during fiscal year	14.24
July 1, 1901, balance unexpended	2,403.37
Amount (estimated) required for completion of existing project	([2])

(See Appendix A A 8.)

9. *Gauging Mississippi River at or near St. Paul, Minn.*—The river and harbor act of August 11, 1888, authorized the gaugings, but none were made until the fall of 1889; from the latter date until 1899, inclusive, gaugings were made as frequently as funds available would permit and the conditions justify. No gaugings were made during the past fiscal year.

Amount expended to June 30, 1900, was $5,720.06.

The records indicate that a rise in the river at St. Paul commences in seven or eight days following the release of the water from the distributing reservoir at Pokegama Falls, and in about five days thereafter the full effect is felt. The mean time is therefore ten days.

(See Appendix A A 9.)

---

[1] The change from amount given in annual report for 1900 was caused by an oversight in not crediting refundments amounting to 80 cents, and an error of 2 cents in transferring figures.
[2] No recognized project in force.

10. *Survey of Red Lake and Red Lake River, Minnesota.*—The survey of Red Lake and Red Lake River, Minnesota, with a view to the construction of a dam with locks at the outlet of said lake for the purpose of improving the navigation of the Red River of the North and said Red Lake River, Minnesota, and estimating the cost of said improvement, required by the river and harbor act approved March 3, 1899, was inaugurated by Maj. Frederic V. Abbot, Corps of Engineers, and a preliminary report thereon was submitted April 27, 1900. Final report can not be made until a sufficiently prolonged record of the run-off has been secured.

The preliminary report was transmitted to Congress and printed in House Doc. No. 671, Fifty-sixth Congress, first session, and on pages 2828-30 of the annual report for 1900. The run-off was measured during the past fiscal year.

Amount expended to June 30, 1900, was $3,506.33.

July 1, 1900, balance unexpended	$1,493.67
June 30, 1901, amount expended during fiscal year	1,083.72
July 1, 1901, balance unexpended	409.95
July 1, 1901, outstanding liabilities	136.50
July 1, 1901, balance available	273.45

(See Appendix A A 10.)

11. *Survey of Otter Tail Lake and Otter Tail River, Minnesota.*—The survey of Otter Tail Lake and Otter Tail River, Minnesota, with a view to the construction of a dam at the outlet of said lake for the purpose of improving the navigation of the Red River of the North, Minnesota, and estimating the cost of said improvement, required by the river and harbor act approved March 3, 1899, was inaugurated by Maj. Frederic V. Abbot, Corps of Engineers, and a preliminary report was submitted thereon April 27, 1900. Final report can not be made until a sufficiently prolonged record of the run-off has been secured.

The preliminary report was transmitted to Congress and printed in House Doc. No. 672, Fifty-sixth Congress, first session, and on pages 2830-33 of the annual report for 1900.

Amount expended to June 30, 1900, was $1,021.89.

The run-off was measured during the past year.

July 1, 1900, balance unexpended	$1,978.11
June 30, 1901, amount expended during fiscal year	513.72
July 1, 1901, balance unexpended	1,464.39
July 1, 1901, outstanding liabilities	55.00
July 1, 1901, balance available	1,409.39

(See Appendix A A 11.)

12. *Survey of Big Stone Lake and Lake Traverse, Minnesota and South Dakota.*—The survey of Big Stone Lake and Lake Traverse, Minnesota and South Dakota, with a view to construct reservoirs therein for the improvement of the navigation of the Minnesota River, and an estimate of the cost of such improvements, required by the river and harbor act approved March 3, 1899, was inaugurated by Maj. Frederic V. Abbot, Corps of Engineers, and a preliminary report thereon was submitted April 26, 1900. Final report can not be made until a sufficiently prolonged record of the run-off has been secured.

RIVER AND HARBOR IMPROVEMENTS. 451

The preliminary report was transmitted to Congress and printed in House Doc. No. 675, Fifty-sixth Congress, first session, and on pages 2833–2836 of the Annual Report of the Chief of Engineers for 1900.
Amount expended to June 30, 1900, was $830.96.
The run-off was measured during the past year.

July 1, 1900, balance unexpended	$4,169.04
June 30, 1901, amount expended during fiscal year	600.86
July 1, 1901, balance unexpended	3,568.18
July 1, 1901, outstanding liabilities	86.75
July 1, 1901, balance available	3,481.43

(See Appendix A A 12.)

SURVEY MADE IN COMPLIANCE WITH RIVER AND HARBOR ACT APPROVED MARCH 3, 1899.

Report dated June 4, 1900, upon survey and investigation to *determine the causes of and the means of preventing the excessive floods in the Mississippi River between the Government dam at Sandy Lake and Brainerd, Minn., and the effect thereof on the interests of navigation* was submitted by Major Abbot through the division engineer. Three plans are presented, estimated to cost, respectively—

1. By means of levees	$750,000
2. By means of a canal	937,000
3. By straightening the present channel by means of cut-offs	1,796,000

The report was transmitted to Congress and printed in House Doc. No. 113, Fifty-sixth Congress, second session. (See also Appendix A A 13.)

The local officer was also charged with the duty of making survey of *flowage lines of Winnibigoshish, Leech Lake, Pokegama Falls, and Pine River Reservoir, Mississippi River*, and, if possible, report thereon will be submitted in time for transmission to Congress at its next session.

EXAMINATIONS MADE IN COMPLIANCE WITH EMERGENCY RIVER AND HARBOR ACT APPROVED JUNE 6, 1900.

Preliminary examinations of the following localities were made by the local officer and reports thereon submitted through the division engineer:

1. Preliminary examination of Warroad Harbor and Warroad River, Minnesota.—Major Abbot submitted report June 21, 1900, with plan and estimate for improvement at an estimated cost of $45,000. The report was transmitted to Congress and printed in House Doc. No. 92, Fifty-sixth Congress, second session. (See also Appendix A A 14.)

2. Preliminary examination of Long Prairie River and its sources, Minnesota.—Major Abbot submitted report August 2, 1900. In his opinion, concurred in by the division engineer and the Chief of Engineers, improvement of the locality by the General Government is not advisable. The report was transmitted to Congress and printed in House Doc. No. 97, Fifty-sixth Congress, second session. (See also Appendix A A 15.)

PLAN AND ESTIMATE OF COST OF RECTIFICATION OF MISSOURI RIVER AT ST. JOSEPH, MO., MADE IN COMPLIANCE WITH CONCURRENT RESOLUTION OF CONGRESS DATED MARCH 1, 1901.

Col. Amos Stickney, Corps of Engineers, president Missouri River Commission, submitted report November 28, 1900. The total sum required for improvement in accordance with the plan presented is $195,000. The report was transmitted to Congress and printed in House Doc. No. 506, Fifty-sixth Congress, second session. (See also Appendix B B.)

ESTIMATE OF COST OF COMPLETION OF LOCK AND DAM NO. 1, BRENNECKES SHOALS, OSAGE RIVER, MISSOURI, MADE IN COMPLIANCE WITH CONCURRENT RESOLUTION OF CONGRESS DATED JANUARY 22, 1901.

Capt. Charles Keller, Corps of Engineers, secretary Missouri River Commission, submitted report November 9, 1900. The estimated cost of completing the lock and dam was given as $20,000 in addition to the balance ($15,800) available November 1, 1900. His report was transmitted to Congress and printed in Senate Doc. No. 109, Fifty-sixth Congress, second session. (See also Appendix C C.)

IMPROVEMENT OF MISSOURI RIVER AT AND ABOVE SIOUX CITY, IOWA.

This district was in the charge of Capt. H. M. Chittenden, Corps of Engineers. Division Engineer Col. J. W. Barlow, Corps of Engineers (now brigadier-general, Chief of Engineers, United States Army, retired), to May 3, 1901, and Col. S. M. Mansfield, Corps of Engineers, since May 9, 1901.

1. *Missouri River between Stubbs Ferry, Montana, and the lower limits of Sioux City, Iowa.*—The river distance between the above points is 1,660 miles. By its physical characteristics this portion of the river is divided into four sections: The first, Stubbs Ferry to Greatfalls, Mont., 130 miles, is the navigable portion above the "Great Falls;" the second, Greatfalls to Fort Benton, Mont., 49 miles, is an unnavigable section, occupied by cataracts and dangerous rapids; the third, Fort Benton to Carroll, Mont., 172 miles, known as the "Rocky River," contains numerous rapids and rock obstructions, but has carried a heavy commerce; the fourth, Carroll to Sioux City, 1,309 miles, known as the "Sandy River," is characterized by muddy water, sand bars, and a shifting channel, with easily eroded and constantly eroding banks. Navigation is difficult at low water, due to the too great width of the river in many places. The upper 158 miles forms a transition portion between the "Rocky" and "Sandy" rivers.

For work above Fort Benton there has been no appropriation since June 3, 1896, and the work has been dropped from the list of those requiring regular reports.

Between Fort Benton and Carroll work has been carried on at the following points:

At Fort Benton, Mont.—The river and harbor act of March 3, 1899, appropriated $5,000 for repairing the levee at Fort Benton and confining the river within its present limits.

No work had been done by the General Government in this locality prior to the passage of this act. The project, approved January 23, 1900, provides for the expenditure of the above appropriation in revetting the bank in front of the town. Under this project 436 linear feet of bank was protected from further erosion by revetment in July-September, 1900.

To June 30, 1900, $150.43 had been expended.

Amount expended during the fiscal year ending June 30, 1901, was $4,843.98.

At Judith, Mont.—The river and harbor act of March 3, 1899, appropriated $5,000 for repairing the south bank of the river at Judith, Mont.

No work had been done by the General Government in this vicinity except the closing of the chute behind Norris Island by a dam constructed in 1891 as a part of the general improvement of the river between Fort Benton and Carroll.

The project, approved July 19, 1899, for the expenditure of the above appropriation provides for the protection by revetment of so much of the south bank as the funds will permit. Under this project 830 linear feet of bank was protected from further erosion by revetment in July-September, 1900.

To June 30, 1900, $115.94 had been expended.

Amount expended during fiscal year ending June 30, 1901, was $4,850.77.

Between Carroll and Sioux City work has been carried on at the following points:

At Bismarck Harbor.—For report on work previous to 1900 see former reports.

The project, adopted May 27, 1899, for expenditure of the allotment of $40,000 from the appropriation of March 3, 1899, provides for repairing existing works, constructing a dike and revetment on the right bank above the bridge, if found necessary, and continuing downstream, so far as funds will permit, the left-bank protection below the bridge.

Under this project, to the close of the fiscal year ending June 30, 1900, on the right bank the group of dikes constructed above the bridge in 1895 had been repaired and 1,913 linear feet of bank had been protected by revetment; on the left bank below the bridge 500 linear feet of bank just above the railroad warehouse and 900 linear feet of bank below the revetment constructed in 1897 had been protected by revetment.

To June 30, 1900, $111,471.54 had been expended at this locality.

Total amount expended during fiscal year ending June 30, 1901, was $1,788.85, of which $250.70 was for maintenance.

By the work done on this reach the tendency of the river to cut through above the bridge to the Heart River has been checked and further erosion at the site of the works has been prevented.

The works constructed on this reach are in fairly good condition, but require slight repairs from time to time.

At Pierre and Fort Pierre.—For report òn work previous to 1900 see former reports.

The project, adopted June 19, 1899, for the expenditure of the allotment of $40,000 from the appropriation of March 3, 1899, provides for protecting the head of Marion Island and closing the chute behind it; for extending the present Marion Island revetment to the foot of the island; for repairing the present works and raising the shore ends of the dikes at Pierre, and for constructing so much of two proposed dikes on the Pierre side.as remaining funds will permit.

Under this project to the close of the fiscal year ending June 30, 1900, the head of Marion Island had been protected by 1,790 linear feet of revetment, the Marion Island dam had been extended 300 feet, and the work of repairing and strengthening the dam, which had been damaged by the high water accompanying the spring break-up of 1900 and of raising the dam and the head of the island above extreme high water, which was thought necessary to insure the permanence of the work at this point, had been begun and half completed.

To June 30, 1900, $106,705.79 had been expended at this locality.

Amount expended for maintenance of improvement during fiscal year ending June 30, 1901, was $737.73.

Total amount expended during fiscal year ending June 30, 1901, was $11,412.27.

The work of raising the Marion Island dam and the head of the island above extreme high water, which was in progress at the end of the last fiscal year, was finished in September, 1900.

The work done in this locality has stopped the flow of water through the chute behind Marion Island.

The works so far constructed in this locality are in fairly good condition, but will require slight repairs from time to time.

At Yankton.—For report on work previous to 1900 see former reports.

The project adopted April 19, 1899, for the expenditure of the allotment of $40,000 from the appropriation of March 3, 1899, provides for continuing the construction of dikes.

Under this project 2,450 linear feet of 3-row dike was constructed during the fiscal year ending June 30, 1900.

To June 30, 1900, $68,305.40 had been expended at this locality.

Amount expended for maintenance of improvement during fiscal year ending June 30, 1901, was $126.40.

Total amount expended during fiscal year ending June 30, 1901, was $2,331.39.

No construction work was done in this locality during the fiscal year except some minor repairs to dikes.

By the work so far done the channel has been forced over considerably toward Yankton, and the portion of the Nebraska bank covered by the dikes has been protected from further erosion. The works so far constructed in this locality are in good condition but will require slight repairs from time to time.

At Elkpoint.—For report on work prior to 1900 see former reports.

The project adopted June 22, 1899, for the expenditure of the allotment of $20,000 from the appropriation of March 3, 1899, together with the balance from the appropriation of June 3, 1896, provides for beginning the protection of the left bank opposite the town, the works to consist of revetment and, where necessary to fair out the shore line, of short permeable dikes.

Under this project 2,124 linear feet of revetment was constructed during the fiscal year ending June 30, 1900.

Congress in the sundry civil act of June 6, 1900, directed that $10,000 additional to the amount already apportioned from the appropriation of March 3, 1899, should be expended at Elkpoint.

The project adopted June 29, 1900, for the expenditure of this additional allotment, provides for the continuation of the revetment.

Under the above projects 2,440 linear feet of revetment was constructed during the fiscal year.

To June 30, 1900, $24,531.72 had been expended at this locality.

Amount expended during the fiscal year ending June 30, 1901, was $18,378.56.

The work thus far done has protected from further erosion the portion of the river bank covered. The works constructed in this locality are in good condition, except some slight damage caused by recent high water, which will be repaired as soon as conditions are favorable. Slight repairs will be needed from time to time.

Opposite Sioux City to opposite Elkpoint.—The Nebraska bank of the Missouri River in front of South Sioux City had been protected for about 4,000 feet upstream from the lower bridge and for about 5,400 feet upstream from the upper bridge by revetments constructed by the owners of the respective bridges. Between these two revetments about 4,270 linear feet of bank was unprotected and was being rapidly eroded. The project, adopted July 24, 1896, contemplated the expenditure of the funds provided by the river and harbor act of June 3, 1896, in revetting this unprotected bank, in repaving the upper bank for 300 feet farther upstream, and in protecting the head of the work by a short pile dike. The work forms part of a general plan, described under report upon work at Sioux City, for the improvement of the river in this vicinity.

The revetment was completed in the fall of 1896 and the dike in March, 1897.

The project adopted December 23, 1899, for the expenditure of the $25,000 appropriated by the river and harbor act of March 3, 1899, provides for protecting the right bank of the river with standard revetment used on this section of the river, from Jackson Chute as far down the river as funds will permit.

Under this project 2,288 linear feet of revetment was constructed during the fiscal year ending June 30, 1900, and 1,600 linear feet during the fiscal year ending June 30, 1901, making a total of 3,888 linear feet of continuous revetment.

To June 30, 1900, $52,658.50 had been expended at this locality.

Amount expended during fiscal year ending June 30, 1901, was $7,351.29.

The works so far constructed in this locality are in good condition, but will require slight repairs from time to time.

At Sioux City.—The river above Sioux City was extremely unstable. Several cut-offs had occurred in recent years, causing radical changes in channel, increased slope, and a large amount of erosion on banks opposite Sioux City. For the purpose of checking this erosion work was begun in 1878 and continued in each succeeding year until 1882. The works constructed were of an experimental type, and have since been destroyed or abandoned by the river.

In 1889 a group of 9 dikes was built at the center of the Sioux City front to check a dangerous erosion and fair out the bank line. In 1895 2 dikes were built just above this group and 2 dikes of the group strengthened. In the same year, under a project for the expenditure of $40,000 appropriated by the sundry civil act of March 2, 1895, a group of 16 short dikes were built near the upper limits of the city to protect the bank there. This latter work formed part of a general plan submitted at the same time for the rectification of the river from about 2¼ miles above the mouth of the Big Sioux River to near the lower limits of the city, at an estimated cost for the portion below the Big Sioux River only of $400,000.

The project, adopted June 10, 1897, for the expenditure of the $40,000 allotted from the appropriation of June 3, 1896, provided for protecting the lower portion of the city front (below the Floyd River), for making necessary repairs to existing dikes, and for applying the balance to such work as might afterwards be found necessary.

Under this project the Iowa bank from the mouth of the Floyd River to a point about 7,400 feet below had been protected by a revetment 824 feet in length and by 20 short pile dikes.

The project, adopted July 2, 1900, for the expenditure of the allotment of $20,000 from the appropriation of March 3, 1899, together with the small balance left over from previous appropriations, provides for revetting the river bank from the Combination Bridge downstream as far as the funds will permit.

Under this project 2,900 linear feet of revetment was constructed. Some minor repairs were made during the fiscal year to the dikes constructed in 1895.

To June 30, 1900, $229,740.77 had been expended at this locality.

Amount expended for maintenance of improvement during fiscal year ending June 30, 1901, was $121.88.

Total amount expended during fiscal year ending June 30, 1901, was $18,399.59.

Ice harbors.—The adopted project provides for the construction of two ice harbors, which were afterwards located at Rockhaven, near Mandan, N. Dak., and on the Big Sioux River (upper limits of Sioux City) near its confluence with the Missouri.

To June 30, 1899, $42,762.75 had been expended, by which the two ice harbors had been completed.

Total expenditures.—Total expenditures on the Missouri River between Stubbs Ferry and Sioux City to June 30, 1900, except for snagging, were about $1,547,096.28. In addition about $10,000 was expended on the general river survey above Stubbs Ferry.

The estimates submitted for construction are intended to be applied in continuing the work begun at the several points. The work at none of these points has been carried far enough so that it can be abandoned without risk of loss of what has already been done.

The estimates for maintenance are intended to be applied in repairing damage to the works due to deterioration or caused by high water, ice, and drifting logs.

July 1, 1900, balance unexpended	a$93,287.50
June 30, 1901, amount expended during fiscal year	69,356.70
July 1, 1901, balance unexpended	23,930.80
July 1, 1901, outstanding liabilities	9,648.78
July 1, 1901, balance available	14,282.02

{ Amount (estimated) required for completion of existing project .... Indefinite.
Amount that can be profitably expended in fiscal year ending June 30, 1903, for works of improvement and for maintenance, in addition to the balance available July 1, 1901................................. 200,000.00
Submitted in compliance with requirements of sundry civil act of June 4, 1897, and of section 7 of the river and harbor act of 1899.

(See Appendix D D 1.)

2. Improving Upper Missouri River by snagging.—In its original condition the "Sandy River" between Carroll and Sioux City was greatly obstructed by snags, and to a less extent by loose rocks.

The original project, adopted in 1890, provides for removing the obstructions and the temporary improvement of the worst shoals, at an estimated cost of $50,000 annually. The work, begun in 1891, has been continued in each subsequent year under allotments and appropriations for this purpose.

The expenditures to June 30, 1900, were $376,144.60. Three snag boats had been constructed or purchased, and had been operated as funds permitted.

The river has been kept fairly clear of snags and obstructions over the portions used by commercial boats.

One boat was in commission 125 days during the past fiscal year. The results were 320 snags and miscellaneous obstructions removed, 330 trees cut on caving banks, and 1,748 miles of river passed over.

A machine shop has been erected at the Sioux ice harbor, and equipped with machinery, principally for use in repairing snag boats.

COMMERCIAL STATISTICS.

Amount of freight carried on the Missouri River above Sioux City, Iowa.

Calendar year—	Tons.	Calendar year—	Tons.
1887	13,961	1894	37,986
1888	12,895	1895	21,264
1889	16,723	1896	10,368
1890	14,072	1897	17,105
1891	14,211	1898	b 26,896
1892	17,292	1899	23,041
1893	19,481	1900	27,179

a Decrease of $210.27 from amount stated in the 1900 report, explained as follows:
Increase:
  Refundment by Capt. H. M. Chittenden, U.S.A., November 16, 1900........................ $1.33
  Refundment by Capt. H. M. Chittenden, U.S.A., June 22, 1901............................ .79
                                                                                          ─────
                                                                                          2.12

Decrease:
  Elimination of balances of works authorized to be dropped from list of duties, as per the 1899 report:
  Allotment for "Between Greatfalls and Stubbs Ferry"..................................... 43.03
  Allotment for "At and near Greatfalls".. 11.86
  Allotment for "In front of Sioux City".. 28.20
  Allotment for ice harbors and river survey.. 129.30
                                                                                          ─────
                                                                                          212.39
  Less.. 2.12
                                                                                          ─────
  Decrease... 210.27

b Includes 700 tons carried above Greatfalls, estimated; also 1,000,000 feet B. M. lumber rafted above Stubbs Ferry, estimated.

458   REPORT OF THE CHIEF OF ENGINEERS, U. S. ARMY.

No new lines of transportation were established during the fiscal year 1901.

July 1, 1900, balance unexpended	[1] $16,917.05
June 30, 1901, amount expended during fiscal year	15,309.34
July 1, 1901, balance unexpended	1,607.71
July 1, 1901, outstanding liabilities	546.67
July 1, 1901, balance available	1,061.04
Amount that can be profitably expended in fiscal year ending June 30, 1903, in addition to the balance available July 1, 1901. Submitted in compliance with requirements of sundry civil act of June 4, 1897.	30,000.00

(See Appendix D D 2.)

EXAMINATION MADE IN COMPLIANCE WITH EMERGENCY RIVER AND HARBOR ACT APPROVED JUNE 6, 1900.

Report upon preliminary examination of *Sioux River, South Dakota, with a view to the construction of a dam for the storage of water of said stream in Lake Kampeska and Lake Poinsett, with an estimate of the capacity of said reservoir and the feasibility of utilizing the same,* was submitted through the division engineer by Captain Chittenden, November 15, 1900. The report was transmitted to Congress and printed in House Doc. No. 93, Fifty-sixth Congress, second session. (See also Appendix D D 3.)

IMPROVEMENT OF CUMBERLAND RIVER, TENNESSEE AND KENTUCKY, AND OF OBION AND FORKED DEER RIVERS, TENNESSEE.

This district was in the charge of Lieut. Col. M. B. Adams, Corps of Engineers, to July 18, 1900, in the temporary charge of Maj. Dan C. Kingman, Corps of Engineers, from July 18, 1900, to September 20, 1900, and in the charge of Lieutenant-Colonel Adams since September 20, 1900.

1. *Obion River, Tennessee.*—This stream is situated in northwestern Tennessee, taking its rise in Henry and Weakley counties. It has a north and south fork that unite about 85 miles above its mouth in the Mississippi River some 5 miles below the Missouri and Arkansas State line. The head of navigation is regarded as at Obion, Tenn., where it is crossed by the Illinois Central Railroad.

The present project provides for the maintenance of a clear channel, free from snags, trees, etc., at a cost of some $2,500 per year. These operations have been productive of an improved channel between Obion, Tenn., and the mouth of the river, by the removal of the drift, snags, and obstructing timber. In 1893 a small steamboat, with tow, was enabled to ascend the river—the first in fifty years.

The amount expended in these operations to the close of the fiscal year ending June 30, 1900, was $19,971.09.

During the fiscal year ending June 30, 1901, the work done was as follows: Leaning trees cut, 5,202; trees deadened, 3,859; logs lying

---

[1] Decrease of $9.18 from amount stated in the 1900 report, explained as follows:
Increase:
　Refundment by Capt. H. M. Chittenden, U. S. A., November 16, 1900.... $2.70
Decrease:
　Elimination of balance turned into the Treasury as per the 1899 report... 11.88

　　　　　　　　　　　　　　　　　　　　　　　　　　　　　11.88
　　　　　　　　　　　　　　　　　　　　　　　　　　　　　 2.70

Decrease.. 9.18

along bank cut up to prevent being carried into channel at high water, 3,625; snags cut, 2,160; snags removed, 1,816.

It is proposed to use the balance of available funds in continuing channel work from Obion, Tenn., to mouth of river and for care of plant.

In view of the fact that operations on the Obion and Forked Deer rivers are of precisely the same nature, as well as owing to some confusion that appears to have existed regarding the proper separation of the work on these streams, with their common channel for 3¼ miles immediately above their common exit into the Mississippi, it is recommended by the officer now in local charge that the two streams be hereafter considered together, being called the "Obion and Forked Deer rivers," and in appropriating for them that a sum equal to what is now separately allowed for the maintenance of each be appropriated as one item for the maintenance of both as one stream. I concur in this recommendation.

The commerce of this stream consists principally of lumber cut by numerous sawmills on or near the river and which reaches a market by way of the Mississippi River. So far as could be ascertained, the commerce during the calendar year 1900 aggregated about 170,113 tons, having an estimated value of $449,822; passengers carried, 900.

It is believed that the improvements have given material aid to navigation.

Comparative statement of traffic for five years.

Fiscal year—	Tons.	Calendar year—	Tons.
1896	66,615	1898	60,269
1897	(¹)	1899	67,852
1898	18,263	1900	170,113

July 1, 1900, balance unexpended	$3,528.91
June 30, 1901, amount expended during fiscal year	2,257.15
July 1, 1901, balance unexpended	1,271.76
July 1, 1901, outstanding liabilities	3.00
July 1, 1901, balance available	1,268.76

Amount that can be profitably expended in fiscal year ending June 30, 1903, for maintenance of improvement, in addition to the balance available July 1, 1901............ 2,500.00

Submitted in compliance with requirements of sundry civil act of June 4, 1897, and of section 7 of the river and harbor act of 1899.

(See Appendix E E 1.)

2. Forked Deer River, Tennessee.—This stream carries off most of the precipitation that falls in Carroll, Gibson, Henderson, Madison, Chester, and Crockett counties, Tenn., and finds its exit now into the Mississippi River through the lower 3¼ miles of the Obion River, and therefore joins its waters to the Mississippi about 5 miles below the Missouri and Arkansas State line.

The project for the improvement of this river provides for continuing the improvement by removing snags, cypress knees, logs, drift, leaning trees, and other surface obstructions, and including the removal of bars and shoals from Dyersburg, Tenn., to the Mississippi River, a distance of about 33 miles, so as to deepen the channel and make it navigable for crafts at a 3-foot stage or higher. This project was approved July 24, 1896, based on the provisions of the act of June 3, 1896. (See Annual Report of the Chief of Engineers for 1898, p. 1873.)

---

[1] Not given.

These operations have been productive of an improved channel, though of course no increased depth of channel has resulted or is to be expected.

The amount expended under the present project to the close of the fiscal year ending June 30, 1900, was $5,448.37, and the total amount expended to that date on improvement of the river and its forks, including the above, was $30,448.37.

During the fiscal year ending June 30, 1901, the channel was cleared from the mouth of the Forked Deer River to Dyersburg, Tenn., the head of navigation on North Fork. The work done was as follows: Leaning trees cut, 3,813; snags cut, 1,595; trees deadened, 996; snags removed, 688; logs lying along banks cut up to prevent being carried into channel at high water, 2,485.

The balance of available funds will be applied to clearing the channel of surface obstructions, reducing bars and shoals where necessary from Dyersburg, Tenn., to mouth of Forked Deer River, and to maintain the improved channel of the North Fork, South Fork, and main stream, and to care of plant.

In view of the fact that operations on the Obion and Forked Deer rivers are of precisely the same nature, as well as owing to some confusion that appears to have existed regarding the proper separation of the work on these streams, with their common channel for 3¼ miles immediately above their common exit into the Mississippi, it is recommended by the officer now in local charge that the two streams be hereafter considered together, being called the "Obion and Forked Deer rivers," and in appropriating for them that a sum equal to what is now separately allowed for the maintenance of each be appropriated as one item for the maintenance of both as one stream. I concur in this recommendation.

The commerce of this stream and its navigable branches consists principally of logs and timber products in rafts. Quite a number of flatboats have been used in connection with steamboats during the year.

So far as could be ascertained, the commerce for the calendar year 1900 aggregates about 43,794 tons, having an estimated value of $175,395; passengers carried, 900.

The improvements thus far have given material aid to the lumber interests involved.

Comparative statement of traffic for five years.

Fiscal year—	Tons.	Calendar year—	Tons.
1896	104,010	1898	56,256
1897	80,258	1899	50,770
1898	21,363	1900	43,794

July 1, 1900, balance unexpended	$2,551.63
June 30, 1901, amount expended during fiscal year	1,368.12
July 1, 1901, balance unexpended	1,183.51
July 1, 1901, outstanding liabilities	21.50
July 1, 1901, balance available	1,162.01
Amount that can be profitably expended in fiscal year ending June 30, 1903, for maintenance of improvement, in addition to the balance available July 1, 1901	2,000.00

Submitted in compliance with requirements of sundry civil act of June 4, 1897, and of section 7 of the river and harbor act of 1899.

(See Appendix E E 2.)

3. *Cumberland River, Tennessee and Kentucky.*—(*a*) *Below Nashville* (*191 miles*).—Operations for the improvement of this section of the river date as far back as 1832. Congress made five appropriations for it prior to 1839, $20,000 of which was to be expended below Nashville, and the balance, $135,000, on the river generally.

A survey of the Cumberland River below Nashville was made under the provisions of act of August 11, 1888, to ascertain whether it was necessary to establish locks and dams thereon.

The existing project is based on the above-named survey and contemplates the extension of the lock and dam system of the upper river over a considerable portion of the river below Nashville by the construction of 7 locks and dams, commencing at or near Harpeth Shoal (Lock A) and ending at Big Eddy Shoal (Lock G); the locks to be 52 feet wide and 280 feet long, with lifts varying from 8½ to 11½ feet, and aggregating some 70 feet. The project also includes the improvement of the Kentucky Chute at the mouth of the river according to the recommendation of the Board of Engineer officers, June 16, 1888 (Annual Report of the Chief of Engineers for 1888, p. 1628), the necessary channel work below Lock G, and the removal of surface obstructions, snags, logs, etc., below Nashville. The total estimated cost of the entire improvement is $1,964,500 (Annual Report of the Chief of Engineers for 1890, pp. 2151–2161).

Inasmuch as the shoals near the mouth of Harpeth River constitute the most formidable obstruction of the Cumberland below Nashville, it is proposed to press the work on Lock A and its accessories to completion at the earliest possible date. Appropriations aggregating $250,000 have been made for this work under the new or canalized river project.

The expenditures to June 30, 1900, under this project amounted to $226,390.28, of which $12,815 was for maintenance. The condition of the work at Lock A at the present time may be briefly stated as follows:

The masonry of the lock and the abutment is completed, except the concrete in the head bay of the lock. Most of the stone filling for the dam, riprapping, and paving is on hand, being the refuse from the quarry in getting out dimension stone.

No funds being available, the work on the Lower Cumberland is entirely suspended, the engineer property, buildings, and floating plant being in charge of a watchman. The small balance still available, $648.87, will be applied to care of plant.

The cost of maintenance of the river in its present condition by the removal of surface obstructions, logs, snags, etc., is about $5,000 per annum, and this amount can be profitably expended for such work during the fiscal year 1903.

The reported tonnage for the calendar year 1900 aggregates 407,088 tons, having an estimated value of $5,140,616.

Comparative statement of traffic for five years.

Fiscal year—	Tons.	Calendar year—	Tons.
1896	40,676	1898	120,232
1897	32,703	1899	263,608
1898	71,674	1900	407,088

July 1, 1900, balance unexpended	$23,609.72
Amount received on account of transfer of public property	161.95
	23,771.67
June 30, 1901, amount expended during fiscal year	22,896.50
July 1, 1901, balance unexpended	875.17
July 1, 1901, outstanding liabilities	226.30
July 1, 1901, balance available	648.87

Amount (estimated) required for completion of existing project	1,714,500.00
Amount that can be profitably expended in fiscal year ending June 30, 1903, for works of improvement and for maintenance, in addition to the balance available July 1, 1901	600,000.00
Submitted in compliance with requirements of sundry civil act of June 4, 1897, and of section 7 of the river and harbor act of 1899.	

(*b*) *Above Nashville (357 miles).*—Operations for the improvement of this river were commenced by the States of Kentucky and Tennessee as early as 1830. Congress made five appropriations for it as early as 1839, aggregating $155,000.

The existing project for the canalization of the Cumberland River above Nashville is based on reports of an examination and survey in 1882 and 1883 (Annual Report of the Chief of Engineers for 1884, p. 1662 et seq.) and on the acts of September 19, 1890, and July 13, 1892.

By act of September 19, 1890, Congress provided that of the general appropriation for improving Cumberland River above Nashville, $50,000 might be expended in commencing the improvement at Smith Shoals, and by acts of July 13, 1892, and August 18, 1894, it was provided that $10,000 of a like general appropriation might be used "in the improvement of the river above the town of Burnside."

This scheme of improvement comprehends the construction of 23 locks and dams below Burnside and 6 locks and dams at Smith Shoals, above Burnside; and it intends to provide a complete system of lockage from Nashville, Tenn., to Rock Castle River, so as to afford a channel depth of 6 feet, the locks to be 52 feet wide and 280 feet long, with lifts varying from 10 to 12 feet, at an estimated cost of $8,500,000 (see Annual Report of the Chief of Engineers for 1896, p. 1916). Of this amount $1,695,000 has been appropriated.

The amount expended to June 30, 1900, under the present project for a system of locks and dams from Nashville, Tenn., to head of Smith Shoals, mouth of Rock Castle River, Kentucky, was $1,521,832.02, of which sum $20,252.94 was expended on the Smith Shoals section.

During the past fiscal year active operations were in progress at Lock No. 1 under contract, and at Lock 5 by hired labor.

At Lock No. 1 the contractors carried on their work of construction of lock approaches and abutment protection until the end of November, 1900, when the season's work was closed on account of high water. Active operations were resumed May 13, 1901, and were in progress at the close of the fiscal year. An extension of time until December 31, 1901, was granted these contractors for completion of their contract.

A statement of the work done under this contract is given in Appendix E E 3 of this report.

There is a balance of $41,799.04 remaining of the appropriation of March 3, 1899, which this contract will practically exhaust.

The masonry of lock walls and abutments Nos. 1, 5, 6, and 7 are completed; Lock No. 2 will require no dam abutment, and the dam abutments of Locks 3 and 4 are still to be provided.

With the completion of the operations now in progress at Locks 1 and 5, the work remaining to be done in order that the seven locks (1 to 7, inclusive) may be made operative is estimated to cost $898,740.15, as per the detailed report referred to in the accompanying appendix.

There is a balance of $16,955.39 applicable to Locks 21 and 22 that is expected to be applied in getting out stone for Lock 21 when further appropriations for this section are made.

The sites of the six locks and abutments of dams of the Smith Shoals section have been approved and authority granted to obtain the lands by voluntary purchase if practicable, otherwise by condemnation. Abstracts of title to all the sites have been procured, the records being brought up to April 18, 1898. No further action has yet been taken to acquire any of the sites. There is a balance of $9,747.06 available for this work.

No operations for clearing the river of surface obstructions were carried on during the year, owing to lack of funds. The annual expenditure for these open-channel operations is estimated at $5,000.

The commerce of the Cumberland River above Nashville for the calendar year 1900, as nearly as could be ascertained, aggregated 289,218 tons, having an estimated value of $8,395,055; passengers carried, 17,906.

The Bowman Transportation Line was established during the fiscal year for business on the Upper Cumberland.

Comparative statement of traffic for five years.

Fiscal year—	Tons.	Calendar year—	Tons.
1896	48,393	1898	124,518
1897	82,675	1899	294,763
1898	89,776	1900	289,218

July 1, 1900, balance unexpended	$173,167.98
June 30, 1900, amount expended during fiscal year	66,177.52
July 1, 1901, balance unexpended	106,990.46
July 1, 1901, outstanding liabilities	1,965.90
July 1, 1901, balance available	105,024.56
July 1, 1901, amount covered by uncompleted contracts	24,027.37
Amount (estimated) required for completion of existing project	6,805,000.00
Amount that can be profitably expended in fiscal year ending June 30, 1903, for works of improvement and for maintenance, in addition to the balance available July 1, 1901	600,000.00

Submitted in compliance with requirements of sundry civil act of June 4, 1897, and of section 7 of the river and harbor act of 1899.

(See Appendix E E 3.)

4. Removing sunken vessels or craft obstructing or endangering navigation.—The steamer *W. K. Phillips* sunk on or about December 14, 1897, on the north bank in the north chute of Dover Island.

Reported as dangerous to navigation, September 10, 1900. Report made on wreck to Chief of Engineers September 26, 1900. Removal authorized October 6, 1900, under provisions of act of March 3, 1899.

Under date of September 26, 1900, the engineer officer in charge reported that it would be economical to the Government to defer work of removal until the United States snag boat could do so in the regular season's work, clearing away obstructions in the river below

Nashville. A snagging party was not sent out owing to the failure of the river and harbor bill to become law. Therefore the wreck, at the close of the fiscal year, had not been removed.

(See Appendix E E 4.)

IMPROVEMENT OF TENNESSEE RIVER AND ITS TRIBUTARIES.

This district was in the charge of Maj. Dan C. Kingman, Corps of Engineers, to May 2, 1901, and in the charge of Maj. John G. D. Knight, Corps of Engineers, since that date. Division Engineer, Col. Henry M. Robert, Corps of Engineers (now brigadier-general, Chief of Engineers, United States Army, retired), to May 2, 1901, and Col. Amos Stickney, Corps of Engineers, since May 9, 1901.

TENNESSEE RIVER SYSTEM.

The Tennessee River and its principal tributaries form a system of internal waterways capable of being navigated more than 1,350 miles by steamboats. In addition to this it is still farther navigable by rafts and flatboats for a distance of more than 1,050 miles, thus making a system of navigable water of the United States 2,400 miles in extent.

Notwithstanding the many obstructions which still exist in the river and the difficulties and dangers of navigation, there were 78 different steamboats of an aggregate tonnage of 10,468 tons and 359 barges with a carrying capacity of 108,274 tons employed during the year 1900 upon the system.

In addition to these a large amount of lumber was transported in rafts and a considerable amount of material was moved in flatboats, of which no record could be obtained. The statistics actually collected show that there were transported upon the river during that year more than 68,000 passengers and 2,140,114 tons of freight, valued at $18,140,508.35.

1. *Tennessee River.*—(a) *above Chattanooga, Tenn.* (188 miles).—In its original condition this section of the river was obstructed by rock reefs, bowlders, gravel bars, and by snags brought down by freshets. The depth of water on the bars varied from 10 inches to 30 inches at low water, and the current was at some places as great as 6 miles an hour.

The present plan of improvement, based upon a survey made in 1891–1893, is to obtain a 3-foot low-water navigation channel between Chattanooga and the mouth of the French Broad River, at an estimated cost of $650,000.

The total amount expended to June 30, 1895, under the original project was $293,255.83.

From the adoption of the present project, to June 30, 1900, $95,033 had been expended.

At ordinary low-water stages boats drawing 2 feet can navigate this section.

The commerce on the river has increased and the cost of water transportation has been reduced. The total value of freight carried on this portion of the river during the calendar year ending December 31, 1900, was $3,847,629.30.

There were not sufficient funds on hand at the beginning of the year to do any work. The unexpended balance of the appropriation was exhausted in caring for floating plant and the property stored thereon.

RIVER AND HARBOR IMPROVEMENTS. 465

July 1, 1900, balance unexpended	$2,711.17
June 30, 1901, amount expended during fiscal year	2,660.04
July 1, 1901, balance unexpended	51.13
July 1, 1901, outstanding liabilities	50.63
July 1, 1901, balance available	.50
Amount (estimated) required for completion of existing project	555,000.00
Amount that can be profitably expended in fiscal year ending June 30, 1903, for works of improvement and for maintenance, in addition to the balance available July 1, 1901	50,000.00

Submitted in compliance with requirements of sundry civil act of June 4, 1897, and of section 7 of the river and harbor act of 1899.

(*b*) *Chattanooga, Tenn., to Riverton, Ala., (237.3 miles).*—The original condition of the river from Chattanooga to Browns Ferry was unfavorable to navigation, the channel being obstructed by rock reefs, bars, bowlders, and projecting rocky points, permitting the passage of vessels from six to nine months annually. From Browns Ferry to Florence it was navigable only at unusual high-water stages, owing to the obstructions known as Big and Little Muscle shoals. Navigation between Florence and Riverton, Ala., was limited to about six months annually, owing to the obstructions known as Colbert and Bee Tree shoals.

The existing project of improvement is as follows:

(1) By blasting and dredging to remove existing obstructions to navigation at Ross Towhead, in the mountain section, at Bridgeport and Guntersville, and elsewhere on the river.

(2) Building a canal 14.5 miles long, 70 to 120 feet wide, and 6 feet deep, to permit navigation past the river obstruction known as Big Muscle Shoals, and a canal 1¼ miles long to enable vessels to avoid the obstruction known as the Elk River Shoals.

(3) Constructing at Little Muscle Shoals a canal about 3 miles long and 6 feet deep.

(4) Constructing a canal 8 miles long, 150 feet wide, and 7 feet deep, past the Colbert and Bee Tree shoals obstructions.

The total amount expended to June 30, 1900, was $4,627,445.04.

This expenditure had resulted in the completion of the Big Muscle Shoals and Elk River Shoals canals and their approaches at a cost of $3,181,726.50, and in the improvement of Little Muscle Shoals by excavation and the construction of wing dams, whereby its navigation was greatly improved; but as the results show that the requisite depth could not be obtained in this manner, the new project for a canal at Little Muscle Shoals was adopted October 29, 1890.

In like manner the Bee Tree and Colbert shoals were temporarily improved at a cost of $62,243.41. This was before the adoption of the present project for the lateral canal.

The masonry of the lift lock at Colbert Shoals has been completed, and the right of way for the canal has been purchased and paid for.

At several localities the channel depth at low water is less than 3 feet, and at four localities it ranges from 1 to 1.8 feet.

The appropriation of March 3, 1899, provided funds for the survey of that portion of the river which had not heretofore been mapped. This portion lies between Shellmound, a short distance above Bridgeport, Ala., and the head of Browns Island, a short distance below Decatur. The total length of this part of the river is 136 miles. This survey was completed March 25, 1901.

At Colbert Shoals, owing to the small balance of funds on hand, the work was limited to quarrying stone for guard lock of canal and preservation and care of property.

July 1, 1900, balance unexpended	$57,080.99
June 30, 1901, amount expended during fiscal year	38,005.71
July 1, 1901, balance unexpended	19,075.28
July 1, 1901, outstanding liabilities	6,658.24
July 1, 1901, balance available	12,417.04

Amount (estimated) required for completion of existing project	5,127,939.81
Amount that can be profitably expended in fiscal year ending June 30, 1903, for works of improvement and for maintenance, in addition to the balance available July 1, 1901	600,000.00
Submitted in compliance with requirements of sundry civil act of June 4, 1897, and of section 7 of the river and harbor act of 1899.	

(c) *Below Riverton, Ala. (226 miles).*—Over the lower 196 miles, a depth of 3½ feet exists at low water; on the remaining and upper 30 miles, not over 24 inches is available.

The existing project of improvement is:

(1) Improving the river by dredging, to obtain a low-water channel not less than 5 feet deep and 150 feet wide; and (2) protecting Livingston Point, Kentucky, and Tennessee Island, and preservation of harbor of Paducah, Ky.

During the year the U. S. dredge *Kentucky* removed from various points in the channel 202,816 cubic yards of gravel, and 400 cubic yards of rock; and a Government snag boat pulled 196 snags, 53 logs and stumps, cut 665 overhanging trees and 760 saplings.

The work at Livingston Point and Tennessee Island is completed.

July 1, 1900, balance unexpended	$47,700.00
June 30, 1901, amount expended during fiscal year	29,951.98
July 1, 1901, balance unexpended	17,748.02
July 1, 1901, outstanding liabilities	2,349.12
July 1, 1901, balance available	15,398.90

Amount that can be profitably expended in fiscal year ending June 30, 1903, for works of improvement and for maintenance, in addition to the balance available July 1, 1901	19,000.00
Submitted in compliance with requirements of sundry civil act of June 4, 1897, and of section 7 of the river and harbor act of 1899.	

(See Appendix F F 1.)

2. *Operating and care of Muscle Shoals Canal, Tennessee River.*—This canal was maintained in a state of efficiency and readiness for use throughout the entire year. The number of commercial steamboats and barges that used it during the calendar year ending December 31, 1900, was 829, and the freight carried was 14,881 tons, worth $297,894.20. The number of lockages was 3,165. So far there has been a steady annual increase in the number of vessels passing through the canal.

During the past five months a steamer of 305 tonnage has carried about 2,901 tons of freight through the canal on regular service between Chattanooga and Paducah, Ky.

The canal is 16 miles in length and has 11 locks. It has a railroad nearly 15 miles in length and a large number of buildings for the occupancy of the employees of the United States and for other purposes.

The amount expended on operating and care during the fiscal year ending June 30, 1901, was $65,546.41.

A dry dock was completed in February, 1897, and since that time has been constantly used in the repair of the Government plant.
(See Appendix F F 2.)

3. *French Broad and Little Pigeon rivers, Tennessee.*—(a) *French Broad River.*—This river is one of the largest tributaries of the Tennessee. It rises in North Carolina, flows generally in a westerly direction, and finally unites with the Holston River, in the State of Tennessee, to form the Tennessee River.

In its original condition the river was obstructed by rock reefs, sand and gravel bars, and by bowlders, snags, and overhanging trees, and numerous islands in the river divided the water and diminished the depth in the navigable channels.

The project for its improvement is based upon a reconnaissance made about thirty years ago. It has for its object the removal of surface obstructions, the excavation of channels through reefs and bars, and the concentration and regulation of its flow by means of wing dams and training walls, so as to secure a channel depth of 2¼ feet at ordinary low water as far up as the town of Leadvale, a short distance below the mouth of the Nolichucky.

The amount expended to June 30, 1900, was $76,591.54. This expenditure resulted in the improvement of navigation below Dandridge, 50 miles from the mouth, by deepening and clearing the channel, removing natural and artificial obstructions, constructing wing dams, sills, and training walls, and revetting the bank where necessary.

The total value of freight carried on the French Broad River during the calendar year 1900 was $1,225,677.50, or more than fifteen times the total amount expended on the river since the improvement was begun by the United States in 1880.

The balance available is too small to permit any extensive work to be undertaken upon the river. It will be used as may be necessary for the repair of existing works and for dredging at such points as may most require it.

(b) *Little Pigeon River.*—This river is formed by the junction of its east fork and south fork at Sevierville, Tenn., and flows in a northwesterly direction for about 5 miles, where it empties into the French Broad about 32 miles above Knoxville.

In its original condition it was obstructed by rock and gravel shoals and by rapids.

The project provides for the removal of the bar near the mouth of the river and the removal of the shoal below Catlettsburg so as to permit light-draft steamers to reach that place.

A channel 30 inches deep at low water has been dredged through the bar at the mouth of the Little Pigeon; the head of McCroskeys Island has been riprapped, and the dam across the island chute repaired.

It is impracticable to separate the freight carried on the Little Pigeon River from that carried on the French Broad, as the same boats are engaged in the trade, and the Little Pigeon practically amounts to an additional landing on the French Broad.

Owing to the great slope of the Little Pigeon River, it is subject to sudden and violent freshets, and these bring down coarse gravel and bowlders, which tend to re-form the two bars which now obstruct the navigable portion of it. Redredging of these bars will be necessary from time to time, and the improvement can never be considered as completed.

The river and harbor act of July 13, 1892, provided that of the $15,000 appropriated for improving French Broad River, Tennessee, $1,000 "may be used in removing bar or shoal in Little Pigeon River."

This is the only separate appropriation ever made for this river. The navigable portion of it is so short, about 2 miles, in reality to amount only to an additional landing for French Broad River boats.

July 1, 1900, balance unexpended	$3,408.46
June 30, 1901, amount expended during fiscal year	941.15
July 1, 1901, balance unexpended	2,467.31
July 1, 1901, outstanding liabilities	156.19
July 1, 1901, balance available	2,311.12

Amount (estimated) required for completion of existing project....... 80,000.00
Amount that can be profitably expended in fiscal year ending June 30, 1903, for works of improvement and for maintenance, in addition to the balance available July 1, 1901 .... 10,000.00
Submitted in compliance with requirements of sundry civil act of June 4, 1897, and of section 7 of the river and harbor act of 1899.

(See Appendix F F 3.)

4. Clinch River, Tennessee.—This river rises in the Cumberland Mountains in Virginia, and after following a southwesterly course empties into the Tennessee River at Kingston, 104 miles above Chattanooga. About 230 miles of the river lies in the State of Tennessee.

In its original condition the channel was obstructed by rock reefs, sand and gravel bars, bowlders, snags, and overhanging trees.

The present project provides for channel excavations, removing surface obstructions, and the construction of wing dams and training walls, so as to secure a navigable channel 2 feet in depth at ordinary low water from the mouth of the river to Clinton, about 70 miles, and of 1½ feet in depth from Clinton to Haynes (or Walkers) Ferry, about 75 miles. From Haynes Ferry to Osborne Ford, in Virginia, a distance of 120 miles, it is proposed simply to remove the loose rock and bowlders, reduce the rock ledges, remove snags, overhanging trees, and similar obstructions, so as to assist raft and flatboat navigation at the stages at which the river is ordinarily used.

The amount expended to June 30, 1900, was $45,977.78, which had resulted in reducing many of the reefs, removing obstructions from the channel, building several wing dams and training walls, whereby the channel was so far improved as to enable the river to be used at stages 2 to 3 feet lower than before the improvement was begun.

The balance of the funds remaining on hand is too small to undertake any extensive work of improvement.

July 1, 1900, balance unexpended	$4,022.22
June 30, 1901, amount expended during fiscal year	732.85
July 1, 1901, balance unexpended	3,289.37
July 1, 1901, outstanding liabilities	137.17
July 1, 1901, balance available	3,152.20

Amount that can be profitably expended in fiscal year ending June 30, 1903, for maintenance of improvement, in addition to the balance available July 1, 1901 .... 3,000.00
Submitted in compliance with requirements of sundry civil act of June 4, 1897, and of section 7 of the river and harbor act of 1899.

(See Appendix F F 4.)

RIVER AND HARBOR IMPROVEMENTS. 469

5. Elk River, Tennessee and Alabama.—Elk River rises on the western slope of the Cumberland Mountains in the south central portion of Tennessee, flows in a southwesterly direction, and finally empties into the Tennessee River about 30 miles above Florence, Ala.

Fayetteville, Tenn., is regarded as the head of possible navigation. Above this the river is too small and the fall too great to admit of improvement. About 56 miles of the navigable portion lies in Tennessee and 34 miles in Alabama.

In its original condition the river was obstructed by low bridges, milldams, fish-trap dams, rock reefs, bowlders, snags, and overhanging trees. The present project for its improvement provides for the removal of surface obstructions below the point where it is crossed by the Louisville and Nashville Railroad, 34 miles above the mouth. There are no milldams below this point. The project also contemplates cutting through the rock reef at the mouth of the river, so as to permit the easy entrance to it from the Tennessee River.

During the year ending December 31, 1900, 6 steamboats and 28 barges navigated the river, carrying 6,937 tons of freight, valued at $109,981.33.

July 1, 1900, balance unexpended $159.77
June 30, 1901, amount expended during fiscal year 159.77

(See Appendix F F 5.)

EXAMINATION AND SURVEYS MADE IN COMPLIANCE WITH RIVER AND HARBOR ACT APPROVED MARCH 3, 1899.

Preliminary examination and surveys of the following localities were made by the local engineer and reports thereon submitted through the division engineer:

1. Final report on survey of Hiwassee River, Tennessee, from its mouth to the mouth of the Ocoee.—Major Kingman submitted report September 13, 1900, with plan for improvement, at an estimated cost of $71,125. The report was transmitted to Congress and printed in House Doc. No. 77, Fifty-sixth Congress, second session. (See also Appendix F F 6.)

2. Preliminary examination and survey of Little Tennessee River, Tennessee, from its mouth to the slate quarries on Abrams Creek.—Major Kingman submitted reports dated May 19, 1899, and May 10, 1900, respectively. The estimated cost of the improvement proposed is $208,505. The reports were transmitted to Congress and printed in House Doc. No. 66, Fifty-sixth Congress, second session. (See also Appendix F F 7.)

3. Final report on survey of Holston River, Tennessee, from its mouth to Kings Ford.—Major Kingman submitted report November 30, 1900. Estimates are submitted for improvement by the usual methods of regulation works and by locks and dams, but, in his opinion, the locality is not worthy of such expensive improvements at this time. He submits an estimate of $5,000 for improvement by removal of channel obstructions and the cutting of overhanging trees. The views of the local officer are fully concurred in by the division engineer and by the Chief of Engineers. The report was transmitted to Congress and printed in House Doc. No. 218, Fifty-sixth Congress, second session. (See also Appendix F F 8.)

4. Final report on survey of Clinch River, Tennessee.—Major Kingman submitted report August 3, 1900, with plan for improvement at an estimated cost of $1,460.000. His report was transmitted to Congress and printed in House Doc. No. 75, Fifty-sixth Congress, second session. (See also Appendix F F 9.)

The local officer was also charged with the duty of making a survey of *Tennessee River between Chattanooga, Tenn., and Riverton, Ala.*, and a report thereon will be submitted in time for transmission to Congress at its next session.

IMPROVEMENT OF OHIO RIVER.

This district was in the charge of Maj. William H. Bixby, Corps of Engineers. Division Engineer, Col. Henry M. Robert, Corps of Engineers (now brigadier-general, Chief of Engineers, United States Army, retired), to May 2, 1901, and Col. Amos Stickney, Corps of Engineers, since May 9, 1901.

1. *Ohio River.*—The Ohio River from Pittsburg, Pa., to its mouth in the Mississippi, near Cairo, Ill., has a length of about 1,000 miles. Its total drainage area is about 210,000 square miles. The total population of the cities and towns situated immediately upon the banks of the Ohio and its principal tributaries is, in round numbers, 1,800,000 (census of 1890).

Original condition.—The first work to improve the navigation of the river was done in 1825. At that time the river was obstructed throughout its entire length by snags, rocks, and gravel and sand bars, and navigation at low stages was exceedingly difficult and dangerous, even for boats of only 1 or 2 feet draft.

Project.—The work on the Ohio River has been carried on in pursuance of a general plan which has been followed ever since the work was first begun in 1825.

In general terms, the design of the work proposed and approved is to aid navigation by increasing the low-water depth in the channel, so as ultimately to secure a minimum channel depth of 6 feet at low water all the year round from Pittsburg to the mouth of the river, 967 miles. This is to be accomplished by low fixed dams at islands, confining the water to a single channel; by dikes where shallow bars exist; by dredging; by the removal of rocks, snags, and other obstructions, and by the further addition in recent years of movable dams in the upper river down as far as Marietta, the construction of which is provided for by special appropriations separate from those for the general improvement, the latter being of course still necessary, although to a lessened extent. From the nature and extent of this work final estimates of cost were practically impossible.

Surveys, fixed dams and dikes, dredging, bank protection, etc., constituting what is known as the general improvement of the river, where of special importance, are covered by subprojects, as follows:

Mouth-of-Licking Bar, opposite Cincinnati, under project approved April 1, 1899, for removal of bar to 200 feet width and 4 feet depth. (Paid for out of general funds.)

Mound City Bar, under provisions of act of March 3, 1899, and under projects of April 1, 1899, and May 4, 1900, for dikes and removal of bar to 300 feet width and 6 feet depth. Unexpended balance July 1, 1900, $13,316.89; July 1, 1901, $13,096.42 (additional work also paid for out of general funds).

RIVER AND HARBOR IMPROVEMENTS. 471

Lawrenceburg (Ind.) embankment repair, under provisions of act of March 3, 1899. Unexpended balance July 1, 1900, $4,588.15; July 1, 1901, nothing.

Shawneetown (Ill.) embankment repair, under provisions of acts of July 1, 1898, and March 3, 1899. Unexpended balance July 1, 1900, $15,321.17; July 1, 1901, $828.04.

Evansville (Ind.) bank protection, under provision of act of August 18, 1894, and under projects of 1896 and 1897. Unexpended balance July 1, 1900, $1,611.22; July 1, 1901, nothing.

Evansville (Ind.) dikes and dredging, under provisions of act of June 3, 1896, and under projects of 1895 and 1896. Unexpended balance July 1, 1900, $3,994; July 1, 1901, nothing.

Evansville (Ind.) harbor dredging, under provisions of act of March 3, 1899. Unexpended balance July 1, 1900, $19,982.91; July 1, 1901, $12,884.08.

Madison (Ind.) harbor dredging and survey, under provisions of act of March 3, 1899. Unexpended balance July 1, 1900, $15,408.03; July 1, 1901, nothing.

Golconda (Ill.) harbor dredging, under provisions of act of March 3, 1899, and under projects of 1899. Unexpended balance July 1, 1900, $6,866.97; July 1, 1901, $6,615.60.

Brooklyn (Ill.) harbor dredging, under provisions of act of March 3, 1899, and under projects of 1899. Unexpended balance July 1, 1900, $9,564.09; July 1, 1901, $1,253.30.

Tradewater Bar (Kentucky and Illinois) below Caseyville, under project approved May 9, 1900, for a third dike. (Paid for out of general funds.)

Surveys.—Marietta to mouth of Big Miami, to determine cost of obtaining 6 feet navigation by movable dams, etc., under provisions of act of March 3, 1899. (The emergency river and harbor act approved June 6, 1900, provides for continuing and completing this survey out of the general-improvement funds, and final report will be submitted, if possible, in time for transmission to Congress at its next session.)

The amount expended up to the close of the fiscal year ending June 30, 1900, was $5,995,868.81.

The work accomplished up to that date has been of great benefit to navigation, but at many localities good results can be obtained only by a large expenditure, and the small amount available yearly for the whole river prevents much desirable work of improvement.

The work done during the year is as follows:

Lawrenceburg embankment.—Contract work completed in July.

Shawneetown embankment.—Contract work completed in December.

Evansville, Ind.—Extension of dikes and repair of bank protection. Contract work completed in September.

Tradewater dike.—Contract work half completed.

Mound City dike.—One thousand yards stone delivered. Work stopped by high water.

Dikes and dams between Pittsburg and Marietta.—Twenty works examined and estimates made for repair; two dams repaired.

Ice piers.—All piers examined and estimates made for repair. Preparations have been made for renewal of ice piers at Middleport and Gallipolis, and for construction of new pier at Big Hocking. Unexpended balance July 1, 1901, $44,044.78.

Operations of United States dredges.—This plant was employed at

Mound City and Brooklyn, Ill., and removed 54,241 cubic yards of material, 116 tons snags, logs, and rocks, and 1 wreck. Repairs of dredges were in progress from July 1 to August 8, 1900.

Hired dredging plants.—Two plants hired under contract were employed at Madison and Evansville, Ind., and removed 125,682 cubic yards of material; at eight other points, removed 32,085 cubic yards; rocks and snags removed, 35 tons.

Survey from Marietta, Ohio, to mouth of Big Miami River.—Work was carried on vigorously in the field from July 20 to December 10; platting and tracing of maps continued to end of year.

Harbor lines.—The principal field work was that of special investigations of encroachments along the river over its entire length, which required notices to the offenders. Notices were issued in many cases through the master of the United States snag boat. Office work in the completion and issue of maps and other data was continued through the year.

Results.—The result of improvement so far has been to enable light-draft boats to run all through the low-water season, where they were often stopped in former years for three or four months per year. The work of the past year was specially effective in this respect and greatly reduced the length of suspension of navigation above Cincinnati as well as below Louisville. The present extreme low-water depths of the Ohio River are 6 feet above Davis Island dam, 1.5 feet thence to Marietta, and 2 feet from thence to its mouth.

Commerce.—The total amount of freight transported during the calendar year was 14,054,322 tons; passengers, 3,881,582. The coal-boat traffic is constantly increasing both as to total quantity of coal and as to size of boats and the number of boats per tow.

A single coal and iron tow from Cincinnati to Louisville January 21, 1901, contained 40 barges and measured 1,170 feet total length and 192 feet width, with about 8.5 feet draft.

No new lines of transportation have been established that would materially affect the aggregate commerce of the river.

Estimates and recommendations.—The general surveys of the year on the upper half of the river show channel dredging to be needed at about seventy-two bars between Pittsburg and Cincinnati, at an estimated cost of $992,000. Such dredging, where not provided for by special appropriations, will be done gradually under appropriations for general improvement. Special provision for continuous dredging by one or more Government plants appears desirable.

July 1, 1900, balance unexpended	$397,173.23
June 30, 1901, amount expended during fiscal year	159,952.38
July 1, 1901, balance unexpended	237,220.85
July 1, 1901, outstanding liabilities	3,818.22
July 1, 1901, balance available	233,402.63
July 1, 1901, amount covered by uncompleted contracts	23,072.60

Amount (estimated) required for completion of existing project....... Indefinite.
Amount that can be profitably expended in fiscal year ending June 30, 1903, for works of improvement and for maintenance, in addition to the balance available July 1, 1901................................. 400,000.00

Submitted in compliance with requirements of sundry civil act of June 4, 1897, and of section 7 of the river and harbor act of 1899.

(See Appendix G G 1.)

2. Operating snag boat on the Ohio River.—The condition of the channel way of the Ohio, the necessity for continuous snag-boat work, and the benefits accruing therefrom to river commerce are plainly shown by the yearly reports of obstructions removed, which obstructions, if permitted to remain, would make navigation highly dangerous at ordinary stages and hazardous at any time.

The project for removing obstructions by a properly equipped snag boat was put in operation in 1876, the boat having been completed at a cost of $125,125.24, and the expense of operating having been borne by appropriations for improving the Ohio River until 1890. The river and harbor act of September 19, 1890, provided $25,000 yearly for this purpose, and the act of June 3, 1896, increased the yearly appropriation to $50,000.

The amount expended on this work up to the close of the fiscal year ending June 30, 1900, was $271,420.39.

As far as practicable, removal of obstructions is carried on whenever permitted by the stage of water and the absence of dangerous ice. The work of the snag boat, in connection with the occasional hire of other boats and the sending out of small parties when the snag boat is not available, maintains a channel as nearly unobstructed as possible; a large and important part of the work being the removal of wrecked coal barges as soon as practicable after the limit permitted by law.

In this way during the year the snag boat went over the entire length (1,000 miles) of river, and, in conjunction with the various hired plants and snagging and wrecking parties, removed the following obstructions: 1,093 snags, 16,764 cubic yards rock, 1,000 cubic yards earth, 40 cords drift, 38 large ice-pier timbers, 15 piles, and 86 wrecks, which latter included the steamboats *Percy Kelsy, Comer B, City of New Orleans, Potomac, Storm, Homer B, W. F. Nisbet, Dick Brown, John Fowler,* and *Charley McDonald.*

The amount expended during the past year was $41,118.47.

(See Appendix G G 2.)

3. Operating and care of Davis Island dam, Ohio River, near Pittsburg, Pa.—This dam is the first of the series for the slack-water improvement of the upper portion of the river. It has been in successful operation since 1885 and has proved to be of great benefit to commerce in general, and especially to coal interests, by allowing the harborage of coal at Pittsburg in large quantities while awaiting stages of water suitable to the passage of the boats down the river to its mouth.

The amount expended up to June 30, 1900, in operating this dam and keeping it in repair was $232,923.09.

During the year the dam was raised once and lowered twice and was up for 146 days.

The power house under contract was completed; a steam boiler, two steam pumps, and a new lock-gate engine were installed; repairs made to wickets, service bridge, and machinery; awards made for rebuilding both guide walls, at a cost of $49,111.10; $40,000 was allotted for renewal of back-channel dam. The next annual estimate includes $20,000 for reconstruction of bear-trap dam and $10,000 for renewals on service bridge and weirs.

The amount expended during the year was $17,662.76.

(See Appendix G G 3.)

4. *Movable dams, Ohio River.*—For 150 miles or more below Pittsburg the narrow channel of the Ohio River is so greatly obstructed by bars and shoals that navigation for ordinary vessels is much interrupted and for the numerous coal fleets of this section is only possible during flood stages. The movable dam at Davis Island (completed in 1885) has greatly relieved these conditions near Pittsburg, and it is evident that the only method of securing the desired 6-foot navigation the year round is by a continuation of this system.

The construction of Dams Nos. 2, 3, 4, and 5 was provided for by the river and harbor act of June 3, 1896, which appropriated funds for the purchase of the sites "in accordance with the project submitted February 3, 1896," by which project (Annual Report of the Chief of Engineers for 1896, p. 2120) the estimated cost of these four dams was placed at $750,000 each, making a total estimated cost of $3,000,000 for the four. Further provision was made in the acts of June 3, 1896, and June 4, 1897, which authorized contracts to be let for so much of the work on Dams Nos. 2, 3, 4, and 5 as could be done within a $2,000,000 limit, which was $1,000,000 less than the total estimated cost. The $2,000,000 has now been entirely appropriated and will be all pledged during the coming year. The estimates of final cost have been revised to agree with the experience of the past four years and are now placed at $900,000 per dam, or $3,600,000 for the four. This still leaves $1,600,000 necessary to be appropriated to provide for the completion of work.

At No. 2 the lock construction under contract was completed June 14, 1900. New contracts for the construction of 500 feet length of navigable pass were entered into April 29, 1901, and work of this contract is now in progress. About three-quarters of an acre of land next to the county road was found necessary as an outlet to property already owned, and its acquisition is in progress.

At No. 3 commencement of work was much delayed by difficulties in acquiring title to the land. Lock construction under contract has been continued through the year and is about three-quarters done. The removal of old dikes in the way of new contract work and in the way of navigation was begun under contract dated August 3, 1900, and is now completed. Dredging, under the same contract, to make a temporary channel for use during construction of the navigable pass is still in progress.

At No. 4 the lock construction under contract at the beginning of the year was completed January 31, 1901. New contracts for the construction of 500 feet length of navigable pass and for dredging of a temporary channel around the pass were awarded in June, 1901, and contract papers are under execution.

At No. 5 commencement of work was much delayed by difficulties in acquiring title to the land. Lock construction under contract has been continued through the year and is about nine-tenths done.

The amount expended on Dams Nos. 2, 3, 4, and 5 up to the close of the fiscal year ending June 30, 1900, was $571,857.99.

The construction of Dam No. 6, now building, was ordered by the river and harbor act of September 19, 1890.

The lock and navigable pass have been built. The contract work on the weirs, piers, and abutment, entered into May 10, 1899, has been continued through the year and is about four-fifths done. The lock gate, maneuvering apparatus (including power-house machinery, boats, etc.), the employees' quarters, storehouses, and grading, paving, riprapping, etc., of banks remain still to be provided for by further appropriations. One hundred and seventy-five thousand dollars in addition to all past and existing appropriations is still needed for such work.

The amount expended on Dam No. 6 up to the close of the fiscal year ending June 30, 1900, was $736,882.50.

The river and harbor act of March 3, 1899, made appropriations for the commencement of work on Dam No. 13, near Wheeling, and Dam No. 18, near Marietta, in accordance with the project of the report of December 28, 1898, for 6 feet of water the year round by movable dams from Pittsburg to Marietta, at a cost of $850,000 per dam. It also provided that continuing contracts might be entered into for the completion of such work at Dams Nos. 13 and 18 not to exceed in the aggregate $850,000 at each place. So far $610,000 has been so appropriated.

At Dam No. 13 title to the land has been acquired and contracts for the lock have been awarded and the contract papers are under execution.

At Dam No. 18, title to land was acquired and plans made for contract work on the lock, but no construction work actually commenced. By this time the surveys in progress on the river below showed the desirability of relocating this dam a few miles farther downstream. Such relocation being approved by the War Department, steps were taken toward the acquisition of title to the new site.

The amount expended on Dams Nos. 13 and 18 up to the close of the fiscal year ending June 30, 1900, was $4,038.15.

Commercial statistics are appended to the report for improving Ohio River.

CONSOLIDATED.

July 1, 1900, balance unexpended	$2,177,221.36
Amount appropriated by sundry civil act approved March 3, 1901	40,000.00
	2,217,221.36
June 30, 1901, amount expended during fiscal year	488,771.95
July 1, 1901, balance unexpended	1,728,449.41
July 1, 1901, outstanding liabilities	3,612.04
July 1, balance available	1,724,837.37
July 1, 1901, amount covered by uncompleted contracts	[1] 399,232.33
Amount (estimated) required for completion of existing project	2,865,000.00
Amount that can be profitably expended in fiscal year ending June 30, 1903, in additional to the balance available July 1, 1901 Submitted in compliance with requirements of sundry civil act of June 4, 1897.	[2] 655,000.00

[1] In July, 1901, additional contracts for $522,556.50.
[2] Of this amount $355,000 is for continuing construction of Dams Nos. 2 to 6 and $300,000 for work on Dams Nos. 13 and 18 under continuing contract.

DAMS NOS. 2, 3, 4, AND 5.

July 1, 1900, balance unexpended	$1,468,475.30
June 30, 1901, amount expended during fiscal year	381,538.00
July 1, 1901, balance unexpended	1,086,937.30
July 1, 1901, outstanding liabilities	2,414.76
July 1, 1901, balance available	1,084,522.54
July 1, 1901, amount covered by uncompleted contracts	[1]350,959.02
Amount (estimated) required for completion of existing project	1,600,000.00

DAM NO. 6.

July 1, 1900, balance unexpended	$142,784.21
June 30, 1901, amount expended during fiscal year	82,121.31
July 1, 1901, balance unexpended	60,662.90
July 1, 1901, outstanding liabilities	675.32
July 1, 1901, balance available	59,987.58
July 1, 1901, amount covered by uncompleted contracts	48,273.31
Amount (estimated) required for completion of existing project	175,000.00

DAMS NOS. 13 AND 18.

July 1, 1900, balance unexpended	$565,961.85
Amount appropriated by sundry civil act approved March 3, 1901	40,000.00
	605,961.85
June 30, 1901, amount expended during fiscal year	25,112.64
July 1, 1901, balance unexpended	580,849.21
July 1, 1901, outstanding liabilities	521.96
July 1, 1901, balance available	580,327.25
July 1, 1901, amount covered by uncompleted contracts	([2])
Amount (estimated) required for completion of existing project	1,090,000.00

(See Appendix G G 4.)

5. *Survey of Licking River, Kentucky.*—The river and harbor act of March 3, 1899, appropriated $10,000 for survey of Licking River, Kentucky, from its mouth, opposite Cincinnati, Ohio, to Falmouth, Pendleton County, Ky., and for estimate of the cost of a lock and dam at or near Three-mile Ripple, about 3 miles from its mouth.

Final report dated April 17, 1900, was transmitted to Congress and printed in House Doc. No. 645, Fifty-sixth Congress, first session, and in the annual report of 1900, at page 3155. Detailed maps have been completed for future reference and use. All work called for by the provisions of the appropriation has been completed.

July 1, 1900, balance unexpended	$5,576.86
June 30, 1901, amount expended during fiscal year	2,621.86
July 1, 1901, balance unexpended	2,955.00

(See Appendix G G 5.)

---

[1] In July, 1901, additional contracts for $238,421.50.
[2] In July, 1901, contracts for $284,135.

EXAMINATION AND SURVEY MADE IN COMPLIANCE WITH EMERGENCY RIVER AND HARBOR ACT APPROVED JUNE 6, 1900.

Reports on examination and survey of the *Ohio River, with a view to the construction of a pier for a harbor of refuge on the south shore at or near Maysville, Ky.*, were submitted through the division engineer by Major Bixby September 5 and November 24, 1900, respectively. He presents a plan for improvement at an estimated cost of $21,000. The reports were transmitted to Congress and printed in House Doc. No. 148, Fifty-sixth Congress, second session. (See also Appendix G G 6.)

IMPROVEMENT OF HARBOR AT PITTSBURG, PA., OF ALLEGHENY RIVER, PENNSYLVANIA, AND OF MONONGAHELA RIVER, WEST VIRGINIA AND PENNSYLVANIA.

This district was in the charge of Maj. Charles F. Powell, Corps of Engineers. Division Engineer, Col. Henry M. Robert, Corps of Engineers (now brigadier-general, Chief of Engineers, United States Army, retired), to May 2, 1901, and Col. Amos Stickney, Corps of Engineers, since May 9, 1901.

1. *Monongahela River, West Virgina.*—Several years ago the United States built Locks and Dams Nos. 8 and 9 on the Upper Monongahela River, which extended an existing slack water upstream to beyond Morgantown, W. Va., and made that place the head of packet navigation. Previously a downstream navigation of flats and small rafts at favorable river stages only was conducted. An inconsiderable amount of rafting continues above Morgantown. Before the improvement, and as now on the unimproved part, the river on low stages was easily forded at numerous shoals and rapids. Locks Nos. 8 and 9 are of sufficient capacity for the largest packets running on the river, and afford minimum sill depths at pool levels of nearly 5¼ feet.

The river and harbor act of 1896 provided for the extension of slack water by the construction of six locks and dams between Morgantown and Fairmont, W. Va., 25 miles upstream, at a limiting cost of $1,200,000.

The locks and dams are to be built of concrete. The total lift, 64 feet, will back the water into the mouths of the forks of the river a few miles above Fairmont. The controlling depth on the lock sills is to be 7 feet, and the chambers are to be made large enough to take in two coal boats abreast, or of the same width, 56 feet, as the large locks at Dams Nos. 1 to 4. This general project was approved March 3, 1897.

A contract made in 1897 for construction of all the locks and dams had been annulled near the end of the preceding year for failure to prosecute it faithfully and diligently. To that time the masonry, part guide cribs, and part grading of Lock No. 10 had been made, Dam No. 10 built except at a middle section of about one-third the full length, and part excavation of lock pit at No. 11 made. Besides this contract work, lock irons for Nos. 10, 11, and 12 had been purchased on offers received under competition. The locks and dams were readvertised in the early part of the year and a contract awarded for all of them. This contract having proved a failure, the works were again readvertised, and then for a fourth time, and a contract entered into for each of the three sets of locks and dams.

In the meantime minor operations by hired labor and job work were conducted at Lock No. 10 and abutment of its dam.

On the new contracts work was begun at Nos. 11, 12, and 13 in the spring or early summer, but progress of actual construction was small, mainly on account of interruptions by continued river rises.

The total amount expended on the improvement, including costs of surveys, examinations, and lands, to the close of the year ending June 30, 1900, not including outstanding liabilities, was $573,815.73.

The traffic at Dam 9, below Morgantown, was:

Fiscal year.	Passengers.	Freight.
	Number.	*Tons.* (a)
1900	21,609	57,211
1901	15,523	32,486

a Tons of 2,000 pounds.

July 1, 1900, balance unexpended	$688,084.27
June 30, 1901, amount expended during fiscal year	45,296.74
July 1, 1901, balance unexpended	642,787.53
July 1, 1901, outstanding liabilities	20,124.75
July 1, 1901, balance available	622,662.78
July 1, 1901, amount covered by uncompleted contracts	494,561.78

{ Amount (estimated) required for completion of existing project 350,000.00
Amount that can be profitably expended in fiscal year ending June 30, 1903, in addition to the balance available July 1, 1901 .... 250,000.00
Submitted in compliance with requirements of sundry civil act of June 4, 1897.

(See Appendix H H 1.)

2. Monongahela River, Pennsylvania.—The act of March 3, 1899, provided for enlargement and improvement at Lock No. 6, for certain accessory structures at Lock No. 3, and for floating plant.

The amount expended on the improvement to close of year ending June 30, 1900, was $3,781,845.15, inclusive of cost ($3,769,073.88) of the slack-water system acquired from the Monongahela Navigation Company.

The project, approved July 22, 1899, provides for lengthening chamber at Lock 6 6 feet, rebuilding its lift wall, lowering upper sills 19 inches and lower sill 12 inches (or as much as practicable), building a concrete guide wall below lock in prolongation of land chamber face, building a guard wall above lock, lengthening dam and building a low movable dam on its fixed part, and making other but smaller improvements at the lock; at Lock 3 to extend upper guide wall 300 feet and build a timber crib deflecting dike above the lock; to build a repair steamer, with snagging appliances and dipper dredge, and two dump scows; all at a cost not exceeding $185,556.

During the year the works at Lock 3 were completed, making the upper entrance to the lock, which had been difficult and dangerous, about the safest and most convenient one on the river. At Lock 6, its enlargement and improvement were completed, thereby making the lock chamber as long as that of the single lock at any dam downstream from the lock, depressing its lower sill from 4 feet depth to 5.5 feet at pool stage, and providing good aid and protection to boats entering and leaving the lock. In the previous year the lift wall had been rebuilt with a lowering of sills of 1.6 feet, or to the same pool depth as at lower sill of lock next upstream, together with erection of new upper gates, floor in head bay, and new valves at filling culverts. These improvements are an accommodation to boats, and especially to loaded coal craft which ply from tipples at new river mines in Pool 6.

Plans and specifications were prepared for a repair steamer.

The structures named in the appropriation act are part of the extensive slack-water system acquired from the Monongahela Navigation Company in 1897. A history of the system and an estimate of cost of its enlargement and improvement for affording adequate accommodation to a large and growing traffic are given in the Annual Report of the Chief of Engineers for 1897, pages 2412-2424. The traffic of the river is hampered and restricted by insufficient capacity and conveniences at the locks and in the pool channels. The tonnage of the river last year was nearly 7,000,000; in the previous year it was about 6,000,000. The least pool-stage depth at sills is 4 feet, and obtains at Lock No. 5; the minimum depth at low water is increased by means of flashboards maintained on Dam No. 4. This temporary expedient is uncertain and otherwise very unsatisfactory.

The reasons for a recommended appropriation for the purchase of a small parcel of land at cost of $12,500, together with the opinion of the engineer officer in charge that $30,000 in addition could advantageously be applied for similar purpose, are given on pages 479 and 480 of the annual report for 1900.

July 1, 1900, balance unexpended	[1]$175,627.67
June 30, 1901, amount expended during fiscal year	73,307.45
July 1, 1901, balance unexpended	102,320.22
July 1, 1901, outstanding liabilities	6,710.57
July 1, 1901, balance available	95,609.65

(See Apendix H H 2.)

3. *Operating and care of locks and dams, Monongahela River.*—The slack-water system of the Monongahela River comprises 9 dams and sets of locks. Locks 1 to 4 are double locks; 5 to 9 are single locks. Controlling depths on sills at the different locks at pool surface vary from 4 to 6.7 feet. Effort is made to provide necessary depths during low stages for 8-foot draft boats running below Dam 6 by putting flashboards on the dams, but this is an uncertain and otherwise unsatisfactory expedient. The locks were operated throughout the year, except that Lock No. 5 was closed three days for repairs; Lock No. 6 for one hundred and fifty-three days (during late fall and winter) for enlargement and improvement, as described in report on Monongahela River, Pennsylvania, and Lock No. 9 for twenty-six days on account of collapse of its lower gates. While work was in progress at Lock 6 freight and passengers were accommodated by means of inclined transfers on the dam. The walls at all the locks were flooded from one

---

[1] The unexpended balance July 1, 1900, reported in annual report for 1900, should have been less by expenditures made from appropriation for "Costs of condemnation, property of Monongahela Navigation Company," not previously reported, viz: January 27, 1900, Treasury settlement 9630, $200; June 6, 1900, Postal Telegraph-Cable Company, telegram, 20 cents; total, $200.20.

day to ten days, and navigation in pools 8 and 9 was closed by ice from two to five days.

From minor to considerable work of repair or renewal at the various locks and dams was done. Four new lock gates were constructed and 6 partly built at the repair yard, and a set of gates at Lock 9 rebuilt; 32,223 cubic yards of material was dredged at lock entrances or pool channels; 229 snags or stumps, 4 old wrecks, and 21 abandoned river coal-tipple or protection cribs were removed from the pools above Pittsburg Harbor.

The amount expended for operating and care of the locks and dams during year ending June 30, 1901, was $159,496.37.

COMMERCIAL STATISTICS.

Fiscal year.	Aggregate number of lockages.	Maximum at any dam. Products.	Maximum at any dam. Passengers.
		Tons. (a)	Number.
1898	80,885	6,117,978	157,098
1899	84,230	6,964,965	163,245
1900	75,834	5,994,975	192,652
1901	77,986	6,856,507	186,762

a Tons of 2,000 pounds.

(See Appendix H H 3.)

4. Harbor at Pittsburg, Pa.—This harbor as defined by harbor lines, established or authorized, extends from the Davis Island dam in the Ohio River to the site of Allegheny River Dam No. 2, and on the Monongahela River to McKeesport, at the mouth of the Youghiogheny River, being an aggregate length of river of 27.5 miles. The part of the harbor most used by waiting coal fleets, and called the lower harbor, lies below Dams Nos. 1 on the Monongahela and Allegheny, and measures 8 miles of river. The general widths in the whole harbor at pool surfaces are: On the Ohio about 1,100 feet, on the Allegheny about 930 feet, and at different parts of the Monongahela from about 750 to 950 feet. The maximum draft which could be carried over the shoalest place in the coal-boat channel before improvement was scant 8 feet at pool stage, and that for a narrow width. The harbor was and is still partly obstructed by fillings and old structures, some submerged, projecting beyond the harbor line. Other parts of the channel are from 10 and 12 to 16 feet and even, in spots, 20 feet in depth. When the movable dam at Davis Island is down, as it unavoidably is sometimes at low stages of river, lower harbor depths become reduced 3 and 4 feet on natural mean low river, to the serious inconvenience of coal-boat traffic, and at still lower stages cause suspension of its movement. Besides harboring coal fleets waiting to descend the Ohio River, a large local commerce is accommodated, and at times with inconvenience. The Monongahela River part serves as a refuge from Allegheny River ice. During seasons of prolonged low stage in the Ohio waiting coal fleets almost block the harbor. Thus, in 1893, according to reliable records, the fleet in the harbor at one time numbered about 50 towboats and some 1,800 craft, carrying more than 1,000,000 tons. In 1895 the fleet contained about 2,000 pieces, having cargoes of 1,250,000 tons. On June 30, 1900, about 520,000 tons of coal was afloat, besides that intended for local consumption. The ordinary maximum draft of loaded boats plying or moored in the harbor is 8 feet. The tendency is to increase the draft. Coal boats have occasionally come into the harbor from the Monongahela River drawing from 8 feet to 8 feet 3 or 4 inches, and sometimes even as much as 8 feet 9 inches.

The act of March 3, 1899, provided for completion of improvement of this harbor upon a certain estimate of cost. The estimate proposed annual maintenance at an expense of $10,000, which item has since been incorporated in the adopted project for the improvement. This project, approved July 11, 1899, consists, first, in dredging a channel throughout the lower harbor, where needed, 10 feet deep at pool level and 500 feet wide below Smithfield Street Bridge, Monongahela River, and above this bridge and in the Allegheny River of a less width and one limited by lines from ends of channel spans of adjoining bridges; second, raising the old riprap stone dam across Brunot Island channel, Ohio River, and protecting its surface by large and flat pieces of stone, but leaving a channel way of 5 feet depth at pool surface; third, removal of abandoned structures and unauthorized and obstructive fillings projecting from the bank beyond the harbor line in cases where it is impossible to secure removal except at expense of the United States; fourth, systematic and extensive marking of harbor lines and conducting inspection and patrol for execution of law for protection and preservation of harbors; and fifth, annual maintenance of the works, making local surveys and measurements, and preparation of harbor-line plats.

During the year the previously dredged channel way of the Monongahela River below the Tenth Street Bridge at Pittsburg was widened, the improvement project being finished from that bridge to the Panhandle Railroad bridge; from thence downstream to deep water, opposite Market street, the required channel of 10 feet pool stage depth was widened to 300 feet. The amount dredged was 80,075 cubic yards, besides removal of several large stones, stubs and riprap of old bridge piers, sunken oak timbers, pipe and large oil tank. The opening of a channel about 1,200 feet long and average width of 150 feet through Garrison Bar, Allegheny River, was completed by directing work of sand diggers operating under permits of the Secretary of War. By the same means the channel at wide shoal in the upper end of the Ohio River was improved. Operations were conducted to secure removal of abandoned river structures; systematic location and marking of established harbor lines progressed. Surveys, patrol, and inspection of the harbor and bank were made; and prevention or stoppage of deposits over the banks or improper dumping in the river and of encroachments of unauthorized structures beyond harbor lines was secured in a large number of cases.

The amount expended on the work to close of year ending June 30, 1900, was $22,488.38.

July 1, 1900, balance unexpended	$88,174.52
June 30, 1901, amount expended during fiscal year	26,961.64
July 1, 1901, balance unexpended	61,212.88
July 1, 1901, outstanding liabilities	8,017.22
July 1, 1901, balance available	53,195.66

{ Amount that can be profitably expended in fiscal year ending June 30, 1903, for maintenance of improvement, in addition to the balance available July 1, 1901.. 10,000.00
Submitted in compliance with requirements of sundry civil act of June 4, 1897, and of section 7 of the river and harbor act of 1899.

(See Appendix H H 4.)

5. *Locks and dams at Herr Island, head of Six-mile Island, and at Springdale, Allegheny River.*—The originally adopted project providing for the Herr Island lock and dam contemplated that the dam should be a fixed one, but in compliance with a request of municipal authorities the plan was changed to a movable dam, and to satisfy local riparian owners the position of the lock was changed so that a slip or basin, 55 feet wide and open at its lower end, is left between the lock and the river bank. The site of the Herr Island works is in the pool of the Davis Island dam of the Ohio River, 6.3 miles below, which gives a pool depth in the Allegheny River channel of 8 to 9 feet as far as Garrison Ripple, above Herr Island dam and about 2 miles above the mouth of the river. The completion of the project will extend the useful part of Pittsburg Harbor 4.5 miles upstream. The sills of the lock have pool depths of 8 feet; the sill of the navigable pass of the dam has 6 feet pool depth.

The river and harbor act of 1896 provided for the construction of two additional locks and dams, which will extend slack water, having 7 feet minimum pool depth on lock sills, from Herr Island 17 miles, or to Natrona.

The locks are of concrete construction. Dams Nos. 2 and 3 are to be fixed timber dams.

The present general projects were approved September 29, 1890, and March 3, 1897.

During the year the building of Herr Island dam by contract so far progressed that its completion is expected by December, 1901. The upper sills at the lock of this dam were depressed 2 feet, and work pertaining thereto was done in order to give the same depth at upper sills as at the lower sill, or 2 feet more than over the sill of the navigable pass of the dam. The contractor for the Six-mile Island and Springdale locks and dams completed the cribs and lower guide wall, except paving of high cribs, at the Springdale lock, and set its sill cushions, valves, and lower sections of oak hollow quoins; also dredged at site of dam and its abutment and built and placed the large abutment and adjoining apron cribs.

A modification of the project as to the Springdale dam, by which it was changed from a comb dam to one with a flat top and of greater depth and weight, was approved April 27, 1901. A supplemental contract providing for the change in plan of construction was entered into with the present contractor, and was approved by the Secretary of War July 13, 1901.

The status at Six-mile Island is the same as given on page 484 of the annual report for 1900, except that effort to obtain satisfactory answer from the city of Pittsburg as to the offer made by the United States for a small strip of shore land desired for the lock and belonging to the city was continued, and that the recorder of the city, its executive, has lately advised that attention to the matter would be given at an early date.

The amount expended on the works to the close of the year ending June 30, 1900, was $488,953.81.

The commerce on the part of river under slack-water improvement for the calendar year 1900 was 1,611,103 tons of freight and 36,525 passengers. These items for the preceding year were 2,570,900 and 16,546, respectively.

RIVER AND HARBOR IMPROVEMENTS. 483

July 1, 1900, balance unexpended	$398,546.19
Amount appropriated by sundry civil act approved March 3, 1901	126,000.00
	524,546.19
June 30, 1901, amount expended during fiscal year	88,346.56
July 1, 1901, balance unexpended	436,199.63
July 1, 1901, outstanding liabilities	32,150.81
July 1, 1901, balance available	404,048.82
July 1, 1901, amount covered by uncompleted contracts	419,819.91

Amount (estimated) required for completion of existing project........ 118,000.00
Amount that can be profitably expended in fiscal year ending June 30, 1903, in addition to the balance available July 1, 1901.............. 118,000.00
Submitted in compliance with requirements of sundry civil act of June 4, 1897.

(See Appendix H H 5.)

6. *Allegheny River, Pennsylvania.*—In its original condition the Allegheny River, having a hard gravel and sand bottom, with an average slope of 2.06 feet per mile for a distance of 126.5 miles between its mouth and French Creek, at Franklin, Pa., and an average slope of 3.4 feet per mile over 132 miles between Franklin and Olean, N. Y., was obstructed by numerous large bowlders, which reduced the low-water navigable depth as much as 2 feet on various ripples, and made navigation over them extremely hazardous at ordinary stages. The river also embraced several wide-spreading shoals, giving an available navigable depth at low water of less than 6 inches. The project of improvement, adopted in 1878 and 1880, which has not since been materially changed, contemplates the removal of bowlders, snags, and other obstructions from the channel and the construction of low dams to close duplicate channels and of dikes to confine the waterway on extensive shoals. There had been expended under this project to the close of the year ending June 30, 1900, the sum of $242,417.29, about two-thirds of which was devoted to the removal of new rock obstructions washed out from the banks and those brought down by the rapid tributaries or moved along the river bed by the action of freshets and ice. The latter is a powerful agent in modifying the river bed. The result had been a marked improvement, furnishing a least depth of 1.4 feet over the shallowest bars at low water, with ample width of channel and a consequent lengthening of the period of practicable navigation, and permitting rafting and floating downstream of coal-boat bottoms to be done on stages a foot lower than formerly. The low stages are valuable for steamboating, as numerous low bridges block such navigation at even mean stage of river.

This improvement is partly lost when maintenance of the channel is omitted for a year.

During the last fiscal year Nicholson dam and Red Bank dike were considerably repaired, and small repairs, as needed, made to the Corydon log chute, Hickory and Pithole dams, and upper Cowanshannock dike; remaining improvement structures were in good condition during the year. Removal of rock and other obstructions from the channel was conducted on the part of the river, 142 miles long, from Hickory, 161 miles above Pittsburg, to New Kensington, near middle of upstream pool of authorized slack-water improvement; about 2,700 cubic yards of bowlders and 350 of gravel and 14 snags were removed from the low-water running channel, restoring it to good condition. The amount expended upon this maintenance of the channel was $3,208.31.

The head of principal navigation on the river for several years has been at Hickory, and hence improvements have been confined almost exclusively to the stream below that point. Urgent requests are now made for improvement of the river from Hickory upstream to near Warren, a distance of about 30 miles, on account of recent establishment of sawmills and a boat yard at Irvinton, near Warren, for furnishing river shipments of lumber, barges, and coal-boat bottoms.

It is intended to devote the available balance of funds to a cleaning of the low-water channel from Hickory to New Kensington, and to minor repairs for temporary maintenance of Nicholson dam and Red Bank dike. The additional appropriation recommended is for openchannel work from Warren to Hickory, maintenance of channel below Hickory, improvement at Nicholson and Red Bank, and minor repairs at the other contraction works.

The principal river traffic consists of rafting, running downstream coal-boat bottoms, and new barges, generally loaded with lumber, hay, or tan bark, and towage of flats of sand, gravel, and stone. A small packet business was conducted between Pittsburg and Kittanning during the fall and spring months. The tonnage on the part of the river above slack-water improvement in progress was, in round numbers, for calendar years:

	Tons (2,000 lbs.).
1897	437,000
1898	294,000
1899	364,000
1900	440,000

July 1, 1900, balance unexpended	$2,582.71
Amount allotted from appropriation contained in emergency river and harbor act approved June 6, 1900	5,000.00
	7,582.71
June 30, 1901, amount expended during fiscal year	5,393.15
July 1, 1901, balance unexpended	2,189.56
July 1, 1901, outstanding liabilities	26.17
July 1, 1901, balance available	2,163.39

{ Amount that can be profitably expended in fiscal year ending June 30, 1903, for works of improvement and for maintenance, in addition to the balance available July 1, 1901 .... 10,000.00
Submitted in compliance with requirements of sundry civil act of June 4, 1897, and of section 7 of the river and harbor act of 1899.

(See Appendix H H 6.)

IMPROVEMENT OF MUSKINGUM RIVER, OHIO, AND OF CERTAIN RIVERS IN WEST VIRGINIA AND KENTUCKY TRIBUTARY TO OHIO RIVER.

This district was in the charge of Maj. H. F. Hodges, Corps of Engineers, to April 30, 1901, and of Maj. E. H. Ruffner, Corps of Engineers, since that date. Division Engineer Col. Henry M. Robert, Corps of Engineers (now brigadier-general, Chief of Engineers, United States Army, retired), to May 2, 1901, and Col. Amos Stickney, Corps of Engineers since May 9, 1901.

1. *Muskingum River, Ohio.*—The original condition of the waterway was as described in the annual report for 1900, page 488.

This report is limited to work carried on under and appropriation of $102,000 by act of August 11, 1888, for the construction of a lock at Taylorsville and the reconstruction of the lock at Zanesville, Ohio, and to work carried on under an appropriation of $6,000 for the repair and extension of the levee at Zanesville, Ohio, which was included in the sundry civil act of July 1, 1898. The river and harbor act of August 18, 1894, provided for the completion of the ice-harbor lock at mouth of Muskingum River, diverting for this purpose a portion of the funds remaining to the credit of the August 11, 1888, appropriation.

Up to the close of the fiscal year ending June 30, 1900, there had been expended on this project the sum of $106,815.81. At that date the lock at Taylorsville had been completed and opened to navigation and the reconstruction of the lock at Zanesville had been indefinitely postponed, as the money available for it had been diverted by Congress to other purposes; the ice-harbor lock and its appurtenances at the mouth of the Muskingum had been practically completed, and the repair and extension of the Zanesville levee had been finished. During the fiscal year ending June 30, 1901, the ice-harbor project at Marietta, Ohio, was completed by making some minor improvements to the grounds and lock house.

The minimum sill depth is the controlling mean low-water depth of the Muskingum River system; this is 6 feet at the Taylorsville lock and 3 feet at the ice-harbor lock. (Lock No. 1 of the Muskingum River.)

For the reasons stated in the Annual Report of the Chief of Engineers for 1899, pages 424 and 2454, the recommendation is renewed that an additional appropriation be made for building five dwellings for lock tenders and for raising the crests of Dams 3 and 9.

The commercial statistics for this work can not be separated from the general commerce of the Muskingum River and are reported under the head of operating and care of locks and dams on the Muskingum River.

Deterioration has occured at Lock and Dam No. 11 above Zanesville to such an extent as to render them useless, and the local engineer estimates that $110,000 will be required to put them in good condition.

July 1, 1900, balance unexpended	$1,184.19
June 30, 1901, amount expended during fiscal year	116.70
July 1, 1901, balance unexpended	1,067.49
July 1, 1901, outstanding liabilities	2.25
July 1, 1901, balance available	1,065.24

{ Amount that can be profitably expended in fiscal year ending June 30, 1903, in addition to the balance available July 1, 1901 .... 10,300.00
Submitted in compliance with requirements of sundry civil act of June 4, 1897.

(See Appendix I I 1.)

2. *Operating and care of locks and dams on Muskingum River, Ohio.*—As originally improved by the State of Ohio, 11 dams and 12 locks were built on the 91 miles of river from its mouth in the Ohio at Marietta to Dresden, where connection was made with the Ohio Canal, which carried the slack-water navigation to Lake Erie at Cleveland. The lock and dam above Zanesville are now in a state of ruin, but the 75 miles of slack water between Zanesville and the Ohio River has been maintained. The locks and dams on this part of the river passed into the hands of the United States in 1887. All the works were in bad repair and much reconstruction was unavoidable.

The existing project is to keep the system in good navigable condition by caring for the locks and dams and maintaining the navigable depth and width of channels by dredging. A statement of the amounts and dates of all allotments for this work is given in the report of the district officer.

Up to the close of the fiscal year ending June 30, 1900, a total sum of $1,310,035.80 had been expended in general repairs and in operating and caring for the works, and an additional sum of $17,190.44 in building a protection wall at Zanesville and altering the bridges at Taylorsville and Marietta.

The expenditures during the fiscal year ending June 30, 1901, amounted to $35,147.83. With this sum the system has been operated and kept in repair, and the necessary depth and width of channels was maintained by dredging. The river was available for boats small enough to pass the locks, which have a width of 36 feet with a length of 180 feet between hollow quoins, and a depth over the sills at mean low water of 6 feet at 9 of the 11 locks, 3 feet at 1, and 5 feet at the other.

The system was in good navigable condition at the close of the fiscal year, but many parts are decayed and worn-out and must be renewed.

The total commerce for the calendar year 1900 was 78,595 tons of freight, valued, approximately, at $4,200,000, and 116,599 passengers.

(See Appendix I I 2.)

3. Little Kanawha River, West Virginia.—A description of the original condition of the river as to depth, width, and availability for purposes of commerce, and the existing project for its improvement are given in the Annual Report of the Chief of Engineers for 1900, page 489.

The amount expended up to June 30, 1900, was $213,246.26. At that date the upper part of the stream had been placed in fair condition for timber-floating purposes and for light-draft boats as far as Glennville, 102¼ miles above Parkersburg. Lock and Dam No. 5, 41 miles from the mouth of the river, were completed and opened to navigation on December 2, 1891; since then the works have been maintained under the indefinite appropriation for operating and care of canals and other works of navigation.

Nothing was done during the fiscal year ending June 30, 1901. The condition of the slack-water system and the maximum draft that could be carried June 30, 1901, over the shoalest part of the locality under improvement, remained as presented in the annual report for 1900, page 489.

It is estimated that it will require an expenditure of $1,500, in addition to the balance remaining on hand from former appropriations, to clear the upper river of obstructions which have re-formed as snags, overhanging trees, etc., and to remove rocks from shoals, so as to aid light-draft steamboat navigation and the floating of timber to market.

A statement of commerce on this river is given in the report for operating and care of lock and dam on Little Kanawha River, West Virginia.

July 1, 1900, balance unexpended	$171.74
July 1, 1901, balance unexpended	171.74
Amount that can be profitably expended in fiscal year ending June 30, 1903, for maintenance of improvement, in addition to the balance unexpended July 1, 1901. Submitted in compliance with requirements of sundry civil act of June 4, 1897, and of section 7 of the river and harbor act of 1899.	1,000.00

(See Appendix I I 3.)

4. Operating and care of lock and dam on Little Kanawha River, West Virginia.—The report upon this lock and dam, known as No. 5 of the system, printed in the annual report for 1900, page 490, presented the original project of the work and its efficiency as an aid to navigation since completion of the work.

The amount expended up to June 30, 1900, was $23,940.29 in operating the lock and making repairs to the lock, dam, and appurtenances. The amount expended during the fiscal year ending June 30, 1901, was $2,355.63. With this sum the lock has been operated and cared for, and necessary repairs have been made.

The lock has a depth of 4 feet over the lower sill and 7.56 feet over the upper sill at mean low water. When the pool below is drained down, by reason of leaks in the dam below, the depth over lower sill is less.

The commerce that has passed Lock No. 5 since it was opened to navigation, and which has consisted almost wholly of timber, is as follows:

Fiscal year—	Tons.	Fiscal year—	Tons.
1890	140,115	1897	176,169
1891	190,688	Calendar year—	
1892	244,254	1897	127,943
1893	137,072	1898	122,405
1894	106,412	1899	138,664
1895	179,240	1900	119,439
1896	105,212		

(See Appendix I I 4.)

5. Kanawha River, West Virginia.—A description of the original condition of this river, of the first and the modified projects, and of work accomplished to June 30, 1900, is given in the report of the Chief of Engineers for 1900, pages 490, 491, and 492. Up to June 30, 1900, there was expended under the first project of 1873 $50,000, and under the modified projects a total of $3,963,011.39.

The work done during the past fiscal year consisted principally in continuing the improvement of the towing channels in the pools by dredging and crane-boat work, completing 4 lock houses, making wells and cisterns for lock hands, and procuring and setting capstans on the lock walls. A contract was also let for building a new towboat, some progress made on its construction, and a new fuel flat built.

The maximum draft which can be carried at the shoalest part of the slack-water system at mean low water is 6 feet.

Commercial statistics are given in the report for operating and care of locks and dams on Kanawha River.

July 1, 1900, balance unexpended	$195,188.61
June 30, 1901, amount expended during fiscal year	12,434.66
July 1, 1901, balance unexpended	182,753.95
July 1, 1901, outstanding liabilities	748.85
July 1, 1901, balance available	182,005.10
July 1, 1901, amount covered by uncompleted contracts	14,000.00

(See Appendix I I 5.)

6.· *Operating and care of locks and dams on Kanawha River, West Virginia.*—Slack-water navigation on the Kanawha River extends from Lock No. 11, at Point Pleasant, 1¾ miles above the Ohio River, to Loup Creek Shoal, 90 miles above the Ohio River. There are 10 locks with dams, 2 of which are fixed and 8 movable, on the Chanoine system. The locations are given in the Annual Report of the Chief of Engineers for 1899, page 428. As these locks and dams have from time to time been opened to navigation, the maintenance of them has devolved upon the indefinite appropriation of July 5, 1884, for operating and care of canals and other works of navigation. At the close of the fiscal year ending June 30, 1900, the entire system was so maintained. The total disbursements up to that date had been $388,009.59, which had been used in the current work of operating and caring for the finished locks and dams, making renewals of those parts of the works which had deteriorated from use and exposure, and in dredging deposits from the lock chambers and entrances and from the channels between the locks, which had been originally formed by dredging, under the appropriations for "Improving Great Kanawha River."

During the year ending June 30, 1901, the system was operated and kept in repair. Navigation was interrupted at the fixed dams twenty-two and one-half days by high water and ice and ten days for repairs, the latter being only at Lock No. 3, for the purpose of removing an old and hanging a new lock gate. There was no notable interruption to navigation at the movable dams, though considerable trouble in operating them was experienced from escaped logs, ties, and drift. Considerable repairs, necessitated by ordinary use and decay, were made at the older works, principally on gates and guide cribs of the locks and on the movable parts—wickets, trestles, etc.—of the movable dams. The Government dredge and crane boat were used, as required, to remove sediment, snags, and wrecks from lock chambers and approaches and made channels in the pools.

The amount expended during the fiscal year ending June 30, 1901, was $44,157.03.

The commerce of the Kanawha River since 1889 has been as follows:

Fiscal year—	Tons.	Fiscal year—	Tons.
1890	1,127,232	1897	1,124,843
1891	1,225,355	Calendar year—	
1892	1,360,750	1897	832,002
1893	1,116,537	1898	1,244,334
1894	1,222,530	1899	1,124,364
1895	1,082,342	1900	1,475,930
1896	1,162,782		

The shipment of coal, which is the principal commodity, has more than quadrupled since 1880, the year the first locks and dams were completed. The coal shipment for 1900 considerably exceeded that of any former year.

(See Appendix I I 6.)

RIVER AND HARBOR IMPROVEMENTS. 489

7. *Elk River, West Virginia.*—A description of the original condition, project, etc., is given in the Annual Report of the Chief of Engineers for 1900, pages 493-494.

Up to June 30, 1900, $30,246.87 had been expended.

No work was done during the past year.

The maximum draft which can be carried at mean low water over the shoalest part of the improved river in push boats or canoes is about 2 feet.

The commercial statistics are given in detail in the report of the local officer. The total tonnage for the year was 96,940, which consisted mainly of saw logs and railroad ties, floated loose or run out in rafts.

July 1, 1900, balance unexpended	$253.13
July 1, 1901, balance unexpended	253.13
Amount (estimated) required for completion of existing project	69,000.00

(See Appendix I I 7.)

8. *Gauley River, West Virginia.*—A description of the original condition, project, etc., is given in the Annual Report of the Chief of Engineers for 1900, page 494.

Up to June 30, 1900, $14,691.30 had been expended.

No work was done during the year ending June 30, 1901.

The maximum draft at mean low water for the first 10 miles (for small push boats) is about 2 feet; above that point, aside from the pools between the shoals, there is no navigation except for floating saw logs in high stages of the river.

The only commerce of any note on the river during 1900 consisted in about 20,000 tons of saw logs floated from 11 to 28 miles to a sawmill in the upper part of the stream.

July 1, 1900, balance unexpended	$308.70
June 30, 1901, amount expended during fiscal year	25.77
July 1, 1901, balance unexpended	282.93
July 1, 1901, outstanding liabilities	4.50
July 1, 1901, balance available	278.43
Amount (estimated) required for completion of existing project	60,000.00

(See Appendix I I 8.)

9. *Guyandot River, West Virginia.*—This stream was first improved by the State of Virginia by the construction of six timber locks and dams, which soon decayed and were abandoned, being finally carried away by floods. At the time the United States began improving the river it was practically closed to navigation by snags, rocks, overhanging trees, and shoal places.

The approved project for the improvement of this river, adopted in 1878, provides for obtaining a clear channel for a distance of 122 miles upstream from its mouth, with a width of from 30 to 50 feet, and with a least depth of 18 inches during five months of the year, the same to be obtained by the removal of obstructions, such as logs, snags, stumps, rocks, and overhanging trees, and by the construction of low stone dikes at shoals, so as to concentrate and increase the depth of water at such points.

The purpose of improvement is to aid light-draft steamboat navigation in the lower portion of the stream and the floating of timber down to the Ohio and thence to market. The work is done by hire of labor.

Up to June 30, 1900, $22,499.78 had been expended, resulting in the partial improvement of the river for the distance of 119 miles upstream from its mouth, removing snags, logs, etc., cutting passageways through old dams, and constructing low dams of loose stones to deepen the water on shoals.

At that date the improvement was available for logs and light-draft steamers. The usefulness of the river was restricted by two dams, Peck's and Lambert's, respectively, about 73 and 54 miles above the mouth.

The last work done was during the fiscal year ending June 30, 1900, under the act of March 3, 1899. It consisted of clearing the channel of obstructions. A full report of this work is given in Annual Report of the Chief of Engineers for 1900, pages 3343-3346.

On June 30, 1901, the conditions as to availability for commerce remained the same as at the close of the preceding fiscal year.

The maximum draft that could be carried June 30, 1901, at mean low water, over the shoalest part of the locality under improvement, was about 20 inches.

COMMERCIAL STATISTICS.

Fiscal year—	Tons.	Fiscal year—	Tons.
1891	61,128	1897	143,300
1892	103,800	Calendar year—	
1893	182,250	1897	190,000
1894	141,221	1898	158,000
1895	247,400	1899	110,000
1896	202,000	1900	130,000

The commerce consists almost entirely of timber, cross-ties, and staves.

July 1, 1900, balance unexpended $0.22
July 1, 1901, balance unexpended .... .22

(See Appendix I I 9.)

10. *Big Sandy River, West Virginia and Kentucky.*—In its original condition this river and its forks were much obstructed by rocks, bars, snags, and leaning trees. During the low-water period of each year navigation was practically suspended.

The original project, providing for the removal of rocks, snags, and overhanging trees from the main stream and the Levisa and Tug forks, which unite at the town of Louisa, Ky., to form the main stream, was for "improving Big Sandy River, from Catlettsburg, Ky., to the head of navigation," and was adopted in 1878 (Annual Report of the Chief of Engineers for 1875, pp. 756-769). This improvement was for the purpose of aiding light-draft steamboat, push-boat, and rafting navigation on the main river and the Tug and Levisa forks.

In 1880 the appropriations for the forks were made distinct from that for the main river and three works resulted. At the same time the project of 1878 for the improvement of the Big Sandy proper was so modified as to provide for the construction of a lock and dam in that stream at Louisa, immediately below the junction of Levisa and Tug forks. A concurrent resolution of Congress of April 14, 1898, required surveys and the preparation of more complete plans and estimates for the improvement of the Big Sandy and the Tug and

Levisa forks of same in Kentucky and West Virginia, with probable cost of same. A report was submitted and is printed as House Doc. No. 456, Fifty-fifth Congress, second session, and found on page 2159 of the Annual Report of the Chief of Engineers for 1898.

The river and harbor act of March 3, 1899, adopted a portion of the extended improvement recommended, and authorized the letting of contracts for completion of two locks and dams on the Big Sandy River, between Louisa and the mouth, at a cost not to exceed $450,000.

Up to June 30, 1900, the expenditures had aggregated $421,902.85, with results as follows:

Under the project for the removal of obstructions the channel had been cleared and maintained from 1878 to 1880.

Under the modified projects of 1880 and 1891 a lock and movable needle dam had been finished and opened to navigation. As this dam is the only one yet built on the river, it has little influence on the general commerce.

The survey provided for in the act of March 3, 1899, had also been completed, except the boring at probable lock sites.

During the fiscal year ending June 30, 1901, obstructions to navigation were removed over the entire length of the river. The amount expended was $1,000, the same being paid from an allotment made July 7, 1900, from the appropriation provided by the emergency river and harbor act approved June 6, 1900. This work left the river in as good navigable condition as it is possible to attain by works of this character. Its maintenance, however, must continue from year to year.

The purchase of sites for Locks 1 and 2 was completed, plans for the locks made and approved, and contracts entered into for the construction of both locks and the construction of a lock house, fences, roadways, etc., at Lock 2. The latter contract has been about completed, and the preparation and delivery of materials for the locks is going on. At No. 1 high water has interfered with the procuring of material to some extent, and no active operations on construction have yet been undertaken. Plans of the dams are now being prepared, and funds for their construction are on hand.

Final report upon the survey was made November 26, 1900, and is printed as House Doc. No. 235, Fifty-sixth Congress, second session, and as Appendix I I 16 of this report, the borings at probable lock sites having been completed.

The maxium draft which can be carried at mean low water over the shoalest part of the river is 20 inches.

The commerce consists of timber and farm products. The amount can not well increase until slack water has been extended by additional dams above and below the single dam now in place. The country bordering Levisa and Tug forks abounds in bituminous, cannel, and coking coal of good quality, but it remains undeveloped for lack of transportation facilities.

The limit of authority given by the act of March 3, 1899, for expenditure in the construction of two locks and dams below Louisa was $450,000. The project of Major Bixby, upon which the legislation authorizing these dams was based, estimated the cost of the lower dams at $250,000 each. It will appear, therefore, that the limit now set by law for these works is less by $50,000 than the estimated cost of the work. An additional appropriation of $50,000 is required in order to be able to give to them certain features which are eminently desirable for their satisfactory operation.

A continuation of the improvement of the main river and its two forks should embrace work as follows, in addition to that already authorized:

Regulating works below Dam No. 1; altering Lock and Dam No. 3, at Louisa; continuing work on Dams 1 and 2, below Louisa, in addition to expenditures already authorized; continuing improvements on forks above Louisa.

COMMERCIAL STATISTICS.

Fiscal year—	Tons.	Fiscal year—	Tons.
1890	268,582	1897	414,500
1891	277,303	Calendar year—	
1892	455,926	1897	406,900
1893	466,723	1898	415,400
1894	297,800	1899	328,272
1895	545,910	1900	300,000
1896	471,382		

The above is the commerce of the three streams: Big Sandy proper, from Louisa, Ky., to its mouth in the Ohio at Catlettsburg, Ky., a distance of 26 miles, and of Levisa and Tug forks, which unite at Louisa to form the main river.

July 1, 1900, balance unexpended	$289,097.15
Amount appropriated by sundry civil act approved March 3, 1901	140,000.00
	429,097.15
June 30, 1901, amount expended during fiscal year	24,983.62
July 1, 1901, balance unexpended	404,113.53
July 1, 1901, outstanding liabilities	1,496.87
July 1, 1901, balance available	402,616.66
July 1, 1901, amount covered by uncompleted contracts	243,736.72
Amount that can be profitably expended in fiscal year ending June 30, 1903, for works of improvement and for maintenance, in addition to the balance available July 1, 1901	51,000.00

Submitted in compliance with requirements of sundry civil act of June 4, 1897, and of section 7 of the river and harbor act of 1899.

(See Appendix I I 10.)

11. Operating and care of lock and dam on Big Sandy River, West Virginia and Kentucky.—This lock and dam, located near Louisa, Ky., was finished during the fiscal year of 1897 under appropriations for improving Big Sandy River, West Virginia and Kentucky.

The lock has a depth of 1 foot 9 inches over the lower sill at mean low water and of 11 feet 9 inches over the upper sill at pool level. When the other dams of the series have been built the minimum depth at pool stage will be 6 feet. The lock is 52 feet wide and 190 feet long between hollow quoins. The navigable pass is 130 feet wide.

The project involves operating and caring for the lock and dam with such funds as may annually be allotted.

The amount expended for this purpose to June 30, 1900, was $8,784.28, the work having continued since July 1, 1897.

On June 30, 1900, the work was in good condition and available for commerce.

The expenditures during the fiscal year ending June 30, 1901, were

$3,477.21, and have resulted in keeping the work in excellent navigable condition, the buildings, walks, and grounds in repair, and in the satisfactory operation of the lock and dam.

Commercial statistics for this work are given in the report for improving Big Sandy River.

(See Appendix I I 11.)

12. Tug Fork of Big Sandy River, West Virginia and Kentucky.—In its original condition this stream was much obstructed by rocks, snags, logs, and overhanging trees.

The original project, adopted in 1880, for improving Big Sandy River and its forks (Annual Report of the Chief of Engineers for 1875, pp. 756–769), provides for removing the natural obstructions in the stream and the construction of low wing dams of loose stones at shoal places, so as to aid the floating of timber and light-draft steamboat navigation.

Until 1880 there was no separation in the appropriations for the Big Sandy River and its forks. Since that year the appropriations have been made separately for the main river and Tug and Levisa forks.

Reckoning from the time of separation of the appropriations to June 30, 1900, the total amount spent on Tug Fork amounts to $29,222.85. This expenditure has resulted in the material improvement of navigation, giving increased facilities for push boats at low water and rafting and light-draft steamboats at moderate stages, for the distance of 100 miles upstream from Louisa, Ky.

During the past fiscal year no work was done. The last work done was during the fiscal year ending June 30, 1900. It consisted of removing channel obstructions.

The maximum draft that could be carried June 30, 1901, at mean low water over the shoalest part of the improvement was about 20 inches.

The commerce for the last four years has been:

Calendar year—	Tons.
1897	135,000
1898	130,400
1899	128,200
1900	120,000

No material increase can be hoped for until the slack-water system has been carried up the fork for some distance above Louisa.

July 1, 1900, balance unexpended	$27.15
July 1, 1901, balance unexpended	27.15

Amount that can be profitably expended in fiscal year ending June 30, 1903, for maintenance of improvement, in addition to the balance unexpended July 1, 1901 .... 1,000.00

Submitted in compliance with requirements of sundry civil act of June 4, 1897, and of section 7 of the river and harbor act of 1899.

(See Appendix I I 12.)

13. Levisa Fork of Big Sandy River, Kentucky.—In its original condition this stream was much obstructed by rocks, snags, logs, and overhanging trees.

The original project, adopted in 1880, for improving Big Sandy River and its forks (Annual Report of the Chief of Engineers for 1875, pp. 756–769) provides for removing the natural obstructions in the stream and the construction of low wing dams of loose stones at shoal places, so as to aid the floating of timber and light-draft steamboat navigation.

Until 1880 there was no separation in the appropriations for the Big Sandy River and its forks. Since that year the appropriations have been made separately for the main river and Tug and Levisa forks.

Reckoning from the time of separation of the appropriations to June 30, 1900, the total amount spent on Levisa Fork amounts to $27,679.59. This expenditure has resulted in the material improvement of navigation, giving increased facilities for push boats at low water, and rafting and light-draft steamboats at moderate stages.

During the fiscal year ending June 30, 1901, obstructions to navigation were removed over the entire length of the river from Louisa to Pikeville. The amount expended was $1,000, the same being paid from an allotment made July 7, 1900, from the appropriation provided by the emergency river and harbor act approved June 6, 1900.

The maximum draft that could be carried June 30, 1901, at mean low water, over the shoalest part of the improvement, was about 20 inches.

The commerce for the last four years has been:

Calendar year—	Tons.
1897	220,800
1898	211,300
1899	158,250
1900	150,000

No material increase can be hoped for until the slack-water system has been carried up the fork some distance above Louisa.

July 1, 1900, balance unexpended	$1,070.41
June 30, 1901, amount expended during fiscal year	1,001.07
July 1, 1901, balance unexpended	69.34

Amount that can be profitably expended in fiscal year ending June 30, 1903, for maintenance of improvement, in addition to the balance unexpended July 1, 1901 .... 1,000.00
Submitted in compliance with requirements of sundry civil act of June 4, 1897, and of section 7 of the river and harbor act of 1899.

(See Appendix I I 13.)

14. Kentucky River, Kentucky.—At the time the project was adopted, in 1879, five locks and dams built by the State of Kentucky many years ago were in a dilapidated condition and had been practically abandoned and allowed to go to ruin. The channel was also much obstructed by snags and leaning trees. Portions of Dams Nos. 1 and 2, on the lower part of the stream, were gone entirely, so that navigation was suspended.

The original and present project was adopted in 1879 (Annual Report of the Chief of Engineers for 1879, pp. 1398-1422), and provided for repairing and rebuilding the five old locks and dams, removing snags, logs, and other obstructions, and extending 6-foot slack-water navigation up the stream to Three Forks, a distance of about 261 miles from the mouth of the river in the Ohio, at Carrollton, Ky.

The amount expended to June 30, 1900, was $1,995,902.37. The result of this expenditure was the repairing and rebuilding of five old locks and dams constructed by the State of Kentucky, the construction and completion of Locks and Dams Nos. 6, 7, and 8, and the construction of a dam at Beattyville.

Ordinary low-water depth through Lock No. 1 and to the Ohio

River, 4 miles below, is 6 feet or more, but at extreme low water only about 2¼ feet can be carried over the lower sill of Lock No. 1.

The old Locks Nos. 1 to 5, inclusive, built by the State, have 145 feet available length and 38 feet width, and can pass coal barges only singly. Locks No. 6, 7, and 8, built by the United States, have 148 feet available length and 52 feet width, and can pass two coal barges at each lockage.

The expenditure during the year ending June 30, 1901, has resulted in finishing the masonry, cribs, and dam at Lock No. 8, clearing the pool of No. 8 of overhanging trees, selecting the site of Nos. 9 and 10, and preparing the papers for purchase and condemnation, and in surveys for Locks Nos. 10, 11, and 12.

The availability for commerce remains the same as at the close of the preceding fiscal year. The maximum draft at mean low water which can be carried over the shoalest part of the slack-water system to Valley View, 158 miles from the mouth, is 5.5 feet. Above the slack-water system no boats can run at low stage.

The cost of the complete improvement will exceed by a large sum the limit of authority for continuing contracts granted by existing legislation, as stated in the Annual Report of the Chief of Engineers for 1899, page 2514. This limit of $1,349,000 will probably be reached while the last three locks and dams are still untouched or incomplete. With the existing balance it is proposed to purchase sites for Locks Nos. 10, 11, and 12; make plans for Nos. 10 and 11; build lock-keepers' houses at Nos. 9 and 10, and commence construction of Nos. 9 and 10. With the amount asked for the fiscal year ending June 30, 1903, it is proposed to clear Pool No. 9 of all obstructions; complete Locks and Dams Nos. 9 and 10; build lock houses and commence construction at Nos. 11 and 12.

Commercial statistics will be found in report for operating and care of Kentucky River.

July 1, 1900, balance unexpended	$391,591.83
Amount appropriated by sundry civil act approved March 3, 1901	150,000.00
	541,591.83
June 30, 1901, amount expended during fiscal year	82,226.81
July 1, 1901, balance unexpended	459,365.02
July 1, 1901, outstanding liabilities	1,303.46
July 1, 1901, balance available	458,061.56
July 1, 1901, amount covered by uncompleted contracts	208,126.25
Amount (estimated) required for completion of existing project	2,335,000.00
Amount that can be profitably expended in fiscal year ending June 30, 1903, in addition to the balance available July 1, 1901. Submitted in compliance with requirements of sundry civil act of June 4, 1897.	200,000.00

See Appendix I l 14.)

15. *Operating and care of locks and dams on Kentucky River, Kentucky.*—The maintenance of these locks devolves upon the indefinite appropriation of July 5, 1884, for operating and care of canals and other works of navigation; the total expended up to June 30, 1900, was $809,973.06.

The amount expended during the fiscal year ending June 30, 1901, was $71,419.10. With this sum the locks were operated and the channels maintained in navigable condition.

On June 30, 1901, the system was in good navigable condition, but many parts are nearly worn-out and must soon be renewed.

The commerce, in tons of freight, at the different locks for the last three years, has been as follows:

Lock.	Calendar year—			Lock.	Calendar year—		
	1898.	1899.	1900.		1898.	1899.	1900.
No. 1	74,175	96,651	113,823	No. 6	46,878	73,300	113,192
No. 2	67,080	83,809	95,353	No. 7	47,642	94,379	127,405
No. 3	55,469	72,370	90,866	No. 8			8,348
No. 4	52,727	72,983	84,005				
No. 5	56,351	83,366	119,711	Average	57,189	82,480	106,336

NOTE.—No. 8, opened October 15, 1900, not included in average.

(See Appendix I I 15.)

SURVEY MADE IN COMPLIANCE WITH RIVER AND HARBOR ACT APPROVED MARCH 3, 1899.

Final report on survey of *Big Sandy River, Kentucky and West Virginia, including Levisa and Tug forks*, was submitted through the division engineer by Captain Hodges November 26, 1900. He presents a plan for continuation of the improvement of the Big Sandy and its forks and states that an appropriation of $150,000, with authority to continue the improvement by the expenditure of $2,080,000 additional, to be provided by future appropriations, will carry the system far enough to open extensive coal fields, and will finish about half of the projected work. The report was transmitted to Congress and printed in House Doc. No. 235, Fifty-sixth Congress, second session. (See also Appendix I I 16.)

IMPROVEMENT OF FALLS OF OHIO RIVER, OF WHITE RIVER, INDIANA, AND WABASH RIVER, INDIANA AND ILLINOIS, AND OF CERTAIN RIVERS IN KENTUCKY.

This district was in the charge of Capt. George A. Zinn, Corps of Engineers, to July 6, 1900, and of Capt. W. L. Sibert, Corps of Engineers, since that date. Division Engineer, Col. Henry M. Robert, Corps of Engineers (now brigadier-general, Chief of Engineers, United States Army, retired), to May 2, 1901, and Col. Amos Stickney, Corps of Engineers, since May 9, 1901.

1. *Falls of the Ohio River at Louisville, Ky.*—Previous to June 4, 1897, the work of improving the falls of the Ohio River was carried on under two heads, each provided for under separate appropriations or allotments, one for the work of enlarging the upper end of the Louisville and Portland Canal and the other for excavation and structures in the main channel over the falls, known as the Indiana Chute. By the sundry civil act of June 4, 1897, the two divisions of the project were combined.

Before the adoption of the original project in 1883 the approach to the canal and its upper end above the railroad bridge was so narrow as to be a source of constant delay to the large coal fleets which came down the river on ordinary rises. The canal proper, from Ninth to Fourteenth streets, was only 100 feet wide and curved between the two points, making progress slow and liability to accident frequent and unavoidable. The greater part of the dike making the north line of the approach was submerged when the river reached a stage of 8.4 feet, upper canal gauge, and at 9 feet and above a strong cross current was created by which many vessels were pulled against the structure, and at high water carried over it to the rock ledges. This approach was 1,800 feet long, 400 feet wide at its upper end, and 100 feet wide at the mouth of the canal, opposite Ninth street. This area did not provide sufficient room for making up or breaking tows preparatory to leaving or entering the canal, and caused much delay to traffic, and often resulted in considerable additional expense by reason of the fact that tows arriving on a falling stage, and at one too low to continue via the Indiana Chute, were unable to get the boats through the locks in time to continue the journey before the water reached a stage too low to float the loaded craft, thus compelling them to lie over and wait for another rise to occur, which involved harboring the boats and consequent expenses.

The projects under which work has been and is now carried on are as follows: The original, adopted in 1883 and slightly modified in 1885, which provided for the enlargement of the canal from its mouth to a point below the railroad bridge and a large harbor or basin above the mouth; that approved January 31, 1890, after having been considered and submitted by a Board of Engineer officers convened for that purpose, which included work and structures at the head of the canal and in the Indiana Chute, to provide a navigable channel through the latter when the stage of the river is at or above 8 feet upper canal gauge. A revision of the latter project, submitted by a Board of Engineer officers and approved April 8, 1899, modified the area to be excavated and determined definitely the character of the structures to be erected in the enlargement at the head of the canal. That portion of the project pertaining particularly to the enlargement of the easterly end of the canal provides for enlarging the canal on its northerly side from a point 725 feet below the railroad bridge near Fourteenth street, where the canal is abruptly increased from 90 to 210 feet in width. This latter width is gradually increased through a distance of nearly 2,800 feet to 325 feet at the head of the canal proper, at which point the enlargement is expanded into a capacious basin 1,200 feet wide, and practically parallel to the Kentucky shore. Along the western line of this basin a movable dam is provided, which will hold the river at stages of 8 feet and less and serve as a sluice for carrying away mud and deposit at stages greater than 8 feet. The dam on the north line of the basin, connecting one end of the movable dam with the present cross dam at the south abutment of the middle chute, is built of concrete, with its crest at 8 feet upper canal gauge, which provides a basin with ample accommodations for the movement of vessels and tows approaching the canal.

At the end of the fiscal year 1900 the work outlined in the projects had been completed with exception of the rock excavation east of the former cross dam, earth and rock excavation, and a new wall and stone revetment on the south side of the canal west of Tenth street to a point about 412 feet east of the Fourteenth Street Bridge. During the fiscal year work was directed toward the removal of disrupted rock within the limits of the enlargement, using for that purpose the dredges, derrick boats, and towboats pertaining to the canal when they could be spared from canal work.

The main channel of the river, by which commerce passes the falls when the stage of the river is such as to permit navigation over them, is known as Indiana Chute. Originally it was very crooked, with swift currents and whirls, filled with dangerous rocky points projecting from the sides and bottom, and navigable by skilled pilots only when the river was up to or above 11 feet on the upper gauge of the Louisville and Portland Canal. About half the distance down was an abrupt turn flanked by two projecting points of rock, the one on the south, a part of Goose Island, known as Wave Rock; the other, on the north and slightly west, a part of the Indiana shore called Willow Point. The channel around and between these points was tortuous, the current swift, and navigation dangerous except at very high stages of water.

Prior to January 31, 1890, there was no specific project for the improvement of the Indiana Chute. The work was carried on with allotments from appropriations for improving Ohio River, and under projects having in view the removal of projecting rocks and straightening the channel between the cross dam and railroad bridge, but no definite limits were prescribed within which work was to be done.

The work previous to the adoption of the definite project resulted in increasing the safe width of the channel between the cross dam and railroad bridge from 60 to 250 feet, and the removal of a large mass of reefs just below the bridge known as Rubels Rocks. The project of January 31, 1890, is not materially changed by the revision approved April 8, 1899. The general object is to make the chute safely navigable for descending traffic when the stage of the river is at or above 8 feet, upper canal gauge, by providing a good channel 400 feet wide between the cross dam and railroad bridge. The top of Wave Rock is to be excavated to ref. 22 and of Willow Point to ref. 19. Below Willow Point a stone dike 1,250 feet long, and below Wave Rock a similar structure 2,300 feet long, curving downstream, will fix the navigable channel at a width of about 700 feet. These dikes are also intended to reduce the area of discharge of the chute so as to maintain the 8-foot depth over Wave Rock and Willow Point as long as that depth exists in the channel at the head.

Operations on this part of the project were directed toward the completion of excavation to grade at Willow Point, Wave Rock, and the channel above the railroad bridge, together with the repair of the Willow Point dike and the continuation of construction of the Wave Rock dike. Of these, the repairs to Willow Point dike, excavation to specified grade in channel above the bridge at Willow Point and Wave Rock were completed, and the Wave Rock dike partly completed. To complete the latter dike it is estimated will require about 4,300 cubic yards stone filling and 7,100 square yards paving.

The amount expended on the combined project up to the close of the fiscal year ending June 30, 1900, was $1,387,432.75. Statistics showing the quantity and character of commerce passing through the canal and over the falls may be seen by reference to the report of operating and care of Louisville and Portland Canal.

During the progress of work near the close of the past season's operations it became evident that the original estimates would be insufficient for the completion of the work included in the approved project. An estimate of the quantities of work remaining to be done on November 1, 1900, and cost thereof was submitted to the Chief of Engineers November 13, 1900, and authority granted to submit the increased cost in this report. This increased cost is attributable largely to the shortness and uncertainty of the working seasons on the falls of the Ohio, a rise of 2 feet being sufficient to stop work at Wave Rock, Willow Point, and the excavation above the bridge. The nature of the rock also necessitated the removal of much more than was anticipated in the estimate, so as to be absolutely certain that no solid rock was left projecting above grade.

July 1, 1900, balance unexpended	$139,817.25
June 30, 1901, amount expended during fiscal year	105,201.88
July 1, 1901, balance unexpended	34,615.37
July 1, 1901, outstanding liabilities	873.93
July 1, 1901, balance available	33,741.44
Amount (estimated) required for completion of existing project	132,389.79
Amount that can be profitably expended in fiscal year ending June 30, 1903, in addition to the balance available July 1, 1901. Submitted in compliance with requirements of sundry civil act of June 4, 1897.	80,000.00

(See Appendix J J 1.)

2. Operating and care of Louisville and Portland Canal.—The present work is the outgrowth of the construction of the canal by a private corporation in 1830, and its transfer to the United States in 1874 by the authority of Congress. The canal is about 2 miles long and 90 feet wide below the enlargement at the head. There are 2 new masonry locks in flight, the chambers of each being 350 feet long and 80 feet wide.

The annual estimates and projects have provided for operation and maintenance in good navigable condition, together with such special work as may from time to time be found necessary to make it sufficient to meet the demands of navigation and commerce.

Expenditures from July 1, 1880, when tolls were abolished and the canal became a direct charge on the Treasury, to June 30, 1900, amounted to $1,493,690.13, not including outstanding liabilities.

The canal is available to commerce at all stages of water less than 12.7 feet, upper gauge, and serves its purpose by permitting free navigation around the falls of the Ohio River at stages of water when the passage can not be made by the open-river channel.

During the fiscal year ending June 30, 1901, expenditures amounted to $75,330.09.

During the fiscal year ending June 30, 1901, 5,581 boats, barges, and small craft passed through the canal; the tonnage of these amounted to 1,275,536, and they carried 1,216,906 tons of freight and 13,090 passengers. The annual average for the past twenty years of traffic and commerce passing this place via canal and open river is as follows: Boats, 6,781+; tonnage, 1,854,053+; freight average for fifteen years, 1,994,788 tons.

(See Appendix J J 2.)

3. Wabash River, Indiana and Illinois.—In its original condition this river was badly obstructed with shoal bars, accumulations of snags, rocky reefs, and numerous secondary channels or cut-offs, which lessened the flow of water through the main channel, and navigation was impossible except at high stages of water.

From the commencement of the work in 1872 to March 31, 1881, the expenditures, all of which were for work below Vincennes, amounted to $324,845.44. Since March, 1881, expenditures for each section of the river are given below separately.

Below Vincennes.—From March, 1881, to June 30, 1900, expenditures for work below Vincennes amounted to $369,808.42, including $25,000 expended for levee work at Grayville, Ill.

Since 1884 the greater part of the appropriations for the section below Vincennes has been applied to the construction of a masonry lock and timber dam, with masonry abutment and timber guide cribs, at Grand Rapids. The lock, dam, abutments, and guide cribs have been completed.

Since the operations and funds have been concentrated to complete the structures just mentioned, and work necessarily suspended elsewhere on the river, the improvements at other places have rotted away or been damaged by ice and freshets. High water has cut its way around them, leaving the river as badly obstructed as it was before its improvement was commenced, and with no improvement to its navigation and commerce other than the channels cut through solid rock, and the lock and dam at Grand Rapids, which latter will be of little benefit unless the river is improved in such manner as to enable boats to reach that point.

Therefore, considered as an entirety, this section of the river at a normal stage is not available for navigation. The obstructions now existing present no unusual features to indicate that they would be difficult to overcome, and with sufficient funds for regular and continuous operations the river could be easily adapted to the requirements of commerce. The improvements, however, should begin at the mouth of the river and be carried continuously upstream. No work was done on this section of the river during the past year.

The only commercial statistics available are those collected at the lock at Grand Rapids and given in the report upon operating and care of that work.

There is in existence no approved project with estimate which adequately provides for the systematic improvement of the Wabash River, and as a prerequisite to the preparation of such a project a detailed survey is necessary. Such survey for that part of the river below the lock at Grand Rapids would cost, approximately, $20,000. The funds now reported as available were appropriated by the river and harbor act of March 3, 1899, with a view of closing the cut-off at New Harmony, to do which it was estimated would require $50,000. However, this is not the only place where improvement work is needed to make the river navigable, and it would appear to be the better plan to defer any work at New Harmony Cut-off until a survey has been made and definite determination arrived at as to the character and extent of improvements necessary. In this connection it is deemed admissible to suggest that, if the funds now available be made applicable to a survey of the river below the lock, only $5,000 in addition thereto will be needed for such purpose.

July 1, 1900, balance unexpended	$15,346.14
July 1, 1901, balance unexpended	15,346.14
July 1, 1901, outstanding liabilities	25.75
July 1, 1901, balance available	15,320.39
Amount (estimated) required for completion of existing project	45,000.00
Amount that can be profitably expended in fiscal year ending June 30, 1903, in addition to the balance available July 1, 1901	5,000.00

Submitted in compliance with requirements of sundry civil act of June 4, 1897.

Above Vincennes.—Since this part of the river became the object of specific appropriations, the sum of $93,075.67 had been expended to June 30, 1900. Formerly a good channel 3 feet in depth was maintained, but for several years past the appropriations have been too small to permit of other than snagging operations at irregular intervals. The channel at present is available for navigation only at high stages of water. At low water the numerous snags, bars, and secondary channels render navigation, even with boats of lightest draft, extremely uncertain. No regular line of steamboats operates upon this section of the river. The only traffic is carried on during high stages of water, when a few light-draft boats make irregular trips to transport corn, wheat, oats, and similar commodities to the nearest railway for shipment. The only operations in progress on this section of the river during the fiscal year consisted in the removal of snags, and embraced that portion between Vincennes and 1 mile above Hutsonville, about 48 miles. Overhanging trees, snags, and similar obstructions, numbering 375 in all, were removed during the period of operations from July 17 to September 22, 1900.

Funds under the former estimate are so nearly exhausted that further field work is not proposed for the ensuing fiscal year. Recommendations as to additional appropriations can not be made until a new project, as suggested in the report upon improvement Below Vincennes, has been decided upon.

The only commercial statistics available are given in the report for operating and care of lock and dam at Grand Rapids.

July 1, 1900, balance unexpended	$2,424.33
June 30, 1901, amount expended during fiscal year	1,857.98
July 1, 1901, balance unexpended	566.35

(See Appendix J J 3.)

4. Operating and care of lock and dam at Grand Rapids, Wabash River.—This lock and dam was built from funds derived from appropriations for improving Wabash River, Indiana and Illinois. The operating expenses were also paid from that appropriation until March 1, 1897, since which date they have been paid from allotments from the indefinite appropriation for operating and care of canals and other works of navigation, act of July 5, 1884. The annual projects and estimates provide for the lock's operation and such repairs thereto and the appurtenant structures as may be necessary to maintain them in good condition. From March 1, 1897, to June 30, 1900, the expenditures amounted to $8,076.21.

The expenditures during the fiscal year ending June 30, 1901, amounted to $10,721.40, which were for lock tender's salary, repairs, material for new gates, cleaning out mud from lock chambers and upper entrance, a small protection crib on the abutment side of the river, and work in connection with placing the new gates.

A synopsis of traffic through the lock during fiscal year 1901 is as follows: Boats, etc., 267; tonnage, 8,976; freight, 1,128¼ tons. Average for five fiscal years: Boats, 279; tonnage, 7,561; freight, 3,044 tons.

(See Appendix J J 4.)

5. White River, Indiana.—Originally this river was, throughout the entire reach embraced within the project, badly obstructed by rock reefs, shoals, remains of old structures, and a very great number of snags. It could be navigated only during high stages of water.

The original project is based upon the report of examination of the White River and its forks in Indiana, submitted December 31, 1878, and the first provision for improvement was made in the river and harbor act of March 3, 1879. The object was to provide a channel as far as might be practicable without constructing locks and dams, at an estimated cost of $150,000. The project has not been amended or revised. Funds under the former estimate are practically exhausted. The river and harbor act of August 18, 1894, provided for a resurvey of the river and certain portions of the forks. Full report of this survey and estimate of cost under alternative plans for improvement will be found on pages 2483 to 2496, report of the Chief of Engineers for fiscal year 1896. The small balance of funds was not sufficient to permit any operations during the past year, and for the same reasons no field operations are proposed for the ensuing year. The total expenditures to June 30, 1900, were $119,296.18. The lower 13 miles of the river are navigable for boats drawing 3 feet; above this to the junction of the two forks and about 5 miles up East Fork boats drawing 18 inches can navigate about one month in the year.

July 1, 1900, balance unexpended $703.82
July 1, 1901, balance unexpended 703.82

(See Appendix J J 5.)

6. *Lock No. 2, Green River, at Rumsey, Ky.*—This lock was originally built by the State of Kentucky and was acquired by the United States, with other locks and dams on Green and Barren rivers, Kentucky, December 11, 1888. The lock was then in a dilapidated and dangerous condition. The deficiency act, approved March 3, 1893, appropriated $65,000 for rebuilding this lock which, in 1892, was reported as no longer safe for navigation. The project for the work, approved in 1893, provided for the construction of a new lock on the river side of the old lock, with certain changes of existing conditions, to make them conform to the new location. The amount expended to June 30, 1900, was $167,739.06.

During the past fiscal year the work remaining to be done at the close of the preceding fiscal year was completed. This work consisted in drilling and blasting the limestone ledge at the lower entrance to the lock, so as to strengthen the approach and facilitate the passage of traffic through the lock; the walk ways were also completed. The work being completed and funds exhausted, this will be the final report under this appropriation.

July 1, 1900, balance unexpended $2,260.94
June 30, 1901, amount expended during fiscal year 2,260.94

(See Appendix J J 6.)

7. *Green River above the mouth of Big Barren River, Kentucky.*—Originally this part of Green River was much obstructed by snags, bowlders, and overhanging trees. Dam No. 4, Green River, afforded slack water for about 18 miles.

The original project is that submitted under date of August 11, 1891 (printed in Annual Report of the Chief of Engineers for 1891, p. 2481), and provided for slack-water navigation from the upper limits of Pool No. 4, to Mammoth Cave, by the construction of two locks and dams, at an estimated cost of $361,346.40 for both. One of the locks and dams has been completed and opened to navigation, thus leaving one more lock and dam to be constructed to complete the project. The amount expended on the work up to the close of the fiscal year ending June 30, 1900, was $174,371.27. The result, as stated above, is the completion of Lock and Dam No. 5, and the extension of slack-water navigation through a part of the rich mineral district bordering on the river, and which heretofore had no conveniently accessible means of transportation. The marked increase in traffic through Pool No. 4 and the new lock during the short period it has been in operation is the most substantial evidence of the benefit that has resulted from the improvement, as well as the great advantage that would result from the completion, of the second lock proposed in the project, and the extension of slack-water navigation to Mammoth Cave.

The only operations in progress during the year consisted of the completion of crib work and bank protection, and construction of a cottage for the lock hand at Lock No. 5. The small balance available will not permit much work beyond the completion of the cottage and clearing up the lock grounds. Work on proposed Lock No. 6 can be commenced promptly after money therefor has been appropriated.

Traffic and commercial statistics are given in the report for operating and care of locks and dams on Green and Barren rivers.

July 1, 1900, balance unexpended	$6,301.93
June 30, 1901, amount expended during fiscal year	1,908.71
July 1, 1901, balance unexpended	4,393.22
July 1, 1901, outstanding liabilities	662.75
July 1, 1901, balance available	3,730.47
Amount (estimated) required for completion of existing project	180,673.20
Amount that can be profitably expended in fiscal year ending June 30, 1903, in addition to the balance available July 1, 1901	135,000.00
Submitted in compliance with requirements of sundry civil act of June 4, 1897.	

(See Appendix J J 7.)

8. *Operating and care of locks and dams on Green and Barren rivers, Kentucky.*—The United States acquired possession of the five locks and dams on Green and Barren rivers on December 11, 1888, by purchase of the unexpired lease of the Green and Barren River Navigation Company, the legislature of the State of Kentucky having ceded them, with land and appurtenances pertaining thereto, to the United States, upon condition that the latter should extinguish the claim of the navigation company to take tolls and to exercise control over the rivers.

At the time of the transfer the river wall of Lock No. 3, Green River, had fallen into the river; the lower end of the land wall of Lock No. 1, Barren River, was badly cracked and liable to fall at any time, and both walls of Lock No. 2, Green River, were in a dangerous condition. The channel of the river was much obstructed by snags and slides.

Since the United States acquired control of the locks and dams navigation throughout the entire system has been restored by either extensive repairs or new work. The expenditures for repairs, operations, and maintenance to June 30, 1900, aggregated $840,032.78. During the fiscal year ending June 30, 1901, the expenditures amounted to $61,816.40, which were for the operation and maintenance of the several locks and dams and for necessary repairs to houses and property.

Following is a synopsis of traffic through the locks:

During fiscal year ending June 30, 1901.

	Boats.		Freight.
	Number.	Tonnage.	
Green River:			*Tons.*
Lock No. 1	3,856	558,680	452,522
Lock No. 2	3,102	483,112	285,744
Lock No. 3	2,410	414,417	183,512
Lock No. 4	2,580	370,845	117,054
Lock No. 5	1,005	124,916	57,058
Barren River:			
Lock No. 1	1,612	195,047	46,445
Coal shipments from mine below Lock No. 1, Green River			43,421

Average for four past fiscal years.

Green River:			
Lock No. 1	3,014	350,126	320,449
Lock No. 2	2,639	322,014	225,687
Lock No. 3	1,957	265,260	137,192
Lock No. 4	2,340	270,623	96,251
Lock No. 5	810	88,305	26,039
Barren River:			
Lock No. 1	1,475	613,669	37,744

(See Appendix J J 8.)

9. *Rough River, Kentucky.*—Originally this river was very much obstructed by snags, sunken logs, and bowlders in the bed, and by overhanging trees on the banks. Backwater from Rumsey Dam No. 2, on Green River, affected the lower 8 miles of the river, but above that distance the stream was very shallow at low water.

The project for the improvement, adopted in 1890, provided for the clearing of the river of obstructions and for the location and construction of a lock and dam, so as to carry slack water to Hartford, Ky., for boats not exceeding 123 feet in length, 27 feet in width, and 4 feet draft.

Expenditures to June 30, 1900, amounted to $99,417.03.

Operations during the year consisted of the removal of two slides below Hartford, removing overhanging trees, snags, stumps, etc., in building a protection crib 45 feet long, 10 feet wide, and 6 feet high below the abutment of the dam at the lock, and grading and riprapping the banks below the abutment and lock. The funds now available are sufficient to keep the improved portion of the river clear of snags during the next fiscal year.

Commercial statistics for the river are given under report for operating and care of lock and dam on Rough River, Kentucky.

July 1, 1900, balance unexpended	$6,082.97
June 30, 1901, amount expended during fiscal year	2,887.78
July 1, 1901, balance unexpended	3,195.19
July 1, 1901, outstanding liabilities	17.27
July 1, 1901, balance available	3,177.92

(See Appendix J J 9.)

10. *Operating and care of lock and dam on Rough River, Kentucky.*—This lock and dam was built from funds provided in appropriations for improving Rough River, Kentucky, and was opened to navigation December 12, 1896. The expenses of their operation and

care since July 1, 1897, have been paid from allotments from the indefinite appropriation for operating and care of canals and other works of navigation, act of July 5, 1884. The total of these expenditures to June 30, 1900, was $2,282.88.

The project and estimate for the past fiscal year provided for nothing further than the operation and care of the lock and such minor current repairs as are usually incident to such structures.

The lock and dam affords slack-water navigation to Hartford, Ky.

Traffic through the lock during the past fiscal year included 657 boats of various kinds, with an aggregate tonnage of 24,407, carrying 20,666 tons of freight.

Annual averages for the past four years are as follows: Boats, 610; tonnage, 14,273.79; freight, 24,849 tons.

(See Appendix J J 10.)

11. Removing sunken vessels or craft obstructing or endangering navigation.—The steamer *Defender*, while bringing a tow of coal to the locks of the Louisville and Portland Canal January 20, 1901, sunk a coal barge at station 25. Dredges *Louisville No. 1* and *Wabash* removed the wreck at a cost of $99.39. This amount was subsequently refunded to the United States by the owners of the coal.

(See Appendix J J 11.)

EXAMINATION MADE IN COMPLIANCE WITH EMERGENCY RIVER AND HARBOR ACT APPROVED JUNE 6, 1900.

Report on preliminary examination of *Ohio River (in Kentucky), with a view to ascertaining the desirability of acquiring the island immediately below the Louisville and Portland Canal in the Ohio River known as Sand Island and the probable cost of purchasing the same*, was submitted through the division engineer by Captain Zinn, June 20, 1900. In his opinion, concurred in by the division engineer and by the Chief of Engineers, the improvement of the locality by the General Government in the manner indicated by the act is not advisable. The report was transmitted to Congress and printed in House Doc. No. 68, Fifty-sixth Congress, second session. (See also Appendix J J 12.)

LAKE RIVERS AND HARBORS.

IMPROVEMENT OF RIVERS AND HARBORS ON LAKE SUPERIOR.

This district was in the charge of Maj. Clinton B. Sears, Corps of Engineers, to February 20, 1901, in the temporary charge of Maj. D. W. Lockwood, Corps of Engineers, from February 20 to March 11, 1901, and in the charge of Capt. D. D. Gaillard, Corps of Engineers, since March 11, 1901. Division Engineer, Col. J. W. Barlow, Corps of Engineers (now brigadier-general, Chief of Engineers, United States Army, retired), to May 3, 1901, and Col. S. M. Mansfield, Corps of Engineers, since May 9, 1901.

1. Harbor at Grand Marais, Minn.—This small natural basin was not originally of sufficient depth, nor was it adequately sheltered, either for commercial purposes or for use as a harbor of refuge. The approved project of 1879 proposed two breakwater piers, each 350 feet long, from the east and west points of the bay, or one pier 700 feet long from the east point, and the dredging to a depth to accommodate the prevailing draft of vessels, which was 14 feet. The original estimated cost was $139,669.40, but for reasons explained in the report of the local officer (Annual Report of the Chief of Engineers for 1898, p. 2217) this was increased to $163,954.63. Up to the close of the fiscal year ending June 30, 1900, there had been expended on this work $133,100.66. With this sum 350 feet of the east pier had been completed and the 16-foot anchorage area increased to 26 acres. The increment of commerce which has accrued since the improvement of this harbor began bears the ratio of 25 entrances and clearances (made by 4 tugs and 5 schooners), with 60 tons of cargo, valued at $6,000, in 1878, to 346 entrances and clearances (nearly all steamers), with 6,203 tons of cargo, valued at $454,360, in 1899. The commercial statistics for 1900 were destroyed by fire. The value of the commerce of the harbor from 1878 to 1900, both inclusive, is roughly estimated at $2,000,000.

The act of March 3, 1899, appropriated $30,000 for completing improvement. With this it is proposed to build a breakwater 350 feet long from the western point and running out in a southeasterly direction.

The contract for this work was awarded at $88.91 per linear foot of stone embankment and crib structure and timber superstructure, to be completed December 1, 1900.

This contract expired before the completion of the work, but operations are being carried on by the former contractors at the same rates, under an implied agreement, and it is expected that the work will be satisfactorily completed by September 1, 1901.

July 1, 1900, balance unexpended	$30,249.34
June 30, 1901, amount expended during fiscal year	9,312.26
July 1, 1901, balance unexpended	20,937.08
July 1, 1901, outstanding liabilities	902.18
July 1, 1901, balance available	20,034.90
July 1, 1901, amount covered by uncompleted contracts	19,978.26
Amount that can be profitably expended in fiscal year ending June 30, 1903, for maintenance of improvement, in addition to the balance available July 1, 1901. Submitted in compliance with requirements of sundry civil act of June 4, 1897, and of section 7 of the river and harbor act of 1899.	2,000.00

(See Appendix K K 1.)

2. Harbor at Agate Bay, Minnesota.—This harbor, 27 miles east of Duluth, is a shipping port for iron ore and is a harbor of refuge.

The project for the improvement was adopted in 1887, and contemplates the erection of two piers projecting from the headlands of the bay and inclosing about 109 acres of water area, natural depth of 20 feet or more; the eastern pier to be 1,050 feet long and the western one 900 feet. Work upon the east pier was commenced in 1887, and at the close of work in November, 1898, besides the 750 feet of east pier built in 1891, there were completed 750 feet of west pier and 160 feet of rock embankment brought to the 20-foot level for foundation of the extension to said pier.

The act of March 3, 1899, appropriated $71,708 to complete the project for this harbor.

With this sum the west pier has been completed to its full length of ⁻⁻⁻ feet, and operations are now in progress upon the extension of the east pier, the work to be completed by September 1, 1901. When this has been done, the balance of the appropriation will be expended in necessary repairs to the old work.

The commerce of this harbor has increased from 236,000 cargo tons, valued at $524,800, in 1885, to 4,723,784 cargo tons, valued at $11,066,026, in 1900. The total valuation of the commerce of this port for sixteen years, 1885 to 1900, is roughly estimated at $51,000,000.

The arrivals and departures of vessels have increased from 174, with a registered tonnage of 295,800 tons, in 1885, to 2,444, with a registered tonnage of 7,087,600 tons, in 1900.

The amount expended to June 30, 1900, was $180,724.93.

July 1, 1900, balance unexpended	$63,483.07
June 30, 1901, amount expended during fiscal year	34,288.97
July 1, 1901, balance unexpended	29,194.10
July 1, 1901, outstanding liabilities	4,415.14
July 1, 1901, balance available	24,778.96
July 1, 1901, amount covered by uncompleted contracts	18,668.49
Amount that can be profitably expended in fiscal year ending June 30, 1903, for maintenance of improvement, in addition to the balance available July 1, 1901	2,000.00

Submitted in compliance with requirements of sundry civil act of June 4, 1897, and of section 7 of the river and harbor act of 1899.

(See Appendix K K 2.)

3. Harbor at Duluth, Minn., and Superior, Wis.—Previous to the annual report of 1897 this harbor was reported on under the separate heads of Duluth, Minn., and Superior, Wis., respectively.

The act of June 3, 1896, unified these harbors under the above title, and provided for continuous contracts for its improvement to the amount of $3,080,553.

This harbor now consists of the Duluth Canal, the Wisconsin Entrance, Superior Bay, Allouez Bay, St. Louis Bay, and St. Louis River to the limits of the cities of Duluth and Superior, about 20 miles from the original natural entry, which before improvement was obstructed by shifting bars, with but 9 feet of water over them. The bays were broad expanses of shallow water, averaging only 8 or 9 feet, except along the channel through them, where the depth was greater, but variable.

The project previous to the present one was for 16-foot navigation. This was practically completed July 1, 1897, and resulted in giving a good 16-foot navigation through the natural or Wisconsin Entry; through the artificial Duluth Canal; over the Duluth Basin, of 104 acres; along and parallel to the dock lines of Duluth and Superior, in Superior and St. Louis bays, and up the St. Louis River to New Duluth, near the head of navigation of the river, with well-defined channels from 85 to 300 feet in width.

The present project, authorized by the act of June 3, 1896, provides for the widening and deepening to a navigable depth of 20 feet of the existing channels, for new channels in Allouez Bay and St. Louis River, for extensive turning and anchorage basins of a navigable depth of 20 feet at the junctions of two or more channels, for widening the Duluth Canal, and for rebuilding the piers at the Duluth Canal and Wisconsin Entry and finishing them off with concrete superstructures built of monolithic blocks.

The total amount expended previous to the commencement of operations under the present project was $1,548,183.

The amount expended on the present project to June 30, 1900, was $1,448,034.65.

The contracts for dredging the channels and basins have been in operation for four seasons, and up to June 30, 1901, 15,626,995 cubic yards of material has been removed.

All the land necessary for the widening of the Duluth Canal has been acquired by deed of gift, purchase, or condemnation, at a cost of $53,919.05.

For the land at the Wisconsin Entry, the mouth of the Nemadji River, and a marshy island in the St. Louis River condemnation proceedings have been instituted in the United States courts. A small parcel of land at the end of Grassy Point, containing 4.6 acres, has been purchased for $1,610.

The south pier of the Duluth Canal has been completed and the substructure of the north pier. All of the footing blocks for the latter have been set and secured in place, and up to June 30, 1901, 80 monolithic blocks, containing 3,512 cubic yards of concrete, have been molded in place on this pier, completing 807 feet of concrete superstructure.

The old south pier was removed under contract in November and December, 1900, for the sum of $15,000. Ninety-eight iron lamp posts for lighting the piers of the Duluth Canal were secured by contract for the sum of $3,235.74.

A contract has been made for furnishing 9,000 tons of stone for use at the Duluth Canal.

During the fiscal year ending June 30, 1901, 9,049 barrels of Portland cement were purchased under contract for use upon the canal piers.

It is believed that dredging operations will be successfully completed by the close of the next working season, giving more than 16 miles of dredged channels from 120 to 600 feet in width, and basins of an aggregate area of about 250 acres, which must be maintained thereafter by dredging as needed.

This work can best be done by plant owned and operated by the United States, the cost of which is estimated at $143,000. With this plant provided the officer in charge estimates that the channels and basins can be maintained for an annual sum equivalent to less than 4 mills per ton for the vessel freight of the harbor each year.

The piers at the Wisconsin Entry were placed about 31 years ago in water of an average depth of 8 to 10 feet, the object then being to secure a depth of 12 feet in the channel. With the growth of commerce the channel depth has been increased to 24 feet, and the crib bottoms are now many feet above the bottom of the channel. Owing to this and other causes considerable displacement has resulted, and the present piers should be replaced by new ones. The estimated cost of this work is $925,000. The estimated balance from the appropriations authorized by the act of June 3, 1896, is $258,717.34, leaving $666,282.66 to be provided outside of the appropriations authorized by this act.

The improvements made are in excellent condition, and the expenditure has been amply justified by the immense commerce which it has readily accommodated.

The lake commerce of this port, Duluth-Superior, during the last season of navigation amounted to over $135,000,000, and since the beginning of improvement by the United States this commerce has amounted to 90,485,000 tons of freight, valued at $1,453,352,000. The total amount expended by the United States on harbor improvements during this period, including outstanding liabilities, was $3,527,072.45, equivalent to less than 4 cents per ton of vessel freight, and less than one-quarter of 1 per cent of the money value of this freight.

The tonnage for 1900, 11,725,245 tons, is the largest in the history of this port.

July 1, 1900, balance unexpended	$902,790.85
Amount appropriated by sundry civil act approved March 3, 1901	320,000.00
	1,222,790.85
June 30, 1901, amount expended during fiscal year	556,931.11
July 1, 1901, balance unexpended	665,859.74
July 1, 1901, outstanding liabilities	155,569.90
July 1, 1901, balance available	510,289.84
July 1, 1901, amount covered by uncompleted contracts	540,200.00
Amount (estimated) required for completion of existing project	459,727.50
Amount that can be profitably expended in fiscal year ending June 30, 1903, in addition to the balance available July 1, 1901	[1] 459,727.50
Submitted in compliance with requirements of sundry civil act of June 4, 1897.	

(See Appendix K K 3.)

4. Harbor at Ashland, Wis.—Ashland Harbor is located at the head of Chequamegon Bay, and originally had no protection from the waves which rolled into the bay, nor from waves generated within the bay itself by storms.

The original project was for the construction of a pile, slab, and rock breakwater 8,000 feet long and for dredging a channel in front of the wharves of the city. The act of March 3, 1899, added to this project by authorizing an extension of the breakwater to the shore, thus requiring the ultimate construction of 10,200 feet of breakwater. The emergency river and harbor act of June 6, 1900, provided for building a shore spur 4,700 feet in length from a point 2,600 feet east of the prolongation of the present breakwater and parallel thereto. This again changed the project, adding greatly to the total length of breakwater to be constructed and largely to the total expense.

The act of March 3, 1899, appropriated $35,000 for continuing the improvement, of which $10,000 was expended in repairs to the old work. The balance was expended under contract with Hugo & Tims during the season of 1900 in constructing 91 linear feet of breakwater next to the shore on the line of the old breakwater, and 842 linear feet of breakwater on the new line, fixed by the act of June 6, 1900.

The total amount expended under approved project and in repairs to June 30, 1900, was $248,752.31.

The breakwater has exerted a marked influence in improving the tranquillity of the harbor.

[1] In addition to this amount $100,000 will be required for work on Superior Entry piers, and $143,000 for a dredging plant for maintenance of improvement, as heretofore explained.

510   REPORT OF THE CHIEF OF ENGINEERS, U. S. ARMY.

The commerce of this port consists principally of iron ore and lumber exported, and coal, mineral oil, and general merchandise imported. The commerce has largely increased during the fourteen years the harbor has been under improvement by the United States, from 892 arrivals and clearances, with cargo tonnage of 1,400,000 tons, in 1887, to 2,335 arrivals and clearances, with cargo tonnage of 3,295,837 tons, in 1900, the total commerce having a valuation, roughly estimated, of $370,000,000.

July 1, 1900, balance unexpended	$25,747.69
June 30, 1901, amount expended during fiscal year	24,799.14
July 1, 1901, balance unexpended	948.55

Amount (estimated) required for completion of existing project	426,500.00
Amount that can be profitably expended in fiscal year ending June 30, 1903, for works of improvement and for maintenance, in addition to the balance unexpended July 1, 1901	40,000.00
Submitted in compliance with requirements of sundry civil act of June 4, 1897, and of section 7 of the river and harbor act of 1899.	

(See Appendix K K 4.)

5. *Harbor at Ontonagon, Mich.*—The entrance to Ontonagon River, which forms the harbor, had but 7 feet depth in 1867, at which time the project for securing 12 feet depth by building parallel piers on either side of the mouth, extending to the 18-foot curve of depth in Lake Superior, and dredging a channel between the piers, was adopted. The west pier was built to a length of 2,675 feet and the east pier to a length of 2,315 feet. This brought the outer end of the west pier very nearly to the 18-foot curve of depth, as proposed. But this curve has advanced since, owing to the very considerable volume of sand carried into the lake by the river, and as it appears probable that the advance of the bar will keep pace with the extension of the piers unless a very considerable extension is made at once, it does not appear that economic considerations would justify any further extension of the piers. It seems that better results will be secured by keeping the piers in repair and by dredging across the bar after each spring freshet.

As far as new work is concerned the project may be said to be completed, and further expenditure will be needed only for keeping a 12-foot channel open by dredging and for the repairs to the piers.

The balance of the $10,000 appropriated by the act of June 3, 1896, $6,845.63, was expended during the season of 1900, under contract with McCurdy Bros., of Houghton, Mich., in repairs to the outer 1,120 feet of the east pier, which was in a very rotten condition.

There is still a good 12-foot channel between the piers and out into the lake, but as this is liable to be impaired each spring by sediment brought down by the high water of the Ontonagon River, a dredging fund of $8,000 should be always available if it be intended to maintain the 12-foot depth.

The total cost of the improvement to June 30, 1900, was $337,306.46. The great fire in 1896 destroyed the principal commercial industry, the plant of the Diamond Match Company, and this company has not rebuilt. In 1867 there were 449 arrivals and departures with 5,000 tons of cargo for this port. In 1900 there were 176 arrivals and departures with 7,352 tons cargo and 1,300,000 feet of logs. In addition there were many tugs and vessels seeking refuge not recorded.

RIVER AND HARBOR IMPROVEMENTS. 511

July 1, 1900, balance unexpended	$7,821.54
June 30, 1901, amount expended during fiscal year	7,354.85
July 1, 1901, balance unexpended	466.69

Amount that can be profitably expended in fiscal year ending June 30, 1903, for maintenance of improvement, in addition to the balance unexpended July 1, 1901... 5,000.00
Submitted in compliance with requirements of sundry civil act of June 4, 1897, and of section 7 of the river and harbor act of 1899.

(See Appendix K K 5.)

6. *Waterway across Keweenaw Point from Keweenaw Bay to Lake Superior, Michigan.*—This work was formerly reported on as the Portage Lake and Lake Superior canals, across Keweenaw Point, Michigan.

In accordance with the provisions of the river and harbor act of September 19, 1890, the United States purchased and assumed the charge and care of these canals on August 3, 1891.

At the time of purchase by the United States there was a very poor 13-foot navigation; the channel was narrow and crooked, with many sharp bends; it was poorly marked and lighted; the entrance piers were in a very bad condition; the revetments were rotten or entirely gone, and there was a tax on the commerce through the canals in the shape of a tonnage charge.

The improvements consist of entrance piers at the harbor entrances on Lake Superior and Keweenaw Bay, canals and canal revetments, and dredged cuts and channel ways. There are no locks.

The approved project is for a 20-foot channel 120 feet wide, a renewal of the canal revetments, a reconstruction of the piers at the upper and lower entrances, and their extension to 30 and 20 feet of water, respectively.

The act of June 3, 1896, authorized continuing contracts to complete the above to the amount of $1,065,000.

Three of these contracts have been completed, and five are still in force.

One for 5,480 feet of breakwater piers at the upper entrance; one for widening the upper canal by dredging; one for revetment work at the upper canal; another for revetment work at the upper canal, and the fifth for dredging in Portage River.

The pier extension at the Keweenaw entrance and the revetment of the canal cuts at the lower entrance have been completed.

With the exception of some dredging, which can easily be done next season with the balance of $10,000 yet unappropriated, provided it becomes available in time, it is expected that the project will be completed during the present working season.

During the navigation season of 1900 the commerce through this waterway amounted to 1,734,136 tons of freight, valued at $57,380,129, and 32,875 passengers. The increase in net freight tonnage over that of the preceding year amounted to 22 per cent.

During the fiscal year ending June 30, 1901, $80,081.27 was expended in dredging, $98,500 in pier work, and $103,022.61 for revetment work, including contingencies, etc.

Amount expended on this work to June 30, 1900, was $740,243.42.

July 1, 1900, balance unexpended $399,751.11
Reimbursement by Quartermaster's Department, October, 1900 .... ¹5.47
Amount appropriated by sundry civil act approved March 3, 1901 ...... 145,000.00

544,756.58
June 30, 1901, amount expended during fiscal year 281,603.88

July 1, 1901, balance unexpended 263,152.70
July 1, 1901, outstanding liabilities 50,897.92

July 1, 1901, balance available 212,254.78

July 1, 1901, amount covered by uncompleted contracts 182,500.42

{ Amount (estimated) required for completion of existing project 10,000.00
Amount that can be profitably expended in fiscal year ending June 30, 1903, in addition to the balance available July 1, 1901 .... 10,000.00
Submitted in compliance with requirements of sundry civil act of June 4, 1897.

(See Appendix K K 6.)

7. *Operating and care of waterway across Keweenaw Point from Keweenaw Bay to Lake Superior, Michigan.*—During the fiscal year ending June, 30, 1901, $8,300 from the permanent-indefinite appropriation of July 5, 1884, was expended in maintaining by dredging a practicable 20-foot stage of water, in superintendence and general operation of the canals, and in guarding against encroachments on the legally established harbor lines, and an allotment of $8,500 from the same source for the same purpose has been made for the fiscal year ending June 30, 1902.

(See Appendix K K 6.)

8. *Harbor at Marquette, Mich.*—Originally this harbor afforded no protection to vessels from easterly or northeasterly storms, and projects were approved for the construction of a breakwater composed of cribs filled with rock and projecting from the shore into the bay a distance of 3,000 feet. This breakwater was finished in 1894, practically as projected, but since its commencement extensive repairs have been made to the superstructure. The harbor has natural deep water of 18 feet or more.

A project for a concrete superstructure was approved in February, 1890. Its estimated cost was $232,936.71.

Work on this concrete superstructure was begun in the spring of 1895, and 1,500 linear feet has been completed.

Owing to lack of funds no construction work was in progress during the fiscal year ending June 30, 1901.

In this latitude the working season is very short, especially for concrete made in place. For this reason it will be decidedly economical to have sufficient funds in hand at one time to utilize the whole of two consecutive seasons.

The breakwater has given complete protection to the harbor, and commerce has grown steadily until it amounts now to some $6,000,000 annually.

During the fiscal year ending June 30, 1872, there were 780 arrivals and clearances of vessels, with a registered tonnage of 370,000 tons. In

---

¹$5.47 credited this appropriation, on account reimbursement by Quartermaster's Department, October, 1900, for mileage paid Michigan Central Railroad in November, 1898, Certificate of Settlement No. 13026, October 24, 1900.

1900 there were 2,060 arrivals and clearances, with a registered tonnage of 2,776,953 tons.

The permanent maintenance of the breakwater by a durable concrete superstructure will do away with the frequent and expensive repairs incident to timber work.

The total cost of the work to June 30, 1900, was $557,492.12, of which $87,759.68 was under present project.

July 1, 1900, balance unexpended	$1,066.57
June 30, 1901, amount expended during fiscal year	528.35
July 1, 1901, balance unexpended	538.22

Amount (estimated) required for completion of existing project	100,000.00
Amount that can be profitably expended in fiscal year ending June 30, 1903, for works of improvement and for maintenance, in addition to the balance unexpended July 1, 1901	45,000.00
Submitted in compliance with requirements of sundry civil act of June 4, 1897, and of section 7 of the river and harbor act of 1899.	

(See Appendix K K 7.)

9. *Harbor of refuge, Marquette Bay, Michigan.*—This is a work authorized by the act of June 3, 1896. Marquette Bay is a small bay within the city limits of Marquette, north of Marquette proper, and distant 1¼ miles therefrom.

A resolution of Congress approved March 20, 1896, directed the Secretary of War to make a survey and submit an estimate for a breakwater in this bay. The results of this survey, with estimates amounting to $20,000 for breakwater 500 feet long and $50,000 for construction of one 1,000 feet long, were published in House Doc. No. 318, Fifty-fourth Congress, first session.

The approved project is to build a breakwater 1,000 feet in length off Presque Isle Point.

With the appropriation of $30,000 made in the act of March 3, 1899, this breakwater was completed to its full length in July, 1900. A recent inspection by the officer in charge shows the work to be in excellent condition.

Arrivals and clearances in 1896 were 414, with tonnage of 347,781 tons, and in 1900 there were 1,048 arrivals and clearances, with freight tonnage of 1,578,603 tons, valued at $3,418,898.

Total expended to June 30, 1900 was $31,205.64.

July 1, 1900, balance unexpended	$18,794.36
June 30, 1901, amount expended during fiscal year	17,957.27
July 1, 1901, balance unexpended	837.09

(See Appendix K K 8.)

10. *Harbor of refuge at Grand Marais, Mich.*—Originally the entrance to this harbor was obstructed by a bar having but 9 feet depth of water upon it. The project for its improvement, adopted in 1881, has for its object a deep and safe channel into the harbor, making it a harbor of refuge. This object is to be attained by building parallel piers projecting into the lake and dredging out a channel between them, connecting the deep water of the lake with that of the harbor, and by closing up the natural entrance, 5,700 feet in width, by a solid pile dike, driven with a slope toward the waves and strongly braced. The proposed length of each pier was 1,800 feet. The west pier has now reached a length of 1,656 feet, and the east pier 1,153 feet.

ENG 1901——33

An examination made in May, 1901, showed a least depth of about 14 feet along the channel between the piers. The pile dike, finished August 5, 1897, has successfully withstood the fall and spring storms and the action of the ice during three years. It is reported to be in good condition, except in two places, aggregating about 150 feet in length, where minor repairs are needed, and is being gradually strengthened by sand accumulating against it.

The act of March 3, 1899, appropriated $25,000 for continuing the improvement of this harbor. Of this amount $10,000 was expended in 1899 in repairs to the piers, and the balance was expended in 1900 in extending the east pier by a crib substructure temporarily decked over at the water surface, under contract, after due advertisement.

The present depth is insufficient to afford refuge to all classes of vessels.

The sand about Grand Marais shifts extensively, and to secure the depth called for in the present project the piers should be rapidly extended to the 22-foot curve, and a channel dredged out between them.

The commerce of this place has increased from 1,910 tons in 1887 to 135,756 tons in 1900. In 1892 310 vessels entered and departed, while in 1900 857 entered and departed. Value of commerce, including logs, $1,626,000.

The total amount expended to June 30, 1900, was $314,989.27. The result has been the creation of a very safe and commodious harbor for vessels drawing 13 feet. It is expected that the completion of the project will make this safely accessible for vessels of 16 feet draft.

July 1, 1900, balance unexpended.. $15,260.73
June 30, 1901, amount expended during fiscal year .... [1]15,253.95

July 1, 1901, balance unexpended..................................... 6.78

Amount (estimated) required for completion of existing project........ 153,401.68
Amount that can be profitably expended in fiscal year ending June 30, 1903, for works of improvement and for maintenance, in addition to the balance unexpended July 1, 1901................................... 70,000.00
Submitted in compliance with requirements of sundry civil act of June 4, 1897, and of section 7 of the river and harbor act of 1899.

(See Appendix K K 9.)

11. Removing sunken vessels or craft obstructing or endangering navigation.—The tug *E. P. Ferry* was burned in Duluth Harbor in January, 1900, and subsequently drifted into the bay. Being a menace to navigation, its removal was authorized June 12, 1901. It is proposed to remove the wreck by contract.

(See Appendix K K 10.)

EXAMINATION AND SURVEY MADE IN COMPLIANCE WITH EMERGENCY RIVER AND HARBOR ACT APPROVED JUNE 6, 1900.

Reports on preliminary examination and survey of *Burlington Bay, Lake County, Minnesota, with a view to improvement of said bay and constructing a harbor therein*, were submitted through the division engineer by Major Sears August 13 and November 10, 1900, respec-

---

[1] In addition, $348.32 was expended on repairs to west pier from allotment of $500 from appropriation contained in emergency river and harbor act approved June 6, 1900.

tively. He presents a plan for improvement at an estimated cost of $435,000. The reports were transmitted to Congress and printed in House Doc. No. 114, Fifty-sixth Congress, second session. (See also Appendix K K 12.)

IMPROVEMENT OF RIVERS AND HARBORS ON WESTERN SHORE OF LAKE MICHIGAN.

This district was in the charge of Maj. J. G. Warren, Corps of Engineers. Division Engineer, Col. J. W. Barlow, Corps of Engineers (now brigadier-general, Chief of Engineers, United States Army, retired), to May 3, 1901, and Col. S. M. Mansfield, Corps of Engineers, since May 9, 1901.

1. *Menominee Harbor, Michigan and Wisconsin.*—The survey made in 1871 with a view to the improvement of the entrance to the Menominee River showed that it had a depth of 5 feet. The present project, adopted March 3, 1899, provides for a channel 20 feet deep between two parallel piers, 400 feet apart.

The amount expended up to June 30, 1900, was $231,556.27.

During the fiscal year ending June 30, 1901, the required depth and width of channel was maintained by dredging.

The channel has a depth of 20 feet below datum and a least width of 300 feet.

The maximum draft that could be carried June 30, 1901, was 19.2 feet.

Commercial statistics for 1900.—Arrivals of vessels, 740; tonnage, 352,440; total approximate imports by way of harbor, 616,210 tons; exports, 553,579 tons.

July 1, 1900, balance unexpended	$3,155.73
June 30, 1901, amount expended during fiscal year	1,275.05
July 1, 1901, balance unexpended	1,880.68

Amount that can be profitably expended in fiscal year ending June 30, 1903, for maintenance of improvement, in addition to the balance unexpended July 1, 1901 .... 3,000.00
Submitted in compliance with requirements of sundry civil act of June 4, 1897, and of section 7 of the river and harbor act of 1899.

(See Appendix L L 1.)

2. *Menominee River, Michigan and Wisconsin.*—The survey made in 1889 with a view to the improvement of the Menominee River showed a governing depth of about 5 feet, and that by private enterprise a tortuous channel had been dredged about 50 feet wide and 14 feet deep, extending up the river a distance of 2 miles.

The present project, adopted June 3, 1896, provides for a channel 17 feet deep, the lower 9,000 feet to be 200 feet wide; thence for 2,600 feet, 100 feet wide; thence for 425 feet, 75 feet wide, and a turning basin 600 feet long and 250 feet wide of same depth as channel.

The total amount expended to June 30, 1900, was $113,691.82. The original and modified projects have been completed. A small amount of dredging for maintenance of channel was done during the fiscal year ending June 30, 1901.

Soundings taken in January, 1900, showed considerable shoaling in channel and basin.

The maximum draft that could be carried June 30, 1901, was 16.2 feet.

The commercial statistics for Menominee River are the same as for Menominee Harbor. (See Menominee Harbor report.)

July 1, 1900, balance unexpended	$808.21
June 30, 1901, amount expended during fiscal year	722.33
July 1, 1901, balance unexpended	85.88
Amount that can be profitably expended in fiscal year ending June 30, 1903, for maintenance of improvement, in addition to the balance unexpended July 1, 1901. Submitted in compliance with requirements of sundry civil act of June 4, 1897, and of section 7 of the river and harbor act of 1899.	6,600.00

(See Appendix L L 2.)

3. *Oconto Harbor, Wisconsin.*—In its natural condition the channel at the entrance to the Oconto River was obstructed by a bar with less than 3 feet of water over it. Previous to 1881, when the first appropriation was made for its improvement, the citizens, by the construction of a small amount of slab pier and dredging, had increased the depth to 4½ feet.

The part of the river between the mouth and the city of Oconto had a width of from 150 to 250 feet and a low-water channel depth of from 4 to 6 feet.

The present project, adopted in 1882 and modified in 1897, provides for a channel 9 feet deep, extending from Green Bay up the river to Spies's mill, a distance of about 1¼ miles.

The total amount expended up to June 30, 1900, was $91,627.31. At that date the south pier was of its projected length, and to complete the north pier to its full length an extension of 875 feet was required.

Soundings taken in May, 1900, showed a channel 9 feet deep below datum with a least width of 70 feet.

The actual depth June 30, 1901, was 8.2 feet.

Commercial statistics for 1900.—Arrivals of vessels, 375; tonnage, 20,000. Exports, 12,953 tons; imports, 61,320 tons.

July 1, 1900, balance unexpended	$1,372.69
June 30, 1901, amount expended during fiscal year	422.74
July 1, 1901, balance unexpended	949.95
Amount (estimated) required for completion of existing project	22,610.00

(See Appendix L L 3.)

4. *Green Bay Harbor, Wisconsin.*—The original channel from Green Bay into the Fox River was circuitous and narrow, with but 11 feet of water at its shoalest point, and the present harbor was available for light-draft vessels only.

The present project, adopted in 1892 and modified in 1897, provides for a dredged channel 16,500 feet long, 200 feet wide, and 17 feet deep, with a revetted cut at Grassy Island, the north end of channel to be 500 feet wide.

The Fox River below Depere, Wis., was included in the Green Bay appropriations of July 13, 1892, and June 3, 1896, and the project adopted in 1896 provides for the same depth as in the other channel.

The total amount expended up to June 30, 1900, was $398,769.52.

At that date the channel from Green Bay into the Fox River had a depth of 17 feet, with a least width of 200 feet.

The channel in the Fox River below Depere had a depth of 17 feet for a width of 150 feet.

Soundings taken in the winter of 1901 showed a channel 17 feet deep below datum from deep water in Green Bay to Depere, Wis.

The maximum draft that could be carried June 30, 1901, from Green Bay into the Fox River was 16.2 feet.

Commercial statistics for 1900.—Arrivals of vessels, 598; tonnage, 281,418; exports, 169,312 tons; imports, 347,960 tons.

July 1, 1900, balance unexpended	$7,432.98
June 30, 1901, amount expended during fiscal year	892.17
July 1, 1901, balance unexpended	6,540.81

{ Amount that can be profitably expended in fiscal year ending June 30, 1903, for maintenance of improvement, in addition to the balance unexpended July 1, 1901 .... 8,000.00
Submitted in compliance with requirements of sundry civil act of June 4, 1897, and of section 7 of the river and harbor act of 1899. }

- (See Appendix L L 4.)

5. Sturgeon Bay and Lake Michigan Ship Canal, Wisconsin.—In its natural condition Lake Michigan was separated from Sturgeon Bay, an arm of Green Bay, by a neck of land about 1⅜ miles wide, having a maximum elevation above the lake level of about 28 feet. The Sturgeon Bay and Lake Michigan Ship Canal and Harbor Company from 1872 to 1881 constructed across this neck a canal without locks or gates 7,200 feet long, 100 feet wide at water surface, and 14 feet deep, and in continuation of the canal dredged a channel in Sturgeon Bay 6,100 feet long, of about the same dimensions as the canal. Of the 14,400 linear feet of canal banks, 8,437 feet was provided with pile revetments. The United States assumed possession of the canal April 25, 1893.

The present project, adopted in 1894 and modified in 1896, provides for completing the revetments; widening the canal to 160 feet, except the westerly 1,000 feet, which is to be 250 feet wide between revetments, with a channel width of 200 feet; and a channel 15 feet deep.

The total amount expended to June 30, 1900, was $153,616.37, of which amount $81,833 was for the purchase of the canal by the United States.

The expenditures during the fiscal year ending June 30, 1901, were chiefly for widening the canal, 93,580 cubic yards of material and 2,300 linear feet of old revetment being removed in so doing.

The canal affords a considerable shortening of distance for many vessels over the natural outlet of Green Bay into Lake Michigan, avoids the dangers of the natural route, and makes Sturgeon Bay available and accessible as a harbor of refuge for vessels on Lake Michigan with a draft of less than 15 feet.

The maximum draft that could be carried June 30, 1901, was 14.2 feet.

July 1, 1900, balance unexpended	$8,216.63
June 30, 1901, amount expended during fiscal year	6,134.14
July 1, 1901, balance unexpended	2,082.49

{ Amount (estimated) required for completion of existing project 33,500.00
Amount that can be profitably expended in fiscal year ending June 30, 1903, in addition to the balance unexpended July 1, 1901 .... 12,000.00
Submitted in compliance with requirements of sundry civil act of June 4, 1897. }

(See Appendix L L 5.)

518   REPORT OF THE CHIEF OF ENGINEERS, U. S. ARMY.

6. Operating and care of Sturgeon Bay and Lake Michigan Ship Canal, Wisconsin.—Under an allotment from the indefinite appropriation of July 5, 1884, for operating and care of canals and other works of navigation, there was expended during the fiscal year ending June 30, 1901, $29,943.56. The principal work was the renewal and repairs to canal revetments and dredging. The riprap protection along the harbor front was repaired with additional stone, the grounds adjacent to the canal buildings were graded and the buildings repaired, the pile driver repaired, and 14,419 cubic yards of material dredged from the canal.

Navigation through the canal opened April 20, 1900, was maintained until practically closed by ice December 18, 1900, and reopened April 18, 1901.

No serious groundings occurred in the canal on account of an insufficient depth of water.

The water reached its lowest stage for the year on January 17, 1901, when it was 5.66 feet below high-water mark of 1838, and its highest stage June 17, 1901, when it was 2.16 feet below that point.

For commercial statistics see report upon improvement of Sturgeon Bay and Lake Michigan Ship Canal.

(See Appendix L L 6.)

7. Sturgeon Bay Canal harbor of refuge, Wisconsin.—Before the construction of this harbor was undertaken the Lake Michigan entrance to the Sturgeon Bay and Lake Michigan Ship Canal was entirely unprotected from storms from northeast to southwest.

The project of constructing a harbor of refuge at this point was adopted in 1873 and modified in 1879 and 1880. The modified project, as carried out and completed in 1884, consisted of two piers, each 1,344 feet long, 850 feet apart at the shore line, protecting the lake entrance to the canal and converging so as to make the harbor entrance 335 feet wide, inclosing an area of about 10 acres, with a depth of at least 17 feet.

The total expenditure at this harbor up to June 30, 1900, was $188,029.95. This expenditure resulted in the completion of the piers as projected and in a dredged channel 17 feet deep and 150 feet wide from the 17-foot contour in Lake Michigan to the canal entrance.

The expenditures during the fiscal year ending June 30, 1901, were for maintenance of channel.

Soundings taken in April, 1900, showed a depth of about 16.8 feet below datum.

Soundings taken in April, 1901, showed a channel 17 feet deep, with a minimum width of 75 feet.

The maximum draft that could be carried June 30, 1901, was 16.2 feet.

The commercial statistics for this harbor will be found in report upon improvement of Sturgeon Bay and Lake Michigan Ship Canal.

July 1, 1900, balance unexpended..	$652.55
June 30, 1901, amount expended during fiscal year.....................	283.74
July 1, 1901, balance unexpended	368.81
Amount that can be profitably expended in fiscal year ending June 30, 1903, for maintenance of improvement, in addition to the balance unexpended July 1, 1901... Submitted in compliance with requirements of sundry civil act of June 4, 1897, and of section 7 of the river and harbor act of 1899.	4,000.00

(See Appendix L L 7.)

RIVER AND HARBOR IMPROVEMENTS. 519

8. *Ahnapee Harbor, Wisconsin.*—Previous to the improvement of this harbor the depth of water at the mouth of the Ahnapee River was only 3 feet and the present harbor was not available for purposes of commerce.

The present project was adopted in 1875 and modified in 1884, 1897, and 1899. It provides for a small artificial harbor connected with the lake by a channel 100 feet wide and 13 feet deep, between two piers, with a 200-foot entrance channel between the pierheads; also for a channel 13 feet deep and 50 feet wide extending up the river a distance of 800 feet.

The total amount expended up to June 30, 1900, was $194,598.75.

Both piers have been built to their projected length.

June, 1900, the depth in the channel at the piers varied from 16$\frac{1}{4}$ feet to 13$\frac{1}{4}$ feet below datum. The channel provided for by project of 1899 is only partially completed. It has a depth of 10 feet and a least width of 30 feet for a length of 520 feet.

The maximum draft that could be carried June 30, 1901, was about 12 feet. During the fiscal year ending June 30, 1901, repairs were made to the United States dredging plant.

Commercial statistics for 1900.—Arrivals of vessels, 819; tonnage, 290,700. Exports and imports were 78,882 and 68,554, respectively, by all ways of transportation, their approximate values being $1,350,000 and $950,000.

July 1, 1900, balance unexpended	$1,621.25
June 30, 1901, amount expended during fiscal year	576.53
July 1, 1901, balance unexpended	1,044.72
Amount (estimated) required for completion of existing project	19,266.00
Amount that can be profitably expended in fiscal year ending June 30, 1903, for works of improvement and for maintenance, in addition to the balance unexpended July 1, 1901	3,000.00

Submitted in compliance with requirements of sundry civil act of June 4, 1897, and of section 7 of the river and harbor act of 1899.

(See Appendix L L 8.)

9. *Kewaunee Harbor, Wisconsin.*—The original entrance to the Kewaunee River was not more than 20 feet wide, with a depth of about 3 feet at its shoalest point, and was obstructed by submerged bowlders. The present harbor was therefore not available for purposes of commerce.

The project for its improvement, adopted in 1881, provided for an artificial entrance channel 15 feet deep, located about 2,000 feet south of the river mouth, protected by two parallel piers 200 feet apart, extending from the shore to the 19-foot contour in the lake.

The total amount expended on this harbor to the close of the fiscal year ending June 30, 1900, was $158,252.60, in addition to which the local harbor commissioners had expended $8,042.72. At that time both piers were of their full projected length. Soundings taken in May, 1900, show a depth of 15 feet, with a least width of 140 feet.

In April, 1901, the depth of channel was 15 feet below datum, with a minimum width of 90 feet.

The actual depth June 30, 1901, was about 14.2 feet.

Commercial statistics for 1899.—Arrivals of vessels, 1,236; tonnage, 712,740. By all ways of transportation: Exports, 473,918 tons; value, $13,673,200. Imports, 190,996 tons; value, $2,826,350.

520   REPORT OF THE CHIEF OF ENGINEERS, U. S. ARMY.

July 1, 1900, balance unexpended	$561.40
June 30, 1901, amount expended during fiscal year	3.50
July 1, 1901, balance unexpended	557.90

Amount that can be profitably expended in fiscal year ending June 30, 1903, for maintenance of improvement, in addition to the balance unexpended July 1, 1901... 11,000.00
Submitted in compliance with requirements of sundry civil act of June 4, 1897, and of section 7 of the river and harbor act of 1899.

(See Appendix L L 9.)

10. Two Rivers Harbor, Wisconsin.—The original depth of the entrance to Twin Rivers was from 3 to 4 feet, and the present harbor was not available for purposes of commerce.

The present project, adopted in 1870 and modified in 1875 and 1897, provides for maintenance of a channel 13 feet deep between parallel piers, the least distance apart to be 230 feet. The piers are of the full projected length.

The amount expended up to June 30, 1900, was $221,176.48.

In June, 1900, there was a channel 13 feet deep and 200 feet wide. In May, 1901, the channel was 13 feet deep for a width of 150 feet.

The maximum draft that could be carried June 30, 1901, was 11.5 feet.

The superstructure of the pile piers is in a dilapidated condition, and the sheet piling does not prevent the passage of sand through the piers into the channel.

Commercial statistics for 1900.—Arrivals of vessels, 1,114; tonnage, 323,354; departures of vessels, 1,114; tonnage, 323,354; exports by all ways of transportation, 254,896 tons; imports by all ways of transportation, 118,896 tons.

July 1, 1900, balance unexpended	$1,323.52
June 30, 1901, amount expended during fiscal year	44.07
July 1, 1901, balance unexpended	1,279.45

Amount that can be profitably expended in fiscal year ending June 30, 1903, for maintenance of improvement, in addition to the balance unexpended July 1, 1901... 7,000.00
Submitted in compliance with requirements of sundry civil act of June 4, 1897, and of section 7 of the river and harbor act of 1899.

(See Appendix L L 10.)

11. Manitowoc Harbor, Wisconsin.—The original depth of water at the mouth of the Manitowoc River was about 4 feet at the shoalest point, and the existing harbor was not available for purposes of commerce.

The present project, adopted in 1896, provides for a channel 20 feet deep. A project adopted in 1890 provided for a breakwater 400 feet long.

The amount expended up to June 30, 1900, was $399,850.66. At that date the breakwater was completed and both harbor piers were of the full length contemplated.

In April, 1900, the channel was 20 feet deep and 100 feet wide. In June, 1901, it was 20 feet deep with a least width of 150 feet.

The maximum draft that could be carried June 30, 1901, was 19.2 feet.

During the fiscal year the required depth and width of channel were maintained by dredging. Minor repairs were made to the north pier.

Commercial statistics for 1899.—Arrivals of vessels, 2,026; tonnage, 1,706,685; total approximate value of imports by way of the harbor, $2,700,000; exports, $2,600,000.

July 1, 1900, balance unexpended	$3,929.84
June 30, 1901, amount expended during fiscal year	1,952.52
July 1, 1901, balance unexpended	1,977.32

Amount that can be profitably expended in fiscal year ending June 30, 1903, for maintenance of improvement, in addition to the balance unexpended July 1, 1901. Submitted in compliance with requirements of sundry civil act of June 4, 1897, and of section 7 of the river and harbor act of 1899.	8,000.00

(See Appendix L L 11.)

12. Sheboygan Harbor, Wisconsin.—The depth of water over the bar at the mouth of the Sheboygan River did not originally exceed 7 feet, and the present harbor was not available for purposes of commerce.

The existing project, adopted in 1881 and modified in 1894 and March 3, 1899, provides for extending the piers to the 21-foot contour in the lake, and dredging to a depth of 19 feet at the outer ends, gradually diminishing to 15 feet at their shore ends; for a uniform width between the piers by reconstructing about 1,200 linear feet of the inner end of the south pier and removing the old pier by dredging, etc.; and for a breakwater 700 feet long.

The amount expended up to the close of the fiscal year ending June 30, 1900, was $396,433.87.

At that date there remained about 100 feet of each pier and 700 feet of breakwater to be built; there was a channel 19 feet deep, with a least width of 155 feet.

Soundings taken in April, 1901, showed a channel 19 feet deep, with a least width of 155 feet, and a bar with a least depth of 18.7 feet extended nearly across the entrance,

The maximum draft that could be carried June 30, 1901, was 18.2 feet.

During the fiscal year 600 feet of breakwater was built, repairs were made to the harbor piers, and the outer bar removed and projected depth of channel maintained by dredging.

Commercial statistics for 1899.—Arrivals of vessels, 1,248; tonnage, 746,914; exports, 466,328 tons; imports, 575,671 tons.

July 1, 1900, balance unexpended	$78,415.04
June 30, 1901, amount expended during fiscal year	73,962.15
July 1, 1901, balance unexpended	4,452.89

Amount (estimated) required for completion of existing project	14,300.00
Amount that can be profitably expended in fiscal year ending June 30, 1903, for works of improvement and for maintenance, in addition to the balance unexpended July 1, 1901	35,000.00
Submitted in compliance with requirements of sundry civil act of June 4, 1897, and of section 7 of the river and harbor act of 1899.	

(See Appendix L L 12.)

13. Port Washington Harbor, Wisconsin.—The natural channel at the mouth of the Sauk River was narrow, and at the shoalest point had a depth of 1 foot, and the present harbor was not available for purposes of commerce.

The present project, adopted in 1869 and modified in 1870 and 1876, provides for a channel 13 feet deep between two parallel piers, and two interior basins having a combined area of 5¾ acres and same depth as channel.

The amount expended thereon up to the close of the fiscal year ending June 30, 1900, was $197,062.10.

The piers were completed in 1893, and the channel and basins had been excavated to their required depth.

Soundings taken in April, 1900, showed a channel 13 feet deep below datum, with a least width of 60 feet, and a bar at entrance with a minimum depth of about 12½ feet.

During the fiscal year ending June 30, 1901, the width of channel was increased and the outer bar removed.

Soundings taken June 12, 1901, showed a depth of 13 feet in channel and basins.

The maximum draft that could be carried June 30, 1901, was 12.2 feet.

Commercial statistics for 1900.—Arrivals of vessels, 100; tonnage, not given. By way of the harbor only: Exports, 9,767 tons; imports, 43,989 tons.

July 1, 1900, balance unexpended	$1,874.40
June 30, 1901, amount expended during fiscal year	766.54
July 1, 1901, balance unexpended	1,107.86
Amount that can be profitably expended in fiscal year ending June 30, 1903, for maintenance of improvement, in addition to the balance unexpended July 1, 1901. Submitted in compliance with requirements of sundry civil act of June 4, 1897, and of section 7 of the river and harbor act of 1899.	4,000.00

(See Appendix L L 13.)

14. Harbor of refuge, Milwaukee, Wis.—Milwaukee Bay, in which the harbor of refuge is located, is protected by the coast from storms excepting those from the northeast to the southeast, and, while the anchorage ground is good, vessels were in danger of dragging their anchors or of failing to effect an anchorage at the proper place.

A Board of Engineers, in its report dated April 21, 1881, recommended a plan for a breakwater to inclose a portion of the bay 417 acres in extent beyond the 19-foot contour, and about twice that area beyond the 13-foot contour. Work began in 1881, and up to June 30, 1900, there had been expended $836,808.56, resulting in the completion of 6,950 feet of substructure and 4,450 feet of superstructure and extensive repairs.

During the past fiscal year the breakwater was extended to the full projected length, all of which is now provided with timber superstructure. A mooring station for harbor tugs was provided. Repairs were made to the superstructure.

It is proposed to renew 3,250 feet of the older timber superstructure with concrete.

The commercial statistics are the same as for Milwaukee Harbor, and are given in the report upon that work.

July 1, 1900, balance unexpended	$118,841.44
June 30, 1901, amount expended during fiscal year	98,132.15
July 1, 1901, balance unexpended	20,709.29
Amount that can be profitably expended in fiscal year ending June 30, 1903, for maintenance of improvement, in addition to the balance unexpended July 1, 1901. Submitted in compliance with requirements of sundry civil act of June 4, 1897, and of section 7 of the river and harbor act of 1899.	125,000.00

(See Appendix L L 14.)

RIVER AND HARBOR IMPROVEMENTS.   523

15. Milwaukee Harbor, Wisconsin.—The original depth of water at the mouth of Milwaukee River was not more than 4½ feet, and the present harbor was not available for purposes of commerce.

The present project, adopted by river and harbor act of March 3, 1899, provides for increasing the depth to 21 feet, width of channel between piers to be 225 feet, and width outside pierheads to be 600 feet.

The amount expended up to the close of the fiscal year ending June 30, 1900, was $370,858.84. The harbor piers were completed to their projected length in 1872; the channel was deepened to 21 feet below datum in 1899.

In April, 1900, there was a channel 21 feet deep with a least width of 180 feet. Soundings taken in April, 1901, showed a channel of same depth and width.

The maximum draft that could be carried June 30, 1901, was 20.2 feet.

Repairs of stone superstructure of the north pier are greatly needed. The present superstructure should be rebuilt with concrete.

Commercial statistics for 1900.—Arrivals of vessels, 5,773; tonnage, 5,026,239. Departures of vessels, 5,783; tonnage, 5,045,899. Receipts from duties on imports, $423,604.34.

July 1, 1900, balance unexpended	$8,566.52
June 30, 1901, amount expended during fiscal year	25.75
July 1, 1901, balance unexpended	8,540.77
Amount that can be profitably expended in fiscal year ending June 30, 1903, for maintenance of improvement, in addition to the balance unexpended July 1, 1901. Submitted in compliance with requirements of sundry civil act of June 4, 1897, and of section 7 of the river and harbor act of 1899.	82,500.00

(See Appendix L L 15.)

16. South Milwaukee Harbor, Wisconsin.—The entrance to this harbor originally varied in depth from absolute closure to about 3 feet. The project of improvement, adopted in 1896, provides for a channel 18 feet deep, 200 feet wide between parallel piers, at an estimated cost of $138,000.

The amount expended thereon up to the close of the fiscal year ending June 30, 1900, was $4,722.84. At that date the north pier had been extended 185 feet. In April, 1897, there was a channel depth varying from 9 feet to nearly absolute closure.

The improvement of this harbor is not yet far enough advanced to make it of any value for purposes of navigation and commerce.

Commercial statistics for 1900.—There are no available statistics of arrivals and departures of vessels.

July 1, 1900, balance unexpended	$277.16
June 30, 1901, amount expended during fiscal year	70.00
July 1, 1901, balance unexpended	207.16
Amount (estimated) required for completion of existing project	133,000.00

(See Appendix L L 16.)

17. Racine Harbor, Wisconsin.—The entrance to this harbor originally varied in depth from absolute closure after storms to about 7 feet, and the present harbor was not available for purposes of commerce.

The present project, adopted March 3, 1899, provides for widening channel and a depth of 21 feet, pier extension, and a breakwater 600 feet long.

The amount expended up to the close of fiscal year ending June 30, 1900, was $366,660.18.

Soundings taken in April, 1900, showed a channel 16¼ feet deep; least width, 40 feet.

May, 1901, there was a channel 20.3 feet deep below datum, with a least width of 140 feet.

The maximum draft that could be carried June 30, 1901, was 19.5 feet.

The present project was completed December 3, 1900.

During the fiscal year ending June 30, 1901, repairs were made to the harbor piers.

Commercial statistics for 1900.—Arrivals of vessels, 1,793; tonnage, 1,208,946. By way of harbor only: Exports, 108,566 tons; imports, 237,835 tons.

July 1, 1900, balance unexpended	$87,774.82
June 30, 1901, amount expended during fiscal year	82,087.73
July 1, 1901, balance unexpended	5,687.09

Amount that can be profitably expended in fiscal year ending June 30, 1903, for maintenance of improvement, in addition to the balance unexpended July 1, 1901 .... 10,000.00

Submitted in compliance with requirements of sundry civil act of June 4, 1897, and of section 7 of the river and harbor act of 1899.

(See Appendix L L 17.)

18. *Kenosha Harbor, Wisconsin.*—The original depth of water at the mouth of Pike Creek varied from nothing to 4 feet, and the present harbor was not available for purposes of commerce.

The present project, adopted by river and harbor act of March 3, 1899, provided for increasing depth in channel and basin to 21 feet and 20 feet, respectively, and for widening channel by pier extension and dredging; also a breakwater 600 feet long.

The amount expended up to the close of the fiscal year ending June 30, 1900, was $330,992.38. Soundings taken in April, 1900, showed a channel 16.5 feet deep; least width, 70 feet. June, 1901, there was a channel 170 feet wide and 21 feet deep below datum, and a depth of 20 feet over about 3 acres in the basin. The maximum draft that could be carried June 30, 1901, was 20.2 feet.

The present project was completed December 3, 1900. Repairs have been made to the south pier.

Commercial statistics for 1900.—Arrivals of vessels, 455; tonnage, 106,308. The approximate exports and imports by way of the harbor only, as reported by Mr. H. S. Van Ingen, were: Exports, 11,943 tons; value, $250,000; imports, 86,456 tons; value, $1,700,000.

July 1, 1900, balance unexpended	$153,315.03
June 30, 1901, amount expended during fiscal year	137,096.08
July 1, 1901, balance unexpended	16,218.95

(See Appendix L L 18.)

19. *Waukegan Harbor, Illinois.*—There was no navigable channel or natural harbor at this place. The project of improvement adopted in 1880 had for its object the construction of an artificial harbor of suf-

ficient capacity for local trade by inclosing a portion of Lake Michigan with pile piers, the entrance channel and inclosed area to be dredged to 13 feet. In 1882 this project was modified by reducing the area of the exterior basin by obtaining the additional space needed by dredging an interior basin connected by a narrow channel with the exterior basin. It has become necessary to abandon the interior basin because the land required was not secured for the purpose, and it is now practically impossible to secure possession. The present project provides for a basin 300 feet wide and 967 feet long.

The amount expended thereon up to the close of the fiscal year ending June 30, 1900, was $215,734.62.

Both piers have been completed to their projected length. In April, 1900, there was a depth in the channel of 13 feet below datum, with a least width of 160 feet.

June 18, 1901, there was a depth of 13 feet for a least width of 150 feet.

Private parties have dredged a channel 17 feet deep and about 90 feet wide.

The maximum draft that could be carried June 30, 1901, was 16.2 feet.

Commercial statistics for 1900.—Arrivals of vessels, 747; tonnage, 153,264. Departures of vessels, 747; tonnage, 153,264. Exports by all ways of transportation, 97,500 tons. Imports by all ways of transportation, 941,799.

July 1, 1900, balance unexpended	$4,765.38
June 30, 1901, amount expended during fiscal year	11.52
July 1, 1901, balance unexpended	4,753.86
Amount that can be profitably expended in fiscal year ending June 30, 1903, for maintenance of improvement, in addition to the balance unexpended July 1, 1901. Submitted in compliance with requirements of sundry civil act of June 4, 1897, and of section 7 of the river and harbor act of 1899.	3,500.00

(See Appendix L L 19.)

20. *Fox River, Wisconsin.*—The Fox and Wisconsin rivers, separated at Portage City, Wis., by a distance of only 2 miles, one flowing into Lake Michigan, the other into the Mississippi River, were the early means of communication between those waters. In 1846 Congress granted to the State of Wisconsin a quantity of land for the purpose of improving the navigation of this route. By means of a board of public works the State began and carried on the improvement until 1853, when it was transferred to a private company. In 1872 the United States acquired possession of the property, with the exception of the water power, water-power lots, and personal property. The earliest project, that of 1848, called for canals 40 feet wide at bottom and 4 feet deep, with locks 125 feet long and 30 feet wide. This project was enlarged subsequently. The present project is that of a Board of Engineers submitted September 17, 1884, and modified May 14, 1886. It provides for deepening and widening the channel of the Fox River from Montello to Green Bay to 6 feet depth and 100 feet width, and from Portage to Montello to 4 feet depth, and for the renovation of 12 old locks.

The amount expended on the Fox and Wisconsin rivers from 1867 to the close of the fiscal year ending June 30, 1900, including $145,000 paid to the Green Bay and Mississippi Canal Company for its property, was $3,070,818.09, of which amount $425,478.49 was appropriated solely for and expended solely upon the Fox River since 1885.

The result of this expenditure upon the Fox River was the construction of 16 new stone locks, 10 composite locks, 16 permanent dams, 12 canals, a head wall and feeder at the old first lock at Appleton, a lock house at Appleton, warehouses at Appleton first lock and Berlin lock, a wing dam and brush and stone shore protection to the portage levee, masonry wasteweirs at Little Chute combined locks and Appleton third lock, masonry culvert at head of Little Chute combined locks, a dry dock at Kaukauna, guard gates at head of Kaukauna Canal; also rebuilding canal banks at Kaukauna, wing walls at Kaukauna fourth lock, and 1,237 linear feet of cement-laid rubble-core wall in canal banks of fourth and fifth levels. A channel 75 feet wide and 450 feet long has been secured by blasting and drilling the rock bar below Depere lock from 4 to 12 inches below the top of the lower miter sill. Channel below Depere has been deepened, and channel deepened at mouth of Fondulac River, Neenah Channel, Fox River at head of Lake Butte Des Morts, Grignon Rapids, below Little Chute and Rapide Croche locks, and in the canals and Upper Fox River. Masonry outlet to wasteweir at Kaukauna second lock, a roadway upon the United States property at Appleton first lock, and fishways in the Eureka, Berlin, White River, Princeton, Grand River, Montello, and Fort Winnebago dams have been constructed. A harbor of refuge has been constructed at Stockbridge Landing, Lake Winnebago, and snags have been removed and bars dredged in Wolf River, making a 4½-foot channel 100 feet wide to New London.

The improvement of the Wisconsin River was abandoned in 1887.

The full depth of 6 feet has now been obtained from Depere to White River lock, with the exception of about three-fourths of a mile between mileposts 34 and 35, a distance of 99 miles from mouth of Fox River. Above this point the projected depth has not yet been obtained.

The expenditures during the fiscal year ending June 30, 1901, were for dredging Upper Fox River.

The relative value of the commerce involved and the cost of the improvement can not be estimated.

Its principal effect so far has been to cause considerable reduction in freight rates to points in the Fox River Valley. Deepening the channel of the Upper Fox by dredging has also had, and will continue to have, the effect of draining the enormous expanse of meadow lands in the Fox River Valley and greatly increasing their availability and value.

The maximum draft that could be carried June 30, 1901, at mean low water over the shoalest part of the improvement was from Depere to White River lock, 6 feet; from that point to Montello, 4 feet, and from Montello to Portage, 3 feet.

July 1, 1900, balance unexpended	$9,271.51
June 30, 1901, amount expended during fiscal year	2,346.19
July 1, 1901, balance unexpended	6,925.32
Amount (estimated) required for completion of existing project	153,366.48
Amount that can be profitably expended in fiscal year ending June 30, 1903, in addition to the balance unexpended July 1, 1901	60,000.00

Submitted in compliance with requirements of sundry civil act of June 4, 1897.

(See Appendix L L 20.)

21. *Operating and care of locks and dams on Fox River, Wisconsin.*—Under an allotment from the indefinite appropriation for operating and care of canals and other works of navigation, there has been expended during the year ending June 30, 1901, the sum of $66,552.85.

The principal work has been dredging bars and channels, making repairs of locks, dams, canal banks, lock houses, dredges, and boats; rebuilding Appleton third lock, wasteweir, and wall, and Appleton second lock; completing dry dock at Kaukauna, and survey of United States works and property along Fox River.

A detailed statement, appended to the report of the local engineer officer in charge, shows the items of expenditures.

Navigation was closed November 21, 1900, and reopened April 25, 1901. The water in Lake Winnebago and the Lower Fox has been maintained at the crests of the dams throughout the year, with the exception of Lake Winnebago during the close of navigation, drawn down by the mills with permission of the Secretary of War.

For commercial statistics, see report upon improvement of Fox River, Wisconsin.

(See Appendix L L 21.)

22. *Removing sunken vessels or craft obstructing or endangering navigation.*—On the evening of November 20, 1900, a flat scow laden with about 150 cords of stone sunk in Sturgeon Bay and Lake Michigan Ship Canal, Wisconsin, about 300 feet from the easterly end of the canal.

Under section 20 of river and harbor act of March 3, 1899, the United States assumed control of the wreck, and operations for its removal were begun at once. All obstructions were removed and the channel cleared November 30, 1900, at a cost of $715.12.

(See Appendix L L 22.)

EXAMINATIONS AND SURVEY MADE IN COMPLIANCE WITH EMERGENCY RIVER AND HARBOR ACT APPROVED JUNE 6, 1900.

Preliminary examinations and survey of the following localities were made by the local engineer and reports thereon submitted through the division engineer.

1. *Preliminary examination and survey of Sturgeon Bay and Lake Michigan Ship Canal, Wisconsin, with a view to deepening the same to 18 feet.*—Captain Warren submitted reports dated June 28 and November 24, 1900, respectively. He presents a plan for improvement at an estimated cost of $218,000. The reports were transmitted to Congress and printed in House Doc. No. 117, Fifty-sixth Congress, second session. (See also Appendix L L 23.)

2. *Preliminary examination of Manitowoc Harbor, Wisconsin, with a view to making a harbor of refuge with a depth of not less than 20 feet.*—Captain Warren submitted report June 23, 1900. In his opinion, concurred in by the division engineer and by the Chief of Engineers, the improvement of the locality by the General Government in the manner indicated by the act is not advisable. The report was transmitted to Congress and printed in House Doc. No. 95, Fifty-sixth Congress, second session. (See also Appendix L L 24.)

3. *Preliminary examination of Milwaukee Harbor, Wisconsin, with a view to necessary enlargement and suitable protection therefor.*—Captain Warren submitted report August 6, 1900. In his opinion, concurred in by the division engineer and b the Chief of En 'neers, ner indicated by the act is not advisable. The report was transmitted to Congress and printed in House Doc. No. 86, Fifty-sixth Congress, second session. (See also Appendix L L 25.)

IMPROVEMENT OF CHICAGO AND CALUMET HARBORS AND CHICAGO AND ILLINOIS RIVERS, ILLINOIS, AND OF CALUMET RIVER, ILLINOIS AND INDIANA; CONSTRUCTION OF ILLINOIS AND MISSISSIPPI CANAL.

This district was in the charge of Maj. J. H. Willard, Corps of Engineers. Division Engineer, Col. J. W. Barlow, Corps of Engineers (now brigadier-general, Chief of Engineers, United States Army, retired), to May 3, 1901, and Col. S. M. Mansfield, Corps of Engineers, since May 9, 1901.

1. Chicago Harbor, Illinois.—The present project was adopted in 1870 and modified in 1878, and contemplated—

(a) The formation of an outer harbor by inclosing a portion of Lake Michigan just south of the entrance to Chicago River by breakwaters, and dredging the same, for the purpose of increasing the harbor facilities of Chicago.

(b) The construction of an exterior breakwater in deep water in Lake Michigan, north of the entrance to Chicago River and about 1 mile distant therefrom, to shelter the approaches to the river and outer harbor and to form a harbor of refuge near the southern end of Lake Michigan.

(c) To keep the entrance to Chicago River dredged for the passage of vessels navigating Chicago River as far as to the original shore line of Lake Michigan, at or near Rush Street Bridge.

The river and harbor act of March 3, 1899, further modified the project of 1870 by providing for dredging the outer basin and harbor entrance to 20 feet depth at low water.

There had been expended upon this project up to June 30, 1900, $1,786,400.25.

All of the work under the projects of 1870 and 1878 has been completed except dredging the outer basin.

A contract has been let for dredging the Chicago River from Rush street eastward, for removing the bar at the entrance to the river, and for dredging the inner harbor or basin so far as the funds will permit. Work under this contract began May 2, 1901, and at the close of the fiscal year an aggregate of 200,256 cubic yards had been removed, practically completing the river channel west of the United States life-saving station, and removing more than one-half of the bar at the approach to this harbor.

July 1, 1900, balance unexpended	$102,875.61
June 30, 1901, amount expended during fiscal year	8,297.01
July 1, 1901, balance unexpended	[1] 94,578.60
July 1, 1901, amount covered by uncompleted contracts	85,158.99
Amount (estimated) required for completion of existing project	409,960.00
Amount that can be profitably expended in fiscal year ending June 30, 1903, for works of improvement and for maintenance, in addition to the balance unexpended July 1, 1901	150,000.00

Submitted in compliance with requirements of sundry civil act of June 4, 1897, and of section 7 of the river and harbor act of 1899.

(See Appendix M M 1.)

---

[1] Includes $500 allotted for expenses of Office Chief of Engineers for the fiscal year ending June 30, 1902.

2. *Chicago River, Illinois.*—This river, as far as its navigable water extends, is entirely within the limits of the city of Chicago, Ill. Prior to the act of June 3, 1896, no work had been done for the improvement of its navigation by the United States. The present project, inaugurated by Congress under the act of June 3, 1896, as modified by the act of June 4, 1897, contemplates the improvement of the river by dredging and minor changes of docks and dock lines to admit passage by vessels drawing 16 feet of water.

The river and harbor act of August 18, 1894, allowed $25,000 from the appropriation made for the improvement of Chicago Harbor to be applied to the improvement of Chicago River between the mouth of the river and the junction of the two branches, of which amount $3,645.70 was expended in the year ending June 30, 1896, in dredging to 18 feet depth as far as to Rush Street Bridge. Since the passage of the act of June 3, 1896, the balance of this amount has been transferred to the Chicago River work.

Up to the close of the fiscal year ending June 30, 1900, there had been expended $346,558.54, excluding the $25,000 allotted as above stated, and during the fiscal year ending June 30, 1901, there was expended $53,449.94. As a result of this expenditure the river has been dredged to a depth of 17 feet below Chicago city datum, from the mouth of the river to Ashland avenue on the South Branch and West Fork, and to the stock yards on the South Fork, South Branch, a distance of about 6 miles, and to Belmont avenue on the North Branch, the head of navigation, a total of 1,873,909 cubic yards of material having been removed; the securing of titles to all of the lands (17 tracts) to be removed under project for widening and deepening the river, at a total cost, including damages, of $91,949.50, and the improvement of fifteen of these tracts, have been completed. Two are still in progress.

July 1, 1900, balance unexpended	$278,441.46
June 30, 1901, amount expended during fiscal year	53,449.94
July 1, 1901, balance unexpended	[1] 224,991.52
July 1, 1901, amount covered by uncompleted contracts	30,948.60

(See Appendix M M 2.)

3. *Calumet Harbor, Illinois.*—This harbor is known on the Great Lakes as South Chicago Harbor.

This improvement was designed to furnish a safe and practicable entrance to Calumet River and the port of South Chicago by the construction of parallel piers 300 feet apart, projecting from the shore into Lake Michigan, and by dredging between them.

The work began in 1870, and all the projected work had been accomplished for 16-foot draft prior to June 30, 1896, resulting in the construction of 3,640 linear feet of north pier and 2,020 linear feet of the south pier and securing and maintaining a channel 16 feet deep and of suitable width from similarly deep water in Lake Michigan to the Calumet River at the roots of the piers, at a cost of $454,483.53. The work included also 476,564 cubic yards of material dredged, increasing the depth in the channel from 7 to 16 feet.

On June 30, 1896, it may be considered that the original project for this locality was terminated and completed.

---

[1] Includes $500 allotted for expenses of Office Chief of Engineers for the fiscal year ending June 30, 1902.

530   REPORT OF THE CHIEF OF ENGINEERS, U. S. ARMY.

Under date of February 21, 1896, a plan for improvement of both the inner and outer harbors was submitted. The estimated cost of this improvement was $1,134,830. (Annual Report of the Chief of Engineers for 1896, p. 2583.)

The expenditures to June 30, 1900, were $543,501.65.

Under the project of February 21, 1896, for construction of the outer harbor of refuge, adopted by Congress in the river and harbor act of March 3, 1899, work was in progress under contract at the close of the fiscal year ending June 30, 1900, and 1,000 feet of foundation had been prepared, 13 cribs constructed, and 8 cribs sunk and filled with stone. During the year ending June 30, 1901, 2,200 linear feet of foundation was prepared, 19 cribs constructed, 24 cribs sunk and filled with stone, 1,700 feet of superstructure built, and 2,529 linear feet of ice guard placed.

July 1, 1900, balance unexpended	$329,248.35
Amount appropriated by sundry civil act approved March 3, 1901	255,000.00
	584,248.35
June 30, 1901, amount expended during fiscal year	144,748.19
July 1, 1901, balance unexpended	439,500.16
July 1, 1901, amount covered by uncompleted contracts	193,554.06
Amount (estimated) required for completion of existing project	419,480.00
Amount that can be profitably expended in fiscal year ending June 30, 1903, in addition to the balance unexpended July 1, 1901	419,480.00

Submitted in compliance with requirements of sundry civil act of June 4, 1897.

(See Appendix M M 3.)

4. Calumet River, Illinois and Indiana.—The project for the improvement of this river, adopted by Congress in 1883, contemplated securing a channel 200 feet in width and 16 feet in depth below low water in Lake Michigan, from the mouth of Calumet Harbor, Illinois, to one-half mile east of Hammond, Ind., with a view to increasing the facilities for handling the commerce of this region and also aiding in providing means for the better accommodation of much of the commerce of Chicago River, which river was and still is much crowded.

The project was modified by the river and harbor act of June 3, 1896, so as to provide for dredging the channel for 2 miles southward from the mouth of the river to 20 feet depth.

Under the project of 1883 there was dredged a channel, measured from the harbor southward, to the full width of 200 feet and depth of 16 feet, 19,518 feet in length, except that over a short portion where rock was encountered the width was reduced to 85 feet.

In addition there was removed 248,516 cubic yards of material from the channel between the forks and one-half mile east of Hammond, Ind., in an effort to secure a practicable channel 10 feet deep and 60 feet wide, resulting in failure, due to rapid refilling of channel.

Under the supplementary project of 1896, there has been 320,405 cubic yards of material removed under contract, completing the channel 20 feet deep a distance of 2 miles, and providing a winding or turning basin 20 feet deep at the first cut-off above the mouth of the river.

The expenditures to June 30, 1900, amounted to $365,824.43.

Winding or turning basins should be provided at intervals of from 1 to 2 miles along the river, to avoid in future the restrictions now imposed in other lake harbors within the shore lines.

RIVER AND HARBOR IMPROVEMENTS. 531

The river and harbor act of March 3, 1899, appropriated $60,000 for the improvement of this stream, and confined the work to the section of river between the mouth and the forks of the Calumet. Dredging under contract was in progress at the close of the fiscal year ending June 30, 1900, and was continued until August 29, 1900, when contract was completed and funds practically exhausted.

July 1, 1900, balance unexpended	$44,175.57
June 30, 1901, amount expended during fiscal year	30,815.27
July 1, 1901, balance unexpended	[1] 13,360.30

Amount (estimated) required for completion of existing project	Indefinite.
Amount that can be profitably expended in fiscal year ending June 30, 1903, in addition to the balance unexpended July 1, 1901	60,000.00
Submitted in compliance with requirements of sundry civil act of June 4, 1897.	

(See Appendix M M 4.)

5. *Illinois River, Illinois.*—The project which contemplates the extension of the slack-water improvement begun by the State of Illinois from Copperas Creek locks to the Mississippi River, and which includes the construction of two locks, 350 feet long between sills, 75 feet width of chamber, with 7 feet of water over sills at low-water level of 1879, and dredging the channel where necessary to obtain 7 feet depth at low water, was adopted in 1880.

The two locks and dams, one at Kampsville, Ill., 31 miles above the mouth of the Illinois River, and the other at Lagrange, 79 miles above the mouth, are completed and have been in use, the former about eight and the latter about twelve years.

On this work the United States expended up to June 30, 1900, $1,402,114.78.

The expenditures during the year ending June 30, 1901, were applied to dredging at points between Kampsville lock and the mouth of the river, and care and repair of plant.

July 1, 1900, balance unexpended	$59,258.43
June 30, 1901, amount expended during fiscal year	28,040.94
July 1, 1901, balance unexpended	31,217.49
July 1, 1901, outstanding liabilities	3,500.00
July 1, 1901, balance available	27,717.49

Amount (estimated) required for completion of existing project	257,000.00
Amount that can be profitably expended in fiscal year ending June 30, 1903, in addition to the balance available July 1, 1901	130,000.00
Submitted in compliance with requirements of sundry civil act of June 4, 1897.	

(See Appendix M M 5.)

6. *Operating and care of Lagrange and Kampsville locks, Illinois River, and approaches thereto.*—These locks and dams have been operated and maintained under the indefinite appropriation provided for in section 4 of the river and harbor act of July 5, 1884.

Lagrange lock and dam.—During the period between December 18 and March 11 there was no navigation through the lock, except four steamboats in January, and from March 17 to April 29, during high

[1] Includes $1,000 allotted for expenses of Office Chief of Engineers for the fiscal year ending June 30, 1902.

water, all boats passed over the dam except a few heavily loaded barges and small steamers.

The tonnage for past fiscal year shows an increase over that for preceding year, ranking fifth in amount since the lock has been in operation, about twelve years. Five thousand three hundred and sixteen dollars and seventy-four cents was expended during the year, exclusive of $402.90 outstanding liabilities June 30.

Kampsville lock and dam.—Between December 16 and March 14 there was no navigation through the lock, and from March 24 to April 28, with the exception of three ice tows and one small steamer, all boats passed over the dam.

Tonnage of steamboats is greater than that of any year since the works have been in operation, and the combined tonnage of steamboats and barges ranks fifth.

The expenditures during the year amounted to $5,338.23, exclusive of $471.97 outstanding liabilities June 30.

(See Appendix M M 6.)

7. *Illinois and Mississippi Canal, Illinois.*—The object of the improvement is to furnish a link in a navigable waterway from Lake Michigan to the Mississippi River at the mouth of Rock River, Illinois.

The canal has been located on the Rock Island route, approved by the Secretary of War October 27, 1888, as directed in the act of Congress of August 11, 1888. It proceeds from the Illinois River at its great bend, 1¾ miles above the town of Hennepin, Ill., thence via Bureau Creek Valley and over the summit to Rock River at the mouth of Green River; thence, by slack water in Rock River and a canal around the lower rapids of the river at Milan, to the Mississippi River at the mouth of Rock River.

The canal is to be at least 80 feet wide at the water surface, 7 feet deep, and with locks 170 feet long and 35 feet width of lock chamber, capable of passing barges carrying 600 tons (maximum) freight.

A report upon the location, with detailed estimates of cost, of this canal was submitted June 21, 1890, and published (without maps) as House Ex. Doc. No. 429, Fifty-first Congress, first session, and is also printed in the Annual Report of the Chief of Engineers for 1890, page 2586.

The river and harbor act of September 19, 1890, made the first appropriation for the construction of the canal and directed work to be begun by the construction of one of the locks and dams in Rock River.

In accord with this act, work was begun in July, 1892, near the mouth of Rock River, on the construction of a canal around the lower rapids of the river, and since that date has been prosecuted as rapidly as appropriation of funds permitted. The survey work in locating the canal on the ground and proceedings for acquiring title to the right of way have been continuous since October, 1890, and the canal has been definitely located on the ground throughout its entire extent.

There had been expended on this work up to the close of the fiscal year ending June 30, 1900, $3,518,797.86, and during the fiscal year ending June 30, 1901, $971,707.35.

The result of this expenditure has been:

First. The acquisition of the right of way for 4¼ miles around the lower rapids of Rock River and the completion of 4¼ miles of canal there, involving the construction of 4¼ miles of earthwork in constructing the canal trunk, 3 locks, 1 railroad and 2 highway swing bridges, 7 sluiceways and gates, 1 arch culvert, 2 dams, 1,392 feet long, across the arms of Rock River, 3 lock keepers' houses, 1 small office building, a thorough riprapping of the canal banks, not estimated for in the original estimates, and construction, by contract, of Moline wagon bridge, at a cost of $25,000, which was also not included in original estimate.

Second. In the location on the ground and preparation of descriptions, plats, and abstracts of title of all land needed for the construction of the canal and feeder and for lands to be overflowed or damaged by the canal at Sterling.

Third. In the completion of all earthwork, miles 1 to 18, except reenforcing high embankments and except part of mile 1, forming the approach from the Illinois River to Lock No. 1; the foundation and masonry for all culverts, Locks 1 to 21; the construction of aqueducts 1, 2, and 3, highway bridges 1 to 10, and 3 railroad bridges; the construction of 9 arch culverts and 11 pipe culverts; the partial completion of earthwork on miles 19, 20, and 24 to 28, inclusive; the erection of 5 houses for superintendents and lock keepers and 1 small house for office use, all on eastern section.

Fourth. In the acquisition, by purchase or condemnation, of all lands required for the canal, except a small amount required for approaches to highway bridges and 3 parcels in Henry County to which title has not yet been perfected.

Fifth. In the putting under contract of earthwork of all the feeder line and of all the pipe culverts and of all arch culverts under the feeder except one, and in the construction of 4,405,566 cubic yards of earthwork along the feeder, resulting in the completion of all earthwork along 17 miles and 85 per cent of the remainder; in constructing 1 12-foot arch culvert and 10 pipe culverts; foundations of 7 arch culverts, except slope paving for one; concrete masonry for 3 arch culverts and flushing devices for 2 pipe culverts; foundations and abutments for 7 highway bridges, and superstructure of one double-track highway and one double-track railroad bridge.

In the placing under contract of about 21 miles of earthwork on the western section, and the construction of 1,297,739 cubic yards of earthwork; construction of 13 pipe culverts and foundations for 3 arch culverts; the building of 5 warehouses, and fencing of 32 miles of right of way. Earthwork on 7 miles completed.

July 1, 1900, balance unexpended	$1,719,728.60
Amount appropriated by sundry civil act approved March 3, 1901	975,000.00
	2,694,728.60
June 30, 1901, amount expended during fiscal year	971,707.35
July 1, 1901, balance unexpended	1,723,021.25
July 1, 1901, outstanding liabilities	95,335.21
July 1, 1901, balance available	1,627,686.04
July 1, 1901, amount covered by uncompleted contracts	175,021.50
Amount (estimated) required for completion of existing project	758,220.00
Amount that can be profitably expended in fiscal year ending June 30, 1903, in addition to the balance available July 1, 1901	758,220.00
Submitted in compliance with requirements of sundry civil act of June 4, 1897.	

(See Appendix M M 7.)

8. *Survey of Upper Illinois and Lower Des Plaines rivers, Illinois, with a view to the extension of navigation from the Illinois River to Lake Michigan at or near Chicago, Ill.*—This survey was required by the river and harbor act of March 3, 1899. Preliminary report of Board of Engineers is printed in the Annual Report of the Chief of Engineers for 1900, page 3855 et seq.

The Board submitted final report November 17, 1900, which was transmitted to Congress and printed in House Doc. No. 112, Fifty-sixth Congress, second session. It is also herewith in Appendix M M 8.

July 1, 1900, balance unexpended $12,509.04
June 30, 1901, amount expended during fiscal year 6,163.85

July 1, 1901, balance unexpended 6,345.19

(See Appendix M M 8.)

EXAMINATIONS MADE IN COMPLIANCE WITH EMERGENCY RIVER AND HARBOR ACT APPROVED JUNE 6, 1900.

Preliminary examinations of the following localities were made and reports thereon submitted:

1. *Preliminary examination of Illinois and Des Plaines rivers, Illinois, with a view to the extension of navigation to Lake Michigan at or near Chicago, with channel depths of 10, 12, and 14 feet.*—A Board of Engineers submitted report dated November 18, 1900, with plan and estimate for improvement at a cost of $30,000,000. The report was transmitted to Congress and printed in House Doc. No. 220, Fifty-sixth Congress, second session. (See also Appendix M M 9.)

2. *Preliminary examination of Rock River, Illinois, at the head of the feeder for the Illinois and Mississippi Canal, with a view to the construction of a lock and dam in the river in connection with said canal.*—Major Willard submitted report dated October 19, 1900. He submits plan for improvement at an estimated cost of $75,000. The report was transmitted to Congress and printed in House Doc. No. 126, Fifty-sixth Congress, second session. (See also Appendix M M 10.)

IMPROVEMENT OF MICHIGAN CITY HARBOR, INDIANA, AND OF RIVERS AND HARBORS ON THE EASTERN SHORE OF LAKE MICHIGAN.

This district was in the charge of Capt. Chester Harding, Corps of Engineers, to April 30, 1901, and of Capt. Charles Keller, Corps of Engineers, since that date. Division Engineer, Col. J. W. Barlow, Corps of Engineers (now brigadier-general, Chief of Engineers United States Army, retired), to May 3, 1901, and Col. S. M. Mansfield, Corps of Engineers, since May 9, 1901.

1. *Michigan City Harbor, Indiana.*—The improvement of this harbor dates from 1836, and has resulted in establishing an inner harbor for local commerce and partly completing an outer harbor, designed to facilitate entrance to the former and afford refuge to vessels engaged in general lake commerce.

The inner harbor has been made by deepening the entrance to Trail Creek and protecting the channel by piers extending to deep water in Lake Michigan, to which operations were limited until 1870. The original condition at the mouth is not definitely known, but at a short distance above the mouth the depth was less than 3 feet and the width varied from 175 feet in the lower portion to 60 feet or less in the upper portion. Since 1882 the entrance channel has been prolonged up the creek by dredging between revetments, as they are built on 'lished dock lines at the expense of the nd' owners as required by city ordinance. No general project for the expenditure of funds has been definitely adopted, but it seems to have been agreed that the improvement should extend upstream between banks revetted, as previously described, as far as the Lake Erie and Western Railroad bridge. A map of this portion of Trail Creek is given opposite page 2270, Report of the Chief of Engineers for 1882.

In recent years the project has been purely one of maintenance, and has resulted in creating, by dredging, a channel 9,159 feet long between revetments from 100 to 175 feet apart, except at the turning basins, where the width is about 350 feet. The upper limit of this improved channel is 100 feet above the upper turning basin in the map above mentioned.

The total expenditure to June 30, 1900, was $435,715.52, at which date the channel depths were 13 feet and more from the harbor entrance to the railroad bridge, a distance of about 4,700 feet, above which point there was 12 feet available.

Operations during the past year were confined to dredging for maintenance. This work was done between May 17 and June 11, and resulted in a channel 100 feet wide and 18 feet deep through the shoal at the harbor entrance, and in improving the upper reaches so as to afford a channnel of navigable width and 15 feet depth between the piers, thence 14 feet deep to the Michigan Central Railroad bridge, and 13 feet from that point to the first bend above the Sixth Street Bridge. Above this latter bridge the channel is 12 feet deep to lower end of the upper basin.

The harbor structures aggregate 3,563 feet in length, of which a length of 735 feet of old cast pier and 1,544 feet of west pier require sheet piling and new superstructure.

Provision should be made for maintaining the required depth of channel by dredging.

July 1, 1900, balance unexpended	$3,543.45
June 30, 1901, amount expended during fiscal year	2,136.73
July 1, 1901, balance unexpended	1,406.72
July 1, 1901, outstanding liabilities	36.67
July 1, 1901, balance available	1,370.05
July 1, 1901, amount covered by uncompleted contracts	198.90
Amount that can be profitably expended in fiscal year ending June 30, 1903, for maintenance of improvement, in addition to the balance available July 1, 1901	68,000.00

Submitted in compliance with requirements of sundry civil act of June 4, 1897, and of section 7 of the river and harbor act of 1899.

The outer harbor.—Michigan City being at the southern end of the lake, is exposed to northerly storms, especially those from west of north, with a clear sweep of practically the entire length of the lake, or, roughly speaking, about 250 miles. As a result, there arose a demand for a harbor of refuge in this vicinity, which was answered in 1870 by the adoption of a project for the creation of an outer harbor at this place which was to consist of an outer basin east of the entrance to the inner harbor; in 1882 this project was extended to include the construction of an exterior breakwater northwest of the entrance. The piers and breakwaters covering the outer basin were completed in 1885 and have a total length of 3,141 feet, viz, a pile pier 1,225 feet long, extending in a northerly direction from the shore and closing the basin on the east; a crib breakwater 1,411 feet long, extending westward from the lake end of the pile pier and closing the basin on the north, and a crib pier, 505 feet long, extending northward from the west end of the crib breakwater. The exterior breakwater contemplated by the project of 1882 was to have a total length of 2,000 feet, but a length of only 700 feet has been built.

The river and harbor act of March 3, 1899, authorized the adoption of the project of the Board of Engineers as printed in the Annual Report of the Chief of Engineers for 1897, pages 2899 to 2904, inclusive, and provided for the completion of the work under the continuing-contract system. This project requires the extension of the breakwater pier by 600 feet, the construction of a new detached breakwater 1,500 feet long, and the removal of the present detached breakwater. Operations are in progress under a contract for the completion of all the work contemplated in the project except one crib 100 feet long in the new detached breakwater. Funds are available for the completion of the contract.

To June 30, 1900, there had been expended $758,033.84, all of which, with the exception of $2,050.39, has gone into work under the projects of 1870 and 1882, with the result that the work above described had been finished; $2,050.39 had been spent in preliminary operations under the project of 1899. The amount expended for maintenance is not known.

During the past year $9,583.59 was expended in work under the new project. Progress under this contract has been unsatisfactory. Dredging upon the site of four cribs has been completed, and the foundation piles for three of them driven, four piles for the foundation of the fourth crib are in place, and three cribs partly built, and 716.19 cords of stone has been placed in the foundation of the detached breakwater.

A map showing this harbor is found opposite page 2904, report of the Chief of Engineers for 1897.

Entrances and clearances.

Calendar year.	Number.	Tonnage.	Calendar year.	Number.	Tonnage.
1888	1,153	208,617	1895	343	91,016
1889	795	169,193	1896	437	106,543
1890	921	172,817	1897	492	118,187
1891	837	168,654	1898	478	127,237
1892	1,391	443,055	1899	601	144,880
1893	1,577	569,863	1900	412	102,323
1894	389	119,929			

Maximum draft, 13 feet in inner harbor.

NOTE.—No record is kept of traffic between Michigan City and Chicago.

July 1, 1900, balance unexpended $278,841.16
June 30, 1901, amount expended during fiscal year 9,583.59

July 1, 1901, balance unexpended 269,257.57
July 1, 1901, outstanding liabilities 236.25

July 1, 1901, balance available 269,021.32

July 1, 1901, amount covered by uncompleted contracts 252,356.80

Amount that can be profitably expended in fiscal year ending June 30, 1903, for maintenance of improvement, in addition to the balance available July 1, 1901................................. 15,000.00
Submitted in compliance with requirements of sundry civil act of June 4, 1897, and of section 7 of the river and harbor act of 1899.

(See Appendix N N 1.)

2. St. Joseph Harbor, Michigan.—This harbor is formed by the junction of the St. Joseph and Pawpaw rivers and extends along the city front of St. Joseph with a natural width of 800 feet, ultimately to be reduced to 300 feet when wharves are fully built upon the approved harbor lines. It has been under improvement by the United States since 1836, previous to which time there was a narrow and crooked channel with depths which varied from 3 to 7 feet.

The present project was adopted in 1866 and amended in 1874, 1875, 1880, 1892, and 1899. As last amended and adopted in the river and harbor act of March 3, 1899, the project provides for an entrance channel 18 feet deep and for an interior channel 18 feet deep and 150 feet wide along the city front of St. Joseph, while the Benton Harbor Canal and the turning basin at the mouth of the St. Joseph River are to be dredged to 15 feet. The north pier is to be extended to the 20-foot contour, a distance of 1,000 feet, and the south pier, upon a line parallel to the north pier, 1,800 feet to the 18-foot contour. The harbor width will be 270 feet. This project is printed in full in the report of the Chief of Engineers for 1898, page 2498. Estimated cost of completion of the revised project of 1899 was $380,000.

The sum of $512,522.95 had been expended up to June 30, 1900, resulting in producing and maintaining a channel whose width at the entrance was 270 feet, protected by a north pier and revetment 2,017 feet long and a south pier and revetment 819 feet long. The Benton Harbor Canal, about 1 mile long, leading from the upper part of the harbor to the town of Benton Harbor, and the harbor, with its entrance, had been repeatedly dredged so as to produce a practicable channel 13.5 feet deep. The amount expended for maintenance can not be stated with precision.

The river and harbor act of March 3, 1899, placed the work of completing the amended project of 1899 under the continuing-contract system. Contracts have been made for all the work involved, and operations are now in progress.

During the past fiscal year $12,760.02 was expended in the repair under contract of a portion of the south pier.

Soundings made May 3–7 showed that the maximum draft that could be carried to the Pere Marquette Railroad bridge was 14 feet, while above the bridge only 11.5 feet could be carried.

Dredging under contract to secure the projected depth and width of channel was begun June 14.

The last published map of the harbor is contained in House Doc. No. 307, Fifty-fifth Congress, second session, and shows the present approved project.

All funds necessary for the completion of the project have been appropriated.

Entrances and clearances.

Calendar year.	Vessels entered. Number.	Vessels entered. Tonnage.	Vessels cleared. Number.	Vessels cleared. Tonnage.
1890	948	131,607	946	131,395
1891	742	215,334	743	215,591
1892	1,726	707,285	1,727	707,785
1893	1,576	1,125,063	1,575	1,125,988
1894	1,100	900,000	1,100	900,000
1895	779	827,384	727	827,837
1896	835	439,031	833	435,033
1897	842	385,915	849	848,040
1898	948	1,216,567	943	1,114,560
1899	858	446,178	851	430,411
1900	940	458,543	934	442,419

Maximum draft, 17 feet to railroad bridge, 11.5 feet throughout.

The Benton Transit Company, doing a general shipping business between this harbor and Chicago, was established during the year.

July 1, 1900, balance unexpended	$284,539.25
Amount appropriated by sundry civil act approved March 3, 1901	38,000.00
	322,539.25
June 30, 1901, amount expended during fiscal year	12,760.02
July 1, 1901, balance unexpended	309,779.23
July 1, 1901, outstanding liabilities	82.50
July 1, 1901, balance available	309,696.73
July 1, 1901, amount covered by uncompleted contracts	288,554.38
Amount that can be profitably expended in fiscal year ending June 30, 1903, for maintenance of improvement, in addition to the balance available July 1, 1901. Submitted in compliance with requirements of sundry civil act of June 4, 1897, and of section 7 of the river and harbor act of 1899.	24,000.00

(See Appendix N N 2.)

3. *St. Joseph River, Michigan.*—This is a crooked stream, obstructed by numerous shoals, with depth in channel crossings of from 24 to 30 inches. The intervening pools are generally from 4 to 8 feet deep. The part under improvement is from the mouth, at St. Joseph, to Berrien Springs, a distance of about 25 miles by river. The improvement of this section to make a low-water channel 3 feet deep has been in progress since 1889, and consists in removing snags and logs and closing secondary channels, or concentrating the flow at other critical points by dams of brush, logs, and stone.

The amount expended to June 30, 1900, was $5,490.11, as a result of which many of the worst places of the stream had been improved to the required extent.

There were no operations in progress during the year, on account of the exhaustion of funds.

The cost of completing an improvement of this character depends entirely on how long the work is to be kept up and the annual cost of doing it. In the present case the average annual expenditure has been $500, and experience shows that it is too little to accomplish what is required for making and maintaining the limited improvement.

Commercial statistics for St. Joseph River, Michigan, calendar year ending December 31, 1900.—The steamers *May Graham* and *Tourist* carried 25,000 passengers and 2,419 tons of miscellaneous freight between St. Joseph and Berrien Springs. The boats draw 34 and 30 inches, respectively.

July 1, 1900, balance unexpended	$9.89
June 30, 1901, amount expended during fiscal year	.80
July 1, 1901, balance unexpended	9.09
Amount that can be profitably expended in fiscal year ending June 30, 1903, for maintenance of improvement, in addition to the balance unexpended July 1, 1901. Submitted in compliance with requirements of sundry civil act of June 4, 1897, and of section 7 of the river and harbor act of 1899.	700.00

(See Appendix N N 3.)

4. *South Haven Harbor, Michigan.*—This harbor is situated at the mouth of Black River. Improvements were begun in 1867, at which time there existed a channel 7 feet deep and 85 feet wide between slab piers. These piers had been built by residents of the vicinity at a

cost of about $18,000. The banks of the river for 500 feet on each side had a rough protection of close piling.

The existing project is that of 1866 as modified in 1869, 1872, and 1888, and provides for constructing parallel piers and revetments 177 feet apart at the mouth of Black River, with the object of procuring a channel 12 feet deep, and to extend the navigable channel one-half mile up Black River to the highway bridge by dredging.

The total expenditure to June 30, 1900, was $264,978.20. A large part of this amount had been applied to maintenance of improvement, but it is impossible definitely to state the exact sum. The work is largely one of maintenance by dredging and by repairs of existing structures.

Operations during the year consisted in completion of two cribs, each 100 by 24 by 16¼ feet, with superstructure 6 feet high, and in replacing the superstructure of the north pier for a length of 254 feet immediately adjoining the above new work, all this work being done under formal contract at a cost of $25,275.77.

This completes all new construction authorized by the existing project, but the navigable depth called for by that project can not be maintained except by considerable annual dredging until further extensions of 100 and 175 feet are made to the north and the south piers, respectively.

The actual depths available for navigation on April 16–19, 1901, when the last survey was made, were 15 feet outside of and at the ends of the piers, 11.5 feet between the piers and in the river, except for a short distance in the river, where available depth was but 10.4 feet.

The most recently published map of this harbor accompanies House Doc. No. 279, Fifty-fourth Congress, second session.

Entrances and clearances.

Calendar year.	Number.	Tonnage.	Calendar year.	Number	Tonnage.
1889 (estimated)	1,080		1895	3,222	238,060
1890	2,246	128,880	1896	1,218	343,016
1891	2,994	201,380	1897	1,256	351,000
1892	3,060	212,160	1898	771	322,620
1893	3,822	251,780	1899	682	276,117
1894	3,246	228,246	1900	1,231	407,289

Maximum draft, 10.4 feet.

During the past spring the Dunkley Line, operating between South Haven and Chicago and doing a daily passenger and freight business, was established.

July 1, 1900, balance unexpended	$32,021.80
Amount allotted from appropriation contained in emergency river and harbor act approved June 6, 1900	1,000.00
	33,021.80
June 30, 1901, amount expended during fiscal year	30,885.10
July 1, 1901, balance unexpended	2,136.70
July 1, 1901, amount covered by uncompleted contracts	2,000.00
Amount that can be profitably expended in fiscal year ending June 30, 1903, for maintenance of improvement, in addition to the balance unexpended July 1, 1901. Submitted in compliance with requirements of sundry civil act of June 4, 1897, and of section 7 of the river and harbor act of 1899.	12,000.00

(See Appendix N N 4.)

5. Saugatuck Harbor, Michigan.—Before the work of improvement was begun by the United States in 1869, this harbor, which is at the mouth of the Kalamazoo River, had been improved by local enterprise by the construction of slab piers 200 feet apart, the north pier being 500 feet long and the south pier 1,575 feet. The channel depth varied from 5 to 7 feet.

The present project was adopted in 1867 and amended in 1869, 1875, and 1882.

The original project of 1867, modified in 1869 and 1875, provided for the construction of piers and revetments 200 feet apart in extension of the existing slab piers, and for dredging a 12-foot channel between them. In 1882 this project was modified to the effect that "future appropriations should be applied merely to maintaining the existing condition of the improvement." The practicable depth at that time was 8 feet. Estimated cost was $175,699.45.

To June 30, 1900, there had been expended upon this harbor $173,871.31. At present there is a north pier 715 feet long, which is entirely unserviceable; separated from the pier by a long stretch of unprotected bank there is a north revetment, partly destroyed and partly covered by sand, and a south pier 3,863 feet long, of which 1,300 feet is in fair condition, while the remainder is ruined. Frequent dredging has been required for maintenance of an 8-foot channel, which rapidly deteriorates. Appropriations since 1882 have been too small to keep the piers in proper repair.

The port of shipment pertaining to this harbor is Saugatuck, 3 miles above the entrance from Lake Michigan, and the natural difficulties of making and maintaining a reliable channel upon the present line led to an alternative project, printed in the report of the Chief of Engineers for 1896, pages 2741 to 2743. This project was adopted by the river and harbor act of June 3, 1896. It is further described in the report upon Kalamazoo River. Until this latter project is completed, funds will be required annually for maintaining the old harbor of Saugatuck. (See Kalamazoo River, below).

The amount expended for maintenance can not be stated, but all funds appropriated since 1882 have been applied to that purpose.

During the past fiscal year, $2,955.59 was expended, under contract, for dredging, $2,500 of this amount being an allotment from the emergency river and harbor act of June 6, 1900. The result was an 8-foot channel, which, as usual, has since greatly deteriorated, so that on May 1, when the harbor was surveyed, only 2.3 feet could be carried over the entrance bar. At the close of the year dredging operations were once more in progress.

For last published map of this harbor see House Document No. 192, Fifty-fourth Congress, first session.

Entrances and clearances.

Calendar year.	Number.	Tonnage.	Calendar year.	Number.	Tonnage.
1888	262	132,400	1895	1,256	134,948
1889	314	76,300	1896	848	153,190
1890	178	42,000	1897	586	70,860
1891	492	120,000	1898	1,329	128,325
1892	(a)	(a)	1899	1,190	88,236
1893	626	162,682	1900	1,850	120,946
1894	862	106,000			

a Not stated.

Maximum draft, 5 feet.

RIVER AND HARBOR IMPROVEMENTS. 541

July 1, 1900, balance unexpended	$567.69
Amount allotted from appropriation contained in emergency river and harbor act approved June 6, 1900	7,500.00
	8,067.69
June 30, 1901, amount expended during fiscal year	2,955.59
July 1, 1901, balance unexpended	5,112.10
July 1, 1901, outstanding liabilities	103.00
July 1, 1901, balance available	5,009.10
July 1, 1901, amount covered by uncompleted contracts	5,000.00

{ Amount that can be profitably expended in fiscal year ending June 30, 1903, for maintenance of improvement, in addition to the balance available July 1, 1901 .... 15,000.00
Submitted in compliance with requirements of sundry civil act of June 4, 1897, and of section 7 of the river and harbor act of 1899. }

(See Appendix N N 5.)

6. *Kalamazoo River, Michigan.*—The portion of the river which it is proposed to improve extends from the mouth to Saugatuck, a distance of a little over 3 miles. No work has yet been done, and the present is the original condition and is described in the report upon Saugatuck Harbor immediately preceding.

The existing project is contained in the report of the Chief of Engineers for 1896, page 2740, and was adopted by the river and harbor act of June 3, 1896. It provides for creating a channel of 12 feet depth and navigable width by dredging the river for a distance of 1¾ miles below Saugatuck and thence making a new cut from the river to the lake, entering the latter about 3,700 feet above the present mouth at the Saugatuck piers.

The original estimate for the work was $150,000, but authority was granted on May 31, 1900, to increase this to $250,000.

In all $15,000 has been appropriated, but as the cut is the principal feature of the work it would be unwise to begin work until sufficient funds are available to insure its permanence.

July 1, 1900, balance unexpended	$14,980.78
June 30, 1901, amount expended during fiscal year	.27
July 1, 1901, balance unexpended	14,980.51

{ Amount (estimated) required for completion of existing project 235,000.00
Amount that can be profitably expended in fiscal year ending June 30, 1903, in addition to the balance unexpended July 1, 1901 .... 150,000.00
Submitted in compliance with requirements of sundry civil act of June 4, 1897. }

(See Appendix N N 6.

7. *Holland (Black Lake) Harbor, Michigan.*—When improvement of this harbor was begun in August, 1867, by the United States, there existed a narrow channel 5¼ feet deep between piers built of brush and of cribs of irregular size and shape. These piers had been built by the harbor commissioners of the adjoining town of Holland. From 1867 to 1880 there were built by the United States piers and revetments aggregating 1,854 feet on the north side and 1,691 feet on the south side. Since the latter date no additions have been made to these structures, which were designed to create a channel 12 feet deep, varying in width from 160 feet inside to 215 feet outside.

The present project was adopted in 1867 and amended in 1873, 1879, 1884, and 1892. As further amended by the adoption in the river and harbor act of March 3, 1899, of the modified project printed in the report of the Chief of Engineers for 1897, page 2950, the existing project provides for securing and maintaining a navigable channel 16 feet deep below the mean low-water level of Lake Michigan, protected by piers and revetments 160 to 215 feet apart. Estimated cost for completion was $240,000.

Up to close of the fiscal year ending June 30, 1900, a total expenditure of $338,181.66 had been made. As a result the piers and revetments above mentioned were completed. Owing to insufficient development of piers the natural depth at entrance is only 7 to 8 feet, and a large part of this total has necessarily been expended upon dredging to maintain temporarily a depth of 13 feet. The total amount expended for dredging and for repairs for maintenance of piers can not be ascertained.

Operations during the past year were confined to dredging for maintenance. Under formal contract, the removal of 20,702 cubic yards resulted in a channel of navigable width from Lake Michigan to Black Lake, with a minimum depth of 13 feet.

Entrances and clearances.

Calendar year.	Number.	Tonnage.	Calendar year.	Number.	Tonnage.
1889	1,087	80,790	1895	809	210,299
1890	(a)	(a)	1896	408	269,182
1891	2,676	178,300	1897	456	153,852
1892	2,800	200,000	1898	538	163,119
1893	2,060	315,150	1899	527	(a)
1894	1,816	159,657	1900	862	354,718

a Not stated.

Maximum draft, 13 feet.

During the year the Pere Marquette Railroad Company established a daily line of steamers between Holland and Milwaukee to do a combined freight and passenger business. Fifteen thousand passengers were carried the first season.

July 1, 1900, balance unexpended	$3,932.46
Amount allotted from appropriation contained in emergency river and harbor act approved June 6, 1900	1,000.00
	4,932.46
June 30, 1901, amount expended during fiscal year	4,205.99
July 1, 1901, balance unexpended	726.47
July 1, 1901, outstanding liabilities	56.33
July 1, 1901, balance available	670.14
July 1, 1901, amount covered by uncompleted contracts	372.63
Amount (estimated) required for completion of existing project	202,500.00
Amount that can be profitably expended in fiscal year ending June 30, 1903, for works of improvement and for maintenance, in addition to the balance available July 1, 1901	73,000.00

Submitted in compliance with requirements of sundry civil act of June 4, 1897, and of section 7 of the river and harbor act of 1899.

(See Appendix N N 7.)

8. *Grand Haven Harbor, Michigan.*—This harbor is at the mouth of Grand River, the largest river in the State of Michigan. Before

any work had been done, the natural depth at the mouth of the river varied from 9 to 12 feet, with greater depths in the inner reaches.

In 1857 the Detroit and Milwaukee Railroad Company (Grand Trunk), whose western terminus is at the town of Grand Haven, built a pile pier 3,185 feet long upon the south side of the entrance, and also revetted, by means of close piles, portions of the bank upon the north side of the river. In 1866, when work by the United States was begun, the pile pier had been partly destroyed by fire and by storms. The available depth was 13 feet.

The present project was adopted in 1866, amended in 1868, 1880, 1890, and 1892. It provides for the construction of parallel piers and revetments 400 feet apart, with the object of creating an entrance channel 18 feet deep. Estimated cost was $804,366.15.

To June 30, 1900, $750,813.88 was expended in the construction and maintenance of 3,538 linear feet of north pier and 5,774 linear feet of south pier, while the channel depth was maintained by dredging. The total cost of maintenance can not be stated.

The expenditures during the past year were for minor repairs of the south pier and for the necessary care and maintenance of public plant now stored in this harbor.

The greatest draft that can be carried into this harbor is 17 feet.

The approved project provides for an extension of 100 feet to the south pier and 150 feet to the north pier, and for expedients for restraining the drift of sands over the piers and revetments.

The latest map of this harbor is found in the report of the Chief of Engineers for 1890.

Entrances and clearances.

Calendar year.	Number.	Tonnage.	Calendar year.	Number.	Tonnage.
1888	1,508	1,405,800	1895	574	482,822
1889	1,110	649,370	1896	883	727,209
1890	1,172	834,089	1897	1,151	1,018,805
1891	819	616,422	1898	934	874,312
1892	815	693,835	1899	1,250	1,090,325
1893	761	613,425	1900	1,151	1,132,861
1894	641	504,609			

Maximum draft, 17 feet.

During the year the Barry Line of steamers, with terminal at Chicago, and doing a daily passenger and freight business, was established.

July 1, 1900, balance unexpended	$18,552.27
June 30, 1901, amount expended during fiscal year	1,522.41
July 1, 1901, balance unexpended	17,029.86
July 1, 1901, outstanding liabilities	195.01
July 1, 1901, balance available	16,834.85
July 1, 1901, amount covered by uncompleted contracts	2,000.00
Amount (estimated) required for completion of existing project	35,000.00
Amount that can be profitably expended in fiscal year ending June 30, 1903, for works of improvement and for maintenance, in addition to the balance available July 1, 1901	40,000.00

Submitted in compliance with requirements of sundry civil act of June 4, 1897, and of section 7 of the river and harbor act of 1899.

(See Appendix N N 8.)

9. *Grand River, Michigan.*—Before any work of improvement was done upon this stream the depth in the crossings over some of the bars did not exceed 2 feet.

Between 1881 and 1886 the sum of $50,000 was expended in securing, by dredging, narrow channels through these bars with a depth of about 4 feet. No further work was done until 1896, but even then, at the expiration of over ten years, traces of the dredged cuts were still apparent.

The present project, upon which work was begun in May, 1897, was adopted by the river and harbor act of June 3, 1896, and is based upon a report upon examination and survey reprinted in report of the Chief of Engineers for 1892, pages 2369 to 2395. The project contemplates dredging a channel a distance of 38 miles, from Grand Haven to Grand Rapids, with a depth of 10 feet and a width of 100 feet. The project also proposes the use of contraction works wherever necessary to increase the effect of the dredging or to render it more permanent. Estimated cost was $670,500.

Up to June 30, 1900, there had been expended upon this project $73,513.12, in dredging 311,254 cubic yards of material and in building 14,073 linear feet of longitudinal training walls. The maximum available depths varied from 2.6 to 5 feet at extreme low water.

During the past year $38,150.69 has been expended in continuing the dredging within the ultimate limits of the proposed channel and the construction of longitudinal training walls. The dredged cut is 30 feet wide at the bottom and 6 feet deep at low water; 72,037.35 cubic yards of material was dredged and 40,468 linear feet of training wall built, the whole of the latter being between the first and tenth miles below Grand Rapids and on the Lamont and Deer Creek bars in the seventeenth and nineteenth miles. On June 30, 1901, the maximum available depths over the shoalest portions of the stream at extreme low water varied from 3 to 5.5 feet, and there were but 6 crossings with depths less than 4 feet.

The project, from its nature, is one of constant repair and maintenance.

Entrances and clearances.

Calendar year.	Number.	Tonnage.
1896	282	46,750
1897	77	30,390
1898	76	86,793
1899	323	64,242
1900	264	59,928

The Grand River Transportation Company was established during the year, operating two steamers between Grand Rapids and Grand Haven, Mich., giving a daily service, freight and passenger.

July 1, 1900, balance unexpended	$51,486.88
June 30, 1901, amount expended during fiscal year	38,150.69
July 1, 1901, balance unexpended	13,336.19
July 1, 1901, outstanding liabilities	1,057.47
July 1, 1901, balance available	12,278.72

{ Amount (estimated) required for completion of existing project.........$545,500.00
Amount that can be profitably expended in fiscal year ending June 30,
  1903, in addition to the balance available July 1, 1901................ 125,000.00
Submitted in compliance with requirements of sundry civil act of June
  4, 1897.

(See Appendix N N 9.)

10. *Muskegon Harbor, Michigan.*—This harbor is the outlet of Muskegon River, one of the largest in Michigan, which before emptying into Lake Michigan expands into Muskegon Lake. The channel between the lakes in 1867, before operations were begun by the United States, was 3,000 feet long and about 12 feet deep except at the entrance, where the depth was 7 feet and the channel fluctuating. By private enterprise the entrance had been protected by converging slab piers 1,450 feet long on the north side and 2,070 feet long on the south side, with a width between them varying from 240 feet inside to 175 feet at the entrance.

The present project was adopted in 1866 and amended in 1869, 1873, 1881, 1884, 1890, and 1892. In its final form it provides for a through channel 15 feet deep, 300 feet wide at the entrance, and 180 feet wide at the shore line, protected by piers and revetments. Estimated cost, amended in 1899 was $596,600.

To June 30, 1900, $479,468.70 was expended in securing a channel whose north pier was 2,579 feet long and south pier 1,989 feet long, with a natural depth of not over 13 feet. The piers and revetments had been maintained and the depth increased by periodical dredging. The exact sum expended on maintenance can not be ascertained.

During the past year $14,299.84 was expended under contracts for dredging and for pier extension, and under an open-market agreement for emergency dredging. Under the contract for dredging, completed September 1, a through channel of 15 feet draft was created, which, having deteriorated, was again restored under an emergency agreement for the necessary work. Under the contract for pier extension two cribs have been sunk in place in the north pier and their superstructure partly completed. On June 17 the new end crib of the north pier was damaged by the steamer *State of Michigan*. Under the contract the cost of repairs will fall upon the contractor. The crib for the south pier is completed, but not yet in place.

The latest map of the harbor is found in House Doc. No. 104, Fifty-sixth Congress, second session.

Entrances and clearances.

Calendar year.	Number.	Tonnage.	Calendar year.	Number.	Tonnage.
1888	2,688	....	1895	887	441,289
1889	4,626	884,869	1896	931	562,757
1890	3,786	649,540	1897	1,244	725,514
1891	2,886	704,046	1898	1,508	1,165,802
1892	4,174	740,021	1899	1,545	1,284,193
1893	2,482	834,049	1900	1,366	904,636
1894	1,423	793,184			

Maximum draft, 15 feet.

During the year the Barry Line of steamers, doing a daily freight and passenger business between Muskegon and Chicago, was established.

July 1, 1900, balance unexpended	$44,531.30
Amount allotted from appropriation contained in emergency river and harbor act approved June 6, 1900	2,500.00
	47,031.30
June 30, 1901, amount expended during fiscal year	14,299.84
July 1, 1901, balance unexpended	32,731.46
July 1, 1901 outstanding liabilities	60.25
July 1, 1901, balance available	32,671.21
July 1, 1901, amount covered by uncompleted contracts	30,904.48
Amount (estimated) required for completion of existing project	72,600.00
Amount that can be profitably expended in fiscal year ending June 30, 1903, for works of improvement and for maintenance, in addition to the balance available July 1, 1901	75,000.00
Submitted in compliance with requirements of sundry civil act of June 4, 1897, and of section 7 of the river and harbor act of 1899.	

(See Appendix N N 10.)

11. *White Lake Harbor, Michigan.*—When the present project was adopted the natural outlet of White Lake, about 3,550 feet north of the present entrance, afforded a channel 5 feet deep and 125 feet wide between slab piers built by local enterprise.

The approved project provided for the abandonment of the old outlet and the creation of a new one, 12 feet deep and 200 feet wide between piers and revetments. This project was adopted in 1866, amended in 1873, 1884, and 1892, the present amended estimated cost being $353,550.

The total expenditure to June 30, 1900, was $293,217.77, and resulted in the construction of a north pier 1,515 feet long, and a south pier 1,854 feet long, with a 10-foot channel between them. Periodical dredging is required to maintain a 12-foot channel.

During the past fiscal year the north pier has been extended 200 feet and the south pier 100 feet, while the old end crib of the south pier was also repaired, all work being done under formal contract.

Dredging to restore the proper depth was also done under contract. The excavation of 5,802 cubic yards restored a straight channel, with depth of not less than 12.5 feet, which has since materially improved through natural causes. The available depth is now 15 feet outside, 16 feet at end of piers, and 12.7 feet inside.

The approved project provides for additional extensions of 50 feet to the north pier and 100 feet to the south pier, but to insure a 12-foot navigation these piers will need still further extensions.

The last published map of this locality is contained in the report of the Chief of Engineers for 1884.

Entrances and clearances.

Calendar year.	Number.	Tonnage.	Calendar year.	Number.	Tonnage.
1888	1,408	147,142	1895	281	34,574
1889	732		1896	245	27,962
1890	579	62,276	1897	247	33,409
1891	405	47,135	1898	175	16,415
1892	392	58,950	1899		
1893	260	1,052,026	1900		
1894	195	18,115			

Maximum draft, 12.7 feet.

No data relative to commercial statistics for calendar year ending December 31, 1900, could be obtained.

RIVER AND HARBOR IMPROVEMENTS. 547

July 1, 1900, balance unexpended	$31,332.23
June 30, 1901, amount expended during fiscal year	30,717.94
July 1, 1901, balance unexpended	614.29
July 1, 1901, outstanding liabilities	482.68
July 1, 1901, balance available	131.61
Amount (estimated) required for completion of existing project	29,000.00
Amount that can be profitably expended in fiscal year ending June 30, 1903, for works of improvement and for maintenance, in addition to the balance available July 1, 1901	17,500.00
Submitted in compliance with requirements of sundry civil act of June 4, 1897, and of section 7 of the river and harbor act of 1899.	

(See Appendix N N 11.)

12. Pentwater Harbor, Michigan.—Before work was begun at this harbor by the United States there existed an irregular channel 4 feet deep and 75 feet wide between slab piers built by local enterprise.

The existing project, adopted in 1867 and amended in 1873, 1884, and 1892, provides for widening the old entrance to 150 feet and to deepen it to 12 feet, the sides being protected by piers and revetments. Estimated cost was $327,713.40.

Up to June 30, 1900, there had been expended $272,126.23. The result was a channel 150 feet wide whose natural depth is from 9 to 10 feet, protected by piers and revetments 2,226 feet long on north side and 2,112 feet long on south side. This channel requires periodical dredging to deepen it to 12 feet. A considerable sum had been expended upon maintenance by repair of piers and by dredging, but its exact amount can not be stated.

Owing to lack of funds no work was done at this harbor during the past fiscal year. Soundings made May 11-13, 1901, showed the following minimum depths: 14 feet outside, 11.8 feet inside, the stage at that time being —0.9 feet.

The approved project contemplates an extension of 200 feet to the south pier.

The last published map of this locality is found in the report of the Chief of Engineers for 1884.

Entrances and clearances.

Calendar year.	Number.	Tonnage.	Calendar year.	Number.	Tonnage.
1888	300	45,000	1895	500	
1889	(a)	(a)	1896	(a)	(a)
1890	27	2,559	1897	(a)	(a)
1891	1,140	71,260	1898	1,208	108,253
1892	(a)	(a)	1899	(a)	(a)
1893	116		1900	(a)	81,721
1894	60				

a Not stated.

Maximum draft, 11.8 feet.

July 1, 1900, balance unexpended	$1,693.77
June 30, 1901, amount expended during fiscal year	342.17
July 1, 1901, balance unexpended	1,351.60
July 1, 1901, outstanding liabilities	28.08
July 1, 1901, balance available	1,323.52
Amount (estimated) required for completion of existing project	53,893.40
Amount that can be profitably expended in fiscal year ending June 30, 1903, for works of improvement and for maintenance, in addition to the balance available July 1, 1901	32,000.00
Submitted in compliance with requirements of sundry civil act of June 4, 1897, and of section 7 of the river and harbor act of 1899.	

(See Appendix N N 12.)

13. Ludington Harbor, Michigan.—This harbor is the outlet of Pere Marquette River, which expands into Pere Marquette Lake before emptying into Lake Michigan. In 1867, before improvement was begun by the United States, the outlet from Pere Marquette Lake to Lake Michigan had a length of 830 feet protected by divergent slab piers. The entering depth was about 7 feet.

The present project was adopted in 1867 and modified in 1885, 1889, 1890, and 1899. In its final form, as adopted by the river and harbor act of March 3, 1899, it provides for a through channel 200 to 250 feet wide and 18 feet deep, protected by the requisite piers and revetments. Estimated amount required to complete revised project was $210,000.

To June 30, 1900, $388,478.02 had been expended in producing a channel whose natural depth was 13 feet, protected by a north pier 1,452 feet long and by a south pier 2,381 feet long. By occasional dredging a depth of 17 to 18 feet is easily maintained. The sum expended upon maintenance can not be stated.

During the past year $17,578.79 was expended under contract in force at beginning of fiscal year for the repair of 444 linear feet of the north pier and 303 linear feet of the south pier. Work was completed November 24, 1900, and resulted in a thorough renewal of this part of the work. A length of 30 feet of the inner end of the south pier was also strengthened by piling.

Soundings made May 14–15 showed that the shoal at the end of the north pier had narrowed the channel, although the full depth of 18 feet was still available. At the close of the year the widening of the channel under contract had almost been completed.

The latest map of this harbor is published in House Doc. No. 273, Fifty-fourth Congress, second session.

Entrances and clearances.

Calendar year.	Number.	Tonnage.	Calendar year.	Number.	Tonnage.
1888	1,778	277,074	1895	1,556	594,124
1889	1,759	....	1896	1,996	952,469
1890	2,270	461,997	1897	2,063	2,944,425
1891	2,420	610,057	1898	2,493	2,014,019
1892	1,969	538,568	1899	2,587	2,254,495
1893	979	211,438	1900	2,637	2,526,244
1894	1,466	426,599			

Maximum draft, 18 feet.

July 1, 1900, balance unexpended	$24,956.08
June 30, 1901, amount expended during fiscal year	17,578.79
July 1, 1901, balance unexpended	7,377.29
July 1, 1901, outstanding liabilities	107.92
July 1, 1901, balance available	7,269.37
July 1, 1901, amount covered by uncompleted contracts	3,000.00
Amount (estimated) required for completion of existing project	185,000.00
Amount that can be profitably expended in fiscal year ending June 30, 1903, for works of improvement and for maintenance, in addition to the balance available July 1, 1901	75,000.00

Submitted in compliance with requirements of sundry civil act of June 4, 1897, and of section 7 of the river and harbor act of 1899.

(See Appendix N N 13.)

14. *Manistee Harbor, Michigan.*—In 1866, previous to the beginning of work by the United States, the entrance to this harbor was improved by slab piers 100 to 150 feet apart built by local enterprise, a navigable depth of 7 to 8 feet being thereby maintained.

The present project was adopted in 1867 and amended in 1871, 1873, 1875, 1884, 1890, and 1892, and provides for a channel of navigable width with a depth of 15 feet, extending from Lake Michigan to Manistee Lake, protected by piers and revetments at the entrance.

Up to June 30, 1900, there had been expended $369,064.85, resulting in a channel protected by piers and revetments 2,906 feet long on the north side and 1,300 feet long on the south side, the width between piers varying from 160 feet inside to 185 feet at the outer end of south pier, which is about 400 feet shorter than the north pier. The depth is maintained by periodical dredging, the total expended for this purpose and for maintaining the piers not being accurately known.

During the fiscal year ending June 30, 1901, $15,096.92 was expended in extending the south pier 100 feet and in renewing the superstructure in parts of both piers.

The maximum draft that can be carried into this harbor is shown by the survey of May 20-24, 1901, to be 14.3 feet at a stage of − 0.8 feet. This occurs in the inner part of the channel, there being 21 feet at the outer end of the north pier.

To complete the project an extension of the south pier of 250 feet is required.

The last published map of this locality is found in the report of the Chief of Engineers for 1890.

Entrances and clearances.

Calendar year.	Number.	Tonnage.	Calendar year.	Number.	Tonnage.
1888	3,595	966,221	1895	3,054	980,645
1889	3,524	945,329	1896	2,855	643,048
1890	3,691	975,049	1897	2,371	666,000
1891	3,617	1,079,818	1898	1,856	528,752
1892	4,044	1,028,629	1899	2,313	698,662
1893	2,831	959,550	1900	2,049	625,630
1894	3,054	956,463			

Maximum draft, 14.3 feet.

July 1, 1900, balance unexpended	$25,935.15
June 30, 1901, amount expended during fiscal year	16,759.45
July 1, 1901, balance unexpended	9,175.70
July 1, 1901, outstanding liabilities	117.08
July 1, 1901, balance available	9,058.62
July 1, 1901, amount covered by uncompleted contracts	3,000.00
Amount (estimated) required for completion of existing project	33,000.00
Amount that can be profitably expended in fiscal year ending June 30, 1903, for works of improvement and for maintenance, in addition to the balance available July 1, 1901	42,000.00

Submitted in compliance with requirements of sundry civil act of June 4, 1897, and of section 7 of the river and harbor act of 1899.

(See Appendix N N 14.)

15. *Harbor of refuge at Portage Lake, Manistee County, Mich.*—In 1879, when work was begun by the United States, there was a channel 4 feet deep and 130 feet wide between slab piers built by local enterprise.

The approved project, adopted in 1879 and amended in 1881 and 1890, contemplates the construction of a harbor of refuge with an entrance from Lake Michigan 370 wide and 18 feet deep, protected by piers and revetments. Estimated cost, revised in 1897 and 1899, was $344,300.

To June 30, 1900, $153,202.27 had been expended in the construction and maintenance of a north pier and revetment 1,500 feet long and a south pier and revetment 1,399 feet long. To complete the project the north pier required an extension of 700 feet and the south pier 900 feet. The river and harbor act of March 3, 1899, placed the work under the continuing-contract system and contract was entered into January 25, 1900, for the above extensions. Operations under this contract to June 30, 1900, resulted in no increase of work in place.

During the past fiscal year $55,304.49 was expended upon above contract for pier extension and upon contract for dredging in force at the beginning of the fiscal year. As a result of this expenditure, the seven cribs for the north pier were sunk in place and their superstructure partly completed and three cribs placed in the south pier. The channel was dredged from lake to lake to a depth of 13 feet and a width of 75 feet. The maximum draft that can be carried through is 12 feet.

When the contract for pier extension is completed the piers will have the length provided in the approved project. Provision remains to be made for the dredging necessary to secure the projected depth of 18 feet, and until this is done the harbor will not be available for purposes of refuge.

The amount that has been expended in maintenance can not be stated with accuracy.

The last published map of this locality is contained in the report of the Chief of Engineers for 1884.

No data relative to entrances and clearances can be obtained. Maximum draft, 12 feet.

July 1, 1900, balance unexpended	$157,297.73
June 30, 1901, amount expended during fiscal year	55,304.49
July 1, 1901, balance unexpended	101,993.24
July 1, 1901, outstanding liabilities	290.08
July 1, 1901, balance available	101,703.16
July 1, 1901, amount covered by uncompleted contracts	96,551.64
Amount (estimated) required for completion of existing project	33,800.00
Amount that can be profitably expended in fiscal year ending June 30, 1903, for works of improvement and for maintenance, in addition to the balance available July 1, 1901	59,000.00

Submitted in compliance with requirements of sundry civil act of June 4, 1897, and of section 7 of the river and harbor act of 1899.

(See Appendix N N 15.)

16. *Frankfort Harbor, Michigan.*—In 1867, when the United States began the work of improvement of this harbor, which is the outlet to Lake Aux Becs Scies, there existed an outlet about 750 feet north of the present channel affording a depth of 3 to 7 feet and 70 to 80 feet wide between slab piers built by local enterprise.

The present project was adopted in 1866, and as amended in 1868, 1879, and 1892, provided for a new outlet with channel 12 feet deep and 200 feet wide, protected by piers and revetments. The estimated cost, revised in 1897 in compliance with the river and harbor act of June 3, 1896, to cover cost of securing channel 18 feet deep, was $413,659.85, further revised in 1899 to $421,938.35.

To June 30, 1900, there had been expended upon this harbor the sum of $345,705.33. This expenditure resulted in the creation of a channel whose natural depth is 12 feet, the channel being 200 feet wide, protected by a north pier and revetment 1,499 feet in length and by a south pier and revetment 1,938 feet long, the outer 400 feet of which was built by the Toledo and Ann Arbor Railroad Company. Annual dredging is needed to maintain the depth required by navigation. The exact sum hitherto expended on repairs and dredging for maintenance can not be stated.

During the past fiscal year the sum of $28,884.41 was expended under contract in extending the north pier 200 feet, in repairing portions of both piers, and in dredging to restore proper width to channel, which had been encroached on by a shoal extending south from the outer end of the north pier.

Soundings made May 27-29 show that this shoal has again extended into the channel so as to reduce its width to 80 feet at its outer end. The 18-foot channel is continuous to the inner lake.

The last published map of this harbor is contained in the report of the Chief of Engineers for 1884.

An additional extension of the piers is desirable to provide and maintain the 18-foot channel called for by the river and harbor act of June 3, 1896. This depth is urgently demanded by the commerce of this port.

Entrances and clearances.

Calendar year.	Number.	Tonnage.	Calendar year.	Number.	Tonnage.
1888	1,342	216,876	1895	1,182	412,951
1889	(a)	(a)	1896	1,374	509,277
1890	443	57,140	1897	1,714	706,546
1891	1,541	258,908	1898	1,681	798,896
1892	910	167,777	1899	1,790	1,405,955
1893	988	278,709	1900	1,480	1,308,722
1894	1,101	337,728			

a Not stated.

Maximum draft, 18 feet.

July 1, 1900, balance unexpended	$32,233.02
June 30, 1901, amount expended during fiscal year	28,884.41
July 1, 1901, balance unexpended	3,348.61
July 1, 1901, outstanding liabilities	131.00
July 1, 1901, balance available	3,217.61
July 1, 1901, amount covered by uncompleted contracts	1,500.00
Amount (estimated) required for completion of existing project	44,000.00
Amount that can be profitably expended in fiscal year ending June 30, 1903, for works of improvement and for maintenance, in addition to the balance available July 1, 1901	54,500.00

Submitted in compliance with requirements of sundry civil act of June 4, 1897, and of section 7 the river and harbor act of 1899.

(See Appendix N N 16.)

17. Charlevoix Harbor, Michigan.—In 1868, when the first estimate for improvement was made, the available channel in Pine River between Lake Michigan and Round Lake was 75 feet wide and 2 to 6 feet deep. Up to 1873 the local authorities, with some assistance from the State, had constructed 468 feet of crib work in the north pier and 80 feet of crib work in the south pier, and the available depth was 6 feet. The first appropriation by the United States was made in 1876, and actual operations were begun in fiscal year 1878 upon the lower channel; the first appropriation for the upper channel was made in in 1882, and actual work begun in 1885. Total estimated cost was $186,000.

The present project was proposed in 1866, and, as amended in 1876 and 1882, provides for a 12-foot channel from Lake Michigan to Round Lake between piers and revetments 100 to 150 feet apart, and from Round Lake to Pine Lake between revetments 83 feet apart.

Up to June 30, 1900, the sum of $143,172.56 had been expended in securing a channel whose natural depth is 10 feet, protected in its two divisions by a north pier and revetment 2,064 feet long, and by a south pier and revetment 2,396 feet long. The total expenditure for maintaining the piers and the channel can not be definitely stated.

During the past fiscal year the sum of $7,940.02 was expended in repairing under contract 402 feet of the south pier.

No dredging was required during the year, the maximum draft capable of being carried clear through the upper channel being 13.5 feet at a stage of −0.7 feet.

All work since 1890 has been for maintenance. The approved project provides for an extension of 200 feet to the south pier.

Last published map of the lower channel is contained in House Doc. No. 54, Fifty-fourth Congress, second session.

Entrances and clearances.

Calendar year.	Number.	Tonnage.	Calendar year.	Number.	Tonnage.
1888	526	92,806	1895	528	92,387
1889	473	....	1896	420	75,268
1890	582	75,224	1897	545	110,474
1891	584	79,618	1898	566	105,797
1892	587	79,966	1899	675	144,400
1893	820	144,976	1900	1,725	350,769
1894	1,701	338,015			

Maximum draft, 13.5 feet.

July 1, 1900, balance unexpended	$12,327.44
June 30, 1901, amount expended during fiscal year	7,940.02
July 1, 1901, balance unexpended	4,387.42
July 1, 1901, amount covered by uncompleted contracts	2,000.00
Amount (estimated) required for completion of existing project	30,500.00
Amount that can be profitably expended in fiscal year ending June 30, 1903, for works of improvement and for maintenance, in addition to the balance unexpended July 1, 1901	30,000.00

Submitted in compliance with requirements of sundry civil act of June 4, 1897, and of section 7 of the river and harbor act of 1899.

(See Appendix N N 17.)

18. Petoskey Harbor, Michigan.—Before work at this harbor was begun by the United States, its landing pier was exposed to winds coming from between west and northwest, and in high gales it was dangerous to attempt a landing.

The present project was adopted in the river and harbor act of August 18, 1894. The approved project provides for constructing a breakwater 600 feet long about 600 feet west of the outer end of the landing pier, and another north of it 500 feet long, or as much longer as may be found necessary to cover the landing from all dangerous seas. Work was begun in 1896. Estimated cost was $170,000.

To June 30, 1900, there had been expended upon this work $52,029.21. Four hundred feet of the west breakwater and 200 feet of the north breakwater had been built of timber cribs resting in deep water upon stone foundation and in shallow water upon the natural bottom. The remaining 200 feet of the west breakwater had been constructed of riprap stone and bowlders of suitable size.

During the past fiscal year $3,234.02 was expended under contract for repairing the south (stone) portion of the west breakwater and the stone foundation of the north breakwater.

The project contemplates no increase in depth, which is sufficient for the needs of commerce.

Available funds are not sufficient for the extension of the north breakwater provided for in the approved project, and an estimate for this purpose is accordingly submitted.

Entrances and clearances.

Calendar year.	Number.	Tonnage.	Calendar year.	Number.	Tonnage.
1893	1,338	8,000	1897	4,362	91,600
1894	4,160	20,000	1898	4,704	76,000
1895	4,360	28,000	1899		
1896	3,156	24,000	1900		

No data relative to the commercial statistics for calendar year 1900 could be obtained.

July 1, 1900, balance unexpended.. $20,970.79
November 9, 1900, deposited on account of disallowance................ 2.86

                                                                              20,973.65
June 30, 1901, amount expended during fiscal year..................... 3,234.02

July 1, 1901, balance unexpended.. 17,739.63

Amount (estimated) required for completion of existing project........ 97,000.00
Amount that can be profitably expended in fiscal year ending June 30, 1903, in addition to the balance unexpended July 1, 1901............ 15,000.00
Submitted in compliance with requirements of sundry civil act of June 4, 1897.

(See Appendix N N 18.)

EXAMINATION MADE IN COMPLIANCE WITH EMERGENCY RIVER AND HARBOR ACT APPROVED JUNE 6, 1900.

Report on preliminary examination of *Muskegon River, Michigan, with a view to obtaining a channel with a depth of 20 feet and a uniform width of 300 feet through the exterior to the interior lake, the plan to provide for sheet piling to prevent erosion along banks not protected by cribs*, was submitted through the division engineer by Captain Harding August 6, 1900. A plan is presented for improvement at an estimated cost of $380,000. The report was transmitted to Congress and printed in House Doc. No. 104, Fifty-sixth Congress, second session. (See also Appendix N N 19.)

IMPROVEMENT OF RIVERS AND HARBORS ON THE EASTERN COAST OF MICHIGAN NORTH OF LAKE ERIE.

The works in this district were in the charge of Col. G. J. Lydecker, Corps of Engineers, to January 3, 1901, and of Maj. W. L. Fisk, Corps of Engineers, since that date. Division Engineer, Col. J. W. Barlow, Corps of Engineers (now brigadier-general, Chief of Engineers, United States Army, retired), from January 18 to May 3, 1901, and Col. S. M. Mansfield, Corps of Engineers, since May 9, 1901.

1. *Cheboygan Harbor, Michigan.*—The present harbor is the result of improvements made at the mouth of Cheboygan Harbor since 1871, when the available depth of water was only 6 feet. The project called for a channel 200 feet wide and 14 feet deep, and the estimated cost of the whole work was $395,335. The project was modified in 1880 to increase the navigable depth to 15 feet and in 1896 to make it 18 feet, and such depth now exists from deep water in the Straits of Mackinac to a point about 2,700 feet below the upper limits of the harbor. A 40-foot square crib was built in 1881 to mark the entrance to the channel, and a light-house was subsequently placed on it by the United States Light-House Establishment.

The total expenditure to June 30, 1900, was $165,280.86, and the available channel depth at that date was 18 feet to a point 2,700 feet below upper limits of the harbor.

During the past fiscal year no work was in progress.

As a result of a survey made in the fiscal year 1900, it was found that $15,500 will be required to complete the channel up to the State road bridge to the depth of 18 feet called for by the present approved project.

The following statement indicates the commerce of this harbor during the past eight calendar years, as shown by data compiled from the most reliable information available:

Year.	Number of vessels.	Freight tonnage.	Year.	Number of vessels.	Freight tonnage.
1893	940	441,087	1897	1,216	340,332
1894	1,083	303,900	1898	1,336	422,741
1895	1,249	326,930	1899	1,368	415,613
1896	1,040	525,373	1900	1,520	504,069

July 1, 1900, balance unexpended	$2,719.14
June 30, 1901, amount expended during fiscal year	283.00
July 1, 1901, balance unexpended	2,436.14
July 1, 1901, outstanding liabilities	13.18
July 1, 1901, balance available	2,422.96
Amount (estimated) required for completion of existing project	15,500.00
Amount that can be profitably expended in fiscal year ending June 30, 1903, in addition to the balance available July 1, 1901	10,000.00

Submitted in compliance with requirements of sundry civil act of June 4, 1897.

(See Appendix O O 1.)

2. *Alpena Harbor (Thunder Bay River), Michigan.*—The city of Alpena occupies both banks of Thunder Bay River at its mouth, and the harbor has been made by dredging the river for a distance of about a mile upstream and through the bar at the mouth to the 16-foot contour in Thunder Bay. The improvement was formerly carried on by the Government under separate appropriations for Thunder Bay Harbor and Thunder Bay River.

The original depth at entrance to the river was only 7 feet, but local enterprise increased it to 12 feet. The work of improvement by the Government was commenced in 1876 and has provided a wider channel and increased the depth to 13, 14, and 16 feet under successive projects, the total of the three separate estimates being $55,851. The last project was completed in 1893, and nothing was done from that time until the summer of 1899.

The total amount expended to June 30, 1900, was $48,814.07.

At the beginning of the fiscal year 1900 the channel had shoaled to such an extent as to limit the safe draft of vessels to scant 13 feet, and a contract was thereupon entered into for redredging it. Work under the contract was commenced September 5, and duly completed November 8, 1899, the total amount of dredging done being 42,497 cubic yards. The result of the work was to give the channel a least depth of 16 feet, and enabled vessels to pass through the harbor drawing 3 feet more than before the work was done. Previous experience indicates that the improvement will have a fair degree of permanence and that little or no expenditure will be required for its maintenance in the near future.

The following statement indicates the commerce of this harbor during the past eight calendar years, as shown by data compiled from the most reliable information available:

Year.	Number of vessels.	Freight tonnage.	Year.	Number of vessels.	Freight tonnage.
1893	940	360,588	1897	1,245	353,962
1894	1,033	465,991	1898	980	270,743
1895	1,249	305,160	1899	802	221,888
1896	1,040	349,754	1900	1,976	478,875

July 1, 1900, balance unexpended	$2,685.93
June 30, 1901, amount expended during fiscal year	360.00
July 1, 1901, balance unexpended	2,325.93

(See Appendix O O 2.)

3. *Saginaw River, Michigan.*—Before improvement the navigable capacity of this stream was limited by the bar at its mouth, where a channel depth of only 8 feet was available, and by many shoal stretches in the river between there and the city of Saginaw, over which still less depth was to be found. Its improvement was commenced in 1867 by dredging a straight cut through the bar at the mouth to a depth of 13 feet. In subsequent years the scope of operations was gradually extended to various shoals higher up, but subject to no general project until 1882, when a comprehensive and connected scheme of improvement covering the entire river was adopted. It called for a navigable channel 14 feet deep and 200 feet wide from Saginaw Bay to the upper limits of Bay City, about 8 miles above the point of beginning, and thence to the head of navigation, some 16 miles farther up, a channel of the same width but only 12 feet deep. The estimated cost of this

project was $446,000, which, added to the estimated cost of the several preceding projects ($294,378), gives $740,378 as the estimate of cost for the whole improvement. These estimates concerned the question of original cost only and took no note of maintenance, which, in a stream of this character, is a matter of great and constant expense, and in the absence of appropriations specifically applicable thereto must be an annual tax of no small magnitude on the successive appropriations for construction. The sum total of appropriations that will have to be made before the work can be completed must therefore largely exceed the orginal estimates for construction only.

The total expenditure to June 30, 1900, was $741,123.23, and the result has only been to obtain a narrow through channel, which has little permanence, and almost constant dredging is needed to maintain it. This has been the case especially as respects the section of river from Bay City to Saginaw and in a somewhat less degree through the bar at the river's mouth in Saginaw Bay.

At the beginning of the fiscal year 1900 the maximum depth available over most shoal places above Bay City was only 10 feet, and the available depth through the bar at mouth 13 feet. Contracts were thereupon entered into for restoring the required depth, and work was in progress under them from August 23, 1899, until August 27, 1900, except during the winter months; the total amount of dredging accomplished was 250,997 cubic yards, of which 125,355 cubic yards was dredged from the channel through the bar at the mouth of the river and 125,642 cubic yards from the river shoals between Bay City and Saginaw. The bar channel was dredged to a depth of 16 feet and the river shoals to 14 feet, but the resultant commercial benefit will be only temporary, as the width of channels dredged through shoals in the river is from 80 to 100 feet only, and with that limited width the depth will diminish very rapidly.

In order to restore and maintain these channels, as required in the interests of navigation the work of dredging should be constant until they have been excavated to a depth of 14 feet and a minimum width of 150 or 200 feet.

The commerce of the river for the past eight calendar years, as compiled from the most reliable information available, is approximately indicated in the following tabular statement:

Year.	Number of vessels.	Freight tonnage.	Year.	Number of vessels.	Freight tonnage.
1893	1,290	393,487	1897	1,034	330,031
1894	226	72,702	1898	996	304,827
1895	226	72,689	1899	889	336,269
1896	189	48,752	1900	798	252,931

July 1, 1900, balance unexpended $46,626.77
June 30, 1901, amount expended during fiscal year 30,409.48

July 1, 1901, balance unexpended.. 16,217.29
July 1, 1901, outstanding liabilities 10.00

July 1, 1901, balance available... 16,207.29

{ Amount that can be profitably expended in fiscal year ending June 30, 1903, in addition to the balance available July 1, 1901 .... 37,500.00
Submitted in compliance with requirements of sundry civil act of June 4, 1897.

(See Appendix O O 3.)

4. Sebewaing River, Michigan.—This stream discharges into the eastern part of Saginaw Bay. In 1875 the river channel was straightened, deepened to 6 feet, and the work of dredging extended to the 6-foot contour in Saginaw Bay. In 1880-81 this channel was deepened to 7 feet. The total expenditure in these operations was $15,000.

The present project of improvement was adopted by the river and harbor act of June 3, 1896, and provides for dredging the entrance channel for a length of about 15,000 feet to a width of 100 feet and depth of 8 feet, the estimated cost being $37,000.

The above-named act appropriated $5,000 for work under the new project, but operations were not commenced, because no useful results could be accomplished by the expenditure of so small a sum. The river and harbor act of March 3, 1899, supplied the necessary additional funds, but no work was done or expenditure made up to June 30, 1899, on which date advertisement was published inviting proposals.

Contract for dredging under the approved project was approved September 13, 1899, but stormy weather prevented the arrival of the contractor's plant until September 29, and it was the middle of October before he was able to do any work. Operations were continued until the end of November, when it became necessary to place the plant in winter quarters. Work was resumed May 1, 1900, and continued until November 15, under an extension of contract to December 31, 1900. A further extension to December 1, 1901, was granted, and under this extension work was resumed on April 24, 1901, and is still in progress. To June 30, 1901, a total of 46,828 cubic yards has been dredged and deposited at designated dumping grounds, and a great amount cast over by the dredge in preparing suitable channels in which to operate and berth the plant.

The total estimated cost of the improvement has been appropriated, and the contract price of work is such that the money now available will suffice for completing it unless the contractor should fail to meet his contract obligation. Accordingly, no estimate for further appropriation is presented in this report.

The total amount expended to June 30, 1900, for improvement of this river was $16,449.66.

July 1, 1900, balance unexpended	$35,550.37
June 30, 1901, amount expended during fiscal year	7,076.22
July 1, 1901, balance unexpended	28,474.15
July 1, 1901, outstanding liabilities	2,085.34
July 1, 1901, balance available	26,388.81
July 1, 1901, amount covered by uncompleted contracts	26,388.81

(See Appendix O O 4.)

5. Harbor of refuge at Sandbeach, Lake Huron, Michigan.—The site for this harbor, selected in 1872 after careful consideration, is on the west shore of Lake Huron, 60 miles north of its outlet into the St. Clair River, and the artificial harbor built there since then is the only safe refuge on that coast from the foot of the lake to Tawas Bay, 115 miles above. The work of construction was commenced in 1873, under a project providing for three sections of breakwater made of stone-filled crib work, so located as to shelter a water area of some 650 acres, and for deepening this area by dredging where necessary.

The estimated cost was $1,442,500. The sheltering breakwaters, with a total length of 8,132 feet, were completed in 1885, at a cost of about $975,000, and since that time expenditures have been applied to keeping them in repair, dredging, regulating and controlling the berthing of vessels entering the harbor for refuge, engineering supervision, and general office expenses.

The total expenditure to June 30, 1900, was $1,210,022.37.

The expenditure for the past fiscal year was applied to making some temporary repairs to superstructures of the main breakwater and to general contingencies, including custody of harbor, supervision, control of vessels, and office expenses.

The number of vessels that entered the harbor for refuge during the past fiscal year was 1,276, with a total tonnage of 804,836. The grand total of vessels that have found shelter there from 1877 to 1900, inclusive, is 28,713, the tonnage of which aggregated 10,427,111. The vessels sheltered in 1877 averaged 289 tons each, and those during the year 1900 603 tons.

During the present fiscal year it is proposed to commence to rebuild the superstructure of the main breakwater in concrete.

July 1, 1900, balance unexpended	$296,084.68
June 30, 1901, amount expended during fiscal year	5,989.06
July 1, 1901, balance unexpended	290,095.62
July 1, 1901, outstanding liabilities	519.11
July 1, 1901, balance available	289,576.51

Amount that can be profitably expended in fiscal year ending June 30, 1903, in addition to the balance available July 1, 1901:
  For works of improvement.......................... $50,000.00
  For maintenance of improvement 7,500.00
                                                                            57,500.00

Submitted in compliance with requirements of sundry civil act of June 4, 1897, and of section 7 of the river and harbor act of 1899.

(See appendix O O 5.)

6. *Mouth of Black River, Michigan.*—An extensive shoal and a bar formerly existed in the St. Clair River adjoining the mouth of the Black. The bar lay close to the American side and obstructed approach to the Port Huron docks, while the shoal forming a "middle ground," nearly 50 acres in extent, crowded the main channel in a sharp curve close to the Canadian shore. In 1871 a project was adopted for dredging the bar and middle ground to a uniform depth of 15 feet; work was commenced in 1872 and completed in 1878. The whole area was redredged between 1889 and 1892, and again in 1897, to a depth of 16 feet. The total expenditure to June 30, 1900, was $92,879.87.

No work was in progress during the past fiscal year, and the total expenditure of $750.01 was for general office and engineering contingencies. An examination of the area made in 1900 to ascertain what work, if any, might be needed showed a small amount of dredging to be desirable to improve the approach to the Port Huron docks.

This examination and all previous experience show that the shoal will re-form gradually, and as vessels of moderate draft habitually pass over this area instead of through the main channel followed by those of deep draft, it is very desirable that means be at hand for maintaining the improvement as the interests of this commerce require.

July 1, 1900, balance unexpended $5,620.13
June 30, 1901, amount expended during fiscal year 750.01

July 1, 1901, balance unexpended 4,870.12

{ Amount that can be profitably expended in fiscal year ending June 30,
1903, for maintenance of improvement, in addition to the balance
unexpended July 1, 1901 .... 2,500.00
Submitted in compliance with requirements of sundry civil act of June
4, 1897, and of section 7 of the river and harbor act of 1899. }

(See Appendix O O 6.)

7. *Black River at Port Huron, Michigan.*—The improvement of this stream was inaugurated by the river and harbor act of September 19, 1890, under a project which contemplated dredging it to a navigable depth of 16 feet from its mouth to the Grand Trunk Railway bridge, at an estimated cost of $75,000, and the act of July 13, 1892, directed that the improvement be extended 1,400 feet farther upstream, to Washington avenue. Operations were commenced in 1891 and continued until the summer of 1893, when the required 16-foot channel had been dredged throughout the designated limits to a width varying between 160 feet near the mouth and 50 or 75 feet in the contracted river sections above. The total length of channel so dredged was 9,700 feet. Before improvement the minimum channel depth was between 8 and 10 feet for about 1 mile from the mouth of the river, but only 6 to 8 feet from there up to Washington avenue. The narrow upstream section and some shoal spots in the wider section below were redredged in 1897.

The total expenditure to June 30, 1900, was $42,486.29.

A thorough examination of the river in April, 1900, showed that every evidence of the dredging done above the Grand Trunk Railway bridge had been obliterated, the maximum available draft that could be carried over the shoalest parts of the channel being scant 9 feet, but up to that bridge a draft of a little over 12 feet could be carried safely. This confirms all previous experience and observation, showing conclusively that the narrow dredged channels in the upper limits of the improvement can have no reasonable degree of permanence.

Advertisement for proposals to redredge the channel to the depth of 16 feet, so far as available funds would permit, was published June 20, 1900, bids opened June 30, 1900, and contract for the work entered into.

Dredging was begun July 14 and completed August 14, 1900, the total amount taken out under the contract being 23,214 cubic yards.

Annual dredging is necessary for maintaining this improvement, and for this reason an estimate for maintenance is submitted below for the fiscal year ending June 30, 1903.

The following statement indicates the commerce of this river during the past eight calendar years, as shown by data compiled from the most reliable information available:

Year.	Number of vessels.	Freight tonnage.	Year.	Number of vessels.	Freight tonnage.
1893	602	182,568	1897	645	98,380
1894	595	120,948	1898	216	82,410
1895	587	111,675	1899	504	110,860
1896	628	189,556	1900	5,796	1,607,356

560   REPORT OF THE CHIEF OF ENGINEERS, U. S. ARMY.

July 1, 1900, balance unexpended $4,513.71
June 30, 1901, amount expended during fiscal year 3,818.68

July 1, 1901, balance unexpended 695.03

{ Amount (estimated) required for completion of existing project 28,000.00
Amount that can be profitably expended in fiscal year ending June 30, 1903, for works of improvement and for maintenance, in addition to the balance unexpended July 1, 1901 .... 14,000.00
Submitted in compliance with requirements of sundry civil act of June 4, 1897, and of section 7 of the river and harbor act of 1899. }

(See Appendix O O 7.)

8. *Pine River, Michigan.*—This river was improved in 1875 by dredging a channel 100 feet wide, 12 feet deep, for a distance of about three-fourths of a mile from the mouth, at a cost of $5,000. This channel shoaled in time, and after an examination of the river, called for by the river and harbor act of July 13, 1892, a project for further improvement was prepared under the act of August 18, 1894, and the act of June 3, 1896, appropriated $5,000 for commencing the work. This project provides for dredging a channel 14 feet deep, extending about 5,800 feet from the mouth, the width to be 100 feet or 75 feet, according to locality. The estimated cost is $10,560. Work on the new project was commenced September 24 and continued until November 16, 1896, when operations were suspended to await further appropriation. Nothing further was done until the summer of 1899.

The total expenditure for improvements on the river to June 30, 1900, was $13,646.89. Of this total, $8,646.89 pertains to the work thus far done under the new project, by which the depth of channel was increased from 9 to 14 feet through nearly one-half of the total distance contemplated by the project.

Operations were resumed August 28, 1899, under the appropriation made by river and harbor act of March 3, 1899, and continued until October 19, when the improvement was completed as proposed, and a balance of the last appropriation, amounting to $1,593.11, is now on hand, which will suffice for all probable contingencies of supervision, maintenance, etc., for some time to come.

The commerce of this river during the past five calendar years, as derived from the best information obtainable, amounted to 2,683 freight tons for 1896, 6,820 for 1897, 107,800 for 1898, 822,660 for 1899, and for 1900, 8,294, the total for the five years being 948,257 freight tons.

July 1, 1900, balance unexpended $1,913.11
June 30, 1901, amount expended during fiscal year 320.00

July 1, 1901, balance unexpended 1,593.11

(See Appendix O O 8.)

9. *Belle River, Michigan.*—This river was improved, 1880–1885, by dredging a channel 50 feet wide, 13 feet deep, to the first bridge and 12 feet deep to the second one, a total distance of 5,400 feet. The total cost was $14,000, and the principal benefit was to provide a winter harbor for vessels.

The river and harbor act of July 13, 1892, called for an examination of the river, and that of August 18, 1894, for survey and estimate of cost of its further improvement. Project for redredging the channel to a width of 75 feet and depth of 15 feet to the first and 14 feet depth to the second bridge was submitted November 30, 1895, the estimated cost being $21,500. The act of June 3, 1896, appropriated $5,000 for beginning the work, and dredging to the extent of about 40,000 cubic yards was done during the summer of 1897, thereby obtaining the required depth and width of channel for a distance of about 2,400 feet above the mouth of the river. Operations were then suspended to await further appropriation, and no further work was done until the summer of 1899.

The total expenditure for all improvements to June 30, 1900, was $24,300.88, of which $10,300.88 was applied to operations under the project now in force.

The river and harbor act of March 3, 1899, having appropriated $10,000 for completing the improvement, operations were resumed August 22, 1899, and the work was completed in accordance with the approved project October 3, 1899. The total cost of the improvement, including all contingencies, was $10,300.88.

No further appropriation is required at present, the unexpended balance of those already made being sufficient to provide for all contingencies of supervision, maintenance, etc., for some considerable time to come.

The following statement indicates the commerce of this river during the past four calendar years, as shown by data compiled from the most reliable information available:

Year.	Number of vessels.	Freight tonnage.
1897	52	3,092
1898	60	23,743
1899	85	33,272
1900	32	2,014

July 1, 1900, balance unexpended	$4,699.12
June 30, 1901, amount expended during fiscal year	639.58
July 1, 1901, balance unexpended	4,059.54

(See Appendix O O 9.)

10. *Clinton River, Michigan.*—This stream empties into Anchor Bay, in the northwesterly part of Lake St. Clair, and before improvement had a channel depth of about 10 feet, except at several shoals, over which but 5 or 6 feet could be carried, and a broad flat at the mouth with a general depth of from 3 to 4 feet. In 1870–71 a channel 9 feet deep, 60 feet wide, and 2,700 feet long was dredged through this flat, but being left without works of protection, it soon filled in again. In 1885 a project of general improvement was adopted, which provided for a through channel 8 feet deep to Mount Clemens (8 miles upstream), for a pile dike extending across the flat at the mouth to the curve of 10 feet depth in the bay, and for revetments as needed above. The estimated cost, as modified in 1889, was $34,564.

The total expenditure to June 30, 1900, was $68,189.06, of which $25,500 was applied to occasional and scattering work done before the adoption of the general project of 1885, leaving $42,689.06 as the amount applied to the latter.

As a result of these expenditures the proposed 8-foot channel was obtained and kept in a fairly navigable condition, but the appropriations were at no time sufficient to permit the construction of protecting works of a permanent character, and in their absence the maintenance of the channel must depend on periodical dredgings.

No work was in progress during the past fiscal year.

An examination made just before the close of the fiscal year 1900 showed a general channel depth of 6 feet or over, and dredging will probably be called for to restore and maintain the depth required for convenient navigation. Funds on hand will suffice for this purpose, but an appropriation is likely to be needed for maintenance of the improvement during the year ending June 30, 1903.

The commerce of the river during the past five calendar years, as derived from the best data obtainable, is indicated in the following table, which shows the number of vessels entered and cleared and their freight, in tons:

Year.	Number of vessels.	Freight tonnage.	Year.	Number of vessels.	Freight tonnage.
1896	420	31,159	1899	384	35,525
1897	420	29,077	1900	161	14,060
1898	263	29,085			

July 1, 1900, balance unexpended $6,874.94
June 30, 1901, amount expended during fiscal year..................... 51.48

July 1, 1901, balance unexpended 6,823.46

Amount that can be profitably expended in fiscal year ending June 30, 1903, for maintenance of improvement, in addition to the balance unexpended July 1, 1901... 3,000.00
Submitted in compliance with requirements of sundry civil act of June 4, 1897, and of section 7 of the river and harbor act of 1899.

(See Appendix O O 10.)

11. *Rouge River, Michigan.*—This stream originally had a channel depth of from 10 to 17 feet from its mouth to the point at which the Wabash Railroad bridge crosses it, a distance of about 3 miles. During the years 1888 to 1892, inclusive, this part was improved by the Government so as to provide a minimum depth of 16 feet in a central channel 240 feet wide for a distance of 800 feet above the mouth, and thence 100 feet wide to the Wabash bridge. The cost of this improvement, originally estimated, was $31,690.39.

The total expenditure to June 30, 1900, was $38,087.14, the result obtained being a 16-foot channel, as called for by the approved project, and its maintenance since 1892 to such extent as was necessary to meet the requirements of local commerce, but a gradual shoaling had taken place in the meantime, such as to limit navigation to vessels drawing 13 feet or less. Congress, by joint resolution approved April 11, 1898, authorized an extension of the improvement up to the Maples road, a distance of about 1½ miles above the Wabash Railroad bridge, limiting the expenditure for that purpose to $5,000.

Just before the close of the fiscal year 1900 proposals were invited, by advertisement, for redredging the channel as far up as the Wabash bridge in order to restore a navigable depth of 16 feet and for dredging a channel 75 feet wide, 13 feet deep, from that point to the Maples road. Under this contract a total of 95,351 cubic yards was removed, exhausting the available funds, and an additional appropriation should be provided by the next river and harbor act for future maintenance of the improvement.

The following statement indicates the commerce of this river during the past eight calendar years, as shown by data compiled from the best information obtainable:

	Tons.		Tons.
1893	73,732	1897	125,373
1894	47,106	1898	127,745
1895	114,090	1899	93,394
1896	123,495	1900	124,312

July 1, 1900, balance unexpended $13,602.86
June 30, 1901, amount expended during fiscal year 13,351.27

July 1, 1901, balance unexpended 251.59

{ Amount that can be profitably expended in fiscal year ending June 30, 1903, for maintenance of improvement, in addition to the balance unexpended July 1, 1901.. 5,000.00
Submitted in compliance with requirements of sundry civil act of June 4, 1897, and of section 7 of the river and harbor act of 1899. }

(See Appendix O O 11.)

IMPROVEMENT OF WATERS CONNECTING THE GREAT LAKES.

The works in this district were in the charge of Col. G. J. Lydecker, Corps of Engineers.

1. Ship channel connecting waters of the Great Lakes between Chicago, Duluth, and Buffalo.—This project was adopted by the river and harbor act of July 13, 1892, the object being to provide a navigable depth of 20 feet by excavating channels to a minimum width of 300 feet through the shoal places in the specified waters. The estimated cost of the improvement was $3,340,000.

Operations were commenced in the spring of 1893, and by 1897 channels of the required depth and with widths of 300 feet or more had been excavated through all the shoal areas that were considered when the project was adopted. The maximum draft that could be carried over these shoals before improvement was from 15 to 16 feet at mean stage of water. Work since that time has been applied to increasing the width of channels at angles and other critical points, and to removing numerous isolated shoals of comparatively small area that have been found in the through line of travel. In many instances there was no knowledge of the existence of the shoals, but in most cases they have been found in the course of surveys or examinations with a sweeping raft. The total amount of material excavated to June 30, 1900, was 10,416,984 cubic yards, and the total expenditure on the improvement up to that date was $2,926,553.65.

During the past fiscal year four shoals were removed from the St. Clair River section of the ship channel, the total amount of material dredged being 76,258 cubic yards. The result of the work was to provide a clear depth of 21 feet where the controlling depths before improvement ranged from 16¼ to 18 feet. In the St. Marys River section 56,324 cubic yards of material was dredged, by which the channel widths at the angles above Sailors Encampment Cut and at the head of Little Mud Lake were increased 35 feet and 90 feet, respectively. Surveys and examinations with sweeping raft were made over considerable areas of the St. Marys and St. Clair rivers.

Proposals were invited May 6, and opened May 28, for time work by dredging plant in removing obstructions to navigation between the head of St. Clair and mouth of Detroit rivers, and contract was entered into June 13 with the Duluth Dredge and Dock Company, of Duluth, Minn., at the rate of $12 per hour working time; but no work was done before the close of the year.

The unexpended balance of previous appropriations will suffice for all work required to complete improvements contemplated by the present approved project, and for this reason no additional appropriation is now needed for this purpose.

The amount of freight carried through the St. Marys River sections of this channel during the navigable season of 1900 was 25,643,073 tons, valued at $267,041,959. Reliable statistics of traffic through the Detroit River are not obtainable, but such as could be procured indicate that about 42,000,000 tons of freight passed during that season.

July 1, 1900, balance unexpended	$416,224.41
June 30, 1901, amount expended during fiscal year	[1] 35,519.14
July 1, 1901, balance unexpended	[2] 380,705.27
July 1, 1901, outstanding liabilities	3,003.47
July 1, 1901, balance available	[2] 377,701.80
July 1, 1901, amount covered by uncompleted contracts	20,000.00

(See Appendix P P 1.)

2. St. Marys River at the falls, Michigan.—Commercial navigation of the falls, or rapids, of this river at Sault Ste. Marie was impracticable until the State of Michigan constructed a canal and lock which provided a convenient navigable channel for vessels whose draft did not exceed 11 feet at mean stage of water. This improvement was completed in 1855, the lock having a double lift with chambers 350 feet long by 70 feet wide, and the canal being about 5,400 feet long, with a general width of 100 feet.

In 1870 the United States entered upon a project for increasing the width of the canal, building a new lock, and providing a navigable depth of 15 feet. The new lock (now known as the Weitzel lock) was opened to traffic in 1881, its chamber being 515 feet long and 80 feet wide. A rapidly increasing commerce developed as a result of these improvements.

The present approved project was presented in a report dated October 18, 1886, which provided for building a new single-lift lock on the site of the old State locks, with a chamber 800 feet long by 100 feet wide and 21 feet of water over miter sills; and the canal, together with its approaches, to be deepened to correspond. The estimated cost was $4,738,865. The essential features of this project were so far completed in 1896 as to permit the new lock to be opened to navigation August 3 of that year; this lock is now known as the Poe lock. Work since that time has consisted in completing the deepening of the canal and its approaches, rebuilding and extending piers, grading and improving canal grounds, etc. The total expenditure to June 30, 1900, was $2,933,013.81.

---

[1] Includes $1.14 paid by Treasury Department account Western Union Telegraph Company.
[2] Includes $500 reserved for expenses of Office Chief of Engineers for the fiscal year ending June 30, 1902.

RIVER AND HARBOR IMPROVEMENTS. 565

Operations during the past year comprised (1) building 240 linear feet of stone-filled crib work, 30 feet wide, in extension of the northeast pier of the Poe lock, thereby providing additional berthing space for vessels when awaiting opportunity to enter the lock; (2) erecting three stone buildings on the lock walls for protecting gate engines and providing shelter for lockmen in stormy weather; (3) improving canal grounds by grading, sodding or seeding, planting trees, and building 4,662 square yards of walks, and (4) quite extensive surveys and examinations with sweeping raft with a view to ascertaining the condition of improved channels and projecting further improvements.

The unexpended balance of previous appropriations will suffice for all work required to complete improvements thus far authorized, and for this reason no additional appropriation is now needed for this purpose.

The commerce passing the falls during the navigation season of 1900, a period of 238 days, comprised 25,643,073 tons of freight, valued at $267,041,959; the number of passengers reported during the same period was 58,555.

July 1, 1900, balance unexpended	$830,890.75
June 30, 1901, amount expended during fiscal year	36,416.24
July 1, 1901, balance unexpended	[1]794,474.51
July 1, 1901, outstanding liabilities	7,616.61
July 1, 1901, balance available	[1]786,857.90

(See Appendix P P 2.)

3. Operating and care of St. Marys Falls Canal, Michigan.—The canal was open to navigation 231 days, the closed season being from December 13, 1900, to April 26, 1901. A total of 14,975 vessels, aggregating 18,345,306 registered tons, and carrying 20,994,320 tons of freight and 35,327 passengers, passed through the locks in 8,875 lockages. The Canadian canal at Sault Ste. Marie, Ontario, passed 3,531 vessels in 2,409 lockages, carrying 2,742,392 tons of freight and 26,900 passengers, making the combined traffic through the two canals 23,736,712 tons of freight and 62,227 passengers. This is a decrease during the year of 3,783,493 tons, or 14 per cent, and an increase of 11,177 passengers, or 22 per cent.

The principal items of freight carried were: Iron ore, 15,302,815 tons; coal, 4,014,558 tons; flour, 6,783,135 barrels; wheat, 30,725,254 bushels; other grain, 16,306,900 bushels, and lumber, 906,455,000 feet B. M.

Other statistics in relation to this traffic and commerce are summarized in the following statements:

Summary of traffic through St. Marys Falls Canal, Michigan, for fiscal year ending June 30, 1901.

Number of vessels through Weitzel lock	6,956
Number of vessels through Poe lock	8,019
Number of lockages through Weitzel lock	3,987
Number of lockages through Poe lock	4,888
Total registered tonnage	18,345,306
Total freight tonnage	20,994,320
Total time occupied in making lockages	3,570 hours 35 min.

[1] Includes $500 reserved for expenses of Office Chief of Engineers for the fiscal year ending June 30, 1902.

Average time occupied in making a lockage........................ 24 min. 14 sec.
Total time spent by vessels in passing locks.................. 8,322 hours 38 min.
Average time spent by vessels in passing locks.................. 33 min. 34 sec.
Cost per lockage $8.60
Cost per passage $5.10
Cost per registered ton .... 4.16 mills
Cost per freight ton .... 3.64 mills

The Weitzel lock was open to navigation 211 days, from July 1 to December 4, 1900, and from May 8 to June 30, 1901.

The time for the Poe lock was 231 days, July 1 to December 12, 1900, and from April 26 to June 30, 1901.

Summary of St. Marys River commerce, via American and Canadian canals, during the season of 1900, viz, from April 19, 1900, to December 16, 1900, a period of seven months and twenty-eight days.

Total mile-tons..	21,179,229,014
Total freight carried, net tons	25,643,073
Total valuation placed on freight carried	$267,041,959
Average value per ton of freight carried..............................	$10.41
Total amount paid for freight transportation	$24,953,314.71
Average distance freight was carried, miles..........................	825.9
Cost per mile per ton, mills	1.18
Average cost per ton for freight transportation.......................	$0.97
Total number registered vessels using canals.........................	879
Total number of passages by unregistered crafts carrying freight.....	454
Time American lock was operated, days.................................	238
Time Canadian lock was operated, days.................................	238
Total valuation placed on registered vessels	$69,735,159
Total number of passengers transported	58,555
Freight carried by—	
Registered vessels, tons..	25,585,934
Unregistered vessels, tons......................................	57,139
American vessels, per cent	97
Canadian vessels, per cent	3
Passengers carried by—	
American vessels, per cent	42
Canadian vessels, per cent	58

This service is provided for from the permanent-indefinite appropriation for operating and care of canals and other works of navigation under section 4 of the river and harbor act of July 5, 1884; the total expenditure on this account from 1881, when the Weitzel lock was first put in service, to June 30, 1901, amounts to $968,773.54, of which $75,475.33 related to operations during the past fiscal year, as follows: For pay rolls, $58,584.88; for repairs, $3,441.67; for general supplies, $5,630.96; for electric lighting, $2,265.68, and for office expenses and general contingencies, $5,552.14. The growth of freight traffic during the same period is shown by the following tabular statement:

Freight traffic.

	Tons.		Tons.
1881	1,567,741	1891	8,888,759
1882	2,029,521	1892	11,214,333
1883	2,267,105	1893	10,796,572
1884	2,874,557	1894	13,195,860
1885	3,256,628	1895	15,062,580
1886	4,527,759	1896	16,239,061
1887	5,494,649	1897	18,982,755
1888	6,411,423	1898	21,234,664
1889	7,516,022	1899	25,255,810
1890	9,041,213	1900	25,643,073

(See Appendix P P 3.)

4. Hay Lake Channel, St. Marys River, Michigan.—On account of rapids and shoals that intervened between the navigable channel of the river and the lake at its head and foot this channel was not navigable for commercial purposes before improvement. The original project of improvement of October 27, 1882, contemplated the excavation of channels 17 feet deep and 300 feet wide through all obstructed portions of the Hay Lake route, but this project was modified in 1886 to provide a depth of 20 feet, the total estimated cost being $2,659,115. The work of improvement was commenced in 1883, and the route opened to commerce June 7, 1894, though full width and depth of channel had not then been obtained at all points; but since then several shoals in the deep-water section of the lake have been removed and the dredged channels have been widened at angles and other critical points.

The amount expended to June 30, 1900, was $2,165,142.47, and the improvement as it stood at that date comprised 10 miles of channel dredged to a depth of 20 or 21 feet, in 6 miles of which the width was 300 feet and in the remaining 4 from 450 to 1,100 feet. The new channel is 11 miles shorter than the old one via Lake George. It can be navigated with reasonable safety at night, which could not be done by the old route, and it is available for vessels drawing 5 feet more water than could be safely carried through the latter.

Operations during the past fiscal year were applied to straightening the Middle Neebish dike by distributing bowlders along its face and thereby protecting it against further erosion, due to the current and to the wash of waves made by vessels while passing through the adjoining channel. Extensive surveys were made with reference to further improvements.

The whole commerce of the St. Marys River passes through this channel, except small river steamers engaged in local traffic and rafts of logs which continue to be taken via the old channel as a measure of safety to general commerce. The following tabular statement indicates the extent and growth of this commerce from the year in which this route was opened to travel:

Season of navigation.	Freight.	Valuation.	Passengers.
1894	13,195,860	$143,114,502	27,236
1895	15,062,580	159,575,129	31,656
1896	16,239,061	195,146,842	37,066
1897	18,982,755	218,235,927	40,213
1898	21,234,664	233,069,739	43,426
1899	25,255,810	281,364,750	51,050
1900	25,643,073	267,041,969	58,555

Funds now available will be applied toward increasing the width of the Little Rapids division of this channel from 300 to 600 feet, and the work will be done under the continuing contracts as authorized by the river and harbor act of March 3, 1899. Specifications for these contracts have been completed and work will be commenced at an early date. The total expenditure authorized is $494,115, toward which $350,000 has been appropriated, and the remaining $144,115 will be required to meet contract obligations that will be incurred during the ensuing fiscal year.

568   REPORT OF THE CHIEF OF ENGINEERS, U. S. ARMY.

July 1, 1900, balance unexpended... $350,000.00
June 30, 1901, amount expended during fiscal year....................... 46,905.78

July 1, 1901, balance unexpended... 303,094.22
July 1, 1901, outstanding liabilities.. 1,176.23

July 1, 1901, balance available.. 301,917.99

{ Amount that can be profitably expended in fiscal year ending June 30,
1903, in addition to the balance available July 1, 1901............... 144,115.00
Submitted in compliance with requirements of sundry civil act of June
4, 1897.

(See Appendix P P 4.)

5. *St. Clair Flats Canal, Michigan.*—This improvement dates back to 1866. It is a dredged cut, connecting the main channel of St. Clair River with deep water in Lake St. Clair. The dredged material was deposited so as to form dikes on each side of the cut, the channel faces of which are sustained by substantial sheet-pile revetments. In its present condition the width of waterway between revetments is 292 feet, depth of water 20 feet at mean stage in channel 260 feet wide, and length of each lateral dike 7,221 feet. Before improvement the general depth of water over the entire area included in the canal was only 6 feet.

The total amount appropriated for this improvement from its beginning is $764,810, and the total expenditure to June 30, 1901, $761,750.61.

No operations were in progress or expenditure made during the past fiscal year.

No specific appropriation has been made for this work since 1890, and there is now an unexpended balance of $3,059.39, which will probably be applied during the ensuing fiscal year to repairing and extending the protecting pile work at the head and foot of the canal dikes.

No further estimate is submitted for work under the present approved project, but the emergency river and harbor act of June 6, 1900, called for survey and estimate with a view to doubling the capacity of the canal, and special reports in the matter, dated July 28 and December 6, 1900, are printed in House Doc. No. 234, Fifty-sixth Congress, second session, and in Appendix P P 10 of this report. The combined freight and passenger traffic that passes through this canal is probably not exceeded at any other place on the Great Lakes, and the channel width now available for this vast commerce is less than 275 feet.

July 1, 1900, balance unexpended... $3,059.39
July 1, 1901, balance unexpended... [1] 3,059.39

(See Appendix P P 5.)

6. *Operating and care of St. Clair Flats Canal, Michigan.*—This service is provided for by the permanent-indefinite appropriation for operating and care of canals and other works of navigation, under the provisions of section 4 of the river and harbor act of July 5, 1884.

Operations during the past fiscal year were of the same routine character as have been carried on since the canal was opened to traffic in 1871, viz, a custodian was present during the season of navigation to watch the passage of vessels, enforce regulations respecting

---
[1] Includes $500 reserved for expenses of Office Chief of Engineers for the fiscal year ending June 30, 1902.

traffic through the canal, and supervise all work required for the care and repair of the canal dikes. The expenditure on this account during the year was $3,053.23.

No record is kept of commerce through this canal, but it is substantially the same as that through the Detroit River, which is reported at about 42,000,000 tons of freight for the year 1900. The passenger traffic is also very great, but no approximate record of it is available at present.

(See Appendix P P 6.)

7. *Detroit River, Michigan.*—Before improvement the shoalest part of the channel through Detroit River was at the Limekiln Crossing, where the normal depth was 13 feet over a bottom of solid rock. The improvement of this crossing was commenced in 1874 and completed in 1890, which provided a straight channel 440 feet wide and 20 feet deep at mean stage of water. The general depth above and below the Limekiln was 20 feet or more, but the bed of the river was studded with large bowlders and rocky shoals, which limited the safe navigable depth to scant 15 feet through a distance of about 12 miles, and a general project of improvement was thereupon adopted in 1892 for the removal of all obstructive shoals between the city of Detroit and Lake Erie, with a view to obtaining a through channel with a least width of 600 feet and navigable depth of 20 feet. Operations under that project are still in progress.

The total estimated cost of these combined projects was $1,554,500, and to June 30, 1900, the total expenditure on the improvement was $797,587.57. As a result of the work done to that date, a channel ranging from 300 to 600 feet in width was obtained, in which the least depth at mean stage of water was 17¼ feet, and from 19 to 21 feet through most of the distance.

Operations were in progress during the past fiscal year under three continuing contracts, and work by hired labor with Government plant, the result of which was to increase the minimum depth of the improved channel to 18 feet. Extensive surveys relating to work in progress and projects for more extensive improvements were also made.

The river and harbor act of March 3, 1899, authorized expenditures for work under the present project to the amount of $661,500, payable from appropriations to be made after that date, and $525,000 has been appropriated for that purpose by the sundry civil acts of June 6, 1900, and March 3, 1901. The remaining $136,500 will be required to meet obligations that will mature before June 30, 1901, under contracts made as authorized by the river and harbor act above referred to.

Congress, in the river and harbor act of March 3, 1899, called for plans and estimates of cost of such improvements in the Detroit River, from Detroit to Lake Erie, "as will secure a safe and convenient channel 21 feet deep between said points." Preliminary report, dated May 29, 1900, was transmitted to Congress and is printed in House Doc. No. 712, Fifty-sixth Congress, first session; also in the Annual Report of the Chief of Engineers for 1900, page 4015. If possible, final report will be submitted in time for transmission to Congress at its next session.

No accurate or complete record of Detroit River commerce is obtainable, but from the best available data it is estimated that not less than 42,000,000 tons of freight passed through during the calendar year

1900, and there is probably no other waterway in the upper lakes through which a larger passenger traffic is found.

July 1, 1900, balance unexpended	$295,522.84
Amount appropriated by sundry civil act approved March 3, 1901	325,000.00
	620,522.84
June 30, 1901, amount expended during fiscal year	130,420.68
July 1, 1901, balance unexpended	490,102.16
July 1, 1901, outstanding liabilities	46,096.00
July 1, 1901, balance available	444,006.16
July 1, 1901, amount covered by uncompleted contracts	477,426.51
Amount (estimated) required for completion of existing project	136,500.00
Amount that can be profitably expended in fiscal year ending June 30, 1903, in addition to the balance available July 1, 1901	136,500.00

Submitted in compliance with requirements of sundry civil act of June 4, 1897.

(See Appendix P P 7.)

8. *Removing sunken vessels or craft obstructing or endangering navigation— Wreck of schooner Leader.*—This vessel was sunk by collision in the main channel of the Detroit River, near the head of Belle Isle. An allotment of $2,500 for its removal was made September 1, 1900. The work was commenced under contract October 3 and completed November 3, 1900, at a total cost of $2,050.06. Nothing of value was recovered from the wreck.

Wrecks of schooners Fontana and Martin.—These vessels were sunk by collisions in the so-called rapids at the head of St. Clair River, the former August 4 and the latter September 21, 1900. The two wrecks lay about 1,250 feet apart, in a rapid current, and combined to make the navigable conditions critically dangerous. Prompt measures were accordingly taken for their removal and provisional allotments aggregating $11,200 were made for that purpose, viz, $10,000 for the *Fontana* and $1,200 for the *Martin.* Operations were in progress from September 23 to November 20, 1900, when careful examination with sweeping bars showed a clear depth of 25 feet at the site of the *Fontana* and 22 feet at the *Martin.* The expenditures on account of the removal of the wrecks aggregated $9,398.40, viz, $8,288.51 for the *Fontana* and $1,109.89 for the *Martin.* The unexpended balance of the allotment, amounting to $1,801.60, will be required to adjust some outstanding claims.

(See Appendix P P 8.)

SURVEY MADE IN COMPLIANCE WITH RIVER AND HARBOR ACT APPROVED MARCH 3, 1899.

Colonel Lydecker submitted preliminary report June 4, 1900, on *survey of waters connecting lakes Superior and Huron, including Hay Lake Channel, St. Marys River, with a view to securing a channel 21 feet deep.*—The maximum total cost of works to be proposed is now estimated by him at $9,000,000. The report was transmitted to Congress and printed in House Doc. No. 128, Fifty-sixth Congress, second session. If possible, final report on this survey will be submitted in time for transmission to Congress at its next session. (See also Appendix P P 9.)

EXAMINATIONS AND SURVEY MADE IN COMPLIANCE WITH EMERGENCY RIVER AND HARBOR ACT APPROVED JUNE 6, 1900.

Examinations and survey of the following localities were made by the local engineer and reports thereon submitted:

1. *Examination and survey of St. Clair Flats Canal, Michigan, with a view to doubling its capacity.*—Colonel Lydecker submitted reports July 28, 1900, and December 6, 1900, respectively. The cost of the proposed improvement is estimated at $330,000. The reports were transmitted to Congress and printed in House Doc. No. 234, Fifty-sixth Congress, second session. (See also Appendix P P 10.)

2. *Preliminary examination of Detroit River, Michigan, with a view to obtaining sufficient depth of water in the channel on west side of Grosse Isle.*—Colonel Lydecker submitted report October 20, 1900. In his opinion, concurred in by the Chief of Engineers, improvement of the locality by the General Government in the manner indicated by the act is not advisable. The report was transmitted to Congress and printed in House Doc. No. 82, Fifty-sixth Congress, second session. (See also Appendix P P 11.)

IMPROVEMENT OF RIVERS AND HARBORS ON LAKE ERIE WEST OF ERIE, PENNSYLVANIA.

This district was in the charge of Col. Jared A. Smith, Corps of Engineers, to December 1, 1900, of Col. S. M. Mansfield, Corps of Engineers, from December 1, 1900, to May 8, 1901, and of Maj. Dan C. Kingman, Corps of Engineers, since May 8, 1901. Division Engineer, Col. S. M. Mansfield, Corps of Engineers, since May 9, 1901.

1. *Monroe Harbor, Michigan.*—The harbor of Monroe, Mich., is within the mouth of the Raisin River, at the western extremity of Lake Erie. In its natural condition the river flowed into the lake through several ponds and winding creeks. The depth of water at the deepest mouth of the river in its natural condition did not exceed 5 feet.

The project for the improvement of this harbor was adopted in 1834 and was practically completed in 1845. It had for its object to dredge a new and direct channel 100 feet wide and 10 feet deep from the lake across the marsh, a distance of 4,000 feet, to the portion of the river ordinarily used as a harbor. The sides of the canal were protected by a revetment and the entrance to the lake was protected by piers extending outward to a depth of 10 feet in the lake.

Subsequently the city of Monroe further improved the river channel by cutting a canal 1,400 feet long across a bend of the river.

The total expenditure to June 30, 1900, was $245,687.03.

At that time a contract was in force for deepening the channel both within and beyond the jetties, and this contract was completed July 20, 1900. This work left a channel about 200 feet wide and 13 feet deep extending outward from the end of the jetties to deep water in the lake, and a channel about 60 feet wide extending inward between the jetties and through the United States canal.

An inspection made June 27, 1901, indicates that the depth in the lake has been generally maintained, and there is no special indication of fill to be found there. Within the jetties, while the depth has in general been maintained the width of the channel is somewhat reduced. The piers are in need of repairs.

From its size and depth of channel this harbor can not accommodate the larger class of vessels used upon the lake, and its commerce is not great. From information furnished by the collector of customs and others, it would appear that the total receipts and shipments during the year 1900 amounted to about 6,500 tons, which was considerably greater than that reported in the previous year. One hundred and nineteen vessels entered the harbor, and one vessel was built there. The draft of largest vessels using the harbor was 10 feet.

July 1, 1900, balance unexpended	4,828.24
June 30, 1901, amount expended during fiscal year	4,828.24

Amount that can be profitably expended in fiscal year ending June 30, 1903, for maintenance of improvement................... 2,000.00
Submitted in compliance with requirements of sundry civil act of June 4, 1897, and of section 7 of the river and harbor act of 1899.

(See Appendix Q Q 1.)

2. Toledo Harbor, Ohio.—The harbor of Toledo is in the Maumee River. The wharf frontage on the river extends over a distance of about 3 miles, the lower end of which is about 4 miles above the mouth of the river, at the head of Maumee Bay.

Originally the channels in the river were much better than in the bay, having minimum depths of 14 to 16 feet, while in the bay the least depths were 8.5 feet and the maximum depth for most of the distance was but 12 feet.

In 1866 a project was adopted to dredge the channels of deepest water in the bay to a depth of 12 feet. The project was amended from time to time until 1887, when the old indirect channel had a minimum depth of 15 feet.

In 1887 a project was adopted for a straight channel through Maumee Bay, with a depth of 17 feet and a bottom width of 200 feet. The estimate of cost, including dikes or other channel protections, was $1,875,000.

The project for straight channel was amended in 1893 by increasing the width of outer section about 3 miles long to 300 feet. Since 1892 the improvement has been extended to include the Maumee River.

The river and harbor act of March 3, 1899, appropriated $150,000 for—

Improving harbor at Toledo, Ohio, by providing a straight channel through Maumee River and Bay four hundred feet in width and twenty-one feet deep, in accordance with the project dated December sixteenth, eighteen hundred and ninety-seven, * * * *Provided*, That a contract or contracts may be entered into by the Secretary of War for such materials and work as may be necessary to complete the said project, to be paid for as appropriations may from time to time be made by law, not to exceed eight hundred thousand dollars, exclusive of the amount herein and heretofore appropriated.

This then is the present project for improving the harbor at Toledo, Ohio.

Of the amount appropriated in the river and harbor act of March 3, 1899, the sum of $100,000 was allotted for operating and maintaining the United States dredge plant to dredge the channels south of the Wheeling and Lake Erie Railroad bridge. A continuous contract authorized by law was entered into with the Lydon & Drews Company, of Chicago, Ill., and was approved September 23, 1899.

The total expenditure for improving and maintaining channels in Maumee River and Bay to June 30, 1900, was $1,660,953.45.

This had sufficed to secure a dredged channel 200 feet wide and not less than 17 feet throughout. At some places it had been necessary to redredge the channel several times, and in some places the width had been increased to 400 feet.

Work has been in progress throughout the fiscal year 1901 by the contractor's plant and by the United States dredge when not required for emergency work elsewhere. The total amount of material excavated by the United States dredge during the year was 184,996 cubic yards; by the contractor's dredges, 961,552 cubic yards; the total for both was 1,146,521 cubic yards. This with the work previously done under the present project amounts in all to 1,490,558 cubic yards.

Work is now being so carried forward as to secure first a channel of full depth and 200 feet in width throughout the entire length of the proposed cut, after which the channel will be increased to the full width provided for by law.

A recent examination of the work already done shows that the channel is maintaining itself fairly well, but it is to be reasonably anticipated that a certain amount of periodical dredging will be necessary to maintain the channel.

Most of the floating plant belonging to the United States in this district has been employed at this locality. The plant consists of an inspection steamer, *Visitor*, dredge *Maumee*, tug *Thos. Spear*, six dump scows, and one flat scow, valued in all at $50,000. This plant is very useful and valuable in the district, and an estimate is included in this report for its operation, care, and maintenance.

The commerce of the harbor shows a material increase over that of the preceding year. The total freight received and shipped amounts to nearly 3,000,000 tons, an increase of more than 450,000 tons over that of 1899. There is every reason to believe that this rate of increase will continue as vessels are able to load to the full depth contemplated for the improved channel.

July 1, 1900, balance unexpended	$243,746.55
Amount appropriated by sundry civil act approved March 3, 1901	8,000.00
	251,746.55
June 30, 1901, amount expended during fiscal year	108,335.04
July 1, 1901, balance unexpended	143,411.51
July 1, 1901, outstanding liabilities	16,744.50
July 1, 1901, balance available	126,667.01
July 1, 1901, amount covered by uncompleted contracts	764,786.14
Amount (estimated) required for completion of existing project	659,500.00
Amount that can be profitably expended in fiscal year ending June 30, 1903, in addition to the balance available July 1, 1901:	
For works of improvement $250,000.00	
For maintenance of plant............ 15,000.00	
	265,000.00

Submitted in compliance with requirements of sundry civil act of June 4, 1897, and of section 7 of the river and harbor act of 1899.

(See Appendix Q Q 2.)

3. Port Clinton Harbor, Ohio.—The harbor of Port Clinton is within the mouth of the Portage River. This river flows into Lake Erie at a point, about 13 miles by land and 22 miles by lake, west of the city of Sandusky. In its natural condition the depth of water on the bar at the mouth of the river rarely exceeded 5 feet.

The project for its improvement was adopted in 1871 and slightly modified in 1872 and 1873. It provided for the construction of two parallel jetties extending outward from the mouth of the river to a depth of 10 feet of water in the lake.

The work done consisted mainly of sheet piling of oak plank, secured and reenforced by oak piles with heavy oak waling pieces. The pierhead of east jetty was a solid construction of piles and stone, and 720 linear feet of west jetty consisted of a substructure of piles with superstructure of timber crib work, both filled with stone.

The jetties were extended to a depth of 10 feet in the lake in 1883, and since then no further extension has been considered necessary. The channel was dredged to a depth of 10 feet over a width of 100 feet between the jetties and a width of 200 feet inside the shore line in 1893 and 1894. The natural conditions prevailing at the mouth of the river have been sufficient to maintain this depth since the dredging was done. The jetties, having become very much decayed, have been partially protected by a riprap of stone piled against them on both sides and given a slope of about one on one.

The present project covers merely the reenforcing of old wooden jetties by banks of small stone covered with heavy pavement.

The total amount expended to June 30, 1900, was $87,663.22.

A contract was entered into with Charles H. Strong & Son on October 4, 1900, for continuing the work of reenforcing the old jetties with stone.

Complaints have been received from time to time of the existence of a detached bowlder, on a line in prolongation of the axis of the jettied channel and some distance out in the lake. An effort will be made to discover and remove this bowlder.

Instead of doing further work upon the jetties at this time, it would be advantageous to dredge the channel to a depth of about 12½ feet. This would require the removal of about 28,000 cubic yards of material and would cost about $7,000.

The commerce of Port Clinton is not large. The total amount reported for the calendar year 1900 was 4,120 tons.

July 1, 1900, balance unexpended	$6,336.78
June 30, 1901, amount expended during fiscal year	455.16
July 1, 1901, balance unexpended	5,881.62
July 1, 1901, outstanding liabilities	977.21
July 1, 1901, balance available	4,904.41
July 1, 1901, amount covered by uncompleted contracts	4,461.45
Amount that can be profitably expended in fiscal year ending June 30, 1903, for maintenance of improvement, in addition to the balance available July 1, 1901	5,000.00

Submitted in compliance with requirements of sundry civil act of June 4, 1897, and of section 7 of the river and harbor act of 1899.

(See Appendix Q Q 3.)

4. Sandusky Harbor, Ohio.—The harbor of Sandusky is in the lower part of Sandusky Bay, along the city front, the part nearest to the lake being about 2 miles from the bar which divides the waters of the bay from those of the lake. In its natural condition the depth was only such as the bay afforded, which was about 10 feet along the city front and from 9 to 12 feet thence to the lake.

A long, flat sand bar divided the bay from the lake, this bar being cut through by a channel, from 1,000 to 2,000 feet in width, near its central portion. The southern part of the bar is called "Cedar Point" and the northern "Sand Point." Between these two points the currents between the bay and the lake, resulting from the action of the wind and from varying barometric pressures, had scoured out the channel to a depth of not less than 18 feet for a distance of a mile or more, the maximum depth being as great as 40 feet. This place has always been known as the "Deep Hole."

The first appropriation was made for a survey in 1826, and the first improvement was made in 1844, consisting in the construction of a dam to close a breach across Sand Point. With this exception all the improvements made previous to 1896 consisted in deepening natural channels and in making a new straight channel from the city front to Cedar Point and in removing sand and bowlders from the dock channel along the city front. Natural causes have washed away a greater part of Sand Point since 1826, and there is now a space of about 7,000 feet between the edge of the Deep Hole and Sand Point in which the water has a depth of from 2 to 6 feet.

The total amount appropriated up to 1896, and expended as above described, was $436,792.

In 1896, and subsequently, the project has been added to so as to provide for the construction of a stone jetty upon a mattress foundation extending from Cedar Point outward, with a view to confining and directing the flow of water to and from the bay. Additional provision was also made for a spur upon the other side of the Deep Hole and a short piece of jetty, and for the protection by a mattress covering of a portion of the bank of the channel and the point of the bar near the light-house.

The total expenditure for improving Sandusky Harbor, from 1844 to June 30, 1900, was $510,516.29.

This expenditure had resulted in the dredging, as above described, and in the construction of a portion of the south jetty, about 180 feet of the north jetty, and 800 feet of a dike extending toward Sand Point.

At the beginning of the fiscal year 1901 dredging was in progress under contract with E. J. Pryor, of Houghton, Mich. This contract was completed by the exhaustion of funds in October, 1900. In addition to this the United States dredge removed 27,355 cubic yards. Work of jetty construction was in progress under contract with Patrick Keohane, of Fayetteville, N. Y., at the beginning of the fiscal year. The contract was closed by the exhaustion of funds October 22. 1900.

The total completed length of the east jetty is now 3,113 feet, measured from the shore. There is a further portion, about 223 feet, which is only partially completed. The finishing of these works will complete the present project.

The commerce of Sandusky is increasing, and would no doubt increase more rapidly if the depth were made that of a first-class lake harbor. The total freight tonnage for 1900 amounted to a million and a quarter tons, an increase of over 100,000 tons over that of the preceding year.

576   REPORT OF THE CHIEF OF ENGINEERS, U. S. ARMY.

July 1, 1900, balance unexpended	$46,275.71
June 30, 1901, amount expended during fiscal year	45,314.65
July 1, 1901, balance unexpended	961.06
July 1, 1901, outstanding liabilities	173.00
July 1, 1901, balance available	788.06

{ Amount (estimated) required for completion of existing project 345,796.00
Amount that can be profitably expended in fiscal year ending June 30, 1903, for works of improvement and for maintenance, in addition to the balance available July 1, 1901 .... 125,000.00
Submitted in compliance with requirements of sundry civil act of June 4, 1897, and of section 7 of the river and harbor act of 1899.

(See Appendix Q Q 4.)

5. *Huron Harbor, Ohio.*—This harbor is situated within the mouth of the Huron River. In its natural condition the mouth was practically closed by a sand bar.

The first project for its improvement was adopted in 1826 and provided for the construction of two parallel jetties 140 feet apart, extending outward from the river banks. The jetties were extended from time to time and repaired as required, and the channel was finally deepened by dredging.

In 1890 the project was modified to provide for the extension of the jetties out to a depth of 16 feet of water in the lake, and to obtain a similar depth between the piers by dredging.

The total amount expended under all projects for all purposes of construction and maintenance to June 30, 1900, was $172,273.71. It was then estimated that $117,500 was necessary to complete the improvement proposed.

In addition to the work done by the United States the Wheeling and Lake Erie Railway Company, under authority granted by the Secretary of War, has excavated and maintained a channel of 20 feet depth between the jetties and outward to deep water in the lake.

The commercial statistics which have been collected for this harbor show that 656,179 tons of iron ore and coal was received and shipped during the year 1900. This is an increase of 45 per cent over the largest amount of tonnage heretofore reported.

For the expenditure of funds available at the beginning of the fiscal year a contract was entered into with I. R. Churchyard, of Buffalo, N. Y., to remove and rebuild a part of the west pier. The contract was annulled April 25, 1901. Preparations were then made to do the work by hired labor.

July 1, 1900, balance unexpended	$25,000.00
June 30, 1901, amount expended during fiscal year	240.69
July 1, 1901, balance unexpended	24,759.31
July 1, 1901, outstanding liabilities	15.10
July 1, 1901, balance available	24,744.21

{ Amount (estimated) required for completion of existing project 117,500.00
Amount that can be profitably expended in fiscal year ending June 30, 1903, for maintenance of improvement, in addition to the balance available July 1, 1901 .... 35,000.00
Submitted in compliance with requirements of sundry civil act of June 4, 1897, and of section 7 of the river and harbor act of 1899.

(See Appendix Q Q 5.)

6. *Vermilion Harbor, Ohio.*—An allotment was made by the Secretary of War of $1,500 from the appropriation for emergencies in river and harbor works, act of June 6, 1900, to be applied to the work of repairing the damage done at shore end of east jetty by a storm. Temporary work was at once undertaken and the break was closed at a cost of $176.27. The balance of the allotment is still held in order to determine what further work, if any, is necessary to complete the repair for which the allotment was made.

Amount allotted from appropriation contained in emergency river and
 harbor act approved June 6, 1900.................................... $1,500.00
June 30, 1901, amount expended during fiscal year 176.27

July 1, 1901, balance unexpended...................................... 1,323.73

(See Appendix Q Q 6.)

7. *Black River (Lorain) Harbor, Ohio.*—This harbor is within the mouth of Black River, where it enters into Lake Erie 26 miles west of Cleveland. In its natural condition the depth of water at the mouth of this river did not exceed 3 feet, but the river itself was navigable for a distance of 4 miles from its mouth for all vessels then in use upon the lake.

The first project provided for the construction of parallel jetties. These jetties have had to be rebuilt and extended from time to time so as to keep pace with increasing requirements, and dredging has been resorted to to secure a greater depth than the natural currents would afford.

In compliance with the requirements of the river and harbor act of June 3, 1896, a survey of this harbor was made and a new project prepared for its improvement. This project provided for the construction of two breakwaters converging toward the lake, having an opening between them 500 feet in width, in prolongation of the axial line in the jettied channel. It also provided for rebuilding the jetties and for dredging the protected areas to a depth of 20 feet.

The river and harbor act of March 3, 1899, provided for the execution of these works by a continuous contract. Proposals were invited separately for the dredging and the construction and repair work. The dredging was done under contract with Edward J. Hingston, of Buffalo, N. Y., the work being completed September 9, 1900, but the lowest bids obtained for the renewal of the jetties and the construction of the breakwaters exceeded the amount allowed by law.

The act of June 6, 1900, authorized contracts to be entered into for such a portion of the work as the funds available would allow, at a cost not to exceed a 10 per cent increase over the original estimates. Such a contract was entered into October 6, 1900, with Patrick Keohane, of Fayetteville, N. Y., and provided for the construction of all of the proposed works except the east breakwater. But little was accomplished by the end of the past fiscal year.

The total expended to June 30, 1900, amounted to $300,600.35.

At this time a good channel of not less than 20 feet depth existed between the jetties and outward to deep water of the lake. An examination made in May, 1901, showed the depth had been perfectly maintained.

To complete the east breakwater will require an expenditure of $190,000 in excess of that now provided for by law. This increase of estimate is due to the increased cost of labor and material which has resulted since first estimates were made.

The commercial statistics for this harbor collected for the year 1900 show that the total amount of freight received and shipped during that period amounted to 1,546,709 tons, an increase of nearly 125,000 tons over that of the previous year. Eight vessels were built in this harbor during the year, with an aggregate burden of 27,730 tons.

July 1, 1900, balance unexpended	$166,604.42
June 30, 1901, amount expended during fiscal year	10,142.49
July 1, 1901, balance unexpended	156,461.93
July 1, 1901, outstanding liabilities	138.25
July 1, 1901, balance available	156,323.68

Amount (estimated) required for completion of existing project		530,350.00
Amount that can be profitably expended in fiscal year ending June 30, 1903, in addition to the balance available July 1, 1901:		
For works of improvement	$300,000.00	
For maintenance of improvement	6,000.00	
		306,000.00

Submitted in compliance with requirements of sundry civil act of June 4, 1897, and of section 7 of the river and harbor act of 1899.

(See Appendix Q Q 7.)

8. *Cleveland Harbor, Ohio.*—The harbor of Cleveland, Ohio, consists of two distinct parts. The main portion, which is used for business purposes, is in the navigable portion of the Cuyahoga River, and a branch known as the "Old River Bed," all inside of the present shore line. All of the channel above the bridge of the Lake Shore and Michigan Southern Railway, which occupies a position practically coincident with the shore line of 1825, has been improved and maintained under the direction of the city authorities.

In 1826, when improvements were first undertaken, the middle of the river was about 700 feet west of its present location. The plan of improvement contemplated rectifying the channel so that it would lead more directly into the lake, and making the new location permanent by jetties to confine the channel and concentrate the action of the current upon the bar.

The piers were repaired and extended, parts were rebuilt, and the channel was made deeper and maintained by dredging as necessities arose, with no change in the general method of improvement until 1875, at which time the total expenditure had been $346,881.61.

In 1875 a project was adopted for a breakwater in 5 fathoms of water. The west breakwater was commenced in 1876 and completed in 1883, a total length of 7,130 feet. The east breakwater was commenced in 1888 and continued at intervals until 1893, when its length was 2,494.5 feet. In 1895 an opening of 200 feet was made in the shore arm of the west breakwater as a sanitary measure. In 1896 a project for completing certain improvements was approved by Congress and contracts for the work were authorized, at a total cost not to exceed $1,354,000. These improvements embodied in the latest project involve the completion of the east breakwater, covering an extension of about 3,000 feet; removing superstructure of the old west breakwater to a depth of 2 to 3 feet below water level and replacing it with a superstructure of concrete masonry; reenforcing the cribs below the masonry; sheathing the face of east breakwater; removing and rebuilding the east and west piers, and widening the mouth of the river.

RIVER AND HARBOR IMPROVEMENTS. 579

The river and harbor act of March 3, 1899, appropriated $75,000 for dredging. A contract for dredging in the harbor to a depth of 21 feet was approved July 7, 1899.

The total of all expenditures for improving Cleveland Harbor from 1825 to June 30, 1900, was $2,215,278.80.

This expenditure covered the cost of construction of the works under the earlier projects and their maintenance up to the time that the project was enlarged, and under the project of 1896 the old superstructure had been removed from the west breakwater over a distance of 2,490 feet and the work completed on all but 100 feet of this length. The west pier had been completed over a length of 821 feet and the substructure completed for the entire length. The foundation for the extension of the east breakwater had been completed and the substructure built for a length of 964 feet and the superstructure completed on all of this but 100 feet. The dredging to a depth of 21 feet had been nearly completed, as far as the funds available would allow.

During the past fiscal year the sum of $254,275.61 was expended, exclusive of outstanding liabilities. Of this sum about $18,000 was applied to dredging and the remainder expended under the contracts for the repair and extension of the breakwater. This expenditure resulted in a further extension of the new concrete superstructure over a length of a little more than 1,400 feet, the completion of concrete superstructure over about 575 linear feet of the west pier, and an extension of the substructure of the east breakwater 1,120 feet, over which about one-half of the superstructure has been completed. Forty thousand cubic yards of material was removed from the harbor.

As the appropriations for the works under continuous contract and for dredging were made under different acts of Congress for different purposes, the money statements are submitted separately.

Dredging is now being carried on to a depth of 21 feet below mean lake level to provide a minimum depth of 20 feet; dredging to a greater depth will be necessary.

During the past year a depth of 21 feet below mean lake level would have furnished a depth for navigation averaging but 19.8 feet, and for at least one month would have afforded but 18.3 feet.

The freight tonnage of Cleveland Harbor is very large. It amounted to more than 7,500,000 tons in the year 1900, an increase over the previous year of 178,000 tons. This increase is considerably less than that in some other harbors in the district, and it would seem to indicate that the present business is now very nearly equal to the maximum capacity of the harbor. Greater accommodations for vessels would appear to be necessary.

PROJECT UNDER CONTINUOUS CONTRACT.

July 1, 1900, balance unexpended	$515,463.93
June 30, 1901, amount expended during fiscal year	236,386.73
July 1, 1901, balance unexpended	279,077.20
July 1, 1901, outstanding liabilities	22,271.96
July 1, 1901, balance available	256,805.24
July 1, 1901, amount covered by uncompleted contracts	296,068.51
Amount (estimated) required for completion of existing project	353,000.00
Amount that can be profitably expended in fiscal year ending June 30, 1903, in addition to the balance available July 1, 1901	100,000.00

Submitted in compliance with requirements of sundry civil act of June 4, 1897.

PROJECT FOR DREDGING TO A DEPTH OF 21 FEET.

July 1, 1900, balance unexpended $17,888.88
June 30, 1901, amount expended during fiscal year 17,888.88

Amount (estimated) required for completion of existing project........ 160,300.00
Amount that can be profitably expended in fiscal year ending June 30, 1903, for works of improvement and for maintenance................ 150,000.00
Submitted in compliance with requirements of sundry civil act of June 4, 1897, and of section 7 of the river and harbor act of 1899.

(See Appendix Q Q 8.)

9. Fairport Harbor, Ohio.—This harbor is situated at the mouth of Grand River where it enters Lake Erie, about 32 miles eastward from the harbor of Cleveland. Before the improvement was undertaken the depth across the bar at the mouth of the river was variable and uncertain and quite insufficient for the needs of commerce.

The first improvement was undertaken in 1825, and the original project provided for the construction of parallel jetties of crib work filled with stone, placed about 200 feet apart and extending outward across the bar and into the lake. The jetties were extended and have been repeatedly repaired and rebuilt as necessities required, and the channel has been deepened and redredged many times.

The last extension to jetties was made in 1893. Since then all expenditures have been for maintenance.

The total amount expended to June 30, 1900, was $386,399.92.

The west jetty is 2,370 feet in length and the east one 1,765 feet in length from the original shore line. The present shore line on the west side of the jetties has advanced about 1,700 feet from its original position. If this rate continues it will soon overlap the end of the jetties. It may be necessary ere long to provide for the construction of one or more groins to the westward of the harbor in order to arrest the movement of sand.

The present project, adopted in 1896, provides for the construction of two breakwaters converging toward the lake, the outer ends being in deep water and sufficient space being left between them to afford an easy entrance to the jettied channel. The west breakwater is to be 2,030 feet in length and the east breakwater 1,350 feet in length.

On the 26th of June, 1899, a contract was entered into for the construction of a portion of the west breakwater, and under this contract 828 linear feet was constructed, at an average cost of $125 per linear foot. The work consisted of timber cribs filled with stone and surmounted by a continuous timber superstructure. Since then the project has been changed and requires that the remaining portion of the breakwaters shall be constructed wholly of stone, in accordance with an approved design, the pierheads alone to be of timber surmounted by concrete.

Owing to the great advance in price of timber, iron, and labor, etc., it has been found necessary to increase the estimate of the amount required for the completion of the project. (See Annual Report of the Chief of Engineers for 1900, pp. 4071–4072.)

In addition to the new work proposed a large amount of work will have to be done soon for the maintenance of the jetties already constructed. The estimated cost of this work, including cost of dredging for one year, is given in the report of the Chief of Engineers for 1900 as $184,825.

The commerce of Fairport during the year 1900 amounted to

1,688,147 tons, received and shipped. This is a trifle less than the amount handled during the previous year, but the tonnage of vessels entering the harbor shows an increase of nearly 1,000,000 tons.

July 1, 1900, balance unexpended	$119,473.61
Amount allotted from appropriation contained in emergency river and harbor act approved June 6, 1900	3,000.00
	122,473.61
June 30, 1901, amount expended during fiscal year	110,919.33
July 1, 1901, balance unexpended	11,554.28
July 1, 1901, outstanding liabilities	9.90
July 1, 1901, balance available	11,544.38

{ Amount (estimated) required for completion of existing project 480,000.00
Amount that can be profitably expended in fiscal year ending June 30, 1903, for works of improvement and for maintenance, in addition to the balance available July 1, 1901 .... 210,000.00
Submitted in compliance with requirements of sundry civil act of June 4, 1897, and of section 7 of the river and harbor act of 1899.

(See Appendix Q Q 9.)

10. Ashtabula Harbor, Ohio.—This harbor is situated at the mouth of the Ashtabula River, where it enters Lake Erie at a point about 54 miles eastward from the harbor of Cleveland. In its natural condition the mouth of the river was obstructed by a bar upon which the depth of water varied according to the prevailing conditions of storms on the lake and freshets in the river. The greatest possible depth on the bar was 9 feet, this being the distance to the underlying rock near the shore line. The minimum depth probably did not exceed 2 feet.

The original project for improvement of this harbor was adopted in 1826, and provided for the construction of two parallel jetties extending outward from the shore line into the lake. The jetties have been repaired from time to time and extended, and the channel has been deepened by dredging.

In 1891 the depth in the channel was 17 feet, and the project was modified to provide for widening the jettied channel to 213 feet and to extend the jetties to 22 feet depth in the lake, and to dredge between them to a depth of 20 feet.

The river and harbor act of 1896 authorized a new project which modifies the previous one in regard to the length of the jetties and provides for the construction of two breakwaters converging toward the la e, the outer ends being about 400 feet apart and in water 29 feet deep.

The river and harbor act of March 3, 1899, authorized a continuous contract to be made for the construction of these breakwaters, at a cost not to exceed $430,000.

The total amount expended to June 30, 1900, was $669,409.38.

At that time the channel between the jetties had been widened to 213 feet from a point northward from the Lake Shore Canal and Slip, and had been dredged to a depth of 20 feet from the county bridge to deep water in the lake. A section of west breakwater 432 feet in length had been completed. A continuous contract, approved June 22, 1900, had been entered into with James B. Donnelly, of Buffalo, N. Y., for the completion of the breakwaters.

The shore westward of this harbor is very sandy and there is a constant tendency of the shore line to advance along the west jetty. The jetties themselves are very short and do not extend outward beyond the effect of beach sand raised and held in suspension temporarily by the action of storm waves. A bar, therefore, constantly tends to form out beyond the jetties, greatly interfering with navigation. Frequent dredging is required to maintain the existing depth.

Two allotments of $3,000 each were made during the past fiscal year from the appropriation for emergencies in river and harbor works, act of June 6, 1900, and applied to the maintenance of this channel.

The dry sand from the beach to the westward is moved by the prevailing westerly winds over the west jetty and carried into the channel. The officer in charge considers it desirable that the United States should acquire the ownership of at least a half mile of the lake shore immediately west of the jetties in order that this sand movement might be stopped or at least controlled by plantations of willows or by the construction of sand fences, which the United States can not at present erect or maintain. The jetties are in great need of repair, and the channel is in danger of being closed at almost any time.

It was estimated in the Annual Report of the Chief of Engineers of 1900 (p. 4078) that the cost of maintaining, repairing, and rebuilding the jetties, revetting the bank, and maintaining the channel for one year would be $205,520.

Ashtabula is one of the greatest harbors of Lake Erie. The receipts and shipments of freight for the year 1900 amounted to more than five and three-quarter million tons, an increase of 1,100,000 tons over that of the previous year.

July 1, 1900, balance unexpended	$152,991.83
Amount appropriated by sundry civil act approved March 3, 1901	2,000.00
Amount allotted from appropriation contained in emergency river and harbor act approved June 6, 1900	6,000.00
	160,991.83
June 30, 1901, amount expended during fiscal year	6,549.94
July 1, 1901, balance unexpended	154,441.89
July 1, 1901, outstanding liabilities	269.28
July 1, 1901, balance available	154,172.61
July 1, 1901, amount covered by uncompleted contracts	407,410.11
Amount (estimated) required for completion of existing project	318,000.00
Amount that can be profitably expended in fiscal year ending June 30, 1903, in addition to the balance available July 1, 1901:	
For works of improvement $300,000.00	
For maintenance of improvement 100,000.00	
	400,000.00

Submitted in compliance with requirements of sundry civil act of June 4, 1897, and of section 7 of the river and harbor act of 1899.

(See Appendix Q Q 10.)

11. Conneaut Harbor, Ohio.—This is the most easterly harbor comprised in the Cleveland district. It is at the mouth of Conneaut Creek in the northeastern part of the State of Ohio. It is about 67 miles eastward from the harbor of Cleveland, and westward about 28 miles from the harbor of Erie, Pa. In its natural condition the creek was obstructed by a bar at its mouth over which the average depth of water did not exceed 2 feet.

The first improvement was undertaken in 1829, and consisted in the construction of parallel jetties of timber and stone extending outward into the lake so as to prolong the natural banks of the river and to confine the current and cause it to wash away the bar.

From 1829 until 1880 there was expended in the construction and maintenance of these works the sum of $112,629.39. No appropriation was made for the harbor from 1880 until 1892.

At that time the jetties were in a decayed and ruinous condition, and the channel had been filled up with sand and silt and was too shallow to be used by any vessel larger than the small sailing craft used for fishing.

A new project was approved in 1892, and provided for the construction of parallel jetties 200 feet apart and of sufficient length to extend outward to a depth of 17 feet in the lake. The project was further modified in 1896 to provide for the construction of two breakwaters converging toward the lake in such a manner as to shelter the entrance into the jettied channel, and possibly to prevent the formation of the bar of sand which the seas were constantly building across it. The project also contemplated a small extension of the east jetty and dredging of the protected areas to a depth of 20 feet.

The estimate of cost of the new project, exclusive of maintenance, was $610,000, and the amount expended in furtherance of it to June 30, 1900, was $124,834.44. It was then estimated that the amount necessary for completion would be $407,000.

A channel 200 feet wide and 20 feet deep has been dredged between the jetties and outward to a corresponding depth in the lake, but it shows a constant tendency under present conditions to refill, and repeated dredging has been necessary to maintain the depth.

The existing jetties do not prevent the sand from washing over them or through them, and they do not extend far enough out into the lake to be beyond the limit of the sand lifted and stirred up by the storm waves. Four hundred feet of the west jetty, 600 feet of the east jetty, and 526 feet of pile revetment inside of shore line were built, and 282 feet of the shore end of the west breakwater completed prior to June 30, 1900.

In the summer of 1898 the Pittsburg, Bessemer and Lake Erie Railroad Company, whose terminal is at this harbor, removed all the old jetty and underlying rock in the channel to a depth of not less than 20 feet.

In August, 1899, a contract was entered into for continuing the construction of the west breakwater as far as the funds available for the purpose would allow.

Under this contract four large cribs have been constructed and sunk in place, extending the breakwater to a total length of about 1,032 feet. The superstructure has not yet been completed upon the new work. This leaves about 222 feet of the west wing of the breakwater to be constructed, including the pierhead. No work has been done upon and no funds have yet been provided for the east breakwater required by the project, which is to be 1,050 feet in length.

On July 2, 1900, an allotment of $3,000 was made from the appropriation for emergencies in river and harbor works, act of June 6, 1900, to dredge away the bar that had formed beyond the jetties.

About 16,000 cubic yards of material was removed and a good channel formed. At the opening of navigation in the spring of 1901 it was found that the bar had re-formed, and an additional allotment of $2,500 was made to remove it. This work was done between May 24 and June 7, furnishing a channel 20 feet in depth and of a width equal to that between the jetties.

Frequent dredging will be necessary until the completion of the works proposed, and even then it may be required periodically.

The growth of commerce at this harbor has been most remarkable. In 1893 it amounted to nothing. In 1900 the receipts and shipments aggregated 3,322,607 tons, and the harbor is scarcely able to hold the number of vessels that desire to enter it. It seems desirable to push the improvement to completion as rapidly as possible, and in the meantime to provide a sufficient sum for maintenance of the channel by dredging.

July 1, 1900, balance unexpended	$95,165.56
Amount allotted from appropriation contained in emergency river and and harbor act approved June 6, 1900	5,500.00
	100,665.56
June 30, 1901, amount expended during fiscal year	47,450.07
July 1, 1901, balance unexpended	53,215.49
July 1, 1901, outstanding liabilities	16,707.91
July 1, 1901, balance available	36,507.58
July 1, 1901, amount covered by uncompleted contracts	31,838.19
Amount (estimated) required for completion of existing project	407,000.00
Amount that can be profitably expended in fiscal year ending June 30, 1903, for works of improvement and for maintenance, in addition to the balance available July 1, 1901	200,000.00
Submitted in compliance with requirements of sundry civil act of June 4, 1897, and of section 7 of the river and harbor act of 1899.	

(See Appendix Q Q 11.)

12. Removing sunken vessels or craft obstructing or endangering navigation.—(a) *Wreck of schooner Benson.*—In June, 1899, the schooner *Benson*, laden with coal, was sunk in Lake Erie, near the outer end of the channel over the outer bar at Sandusky, Ohio. The wreck was removed during the fiscal year ending June 30, 1900, but the inspection and final payment was not made until the past fiscal year.

The total cost of removal was $2,572.92.

(b) *Wreck of schooner Dundee.*—The schooner *Dundee*, a large vessel 211 feet long, 35 feet beam, and 16¼ feet depth, was wrecked in the night of September 11-12, 1900, about 13 miles off the harbor of Cleveland, Ohio. It went down in 68 feet of water and rested on an even keel. Two of its masts were standing and showed well above water, and with the attached wreckage formed an obstruction to navigation.

An allotment for the removal of the dangerous portions of the wreck was made and the work was completed September 15, 1900, the total cost being $500.

(c) *Wreck of dump scow in Cleveland Harbor, Ohio.*—In the night of September 18-19, 1900, a dump scow belonging to the L. P. & J. A. Smith Company sunk in the harbor of Cleveland, about 500 feet north of the Lake Shore bridge. It was a dangerous obstruction to navigation and preparations were made for its removal, but it was finally raised and removed by its owners on December 3, 1900, without cost to the United States.

(See Appendix Q Q 12.)

EXAMINATIONS AND SURVEYS MADE IN COMPLIANCE WITH EMERGENCY RIVER AND HARBOR ACT APPROVED JUNE 6, 1900.

Preliminary examinations and surveys of the following localities were made by the local engineer and reports thereon submitted:

1. Preliminary examination and survey of Sandusky Harbor, Ohio, with a view to maintaining a channel 21 feet deep at mean lake level with a width of 400 feet in the approaches to the harbor front and 300 feet in the harbor channel.—Colonel Smith submitted reports, dated August 22 and November 17, 1900, respectively. He submits a plan for improvement at an estimated cost of $781,000 and $10,000 annually for maintenance for the first five years. The reports were transmitted to Congress and printed in House Doc. No. 120, Fifty-sixth Congress, second session. (See also Appendix Q Q 13.)

2. Preliminary examination and survey of Cleveland Harbor, Ohio, with a view to the further improvement, etc.—Colonel Smith submitted reports, dated August 17 and November 17, 1900, respectively. He presents projects for improvement as follows:

For construction of breakwater, etc., to provide a safer and better entrance, estimated to cost according to one plan	$695,587
According to alternate plan	1,001,727
For extension eastward of breakwater now under construction to provide additional harbor room, according to one plan	3,785,869
According to alternate plan	3,853,069

The reports were transmitted to Congress and printed in House Doc. No. 118, Fifty-sixth Congress, second session. (See also Appendix Q Q 14.)

IMPROVEMENT OF ERIE HARBOR, PENNSYLVANIA, AND OF CERTAIN RIVERS AND HARBORS IN WESTERN NEW YORK.

This district was in the charge of Maj. T. W. Symons, Corps of Engineers. Division Engineer, Col. G. L. Gillespie, Corps of Engineers (now brigadier-general, Chief of Engineers, United States Army), to May 3, 1901, and Col. Charles R. Suter, Corps of Engineers, since May 9, 1901.

1. Harbor at Erie, Pa.—In its original condition the harbor of Erie was landlocked, the only entrance being to the east. The channel was narrow and tortuous, variable in position, with a depth of about 6 feet.

The original project approved March 26, 1824, provided for closing the eastern end of the harbor by means of a breakwater in which there should be an opening 200 feet wide, and for extending to deep water in the lake two parallel piers, one on each side of the opening. The project also includes the necessary work of dredging to keep the channel open, making the necessary repairs to existing structures, and maintaining Presque Isle Peninsula.

This project was modified by the river and harbor act of March 3, 1899, and now requires the harbor and entrance to be dredged to a depth of 20 feet, the north and south piers to be extended 500 and

1,000 feet, respectively, and four protection jetties to be built along the outer edge of Presque Isle Peninsula.

The estimated cost of completing the modified project was $377,000.

At the close of the fiscal year 1,210 feet of wooden superstructure on north pier had been replaced with concrete, the pier had been extended 510 feet, one protection jetty had been built, the channel dredged 20 feet deep, and the basin partly dredged.

The total amount expended on the harbor to June 30, 1900, was $1,021,271.17. It is impracticable to separate the cost of construction and maintenance.

The maximum draft that could be carried June 30, 1901, at mean low water over the shoalest part of the locality under improvement was 18½ feet.

The following table gives the total arrivals and departures, including tonnage for the past ten years, as compiled from Annual Reports of the Chief of Engineers:

Year.	Number.	Tonnage.	Year.	Number.	Tonnage.
1891	2,437	2,480,853	1896	3,100	3,323,672
1892	2,180	2,409,945	1897	3,133	4,051,964
1893	1,677	1,701,542	1898	2,939	3,939,019
1894	2,687	3,069,545	1899	3,200	3,961,794
1895	2,936	3,323,672	1900	2,709	3,403,812

July 1, 1900, balance unexpended $50,312.95
June 30, 1901, amount expended during fiscal year 30,702.08

July 1, 1901, balance unexpended 19,610.87

{ Amount (estimated) required for completion of existing project........ 252,000.00
Amount that can be profitably expended in fiscal year ending June 30, 1903, for works of improvement and for maintenance, in addition to the balance unexpended July 1, 1901 .... 125,000.00
Submitted in compliance with requirements of sundry civil act of June 4, 1897, and of section 7 of the river and harbor act of 1899.

(See Appendix R R 1.)

2. Harbor at Dunkirk, N. Y.—The harbor at Dunkirk is naturally a simple indentation of the south shore of Lake Erie. It lies between Point Gratiot on the west and Battery Point on the east. Between the two points is a distance of 9,600 feet, and the maximum breadth of the bay behind the line of the two headlands is 3,600 feet. The general depth of water in the bay was about 10 feet. The bay is underlaid with rock at an average depth of 15 to 16 feet. The object of the improvement is to form an artificially protected harbor in this indentation or bay.

The existing project, approved November 30, 1870, provides for a detached breakwater 2,860 feet long, one part of which, 2,300 feet long, was to be nearly parallel with the shore; the other part, 560 feet long, to be nearly parallel with the axis of the channel entrance.

This breakwater and the pier already built were to form the harbor, and the old channel was to be enlarged to 170 feet wide and 13 feet deep.

All the works now existent at Dunkirk have been built according to this plan. The project adopted by Congress and provided for by the river and harbor act of June 3, 1896, consisted in completing the breakwater, as before planned, by the addition of 360 feet to its eastern end and adding the channel arm, 560 feet long, and in addition thereto dredging an entrance channel and a harbor basin, containing in all about 65 acres, to a depth at mean lake level suitable for vessels drawing 16 feet. This work was completed in 1898 at a total cost of $389,060.55.

The total amount expended on the harbor to June 30, 1900, was $960,643.28.

It is impracticable to separate the cost of construction and maintenance. No work was done during the past fiscal year.

The old timber breakwater and pier will soon need repair, to provide for which an estimate is submitted.

The maximum draft that could be carried June 30, 1901, at mean low water over the shoalest part of the locality under improvement was 16 feet.

The following table gives the total arrivals and departures, including tonnage, for the past ten years, as compiled from the Annual Reports of the Chief of Engineers:

Year.	Number.	Tonnage.	Year.	Number.	Tonnage.
1891	96	24,465	1896	42	12,160
1892	58	13,756	1897	197	14,745
1893	187	19,158	1898	180	22,005
1894	76	18,763	1899	192	82,783
1895	69	15,650	1900	278	107,316

July 1, 1900, balance unexpended $1,694.10
June 30, 1901, amount expended during fiscal year 323.49

July 1, 1901, balance unexpended 1,370.61

Amount that can be profitably expended in fiscal year ending June 30, 1903, for maintenance of improvement, in addition to the balance unexpended July 1, 1901 .... 25,000.00
Submitted in compliance with requirements of sundry civil act of June 4, 1897, and of section 7 of the river and harbor act of 1899.

(See Appendix R R 2.)

3. *Harbor at Buffalo, N. Y.*—Buffalo Creek was the original harbor of the port of Buffalo. In its original condition it was shallow and closed by a gravel bar for most of the year. The original Governmental project for the improvement of this harbor was adopted in 1826, and provided at first for the construction of piers on the north and south sides of Buffalo Creek. Subsequently a masonry sea wall, running south from the shore end of the south pier, was proposed and built. In 1868 a detached breakwater, about 2,500 feet lakeward from the light-house, to extend south a distance of 4,000 feet, was proposed and adopted. In 1874 it was determined to extend this breakwater to a total length of 7,600 feet. This breakwater has now its full proposed length, the final extension of 806 feet having been built in 1893. It runs parallel with the shore and about half a mile distant from it. In 1874 it was also proposed to build a shore arm to the breakwater, the inshore end to consist of pile work near shore and crib work in deeper water. Upon reaching the 16-foot contour line in the lake this shore arm was planned to continue in a direction making an angle of 45

degrees with the shore and to overlap the south end of the breakwater, leaving an opening of 150 feet. In 1886 a project was approved for replacing with concrete the wooden superstructure as soon as it became badly decayed. To date 4,894.13 feet has been so replaced.

In 1895 a new project was adopted for the improvement of Buffalo Harbor. The project consists of the abandonment of the shore arm and the extension of the breakwater from its present southern end to Stony Point. The report of the Board and details of its plans are published in the Annual Report of the Chief of Engineers for 1895, page 3153 et seq. The river and harbor act of June 3, 1896, added to the project of the Board of Engineers by providing for the construction of a further length of the sand-catch pier, extending it to the established pierhead line.

The project now in force for the improvement of Buffalo Harbor is:

(*a*) To maintain existing structures, making the requisite minor repairs, and replacing the wooden superstructure of the breakwater with concrete when necessary.

(*b*) To build an extension of the breakwater from its present southern end to Stony Point, leaving the necessary openings for the convenience of commerce.

(*c*) To extend the sand-catch pier to the established pierhead line.

A new concrete superstructure will be placed on 1,400 feet of the south pier during the present season, a contract having been made with the Buffalo Dredging Company for the work.

About 1,800 feet of timber crib superstructure on the south harbor section of the breakwater will be replaced with a concrete superstructure during the present year, having been wrecked by the severe storms of last fall. A contract was made with the Buffalo Dredging Company for the work April 10, 1901, and they have commenced operations.

The total amount expended by the United States on the improvement of Buffalo Harbor to June 30, 1900, was $3,626,906.20. It is impracticable to separate the cost of construction and maintenance.

A very good harbor has been obtained. The principal features are north and south piers at the mouth of Buffalo Creek, in which most of the business of the port is done; also an outer breakwater 7,608.6 feet long, built of timber and stone; the new north breakwater, 2,200 feet long, and the main breakwater extension now under way.

A sea wall 5,400 feet long was built along the lake shore south of the harbor entrance, and a sand-catch pier of piles and stone, 1,147 feet long, built out from the shore.

The maximum draft that could be carried June 30, 1901, at mean low water over the shoalest part of the locality under improvement was 20 feet. The commerce of Buffalo is enormous. During the year the arrivals and departures of vessels by lake and river aggregated in number 9,973 and in tonnage 10,701,228.

The arrivals and departures of canal boats by the Erie Canal were 6,842. The principal receipts by lake and river were wheat, corn, flour, oats, iron ore, lumber, copper, pig iron, glucose, lard, and pork. The total receipts amounted to 7,425,876 tons.

The shipments by lake were principally coal, sugar, salt, and cement, and aggregated 2,790,533 tons.

For comparison the following table is given, showing arrivals and departures by lake and canal and the tonnage for the past five years:

RIVER AND HARBOR IMPROVEMENTS.

	Lake.		Canal.	
	Number.	Tonnage.	Number.	Tonnage.
1896	10,446	11,063,206	11,576	1,570,743
1897	10,778	11,299,091	9,218	1,207,964
1898	10,708	12,040,993	8,338	1,115,407
1899	10,417	10,481,043	7,506	1,083,170
1900	9,973	10,216,407	6,842	888,318

The grand total of the commerce of Buffalo carried on by lake, river, and canal for the seasons of 1899 and 1900 is as follows:

	Arrivals and departures.		Receipts of freight.		Shipments of freight.	
	1899.	1900.	1899.	1900.	1899.	1900.
			Tons.	Tons.	Tons.	Tons.
Lake and river	10,417	9,973	7,161,166	7,425,874	3,415,491	2,790,533
Canal	7,506	6,842	341,736	365,725	691,434	522,593
Total	17,923	16,815	7,502,902	7,791,601	4,106,925	3,313,126

Total receipts and shipments 1899, 11,609,827 tons; 1900, 11,104,727 tons. The amount of wheat and breadstuffs going east by canal in 1895 was the lowest for many years, and the canal freights were the lowest ever known, the average rate, Buffalo to New York, for wheat and corn having been only 2.2 cents.

The business on the canal picked up during 1896, but it has gradually decreased since to nearly the amounts of freight and rates reached in 1895.

July 1, 1900, balance unexpended	$742,583.17
Amount appropriated by sundry civil act approved March 3, 1901	400,000.00
	1,142,583.17
June 30, 1901, amount expended during fiscal year	382,184.46
July 1, 1901, balance unexpended	760,398.71
July 1, 1901, amount covered by uncompleted contracts	919,528.65
Amount (estimated) required for completion of existing project	343,506.00
Amount that can be profitably expended in fiscal year ending June 30, 1903, in addition to the balance unexpended July 1, 1901:	
For works of improvement $200,000.00	
For maintenance of improvement 25,000.00	
	225,000.00

Submitted in compliance with requirements of sundry civil act of June 4, 1897, and of section 7 of the river and harbor act of 1899.

(See Appendix R R 3.)

4. Buffalo entrance to Erie Basin and Black Rock Harbor, New York.—The first appropriation, $50,000, for this improvement was made March 3, 1899, the item of the act being as follows:

For improvement of the Buffalo entrance to Erie Basin and Black Rock Harbor, New York, fifty thousand dollars: *Provided,* That a contract or contracts may be entered into by the Secretary of War for such materials and work as may be necessary for the completion of said project, in accordance with the recommendation of the Secretary of War, House Document Number Seventy-two, Fifty-fifth Congress, first session, to be paid for as appropriations may from time to time be made by law, not to exceed in the aggregate one hundred and ninety-eight thousand one hundred and thirteen dollars and eighty cents, exclusive of the amount herein appropriated.

An appropriation of $191,701.25 was made June 3, 1896, to complete the work.

The adopted project is to build a breakwater about 2,200 feet long, covering and protecting the entrance to Erie Basin and Black Rock Harbor and the lake front of Buffalo Harbor between the State structures known as the Erie Basin breakwater and the Bird Island pier.

Contract was made with James B. Donnelly on August 4, 1900, for building the breakwater, and work commenced at once. The structure was completed June 4, 1901.

The amount expended to June 30, 1900, was $96,152.54, all for construction.

The maximum draft that could be carried over the shoalest part of the locality under improvement at mean low water June 30, 1901, was 17 feet.

For commercial statistics see report on Buffalo Harbor.

July 1, 1900, balance unexpended	$145,548.71
June 30, 1901, amount expended during fiscal year	140,125.56
July 1, 1901, balance unexpended	5,423.65

(See Appendix R R 4.)

5. *Tonawanda Harbor and Niagara River, New York.*—In its original condition the navigation of Niagara River from Lake Erie to Tonawanda was obstructed by several reefs and shoals, which materially limited the draft of vessels traversing it. The water in the harbor between Tonawanda Island and the mainland was shoal, and the river in some places had a very swift current.

The object of the project undertaken is to provide a navigable channel from the head of Niagara River at Lake Erie to the north line of the village of North Tonawanda, and to dredge Tonawanda Harbor to a depth permitting its use by vessels of 16 feet draft.

The adopted project of April 11, 1888, is to remove obstructions so as to make a channel 400 feet wide and 18 feet deep, which includes work at the following places:

(a) On the Horseshoe Reef, at the entrance to Niagara River.
(b) On the shoal at the head of Strawberry Island.
(c) At a few shoal places abreast of the lower end of Rattlesnake Island.
(d) The full width of the river between Tonawanda Island and the mainland along the entire front of Tonawanda.

The cost of the work estimated in 1891 was $1,152,987.93. This does not include the work necessary between Tonawanda Island and the north line of the village of North Tonawanda. The amount expended on the general project up to June 30, 1900, was $413,671.28, all for excavation.

At this time the channels through the Horseshoe Reef and the channel through the reef at Strawberry Island had been completed to a depth of 18 feet and width of 400 feet. No change in depth was made during the past year.

Tonawanda Harbor has been dredged 20 feet wide to a depth of 18 feet along nearly all the length of Tonawanda Island and mainland front, and a shoal at the foot of Tonawanda Island removed.

The commerce of Tonawanda is large. During the year 1900 there were entered and cleared 1,893 lake craft, with a tonnage of 953,613 tons. The receipts were principally lumber, iron ore, and limestone, and aggregated 961,573 tons. The shipments from Tonawanda amount to very little.

The maximum draft that could be carried June 30, 1901, at mean low water over the shoalest part of the locality under improvement was 15 feet.

July 1, 1900, balance unexpended	$11,328.77
June 30, 1901, amount expended during fiscal year	9,614.06
July 1, 1901, balance unexpended	1,714.71

{ Amount (estimated) required for completion of existing project....... 727,987.93
Amount that can be profitably expended in fiscal year ending June 30, 1903, in addition to the balance unexpended July 1, 1901 .... 150,000.00
Submitted in compliance with requirements of sundry civil act of June 4, 1897.

(See Appendix R R 5.)

6. *Niagara River from Tonawanda to Port Day, New York.*—Port Day is the inlet to the old hydraulic-power canal at Niagara Falls. It is not and never has been a practicable port of commerce, owing to its shallow water and its proximity to the head of Niagara Falls.

From Port Day up the river in front of the city of Niagara Falls is very shallow and with rock bed until Conners Island is reached. Between Conners Island and the main shore is a snug little harbor of about 5 acres, with a depth of 12 feet at mean river stage and with a maximum depth of about 18 feet.

By act of Congress of August 18, 1894, provision was made for improving Niagara River from Tonawanda to Port Day, with a view to obtaining a channel of 12 feet depth to Schlosser's dock.

The project as it now stands is, therefore, to provide a channel 12 feet in depth at low water and 200 feet in width from Schlosser's dock, back of Conners Island, through to Tonawanda by the American channel of the Niagara River. This project is recognized by the river and harbor act of June 3, 1896. The total cost of the work contemplated by the project is $95,000.

Up to June 30, 1900, there had been expended on the project $58,210.86, all for excavation. A channel 12 feet deep at mean river level and 200 feet wide has been completed the entire length of the Conners Island shoal, about 1,700 feet, and a channel 12 feet deep and 150 to 170 feet wide through the Cayuga Island shoal. No work has been done during the past year.

The commerce involved in the improvement is very small. During the year the total arrivals and departures were 110, most of which were small excursion boats. Whatever benefit the work confers will be upon future commerce.

The maximum draft that could be carried June 30, 1901, at mean low water over the shoalest part of the locality under improvement was 12 feet.

July 1, 1900, balance unexpended	$1,789.14
June 30, 1901, amount expended during fiscal year	1,430.65
July 1, 1901, balance unexpended	358.49

{ Amount (estimated) required for completion of existing project 35,000.00
Amount that can be profitably expended in fiscal year ending June 30, 1903, in addition to the balance unexpended July 1, 1901............ 10,000.00
Submitted in compliance with requirements of sundry civil act of June 4, 1897.

(See Appendix R R 6.)

EXAMINATION AND SURVEY MADE IN COMPLIANCE WITH EMERGENCY RIVER AND HARBOR ACT APPROVED JUNE 6, 1900.

Reports on preliminary examination and survey of *Lake Erie entrance to Black Rock Harbor and Erie Basin, New York*, were submitted through the division engineer by Major Symons under date of July 6 and November 8, 1900, respectively. He submits a plan for improvement estimated to cost as follows:

For channel of Erie Basin	$188,743
For branch channel and basin to Black Rock Harbor	625,900
Total	814,643

The reports were transmitted to Congress and printed in House Doc. No. 125, Fifty-sixth Congress, second session. (See also Appendix R R 7.)

IMPROVEMENT OF HARBORS ON LAKE ONTARIO AND OF ST. LAWRENCE RIVER AND HARBORS THEREON, NEW YORK.

This district was in the charge of Capt. Graham D. Fitch, Corps of Engineers, to April 24, 1901, and in the temporary charge of Maj. T. W. Symons, Corps of Engineers, since that date. Division Engineer, Col. G. L. Gillespie, Corps of Engineers (now brigadier-general, Chief of Engineers, United States Army), to May 3, 1901, and Col. Charles R. Suter, Corps of Engineers, since May 9, 1901.

1. Harbor at Wilson, N. Y.—This harbor is at the mouth of Twelvemile Creek. In its original condition there was a depth on the bar of 1 foot. In 1846 two piers were built by private enterprise about 400 feet into the lake.

The original project of 1873 for improvement by the General Government was to extend the piers to the 12-foot curve in Lake Ontario and to dredge a channel 12 feet deep between the piers and to deep water in the creek, at an estimated cost of $90,000, increased in 1877 to $100,000. January 10, 1900, the project was modified to obtain and maintain a depth of 10 feet at extreme low water without further extension of the piers, at least for the present.

The amount expended to June 30, 1900, was $71,793.19, of which $14,405.74 was applied to maintenance of improvement.

At that date there was a minimum depth of 9.3 feet below extreme low water, but the channel is not stable and fills rapidly with sand driven by storms.

During the fiscal year ending June 30, 1901, the most necessary repairs were made to the decks of both piers and 44 linear feet of Wakefield sheet piling was driven to close a hole under two cribs in the west pier.

The maximum draft that could be carried into this harbor at mean low water June 30, 1901, was 8 feet.

The following is a statement of the commerce at this port for the years given:

	Tons.		Tons.
1890	1,258	1899	124
1891	1,296½	1900	653
1898	294½		

July 1, 1900, balance unexpended $707.31
June 30, 1901, amount expended during fiscal year 707.31

{ Amount that can be profitably expended in fiscal year ending June 30,
  1903, for maintenance of improvement............................. 2,500.00
  Submitted in compliance with requirements of sundry civil act of June
  4, 1897, and of section 7 of the river and harbor act of 1899. }

(See Appendix S S 1.)

2. Harbor at Charlotte, N. Y.—This harbor is at the mouth of the Genesee River. In its original condition vessels could carry only 8 feet across the bar.

The original project of 1829 was to scour a channel 12 feet deep across the bar by constructing parallel piers to confine and direct the action of spring freshets. The present project of 1882 is to obtain a depth of 15 feet by extending the two piers a total of 3,250 feet and by dredging (see Annual Report of the Chief of Engineers for 1881, p. 2457). After the piers had been extended 1,444 feet the project was modified July 18, 1896, to preserve the depth by dredging without further extension of the piers for the present, and March 2, 1897, it was again modified to obtain and maintain not less than 16 feet and not more than 16¼ feet at extreme low water.

The amount expended to June 30, 1900, was $527,770.42. It was impracticable to separate the cost of construction and of maintenance.

At that date there was a minimum depth of 15 feet below extreme low water in a channel width of 100 feet.

During the fiscal year ending June 30, 1901, two allotments were made by the Secretary of War from the appropriation for emergencies in river and harbor works—one of $1,000 on August 4, 1900, for repairs to piers, and one of $2,500, May 24, 1901, for dredging the entrance to the harbor. Under the former allotment 144¾ cords of stone was placed in depleted pockets in the west and east piers, and dredging under the latter was in progress at the close of the fiscal year. June 30, 1901, the minimum depth that could be carried at mean low water was 15 feet.

The following is a statement of the commerce at this port during the last ten years:

	Tons.		Tons.
1891	480,407	1896	444,557
1892	460,956	1897	385,981
1893	347,288	1898	483,850
1894	400,492	1899	447,428
1895	369,417	1900	399,605

July 1, 1900, balance unexpended $557.98
Amount allotted from appropriation contained in emergency river and
  harbor act approved June 6, 1900............................... 3,500.00

                                                                 4,057.98
June 30, 1901, amount expended during fiscal year 2,109.35

July 1, 1901, balance unexpended 1,948.63

{ Amount that can be profitably expended in fiscal year ending June 30,
  1903, for maintenance of improvement, in addition to the balance unexpended July 1, 1901 .... 15,000.00
  Submitted in compliance with requirements of sundry civil act of June
  4, 1897, and of section 7 of the river and harbor act of 1899. }

(See Appendix S S 2.)

594   REPORT OF THE CHIEF OF ENGINEERS, U. S. ARMY.

3. Harbor at Pultneyville, N. Y.—This harbor is in Salmon Creek, Wayne County, N. Y. In its original condition the depth was only 20 inches at its mouth.

The project of 1871-72 was to protect the approach to the creek by building two piers in the lake of timber cribs filled with stone, and to dredge a channel 10 feet deep from the 10-foot curve in the lake to the mouth of the creek, at an estimated cost of $59,000, increased in 1875 to $71,000 on account of the difficult character of the dredging.

The amount expended to June 30, 1900, was $78,263.61, of which $7,655.65 was applied to maintenance of improvement.

At that date the governing depth was 3.5 feet at extreme low water.

The work done during the fiscal year consisted in the removal of 3,390 cubic yards of sand and gravel from a cut 960 feet long, 20 feet wide, and 8 feet deep below extreme low water.

The maximum draft that could be carried over the improvement at mean low water June 30, 1901, was 3 feet.

July 1, 1900, balance unexpended	$736.39
June 30, 1901, amount expended during fiscal year	736.39

(See Appendix S S 3.)

4. Harbor at Great Sodus Bay, New York.—In its original condition, the channel connecting this bay with Lake Ontario was wide and impracticable for vessels drawing over 8 feet.

The original project of 1829 was to narrow the entrance by constructing two converging breakwaters and deepen it to 12 feet by building two parallel piers and by dredging. The present project of 1882 is to obtain a depth of 15 feet at extreme low water by extending the two piers a total of 1,100 feet and by dredging. (See Annual Report of the Chief of Engineers for 1881, p. 2442.) After the piers had been extended 519 feet the project was modified July 18, 1896, to restore and maintain the requisite depth of 15 feet by dredging, without further extension of the piers for the present.

The amount expended to June 30, 1900, was $483,037.30, of which $74,785.50 was applied to maintenance of improvement.

At that date there was a minimum depth of 13 feet at extreme low water in a channel width of 60 feet.

The channel was redredged in the summer and early fall of 1900 and the harbor was surveyed. The maximum draft that could be carried in at mean low water June 30, 1901, was 12 feet.

The following is a statement of commerce at this port for the last ten years:

Year	Tons	Year	Tons
1891	36,032	1896	36,361
1892	62,276	1897	53,548
1893	14,277	1898	79,709
1894	77,471	1899	78,885
1895	43,566	1900	84,379

July 1, 1900, balance unexpended	$6,610.50
June 30, 1901, amount expended during fiscal year	3,598.54
July 1, 1901, balance unexpended	3,011.96

Amount that can be profitably expended in fiscal year ending June 30, 1903, for maintenance of improvement, in addition to the balance unexpended July 1, 1901 .... 7,000.00

Submitted in compliance with requirements of sundry civil act of June 4, 1897, and of section 7 of the river and harbor act of 1899.

(See Appendix S S 4.)

RIVER AND HARBOR IMPROVEMENTS. 595

5. *Harbor at Little Sodus Bay, New York.*—In its original condition the channel connecting this bay with Lake Ontario was about 150 feet wide and 18 inches deep.

The original project of 1854 was to deepen the channel by building two parallel piers across the bar to the 15-foot curve in the lake and to connect them with the shore by riprap. In 1867 this project was modified to provide for dredging to the depth of 12 feet. The present project of 1882 is to obtain a depth of 15 feet by extending the piers to the 15-foot curve in the lake and by dredging. (See Annual Report of the Chief of Engineers for 1882, p. 2449.) After the piers had been extended 835 feet the project was modified June 29, 1898, to restore and maintain the requisite depth of 15 feet by dredging without further extension of the piers for the present.

The amount expended to June 30, 1900, was $335,722.51, of which $55,274.25 was applied to maintenance of improvement.

At that date there was a depth in the channel between the piers of 13 feet at extreme low water in a channel width of 100 feet.

The channel was redredged in the fall of 1900, and the maximum draft that could be carried over the shoalest part of the locality under improvement June 30, 1901, was 12 feet.

The following is a statement of the commerce at this port for nine years:

	Tons.		Tons.
1891	134,241	1896	65,418
1892	101,324	1897	68,888
1893	66,345	1898	50,339
1894	63,595	1899	81,969
1895	63,708		

On account of increased commercial activity and the difficulty experienced by vessels in safely entering the channel between the piers in their present condition, work under the permanent project for pier construction should be resumed. It is proposed to extend the east pier 300 feet, and an appropriation of $20,000 for the purpose will be required.

July 1, 1900, balance unexpended	$2,720.26
June 30, 1901, amount expended during fiscal year	1,646.18
July 1, 1901, balance unexpended	1,074.08

Amount that can be profitably expended in fiscal year ending June 30, 1903, for maintenance of improvement, in addition to the balance unexpended July 1, 1901... 6,500.00
Submitted in compliance with requirements of sundry civil act of June 4, 1897, and of section 7 of the river and harbor act of 1899.

(See Appendix S S 5.)

6. *Harbor at Oswego, N. Y.*—In its original condition this harbor, consisting of an inner part in the Oswego River which was navigable by vessels of light draft only, and of an outer part forming a cove in the lake, had no protection against the seas.

The original project of 1827 (completed in 1829) was to build across the cove a breakwater of timber cribs filled with stone. Between 1830 and 1838 a superstructure of masonry was built on 500 feet of the breakwater. Between 1866 and 1869, $41,000 was expended in dredging the harbor to the depth of 12 feet at extreme low water. Between 1868 and 1870 the light-house pier was extended north 437 feet. In 1881 an outer breakwater was completed, having a lake face 4,870 feet long, a westerly shore return 916 feet long, and an easterly return 246 feet long. In 1881 a project was adopted to build an east breakwater, 248 feet of which was constructed in 1881 and removed in 1889. In 1885 and 1889 two spurs to the outer breakwater, 100 and 150 feet long, respectively, were completed. In 1893 (sundry civil act of March 3) the excavation of rock in the river was added to the project.

The present project of 1896, as subsequently modified, is: First, to build an east breakwater 1,435 feet long, at an estimated cost of $197,000 (acts of March 3, 1895, and June 3, 1896); second, to narrow the breach made in the outer breakwater in 1884 from 175 to about 75 feet, at an estimated cost of $18,500 (June 20, 1896); third, to carry the rock excavation in the Oswego River farther upstream (March 3, 1897); fourth, to remove part of the island between Schuyler and Van Buren streets to a depth of 15 feet, also to excavate rock and dredge to a small extent between the island and the west bank, at an estimated cost of $12,000 (March 6, 1897, and act of March 3, 1899).

The amount expended to June 30, 1900, was $1,934,208.19. It is impracticable to separate the cost of construction and of maintenance. At that date there were 5,857 feet of outer breakwater and 1,963 feet of inner breakwater, forming an outer harbor containing 38.9 acres and an inner harbor containing 9.35 acres (including the Oswego River), both having a controlling depth of 14.5 feet at extreme low water.

During the fiscal year ending June 30, 1901, the 1884 breach was reduced from about 175 feet to about 125 feet by placing on its west side a 50-foot crib; the removal of part of the upper island in the Oswego River was commenced, and general repairs were made to the outer breakwater. The repairs to that structure from the opening of the season in 1901 to June 30, 1901, were made under an allotment of $10,000 from the appropriation for emergencies in river and harbor works.

June 30, 1901, the harbor areas remained the same as in 1900, and the maximum draft that could be carried at extreme low water over the shoalest part of the locality under improvement was 14 feet.

The following is a statement of the commerce at this harbor for the last ten years:

	Tons.		Tons.
1891	826,813	1896	783,972
1892	964,240	1897	706,805
1893	947,688	1898	615,503
1894	829,469	1899	716,753
1895	749,575	1900	575,160

July 1, 1900, balance unexpended	$28,404.68
Amount allotted from appropriation contained in emergency river and harbor act approved June 6, 1900	10,000.00
	38,404.68
June 30, 1901, amount expended during fiscal year	27,515.43
July 1, 1901, balance unexpended	10,889.25
Amount that can be profitably expended in fiscal year ending June 30, 1903, for works of improvement and for maintenance, in addition to the balance unexpended July 1, 1901. Submitted in compliance with requirements of sundry civil act of June 4, 1897, and of section 7 of the river and harbor act of 1899.	150,000.00

(See Appendix S S 6.)

RIVER AND HARBOR IMPROVEMENTS. 597

7. *Harbor at Cape Vincent, N. Y.*—This harbor is an open roadstead on the St. Lawrence River, 2½ miles from Lake Ontario, and is a convenient location for vessels to lie during storms at night and in thick weather.

The original project of 1896 was to build a breakwater parallel to and 600 feet from the railroad wharf 1,600 feet long, at an estimated cost of $320,000. On May 13, 1899, this project was modified to build a breakwater parallel to and 500 feet from the railroad wharf 1,500 feet long, at an estimated cost of not over $200,000.

The amount expended to June 30, 1900, was $854.39. At that date a trench had been dredged to receive 410 linear feet of breakwater and partly filled with stone.

During the fiscal year ending June 30, 1901, the filling of the trench was completed and 410 linear feet of breakwater built. The maximum draft that could be carried over the locality under improvement at mean low water June 30, 1901, was 19 feet.

July 1, 1900, balance unexpended $49,145.61
June 30, 1901, amount expended during fiscal year 47,316.26

July 1, 1901, balance unexpended 1,829.35

Amount (estimated) required for completion of existing project....... 150,000.00
Amount that can be profitably expended in fiscal year ending June 30,
  1903, in addition to the balance unexpended July 1, 1901 .... 100,000.00
Submitted in compliance with requirements of sundry civil act of June
  4, 1897.

(See Appendix S S 7.)

8. *Shoals in the St. Lawrence River between Ogdensburg and the foot of Lake Ontario.*—In its original condition the channel of the St. Lawrence River from Sister Island light down to the head of Brockville Narrows was obstructed by 12 ledges, on which the depth was 9½ feet to 16 feet at low water.

The original project, act of September 19, 1890, was to remove to 18 feet below the zero of the Ogdensburg gauge ledges between Sister Island and Crossover lights, at an estimated cost of $43,305. In 1893, owing to the discovery of several outlying spurs, the estimated cost was increased to $54,772. By the act of June 3, 1896, the project was extended to embrace ledges in the St. Lawrence between Ogdensburg and the foot of Lake Ontario.

April 13, 1897, the removal of the obstructions to a depth of 1.4 feet greater, i. e., to 18 feet below the zero of the Oswego gauge, was included in the project, thereby increasing the total estimated cost to $108,000.

The amount expended to June 30, 1900, was $60,977.60.

At that date three of the ledges had been removed to 18 feet below the zero of the Oswego gauge and five to 18 feet below the zero of the Ogdensburg gauge.

During the past fiscal year six ledges were removed to 18 feet below the zero of the Oswego gauge.

The maximum draft that could be carried over the locality under improvement at mean low water June 30, 1901, was 16 feet.

598   REPORT OF THE CHIEF OF ENGINEERS, U. S. ARMY.

July 1, 1900, balance unexpended $7,022.40
June 30, 1901, amount expended during fiscal year 5,911.66

July 1, 1901, balance unexpended 1,110.74

Amount (estimated) required for completion of existing project 40,000.00
Amount that can be profitably expended in fiscal year ending June 30,
  1903, in addition to the balance unexpended July 1, 1901 .... 40,000.00
Submitted in compliance with requirements of sundry civil act of June
  4, 1897.

(See Appendix S S 8.)

9. *Harbor at Ogdensburg, New York.*—In its original condition the low-water depth in this harbor was 9 feet in the channel leading to the Oswegatchie River, 10 to 12 feet in the two lower entrance channels, and 6 to 12 feet along the city front.

The original project of 1868 was to dredge to the depth of 12 feet, and to build, if necessary, 5,500 linear feet of piers, at an estimated cost of $100,000. (See Annual Report of the Chief of Engineers for 1868, p. 271.) The piers were never built. The project of 1882 provided for dredging the channel across the shoal to the mouth of the Oswegatchie to 16 feet and all other channels to 15 feet at extreme low water, at an estimated cost of $76,000. (See Annual Report of Chief of Engineers for 1882, p. 2461.) The present project (see Annual Report of the Chief of Engineers for 1890, p. 2872) provided for dredging all the channels to a depth of 16.5 feet below the zero of the Ogdensburg gauge (15 feet below the zero of the Oswego gauge), at an estimated cost of $158,950. The project was modified February 27, 1897, to deepen the two lower entrance channels to 16 feet below the zero of the Oswego gauge, and by act of March 3, 1899, further modified to dredge 900 feet of the channel along the front of Ogdensburg above Franklin street to but 14 feet below the same zero, elsewhere the projected depths to remain 15 feet.

The amount expended to June 30, 1900, was $290,548.45, of which $33,301.15 was applied to maintenance of improvement.

At that date the controlling depths were: In the two lower entrance channels and in the basin in front of the Ogdensburg Terminal Company's elevator, 16 feet; in the channel between the two lower entrance channels, 15 feet; in the channel along the city front between the Oswegatchie and the lower harbor, 12 feet; and elsewhere, 14.5 feet.

Twenty thousand cubic yards of sand, etc., was redredged in October and November, 1900, from the city front channel, to the depth of 15 feet below the zero of the Oswego gauge. This work was done by William J. Daly, of Ogdensburg, N. Y., under supplemental contract.

The maximum draft that could be carried over the improvement at mean low water June 30, 1901, was as follows: In the lower entrance channels, 15 feet; in the channel along the city front, 12 feet; elsewhere, 15 feet. The following is a statement of the commerce at this port for the last ten years:

	Tons.		Tons.
1891	699,748	1896	886,438
1892	625,846	1897	866,035
1893	908,048	1898	645,201
1894	736,084	1899	670,363
1895	693,825	1900	646,248

RIVER AND HARBOR IMPROVEMENTS. 599

July 1, 1900, balance unexpended $6,807.11
June 30, 1901, amount expended during fiscal year 6,170.58

July 1, 1901, balance unexpended 636.53

{Amount that can be profitably expended in fiscal year ending June 30, 1903, for works of improvement and for maintenance, in addition to the balance unexpended July 1, 1901 .... 15,000.00
Submitted in compliance with requirements of sundry civil act of June 4, 1897, and of section 7 of the river and harbor act of 1899.

(See Appendix S S 9.)

EXAMINATIONS AND SURVEYS MADE IN COMPLIANCE WITH EMERGENCY RIVER AND HARBOR ACT APPROVED JUNE 6, 1900.

Preliminary examinations and surveys of the following localities were made by the local engineer and reports thereon submitted through the division engineer:

1. Preliminary examination and survey of Grass River, New York, from its confluence with St. Lawrence River to Massena, with the view of obtaining a depth of 21 feet.—Captain Fitch submitted reports dated August 2 and November 29, 1900, respectively. He presents a project for improvement at an estimated cost of $200,000. The reports were transmitted to Congress and printed in House Doc. No. 151, Fifty-sixth Congress, second session. (See also Appendix S S 10.)

2. Preliminary examination and survey of St. Lawrence River, New York, with a view to securing a navigable depth of 20 feet in the south channel at the head of Long Sault Island.—Captain Fitch submitted reports dated August 2 and December 1, 1900, respectively. The estimated cost of the improvement proposed is $48,000. The reports were transmitted to Congress and printed in House Doc. No. 201, Fifty-sixth Congress, second session. (See also Appendix S S 11.)

PACIFIC COAST.

IMPROVEMENT OF HARBORS IN CALIFORNIA SOUTH OF SAN FRANCISCO.

This district was in the charge of Capt. James J. Meyler, Corps of Engineers. Division Engineer, Col. S. M. Mansfield, Corps of Engineers, to November 23, 1900, and Col. Jared A. Smith, Corps of Engineers, since December 15, 1900.

1. San Diego Harbor, California.—San Diego Harbor is just to the northward of the national boundary of Mexico and 482 nautical miles to the southward of San Francisco.

Before the adoption of the present project the work carried on had for its object the preservation of the harbor, which was being injured by the deposit of material brought down the San Diego River during flood stages, and for this purpose a dike was built across the mouth of the river and a new channel excavated, causing the river to empty into False Bay. This work was completed in 1876, at a cost of $79,798.72.

The present project for the improvement of the harbor, approved December 8 and 30, 1890, has for its object the construction of a jetty on Zuninga Shoal, at the entrance to the harbor; the maintaining of a channel 24 feet deep at mean low tide and 500 feet wide through the middle ground, and the repairs of the dike. The jetty was to be about 7,500 feet long, extending from Coronado Island out on Zuninga Shoal, with a view to gaining 26 feet at mean low tide on the outer bar, where the survey of 1887 showed a depth of 21 feet.

The original estimated cost of this improvement was $394,400, but as work on the inner half of the jetty progressed under the different contracts it became evident that this sum would be inadequate. Therefore, under date of June 20, 1900, the local officer was authorized to change this estimated cost to $542,850.

The amount expended up to the close of the fiscal year ending June 30, 1900, was $298,733.61, and the jetty had been carried a distance of 3,347 feet seaward up to high water, and a foundation course of brush and stone 1,678 feet farther.

Under a contract for extending the jetty, 22,408 tons of riprap stone was delivered and put in place during the fiscal year ending June 30, 1901. On that date the jetty had been completed for a distance of 4,595 feet, and the foundation course extended 430 feet farther.

No material results in the way of increased depth or width of channel over the outer bar are as yet apparent from the expenditures made during the past fiscal year, the least depth still being 22¼ feet.

The commerce of this harbor was 152,777 tons for the year 1900, this being an increase of about 13 per cent over that of the previous year. The effect on commerce of this work of improvement will be to admit of the entrance of deeper-draft vessels, and to make their passage safer by straightening out the channel.

Deterioration of channel depth has occurred in the cut through the middle ground, and the local officer estimates the cost of restoration at $6,000.

July 1, 1900, balance expended... $58,766.39
June 30, 1901, amount expended during fiscal year 57,048.07

July 1, 1901, balance unexpended 1,718.32

{ Amount (estimated) required for completion of existing project....... 267,850.00
Amount that can be profitably expended in fiscal year ending June 30, 1903, in addition to the balance unexpended July 1, 1901............ 200,000.00
Submitted in compliance with requirements of sundry civil act of June 4, 1897.

(See Appendix T T 1.)

2. Deep-water harbor at San Pedro Bay, California.—The river and harbor act of June 3, 1896, provided for the appointment of a Board to determine upon the location of a deep-water harbor for commerce and refuge in Santa Monica Bay, California, or at San Pedro, in the same State, the decision of a majority of the Board as to location to be final. The Board was to make plans, specifications, and estimates for said improvement. After the Board had rendered its decision and submitted its report the Secretary of War was empowered to make contracts for the completion of the selected harbor in accordance with the project of the Board, at a cost not exceeding in the aggregate $2,900,000.

In accordance with the provisions of this act a Board was appointed, which submitted its report March 1, 1897, deciding in favor of San Pedro Bay. The report of the Board is printed in Senate Doc. No. 18, Fifty-fifth Congress, first session.

On August 12, 1898, a contract was entered into with Messrs. Heldmaier & Neu, of Chicago, Ill., for the construction of the entire breakwater, the price bid by them being $1,303,198.54. The contractors were to commence work on or before November 12, 1898, and they were to so prosecute it as to earn each year the money appropriated by Congress.

This contract was annulled on March 19, 1900, the contractors having failed to attain the rate of progress required by the specifications.

Up to the close of the fiscal year ending June 30, 1900, $51,537.43 had been expended, and the construction of the breakwater was continued during the year by the deposit of about 79,020 tons of stone, making the total amount deposited to that date 84,581 tons.

On June 7, 1900, a contract for continuing and completing the construction of the breakwater was entered into with the California Construction Company, of San Francisco, Cal., and the same was approved by the Chief of Engineers on June 27, 1900; time of commencement of work to be August 4, 1900; rate of progress to be as required by the specifications.

Under this contract 190,260 tons of stone has been delivered and placed in the substructure in the west arm of the breakwater, and the breakwater has been more or less built up for a distance of 2,700 feet from its westerly extremity.

The commerce of San Pedro Harbor, heretofore simply an anchorage ground in open roadstead, is so intimately connected with that of Wilmington Harbor that reference is made thereto for statistics on same. The effect on commerce of this work will be to afford a place of refuge, easy of access and secure from storms, for coastwise and deep-draft vessels, and a protected harbor of about 1 square mile in area for the commerce of the latter class of vessels. Vessels, while waiting for a favorable tide in order to enter the inner harbor of San Pedro, are now anchoring in the lee of the 2,700 feet of the more or less built-up portion of the breakwater.

July 1, 1900, balance unexpended	$562,607.23
Amount appropriated by sundry civil act approved March 3, 1901	146,000.00
	708,607.23
June 30, 1901, amount expended during fiscal year	133,753.89
July 1, 1901, balance unexpended	574,853.34
July 1, 1901, outstanding liabilities	24,691.20
July 1, 1901, balance available	550,162.14
July 1, 1901, amount covered by uncompleted contracts	2,454,655.57
Amount (estimated) required for completion of existing project	1,904,493.43
Amount that can be profitably expended in fiscal year ending June 30, 1903, in addition to the balance available July 1, 1901	400,000.00

Submitted in compliance with requirements of sundry civil act of June 4, 1897.

(See Appendix T T 2.)

3. Wilmington Harbor, California.—Wilmington is situated at the head of a small estuary which has its outlet in the bay of San Pedro, and is 393 nautical miles to the southward of San Francisco.

Previous to the commencement of the improvement, in 1871, there was a depth of less than 2 feet of water at low tide at the entrance.

The original project, approved July 1, 1871, contemplated gaining a depth of 10 feet at mean low tide.

In 1881 a further project to increase depth of channel from 10 to 15 feet at mean low tide by dredging a reef and between the jetties, raising existing works, and extending the jetties to 18 feet of water in San Pedro Bay was submitted.

In 1894 a project was submitted by the local officer in charge for a channel 18 feet deep at mean low tide, which would permit drafts of 22 to 24 feet at high tide, at an estimated cost of $392,725, and, in obedience to a resolution of the United States Senate, the Chief of Engineers submitted this report on February 7, 1895. The river and harbor act of June 3, 1896, appropriated $50,000 for improving the harbor in accordance with this plan, but provided for the appointment of a Board to decide whether a harbor of refuge should be established at Santa Monica or San Pedro (outer harbor of Wilmington), with the condition that if San Pedro was chosen existing appropriations for the Wilmington Harbor should not be expended. The Board having selected San Pedro the expenditure of existing appropriations was prohibited, and without further action of Congress the presenting of an estimate for the additional sum required for the completion of the improvement of this harbor is not permissible.

Up to the close of the fiscal year ending June 30, 1900, the amount expended on this improvement was $954,496.76, though no work had been done since 1894.

By this expenditure the available channel depth had been increased from 2 feet to 15.5 feet at mean low tide; and as the high tides average nearly 6 feet, vessels drawing over 21 feet could make the entrance.

The river and harbor act of March 3, 1899, provided for an examination and survey of this harbor, under the name of inner harbor at San Pedro, with a view to its further improvement. A map of this survey, together with a project for further improvement of this harbor, was submitted to Congress and printed in House Doc. No. 357, Fifty-sixth Congress, first session, and also in report of the Chief of Engineers for 1900, pages 4194-4211.

At the close of the fiscal year the least channel depth at the entrance was 15.5 feet.

The commerce of this harbor was 253,855 tons for the year 1900, an increase of 6 per cent over the previous year. No new steamship lines have been established during the year.

The local engineer reports deterioration of the east jetty, the restoration of which he estimates will cost $15,000.

July 1, 1900, balance unexpended	$50,503.24
June 30, 1901, amount expended during fiscal year	.92
July 1, 1901, balance unexpended	50,502.32

(See Appendix T T 3.)

4. San Luis Obispo Harbor, California.—San Luis Obispo Harbor is 9 miles to the southward and westward of the town of San Luis Obispo, 216 nautical miles from San Francisco.

It is a bight of the coast about 18 miles long between Point San Luis on the north and Point Sal on the south. The upper end, where Port Harford is situated, has a wharf and is the part used for commercial purposes. Whaler Reef, extending nearly half a mile to the southward and eastward of Point San Luis, forms more or less of a natural breakwater, but during the winter season it is exposed to the heavy swell caused by southerly gales.

The original project, approved September 22, 1888, was to construct a breakwater of rough stone on Whaler Reef, extending from Point San Luis to Whaler Island and thence to a point where the outer reef rises above high water. Its length when completed, including the island, was to be nearly 2,000 feet, and it was to be brought up to the plane of mean low water. This project was subsequently modified, January 17, 1893, so as to raise the structure up to a height of 6 feet above high water, with a thickness on top of 20 feet and such side slopes as may be assumed under the action of the sea.

The amount expended up to the close of the fiscal year ending June 30, 1900, was $188,455.34.

The contract for the extension of the breakwater, which was in force at that time, was completed September 29, 1900. Under this contract 18,180 tons of stone was delivered and placed in the breakwater during the first part of the past fiscal year. The completed breakwater was extended to a distance of 745 feet from Whaler Island, and a section, more or less built up, was extended 455 feet farther. The result has been to give increased security to vessels at the landing and anchorage against heavy swells.

The commerce of this harbor was 35,499 tons for 1900, a decrease of 31 per cent over that of the previous year.

July 1, 1900, balance unexpended	$41,544.66
June 30, 1901, amount expended during fiscal year	40,343.72
July 1, 1901, balance unexpended	1,200.94
Amount (estimated) required for completion of existing project	338,680.00
Amount that can be profitably expended in fiscal year ending June 30, 1903, in addition to the balance unexpended July 1, 1901	65,000.00
Submitted in compliance with requirements of sundry civil act of June 4, 1897.	

(See Appendix T T 4.)

EXAMINATION MADE IN COMPLIANCE WITH EMERGENCY RIVER AND HARBOR ACT APPROVED JUNE 6, 1900.

Report on preliminary examination of *Colorado River between El Dorado Canyon and Rioville, Nev.*, was submitted through the division engineer by Captain Meyler September 29, 1900. In his opinion, concurred in by the division engineer and by the Chief of Engineers, improvement of the locality by the General Government in the manner indicated by the act is not advisable. The report was transmitted to Congress and printed in House Doc. No. 67, Fifty-sixth Congress, second session. (See also Appendix T T 5.)

IMPROVEMENT OF ALVISO, SAN FRANCISCO, AND OAKLAND HARBORS, CALIFORNIA, OF SAN JOAQUIN AND SACRAMENTO RIVERS AND THEIR TRIBUTARIES, OF RIVERS AND HARBORS IN CALIFORNIA NORTH OF SAN FRANCISCO, AND OF PEARL HARBOR, HAWAII.

This district was in the charge of Lieut. Col. W. H. Heuer, Corps of Engineers.

1. *Harbor at Alviso, Cal.*—Alviso Slough is a small tidal estuary about 3¼ miles in length, from 60 to 800 feet in width, and from

3 to 7 feet in depth at low water. The range of the tide varies from 7 to 11 feet. The village of Alviso is situated at the head of the slough. It is an outlet for the commerce of the Santa Clara Valley, of which San Jose, distant by wagon road about 9 miles from Alviso, is the principal town.

Congress required preliminary examination of this slough in 1890 and again in 1892, and a survey, with estimate for improvement, in 1896. All reports of examinations made stated that the slough was unworthy of improvement by the General Government. The report of 1896 submitted plan for a dredged channel 7 feet deep at low water, 60 feet wide generally, and 80 feet wide opposite the wharves, and for a V-shaped basin in front of the village, so that boats could turn around. The estimated cost of the project was about $48,000. In March, 1899, Congress appropriated $48,000 to carry out the above-outlined project.

The work was completed on June 19, 1901, and a practicable channel of 7 feet least depth at low water, 60 feet of least width, and 80 feet wide abreast the wharves, with a turning basin, has been obtained, in accordance with the project approved by Congress. The total length of channel dredged was about 11,000 linear feet, 166,263 cubic yards of material was removed, and the total cost was $26,378.09, which may be reduced by $10,000, the amount of the bond furnished by the surety company on account of a failing contractor.

There is no tidal reservoir of any value above the dredged channel, and it will probably refill. As the work has just been completed, it as yet has had no effect in increasing the commerce of that section of the country.

The commerce of Alviso Slough is carried on one steamer, the *F. M. Smith*, 295 tons gross tonnage, which is reported to have carried 7,839 tons of freight and 21,840 passengers during the year 1900. From October 3, 1900, until the end of the year she did not run, because, it is reported, she did not pay her expenses, about $65 per day.

July 1, 1900, balance unexpended	$47,455.62
June 30, 1901, amount expended during fiscal year	25,833.71
July 1, 1901, balance unexpended	21,621.91
July 1, 1901, outstanding liabilities	457.50
July 1, 1901, balance available	21,164.41

(See Appendix U U 1.)

2. Harbor at San Francisco, Cal.—The improvement adopted by the river and harbor act of March 3, 1899, is the removal of three rocks, known as Arch Rock, Shag Rock No. 1, and Shag Rock No. 2, which were considered a menace to navigation.

Up to June 30, 1900, $3,329.83 had been spent on this work, but as the removal of Shag Rock No. 1, to which work had been confined up to that time, had not been completed, no practical results had been obtained.

Work was continued during the past fiscal year. The removal of Shag Rock No. 1 was completed by July 30, 1900, Shag Rock No. 2 was removed by April 5, 1901, and work on Arch Rock commenced. A platform resembling a wharf has been built over the latter and 171 holes, 10 inches in diameter, drilled in the rock to a depth of 5 feet below the level of the grade plane.

July 1, 1900, balance unexpended	$266,670.17
June 30, 1901, amount expended during fiscal year	52,181.31
July 1, 1901, balance unexpended	214,488.86
July 1, 1901, outstanding liabilities	285.00
July 1, 1901, balance available	214,203.86
July 1, 1901, amount covered by uncompleted contracts	205,118.26

(See Appendix U U 2.)

3. Oakland Harbor, California.—In its original condition the depth of the entrance to San Antonio Estuary, which is now Oakland Harbor, was 2 feet at low tide and admitted vessels of from 5 to 8 feet draft at high tide.

The principal features of the project for its improvement, which was approved February 15, 1874, are: (1) Two mid-tide training walls of rubblestone extended from the shore westward into San Francisco Bay about 2 miles; (2) a connection, by a canal 1½ miles long, with San Leandro Bay; (3) a dam at the entrance to San Leandro Bay; (4) dredging basin and a channel, the latter to have a depth of 20 feet at low water.

Two modifications were later adopted, namely, to increase width of tidal canal to 400 feet, and to raise the training walls to full tide height.

Up to the present time $2,450,000 has been appropriated for this work.

Up to June 30, 1900, the sum of $1,944,925.98 had been expended on this improvement, which had resulted in a channel 300 feet wide and 20 feet deep at low water from the bay of San Francisco to Webster Street Bridge; two stone jetties, one 12,000 feet long and the other 10,000 feet long, built into San Francisco Bay on the north and south sides of the jetty channel; a tidal basin, about 2 feet deep at low water, covering about 300 acres; a tidal basin channel in front of Brooklyn 6 feet deep at low water, 200 feet wide, and 5,000 feet long; portion of the tidal canal excavated both at the Oakland and San Leandro ends, and a bridge built over the tidal canal at Park street between East Oakland and Alameda,

Bridges were also being built over the tidal canal at High street, and Fruitvale avenue, near Alameda, Cal., and a diverting channel for Sausal Creek, to prevent deposits in the tidal canal, was in course of construction.

During the past fiscal year $170,135.98 was spent, making the total expended on this work to June 30, 1901, $2,115,061.96.

The result of the expenditures during the past fiscal year has been the completion of the bridge at High street and the diverting channel for Sausal Creek. The bridge at Fruitvale avenue is completed, but the lifting apparatus for the draw does not work satisfactorily, and the bridge has not been accepted.

The bridges were built in the dry, or before the canal was completed, partly to save expense in construction and to avoid the erecting of temporary trestle bridges, and principally so as not to interfere with railway and highway traffic.

A release has also been obtained from the obligation to build a bridge across the tidal canal at Washington avenue, which was imposed by the decree of the court condemning the site for the tidal canal, by the payment of $50,000 to the Central Pacific Railway Company.

As these works are in reality only preparatory to digging the tidal canal, no changes have resulted during the fiscal year.

On June 15, 1901, contract was signed with the Atlantic, Gulf and Pacific Company to dig the tidal canal. When this work is finished, all the essential items in the project adopted by Congress will have been completed.

The emergency river and harbor act of June 6, 1900, directed an examination and survey of—

Oakland Harbor: With a view to the improvement of said harbor to meet the needs of present and prospective commerce from the western end of the tidal canal to deep water in San Francisco Bay, including the excavation of a tidal basin.

The examination was made, and to determine the character of the bottom, borings were made to a depth of 30 feet below the low-water plane.

Reports of the survey and examination, with estimate of cost, were submitted to Congress by the Secretary of War on December 28, 1900, and are printed as House Doc. No. 262, Fifty-sixth Congress, second session, and are herewith as Appendix U U 12.

The commerce passing into and out of Oakland Harbor is large and increasing, as the whole of the transcontinental freight to and from San Francisco is carried across the bay on steam ferries and landed at the railroad slips at the upper end of the jetty channel. During the year 1900 the total tonnage of the harbor was 3,600,508 tons, of which 3,432,764 was landed and shipped below the bridges. This leaves the tonnage of the upper harbor, between and above the bridges, as 167,744 tons.

July 1, 1900, balance unexpended $505,674.02
June 30, 1901, amount expended during fiscal year 170,135.98

July 1, 1901, balance unexpended 335,538.04
July 1, 1901, outstanding liabilities 445.00

July 1, 1901, balance available 335,093.04

July 1, 1901, amount covered by uncompleted contracts................ 5,375.90

(See Appendix U U 3.)

4. San Joaquin River, California.—Before improvement the low-water channel to Stockton was only 6 feet in depth and contained several sharp bends where navigation was difficult, while the upper river, above Stockton, was navigable for but few months in the year, during the high-water stage, and part of that time for boats drawing not more than 2 feet of water.

The plan for improvement adopted in 1877, and slightly modified in 1881 and 1888, had for its object the securing and maintaining, by dredging, of a channel 9 feet deep at low water and 100 feet wide through the tidal portions of the river and Stockton Channel to Stockton, and a channel in Mormon Slough 4 feet deep at low water and 80 feet wide to Miller's warehouse; also temporary improvement of the low-water channel of the upper river by dredging, scraping, removal of snags, and the closure of Paradise Cut and Laird Slough.

The amount expended on the improvement of this river to June 30, 1,900 was $407 379.54.

The results obtained to June 30, 1900, were the maintenance of a channel to Stockton practically 9 feet in depth, the result of dredging carried on each year since 1877; the shortening of the river 4½ miles by cut-offs which have been made, three of which are near Devils Elbow, one at Head Reach, and a double cut-off in the narrows below Stockton; a double cut-off at Twenty-one Mile Slough, and the improvement of the navigation of the upper river by the removal of snags and the partial closure of Laird Slough and Paradise Cut by dams.

The work done during the past fiscal year has been dredging in Stockton and Mormon channels. The contract for dredging which was in progress at the end of the preceding fiscal year was completed in November, 1900.

During the work 246,222 cubic yards of material was excavated, giving in both channels the full width and depth required by the approved project. The enormous amount of detritus, however, brought during the winter freshets through Mormon Slough from the Calaveras River refilled Mormon Slough entirely and deposited over 100,000 cubic yards in Stockton Channel, threatening interruption of navigation unless it was again dredged before the river fell. Contract was therefore entered into to redredge Stockton Channel and work under it was commenced on June 22, 1901. Work was in progress at the end of the fiscal year.

Navigation to Stockton has been uninterrupted during the fiscal year, but there has been practically no navigation on the upper river.

The commerce on the lower San Joaquin River (below Stockton) is large and important. It is carried on 13 steamers, averaging 550 tons each; 14 barges, averaging at least 100 tons each, and many scow schooners. During 1900 it amounted to 248,887 tons of freight and 108,637 passengers, all carried on the lower river.

The maximum draft that can be carried to Stockton at mean low water is 9 feet.

The amount required for the completion of the existing project is indeterminate.

July 1, 1900, balance unexpended	$44,120.46
June 30, 1901, amount expended during fiscal year	13,593.42
July 1, 1901, balance unexpended	30,527.04
July 1, 1901, outstanding liabilities	200.00
July 1, 1901, balance available	30,327.04
July 1, 1901, amount covered by uncompleted contracts	5,024.00
Amount that can be profitably expended in fiscal year ending June 30, 1903, in addition to the balance available July 1, 1901. Submitted in compliance with requirements of sundry civil act of June 4, 1897.	18,000.00

(See Appendix U U 4.)

5. *Mokelumne River, California.*—This river, a tributary of the San Joaquin, is a tidal stream, and is navigable to New Hope Landing, 13 miles above its mouth.

Originally navigation was difficult on account of overhanging trees, numerous snags, and a shoal opposite New Hope Landing.

In 1884 project was made to remove snags and overhanging trees, and in 1892 to dredge shoal and remove point of land opposite New Hope Landing. Appropriations aggregating $18,000 were made in

1884, 1886, 1888, 1892, and 1894, and up to date $17,111.66 has been expended, as appropriations became available, in accordance with the project, which has been completed.

The commerce of the river is handled by one steamer of 385 tons capacity and a few scow schooners. The total tonnage carried in 1900 is reported as 86,989.

There has been no improvement in the depth of the stream. It has been widened by the removal of overhanging trees, and there is now no obstacle to navigation for such craft as use this river. The amount of commerce varies with the crops grown. Practically all that grows on and near the banks of the river is transported by the water route.

No work has been done on the river since 1896, and none is required until other snags shall lodge in the river. No deterioration of channel has been reported since work was completed in 1896, and it is not known that the work has increased the tonnage of the river. The maximum draft that can be carried at mean low water is fully 3 feet.

July 1, 1900, balance unexpended.................................... $888.34
July 1, 1901, balance unexpended.................................... 888.34

(See Appendix U U 5.)

6. *Sacramento and Feather rivers and tributaries, California.*—Before improvement navigation on these streams was difficult and dangerous above Sacramento on account of snags, shoals, and rapids. The channel of the stream below the mouth of the Feather and of the tributaries has been injured by the deposits of mining débris.

In 1874 a project was adopted having for its object the improvement of the low-water channels of the Upper Sacramento and Feather rivers by removing snags, scraping bars, and construction of temporary wing dams. In 1890 and 1892 the project was extended to include closure of certain crevasses and the treatment of the Yuba River near and above Marysville.

The river and harbor act of June 3, 1896, provided for the appointment of a Board of three engineer officers to make surveys, submit plans for improvement, and take charge of the work.

The Board submitted a preliminary report upon the improvement of the Sacramento River below Sacramento, December 14, 1897, printed as House Doc. No. 186, Fifty-fifth Congress, second session, and found on page 2944, report of the Chief of Engineers for 1898. A report upon the Sacramento and Feather rivers was submitted by the Board October 11, 1898, printed as House Doc. No. 48, Fifty-fifth Congress, third session, and found on page 3173, report of the Chief of Engineers for 1899. The Board reports that the Sacramento River below Sacramento can be improved by a system of wing dams at or near shoals, supplemented by dredging, if necessary, so as to give a least channel depth of 7 feet, at an estimated cost of $280,000; that a 4-foot depth can be maintained above Sacramento to Colusa, and a 3-foot depth thence to Red Bluff by removal of snags and concentration of channel widths by temporary works, as heretofore, at an estimated annual expense of $25,000, and that such depths are believed to be sufficient for all present demands of commerce. No work on the Feather River was provided for.

The river and harbor act of March 3, 1899, provided for—

Improving Sacramento River, California, from the city of Sacramento to the mouth: Continuing improvement, thirty thousand dollars: *Provided*, That a contract or contracts may be entered into by the Secretary of War for such materials and work as may be necessary to carry out the revised project printed in House Document Number One hundred and eighty-six, Fifty-fifth Congress, second session, and House Document Number Forty-eight, Fifty-fifth Congress, third session, to be paid for as appropriations may from time to time be made by law, not to exceed in the aggregate the sum of two hundred and fifty thousand dollars, exclusive of amount herein and heretofore appropriated. * * *

The work done to June 30, 1900, resulted in a low-water channel in the Sacramento with a least depth of 7 feet from Suisun Bay to Sacramento, 4 feet from Sacramento to Butte City, 3 feet from Butte City to Tehama, and 2½ feet from Tehama to Red Bluff.

The snag boat *Seizer* worked during the past year, from July 10 until November 3, 1900, removing snags and building wing dams.

In 1899 a project was submitted by the Board of Engineers for a series of wing dams opposite the city of Sacramento. Such work was put under contract and completed November 1, 1900. Plans for additional dams between the city of Sacramento and the mouth of the river have been approved and work put under contract, but not yet commenced.

The maximum draft that could be carried on June 30, 1901, on the Sacramento River was, from Suisun Bay to Sacramento, 8 feet; thence to Butte City, 5 feet; thence to Tehama, 3½ feet, and thence to Red Bluff, the head of navigation, 3 feet; the river not having at that date reached its low-water stage.

In addition to the amounts appropriated for work below Sacramento, there will be required to operate the snag boat, so as to keep navigation open on the upper river, the sum of $25,000 annually.

The total freight carried on the Sacramento River during 1900 was 461,314 tons and on the Feather 4,411.

Work of improvement on these rivers is also carried on by the State of California.

SACRAMENTO AND FEATHER RIVERS.

July 1, 1900, balance unexpended	$14,138.79
June 30, 1901, amount expended during fiscal year	13,505.26
July 1, 1901, balance unexpended	633.53
July 1, 1901, outstanding liabilities	75.00
July 1, 1901, balance available	558.53

Amount (estimated) required for completion of existing project.... Indeterminate.
Amount that can be profitably expended in fiscal year ending June 30, 1903, in addition to the balance available July 1, 1901.............. 18,000.00
Submitted in compliance with requirements of sundry civil act of June 4, 1897.

SACRAMENTO RIVER BELOW SACRAMENTO, CAL.

July 1, 1900, balance unexpended	$87,656.64
June 30, 1901, amount expended during fiscal year	5,798.39
July 1, 1901, balance unexpended	81,858.25
July 1, 1901, amount covered by uncompleted contracts	25,306.00

(See Appendix U U 6.)

7. *Napa River, California.*—Napa River before improvement had an average low-water depth of 5 feet, with the exception of the bars,

where the depth was reduced to less than 1 foot on the crests. The ordinary rise of the tides being 5 feet, there was each day a practicable depth of 6 feet.

The approved project consists in dredging the bars between Carr Bend and Vernon Mills, in the immediate vicinity of Napa City, cutting off projecting points of land so as to obtain a channel 75 feet wide and 4 feet deep at mean low water, and removing obstructions, such as snags, logs, etc.

Work upon this improvement was begun in 1889, and in that year a channel was dredged through the different bars between Carr Bend and the highway bridge at Third street, Napa City, and the river was cleared of snags. The channel was again dredged in 1891.

Up to June 30, 1900, $21,455.09 had been expended on this improvement, the result being that the width and depth of the channel had been generally maintained and all dangerous snags, logs, etc., had been removed from the channel.

During the past fiscal year $3,621.42 was spent in redredging the bars which had formed in the river.

The commerce of the stream is carried on two steamboats, which make regular daily trips, and several scow schooners. The amount of tonnage reported for the year 1900 was 81,536 tons.

This channel, being a tidal portion of a silt-bearing stream, requires occasional dredging. The amount required for the completion of the project is consequently indeterminate.

The maximum draft that can be carried to the town of Napa, the head of navigation, is 8 feet at high water. At mean low water the maximum draft is 2.6 feet, the freshets of last winter having caused considerable deposit on some of the bars.

July 1, 1900, balance unexpended	$4,044.91
June 30, 1901, amount expended during fiscal year	3,621.42
July 1, 1901, balance unexpended	423.49

{ Amount (estimated) required for completion of existing project.... Indeterminate.
Amount that can be profitably expended in fiscal year ending June 30, 1903, for maintenance of improvement, in addition to the balance unexpended July 1, 1901.. 4,000.00
Submitted in compliance with requirements of sundry civil act of June 4, 1897, and of section 7 of the river and harbor act of 1899. }

(See Appendix U U 7.)

8. *Petaluma Creek, California.*—This creek is an estuary of San Pablo Bay, and is navigable for 16 miles of its length to Petaluma, a town of about 4,000 inhabitants, which is at the head of navigation.

Before improvement it was very crooked, dry in places at low water, and navigation was dependent entirely upon the tide.

In 1880 project was made for straightening the stream by making cut-offs, and dredging to obtain a channel 50 feet wide and 3 feet deep at low tide. In 1892 the project was extended to dredge the channel as deep as funds would permit.

Up to June 30, 1900, $60,968.04 had been expended on this improvement, with the result that the creek had been shortened 2.5 miles, and a channel dredged having a least width of 50 feet and a least depth of 4 feet near the town of Petaluma and of 6 feet in the lower portion at mean low stages of tide.

No work was done during the past fiscal year and no funds expended. Traffic was uninterrupted.

The maximum draft that can be carried to Petaluma, at the head of navigation, is 4 feet at mean low water.

The commerce of this creek, which is valuable and important, is carried on one steamboat (294 tons) and numerous scow schooners, which carry the heavier freight. The tonnage during 1900 was large, but as much of it was carried on scow schooners it can not be reliably stated.

The drainage area of this stream is about 83 square miles of land, principally agricultural; consequently large quantities of detritus are annually carried into the channel, which the tide waters are unable to carry out; hence redredging will be required about every two years to maintain navigation.

July 1, 1900, balance unexpended $313.03
July 1, 1901, balance unexpended 313.03

{ Amount (estimated) required for completion of existing project...... Indeterminate.
Amount that can be profitably expended in fiscal year ending June 30, 1903, for maintenance of improvement, in addition to the balance unexpended July 1, 1901... 4,000.00
Submitted in compliance with requirements of sundry civil act of June 4, 1897, and of section 7 of the river and harbor act of 1899. }

(See Appendix U U 8.)

9. Humboldt Harbor and Bay, California.—Before improvement the harbor was obstructed by a troublesome and variable sand bar inclosing the entrance about a mile distant. Across the submerged bar was a channel which was exceedingly shifting, uncertain, and dangerous. Its low-water depth has been occasionally as much as 25 feet and frequently as little as 9 feet. The bar constantly changed in position, the greatest range being about $1\frac{1}{4}$ miles. Vessels were often storm bound in the harbor for long periods. There were also numerous shoals within the harbor close to the wharves, rendering it difficult for vessels to reach Eureka, Arcata, and Hookton, the main shipping points on the bay.

In 1882 a project was adopted for improving the entrance, with the object of increasing the depth of water over the bar by constructing a low-tide brush and stone jetty, extending seaward from the end of the south spit for a distance of 6,000 feet. Its estimated cost was $600,000. In 1891 a Board of Engineer officers recommended the raising of this jetty to high tide and the addition of another, making two stone and brush jetties, nearly parallel, about 2,100 feet apart, starting from the north and south spits, respectively, and extending seaward to the 18-foot contour, with such groins as might be found necessary during the progress of the work. The north jetty was not to be begun until the completion of the south. The total cost of these jetties and the necessary bank protection was estimated at $1,715,115 in addition to the sum which had already been appropriated. In 1892 the project was slightly modified so as to start the north jetty from the end of the dike already built for shore protection, making that a part of the jetty. The construction of the north jetty, so far as thought necessary to prevent erosion, without waiting for the completion of the south jetty, was also authorized. The river and harbor act of July 13, 1892, placed the improvement under the continuous-contract system.

The amount expended on this work to June 30, 1900, was $2,171,842.54, of which $130,884.69 was for dredging in the inner harbor and $2,040,957.85 for improving the entrance.

The result was the completion of both the project for improving the entrance and that for dredging the inner harbor. A channel between the jetties 1,350 feet wide and 28 feet deep at low water was procured immediately on the completion of the jetties, but as they became somewhat beaten down by the action of the sea it is probable this depth has been somewhat, but not materially, reduced. The channel width has been maintained.

The completion of the dredging project gave a channel in front of the town of Eureka 8,900 feet long, 200 feet wide, and 15 feet deep at low water.

The expenditures during the past fiscal year have been for services of a custodian to care for the property on the site, moving some of the buildings to prevent their destruction by the sea, and a few minor repairs.

During the year 1900 1,169 vessels, having a gross tonnage of 478,188 tons, passed over Humboldt bar; but large and important as this traffic is, the improvements made are believed to have provided a harbor in every way adequate to the demands of the commerce of the port.

July 1, 1900, balance unexpended	$15,772.46
June 30, 1901, amount expended during fiscal year	1,369.06
July 1, 1901, balance unexpended	14,403.40
July 1, 1901, outstanding liabilities	75.00
July 1, 1901, balance available	14,328.40

(See Appendix U U 9.)

10. Pearl Harbor, Hawaii.—Pearl Harbor is situated on the island of Oahu, about 8 miles west of the city of Honolulu. It is a safe and commodious harbor, with deep water, but the entrance is obstructed by a bar about 1,900 feet through, having at low water only about 10 feet of water over it at its shoalest place.

A full description of the harbor was printed as Senate Ex. Doc. No. 42, Fifty-third Congress, third session.

The river and harbor act of March 3, 1899, provided as follows:

Improving Pearl Harbor, Hawaii, in accordance with the report submitted by Rear-Admiral Walker, July eleventh, eighteen hundred and ninety-four, and contained in Senate Executive Document Number Forty-two, Fifty-third Congress, third session: Completing improvement, one hundred thousand dollars.

The project made for the expenditure of the funds appropriated, which was approved on December 5, 1900, provided for dredging a channel through the bar, by contract, 30 feet deep at low water and as wide as the funds would permit. Bids were opened on February 27, 1901, and all were rejected. The work was readvertised and bids again opened on June 24, 1901. The lowest bid was 44½ cents per cubic yard, and a contract was entered into and was approved July 25, 1901. No work has yet been done.

July 1, 1900, balance unexpended	$100,000.00
June 30, 1901, amount expended during fiscal year	230.49
July 1, 1901, balance unexpended	99,769.51

(See Appendix U U 10.)

11. *Removing sunken vessels or craft obstructing or endangering navigation.*—On September 8, 1900, the iron ship *May Flint*, 3,576 tons register, laden with coal, collided with the U. S. battle ship *Iowa* and immediately thereafter sunk in San Francisco Bay, California, in about 60 feet of water, where she was a menace and serious danger to navigation.

The matter was reported to the Secretary of War, and on October 10, 1900, an arrangement was made with the owner of the wreck by which he was to remove the same to a depth of 35 feet below low water, free of expense to the United States. A bond for $20,000 was given for the proper fulfillment of the agreement.

Most of the coal in the wreck has been removed by the owner, and the vessel itself partly broken up and removed. It is expected that the work will be completed in September next, without any expense to the United States other than the sum of $1.34 paid for telegraph tolls.

(See Appendix U U 11.)

EXAMINATIONS AND SURVEYS MADE IN COMPLIANCE WITH EMERGENCY RIVER AND HARBOR ACT APPROVED JUNE 6, 1900.

Preliminary examinations and surveys of the following localities were made by the local engineer and reports thereon submitted:

1. *Preliminary examination and survey of Oakland Harbor, California, with a view to its improvement from the western end of the tidal canal to deep water in San Francisco Bay, including the excavation of tidal basin.*—Lieutenant-Colonel Heuer submitted reports dated July 26 and December 19, 1900, respectively. Three plans for improvement are presented, estimated to cost $646,293, $1,687,818, and $968,203, respectively. The reports were transmitted to Congress and printed in House Doc. No. 262, Fifty-sixth Congress, second session. (See also Appendix U U 12.)

2. *Preliminary examination and survey of San Joaquin River, California, and the waters connecting the same with the strait of Karquines, extending from the town of Antioch to Suisun Point, California.*—Lieutenant-Colonel Heuer submitted reports dated August 21 and December 12, 1900, respectively. For the reasons presented by him, it is his opinion that improvement of the locality is not necessary to be undertaken by the General Government. The reports were transmitted to Congress and printed in House Doc. No. 261, Fifty-sixth Congress, second session. (See also Appendix U U 13.)

3. *Preliminary examination of San Joaquin River, California, above the mouth of the Stanislaus River, with a view to determining the advisability of closing the mouths of the more important blind sloughs, especially Finegan, Amphlet, and Walden sloughs, etc.*—Lieutenant-Colonel Heuer submitted report September 11, 1900. In his opinion, concurred in by the Chief of Engineers, improvement of the locality by the General Government in the manner indicated by the act is not advisable. The report was transmitted to Congress and printed in House Doc. No. 69, Fifty-sixth Congress, second session. (See also Appendix U U 14.)

IMPROVEMENT OF RIVERS AND HARBORS IN WESTERN OREGON, OF UPPER COLUMBIA AND SNAKE RIVERS, OREGON AND WASHINGTON, AND OF CLEARWATER RIVER, IDAHO.

This district was in the charge of Capt. William W. Harts, Corps of Engineers, to March 19, 1901, and in the temporary charge of Capt. William C. Langfitt, Corps of Engineers, since that date. Division Engineer, Col. S. M. Mansfield, Corps of Engineers, to November 23, 1900, and Col. Jared A. Smith, Corps of Engineers, since December 15, 1900.

1. Coquille River, Oregon (general improvement).—This stream empties into the Pacific Ocean at Bandon, Coos County, Oreg., about 375 miles north of San Francisco. Once safely across the bar in the ocean at the mouth of the river vessels drawing about 11 feet of water experience no special difficulty in ascending the stream at high tide to the town of Coquille, about 25 miles above Bandon.

Before improvement the channel at the mouth of the river skirted the south headland for some distance, as shown on map opposite page 2682 of the Annual Report of the Chief of Engineers for 1882, and was shoal, shifting, and studded with dangerous rocks. The depth of the water on the ocean bar at the original mouth of the river was usually about 3 feet at low tide, or a little over 7 feet at high tide.

The original plan for improvement (report printed in the Annual Report of the Chief of Engineers for 1879, p. 1806) provided for the construction of two converging high-tide jetties, built of rubblestone, 800 feet apart so located as to cause the river to empty into the sea about one-half mile north of the original mouth of the river, these jetties to run out to sea a sufficient distance to create and maintain a channel 12 feet deep at low tide. In 1880 the proposed depth of 12 feet at low tide to be obtained in the channel at the new mouth of the river was reduced to 10 feet; in 1888 it was reduced to 8 feet, and in 1891 the plan was changed to provide that the jetties should be 600 feet apart at their outer ends, instead of 800 feet. In 1892 the estimate of cost for completing the improvement, including previous appropriations (and including $6,883.90 expended in removing snags in the river between Coquille and Myrtle Point, under the acts of Congress of August 11, 1888, and September 19, 1890), was increased from $164,200 to $285,000. (Annual Report Chief of Engineers, 1892, pp. 2664-2665.)

The expenditures to June 30, 1900, $184,294.67, resulted in practically completing the south jetty throughout its projected length of about 2,700 feet, in constructing the proposed 1,500-foot north jetty for the distance of about 510 feet, and in removing some of the principal snags between Coquille and Myrtle Point. The jetty work resulted in closing up the dangerous old channel at the mouth of the river and in opening up a new channel running straight out to sea, the depth obtained in the new channel ranging ordinarily from 4 to 10 feet at low tide.

The expenditures during fiscal year ending June 30, 1901, were, for works of improvement, $2,882.74; for maintenance of improvement, $19,441.73; total, $22,324.47; and resulted in completing, under a contract dated August 15, 1899, all work connected with the 2,700-foot south jetty and in rebuilding the 510-foot section of the incomplete north jetty, which had been practically destroyed by heavy seas. This resulted in obtaining a depth ranging from 7 to 13 feet at mean low

RIVER AND HARBOR IMPROVEMENTS. 615

tide. It is not expected, however, that these favorable conditions can be maintained until the north jetty is extended farther seaward.

The maximum draft that could be carried June 30, 1901, at mean low tide in the new channel at the mouth of the river was about 7 feet.

The principal articles of commerce carried over the bar in the ocean at the mouth of the river are lumber and coal. This commerce is loaded on small coasting vessels along the 25 miles of the river between its mouth and Coquille, and by them taken to San Francisco for market. The river and ocean form the only practicable means for transporting the commerce of the region to market.

COMMERCIAL STATISTICS.

	Tons.		Tons.
1879	7,000	1892	19,362
1882	6,630	1893	14,491
1883	9,438	1894	14,180
1884	13,100	1895	16,256
1885	7,649	1896	21,106
1886	9,080	1897	25,620
1887	6,631	1898	24,556
1888	29,197	1899	26,654
1889	29,309	1900	30,727
1891	15,994		

The statistics for 1895–1900, inclusive, are for calendar years; those for years prior to 1895 are for fiscal years ending June 30.

Statistics for years not named are not available.

July 1, 1900, balance unexpended	$25,705.33
June 30, 1901, amount expended during fiscal year	22,324.47
July 1, 1901, balance unexpended	3,380.86
July 1, 1901, outstanding liabilities	126.50
July 1, 1901, balance available	3,254.36

Amount (estimated) required for completion of existing project	75,000.00
Amount that can be profitably expended in fiscal year ending June 30, 1903, in addition to the balance available July 1, 1901	40,000.00
Submitted in compliance with requirements of sundry civil act of June 4, 1897.	

(See Appendix V V 1.)

2. Coquille River, Oregon, between Coquille and Myrtle Point.—When there is sufficient water small steamboats and launches navigate the 13 miles of the Coquille River between Coquille and Myrtle Point. During a portion of each year, however, navigation is impracticable above a point 8¼ miles above Coquille on account of the small volume of the river and a number of shoals.

The project for improvement adopted in 1892 (report printed in the Annual Report of the Chief of Engineers for 1891, pp. 3280–3283), as amended consequent to survey made in 1894 (report of survey printed in Annual Report of the Chief of Engineers for 1895, pp. 3350–3351), provides for deepening the channel between Coquille and Myrtle Point to 4 feet at mean low water by removing snags and dredging and constructing deflecting dikes at shoals.

The amount expended to June 30, 1900, $27,144.50, was for works of improvement, and was for removing snags, dredging shoals, constructing two deflecting dikes, and confining the channel for the distance of about five-eighths of a mile between two rows of pile dikes 60 feet apart.

616   REPORT OF THE CHIEF OF ENGINEERS, U. S. ARMY.

The expenditures during fiscal year ending June 30, 1901, were for removing obstructing snags and dredging obstructing shoals, and resulted in providing, temporarily, a channel of the projected depth and width, so that the small steamboats and launches could reach Rackliffs Landing, about 11¼ miles above Coquille, at low-water stages.

The maximum draft that could be carried June 30, 1901, at mean low water in the 11¼ miles from Coquille up to Rackliffs Landing was about 4 feet, while at places in the 1¼ miles from Rackliffs Landing up to Myrtle Point the depth of the stream at low water was only a few inches.

The officer in local charge of the improvement reports that the conditions have changed since the adoption of the present project for improvement, and that a revision of the project therefore appears to be advisable.

The commerce carried by the several small boats and launches plying above Coquille consists principally of farm products and is inconsiderable in volume. A railroad parallels the stream between Coquille and Myrtle Point.

COMMERCIAL STATISTICS.

	Tons.		Tons.
1893	1,242	1897	4,293
1894	1,692	1898	4,915
1895	1,409	1899	3,399
1896	3,205	1900	3,783

The statistics for 1893–1895 are for fiscal years ending June 30; for 1896–1900 they are for calendar years.

July 1, 1900, balance unexpended	$3,855.50
June 30, 1901, amount expended during fiscal year	3,820.68
July 1, 1901, balance unexpended	34.82
July 1, 1901, outstanding liabilities	24.55
July 1, 1901, balance available	10.27
Amount (estimated) required for completion of existing project	19,980.77

(See Appendix V V 2.)

3. Entrance to Coos Bay and Harbor, Oregon.—Coos Bay is a tidal estuary on the Pacific coast in Oregon, about 400 miles north of San Francisco. It is the principal harbor between the mouth of the Columbia River and San Francisco. Before improvement the obstructions consisted of the usual bar in the ocean at the entrance to the bay and shoals inside the bay near its entrance, formed by sands which accumulated during northwesterly winds. Under the influence of these winds the sand spit on the north side of the entrance advanced toward the south, contracting the channel under the high stone headland, known as Coos Head, on the south side of the entrance, to a very narrow width, and usually causing the channel across the bar in the ocean at the entrance to follow the west side of the north spit in a tortuous course. The depth on the ocean bar was often but 10 feet at low tide. The mean rise of the tide at this place is about 5.6 feet.

Under the original project for improvement there was constructed a deflecting jetty about 1,760 feet long, running westerly from a point on the south shore near Fossil Point a short distance inside the entrance to the bay, designed to cause the currents to scour away the southern end of the north sand spit, to prevent an undue contraction of the width of the channel at the entrance.

The present approved project (printed in the Annual Report of the Chief of Engineers for 1890, pp. 2936-2965) provides for obtaining and maintaining a channel 20 feet deep at low tide, through the bar in the ocean at the entrance to the bay, by confining the entrance between two high-tide rubblestone jetties, the north jetty to be 9,600 feet long and the south jetty 4,200 feet long. The estimated total cost of this improvement, exclusive of the amount expended on the original project, is $2,466,412.20.

The amount expended under both projects up to June 30, 1900, was, for works of improvement, $738,750, and for maintenance of improvement, $53,983.01, or a total of $792,733.01, and resulted in the construction of the jetty near Fossil Point, under the original project, and in completing the 9,600-foot north jetty running out to sea from the southern end of the north sand spit, provided for in the present project. This has resulted in obtaining a channel through the ocean bar having ordinarily 18 to 22 feet at low tide.

The expenditures during fiscal year ending June 30, 1901, were for maintenance of improvement, and consisted of placing additional rubblestone in the north jetty, principally at the sea end.

Inasmuch as the projected depth of 20 feet at low tide was practically obtained in 1895, and has been maintained with but rare exceptions since, by means of the north jetty alone, the necessity for constructing the proposed south jetty is not at this time apparent.

A comparison of the maps printed in Annual Reports of the Chief of Engineers for 1884 (p. 2264) and for 1900 (p. 4278) will show the improved condition of the entrance to the bay.

The commerce that crosses the bar at the entrance to Coos Bay consists principally of lumber and coal, originating at points on and adjacent to the bay. Practically all of the commerce is marketed in San Francisco, to which point it is taken by coasting vessels. The bay and ocean form the only practicable means of transporting the commerce to market.

COMMERCIAL STATISTICS.

	Tons.		Tons.
1883	93,380	1895	128,544
1885	75,718	1896	144,934
1886	109,988	1897	115,896
1890	242,329	1898	103,039
1892	136,065	1899	116,567
1893	109,044	1900	104,294
1894	109,152		

The statistics for 1895-1900 are for calendar years; those prior to 1895 are for the fiscal years ending June 30. Statistics for years not named are either not available or are incomplete.

July 1, 1900, balance unexpended	$96,016.99
November 10, 1900, refundment of overpayment	.56
	96,017.55
June 30, 1901, amount expended during fiscal year	85,417.56
July 1, 1901, balance unexpended	10,599.99
July 1, 1901, outstanding liabilities	346.73
July 1, 1901, balance available	10,253.26
Amount (estimated) required for completion of existing project	1,791,412.20

(See Appendix V V 3.)

4. Harbor at Coos Bay, Oregon (dredging).—The acts of Congress of August 18, 1894, and June 3, 1896, appropriated $27,390 for the purchase of a dredger and two hopper scows and for operating same in dredging channels through several shoals in Coos Bay, opposite and near Marshfield, the chief town on the bay. These shoals, having only 5 to 8 feet of water on them at low tide, delayed the coasting vessels, drawing about 17 feet of water, which called at Marshfield, for the vessels were compelled to wait until full high tide.

The sundry civil act approved July 1, 1898, provided that the appropriations of August 18, 1894, and June 3, 1896, for the purchase of a dredger and two scows, could be used in carrying on the required dredging by contract or in any other manner that in the judgment of the Secretary of War would be most economical and advantageous to the Government.

The amount expended to June 30, 1900, $27,329.03, was for works of improvement, and resulted in dredging, under a contract, channels about 13 feet deep at mean low tide through four shoals opposite and near Marshfield, known as Hogsback Shoal, Webster Point Shoal, Stave Mill Shoal, and Bunker Shoal (as shown on map following page 3206 of the Annual Report of the Chief of Engineers for 1899), and in dredging with Government plant a channel about 7 feet deep at mean lower low tide through a shoal in the bay at the mouth of Coos River, opposite Marshfield, this latter channel being dredged for the benefit of the light-draft steamboats which ply between Marshfield and points on Coos River.

There were no expenditures in fiscal year ending June 30, 1901.

The project for improvement having been completed in fiscal year ending June 30, 1900, the unexpended funds were returned to the Treasury July 18, 1900.

The maximum draft that could be carried June 30, 1901, at mean low tide in the channels dredged through Hogsback Shoal, Webster Point Shoal, Stave Mill Shoal, and Bunker Shoal is about 13 feet, and through the shoal at mouth of Coos River about 5 feet.

Practically all of the commerce of Coos Bay and Coos River is benefited by the improvements in the bay, as the commerce is carried in vessels using one or more of the dredged channels. This commerce during the past thirteen years has averaged about 125,000 tons per annum.

July 1, 1900, balance unexpended $70.72
July 1, 1901, balance unexpended 70.72

(See Appendix V V 4.)

5. Coos River, Oregon.—Coos River is the principal tributary of Coos Bay, and empties into the bay at its head, opposite the town of Marshfield. At a point 5½ miles from its mouth the river divides into two branches, known as the North and South forks, up each of which tidal influence extends for about 8¼ miles. Before improvement was commenced the small light-draft steamboats and launches plying between Marshfield and the head of tide on each fork experienced considerable difficulty in navigating on account of the many snags, bowlders, etc., in the stream.

The project adopted in 1896 provides for removing snags and bowlders, cutting through bars, etc., where necessary to secure a channel 50 feet wide throughout the 5½ miles in the main river and 8¼ miles of each fork.

The amount expended to June 30, 1900, $7,857.92, was for works of improvement, and resulted in the removal of the obstructing snags and bowlders in the main river and the two forks, so that light-draft boats could navigate the stream with greater ease than formerly.

The expenditures during the fiscal year ending June 30, 1901, were in connection with maintaining the improvement.

The maximum draft that could be carried June 30, 1901, at mean low tide over the shoalest parts of the locality under improvement varied from 2 to 4 feet.

Coos River flows through a narrow but productive valley. The commerce carried on the small boats plying the stream consists principally of farm and dairy products, which are brought to Marshfield, where ocean vessels touch, for market. On account of the formation of the country the stream is the only means of transporting the commerce to market.

COMMERCIAL STATISTICS FOR CALENDAR YEARS.

	Tons.		Tons.
1896	13,204	1899	[1] 70,007
1897	16,534	1900	[2] 229,225
1898	22,674		

July 1, 1900, balance unexpended	$142.08
June 30, 1901, amount expended during fiscal year	47.25
July 1, 1901, balance unexpended	94.83
Amount that can be profitably expended in fiscal year ending June 30, 1903, for maintenance of improvement, in addition to the balance unexpended July 1, 1901	2,000.00

Submitted in compliance with requirements of sundry civil act of June 4, 1897, and of section 7 of the river and harbor act of 1899.

(See Appendix V V 5.)

6. *Mouth of Siuslaw River, Oregon.*—The Siuslaw River empties into the Pacific Ocean at a point about 475 miles north of San Francisco, Cal. It enters the sea through a shifting sand beach, without headlands or other fixed points to mark the entrance, which is obstructed by a shoal outer bar. Before the work of improvement was commenced the channel across this outer bar frequently shifted its position up or down the coast as much as 1 mile, and the depth of water on the bar varied from 5 to 12 feet at low tide.

The project for improvement, approved by the Secretary of War August 4, 1891 (report printed in the Annual Report of the Chief of Engineers for 1891, pp. 3175-3182), provides for confining the mouth of the river in the ocean between two high-tide rubblestone jetties, the north jetty to be 7,500 feet long, including a tramway approach at its shore end 3,000 feet long, and the south jetty to be 5,600 feet long, including a tramway approach at its shore end 2,400 feet long.

These jetties are designed to hold the channel across the bar in the ocean at the mouth of the river in one position and to maintain the depth of 8 feet at low tide in the bar channel. The estimated cost of the improvement is $700,000. The charts opposite page 3174 and page 3178 of the Annual Report of the Chief of Engineers for 1891 show

---

[1] Includes 21,852 tons of stone for the Government jetty at the entrance to Coos Bay, Oregon.
[2] Includes 170,400 tons of stone for the Government jetty at the entrance to Coos Bay, Oregon.

the positions of the proposed jetties. A map of the latest survey of the mouth of the river appears opposite page 4290 of the Annual Report of the Chief of Engineers for 1900.

The amount expended to June 30, 1900, $128,516.85, was for works of improvement, and resulted in the partial construction of about 4,045 feet of the north jetty, which includes a tramway 3,029 feet long at the shore end of the jetty. This checked somewhat the tendency of the bar channel to shift its position as far to the north as often occurred before the work of improvement was commenced.

The expenditures during the fiscal year ending June 30, 1901, resulted in extending the north jetty seaward about 45 feet. This short extension was too limited to produce any appreciable improvement. The great depths of the water (50 to 55 feet) through which the jetty was necessarily extended during the past year rendered it impracticable to add much to its former length with the comparatively small sum appropriated March 3, 1899.

Nothing has been done toward constructing the south jetty, the project providing that the north jetty shall be constructed first, at least in part.

During the past fiscal year the maximum draft that could ordinarily be carried at mean low tide over the shoalest part of the locality under improvement was about 7¼ feet.

The present commerce of the Siuslaw River is limited, the country being but thinly settled. There is much timber of good quality in the vicinity, and lumber is the principal article of commerce at present. It is taken from the river to San Francisco in small coasting vessels. The river and ocean form the only means for transporting such commerce as there is, there being no railroad in the vicinity.

COMMERCIAL STATISTICS.

	Tons.		Tons.
1892	2,381	1897	2,239
1893	7,000	1898	4,350
1894	8,050	1899	4,907
1895	15,296	1900	18,675
1896	7,184		

The statistics for 1896–1900 are for calendar years; for years prior to 1896 they are for fiscal years ending June 30.

July 1, 1900, balance unexpended	$23,483.15
June 30, 1901, amount expended during fiscal year	22,412.68
July 1, 1901, balance unexpended	1,070.47
July 1, 1901, outstanding liabilities	50.00
July 1, 1901, balance available	1,020.47

Amount (estimated) required for completion of existing project 548,000.00
Amount that can be profitably expended in fiscal year ending June 30, 1903, for works of improvement and for maintenance, in addition to the balance available July 1, 1901 .... 35,000.00
Submitted in compliance with requirements of sundry civil act of June 4, 1897, and of section 7 of the river and harbor act of 1899.

(See Appendix V V 6.)

7. *Yaquina Bay, Oregon.*—Yaquina Bay is a small tidal estuary of about 5 square miles area. It lies on the Oregon coast, about 110 miles south of the mouth of the Columbia River. The usual bar exists in the ocean opposite the entrance to the bay. The mean range of tide

is about 7 feet. Prior to improvement the prevailing depth over this bar was only about 7 or 8 feet at low tide, and three distinct channels existed at the entrance to the bay. Under a project for improvement adopted in 1880, as amended in 1882, 1888, and 1892, there were constructed a rubblestone jetty running out to sea about 3,500 feet from the south side of the bay, and a rubblestone jetty running out to sea about 2,800 feet from the north side of the bay. The construction of these jetties resulted in filling up two of the three channels which formerly existed at the entrance to the bay, in developing the third channel, and in obtaining from 14 to 15 feet of water on the ocean bar at mean lower low tide, or from 21 to 22 feet at high tide. The project for improvement called for only 17 feet at high tide. This original project has therefore been satisfactorily completed.

The river and harbor act of June 6, 1900, provides for removing a cluster of rocks located about 2,000 feet beyond the sea end of the south jetty, at an estimated cost of $20,000, in accordance with report submitted by a Board of Engineers November 14, 1899 (report printed as House Doc. No. 110, Fifty-sixth Congress, first session, and in Annual Report of the Chief of Engineers for 1900, pp. 4293–4314).

The expenditures to June 30, 1900, $690,027.68, resulted in completing the two jetties provided for by the original project, as stated above, and in preparing to remove the cluster of rocks as provided for in the present project.

The expenditures during fiscal year ending June 30, 1901, resulted in increasing the depth of water over a portion of the cluster of rocks beyond the sea end of the south jetty from 6 feet to 12¼ feet at mean lower low tide, which latter is equivalent to about 17 feet at high tide.

It is estimated that the remainder of the cluster of rocks may be removed during the present summer with the funds available.

The maximum draft that could ordinarily be carried during the fiscal year ending June 30, 1901, at mean low tide over the shoalest part of the bar channel proper was 14 feet, and over the shoalest part of the cluster of rocks at one side of the channel beyond the sea end of the south jetty about 6 feet.

COMMERCIAL STATISTICS.

	Tons.		Tons.
1882	1,830	1892	27,111
1883	1,359	1893	24,767
1884	4,995	1894	23,345
1885	9,951	1895	24,589
1886	6,249	1896	17,883
1887	24,694	1897	15,364
1888	23,431	1898	10,380
1889	32,921	1899	5,990
1890	40,074	1900	691
1891	27,540		

The statistics for 1882–1894 are for the fiscal years ending June 30; for 1895–1900 they are for calendar years.

July 1, 1900, balance unexpended	$19,972.32
June 30, 1901, amount expended during fiscal year	7,067.83
July 1, 1901, balance unexpended	12,904.49
July 1, 1901, outstanding liabilities	170.00
July 1, 1901, balance available	12,734.49

(See Appendix V V 7.)

8. Yaquina Bay, Oregon, examination.—The river and harbor act of March 3, 1899, provided for a Board of three engineers to make an examination of the bay with a view to ascertaining the desirability of further prosecution of work.

The expenditures up to June 30, 1900, $4,689.60, were for the required examination. The report of the Board was submitted November 14, 1899 (report printed in House Doc. No. 110, Fifty-sixth Congress, first session; also in Annual Report of the Chief of Engineers for 1900, pp. 4293–4314). The report was to the effect that the bay is unworthy of further improvement with the exception of removing to the level of the surrounding bottom a cluster of rocks on the side of the channel about 2,000 .feet beyond the end of the south jetty.

This work was estimated to cost $20,000, and provision for its execution was made by the emergency river and harbor act of June 6, 1900, as stated in the report for the improvement of Yaquina Bay.

The expenditures during fiscal year ending June 30, 1901, were in settlement of liabilities incurred during the previous year.

The Board having completed its work, the unexpended balance of the appropriation of $5,000 made by the act of March 3, 1899, for the examination was returned to the Treasury July 18, 1900.

July 1, 1900, balance unexpended	$310.40
June 30, 1901, amount expended during fiscal year	[1].64
July 1, 1901, balance unexpended	309.76

(See Apprendix V V 8.)

9. Tillamook Bay and Bar, Oregon.—Tillamook Bay is an indentation of the Oregon coast about 6 miles long by about 3 miles wide and lies about 50 miles south of the mouth of the Columbia River. The mean range of tide in the bay is about 6.5 feet. The usual bar exists in the ocean opposite the entrance to the bay, but generally has from 10 to 15 feet of water over it at low tide. At low tide the bay inside is a succession of sand and mud flats, separated by four channels, which latter shoal to a low-tide depth of but 1 or 2 feet near the east end of the bay. A number of streams empty into the bay from the east. These are mountain streams in their upper portions and tidal sloughs in their lower portions. Coasting vessels drawing up to about 14 feet of water, engaged in transporting lumber from the bay to San Francisco, do not go above Hobsonville, a short distance inside the entrance to the bay.

Tillamook City is on Hoquarten Slough, about 12 miles from the entrance to the bay, and is the distributing point for a very fertile valley lying between the Pacific Ocean and the Coast Range of mountains.

The projects for improvement adopted consequent to reports printed in the Annual Reports of the Chief of Engineers for 1888 (pp. 2152–2154) and 1892 (pp. 2742–2752) provided for aiding the smaller class of coasting vessels to reach Tillamook City by obtaining a channel 9 feet deep at mean high tide from Hobsonville up to Tillamook City, at an estimated cost of $105,700.

The expenditures to June 30, 1900, $66,023.56, resulted in obtaining the projected channel 9 feet deep at mean high tide from Hobsonville up to Tillamook City, many snags being removed, shoals dredged, and deflecting dikes being built between those points.

---

[1] Expended by Treasury Department in making settlement with the Southern Pacific Company.

RIVER AND HARBOR IMPROVEMENTS. 623

The expenditures during the fiscal year ending June 30, 1901, were for completing and maintaining the work in progress at the close of the preceding fiscal year, which consisted of dredging shoals and finishing several deflecting dikes.

Although a channel of the projected depth has been obtained up to Tillamook City, it will be necessary to strengthen and perhaps extend some of the existing dikes in order to maintain the channel.

There is a large quantity of timber of good quality in the vicinity of Tillamook Bay, also some very fertile valley lands. The lumber is marketed almost exclusively in San Francisco, and the agricultural products are marketed in both San Francisco and Portland. There being no railroads in the vicinity, the country is dependent upon the bay and ocean for transporting the products to market.

COMMERCIAL STATISTICS.

	Tons.		Tons.
1889	3,571	1896	25,977
1890	27,427	1897	29,405
1891	28,292	1898	35,885
1892	33,220	1899	36,835
1893	18,316	1900	17,640
1895	29,742		

The statistics for years prior to 1896 are for fiscal years ending June 30; since 1896 they are for calendar years.

July 1, 1900, balance unexpended	$12,676.44
November 10, 1900, refundment of overpayments[1]	4.68
	12,681.12
June 30, 1901, amount expended during fiscal year	11,949.81
July 1, 1901, balance unexpended	731.31
July 1, 1901, outstanding liabilities	63.25
July 1, 1901, balance available	668.06
Amount that can be profitably expended in fiscal year ending June 30, 1903, for maintenance of improvement, in addition to the balance available July 1, 1901	5,000.00

Submitted in compliance with requirements of sundry civil act of June 4, 1897, and of section 7 of the river and harbor act of 1899.

(See Appendix V V 9.)

10. *Upper Columbia and Snake rivers, Oregon and Washington.*—The designation "Upper Columbia and Snake rivers, Oregon and Washington," covers the 125 miles of the Columbia River from Celilo up to the mouth of Snake River, at Ainsworth, Wash., and the 145 miles of the Snake River from its mouth up to Asotin, Wash., a small settlement about 5 miles above the town of Lewiston, Idaho.

Both the Columbia and Snake rivers between Celilo and Asotin are more or less obstructed by rock and gravel bars, which cause rapids, the ruling depth over some of which at low water being from 2 to 3 feet, while some (particularly in the 67 miles of the Snake between its mouth and Riparia, Wash.,) are impassable at extreme low-water stages. These bars, together with the narrow and crooked channel at many places, render navigation by light-draft steamboats between Celilo and Asotin more or less difficult at some points and dangerous at others.

A formal plan for improving the two streams throughout the 270 miles between Celilo and Asotin has never been adopted by Congress.

[1] Overpayment of $3.12 made on voucher No. 31, February, 1900, and overpayment of $1.56 made on voucher No. 36, March, 1900.

The Snake River has been surveyed throughout the 140 miles between its mouth and Lewiston, but a continuous survey of the Columbia between Celilo and the mouth of Snake River has never been authorized or made.

From 1872 to 1882 the work of removing obstructions was carried on with the view of obtaining a low-water channel depth of about 5¼ feet in the Columbia between Celilo and the mouth of Snake River, and a low-water channel depth of about 4½ feet in the Snake between its mouth and Lewiston. Owing to the construction of railroads along and adjacent to both streams, and the difficulties of navigating the Snake below Riparia and some portions of the Columbia between Celilo and the mouth of the Snake, steamboats abandoned the streams between Celilo and Riparia for purposes of regular navigation in about 1882.

Since then work of improvement has been confined to the 78 miles of the Snake River between Riparia and Asotin, although Lewiston is at present the head of regular navigation on Snake River.

The expenditures to June 30, 1900—$284,851.92—resulted in removing some of the worst obstructions to steamboat navigation between Celilo and Asotin and in the construction of several dikes to deflect and concentrate the flow over shoals.

The expenditures during the fiscal year ending June 30, 1901, were principally for making a survey of the 73 miles of the Snake River between Lewiston and Riparia.

The maximum draft that could be carried at mean low water during the fiscal year ending June 30, 1901, over the shoalest point in Snake River between Riparia and Lewiston (the limits of regular navigation) was about 4½ feet.

The principal commerce of the upper Columbia and Snake River country is wheat. At present the wheat of the Snake River country is taken to Riparia by steamboats, at which place it is transferred to cars and transported by rail to Portland, Oreg., where it is placed aboard ocean vessels for export to Europe and Asia. It is not expected that the commerce handled on the rivers between Celilo and Asotin will materially increase until some feasible plan is adopted by Congress for passing steamboats around the obstructions in the 12 miles of the Columbia River between the The Dalles and Celilo, and thus give, during a portion of each year at least, an all-water route of transportation from Asotin to the Pacific Ocean, a distance of about 468 miles. For information in detail concerning the immense territory drained by and tributary to the Columbia and Snake rivers, the commerce of the country, and the present means for transporting it, attention is particularly invited to House Doc. No. 228, Fifty-sixth Congress, second session. (See Appendix V V 16, herewith.)

COMMERCIAL STATISTICS.

	Tons.		Tons.
1875	18,230	1895	37,100
1879	65,975	1896	25,977
1884	30,260	1897	31,531
1891	31,400	1898	36,923
1892	19,167	1899	45,654
1893	19,364	1900	35,920
1894	9,902		

The above statistics, since 1896, are for the calendar years; for years prior to 1896 they are for fiscal years ending June 30. Statistics for years not named are not available.

July 1, 1900, balance unexpended $4,427.08
January 29, 1901, reimbursement for property 43.70
                                                                    ─────────
                                                                    4,470.78
June 30, 1901, amount expended during fiscal year 4,173.37

July 1, 1901, balance unexpended 297.41
July 1, 1901, outstanding liabilities 50.00

July 1, 1901, balance available 247.41

Amount (estimated) required for completion of existing project .... Indefinite.
Amount that can be profitably expended in fiscal year ending June 30,
  1903, for works of improvement and for maintenance, in addition to
  the balance available July 1, 1901 .... 10,000.00
Submitted in compliance with requirements of sundry civil act of June
  4, 1897, and of section 7 of the river and harbor act of 1899.

(See Appendix V V 10.)

11. Columbia River at Three-mile Rapids, and the construction and equipment of a boat railway from the foot of The Dalles Rapids to the head of Celilo Falls, Oregon and Washington.—Vessels drawing 23 feet of water easily ascend the Columbia River from its mouth in the Pacific Ocean to the mouth of the Willamette River, a distance of about 98 miles, and river steamers drawing about 8 feet of water navigate the Columbia up to the town of The Dalles, Oreg., a farther distance of about 88 miles. Between the towns of The Dalles and Celilo, Oreg., 12 miles, navigation is completely obstructed at all times by rapids and strong currents caused by falls, the steep slope of the river, and the gorged character of the channel.

From Celilo up to the foot of Priest Rapids, in the southern portion of Douglas County, Wash., 198 miles, the Columbia is navigable for boats drawing 3¼ to 4¼ feet, although with some difficulty at low-water stages, on account of rocks and shoals. The Snake River, which empties into the Columbia at Ainsworth, Wash., 125 miles above Celilo, is navigable for light-draft boats up to Asotin, Wash., 145 miles above Ainsworth, although the 67 miles between Ainsworth and Riparia are not navigable during the lower stages. There is, therefore, 384 miles of the Columbia between its mouth in the Pacific Ocean and the foot of Priest Rapids, and 145 miles of the Snake River next above its mouth, or a total of 529 miles, which are navigable throughout during at least a portion of each year, while in all that distance there is but 12 miles where navigation is totally obstructed. These 12 miles consist of the Columbia River between The Dalles and Celilo, Oreg. In these 12 miles are four principal obstructions. They are known as Three-mile Rapids, Five-mile (or the The Dalles) Rapids, Ten-mile Rapids, and Celilo Falls.

The act of Congress of August 18, 1894, provided for the improvement of Three-mile Rapids and for the construction and equipment of a boat railway from the foot of Five-mile (or The Dalles) Rapids to the head of Celilo Falls, at an estimated cost of $2,264,467. The object of the proposed boat railway is to carry boats overland between the foot of Five-mile Rapids and Celilo, a distance of about 9 miles.

The expenditures to June 30, 1900, $29,708.51, resulted in a survey of the line of the proposed boat railway, in acquiring title to a part of the land required for it, and in partially preparing the necessary plans.

The expenditures during the fiscal year ending June 30, 1901, were principally for making a survey of the 12 miles of the river between

ENG 1901——40

The Dalles and Celilo with the view to the construction of canals and locks to overcome the obstructions to navigation.

Work has been suspended until Congress may determine whether the construction of the boat railway shall continue or some other form of improvement shall be adopted.

July 1, 1900, balance unexpended	$220,291.49
June 30, 1901, amount expended during fiscal year	5,712.23
July 1, 1901, balance unexpended	214,579.26
Amount (estimated) required for completion of existing project	2,014,467.00

(See Appendix V V 11.)

12. Canal at the Cascades, Columbia River, Oregon.—In passing through the Cascade Mountain Range the channel of the Columbia River for the distance of about 4¼ miles (see map opposite p. 2246, Annual Report of the Chief of Engineers for 1884) is so contracted in width that that portion of the stream partakes of the nature of a gorge. In the upper 2,500 feet of this gorge (shown in photograph No. 409, following p. 3224, Annual Report of the Chief of Engineers for 1899) there is a fall of about 24 feet at low water, which, on account of the rapids and huge bowlders, can not be navigated. Throughout the lower portion of the gorge, about 4 miles, the channel, while not as contracted nor of as steep slope as the upper 2,500 feet, is nevertheless so contracted and of such slope that rapids are formed that can not be navigated at the higher stages. This lower portion of the gorge, also, was originally much obstructed by large bowlders and reefs.

Under the original project for improvement, as modified in 1880, and as further modified in 1888 (report of Board of Engineer officers, printed in the Annual Report of the Chief of Engineers for 1889, pp. 2551–2559), work was prosecuted on a canal about 3,000 feet long on the Oregon shore, around the upper or principal rapid at the Cascades, and a lock in the canal 462 feet long, 90 feet wide, and designed for an extreme low-water draft of 8 feet. Also, many obstructing rocks and reefs in the rapids below the canal and lock were removed.

In 1894 (report of Board of Engineer officers, printed in the Annual Report of the Chief of Engineers for 1895, pp. 3571–3582) the present project was adopted, which provided for utilizing 462 feet of the incomplete canal above the upper lock gates as a second lock, by putting in a concrete floor and the necessary side walls. This modification also provided for raising the protection works of the canal, the height of which had been based on the flood of 1876, the highest water known previous to 1894, to make them conform to the flood height of the latter year, which was 6 feet above that of 1876.

There has been $3,748,000 appropriated for this work, and the amount (estimated) required to be appropriated for its completion is $259,260, thus making the estimated total cost $4,007,260.

The expenditures up to June 30, 1900, $3,697,348.26, resulted in the construction of the canal and locks, as projected, to a point where navigation through them is permitted. Although incomplete, the works were opened to navigation on November 5, 1896, and have been used since that time by boats, except when high water made it impracticable.

The expenditures during fiscal year ending June 30, 1901, were for works of improvement and consisted principally of relaying, under a contract dated September 19, 1899, a portion of the slope wall on the south side of the lower entrance to the canal, which was damaged by the high water of 1894, and in placing additional paving on both sides of the canal.

The commerce that has passed through the canal is as follows: 1898, 18,812 tons; 1899, 16,700 tons; 1900, 17,710 tons; 1901, 22,426 tons. These statistics are for fiscal years ending June 30.

July 1, 1900, balance unexpended	$50,651.74
June 30, 1901, amount expended during fiscal year	45,005.01
July 1, 1901, balance unexpended	5,646.73
July 1, 1901, outstanding liabilities	228.00
July 1, 1901, balance available	5,418.73

{ Amount (estimated) required for completion of existing project........ 259,260.00
Amount that can be profitably expended in fiscal year ending June 30, 1903, in addition to the balance available July 1, 1901............... 90,000.00
Submitted in compliance with requirements of sundry civil act of June 4, 1897.

(See Appendix V V 12.)

13. Operating and care of canal and locks at the Cascades of the Columbia River, Oregon.—The obstructions in the Columbia River at the Cascades are described in the preceding report. The canal and locks which pass steamboats around these obstructions were opened to navigation on November 5, 1896, although incomplete in many details, and have been in condition to be used ever since that date, with the exception of a few days when minor repairs were in progress.

The expenditures up to June 30, 1900, $18,948.26, were principally in payment of salaries of employees engaged in operating and caring for the canal and locks, for a new valve for the main culvert on the south side of the lower lock, and for partially repainting the steel lock gates.

The expenditures during the fiscal year ending June 30, 1901, amounting to $5,433.91, were in payment of salaries of employees engaged in operating and caring for the canal and locks and in continuing the work of cleaning and repainting the steel lock gates.

The commerce that has passed through the canal and locks during fiscal years ending June 30 is as follows:

	Tons.
1898	18,812
1899	16,700
1900	17,710
1901	22,426

(See Appendix V V 13.)

14. Columbia River, between Vancouver, Wash., and the mouth of Willamette River.—The city of Vancouver, Wash., is located on the Columbia River about 103 miles above its mouth and 5 miles above the mouth of the Willamette River in the Columbia. Vessels drawing up to about 23 feet of water ascend the Columbia from its mouth up to a point 2¼ miles below Vancouver, where there is a bar which had, originally, but 9 feet of water over it.

The project adopted in 1892 (reports printed in Annual Reports of the Chief of Engineers for 1892, pp. 2865–2869, and for 1896, pp. 3264–3265) provided for constructing a pile, brush, and rubblestone dike about 3,000 feet long from the Oregon shore to the head of Hayden Island, opposite Vancouver, at an estimated cost of $100,000, to stop the flow south of the island during low-water stages and deflect it down the main channel north of the island, so as to scour the bar below Vancouver and obtain a depth over it sufficient to permit ascending vessels drawing 20 or more feet to reach Vancouver.

The expenditures to June 30, 1900, were $85,533.16 for works of improvement up to May 2, 1899, and $9,007.82 for maintenance of improvement from May 2, 1899, to June 30, 1900, or a total of $94,540.98, and resulted in completing the dike and in revetting the head of Hayden Island to prevent erosion. The map following page 3230 of the Annual Report of the Chief of Engineers for 1899 shows the work as completed May 2, 1899.

The expenditures during fiscal year ending June 30, 1901, were for maintenance of improvement, small quantities of brush and rubblestone being placed in the dike and on the head of Hayden Island to compensate for settlement caused by the all-summer high water of 1900.

On June 18, 1901, the sum of $8,000 was allotted, from the appropriation of June 6, 1900, for emergencies in river and harbor works, to be applied to repairing the dike during the low-water period of the autumn of 1901.

It has not been practicable to make a survey recently to determine to what extent the dike has up to the present time caused scour on the bar in the main channel north of the island. It is proposed to make the necessary survey during the next low-water period.

Whether the industries of Vancouver could offer vessels drawing 20 feet of water sufficient inducements in the way of cargoes to make it an object for them to call at that place is questionable, but can not be definitely determined until the project depth is secured. To accomplish this may require dredging, and the estimate submitted includes $10,000 for such dredging and $12,000 for repair work which may be necessary.

July 1, 1900, balance unexpended	$5,460.02
Amount allotted from appropriation contained in emergency river and harbor act approved June 6, 1900	8,000.00
	13,460.02
June 30, 1901, amount expended during fiscal year	5,422.02
July 1, 1901, balance unexpended	8,038.00

Amount that can be profitably expended in fiscal year ending June 30, 1903, for maintenance of improvement, in addition to the balance unexpended July 1, 1901 .... 22,000.00
Submitted in compliance with requirements of sundry civil act of June 4, 1897, and of section 7 of the river and harbor act of 1899.

(See Appendix V V 14.)

15. Clearwater River, Idaho.—This stream empties into the Snake River at Lewiston, Idaho. It is a mountain stream with steep slope and many rapids, the average fall of the stream from Kamiah, Idaho, down to Lewiston being about 7 feet per mile.

The original project for improvement, adopted in 1879, provided for obtaining a low-water channel depth of 4½ feet for small steamboats in the 40 miles next above Lewiston by removing obstructing rocks.

The last project for improvement was approved by the Secretary of War, July 23, 1897, and provided for improving the 75 miles of the river next above Lewiston for steamboat navigation during only high stages by removing obstructions to high-water navigation.

The expenditures to June 30, 1900, $37,126.32, were for works of improvement, and resulted in removing, under the original project, some of the rocks which obstructed low-water navigation, and in removing, under the later project, some of the worst obstructions to high-water navigation from Kamiah, 67 miles above Lewiston, down to Big Eddy, 27 miles above Lewiston.

The officer in local charge of the improvement reported that the construction a year or two ago of a branch of the Northern Pacific Railroad, paralleling the stream at all points between Lewiston and Kamiah and affording ample transportation facilities for the somewhat limited commerce of the region, and the difficulties and dangers connected with navigating the stream, caused steamboats to abandon the river. These conditions were reported to the Secretary of War, July 6, 1899, who authorized, July 8, 1899, that the appropriation of $10,000 of March 3, 1899, be held in the Treasury to await future developments regarding the necessity for further improving the stream.

The expenditures in 1901 were in connection with properly caring for the Government plant used in the work of improvement in former years.

The stream was not visited by a steamboat during the calendar year 1900, therefore no commerce was carried on the river during that year.

COMMERCIAL STATISTICS.

	Tons.
1896	2,900
1898	756
1899	176
1900	None.

The above statistics are for calendar years. Statistics for years not named are not available.

July 1, 1900, balance unexpended	$12,876.18
June 30, 1901, amount expended during fiscal year	121.36
July 1, 1901, balance unexpended	12,754.82

(See Appendix V V 15.)

EXAMINATIONS AND SURVEYS MADE IN COMPLIANCE WITH EMERGENCY RIVER AND HARBOR ACT APPROVED JUNE 6, 1900.

Preliminary examinations and surveys of the following localities were made by the local engineer and reports thereon submitted through the division engineer:

1. Preliminary examination and survey of Columbia River between the foot of The Dalles Rapids and the head of Celilo Falls, Oregon and Washington, with a view to the construction of canals and locks.—Captain Harts submitted reports dated June 22 and November 30, 1900, respectively. The estimated cost of the necessary work in round numbers is $4,000,000. The reports were transmitted to Congress and printed in House Doc. No. 228, Fifty-sixth Congress, second session. (See also Appendix V V 16.)

2. Preliminary examination and survey of Snake River, Idaho and Washington, from the head of navigation on said river to its junction with the Columbia River.—Captain Harts submitted reports dated

June 25 and November 15, 1900. The cost of the work proposed is estimated at $23,000 and $5,000 for maintenance every two years. The reports were transmitted to Congress and printed in House Doc. No. 127, Fifty-sixth Congress, second session. (See also Appendix V V 17.)

IMPROVEMENT OF WILLAMETTE AND LOWER COLUMBIA RIVERS AND THEIR TRIBUTARIES, OREGON AND WASHINGTON.

This district was in the temporary charge of Capt. William W. Harts, Corps of Engineers, to August 18, 1890, and in the charge of Capt. William C. Langfitt, Corps of Engineers, since that date. Division Engineer, Col. S. M. Mansfield, Corps of Engineers, to November 23, 1900, and Col. Jared A. Smith, Corps of Engineers, since December 15, 1900.

1. Long Tom River, Oregon.—The Long Tom River is a tributary of the Willamette. It rises on the eastern slope of the Coast Range, drains an area of about 430 square miles, including a large amount of very productive valley land, and empties into the Willamette River 122 miles distant from Portland by river.

Before improvement the river was almost impassable on account of the numerous brush-covered shoals and overhanging trees. It is very narrow and runs so low during the spring and summer that scarcely 6 inches of water is found on the bars, but during the winter or rainy season a depth of 5 or 6 feet is found, and the improvement was intended to furnish relief during such parts of the year as high water prevails.

The present project for improvement was adopted in 1898. It provided for the removal of snags, overhanging trees, etc., with a view to obtaining a channel for high-water navigation during a few months in the rainy season. This project is now satisfactorily completed.

The river and harbor act of March 3, 1899, transferred $3,000 from funds previously appropriated for improvement of Willamette and Yamhill rivers to this work. All of this amount was expended during the fiscal year ending June 30, 1900.

The desired results have been accomplished, affording high-water transportation for considerable quantities of grain and produce. This traffic, however, has not been as large as was anticipated.

The sum of $500 will probably be required for annual maintenance, which will allow of removing snags, logs, and other obstructions. The expenditure of this amount may not be proportionate to the small traffic involved, as the commerce for the year was only 275 tons as against 300 tons the previous year. Owing to this reason and to the uncertainty of any great benefit derived from previous expenditures, this amount should not be expended unless future traffic and conditions would seem to warrant it.

It is therefore recommended that definite appropriations be discontinued, and that the amount estimated for, or so much thereof as the needs of commerce may demand, be expended from the general appropriation for improving Willamette and Yamhill rivers.

Amount (estimated) required for completion of existing project .... Indefinite.
Amount that can be profitably expended in fiscal year ending June 30, 1903, for maintenance of improvement.............................. $500.00
Submitted in compliance with requirements of sundry civil act of June 4, 1897, and of section 7 of the river and harbor act of 1899.

(See Appendix W W 1.)

2. *Willamette River above Portland, and Yamhill River, Oregon.*—
The Willamette River rises in the Cascade Range, about 150 miles
southward of the Columbia River, and flows northerly, generally
parallel and about 50 miles east of the coast line. It enters the Columbia about 105 miles above its mouth and 12 miles north of the city of
Portland.

The Yamhill River rises in the Coast Range, flows in a northeasterly
direction, and enters the Willamette about 40 miles above its mouth.

A detailed description of the Willamette River, together with that
of its condition prior to improvement, may be found in the Annual
Reports of the Chief of Engineers for 1876, page 654, and for 1880,
page 2280.

The Yamhill River drains an exceedingly fertile valley, which has
been settled for years. Prior to improvement the channel was
obstructed by snags and rocks, which were removed under the project
of 1892, and boats could then reach Dayton (about 5 miles) at all
seasons on a draft of about 2¼ feet. Above Dayton and about 1 mile
below Lafayette the channel was obstructed by rapids, so that boats
could reach Lafayette (9 miles) and McMinnville (about 18 miles) only
during extreme high water.

The original project for improvement of the Willamette was adopted
in 1870 and modified in 1878 and 1879, and in 1892 it was extended to
include the removal of obstructions in the Yamhill to McMinnville.

The approved project (Annual Reports of the Chief of Engineers for
1896, p. 3310, and for 1897, p. 506) proposed the improvement of the
Willamette River from Portland to Eugene by the removal of obstructions and the building of controlling works, with a view of obtaining
a depth of 12 feet or more from Portland to the foot of Clackamas
Rapids (11 miles); of 3 to 3¼ feet thence to Corvallis (107 miles), and
of from 2 to 2¼ feet from Corvallis to Eugene (53 miles); estimated
cost, $131,697. On the Yamhill River the project contemplated the
construction of a lock and dam near Lafayette and the removal of
obstructions, to provide a draft of 3¼ feet throughout the year from
the mouth of the river to McMinnville; estimated cost, $69,000.

The funds appropriated for completion of above project are
exhausted and a further allotment of $5,000 was made under date of
July 9, 1900, from appropriation provided by the emergency river
and harbor act of June 6, 1900, nearly all of which was expended in
repairs and maintenance of existing works.

The amount expended on this improvement up to the close of the
fiscal year ending June 30, 1900, was $429,718.83, of which amount
$4,612,32 was applied to maintenance.

The construction of controlling works under the existing project
has, without doubt, afforded relief and alone made navigation possible
during recent years. However, it is believed that the physical features of the river are such as to make impracticable the attainment in
all sections, at any reasonable cost, of the depths proposed by the
project.

It is proposed, if sufficient funds are made available, to construct
and equip a dredge and accessories, at an estimated cost of $20,000, for
use in creating and maintaining such depths as may be found reasonably practicable, this amount being included in the estimate as well as
the amount which it is proposed to apply to operation of dredge, snagging, and the maintenance of old and construction of new dams and

revetments only at such points where they may be of permanent use. This is practically a continuation of previous operations, with the addition of a dredging plant to aid the work below Corvallis, and confining operations on the stretch above Corvallis to snagging for aid to high-water navigation.

The Yamhill River has been thoroughly cleared of snags, logs, and overhanging trees, and boats are running regularly to McMinnville. The contract for construction of lock and dam was completed and the work turned over to the United States in September, 1900.

Operations under allotment from emergency act of June 6, 1900, were confined to snagging and making repairs to existing works in the Willamette River. Quite extensive repairs were made to the revetment at Corvallis, considerable work was done at Eldridge bar and repairs made at Lamberts Slough, Ash Island, and Feasters Bend, where dams had previously been constructed. All active operations were suspended October 9, owing to the exhaustion of funds.

The traffic of the upper river is handled by from four to six steamers and regular trips are now being made to Salem, with some difficulty at shoal places, where the maximum draft carried over the shoalest place is probably about 2 feet. The Willamette is now at low-water stage and the regular boats are unable to reach Corvallis, the principal obstruction being at Eola Bar. Eugene can be reached only on a 6-foot stage.

Comparative statement of the tonnage carried by river boats on the Willamette River above Portland.

Calendar year.	Merchandise.	Passengers.	Calendar year.	Merchandise.	Passengers.
	Tons.	*Number.*		*Tons.*	*Number.*
1894	74,615	56,368	1898	112,154	67,524
1895	130,870	57,376	1899	117,782	50,738
1896	218,480	48,465	1900	182,458	47,324
1897	186,621	87,960			

July 1, 1900, balance unexpended	$15,718.17
Amount allotted from appropriation contained in emergency river and harbor act approved June 6, 1900	5,000.00
	20,718.17
June 30, 1901, amount expended during fiscal year	19,777.47
July 1, 1901, balance unexpended	940.70
July 1, 1901, outstanding liabilities	50.00
July 1, 1901, balance available	890.70

{ Amount that can be profitably expended in fiscal year ending June 30, 1903, for maintenance of improvement, in addition to the balance available July 1, 1901 .... 30,000.00
Submitted in compliance with requirements of sundry civil act of June 4, 1897, and of section 7 of the river and harbor act of 1899.

(See Appendix W W 2.)

3. Operating and care of lock and dam in Yamhill River, Oregon.— The funds for operation and care during fiscal year 1901 were provided by allotments of September 19, 1900, and January 18, 1901, and amounted to $2,9u0. The total amount expended during the fiscal year was $2,313.40, which was applied to payment of services of employees and for expense of making repairs to embankments.

Considerable further damage has been caused to the newly completed riprap and slopes by freshets, and additional funds were necessary for repairs. The estimated cost of these repairs is $23,200. The funds have been allotted and at the close of the fiscal year the work was in progress.

The total traffic passed through the lock since it was opened in September amounted to 1,738 tons of miscellaneous freight and 2,170 passengers.

(See Appendix W W 3.)

4. Columbia and Lower Willamette rivers below Portland, Oreg.—The Columbia River is the great river of the Pacific coast. It rises in British Columbia, flows southerly and westerly, and forms in its lower portions for 330 miles the boundary between Oregon and Washington, emptying into the Pacific Ocean between these two States.

The Willamette River rises in the Cascade Range about 150 miles southward of the Columbia River, flows northerly, entering the Columbia about 105 miles above its mouth and 12 miles north of the city of Portland.

The portions of these rivers covered by this improvement include the 12 miles of the Willamette between Portland and its mouth and 98 miles of the Columbia from the mouth of the Willamette to the sea.

The original condition of these rivers from Portland to the sea was such that only from 10 to 15 feet could be carried over the shoal places at low water. Numerous sand bars obstructed navigation to deepwater craft and distributed the water over an extended area, so that the greatest depth could be carried over them in only a comparatively narrow channel.

The value and the availability of this waterway for purposes of commerce is proven by the quantities of grain and produce that through it find an outlet to the markets of the world from Oregon, Washington, and Idaho. Its improvement to navigation for deep-water craft is of the utmost importance to the entire northwest section of the country, whose inhabitants find the natural outlet for their produce through the valley of the Columbia.

The original project was adopted in 1877, and was prepared by the Board of Engineers for the Pacific coast with a view of obtaining a channel depth of 20 feet. Prior to this, dredging had been done at shoal places for temporary relief. In 1891 (Annual Report of the Chief of Engineers for 1892, p. 2850) the project was extended to provide for a low-water channel depth of 25 feet, and the Port of Portland Commission, a corporation existing under the laws of the State of Oregon, was granted permission to assist in carrying it into execution.

A further project for securing a 25-foot channel to the sea was prepared, based on survey authorized by act of March 3, 1899, report of which is printed in House Doc. No. 673, Fifty-sixth Congress, first session, and also in the Annual Report of the Chief of Engineers for 1900, page 4418 et seq. The estimated cost of completing the work provided for in this report is $2,796,300, with $175,000 as cost of new dredge and accessories and $50,000 for maintenance.

The amount expended up to the close of the fiscal year ending June 30, 1900, was $1,215,950.22.

Dredging, which has been the only work of improvement for several years, has been continued throughout the year, except for a short period in July, when the dredge was undergoing repairs. The total amount excavated was 483,306 cubic yards.

The operations of the Port of Portland Commission have also been confined to dredging, and its 20-inch Bowers's dredge has been in operation during a portion of the year, but is now undergoing repairs. The Commission reports having excavated 1,869,667 cubic yards, with a total expenditure of $55,065.70.

The depths obtained are believed to be only temporary, and it is anticipated that redredging will be required.

The maximum draft that can be carried over the shoalest part at low water is from 18 to 19 feet, but by taking advantage of the tides ships are towed to sea drawing 23 to 24 feet.

Comparative statement of traffic.

Calendar year.	Handled by river craft.	Foreign and coastwise to and from Portland.	
		Receipts.	Shipments.
	Tons.	*Tons.*	*Tons.*
1893	1,310,866		312,790
1894	1,347,155	52,272	340,792
1895	1,040,022	40,238	395,954
1896	1,129,673	49,011	829,102
1897	1,499,337	47,345	290,412
1898	1,121,161	27,776	488,818
1899	1,489,708	86,258	336,134
1900	1,287,582	82,905	489,385

A new transportation line, known as the Portland and Asiatic Steamship Company, has been established between this port and Asiatic points. The company operates three ships on this line of 2,620, 3,152, and 3,152 tons register, respectively. Under the advertised schedule one steamer leaves Portland every thirty days.

July 1, 1900, balance unexpended	$114,414.98
Refunded account difference sheet No. 42	1.56
	114,416.54
June 30, 1901, amount expended during fiscal year	39,862.73
July 1, 1901, balance unexpended	74,553.81
July 1, 1901, outstanding liabilities	1,763.74
July 1, 1901, balance available	72,790.07

Amount (estimated) required for completion of existing project	2,898,509.93
Amount that can be profitably expended in fiscal year ending June 30, 1903, for works of improvement and for maintenance, in addition to the balance available July 1, 1901.	325,000.00
Submitted in compliance with requirements of sundry civil act of June 4, 1897, and of section 7 of the river and harbor act of 1899.	

(See Appendix W W 4.)

5. *Columbia River, Oregon, below Tongue Point.*—This improvement covers a stretch of the river about 5¼ miles long, beginning just below Tongue Point and extending down along the water front of

Astoria. The principal obstruction is a rocky point known as the Sylvia de Grasse Reef, about 1 milé below Tongue Point, and around which ships are obliged to make a short turn to avoid striking it. The ledge induces shoaling, with consequent narrowing of the passage.

The original and present project, adopted in 1896 (Annual Report of the Chief of Engineers for 1895, pp. 3605–3608), contemplates the removal of the wreck of the *Sylvia de Grasse* and the outer portion of the reef, supplemented by dredging to obtain a 25-foot channel 250 feet in width, extending along the water front of Astoria.

The amount expended on this work up to the close of the fiscal year ending June 30, 1900, was $10,811.38. At that time no work had been done except dredging for temporary relief.

Under date of October 20, a contract for doing the work was made with Mr. E. T. Johnson. Work under this contract began January 7, 1901; was suspended in February on account of incapacity of dredge; resumed in April with plant of better design, and has since been in progress. At the close of the fiscal year 573 cubic yards of rock had been excavated, practically all of which was taken out in May and June.

The work is not yet sufficiently advanced to determine actual results in the way of increased depths or benefit to navigation.

The maximum draft that could be carried June 30, 1901, at mean low water over the shoalest part of the locality under improvement was about 19 feet.

For commercial statistics see report on improving Columbia and Lower Willamette rivers, below Portland, Oreg.

July 1, 1900, balance unexpended	$110,188.62
June 30, 1901, amount expended during fiscal year	9,206.36
July 1, 1901, balance unexpended	100,982.26
July 1, 1901, outstanding liabilities	2,553.90
July 1, 1901, balance available	98,428.36
July 1, 1901, amount covered by uncompleted contracts	63,744.90

(See Appendix W W 5.)

6. *Mouth of Columbia River, Oregon and Washington.*—Prior to commencing the work of construction, in 1885, there were from one to three channels across the bar at the mouth of Columbia River, and these channels varied both in location and depth, the latter being usually from 19 feet to 21 feet, while the location shifted through nearly 180 degrees from Cape Disappointment to Point Adams. A map of this locality before improvement is printed in the Annual Report of the Chief of Engineers for 1886, page 1978.

The project for improvement adopted in 1884 (Report of Board of Engineers, Annual Report of the Chief of Engineers for 1883, p. 2012 et seq.) contemplated securing a low-water channel depth of 30 feet across the bar at the mouth of the river by the construction of a jetty to extend from the shore near Fort Stevens across Clatsop Spit in the direction of a point about 3 miles south of Cape Disappointment, the jetty to be built of rubble and random blocks of large size, resting upon mattresses of brush.

The original project, adopted in 1884, provided for a single jetty on the south side of the entrance, built to low-water level and about 4½ miles long. This was modified in 1893 (Annual Report of the Chief of Engineers for 1893, p. 3489 et seq.) to provide for practically a high-tide jetty, in which was included the construction of four low groins built out from the main jetty. The estimated cost of the jetty in the original project was $3,710,000.

The amount expended to June 30, 1899, was $1,965,022.76 (exclusive of the sum of $50,000 authorized by the river and harbor act of June 3, 1896, to be applied to the improvement below Tongue Point), with the result that the jetty was completed in 1895 to the length of 4¼ miles and full projected height, with four low-tide groins 1,000 feet, 1,000 feet, 600 feet, and 500 feet long, respectively. Map showing completed work is printed in the Annual Report of the Chief of Engineers for 1895. This work caused an increase in depth over the bar from 20 feet to 31 feet at mean lower low water from 1885 to 1895.

Annual surveys since 1896 have shown each year marked shoaling of the depths over the bar, the greatest depth obtained having been 31 feet in 1895, being 1 foot in excess of the depth proposed by the original project.

A detailed survey was made in 1899, and report submitted by the district officer under date of November 6, 1899, with project and estimate for deepening the channel to 40 feet, at a cost of $2,531,140.51. The report is printed in House Doc. No. 94, Fifty-sixth Congress, first session, and also in Annual Report of the Chief of Engineers for 1900, Part VI, page 4430 et seq., to which attention is invited for further details, maps, etc.

Operations during the fiscal year and contemplated work of extending the jetty to obtain increased depths are based on this report.

The sundry civil act approved June 6, 1900, appropriated $250,000 "for the repair of the jetty at the mouth of the Columbia River, Oregon and Washington, including repairs to wharves, approaches, tramway, plant, quarters, and buildings, and contingent expenses."

During the year operations were carried on with above funds. The standing portion of the jetty tramway was thoroughly overhauled, all decayed piling and timbers renewed, and tracks put in first-class condition. The plant, quarters, and buildings have been repaired and pile driving commenced on the washed away portions of the tramway.

The annual survey of the entrance to the Columbia River was completed July 8, 1901. As a rule, very few changes in depths have taken place in the channel between Fort Stevens and the end of the jetty. A depth of only 23 feet across the bar was found at the average of lowest low water through a channel 1,500 feet wide. Last year's survey showed 24 feet over a channel of same width.

Peacock Spit shows considerable movement due west, with a decided shoaling on its extension. On the channel side of the jetty, and near its outer end, Clatsop Spit has built up more and moved farther into the channel than at any previous time. The harbor throat is consequently much reduced in width, but shows an increase in depth of from 10 to 12 feet. Around the end of the jetty and in its prolongation for some distance greater depths are noticed than last year.

For commercial statistics see report on improving Columbia and Lower Willamette rivers.

RIVER AND HARBOR IMPROVEMENTS.

July 1, 1900, balance unexpended	$256,926.86
Refunded account difference sheet No. 21	2.00
	256,928.86
June 30, 1901, amount expended during fiscal year	160,745.62
July 1, 1901, balance unexpended	96,183.24
July 1, 1901, outstanding liabilities	5,670.90
July 1, 1901, balance available	90,512.34
Amount (estimated) required for completion of existing project	2,276,181.46
Amount that can be profitably expended in fiscal year ending June 30, 1903, in addition to the balance available July 1, 1901. Submitted in compliance with requirements of sundry civil act of June 4, 1897.	600,000.00

(See Appendix W W 6.)

7. *Clatskanie River, Oregon.*—The Clatskanie River rises in the Coast Range and is a tributary of the Columbia, which it enters by means of connecting sloughs at a point on the south bank about 65 miles below Portland.

At the time of the adoption of the present and original project (Annual Report of the Chief of Engineers for 1898, p. 3050) a depth of 5 feet could be carried to Clatskanie, except over a shoal near the latter place, where but 2 to 3 feet is found. Large quantities of lumber and shingles find a market through this natural outlet. The channel is very narrow and exceedingly winding. Its improvement will be of benefit to those interested.

The project for expenditure of $13,000 (act of March 3, 1899) contemplated cutting a short channel across the bend immediately below Manzanillo, and another from the bend above this point to the first bend below the town of Clatskanie, and by dredging below the latter point, the work to be done by contract. It is expected to secure thereby a depth of 6 feet to the town of Clatskanie, 3 miles from the mouth.

The amount expended up to the close of fiscal year 1900 was $134.11, which was applied principally to survey work. Great delay has been caused in securing title to land required, and no contract could be made until the land and right of way had been bought. The land has now been purchased, the work advertised, and proposals opened May 30. The lowest bid, that of Robert Wakefield, of Portland, Oreg., at 14 cents per cubic yard, was accepted. It provides for the excavation of 56,000 cubic yards, more or less, of material, the whole work to be completed within five months from date of commencement of work.

For this improvement it is thought that a dredging plant would prove of great advantage in securing and maintaining depths. Such a plant for use on this and other tributaries of the Columbia is estimated for in a separate report (see p. 640).

No results in the way of increased depths have been attained, as no work has been done, and the conditions are as previously reported.

Comparative statement of the tonnage carried by river boats on the Clatskanie River for the past five years.

Calendar year.	Merchandise.	Passengers.	Calendar year.	Merchandise.	Passengers.
	Tons.	*Number.*		*Tons.*	*Number.*
1896	117,242	8,460	1899	68,126	5,210
1897	112,803	11,545	1900	88,622	5,305
1898	153,257	12,250			

638   REPORT OF THE CHIEF OF ENGINEERS, U. S. ARMY.

July 1, 1900, balance unexpended $12,865.89
June 30, 1901, amount expended during fiscal year 277.42

July 1, 1901, balance unexpended 12,588.47
(See Appendix W W 7.)

8. *Lewis River, Washington.*—The Lewis River rises in the Cascade Range. It is a tributary of the Columbia, drains an exceedingly fertile valley, and enters the Columbia from the north about 14 miles below the mouth of the Willamette, or 25 miles from Portland, Oreg.

At the time of the adoption of the present and original project (Annual Report of the Chief of Engineers for 1897, p. 3475) 4 feet could be carried at low water to the forks, 3¼ miles from the mouth, and 2 feet to Lacenter, on the East Fork and about 7 miles from the mouth. The channel was obstructed by trees, snags, and occasional shoals. Its improvement will be of benefit to the farmers and the large adjacent lumbering interests.

The project for expenditure of $10,000, the first appropriation for this river (act of March 3, 1899), contemplates, so far as funds will permit, the removal of snags and obstructions, dike and dam work, and dredging with a view of obtaining a depth of 6 feet in the main river to the forks and 4 feet thence to Lacenter.

The amount expended on the work up to the close of the fiscal year 1900 was $4,284.95.

Operations during the year were confined to the completion of Cowley Bar dike by its extension to a total length of 455 feet. The wor was completed on August 10, since which time nothing has been done.

The results accomplished have been of benefit to commerce and navigation, the depths obtained the previous year by dredging near the forks have not deteriorated to any great extent, and regular river boats have navigated this portion of the stream without interruption. During extreme low water a transfer to a smaller boat was made necessary at one of the crossings above the forks in order to reach Lacenter.

The lower reaches of this stream are of a tidal nature and bars are formed in the sluggish waters during the freshets, which it is believed can best be overcome by dredging. A dredging plant is estimated for in separate report (see p. 640), for use on this and other tributaries of the Lower Columbia, and should funds be made available for its construction it is thought that more economical results can be attained.

The maximum draft that can be carried over the shoalest place at low water is probably about 2 feet.

Comparative statement of the tonnage carried by river boats on the Lewis River for the past five years.

Calendar year.	Merchandise.	Passengers.	Calendar year.	Merchandise.	Passengers.
	Tons.	*Number.*		*Tons.*	*Number.*
1896	2,374	12,990	1899	6,549	12,351
1897	3,881	15,306	1900	12,638	14,129
1898	6,303	15,938			

The above does not include large quantities of logs which are annually floated out of this stream.

July 1, 1900, balance unexpended.. $5,715.05
June 30, 1901, amount expended during fiscal year..................... 342.54

July 1, 1901, balance unexpended 5,372.51

Amount (estimated) required for completion of existing project........ 10,460.00
Amount that can be profitably expended in fiscal year ending June 30, 1903, for works of improvement and for maintenance, in addition to the balance unexpended July 1, 1901 .... 8,000.00
Submitted in compliance with requirements of sundry civil act of June 4, 1897, and of section 7 of the river and harbor act of 1899.

(See Appendix W W 8.)

9. *Cowlitz River, Washington.*—The Cowlitz River rises in the Cascade Range; it is a tributary of the Columbia and flows into it from the north and about 64 miles from its mouth.

Prior to improvement the ruling depth at low water to Toledo, 40 miles above the mouth, was 14 inches. The channel was narrow and tortuous and obstructed by sand bars, numerous snags, drift, logs, etc. The valley is exceedingly fertile, and any improvement of the river is a direct benefit to the farmers, who ship great quantities of produce to market by boat.

The original project, adopted in 1880 (report dated December 15, 1879), contemplated the removal of sand bars and other obstructions to a point about 50 miles above the mouth, at a cost of $5,000 for the first year and an annual expenditure thereafter of $2,000 for maintenance.

The amount expended on the work up to the close of the fiscal year 1900 was $30,983.50, at which time the available funds had been exhausted, and no work has since been done.

The conditions are now such that boats ascend to Toledo regularly, the principal difficulty experienced being at the bar below Toledo, where lining over this shoal becomes necessary at low water. Three or four bars below this point are also giving trouble.

No results in the way of increased depths since last report have been attained. It may be stated, however, that the river is in as good, if not better, condition than the previous year, aside from the snagging which will be annually necessary.

In connection with this improvement, it is thought that dredging in the lower tidal reaches will prove advantageous in securing and maintaining depths. A dredging plant is estimated for in a separate report (see p. 640), for use on this and other tributaries of the Columbia, and if construction of this dredge is authorized and funds provided for its operation it is thought that better and more economical results can be attained.

The maximum draft that can be carried over the shoalest part at low water is about 2 feet.

Comparative statement of traffic.

Calendar year—	Tons.	Calendar year—	Tons.
1894	17,923	1898	16,210
1895	17,940	1899	26,511
1896	14,776	1900	17,279
1897	17,582		

This statement does not include large quantities of logs that are annually floated down this stream.

July 1, 1900, balance unexpended $16.50
June 30, 1901, amount expended during fiscal year 12.60

July 1, 1901, balance unexpended 3.90

{ Amount (estimated) required for completion of existing project........ Indefinite.
Amount that can be profitably expended in fiscal year ending June 30,
1903, for works of improvement and for maintenance, in addition to
the balance unexpended July 1, 1901 .... 3,000.00
Submitted in compliance with requirements of sundry civil act of June
4, 1897, and of section 7 of the river and harbor act of 1899. }

(See Appendix W W 9.)

10. Improving the tributaries of the Columbia River, Oregon and Washington, below the mouth of the Willamette River, by the construction and equipment of a dredging plant for use thereon.—The streams under improvement at present are the Lewis and Cowlitz rivers, Washington, and the Clatskanie River, Oregon. In view of the tidal nature of these streams in their lower reaches, and owing to the sediment brought down by freshets, it is thought that if a small, light-draft dredge and tender were available cheaper and quicker results could be obtained. There is no such plant in this district, and the division engineer and district officer, concurred in by the Chief of Engineers, recommend the construction of a suitable dredge and appliances, the estimated cost of which is $40,000; the funds for construction and equipment to be provided by special appropriation, the operating expenses to be paid from funds available for maintenance or improvement of the stream upon which used; construction of plant to be done by contract.

(See Appendix W W 10.)

11. Gauging waters of Columbia River, Oregon and Washington.— The object of this gauging is to obtain data for use in connection with the improvement of the river and to supply information to persons interested in its navigation.

The self-registering gauge was reestablished at Astoria in November, 1888, where it was kept in operation up to August, 1899, and then moved to Fort Stevens, where it could be more economically maintained. Daily bulletins have been exhibited for the benefit of shipping interests, and in view of the benefit to commerce its maintenance is considered a worthy object.

The amount expended on this work to June 30, 1900, was $7,196.63.

July 1, 1900, balance unexpended $803.37
June 30, 1901, amount expended during fiscal year 20.25

July 1, 1901, balance unexpended 783.12
July 1, 1901, outstanding liabilities 10.00

July 1, 1901, balance available 773.12

{ Amount that can be profitably expended in fiscal year ending June 30,
1903, in addition to the balance available July 1, 1901............... 1,000.00
Submitted in compliance with requirements of sundry civil act of June
4, 1897. }

(See Appendix W W 11.)

IMPROVEMENT OF CERTAIN RIVERS AND HARBORS IN WASHINGTON, IDAHO, AND MONTANA.

This district was in the charge of Capt. Harry Taylor, Corps of Engineers, to November 30, 1900, and of Maj. John Millis, Corps of Engineers, since that date, the officer in charge having under his immediate orders Lieut. Meriwether L. Walker, Corps of Engineers, to January 19, 1901. Division Engineer, Col. S. M. Mansfield, Corps of Engineers, to November 23, 1900, and Col. Jared A. Smith, Corps of Engineers, since December 15, 1900.

1. *Willapa River and Harbor, Washington.*—Willapa Harbor, formerly known as Shoalwater Bay, connects with the Pacific Ocean in the extreme southwestern part of the State of Washington. The portion of the harbor which has been improved is that in the vicinity of Southbend, the principal city of the harbor and the terminus of the branch railroad from the main line of the Northern Pacific at Chehalis.

Southbend is situated very near the mouth of the Willapa River. Just at the upper limits of the town the river divides into a main channel and a secondary channel, the latter known as Mailboat Slough. This division caused bars to form in the main channel at both the upper and lower ends of the slough. There were also several bars in the river proper between Southbend and Willapa City.

The plan of improvement adopted consists in building a dike of piles, brush, and stone across the head of Mailboat Slough, in order to concentrate the ebbing and flooding currents into the main channel, and thereby produce as great a scour as possible on the shoals at the head and foot of the slough; also to dredge a channel 100 feet wide and 8 feet deep at low water through the reef just below Willapa City, and to close Louderback Slough with a pile, brush, and stone dike, with the object of compelling the currents to scour a channel through the bar in the river at its lower end. This was approved May 2, 1891. The estimated cost of the work is $36,350.

The act of August 18, 1894, authorized the expenditure of not to exceed $2,500 from the appropriation for this improvement for cutting a channel through a log jam in the North River, and the act of March 3, 1899, authorized the expenditure of so much of that appropriation for this improvement as might be necessary to more thoroughly clear this same jam.

The amount expended to June 30, 1900, was $31,227.96.

Up to June 30, 1900, the dike work in the river and harbor and the work of dredging through the shoal just below Willapa City had been completed and the jam in the North River partly cleared away.

During the fiscal year ending June 30, 1901, the channel through the North River jam was cleared out and widened to a uniform width of 100 feet at high water.

The work called for by the project has all been completed. The object of the improvement, so far as to give a channel 8 feet deep at mean lower low water to Willapa City, has been practically accomplished.

The dikes at Mailboat Slough have caused a general deepening of the shoals in their vicinity of about 2 feet, so that the least depth to Southbend, the principal city on Willapa Harbor, is now 15 feet at mean lower low water.

It is believed that the effect of the Mailboat Slough dikes has been about as great as can be expected.

The dikes already built need some repairs, which will be made with the balance available.

No recommendation for future appropriations is made.

Exports and imports.

Year.	Tons.	Value.
Fiscal year:		
1894	66,908	$639,280
1895	61,858	705,570
1896	48,960	600,800
Calendar year:		
1896	27,542	351,175
1897	37,815	313,163
1898	32,399	374,050
1899	51,150	755,682
1900	42,090	266,080

July 1, 1900, balance unexpended $5,122.04
June 30, 1901, amount expended during fiscal year 915.10

July 1, 1901, balance unexpended 4,206.94

(See Appendix X X 1.)

2. Grays Harbor and bar entrance, Washington.—Grays Harbor is a large bay in the southwestern part of the State of Washington, connecting with the Pacific Ocean. It has a total length from east to west of 17 miles, and its greatest breadth north and south is 14 miles.

A large part of the bay is occupied by tide flats, bare at low water. At low tide the area covered by water is estimated at 30.6 square miles, or less than one-third of the total area. The average range of the tide is 8.4 feet, with a maximum range of 12.9 feet. There are two main channels crossing the bay from east to west. The north channel is the principal one, and this has been improved. A short distance within the harbor entrance are large areas affording sheltered anchorages for deep-draft vessels.

The harbor entrance is between two low sandy peninsulas, which are about 12,500 feet apart, measured between high-tide lines.

Through this entrance there is a channel having a maximum depth of 100 feet or more. A single broad waterway extends for more than 2 miles out to sea from the entrance, with depths gradually diminishing to 30 feet. At the outer end of this deep waterway lies a bar convex to the sea and extending each way to the sand spits on the two sides of the harbor throat.

Across the bar there was no good permanent channel, but there were several variable shifting channels having depths of about 12 or 13 feet. The general average width of the bar between the inner and outer 18-foot curve is one-half mile.

The first appropriation for this work was made in the river and harbor act of June 3, 1896.

The plan of improvement is to control, by means of a single jetty extending out to sea from the point on the south side of the harbor throat, a distance of about 3¼ miles, the ebbing and flooding waters to a sufficient extent to concentrate and direct upon the bar a much greater portion thereof than would naturally go there. It is expected that a depth of 24 feet at mean low water will be obtained across the bar. This was approved March 20, 1895.

The jetty is to be of rubblestone, built above high-tide level. The estimated cost of the work is $1,000,000.

A full description of this work, with plan, is published in the Annual Report of the Chief of Engineers for 1895, pages 3517-3528.

The act making the first appropriation for this work authorized the making of a contract or contracts for the completion of the project. In accordance with this authority a contract for the entire work was entered into after due advertisement. This contract was approved by the Chief of Engineers February 23, 1898, and work under it commenced in March, 1898.

The amount expended to June 30, 1900, was $370,019.55.

At the end of June, 1900, the jetty trestle had been completed 7,736 feet outside the high-water line on the ocean side of the spit and the foundation of the jetty had been completed 7,656 feet outside the high-water line. The enrockment had been completed to or above the high-water level for a distance of 7,200 feet.

Construction work continued from July 1 until November 16, when it was suspended for the winter. Work was resumed April 11 and actively prosecuted during the remainder of the fiscal year. The progress has been in advance of contract requirements.

During the fiscal year ending June 30, 1901, the jetty trestle was advanced 3,232 feet, the completed foundation advanced 3,200 feet, and the enrockment completed to the level of ordinary high water for an additional distance of 1,992 feet. At the end of June, 1901, the jetty trestle had been completed 10,968 feet outside the high-water line on the ocean side of the spit, the foundation had been completed 10,840 feet, and enrockment raised to or above the level of ordinary high water 9,192 feet from the shore line.

During the year the following materials were received from the contractor:

	Quantity.	Cost per unit.	Amount.
Piles..lin. ft..	105,565	$0.11	$11,612.15
Lumber...ft. B. M..	354,403	11.00	3,896.43
Steel railroad rails, etc.............................tons..	75.017	40.00	3,000.68
Iron..lbs..	56,595	.04	2,263.80
Brush..cu. yds..	13,885.91	1.20	16,663.09
Stone..tons..	184,240.2	1.10	202,664.22
Total...			240,102.37

The available depth of channel across the bar is materially greater than before the work commenced. The minimum channel depth over the bar last reported was 18 feet.

Exports and imports.

Year.	Tons.	Value.
Fiscal year—		
1893...	296,286	$4,431,743
1894...	302,102	3,221,500
1895...	159,744	848,591
1896...	227,351	1,420,055
Calendar year—		
1896...	110,748	629,677
1897...	150,908	1,071,747
1898...	168,468	1,252,089
1899...	265,918	1,979,998
1900...	259,692	2,077,037

644   REPORT OF THE CHIEF OF ENGINEERS, U. S. ARMY.

July 1, 1900, balance unexpended $334,980.45
Amount appropriated by sundry civil act approved March 3, 1901 ...... 138,225.00

    473,205.45
June 30, 1901, amount expended during fiscal year 207,055.37

July 1, 1901, balance unexpended 266,150.08
July 1, 1901, outstanding liabilities 4,628.17

July 1, 1901, balance available 261,521.91

July 1, 1901, amount covered by uncompleted contracts 256,246.64

Amount (estimated) required for completion of existing project 156,775.00
Amount that can be profitably expended in fiscal year ending June 30,
  1903, in addition to the balance available July 1, 1901 .... 156,775.00
Submitted in compliance with requirements of sundry civil act of June
  4, 1897.

(See Appendix X X 2.)

3. Chehalis River, Washington.—This river is in the southwestern part of Washington. It has a westerly course and empties into Grays Harbor Bay at its eastern extremity.

From the mouth to Montesano, 15 miles, there is about 10 feet of water at high tide. From Montesano to Elma, 16 miles, there is generally sufficient water for light-draft boats. There is practically no navigation above Elma.

The plan of improvement contemplates the removal of snags, overhanging trees, jams, drift heaps, shoals, and other obstructions to navigation which may from time to time accumulate in the portion of the river regularly used by boats. This was approved January 25, 1882.

The cost of the work is indefinite.

The amount expended to June 30, 1900, was $16,921.09.

The lower section of the river had been cleared of snags from time to time as they accumulated.

No work was done during the past fiscal year until about the middle of June, when a boat was hired to clear certain obstructions below Montesano.

Exports and imports.

Year.	Tons.	Value.
Fiscal year—		
1895	4,354	$233,691
Calendar year—		
1896	2,561	246,498
1897	2,401	245,387
1898	2,780	295,610
1899	2,282	352,316
1900	4,376	182,157

July 1, 1900, balance unexpended $2,078.91
June 30, 1901, amount expended during fiscal year 490.50

July 1, 1901, balance unexpended 1,588.41

Amount (estimated) required for completion of existing project .... Indefinite.
Amount that can be profitably expended in fiscal year ending June 30,
  1903, in addition to the balance unexpended July 1, 1901 .... 3,000.00
Submitted in compliance with requirements of sundry civil act of June
  4, 1897.

(See Appendix X X 3.)

4. *Puget Sound and its tributary waters, Washington.*—Formerly the streams and channels tributary to Puget Sound, to which the appropriation was to be applied, were specified in the act, but since August 4, 1892, the appropriation has been made under the above general title, with great advantage to the work. The funds have been applied almost exclusively to the improvement of navigable streams flowing into Puget Sound from the eastward. In their original condition these streams were available for purposes of commerce so far as depth and width were concerned, but they were all obstructed by the débris generally found in streams flowing through a heavily wooded country.

The plan of improvement approved July 17, 1891, contemplates removal of snags and other similar obstructions, this work being done mainly by a snag boat owned and operated by the Government.

The amount expended to June 30, 1900, was $160,778.13.

During the past fiscal year snagging operations were continued and the streams available for navigation were maintained in proper condition.

The streams worked on were the Skagit, Stilaguamish, Snohomish, and North Fork of the Skagit.

The Nooksak is now entirely closed to navigation by a log boom in Bellingham Bay, near the mouth, and by an extensive log jam in the lower part of the river. In view of the increasing number of fish traps and log booms in Puget Sound and tributary waters, an estimate for maintenance is submitted.

Exports and imports.

Calendar year.	Tons.	Value.
1896	18,600	$358,600
1897	11,922	325,280
1898	12,676	539,406
1899	13,500	577,566
1900	35,066	1,324,926

July 1, 1900, balance unexpended	$32,721.87
June 30, 1901, amount expended during fiscal year	12,502.72
July 1, 1901, balance unexpended	20,219.15
July 1, 1901, outstanding liabilities	1,959.66
July 1, 1901, balance available	18,259.49

Amount (estimated) required for completion of existing project .... Indefinite.
Amount that can be profitably expended in fiscal year ending June 30, 1903, for works of improvement and for maintenance, in addition to the balance available July 1, 1901 .... 20,000.00
Submitted in compliance with requirements of sundry civil act of June 4, 1897, and of section 7 of the river and harbor act of 1899.

(See Appendix X X 4.)

5. *Harbor at Olympia, Wash.*—Olympia is situated at the extreme southern point of Puget Sound at the head of Budd Inlet. The upper end of this inlet is shoal. The shoal extends northward from the Fourth Street Bridge for a distance of 8,750 feet to a depth of 12 feet at mean lower low water in Budd Inlet. The shoals necessitated the building of long wharves out to deep water. The maintenance of the wharves, due to the ravages of the teredo, was very expensive.

It is proposed by the plan of improvement adopted to dredge a channel 250 feet wide and 12 feet deep at the mean of the lower low waters from the vicinity of the Fourth Street Bridge to deep water in Budd Inlet. Near its inner end the channel is to be widened out to 500 feet, so as to provide a turning basin for boats using it. This project was approved September 19, 1891.

The estimated cost of the work is $147,000.

The amount expended to June 30, 1900, was $121,883.25.

The channel had been dredged to the full depth contemplated, 12 feet at mean lower low water, for the full width of 250 feet over a part of its length, and for a width of 150 feet throughout the remainder. No work was in progress during the past year, owing to lack of funds.

Some shoaling of the channel already dredged may be expected, and to remove this and complete the project it is estimated that $25,000 will be required.

Exports and imports.

Year.	Tons.	Value.
Fiscal year—		
1893	95,011	$2,067,825
1894	55,148	421,225
1895	25,125	239,400
1896	28,480	266,700
Calendar year—		
1896	36,099	191,300
1897	29,800	430,900
1898	52,335	1,203,226
1899	42,694	1,173,684
1900	35,466	848,703

July 1, 1900, balance unexpended.. $116.75
June 30, 1901, amount expended during fiscal year.................... 10.50

July 1, 1901, balance unexpended 106.25

Amount (estimated) required for completion of existing project........ 25,000.00
Amount that can be profitably expended in fiscal year ending June 30, 1903, in addition to the balance unexpended July 1, 1901............ 15,000.00
Submitted in compliance with requirements of sundry civil act of June 4, 1897.

(See Appendix X X 5.)

6. *Waterway connecting Puget Sound with lakes Union and Washington, Washington.*—Lake Washington is about 19 miles long, north and south, with an average breadth of 2¼ to 3 miles. It lies parallel to the eastern shore of Puget Sound at an average distance of 4 to 6 miles. The city of Seattle occupies the central portion of the area between the lake and the sound. Lake Union is a small lake of irregular shape, some 2 miles in extent east and west, which lies between Lake Washington and the Sound, immediately north of the main portion of the city, but within the city limits. Lake Samamish is a small lake 5 miles east of Lake Washington. The water of all these lakes is fresh, and they have moderate elevations above tide water in Puget Sound. Lake Washington has ample depths for the largest vessels over almost its entire area. The same is true of more than half the area of Lake Union. The lakes never freeze over and there is rarely more than a slight formation of ice near shore. The natural outlet of Lake Washington is at its southern extremity, that of Lake Union is at its western end through a small stream flowing into Salmon Bay, a

small arm of Puget Sound. From the eastern end of Lake Union to Lake Washington is only about 1,800 feet. A small canal was cut through the dividing ridge at this point some years ago for the use of small boats and for passing logs. The shores of these lakes are generally bold, the land rising quite abruptly to heights of several hundred feet, but railroads have been constructed along a considerable portion of the shore line, and there are many low-lying, level areas available for terminal facilities. Wharves can readily be constructed at almost any point along shore. The tidal oscillation in the Sound at Seattle is extremely irregular, and it has a range of about 17 feet. The depths along the Sound water front are very great, and there is practically no available anchorage for vessels on this account. The great depths and the ravages of the teredo, which are unusually destructive in Puget Sound, render the construction and maintenance of wharves unusually expensive on the salt-water front of Seattle, and much inconvenience and expense results from the great and irregular tidal movement.

The town of Ballard, on Salmon Bay, has a large and increasing business in the manufacture and shipment of lumber and shingles by water, and in shipbuilding, but the water front is at present only accessible to vessels at high tide. The existing water traffic on Lake Union is principally towing logs received through the small canal from Lake Washington to the lumber and shingle mills on the lake shores. Lake Washington has a considerable business in log towing and transportation of coal from the mines near the eastern shore, besides the small traffic engaged in by ferryboats and boats running from the Seattle lake front to various points on the lake shores.

The river and harbor act of September 19, 1890, contained an item directing the appointment of a Board of three officers of the Corps of Engineers to select and survey the most feasible location and to estimate the expense of constructing a ship canal to connect the waters of lakes Union, Washington, and Samamish with Puget Sound. The sum of $10,000 was appropriated for the necessary expenses. The report of this Board is contained in House Ex. Doc. No. 40, Fifty-second Congress, first session, and also in the Annual Report of the Chief of Engineers for 1892, page 2762 et seq.

This Board did not consider that part of the proposed waterway connecting with Lake Samamish as of sufficient importance or value to justify the cost, and the connection of Lake Samamish with Puget Sound has not been seriously considered since that date.

Subsequently a detailed survey and location of the proposed canal were made in compliance with a clause in the sundry civil act of March 2, 1895, under direction of Capt. Thomas W. Symons, Corps of Engineers. This report, dated August 29, 1895, is published in the Annual Report of the Chief of Engineers for 1896, page 3356.

The western end of the canal through Salmon or Shilshole Bay, instead of through Smiths Cove, as once proposed, and a modification in the location of the lower lock were recommended by a Board of Engineer officers and approved by the Secretary of War August 14, 1898.

The general project for this work so far as adopted contemplates the construction of a ship canal from the waters of Puget Sound through Salmon Bay to Lake Union and thence to Lake Washington. It includes dredging through the flats immediately outside of Salmon Bay to a lock in the lower end of Salmon or Shilshole Bay, the construction of this lock, dredging inside of the lock through Salmon Bay, the digging of a canal from the upper end of Salmon Bay to Lake Union, dredging to the eastern end of Lake Union, and the construction of a canal and lock between lakes Union and Washington.

The maximum lift of the lower lock at low tide will be about 25 feet. The average lift of the upper lock will be about 8½ feet. The canal section and the lock dimensions are to be such as will accommodate the the largest merchant vessels and ships of war.

The amount expended to June 30, 1900, was $5,000.

A detailed survey of the route had been made and maps prepared showing boundaries of all real estate to be acquired.

The two appropriations already made for this work contained the proviso that none of the money should be expended until the entire right of way and a release from all liability to adjacent property owners should have been secured to the United States free of cost. To comply with these restrictions of law, King County, in which the canal is located, obtained the right of way and release from liability and deeded the same to the United States. The deed to the right of way and the release from liability was accepted by the United States and filed for record June 22, 1900.

The operations during the past year comprised making contract for preliminary dredging from Puget Sound to the site of the lower lock site, a distance of about 6,000 feet; making contracts and beginning work on excavation between Lake Union and Salmon Bay; clearing site of lower lock and dam; establishing and observing a number of gauges to determine variations of water level in the lakes and the principal streams connecting with them; the establishment of a self-recording tide gauge at the lower lock site, and discharge measurements. Borings were made along the line of the canal to the head of Salmon Bay, and the site of the lower lock was explored in detail by borings. Preparation of detailed plans and estimates was in progress.

Exports and imports.

Calendar year.	Tons.	Value.
1897	563,901	$19,114,111
1898	804,867	32,665,866
1899	832,942	33,068,012
1900	1,100,099	48,162,383

July 1, 1900, balance unexpended	$170,000.00
June 30, 1901, amount expended during fiscal year	7,022.34
July 1, 1901, balance unexpended	162,977.66
July 1, 1901, outstanding liabilities	672.74
July 1, 1901, balance available	162,304.92
July 1, 1901, amount covered by uncompleted contracts	92,460.00
Amount (estimated) required for completion of existing project	6,500,000.00

(See Appendix X X 6.)

7. *Everett Harbor, Washington.*—The city of Everett is on the east shore of Puget Sound, about 30 miles north of Seattle. The southern part of the water front has ample depth and is accessible for vessels of the deepest draft. The northern portion is at present inaccessible

on account of the delta formation or tide flats off the mouth of the Snohomish River. This river approaches from the southeast, and at a point about a mile and a half back of the Sound water front of Everett divides into several channels. One of these, called Old River, flows north and then west, entering the Sound north of the town. The others reach the Sound still farther to the north. The principal branch, Steamboat Slough, and the Snohomish River proper have sufficient depths for steamboat navigation. Old River is not passable for steamboats except at high tide.

Under date of November 4, 1893, the Acting Secretary of War granted to the Everett Land Company authority to construct certain works designed to produce a fresh-water basin at Everett that would be available for all commercial shipping. These works comprised a dike running south from the lower end of Smiths Island 3,500 feet from shore and about 4¼ miles long, with cross dike and lock at the lower end. The lock was to have a chamber 50 feet by 400 feet and 35 feet deep. At the upper end of Old River there was to be a dam with a lock having a chamber 30 by 150 feet and 25 feet deep and a tide gate 80 feet wide. Between the lower and the upper lock was to be dredged through Old River a channel or harbor basin about 6¼ miles long, 500 feet wide for 4¼ miles and 300 feet wide for the remaining length. Around a large part of this fresh-water basin was to be a roadway 200 feet wide and about 12 miles long, and an extensive system of wharves was projected. The Everett Land Company owned all the tide lands involved in the project, as well as a large part of the other lands adjacent to the proposed work. No work was ever done in carrying out the project by the Everett Land Company. The property of the Everett Land Company has since been acquired by the Everett Improvement Company.

The first appropriation for the improvement of Everett Harbor was in the act of August 18, 1894, "For dredging Everett Harbor, including mouth of Snohomish River, and Snohomish River from mouth to Lowell, in the State of Washington, the sum of $10,000."

It was decided that no dike or bulkhead construction could be done under this appropriation, and that dredging alone would not be of value, so the funds were not applied. Subsequently the dike construction was authorized by resolution of Congress dated February 1, 1895, and the project under which the original and subsequent appropriations have been applied may be stated as follows:

First, to excavate a harbor basin in the shallows and tide lands adjoining deep water near the river's mouth; second, to dredge a channel from this through the tide flats and the Old River mouth to deep fresh water in the Snohomish River, this channel being designed to bring fresh water to the harbor basin and to afford facilities for navigation about the peninsula and into the deep water bounding the peninsula on the east, and, third, to protect and maintain this harbor and channel across the tide flats by a bulkhead interposed between them and the open waters of the Sound, the bulkhead to act as a retaining wall for the material dredged from the harbor. The date of approval of this plan was February 14, 1895.

The estimated cost of the improvement is $422,000, the total expenditure authorized by the act of March 3, 1899.

The amount expended on the project to June 30, 1900, was $34,134.02.

A dike for the purpose of retaining the dredged material had been built from the lower end of Smiths Island along the established bulkhead line for a distance of 14,436 feet, a channel 50 feet wide at the bottom and 6 feet deep at mean low water had been dredged from the deep water on the outside in toward the deep water in the river for a distance of 2,885 feet, a continuing contract for the completion of the project had been made, and the contractor had begun construction of the dredging plant.

Some modifications of details in the bulkhead construction were authorized on April 16, 1901, with a view to a more substantial structure, though at some increase in cost.

Bulkhead construction under the contract began October 17, 1900, and dredging began December 10, 1900.

The amount of dredging done during the year and the quantities of material placed in the bulkhead, with cost, are as follows:

	Quantity.	Cost per unit.	Amount.
Dredging...................cu. yds..	789,179.76	$0.09	$66,526.78
Piles.........................lin. ft..	56,109	.08	4,488.72
Lumber.......................ft. B. M..	81,396	14.00	1,139.54
Fascines......................cords..	19,787.18	3.00	59,361.54
Stone.........................tons..	5,723.32	.95	5,437.15
Total			136,953.73

Until the improvement is practically completed no material benefit will be derived from it, as sand flats which rise several feet above mean low water extend entirely across the proposed channel, so that no boats of any kind can use the channel at or near that stage.

Some modifications of the project now appear to be desirable.

Exports and imports.

Year.	Tons.	Value.
Fiscal year—		
1895...	79,919	$1,845,282
1896...	144,541	2,724,789
Calendar year—		
1896...	210,547	5,384,831
1897...	74,960	2,974,526
1898...	55,460	2,545,054
1899...	42,713	1,477,120
1900...	55,094	1,820,561

July 1, 1900, balance unexpended $180,865.98
Amount appropriated by sundry civil act approved March 3, 1901 ...... 90,000.00

270,865.98
June 30, 1901, amount expended during fiscal year 114,066.68

July 1, 1901, balance unexpended 156,799.30
July 1, 1901, outstanding liabilities.................................. 331.00

July 1, 1901, balance available.. 156,468.30

July 1, 1901, amount covered by uncompleted contracts................. 169,988.06

Amount (estimated) required for completion of existing project 117,000.00
Amount that can be profitably expended in fiscal year ending June 30, 1903, in addition to the balance available July 1, 1901 .... 117,000.00
Submitted in compliance with requirements of sundry civil act of June 4, 1897.

(See Appendix X X 7.)

8. *Swinomish Slough, Washington.*—This slough affords an inland-sheltered passage for small vessels from Puget Sound proper northward to Bellingham Bay and the Gulf of Georgia. The total distance by way of the slough from good water in Skagit Bay to navigable depths in Padilla Bay is about 11 miles. The rise and fall of the tide is about 8 feet.

At the northern end the slough opens out into the flats forming the southern portion of Padilla Bay, in the midst of diked land and marshes.

At the southern end of the slough there were two passages connecting the slough with the waters of Skagit Bay. These passages were separated by a rocky island called McGlinns Island.

The east passage was wide and shallow, having nowhere more than 2 feet depth at low water. The west passage between McGlinns and Fidalgo islands is at the narrowest place 220 feet wide, with an ample depth of water for all purposes.

This short and crooked passage has high and rocky bluffs on either side and is called the "Hole in the Wall."

This is the passage used exclusively by steamers.

Between the Hole in the Wall and deep water in Saratoga Passage there were extensive flats which were almost bare at low water.

The plan of improvement adopted is to dredge a channel 4 feet deep and 100 feet wide from deep water in Saratoga Passage across Skagit Flats, through the shoals of the slough proper, and across the flats of Padilla Bay to deep water, and to build dikes in Skagit and Padilla bays to direct the ebbing and flooding waters through the dredged channels.

The estimated cost of this work is $122,000.

A report of a survey of Swinomish Slough, upon which the plan of improvement is based, is printed with a general map in House Ex. Doc. No. 31, Fifty-second Congress, first session, and reprinted without map in the Annual Report of the Chief of Engineers for 1892, pages 2753–2762.

A map showing parts of the improvement was published in the Annual Report of the Chief of Engineers for 1900, opposite page 4488.

The amount expended to June 30, 1900, was $90,408.93.

At that date a wattled pile dike 6,166 feet long had been constructed from a point 400 feet west of the entrance to the Hole in the Wall westerly to a point 300 feet distant from the northwest point of Goat Island; a dike consisting of a single row of piles had been built between Goat and Ika islands, and a pile, brush, and stone dike 2,745 feet long had been built between McGlinns Island and Gallahers Point, and subsequently repaired. The wattled dike having shown signs of weakness at exposed points, 3,486 feet of it had been strengthened by adding a second row of piles and filling in between the two rows with brush and stone. The remainder of the dike had been thoroughly repaired. A channel 100 feet wide at the bottom and 4 feet deep at mean low water had been dredged parallel to and 75 feet from the wattled dike for a distance of 6,120 feet, and across the tide flat just inside the Hole in the Wall, between McGlinns Island and Laconner, and from Laconner north about halfway to the northern end of the slough. Boats drawing 4 feet can now reach Laconner from the south at mean low water, but not to exceed 2 feet can be carried through the slough.

No work was done during the past year, owing to insufficient funds.

As no work has been done on the northern part of the slough, no increase of depth over the original condition has been obtained for through traffic. The part of the channel that has been improved is used only by vessels running from southern ports on the Sound to Laconner.

The required depth of 4 feet in the part where work has been done has been secured in part, but on account of local shoal spots not over 2 feet can be carried to Laconner at lowest water.

The work yet to be done, according to the original estimate, includes 6,000 linear feet of dike in Padilla Bay, 6,000 linear feet of dike in the slough proper, 90,000 cubic yards of dredging in Padilla Bay, and 30,000 cubic yards of dredging in the slough proper. Some of the channels which have heretofore been dredged have shoaled and the dikes which have been built have deteriorated so as to need additional repairs.

Exports and imports.

Year.	Tons.	Value.
Fiscal year—		
1893	55,700	$1,510,000
1894	64,050	1,637,000
1895	114,917	1,713,020
1896	131,370	1,709,700
Calendar year—		
1896	65,375	1,847,664
1897	64,497	1,190,000
1898	19,625	832,345
1899	76,636	2,028,454
1900	74,516	1,611,460

July 1, 1900, balance unexpended	$4,591.07
June 30, 1901, amount expended during fiscal year	17.50
July 1, 1901, balance unexpended	4,573.57
Amount (estimated) required for completion of existing project	47,000.00
Amount that can be profitably expended in fiscal year ending June 30, 1903, for works of improvement and for maintenance, in addition to the balance unexpended July 1, 1901	35,000.00

Submitted in compliance with requirements of sundry civil act of June 4, 1897, and of section 7 of the river and harbor act of 1899.

(See Appendix X X 8.)

9. *Okanogan River, Washington.* This river rises in Canadian territory, flows in a southerly direction, and empties into the Columbia. The lower portion, for a distance of 87 miles, lies in the northeastern part of Washington.

The first appropriation for this work was made by the river and harbor act of March 3, 1899. The river has a general width of 300 to 400 feet through its entire length in the United States and as a rule has sufficient depth for light-draft navigation throughout the year, but it is obstructed in places by shoals and rocks which prevent any navigation except during the summer high water. The upper stretches are also obstructed by snags.

The plan of improvement contemplates rock removal, the construction of wing dams and snagging, and was approved April 18, 1900. The estimated cost is $30,000.

Descriptions of the river and the plan of improvement are given in the Annual Report of the Chief of Engineers for 1898, page 3121.

The amount expended up to June 30, 1900, was $12,874.37.

RIVER AND HARBOR IMPROVEMENTS. 653

During the months of November and December, 1900, a small force was employed removing bowlders at Crazy Rapids and in the vicinity of Rapids Nos. 18 and 20. A wing dam was built at Rapid No. 20. Some posts to assist vessels were placed at Rapid No. 18. The work resulted locally in removing difficulties of navigation, but there was no general increase in depth except in the immediate locality of the work.

The country adjacent to the Okanogan River is rapidly developing and filling up with settlers, and it is important that the improvement should be completed as early as practicable.

Exports and imports for the year 1899: Tons, 1,733; value, $151,415.

July 1, 1900, balance unexpended	$2,125.63
June 30, 1901, amount expended during fiscal year	1,895.42
July 1, 1901, balance unexpended	230.21

Amount (estimated) required for completion of existing project	15,000.00
Amount that can be profitably expended in fiscal year ending June 30, 1903, in addition to the balance unexpended July 1, 1901	12,000.00
Submitted in compliance with requirements of sundry civil act of June 4, 1897.	

(See Appendix X X 9.)

10. *Pend Oreille River, Washington.*—This river forms the outlet of Pend Oreille Lake, in the northern part of Idaho. It flows in a northwesterly direction through the northeast corner of Washington, crosses the boundary, and connects with the Columbia in Canadian territory. From Lake Pend Oreille to the boundary the distance is about 100 miles.

The first appropriation for this work was made in the river and harbor act of March 3, 1899. The river from Lake Pend Oreille down to Priest River has unobstructed low depths of upward of 25 feet and from Priest River to Albany Falls sufficient depth for river boats. Albany Falls totally obstruct navigation. Below Albany Falls there is sufficient depth for light-draft navigation as far as Box Canyon, about 55¼ miles, but it is somewhat interfered with by shoals and isolated rocks. Navigation is entirely prevented from passing through Box Canyon by swift currents passing over submerged rocks and by projecting rocky points.

The plan of improvement contemplates the improvement of Box Canyon by the removal of submerged rocks, the blowing off of projecting rocky points, and the removal of submerged rocks between Box Canyon and Albany Falls, and was approved April 18, 1899. The estimated cost is $30,000.

Descriptions of the river and the plan of improvement are given in the Annual Report of the Chief of Engineers for 1898, page 3124. The work done previous to June 30, 1900, resulted in partly clearing away the obstructions in Box Canyon, but this resulted in little or no benefit to navigation. On account of the character of the improvement, no benefit is to be expected until the improvement is completed.

Exports and imports.

Year.	Tons.	Value.
1899	2,617	$129,677
1900	1,921	97,125

July 1, 1900, balance unexpended $1,260.29
July 1, 1901, balance unexpended 1,260.29

Amount (estimated) required for completion of existing project 20,000.00
Amount that can be profitably expended in fiscal year ending June 30, 1903, in addition to the balance unexpended July 1, 1901 .... 7,500.00
Submitted in compliance with requirements of sundry civil act of June 4, 1897.

(See Appendix X X 10.)

11. Kootenai River, Idaho, between Bonners Ferry and the international boundary line.—The Kootenai River is a tributary of the Columbia. Its middle portion only is in the United States, in the extreme northwestern part of Montana and northern part of Idaho. Both the upper and the lower portion, including its junction with the Columbia, lie in Canadian territory.

The part that has been improved, between Bonners Ferry and the international boundary line, is about 80 miles in length. It was originally navigable, with difficulty, by small, light-draft steamers.

A description of this part of the river is published in the Annual Report of the Chief of Engineers for 1893, pages 3456–3458.

The plan of improvement is to remove the snags in the river and the leaning trees on the banks which were liable to fall in and become obstructions, and was approved January 1, 1895. The estimated cost of the improvement was $5,000.

The amount expended to June 30, 1900, was $4,254.54.

The entire stretch of river included within the limits of the project had been gone over and cleared of snags.

No work was done nor expenditures made during the fiscal year ending June 30, 1901.

At the time snagging operations were suspended the channel had been practically cleared of snags.

An examination of the Kootenai River between Jennings, Mont., and the international boundary line, a length of about 80 miles, was authorized by the emergency river and harbor act of June 6, 1900. This examination was made by Capt. Harry Taylor, Corps of Engineers, the local engineer, and report submitted under date of June 21, 1900. It was the opinion of Captain Taylor, concurred in by the division engineer and the Chief of Engineers, that this portion of the Kootenai River was not worthy of further improvement by the Government, for the reason that on account of the improved railroad facilities navigation on the river had practically ceased.

Exports and imports.

Calendar year.	Tons.	Value.
1896	1,600	$42,815
1897	2,212	49,025
1898	....	40,699
1899	....	30,508
1900	....	14,585

July 1, 1900, balance unexpended $745.46
July 1, 1901, balance unexpended 745.46

(See Appendix X X 11.)

12. Flathead River, Montana.—This river lies in the northwestern part of Montana. It has a southerly course through Flathead Lake and belongs to the Columbia River system. The portion of the river included within the limits for which this appropriation is available extends from Demarsville to Flathead Lake, and is about 27 miles in length. This portion of the river is of very gentle slope, running with many turns through a large area of low-lying lands, and has a minimum depth of about 10 feet, but is obstructed by a large number of snags which have accumulated in the river.

The plan of improvement is to remove the snags, and was approved August 5, 1896.

No estimate of the cost of this improvement has been made, and from its nature none can be made, since snags are constantly accumulating.

A description of this work is given in the Annual Report of the Chief of Engineers for 1895, pages 3480–3484.

The amount expended to June 30, 1900, was $8,519.51.

Snagging operations were carried on with a hired boat during portions of September and October, 1900. About 280 snags were taken out and a large jam of driftwood was removed from the channel.

There appears to have been ample depth on June 30, 1901, for the only steamer of consequence now running on the river. This vessel draws 24 inches of water.

This portion of the Flathead River is wholly isolated from any navigable water outside the State of Montana. Its navigation is a matter of local interest only and is of very limited extent.

Exports and imports.

	Tons.
1898	78
1899	368
1900	456

July 1, 1900, balance unexpended	$1,480.49
June 30, 1901, amount expended during fiscal year	1,291.26
July 1, 1901, balance unexpended	189.23
Amount (estimated) required for completion of existing project	Indefinite.

(See Appendix X X 12.)

EXAMINATIONS AND SURVEY MADE IN COMPLIANCE WITH EMERGENCY RIVER AND HARBOR ACT APPROVED JUNE 6, 1900.

Preliminary examinations and survey of the following localities were made by the local officer and reports thereon submitted through the division engineer:

1. Preliminary examination and survey of Tacoma Harbor, Washington.—Captain Taylor submitted reports dated June 22 and November 13, 1900, respectively. He submits a plan for improvement at an estimated cost of $444,000. The reports were transmitted to Congress and printed in House Doc. No. 76, Fifty-sixth Congres, second session. (See also Appendix X X 13.)

2. Preliminary examination of Kootenai River between Jennings, Mont., and the international boundary line, with the view of removing obstructions to navigation.—Captain Taylor submitted report June 21, 1900. In his opinion, concurred in by the division engineer and by the Chief of Engineers, improvement of the locality by the General Government in the manner indicated by the act is not advisable. The report was transmitted to Congress and printed in House Doc. No. 98, Fifty-sixth Congress, second session. (See also Appendix X X 14.)

EXAMINATIONS, SURVEYS, AND CONTINGENCIES OF RIVERS AND HARBORS.

For examinations, surveys, and contingencies of rivers and harbors an appropriation of $300,000 should be made, as follows:

For examinations, surveys, and contingencies, and for incidental repairs for rivers and harbors, for which there may be no special appropriation; for all expenses connected with the inspection of bridges reported as obstructions to navigation, with the service of notices required in such cases, with the location of harbor lines under the act of March 3, 1899; and for expenses connected with the examinations and reports by officers of the Corps of Engineers and by Boards of Engineers upon plans for bridges authorized by law to be built, and upon bridge bills, reports on which may be called for by Congress, $300,000.

SUPERVISION OF THE HARBOR OF NEW YORK.

The supervisor of the harbor during the past year was Lieut. Commander John C. Fremont, United States Navy, to July 2, 1900, and Lieut. Commander H. M. Hodges, United States Navy, since that date.

The office of supervisor of the harbor of New York was created by act of Congress approved June 29, 1888, entitled "An Act to prevent obstructive and injurious deposits within the harbor and adjacent waters of New York City, by dumping or otherwise, and to punish and prevent such offenses." This act has been amended by section 3 of the act of August 18, 1894, entitled "An Act Making appropriations for the construction, repair, and preservation of certain public works on rivers and harbors, and for other purposes," by which amendment the functions and powers of the officer have been greatly enlarged. Additional duties are also conferred on the supervisor by section 2 of the last-named act.

Under the provisions of section 5 of the act of June 29, 1888, a line officer of the Navy is designated to discharge the duties created by the act under the direction of the Secretary of War. On May 23, 1889, the Secretary of War directed that all communications in connection with these duties should be addressed to him through this office, and on February 1, 1890, he further directed that the powers conferred upon him by the act should be exercised through the Chief of Engineers.

The report of Lieutenant-Commander Hodges for the fiscal year ending June 30, 1901, is submitted as Appendix Y Y.

Estimates for the fiscal year ending June 30, 1903.—The estimates of funds required for this service for the fiscal year ending June 30, 1903, are given in the above-mentioned report, as follows:

For pay of inspectors, deputy inspectors, office force, and expenses of office $10,260.00
For pay of crews and maintenance of five steam tugs and three launches 60,000.00

Total 70,260.00

CALIFORNIA DÉBRIS COMMISSION.

Act of Congress approved March 1, 1893, provided for the establishment of the California Débris Commission, to consist of three officers of the Corps of Engineers, appointed by the President, with the concurrence of the Senate, whose functions relate to hydraulic mining in the territory drained by the Sacramento and San Joaquin river systems in California. The Commission is empowered and required to adopt plans for improving the navigation of the rivers in the systems mentioned, to project and construct works for impounding detritus and preventing the deterioration of the rivers from the deposit of hydraulic mining and other débris, and to devise means and issue permits for resuming and carrying on hydraulic mining operations under conditions that will not injure other interests in the State. The powers of the Commission, methods of procedure, etc., are prescribed in the act in detail.

The Commissioners during the past fiscal year were Col. S. M. Mansfield to February 8, 1901; Col. Jared A. Smith from February 18, 1901; Lieut. Col. W. H. Heuer, and Capt. Herbert Deakyne, Corps of Engineers.

During the year the Commission has permitted hydraulic mining to be carried on subject to the restrictions imposed by law, and has been engaged in negotiations for the lands required as sites for the restraining works to be constructed in the Yuba River for the purpose of protecting the Sacramento and Feather rivers from injury by the débris now in the Yuba.

The report of the Commission upon its operations during the fiscal year ending June 30, 1901, is submitted herewith as Appendix Z Z.

Estimate for the fiscal year ending June 30, 1903.—The Commission submits an estimate of $15,000 as the amount required for payment of the necessary expenses connected with the work under its charge during the fiscal year ending June 30, 1903.

REMOVAL OF WRECK OF STEAMBOAT CRISTOBAL COLON IN SAN JUAN HARBOR, PORTO RICO.

This work was in the charge of Capt. W. V. Judson, Corps of Engineers, to September 26, 1900, and of Capt. C. A. F. Flagler, Corps of Engineers, since that date.

Under allotment made by the Secretary of War from the permanent-indefinite appropriation for removing sunken vessels or craft obstructing or endangering navigation, the wreck of the iron-hull steamboat *Cristobal Colon* in the entrance to San Juan Harbor was removed to a minimum depth of 36 feet at mean low water, during March, April, and May, 1901.

The total cost of removing this wreck was $7,759.27.

(See Appendix A A A.)

MISSISSIPPI RIVER COMMISSION.

The Mississippi River Commission, constituted by act of Congress of June 28, 1879, is in the charge of the improvement of the Mississippi River from Head of Passes to the mouth of the Ohio River, including the rectification of Red and Atchafalaya rivers at their junction with the Mississippi, the building of levees, and the improvement of the several harbors for which specific appropriations have been made, with the exception of the harbor of Vicksburg and the mouth of Yazoo River.

It is also charged with the survey of the Mississippi River from Head of Passes to its head waters.

The Commissioners during the past fiscal year were: Col. G. L. Gillespie, Corps of Engineers (now brigadier-general, Chief of Engineers United States Army), president, to May 13, 1901; Col. Amos Stickney, Corps of Engineers, president, since May 13, 1901; Lieut. Col. Thomas H. Handbury, Corps of Engineers; Lieut. Col. H. M. Adams, Corps of Engineers, since May 13, 1901; B. M. Harrod, Robert S. Taylor, Henry L. Marindin, assistant United States Coast and Geodetic Survey, and J. A. Ockerson.

The report of the Commission upon the operations under its charge during the fiscal year ending June 30, 1901, was submitted to the Secretary of War August 20, 1901, and is printed in a supplement to this report.

Reports on preliminary examination and survey of the Mississippi River between the highlands near the city of Hickman, in the State of Kentucky, and Slough Landing, in Lake County, in the State of Tennessee, required by the emergency river and harbor act of June 6, 1900, were made by the president of the Commission under date of July 3 and November 24, 1900, respectively. The reports were transmitted to Congress and printed in House Doc. No. 130, Fifty-sixth Congress, second session, and are also herewith as Appendix X.

Estimates for the fiscal year ending June 30, 1903.—The following estimates of funds required for carrying on the works under its charge for the year ending June 30, 1903, are submitted by the Commission:

For continuing the improvement of the Mississippi River from Head of Passes to the mouth of the Ohio River, including salaries and clerical, office, traveling, and miscellaneous expenses of the Mississippi River Commission	$3,000,000
Protection of banks at or near Caruthersville, Mo	50,000
Improving harbor at Memphis, Tenn. (including Hopefield Bend)	50,000
Improving harbor at Memphis, Tenn. (at Wolf River)	30,000
Improving harbor at Helena, Ark	20,000
Improving harbor at Greenville, Miss	25,000
Delta Point, La. (preservation of existing works)	20,000
Improving harbor at Natchez, Miss., and Vidalia, La	150,000
Rectification of Red and Atchafalaya rivers, Louisiana	50,000
Improving harbor at New Orleans, La	300,000
Total	3,695,000

MISSOURI RIVER COMMISSION.

The Missouri River Commission, constituted by act of Congress of July 5, 1884, is in the charge of the improvement and surveys of the Missouri River below Sioux City, Iowa.

The Commissioners during the past fiscal year were: Col. Amos Stickney, Corps of Engineers, president; Lieut. Col. Thomas H. Handbury, Corps of Engineers; Maj. W. L. Marshall, Corps of Engineers; Garland C. Broadhead and C. L. Chaffee.

The river and harbor act of August 18, 1894, in making appropriations for improvement of Gasconade and Osage rivers, Missouri, provided that the funds should be expended by the Missouri River Commission, and the work of improving these streams has since been carried on under its direction.

The report of the Commission upon operations under its charge

BRIDGING NAVIGABLE WATERS. 659

during the fiscal year ending June 30, 1901, was submitted to the Secretary of War August 20, 1901, and is printed in a supplement to this report.

Estimates for the fiscal year ending June 30, 1903.—The following estimates of funds required for carrying on the works under its charge for the year ending June 30, 1903, are submitted by the Commission:

Improving Missouri River from mouth to Sioux City, Iowa, including office and traveling expenses and salaries of Commission, surveys, gauges, physical data and publications, operating snag boat, and systematic improvement of first reach		$1,000,000
Improving Osage River, Missouri:		
For works of improvement	$45,200	
For maintenance of improvement	5,000	
		50,200
Improving Gasconade River, Missouri:		
For works of improvement	10,000	
For maintenance of improvement	5,000	
		15,000
		1,065,200

BRIDGING NAVIGABLE WATERS OF THE UNITED STATES.

Plans and maps of locations of the following bridges, proposed to be erected under the authority of special acts of Congress, have been examined, with a view to protection of the interests of navigation, and have been approved by the Secretary of War, as provided by the acts; and the local engineer officers have been furnished with copies of the instruments of approval and drawings showing plans and locations, and charged with the supervision of the construction of the bridges so far as necessary to see that they are built in accordance with the approved plans:

1. *Bridge of the New York and New Jersey Bridge Company over Hudson River from New York City to New Jersey.*—Detailed plans of this bridge were approved by the Secretary of War May 24, 1899 (see Annual Report of the Chief of Engineers for 1899, p. 619). Plans showing proposed modification of approved detailed plans were approved by the Secretary of War July 3, 1900.

2. *Bridge of Dawson County, Mont., over Yellowstone River at Glendive.*—Plans for reconstructing the bridge at this place under authority of the sundry civil act approved June 6, 1900, were approved by the Secretary of War July 19, 1900.

3. *Bridge of the Alexandria and Pineville Bridge Company over Red River from Alexandria to Pineville, La.*—Plans and map of location of a bridge proposed to be built at this place under authority of act of Congress of June 6, 1900, were approved by the Secretary of War August 8, 1900.

4. *Bridge of Muskingum County, Ohio, over Muskingum River ("Y" Bridge) at Zanesville, Ohio.*—Plans for reconstruction of this bridge were considered at a public hearing in accordance with requirements of act of Congress of April 2, 1888, and were approved by the Secretary of War August 18, 1900.

5. *Bridge of the city of Biloxi, Miss., over Back Bay.*—Plans and map of location of a bridge to be constructed at this locality under authority of act of Congress of May 10, 1900, were approved by the Secretary of War September 4, 1900.

6. Bridge of the Ohio River Bridge and Ferry Company over Ohio River from Williamstown, W. Va., to Marietta, Ohio.—Plans and map of location of a bridge proposed to be built at this place received consideration by a Board of Engineers in accordance with requirements of acts of Congress of December 17, 1872, and February 14, 1883, and plans conforming to requirements recommended by the Board were approved by the Secretary of War December 13, 1900.

7. Bridge of the Dubuque and Wisconsin Bridge Company over Mississippi River in vicinity of Eagle Point, Dubuque, Iowa.—Plans and map of location of a bridge proposed to be built at this place under authority of act of Congress approved March 6, 1900, as amended by act of December 21, 1900, were approved by the Secretary of War January 4, 1901.

8. Bridge of the Indiana, Illinois and Iowa Railroad Company over St. Joseph River at St. Joseph, Mich.—Plans and map of location of a bridge proposed to be built at this place under authority of act of Congress of February 18, 1901, were approved by the Secretary of War February 27, 1901.

9. Bridge of the Kansas City Southern Railway Company over Sulphur River, Arkansas.—Plans for reconstructing the existing bridge at this place under authority of act of Congress of February 8, 1897, were approved by the Secretary of War March 25, 1901.

10. Bridge of Grenada County, Miss., over Yalobusha River at mouth of Martins Creek, Mississippi.—Plans and map of location of a bridge at this place to be built under authority of act of Congress of February 12, 1901, were approved April 1, 1901.

11. Bridge of the Ashland and Ironton Bridge Company over Ohio River from Ironton, Ohio, to Ashland, Ky.—Plans and map of location of a bridge proposed to be built at this place received consideration by a Board of Engineers in accordance with provisions of acts of Congress of December 17, 1872, and February 14, 1883, and new plans conforming to the requirements recommended by the Board were approved by the Secretary of War April 22, 1901.

12. Bridge of the New Orleans and Northwestern Railway Company over Bayou Bartholomew, Louisiana.—Plans and map of location of a bridge proposed to be built at this place under authority of act of Congress of May 4, 1900, were approved by the Secretary of War April 30, 1901.

13. Bridge of the Georgia, Florida and Alabama Railway Company over Flint River in Decatur County, Ga.—Plans and location of this bridge to be constructed under authority of act of Congress of March 1, 1899, amended by act of March 2, 1901, were approved by the Secretary of War May 22, 1901.

14. Bridge of Washington County, Ohio, over Muskingum River Canal above Lowell, Ohio.—Plans and map of location of a bridge proposed to be built at this place under authority of act of Congress of April 2, 1888, were approved by the Secretary of War May 28, 1901.

15. Bridge of the Kingston Bridge and Terminal Railway Company over Clinch River at Kingston, Tenn.—Plans and map of location of a bridge proposed to be built at this place under authority of act of Congress of February 8, 1901, were approved by the Secretary of War June 3, 1901.

16. Bridge of the Bellaire, Benwood and Wheeling Bridge Company over Ohio River from Bellaire, Ohio, to Benwood, W. Va.—Plans and map of location of a bridge proposed to be built at this place were referred to a Board of Engineers in accordance with requirements of acts of Congress of December 17, 1872, and February 14, 1883, and plans conforming to the requirements specified by the Board were approved by the Secretary of War June 14, 1901.

17. *Bridge of the Pennsylvania Railroad Company over Delaware River at Trenton, N. J.*—Plans and map of location of a bridge proposed to be built at this place under authority of act of Congress of February 15, 1901, were approved by the Secretary of War June 14, 1901.

18. *Bridge of the Glassport Bridge Company over Monongahela River from Port Vue to Jefferson, Pa.*—Plans and map of location of a bridge proposed to be built at this place under authority of act of Congress of February 18, 1901, were approved by the Secretary of War June 18, 1901.

19. *Bridge of the Williamstown and Marietta Bridge and Transportation Company over Ohio River from Williamstown, W. Va., to Marietta, Ohio.*—Plans and map of location of a bridge proposed to be built at this place received consideration by a Board of Engineers as required by acts of Congress of December 17, 1872, and February 14, 1883, and were approved by the Secretary of War June 25, 1901.

Under the provisions of section 9 of the river and harbor act approved March 3, 1899, bridges may be built over navigable waters entirely within the limits of any State, under the authority of legislative enactment of such State, when the plans and locations of the structures are approved by the Secretary of War. Plans and maps of locations of the following bridges proposed to be erected under these provisions have been examined, with a view to protection of the interests of navigation, and have been approved by the Secretary of War; and the local engineer officers have been furnished with copies of the drawings and instruments of approval, and charged with the supervision of construction of the bridges so far as necessary to see that they are built in accordance with the approved plans:

1. *Bridge of Clarke County, Wash., over Lewis River at Lacenter, Wash.*—Plans for reconstruction of this bridge were approved by the Secretary of War July 3, 1900.

2. *Bridge of Pender County, N. C., over Black River at Still Bluff, N. C.*—Plans and map of location of a bridge proposed to be built at this place were approved by the Secretary of War July 5, 1900.

3. *Bridge of the city of Milwaukee, Wis., over Milwaukee River at Chestnut street.*—Plans for reconstruction of this bridge were approved by the Secretary of War July 5, 1900.

4. *Bridge of the city of Boston, Mass., over Fort Point Channel at Cove street.*—Plans and location of a bridge to be built at this place were approved by the Secretary of War July 10, 1900.

5. *Bridge of San Joaquin County, Cal., over San Joaquin River at Brandts Ferry, California.*—Plans and map of location of a bridge proposed to be built at this place were approved by the Secretary of War July 18, 1900.

6. *Bridge of the Pittsburgh and Lake Erie Railroad Company over the back channel of Ohio River at the lower end of Neville Island.*—A new instrument was executed by the Secretary of War July 24, 1900, in lieu of a former instrument dated June 12, 1900, expressing the approval of plans and map of location of proposed bridge at this place.

7. *Bridge of Brown County and the town of Wrightstown, Wis., over Fox River at Wrightstown.*—Plans for the partial rebuilding of this bridge were approved by the Secretary of War July 25, 1900.

8. *Bridge of the Carrollton and Prestonville Bridge Company over Kentucky River at Carrollton, Ky.*—Plans of the Carrollton Electric Railway and Bridge Company for a bridge at this place were approved by the Secretary of War November 10, 1899 (see Annual Report of the Chief of Engineers for 1900, p. 699). The rights and franchises of the original company having been transferred to the Carrollton and Prestonville Bridge Company, application was made for approval of the plans in that name and they were so approved by the Secretary of War July 25, 1900, the former approval being canceled.

9. *Bridge of the city of Chicago, Ill., over the North Branch Canal of Chicago River at Division street.*—Plans for reconstruction of this bridge were approved by the Secretary of War July 28, 1900.

10. *Bridge of the Boston and Albany Railroad Company over Chelsea Creek from Boston to Chelsea, Mass.*—Plans for reconstruction of this bridge were approved by the Secretary of War July 28, 1900.

11. *Bridge of the Chicago, Milwaukee and St. Paul Railway Company over Mississippi River near Minneapolis, Minn.*—Plans for reconstruction of the existing bridge at this place were approved by the Secretary of War August 4, 1900.

12. *Bridge of Camden County, N. J., over Cooper Creek at Browning road, near Camden, N. J.*—Plans for rebuilding this bridge were approved by the Secretary of War August 17, 1900.

13. *Bridge of the Moodus and East Hampton Railway Company over Salmon River below Leesville, East Haddam, Conn.*—Plans and map of location of a bridge proposed to be built at this place were approved by the Secretary of War August 20, 1900.

14. *Bridge of Suffolk County, N. Y., over inlet connecting Sag Bay and Sag Harbor Cove, New York.*—Plans for rebuilding this bridge were approved by the Secretary of War August 29, 1900.

15. *Bridge of the city of Pittsburg, Pa., over Monongahela River at South Tenth street.*—Plans for reconstruction of existing structure at this place were approved by the Secretary of War August 29, 1900.

16. *Bridge of the Pittsburgh, Fort Wayne and Chicago Railway (Fort Wayne Bridge) over Allegheny River from Pittsburg to Allegheny, Pa.*—Plans for reconstruction of the existing bridge at this place were approved by the Secretary of War September 1, 1900.

17. *Bridge of the city of Manitowoc, Wis., over Manitowoc River to connect State and Center streets.*—Plans for construction of a temporary bridge at this place were approved by the Secretary of War September 6, 1900.

18. *Bridge of the Chicago and Northwestern Railway Company over the Fox River Canal at Lock No. 2, Kaukauna, Wis.*—Plans for reconstruction of this bridge were approved by the Secretary of War September 7, 1900.

19. *Bridge of the Southern Railway Company over Tennessee River at Decatur, Ala.*—Plans for reconstruction of the bridge at this place were approved by the Secretary of War September 8, 1900.

20. *Bridges of the Sanitary District of Chicago over Chicago River at Harrison street, Throop street, and Ashland avenue, Chicago, Ill.*—Plans for reconstruction of existing bridges at these points were approved by the Secretary of War September 14, 1900.

21. Bridge of the Princeton and Northwestern Railway Company over Fox River at Princeton, Wis.—Plans and map of location of a bridge proposed to be built at this place were approved by the Secretary of War September 14, 1900.

22. Bridge of the Cleveland, Cincinnati, Chicago and St. Louis Railway Company over Cuyahoga River at Cleveland, Ohio.—Plans for rebuilding this bridge were approved by the Secretary of War September 20, 1900.

23. Bridge of the city of New York over Harlem River between One hundred and forty-fifth street and One hundred and forty-ninth street.—Plans for construction of a bridge at this place were approved by the Secretary of War November 11, 1897. (See Annual Report of the Chief of Engineers for 1898, p. 533.) Plans in lieu of those heretofore approved were submitted by the city July 10, 1900, and were approved by the Secretary of War October 6, 1900.

24. Bridge of King County, Wash., over Duwamish River.—Under date of October 11, 1900, the Secretary of War approved plans and map of location of a bridge proposed to be built at this place, said plans to be in lieu of plans approved by the Secretary March 29, 1900.

25. Bridge of the city of Chicago, Ill., over North Branch of Chicago River at Clybourne place.—Plans and map of location of a bridge proposed to be built at this place were approved by the Secretary of War October 23, 1900.

26. Bridge of the Brooklyn and Jamaica Bay Turnpike Company over the waters of Jamaica Bay, New York.—Plans for construction of a bridge at this place were approved by the Secretary of War December 21, 1898 (see Annual Report of the Chief of Engineers for 1899, p. 621), and plans providing for certain modifications in the original plans were approved by the Secretary of War October 26, 1900.

27. Bridge of the Pittsburgh, Cincinnati, Chicago and St. Louis Railway Company over West Fork of South Branch of Chicago River (Mud Lake) at Chicago, Ill.—Plans for rebuilding this bridge were approved by the Secretary of War November 12, 1900.

28. Bridge of the Oil City Station Railway Company over Allegheny River at Franklin, Pa.—Plans and map of location of a bridge proposed to be built at this place were approved by the Secretary of War November 26, 1900.

29. Bridge of the Seattle and Montana Railroad Company over Whatcom Creek Waterway at New Whatcom, Wash.—Plans for rebuilding the existing bridge at this place were approved by the Secretary of War November 27, 1900.

30. Bridge of Monmouth County, N. J., over Shrewsbury River at Seabright, N. J.—Plans for rebuilding this bridge were approved by the Secretary of War December 8, 1900.

31. Bridges of the Philadelphia and Chester Railway Company over Darby Creek and Crum Creek in Delaware County, Pa.—Plans and map of location of bridges proposed to be built over these creeks were approved by the Secretary of War December 11, 1900.

32. Bridge of the Oil City, Rouseville and Franklin Railroad Company over Allegheny River from Oil City to Franklin, Pa.—Plans and map of location of a bridge proposed to be built at this place were approved by the Secretary of War December 13, 1900.

33. Bridge of Bladen County, N. C., over Black River, near Beattys Bridge, North Carolina.—Plans and map of location of a bridge proposed to be built at this locality were approved by the Secretary of War December 26, 1900.

34. Bridge of San Joaquin County, Cal., over Burns Cut-off (San Joaquin River), California.—Plans and map of location of a bridge proposed to be built at this place were approved by the Secretary of War January 2, 1901.

35. Bridge of San Joaquin County, Cal., over San Joaquin River, at Durhams Ferry, California.—Plans and map of location of a bridge proposed to be built at this place were approved by the Secretary of War January 2, 1901.

36. Bridge of Atlantic County, N. J., over the Inside Thoroughfare, at westerly end of Albany avenue, Atlantic City, N. J.—Plans and map of location of a bridge proposed to be built at this locality were approved by the Secretary of War January 3, 1901.

37. Bridge of Houghton County, Mich., over Portage Lake, between Houghton and Hancock, Mich.—Plans for reconstruction of this bridge were approved by the Secretary of War January 7, 1901.

38. Bridge of the Navy Department over channel between Portsmouth Navy-Yard, N. H., and Kittery, Me.—Plans and map of location of a bridge proposed to be built at this place were approved by the Secretary of War January 14, 1901.

39. Bridge of the Baltimore and Ohio Railroad Company over Ohio River at Parkersburg, W. Va.—Plans for reconstruction of spans 35, 36, 37, and 40 of this bridge were approved by the Secretary of War January 15, 1901.

40. Bridge of the New York Connecting Railroad Company over East River at Hell Gate, near Astoria, N. Y.—Plans and map of location were approved by the Secretary of War January 16, 1901.

41. Bridge of Hillsboro County, Fla., over Alafia River, at Riverview, Fla.—Plans and map of location of a bridge proposed to be built at this place were approved by the Secretary of War January 16, 1901.

42. Bridge of the city of Appleton, Wis., over Fox River Canal, at South Division street.—Plans for reconstruction of this bridge were approved by the Secretary of War January 24, 1901.

43. Bridge of the Illinois Central Railroad Company over Little Calumut River, at Riverdale, Ill.—Plans and map of location of a bridge proposed to be built at this place were approved by the Secretary of War January 30, 1901.

44. Bridge of the towns of Buffalo, Moundville, and Douglas, Wis., over Fox River, in Marquette County.—Plans and map of location of a bridge proposed to be built at this place were approved by the Secretary of War January 30, 1901.

45. Bridge of the city of New York over Bronx River, at Westchester avenue.—Plans for a bridge at this place were approved by the Secretary of War December 2, 1897. (See Annual Report of the Chief of Engineers for 1898, p. 534.) Plans to be in lieu of those heretofore approved were submitted by the city January 17, 1901, and were approved by the Secretary of War January 30, 1901.

46. Bridge of the townships of Springwells and Ecorse, Mich., over Rouge River, at Dix avenue.—Plans and map of location of a bridge proposed to be built at this place were approved by the Secretary of War February 5, 1901.

47. Bridge of the Louisville and Nashville Railroad Company over Alabama River, at Selma, Ala.—Plans and map of location of a bridge proposed to be built at this place were approved by the Secretary of War February 7, 1901.

48. Bridge of the Philadelphia, Wilmington and Baltimore Railroad Company over Schuylkill River, at Grays Ferry, Philadelphia, Pa.—Plans for rebuilding the existing bridge at this place were approved by the Secretary of War February 8, 1901.

49. Bridge of Hudson and Bergen counties, N. J., over Hackensack River.—Plans and map of location of a bridge proposed to be built at this place were approved by the Secretary of War February 18, 1901.

50. Bridge of the Chicago, Milwaukee and St. Paul Railway Company over North Branch Canal, at north end of Goose Island, Cherry street, Elston Addition, Chicago, Ill.—Plans for reconstruction of this bridge were approved by the Secretary of War February 19, 1901.

51. Bridge of Rudolph Benz over Dog River, in Mobile County, Ala.—Plans and map of location of a bridge proposed to be built at this place were approved by the Secretary of War February 20, 1901.

52. Bridge of the city of New York over East River from Sixtieth street, borough of Manhattan, to Long Island City, N. Y., via Blackwells Island.—Plans and location of bridge to be built at this place were approved by the Secretary of War February 21, 1901.

53. Bridge of the New York Connecting Railroad Company over Little Hell Gate and Bronx Kills, New York.—Plans and map of location of a bridge proposed to be built at this place were approved by the Secretary of War March 2, 1901.

54. Bridges of the city of New Bedford, Mass., over Acushnet River from New Bedford to Fish Island.—Plans for reconstructing this portion of the New Bedford and Fairhaven bridge, including a temporary structure for use while the permanent bridge is being built, were approved by the Secretary of War March 8, 1901.

55. Bridge of the Chesapeake Transit Company over Lynn Haven Inlet, Virginia.—Plans and map of location of a bridge proposed to be built at this place were approved by the Secretary of War March 13, 1901.

56. Bridge of the Queen Anne's Railroad Company over Kent Island Narrows, at Kent Island, Maryland.—Plans and map of location of a bridge proposed to be built at this place were approved by the Secretary of War March 13, 1901.

57. Bridge of the Southern Branch Drawbridge Company over Southern Branch of Elizabeth River, Virginia.—Plans for construction of a bridge at this place were approved by the Secretary of War March 10, 1899. (See Annual Report of the Chief of Engineers for 1899, p. 622.) New plans, to be in lieu of those originally approved, were approved by the Secretary of War March 14, 1901.

58. Bridge of the Union Bridge Company over Wisconsin River, Wisconsin.—Plans and map of location of a bridge proposed to be built at this place were approved by the Secretary of War March 19, 1901.

59. Bridge of the town of Charlevoix, Mich., over Pine River.—Plans and map of location of a bridge proposed to be built at this place were approved by the Secretary of War March 19, 1901.

60. Bridge of the Eureka and Klamath River Railroad Company over Eureka Slough, California.—Plans and map of location of a bridge proposed to be built at this place were approved by the Secretary of War March 20, 1901.

61. *Bridge of the Philadelphia, Wilmington and Baltimore Railroad Company over Broad Creek River, at Laurel, Del.*—Plans for reconstruction of this bridge were approved by the Secretary of War March 21, 1901.

62. *Bridge of the Camden, Gloucester, and Woodbury Railway Company over Big Timber Creek, below Gloucester, N. J.*—Plans for reconstruction of this bridge were approved by the Secretary of War March 30, 1901.

63. *Bridge of the Newark Plank Road Company over Passaic River, New Jersey.*—Plans for rebuilding this bridge were approved by the Secretary of War April 11, 1901.

64. *Bridge of the Granite State Land Company over Hampton River from Seabrook Beach to Hampton Beach, Maine.*—Plans and map of location of a bridge proposed to be built at this place were approved by the Secretary of War April 15, 1901.

65. *Bridge of the town of South Arm, Mich., over South Arm of Pine Lake.*—Plans for reconstruction of this bridge were approved by the Secretary of War May 1, 1901.

66. *Bridge of the Detroit, Mount Clemens, and Marine City Railway over Belle River, in St. Clair County, Mich.*—Plans and map of location of a bridge proposed to be built at this place were approved by the Secretary of War May 9, 1901.

67. *Bridge of the city of Chicago over North Branch of Chicago River, at Division street.*—Plans and map of location of a bridge proposed to be built at this locality were approved by the Secretary of War May 10, 1901.

68. *Bridge of J. P. Vining et al. over Halifax River, at Dayton, Fla.*—Plans and map of location of a bridge proposed to be built at this place were approved by the Secretary of War May 15, 1901.

69. *Bridge of Jackson County, Miss., over Fort Bayou, at Franco Ferry, Mississippi.*—Plans and map of location of a bridge proposed to be built at this place were approved by the Secretary of War May 21, 1901.

70. *Bridge of the Southern Pacific Company over Sacramento River, at Tehama, Cal.*—Plans for reconstruction of the drawspan of this bridge were approved by the Secretary of War February 23, 1898. (See Annual Report of the Chief of Engineers for 1898, p. 537.) Plans for rebuilding the remainder of the bridge were approved by the Secretary of War May 22, 1901.

71. *Bridge of Stanislaus and Merced counties, Cal., over San Joaquin River, at Hills Ferry.*—Plans for a bridge at this place were approved by the Secretary of War July 27, 1899. (See Annual Report of the Chief of Engineers for 1899, p. 623.) This approval having become null and void, new plans for the bridge were subsequently submitted and were approved by the Secretary of War May 27, 1901.

72. *Bridge of the city of Tacoma, Wash., over Puyallup River.*—Plans and map of location of a bridge proposed to be built at this place were approved by the Secretary of War May 29, 1901.

73. *Bridge of Morgan County, Ohio, over Muskingum River from McConnelsville to Malta, Ohio.*—Plans for reconstruction of this bridge were approved by the Secretary of War May 29, 1901.

74. *Bridge of the town of Boothbay Harbor, Me., over tide waters of Boothbay Harbor.*—Plans and map of location of a bridge proposed to be built at this place were approved by the Secretary of War June 5, 1901.

75. *Bridge of the Florida East Coast Railway Company over Lake Worth, Florida, from Palmbeach to West Palmbeach.*—Plans and map of location of a bridge proposed to be built at this place were approved by the Secretary of War June 14, 1901.

76. *Bridges of the State of Massachusetts over Weweanititt River, at Wareham and Marion, Mass.*—Plans for reconstruction of these bridges were approved by the Secretary of War June 14, 1901.

77. *Bridge of the city of Kenosha, Wis., over Pike Creek, at Main street.*—Plans and map of location of a bridge proposed to be built at this place were approved by the Secretary of War June 14, 1901.

78. *Bridge of the St. Louis and Southern Illinois Railway Company over Kaskaskia River, near Missouri Junction, Illinois.*—Plans and map of location of a bridge proposed to be built at this place were approved by the Secretary of War June 14, 1901.

79. *Bridge of the Seattle and International Railway Company over Stilaguamish River, near Arlington, Wash.*—Plans and map of location of a bridge proposed to be built at this place were approved by the Secretary of War June 14, 1901.

80. *Bridge of the city of New York over Newtown Creek, from Vernon avenue to Manhattan avenue.*—Plans for construction of a temporary bridge at this place for use pending completion of a permanent structure were approved by the Secretary of War June 15, 1901.

81. *Bridge of Dyer County, Tenn., over Obion River, near Lanes Ferry, Tennessee.*—Plans and map of location of a bridge proposed to be built at this place were approved by the Secretary of War June 17, 1901.

82. *Bridge of Muskingum County, Ohio, over the lateral canal along Muskingum River, at Zanesville, Ohio.*—Plans for rebuilding the existing structure at this place were approved by the Secretary of War June 18, 1901.

83. *Bridges of the Maumee Railway Bridge Company over Maumee River, near Toledo, Ohio.*—Plans for two bridges, Nos. 1 and 2, at this place were approved by the Secretary of War August 17, 1900. Modified plans for the "upper bridge" were approved by the Secretary of War June 24, 1901.

84. *Bridges of the Wisconsin Central Railway Company over east channel of Mississippi River from east bank to Nicollet Island and from Nicollet Island to Boom Island, Minneapolis, Minn.*—Plans and map of location of proposed bridges at the localities mentioned were approved by the Secretary of War July 24, 1901.

BRIDGES OBSTRUCTING NAVIGATION.

Under the requirements of section 18 of the river and harbor act approved March 3, 1899, the Secretary of War notified the persons, corporations, or associations owning or controlling certain bridges obstructing navigation, after giving them a reasonable opportunity to be heard, to so alter said bridges as to render navigation through or under them reasonably free, easy, and unobstructed, specifying in the notice the alterations required to be made and prescribing a reasonable time in which to make them, as follows:

1. *Bridge of the town of York, Me. (Sewells Bridge), over York River.*—Notice dated October 10, 1900, served on the board of selectmen October 19, 1900. Specified alterations to be completed within three months from date of service of notice.

2. *Bridge of the city of Depere, Wis., over Fox River Canal, at Main street.*—Notice dated October 25, 1900, served on the mayor of the city November 2, 1900. Specified alterations to be completed on or before May 1, 1901.

3. *Bridges of the city of Menasha, Wis., across the Fox River Canal, at Mill street and Tayco street.*—Notice dated October 25, 1900, served on the mayor of the city November 2, 1900. Specified alterations to be completed on or before May 1, 1901.

4. *Bridges of the city of Kaukauna, Wis., over Fox River Canal, at Lawe street and Wisconsin avenue.*—Notice dated October 25, 1900, served on the mayor of the city November 2, 1900. Specified alterations to be completed on or before May 1, 1901.

5. *Bridge of the Boston and Maine Railroad Company over Fore River, at Portland, Me.*—Notice dated December 5, 1900, served on the company December 15, 1900. Specified alterations to be completed on or before September 1, 1902.

6. *Bridge of the city of Portland and town of Cape Elizabeth, Me. (Vaughan Bridge), over Fore River, at Portland.*—Notice dated December 5, 1900, served on the mayor of the city of Portland December 15, 1900. Specified alterations to be completed on or before September 1, 1902.

7. *Bridge of the towns of Newfields and Stratham, over Exeter River, New Hampshire, from Stratham to Newmarket.*—Notice dated December 14, 1900, served on the respective chairmen of the boards of selectmen of the towns of Stratham and Newfields January 2, 1901. Specified alterations to be completed on or before May 15, 1901.

8. *Bridges (2) of the city of Benton Harbor and township of Benton, Mich., over Pawpaw River near Benton Harbor.*—Notices dated February 28, 1901, served on the mayor of the city of Benton Harbor and the highway commissioner of the town of Benton March 11, 1901. Specified alterations to be completed within six months from the date of service of notice.

9. *Bridge of the Cleveland, Cincinnati, Chicago and St. Louis Railway Company over Pawpaw River near Benton Harbor, Mich.*—Notice dated February 28, 1901, served on the company March 11, 1901. Specified alterations to be completed within six months from date of service of notice.

10. *Bridges (2) of the Pere Marquette Railroad Company over Pawpaw River near Benton Harbor, Mich.*—Notice dated February 28, 1901, served on the company March 18, 1901. Specified alterations to be completed within six months from date of service of notice.

11. *Bridge of the Atlanta, Knoxville and Northern Railway Company over Little Tennessee River near Niles Ferry, Tennessee.*—Notice dated March 14, 1901, served on the company April 8, 1901. Specified alterations to be completed on or before one year after date of service of notice.

12. *Bridge of the city of Portland, Me. (Tukeys Bridge), over entrance to Back Cove, Portland Harbor.*—Notice dated March 30, 1901, served on the mayor of the city April 6, 1901. Specified alterations to be completed on or before July 1, 1901.

13. *Bridge of the parish of Iberville, La., over Bayou Plaquemine.*—Notice dated April 19, 1901, served on the president of the police jury of the parish of Iberville April 29, 1901. Specified alterations to be completed on or before November 1, 1901.

14. Bridge of the Delaware and Hudson Company (Rensselaer and Saratoga Railroad bridge) over Hudson River, at Troy, N. Y.—Notice dated April 22, 1901, served on the company April 29, 1901. Specified alterations to be completed on or before one year from date of service of notice.

15. Bridge of the city of Bath, Me. (Bull Rock Bridge), over New Meadows River.—Notice dated May 10, 1901, served on the mayor of the city May 31, 1901. Specified alterations to be completed on or before thirty days from date of service of notice.

MISCELLANEOUS.

[Public works not provided for in acts making appropriations for the construction, repair, and preservation of works on rivers and harbors.]

BRIDGES AT WASHINGTON, D. C.

Operations under this head were in the charge of Lieut. Col. Chas. J. Allen, Corps of Engineers.

1. Repair of the Aqueduct Bridge across Potomac River.—In compliance with Senate resolution, January 21, 1893, an examination of the piers of this bridge was made with the aid of a diver. A report in detail of the examination was rendered June 21, 1893, and on the 17th of July following an estimate of the cost of repairs was submitted. By act of August 18, 1894, an appropriation of $51,070 was made for the repairs. Under this appropriation Piers Nos. 2, 3, 5, 6, 7, and 8 were repaired by means of Portland cement concrete in bags, placed by a diver, and the repair of Pier No. 4 was made by means of a cofferdam within which new masonry was laid in a large eroded cavity at the upstream end of the pier. This work was completed in August, 1895.

As the work of repairs proceeded it was found that the old masonry of Pier No. 4, which was built about 1838, had not been started from solid rock and that part of it was of poor quality. There was also a crack in the masonry extending nearly throughout the entire height of the pier. It was decided that it would be necessary to remove the defective masonry in the remainder of the pier and replace it by masonry of proper quality founded on the solid rock. The existing appropriation was insufficient for this purpose, and it was therefore necessary to ask a further appropriation.

A full report and estimate of the cost of removing all the old masonry of the pier from the coping down to the bottom and rebuilding from the bottom up was rendered under date of November 30, 1895, and printed in House Doc. No. 158, Fifty-fourth Congress, first session, and in the Annual Report of the Chief of Engineers for 1896, page 3886. The cost was estimated at $65,000, which sum was appropriated for reconstruction of Pier No. 4 by act of Congress of June 8, 1896.

A contract for the work of reconstruction of that pier was made May 17, 1897.

The contract work was to have been completed by November 1, 1897, but the contractors, at their request, were granted an extension of time to June 30, 1898.

The contractors abandoned the work on the 30th of April, 1898, and in consequence their contract was annulled May 27, 1898. For account of this proceeding reference is made to the Annual Report of the Chief of Engineers for the fiscal year ending June 30, 1898, page 3573.

On May 12, 1899, a contract was made with the Central Contracting Company of New York for reconstruction of the pier, the work to be completed on or before November 1, 1899. The time for completion, however, has been several times extended, in all, to July 15, 1901.

The amount expended under the last appropriation to June 30, 1900, was $11,347.63. At that time the contractors had obtained practically all of the dimension stone required for the pier, and installed pumps and derricks, repaired the false works, and tightened the cofferdam.

During the fiscal year ending June 30, 1901, the old masonry of Pier No. 4 was taken down and removed, all débris removed from the foundation area, the rock bed leveled up with concrete, the projecting points of rock cut off, the new pier completed, except a small amount of cleaning, the trusses repaired and secured in the proper position upon the pier, and the false work entirely and the cofferdam mainly removed. There remain but about ten or fifteen days' more work in which to complete the contract.

Congress, by the deficiency act approved March 3, 1901, provided—

That of the unexpended balance of the appropriations for repairs to the Aqueduct Bridge, District of Columbia, the sum of one thousand four hundred and sixty-five dollars may be used under the direction of the Secretary of War for the temporary protection of said bridge.

Under the provisions of this act all the cavities discovered in all the other piers of the bridge were filled with concrete in bags and protected with riprap after being so filled. This protection work is, however, only of a temporary nature.

July 1, 1900, balance unexpended	$53,652.37
June 30, 1901, amount expended during fiscal year	27,295.70
July 1, 1901, balance unexpended	26,356.67
July 1, 1901, outstanding liabilities	222.00
July 1, 1901, balance available	26,134.67
July 1, 1901, amount covered by uncompleted contracts	11,000.00

(See Appendix B B B 1.)

2. Memorial Bridge.—The sundry civil act, approved June 4, 1897, provided for a survey, examination, etc., as follows:

Memorial bridge across Potomac River: To enable the Chief of Engineers of the Army to make the necessary surveys, soundings, and borings, and for securing designs and estimates for a memorial bridge from the most convenient point of the Naval Observatory grounds, or adjacent thereto, across the Potomac River to the most convenient point of the Arlington estate property, two thousand five hundred dollars.

The report of this survey, with maps, was published in House Doc. No. 388, Fifty-fifth Congress, second session. (See Annual Report of the Chief of Engineers for 1898, p. 3573.)

By act approved March 3, 1899, Congress made the following appropriation:

Memorial bridge across Potomac River: To enable the Chief of Engineers of the Army to continue the examination of the subject and to make or secure designs, calculations, and estimates for a memorial bridge from the most convenient point of the Naval Observatory grounds, or adjacent thereto, across the Potomac River to the most convenient point of the Arlington estate property, the sum of five thousand dollars.

Competitive designs with estimates for the bridge were obtained from four of the most distinguished American bridge engineers, each of whom associated with himself at least one architect of established reputation and ability. The designs were all very complete, the estimates accurately and carefully made, and the competition in every way gratifying.

The report of the Board of officers of the Corps of Engineers and of architects appointed by order of the Secretary of War to consider and report upon the relative merits of these designs was submitted March 28, 1900, and it is to be regretted that time admitted of but a very few of the numerous and valuable drawings obtained being reproduced in it.

The Board recommended that design No. 2 of those submitted by Mr. W. H. Burr be adopted, with minor modifications taken mainly from his design No. 1, the cost of which modifications the detail in which his plans had been worked up rendered susceptible of easily and accurately estimating. The estimated cost of the design as recommended is $4,860,000.

This report of the Board was transmitted to Congress and published in House Doc. No. 578, Fifty-sixth Congress, first session. (Also printed in the Annual Report of the Chief of Engineers for 1900, p. 5126.)

There are no operations to report for the year ending June 30, 1901, there having been no appropriation for constructing the bridge.

July 1, 1900, balance unexpended	$227.24
June 30, 1901, amount expended during fiscal year	6.54
July 1, 1901, balance unexpended	220.70

(See Appendix B B B 2.)

MAINTENANCE AND REPAIR OF WASHINGTON AQUEDUCT; INCREASING THE WATER SUPPLY OF WASHINGTON, D. C., AND WASHINGTON AQUEDUCT, DISTRICT OF COLUMBIA, FILTRATION PLANT.

These works were in the charge of Lieut. Col. Alexander M. Miller, Corps of Engineers, having under his immediate orders Lieut. George M. Hoffman, Corps of Engineers.

1. Washington Aqueduct.—Small repairs were made to the riprap backing of the dam at Great Falls. Gatehouses, storehouses, and watchmen's houses were kept in repair and whitewashed or washed with Portland cement.

The grounds at all the reservoirs were kept in good order and the fences whitewashed. The channels around the Dalecarlia Reservoir were cleaned, and concrete steps constructed from the Conduit road to the north connection. The paving on the embankment at the distributing reservoir was repaired.

During the past year the extreme fluctuation of the water level in the distributing reservoir was 4.89 feet.

The Conduit road has been repaired, and the gutters, etc., repaired and cleaned. About 25 cubic yards of deposit was removed from the mouth of the conduit at Great Falls.

A rubble masonry wall has been built at Great Falls, just inside the Government line and along the bank of the Chesapeake and Ohio Canal and the river bank, for the protection of the inlet to the conduit.

The by-conduit at the Dalecarlia Reservoir has been repaired by constructing a 1-ring brick lining inside the old rubble masonry conduit in that portion of the conduit between the north connection and the tunnel, and grouting a portion of the old rubble masonry conduit between the tunnel and the south connection.

Small repairs were made to the pavement of Bridge No. 3 and Cabin

John Bridge, and to the floor of the bridge at the Dalecarlia Reservoir. All the bridges are now in excellent condition.

Measurements of the daily and hourly consumption and waste of water were made each month and gave a daily average of 49,075,940 gallons. The consumption and waste, measured on June 26, 1901, were found to be 53,960,998 gallons per diem. This is the largest June measurement ever taken, and, estimating the population of the District of Columbia as 279,293, gives a daily per capita consumption and waste of 193 gallons. This shows that there is an exceedingly high rate of consumption of water in the District.

Careful and trustworthy investigations made in various cities in the United States show clearly that a daily per capita consumption of 100 gallons is ample for all domestic, business, and public purposes, and that any considerable increase above this amount must be attributed to waste.

This extravagant use of water has become a serious menace to the supply of water by the Washington Aqueduct with its present capacity—76,000,000 gallons—and at the rate of increase the ultimate limit would be reached in about twelve years.

The present consumption and waste have also an important bearing on the subject of filtration. A report on this subject was called for by Congress and was submitted March 28, 1900. (See Senate Doc. No. 259, Fifty-sixth Congress, first session.) It is probable that the cost of filtration will be about $6 per million gallons, or at the present rate of consumption about $300 per day, or $110,000 annually. This is a large charge and can be reduced only by a reduction in consumption.

In the opinion of the local engineer officer in charge of the aqueduct the existing conditions suggest two remedies—either the reduction of the consumption to a reasonable rate, 100 gallons per capita per diem, by the use of meters, or the increase of the present supply to keep up with the present demand by the building of a second conduit from the Great Falls of the Potomac. The necessary surveys of practicable routes for this conduit should be taken in hand at once, and an estimate for this work is submitted by the officer in charge.

Estimates are submitted for building a combined storehouse and stable at Great Falls, for preliminary surveys for an additional conduit from Great Falls, and for operation, maintenance, and repair of the Washington Aqueduct and its accessories, all of which have my approval and of which full explanations will be found in the report of the officer in charge.

The estimates for the fiscal year ending June 30, 1903, are as follows:

For building combined storehouse and stable at Great Falls	$3,000.00
For preliminary surveys for additional conduit from Great Falls	8,000.00
For operation, maintenance, repair, etc., of the aqueduct and its accessories, including the Conduit road, the new reservoir, and the Washington Aqueduct Tunnel	33,000.00
Total	44,000.00

WASHINGTON AQUEDUCT, DISTRICT OF COLUMBIA, 1901.

Amount appropriated by act of June 6, 1900	$22,000.00
June 30, 1901, amount expended during fiscal year	19,242.35
July 1, 1901, balance unexpended	2,757.65
July 1, 1901, outstanding liabilities	2,757.65
Amount that can be profitably expended in fiscal year ending June 30, 1903	33,000.00

WASHINGTON AQUEDUCT, DISTRICT OF COLUMBIA, 1901—PROTECTION TO INLET AT GREAT FALLS.

Amount appropriated by act of June 6, 1900	$5,000.00
June 30, 1901, amount expended during fiscal year	3,184.44
July 1, 1901, balance unexpended	1,815.56
July 1, 1901, outstanding liabilities	701.79
July 1, 1901, balance reverted to Treasury	1,113.77

WASHINGTON AQUEDUCT, DISTRICT OF COLUMBIA, 1901—REPAIRING BY-CONDUIT.

Amount appropriated by act of June 6, 1900	$10,000.00
June 30, 1901, amount expended during fiscal year	8,803.09
July 1, 1901, balance unexpended	1,196.91
July 1, 1901, outstanding liabilities	836.66
July 1, 1901, balance reverted to Treasury	360.25

(See Appendix C C C 1.)

2. *Increasing the water supply of Washington, D. C.*—This work is being prosecuted under an act approved June 30, 1898, making appropriations for the expenses of the government of the District of Columbia for the fiscal year ending June 30, 1899, and for other purposes, which authorizes and directs the Secretary of War to resume work on the Washington Aqueduct Tunnel and its accessories and the Howard University Reservoir, and to prosecute and complete the same, the work to be carried on in accordance with the plans of the board of experts as set forth in its report dated January 17, 1896.

The work recommended by the board of experts and the progress made during the fiscal year ending June 30, 1901, under the different heads, may be classified as follows:

Lining unlined portions of tunnel.—During the year a total of 825 linear feet of lining has been completed, completing this work.

Construction of invert in part of tunnel formerly lined.—A total length of 860 feet of this work has been done during the year, completing this work.

Repairing the defective lining.—A total of 2,250 feet was repaired during the year, completing this work.

Arranging drainage of tunnel west of Rock Creek.—This work was completed during the previous fiscal year.

Iron lining of tunnel at Rock Creek.—This work was completed during the previous fiscal year.

Filling voids in dry rubble backing.—This work was completed during the previous fiscal year. After completing a section of the tunnel it has been given a wash coat of Portland cement; 13,901 feet of the tunnel has been thus treated during the year, completing this work.

Accessory works.—The west gatehouse is completed so far that it is now in condition to supply the tunnel through the by-conduit of the distributing reservoir. The east gatehouse is in an advanced stage toward completion, and will probably be ready for service in three months.

The air shafts are completed except surface construction. The power house at the east shaft for the Bacon air-lift pumping plant is nearly completed. The working shaft at Foundry Branch has been closed. Rock Creek shaft has been lined with iron and is completed with the exception of the top section. The blow-off at Rock Creek shaft is nearly completed. The pump pit and connections are completed, ready to receive the centrifugal pumps. The boiler for these pumps is in place. At Champlain Avenue shaft the power house is under way, and the shaft for a distance of 66 feet has been filled with concrete and lined. At the east shaft a new brick lining 12 inches thick has been placed inside of the old lining.

Howard University Reservoir.—The reservoir has been cleaned up, the circulating conduit completed, a line of four 48-inch pipe laid connecting the east gatehouse with the filter gatehouse, and the revetment of the banks completed except in front of the gatehouses.

It is expected that the new reservoir will be placed in service during the coming fall.

Present condition of tunnel.—The tunnel is now completed from the west shaft to Howard University Reservoir.

The funds available are considered sufficient to complete the work, and the estimate for care and maintenance is included in the estimate for the Washington Aqueduct.

July 1, 1900, balance unexpended	[1] $480,406.45
Amount appropriated by act of March 1, 1901	162,222.97
	642,629.42
June 30, 1901, amount expended during fiscal year	357,603.53
July 1, 1901, balance unexpended	285,025.89
July 1, 1901, outstanding liabilities	58,139.11
July 1, 1901, balance available	226,886.78
July 1, 1901, amount covered by uncompleted contracts	108,964.12
Amount available for completion of existing project	117,922.66

(See Appendix C C C 2.)

3. *Washington Aqueduct, District of Columbia, filtration plant.*— By act approved June 6, 1900, $200,000 was appropriated "For establishing those portions of a filtration plant which are essential to the operation of either system of filtration adopted, including necessary land, grading, masonry, and appurtenances," and by act approved March 1, 1901, $500,000 was appropriated "toward establishing a slow sand filtration plant."

With this appropriation 1,377,619 square feet of land in the vicinity of the new reservoir have been purchased at the uniform price of 45 cents per square foot, amounting to $619,928.55, drawings of various details of the filtration plant have been made, buildings and a derrick erected, excavations made for the clear-water reservoir and forms for the same, and excavations made for the intake for the pumps to supply water to the filter beds. A topographical survey of the site for the filtration plant was also begun. Four 48-inch pipe lines were laid from the east shaft gatehouse of the new reservoir to the filtration gatehouse.

As Congress has stipulated that the slow sand system of filtration shall be adopted, an estimate of $1,000,000, which has my approval, is submitted by the officer in charge to continue the work during the fiscal year ending June 30, 1903.

---
[1] Including 75 cents disallowed in vouchers for June, 1900, and deposited in Treasury July 23, 1900.

July 1, 1900, balance unexpended $200,000.00
Amount appropriated by act of March 1, 1901 .... 500,000.00

700,000.00
June 30, 1901, amount expended during fiscal year 666,269.60

July 1, 1901, balance unexpended 33,730.40
July 1, 1901, outstanding liabilities 8,944.98

July 1, 1901, balance available 24,785.42

Amount (estimated) required for completion of existing project....... 1,786,123.42
Amount that can be profitably expended in fiscal year ending June 30,
 1903, in addition to the balance unexpended July 1, 1901 .... 1,000,000.00

(See Appendix C C C 3.)

IMPROVEMENT AND CARE OF PUBLIC BUILDINGS AND GROUNDS AND CARE AND MAINTENANCE OF THE WASHINGTON MONUMENT IN THE DISTRICT OF COLUMBIA.

Officer in charge, Col. Theo. A. Bingham, United States Army.

The Executive Mansion has received the usual care and such repairs and improvements as the funds available would admit. The arrangement of water supply, waste, and soil pipes has been improved by removing the old pipes and replacing them in a better way with new pipes. The private dining room has been repapered, redecorated, and repainted; the main corridor, first floor, redecorated and repainted; papering and painting done in other apartments, and the north and south porticos repainted. An automatic fire-alarm system has been placed in the attic, and some new carpets, furniture, and furnishings purchased. Plans, with estimates of cost, for extending the mansion have been prepared in accordance with Congressional action. The conservatory was repainted; repairs made to that building, to the greenhouses, and to the stable.

At the Washington National Monument the usual care required for maintenance has been extended, an addition to the boiler house constructed, and a new electric elevator installed. The work of stiffening the tie-rods of the iron columns within which the elevator car runs was completed, and the 70-volt lamps in the shaft replaced with lamps of 110 volts.

Inspections have been made from time to time of the various buildings occupied as offices by the War Department, except the State, War, and Navy Departments building, in connection with their care, repair, and safety.

At the propagating gardens necessary repairs were made to the greenhouse structures, an additional propagating house constructed, the framework of one of the greenhouses rebuilt, a new office building erected and the grounds around it improved, some old iron fencing erected, part of the Fifteenth street roadway graded, and the work of filling up low portions of the nursery grounds continued. A new brick and iron building for a storehouse has been constructed and work commenced and well advanced for the erection of a brick building for shops. About 984,000 plants were propagated for stock and park decoration.

The care required to maintain them in good condition has been extended to the improved parks and park places. Twenty of the small unimproved reservations, containing 2.91 acres, have been brought to the first stage of improvement, and three of the small improved reservations have been further improved. Marking stones were placed at the corners of seventy reservations, and Truxtun circle, hitherto unimproved, has been highly improved. A new entrance has been constructed to one of the main roadways in the Monument grounds.

The asphalt pavements in the parks have been extended by the construction of 2,410 square yards of foot walk, and 240 square yards of asphalt roadway and 455 square yards of asphalt foot walk have been repaired and resurfaced. Fifty-six feet of cobblestone gutter has been constructed, and 438 feet of drainpipe and 1,092 feet of water pipe laid.

A plan, with estimates of cost for improving that section of the city south of Pennsylvania avenue and north of B street SW., and for a suitable connection between the Potomac and Zoological parks was prepared and submitted to the Secretary of War for transmittal to Congress.

The statues of General Logan and Albert Pike have been completed, and the former unveiled on April 9, 1901. Granite coping has been set in position about two-thirds of the way around the site of the statue of General Sherman, and work in connection with the construction of that statue continued.

Attention has been given to the telegraph line connecting the Capitol with the Departments and Government Printing Office, and an electric storage battery, in duplicate, has been purchased to replace the old style gravity battery hitherto used for supplying current to the line. The desirability of replacing the present overhead system of wires with underground conduits and cables is submitted for the action of Congress and printed in House Doc. No. 135, Fifty-sixth Congress, second session.

The damage done by the storm in February, 1897, and by high tide and wind in October, 1898, to the iron pile wharf at Bridge Creek Landing, Virginia, near Wakefield, the birthplace of Washington, has not yet been repaired, there being no funds available for the work.

Attention is invited to the detailed report of the officer in charge and to his estimates and recommendations for the fiscal year ending June 30, 1903.

The estimates are as follows:

For the improvement and care of public buildings and grounds in charge of the Chief of Engineers	$145,789.30
For compensation of persons employed on public buildings and grounds	66,620.00
For repair of existing telegraph lines connecting Capitol and Departments	1,500.00
For contingent and incidental expenses of public buildings and grounds	600.00
For care of Washington Monument and maintenance of elevator:	
Salaries of employees...........$8,520.00	
Fuel, lights, contingencies, etc....2,500.00	11,020.00
Total	225,529.30

(See Appendix D D D.)

NORTHERN AND NORTHWESTERN LAKES—CORRECTING AND ISSUING CHARTS—SURVEYS—WATER LEVELS.

As early as 1817, local surveys of the Great Lakes for special purposes were made by Engineer officers, but the "Lake Survey" as a systematic work was commenced in 1841. It was diligently prosecuted thereafter until 1882, when, for a time, extended field operations were suspended. The correction, printing, sale, and issue of charts continued without cessation, however, the additions and corrections being largely based upon local surveys and reports by Engineer officers in charge of river and harbor improvements on the lakes.

Systematic field work was resumed in 1889, and has since been prosecuted with increased vigor. In 1898 operations were extended to include the cognate work of observing and investigating the levels of the Great Lakes and their connecting waters, with a view to their regulation in the interest of commerce. The survey proper has from the beginning been carried on under the War Department, being at first conducted by the Chief of Topographical Engineers, and by the Chief of Engineers after the consolidation of the Topographical Engineers with the Corps of Engineers.

The first regular appropriation for the survey was made in 1841, and annual appropriations followed, with the single exception of 1847. The appropriations to date for all purposes of the survey during the sixty-one years of its existence have aggregated $3,361,879, of which $2,411.81 has reverted to the Treasury.

The following extract from Professional Papers of the Corps of Engineers, United States Army, No. 24, describes the conditions governing the navigation of the Great Lakes in 1841:

1. The lake survey was begun in 1841, under an appropriation of $15,000, made in May of that year. At this time the country bordering on the lower lakes was already pretty well settled, and works for the improvement or formation of harbors had been commenced at most of the important points on Lakes Erie and Ontario. The Upper Lake region was but thinly settled, and there were no good harbors on Lake Huron, and but one (the harbor of Chicago) on Lake Michigan. Settlers were, however, pouring in rapidly, and there was even then a large and constantly increasing commerce between the lake ports, especially from Buffalo to Detroit and Chicago. Communication with Lake Superior could only be had by portage around the Sault Ste. Marie, but the great mineral wealth of the Lake Superior country was attracting attention, and a survey for a ship canal had been made in 1840 by officers of the Topographical Engineers. The lake commerce was carried on under many difficulties, which caused much loss of life and property each year.

There were no charts of the lakes except the Admiralty charts compiled from the surveys of Capt. H. W. Bayfield, of the royal navy (English), and these were not in general use by the masters of American vessels. These charts were the results of rapid reconnaissances, and although they showed the coast lines with an accuracy which is remarkable considering the rough methods of surveying employed, they were of little value as hydrographical charts of the American coast, because they showed the depths of water in comparatively few places and but a small number of the many reefs and shoals which are found along the lake shores.

There were few light-houses and beacons to indicate the positions of dangers to navigation, and in the absence of charts, pilots were obliged to rely upon their own knowledge, which was frequently only acquired by the vessel's grounding on a shoal or striking a hidden rock.

The navigation of the lakes is attended with peculiar dangers, because while violent gales are frequent and the storms rival those of the ocean itself, a vessel is never more than a few hours' run from the shore, and can not, as is generally the case at sea, drift before the wind until the storm is over, but in a long-continued gale must be thrown upon the shore, unless a port or harbor of refuge can be entered. In 1841 a vessel leaving Chicago found no harbor or shelter in storms until the Manitou or

Beaver Islands were reached, and after passing the Straits of Mackinac it was again exposed without refuge on Lake Huron, except in the vicinity of Presque Isle, until the head of the St. Clair River was reached. In sailing from Chicago to Buffalo the greatest difficulties were encountered in the vicinity of the Straits of Mackinac and in the west end of Lake Erie, on account of the many islands, shoals, and reefs found in those localities, and at the mouth of the St. Clair River, at which no improvements had been made in 1841, and where the channels were not only circuitous and narrow, but so shoal that vessels in low-water seasons frequently were compelled to have their cargoes taken over the bars in lighters.

It was therefore with the double object of furnishing reliable charts to lake vessels and of determining from the surveys the works of improvement which were necessary to the prosperity of the lake commerce that Congress in 1841 directed a survey of the lakes, and that annual appropriations, with the single exception of the year 1847, have since been made for carrying on the survey. Some idea of the magnitude of the work may be had from the following dimensions:

"The American shore line of the Great Lakes and their connecting rivers, if measured in steps of 25 miles, is about 3,000 miles, but if the indentations of the shore and the outlines of the islands be included the developed shore line is about 4,700 miles in length.

"Along rivers and where a lake is narrow it is necessary for navigation that both shores be mapped. This increases the length of the shore line to be surveyed betwen St. Regis, N. Y., and Duluth, Minn., to about 6,000 miles." [1]

During the first ten years of the survey, whilst a general geodetic survey of the entire chain of lakes was contemplated for the future, the actual operations were mainly confined to surveys of special localities where improvements were called for, or where the navigation was difficult, and where the surveys were more extended they were little more than reconnaissances. This course was made necessary because the appropriations were inadequate to the purchase of the finer instruments and the support of the larger force necessary for more extensive and more exact surveys, and also because of the pressing need of improvements at particular localities, for which preliminary surveys were essential.

The execution of the survey involved a great quantity of astronomic, topographic, and hydrographic work, all of which was performed with a high degree of skill and accuracy. The result was the completion of a series of reliable charts for lake vessels and the furnishing of a basis for works of channel improvement upon the lakes themselves and their connecting waters.

The original series consisted of 76 charts, all of which were printed from copperplates. As a result of revisions, additions, and cancellations there are now in force 76 lake survey charts, of which 63 are printed from copperplates, 11 are photolithographs in colors, and 2 are lithographs in colors.

The charts issued in colors have all depths of 18 feet and less in blue, showing at a glance where vessels may proceed with safety, and are considered by vessel men much preferable to the old style printed in plain black and white.

From 1882 to June 30, 1901, a total sum of $15,839.94 was derived from the sale of charts and deposited in the United States Treasury.

Up to February 20, 1890, one full set of charts was issued free to each United States registered vessel; any additional charts furnished such vessels, and all furnished for other unofficial use, were sold at the uniform price of 30 cents each. On the date above mentioned the free issue, except for official purposes of the Government, was discontinued pursuant to law, and since then the charts have been sold for all private and unofficial use at prices ranging from 5 cents to 31 cents each, the price being intended in each instance to cover only the cost of paper and printing.

---

[1] From memoranda respecting the lake survey by Gen. C. B. Comstock, published in the Report of the Chief of Engineers for 1875.

NORTHERN AND NORTHWESTERN LAKES. 679

The principal office of the survey is at Detroit, Mich., and nearly the whole work of conducting surveys and water-level observations and reducing the results thereof, and of correcting and issuing charts, is devolved upon that office. Important aid is given from time to time in making local surveys by the District Engineer Officers, who also regularly supply valuable information for correcting the charts and bulletins. These district officers are located at Duluth, Minn., Milwaukee, Wis., Chicago, Ill., Grand Rapids, Mich., Detroit, Mich., Cleveland, Ohio, and Buffalo, N. Y., with suboffices at Sault Ste. Marie, Mich., and Oswego, N. Y.

Charts can now be purchased at the main office at Detroit and at the canal office at Sault Ste. Marie, Mich., and will shortly be placed on sale also at the United States Engineer office in Buffalo, N. Y. Complete sample sets can now be seen at the United States Engineer offices at Duluth, Minn., Milwaukee, Wis., Chicago, Ill., Cleveland, Ohio, and Oswego, N. Y., enabling purchasers to select exactly the charts they wish to order. It is hoped eventually to be able to furnish all the United States Engineer offices mentioned with supplies of the charts for sale.

During the fiscal year ending June 30, 1901, the total number of charts sold was 6,861, the proceeds of the sales, amounting to $1,445.49, being deposited to the credit of the Treasurer of the United States. One thousand five hundred and sixty-four charts were issued for official use. To date more than 240,000 of these charts have been sold and issued for actual service.

During the year important corrections and additions were made in the Detroit office to 37 of the old charts for use in the office of the Chief of Engineers in bringing the electrotype plates up to date. From these corrected plates new editions of many of the charts have been printed in Washington.

Besides the above-mentioned revisions of the copperplate charts, one photolithograph chart was revised to date, photolithographed again, and a new edition in colors issued; one new chart, which had been photolithographed just at the close of the fiscal year 1900, was printed in colors and issued; six other new charts were completed and issued in colors during the year, four of them being photolithographs and two lithographs; three preliminary maps were photolithographed; another new chart has been completed, but has been held back awaiting results of surveys now in progress; three more entirely new charts are just ready for publication in colors, and will be out by August 15, two being lithographs and one a photolithograph; three additional new charts are well under way, and the reductions for four more well in hand.

In the field there are now six parties, as follows:

One engaged on resurvey of Apostle Islands and vicinity, Lake Superior.

One engaged on resurvey of the northern end of Lake Michigan and the Straits of Mackinac.

One about to begin observing discharge of the St. Marys River at the International Bridge at Sault Ste. Marie.

One observing discharge of St. Clair River at Port Huron and now about to undertake the same work on Detroit River, together with a resurvey of that river.

One observing discharge of St. Lawrence River below Ogdensburg,

N. Y., and collecting information for revision of the St. Lawrence River charts.

One precise-level party which has connected Lake Erie at Buffalo with Lake Ontario at Olcott, N. Y., is now extending the precise-level line from Fort Gratiot to Lexington, Mich., and will then connect Lake Huron at Detour with Lake Superior at Point Iroquois.

Of these the party on the St. Lawrence River and that at Port Huron were in the field last season, the former taking discharges only and the latter taking discharges and making a resurvey of the St. Clair River. The other four parties are newly organized and owing to the late opening of the season are now only well settled at their work.

Several local surveys and examinations were made to provide data for projecting new charts and correcting old ones. A considerable revision of the charts now under way has for its object to show to date certain changes which have taken place, due to natural and artificial agencies, to better serve the deeper draft vessels now engaged in lake commerce, and to indicate the somewhat reduced depths of water which now prevail during the season of navigation. Many of the original charts were prepared with reference to a navigation calling for a draft not exceeding 12 feet; the soundings were referred to planes representing mean or average stages of water, and general depths exceeding 18 feet below such planes were not closely developed. Present conditions of commerce demand, however, that the bottom be accurately charted to depths of not less than 30 feet in the open lakes, or 25 feet in their connecting rivers or straits, and these depths should relate to ordinary "low-water" stages, instead of to the "mean stages" referred to above. This will call for extensive surveys and a vast quantity of office work, all of which must be done with great care and accuracy. To secure a satisfactory rate of progress will require an expenditure of at least $150,000 during the year ending June 30, 1903.

In addition to work relating to charts, the Detroit office was engaged during the year under the project adopted in 1898 for an exhaustive investigation of lake levels, as described in the Annual Report of the Chief of Engineers for that year, pages 3774–3776. The principal field work comprised an accurate series of discharge measurements in the Niagara, St. Clair, and St. Lawrence rivers, together with local surveys related to these measurements; also the maintenance of fifteen self-registering water gauges on the several lakes, from Ontario to Superior and Michigan, which supply an accurate and continuous record of the most minute changes in the elevation of the water surface. This work is now fully organized, and it is highly important that it be pushed to completion as rapidly as possible. For this purpose the sum of $50,000 should be made available for expenditure during the year ending June 30, 1903.

It is therefore recommended that the appropriation for that year be made to include the two amounts indicated above, and that it be formulated as in the act of March 3, 1901, as follows:

Estimate for the fiscal year ending June 30, 1903.

For survey of Northern and Northwestern Lakes, including all necessary expense of preparing, correcting, extending, printing, and issuing charts and bulletins, and of investigating lake levels with a view to their regulation, to be available immediately and until expended.... $200,000.00

NORTHERN AND NORTHWESTERN LAKES. 681

SURVEYS, ADDITIONS TO, AND CORRECTING ENGRAVED PLATES.

July 1, 1900, balance unexpended	$83,236.85
June 30, 1901, amount expended during fiscal year	48,816.44
June 30, 1901, balance unexpended	34,420.41
Amount appropriated by sundry civil act March 3, 1901 (including printing and issuing charts)	100,000.00
July 1, 1901, balance unexpended	134,420.41

PRINTING AND ISSUING CHARTS.

July 1, 1900, balance unexpended		$3,482.29
June 30, 1901, amount expended during fiscal year	$1,989.81	
Reverted to Treasury	29.29	
		2,019.10
June 30, 1901, balance unexpended		1,463.19

(See Appendix E E E 1.)

Annual water levels of the Northern and Northwestern Lakes.—A table showing the monthly water levels from July 1, 1900, to June 30, 1901, at Charlotte and Oswego, N. Y., on Lake Ontario; at Erie Harbor, Pa.; Ashtabula and Cleveland, Ohio, on Lake Erie; at Milwaukee, Wis., on Lake Michigan, and Escanaba, Mich., on Green Bay; at Sand Beach, Mich., on Lake Huron, and Marquette and Sault Ste. Marie, Mich., on Lake Superior, being a continuation of that published in the Annual Report of the Chief of Engineers for 1900, will be found in Appendix E E E 2.

Charts.—Under the supervision of this office during the fiscal year additions have been made to the engraved plates of—

Lake Superior, No. 1.	Coast Chart, No. 6, Lake Michigan.
Ontonagon Harbor, Lake Superior.	Coast Chart, No. 7, Lake Michigan.
Copper Harbor, Lake Superior.	Coast Chart, No. 8, Lake Michigan.
Portage Lake and River, Lake Superior.	Coast Chart, No. 9, Lake Michigan.
L'Anse and Keweenaw Bay, Lake Superior.	Lake Huron.
	St. Clair River.
Grand Island, Lake Superior.	Lake St. Clair.
Straits of Mackinac.	Detroit River.
North End of Lake Michigan.	Lake Erie.
Beaver Island Group, Lake Michigan.	Coast Chart, No. 1, Lake Erie.
North End of Green Bay, Lake Michigan.	Coast Chart, No. 2, Lake Erie.
South End of Green Bay, Lake Michigan.	Coast Chart, No. 5, Lake Erie.
Coast Chart, No. 1, Lake Michigan.	Coast Chart, No. 7, Lake Erie.
Coast Chart, No. 2, Lake Michigan.	Lake Ontario.
Coast Chart, No. 3, Lake Michigan.	Coast Chart, No. 1, Lake Ontario.
Coast Chart, No. 4, Lake Michigan.	St. Lawrence River, No. 5.
Coast Chart, No. 5, Lake Michigan.	

An edition of each of the following charts has been photolithographed and printed in colors:

Lake Michigan (revised to July 1, 1901).
Lake Front, Chicago, Ill., including Calumet Harbor. (New.)
Buffalo Harbor and Niagara River to the Falls. (New.)
Erie Harbor and Presque Isle, Pa. (New.)
Dunkirk Harbor, New York. (New.)

Originals of the following charts have been engraved on stone and an edition of each printed in colors:

Agate and Burlington Bays (Two Harbors), Minn. (New.)
Sturgeon Bay, Canal, and Harbor of Refuge, Lake Michigan. (New.)

682   REPORT OF THE CHIEF OF ENGINEERS, U. S. ARMY.

Three photolithograph editions of preliminary maps were also issued:

Burlington Bay, Minn.
Harbor of Refuge at Entrance to Sturgeon Bay and Lake Michigan Ship Canal.
Muskegon Harbor, Mich.

The following-named charts were canceled by new editions during the fiscal year:

No. 77. Lake Front, Chicago, Ill.
No. 78. Duluth and Superior Harbors.
No. 79. Buffalo Harbor and Head of Niagara River.
No. 82. Erie Harbor and Presque Isle.
No. 88. Harbor of Refuge at Entrance to Sturgeon Bay and Lake Michigan Ship Canal (preliminary map).
Burlington Bay, Minn. (preliminary map).

IMPROVEMENT OF THE YELLOWSTONE NATIONAL PARK, INCLUDING THE CONSTRUCTION, REPAIR, AND MAINTENANCE OF ROADS AND BRIDGES.

Officer in charge, Capt. Hiram M. Chittenden, Corps of Engineers.
The work has been in the charge of the Engineer Department since 1883, except during the period from August, 1894, to March, 1899.

The present project, adopted August 27, 1900, embraces the construction of a belt-line road, including all the important centers of interest in the Park, viz: Mammoth Hot Springs, Norris Geyser Basin, the Firehole Geyser Basins, the Yellowstone Lake, the Canyon and Falls of the Yellowstone, and the section near Tower Falls; also four approaches leading from the boundary of the park to different points on the belt line, and numerous side roads to isolated objects of interest as well as bridle trails for use by exploring parties and by troops and scouts in patrolling the park. The estimated total mileage of the completed system is about 306 miles in the park proper and 417 miles including the roads in the forest reserve.

Estimated total cost of the project exclusive of annual maintenance and repairs and of macadamization is $870,000. Of this sum $472,000, in round numbers, has been expended, about $88,000 ($113,000, act March 3, 1901, less $25,000 annual repairs) is available, and $310,000 is required. The cost of annual maintenance and repairs has been about $174,000. The figures for expenditures do not include the current appropriation which is now being expended, it being impracticable to make a division in the midst of the working season.

The result of the expenditure thus far, after certain portions of the road are rebuilt, will be about 190 miles of road and 80 bridges constructed. There remain to be built about 144 miles and 11 costly bridges.

The work done during the fiscal year, omitting that done under the current appropriation act of March 3, 1901, which is now in progress, is as follows:

The work in the Golden Gate Canyon, including the reconstruction of the viaduct, was completed; a single-track road built from Golden Gate to the Middle Gardiner Falls; material for 3 steel bridges in the Gardiner Canyon was purchased and 1 abutment erected; 10 miles of road was opened up on the eastern approach and nearly the whole line located, and extensive repairs were carried on over the entire system. Of the $60,000 appropriated $6,438.60 was spent for administration and protection, $20,000 on the road from the outlet of the Yellowstone

Lake to the east boundary of the Yellowstone Forest Reserve, and the balance on the general circuit and approaches within the park.

Owing to the growth of the dust nuisance with the increase of travel and the necessity of securing some relief from it, the existing general project has been amended to include the macadamization of 150 miles of the most important roads. The estimated cost of this work is $2,000 per mile, or a total of $300,000.

The estimate for the fiscal year ending June 30, 1903, is as follows:

New work	$165,000
Macadamization of existing roads	60,000
Annual maintenance and repairs	25,000
Total	250,000

It is desirable that the appropriation be made in the same terms as that for the current year, viz, that it be made immediately available from date of passage, and that it remain available until expended; also that separate provision be made for administration and protection.

Full details as to work done and estimates for new work are given in the report of the officer in charge.

July 1, 1900, balance unexpended		[1]$56,738.88
Amount appropriated by sundry civil act approved March 3, 1901		113,000.00
		169,738.88
June 30, 1901, amount expended during fiscal year	$81,572.26	
Deduct refundment October 27, 1900, by N. P. Rwy. Co	17.85	
		81,554.41
July 1, 1901, balance unexpended		88,184.47
July 1, 1901, outstanding liabilities		36,288.82
July 1, 1901, balance available		51,895.65
Amount (estimated) required for completion of existing project, in addition to the balance available July 1, 1901		610,000.00
Amount that can be profitably expended in fiscal year ending June 30, 1903:		
For works of improvement	$225,000.00	
For maintenance of improvement	25,000.00	
		250,000.00

(See Appendix F F F.)

RECONNAISSANCES, EXPLORATIONS, AND WORK IN THE FIELD.

Engineer officers and acting engineer officers on the staffs of commanding generals of military divisions and departments have been engaged during the year in building and repairing wagon roads and bridges, making surveys in the field, making and distributing maps, and in other duties incidental to the work of engineers in the field.

Reports of such work have been submitted by the following officers:

Lieut. Col. W. P. Richards, Seventh United States Infantry, at Department of the Columbia.

Capt. Clement A. F. Flagler, Corps of Engineers, at Department of the East.

First Lieut. Lytle Brown, Corps of Engineers, at headquarters, provost-marshal-general, office city engineer, Manila, P. I.

---

[1] Increase of $8.66 over amount stated in the 1900 report, explained as follows: Refundment of $6.50 by Capt. H. M. Chittenden, United States Army, October 18, 1900; refundment of $2.16 by Capt. H. M. Chittenden, United States Army, November 16, 1900.

First Lieut. James F. McKinley, Eleventh United States Cavalry, at Department of California.

Lieut. Col. W. P. Richards, Seventh United States Infantry, acting engineer officer, Department of the Columbia, reports that the fieldwork consisted of a survey at Vancouver Barracks, Wash., for the purpose of showing the feasibility of running a railroad in a part of the reservation which would be less detrimental to the post than the route surveyed by the railroad company. That office work consisted of preparation of map and tracing of proposed change of route of railroad through Vancouver Barracks reservation; tracings of military reservations at Forts Lawton and Columbia, Wash.; profile of water-supply pipes at Fort Liscum, Alaska; revision of map showing the location of sewers and water-supply pipes at Vancouver Barracks, and making estimate of the cost of the repairs of the reservoir at the post. Eleven solar prints were made, 10 maps mounted on muslin, and 4 maps were issued. In addition work pertaining to the Adjutant-General's Office was done in the engineer office.

(See Appendix G G G 1.)

Capt. Clement A. F. Flagler, Corps of Engineers, engineer officer, Department of the East, reports that from July 1 to December 15, 1900, the engineer officer in charge of the office was on the staff of Brig. Gen. George W. Davis, commanding the Department of Porto Rico. Since December 15, 1900, he has been on the staff of Maj. Gen. John R. Brooke, commanding the Department of the East. Capt. William V. Judson, Corps of Engineers, was engineer officer of the Department until August 6, 1900; Lieut. H. E. Eames, Eleventh Infantry, from August 6 to October 19, 1900, and Captain Flagler since that date. Numerous practice marches were made by the troops of the Department in Porto Rico during the year. Instruments and materials for making route sketches of these marches were issued from the office and the sketches received corrected, if necessary, and filed. Research was made into the ownership of public lands and buildings in many cases, and numbers of maps collected and filed. The principal work done during the year was the construction of public roads on the island of Porto Rico. Captain Flagler's report is printed in full in the Annual Report of the Commanding General of the Army.

First Lieut. Lytle Brown, Corps of Engineers, city engineer of Manila, Philippine Islands, reports upon work of the department of city public works and water supply. The work of the department is comprised under the heads of city markets, city bridges, Bridge of Spain, Ayala Bridge, Santa Cruz Bridge, Luneta sea wall, crematories, slaughterhouse, Bilibid prison, projects, estimates, surveys, and miscellaneous. Lieutenant Brown's report is printed in full in the Annual Report of the General Commanding, Division of the Philippines.

First Lieut. James F. McKinley, Eleventh United States Cavalry, aid, acting engineer officer, Department of California, reports that no field work was performed during the year; that the routine work of the office was carried on; many maps were mounted and distributed, notably those of the Philippine Islands; tracings and blue prints were made when required, and considerable time was consumed in the care and preservation of the numerous and valuable astronomical and surveying instruments belonging to the office.

(See Appendix G G G 2.)

ESTIMATE FOR AMOUNT REQUIRED FOR MAPS, INCLUSIVE OF WAR MAPS.

For publication of maps for use of the War Department, inclusive of war maps, $5,000.

Paragraph 393 of the Army Regulations requires that the commanding officer of each post where there are fixed batteries bearing upon a channel will call upon the Engineer Department for accurate charts showing the soundings to the extent of the ranges of the guns. Calls upon this Department to perform its duty under this regulation are now being honored as rapidly as possible. To further the work $5,000 should be appropriated for the fiscal year ending June 30, 1903.

NEW BUILDING FOR GOVERNMENT PRINTING OFFICE.

Officer in charge, Capt. John S. Sewell, Corps of Engineers.

The sundry civil appropriation act approved March 3, 1899, authorized the construction, under the direction and supervision of the Chief of Engineers of the Army, of a fireproof building for the use of the Government Printing Office, upon plans and specifications to be prepared by the Chief of Engineers and approved by the Public Printer, and at a total cost, including approaches, elevators, lighting and heating apparatus, not exceeding $2,000,000, and appropriated $350,000 toward the execution of the work. This act also provided that the selection and appointment of a competent architect to prepare the plans and specifications for the elevations of said building should be made by the Chief of Engineers and the Public Printer jointly.

By joint resolution of Congress approved February 17, 1900, the limit of cost of the building was increased to $2,429,000 to meet the increased prices of building materials, and to permit of making the south end of the power-house extension, for a depth of about 45 feet from G street NW., of the same height as the main building.

The sum of $775,000 was appropriated in the sundry civil act of June 6, 1900, toward the construction of the building, and in the sundry civil act of March 3, 1901, $1,304,000 was appropriated for its completion.

Immediately upon the receipt of a copy of the law authorizing the construction of the building under the direction of the Chief of Engineers Captain (then Lieutenant) Sewell was assigned, by authority of the Secretary of War, to the direct charge of the work. After consultation with the Public Printer, and with his approval, Mr. J. G. Hill was appointed architect of the building.

The original plan provided for the construction of the building on a site at the northwest corner of North Capitol and G streets west, separated from the present printing-office building by Jackson alley. It included the extension to G street of the power house, with its height and width as then existing, and the erection of a main building, fronting 278 feet on G street, 278 feet on Jackson alley, and 175¼ feet on North Capitol street, with interior court about 29 feet by 168 feet. After careful study of the subject the Public Printer decided that the necessities of his department demanded that the south extension of the power house should be carried to the same height as the main building, and the plans were modified accordingly. The building is to be fireproof, constructed mainly of brick, and to be thoroughly modern in every particular. It is to have seven stories, a basement, and an attic, with a vault for storage purposes under the G street and North Capitol street sidewalks, the basement to extend under the interior court and driveway. The original project provided for only two stories in the south extension of the present power house.

Actual work upon the ground was commenced within a few days after notification was received of the transfer of the land to the United States. By July 6, 1899, all old buildings were removed from the site. On July 10 proposals were opened and the contract for excavation work was awarded. The work of laying the concrete foundations was commenced as soon as the excavation was sufficiently advanced.

Work was pushed during the year 1900 as rapidly as circumstances would permit. On November 30 of that year all structural and architectural plans had been completed, except some details of interior finish; plans for mechanical equipment (plumbing, wiring, elevators, etc.), were well advanced and most of them completed; the steel frame as high as the third story was nearly all in place; the masonry of the basement story and the underground sewerage work were nearly finished, and the fireproof construction had been satisfactorily begun.

At the close of the fiscal year 1901 the foundations, the steel work, and the underground drains were practically completed; the walls were at an average height about equivalent to that of the second floor, or a little higher; the power-house extension was under roof and nearly completed; about 80 per cent of all plans and drawings were completed, and good progress had been made on such parts of the mechanical equipment as could be begun before the building is closed in. The building will probably be practically complete by July 1, 1902, and its completion in all details and the winding up of all business connected with it will probably be not later than September 30, 1902. Everything indicates that the entire work will be finished within the authorized limit of cost.

Full details of the work are given in the report of the officer in charge.

Amount appropriated by act of March 3, 1899	$350,000.00
Amount appropriated by act of June 6, 1900	775,000.00
Amount appropriated by act of March 3, 1901	1,304,000.00
	2,429,000.00
June 30, 1901, amount expended to date	955,158.61
	1,473,841.39
July 1, 1901, balance unexpended	
July 1, 1901, outstanding liabilities $119,614.02	
July 1, 1901, amount covered by uncompleted contracts 391,539.38	
	511,153.40
July 1, 1901, balance available	962,687.99

(See Appendix H H H.)

CONSTRUCTION OF MILITARY ROAD FROM FORT WASHAKIE TO MOUTH OF BUFFALO FORK OF SNAKE RIVER, WYOMING.

Officer in charge, Capt. Hiram M. Chittenden, Corps of Engineers.

The first appropriation for this work was made by act of June 4, 1897; construction was commenced in August, 1898, and finished in October of the same year so far as funds would permit. For description of the locality, character and value of the road, and work done to

June 30, 1899, see Annual Report of the Chief of Engineers, 1899, Part VI, pages 3881-3900.
Amount expended to June 30, 1900, $9,974.88
Amount expended during fiscal year ending June 30, 1901, $8,392.97.
The sundry civil act of June 6, 1900, appropriated $10,000 for repair and completion of the road. A project was submitted June 17, 1900, and approved June 22, 1900. Work began immediately after the 1st of July and continued until the 13th of September. It consisted entirely in completing and repairing the road built in 1898. The most important item of the work was the construction of a large bridge (117 feet long) over Buffalo Fork of Snake River. In the month of October a reconnaissance was made along Wind River Valley to determine the best location for a road along that stream, if there should be an appropriation for completing the road.

July 1, 1900, balance unexpended	$10,025.12
June 30, 1901, amount expended during fiscal year	8,392.97
July 1, 1901, balance unexpended	1,632.15
July 1, 1901, outstanding liabilities	19.19
July 1, 1901, balance available	1,612.96

(See Appendix I I I.)

ERECTION OF MONUMENT TO SERGEANT CHARLES FLOYD.

Officer in charge, Capt. Hiram M. Chittenden, Corps of Engineers.
The deficiency act of March 3, 1899, appropriated $5,000 for the erection, in cooperation with the Floyd Memorial Association, of a monument near Sioux City, Iowa, over the remains of Sergeant Charles Floyd, of the Lewis and Clarke expedition. This sum has been expended in conjunction with other sums appropriated by the State of Iowa, the county of Woodbury, Iowa, the city of Sioux City, Iowa, and contributions from various other sources, the total amounting to nearly $20,000. The work has been conducted entirely under the supervision of the United States engineer office in Sioux City.

At the close of the last fiscal year the foundation for the monument had been completed, a contract had been let on the part of the State of Iowa for the stone in the shaft, and advertisements were out for the erection of the monument, this part of the work to be done from the United States appropriation.

Since that date the work has progressed steadily except during the winter season, and is now completed. The monument was formally dedicated May 30, 1900.

The foundation is a solid monolith of concrete, approximately of the form of a frustum of a pyramid, with 484 square feet bearing surface. It weighs 278 tons.

The style of the shaft is that of the Egyptian obelisk. The base is 9.42 feet square and the height is 100.174 feet. The material is cut stone from the Kettle River sandstone quarries of Minnesota. The cut stone comprises the greater part of the volume of the shaft, there being a small core composed of concrete. Upon the east and west faces of the shaft are two large bronze tablets with suitable inscriptions. The monument is protected from defacement by a steel picket fence 7½ feet high. A concrete pavement in the form of a terrace and roadway extends around the monument to the circumfrence of a circle of nearly 50 feet radius. The grounds in the immediate vicinity have been graded, and a roadway has been constructed from the monument to the nearest public highway.

The monument and 1 acre of ground around it are now the property of the Floyd Memorial Association.

A detailed report upon the erection of the monument is given in the report of the officer in charge.

Amount expended to June 30, 1900, $1,231.92. (Decrease of $95.25 from amount stated in 1900 report, on account of sale of tools.)

July 1, 1900, balance unexpended .... [1]$3,768.08
June 30, 1901, amount expended during fiscal year 3,768.08

(See Appendix J J J.)

OFFICE OF THE CHIEF OF ENGINEERS.

During the fiscal year ending June 30, 1901, the following-named officers were on duty in this office as assistants:

Col. Alexander Mackenzie.
Maj. James L. Lusk.
Maj. Frederic V. Abbot, since August 13, 1900.
Capt. Joseph E. Kuhn, until August 21, 1900.
Capt. Charles S. Bromwell.

Very respectfully, your obedient servant,

G. L. GILLESPIE,
Brig. Gen., Chief of Engineers,
U. S. Army.

Hon. ELIHU ROOT,
Secretary of War.

---

[1] Increase of $95.25 over amount stated in 1900 report. Treasury transfer settlement No. 15608, June 28, 1900, credited to appropriation November 19, 1900.

APPENDIXES

TO THE

REPORT OF THE CHIEF OF ENGINEERS,

UNITED STATES ARMY.

APPENDIXES

TO THE

REPORT OF THE CHIEF OF ENGINEERS,

UNITED STATES ARMY.

FORTICATIONS, ETC.

APPENDIX No. 1.

REPORT OF THE BOARD OF ENGINEERS.

THE BOARD OF ENGINEERS, ARMY BUILDING,
New York City, July 8, 1901.

GENERAL: 1 have the honor to submit the annual report recounting the operations of The Board of Engineers for the year ending June 30, 1901.

The following changes in the personnel of the Board has taken place since the date of the last annual report:

On April 30, 1901, Col. Henry M. Robert, Corps of Engineers, was appointed brigadier-general and Chief of Engineers, and retired from active service May 2, 1901.

On May 2, 1901, Col. J. W. Barlow, Corps of Engineers, was appointed brigadier-general and Chief of Engineers, and retired from active service May 3, 1901.

On May 3, 1901, Col. G. L. Gillespie, Corps of Engineers, was appointed brigadier-general and Chief of Engineers.

The following details as members of the Board have been made:

Col. S. M. Mansfield, Corps of Engineers, by Special Orders, No. 73, Headquarters of the Army, A. G. O., March 29, 1901.

Col. Charles R. Suter and Lieut. Col. C. W. Raymond, Corps of Engineers, by Special Orders, No. 18, Headquarters Corps of Engineers, May 6, 1901.

Maj. Sedgwick Pratt, Artillery Corps, by Special Orders, No. 129, Headquarters of the Army, A. G. O., June 4, 1901.

As at present constituted the Board of Engineers consists of the following-named officers: Col. Chas. R. Suter, Corps of Engineers, president; Col. S. M. Mansfield, Corps of Engineers; Lieut. Col. C. W. Raymond, Corps of Engineers; Maj. Sedgwick Pratt, Artillery Corps; Capt. Edgar Jadwin, Corps of Engineers, recorder and disbursing officer.

In addition Col. Peter C. Hains, Corps of Engineers, Division Engineer of the Southeast Division; Col. Jared A. Smith, Corps of Engineers, Division Engineer of the Pacific Division, and Col. Amos Stickney, Corps of Engineers, Division Engineer of the Southwest Division, are members of the Board of Engineers when matters pertaining to defensive works in their respective divisions are under consideration by the Board.

In the past fiscal year the following officers of the Corps of Engineers in charge of engineering districts were associated with the Board during the consideration of the defenses of the localities indicated: Col. Chas. R. Suter: San Francisco, Cal. Maj. S. S. Leach: Eastern Entrance to Long Island Sound. Maj. S. W. Roessler: Portland, Me. Capt. Harry Taylor: Portsmouth, N. H. Capt. W. V. Judson: San Juan, P. R.

The Board has considered the various subjects referred to it during the past fiscal year by the Chief of Engineers, and the following is a brief summary of the reports rendered thereon:

1900.
July 3. On mounting twelve high-power guns projected under the appropriations made by act of May 25, 1900.
July 6. On general storage magazines at military posts.
July 9. On area required for defenses at Fort Mason, Cal.
July 11. Annual report recounting the operations of the Board of Engineers for the year ending June 30, 1900.
July 25. Suggestions with regard to the character of mounts to be used for high-power guns at certain localities.
Aug. 6. Relative to central storage magazines in seacoast forts.
Aug. 6. On proposed design for 10-inch B. L. rifles, mounted on disappearing carriage, model 1896.
Sept. 14. On rapid-fire guns for defense of seacoast fortifications.
Sept. 15. On revision of project for the defense of San Francisco, Cal.
Sept. 18. On revision of project for defense of Portland, Me.
Sept. 19. On construction of two emplacements for 15-pounder guns at Fort Winfield Scott, Cal.
Sept. 21. On revision of project for artillery defense of the Columbia River.
Sept. 25. Preliminary report relative to naval maneuvers in Narragansett Bay.
Oct. 9. On acquisition of sites for defenses at Nortons Point, Coney Island, N. Y.
Dec. 3. On revised project for the defense of Galveston, Tex.
Dec. 24. On project of Capt. W. V. Judson, Corps of Engineers, for the submarine-mine defense of San Juan, P. R.
Dec. 26. On the naval maneuvers against coast defenses at the entrance to Narragansett Bay, R. I., on September 24, 1900.
Dec. 28. Relative to maps to accompany the Board's revised project for defense of San Francisco Harbor.
Dec. 31. On defense by rapid-fire guns of Upper New York Harbor.
1901.
Jan. 11. Relative to necessity of raising the height of trunnions of the Emery gun carriage.
Jan. 11. Relative to ammunition to be used in testing the 6-inch chain hoist.
Jan. 11. Relative to additional land at Cushings Island, Me., for defense of Portland Harbor.
Jan. 15. On project of Lieut. Edward M. Adams, Corps of Engineers, for submarine-mine defense of New Orleans, La.
Jan. 15. On searchlights for use in defense of Pensacola Harbor, Florida.
Jan. 19. On inspection report of Col. John I. Rodgers, Fifth Artillery, on works under construction for artillery defense at Fort Hamilton, N. Y.
Jan. 23. Detailed project for the defense of the entrance to Chesapeake Bay at Cape Henry, Virginia.
Jan. 28. Recommendation relative to submarine-mine defense of the entrance to Chesapeake Bay at Cape Henry, Virginia.
Feb. 2. Specifications and plans for type storage magazines for peace storage of powder and fixed ammunition.

APPENDIX 1—THE BOARD OF ENGINEERS.

1901.
Feb. 5. Recommendations relative to location of two 12-inch guns at Point Bonita and two 15-pounder guns at Presidio, San Francisco, Cal.
Feb. 26. Drawings to illustrate Board's project of April 6, 1900, for defense of Portsmouth, N. H.
Mar. 5. Foundations for high-power gun emplacements.
Mar. 5. Method of piling ammunition in peace storage magazine.
Mar. 8. Searchlights required for defense of the seacoast of the United States.
Mar. 19. Necessity of further defenses at Port Royal in view of transfer of naval station to Charleston, S. C.
Mar. 19. Lieutenant Adams's project for submarine defense of New Orleans.
Mar. 28. Distribution of rapid-fire guns for defense of eastern entrance to Long Island Sound.
Apr. 3. Project for the rapid-fire defense of Puget Sound.
Apr. 5. Project for the submarine-mine defense of New Orleans, La.
Apr. 8. Type emplacement for 6-inch rapid-fire gun on ordnance pedestal mount, model 1900.
Apr. 25. Revised project for defense of the eastern entrance to New York Harbor.
Apr. 29. Revised project for defense of the southern entrance to New York Harbor.
Apr. 29. Ammunition supply for the 12-inch barbette carriage.
Apr. 29. Inspection report of Col. Jared A. Smith, Corps of Engineers, relative to defensive sites at San Diego, Cal.
Apr. 29. Drawings to illustrate the revised project for defense of Galveston, Tex.
Apr. 30. Indorsement of the Engineer Department of April 29, 1900, relative to the emplacement of 12-inch guns.
May 15. Drawings to illustrate revised project of the Board for defense of Portland, Me.
May 29. Relative to armament for defense of Fort Barrancas, Fla.
June 3. On necessity of project for defense of St. Augustine, Fla.
June 3. On rapid-fire armament for defense of Charleston, S. C.
June 3. On total armament for defense of Pensacola, Fla.
June 28. On the necessity of a project for defense of Port Angeles, Wash.
June 28. Acquisition of land at Popham Beach, Me., for the defenses of the Kennebec River.
June 29. On the submarine-mine defense of the entrance to Chesapeake Bay at Cape Henry, Va.

The following personal inspections connected with the duties of the Board in the past fiscal year were made:

On August 17, 1900, a committee of the Board, consisting of Col. J. W. Barlow and Capt. Edgar Jadwin, Corps of Engineers, inspected defensive sites in the harbor of Portland, Me., under orders from the Chief of Engineers dated August 13, 1900.

On September 24 and 25, 1900, a committee of the Board, consisting of Col. Henry M. Robert and Capt. Edgar Jadwin, Corps of Engineers, witnessed the naval maneuvers against coast defenses in Narragansett Bay under orders from the Chief of Engineers dated September 19, 1900.

On February 1, 1901, Capt. Edgar Jadwin, Corps of Engineers, visited the Dupont Powder Works at Wilmington, Del., in connection with the Board's plans for central storage magazines, under orders from the Chief of Engineers dated January 24, 1901.

In addition to their duties with The Board of Engineers, the officers composing the same have been otherwise engaged during the period they have been members in the past fiscal year as follows:

Col. Chas. R. Suter, Corps of Engineers, the president of the Board, was in charge of the fortifications, of the river and harbor improvements, and of the construction of certain bridges in Boston Harbor, Massachusetts, and in the district embraced in his duties while stationed at Boston, Mass., until May 31, 1901. He continues as division engineer of the Northeast Division and president of the following Boards: (*a*) On harbor lines for the harbor of New York and its adjacent waters;

(b) for the examination of officers of the Corps of Engineers with the view to their promotion, and (c) for examination of officers of the line of the Army with the view to their transfer to the Corps of Engineers, under the provisions of the act of Congress approved February 2, 1901.

Col. S. M. Mansfield, Corps of Engineers, was in charge of river and harbor improvements and of the construction of certain bridges in the district embraced in his duties while stationed at Cleveland, Ohio, until May 8, 1901. He is division engineer of the Northwest Division and is in charge of improvements in the Hudson River and harbors thereon, of rivers and harbors in New Jersey and New York, and has the supervision of various bridges in the city of New York and of the removal of various wrecks. He is also a member of the Board on harbor lines for the harbor of New York and its adjacent waters, and of the Board for examination of officers of the Corps of Engineers with a view to their promotion.

Lieut. Col. C. W. Raymond, Corps of Engineers, is in charge of the works of defense and of river and harbor improvements and the construction of bridges in the Delaware River at Philadelphia, Pa., and is a member of the Board on harbor lines for the harbor of Philadelphia.

Maj. Sedgwick Pratt, Artillery Corps, is stationed at Fort Wadsworth, N. Y., and continues in the performance of his duties at that post.

Capt. Edgar Jadwin, Corps of Engineers, has continued as the recorder and disbursing officer of the Board of Engineers. He served as a member of a Board to examine and report upon the condition of jetties and fortifications at Galveston, Tex., and to submit projects for their repair and reconstruction, and continues as a member of the Board appointed under the provisions of the act of Congress approved February 2, 1901, for examination of officers of the line of the Army with a view to their transfer to the Corps of Engineers.

For the Board:

Very respectfully, your obedient servant,

CHAS. R. SUTER,
Colonel, Corps of Engineers, President of the Board.

Brig. Gen. G. L. GILLESPIE,
Chief of Engineers, U. S. A.

APPENDIX No. 2.

REPORT OF THE BOARD ON TORPEDO SYSTEM.

BOARD FOR REVISION OF THE
EXISTING TORPEDO SYSTEM,
Willets Point, N. Y., July 24, 1901.

GENERAL: I have the honor to submit herewith annual report and summary thereof, in duplicate, upon the operations of the Board on existing torpedo system for the fiscal year ending June 30, 1901.
Very respectfully,

W. M. BLACK,
Major, Corps of Engineers, U. S. A.,
President of the Board.

Brig. Gen. GEO. L. GILLESPIE,
Chief of Engineers, U. S. A.

REPORT OF OPERATIONS OF THE BOARD FOR THE CONSIDERATION OF THE EXISTING TORPEDO SYSTEM FOR THE FISCAL YEAR ENDING JUNE 30, 1901.

The Board was constituted January 30, 1896.
By direction of the Chief of Engineers, United States Army, it examined and reported upon papers as follows:

1900.
Aug. 3. A report of the action, to date, of the Board in the case of the Halpire torpedo was submitted.
Sept. 8. An additional report upon the Halpine torpedo was submitted, in which the Board recommended that if further opportunity were allowed Lieutenant Halpine to furnish a torpedo the specifications should state full requirements.
Nov. 28. A model of a floating torpedo, submitted by Messrs. Leins and Smith, Alto Pass, Ill.
Dec. 22. Report upon certain modifications in the adopted method of submarine-mine defense for New Orleans, La., proposed by the officer in charge.
Dec. 22. Special report upon the corrosion of the aluminum parts of circuit regulators.
1901.
Mar. 4. Report upon a device for automatically signaling the approach of a vessel to a mine proposed by Lieut. George Van Horn Moseley, Ninth United States Cavalry.
Mar. 4. An additional report upon the submarine-mine defense of New Orleans, La.
Mar. 19. After consultation with The Board of Engineers in New York City, a report upon the submarine-mine defense of Cape Henry, Virginia, was submitted.

The Board still has under consideration a new pattern of jointing box and a new pattern of circuit-regulator plug, proposed by Maj. John G. D. Knight, Corps of Engineers, and a report of Maj. W. T.

Rossell, Corps of Engineers, calling attention to defects in circuit closers and regulator plugs.

A recommendation for a reconstitution of the Board was forwarded by the president June 4.

Changes in personnel.—March 18, 1901: Capt. Henry Jervey, Corps of Engineers, was relieved from duty as member of the Board; Capt. James F. McIndoe, Corps of Engineers, was detailed in his stead. April 29, 1901: Maj. John G. D. Knight, Corps of Engineers, was relieved from duty as president of the Board, and Maj. W. M. Black, Corps of Engineers, was detailed in his stead.

The Board now consists of the following officers of the Corps of Engineers, all stationed at Fort Totten, N. Y.:

Maj. W. M. Black.
Capt. James F. McIndoe.
Capt. George P. Howell.

APPENDIX No. 3.

FORTIFICATIONS.

FISCAL YEAR 1900-1901.

3 A.

DEFENSES OF COAST OF MAINE.

Officer in charge, Maj. Solomon W. Roessler, Corps of Engineers; assistants, Lieut. Thomas H. Jackson, Corps of Engineers, to September 20, 1900, and Lieut. Charles W. Kutz, Corps of Engineers, since August 31, 1900; Division Engineers, Col. George L. Gillespie, Corps of Engineers (now brigadier-general, Chief of Engineers, United States Army), to April 30, 1901, and Col. Charles R. Suter, Corps of Engineers, since May 9, 1901.

BAR HARBOR, ME.

Two 8-inch converted rifles and two 10-inch smoothbore guns were mounted on temporary wooden platforms for the defense of this point during the war with Spain in 1898. No repairs have been made during the year.

The two 10-inch guns were condemned in April last and sold. The two 8-inch converted rifles are to be removed to the nearest Government reservation, and the remaining ordnance stores are to be sent to Watertown Arsenal.

PENOBSCOT RIVER, MAINE.

The only work during the year in connection with the fort proper has been a few small repairs and removing accumulated débris. Three old dilapidated buildings were sold. Under an allotment of funds from the appropriation for "Torpedoes for Harbor Defense," a brick storehouse, 56 feet by 27 feet, with traveling crane, for storage of submarine-mining material was constructed during the year. Only a small quantity of grading remains to be done. Plans and estimates for two emplacements for 6-inch rapid-fire guns on pedestal mounts have been called for.

Money statements.

PRESERVATION AND REPAIR OF FORTIFICATIONS.

July 1, 1900, balance unexpended	$694.61
June 30, 1901, amount expended during fiscal year	176.43
July 1, 1901, balance unexpended	518.18

TORPEDOES FOR HARBOR DEFENSE.

Allotted July 13, 1900	$3,000.00
June 30, 1901, amount expended during fiscal year	2,414.63
July 1, 1901, balance unexpended	585.37

ALLOTMENTS.

Preservation and repair of fortifications.

April 20, 1898, act March 3, 1897	$150.00
July 19, 1898, act May 7, 1898	600.00

Torpedoes for harbor defense.

July 13, 1900, act May 25, 1900	3,000.00

KENNEBEC RIVER, MAINE.

The only work done during the year consisted in repairs. The slopes and retaining walls, etc., of the emplacement for one 8-inch B. L. rifle mounted on 15-inch smoothbore carriage, were practically rebuilt.

Plans and estimates for the construction of two emplacements for 6-inch rapid-fire guns on pedestal mounts have been called for.

The submarine-mining material stored here has been overhauled and cleaned.

Money statement.

PRESERVATION AND REPAIR OF FORTIFICATIONS.

July 1, 1900, balance unexpended	$788.09
June 30, 1901, amount expended during fiscal year	349.37
July 1, 1901, balance unexpended	438.72
July 1, 1901, outstanding liabilities	59.68
July 1, 1901, balance available	379.04

ALLOTMENT.

Preservation and repair of fortifications.

July 24, 1899, act March 3, 1899	$1,200.00

PORTLAND, ME.

Fort Gorges, Me.—No work was done during the fiscal year. A watchman was on duty throughout the year. All the armament has been either condemned or donated.

Money statement.

PRESERVATION AND REPAIR OF FORTIFICATIONS.

July 1, 1900, balance unexpended	$870.22
Allotted May 10, 1901	600.00
	1,470.22
June 30, 1901, amount expended during fiscal year	611.22
July 1, 1901, balance unexpended	859.00
July 1, 1901, outstanding liabilities	50.00
July 1, 1901, balance available	809.00

APPENDIX 3—FORTIFICATIONS.

ALLOTMENTS.

June 9, 1899, act May 7, 1898	$600.00
June 7, 1900, act May 25, 1900	800.00
May 10, 1901, act March 1, 1901	600.00

Fort Scammel, Me.—No work has been done during the past fiscal year. No regular watchman was kept, the place being visited daily from other work in the vicinity until the armament was condemned and sold. During the time the purchasers are engaged in removing the old ordnance a man is kept at the fort to see that no damage is done to slopes, etc.

Money statement.

PRESERVATION AND REPAIR OF FORTIFICATIONS.

July 1, 1900, balance unexpended	$481.44
June 30, 1901, amount expended during fiscal year	95.61
July 1, 1901, balance unexpended	385.83
July 1, 1901, outstanding liabilities	30.80
July 1, 1901, balance available	355.03

ALLOTMENTS.

October 4, 1898, act May 7, 1898	$500.00
June 9, 1899, act May 7, 1898	250.00

SITE NO. 1.

Battery for sixteen 12-inch B. L. mortars.—At the beginning of the fiscal year all carriages were assembled and mortars mounted, but work was in progress on the grading and sodding of the slopes, and the construction of concrete floors in pits A and B and concrete retaining walls. This work was completed during the season of 1900.

A subsequent allotment of $5,000 was made for the purposes of lining the shell rooms and magazines in order to collect the moisture due to infiltration, and for raising and grading the floors in the east half of the battery.

This work has been partially completed at the close of the year.

In the east half of the battery the wall lining consists of a 4-inch wall of hollow brick separated from the concrete by a layer of asbestus felt. In the other half of the battery, it consists of galvanized corrugated sheet steel supported on kyanized furring strips.

The roof lining in both cases is galvanized corrugated sheet steel.

This battery was transferred to the artillery March 8, 1901.

Money statements.

GUN AND MORTAR BATTERIES.

July 1, 1900, balance unexpended	$18,469.04
Allotted April 8, 1901	5,000.00
	23,469.04
June 30, 1901, amount expended during fiscal year	18,575.84
July 1, 1901, balance unexpended	4,893.20
July 1, 1901, outstanding liabilities	1,655.11
July 1, 1901, balance available	3,238.09

TORPEDOES FOR HARBOR DEFENSE.

July 1, 1900, balance unexpended	$732.73
Allotted September 5, 1900	9.78
	742.51
June 30, 1901, amount expended during fiscal year	42.51
July 1, 1901, balance unexpended	700.00

ALLOTMENTS.

Gun and mortar batteries.

July 3, 1896, act June 6, 1896	$100,000.00
December 14, 1896, act June 6, 1896	25,000.00
November 16, 1897, act June 6, 1896	10,000.00
February 9, 1898, act June 6, 1896	40,000.00
June 20, 1898, act May 7, 1898	17,000.00
December 27, 1898, act March 2, 1895	517.29
December 27, 1898, act June 6, 1896	1,336.36
December 27, 1898, act May 7, 1898	11,146.35
June 16, 1899, act March 3, 1899	1,050.00
May 4, 1900, act July 7, 1898	19,000.00
April 8, 1901, act May 25, 1900	5,000.00

Torpedoes for harbor defense.

May 1, 1897, act March 3, 1897	$3,200.00
September 5, 1900, act March 3, 1897	9.78

Battery commander's station.—Work was begun in October, 1900, and practically completed at the close of the fiscal year. A little painting and carpenter work remain to be done.

Money statement.

Allotted September 26, 1900	$4,600.00
June 30, 1901, amount expended during fiscal year	2,194.62
July 1, 1901, balance unexpended	2,405.38
July 1, 1901, outstanding liabilities	915.80
July 1, 1901, balance available	1,489.58

ALLOTMENT.

Gun and mortar batteries.

September 26, 1900, act May 25, 1900	$4,600.00

Preservation and repair of fortifications.—An allotment of $1,000 was made April 19, 1901, for the repair of slopes that had been badly washed by the heavy spring rains, and for the loaming and seeding of the front slopes of the east half of the battery, which had been left in an unfinished condition.

This work has been completed.

A subsequent allotment of $600 was made May 10, 1901, for minor repairs that will be necessary from time to time during the ensuing year.

APPENDIX 3—FORTIFICATIONS. 701

Money statement.

July 1, 1900, balance unexpended	$430.00
Allotted during fiscal year	1,630.00
	2,060.00
June 30, 1901, amount expended during fiscal year	987.65
July 1, 1901, balance unexpended	1,072.35
July 1, 1901, outstanding liabilities	373.15
July 1, 1901, balance available	699.20

ALLOTMENTS.

August 23, 1899, act March 3, 1899	$1,400.00
April 4, 1901, act May 25, 1900	30.00
April 19, 1901, act March 1, 1901	1,000.00
May 10, 1901, act March 1, 1901	600.00

SITE NO. 2.

Emplacements for five 10-inch B. L. rifles on disappearing carriages.—Guns and carriages are mounted and in the hands of the artillery garrison.

On November 8, 1900, an allotment of $700 was made for installing speaking-tube communication between platforms and magazines and telephone connection between battery commanders' stations and the telephone booths. The speaking tubes have been placed and material is on hand for the telephone lines, which are to consist of iron-armored lead-covered cables laid under ground.

Money statement.

GUN AND MORTAR BATTERIES.

July 1, 1900, balance unexpended	$500.00
Allotted November 8, 1900	700.00
	1,200.00
June 30, 1901, amount expended during fiscal year	596.03
July 1, 1901, balance unexpended	603.97

ALLOTMENTS.

Gun and mortar batteries.

November 5, 1892, act July 23, 1892	$110,000.00
September 27, 1894, act August 1, 1894	5,000.00
September 25, 1895, act March 2, 1895	5,000.00
July 3, 1896, act March 2, 1895, and June 6, 1896	65,000.00
September 16, 1896, act June 6, 1896	18,000.00
August 31, 1897, act June 6, 1896	21,000.00
June 14, 1900, act July 7, 1898	500.00
November 8, 1900, act July 7, 1898	700.00

Emplacements for two 12-inch B. L. rifles on disappearing carriages.—Work was begun on the battery in March, 1901. The excavation is now practically completed, the plant is in operation, and 617 cubic yards of concrete have been placed. The excavation consists of 1,331 cubic yards of earth and 839 cubic yards of rock.

The plant includes a stone bin 18 by 40 feet inside and 31 feet high, a sand bin 18 by 18 feet inside and 31 feet high, a cement shed with a capacity of 4,000 barrels, a 5-foot cylindrical mixer, two 60-foot boom derricks, and one 75-foot crane derrick.

Sand and stone are delivered in dump carts and placed in the bins by means of bucket conveyors. Materials are conveyed to the top of the mixer frame by vertical bucket elevators, the same elevator being fed by a horizontal belt conveyor running beneath the stone bin.

A 25-horsepower engine is used to run all elevators and a second engine of the same capacity is used to run the mixer. Both engines are fed from a single boiler so placed that the cement barrel staves may be conveniently used as fuel.

The cost of the plant has been $12,614.49, which does not include the mixer and the two engines used for mixer and elevators, the excluded items having been transferred from other works.

Cement has to unload from vessels at a point 3 miles distant and be hauled to the site of the work in teams, thereby adding 15 cents to the cost of each barrel.

Sand used for concrete and fill has to be hauled about 3 miles.

Crushed rock is obtained from a quarry recently opened in the vicinity of the work.

Money statement.

GUN AND MORTAR BATTERIES.

Allotted November 9, 1900	$130,000.00
June 30, 1901, amount expended during fiscal year	17,248.75
July 1, 1901, balance unexpended	112,751.25
July 1, 1901, outstanding liabilities	12,414.17
July 1, 1901, balance available	100,337.08

ALLOTMENT.

Gun and mortar batteries.

November 9, 1900, act May 25, 1900	$130,000.00

Electric light and power plant.—The preparation of plans and specifications for a central plant to be used jointly for emplacement service and post lighting has been completed. Contracts have been entered into for storage batteries and switchboards. All bids for boiler and generator were rejected and new proposals invited which are to be opened July 5, 1901.

Work on the power house has been started and the excavation therefor 80 per cent completed. One hundred and seventy-eight cubic yards of earth and 709 cubic yards of rock have been removed, the former costing 68 cents per cubic yard and the latter $1.19 per cubic yard, which, however, does not include any cost for plant.

Money statement.

GUN AND MORTAR BATTERIES.

Allotted January 3, 1901		$34,500.00
June 30, 1901, amount expended during fiscal year		2,173.79
July 1, 1901, balance unexpended		32,326.21
July 1, 1901, outstanding liabilities	$386.72	
July 1, 1901 amount covered by uncompleted contracts	5,377.00	
		5,763.72
July 1, 1901, balance available		26,562.49

APPENDIX 3—FORTIFICATIONS.

ALLOTMENT.

Gun and mortar batteries.

January 3, 1901, act May 25, 1900... $34,500.00

Contracts in force during fiscal year ending June 30, 1901.

    Name of contractor: H. B. Coho & Co. (For switchboards.)
    Date of contract: May 2, 1901.
    Date of approval: May 16, 1901.
    Time for completion: July 19, 1901.
    Price, $1,677.
    Name of contractor: Sipe & Sigler. (For accumulators.)
    Date of contract: May 8, 1901.
    Date of approval: May 28, 1901.
    Time for completion: October 10, 1901.
    Price, $3,700.

Emplacements for two 6-inch B. L. rifles on pedestal mounts.—The preparation of plans for this battery is in progress and will be completed at an early date.

Money statement.

Allotted November 9, 1900... $30,000.00
July 1, 1901, balance unexpended 30,000.00

ALLOTMENT.

Gun and mortar batteries.

November 9, 1900, act May 25, 1900....................................... $30,000.00

Mining casemate.—Plans have been completed and approved, but no field work has yet been started. The only expenditures have been for tools.

Money statement.

Allotted October 20, 1900 .... $5,000.00
June 30, 1901, amount expended during fiscal year 15.04
                                                                                       —————
July 1, 1901, balance unexpended 4,984.96

ALLOTMENT.

Torpedoes for harbor defense.

October 20, 1900, act May 25, 1900.. $5,000.00

Preservation and repair of fortifications.—An agreement has been entered into with George Lanzendoerfer for glazing the walls and ceilings of the magazine in the five 10-inch emplacements in order to render them impervious to moisture. Owing to the continued illness of Mr. Lanzendoerfer the work has not yet been started.

The work at this site has been in charge of Charles P. Williams, junior engineer inspector.

Money statement.

July 1, 1900, balance unexpended $114.67
Allotted September 21, 1900.. 1,000.00
                                                                                       —————
                                                                               1,114.67
June 30, 1901, amount expended during fiscal year .... .49
                                                                                      —————
June 1, 1901, balance unexpended... 1,114.18

ALLOTMENTS.

Preservation and repair of fortifications.

August 18, 1899, act March 3, 1899	$12,000.00
September 21, 1900, act May 7, 1898	543.20
September 21, 1900, act March 3, 1899	456.80

SITE NO. 3.

Eight emplacements for 8-inch B. L. rifles on disappearing carriages, model 1896.—These emplacements are divided into three batteries.

Three-gun battery (first battery): At the beginning of the fiscal year work was completed, except the sand portions of the parapet and some minor details. Carriages had been assembled. Guns were on hand, but not mounted.

During the year work was completed, guns mounted, and battery turned over to the artillery January 22, 1901.

Shrinkage cracks appearing on the platforms, a V-shaped groove was cut along the line of the cracks and filled with bitumen.

Two-gun battery: At the beginning of this fiscal year this battery was completed, except placing loam and minor details. Carriages had been assembled and guns were on hand, but not mounted.

During the year work was completed, guns mounted, and battery turned over to the artillery under date of January 22, 1901.

Three-gun battery (second battery): At the beginning of the fiscal year emplacement No. 2 was practically completed, No. 1 nearly so, and No. 3 about 30 per cent completed. Three carriages and one gun were on hand, but not mounted.

During the year the battery was practically completed. Slopes have not yet been covered with loam and some excavation remains to be done in the roadway in rear.

Three gun carriages were assembled and one gun mounted. A second gun is on hand and was placed on the parapet ready for mounting as soon as certain ordnance work on its carriage is completed.

The principal items of work on this battery during the year were 2,126 cubic yards concrete, 349 cubic yards stone masonry, and 2,846 cubic yards earth fill.

The rubble masonry was used in the 2-foot walls. It was laid in natural cement mortar 1 to 2, and cost in place $6.76 per cubic yard. The cost of concrete, which was machine mixed, was as follows:

Platform, 1:3:5 (Portland) per cubic yard	$5.75
Parapet and traverses, 1:3:5 do	5.58
Parapet and traverses, 1:4:7 (Portland) do	4.74
Parapet and traverses, 1:3:5 (Rosendale) do	4.25
Cement mortar finish, 1:2 (Portland) do	11.70

These prices do not include the cost of sheathing.

Permanent water supply.—During the year a wooden water tank having a capacity of 21,000 gallons was erected and it was connected with the artesian well and pump and with the first three-gun battery and the two-gun battery by means of a 4-inch cast-iron main.

APPENDIX 3—FORTIFICATIONS.

Money statements.

GUN AND MORTAR BATTERIES.

For six 8-inch emplacements.

July 1, 1900, balance unexpended	$18,423.43
June 30, 1901, amount expended during fiscal year	15,403.28
July 1, 1901, balance unexpended	3,020.15
July 1, 1901, outstanding liabilities	136.09
July 1, 1901, balance available	2,884.06

For two 8-inch emplacements.

July 1, 1900, balance unexpended	$8,598.75
Allotted July 31, 1900	12,000.00
	20,598.75
June 30, 1901, amount expended during fiscal year	17,603.98
July 1, 1901, balance unexpended	2,994.77
July 1, 1901, outstanding liabilities	767.19
July 1, 1901, balance available	2,227.58

ALLOTMENTS.

For six 8-inch emplacements.

"National Defense:"
March 18, 1898, act March 9, 1898	$150,000
August 16, 1898, act March 9, 1898	90,691
February 27, 1899, act March 9, 1898	4,309
March 16, 1899, act March 9, 1898	30,000

Gun and mortar batteries:
June 29, 1899, act March 3, 1899	25,000
February 26, 1900, act July 7, 1898	17,000

For two 8-inch emplacements.

Gun and mortar batteries:
July 16, 1898, act May 7, 1898	$70,000
July 31, 1900, act July 7, 1898	12,000

Emplacements for two 12-inch B. L. rifles on disappearing carriages.—At the beginning of the fiscal year the battery was nearly completed and guns mounted.

During the year work was completed and the battery turned over to the artillery under date of April 16, 1901. Prior to the transfer one of the guns was dismounted in order that certain defects in the mechanism of the carriage could be remedied by the Ordnance Department.

Money statement.

GUN AND MORTAR BATTERIES.

July 1, 1900, balance unexpended	$1,424.56
June 30, 1901, amount expended during fiscal year	1,424.56

ALLOTMENTS.

Gun and mortar batteries.

March 16, 1897, act June 6, 1896	$200.00
March 27, 1897, act June 6, 1896	800.00
March 27, 1897, act March 3, 1897	70,000.00
August 13, 1897, act March 3, 1897	2,200.00
August 16, 1898, act March 3, 1897	36,800.00
October 30, 1899, act May 7, 1898	9,000.00

Battery for eight 12-inch B. L. mortars.—At the beginning of the fiscal year 80 per cent of the excavation had been made and about 15 per cent of the concrete placed. During the year the eastern and middle traverses have been completed except the loam surfacing and part of the sand fill, both mortar pits have been completed, and eight mortar carriages have been assembled.

In addition floors have been laid in the western traverse and the heavy wall of this traverse brought up to ceiling level.

The principal items of work during the year were 1,725 cubic yards rock excavation, 2,186 cubic yards earth excavation, 5,892 cubic yards concrete, 4,407 cubic yards sand fill, and 2,345 square yards asphalt waterproofing three-fourths inch thick.

The waterproofing cost $1.56 per square yard. The cost of concrete mixed in a 5-foot cylindrical mixer and placed by derricks was as follows:

Walls, 1:4:8 (Portland)	per cubic yard..	$4.30
Roof, 1:3:6 (Portland)	do....	5.39
Roof, 1:2:4 (Rosendale)	do....	[1] 4.33
Mortar finish, 1:2 (Portland)	do....	10.26

These prices do not include the cost of sheathing.

Money statement.

GUN AND MORTAR BATTERIES.

July 1, 1900, balance unexpended	$61,533.54
Allotted January 14 and April 8, 1901	21,000.00
	82,533.54
June 30, 1901, amount expended during fiscal year	62,771.96
July 1, 1901, balance unexpended	19,761.58
July 1, 1901, outstanding liabilities	3,252.57
July 1, 1901, balance available	16,509.01

ALLOTMENTS.

Gun and mortar batteries.

July 30, 1898, act May 7, 1898	$116,000.00
January 14, 1901, act May 25, 1900	20,000.00
April 8, 1901, act May 25, 1900	1,000.00

Emplacements for two 6-inch B.L. rifles on disappearing carriages.—At the beginning of the fiscal year the excavation had been completed. During the year the concrete portion of one emplacement was completed and the masonry of the other brought up to ceiling level, except the gun platform, which was completed.

One carriage is on hand but not mounted. No fill has yet been placed. The principal item of work during the year was 3,386 cubic yards of concrete. The cost of concrete was as follows:

Walls, 1:4:8 (Portland)	per cubic yard..	$4.66
Platform, 1:3:5 (Portland)	do....	6.35
Parapet and traverse, 1:3:5 (Portland)	do....	6.43
Platforms, 1:3:6 (Portland)	do....	4.79
Parapet and traverse, 1:2:4 (Rosendale)	do....	[2] 4.29
Mortar finish, 1:2 (Portland)	do....	10.32

These prices do not include the cost of sheathing.

---

[1] Thirteen per cent of the mass was deflectors.
[2] Twenty-two per cent of the volume was deflectors.

APPENDIX 3—FORTIFICATIONS.

Money statement.

GUN AND MORTAR BATTERIES.

July 1, 1900, balance unexpended	$49,612.11
June 30, 1901, amount expended during fiscal year	31,288.50
July 1, 1901, balance unexpended	18,323.61
July 1, 1901, outstanding liabilities	3,427.44
July 1, 1901, balance available	14,896.17

ALLOTMENT.

Gun and mortar batteries.

March 17, 1899, act July 7, 1898	$56,000.00

Emplacements for two 15-pounder rapid-fire guns on balanced-pillar mounts (first battery.)—At the beginning of the fiscal year most of the excavation had been completed.

During the year the gun platforms were built and floors of magazines and rooms laid. Two guns and mounts are on hand not mounted except the base castings.

Money statement.

GUN AND MORTAR BATTERIES.

July 1, 1900, balance unexpended	$9,554.58
June 30, 1901, amount expended during fiscal year	1,125.09
July 1, 1901, balance unexpended	8,429.49
July 1, 1901, outstanding liabilities	1,074.36
July 1, 1901, balance available	7,355.13

ALLOTMENT.

Gun and mortar batteries.

March 27, 1899, act July 7, 1898	$10,000.00

Emplacements for two 15-pounder rapid-fire guns on balanced-pillar mounts (second battery).—Work was begun in April, 1901. The excavation has been completed, a concrete mixer partly erected (to be run in connection with other work), and track laid to connect mixing plant and battery. Cement has been received and stored.

No guns or mounts are on hand.

Money statement.

GUN AND MORTAR BATTERIES.

Allotted during fiscal year	$9,103.10
June 30, 1901, amount expended during fiscal year	1,055.99
July 1, 1901, balance unexpended	8,047.11
July 1, 1901, outstanding liabilities	1,485.41
July 1, 1901, balance available	6,561.70

ALLOTMENTS.

Gun and mortar batteries.

November 9, 1900, act May 25, 1900	$8,625.00
May 1, 1901, act March 1, 1901	[1]478.10

---
[1] To cover cost of triangulation of Portland Harbor.

708   REPORT OF THE CHIEF OF ENGINEERS, U. S. ARMY.

Mining casemate, No. 1.—Work was begun April, 1901, and has consisted of earth and ledge excavation and the removal of parts of the old casemate that interfered with the new. Excavation is completed.

Money statement.

TORPEDOES FOR HARBOR DEFENSE.

Allotted March 1, 1901	$5,500.00
June 30, 1901, amount expended during fiscal year	107.07
July 1, 1901, balance unexpended	5,392.93
July 1, 1901, outstanding liabilities	344.10
July 1, 1901, balance unexpended	5,048.83

ALLOTMENT.

Torpedoes for harbor defense.

March 19, 1901, act March 1, 1901 .... $5,500.00

Mining casemate, No. 2.—Work was begun in June, 1901, and has consisted of earth excavation and the removal of parts of the old casemate that interfered with the new. About half the excavation is completed.

Money statement.

Allotted June 15, 1901	$4,500.00
July 1, 1901, outstanding liabilities	102.15
July 1, 1901, balance available	4,397.85

ALLOTMENT.

Torpedoes for harbor defense.

June 15, 1901:
Act March 3, 1899	$76.49
Act March 1, 1901	4,423.51

Emplacements for two 6-inch B. L. rifles on pedestal mounts.—Plans for this battery have been completed and approved, but no field work has yet been started.

Money statement.

GUN AND MORTAR BATTERIES.

Allotted June 6, 1901	$25,000.00
July 1, 1901, balance unexpended	25,000.00

ALLOTMENT.

Gun and mortar batteries.

June 26, 1901, act March 1, 1901 .... $25,000.00

SITE NO. 4.

Emplacements for three 15-pounder rapid-fire guns on balanced-pillar mounts.—Plans for this battery have been completed and forwarded for approval. No funds have yet been allotted.

Work at this site was in charge of Mr. Charles P. Williams, junior engineer inspector, until January 1, 1901; since that date in charge of Mr. Charles R. Hall, overseer.

APPENDIX 3—FORTIFICATIONS. 709

SITE NO. 5.

Emplacements Nos. 3 and 4 for two 12-inch rifles on disappearing carriages.—At the beginning of the fiscal year Emplacement No. 4 was practically completed to the platform level. At Emplacement No. 3 the excavation was completed and drains laid. Emplacement No. 4 is now completed, except placing loam on parapet and grading roadway. Carriage is assembled and gun mounted. Emplacement No. 3 is nearly completed. Three hundred and twenty-five cubic yards of concrete and part of the sand parapet are yet to be placed, and the erection of trolley rails and ammunition hoists is not completed.

Including deflectors and mortar finish, 5,558 cubic yards of concrete was placed in these two emplacements during the year. Six hundred and fifty square yards of asphalt was laid, and 2,324 cubic yards of rock waste and sand were placed as fill.

Money statement.

GUN AND MORTAR BATTERIES.

July 1, 1900, balance unexpended	$43,939.72
Allotted February 13, 1901	10,000.00
	53,939.72
June 30, 1901, amount expended during fiscal year	35,916.48
July 1, 1901, balance unexpended	18,023.24
July 1, 1901, outstanding liabilities	8,873.63
July 1, 1901, balance available	14,149.61

ALLOTMENTS.

Gun and mortar batteries.

July 13, 1898, act May 7, 1898	$110,000.00
May 4, 1900, act July 7, 1898	17,000.00
February 13, 1901, act May 25, 1900	10,000.00

Emplacement No. 2, for one 12-inch rifle on disappearing carriage.—At the beginning of the fiscal year most of the excavation and about half the drainage system was completed.

During the year the following work was done: Four hundred and fifty-nine cubic yards rock excavation, 98 linear feet drains, 230 cubic yards loose rock fill, and 337 cubic yards concrete in floors and wall foundations. Forms for building the rooms have been erected over half the area of the emplacement.

Money statement.

GUN AND MORTAR BATTERIES.

July 1, 1900, balance unexpended	$35,231.93
Allotted February 13, 1901	10,500.00
	45,731.93
June 30, 1901, amount expended during fiscal year	8,175.58
July 1, 1901, balance unexpended	37,556.35
July 1, 1901, outstanding liabilities	1,151.60
July 1, 1901, balance available	36,404.75

ALLOTMENTS.

Gun and mortar batteries.

May 23, 1899, act March 3, 1899	$52,000.00
February 13, 1901, act May 25, 1900	10,500.00

Emplacements Nos. 3 and 4, for 10-inch rifles on disappearing carriages.—At the beginning of the fiscal year Emplacement No. 4 had been brought up to roof level. The battery is now practically completed, barring the right flank traverse, the construction of which has been, for reasons of economy, postponed until work on the adjacent 6-inch battery is begun.

Both carriages are assembled and both guns in their trunnions.

The work of the year included 4,631 cubic yards of concrete, 523 square yards of asphalt, and 5,133 cubic yards of sand fill.

Work on the above-mentioned emplacements at Site No. 4 was carried on simultaneously by means of a central stone-crushing and concrete-mixing plant, and unit prices have been computed for the work as a whole.

The following table shows the cost of the principal items of work during the year. Prices do not include first cost of plant:

1,245 square yards asphalt mastic three-fourths inch thick...per square yard..	$1.02
262 square yards P. and B. paint ....do....	.20
9,351 cubic yards rock (crushing)............per cubic yard..	.43
1,716 cubic yards concrete (Rosendale) ....do....	3.78
7,567 cubic yards concrete (Portland)............do....	4.52
499 cubic yards deflectors............do....	1.02
744 cubic yards mortar (Portland) ....do....	8.32

Money statement.

GUN AND MORTAR BATTERIES.

July 1, 1900, balance unexpended	$37,658.57
June 30, 1901, amount expended during fiscal year	30,340.02
July 1, 1901, balance unexpended	7,318.55
July 1, 1901, outstanding liabilities	5,395.03
July 1, 1901, balance available	1,923.52

ALLOTMENTS.

Gun and mortar batteries.

July 25, 1898, act July 7, 1898	$92,000.00
May 4, 1900, act July 7, 1898	26,000.00

Three emplacements for 15-pounder rapid-fire guns on balanced-pillar mounts.—At the beginning of the fiscal year the excavation was completed, some fill placed, drains laid and parts of the foundations built.

The battery has been completed.

The following table shows the cost of the work. There were practically no expenditures for plant, use having been made of plant purchased for construction of the 10-inch and 12-inch batteries.

APPENDIX 3—FORTIFICATIONS.

Materials and labor.

Roadway	$923.70
Drains, including 68¼ cubic yards rock excavation	453.44
Earth excavation, 290 cubic yards, at $0.683	198.24
Rock excavation, exclusive of drains, 1,932 cubic yards, at $2.442	4,717.95
Concrete, 921 cubic yards, at $6.893	6,348.68
Asphalt, 72 square yards, at $0.9622	69.28
Iron work (stairs, beams, hand rails, etc.)	1,175.65
Doors	118.71
Armament (receiving, mounting, and care of guns)	94.57
Earthwork fill, 893 cubic yards, at $0.594	530.45
Earthwork grading and turfing, 356 square yards, at $0.355	126.36
Removing plant and clearing up	60.79
June 30, 1901, total expended	14,817.82
Balance	182.18
	15,000.00

Money statement.

GUN AND MORTAR BATTERIES.

July 1, 1900, balance unexpended	$5,021.20
Allotted July 31, 1900	2,000.00
	7,021.20
June 30, 1901, amount expended during fiscal year	6,835.27
July 1, 1901, balance unexpended	185.93
July 1, 1901, outstanding liabilities	3.75
July 1, 1901, balance available	182.18

ALLOTMENTS.

Gun and mortar batteries.

February 1, 1899, act July 7, 1898	$13,000.00
July 31, 1900, act July 7, 1898	2,000.00

Armament.—The following table shows the cost of handling, caring for, and mounting guns and carriages:

Twelve-inch rifle, No. 28, model 1895:
- Receiving and placing on blocks $60.00
- Cleaning and care, seven months 50.25
- Appliances for moving 143.59
    - $253.84

Twelve-inch rifle, No. 13, model 1895:
- Receiving and placing on blocks 60.00
- Moving and mounting 280.87
- Cleaning and care, seven months 50.25
    - 391.12

Twelve-inch disappearing carriage, No. 18:
- Receiving and placing on blocks 175.04
- Cleaning and care, seven months 332.25
    - 507.29

Twelve-inch disappearing carriage, No. 13:
- Receiving and placing on blocks 169.38
- Moving and assembling 759.99
- Cleaning and care, eighteen months 394.84
    - 1,324.21

Ten-inch rifle, No. 19, model 1895:
- Receiving and placing on blocks 71.81
- Moving and mounting 152.25
- Cleaning and care, fifteen months 36.16
    - 260.22

Ten-inch rifle, No. 17, model 1895:
Receiving and placing on blocks	$71.81	
Moving and mounting	117.05	
Cleaning and care, fifteen months	21.46	
		$210.32

Ten-inch disappearing carriage, No. 67:
Receiving and placing on blocks	199.10	
Moving and assembling	460.45	
Cleaning and care, twenty-one months	210.60	
		870.15

Ten-inch disappearing carriage, No. 68:
Receiving and placing on blocks	202.46	
Moving and assembling	417.60	
Cleaning and care, eighteen months	225.30	
		845.36

Work at this site was in charge of Lieut. Thomas H. Jackson, Corps of Engineers, until September 20, 1900; since that date in charge of Mr. Thomas Robinson, assistant engineer.

RANGE-FINDING STATIONS.

Battery commanders' stations.—At Sites No. 1 and No. 3, seven high-site range and position finder stations have been authorized and the plans therefor approved.

The two at Site No. 1 are entirely completed. At Site No. 3 the excavation has been completed for the five stations and the foundation of one of them is completed.

Money statement.

GUN AND MORTAR BATTERIES.

July 1, 1900, balance unexpended	$5,568.00
Allotted December 20, 1900	4,000.00
	9,568.00
June 30, 1901, amount expended during fiscal year	95.59
July 1, 1901, balance unexpended	9,472.41
July 1, 1901, outstanding liabilities	391.30
July 1, 1901, balance available	9,081.11

ALLOTMENTS.

Gun and mortar batteries.

April 8, 1899, act July 7, 1898	$9,000.00
December 20, 1900:	
Act July 7, 1898	1,500.24
Act May 25, 1900	2,499.76

Temporary stations for range and position finders.—By Department indorsement of June 11, 1901, the construction of two temporary stations was authorized, one at Site No. 4, for Lewis type A instrument, and one at Site No. 1, for base-end instruments. The former is completed, and the latter will be constructed in the near future.

APPENDIX 3—FORTIFICATIONS.

Money statement.

GUN AND MORTAR BATTERIES.

Allotted June 11, 1901	$100.00
July 1, 1901, outstanding liabilities	30.50
July 1, 1901, balance available	69.50

TORPEDO DEFENSE.

Torpedo material.—The torpedo material for the district has been cared for, and, as needed, overhauled and cleaned, under allotments from appropriation for "Preservation and Repair of Fortifications."

Money statement.

July 1, 1900, balance unexpended	$35.49
Allotted May 10, 1901	150.00
	185.49
June 30, 1901, amount expended during fiscal year	91.47
July 1, 1901, balance unexpended	94.02
July 1, 1901, outstanding liabilities	68.58
July 1, 1901, balance available	25.44

Torpedoes for harbor defense, January 1, 1899.—An allotment of $2.01 was made September 5, 1900, from this appropriation to provide for payment of outstanding liabilities for telegrams.

Money statement.

Allotted September 5, 1900	$2.01
June 30, 1901, amount expended during fiscal year	2.01

Two Treasury settlements, aggregating $1.41, for accounts for telegrams were also made from this appropriation during the year.

SUPPLIES FOR SEACOAST DEFENSES.

Under funds allotted for the purpose, a small quantity of supplies has been furnished post commanders on requisitions approved by the Chief of Engineers.

Money statement.

July 1, 1900, balance unexpended	$600.00
June 30, 1901, amount expended during fiscal year	30.68
July 1, 1901, balance unexpended	569.32

---

3 B.

DEFENSES OF PORTSMOUTH, N. H.

Officers in charge, Maj. Walter L. Fisk, Corps of Engineers, until December 15, 1900, and Capt. Harry Taylor, Corps of Engineers, since that date; Division Engineers, Col. George L. Gillespie, Corps of Engineers (now brigadier-general, Chief of Engineers, United States

Army), until April 30, 1901, and Col. Charles R. Suter, Corps of Engineers, since May 9, 1901.

Emplacements for two 8-inch guns on disappearing carriages.—This battery, which was built under contract, was completed with the exception of the electric-lighting plant and turned over to the troops during the fiscal year 1899. A mining casemate which had been built in connection with the battery had also been completed at a total cost of $3,833.60.

Money statement.

July 1, 1900, balance unexpended	$4,088.81
June 30, 1901, amount expended during fiscal year	1.61
July 1, 1901, balance unexpended	4,087.20
July 1, 1901, outstanding liabilities	15.04
July 1, 1901, balance available	4,072.16

Emplacements for three 10-inch guns on disappearing carriages.— At the beginning of the fiscal year a wharf had been built and a railroad, 36-inch gauge, connecting the wharf with all parts of the work had been laid. The necessary buildings had been built and the plant installed. The excavation was completed, about one-third of the earth fill was in place, and about one-third of the concrete was in place.

The work was carried on continuously through the summer and fall months, although it was delayed somewhat on account of the failure of the water supply due to the extreme dryness of the season. The water supply on the reservation is insufficient and the water used was obtained from a small pond near the work until it failed, when water was bought in Portsmouth and transported by boat to the work.

The concrete work was completed the last of October with the exception of about 15 cubic yards for floors under the ammunition hoists.

During the months of November and December, 1900, and January and February, 1901, a small force of men was employed in erecting ironwork, such as trolly beams and railings, and in hanging the doors and in covering the loading platforms, parapet wall, and rear wall of the emplacements with a waterproof solution, moving the carriages, and storing the plant. Work was closed on the last of February for the season. Mr. J. W. Walker, overseer, was in local charge of the work up to February 28, 1901.

Work was resumed the last of March, 1901, and has been carried on without delay up to June 30, 1901. The work consisted in erecting the ammunition hoists, completing the earth fill in the parapet, assembling and mounting the gun carriages, demolishing two concrete magazines of the old work which were in the field of fire of the present battery, cleaning up and grading in front and rear of the battery, grading the slope in rear of the battery, and taking down and storing the plant used on the work. On June 30 the above had nearly all been accomplished and the battery itself was practically completed, with the exception of seeding the slopes and some cleaning up of the site of the plant and grounds near the work and making a road to connect with the roadway in rear of the battery.

Two 10-inch B. L. rifles have been received, and the carriages are ready to receive them when some changes which are being made by the Ordnance Department are completed.

The cost of the work, excluding the expenses of the general office

APPENDIX 3—FORTIFICATIONS.

chargeable against this work, up to June 30, 1901, was $146,830.86, and this amount is made up from the following items:

Superintendence	$9,330.50
Permanent plant, tools, etc.	21,991.02
Installation of plant	2,580.56
Temporary structures	4,295.98
Buildings	2,859.84
Excavation	9,193.99
Drainage system	2,687.53
Rock filling under floors	715.56
Concrete, 9,870 cubic yards	63,148.69
Embankment	5,746.47
Doors	486.91
Steel beams, railings, etc.	6,956.89
Ammunition hoists	4,688.92
Painting ironwork and waterproofing concrete	436.81
Wharf	5,325.56
Moving and assembling carriages	1,519.41
Maintenance of plant	4,866.22
Total	146,830.86

The cost per cubic yard of concrete in place was $6.397+, and was made up of the following items:

Cement	$3.493+
Sand	.476+
Stone	.568+
Coal, water, oil, etc.	.232+
False work (forms)	.548+
Mixing	.266+
Placing	.510+
Ramming	.147+
Testing cement	.143+
Trimming and dressing concrete	.014+
Total	6.397+

Since work was resumed in March, 1901, it has been under the immediate charge of Mr. W. F. Robinson, assistant engineer, with Mr. C. F. Woodbury, overseer, in local charge.

Money statement.

July 1, 1900, balance unexpended	$68,020.28
November 26, 1900, additional allotment	12,000.00
	80,020.28
June 30, 1901, amount expended during fiscal year	73,655.61
July 1, 1901, balance unexpended	6,364.67
July 1, 1901, outstanding liabilities	2,971.75
July 1, 1901, balance available	3,392.92

Contract in force during fiscal year.

Contractor.	Article.	Price per barrel.	Entered into.	Approved.	Commence.	Complete.
Waldo Bros., Boston, Mass.	"Atlas" Portland cement.	$2.24	Apr. 28, 1900	May 14, 1900	At once...	Nov. 1, 1900

Emplacements for two 12-inch guns on disappearing carriages.—A preliminary allotment of $2,000 was made April 15, 1901, for drilling an artesian well for obtaining water for use in construction of these emplacements, and at the close of the fiscal year the well had been drilled to a depth of 185 feet. Plans and estimates for the battery were submitted and at the close of the year were awaiting the action of the Department.

Money statement.

April 15, 1901, amount allotted	$2,000.00
July 1, 1901, outstanding liabilities	925.00
July 1, 1901, balance available	1,075.00

Cable tank.—At the close of the last fiscal year a cable tank had been completed, with the exception of gutters and providing means for filling the tank. During the year the gutters have been placed and a cistern for a water supply for the tank has been built under the torpedo storehouse. The installation of a pump for transferring water to the tank yet remains to be done.

Money statement.

July 1, 1900, balance unexpended	$317.90
April 2, 1901, additional allotment	300.00
	17.90
June 30, 1901, amount expended during fiscal year	12.53
July 1, 1901, balance unexpended	605.37
July 1, 1901, outstanding liabilities	505.37
July 1, 1901, balance available	100.00

Torpedo storehouse.—An allotment was made July 13, 1900, for the construction of a torpedo storehouse, and at the close of the fiscal year the building was completed with the exception of a few minor details and the installation of a traveling crane for handling the torpedo material. The building is of brick, 72 by 32 feet, with slate roof, and has a cistern underneath of about 15,000 gallons capacity for the storage of water for the cable tank.

Money statement.

July 13, 1900, amount allotted	$5,000.00
April 2, 1901, additional allotment	700.00
	5,700.00
June 30, 1901, amount expended during fiscal year	10.00
July 1, 1901, balance unexpended	5,690.00
July 1, 1901, outstanding liabilities	4,910.63
July 1, 1901, balance available	779.37

Fort McClary, Me.—The work under allotments for preservation and repair pertaining to this fort consisted in overhauling and caring for the torpedo material and in preparing the surplus and unserviceable material for shipment to the Engineer Depot preparatory to transferring the serviceable material to the artillery.

Money statement.

July 1, 1900, balance unexpended	$534.71
June 30, 1901, amount expended during fiscal year	198.46
July 1, 1901, balance unexpended	336.25

Fort Constitution, N. H.—The work done at this fort under allotments for preservation and repair consisted in repairing the wharf and constructing a landing stage, reshingling and painting engineer office building, and repairing roadway to reservation.

Money statement.

July 1, 1900, balance unexpended	$914.51
August 20, 1900, amount allotted	345.00
	1,259.51
June 30, 1901, amount expended during fiscal year	832.56
July 1, 1901, balance unexpended	426.95

---

3 C.

BOSTON HARBOR, MASSACHUSETTS.

Officers in charge, Col. Charles R. Suter, Corps of Engineers, until May 31, 1901, after which date in charge of Capt. Harry Taylor, Corps of Engineers, to whom the works were transferred through Lieut. Col. William S. Stanton, Corps of Engineers; assistant, Lieut. Robert R. Raymond, Corps of Engineers; Division Engineer, Col. Charles R. Suter, Corps of Engineer, since May 31, 1901.

SITE NO. 1.

Emplacements for five 10-inch guns on disappearing carriages.—Funds have been allotted as follows:

September 8, 1890	$50,000.00
December 12, 1891	106,194.05
August 16, 1895	35,138.16
August 16, 1895	7,000.00
August 16, 1895	9,000.00
August 16, 1895	2,000.00
August 2, 1898	3,800.00
May 15, 1899	3,000.00
May 31, 1899	2,500.00
Total	218,632.21
Withdrawn March 29, 1894	4,300.00
	214,332.21

Of this amount $214,147.50 has been expended up to July 1, 1900, leaving a balance available of $182.71.

Emplacements Nos. 3 and 4 were begun and partially completed under the appropriation for "National Defense."

At the beginning of the fiscal year the guns were mounted and the emplacements were complete with the exception of the road in rear of the battery. During the year the concrete plant used for constructing these and other emplacements was removed, but the completion of the road was postponed to await the result of a study of the general problem of grading the post.

Money statement.

July 1, 1900, balance available	$182.71
Expended during the fiscal year	129.64
Deposited to the credit of United States Treasurer	53.07

Emplacements for two 12-inch guns on disappearing carriages.—These emplacements were authorized June 4, 1898. Plans were submitted to the Chief of Engineers October 19, 1898, and resubmitted, changed in some details, December 28, 1898.

The gun platforms rest upon concrete masses placed upon natural ground in front of the old scarp wall, the magazines and other rooms being placed in the casemates of the old work.

At the beginning of the fiscal year the concrete was completed except the gun platforms, which were omitted to allow the mass of concrete upon which they stand to settle and come to a position of rest. The earth cover of the parapet was also nearly complete.

During the year the platforms were completed and the armament was mounted by hired labor.

No settlement has taken place. The earth parapet was completed, but is still settling and will probably require grading in the future. On account of the large drainage area of the superior slope trouble was experienced with slides on the exterior slope. To remedy this a trench was cut just above the exterior crest, in which tile drain with open joints was laid. The trench was then filled with gravel and sand. No slides have occurred since this drain was completed.

Two ammunition cranes were installed for each gun. These consist of davits of steel I-beam section with cast-iron gudgeons and bushings, resting in cast-iron steps and wrought-iron collars bolted to the face of the parade wall. The general form is similar to that of the usual crane, but the weight is much less, while the strength and rigidity are greater and the cost is less than one-half. (See report on technical details of fortification works in Boston Harbor, Appendix 4 B.)

The following allotments for the work have been made:

January 3, 1899, act of May 7, 1898	$123,000
March 3, 1900, act of March 3, 1897	5,772
May 4, 1900, act of July 7, 1898	7,488
June 27, 1900, act of July 7, 1898	1,027
June 27, 1900, act of May 25, 1900	1,473
August 16, 1900, act of May 25, 1900	3,400
November 20, 1900, act of July 7, 1898	2,000
Total	144,160

Money statement.

July 1, 1900, balance available	$10,917.26
Allotted since	5,400.00
	16,317.26
Expended during the fiscal year	16,280.16
July 1, 1901, balance available	37.10

APPENDIX 3—FORTIFICATIONS. 719

Battery of three 15-pounder rapid-fire guns.—This battery was authorized by the Chief of Engineers November 1, 1898, and the plans were approved June 23, 1899.

The following allotments for its construction were made from the appropriation for "Gun and Mortar Batteries:"

June 23, 1899, act of July 7, 1898	$9,300
October 20, 1899, act of July 7, 1898	2,200
December 6, 1899, act of July 7, 1898	800
February 19, 1900, act of July 7, 1898	450
Total	12,750

At the beginning of the fiscal year the battery was complete, the armament mounted, and the work was turned over to the artillery. During the year all outstanding liabilities were settled.

Money statement.

July 1, 1900, balance available	$11.62
Expended during the fiscal year	11.62

Range-finder stations.—A plan and estimate for a range-finder station was submitted to the Chief of Engineers July 5, 1899. This was returned approved July 8, 1899. The station was intended to be built for the control of one battery, but as this location was found to interfere with the future construction of a gun emplacement contemplated by the existing project for the defense of Boston Harbor the construction of the fire commander's station was authorized July 24, 1899.

The construction of two additional range-finder stations was authorized June 13, 1900.

The following allotments were made from the appropriation for "Gun and Mortar Batteries:"

July 8, 1899, act of July 7, 1898	$4,180
February 19, 1900, act of July 7, 1898	425
June 13, 1900, act of May 25, 1900	8,400
October 18, 1900, act of May 25, 1900	3,600
February 11, 1901, act of May 25, 1900	420
Total	17,025

At the beginning of the fiscal year one station was complete. This station was turned over to the artillery October 24, 1900.

During the year the other two stations were completed. These stations are of brick, with independent concrete piers for the instrument foundations. The roofs are of concrete and glass sidewalk construction. Floors are of concrete, supported on beams of concrete and twisted steel.

Money statements.

ONE STATION.

July 1, 1900, balance available	$89.57
Expended during the fiscal year	89.57

TWO STATIONS.

July 1, 1900, balance available	$8,400.00
Allotted since	4,020.00
	12,420.00
Expended during the fiscal year	12,420.00

Underground conduit system.—The construction of this system of conduits was authorized by the Chief of Engineers October 9, 1899.

The system consists of four vitrified ducts set in concrete at a depth of at least 3 feet, with manholes at convenient intervals for drawing in the wires. A manhole is placed in the immediate vicinity of each emplacement or range-finder station, from which branches are conveniently run. An open-joint tile drain running below the ducts and connecting and draining the manholes has proved of great value. Plans were approved October 9, 1899.

Allotments for the work were made as follows from the appropriation for "Gun and Mortar Batteries:"

October 9, 1899, act of July 7, 1898	$7,000
June 14, 1900, act of May 25, 1900	2,250
Total	9,250

At the beginning of the year about 3,000 feet of the system was complete.

During the year the system was completed.

Money statement.

July 1, 1900, balance available	$2,687.95
Expended during the fiscal year	2,687.95

Central electric-lighting plant.—The plans for this work were approved November 15, 1899, and the expenditure of $10,000 for the installation of the plant was authorized. A description of the plant is contained in the last annual report. At the beginning of the fiscal year the plant was complete in all respects. It was turned over to the artillery December 1, 1900.

Money statement.

July 1, 1900, balance available	$44.14
Expended during the fiscal year	44.14

Mounting guns.—This work consisted in mounting two 12-inch B. L. rifles on disappearing carriages, model 1897.

The following allotments were made from the appropriation for "Gun and Mortar Batteries:"

June 27, 1900, act of July 7, 1898	$1,027
June 27, 1900, act of May 25, 1900	1,473
February 11, 1901, act of March 3, 1899	440
Total	2,940

At the beginning of the fiscal year nothing had been done. During the year the guns and carriages were moved from the position near the wharf, where they had been placed by the contractor for their transportation, and mounted in the emplacements ready for service. The work was performed by hired labor, ordinary methods being employed.

Money statement.

July 1, 1900, balance available	$2,500.00
Allotted since	440.00
	2,940.00
Expended during the fiscal year	2,897.52
July 1, 1901, balance available	42.48

APPENDIX 3—FORTIFICATIONS. 721

SITE NO. 2.

Emplacements for five 10-inch guns on disappearing carriages.—Allotments for these emplacements were made as follows:

November 17, 1892, act of July 23, 1892	$58,000.00
August 16, 1895, act of March 2, 1895	16,174.75
August 16, 1895, act of March 2, 1895	5,500.00
June 30, 1896, act of June 6, 1896	100,000.00
November 7, 1896, act of June 6, 1896	52,200.00
June 23, 1897, act of March 3, 1897	45,000.00
June 25, 1901, act of March 1, 1901	10,500.00
Total	287,374.75
March 3, 1900, withdrawn	960.30
Balance	286,414.45

At the beginning of the year the work was complete, except in rear of Emplacement 4, where the ground was occupied by the light-house, and all armament was mounted.

During the year the light-house was removed by the Treasury Department, and the grading of the roadway was begun.

The works were turned over to the artillery on October 21, 1899.

Money statement.

July 1, 1900, balance available	$2,282.34
Allotted since	10,500.00
	12,782.34
Expended during the fiscal year	1,978.67
July 1, 1901, balance available	10,803.67

Battery commander's station.—This statement resembles in its general features the stations described in the report for Site No. 1.

The following allotments were made:

June 7, 1899, act of July 7, 1898	$4,000
October 20, 1899, act of July 7, 1898	1,200
February 19, 1900, act of July 7, 1898	185
Total	5,385

At the beginning of the fiscal year the work was complete. The station was turned over to the artillery November 19, 1900.

Money statement.

July 1, 1900, balance available	$46.87
Expended during the fiscal year	46.87

Emplacements for two 15-pounder rapid-fire guns.—The plans of this battery were approved by the Chief of Engineers, July 19, 1899.

The following allotments were made from the appropriation for "Gun and Mortar Batteries:"

July 19, 1899, act of July 7, 1898	$9,000
October 20, 1899, act of July 7, 1898	2,700
December 8, 1899, act of July 7, 1898	1,500
August 16, 1900, act of May 25, 1900	5,300
February 11, 1901, act of March 3, 1899	280
Total	18,780

ENG 1901——46

At the beginning of the fiscal year the work was complete, except sodding the slopes and providing ammunition lifts.

During the year ammunition lifts were installed, the slopes were sodded, the bank in rear of the battery was graded and sodded, a large intercepting drain was built to prevent snow and water from entering the battery, and the armament was received and mounted. The battery was turned over to the artillery March 6, 1901.

Money statement.

July 1, 1900, balance available	$14.77
Allotted since	5,580.00
	5,594.77
Expended during the fiscal year	5,583.87
July 1, 1901, balance available	10.90

Central electric-lighting plant.—A description of this plant is contained in the last annual report. No work was done during the fiscal year. The plant was turned over to the artillery November 19, 1900.

Money statement.

July 1, 1900, balance available	$0.41
Expended during the fiscal year	.41

SITE NO. 3.

Emplacements for three 12-inch guns on disappearing carriages.—This battery was essentially completed with funds allotted from the appropriation for "National Defense." The following allotments were made from the appropriation for "Gun and Mortar Batteries:"

June 9, 1899, act of March 3, 1899	$9,000.00
August 19, 1899, act of July 7, 1898	6,000.00
June 1, 1900, act of July 7, 1898	5,800.00
December 14, 1899, act of March 3, 1899	2,500.00
March 30, 1900, act of June 6, 1896	19.50
March 30, 1900, act of May 7, 1898	376.68
March 30, 1900, act of March 3, 1899	103.82
Total	23,800.00

At the beginning of the fiscal year the battery was complete except in the following details: Speaking tubes, electric-light wiring, guardroom window shutters, water supply, road in rear of battery, and painting. The guns and carriages were mounted ready for service.

During the year the battery was completed in all respects, and the necessary steps were taken to turn it over to the artillery.

Money statement.

July 1, 1900, balance available	$5,734.25
Expended during the fiscal year	5,734.25

Range-finder stations.—The construction of these stations was authorized by the Chief of Engineers September 25, 1899. The following allotments were made from the appropriation for "Gun and Mortar Batteries:"

September 25, 1899, act of July 7, 1898	$6,400
August 23, 1900, act of July 7, 1898	2,600
Total	9,000

These stations resemble in their general features those described in the last annual report for Site No. 1.

At the beginning of the fiscal year the foundations were laid and the walls begun. During the year the work was completed in all respects.

Money statement.

July 1, 1900, balance available	$6,037.66
Allotted since	2,600.00
	8,637.66
Expended during the fiscal year	8,637.66

Underground conduit.—This work was authorized by the Chief of Engineers August 16, 1900, and an allotment of $780 was made on that date from the appropriation for "Gun and Mortar Batteries," act of May 25, 1900.

The conduit consists of vitrified ducts laid in concrete, brick manholes being constructed where needed for drawing in cables.

At the beginning of the fiscal year nothing had been done. During the year the work was completed, connecting the fire and battery commanders' stations with each other and with the gun emplacements.

Money statement.

Allotted August 16, 1900	$780.00
Expended during the fiscal year	780.00

SITE NO. 4.

Mortar battery.—On March 20, 1901, an allotment of $6,750 was made by the Chief of Engineers from the appropriation for "Gun and Mortar Batteries," act of May 25, 1900, for the construction of ventilators and drains and reconstruction of pavements in mortar pits.

At the beginning of the fiscal year the battery was complete, but the additional work above was required to place it in a serviceable condition. During the year the ventilators and drains were nearly completed, and the removal of the old pavements was begun. The system of ventilation adopted provides two ventilators for each magazine, the openings being placed as far apart as possible. Ordinary movements of the external atmosphere do not affect both openings alike, and a constant and gentle circulation is set up. This result has been found to have been attained in recent works.

The original drainage system provided two sumps for the surface drainage from the mortar pits. No outlets were provided, the water being absorbed by the earth. This system was inadequate, and ordinary rains flooded the passages and even the magazines of the battery. The floor level being no higher than the surrounding land, ordinary drains were not practicable. A trial pit developed the fact that the ground water level near the battery was about 5 feet below the floors, and the subsoil was a porous gravel. A cesspool 25 feet square was therefore built to receive the drainage. This provides for all water liable to fall upon the area drained in severe rainstorms, and the bottom of the cesspool being unpaved, the water is rapidly absorbed by the earth.

Money statement.

Allotted March 20, 1901	$6,750.00
Expended during the fiscal year	1,082.94
July 1, 1901, balance available	5,667.06

SITE NO. 5.

The Commonwealth of Massachusetts ceded jurisdiction over this site to the National Government by act approved April 6, 1897.

Mortar battery.—First half: A contract with Messrs. Yates & Triest, of New York, was entered into on June 9, 1898. Excavation was begun June 15, 1898. The contractors having failed to complete the work before November 1, 1898, as required by the contract, an extension of time was granted at their request October 26, 1898, requiring the work to be completed by June 1, 1899, on which date the contract expired by limitation.

An allotment of $108,000 was made July 22, 1897, from the appropriation for "Gun and Mortar Batteries."

The following funds were withdrawn for use elsewhere:

November 9, 1899	$3.10
November 15, 1899	16,300.00
March 1, 1900	375.00
March 3, 1900	5,772.00
March 3, 1900	1,000.00
	23,450.10

At the beginning of the fiscal year the battery was completed, except the installation of the electric-light plant. The armament was mounted.

During the year the electric-light conduits were installed, but the generating plant was not purchased, as the plant for the second half of the battery will provide the necessary power for all works on the post.

Money statement.

July 1, 1900, balance available	$1,514.00
Expended during the fiscal year	1,514.00

Second half: This work provides emplacements for eight 12-inch mortars. Allotments were made from the appropriation for "Gun and Mortar Batteries," as follows:

September 1, 1900, act of May 25, 1900	$75,000
February 26, 1901, act of May 25, 1900	38,000
Total	113,000

At the beginning of the fiscal year nothing had been done. During the year plans were submitted and approved, the working plant and quarters for the working force were installed, materials were purchased, the excavation was completed, drains were laid, about one-half of the foundations were placed, and the construction of forms was begun. (See report on technical details of fortification works in Boston Harbor, Appendix 4 B.)

No armament for this work has been received.

Money statement.

Allotted during the fiscal year	$113,000.00
Expended during the fiscal year	54,900.93
July 1, 1901, balance available	58,099.07

Emplacements for two 5-inch rapid-fire guns.—This work provides emplacements for two wire-wound rapid-fire guns on pedestal mounts.

APPENDIX 3—FORTIFICATIONS. 725

Allotments were made from the appropriation for "Gun and Mortar Batteries," as follows:

November 28, 1899, act of July 7, 1898	$20,000
August 16, 1900, act of May 25, 1900	3,800
Total	23,800

At the beginning of the fiscal year the concrete was practically completed and the earth parapet was in place, requiring only to be graded.

During the year the work was completed in all respects. No armament was received.

(See report on the technical details of fortification works in Boston Harbor, Appendix 4 B.)

Money statement.

July 1, 1900, balance available	$7,011.58
Allotted since	3,800.00
	10,811.58
Expended during the fiscal year	10,809.08
July 1, 1901, balance available	2.50

Emplacements for two 6-inch rapid-fire guns.—This battery provides emplacements for two 6-inch rapid-fire guns on pedestal mounts. A double magazine serves both guns.

An allotment of $27,000 was made by the Chief of Engineers from the appropriation for "Gun and Mortar Batteries," act of March 1, 1901, on June 13, 1901.

At the beginning of the fiscal year nothing had been done. During the year plans were prepared and submitted to the Chief of Engineers June 6, 1901, and approved June 13, 1901. Active operations were not begun, as the site was occupied by the supply of crushed stone stored for use in the construction of the mortar battery.

Money statement.

Allotted June 13, 1901	$27,000
July 1, 1901, balance available	27,000

SITE NO. 6.

Emplacements for two 12-inch guns on nondisappearing carriages.—This battery consists of two emplacements for 12-inch rifles mounted upon nondisappearing carriages, model 1892, and its construction was begun with funds allotted from the appropriation for "National Defense."

The following allotments have been made from the appropriation for "Gun and Mortar Batteries:"

July 6, 1899, act of March 3, 1899	$5,000.00
March 3, 1900, by transfers	1,960.30
Total	6,960.30

At the beginning of the year the battery was complete, excepting trolleys, cranes, and railings. These items were completed during the fiscal year, and on January 26, 1901, the work was turned over to the artillery.

Money statement.

July 1, 1900, balance available $1,125.94
Expended during the fiscal year... 1,125.94

Mounting 12-inch guns and carriages.—An allotment of $1,200 was made by the Chief of Engineers on December 14, 1899, from the appropriation for "Gun and Mortar Batteries," act of March 3, 1899, for this work.

At the beginning of the fiscal year the carriages had been mounted ready to receive the guns. No guns have as yet been received. All funds on hand were deposited to the credit of the United States Treasurer.

Money statement.

July 1, 1900, balance available $821.43
Deposited to credit of United States Treasurer........................... 821.43

Emplacements for two 5-inch rapid-fire guns.—This battery provides emplacements for two 5-inch rapid-fire guns on balanced-pillar mounts. The plans were approved March 30, 1899. The following allotments were made from the appropriation for "Gun and Mortar Batteries:"

March 30, 1899, act of July 7, 1898... $11,500
March 3, 1900, act of July 7, 1898 2,550

Total 14,050

At the beginning of the fiscal year the battery was complete, except the hand rails. The carriages were mounted ready to receive the guns. During the year the hand rails were completed, and the battery was turned over to the artillery on January 26, 1901.

Money statement.

July 1, 1900, balance available $377.15
Expended during the fiscal year... 377.15

SITE NO. 7.

Emplacements for three 6-inch rapid-fire guns.—This battery consists of three emplacements for 6-inch rifles on disappearing carriages, and was originally projected for Site No. 8. The change of site was approved May 26, 1899.

The following allotments were made from the appropriation for "Gun and Mortar Batteries:"

June 1, 1899, act of July 7, 1898 .... $65,000
August 16, 1900, act of May 25, 1900.. 14,000
February 11, 1901, act of May 25, 1900..................................... 12,000

Total 91,000

At the beginning of the fiscal year about one-half the concrete was in place; the drainage system was complete and two disappearing carriages for 6-inch rifles were on hand.

During the fiscal year the concrete was completed, the earth parapet was constructed and graded, the electric plant was installed, the parados was nearly completed, the water supply was nearly completed, the trolleys, hand rails, and doors were placed, one disappearing carriage was received, and the three carriages were mounted. No guns were received. A portion of the working plant was removed. (See report on the technical details of fortification works in Boston Harbor, Appendix 4 B.)

Money statement.

July 1, 1900, balance available	$17,685.92
Allotted since	26,000.00
	43,685.92
Expended during the fiscal year	35,499.86
July 1, 1901, balance available	8,186.06

Emplacements for three 15-pounder rapid-fire guns.—On June 20, 1900, the Chief of Engineers authorized the construction of two of these emplacements and allotted the sum of $12,000 from the appropriation for "Gun and Mortar Batteries," act of May 25, 1900. These emplacements form part of a three-gun battery. The guns will be mounted on balanced-pillar mounts. No armament has yet been received.

At the beginning of the fiscal year no work had been done in the field. During the year the work was completed, except the final grading of the parapet. This was postponed in order to complete the third emplacement, and to await the completion of the 6-inch battery, which was receiving all the earth obtainable for fill, there being but one locomotive available for hauling. (See report on the technical details of fortification works in Boston Harbor, Appendix 4 B.)

Money statement.

July 1, 1900, balance available	$12,000.00
Expended during the fiscal year	11,999.78
July 1, 1901, balance available	.22

The construction of the third emplacement of this battery was authorized April 11, 1901, on which date an allotment of $9,000 was made from the appropriation for "Gun and Mortar Batteries," act of March 1, 1901. At the beginning of the fiscal year nothing had been done, but the plans had been approved with those of the other two emplacements. During the year the concrete work was completed. The fill and grading were not begun, as the locomotive was still occupied elsewhere.

There remained to complete hanging the doors and constructing the earth parapet.

Money statement.

Allotted April 11, 1901	$9,000.00
Expended during the fiscal year	2,826.83
July 1, 1901, balance available	6,173.17

Emplacements for four 15-pounder rapid-fire guns.—The construction of a battery for four 15-pounder rapid-fire guns was authorized April 24, 1901, and an allotment of $19,000 for its construction was made from the appropriation for "Gun and Mortar Batteries," act of March 1, 1901. (See report on the technical details of fortification works in Boston Harbor, Appendix 4 B.)

At the beginning of the fiscal year nothing had been done. During the year a railroad was constructed from the wharf, the derrick and engine installed, the excavation completed, drains laid, forms erected, and concrete work begun.

Money statement.

Allotted April 24, 1901	$19,000.00
Expended during the fiscal year	1,590.19
July 1, 1901, balance available	17,409.81

Emplacements for two 6-inch rifles.—This battery provides emplacements for two 6-inch rapid-fire guns on pedestal mounts. . The plans were approved by the Chief of Engineers May 23, 1901. A provisional allotment of $30,000 was made November 9, 1900, from the appropriation for "Gun and Mortar Batteries," act of May 25, 1900, for this work, but no expenditures were authorized until plans had been approved by the Chief of Engineers. On May 23, 1901, $5,000 of this sum was withdrawn, the estimated cost of the battery being only $25,000.

At the beginning of the fiscal year the site had been surveyed. During the year the site was prepared for work, the drains were laid, forms erected, and foundations placed.

Money statement.

Allotted November 9, 1900	$30,000.00
Withdrawn	5,000.00
July 1, 1901, balance available	25,000.00

Emplacements for 10-inch rifles.—This battery provides emplacements for four 10-inch B. L. rifles on disappearing carriages.

The construction of three of these emplacements was authorized by the Chief of Engineers March 30, 1901.

The plans of the battery were approved May 10, 1901.

The following allotments were made from the appropriation for "Gun and Mortar Batteries:"

March 30, 1901, act of March 1, 1901	$10,000
May 10, 1901, act of March 1, 1901	182,500
Total	192,500

At the beginning of the fiscal year nothing had been done. During the year the plans were prepared, materials and plant were purchased, a railroad from the wharf built, and the excavation was begun, about 5,500 cubic yards of earth being handled.

No armament has been received.

Money statement.

Allotted during the fiscal year	$192,500.00
Expended during the fiscal year	3,533.50
July 1, 1901, balance available	188,966.50

Construction of storehouses.—On January 2, 1901, the Secretary of War set aside a portion of this site as an engineer reservation, to be used for the storage and care of engineer property not in use in construction work.

An allotment of $3,500 was made by the Chief of Engineers on January 5, 1901, from the appropriation for "Gun and Mortar Batteries," act of May 25, 1900, for the construction of two storehouses upon this reservation.

At the beginning of the fiscal year nothing had been done. During the year a large storehouse was nearly completed. A spur track was run from the railroad through the building to enable heavy machinery to be handled readily.

Materials were purchased for the second building and the site was prepared.

Money statement.

Allotted January 5, 1901	$3,500.00
Expended during the fiscal year	2,768.02
July 1, 1901, balance available	731.98

CONSTRUCTION OF LIGHTER.

Authority for the construction or purchase of a steam lighter for use in connection with the fortification work in Boston Harbor was authorized by the Chief of Engineers May 15, 1901.

The following allotments were made from the appropriation for "Gun and Mortar Batteries:"

May 15, 1901, act of March 1, 1901	$10,000
June 6, 1901, act of March 1, 1901	10,000
Total	20,000

During the fiscal year plans and specifications were prepared by a naval architect. The construction of the vessel was not begun.

Money statement.

Allotted during the fiscal year	$20,000.00
July 1, 1901, balance available	20,000.00

TORPEDOES FOR HARBOR DEFENSE.

The following allotment was made for the construction of a submarine-mining casemate:

December 18, 1899, act of May 7, 1898	$2,000
Withdrawn December 18, 1899	600
Balance available	1,400

At the beginning of the year the casemate was nearly complete. During the year it was completed.

Money statement.

July 1, 1900, balance available	$99.49
Expended during the fiscal year	99.49

The following allotments have been made from the appropriation for "Torpedoes for Harbor Defense" for the construction of a cable tank and an extension of the same:

January 13, 1897, act of June 6, 1896	$4,300
August 11, 1900, act of March 3, 1899	7,000
Total	11,300

At the beginning of the fiscal year the cable tank had been completed except for a device for handling cable drums.

During the year an extension of the tank was built, a frame shed was constructed over the tank, and a hoisting device was designed and partially constructed.

Money statement.

Allotted August 11, 1900	$7,000
Expended during the fiscal year	3,615
July 1, 1901, balance available	3,385

The following allotments were made for the construction of a mining casemate:

October 8, 1898, act of May 7, 1898	$2,700
December 18, 1899, act of June 6, 1896	250
December 18, 1899, by transfer	600
Total	3,550

At the beginning of the fiscal year the work had been completed. No work has been done since.

Money statement.

July 1, 1900, balance available	$17.97
Expended during the fiscal year	17.97

PRESERVATION AND REPAIR OF FORTIFICATIONS.

The following allotments have been made from the appropriation for "Preservation and Repair of Fortifications" for work at Site No. 1:

June 9, 1899, act of May 7, 1898	$800
February 13, 1900, act of March 3, 1899	175
June 9, 1900, act of May 25, 1900	500
May 16, 1901, act of March 1, 1901	230
Total	1,705

During the fiscal year repairs were made to the lighting system in one 10-inch emplacement, to ammunition lifts, to the cover of the well in the parade, to earth slopes, to the searchlight, to locks of doors, to ventilator in the power house, and to a switch in the electric system. The walls of the power room were painted, a leak in the roof of the fire commander's station was stopped, a leaky cell of the electric accumulator was repaired, and swollen wooden doors throughout the works were eased.

Money statement.

July 1, 1900, balance available	$821.03
Allotted since	230.00
	1,051.03
Expended during the fiscal year	739.59
July 1, 1901, balance available	311.44

For work at Site No. 2 the following allotments have been made:

June 9, 1899, act of May 7, 1898	$500
June 9, 1900, act of May 25, 1900	300
August 15, 1899, act of March 3, 1899	4,000
December 6, 1899, act of March 3, 1899	250
June 8, 1900, act of March 3, 1899	210
April 10, 1901, act of March 1, 1901	250
May 16, 1901, act of March 1, 1901	540
Total	6,050

During the fiscal year an old engineer building was demolished and removed, the ammunition trolleys were overhauled and oiled, a roof was built over the electric accumulator to prevent water from dripping into the cells, the feed-water heater was repaired, and the piping of the power plant was repaired and rearranged.

Money statement.

July 1, 1900, balance available	$599.44
Allotted since	790.00
	1,389.44
Expended during the fiscal year	849.41
July 1, 1901, balance available	540.03

An allotment of $175 was made June 9, 1899, for repairing the bridge leading to the keep and the roof and windows of the keep of one of the works of older type. At the beginning of the fiscal year the work had been completed. Nothing has been done since.

Money statement.

July 1, 1900, balance available	$54.38
July 1, 1901, balance available	54.38

On July 19, 1898, an allotment of $2,200 was made for repairs to the wharf at another work of older type. The site of the wharf having been loaned to the Treasury Department for use as a depot for the Light-House Establishment, which would necessitate the construction of a new and larger wharf, no repairs were made.

Money statement.

July 1, 1900, balance available	$2,173.20
Deposited to the credit of the appropriation	2,173.20

The following allotments were made for the care of the torpedo material:

January 15, 1900, act of March 3, 1899	$1,500.00
June 9, 1900, act of May 25, 1900	100.00
May 16, 1901, act of March 1, 1901	55.00
April 21, 1901, act of June 6, 1896	12.44
April 21, 1901, act of May 7, 1898	159.06
April 21, 1901, act of May 25, 1900	28.50
May 29, 1901, act of March 1, 1901	350.00
Total	2,205.00

During the fiscal year the property was overhauled and listed and old and unserviceable material was sorted out and shipped to the engineer depot at Willets Point.

Money statement.

July 1, 1900, balance available	$177.37
Allotted since	605.00
	782.37
Expended during the fiscal year	443.94
July 1, 1901, balance available	338.43

The following allotments were made for work at Site No. 3:

June 9, 1900, act of May 25, 1900	$800
February 9, 1901, act of May 25, 1900	600
May 16, 1901, act of March 1, 1901	520
Total	1,920

During the fiscal year two watchmen were maintained at this post until the arrival, June 1, 1901, of a detachment of troops. Minor repairs were made to the electric system, signs warning unauthorized persons against trespassing were set up, and the guns and carriages were cared for.

Money statement.

July 1, 1900, balance available	$800.00
Allotted since	1,120.00
	1,920.00
Expended during the fiscal year	1,397.22
July 1, 1901, balance available	522.78

Allotments were made as follows for work at Site No. 4:

June 9, 1899, act of May 7, 1898	$415
February 19, 1900, act of March 3, 1899	180
June 9, 1900, act of May 25, 1900	150
May 16, 1901, act of March 1, 1901	110
Total	855

During the fiscal year repairs were made to the electric-generating plant, the steam piping, the switchboard, and the storage battery. A test of forced ventilation in the battery was made without useful results. Outdoor protection for meteorological instruments was set up.

Money statement.

July 1, 1900, balance available	$201.77
Allotted since	110.00
	311.77
Expended during the fiscal year	201.64
July 1, 1901, balance available	110.13

Allotments have been made as follows for work at Site No. 5:

June 9, 1899, act of May 7, 1898	$365
June 9, 1900, act of May 25, 1900	1,000
May 16, 1901, act of March 1, 1901	425
Total	1,790

During the year general care was taken of the reservation and batteries. The guns and carriages were cleaned, oiled, and traversed.

Money statement.

July 1, 1900, balance available	$1,017.48
Allotted since	425.00
	1,442.48
Expended during the fiscal year	1,003.73
July 1, 1901, balance available	438.75

Allotments have been made as follows for work at Site No. 6:

June 9, 1899, act of May 7, 1898	$365
March 1, 1900, act of March 3, 1899	360
June 9, 1900, act of May 25, 1900	1,500
May 16, 1901, act of March 1, 1901	220
Total	2,445

During the year care was taken of the reservation, armament, and machinery. The electric accumulator, not being required for use, was placed out of commission. Minor repairs to the batteries were made.

Money statement.

July 1, 1900, balance available	$1,510.25
Allotted since	220.00
	1,730.25
Expended during the fiscal year	1,256.10
July 1, 1901, balance available	474.15

Allotments have been made as follows for work at site No. 7:

June 9, 1900, act of May 25, 1900	$250
May 16, 1901, act of March 1, 1901	100
Total	350

During the year the ironwork of the battery was painted and general care was taken of the reservation and armament.

Money statement.

July 1, 1900, balance available	$250.00
Allotted since	100.00
	350.00
Expended during the fiscal year	160.89
July 1, 1901, balance available	189.11

SITES FOR FORTIFICATIONS AND SEACOAST DEFENSES.

During the fiscal year negotiations were in progress for the purchase of two lots to complete the acquisition of the required tract at one site. These lots were acquired by condemnation. The following allotments have been made from the appropriation for "Sites for Fortifications and Seacoast Defenses":

June 12, 1897, act of June 6, 1896	$185,160.79
June 12, 1897, act of March 3, 1897	64,839.21
June 17, 1897, act of March 3, 1897	1,248.85
Total	251,248.85

Money statement.

July 1, 1900, balance available	$9,198.62
Expended during the fiscal year	8,874.78
July 1, 1901, balance available	323.84

This balance will be deposited to the credit of the appropriation.

Allotments for the examination and appraisal of the land required at a second site were as follows:

September 8, 1898, act of May 7, 1898	$100
September 9, 1899, act of May 7, 1898	1,400
Total	1,500

At the beginning of the fiscal year the appraisal had been completed.

Money statement.

July 1, 1900, balance available	$71.43
Deposited to the credit of the appropriation	71.43

An allotment of $1,000 was made September 22, 1899, for a survey of this site.

At the beginning of the year the survey had been completed.

Money statement.

July 1, 1900, balance available	$745.30
Deposited to the credit of the appropriation	745.30

An allotment was made September 13, 1899, for the purchase of about 48 acres of land at the same site:

Act of May 7, 1898	$142,517.06
Act of March 3, 1899	142,982.94
Total	285,500.00

At the beginning of the fiscal year offers for 73 parcels had been accepted by 39 owners, amounting to $178,079.37, against an appraised value of $196,291.37, aggregating 1,584,033.1 square feet out of a total of 1,970,044 square feet. No land had been paid for. Abstracts of titles were prepared by Mr. George A. Dary under authority of the Secretary of War.

During the year negotiations were continued. About 239,078.9 square feet of land was acquired at a cost of $35,768.19, against an appraised value of $36,697.68.

Forty-nine lots, aggregating 1,116,095.4 square feet, acquired from 24 owners, were paid for.

Money statement.

July 1, 1900, balance available	$285,500.00
Expended during the fiscal year	148,613.62
July 1, 1901, balance available	136,886.38

SUPPLIES FOR SEACOAST DEFENSES.

On June 9, 1900, an allotment of $1,000 was made from the appropriation for "Supplies for Seacoast Defenses," act of May 25, 1900, for the purchase of electrical supplies upon requisitions of post commanders, under the provisions of General Orders, No. 66, Adjutant General's Office, 1900.

During the fiscal year supplies were purchased and issued.

Money statement.

July 1, 1900, balance available	$1,000.00
Expended during the fiscal year	619.29
July 1, 1901, balance available	380.71

3 D.

DEFENSES OF SOUTHEAST COAST OF MASSACHUSETTS AND RHODE ISLAND AT NEW BEDFORD, MASSACHUSETTS, AND NEWPORT, RHODE ISLAND.

Officers in charge, Maj. Daniel W. Lockwood, Corps of Engineers, until July 25, 1900; Lieut. Robert P. Johnston, Corps of Engineers, from July 25 until August 31, 1900, and Maj. George W. Goethals, Corps of Engineers, since August 31, 1900; assistant, Lieut. Robert P. Johnston, Corps of Engineers, until July 25, 1900, and since August 31, 1900; Division Engineer, Col. George L. Gillespie, Corps of Engineers (now brigadier-general, Chief of Engineers, United States Army), until April 30, 1901, and Col. Charles R. Suter, Corps of Engineers, since May 9, 1901.

NEW BEDFORD, MASSACHUSETTS.

Emplacements for two 8-inch guns on disappearing carriages.—During the last fiscal year these emplacements have been under the charge of and in use by a detachment of 20 men belonging to the artillery corps, and no work was done on these emplacements other than a few needed repairs, as reported under preservation and repair.

Money statement.

July 1, 1900, balance unexpended $206.86
June 30, 1901, amount returned to United States Treasury 206.86

Emplacements for two 5-inch rapid-fire guns.—Under the provisions of the deficiency act of Congress approved July 7, 1898, funds were allotted for the purpose of constructing emplacements on which to mount two 5-inch rapid-fire guns of the navy pattern, Brown segmental wire type. These allotments consisted of $13,300 from the above act made under date of August 30, 1898, and $4,200 from the same appropriation on September 6, 1899. On August 3, 1900, an additional amount was requested for completing these emplacements, and under date of August 7, 1900, the sum of $4,000 was allotted from the same act for the purpose.

Under date of August 25, 1898, plans and estimates were submitted for two emplacements and approved in September, but no work of construction was undertaken until the spring of 1900, owing to the difficulty of obtaining cement. The necessary excavation, however, was made, and a few yards of concrete foundation were placed for magazines and bomb proofs, in addition to laying certain drain pipes. Active operations were resumed in May, 1900, and carried forward until work was suspended by reason of inclement weather, when all the concrete was completed and embankments finished, except grading and sodding of embankments and paving of magazine floors. All this work has since been completed, and the emplacements, with the exception of a slight amount of grading in their rear, are completed ready for the guns and the electric lighting. Under date of September 6, 1900, in compliance with Engineer Department letters of May 16 and June 13, 1900, plans and estimates were submitted for the construction of emplacements for two additional 5-inch rapid-fire guns on pedestal mounts, but upon the recommendation of the division engineer, on September 11, 1900, the Chief of Engineers decided to drop these two 5-inch gun emplacements from the project, substituting four 15-pounder rapid-fire guns.

Money statement.

July 1, 1900, balance unexpended	$10,061.63
June 30, 1901, amount allotted since	4,000.00
	14,061.63
June 30, 1901, amount expended during fiscal year	12,392.97
July 1, 1901, balance unexpended	1,668.66

Emplacements for four 15-pounder rapid-fire guns.—In compliance with instructions received from the Chief of Engineers, dated September 11, 1900, plans and estimates for the construction of emplacements for four 15-pounder rapid-fire guns were submitted on October 8, and under date of October 26, 1900, an allotment of $18,300 was made from the appropriation for "Gun and Mortar Batteries," act of May 25, 1900. These guns are to be disposed in two batteries of two guns each, and work on the emplacements was commenced in November. Owing to the difficulty of procuring cement, the contract for which was annulled, work was suspended in December and nothing further was done until April, 1901, when active operations were resumed. At the close of the fiscal year both batteries are practically completed. There remains to be done the completion of the platforms and the top steps leading to the platforms, which work will not be undertaken until the receipt of the base rings, the paving of the magazines, the electric wiring, hanging of doors and shutters, etc.

Money statement.

Amount allotted October 26, 1900	$18,300.00
June 30, 1901, amount expended during the year	13,458.63
July 1, 1901, balance unexpended	4,841.37
July 1, 1901, outstanding liabilities	2,284.33
July 1, 1901, balance available	2,557.04

Abstract of awards made for furnishing material for construction of emplacements for four 15-pounder guns after receipt of sealed proposals invited by circular notices.

Awarded to—	Class of material.	Per—	Rate.	Where delivered.
Hudson River Stone Supply Co., New York, N. Y.	Crushed stone	Cubic yard	$1.75	Alongside wharf.
E. B. Tripp, Fairhaven, Mass	Sand	do	1.30	At site of work.
		Barrel	2.26	On wharf November, 1900.
S. S. Paine & Bro., New Bedford, Mass.	Giant Portland cement.	do	1.80	On wharf Mar. 1, 1901.
Greene & Wood, New Bedford, Mass.	Spruce, planed	M. feet	21.00	At site of work.
	Spruce, rough	do	17.00	Do.

Preservation and repair of fortifications.—Under date of June 13, 1900, an allotment of $420 was made from the appropriation for "Preservation and Repair of Fortifications," act of May 25, 1900, for necessary miscellaneous repairs needed at this post up to June 30, 1901. On June 21, 1900, $350 was allotted from the same appropriation ($234.43 from act of March 3, 1899, and $115.57 from act of May 25,

1900) for wiring mining casemate at this post and for care and preservation of torpedo material pertaining to the defense of New Bedford Harbor for the fiscal year ending June 30, 1901. On July 20, 1899, $150 was allotted from the act of March 3, 1899, to correct dampness in the rooms of the new 8-inch gun emplacements; May 15, 1901, $150 was allotted for the preservation and repairs needed to June 30, 1902, from the act of March 1, 1901; and May 20, 1901, $35 from the same act for the repair of hoists and doors.

The only work during the past fiscal year under these several allotments has been the painting and scraping of the I-beams and the iron work connected with the battery and investigations as to cause of dampness. The wet condition of the magazines in the 8-inch gun emplacements is due primarily to leakage, though condensation does its share during the warmer season. The platforms hold water during and after rains, which gradually seeps through to the rooms below. From experience gained in other magazines, it is not considered possible to stop these leaks by the application of any material on the top surfaces, since any layer of material put there must necessarily be thin, due to the excessive cost of digging out hardened concrete, and thin layers crack and scale so as to become useless in a short time. An effort will be made, however, by lining the magazines and by providing ample drainage to carry away the water that may get to the outside of this lining, to keep a dry place for the storage of powder.

The guides of the hoists and drums of the 8-inch battery have been thoroughly overhauled and repaired. The openings remaining above the doors on gun platforms after the doors are closed have been lessened by the addition of angle irons.

All the torpedo material for the defense of New Bedford Harbor has been overhauled, cleaned up, and put in good condition, as well as the materials of large invoices received during the year from the Engineer Depot.

Money statements.

GENERAL WORK OF REPAIR.

July 1, 1900, balance unexpended	$820.00
June 30, 1901, amount allotted since	185.00
	1,005.00
June 30, 1901, amount expended during fiscal year	195.07
July 1, 1901, balance unexpended	809.93
July 1, 1901, outstanding liabilities	33.04
July 1, 1901, balance available	776.89

PREVENTION OF DAMPNESS IN BATTERIES.

July 1, 1900, balance unexpended	150.00
July 1, 1901, balance unexpended	150.00

CARE OF TORPEDO MATERIAL.

July 1, 1900, balance unexpended	350.00
June 30, 1901, amount expended during fiscal year	332.85
July 1, 1901, balance unexpended	17.15
July 1, 1901, outstanding liabilities	2.50
July 1, 1901, balance available	14.65

Mining casemate.—Under the provisions of the fortification appropriation act of May 7, 1898, an allotment of $13,500 was made May 31, 1899, for the construction of a mining casemate. This mining casemate was completed except the wiring, but leaks so badly that no effort has been made to do this work. The engine has been placed in a temporary building, and will be kept there until some means is adopted for securing a dry room, which it is hoped may be accomplished by an interior lining in the existing casemate and by proper drainage.

Money statement.

TORPEDOES FOR HARBOR DEFENSE.

July 1, 1900, balance unexpended	$1,679.06
June 30, 1901, amount expended during fiscal year	683.24
July 1, 1901, balance unexpended	995.82
July 1, 1901, outstanding liabilities	88.88
July 1, 1901, balance available	906.94

Torpedo storehouse.—Under date of March 19, 1901, an allotment of $4,500 was made from the appropriation for "Torpedoes for Harbor Defense," act of March 1, 1901, for the construction of a torpedo storehouse. This building is of brick with a slate roof supported by steel trusses, and with the exception of hanging the doors and shutters, building the racks for mines, placing traveler and trolley, and connecting the railroad within the building to that on the wharf the work is completed.

Money statement.

Amount allotted since July 1, 1900	$4,500.00
June 30, 1901, amount expended during fiscal year	2,404.34
July 1, 1901, balance unexpended	2,095.66
July 1, 1901, outstanding liabilities	450.65
July 1, 1901, balance available	1,645.01

Torpedo material.—Under date of March 16, 1901, $150 was allotted from the appropriation for "Torpedoes for Harbor Defense," as follows: Act May 7, 1898, $51.40; act of May 25, 1900, $23.30; and act of March 1, 1901, $75.30, for the purpose of transferring the torpedo material to the artillery in compliance with instructions from the Chief of Engineers dated February 1, 1901. This transfer was made during the month of June, 1901, with the exception of the cable, which remains to be tested.

Money statement.

Amount allotted since July 1, 1900	$150.00
July 1, 1901, balance unexpended	150.00

NARRAGANSETT BAY, RHODE ISLAND.

Electric-light plant.—On November 27, 1900, an allotment of $22,700 was made for the installation of a central electric-light plant at the defenses to the eastern entrance, from the appropriation for "Gun and Mortar Batteries," act of May 25, 1900. The plans and estimates submitted on which this allotment was based contemplated supplying sufficient power for the battery lighting, searchlights, and post and building lighting, but did not contemplate the laying of any wires for the post and building lighting. As under existing Army Regulations, this is contemplated, an additional allotment of $25,500 was requested, which sum was set aside for the purpose on May 4, 1901, from the appropriation for "Gun and Mortar Batteries," act of March 1, 1901. The power house has been practically completed. Bids have been invited for the plant and contracts made. The conduit provided for in the first allotment has been received and laid. Eleven hundred linear feet of 4-inch cast-iron water main was laid to the power house.

Money statement.

Amount allotted since July 1, 1900	$48,200.00
June 30, 1901, amount expended during fiscal year	4,392.40
July 1, 1901, balance unexpended	43,807.60
July 1, 1901, outstanding liabilities	$4,962.15
July 1, 1901, amount covered by uncompleted contracts	8,409.62
	13,371.77
July 1, 1901, balance available	30,435.83

CONTRACTS IN FORCE.

Materials.	Contractor.	Date of approval.	To commence—	To complete—
		*1901.		
Vitrified and armored conduit, switches, junction boxes, lamps, etc.	The Burnet Co., New York, N. Y.	Apr. 25	Within 30 days	Within 60 days.
Generator and accumulator switchboards.	H. B. Cohe & Co., New York, N. Y.	May 1	....do............	Within 45 days (extended 30 days).
Lead and rubber covered cable.	Standard Underground Cable Co.	May 4	....do............	Within 30 days.
Two 30-kilowatt generating sets.	McCay Engineering Co., Baltimore, Md.	May 11		Within 10 weeks.
One 60-cell accumulator.	Sipe & Sigler, Cleveland, Ohio.	May 16		To be delivered when ordered.

Sea walls and embankments.—An allotment of $13,000 from the appropriation for "Sea Walls and Embankments," act of March 1, 1901, has been made for rebuilding a sea wall. Proposals were invited for doing the work by contract, and the contract awarded to Mr. Eugene S. Belden, of Hartford, Conn.

Money statement.

June, 30, 1901, amount allotted since July 1, 1900	$13,000.00
July 1, 1901, balance unexpended	13,000.00
July 1, 1901, outstanding liabilities	44.62
July 1, 1901, balance available	12,955.38

Battery commander's station.—The station for the 10-inch guns was painted and an iron ring put around the base to give sufficient surface for the instrument.

Money statement.

July 1, 1900, balance unexpended		$66.43
June 30, 1901, amount expended during fiscal year	$55.16	
Returned to United States Treasury	11.27	
		66.43

Preservation and repair of fortifications.—Allotments have been made as follows from the appropriation for "Preservation and Repair of Fortifications:" July 29, 1899, act of March 3, 1899, $245, for correcting dampness in the rooms of the new works; June 13, 1900, act of May 25, 1900, $865, for necessary miscellaneous expenses for repairs needed to June 30, 1901; June 21, 1900, same act, $600, for care and preservation of torpedo material for defense of Narragansett Bay, Rhode Island, of which $75 is to be used for wiring a casemate; February 26, 1901, same act, $1,000, for part of expense of rebuilding dangerous casemate wall; May 15, 1901, act of March 1, 1901, $2,760, for necessary miscellaneous repairs needed to June 30, 1902, including the relaying of ashlar wall.

During the last winter and spring careful observations were made for the purpose of determining the cause of the dampness in the mortar battery, and the conclusion reached is that the greater portion of the dampness is due to leakage, though condensation during the warmer season will account for a portion of the moisture that accumulates during dry weather. No effort has been made to correct the dampness, as it is not believed expedient to expend funds in trying to correct it by the application of exterior coverings. Plans and estimates will be submitted for an interior lining of the mortar-battery magazines.

The 10-inch battery has been dry as to its interior rooms, but the outer gallery is wet when rain falls. This has been to some extent remedied by filling the horizontal cracks on the exposed wall with elastic cement and by coating the wall with hot paraffin and with the Sylvester waterproof mixture. In addition, the repairs to the 10-inch battery consisted in the construction of penthouses to prevent snow from being piled up in the passage and stairways leading to the gun platforms and in making racks for rammer and sponge staffs.

The casemate wall on the east side of the old fort, due to the action of frost, had bulged out to such an extent as to become dangerous, and under authority of the Chief of Engineers, from funds allotted for the purpose, scaffolding has been erected and the dangerous portion of the wall removed. Funds now on hand will permit the rebuilding of the portion removed and the straightening up of other portions of the wall that are out of plumb.

Care of torpedo material.—An allotment was made in June, 1900, for the care and preservation of torpedo material for the defense of Narragansett Bay for the year ending June 30, 1901, and in December the authority of the Chief of Engineers was received to expend about $265 of the funds for the care of torpedo material for painting the buildings used in connection with the mining defense of this place and for transferring five reels of cable.

Money statements.

GENERAL WORK OF REPAIR.

July 1, 1900, balance unexpended	$879.59
June 30, 1901, amount allotted during year	3,760.00
	4,639.59
June 30, 1901, amount expended during fiscal year	573.01
July 1, 1901, balance unexpended	4,066.58
July 1, 1901, outstanding liabilities	83.15
July 1, 1901, balance available	3,983.43

CARE OF TORPEDO MATERIAL.

July 1, 1900, balance unexpended	$600.00
June 30, 1901, amount expended during fiscal year	565.59
July 1, 1901, balance unexpended	34.41

PREVENTION OF DAMPNESS IN BATTERIES.

July 1, 1900, balance unexpended	$245.00
June 30, 1901, amount expended during fiscal year	69.00
July 1, 1901, balance unexpended	176.00

Torpedoes for harbor defense.—An allotment of $250 from the appropriation for "Torpedoes for Harbor Defense," act of May 25, 1900, was made for overhauling, with a view of its transfer to the artillery, all torpedo material on hand. Everything on hand was carefully gone over, as well as the material making up large invoices received from the Engineer Depot during the winter, and all placed in good condition. Under instructions received from the Chief of Engineers, dated February 23, 1901, all of this material has been transferred to the Artillery Corps, with the exception of the cables, which have not yet been tested.

Money statement.

Amount allotted since July 1, 1900	$250.00
June 30, 1901, amount expended during fiscal year	80.00
July 1, 1901, balance unexpended	170.00

Two 10-inch gun emplacements.—A survey of the land, acquired by condemnation proceedings for the construction of the high-power gun emplacements, was completed, plans and estimates were submitted for the construction of two 10-inch gun emplacements, and allotments were made, under dates of November 9 and 24, 1900, from the appropriation for "Gun and Mortar Batteries," act of May 25, 1900, amounting to $122,500 for the construction of these works, with the understanding that none of the funds were to be expended until the question of damages based on negative easements was decided by the United States court. Though the case was argued in November, 1900, and taken under advisement by the judge of the circuit court, a decision has not yet been rendered. Under date of May 28, 1901, telegraphic instructions were received from the Chief of Engineers to proceed with the construction of the batteries, and work was commenced at once. A road has been built from the wharf to connect with the county road, and objectionable grades in the county road have been reduced. Temporary structures were begun for the storage of cement, storage of tools, etc., and at the close of the fiscal year these were well under way. Bids have been received and opened for the necessary materials to be used in the construction of the work, and contracts awarded.

Money statement.

Amount allotted since July 1, 1900	$122,500.00
June 30, 1901, amount expended during fiscal year	503.00
July 1, 1901, balance unexpended	121,997.00
July 1, 1901, outstanding liabilities	2,698.41
July 1, 1901, balance available	119,298.59

Emplacements for two 6-inch rapid-fire guns.—A provisional allotment of $30,000 for the construction of two 6-inch rapid-fire gun emplacements was made November 9, 1900, from the appropriation for "Gun and Mortar Batteries," act of May 25, 1900. Plans and estimates were not submitted until May 7, 1901, and upon their approval by the Chief of Engineers on June 19, 1901, the sum of $35,000 was allotted from the act of March 1, 1901, the previous allotment being withdrawn. As the restrictions had been removed at the time this allotment was made, work on the 6-inch gun emplacements consists practically of that reported under the 10-inch gun emplacements. The emplacements for the 10-inch, 15-pounder, and 6-inch guns, will be carried forward simultaneously.

Money statement.

Amount allotted since July 1, 1900	$35,000.00
July 1, 1901, balance unexpended	35,000.00
July 1, 1901, outstanding liabilities	1,579.24
July 1, 1901, balance available	33,420.76

Emplacements for two 15-pounder rapid-fire guns.—Under the appropriation for "Gun and Mortar Batteries," act of May 25, 1900, two 15-pounder rapid-fire gun emplacements are to be constructed, and allotments amounting to $15,000 have been made from the above act under dates of November 9 and 24, 1900. This work is in the same category as that of the 10-inch gun emplacements; the work was authorized by telegram of the Chief of Engineers under date of May 28, 1901.

Money statement.

Amount allotted since July 1, 1900	$15,000.00
July 1, 1901, outstanding liabilities	1,646.24
July 1, 1901, balance available	13,353.76

Constructing wharf.—In 1898, when the 12-inch gun battery was commenced, a temporary pile wharf was constructed for the landing of materials, supplies, etc. This wharf consisted of piles driven down into the hard bottom, and filled with broken stone, clay, etc., taken from the site of the batteries. The whole was inclosed with sheet piling so as to hold the riprap. The sheet piling soon decayed, opening up a way for the filling to escape, and at the beginning of the fiscal year the wharf had deteriorated to such an extent as to necessitate its reconstruction. When allotments were made for the construction of the batteries, estimates were submitted for the construction of a permanent wharf and allotments from the acts of July 7, 1898, and May 25, 1900, aggregating $28,500, were made for this purpose. The site consists of hard bottom covered by 6 or 7 feet of soft material, and it was decided to remove the piles of the old structure, excavate the soft material from the bottom, fill in the excavated area with riprap already in the existing wharf up to a grade of 10 feet below mean low water, and use this foundation for a stone structure. All the material has been removed that is to be taken out and about 2,700 tons of stone and 400 yards of rock fill have been placed. The material obtained from excavating the road from the wharf to the county road has been used as fill, the remainder of the filling to be obtained from the excavation for the 15-pounder and 6-inch rapid-fire gun emplacements.

Money statement.

Amount allotted since July 1, 1900	$28,500.00
June 30, 1901, amount expended during fiscal year	7,606.06
July 1, 1901, balance unexpended	20,893.94
July 1, 1901, outstanding liabilities	7,409.60
July 1, 1901, balance available	13,484.34

Preservation and repair of fortifications.—The following allotments from the appropriation for "Preservation and Repair of Fortifications" have been made: June 5, 1900, $750, for repair of dynamo room, act of March 3, 1899; June 13, 1900, $225, for the necessary miscellaneous repairs needed to June 30, 1901, act of May 25, 1900; December 20, 1900, $243.20, for additional cost of caring for batteries at this place until January 15, 1901, act of May 25, 1900; May 15, 1901, $300, for necessary miscellaneous repairs needed to June 30, 1902, act of March 1, 1901.

The engine room leaked very badly and the work of waterproofing the room was begun June 20, 1900. During the fiscal year earth and concrete were removed from the portion showing leakage, the surface recovered with asphalt, the concrete replaced and finished with trowels, and the earth put in position and covered with sod. The work was completed in July and the room is practically water tight.

Other work consisted in painting and scraping the iron work of the 12-inch and 15-pounder gun emplacements. This battery was cared for by the Engineer Department until February 15, 1901, when, under orders from the War Department, it was transferred to the artillery.

Money statement.

July 1, 1900, balance unexpended	$975.00
June 30, 1901, amount allotted since	543.20
	1,518.20
June 30, 1901, amount expended during fiscal year	1,217.92
July 1, 1901, balance unexpended	300.28

Emplacements for 12-inch guns and 6-inch rapid-fire guns.—Toward the close of the fiscal year plans and estimates were called for by the Chief of Engineers for the construction of three 12-inch gun emplacements and two 6-inch rapid-fire gun emplacements for the defense of the western passage. This necessitated a topographical survey of the land owned by the United States and an allotment for this purpose was made March 26, 1901, of $500, from the appropriation for "Gun and Mortar Batteries," act of March 1, 1901. The survey has been completed and plans and estimates for the 12-inch gun emplacements submitted.

Money statement.

Amount allotted since July 1, 1900	$500.00
June 30, 1901, amount expended during fiscal year	376.00
July 1, 1901, balance unexpended	124.00
July 1, 1901, outstanding liabilities	68.50
July 1, 1901, balance available	55.50

Battery for eight 12-inch mortars.—Under allotments from the appropriation for "Gun and Mortar Batteries," act of May 7, 1898, $143,400 were allotted for the construction of emplacements for eight 12-inch mortars. Work was commenced in September, 1898, and by the end of November, 1900, all construction work was practically completed, including the installation of the trolley system, roadway approach to the battery, water-service piping—in short, all but the electric-light fixtures. The mortar carriages, base rings, and racers, which were received in June and July, 1898, have been assembled and mounted in place, ready for the reception of the mortars which have recently been received from the Ordnance Department. The battery was formally transferred to the artillery for its use and care January 22, 1901, and the only work that remains is the clearing up of the grounds in the vicinity as soon as the mortars, which are on hand, are mounted.

Money statement.

July 1, 1900, balance unexpended		$12,120.32
June 30, 1901, amount expended during the fiscal year	$9,566.59	
Returned to United States Treasury	2,000.00	
Transferred to other work	53.98	
		11,620.57
July 1, 1901, balance unexpended		499.75

Battery commander's station.—The small amount of work necessary to complete the battery commander's station was done early in the year.

Money statement.

July 1, 1900, balance unexpended	$1,038.64
June 30, 1901, amount expended during fiscal year	271.86
Returned to United States Treasury	766.78

Electric-light plant.—Plans and estimates having been submitted, by Department indorsement of March 2, 1900, $6,930 were allotted from the appropriation for "Gun and Mortar Batteries," act of May 25, 1900, to be applied to installing the part of the electric-lighting outfit at the mortar battery, and on March 15, 1901, $31,020 were allotted from the appropriation for "Gun and Mortar Batteries," act of March 1, 1901, for completion. A survey of the proposed site was made and plans prepared. Specifications were approved and proposals invited for furnishing the material for the various parts of the system and opened June 19, since which date the awards of contracts have been authorized, though no contracts have yet been made.

Money statement.

Amount allotted since July 1, 1900	$37,950.00
June 30, 1901, amount expended during fiscal year	54.75
July 1, 1901, balance unexpended	37,895.25
July 1, 1901, outstanding liabilities	197.74
July 1, 1901, balance available	37,697.51

Preservation and repair of fortifications.—The roadway in rear of the three 10-inch gun battery was macadamized and thoroughly rolled, funds for the purpose being especially allotted by the Department;

brackets for sponge and rammer staffs were put up; locking devices for shot lifts repaired, and the ironwork scraped and painted.

At the 6-inch battery, the magazines leaking badly, an effort was made to stop the leaks by removing the top surface of concrete to a depth of about 6 inches, covering the surface with asphalt and putting on four layers of tarred paper, over which was to be placed from 4 to 6 inches of concrete. This asphalt was placed in position and accomplished the object desired, but, due to the action of frost followed by warmer weather, the asphalt caked, cracked, and began to peal, opening up seams through which the water passed as easily as before this work was done. The blasts of the gun firing salutes caused a curling up of the covering, injuring it still more. Unless such a protection be covered by a sufficiently thick layer of concrete to form a heavy and solid mass, it is not believed that this method of waterproofing can do satisfactorily what is required of it, and the excessive cost of digging out the old concrete makes it practically prohibitory. It was proposed to apply the same method of waterproofing to the 10-inch gun emplacements, but as the results were so unsatisfactory nothing has been done in this connection, it being decided to resort to interior linings rather than the application of these exterior layers.

At the 6-inch battery the ironwork has been scraped and painted, the wooden doors painted, the vertical walls covered with three coats of Sylvester process, and a cement hood placed over the magazine doors.

Money statement.

July 1, 1900, balance unexpended	$2,261.55
June 30, 1901, amount allotted since	1,015.00
	3,276.55
June 30, 1901, amount expended during fiscal year	1,080.88
July 1, 1901, balance unexpended	2,195.67

Torpedo storehouse.—The material for the torpedo defense of Narragansett Bay has all been stored in one place. The storage capacity was more than reached, and with the transfer of the torpedo material to the artillery branch of the service it was concluded to separate this material into that pertaining to the eastern and western passages, transferring that for the western passage for storage in a torpedo storehouse to be constructed. On March 19, 1901, an allotment of $4,000 was made for the construction of this storehouse from the appropriation for "Torpedoes for Harbor Defense," act of March 1, 1901. Plans and estimates have been submitted and approved, foundation course laid, and the brickwork is now in process of construction.

Money statement.

Amount allotted since July 1, 1900	$4,000.00
June 30, 1901, amount expended during fiscal year	299.00
July 1, 1901, balance unexpended	3,701.00
July 1, 1901, outstanding liabilities	1,052.24
July 1, 1901, balance available	2,648.76

Cable tank.—Plans and estimates for the erection of a cable tank for the storage of cable required for the torpedo defense of the western passage were submitted March 7 and approved March 19, 1901, when an allotment of $4,000 was made from the appropriation for "Torpedoes for Harbor Defense," act of March 1, 1901, for the construction of the tank. At the close of the fiscal year the tank was practically completed.

Money statement.

Amount allotted since July 1, 1900	$4,000.00
June 30, 1901, amount expended during fiscal year	392.08
July 1, 1901, balance unexpended	3,607.92
July 1, 1901, outstanding liabilities	1,391.49
July 1, 1901, balance available	2,216.43

Supplies for seacoast defenses.—Under the provisions of the appropriation for "Supplies for Seacoast Defenses," act of May 25, 1900, an allotment of $800 was made June 7, 1900. These funds are expended in furnishing supplies on approved requisitions of the coast artillery.

Money statement.

July 1, 1900, balance unexpended	$800.00
June 30, 1901, amount expended during fiscal year	48.00
July 1, 1901, balance unexpended	752.00

Sites for fortifications and seacoast defenses.—Under the provisions of the act of Congress of May 25, 1900, the Chief of Engineers, on August 18, 1900, directed that a report be submitted showing what land was needed at one of the sites selected for the defenses projected for the western passage. The report was submitted October 24, 1900, and by Department indorsement of October 30, 1900, authority was received to enter into negotiations for the purchase of 25 acres of land.

In November negotiations were entered into with the owner of the land desired, an agreement made as to price, $65,000 for the tract required, and by Department indorsement of November 20, 1900, authority was received and an allotment of funds made for the purchase of the land. In December a survey of the land was made, an allotment of $1,000 from the appropriation for "Sites for Fortifications and Seacoast Defenses," act of March 3, 1899, being made for the purpose. In January an abstract of title was forwarded to the United States district attorney, and during the same month information was received that the Secretary of War had authorized the acquisition of the land by condemnation proceedings. Decree of condemnation was entered March 2, 1901, in the United States circuit court. Payment for the land has not yet been made, as there has been some question as to the necessity or advisability of acquiring a larger tract for the use of the troops.

Money statements.

PURCHASE OF LAND.

Amount allotted since July 1, 1900	$65,000.00
July 1, 1901, balance unexpended	65,000.00

SURVEY OF LAND.

Amount allotted since July 1, 1900	1,000.00
June 30, 1901, amount expended during fiscal year	686.79
July 1, 1901, balance unexpended	313.21

3 E.

DEFENSES OF EASTERN ENTRANCE TO LONG ISLAND SOUND AND COAST OF CONNECTICUT.

Officer in charge, Maj. Smith S. Leach, Corps of Engineers; assistant, Lieut. Edward H. Schulz, Corps of Engineers; Division Engineer, Col. George L. Gillespie, Corps of Engineers (now brigadier-general Chief of Engineers, United States Army), to April 30, 1901, and Col. Charles R. Suter, Corps of Engineers, since May 9, 1901.

DEFENSES OF NEW LONDON.

The defenses of New London consist of Fort Trumbull, on the western side of the harbor, and Fort Griswold, on the eastern side.

Fort Trumbull.—Fort Trumbull occupies a small peninsula jutting out into the Thames River just below the heart of the city. During the past year it has been garrisoned by artillery troops. The fort contains no modern guns or carriages.

There have been no funds on hand during the fiscal year. No work has been done by the Engineer Department. Nothing is contemplated.

Fort Griswold.—Fort Griswold is an earthwork mounting barbette guns, situated on the heights opposite Fort Trumbull. The fort is not garrisoned. During the year an ordnance sergeant has been in immediate charge. The armament is all of old type.

An allotment of $185 was made May 28, 1901, for necessary repairs to the ordnance sergeant's quarters. This work will be done during the coming year.

Money statement.

PRESERVATION AND REPAIR OF FORTIFICATIONS.

May 28, 1901, amount transferred from allotment for other works	$185.00
July 1, 1901, balance available	185.00

DEFENSES OF EASTERN ENTRANCE TO LONG ISLAND SOUND.

Emplacements for two 12-inch B. L. rifles on disappearing carriages, model 1897.—The contract for this battery was entered into December 11, 1896, and included the construction of a crib wharf at the island. The work was begun in the spring of 1897. By July, 1899, the emplacements were practically completed. The electric system is installed and the armament mounted. This battery was the first constructed in this district. There has been considerable trouble from dampness, as no damp proofing was introduced. The means used to overcome this were, first, to paint the superior slope and breastheight with two coats of alum and potash solution, and, second, to cover the loading platform with a coating of asphalt put on hot with sand. Experience has shown that this method of covering platforms is not satisfactory. During the past year a false slab ceiling has been installed in one of the magazines, which method has given good results as regards percolation, but has not reduced condensation as much as desired. To overcome the latter difficulty, it is intended to heat the room artificially by steam.

During the year the base ring of the 12-inch carriage, No. 1 emplacement, has been releveled and reset.

This battery was transferred to the artillery May 12, 1900.

Money statements.

GUN AND MORTAR BATTERIES.

Mounting guns.

July 1, 1900, balance unexpended		$141.89
June 30, 1901, amount expended during fiscal year	$124.20	
May 9, 1901, amount deposited to credit of Treasurer of United States	17.69	
		141.89

PRESERVATION AND REPAIR OF FORTIFICATIONS.

Slopes, etc.

July 1, 1900, balance unexpended	$260.00
June 30, 1901, amount expended during fiscal year	260.00

Care of fortifications.

July 1, 1900, balance unexpended	$0.98
June 30, 1901, amount expended during fiscal year	.98

Waterproofing.

July 1, 1900, balance unexpended	$535.43
June 30, 1901, amount expended during fiscal year	535.43

Emplacements for two 10-inch B. L. rifles on disappearing carriages, model 1896.—The construction of this battery was begun in March, 1898. By July, 1898, the platforms were ready for the armament, and the completed battery, with installation for light and power, was transferred to the artillery on May 12, 1900. During the present year some sodding has been done on the slopes. No other work has been done except furnishing minor supplies for the electric system.

Money statement.

GUN AND MORTAR BATTERIES.

November 13, 1900, amount allotted	$500.00
July 1, 1901, outstanding liabilities	500.00

Emplacements for two 6-inch rapid-fire guns on pedestal mounts.—An allotment for this work was made June 26, 1901. At the close of the fiscal year no work had been done except preparation of drawings.

Money statement.

June 26, 1901, amount allotted	$25,000.00
July 1, 1901, balance available	25,000.00

Range-finder station for 12-inch battery.—An allotment of $7,000 was made August 16, 1900, for the construction of this station. Active field work was begun in April, 1901. Foundation and concrete column were constructed by the United States. All other work was done by contract. The station is the typical low-site, instrument axis 60 feet above mean low water. Owing to the lowness of the site and exposure

APPENDIX 3—FORTIFICATIONS. 749

to wind and sea the foundation was carried to low water. At the close of the fiscal year the station is practically complete, except minor details of painting and finishing up.

Money statement.

August 16, 1900, amount allotted	$7,000.00
June 30, 1901, amount expended during fiscal year	1,722.44
July 1, 1901, balance unexpended	5,277.56
July 1, 1901, outstanding liabilities	3,792.81
July 1, 1901, balance available	1,484.75

Construction of sea wall.—On September 8, 1900, an allotment of $12,000 was made for the construction of a random rubble wall for the protection of the exposed portion of one of the sites. This exposed part is practically the entire central portion of the southern shore. The work was begun near the western end, and the portion in front of the barracks and quarters has now been protected. The heavy footing stones were obtained from the quarry by purchase, and the remaining stones from another reservation. The United States steam lighter transported all stone and loaded it on cars. It was then hauled by stationary engine and placed in the work by derrick. At the close of the fiscal year 5,050 tons have been placed in the wall and 330 linear feet of wall have been completed. This is much the heaviest part of the work owing to height of bank. The exposed banks are subject to disintegration by frost action. The sea wall is constructed as a revetment, holding the bank in place so that further disintegration and falling away are prevented. The work is about one-quarter completed as to length and half as to volume and cost.

Money statements.

SEA WALLS AND EMBANKMENTS.

September 8, 1900, amount allotted	$12,000.00
June 30, 1901, amount expended during fiscal year	6,276.22
July 1, 1901, balance unexpended	5,723.78
July 1, 1901, outstanding liabilities	787.94
July 1, 1901, balance available	4,935.84

PRESERVATION AND REPAIR OF FORTIFICATIONS.

May 28, 1901, amount transferred from another allotment:	
For repairing electric plant of 12-inch battery, including new switchboard and rewiring	$750.00
For continuing damp proofing of magazines in 12-inch emplacements	1,000.00
For repairing slopes, painting ironwork, etc	150.00
	1,900.00
July 1, 1901, balance available	1,900.00

Emplacements for two 10-inch B. L. rifles on disappearing carriages, model 1896, and a mining casemate.—This work was done under contract with Mairs & Lewis, entered into August 11, 1897, and included the construction of a crib wharf. The battery commander's station for this battery was subsequently built by the United States. The battery and station were completed and transferred to the troops on

750   REPORT OF THE CHIEF OF ENGINEERS, U. S. ARMY.

March 31, 1900. During the present year the casemate has been wired and partition wall installed separating the operating from the accumulator room. It is now complete, but not equipped, and was transferred to the troops April 30, 1901.

Minor repairs to the battery have been made during the year.

Money statement.

PRESERVATION AND REPAIR OF FORTIFICATIONS.

July 1, 1900, balance unexpended	$250.00
June 30, 1901, amount expended during fiscal year	250.00

Emplacements for eight 12-inch B. L. steel mortars.—Plans for this battery were made and approved in the early part of 1898. The work was begun about July 1, 1898. At the beginning of the fiscal year the battery was complete except earthwork, sodding, concreting terreplein, and electric system. The battery commander's station was completed. During the present year the battery has been completed and the electric plant installed. The plant was tested in January and February. This plant furnishes current to the 6-inch battery, the 5-inch and 4.7-inch emplacements, and to the mining casemate. The electric system includes a 64-cell, 70-ampere Willard accumulator, in lead-lined tanks. The first test of this accumulator not being entirely satisfactory, the company decided to replace the positive plates with new ones. The accumulator was again tested in May, and was accepted as satisfactory. The mortar battery and battery commander's station, with all engineer and ordnance property, were transferred to the artillery on March 4, 1901. The armament is all on hand. Two mortars and two carriages in the right pit are mounted.

Money statement.

GUN AND MORTAR BATTERIES.

July 1, 1900, balance unexpended	$7,121.64
June 30, 1901, amount allotted during the fiscal year	2,000.00
	9,121.64
June 30, 1901, amount expended during fiscal year	8,869.64
July 1, 1901, balance unexpended	252.00
July 1, 1901, outstanding liabilities	252.00

Emplacements for two 6-inch rapid-fire guns on disappearing mounts.—This work was begun about June, 1899. At the beginning of the fiscal year the battery was practically complete except consolidation of slopes, roadways, and electric lighting.

On July 30 an allotment of $2,000 was made for the adaptation of the room in the rear traverse of this battery for a power room and the construction of a casemate shelter on the left flank of the battery for a 30-inch projector. A track for drill purposes was also built. The searchlight is the 30-inch type, electrically controlled. Power is furnished by a 16-horsepower oil engine and a 7.9-kilowatts dynamo. The battery and shelter room were completed in December. The electric system was installed and tested, and the entire battery, with searchlight, ordnance, and engineer property, transferred to the artillery March 4, 1901.

Carriages for this battery are on hand, not mounted; guns not yet received.

APPENDIX 3—FORTIFICATIONS.

Money statements.

GUN AND MORTAR BATTERIES.

6-inch battery.

July 1, 1900, balance unexpended	$21,501.60
June 30, 1901, amount expended during fiscal year	21,501.60

Installation of searchlight, etc.

July 30, 1900, amount allotted	$2,000.00
June 30, 1901, amount expended during fiscal year	2,000.00

Emplacement for a 4.7-inch Armstrong rapid-fire gun.—This emplacement was finished in July, 1898. The armament is complete. Electric wiring is installed. The emplacement was transferred to the troops March 26, 1900.

Emplacement for 5-inch rapid-fire wire-wound gun.—At the beginning of the fiscal year this emplacement was nine-tenths completed. During the year the work was finished, electric wiring installed, and emplacement transferred to the artillery March 4, 1901.

Money statements.

GUN AND MORTAR BATTERIES.

July 1, 1900, balance unexpended	$1,652.61
June 30, 1901, amount expended during fiscal year	1,652.61

PRESERVATION AND REPAIR OF FORTIFICATIONS.

Repairing slopes, painting ironwork, etc.

May 28, 1901, amount allotted	$150.00
July 1, 1901, balance available	150.00

Emplacements for two 8-inch B. L. rifles on disappearing carriages, model 1896, and two 5-inch rapid-fire guns on balanced-pillar mounts.—Plans for these emplacements were drawn early in 1898. Work was begun on a pile dock in August of the same year. At the beginning of the fiscal year the batteries were completed and electric system installed. Two carriages and one gun of the 8-inch battery had been mounted and two carriages for the 5-inch battery were mounted. During the year the electric system has been maintained and painting of ironwork, etc., has been done. The batteries were in charge of two watchmen until their transfer to the troops on February 18, 1901. The asphalt waterproof covering on the 8-inch platforms has proved unsatisfactory. On April 27 an allotment of $1,500 was made for the thorough waterproofing of these platforms. The plan to be followed consists in cutting away the asphalt and granolithic surface and placing a layer of tar paper and asphalt, to be followed by 4 to 6 inches of concrete and granolithic covering. In addition, a more positive drainage will be given to the terreplein.

The remaining 8-inch B. L. rifle is now on hand, not mounted.

Money statements.

GUN AND MORTAR BATTERIES.

Two 8-inch gun emplacements.

July 1, 1900, balance unexpended	$556.60
July 30, 1901, amount expended during fiscal year	556.60

PRESERVATION AND REPAIR OF FORTIFICATIONS.

For waterproofing, drainage, etc.

April 27, 1901, amount allotted	$1,500.00
July 1, 1901, balance available	1,500.00

Emplacements for two 5-inch rapid-fire wire-wound guns.—This battery was begun in the fall of 1899. At the beginning of the fiscal year it was about nine-tenths complete. During the present year the electric wiring has been installed and slopes completed and sodded. Current for lighting is obtained by underground cable from the power plant at the 8-inch battery. The battery was transferred to the troops February 18, 1901.

No armament is on hand.

Money statement.

July 1, 1900, balance unexpended	$4,642.46
June 30, 1901, amount expended during fiscal year	4,642.46

Bank revetment.—On May 1 an allotment of $2,600 was made for the construction of a bank revetment of piles and sheet piling. This revetment is to be in front of the temporary barracks and is to be about 400 feet long. It is intended to prevent the erosion of the bank and also to raise the general level of the shore line. At the end of the fiscal year proposals had been called for and received, and it is probable that award will be made and the work executed this summer.

Money statements.

SEA WALLS AND EMBANKMENTS.

May 1, 1901, amount allotted	$2,600.00
June 30, 1901, amount expended during fiscal year	16.97
July 1, 1901, balance available	2,583.03

PRESERVATION AND REPAIR OF FORTIFICATIONS.

General works of repair.

July 1, 1900, balance unexpended		$1,650.00
June 30, 1901, amount expended during fiscal year	$822.00	
June 30, 1901, amount deposited to credit of Treasurer United States	28.00	
May 28, 1901, amount transferred to other works	800.00	
		1,650.00

Repairing slopes, painting ironwork, etc.

May 28, 1901, amount transferred from allotment for other work	$100.00
July 1, 1901, balance available	100.00

Emplacements for two 8-inch B. L. rifles.—This battery is located on an exposed, low, sandy site. The work was begun in 1898 and sufficiently completed for use by the spring of 1899. It was intended (and so constructed) to temporarily mount the rifles on 15-inch smoothbore converted barbette carriages. The carriages and rifles are on hand, but not mounted. It is now proposed to modify the platforms for disappearing carriages, model 1896, which change was considered and provided for in the original construction. The platforms will at the same time be made thoroughly waterproof. During the year

APPENDIX 3—FORTIFICATIONS. 753

minor repairs have been made. The work has been in charge of two watchmen.

Emplacements for two 5-inch rapid-fire wire-wound guns, with parados.—Operations began in the fall of 1898. The emplacements are completed; armament not on hand. No garrison is present.

In conjunction with the 8-inch battery improvement a thorough system of damp proofing will be introduced on the platforms.

The site of this work is a bar of gravel and sand, about 250 feet wide, 1,200 feet long, and 5 feet above high-water level. The exposure is very great, and a sea wall was imperative. During the present year the sea wall has been strengthened and extended. The project includes filling in the area within the wall to high water by gravel or otherwise. The work is about seven-tenths complete. Actual work under the present allotment was begun in August, 1900. At the end of the fiscal year 3,450 tons had been placed.

Money statements.

GUN AND MORTAR BATTERIES.

Emplacements for two 5-inch rapid-fire wire-wound guns.

July 1, 1900, balance unexpended	$1,256.61
June 30, 1901, amount expended during fiscal year	864.50
July 1, 1901, balance available	392.11

SEA WALLS AND EMBANKMENTS.

July 5, 1901, amount allotted	$8,000.00
June 30, 1901, amount expended during fiscal year	6,197.88
July 1, 1901, balance available	1,802.12

PRESERVATION AND REPAIR OF FORTIFICATIONS.

July 1, 1900, balance unexpended		$2,432.68
May 28, 1901, amounts allotted:		
For watchmen, laborers	$1,495.00	
For supplies for maintenance and operation of electrical installation	100.00	
		1,595.00
May 28, 1901, amounts transferred from another allotment, to be applied as follows:		
For repairing slopes, painting ironwork, etc	$150.00	
For watchmen, laborers	65.00	
		215.00
		4,242.68
June 30, 1901, amount expended during fiscal year	1,510.36	
June 30, 1901, amount withdrawn	200.00	
June 30, 1901, amount deposited to credit of Treasurer United States	122.32	
		1,832.68
July 1, 1901, balance avalable		2,410.00

Emplacements for two 12-inch B. L. rifles on disappearing carriages, model 1897; two 10-inch B. L. rifles on disappearing carriages, model 1896; and three 6-inch rapid-fire guns on disappearing mounts.—The 12-inch and 10-inch emplacements: Work was begun in December, 1898. A cut was dredged through the beach into a pond, thus forming a sheltered harbor. A breakwater jetty was built to protect the cut, and a dock was constructed on the shore of the pond.

At the beginning of the fiscal year the power room at the two 10-inch emplacements and the casemates in rear of them had been completed, and the 12-inch emplacements were well advanced, the anchor bolts set, and concreted up to loading platform. The entire battery was completed, except electric installation, by December, 1900. Test of the electric system is now in hand. This has been somewhat delayed on account of quarantine restrictions from May 4 to 20, due to a case of smallpox. In installing the electric system the report of the board of officers on electric installations has been closely followed. The electric plant includes two 40-horsepower upright boilers, one 50-kilowatt generating set, an 80-ampere, 58-cell, chloride accumulator in lead-lined tanks.

During the year the chain ammunition lifts for the four emplacements have been purchased and placed.

Three temporary range-finder stations and a tide gauge have been built, to be used by the troops in target practice with the above battery.

The battery was transferred to the troops on March 7, 1901.

The three 6-inch emplacements: Preliminary work was begun in December, 1898. At the beginning of the fiscal year excavation had been made and concrete well advanced. The battery was completed in December, 1900. The electric wiring is now being installed. The system includes a 35-ampere chloride accumulator, to be charged from the main plant of the 10-inch and 12-inch battery. During the year chain ammunition lifts have been installed. The three carriages are mounted; the guns are not on hand. The battery was transferred to the troops March 7, 1901.

Money statements.

TWO 12-INCH AND TWO 10-INCH GUN EMPLACEMENTS.

July 1, 1900, balance unexpended	$40,044.02
June 30, 1901, amount expended during fiscal year	38,325.60
July 1, 1901, balance unexpended	1,718.42
July 1, 1901, outstanding liabilities	1,718.42

THREE 6-INCH GUN EMPLACEMENTS.

July 1, 1900, balance unexpended	$52,943.48
June 30, 1901, amount expended during fiscal year	50,638.35
July 1, 1901, balance unexpended	2,305.13
July 1, 1901, outstanding liabilities	2,305.13

Emplacements for eight 12-inch B. L. steel mortars.—Allotment for this battery was made July 7, 1900. Material was purchased and track laid in October and November. Excavation began in December. At the end of the fiscal year the middle traverse was completed and the right one well advanced. The plant comprises a radial cable way of about 750 feet span, two locomotives, a steam crane, and two gravity concrete mixers. Excellent sand has been obtained on the site. Gravel is obtained from the beach, and grout was taken from various parts of the reservation. The rooms of this battery will be completely damp-proofed by paper and asphalt both over the ceiling and under the floors. I-beams are spanned by 6-inch thick, flat, hollow-tile arches; I-beams not exposed. A system of steam heating has been provided for. The electric system will include wiring, switchboard, and a 50-ampere accumulator.

Money statement.

July 7, 1900, amount allotted	$105,000.00
February 18, 1901, amount allotted	10,000.00
	115,000.00
June 30, 1901, amount expended during fiscal year	52,269.15
July 1, 1901, balance unexpended	62,730.85
July 1, 1901, outstanding liabilities	2,507.63
July 1, 1901, balance available	60,223.22

Protection of dynamite battery.—On August 1, 1900, an allotment of $66,000 was made for protection to the dynamite battery. During the year structural steel and other materials have been purchased and delivered. Actual work is deferred until completion of the test of this gun by the Ordnance Department.

Money statements.

GUN AND MORTAR BATTERIES.

August 1, 1900, amount allotted	$66,000.00
June 30, 1901, amount expended during fiscal year	3,675.82
July 1, 1901, balance available	62,324.18

PRESERVATION AND REPAIR OF FORTIFICATIONS.

General works of repair.

July 1, 1901, balance unexpended	$2,000.00
May 28, 1901, amount transferred to other works	2,000.00

Specific allotments.

May 28, 1901, amounts transferred from another allotment, to be applied as follows:

For repair of slopes, painting ironwork, etc	$250.00
For supplies for maintenance and operation of electrical installations prior to transfer to artillery	150.00
July 1, 1901, balance available	400.00

Preservation and repair of fortifications.—During the past year an electrician has been employed in keeping in repair the several electric plants pertaining to the batteries. From a special allotment incidental supplies and repairs have been made to the various fortifications and electric systems.

Money statements.

PRESERVATION AND REPAIR OF FORTIFICATIONS.

For electrician.

October 15, 1900, amount allotted.................................		$900.00
June 30, 1901, amount expended during fiscal year	$538.75	
June 30, 1901, amount withdrawn.............................	300.00	
June 30, 1901, amount deposited to credit of Treasurer United States	61.25	
		900.00
May 28, 1901, amount allotted..................................		$900.00
July 1, 1901, balance available		900.00

Civilian electrician.

July 1, 1900, balance unexpended	$225.00
June 30, 1901, amount expended during fiscal year	225.00

SUPPLIES FOR SEACOAST DEFENSES.

July 1, 1900, balance unexpended	$800.00
June 30, 1901, amount expended during fiscal year	184.15
July 1, 1901, balance unexpended	615.85
July 1, 1901, outstanding liabilities	73.86
July 1, 1901, balance available	541.99

Submarine-mining material.—This material has been inspected and overhauled, and was invoiced and transferred to the artillery May 20, 1901. A torpedo casemate was transferred to the artillery on April 30, 1901

Money statements.

PRESERVATION AND REPAIR OF FORTIFICATIONS.

Care of torpedo material.

July 1, 1900, balance unexpended	$177.79
June 30, 1901, amount expended during fiscal year	177.79

Inspection of torpedo material.

December 21, 1900, amount allotted	$50.00
June 30, 1901, amount expended during fiscal year	50.00

Approximate value of plant belonging to the United States and used upon the construction of fortifications under the appropriation for " Gun and Mortar Batteries."

Class of property.	Approximate value June 30, 1901.
Hoisting and conveying machinery.......................	$3,000.00
Railroad plant...	1,500.00
Tools, appliances, etc...	500.00
Cement tester, concrete mixers, etc........................	500.00
Office furniture...	85.00
Surveying instruments...	100.00
Typewriter...	50.00
Drawing instruments...	10.00
Steam lighter Panuco...	5,500.00
Derricks...	25.00
Boilers, engines, and pumps..................................	900.00
Outfit for quarters...	25.00
Total...	12,195.00

3 F.

DEFENSES OF NEW YORK HARBOR.

Officer in charge of artillery defense and of torpedo defense of southern entrance to harbor, Maj. William L. Marshall, Corps of Engineers; assistants, Lieut. James A. Woodruff, Corps of Engineers, until September 19, 1900, and Lieut. James F. McIndoe, Corps of Engineers, until March 9, 1901. Officers in charge of torpedo defense of eastern entrance to harbor, Maj. John G. D. Knight, Corps of Engineers, until April 29, 1901, and since that date Maj. William M. Black, Corps of Engineers. Division Engineers, Col. George L. Gillespie, Corps of Engineers (now brigadier-general, Chief of Engineers, United States Army), until April 30, 1901, and Col. Charles R. Suter, Corps of Engineers, since May 9, 1901.

AT EASTERN ENTRANCE TO HARBOR.

Mortar battery for sixteen 12-inch mortars.—At the beginning of the fiscal year the mortar battery had been completed, mortars mounted, and the battery lighted by electricity.

An earthen parapet and temporary magazines had been constructed for the practice battery, where one 8-inch B. L. rifle on altered 15-inch carriage and one 8-inch converted rifle were mounted.

Two emplacements for 5-inch rapid-fire guns, begun in August, 1899, were nearly completed.

During the past fiscal year the following work was done:

Two emplacements for 5-inch rapid-fire guns.—The emplacements were completed and turned over to the commanding officer February 26, 1901. They are not yet armed.

Two emplacements for 6-inch rapid-fire guns.—Construction was authorized in June, 1901, and on June 17 excavating and clearing the site was begun.

Preservation and repair of fortifications.—During the past fiscal year the following work was done at the mortar battery: A retaining wall was built at the entrance to the northwest pit, where the embankment was falling; a new manhole was built and drains cleaned; repairs were made to the embankment. Total cost, $149.20.

Armament.—No changes during the year.

Sea walls and embankments.—Under an allotment for sea-wall construction a project was approved for building a sea wall about 300 feet long on the northeast side of the site. Work under this allotment was begun June 4. Materials have been purchased and derrick and plant prepared for construction.

Money statements.

GUN AND MORTAR BATTERIES.

July 1, 1900, balance unexpended		$5,419.65
Allotted since		27,500.00
		32,919.65
June 30, 1901, amount expended during fiscal year	$3,812.38	
Restored to appropriation	1,457.27	
		5,269.65
July 1, 1901, balance unexpended		27,650.00
July 1, 1901, outstanding liabilities		705.76
July 1, 1901, balance available		26,944.24

PRESERVATION AND REPAIR OF FORTIFICATIONS.

July 1, 1900, balance unexpended	$223.92
Allotted since	400.00
	623.92
June 30, 1901, amount expended during fiscal year	103.77
July 1, 1901, balance unexpended and available	520.15

SEA WALLS AND EMBANKMENTS.

Amount allotted	10,000.00
June 30, 1901, amount expended during fiscal year	175.00
July 1, 1901, balance unexpended	9,825.00
July 1, 1901, outstanding liabilities	985.00
July 1, 1901, balance available	8,840.00

On the northern side of eastern entrance.—These works consist of an old stone fort and outlying batteries, with modern batteries.

At the beginning of the fiscal year, July 1, 1900, the battery of two 10-inch guns had been completed and armed; two 12-inch emplacements had been completed and armed; two emplacements for 5-inch rapid-fire guns had been completed and base rings set, guns not mounted; two emplacements for 15-pounder rapid fire guns had been completed, but not armed; an electric-light plant had been installed in one of the casemates of the stone fort and connected with the complete emplacements; two range-finder stations, type A, had been constructed, and a searchlight had been mounted and connected.

During the past fiscal year the following work has been done:

One emplacement for 12-inch gun (No. 2); a small amount of grading was done in rear of platform and surface drains were made; the emplacement was turned over to the commanding officer August 15, 1900.

Two emplacements for 15-pounder rapid-fire guns: Base rings were received and set and the emplacements turned over to the commanding officer December 22, 1900. The guns were received and mounted.

Iron gallery to connect loading platforms of 10-inch battery: This was authorized May 8, 1900. Material was purchased and the gallery erected, painted, and completed in November, 1900. The length of the gallery is 55 feet. Its total cost was $608.24, of which $404.74 was for structural materials and $203.50 for labor, painting, etc.

Electric tide indicator: This consists of a box tide gauge with float and electric connections to the range-finder stations, to record there the height of tide. The construction was completed and was turned over to the commanding officer May 11, 1901.

Cost of tide indicator	$325.00
Cable and materials for connections	58.90
Labor setting up the system	91.10
Total cost	475.00

Preservation and repair of fortifications: The rooms, magazines, and galleries of the 10-inch and 12-inch emplacements were rewired, armored cable being substituted for iron conduits. Cost:

Materials	$391.46
Labor	315.26
Total cost	706.72

The 10-inch and 12-inch batteries were waterproofed (Sylvester process), a doorway in the stone fort was cut out, doors were painted, and repairs were made to slopes, hand rails, and electric-light wires.

Sea walls: At the beginning of the year $10,904.47 were available for building a sea wall on the north shore of the reservation. A wall was built along the line of half tide on the beach from a point 360 feet west from 12-inch emplacement No. 2 to about 700 feet from the west line of the reservation.

The wall was built of rubble stone, laid in cement mortar, the voids filled with concrete; most of the wall was covered with a coping course made from old stone on hand. The length of wall built was 1,343 feet, and the total cost, including labor and materials purchased for shore protection, was $12,262.81.

In May, 1901, $15,000 were allotted for the construction of about 800 linear feet of sea wall on the south shore of the reservation, the wall to be built of rubble masonry, with capping at 14 feet above mean low water.

Material has been purchased and up to the close of the fiscal year 50 linear feet of wall have been built, but no coping yet put on.

Money statements.

GUN AND MORTAR BATTERIES.

July 1, 1900, balance unexpended		$15,308.92
Allotted since		475.00
		15,783.92
June 30, 1901, amount expended during fiscal year	$2,509.03	
Restored and deposited to credit of appropriation	13,274.89	
		15,783.92

PRESERVATION AND REPAIR OF FORTIFICATIONS.

July 1, 1900, balance unexpended	$1,572.57
Allotted since	1,700.00
	3,272.57
June 30, 1901, amount expended during fiscal year	1,624.30
July 1, 1901, balance unexpended	1,648.27
July 1, 1901, outstanding liabilities	33.75
July 1, 1901, balance available	1,614.52

SEA WALLS AND EMBANKMENTS.

July 1, 1900, balance unexpended	$11,173.05
Allotted since	15,000.00
	26,173.05
June 30, 1901, amount expended during fiscal year	10,853.04
July 1, 1901, balance unexpended	15,320.01
July 1, 1901, outstanding liabilities	1,393.99
July 1, 1901, balance available	13,926.02

On southern side of eastern entrance.—These fortifications consist of an old casemated stone fort with old batteries and modern defenses.

At the beginning of the fiscal year, July 1, 1900, a mortar battery containing eight positions for 12-inch B. L. mortars had been completed and armed; at the gun battery (six positions for disappearing guns) two 10-inch and two 8-inch emplacements had been completed and armed, and two 12-inch emplacements had been completed, except some minor fittings, and were armed; two emplacements for 15-pounder rapid-fire guns had been completed and were armed; two emplacements for 5-inch rapid-fire guns had been nearly completed and were ready for armament; an electric-light plant, with underground conduits for connections, was under construction; a mining casemate had been built and turned over to the commanding officer.

During the past fiscal year the following work was done:

Two emplacements for 5-inch rapid-fire guns: The carriages were received, set in place, and grouted, and the pavements finished. The emplacements were turned over to the commanding officer December 11, 1900.

Disappearing gun battery: The two emplacements for 12-inch guns were completed, the ammunition hoists and magazines were painted, shutters placed in doors, and electric connections finished. Cost, $623.71.

The roads in rear of and near the battery were graded, macadamized, and drained, and side slopes sodded; iron stairways and concrete steps were placed; and minor repairs made, at a cost of $1,127.52.

Iron galleries were built to connect the loading platforms of emplacements 1 and 2 of the gun battery, at a total cost of $1,548.93.

Electric-light plant: This consists of a 55-horsepower Worthington boiler; a 33-kilowatt dynamo, direct connected; a storage battery of 64 cells, type 13 G chloride accumulator. The installation has been completed, and the plant was turned over to the commanding officer October 30, 1900.

Preservation and repair of fortifications: Under allotments from this appropriation rooms and galleries have been painted, the engineer wharf has been repaired, watchmen have been employed to care for property, slopes have been mowed, and minor repairs have been made to embankments, drains, slopes, walls, etc., at a total cost of $730.27.

Armament: Two 5-inch rapid-fire guns and carriages mounted on pillar mounts; two 12-inch guns mounted on disappearing carriages.

Money statements.

GUN AND MORTAR BATTERIES.

July 1, 1900, balance unexpended		$13,127.62
Allotted since		5,600.00
		18,727.62
June 30, 1901, amount expended during fiscal year	$17,413.33	
Deposited to credit of appropriation	154.19	
		17,567.52
July 1, 1901, balance unexpended		1,160.10
July 1, 1901, outstanding liabilities		168.89
July 1, 1901, balance available		991.21

PRESERVATION AND REPAIR OF FORTIFICATIONS.

July 1, 1900, balance unexpended	$949.58
Allotted since	600.00
	1,549.58
June 30, 1901, amount expended during fiscal year	940.85
July 1, 1901, balance unexpended	608.73
July 1, 1901, outstanding liabilities	18.92
July 1, 1901, balance available	589.81

APPENDIX 3—FORTIFICATIONS. 761

Torpedo defense of eastern entrance to harbor.—A complete list showing all the materials needed for the approved project of this defense is on file.

Forty-three 1,000-pound anchors and 43 buoyant mine cases that were stored at another locality were removed to Willets Point, N. Y.

Anchors and mine cases belonging to the material for this defense are now stored at Willets Point, N. Y.

The removal of mine caps of old-pattern mine cases and the fitting out of the same with pins for jointing boxes was begun.

All other materials are in good condition.

A storeroom has been selected for the reception of all of the necessary material for this locality, excepting the anchors and cables, and partly fitted up. The heavier materials have been stored there.

Two railroad transits have been added to the supply of materials by purchase.

April 22, 1901, a report was forwarded to the Chief of Engineers, United States Army, as to the submarine-mine work proposed at the eastern entrance to New York Harbor, accompanied by a tracing showing the location of the mining casemate, cable tanks, and of the cables leading to the mines; also accompanied by a list of materials on hand and to be supplied from depot. By letter of May 7, 1901, from the Office of the Adjutant-General United States Army, this material was ordered to be placed under the charge of the commanding officer of the post.

AT SOUTHERN ENTRANCE TO HARBOR.

Fort Columbus, Castle Williams, and South Battery.—No modern works of defense are at this point, and no work was done during the fiscal year ending June 30, 1901.

Sea wall at Governors Island, New York Harbor.—This wall, completed in 1893, incloses the entire island. It is in good repair and no work upon it is required at present.

During the past fiscal year the embankment on the southwest side of the island and close against the sea wall was washed out in places to a depth of from one-half to 2 feet, occasioned for the most part by seas washing over the wall; this is the most exposed place of the island. The excavation was filled with about 10 yards of large stone and 30 yards of broken stone, rammed into the hollows. The total cost was $90.94, and was paid by an allotment from the appropriation for "Preservation and Repair of Fortifications," act of May 7, 1898.

Money statement.

PRESERVATION AND REPAIR OF FORTIFICATIONS.

Amount allotted		$250.00
June 30, 1901, amount expended during fiscal year	$90.94	
Deposited to credit of appropriation	159.06	
		250.00

Fort Lafayette, New York.—This work is situated on Hendricks Shoal, in the Narrows, New York Harbor, about 1,000 feet from the Long Island shore. The area inclosed by a sea wall is about 270 feet square.

The fort is a circular casemated structure in three tiers, built of

Newark red sandstone founded on riprap. It was injured by fire in 1868, since which time it has been abandoned as a work of defense.

No work has been done during the past fiscal year.

Fort Wood.—The fortifications consist of a stone fort and outer earthen batteries. No work was done upon the fortifications during the fiscal year ending June 30, 1901.

Sea wall at Bedloes Island, New York Harbor.—The island is surrounded by masonry sea walls from the north angle around the east and south sides to the west side, leaving a length of about 715 feet on the northwest side with no protection.

May 2, 1901, a project was submitted for completing the west front of the island by building a wall of rubble masonry, with coping, and filling in behind it; the wall to be built along the contour of 2 feet above mean low water, to be 714 feet long and 8.4 feet above mean low-water level; estimated cost, $20,000.

By indorsement of the Chief of Engineers, dated May 6, 1901, an allotment of $20,000 from the appropriation for "Sea Walls and Embankments," act of March 1, 1901, was made for the purpose of building a sea wall along this exposed section and filling and grading behind the wall.

Proposals for doing this work by contract were invited, and opened June 24, 1901. The lowest bidder was Harry L. Smith, 240 Purdy street, Long Island City, N. Y. The contract is not yet awarded.

Money statement.

Amount allotted	$20,000.00
June 30, 1901, amount expended during fiscal year	32.49
July 1, 1901, balance unexpended and available	19,967.51

Defenses on Long Island.—These fortifications consist of an old casemated stone fort and outlying batteries, with modern batteries.

During the past fiscal year the following work has been done:

Battery of seven 10-inch guns: The rear ditch has been widened, slopes sodded, and a concrete retaining wall built; water supply has been carried to the gun platforms; and electric-light conduits have been laid; all at a total cost of $3,500.

Battery of four 12-inch guns: Emplacements Nos. 3 and 4 were graded and sodded, doors were hung, electric lights installed, iron work painted, and water supply carried to the platforms. The emplacements are completed. Guns were mounted in emplacements Nos. 3 and 4. Total expenditures, $3,966.77.

Mortar battery: Six hundred and fifty-six cubic yards of concrete were placed, and 5,529 cubic yards of earth in parapet and slopes; the embankment was sodded, the ditch macadamized, and gutters paved; water supply was carried to the mortar pits; an electric-lighting system was installed, and ammunition trolleys put in and stairs erected. The battery is completed; it was turned over to the artillery March 4, 1901. Total expenditures, $12,041.46.

Two 12-inch emplacements: Eight thousand four hundred and ninety-three cubic yards of concrete were placed, parapet graded, doors hung, electric lights partly installed, ammunition cranes, ladders, and hand rails erected, and water supply carried to the platforms. The platforms are completed and ready for armament. Total expenditures, $49,578.45.

Two 6-inch emplacements: Four hundred and twenty-eight cubic yards of obstructing masonry were removed and 4,317 cubic yards of concrete placed; parapets were graded, doors hung, electric lights partly installed, cranes, ladders, and hand rails erected, and water supply carried to the platforms. The emplacements are nearly completed; the platforms are ready for armament. Total expenditures, $28,512.14.

One fire commander's station and two battery commanders' stations: Construction has been authorized, materials purchased, and work is in progress.

Installation of electric-light plants: The project is for two direct-connected steam engines and generating sets of 37½-kilowatt and 62¼-kilowatt capacity at 110 volts, each to have independent steam boilers; two sets of storage batteries with switchboard; a brick power house, and lead-covered insulated distributing cables. Estimated cost, $41,500. Allotments were made in May, 1901. Machinery has been ordered and construction of power house begun.

Four emplacements for 6-inch rapid-fire guns, pedestal mounts, model 1900: Under an allotment of $40,000, made May 15, 1901, from the appropriation for "Gun and Mortar Batteries," act of March 1, 1901, advertisement was made and specifications were issued for cement and stone, and bids were opened June 20, 1901; contracts were entered into and forwarded to the Chief of Engineers. They are not yet approved.

Preservation and repair of fortifications: Under allotments available during the past fiscal year work was done as follows:

At the seven-gun battery: Slopes and doors were repaired, iron shutters built, covers supplied for hygrometers and thermometers, supports for sponges and rammers built, and leakage in ceilings repaired.

At the battery of four 12-inch guns: Slopes were repaired, leakage in ceilings stopped, supports made for sponges and rammers, and skids for shot built.

At the mortar battery: Slopes were repaired, supports made for sponges and rammers, and skids for shot.

Armament: One 12-inch gun mounted on Emplacement No. 3, and one 12-inch gun mounted on Emplacement No. 4 of the 12-inch battery.

Money statements.

GUN AND MORTAR BATTERIES.

Battery construction.

July 1, 1900, balance unexpended		$173,890.58
Alloted since		53,800.00
		227,690.58
June 30, 1901, amount expended during fiscal year	$122,764.00	
Restored and deposited to credit of appropriation	14,255.59	
Transferred to allotment for electric plant	17,000.00	
		154,019.59
July 1, 1901, balance unexpended		73,670.99
July 1, 1901, outstanding liabilities		10,738.62
July 1, 1901, balance available		62,932.37

Electric plant.

Allotted	$30,000.00
June 30, 1901, amount expended during fiscal year	2,465.40
July 1, 1901, balance unexpended	27,534.60
July 1, 1901, outstanding liabilities	26,491.75
July 1, 1901, balance available	1,042.85

SEARCHLIGHTS FOR NEW YORK HARBOR.

Allotted	$11,500.00
July 1, 1901, outstanding liabilities	11,500.00

PRESERVATION AND REPAIR OF FORTIFICATIONS.

July 1, 1900, balance unexpended	$3,089.03
Allotted since	2,500.00
	5,589.03
June 30, 1901, amount expended during fiscal year	2,381.77
July 1, 1901, balance unexpended and available	3,207.26

Defenses on Staten Island.—These fortifications consist of two old casemate stone forts and outlying batteries with modern defenses.

During the past fiscal year the following work has been done:

Two emplacements for 12-inch guns: The emplacements were completed and transferred to commanding officer August 18, 1900; mounting guns and carriages not yet completed.

Two emplacements for 6-inch guns on disappearing carriages: The emplacements were completed and transferred to commanding officer, October 29, 1900; guns and carriage are not yet mounted.

Two emplacements for 12-inch guns: The first allotment for construction was made July 9, 1900; work was begun at once, and up to June 30, 1901, excavation for foundations had been made and 6,717 cubic yards of concrete had been placed, building the concrete structure up to an average height of 3 feet above the loading platforms. The total amount of concrete in the battery, when completed, is estimated at 10,256 cubic yards.

New central electric power station: Excavation was begun June 1, and construction of brick walls is under way; awards have been made for furnishing boiler, engines, generators, cables, and other supplies.

Steel galleries were built to connect adjacent loading platforms at three batteries.

Preservation and repair of fortifications: Under several allotments the submarine-mining material was cared for, cleaned, and stored; the mining casemate, torpedo storage building, three cable tanks, and submarine-mining material were transferred to the artillery May 6, 1901; roofs of torpedo-storage building and of cable tanks were scraped and painted; electric-light systems, with conduits laid for cables, were installed; removing an arch in south cliff battery was begun; hygrometric shelters were built, and minor repairs were made to sodding, doors, etc.

APPENDIX 3—FORTIFICATIONS.

Following is a detailed statement of cost of work done upon two 12-inch emplacements during the past fiscal year:

Description.	Number.	Cost.	Unit.	Remarks.
Plant.				
Locomotive (H. K. Porter make)	1	$2,500.00		On hand from former construction; not charged against battery. Unit of cost on 10,256 cubic yards.
Engines and boilers, hoisting	4	3,468.00		
Mixer, concrete, cubical, 4 by 4 feet	1	239.00		
Derricks, guys, cables, stone cars, cement cars, push cars, and steel and wood trays, etc	3	2,550.00		
Steel rails, 30 pounds to yard, 23 tons at $30 per ton ....feet..	2,500	690.00		
Rails, fastenings, frogs, etc		440.00		
Picks, barrows, shovels, and tackle		400.00		
		10,287.00	$1.00	
Railway construction.				
Earth excavation at 21 cents per cubic yard ....cubic yards..	3,440	729.00		Materials on hand from former construction. Unit of cost on 10,256 cubic yards.
Laying and surfacing track		345.00		
Car wheels, spikes, bolts, etc		241.00		
Stone cars, complete	2	130.00		
Flat cars, complete	2	40.00		
Sawing railroad ties		60.00		
Survey		24.00		
Receiving steel rails from Sandy Hook		8.00		
Building drain boxes under track		6.00		
		1,623.00	.157	
Buildings and plant.				
Cement shed, 40 by 18 feet by 8 feet, labor..	1	$176.00		Materials on hand from former construction. Unit of cost on 10,256 cubic yards.
Stone bin, 89 by 18 feet, labor	1	194.00		
Engine houses	2	101.00		
Erecting derricks		120.00		
		591.00	.057	
Excavation for foundation.				
Earth excavation, at 25 cents per cubic yard ....cubic yards..	11,500	2,840.00		Cost includes haul on earth to parapet. Unit of cost on 6,717 cubic yards.
Clearing and grubbing....acre..	1	60.00		
		2,900.00	.47	
Concrete construction, including cost of unloading and hauling.				
Broken trap rock ....cubic yards..	6,720	5,123.00		Unit of cost on 6,717 cubic yards in battery to date.
Unloading and hauling above		681.00		
Portland and Rosendale cement...barrels..	9,740	13,752.00		
Unloading and hauling same		651.00		
Sand, delivered at bin....cubic yards..	3,635	876.00		
		21,083.00	3.14	
Forms (all materials purchased).				
Lumber and timber....feet B. M..	153,305	3,277.00		Form work completed for 9,000 cubic yards. Unit of cost on this amount.
Carpenters and laborers		4,315.00		
		7,592.00	.84	
Mixing.				
Concrete, mixed, at 28 cents..cubic yards..	6,472	1,811.00		Average: Cement, 1; sand, 4; stone, 8.
Mortar (by hand, at $1.22)....cubic yards..	245	299.00		Average: Cement, 1; sand, 2,5.
		2,110.00	.31	
Placing and ramming.				
Rammed in place....cubic yards..	6,717	4,078.00	.60	
Steel ceiling beams, etc.				
Steel ceiling beams, etc ....tons..	162	3,198.00		Unit of cost on 10,256 cubic yards.
Hauling and placing		155.00		
Blacksmith, etc		225.00		
		3,578.00	.84	

Description.	Number.	Cost.	Unit.	Remarks.
Waterproofing course over rooms and passages. a				
423 rolls, at 82 cents per roll..square yards..	923	$352.00		4 layers of H. W. John's asbestus paper, covered with H. W. John's black coating.
Labor		128.00		
		480.00		
Paving in rooms.				
Square yards	640	281.00		½-foot thick blocks, 4 by 6 feet, 20 inches thick, size 4 by 6 feet.
In loading platform blocks, including steps .....square yards..	923	277.00		
		558.00	$0.08	Unit of cost on 6,717 cubic yards.
Superintendence and contingencies.				
Superintendent	1	1,639.00		
Recorder	1	451.00		
Messenger	1	330.00		Unit of cost on 6,717 cubic yards.
Watchman	1	438.00		
		2,808.00	.04	

a Waterproofing 50 per cent completed.

Master laborers, blacksmith, rigger, engineers, masons, etc., included in cost of items above noted.

Armament: Two 6-inch disappearing carriages mounted; two 12-inch guns and disappearing carriages received, mounting not yet completed; one 12-inch gun and two disappearing carriages received; two 100-pounder Parrotts dismounted and one each sent to South Bend, Ind., and St. Johnsville, N. Y.; one 300-pounder Parrott dismounted and sent to Louisville, Ky.

Sites for fortifications and seacoast defenses: Condemnation proceedings have been instituted for the acquisition of two properties. An allotment of $50,000 was made for this purpose November 24, 1899. By authority of the Secretary of War, one of the properties was purchased, under offer of attorneys, for the sum of $30,000, February 14, 1901, and jurisdiction over this property was ceded to the United States by the Governor of the State of New York May 9, 1901. The matter of acquisition of the other property is in the hands of the United States attorney for the eastern district of New York.

Under allotment of $45,000 made June 19, 1900, tract No. 2 of another estate near by was purchased October 18, 1900, for the sum of $43,226, and jurisdiction over this land was ceded to the United States by the Governor of the State of New York December 19, 1900. The appraised valuation of $45,000 was diminished by $1,774, on account of the burning of a barn on the premises, which was covered by insurance.

CONTRACTS IN FORCE.

With Jacob E. Conklin, for broken trap rock; dated April 24, 1901; approved by the Chief of Engineers April 29, 1901; approximate amount, 6,000 cubic yards, at 79 cents per cubic yard, measured in scows; to be completed October 1, 1901.

With the Commercial Wood and Cement Company for American Portland cement, Saylor's brand; dated May 8, 1901; approved by the Chief of Engineers, May 23, 1901; approximate amount, 6,500 barrels, at $1.532 per barrel in bags, 4 bags to the barrel, with a rebate of 7 cents per bag for each bag returned; to be completed October 1, 1901.

APPENDIX 3—FORTIFICATIONS.

Money statements.

GUN AND MORTAR BATTERIES.

July 1, 1900, balance unexpended		$5,277.65
Allotted since		99,015.00
		104,292.65
June 30, 1901, amount expended during fiscal year	$62,335.21	
Amount deposited to credit of appropriation	1,239.91	
July 1, 1901, outstanding liabilities	8,605.61	
July 1, 1901, amount covered by uncompleted contracts	7,595.00	
		79,775.73
July 1, 1901, balance available		24,516.92

ELECTRIC PLANT.

Gun and mortar batteries.

Amount allotted	$20,000.00
June 30, 1901, amount expended during fiscal year	455.02
July 1, 1901, balance unexpended	19,544.98
July 1, 1901, outstanding liabilities	18,432.70
July 1, 1901, balance available	1,112.28

Searchlights for New York Harbor.

Amount allotted	$21,000.00
June 30, 1901, amount expended during fiscal year	366.33
July 1, 1901, balance unexpended	20,633.67
July 1, 1901, outstanding liabilities	20,633.67

SITES FOR FORTIFICATIONS AND SEACOAST DEFENSES.

July 1, 1900, balance unexpended		$95,000.00
November 2, 1900, amount deposited with Assistant Treasurer United States, New York	$1,771.75	
June 30, 1901, amount expended during fiscal year	73,230.35	
		75,002.10
July 1, 1901, balance unexpended and available		19,997.90

PRESERVATION AND REPAIR OF FORTIFICATIONS.

July 1, 1900, balance unexpended	$1,595.83
Allotted since	3,900.00
	5,495.83
June 30, 1901, amount expended during fiscal year	3,077.16
July 1, 1901, balance unexpended	2,418.67
July 1, 1901, outstanding liabilities	439.41
July 1, 1901, balance available	1,979.26

Defenses at Sandy Hook.—This fortification, on the south side of the main entrance to New York Harbor, consists of an old casemated stone fort with modern batteries.

The following work was done during the fiscal year:

Battery No. 2, for 15-pounder rapid-fire guns: Work on this battery was begun in July and completed in November, 1900, except setting the base castings, which have not been received; guns and carriages are not yet received.

Pneumatic dynamite gun battery: The temporary sand-bag parapet and timber magazines have been removed and replaced by a permanent sand parapet with concrete retaining walls and concrete magazines.

Two range-finder towers: Construction of two towers was authorized August 8, 1900; the towers are of steel on a concrete foundation, with frame instrument room covered with galvanized iron. The tower at the seven-gun battery has been completed; the tower at the mortar battery is built, but the instrument room is not yet finished. The steel structures were built by contract.

Water-supply system: An allotment of $4,500 was made August 22, 1900, for supplying water at all the batteries. Work was begun in September, 1900, and completed in February, 1901. A 3-inch main was laid from the post water supply, with 2-inch branches, and 1-inch delivery pipes to the several emplacements. Frost-proof hydrants were put at the rear of each 10-inch and 12-inch emplacement, at the gun-lift battery, in each pit of the mortar battery, at each 15-pounder battery, and two at the dynamite-gun battery. Total cost, $3,208.47.

Galleries: Construction of galleries for the 10-inch emplacements was authorized July 24, 1900. Work was begun in October, 1900, and completed in May, 1901. The galleries are for the purpose of connecting the loading platforms of adjacent emplacements. They consist of a wooden floor on steel columns, with gas-pipe hand rails, and have a total length of 241½ feet. Total cost, $2,220.68.

Implement racks: Allotments aggregating $450 were made for construction and erection of steel implement racks for the mortar battery, the 10-inch and 12-inch emplacements, and the gun-lift battery. All have been made and erected, except those for the gun-lift battery.

Preservation and repair of fortifications: Gun-lift battery: An allotment of $5,000 was made December 4, 1900, for taking up the flagstone pavement on the parapet and replacing it with a waterproof course. Work was begun in April, and is about seven-eighths completed.

An engineman has been employed to care for the gun-lift mechanism.

At the mortar battery a new electric-light equipment has been installed, with a 52-cell accumulator in one of the bombproofs, with armored distributing wires and with moisture-proof fixtures.

Repairs were made to the drains.

At the seven-gun battery minor repairs were made to floor drains, to superior slopes, and to electric-lighting system.

Care of submarine-mining material: This material was stored and kept in order until May 14, 1901, when it was transferred to the artillery.

Sea wall, north shore: An allotment of $2,000 was made for continuing this sea wall, which, with previous balance, made about $3,550 available. A project was approved for extending the present wall westward about on high-water line for a distance of 450 feet, more or less, to protect the shore along and near the front slopes of the dynamite-gun battery; 157 linear feet of wall have been built, and work is in progress.

Stone is purchased, and construction done by hired labor.

APPENDIX 3—FORTIFICATIONS.

Money statements.

GUN AND MORTAR BATTERIES.

July 1, 1900, balance unexpended	$39,304.74
Allotted since	54,958.37
	94,263.11
June 30, 1901, amount expended during fiscal year...... $57,432.36	
Deposited to credit of appropriation............ 1,291.63	
	58,723.99
July 1, 1901, balance unexpended	35,539.12
July 1, 1901, outstanding liabilities	331.36
July 1, 1901, balance available	35,207.76

PRESERVATION AND REPAIR OF FORTIFICATIONS.

July 1, 1900, balance unexpended	$2,846.28
Allotted since	11,630.00
	14,476.28
June 30, 1901, amount expended during fiscal year	8,628.52
July 1, 1901, balance unexpended	5,847.76
July 1, 1901, outstanding liabilities	1,510.83
July 1, 1901, balance available	4,336.93

SEA WALLS AND EMBANKMENTS.

Sea wall, north shore, Sandy Hook, N. J.

July 1, 1900, balance unexpended	$2,201.97
June 30, 1901, amount expended during fiscal year	420.97
July 1, 1901, balance unexpended	1,781.00
July 1, 1901, outstanding liabilities	675.95
July 1, 1901, balance available	1,105.05

Riprap wall, east shore, Sandy Hook, N. J.

July 1, 1900, balance unexpended	$135.17
Allotted since	2,000.00
July 1, 1901, balance unexpended and available	2,135.17

Searchlights, New York Harbor.—Under the project approved by the Chief of Engineers, April 9, and modified April 13, 1901, the sum of $68,700 was allotted for the purpose of purchasing searchlights for fortifications at the southern entrance to New York Harbor.

This project also authorized the purchase of special trucks, reels, cables, etc.

The searchlights were ordered from the General Electric Company, the lowest bidders, for the sum of $26,750.

Money statement.

Amount allotted	$68,700.00
Amount transferred to electric plant	26,900.00
July 1, 1901, balance unexpended	41,800.00
July 1, 1901, outstanding liabilities	26,750.00
July 1, 1901, balance available	15,050.00

Reassembling searchlights.—The Chief of Engineers allotted the sum of $3,000 May 29, 1900, from the appropriation for "Gun and Mortar Batteries," act July 7, 1898, to be applied to reassembling the parts of the searchlights proper.

This was done and the four complete portable searchlight outfits were transferred to the Quartermaster's Department for shipment to each of the four service schools, at Willets Point, N. Y., Fort Monroe, Va., and Forts Leavenworth and Riley, Kans., during November and December, 1900.

Money statement.

July 1, 1900, balance unexpended		$3,000.00
June 30, 1901, amount expended during fiscal year	$2,864.37	
June 30, 1901, amount deposited to credit of appropriation	135.63	
		3,000.00

Supplies for seacoast defenses.—The sum of $1,000 was available from the appropriation for "Supplies for Sea Coast Defenses," act May 25, 1900.

An allotment of $1,000 was made by the Chief of Engineers, August 29, 1900, from the same appropriation, to be applied to the purpose of purchasing supplies authorized by the Chief of Engineers.

Duly approved purchases were made and the articles issued to the engineer officers at the various posts making requisitions for the same.

Money statement.

July 1, 1900, balance unexpended	$1,000.00
August 29, 1900, amount allotted	1,000.00
	2,000.00
June 30, 1901, amount expended during fiscal year	1,554.19
July 1, 1901, balance unexpended	445.81
July 1, 1901, outstanding liabilities	272.95
July 1, 1901, balance available	172.86

3 G.

DEFENSE OF THE DELAWARE RIVER.

Officer in charge, Lieut. Col. Charles W. Raymond, Corps of Engineers; assistants, Capt. Spencer Cosby, Corps of Engineers, and Lieut. James B. Cavanaugh, Corps of Engineers, to July 13, 1900.

Battery for three 10-inch and three 12-inch disappearing guns.—This battery was completed and the guns and carriages mounted in 1898. It was turned over to the artillery on January 6, 1899. A detailed account of the progress of the work is contained in the Annual Reports of the Chief of Engineers for 1897, 1898, 1899, and 1900.

Under authority of the Chief of Engineers, dated October 27, 1900, $2.07 was transferred to the allotment for this work from the allotment for the construction of the mortar battery, to balance the account.

The work done on the battery during the fiscal year was under various allotments from appropriations for "Preservation and Repair of Fortifications" and for "Supplies for Sea Coast Defenses." The galvanized-metal ceilings at the entrances of the shot hoists were painted with cork paint. The concrete and earth of the superior slope of one of the emplacements, damaged by the repeated firing of a 12-inch gun in one position, were repaired. Repairs were made at various times to the slopes of the parados, which had been gullied by storms, and to the earthen parapet of the battery, which had settled in places from 3 to 6 inches. The sluice gate at the outlet into the river from the parados ditch was repaired and new hinges put on it.

Trees were set out to make the battery less easily visible. One hundred and thirty feet of 1½-inch wrought-iron pipe were laid, connecting the 4-inch main of the permanent water-supply system of the post with the water pipe supplying water to the batteries and to the boilers of the electric plant.

Lead flashing, 6 inches in width, was placed over the joints at each side of the three 10-inch platforms where they join the traverses, to prevent leakage into the shot chambers underneath.

Electric lights were placed around the platforms of the six emplacements for use at night. Four 16-candle-power stationary and one 32-candle-power portable lamps were placed on each 12-inch platform, and four 16-candle-power stationary and two 16-candle-power portable lamps on each 10-inch platform. This work was completed in May, 1901. The lights were tested at night drill by the artillery troops and were found to give sufficient light for working the guns under service conditions.

Emplacements for two 5-inch rapid-fire guns on balanced-pillar mounts.—This battery was completed in August, 1897, ready for the guns and carriages, but was not turned over to the artillery until December 19, 1900.

The carriages were received on July 6, 1900, and were mounted by the artillery troops in August, 1900; the work of grouting in the curbings in the platforms and cutting drains under the bases was done by the engineers. One gun was received on June 26, 1901. This gun will be mounted by the artillery troops.

The ammunition hoists, electric wires, conduit and ceiling beams were painted,

Emplacements for two 5-inch rapid-fire guns on pedestal mounts.— The project for the construction of this battery and an account of the beginning of the work are given in the Annual Report of the Chief of Engineers for 1900, page 845.

The only work done during the preceding fiscal year was to set up two derricks and to receive and store construction materials.

At the beginning of the present fiscal year a small concrete plant was erected, including a cable way for hauling construction materials from the wharf to the site of the battery (1,300 feet), and a boiler and pump for water supply. Some necessary repairs were made to the end of the wharf.

Three hundred and eighty cubic yards of material were excavated for the foundations of the battery and 204 cubic yards of sod and topsoil were dug out over part of the surface to be covered by the embankment. All of this material was deposited by the derrick just outside the limits of the embankment for use later in facing the slopes.

Concrete construction began on August 1, 1900, and was completed on November 30, with the exception of a small amount of pavement work in the east magazine, which was finished in December. The completed battery contains 1,718 cubic yards of concrete, of which 1,640 cubic yards are Portland concrete mixed in the proportions of 1 part cement, 6 parts sand, and 15 parts (1½-inch) broken stone; 68 cubic yards are Portland concrete (1:3:7½) on the superior slope, and 10 cubic yards are Rosendale concrete (1:2:5). The pavement on the superior slope is laid in slabs 16 inches thick, faced with Portland mortar, 1 to 3, and troweled to a smooth finish. The foundation bolts for the gun mounts were set in place.

Sand filling was begun on September 5 and was completed for the whole battery on November 28, 1900. The slopes were then graded and faced with earth 1 foot thick. The embankment contains 8,050 cubic yards, of which 6,558 cubic yards are purchased sand and 1,492 cubic yards are earth facing on the slopes. Eighty square yards of sod were placed on the steep slopes in rear of the battery.

The ceilings of the magazines consist of steel beams built in between with flat arches of 6-inch hollow tile, which conceal the bottom of the beams. The vertical walls are covered with 2-inch hollow-tile furring. Both ceilings and side walls are plastered with a thin layer of Portland mortar, 1 to 3.

The outside walls of the battery were roughly plastered and then waterproofed with paraffin paint No. 3 and coal tar. A 2-inch porous-tile drain was laid around the foundations of each emplacement and covered with a thin layer of broken stone.

Three hundred and fifty-nine feet of vitrified tile and wooden pump log conduit were laid under ground from the main battery to carry the cables for electric light and power. Lead-covered insulated conductors (No. 12 wire) were run through the underground conduit and connected with the electric circuits of the main battery; insulated iron-armored conduit and lamps with Navy standard globes and guards were put up in each magazine. An electric ventilating fan was set up for each magazine.

The iron stairways, railings, ammunition platforms and cranes, ladders to the platforms, and iron doors in the magazines and lamp recesses were put in place and painted.

Part of the permanent railroad track and roadway were moved in close to the exterior slope at the end of the main battery, and the roadway was covered with small broken stone.

In March and April, 1901, samples of the 1:6:15 Portland concrete, of which this battery is constructed, were excavated from the walls of the battery at four different places. The concrete everywhere was found to be hard, compact, and uniform, and superior to Rosendale concrete mixed in the proportions of 1:2:5.

In March, 1901, the earth slopes, which were only slightly washed during the winter, were raked over and seeded with rye and grass seeds.

The battery, having been completed in all respects, was turned over to the artillery on June 7, 1901. No guns or carriages have yet been received.

The following contracts were in force during the year:

With Charles Warner Company, Wilmington, Del., dated January 27, and approved February 12, 1900, for about 900 cubic yards washed sand, at 28 cents per cubic yard, and 9,000 cubic yards unwashed sand, at 22 cents per cubic yard. This contract was satisfactorily completed on November 15, 1900, 804 cubic yards of washed sand and 6,558 cubic yards of unwashed sand having been delivered under it.

With the Brandywine Granite Company, Wilmington, Del., dated January 27, and approved February 16, 1900, for about 1,700 cubic yards small broken stone, at $1.37 per cubic yard. This contract was satisfactorily completed on October 26, 1900, 1,887 cubic yards having been delivered under it.

With William J. Donaldson, Philadelphia, Pa., dated April 30, and approved May 12, 1900, for about 1,400 barrels Alpha brand American Portland cement, of which about 400 barrels are to be delivered elsewhere, at $2.21 per barrel. This contract was satisfactorily completed on September 18, 1900, 1,425 barrels having been delivered under it.

The following table shows the total cost of the work in detail:

1,718 cubic yards of concrete in place, at $4.6658 per cubic yard	$8,015.84
6,558 cubic yards of sand filling in embankment, at $0.48724 per cubic yard	3,195.34
1,492 cubic yards of earth facing on slopes of embankment, at $0.472 per cubic yard	704.22
584 cubic yards of excavation for foundations, at $0.3287 per cubic yard	191.96
Maintenance of plant	149.99
Construction track	159.18
Erection of construction plant	540.09
Derrick and rigging work	267.86
Tile furring in place	308.88
Waterproofing exterior walls of battery	155.16
Steel I-beams and channels in place	453.79
Finishing face walls	84.66
Time allowed employees for legal holidays	148.20
Anchor bolts in place	191.13
Ammunition cranes and platforms in place	394.23
Stairways and railings in place	853.30
Doors and windows in place	212.63
Lighting system	123.97
Drainage system	61.93
Ventilating system	365.85
Maintenance of launch for mail service	30.93
Tearing down and storing construction plant	191.10
Removing samples of Portland concrete	16.10
Mileage paid United States officers	5.60
Philadelphia office expenses	171.53
Superintendence and office expenses	506.53
Total	17,500.00

Converting two old magazines into casemates for 15-pounder rapid-fire guns.—On February 18, 1901, the Chief of Engineers allotted the sum of $3,500 from the appropriation for "Gun and Mortar Batteries," act of May 25, 1900, for the purpose of converting two old magazines into casemates for 15-pounder rapid-fire guns in accordance with the approved design.

Work began on March 25, 1901, and at the end of the fiscal year the following had been accomplished:

The excavation in front of the two casemates, amounting to 1,350 cubic yards, had been practically completed; the side slopes had been graded, faced with earth 1 foot thick, and seeded except near the casemates, where the slopes can not be finished until the masonry is completed; and 140 cubic yards of concrete had been blasted from the fronts of the two old magazines.

The work of rebuilding was delayed, as the anchor bolts, which were to have been delivered on April 30, were not received until June 22. The bolts were set in both casemates and 7 cubic yards of Portland concrete were placed. One hundred cubic yards of small broken stone, left over from another work, were transferred across the river, to be used on this work.

Money statements.

MAIN BATTERY, AND BATTERY FOR TWO 5-INCH GUNS ON BALANCED-PILLAR MOUNTS.

July 1, 1900, balance unexpended	$114.85
October 27, 1900, amount transferred from allotment for construction of mortar battery	2.07
	116.92
June 30, 1901, amount expended during fiscal year	.38
July 1, 1901, balance unexpended	116.54
July 1, 1901, outstanding liabilities	116.54

EMPLACEMENTS FOR TWO 5-INCH RAPID-FIRE GUNS ON PEDESTAL MOUNTS.

July 1, 1900, balance unexpended	$15,423.04
June 30, 1901, amount expended during fiscal year	15,423.04
Amount expended to June 30, 1900	$2,076.96
Amount expended during fiscal year ending June 30, 1901	15,423.04
Total cost of work	17,500.00

CONVERTING OLD MAGAZINES INTO CASEMATES.

February 18, 1901, amount allotted	$3,500.00
June 30, 1901, amount expended during fiscal year	1,360.39
July 1, 1901, balance unexpended	2,139.61
July 1, 1901, outstanding liabilities	764.89
July 1, 1901, balance available	1,374.72

Battery for three 12-inch guns on disappearing carriages.—The preliminary work on this battery began on December 11, 1894.

The projects under which this battery was constructed, a detailed account of the progress of the work, and a description of the battery are contained in the Annual Reports of the Chief of Engineers for 1895 to 1900, inclusive.

At the close of the last fiscal year the battery was completed with the exception of a few minor details, and the guns and carriages had been mounted.

During the fiscal year a 60-horsepower boiler and a new switch board were set up; the completed electric plant was tested on September 20, 1900. The storage battery was received on June 30, 1900, but it was not set up and charged until June, 1901, as it was not needed previous to this time. A hollow-tile partition was constructed between the boiler and dynamo rooms. The 60-horsepower boiler and steam piping were covered with magnesia covering. The steam pump and the Westinghouse engines, which had been in use for construction purposes, were overhauled and thoroughly repaired.

The hanging of the iron doors, the grading and seeding of the parade, and the placing of interior fittings for the latrines were completed in September, 1900. Wooden shelters were built over the openings of the three circular stairways on the platforms.

The installation of the three chain ammunition hoists was completed in October, 1900, and the hoists were satisfactorily tested with full load. A steel highway bridge, 57 feet clear span and 8 feet clear width, was erected over the moat; it takes the place of an old wooden bridge and connects with the roadway leading to the wharves. The interior iron stairways, the trolley rails, and the electric conduit were painted in January, 1901.

The electric plant was cared for from January 1 to June 30, 1901, by a steam engineer of the classified service, paid from the appropriation for "Preservation and Repair of Fortifications." The guns and carriages were cleaned and cared for until a detachment consisting of 1 sergeant, 2 corporals, and 17 privates arrived on April 18, 1901, when the battery was formally transferred to the artillery. The total cost of the battery was $350,500. It has been completed in all respects.

Though the battery is built on a heavy pile and concrete foundation, necessitated by the treacherous nature of the soil, no appreciable settlement or cracks have occurred in any part of it.

The following contracts were in force during the year:

With Messrs. L. Schutte & Co., Philadelphia, Pa., dated March 22, 1900, and approved April 4, 1900, for three chain ammunition hoists for the 12-inch guns, at the price of $1,080 each; delivery to be made within three months from April 6, 1900. This contract expired by its own limitation on July 6, 1900. The hoists were delivered by Messrs. L. Schutte & Co. under an implied agreement at the prices named in the original contract. This was satisfactorily completed on October 31, 1900, the hoists having been erected, tested, and accepted.

The following table shows the total cost of the work in detail:

28,063 cubic yards of masonry in walls of magazines and galleries, at $3.42294 per cubic yard	$96,058.09
1,002 cubic yards of masonry in the three platforms, at $6.315888 per cubic yard	6,328.52
1,286 cubic yards of masonry in pavement on superior slope, at $5.9456 per cubic yard	7,646.04
460 cubic yards of masonry in pavement on barbette of old fort, at $5.29515 per cubic yard	2,435.77
19,600 cubic yards of excavation for foundations, at $0.428414 per cubic yard	8,396.92
17,646 cubic yards of sand and earth placed in sand cores, at $0.535519 per cubic yard	9,449.78
4,627 piles in foundations, at $11.41708 each	52,826.83
Removing earth from barbette of old fort	2,273.67
Tearing down barracks, cisterns, and arches	4,958.37
Taking up flagstone pavement	471.47
Moving old guns and carriages	1,693.28
Lift mechanism (tubes)	492.63
Test borings	196.09
Repairs and maintenance of quarters	2,106.34
Repairs to landing piers	8,970.94
Cleaning out moat	2,130.87
Preliminary survey	494.12
Handling submarine-mining materials	326.21
Purchase, construction, and installation of electric and steam construction plant	22,691.09
Electric light and power plant	5,552.75
Plant and permanent water supply	495.75
Repair and maintenance of construction plant	12,440.97
Auxiliary lights for magazines	318.86
Cost of I-beams and channels in place, 197,098 pounds	3,932.30
Unloading, mounting, and caring for guns and carriages	5,014.75
Drainage system	1,351.36
Telephone system	6.85
Cleaning and grading inside and outside of fort	1,839.65
Extinguishing fire in room of barracks and repairing same	184.07
Derrick and rigging work	6,209.80
Construction track	4,761.71
Changes made in plans (west passage)	691.06
Speaking-tube system	24.47
Three ammunition cranes in place	996.75

776   REPORT OF THE CHIEF OF ENGINEERS, U. S. ARMY.

Trolley system for ammunition service	$1,288.78
Stairways, balconies, and hand railing in place	1,444.51
Observation stations	32.82
Iron ladders in place	178.71
Ventilating system	1,300.36
Transferring and storing engineer property	488.98
Repairs to walls of old fort	753.63
Doors, windows, and shutters in place	3,600.40
Laying flagstone pavements on parade and in casemates of old fort	1,008.84
Waterproofing exterior wall with coal tar	259.34
Finishing face walls	1,646.20
Asphalt in place on platforms and roof of boiler room	2,391.02
Metal flashing on platforms and power house in place	190.37
Tile ceilings of magazines and passages	2,893.96
Tile furring on walls of magazines and casemates	1,312.64
Expanded metal in place	683.39
Watching Government property	52.00
Latrines	1,180.30
Coal bin	210.09
Permanent railroad track	203.29
Stair shelters	264.83
Three ammunition hoists in place	3,710.42
Repairs to and caring for battery	226.76
Storage battery	1,244.37
Completing erection of 15-pounder hoists, right and left flanks	268.56
Building thermometer shelters	5.00
Highway bridge, including part cost of erection	569.88
Taking down plant	188.75
Time allowed employees for legal holidays	2,380.29
Instruments and office furniture	936.75
Printing and advertising	697.72
Mileage paid United States officers	789.01
Philadelphia office expenses	8,627.25
Maintenance of launch for mail service	9,644.02
Superintendence and office expenses	23,576.21
Material transferred to other works	2,482.17
Held in Treasury United States	.25
Total	350,500.00

Emplacements for 15-pounder rapid-fire guns (right and left flanks).—The project under which these batteries were constructed and an account of the progress of the work are contained in the Annual Reports of the Chief of Engineers for 1899 and 1900.

At the end of the last fiscal year these batteries had been completed in all details except for the installation of the ammunition hoists and the mounting of the guns and carriages. The installation of the hoists was completed in January, 1901, and they were satisfactorily tested under full load. The installation of these hoists was very slow and expensive on account of the confined space in the hoist wells in which only one man could work at a time. The balance of the allotment was not quite sufficient to complete the work. Payment was made from the allotment for the 12-inch battery in the flanks of which these emplacements are built. Details of the hoists are shown on tracing herewith.

The following contract was in force during the year:

With the Ellicott Machine Company, Canton, Baltimore, Md., dated March 22, 1900, and approved April 11, 1900, for two double-chain ammunition hoists for the right and left flank guns, at the price of $984 each. Extension of time, 90 days, was granted on account of the company's plant being destroyed by fire. This was further extended 30 days from October 8, 1900. The contract was satisfactorily completed in February, 1901, the hoists having been tested and accepted.

On October 25, 1900, the Chief of Engineers allotted the sum of $400 from the appropriation for "Gun and Mortar Batteries," act of July 7, 1898, to be applied to the expense of mounting the four 15-pounder rapid-fire guns on balanced-pillar mounts on the right and left flanks of the 12-inch battery. Request for authority to mount these guns was approved by the Department under date of October 23, 1900.

The four guns, with mounts, accessories, and spare parts, were received on August 17 and 18, and the parts of the carriages which set in the concrete platforms on October 16, 1900.

The mounting of the four guns and carriages was completed on November 23, 1900. Twenty-four cubic yards of concrete were placed around the outer bases of the carriages and for completing the platforms. After mounting, the guns and carriages were thoroughly cleaned and painted. The total cost was $344.92, and the balance of $55.08 was returned to the credit of the appropriation from which it was allotted.

These four emplacements, with their armament, being in all respects complete, were turned over to the artillery on April 18, 1901.

Emplacements for two 4.72-inch rapid-fire guns.—These emplacements were completed in December, 1898, and were turned over to the artillery on January 28, 1899. The armament was turned over on January 23, 1901. Prior to that time the guns and carriages were cared for and some necessary work of maintenance and repair was done on the battery proper.

On February 14, 1901, the Chief of Engineers allotted the sum of $600 from the appropriation for "Preservation and Repair of Fortifications," act of May 25, 1900, to be applied to repairs to the walls on either side of the two entrances to the 4.72-inch battery and to recovering the entrances with concrete and earth.

The battery proper was built in 1898, on pile foundations, and has not settled. The retaining walls on each side of the two entrances were built on heavy grillage foundations and settled so much that the walls near the magazines were badly broken. The earth and concrete covering was removed to lessen the weight on the foundations, but the settlement still continued.

Under this allotment the broken parts of the walls, aggregating 25 cubic yards, were removed; they were rebuilt with steel beams placed in them at three different levels and anchored into the unbroken parts of the walls. The side walls were then raised 2 feet, decreasing in thickness from 30 to 12 inches, and were covered with I-beams and about 12 inches of concrete. Sixty-six cubic yards of Portland concrete were placed. The top was then waterproofed with a ¾-inch layer of asphalt.

The earth covering, aggregating 225 cubic yards, was replaced. In addition 180 cubic yards of earth were placed on the top of the earth embankment around the platforms and magazines where it had settled from 14 to 18 inches.

The floors in the galleries were made of broken stone and sand. Concrete pavements will be put in if no further settlement is shown. This work was completed on June 25, 1901.

Emplacements for two 15-pounder rapid-fire guns.—On June 28, 1900, the Chief of Engineers allotted the sum of $16,000 from the appropriation for "Gun and Mortar Batteries," act of May 25, 1900, for the construction of emplacements for two 15-pounder rapid-fire guns on balanced-pillar mounts.

Construction work began on this battery on September 1, 1900. A railroad track and trolley line, 800 feet in length, were constructed from the wharf to the site of the battery. An 80-foot derrick was set up and an electric hoist placed for operating it.

Eight hundred and fifteen cubic yards of material were excavated for the foundations, and placed by the derrick just outside the limits of the embankment, to be used later for facing it. One hundred and fifty-five piles, 50 to 51 feet in length, were driven for the foundations and a heavy timber grillage was built on top of them.

Concrete construction was begun on November 7, 1900, and completed for the whole battery on April 29, 1901. Work was stopped by cold weather for four months. The completed battery contains 980 cubic yards of concrete masonry, of which 769 cubic yards are Portland concrete mixed in the proportions of 1 cement, 6 river sand, and 15 small (1½-inch) broken stone; 128 cubic yards are Portland concrete, 1:3:7½; 60 cubic yards are Rosendale concrete; and 23 cubic yards are large stone. In the spring of 1901, samples of the Portland concrete, 1:6:15, placed in November, 1900, were excavated and found to be hard and compact, and superior to Rosendale concrete mixed in the proportions of 1:2:5.

The ceilings of the magazines and postern were constructed with steel beams built in between with flat arches of 6-inch hollow tile, and the side walls of the magazines were covered with 2-inch hollow tile furring; both were plastered with a thin coat of Portland mortar, 1:3. The outside walls of the magazines were roughly plastered and then waterproofed with paraffin paint No. 3 and coal tar. The earth embankment around the battery was completed with the exception of a small part where the derrick stands; 3,211 cubic yards of material were placed, of which 2,625 cubic yards are purchased sand and 586 cubic yards are earth removed from the excavation and placed in a layer 12 to 18 inches thick over the sand.

Money statement.

MAIN BATTERY.

July 1, 1900, balance unexpended	$18,363.01
June 30, 1901, amount expended during fiscal year	18,315.29
July 1, 1901, balance unexpended	47.72
July 1, 1901, outstanding liabilities	47.72
Amount expended to June 30, 1900	$332,136.99
Amount expended during fiscal year ending June 30, 1901	18,315.29
Amount of outstanding liabilities	47.72
Total cost of work	350,500.00

15-POUNDER RAPID-FIRE BATTERIES, RIGHT AND LEFT FLANKS OF MAIN BATTERY.

July 1, 1900, balance unexpended	$2,406.70
June 30, 1901, amount expended during fiscal year	2,406.70
Amount expended to June 30, 1900	$5,393.30
Amount expended during fiscal year ending June 30, 1901	2,406.70
Total cost of works	7,800.00

Mounting guns for above batteries.

October 25, 1900, amount allotted		$400.00
June 30, 1901, amount expended during fiscal year	$344.92	
December 19, 1900, balance redeposited to credit of the appropriation	55.08	
		400.00

15-POUNDER RAPID-FIRE BATTERY, LEFT FLANK 4.72-INCH RAPID-FIRE BATTERY.

July 1, 1900, balance unexpended	$16,000.00
June 30, 1901, amount expended during fiscal year	13,827.37
July 1, 1901, balance unexpended	2,172.63
July 1, 1901, outstanding liabilities	528.46
July 1, 1901, balance available	1,644.17

Battery for sixteen 12-inch breech-loading mortars.—This battery was completed in all details and turned over to the artillery on May 2, 1900. No work was done on the battery during the fiscal year except from allotments for preservation and repair.

At the beginning of the fiscal year eight of the mortars had not been mounted. Four were received during the year and were being mounted by the artillery at its close.

The bedplates of six mortar carriages, which were being reset by an ordnance machinist, were grouted in. These carriages were mounted before the retaining walls and embankments around the mortar pits were constructed. Settlement threw the carriages out of level.

Of the available balance from the allotment for the battery—$6.13 on July 1, 1900—$2.07 was transferred to the 10-inch and 12-inch emplacements, and the balance, $4.06, was withdrawn from the allotment by authority of the Chief of Engineers dated October 27, 1900.

The storage battery was cared for by an attendant until December 31, 1900, when the artillery took charge of the plant.

Emplacements for two 8-inch and two 12-inch breech-loading rifles.—Two emplacements for 8-inch disappearing guns, with carriages and guns mounted, and two emplacements for 12-inch guns on nondisappearing carriages were completed and turned over to the artillery on January 12, 1899. The two 12-inch guns and barbette carriages were mounted in 1899. These four emplacements were constructed under an allotment from the appropriation for "National Defense."

The following operations were carried on during the fiscal year under allotments from the appropriation for "Preservation and Repair of Fortifications."

The electric light and power plant at the battery was cared for and operated by a steam engineer of the classified service until December 31, 1900, when an electrician sergeant took charge of the plant.

Three hundred and ten linear feet of lead flashing were placed along the sides of the platforms of the emplacements to prevent leakage through the vertical joints where the platforms meet the traverses.

Parts of the top surfaces of emplacements Nos. 3 and 4 were waterproofed with two coats of linseed oil and naphtha.

Assistance was rendered the artillery in replacing the defective tubes in the boiler of the electric plant. Under authority of the Chief of

Engineers repairs were made to the water legs and blow-off of this boiler, and a sample of the water used was analyzed by a chemist.

Emplacements for two 5-inch rapid-fire guns.—The approved project under which these emplacements were constructed and an account of the progress of the work are contained in the Annual Report of the Chief of Engineers for 1900, page 863.

At the end of the last fiscal year the masonry of the south emplacement had been completed, including the pavement of the superior slope, and that of the north emplacement had reached the level of the platform. The anchor bolts had been set in both platforms.

At the beginning of the fiscal year work was continued, and on September 30, 1900, the battery had been completed in all details. The completed battery contains 1,615 cubic yards of concrete, of which 468 cubic yards are Rosendale concrete, 1:2:5; 1,110 cubic yards are Portland concrete, 1:6:15; and 37 cubic yards are Portland concrete, 1:3:7½, on the superior slope.

The embankment contains 9,025 cubic yards of sand and earth, of which 5,816 cubic yards are purchased sand, 2,659 cubic yards are sand from the parapet of an old earthen battery, and 550 cubic yards are mud and earth placed 1 foot thick on the slopes of the embankment.

The iron doors, stairways, ammunition platforms, and railings were put in place and painted. On completion of the work the 80-foot derrick was taken down, the concrete plant was dismantled, and lumber and other materials around the battery were removed and stored. A frame for the detailed drawing of the battery was constructed and hung inside.

The battery and the engineer property pertaining to it were turned over to the artillery on December 19, 1900. No guns or carriages have yet been received.

In March and April, 1901, samples of the Portland concrete mixed in the proportions of 1 part cement, 6 parts sand, and 15 parts broken stone, of which concrete the greater part of this battery is constructed, were excavated from the front of the parapet. The concrete was found to be hard and uniform and superior to Rosendale concrete mixed in the proportions of 1:2:5.

In May, 1901, the earth slopes facing the river, which had been badly washed and undermined by high tides and waves, were repaired and faced with stone set on edge from an old sea wall running along the front of the battery. A total of 2,252 square feet were covered with stone, extending 260 feet around the foot of the earth slope. The available balance was entirely expended on this work.

The following contracts were in force during the year:

With the Charles Warner Company, Wilmington, Del., dated January 27, 1900, and approved February 12, 1900, for about 900 cubic yards of washed sand at 28 cents per cubic yard, and 6,000 cubic yards of unwashed sand at 22 cents per cubic yard. This contract was satisfactorily completed on August 13, 1900, 704 cubic yards of washed sand and 5,816 cubic yards of unwashed sand having been delivered under it.

With the Brandywine Granite Company, Wilmington, Del., dated January 27, 1900, and approved February 16, 1900, for about 1,600 cubic yards of small broken stone at $1.56 per cubic yard. This contract was satisfactorily completed on July 14, 1900, 1,622 cubic yards having been delivered under it.

With William J. Donaldson, Philadelphia, Pa., dated April 30, 1900, and approved May 12, 1900, for about 1,400 barrels Alpha brand American Portland cement (of which about 1,000 barrels were to be delivered elsewhere), at $2.21 per barrel. This contract was satisfactorily completed on September 18, 1900, 1,425 barrels having been delivered under it.

APPENDIX 3—FORTIFICATIONS.

The following table shows the total cost of the work in detail:

1,615 cubic yards of concrete in place, at $5.05118 per cubic yard	$8,157.66
8,475 cubic yards of sand filling in embankment, at $0.4414 per cubic yard	3,740.88
550 cubic yards of earth facing on slopes of embankment, at $0.8727 per cubic yard	480.02
360 cubic yards of excavation for foundations, at $0.4863 per cubic yard	175.08
Maintenance and repairs to plant	484.47
Construction track	265.96
Erection of construction plant	379.70
Watching Government property	156.00
Derrick and rigging work	395.45
Tile furring in place	274.91
Waterproofing exterior walls of battery	61.70
I-beams and channels in place	332.84
Finishing face walls	105.04
Time allowed employees for legal holidays	194.95
Anchor bolts in place	211.88
Ammunition service	129.00
Stairways and railings in place	121.00
Doors and windows in place	192.90
Observation stations	53.00
Lighting system	17.00
Tearing down and storing plant	199.02
Removing samples of Portland concrete	14.10
Blue-print frames in place	16.32
Repairing slopes of embankment	77.07
Mileage paid United States officers	12.04
Philadelphia office expenses	112.09
Superintendence and office expenses	439.92
Total	16,800.00

Money statements.

MORTAR BATTERY

July 1, 1900, balance unexpended		$68.42
June 30, 1901, amount expended during fiscal year	$41.60	
October 27, 1900, amount transferred to battery for three 10-inch and three 12-inch disappearing guns	2.07	
October 27, 1900, amount withdrawn from the allotment	4.06	
		47.73
July 1, 1901, balance unexpended (in Treasury of the United States to credit of the appropriation)		20.69
July 1, 1901, outstanding liabilities		20.69

5-INCH RAPID-FIRE BATTERY.

July 1, 1900, balance unexpended	$7,373.21
August 13, 1900, additional allotment	900.00
	8,273.21
June 30, 1901, amount expended during fiscal year	8,272.51
July 1, 1901, balance unexpended	.70
July 1, 1901, outstanding liabilities	.70
Amount expended to June 30, 1900	$8,526.79
Amount expended during fiscal year ending June 30, 1901	8,272.51
Outstanding liabilities	.70
Total cost of work	16,800.00

CLEARING UP GROUND ADJACENT TO MORTAR BATTERY.

February 20, 1901, amount allotted	$400.00
June 30, 1901, amount expended during fiscal year	400.00

Battery commanders' stations.—Under date of September 26, 1900, the Chief of Engineers allotted $5,700 and $5,600 from the appropriation for "Gun and Mortar Batteries," act of May 25, 1900, to be applied to the construction of battery commanders' stations for one 12-inch gun battery and the mortar battery, respectively.

Proposals were issued for the two steel instrument towers, and the order was given to the lowest bidder in October, delivery being called for on or before February 20, 1901. The erection was to be done by the United States.

Preliminary work for the construction began on November 13, 1900. The foundations were completed, including the setting of the foundation bolts and lower sections of the inner cylinders, in December, 1900. One hundred and ninety-six cubic yards of material were excavated for the foundations of the 12-inch station, and 102 cubic yards for the mortar-battery station.

The first delivery of materials was made on March 5, 1901, for each station.

The erection of the towers was then continued. At the end of the fiscal year the framework and the inner and outer cylinders of each tower had been carried up to the floor of the instrument room, and the inner cylinders filled with concrete. The concrete was made of Portland cement, 1:3:7½, and was all hand mixed, except that for the foundations of the 12-inch station, which was mixed in the plant used for the construction of the left-flank 5-inch battery. One hundred and seventeen cubic yards of concrete were placed for the 12-inch station and 109 cubic yards for the mortar-battery station.

The work of assembling the towers was delayed for weeks at a time while waiting for materials to be delivered, and also by the parts not fitting together properly. About 50 per cent of all the holes for bolting the parts together had to be reamed out or redrilled. Parts of the stairways and tie-rods were rejected. At the end of the fiscal year none of the woodwork for the instrument rooms had been delivered.

Money statement.

September 26, 1900, amount allotted	$11,300.00
June 30, 1901, amount expended during fiscal year	3,866.35
July 1, 1901, balance unexpended	7,433.65
July 1, 1901, outstanding liabilities	$244.84
July 1, 1901, amount covered by existing contracts	5,144.00
	5,388.84
July 1, 1901, balance available	2,044.81

Stations for Rafferty range finders.—Under authority of the Chief of Engineers, the construction of two stations for Rafferty range finders, one for the mortar battery and one for the 8-inch and 12-inch battery, was begun on June 19, 1901. They are erected on the sites formerly occupied by the Lewis type B range finders, but the plane of the instrument is made 2 feet higher. The stations consist of a brick pier inclosed by a circular brick wall 13 inches thick, with an earth embankment outside of it. At the end of the fiscal year the brick work of the stations was completed, but the earth embankment was not entirely finished.

Two bases for Rafferty range finder for the three 12-inch gun battery were set on the edge of the parapet in front of two of the observation stations of the battery. The cost of all this work was paid for from the allotment for the two 15-pounder emplacements.

Preservation and repair of submarine-mining material.—The semiannual inspection of all material was made in November, 1900, and all work done necessary to preserve it in good condition. The roof, shutters, and doors of the torpedo shed were painted. Each reel of cable in the tank was tested, with the result that all were found to be in serviceable condition.

All wires leading to the mining casemate, searchlight station, and base-line stations were removed from the poles, placed on reels, and stored in the torpedo shed.

Under authority of the Chief of Engineers a number of materials were sent to the Engineer Depot for repairs, certain materials were supplied by the depot or by purchase to replace others which had been broken, worn-out, or lost, and all obsolete torpedo property was shipped to the depot.

The torpedo property was listed and put in good condition for transfer to the artillery. The Hornsby-Akroyd oil engine shipped to Fort Monroe in June, 1900, was returned in May, 1901, and was set up in the mining casemate and painted.

On January 16, 1901, the Chief of Engineers allotted the sum of $1,500 from the appropriation for "Preservation and Repair of Fortifications," act of May 25, 1900, to line the torpedo cable tank with steel sheets.

This tank was designed to hold only one layer of reels of a designated size, but those furnished were so large as to require to be stored in two layers in the tank, and water could not be kept at a sufficient height to cover the upper layer.

The steel lining was delivered on May 15, 1901, and at the end of the fiscal year the sheets had been riveted together ready for lowering into the tank.

Money statement.

July 1, 1900, balance unexpended	$194.98
June 30, 1901, amount expended during fiscal year	192.36
July 1, 1901, balance unexpended	2.62
July 1, 1901, outstanding liabilities	2.62

Preservation and repair of fortifications.—Mention has already been made under different heads of much of the work carried on during the fiscal year under various allotments from the appropriations for "Preservation and Repair of Fortifications." In addition, the following work was also done during the year.

Necessary repairs were made to river banks, wharfs, and sea walls. A section of the river bank, 340 feet in length, had its height increased 18 to 20 inches, and its top width from $2\frac{1}{4}$ feet to $4\frac{1}{4}$ feet. The stone sea wall was extensively repaired.

The electric plants of the various batteries were cared for and operated until electrician sergeants were appointed to take charge of them. The guns, carriages, ironwork, and drainage systems of the batteries were cleaned and kept in good condition until the transfer of the batteries to the artillery. Frames for holding blue prints of the transferred batteries were constructed and hung.

Unserviceable property and miscellaneous old iron were collected and listed for condemnation. Part of the cost of erecting a steel bridge was paid for. Slight repairs were made to the superior slope of one of the batteries.

An old cement shed between the wharf and the mortar battery was torn down, the material stored in it was removed to another building, and the site was graded.

Money statement.

July 1, 1900, balance unexpended	$3,401.71
August 10, 1900, amount allotted	150.00
January 16, 1901, amount allotted	1,500.00
February 14, 1901, amount allotted	600.00
May 16, 1901, amount allotted	4,000.00
	9,651.71
June 30, 1901, amount expended during fiscal year	3,918.00
July 1, 1901, balance unexpended	5,733.71
July 1, 1901, outstanding liabilities	1,413.35
July 1, 1901, balance available	4,320.36

Supplies for coast defenses.—Materials called for on requisitions of the acting engineer officers at the different forts, duly approved by the Chief of Engineers, were purchased and turned over to them.

Three thermometer shelters were constructed for the artillery. Twenty-four brackets for rammers and staves and four hose hooks were also constructed of 1-inch wrought iron and placed in the 8-inch and 12-inch battery.

An allotment of $500 was made by the Chief of Engineers from the appropriation for "Supplies for Sea Coast Defenses," act of May 25, 1900, to be applied to the installation of electric night lights around the platforms of the six emplacements of the 10-inch and 12-inch battery. This work was practically completed at the end of the fiscal year.

Money statement.

July 1, 1900, balance unexpended	$1,000.00
December 15, 1900, amount allotted	500.00
February 8, 1901, amount allotted	500.00
June 26, 1901, amount allotted	1,000.00
	3,000.00
June 30, 1901, amount expended during fiscal year	1,656.56
July 1, 1901, balance unexpended	1,343.44
July 1, 1901, outstanding liabilities	156.32
July 1, 1901, balance available	1,187.12

3 H.

DEFENSES OF BALTIMORE, MARYLAND.

Officer in charge, Lieut. Col. Oswald H. Ernst, Corps of Engineers; assistant, Lieut. Charles W. Kutz, Corps of Engineers, until August 30, 1900.

Fort McHenry, Md.—This is a fort of historic interest only, being almost useless for defensive purposes. No funds were expended during the fiscal year.

APPENDIX 3—FORTIFICATIONS.

RESERVATION NO. 1.

Emplacements for one 12-inch and three 8-inch B. L. rifles on disappearing carriages.—This battery was complete, garrisoned, and guns mounted at the beginning of the fiscal year.

Emplacements for two 4.7-inch rapid-fire guns.—This battery was complete, garrisoned, and guns mounted at the beginning of the fiscal year.

Emplacements for two 15-pounder rapid-fire guns.—These were complete and garrisoned at the beginning of the fiscal year, but no guns or mounts were on hand. During the fiscal year the armament was received and mounted by the troops.

Mining casemate.—Plans for constructing a mining casemate at this reservation, at an estimated cost of $9,550, were submitted April 28, 1900, and an allotment of $9,000 was made March 19, 1901. At the close of the fiscal year excavations had been made and the concrete brought up to the height of the roof beams.

Money statement.

TORPEDOES FOR HARBOR DEFENSE.

March 19, 1901, allotted	$9,000.00
June 30, 1901, amount expended during fiscal year	4,400.97
July 1, 1901, balance unexpended	4,599.03
July 1, 1901, outstanding liabilities	1,008.42
July 1, 1901, balance available	3,590.61

Coal storage.—An allotment of $1,400 was made May 3, 1901, to enlarge the existing coal bin in rear of the 12-inch emplacement on this reservation, cover it with a roof, and make it of easier access.

At the close of the fiscal year partial excavation had been made.

Money statement.

SUPPLIES FOR SEACOAST DEFENSES.

May 3, 1901, allotted	$1,400.00
June 30, 1901, amount expended during fiscal year	25.00
July 1, 1901, balance unexpended	1,375.00
July 1, 1901, outstanding liabilities	180.54
July 1, 1901, balance available	1,194.46

Surface drainage.—An allotment of $295.21 and a transfer of $1,617.69 October 5, 1900, were made to construct a system of surface drains on the part of this reservation occupied by the batteries, with catch-basins and underground conduits. This work was completed in December, 1900.

Money statement.

GUN AND MORTAR BATTERIES.

October 5, 1900, allotted	$295.21
October 5, 1900, amount transferred from other allotments	1,617.69
	1,912.90
June 30, 1901, amount expended during the fiscal year	1,912.90

Sea walls and embankments.—The reservation containing the foregoing batteries is protected from encroachments of the Patapsco River by a rubble sea wall built before 1900; but the supporting fill behind it was partially washed out and the stability of the wall threatened. An allotment of $3,000 was made April 12, 1901, to place a light backing of concrete to the wall and to replace the fill behind it. At the close of the fiscal year 1,200 linear feet of the 1,600 linear feet of wall had been reenforced with concrete.

Money statement.

April 12, 1901, allotted	$3,000.00
June 30, 1901, amount expended during fiscal year	1,314.02
July 1, 1901, balance unexpended	1,685.98
July 1, 1901, outstanding liabilities	1,057.27
July 1, 1901, balance available	628.71

Preservation and repair of fortifications.—All the batteries and electric-lighting and power plants on the reservation containing the above emplacements were kept in repair and good condition with funds from the appropriation for "Preservation and Repair of Fortifications."

Money statement.

July 1, 1900, balance unexpended	$1,000.00
February 21, 1901, allotted	200.00
May 13, 1901, allotted	1,500.00
	2,700.00
June 30, 1901, amount expended during fiscal year	1,168.13
July 1, 1901, balance unexpended	1,531.87
July 1, 1901, outstanding liabilities	5.25
July 1, 1901, balance available	1,526.62

RESERVATION NO. 2.

Emplacements for two 12-inch B. L. rifles on nondisappearing carriages.—These were complete with their armament at the beginning of the fiscal year, and were turned over to the artillery July 5, 1900.

Emplacements for two 5-inch rapid-fire guns on balanced-pillar mounts.—These were complete at the beginning of the fiscal year, except a small quantity of concrete for one platform that awaited the arrival of the mount. The cylinder of one mount had been concreted in. In July, 1900, the top part of that carriage was mounted on the cylinder already set, and the cylinder of the second mount concreted in, completing the platforms. The top part of the carriage of the second mount is not on hand. The battery was turned over to the artillery August 1, 1900.

Money statement.

MOUNTING TWO 5-INCH GUN CARRIAGES.

July 1, 1900, balance unexpended	$289.71
June 30, 1901, amount expended during the fiscal year	289.71

Emplacements for two 15-pounder rapid-fire guns.—These were complete at the beginning of the fiscal year, but no guns or mounts were

APPENDIX 3—FORTIFICATIONS.

on hand. The emplacements were turned over to the artillery August 1, 1900. The guns were mounted by the troops during the fiscal year.

Remodeling old work.—These operations were not complete at the close of the last fiscal year, and have been continued in the present year by constructing a granolithic pavement and runway 12 feet wide on the terreplein in rear of fronts 2, 3, and 4 and in front of the power house, by placing an asphalt cover on a cement mortar foundation on the roof over the first tier of old casemates, quarters, and storerooms on fronts 2, 3, and 4, and by setting a granite coping on the inside of the wall. The casemate piers on the same fronts were refaced with brick. Work on remodeling was still in progress at the close of the fiscal year.

Money statement.

GUN AND MORTAR BATTERIES.

July 1, 1900, balance unexpended	$3,052.12
January 18, 1901, allotted	4,925.00
	7,977.12
June 30, 1901, amount expended during fiscal year	5,738.15
July 1, 1901, balance unexpended	2,238.97
July 1, 1901, outstanding liabilities	1,969.21
July 1, 1901, balance available	269.76

Preservation and repair of fortifications.—The batteries and the electric light and power plant at this post have been kept in repair and good condition during the fiscal year with funds from the appropriation for "Preservation and Repair of Fortifications."

Money statement.

July 1, 1900, balance unexpended	$1,000.00
May 13, 1901, allotted	1,200.00
	2,200.00
June 30, 1901, amount expended during fiscal year	957.06
July 1, 1901, balance unexpended	1,242.94
July 1, 1901, outstanding liabilities	4.05
July 1, 1901, balance available	1,238.89

RESERVATION NO. 3.

Battery for eight 12-inch B. L. mortars.—This was complete and garrisoned at the close of the fiscal year ended June 30, 1900, but the galleries and rooms proving to be wet, an allotment of $13,500 was made February 23, 1901, to finish one magazine, two shot rooms, one shot passage, one central passage, one entrance passage, one storeroom, and two relocater rooms by placing a layer of asphalt all about the sides and roofs, that at the sides to be held in place by a light 4-inch wall and that at the roofs by a layer of concrete reenforced by iron bars resting on the I-beams, and to provide air spaces by a thin layer of plaster on expanded-metal lathing set 2 inches from the sides and roofs. This plan had been applied to one magazine with encouraging results. The work is in progress at the close of the fiscal year, but has been delayed by water percolating through during the exceptional rainy season since the allotment was made, and by the desire to observe results, under varied atmospheric conditions, in the magazine already treated. Those results may determine that slight changes in details of construction would be desirable. A base for one Rafferty range finder was set.

Money statement.

GUN AND MORTAR BATTERIES.

February 23, 1901, allotted	$13,500.00
June 30, 1901, amount expended during fiscal year	1,217.45
July 1, 1901, balance unexpended	12,282.55
July 1, 1901, outstanding liabilities	556.95
July 1, 1901, balance available	11,725.60

Emplacements for two 12-inch B. L. rifles on disappearing carriages.—These were complete with their armament and garrisoned at the close of the last fiscal year. During the fiscal year a base for one Rafferty range finder was set.

Emplacements for two 5-inch rapid-fire guns.—These were complete and carriages mounted at the close of the last fiscal year. They were turned over to the artillery October 27, 1900. No guns are on hand.

Emplacements for two 15-pounder rapid-fire guns.—These were complete and garrisoned at the close of the last fiscal year. No guns or mounts are on hand.

Emplacements for two 6-inch B. L. rifles on disappearing carriages.—These were complete with the exception of some minor details at the close of the last fiscal year, carriages mounted, and garrisoned. Trolleys and blocks were put in during the fiscal year and soap-and-alum wash applied to the platforms. No guns are on hand. The balance of funds remaining was transferred to construct a surface drainage system at Reservation No. 1.

Money statement.

July 1, 1900, balance unexpended		$1,366.09
October 8, 1900, amount transferred to another allotment	$981.02	
June 30, 1901, amount expended during fiscal year	385.07	
		1,366.09

Emplacements for two 15-pounder rapid-fire guns.—Two allotments aggregating $10,460 were made for constructing this battery and a roadway to it. Only the preliminary steps had been taken at the close of the last fiscal year. During the present fiscal year the emplacements and roadway were constructed and turned over to the artillery January 15, 1901. The emplacements follow the type plans. No guns or mounts are on hand. The cost of the battery is the amount of the allotments.

Money statement.

July 1, 1900, balance unexpended	$10,000.00
November 22, 1900, allotted	460.00
June 30, 1901, amount expended during fiscal year	10,460.00

Mining casemate.—This was practically completed at the close of the last fiscal year. During the present fiscal year a telephone conduit between the casemate and the storehouse was completed, a con-

APPENDIX 3—FORTIFICATIONS. 789

crete gutter placed over the entrance to the casemate, some trees grubbed out, and a connecting roadway constructed, completely finishing the work. It was turned over to the artillery April 29, 1901.

Money statement.

TORPEDOES FOR HARBOR DEFENSE.

July 1, 1900, balance unexpended	$1,484.64
June 30, 1901, amount expended during fiscal year	1,484.64

Storehouse for torpedo material.—This was complete at the close of the last fiscal year, and was turned over to the artillery April 29, 1901.

Cable tank.—This was complete at the close of the last fiscal year, and was turned over to the artillery April 29, 1901.

Sea walls and embankments.—This work is for the protection of that part of the reservation containing the last six batteries reported upon, together with the mining casemate, storehouse, and cable tank. At the close of the last fiscal year the work was complete except for about 151 linear feet of concrete wall and filling behind 1,275 linear feet of concrete wall. During the fiscal year the concrete wall was completed and 3,350 cubic yards of fill placed behind it, exhausting the balance available July 1, 1900.

An allotment of $18,000 was made April 18, 1901, to complete the fill behind the concrete wall; to place a light backing of concrete to the sea wall built of open rubble prior to 1900; to stay the washing of the supporting fill in progress there, which was threatening the stability of the wall, and to place a riprap foundation for a length of about 1,195 feet for the extension of the sea wall westward on that part of the reservation occupied by garrison buildings. At the close of the fiscal year all the rubble wall had been backed with concrete, 9,800 cubic yards of material excavated and placed in fill behind the concrete sea wall, and 200 linear feet of riprap foundation placed for the extension of the sea wall westward. It is estimated that $14,200 additional will be required to complete the extension of the sea wall westward.

Money statement.

July 1, 1900, balance unexpended	$2,040.24
April 18, 1901, allotted	18,000.00
	20,040.24
June 30, 1901, amount expended during fiscal year	4,972.32
July 1, 1901, balance unexpended	15,067.92
July 1, 1901, outstanding liabilities	3,037.47
July 1, 1901, balance available	12,030.45

Peace storage magazine.—Plans for this at an estimated cost of $4,500 were submitted April 6, 1901.

Roadway.—An allotment of $3,316.50 was made April 18, 1901, to construct a road between the mortar battery and the 12-inch battery. Owing to the unusual wet weather, combined with waiting for the completion of some grading at the site, nothing had been done on this at the close of the fiscal year.

Money statement.

GUN AND MORTAR BATTERIES.

April 18, 1901, allotted	$3,316.50
July 1, 1901, balance available	3,316.50

Preservation and repair of fortifications.—The batteries, mining casemate, storehouse, cable tank, and electric-light and power plants located on Reservation No. 3, have been kept in repair and good condition during the present fiscal year with funds derived from the appropriation for "Preservation and Repair of Fortifications."

Money statement.

July 1, 1900, balance unexpended	$2,136.70
Allotted January 4 and May 13, 1901	2,500.00
	4,636.70
June 30, 1901, amount expended during fiscal year	2,236.70
July 1, 1901, balance available	2,400.00

RESERVATION NO. 4.

Emplacements for two 6-inch B. L. rifles on disappearing carriages.—These were completed at the close of the last fiscal year, except installation of electric plant, wiring, and furnishing trolleys and blocks; carriages were mounted and the work was garrisoned. During the present fiscal year trolleys and blocks were put in and the balance of funds transferred to complete a surface drainage system at Reservation No. 1. No guns are on hand. It is proposed to defer the installation of the electric plant for the present.

Money statement.

July 1, 1900, balance unexpended	$784.46
October 8, 1900, amount transferred to another allotment	636.67
	147.79
June 30, 1901, amount expended during fiscal year	147.79

Sea walls and embankments.—Eight thousand dollars were allotted June 26, 1900, to build a concrete sea wall on a riprap foundation to protect the site of the foregoing battery. Only preliminary arrangements for work had been made at the close of the last fiscal year. During the present fiscal year there have been constructed 1,266 linear feet of concrete wall 2 feet wide on top, 4 feet at base, and 5 feet in height, and part of the supporting fill placed behind it. At that point funds were exhausted. April 12, 1901, an additional allotment of $3,000 was made to complete the fill, but operations have been delayed to finish other work.

Money statement.

July 1, 1900, balance unexpended	$8,000.00
April 12, 1901, allotted	3,000.00
	11,000.00
June 30, 1901, amount expended during fiscal year	8,000.00
July 1, 1901, balance available	3,000.00

APPENDIX 3—FORTIFICATIONS.

Preservation and repair of fortifications.—The battery and property on the reservation have been kept in good condition during the present fiscal year with funds from the appropriation for "Preservation and Repair of Fortifications."

Money statement.

July 1, 1900, balance unexpended	$320.00
February 21, 1901, allotted	250.00
May 13, 1901, allotted	400.00
	970.00
June 30, 1901, amount expended during fiscal year	433.89
July 1, 1901, balance unexpended	536.11
July 1, 1901, outstanding liabilities	75.00
July 1, 1901, balance available	461.11

Supplies for seacoast defenses.—Electrical supplies for all the electric installations pertaining to the defenses of Baltimore, Md., have been furnished the artillery on requisitions approved by the Chief of Engineers.

Money statement.

July 1, 1900, balance unexpended	$1,000.00
June 14, 1901, allotted	1,000.00
	2,000.00
June 30, 1901, amount expended during fiscal year	997.35
July 1, 1901, balance available	1,002.65

SUBMARINE-MINE DEFENSE.

During the fiscal year all the material was kept in the storehouse and cable tank at Reservation No. 3, where it was cared for, repaired, and kept clean and in excellent condition by an electrician, mechanic, and watchman until April 29, 1901, when it was transferred to the artillery. The funds for these operations were derived from the appropriation for "Preservation and Repair of Fortifications."

Money statement.

July 1, 1900, balance unexpended	$500.00
June 30, 1901, amount expended during fiscal year	500.00

SEARCHLIGHTS.

A project for searchlights for the defenses of Baltimore, Md., at an estimated cost of $78,821.05, was submitted May 13, 1901.

3 I.

DEFENSES OF WASHINGTON, DISTRICT OF COLUMBIA.

Officer in charge, Lieut. Col. Charles J. Allen, Corps of Engineers.

Fort Foote, Potomac River, Maryland.—For some repairs to the wharf and roadway and for some shore protection an allotment of $50 was made May 20, 1901.

792 REPORT OF THE CHIEF OF ENGINEERS, U. S. ARMY.

Money statement.

June 30, 1901, amount allotted during the fiscal year	$50.00
July 1, 1901, balance available	50.00

ALLOTMENT.

May 20, 1901, "Preservation and Repair of Fortifications," act of March 1, 1901	$50

LEFT BANK POTOMAC RIVER.

The progress and general condition of the work at the close of the fiscal year ended June 30, 1899, were as follows:

A battery for two 10-inch guns on disappearing carriages, L. F., model of 1894, was completed by the close of 1896. The guns were mounted in the winter of 1896–97. During the fiscal year ended June 30, 1899, an electric-light plant was installed in this battery.

A second battery for two 10-inch guns was completed and had an electric light and power plant installed in it. One of the guns was mounted in 1897 on a disappearing carriage, L. F., model of 1894; the other was mounted in May, 1898, on a disappearing carriage, L. F., model of 1896.

A third battery for two 10-inch guns was also completed. The guns were mounted in 1898 on disappearing carriages, model of 1896. This battery was commenced in the latter part of March, 1898, and built with funds from the appropriation of March 9, 1898, for "National Defense."

Emplacements for two 4-inch Driggs-Schroeder rapid-fire guns were also completed. The guns were mounted by the early part of July, 1898.

These three 10-inch gun batteries and the 4-inch rapid-fire gun battery were turned over to the officer of artillery commanding the post on July 6, 1899, in accordance with paragraph 1486, Army Regulations, 1895.

The following work has been carried on during the past fiscal year:

Mortar battery for eight 12-inch mortars on carriages, model of 1896.—Under an allotment of $113,000 made August 8, 1898, for the construction of emplacements for eight 12-inch mortars, work was commenced August 25, 1898. At the close of the fiscal year 1900 about 12 per cent of the work of construction remained to be done, consisting of relaying asphalt roof protection of middle traverse, remodeling and finishing of earth parapet, making and hanging doors, laying granolithic sidewalks and flooring about mortar pits, grading roadway in rear of the battery, constructing an intercepting drain in front of the battery, resetting observation stations, soil covering and seeding slopes, laying terra-cotta electric conduit, cutting trees in front of battery, installing ammunition trolley system, and also the electric-light plant, erecting iron stairs and railings, and mounting the mortars.

All of the foregoing work was completed during the past fiscal year, the trolley system, stairs, and railings, which are nearly done, and installing the electric-light plant and mounting the mortars excepted. The stairs and railings will be completed early in the coming fiscal year, and it is expected that the electric-light plant, bids for which were invited by public advertisement under date of June 27, 1901, will also be installed at an early day.

APPENDIX 3—FORTIFICATIONS. 793

The base rings for mortar platforms were reset during the year on account of a slight settlement of the platforms. The platforms were tested in the fall of 1900 by loading them for from two to three weeks with earth weighing about one-third more than the total weight of mortar and carriage combined, the weighting not producing any settling whatever. But in May last, slight settling having been observed at several of the front platforms, their rings were again releveled.

This battery is about 97 per cent completed. Its full completion, sodding excepted, is expected this summer. The mortars have not yet arrived.

For account of this battery see pages 876–878, Appendix 3, Annual Report for 1900.

Money statement.

July 1, 1900, balance unexpended		$16,107.67
Allotment during year		4,000.00
		20,107.67
June 30, 1901, amount expended during fiscal year		11,586.81
July 1, 1901, balance unexpended		8,520.86
July 1, 1901, outstanding liabilities	$1,082.00	
July 1, 1901, amount covered by uncompleted contracts	1,657.00	
		2,739.00
July 1, 1901, balance available		5,781.86

ALLOTMENTS.

"Gun and mortar batteries:"
August 8, 1898, act of May 7, 1898...... $113,000
March 11, 1901, act of May 25, 1900 4,000

117,000

Battery for two 6-inch rapid-fire guns on disappearing carriages.— This work was commenced in June, 1899, under an allotment of $59,180, made April 26, 1899, by the Chief of Engineers.

For an account of difficulties in the prosecution of this work in the season of 1899, owing to advance in prices of material, etc., reference is made to the Annual Report for 1900.

At the close of the fiscal year 1900 this battery was about one-fourth completed.

By the beginning of the fiscal year 1901 most of the materials of construction, such as sand, gravel, stone, cement, tile, steel beams, and lumbers had been received, 3,000 cubic yards of excavation made, and 395 cubic yards of concrete constructed. The gun carriages had arrived. During the summer and fall of 1900 the remaining materials of construction were delivered. Concrete construction was carried forward without interruption. When the working season closed there were but a few yards of concrete remaining to be built, and that was delayed only on account of the nondelivery of the iron work. The installation of the ammunition hoists was completed in November, 1900. During the winter the iron stairs, railing, and ladders were delivered, and their erection was completed in April, 1901. Concrete construction was completed in May. Base rings have been set and gun carriages mounted, the latter having been done by the artillery. The earth embankments have been built, the roadway and gutters partly constructed, and the doors made and hung.

The end of the fiscal year 1901 finds the battery 92 per cent completed. The work remaining to be done is to construct an electric conduit leading from the mortar battery, and to install a plant to provide for lighting the battery by electricity, obtained from the central generating plant. The trolley beams are yet to be installed, and the roadway and gutters completed. The guns when delivered are to be mounted by the artillery.

Money statement.

July 1, 1900, balance unexpended	$25,085.35
Allotment during year	5,450.00
	30,535.35
June 30, 1901, amount expended during fiscal year	24,404.94
July 1, 1901, balance unexpended	6,130.41
July 1, 1901, outstanding liabilities	850.00
July 1, 1901, balance available	5,280.41

ALLOTMENTS.

"Gun and Mortar Batteries:"
April 26, 1899, act of May 7, 1898	$59,180.00
June 21, 1901, act of March 1, 1901	5,450.00
	64,630.00

Battery for two 15-pounder rapid-fire guns.—An allotment of $9,500 was made December 28, 1898, for emplacements for two 15-pounder rapid-fire guns. By October, 1899, the work was about completed, excepting the construction of the gun platforms, which can not advantageously be undertaken until the gun mounts arrive, and setting the railing. The railing was set during the past fiscal year, but the platforms remain unbuilt, the gun mounts not having yet arrived.

Money statement.

July 1, 1900, balance unexpended	$1,909.98
June 30, 1901, amount expended during fiscal year	59.89
July 1, 1901, balance unexpended and available	1,850.09

Battery commanders' stations.—Under allotments of June 17 and 29, 1899, aggregating $12,206, work was commenced in September, 1899, on three stations. One is a low-type and the other two are high-type stations. They are built of concrete, with walls 2 feet to 2¼ feet thick, with concrete pedestals for the instruments, with concrete floors and steel roofs, and the low-type station is protected with an earth embankment.

Concrete work was carried on during the fall of 1899 and was continued during the following spring. By the beginning of the past fiscal year concrete work was practically completed, a few cubic feet being left to construct after the installation of the iron work. Some of the doors were made. The earth embankment at the low-type station was finished. The steel roofs, stairs, and railing had been purchased, but not delivered. Materials had been hauled by carts and wagons from the nearest points of the railroad. Concrete had been mixed by hand and placed mostly by wheelbarrows. A small derrick was erected to build the higher parts of the high-type stations.

APPENDIX 3—FORTIFICATIONS.

During the past fiscal year the stations have been practically completed. The delivery of steel roofs was commenced in October, 1900, but was not completed till May, 1901. They were purchased by contract with Whitehead & Kales, Detroit, Mich. The railing and stairs were purchased by contract with the North Penn Iron Company, North Penn Junction, Pa. They commenced delivery in November, 1900, but did not complete till March, 1901. The roofs, stairs, and railings have been erected and built into place. The doors, shutters, and windows have been completed, hung, and fitted, the ceilings of wood were constructed, and most of the woodwork painted.

The close of the fiscal year 1901 finds two stations completed and ready to turn over to the artillery; the third lacks a little painting and a little work in completing shutters. This will probably be completed during the first few days of July, 1901.

Money statement.

July 1, 1900, balance unexpended		$7,620.93
June 30, 1901, amount expended during fiscal year		4,262.58
July 1, 1901, balance unexpended		3,358.35
July 1, 1901, outstanding liabilities	$340.00	
July 1, 1901, amount covered by uncompleted contracts	1,185.00	
		1,525.00
July 1, 1901, balance available		1,833.35

ALLOTMENTS.

"Gun and Mortar Batteries," act of July 7, 1898:

June 17, 1899	$3,692.00
July 29, 1899	3,844.00
July 29, 1899	4,670.00
	12,206.00

Experimental parapet.—The construction of the parapet and shield was completed in June, 1898, and the firing tests were made in June, 1899. The work done during the past fiscal year was as follows: In September, 1900, the gun and carriage were dismantled, packed, and shipped away. In November the pit occupied by the gun platform was filled up and graded to its former condition. The cost was as follows:

Dismantling, packing, and shipping away the gun and carriage	$257.30
Filling and grading cut in the bank	84.97
	342.27

Money statement.

July 1, 1900, balance unexpended		$400.23
June 30, 1901, amount expended during fiscal year	$342.27	
July 1, 1901, balance (deposited in the Treasury of the United States)	57.96	
		400.23

ALLOTMENTS.

October 28, 1897, "Board of Ordnance and Fortification"	$10,000.00
October 29, 1897, "Gun and Mortar Batteries," act of March 3, 1897	8,550.00
June 11, 1898, "Gun and Mortar Batteries," act of May 7, 1898	1,700.00
September 21, 1898, "Gun and Mortar Batteries," act of May 7, 1898	1,500.00
	21,750.00

Elevated rear passageways, 10-inch batteries.—Under an allotment of $2,600, dated February 25, 1901, material has been purchased, some of it delivered and some of the construction work done. The project contemplates connecting the gun platforms of two batteries together and with their observing station, with a platform of the same elevation. The steel beams and columns were delivered in April, also the Portland cement. The railing has been purchased, but not yet delivered, and only a limited amount of the construction can be done till the receipt of the railing.

At both batteries some of the old concrete has been cut away, ready to receive the beams, and at one battery some of the concrete footings and piers have been built and part of the passage constructed. The work is about 30 per cent completed.

Money statement.

Allotment during year	$2,600.00
June 30, 1901, amount expended during fiscal year	843.41
July 1, 1901, balance unexpended	1,756.59
July 1, 1901, outstanding liabilities	812.00
July 1, 1901, balance available	944.59

ALLOTMENTS.

February 25, 1901, "Gun and Mortar Batteries:"	
Act of July 7, 1898	$30.45
Act of May 25, 1900	2,569.55
	2,600.00

Supplies for coast defenses.—An allotment of $600 was made June 7, 1900, from the appropriation for "Supplies for Sea Coast Defenses," act of May 25, 1900, for furnishing material for the service of the coast artillery in this engineer district under the provisions of General Orders, No. 66, Adjutant-General's Office, 1900. A quantity of supplies for electric plant at this point was purchased and issued during the year.

Money statement.

July 1, 1900, balance unexpended	$600.00
June 30, 1901, amount expended during fiscal year	394.51
July 1, 1901, balance unexpended and available	205.49

ALLOTMENT.

June 7, 1900, "Supplies for Sea Coast Defenses," act of May 25, 1900	$600.00

Preservation and repair of fortifications.—During the past fiscal year repairs have been made as follows: To the ammunition lifts and motors, to the boiler of the electric-light and power plant, and to the engineer buildings to a slight extent. Two semiannual inspections have been made of the submarine-mine material. Shutters have been placed over the embrasures of caponnières. Brush and rubbish were hauled away from the vicinity of the engineer buildings. The mining casemate was cared for in the interests of its preservation, and slight repairs were made to the drains. The 1,000-pound torpedo anchors were moved from the quartermaster's to the engineer wharf and painted. The oil engine was moved from the mining casemate to the torpedo storehouse, where it is less endangered by dampness. A water pipe was laid to the new position of the engineer house and office in the interest of security from fire. The searchlight engine was tested for efficiency. Some of the submarine-mine material was painted and some of the surplus and obsolete material was packed to be shipped to Willets Point. Some sanitary work was done.

The most extensive work of repair that was done during the past year was to line the magazines and corridors of one of the 10-inch batteries with hollow tile. This was found to be very difficult work, and considerable experimenting was done before the practical difficulties were surmounted, as laborers could not be found who were skilled in this particular class of work.

The first room lined with tile was found to leak quite badly as before. After that experience the rest of the tile was placed with a layer of tarred felt intervening between the wall and the tile. Observation during the rainy months of spring indicated that this was successful in intercepting water, and the first room was afterwards relined in the same manner. The walls are all much dryer than formerly, and except during or immediately after long-continued heavy rains the rooms are quite dry. There are, however, a few imperfectly made joints in the tarred felt and some places where the felt was punctured by anchor bolts that show slight leakage.

Money statement.

July 1, 1900, balance unexpended	$3,241.62
Allotment during year	1,225.00
	4,466.62
June 30, 1901, amount expended during fiscal year	3,072.63
July 1, 1901, balance unexpended	1,393.99
July 1, 1901, outstanding liabilities	226.00
July 1, 1901, balance available	1,167.99

ALLOTMENTS.

"Preservation and Repair of Fortifications:"

June 9, 1899, act of March 3, 1899	$978.00
July 17, 1899, act of March 3, 1899	125.00
September 22, 1899, act of March 3, 1899	1,892.00
June 11, 1900, act of May 25, 1900	875.00
May 20, 1901, act of March 1, 1901	1,225.00
	5,095.00

All the work during the fiscal year ended June 30, 1901, was done by hired labor, excepting erection of lifts and cranes, which was done under contract with Charles E. Ellicott, of Baltimore, Md.

The following contracts were in force during the year:

With Whitehead & Kales, of Detroit, Mich., for furnishing and delivering iron and steel roofs. Amount of contract, $1,185; date of contract, July 3, 1900; approved, July 14, 1900; date for completion (including furnishing and delivering additional roof), August 26, 1900—extended to September 9, 1900.

With the North Penn Iron Company, of North Penn Junction, Philadelphia, Pa., for furnishing and delivering stairs, railings, and ladders. Amount of contract, $1,460.43; date of contract, July 7, 1900; approved, July 27, 1900; date for completion (including furnishing and delivering stairs at another site), September 6, 1900—extended to September 27, 1900.

With New Jersey Foundry and Machine Company, of New York, N. Y., for furnishing and delivering tram rails, trolleys, and hoists. Amount of contract, $1,450; date of contract, July 16, 1900; approved, August 3, 1900; date for completion, September 12, 1900—extended to October 12, 1900.

With Charles E. Ellicott, of Baltimore, Md., for furnishing and erecting lifts and cranes. Amount of contract, $1,730; date of contract, July 19, 1900; approved August 9, 1900; date for completion, October 9, 1900—extended to November 15, 1900, and again to November 29, 1900.

RIGHT BANK POTOMAC RIVER.

Emplacements for three 8-inch guns on disappearing carriages L. F., model of 1894.—This battery was built by contract dated December 16, 1896, with Douglas & Andrews, of Baltimore, Md., under the provisions of the act of Congress of June 6, 1896, providing for the construction of fortifications by contract, to be paid for as appropriations might be made from time to time therefor.

An allotment of $100,000, to be expended under the contract, was made March 27, 1897. The contract work was finally completed August 15, 1898.

The guns were mounted and ready for service by April 1, 1898.

The battery was formally turned over to the commanding officer of the post on January 13, 1900.

No work on the battery other than some repairs and some preparations for constructing an elevated continuous rear passageway to connect gun platforms and emplacement observing stations, and which will be noted further on, was done during the past fiscal year.

The armament is in good condition.

Emplacements for two 5-inch rapid-fire guns.—Under an allotment of $14,500, October 4, 1898, for constructing two emplacements for 5-inch rapid-fire guns on balanced-pillar mounts, work was begun in November, 1898.

By September 6, 1899, the allotment was exhausted. The concrete work for both emplacements was about completed, gun platforms excepted, which could not be built until the arrival of the gun mounts. The embankments were about one-half completed and the doors partly constructed.

On December 29, 1900, the gun mounts were delivered. A further allotment of $2,700 was made February 7, 1901, and the work of finishing the batteries was resumed in March. The gun platforms and earth parapets were completed, the cylinders of gun mounts set, and the batteries practically finished by June 30, 1901. The only work remaining to be done is to set the railing as soon as it shall be delivered by the contractor. The mounting of the guns will be the work of the artillery whenever the guns shall be delivered.

Money statement.

July 1, 1900, balance unexpended	$7.89
Allotment during year	2,700.00
	2,707.89
June 30, 1901, amount expended during fiscal year	2,139.52
July 1, 1901, balance unexpended	568.37
July 1, 1901, outstanding liabilities	324.00
July 1, 1901, balance available	244.37

APPENDIX 3—FORTIFICATIONS. 799

ALLOTMENTS.

October 4, 1898, "Gun and Mortar Batteries," act of July 7, 1898	$14,500.00
February 7, 1901, "Gun and Mortar Batteries," act of May 25, 1900	2,700.00
	17,200.00

Battery for three 15-pounder rapid-fire guns.—An allotment of $15,100 was made June 25, 1900, to be applied to the construction of emplacements for three 15-pounder rapid-fire guns in accordance with plans submitted.

Materials were purchased and the work of construction commenced in August, 1900. A railroad was built to the site from the engineer wharf, a distance of about 3,000 feet; the locomotive and cars were transported from another locality; and a working plant of simple construction built. The materials of construction, such as sand, gravel, stone, cement, tile, steel beams, and lumber, were delivered and hauled to the site before the end of the working season. The drainage system was partly constructed, but otherwise construction was not begun till the spring of 1901. Since that time most of the excavation has been made and the concrete magazines have been built. Concrete was mixed by hand and conveyed in wheelbarrows. About 60 per cent of the concrete has been laid and the entire work of construction is about one-half done.

Money statement.

July 1, 1900, balance unexpended	$15,100.00
June 30, 1901, amount expended during fiscal year	9,688.36
July 1, 1901, balance unexpended	5,411.64
July 1, 1901, outstanding liabilities	1,111.00
July 1, 1901, balance available	4,300.64

ALLOTMENT.

June 25, 1900, "Gun and Mortar Batteries," act of May 25, 1900	$15,100.00

Electric light and power plant.—Under an allotment of $9,032.93 of October 7, 1898, for the construction of a power house and installation of a light and power plant, work of construction was commenced November 7, 1898. By the end of June, 1899, the cistern and power house were built in so far as they could be done before installation of the plant. The floor, doors, and windows are yet to be constructed. No construction work was done during the past year.

Plans and specifications for an electric light and power plant, 25-kilowatt generator, have been approved, and public advertisement will be issued immediately inviting proposals for furnishing and installing the plant, which, it is expected, will be done early in the coming fiscal year.

A further allotment of $4,800 was made for this plant by indorsement of the Chief of Engineers, June 26, 1901.

Money statement.

July 1, 1900, balance unexpended	$5,403.78
Allotment during year	4,800.00
	10,203.78
June 30, 1901, amount expended during fiscal year	58.33
July 1, 1901, balance unexpended	10,145.45
July 1, 1901, outstanding liabilities	84.00
July 1, 1901, balance available	10,061.45

800   REPORT OF THE CHIEF OF ENGINEERS, U. S. ARMY.

ALLOTMENTS.

October 7, 1898, "Gun and Mortar Batteries":	
Act of March 3, 1897	$4,732.93
Act of May 7, 1898	4,300.00
June 26, 1901, "Gun and Mortar Batteries," act of March 1, 1901	4,800.00
	13,832.93

Battery commander's station.—Under an allotment of $4,259, July 29, 1899, for the construction of a high-type station near the 8-inch battery for mounting a type-A range finder, materials were purchased and the construction work was commenced October 5. By June 30, 1900, the concrete walls and pillars had been constructed and the entire work about two-thirds completed. Concrete was mixed by hand and about two-thirds of it placed by wheelbarrows; that for the higher portions of the structure was placed by derrick. All materials were hauled to site from the wharf, nearly a mile distant, with carts and wagons. The iron railing and stairs were purchased in June, 1900, under contract with the North Penn Iron Company. None of it was delivered until late in the fall, and the delivery was not completed until March, 1901. The steel roofs were purchased in June, 1900, under contract with Whitehead & Kales, Detroit, Mich. Delivery commenced in October, but was not completed until May, 1901.

The ironwork has been erected and the station was practically completed during the spring of 1901. The only work that remains to be done is some painting of wood and iron work, a little brickwork to be constructed, and some fitting of windows to be done. This will probably be finished by July 15, ready to turn over to the artillery.

Money statement.

July 1, 1900, balance unexpended		$3,568.86
June 30, 1901, amount expended during fiscal year		1,764.90
July 1, 1901, balance unexpended		1,803.96
July 1, 1901, outstanding liabilities	$192.00	
July 1, 1901, amount covered by uncompleted contracts	395.00	
		587.00
July 1, 1901, balance available		1,216.96

Elevated passage to connect gun platforms, 8-inch battery.—An allotment of $1,485 was made January 16, 1901, for this work. Detailed designs were made as soon as practicable and materials purchased. The floor beams and columns and 35 barrels of Portland cement were received in April. The railing and other ironwork have been purchased, but not yet delivered. Construction work was commenced in June. Concrete piers and footings for columns have been built, and the columns and some floor beams erected. Some drilling and cutting of old concrete to receive the beams has been done and some excavation made. The entire work is about 25 per cent completed.

Money statement.

Allotment during year	$1,485.00
June 30, 1901, amount expended during fiscal year	468.25
July 1, 1901, balance unexpended	1,016.75
July 1, 1901, outstanding liabilities	405.00
July 1, 1901, balance available	611.75

APPENDIX 3—FORTIFICATIONS. 801

ALLOTMENT.

January 16, 1901, "Gun and Mortar Batteries," act of July 7, 1898 ..... $1,485.00

Preservation and repair of fortifications.—The work of the past fiscal year was as follows: During the fall and winter of 1900 a watchman was employed to care for engineer property and maintain a light on the wharf at night. Repairs have been made to ammunition lifts, drains, and doors. One broken bracket has been replaced. Small cracks in the concrete were pointed up and some repairs to earth slopes after storms were made. Storm doors were built and hung and iron lintels were placed over exterior doors to keep out water. The drains of the 5-inch batteries were cleaned out previous to the resumption of work. The searchlight has been run, tested, and cleaned when necessary. The engineer buildings were given a coat of whitewash and were repaired slightly. Some cutting of weeds and removing of rubbish from the vicinity were done.

Money statement.

July 1, 1900, balance unexpended	$1,055.32
Allotment during year	725.00
	1,780.32
June 30, 1901, amount expended during fiscal year	1,024.33
July 1, 1901, balance unexpended	755.99
July 1, 1901, outstanding liabilities	2.00
July 1, 1901, balance available	753.99

ALLOTMENTS.

"Preservation and Repair of Fortifications:"

June 9, 1899, act of March 3, 1899	$454.00
June 11, 1900, act of May 25, 1900	900.00
May 20, 1901, act of March 1, 1901	725.00
	2,079.00

All the work during the fiscal year ended June 30, 1901, was done by hired labor.

The following contracts were in force during the year:

With Whitehead & Kales, Detroit, Mich., for furnishing and delivering roof. Amount of contract, $395; date of contract, July 3, 1900; approved July 14, 1900; date for completion (including furnishing and delivering additional roofs), August 26, 1900, extended to September 9, 1900.

With North Penn Iron Company, of North Penn Junction, Philadelphia, Pa., for furnishing and delivering stairs. Amount of contract, $80; date of contract, July 7, 1900; approved July 27, 1900; date for completion (including furnishing and delivering stairs, railings, and ladders at another site), September 6, 1900, extended to September 27, 1900.

3 J.

DEFENSES OF HAMPTON ROADS, VIRGINIA.

Officer in charge, Maj. James B. Quinn, Corps of Engineers; Division Engineer, Col. Peter C. Hains, Corps of Engineers.

Emplacement for 10-inch gun on spit.—With the exception of electric-light wiring, this work had been finished June 30, 1900. The contractor for this work completed the system of wiring early in the fiscal year and on January 3, 1901, the emplacement was turned over to the artillery.

Money statement.

July 1, 1900, balance unexpended	$592.53
June 30, 1901, amount expended during fiscal year	592.53

ALLOTMENT.

Appropriation for "Gun and Mortar Batteries," act March 3, 1897...... $50,000.00

Emplacement for 10-inch gun in bastion.—This work is entirely finished, with the exception of connecting storage battery with the generating plant.

During the fiscal year work of minor importance has been done, such as setting railing at outer edge of the loading platform, walls and ceilings of all rooms whitewashed, hoods built over all outside doors, open drains cut in surface of loading platform, painting woodwork and trolley track, system of speaking tubes installed, and wires for electric lights placed.

A walkway of concrete from the southern part of this emplacement to the 4.72-inch rapid-fire battery on parapet of main work was laid at a cost of $144.94.

Money statement.

July 1, 1900, balance unexpended	$7,042.62
June 30, 1901, amount expended during fiscal year	2,776.38
July 1, 1901, balance unexpended	4,266.24
July 1, 1901, outstanding liabilities	155.63
July 1, 1901, balance available	4,110.61

ALLOTMENT.

Appropriation for "Gun and Mortar Batteries," act July 7, 1898 .... $38,000.00

Three 10-inch gun emplacements.—When the contractor had placed the wires for lighting these emplacements, they were turned over to the troops, the transfer being made January 3, 1901. The expenditures were made on account of the electric-light installation.

Money statement.

July 1, 1900, balance unexpended	$1,845.76
June 30, 1901, amount expended during fiscal year	1,845.76

ALLOTMENTS.

Appropriations:	
"National Defense," act March 9, 1898	$116,000.00
"Gun and Mortar Batteries," act May 7, 1898	5,000.00
Total	121,000.00

Emplacements for three 12-inch guns.—In the fiscal year 1901 work was confined to completing the emplacements as far as possible. The parts of the carriages having been moved by the troops, the southern slope was finished with 135 cubic yards of sand, 128 cubic yards of clay, 187 cubic yards of soil, and 590 square yards of sod.

The contractor finished the electric wiring early in the fiscal year and the same was tested and accepted. Cable lines were laid underground from the storage battery to each emplacement.

Over the top surface of the concrete covering the magazines Portland cement mortar was spread, the area covered being 759 square yards. The trolley system, ammunition hoists, and loading platform stanchions were painted, and walls and ceilings of all rooms whitewashed. Open drains were cut in the concrete at each of the loading platforms and conductor pipes placed for carrying off the water.

The troops had mounted two of the carriages and guns for the battery at the close of the fiscal year, and after the other gun is mounted the battery can be finished in about three months' time.

Money statement.

July 1, 1900, balance unexpended	$33,965.53
June 30, 1901, amount expended during fiscal year	14,184.60
July 1, 1901, balance unexpended	19,780.93
July 1, 1901, outstanding liabilities	332.85
July 1, 1901, balance available	19,448.08

ALLOTMENT.

Appropriation for "Gun and Mortar Batteries," act May 7, 1898....... $150,000.00

Emplacements for two 12-inch guns.—Plans for a battery as noted to be built on the beach front were approved, with modifications, April 8, 1901. A riprap sea wall has also been authorized to be built along the stretch of beach between Jetties Nos. 1 and 2 for the protection of this battery. The sum provided for the battery and sea wall is $188,000. For preparing plans and making borings at the site, $500 were provided and expended.

The work done to the close of the fiscal year consisted in grading the site, laying out the battery, and driving 179 linear feet of double-lap sheet piling to protect the foundation from being undermined by high tides.

The sand removed in grading amounted to 263 cubic yards and was deposited so that it will be included in the sand cover of the battery. A switch has been put down and 373 feet of railroad track laid for handling material to be delivered for the battery. Proposals have been invited for the cement, broken stone, steel beams, etc., for the foundation, and specifications drawn up for constructing the sea wall.

Money statement.

June 30, 1901, allotted during fiscal year	$188,500.00
June 30, 1901, expended during fiscal year	1,174.89
July 1, 1901, balance unexpended	187,325.11
July 1, 1901, outstanding liabilities	265.44
July 1, 1901, balance available	187,059.67

ALLOTMENTS.

Appropriation for "Gun and Mortar Batteries:"
Act May 25, 1900	$500.00
Act May 25, 1900	125,000.00
Act March 1, 1901	63,000.00
Total	188,500.00

Emplacements for two 6-inch rapid-fire guns.—With funds from the appropriation act of May 25, 1900, for "Gun and Mortar Batteries," it is proposed to construct emplacements for the armament above noted. At the close of the fiscal year the plans and estimate were well under way.

Money statement.

June 30, 1901, allotted during fiscal year	$30,000.00
July 1, 1901, balance unexpended	30,000.00

ALLOTMENT.

Appropriation for "Gun and Mortar Batteries," act of May 25, 1900..... $30,000.00

Emplacements for four 15-pounder rapid-fire guns.—Work on this battery has been delayed awaiting arrival of armament.

During the fiscal year 93 cubic yards of sand, 21 cubic yards of clay, 43 cubic yards of soil, and 120 square yards of sod were used in completing the slope. The doors for the magazines were made, hung, and painted, and 4 shot racks erected, one in each magazine. For steps to the platforms 3 cubic yards of concrete were used and the surface of steps covered with 8 square yards of granolithic finish. All the exposed concrete surface of the battery was coated with a mixture of Portland cement and lampblack.

The battery has been finished as far as possible until after the armament is placed.

Money statement.

July 1, 1900, balance unexpended	$5,699.28
June 30, 1901, expended during fiscal year	2,874.34
July 1, 1901, balance unexpended	2,824.94

ALLOTMENT.

Appropriation for "Gun and Mortar Batteries," act July 7, 1898........ $12,500.00

Battery commander's station.—At a cost of $6,000 the construction of the battery commander's station for the mortar battery was authorized July 27, 1900, and the structural steel and castings for the same were contracted for November 8, 1900.

The foundation for tower was started September 13, 1900, and this, with the concrete placed in the steel cylinder, required 105 cubic yards. At the base a fill was made to reference 14 feet above mean low water, for which 441 cubic yards of sand were used, and on the slopes 24 cubic yards of clay, 27 cubic yards of soil, and 46 square yards of sod were placed.

All the metal structural material was delivered during January, 1901, with the exception of the stairs, and the frame and other parts were fitted, riveted, and placed in position as rapidly as possible.

APPENDIX 3—FORTIFICATIONS. 805

After this the shelter was framed and covered with galvanized sheet iron and floor laid. The interior of the shelter has been given two coats of hard-oil finish, and the exterior of same, the steel cylinder, and framework of shelter support painted.

At the close of the fiscal year the station was entirely finished and ready for transfer to the troops.

Money statement.

June 30, 1901, allotted during fiscal year	$6,000.00
June 30, 1901, expended during fiscal year	5,805.18
July 1, 1901, balance unexpended	194.82
July 1, 1901, outstanding liabilities	41.63
July 1, 1901, balance available	153.19

ALLOTMENT.

Appropriation for "Gun and Mortar Batteries," act May 25, 1900....... $6,000.00

Abstract of contract in force.

Name of contractor, West Side Foundry Co.; date of approval, November 27, 1900; material to be delivered on or before January 4, 1901. (Time extended 60 days.) Date of expiration, March 5, 1901; price, $2,695.

Concrete walk.—Under the allotment of June 22, 1900, referred to in the last Annual Report, a walkway of concrete was laid 4 feet wide for a distance of 376 feet, at a cost of $503.81.

Money statement.

July 1, 1900, balance unexpended		$626.00
June 30, 1901, expended during fiscal year	$503.81	
June 30, 1901, repaid to appropriation during fiscal year	122.19	
		626.00

ALLOTMENT.

Appropriation for "Gun and Mortar Batteries," act of July 7, 1898..... $626.00

Gallery, etc.—Under an allotment of July 26, 1900, the platforms of certain emplacements were connected by a platform supported by steel I-beams let into the vertical concrete wall and braced. The allotment also covered the placing of hand rails for the loading platforms, which were provided.

Money statement.

June 30, 1901, allotted during fiscal year	$165.00
June 30, 1901, expended during fiscal year	165.00

ALLOTMENT.

Appropriation for "Gun and Mortar Batteries," act July 7, 1898........ $165.00

Installing type-B emergency range and position finders.—During the fiscal year 13 stations for emergency range finders were provided for the several modern batteries at this point under an allotment made July 2, 1900, for that particular purpose.

Money statement.

June 30, 1901, allotted during fiscal year		$172.00
June 30, 1901, expended during fiscal year	$142.75	
June 30, 1901, repaid to appropriation during fiscal year	29.25	
		172.00

ALLOTMENT.

Appropriation for "Gun and Mortar Batteries," act May 25, 1900....... $172.00

Tide gauge.—An allotment of $30 was made July 6, 1900, for erecting a tide gauge on the engineer wharf for use in conjunction with the range-finding system. The gauge established is of the float type, and to prevent inaccurate indications in stormy weather the float was placed in a metal pipe 1 foot in diameter.

A shelter was constructed for the gauge and the same painted.

Money statement.

June 30, 1901, allotted during fiscal year	$30.00
June 30, 1901, expended during fiscal year	30.00

ALLOTMENT.

Appropriation for "Gun and Mortar Batteries," act July 7, 1898........ $30.00

Systems of speaking tubes.—Allotments aggregating $505 were made in the fiscal year 1901 for the purpose indicated above.

At one 10-inch battery the relocator room was made the central station and a line of tubes thereto was run from each of the platforms and magazines of the battery. The aggregate length of the four lines of tubes at this work is 596.5 feet. The system cost $140.

At another 10-inch battery a system similar in every respect to the above was provided at a cost of $100. The total length of the lines laid was 402 feet.

At the mortar battery tubes were provided to the relocator room from each of the four pits and from each of the temporary magazines and the observation tower. The pipe laid for these lines amounted to 1,503 feet, and the work cost $265.

Money statement.

June 30, 1901, allotted during fiscal year	$505.00
June 30, 1901, expended during fiscal year	505.00

ALLOTMENTS.

Appropriation for "Gun and Mortar Batteries," act July 7, 1898........	$365.00
Appropriation for "Gun and Mortar Batteries," act May 25, 1900.......	140.00
Total...	505.00

Hand rails.—The sum of $100 was provided January 28, 1901, for placing hand rails on the loading platforms of certain of the works. The railings were provided during the month of February, 1901, at a cost of $90.08. For this work 425 feet of galvanized-iron pipe was purchased, with necessary fittings and iron for stanchions, the latter being made from 1-inch round iron.

Money statement.

June 30, 1901, allotted during fiscal year		$100.00
June 30, 1901, expended during fiscal year	$90.08	
June 30, 1901, repaid to appropriation during fiscal year	9.92	
		100.00

ALLOTMENT.

Appropriation for "Gun and Mortar Batteries," act March 3, 1899...... $100.00

New azimuth circles at mortar battery.—Under an allotment amounting to $400, the azimuth circles of the four carriages of model 1891 at the mortar battery were removed and the concrete cut away so as to receive circles like those supplied with the carriage of model 1896.

The four platforms had been made ready for the reception of the new circles at the close of the fiscal year, and they will be set as soon as received.

Money statement.

June 30, 1901, allotted during fiscal year		$400.00
June 30, 1901, expended during fiscal year	$149.53	
July 1, 1901, balance unexpended	250.47	
		400.00

ALLOTMENT.

Appropriation for "Gun and Mortar Batteries," act May 25, 1900 .... $400.00

Electric plant.—Plans for increasing the electric generating plant at one of the 10-inch batteries to a capacity sufficient to furnish current for lighting that work, the emplacement at the place of arms and another 10-inch battery, and for a building for the said plant and the electric storage batteries at these works were approved April 16, 1901. Allotments aggregating $10,160 were made to cover the estimated cost of the new plant and structure.

Work at the site of the building was started May 1, 1901. The site selected is in the center traverse of the battery, and before the foundation could be laid 307 square yards of sod, 31 cubic yards of soil, 34 cubic yards of clay, and 1,342 cubic yards of sand were removed.

In building the retaining walls at sides and ends of the excavation 98 cubic yards of Rosendale concrete were mixed and placed, which completed them. In the rear of these walls 289 cubic yards of the sand removed were replaced, and 17 cubic yards each of clay and soil and 160 square yards of sod used to finish slopes.

For the foundation of building 16 cubic yards of Portland cement concrete were mixed and placed. This is as far as the building proper was advanced during the fiscal year.

Money statement.

June 30, 1901, allotted during fiscal year	$10,160.00
June 30, 1901, expended during fiscal year	608.25
July 1, 1901, balance unexpended	9,551.75
July 1, 1901, outstanding liabilities	389.05
July 1, 1901, balance available	9,162.70

ALLOTMENTS.

Appropriation for "Gun and Mortar Batteries," act March 1, 1901	$5,505.00
Appropriation for "Supplies for Sea Coast Defenses," act May 25, 1900	4,655.00
Total	10,160.00

Building for mortar-battery electric plant.—The storage battery for lighting this work is set up in a small room partitioned off by a 9-inch brick wall from the passageway in front of Pit No. 2. It being considered desirable to change its location on account of the damp condition of the room and to prevent injury to ammunition and material stored in the passageway by the fumes from the fluid in the battery jars, an estimate for transferring the storage battery to a specially constructed building to be erected in the southern traverse was submitted, and an allotment of $2,900 was made for the work April 19, 1901.

The excavation to be made in the traverse for the storage-battery building was commenced May 1, 1901, and after the sod, soil, and clay had been removed from the slope 1,675 cubic yards of sand were taken out. For the walls to retain sand in the traverse 65 cubic yards of Rosendale concrete were necessary, and for the building 117 cubic yards of Portland concrete were used. The floor of the room was covered with granolithic finish, the surface covered being 32 square yards, and the concrete roof was given a coating of asphalt and coarse broken stone spread over it.

After the building was completed, 1,120 cubic yards of the sand excavated from the site were replaced behind the retaining walls and the top surface covered with 3-inch layers of clay and soil and 116 square yards of sod laid.

On June 30, 1901, the building was ready for the placing of doors and windows, and as soon as they have been provided the transfer of the storage battery to the new building will be made.

Money statement.

June 30, 1901, allotted during fiscal year	$2,900.00
June 30, 1901, expended during fiscal year	604.20
July 1, 1901, balance unexpended	2,295.80
July 1, 1901, outstanding liabilities	728.32
July 1, 1901, balance available	1,567.48

ALLOTMENT.

Appropriation for "Gun and Mortar Batteries," act May 25, 1900....... $2,900.00

Mortar battery.—The sum of $1,000 was provided by allotment, April 17, 1901, for removing the switches, stone bins, cement houses, and other plant, and cleaning up in the vicinity of this battery.

At the close of the fiscal year one of the cement houses had been torn down, and the stone bins and inclined railroad trestle thereto removed.

Money statement.

June 30, 1901, allotted during fiscal year	$1,000.00
July 1, 1901, outstanding liabilities	340.39
July 1, 1901, balance available	659.61

ALLOTMENT.

Appropriation for "Gun and Mortar Batteries," act May 25, 1900....... $1,000.00

Sea wall.—Plans for a concrete sea wall to extend from the engineer wharf to the first jetty on the beach were approved early in the fiscal year 1901, and the sum of $12,000 allotted for constructing a portion of the structure, commencing at the jetty. From funds appropriated for "Sea Walls and Embankments," by the act of March 1, 1901, an additional sum of $11,000 was provided to complete the sea wall between the points stated and for filling in rear of same.

In August, 1900, work was started on the wall at Jetty No. 1, and was discontinued in November of the same year, as the winter season was unfavorable for carrying on the work. When work was suspended 113 feet of the wall had been finished.

Since work on the wall was resumed, in May of the present year, it has been seriously retarded by easterly storms, so that to the close of the fiscal year only 62 feet had been added to the section built in the previous period during which operations were in progress.

Money statement.

June 30, 1901, allotted during fiscal year	$23,000.00
June 30, 1901, expended during fiscal year	4,987.19
July 1, 1901, balance unexpended	18,012.81
July 1, 1901, outstanding liabilities	558.71
July 1, 1901, balance available	17,454.10

ALLOTMENTS.

Appropriation for "Sea Walls and Embankments:"

Act May 25, 1900	$12,000.00
Act March 1, 1901	11,000.00
Total	23,000.00

Supplies for seacoast defenses.—Allotments aggregating $1,500 were made for the purchase of supplies required by the artillery for the defenses at this locality during the fiscal year 1901.

All duly approved articles estimated for by the acting engineer officer of the post for the period above noted have been procured and issued, with the exception of rheostats and wire lamp guards, on requisition for quarter ending with the fiscal year. These articles are of special make, and the manufacturers were unable to make prompt delivery on that account.

Money statement.

June 30, 1901, allotted during fiscal year	$1,500.00
June 30, 1901, expended during fiscal year	495.62
July 1, 1901, balance unexpended	1,004.38
July 1, 1901, outstanding liabilities	848.61
July 1, 1901, balance available	155.77

ALLOTMENTS.

Appropriation for "Supplies for Sea Coast Defenses:"

Act May 25, 1900	$1,000.00
Act May 25, 1900	500.00
Total	1,500.00

Destruction of mine at Picketts Harbor, Va.—The owners of a fishery at the above-mentioned locality, under date of August 31, 1900, reported the capture of a loaded mine case in one of their fish traps, and the Chief of Engineers ordered its destruction, for which the sum of $25 was allotted to cover the expenses incurred.

The mine was exploded March 26, 1901, on the beach about 6 miles south of Cape Charles Harbor, Va. The expenses connected with its destruction amounted to $23.58.

Money statement.

June 30, 1901, allotted during fiscal year	$25.00
June 30, 1901, expended during fiscal year	23.58
July 1, 1901, balance unexpended	1.42

ALLOTMENT.

Appropriation for "Torpedoes for Harbor Defense," act May 25, 1900	$25.00

Preservation and repair of fortifications.—Under allotments which aggregated $7,661, the work indicated hereafter was performed during the fiscal year ending June 30, 1901.

The allotment for general preservation and repair work was $1,175, which was applied to renewing decayed timbers in the bridges at the main and north and south entrances to the enceinte, to painting the railings, and whitewashing the arches and walls of entrances. The roadways, ramps, and drains inside the main work were repaired where required.

The roof of the power plant at one 10-inch battery and the shot gallery doors at the same battery and at the 8-inch barbette rifle magazine were also repaired.

During target practice last season, the concrete of the parapets of one of the 10-inch batteries and the place of arms was damaged and was replaced by 9 cubic yards of new concrete, and gullies washed in the slope at the former work were filled and resodded, requiring 32 cubic yards of clay and 463 square yards of sod.

At the batteries mentioned in the preceding paragraph, surface drains were cut on the loading platforms, and trolley tracks for ammunition service painted.

The allotment for preservation and repair of the torpedo material was $1,000, and that amount was expended in cleaning and painting junction boxes, cleaning and greasing plugs for same, turks-head collars, shackles, sockets, sister hooks, and compound plugs. The anchors were cleaned and tarred, and cable drums, axles, and anvils cleaned and painted, and all the other material overhauled.

At the cable-storage tank the overhead traveler, rail, and support columns were painted.

Shelter boxes for hygrometers at six of the works were made and placed, under an allotment of $36 for that purpose.

Under allotments aggregating $1,725, the base rings of the carriages at the mortar battery were releveled. The carriages of Pit No. 2 were found to be more out of level than any of the others; the variation was one-fourth of an inch in the worst instance.

In removing the base rings the mortars were jacked clear of the carriages and the carriages blocked up so that the racer was sufficiently high to admit the maneuvering of a steel straightedge and machinist level on the base ring. To relieve the friction which was apparent when the carriages were revolved, the distance ring was raised, rollers removed, and the roller path and rollers cleaned, and the parts where binding was evident were filed.

The sum of $100 was allotted for emergency repairs, and this was expended in repairing blocks and hoists of the ammunition service and doors and fastenings at the different batteries.

For correcting the faulty drainage system at two of the 10-inch batteries an allotment of $405 was made, and the work done included the cutting of open-surface drains on the loading platforms, providing conductors to carry off the water therefrom, and the placing of hoods over all doors and other openings to prevent rain beating into rooms and passageways. To reduce the glare of sunlight on the battery, the exterior surfaces of the concrete walls at both redoubts were washed with a solution of lampblack and Portland cement.

The work contemplated under the allotment will be completed when pipes have been run underneath each emplacement for the purpose of carrying off water running into the counterweight wells. This work will not be performed, however, unless it becomes evident that, with proper care, the present arrangement of pipes in the bottom of wells terminating in the sand below are unsatisfactory.

For repairing the parapet and slopes of a 10-inch battery, which were damaged by firing the guns, $775 were allotted.

When this battery was under construction plates of boiler iron were bolted to the concrete mass on the parapet of each emplacement at this work to prevent erosion by the discharge of the guns. The firing in the early spring loosened these plates and broke up the concrete underneath considerably. The plates and broken concrete were removed, and in lieu thereof bolts with anchor plates were set in the solid concrete and surrounded by Portland concrete, which was mixed by hand.

The sand cover of this battery settled somewhat and the sod, soil, and clay over the settled portion were removed and about 80 cubic yards of sand were placed to bring it up to the proper reference. The clay, soil, and sod were then replaced, completing the work.

Under allotments aggregating $1,355 an investigation was made to determine the cause of the leakage of water into the shot galleries at the mortar battery and some work was done toward overcoming this difficulty.

The investigation developed that the leakage was due to the clogging of the blind drains in the valleys formed by the junction of the main work with the revetment walls over each pit, causing the water collected therein to percolate through the concrete to the rooms underneath.

To prevent this a hole 2 by 3 feet was cut through the revetment wall of each pit and a mine gallery run each way to the ends of the revetment walls at the sides of each pit. The interior sides of the walls were cleansed of sand and the valleys filled with Portland cement mortar. As soon as the walls dry out, asphalt will be applied and well ironed with a hot float, after which the valley will be filled level with broken stone and brick and the apertures in the walls closed.

The allotment for purposes of preservation and repair during the fiscal year 1902 was made May 10, 1901. The amount provided was $1,100.

Money statement.

July 1, 1900, balance unexpended	$1,078.77
June 30, 1901, allotted during fiscal year	6,625.00
	7,703.77
June 30, 1901, expended during fiscal year	4,717.40
July 1, 1901, balance unexpended	2,986.37
July 1, 1901, outstanding liabilities	254.86
July 1, 1901, balance available	2,731.51

ALLOTMENTS.

Act June 6, 1896	$125.00
Act May 25, 1900	4,049.30
Act March 1, 1901	2,450.70
Total	6,625.00

Fort Wool, Va.—This is an inclosed casemated fort, is in an uncompleted state, and has no armament.

Until December 31, 1900, a fort keeper was engaged to look after the public property about the place, when his service was discontinued. The expenditures reported below were made in payment of the fort keeper's salary to the date noted and for outstanding liabilities at the close of the previous fiscal year.

Money statement.

PRESERVATION AND REPAIR OF FORTIFICATIONS.

July 1, 1900, balance unexpended	$72.74
June 30, 1901, allotted during fiscal year	300.00
	372.74
June 30, 1901, expended during fiscal year	372.50
July 1, 1901, balance unexpended	[1].24

ALLOTMENT.

Appropriation for "Preservation and Repair of Fortifications," act May 25, 1900	$300.00

3 K.

DEFENSES OF THE COAST OF NORTH CAROLINA.

Officer in charge, Capt. Eugene W. Van C. Lucas, Corps of Engineers; Division Engineer, Col. Peter C. Hains, Corps of Engineers.

Defense of entrance to Beaufort Harbor.—No work was done during the year.

Reservation at Southport.—No work was done during the year. New fences and minor repairs to building are needed. The building has been used for office and storage purposes, as heretofore.

---

[1] Covered by outstanding telegraph account. Amount deposited to credit of Treasurer United States June 30, 1899.

APPENDIX 3—FORTIFICATIONS. 813

The suits for possession of the reservation or parts thereof are still pending, but negotiations in progress promise an early settlement.

Defense of mouth of Cape Fear River.—At the beginning of the fiscal year the emplacements for eight 12-inch mortars had been completed and the carriages and mortars mounted, and only the installation of electric-firing apparatus needed to complete the battery ready for transfer to the garrison. As a result of the overflow during the storm of October, 1899, serious settlement of the mortars in the east pit was detected, and by authority of the Chief of Engineers the transfer of this battery is deferred until completion of the sea wall and fill, when probable settlement will have ceased and the mortars can be properly releveled before transfer.

During the year one of the two emplacements for 5-inch rapid-fire guns was provided with a carriage, which has been mounted, and this emplacement is now ready for transfer to the garrison.

The overflow caused by the storm of October, 1899, having crippled communications (see House Doc. No. 204, Fifty-sixth Congress, first session), a special item of $150,000 was included in the fortification appropriation act of May 25, 1900, for a sea wall and fill at Fort Caswell, N. C., and with funds so provided a concrete sea wall has been built 6,612 feet in length, inclosing the three exposed sides of the post, and a contract has been been made with the Atlantic, Gulf and Pacific Company, of New York, to fill the interior to a level of 12 feet above mean low water, which is higher than the highest recorded storm tides. Work under this contract, calling for about 500,000 cubic yards of fill, will be started in October and completed probably in February next. Details of a technical nature concerning sea wall are given in separate appendix.

In accordance with instructions from the Chief of Engineers, plans for emplacements for a battery of two 15-pounder and one 5-inch rapid-fire guns were prepared and approved and the construction of the 15-pounder emplacements and magazines, with magazine for the 5-inch gun, was authorized and is well under way. The completion of the 5-inch emplacement will await the adoption by the Ordnance Department of an acceptable type of mounting for the 5-inch rapid-fire gun.

By authority of the Chief of Engineers, work has been started for a fire commander's station according to type plans designed by The Board of Engineers for the Lewis range finder at low sites. Work on foundation for this structure is well advanced and a contract has been made for the construction of superstructure.

With allotments from the appropriation for "Preservation and Repair of Fortifications" the carriages at Emplacements 1, 2, and 3 of battery for four 8-inch B. L. rifles have been satisfactorily releveled. Safety stops have also been provided for the electric ammunition hoists in the 12-inch battery. The submarine-mining equipment has been cared for and kept in serviceable condition, and is ready for transfer to the garrison. Telephone boxes have been provided for the gun platforms of batteries, and considerable minor work necessary for keeping the emplacements and equipment in serviceable condition has been done.

CONTRACTS IN FORCE IN CONNECTION WITH SEA WALL AND FILL.

(1) With W. R. Bonsal & Co., Hamlet, N. C.; entered into September 1, 1900; approved by the Chief of Engineers September 19, 1900; for 6,000 long tons of broken stone, at $1.73 per ton, and 7,000 long tons of large stone, at $1.53 per ton, delivered

on wharf at Wilmington, N. C.; deliveries beginning October 1, 1900, and continuing as called for, not exceeding 100 tons per day.

(2) With W. A. Sanders, Wilmington, N. C.; entered into September 1, 1900; approved by Chief of Engineers September 12, 1900; for unloading and transporting from cars on wharf at Wilmington, N. C., 6,000 long tons of broken stone, at 41 cents per ton, and 7,000 long tons of large stone, at 40 cents per ton, as called for after September 24, 1900, not exceeding 100 tons per day.

(3) With Atlantic, Gulf and Pacific Company, New York, N. Y.; entered into September 12, 1900; approved by Chief of Engineers October 10, 1900; for filling in at Fort Caswell, N. C., approximately 500,000 cubic yards of material, at 13.7 cents per cubic yard; to be begun, under terms of contract, June 17, 1901, and completed within seven months thereafter; date of beginning extended, by authority of Chief of Engineers, to October 17, 1901.

CONTRACT IN FORCE FOR FIRE COMMANDER'S STATION.

With North Penn Iron Company, North Penn Junction, Philadelphia, Pa.; entered into April 4, 1901; approved by Chief of Engineers April 20, 1901; for the erection of a steel observation tower; contract price, $3,400; work to begin July 25, 1901, and be completed within seven months thereafter.

Money statements.

GUN AND MORTAR BATTERIES.

Installing ammunition lift in 4.7-inch rapid-fire emplacement.

July 1, 1900, balance unexpended		$126.64
June 30, 1901, amount expended during the fiscal year	$36.92	
November 16, 1900, amount restored to the appropriation	89.72	
		126.64

Mounting eight 12-inch mortars and carriages.

July 1, 1900, balance unexpended	$106.38
June 30, 1901, amount expended during the fiscal year	63.32
July 1, 1901, balance unexpended	43.06
July 1, 1901, outstanding liabilities	26.44
July 1, 1901, balance available	16.62

Emplacements for two 5-inch rapid-fire guns.

July 1, 1900, balance unexpended	$569.29
June 30, 1901, amount expended during the fiscal year	439.62
July 1, 1901, balance unexpended	129.67
July 1, 1901, outstanding liabilities	129.67

Mortar battery.

July 1, 1900, balance unexpended	$402.59
June 30, 1901, allotted during the fiscal year	1,400.00
September 2, 1900, received from the Quartermaster's Department as a reimbursement	57.65
	1,860.24
June 30, 1901, amount expended during the fiscal year	144.05
July 1, 1901, balance unexpended	1,716.19
July 1, 1901, outstanding liabilities	10.30
July 1, 1901, balance available	1,705.89

APPENDIX 3—FORTIFICATIONS.

Contract work—8-inch emplacements.

July 1, 1900, balance unexpended	$10.41
July 1, 1901, outstanding liabilities	10.41

Communicating gallery—8-inch battery.

June 30, 1901, allotted during the fiscal year		$700.00
June 30, 1901, amount expended during the fiscal year	$660.46	
June 17, 1901, deposited to the credit of appropriation	39.54	
		700.00

Fire commander's station.

June 30, 1901, amount allotted during the fiscal year		$8,800.00
June 30, 1901, amount expended during the fiscal year	$1,552.05	
April 11, 1901, amount withdrawn	2,000.00	
		3,552.05
July 1, 1901, balance unexpended		5,247.95
July 1, 1901, outstanding liabilities	$59.95	
July 1, 1901, amount covered by uncompleted contracts	3,480.00	
		3,539.95
July 1, 1901, balance available		1,708.00

Emplacements for one 5-inch and two 15-pounder rapid-fire guns.

June 30, 1901, amount allotted during the fiscal year		$20,000.00
June 30, 1901, amount expended during the fiscal year	$9,378.60	
April 9, 1901, amount withdrawn	5,500.00	
		14,878.60
July 1, 1901, balance unexpended		5,121.40
July 1, 1901, outstanding liabilities		1,632.05
July 1, 1901, balance available		3,489.35

PRESERVATION AND REPAIR OF FORTIFICATIONS.

July 1, 1900, balance unexpended	$1,800.35
June 30, 1901, amount allotted during the fiscal year	2,070.00
	3,870.35
June 30, 1901, amount expended during the fiscal year	2,235.66
July 1, 1901, balance unexpended	1,634.69
July 1, 1901, outstanding liabilities	84.74
July 1, 1901, balance available	1,549.95

SEA WALL.

July 1, 1900, balance unexpended		$149,973.68
June 30, 1901, amount expended during the fiscal year		65,356.05
July 1, 1901, balance unexpended		84,617.63
July 1, 1901, outstanding liabilities	$2,636.29	
July 1, 1901, amount covered by uncompleted contracts	75,108.12	
		77,744.41
July 1, 1901, balance available		6,873.22

SUPPLIES FOR SEA COAST DEFENSES.

July 1, 1900, balance unexpended	$700.00
July 1, 1901, outstanding liabilities	127.84
July 1, 1901, balance available	572.16

3 L.

DEFENSES OF THE COAST OF SOUTH CAROLINA.

Officer in charge, Capt. James C. Sanford, Corps of Engineers; assistant, Lieut. Edwin R. Stuart, Corps of Engineers, after February 22, 1901; Division Engineer, Col. Peter C. Hains, Corps of Engineers.

CHARLESTON HARBOR, SOUTH CAROLINA.

Mortar battery.—For history of work, see pages 508–513, Annual Report for 1896; pages 675–693, Annual Report for 1897; pages 697–698, Annual Report for 1898; pages 859–860, Annual Report for 1899; pages 911–912, Annual Report for 1900.

No work was done under the appropriation for "Gun and Mortar Batteries" during the year and the balance available was turned in to the Treasury October 31, 1900. All work done on this battery during the year will be described under "Preservation and Repair of Fortifications."

Total allotments for this battery	$179,000.00
Total expenditures to June 30, 1901	178,380.69

Money statement.

July 1, 1901, balance unexpended		$661.48
June 30, 1901, amount expended during fiscal year	$42.17	
October 31, 1901, deposited to credit Treasurer United States.	619.31	
		661.48

Emplacement for 6-inch rapid-fire gun on disappearing carriage.—For history of work, see page 862, Annual Report for 1899, and page 913, Annual Report for 1900. No work of construction was done during the fiscal year 1901, and the balance of the allotment was turned into the Treasury February 19, 1901.

Total allotments for this battery	$20,000.00
Total expenditures to June 30, 1901	19,118.07

Money statement.

July 1, 1900, balance unexpended	$881.93
February 28, 1901, balance deposited to credit Treasurer United States..	881.93

Three emplacements for 15-pounder rapid-fire guns.—For history of this work prior to June 30, 1900, see page 861, Annual Report for 1899, and page 913, Annual Report for 1900. During the fiscal year 1901 the base castings, guns, and mounts were received. The base castings were set by the Engineer Department, and the guns were mounted by the artillery garrison. The battery has been reported ready for transfer to the artillery, but at the close of the year the necessary authority had not been received.

Total allotments for this battery	$9,500.00
Total expenditures to June 30 1901	9,500.00

Money statement.

July 1, 1900, balance unexpended	$109.21
July 30, 1901, amount expended during fiscal year	109.21

APPENDIX 3—FORTIFICATIONS.

Preservation and repair of fortifications.—During the fiscal year 1901 the work was as follows: At the 10-inch battery the base rings of guns Nos. 1, 3, and 4 were releveled and grouted; cracks over magazine were grouted to stop leaks, without much success; the gutters carrying water from the superior slope to the cisterns were repaired from time to time; gutters for drainage of gun platform were cut; the battery was painted; experiments were made with a brake for the trolleys, and part of the work of equipping the trolleys with brakes was done; concrete steps were put in the passageways where needed; material was purchased for a hand railing at the rear of the gun platforms, and part of the work of erection was done, and repairs were made to the ammunition hoists.

At the mortar battery a pipe to connect the slopes of the battery with the cable tanks was laid, and the boiler of the electric-lighting plant was repaired. The work of painting the battery was begun, as was also the removal of the level battens used in construction of the floors of the pits. The torpedo material was cared for. The sides of the cable tank were raised and the cable rearranged and stored. Necessary repairs, alterations, etc., preparatory to the transfer to the artillery were made and the property transferred.

In addition to the above, the property was cared for, the ironwork at the rapid-fire batteries was painted, concrete gutters were put in at the 6-inch battery to prevent the slopes being washed by rain, and minor necessary repairs made as needed.

Money statement.

July 1, 1900, balance unexpended	$3,663.65
May 14, 1901, amount allotted	2,000.00
	5,663.65
June 30, 1901, amount expended during fiscal year	3,362.34
July 1, 1901, balance unexpended	2,301.31
July 1, 1901, outstanding liabilities	316.06
July 1, 1901, balance available	1,985.25

Repairs to ammunition hoists, 10-inch battery.—The ammunition hoists installed at the 10-inch battery proved unsatisfactory and have frequently been the cause of complaint on the part of the artillery garrison in charge. Various repairs were made from time to time, but no permanent improvement secured. Based on the recommendation of this office, an allotment of $500 was made on May 4, 1901, from the appropriation for "Preservation and Repair of Fortifications," act of March 1, 1901, for the installation of the Lockwood locking device, to be applied in a modified form, subject to the results of experiments to be made. At the close of the fiscal year the experimental work had not been completed.

Money statement.

May 4, 1901, amount allotted	$500.00
July 1, 1901, balance unexpended and available	500.00

Bracketed galleries.—On October 15, 1900, an allotment of $825 was made from the appropriation for "Gun and Mortar Batteries," act of May 25, 1900, for the construction of galleries connecting the gun platforms at the 10-inch battery. These galleries are supported by brackets made from old railroad iron. The hand railing and sheet steel for flooring were purchased. In the prosecution of the work difficulty was encountered in the insertion of the brackets, due to the blocks of granite embedded in the concrete, and the cost of the work exceeded the original estimate. On March 23, 1901, an additional allotment of $300 was made from the appropriation for "Gun and Mortar Batteries," act of March 1, 1901, with which the galleries were completed.

Money statement.

October 15, 1900, amount allotted	$825.00
March 23, 1901, amount allotted	300.00
	1,125.00
June 30, 1901, amount expended during fiscal year	1,125.00

Electric-light plant, 12-inch battery.—For history of work see page 864 Annual Report for 1899, and page 914 Annual Report for 1900.

During the fiscal year 1901 no work was done. A recommendation that no storage battery be installed was approved by the Chief of Engineers. An estimate was submitted for a central electric plant and for replacing the present boiler, and building a permanent boiler house. The balance of the allotment, except $900 needed to replace the boiler and build a permanent boiler house, was withdrawn on May 9, 1901.

Money statement.

Total amount alloted for this work	$5,000.00
Total expenditures to June 30, 1901	3,015.58
July 1, 1900, balance unexpended	1,984.42
May 9, 1901, amount restored to appropriation	1,084.42
July 1, 1901, balance unexpended and available	900.00

Preservation and repair of fortifications.—During the fiscal year 1901 paint was purchased for painting the ironwork of the 12-inch battery, but the painting has not yet been done.

Money statement.

July 1, 1900, balance unexpended	$340.00
May 14, 1901, amount allotted	800.00
	1,140.00
June 30, 1901, amount expended during fiscal year	7.94
July 1, 1901, balance unexpended and available	1,132.06

Torpedo storehouse.—On October 18, 1900, an allotment of $6,500 was made from the appropriation for "Torpedoes for Harbor Defense" ($521.79, act of March 3, 1897; $763.99, act of May 7, 1898; $5,214.22, act of May 25, 1900) for the construction of a torpedo storehouse.

Plans and specifications were prepared and submitted, and approved by the Chief of Engineers. The United States assistant district attorney delivered an opinion that valid title could not be given to the lot on which it was proposed to build the storehouse. After consultation with the post commander, a site which was satisfactory to him and to this office was recommended and approved by the Chief of Engineers. Bids were opened on May 10, 1901, for the construction of the storehouse, and the contract has been awarded to the lowest bidder, Mr.

George H. Crafts, of Atlanta Ga. At the close of the fiscal year, due to delay incident to ascertaining the standing of the lowest bidder, and to errors by the contractor in executing the papers, the contract had not been completed and no work of construction had been done.

Money statement.

October 18, 1900, amount allotted	$6,500.00
June 30 1901, amount expended during fiscal year	131.70
July 1, 1901, balance unexpended and available	6,368.30

Preservation and repair of torpedo material.—The balance available at the close of the fiscal year 1900 for the preservation and repair of torpedo material at Charleston, S. C., was applied to the necessary care of the material.

Money statement.

July 1, 1900, balance unexpended	$161.92
June 30, 1901, amount expended during fiscal year	161.92

Battery commander's station.—On August 18, 1900, an allotment of $5,100 was made from the appropriation for "Gun and Mortar Batteries," act of May 25, 1900, for the construction of a battery commander's station.

During the fiscal year 1901 plans and specifications for the necessary ironwork were prepared and submitted, but have not yet been returned.

Money statement.

August 18, 1900, amount allotted	$5,100.00
June 30, 1901, amount expended during fiscal year	138.34
July 1, 1901, balance unexpended and available	4,961.66

Plotting and observation station.—On December 10, 1900, an allotment of $160 was made from the appropriation for "Gun and Mortar Batteries," act of July 7, 1898, for constructing plotting and observation stations.

During the fiscal year 1901 the buildings were constructed, the material being furnished by the Engineer Department and the labor by the post quartermaster. On January 31, 1901, the balance was turned in to the Treasury.

Money statement.

December 10, 1901, amount allotted		$160.00
June 30, 1901, amount expended during fiscal year	$90.06	
January 31, 1901, balance deposited to credit Treasurer United States	69.94	
		160.00

Supplies for coast defenses.—An allotment of $800 was made on June 7, 1900, from the appropriation for "Supplies for Sea Coast Defenses," act of May 25, 1900, for filling requisitions, etc., duly approved by the Chief of Engineers.

One requisition for supplies was received and filled.

Money statement.

July 1, 1900, balance unexpended	$800.00
June 30, 1901, amount expended during fiscal year	33.37
July 1, 1901, balance unexpended and available	766.63

PORT ROYAL, S. C.

Emplacement for one 10-inch B. L. rifle.—For history of work prior to June 30, 1900, see page 705, Annual Report for 1898; page 865, Annual Report for 1899, and page 915, Annual Report for 1900.

During the fiscal year 1901 the sand and stone bins and the tank used in construction were taken down and stored. Some work on the specifications for a storage battery was done, but a recommendation was afterwards made and approved that no storage battery be installed. On May 17, 1901, the balance remaining in the Treasury was withdrawn, and on May 27 the balance in hand was turned into the Treasury.

Total amount allotted for this emplacement	$50,000.00
Total amount expended to June 30, 1901	35,293.85

Money statement.

July 1, 1900, balance unexpended		$14,985.91
June 30, 1901, amount expended during fiscal year	$279.76	
May 17, 1901, amount restored to appropriation	14,500.00	
May 27, 1901, amount deposited to credit Treasurer United States	206.15	
		14,985.91

Dynamite battery.—On November 9, 1900, a provisional allotment of $50,000 was made from the appropriation for "Gun and Mortar Batteries" for the pneumatic dynamite battery for the defense of this harbor, and on January 15, 1901, this allotment was made available and an additional allotment of $14,800 was made from the same appropriation.

During the fiscal year 1901 plans were submitted and approved. No work of construction was done, the work under the supervision of the Ordnance Department not having reached such a stage as to permit the construction of the parapet to be begun.

Money statement.

November 9, 1900, amount allotted	$50,000.00
January 15, 1901, amount allotted	14,800.00
July 1, 1901, balance unexpended and available	64,800.00

Preservation and repair of fortifications.—During the fiscal year 1901 repairs were made to the ammunition hoists at the 10-inch battery. The office, traveling derrick, cable tank, the roofs of all buildings, and the ironwork at the batteries were painted. The walls of buildings were whitewashed. The smokestack of the boiler of the electric-light plant was replaced by a better one. Minor repairs were made to wharf. All property was watched and cared for. The care of the torpedo property was continued under the allotment from the appropriation for "Preservation and Repair of Fortifications," after the exhaustion of the allotment applicable to care of torpedo property only.

Money statement.

July 1, 1900, balance unexpended	$1,600.00
June 30, 1901, amount expended during fiscal year	1,353.18
July 1, 1901, balance unexpended	246.82
July 1, 1901, outstanding liabilities	71.25
July 1, 1901, balance available	175.57

Cable tank.—For history of work prior to June 30, 1900, see page 869, Annual Report for 1899, and page 915, Annual Report for 1900. During the fiscal year 1901 no work was done, and on October 31, 1900, the balance was turned into the Treasury.

Total amount allotted for this work	$3,000.00
Total amount expended to June 30, 1901	2,662.78

Money statement.

July 1, 1900, balance unexpended	$337.22
October 31, 1900, amount deposited to credit Treasurer United States	337.22

Preservation and repair of torpedo material.—The balance available at the close of the fiscal year 1900 was expended in general care of the torpedo property. The material was kept in proper condition and inspected as required. The 25-horsepower oil engine was overhauled, and the property prepared for transfer to the artillery. This balance having been exhausted in the spring of 1901, the care of the torpedo material was continued under the allotment from appropriation for "Preservation and Repair of Fortifications," which was available for this purpose.

Money statement.

July 1, 1900, balance unexpended	$401.38
June 30, 1901, amount expended during fiscal year	401.38

Sites for fortifications and seacoast defenses.—For history of work prior to June 30, 1900, see pages 916–917, Annual Report for 1900.

During the fiscal year 1901 lots Nos. 58 and 59 were paid for, and deeds recorded. An order of the court vesting title to these lots in the United States was obtained, recorded, and forwarded to the Chief of Engineers.

Total amount allotted for this purpose	$2,215.95
Total amount expended to June 30, 1901	2,193.42

Money statement.

July 1, 1900, balance unexpended	$719.75
October 6, 1900, amount allotted	40.95
	760.70
June 30, 1901, amount expended during fiscal year	738.17
July 1, 1901, balance unexpended and available	22.53

3 M.

DEFENSES OF THE COAST OF GEORGIA AND OF CUMBERLAND SOUND, GEORGIA AND FLORIDA.

Officer in charge, Capt. Cassius E. Gillette, Corps of Engineers; Division Engineer, Col. Peter C. Hains, Corps of Engineers.

Emplacements for two 15-pounder rapid-fire guns at Site No. 1.—Allotments aggregating $9,530 were made for the construction of this battery. For a summary of operations prior to July 1, 1900, see Annual Report of the Chief of Engineers for 1900, page 920.

No work was done during the fiscal year.

The guns and their mounts have not yet been furnished by the Ordnance Department.

On June 24, 1901, the unexpended balance on hand of $1.56 was deposited to the credit of the appropriation.

Money statement.

July 1, 1900, balance unexpended	$1.56
June 30, 1901, amount returned to the Treasury during the fiscal year	1.56

Mortar battery.—On February 18, 1901, an allotment of $1,800 was made for the purpose of supplying an electric-light plant for the mortar battery, and to place the grounds in the vicinity of that battery in a sightly condition. On April 23, 1901, an additional allotment of $3,000 was made for the purpose of installing an electric plant to be provided with an independent source of power.

During the fiscal year the pavement in the rear of the battery was repaired, drain pipes taken out and lowered, the plant used in the construction of the battery removed and stored, and the grounds in the vicinity cleaned up.

The plans for electric lighting, including the general subject of electric lighting of the post, have not yet been completed.

Money statement.

June 30, 1901, amount allotted during fiscal year	$4,800.00
June 30, 1901, amount expended during fiscal year	406.73
July 1, 1901, balance unexpended	4,393.27
July 1, 1901, outstanding liabilities	151.53
July 1, 1901, balance available	4,241.74

Construction of bracketed galleries to connect adjacent gun emplacements.—On October 15, 1900, an allotment of $1,600 was made for the purchase and installation of bracketed galleries to connect adjacent gun emplacements. The necessary ironwork was ordered in November, 1900; work of installing the galleries was begun in March, 1901, and completed in April, 1901. The unexpended balance of $295.57 was deposited to the credit of the appropriation on May 10, 1901.

Money statement.

June 30, 1901, amount allotted during fiscal year		$1,600.00
June 30, 1901, amount expended during fiscal year	$1,304.43	
June 30, 1901, amount deposited during fiscal year	295.57	
		1,600.00

Preservation and repair of fortifications.—There were allotted during the fiscal year $4,600 for work of preservation and repair. The following work was done:

Thirty cars of manure and 13 cars of brush were spread over blowing-sand areas. Five thousand and thirty-six feet of iron pipe were laid and connections made for use in watering grass on slopes of the parapets of the different batteries. Interlocking devices were added to some of the ammunition hoists and a broken sheave replaced. Drains were repaired and extra drain pipes cut off. All electrical machinery stored at the mortar battery was overhauled and cleaned up. A carload of torpedo material was received. A set of concrete steps was added to one of the wing walls. Three hundred and fifty cubic yards of sand were removed in grading at various places.

Experiments were made in covering interior walls for dryness and also for light, and in tinting the concrete surfaces of parapets.

Numerous minor repairs were made.

Condition June 30, 1901: The wharf is in poor condition, having settled considerably about 150 feet from the end. A great many of the piles in the wharf itself have been eaten by the teredo in spite of having been protected by what is known as the "Galinowski process." The shore line has moved out near the wharf until at present there is only a few feet of water at low tide at the northeastern corner. A good wharf is needed here. for the planting of torpedoes and the landing of coal to supply the electric-light plant. The present wharf can be extended and repaired properly for about $16,000.

The blowing-sand nuisance has been practically overcome. Bermuda grass is growing over the greater part of the previous sand areas and will ultimately doubtless cover the entire reservation where it has been started.

There is a good water supply at the post, besides artesian wells at the more distant batteries.

Armament: There has been no change in the armament during the fiscal year. All the armament is in good condition. It is under charge of the artillery.

Money statement.

July 1, 1900, balance unexpended	$2,951.90
June 30, 1901, amount allotted during fiscal year	4,600.00
	7,551.90
June 30, 1901, amount expended during fiscal year	5,951.05
July 1, 1901, balance unexpended	1,600.85
July 1, 1901, outstanding liabilities	320.02
July 1, 1901, balance available	1,280.83

Mining casemate.—There was allotted on July 13, 1900, $9,000 for the construction of a mining casemate. Work of construction was begun August 7, 1900, and the casemate was completed in December, 1900. Dynamo, oil engine, cooling tank, storage battery, and other appliances were installed and all connections made.

The unexpended balance of $83.97 was deposited to the credit of the appropriation on June 24, 1901.

At the close of the fiscal year the casemate was in good condition. It, together with all the torpedo material on hand, was transferred to the artillery on June 29, 1901.

Money statement.

June 30, 1901, amount allotted during the fiscal year		$9,000.00
June 30, 1901, amount expended during fiscal year	$8,916.03	
June 30, 1901, balance deposited during the fiscal year	83.97	
		9,000.00

Torpedo storehouse.—On March 19, 1901, an allotment of $4,000 was made for the construction of a fireproof torpedo storehouse. Bids for its construction were called for and opened, but the lowest bid received was much in excess of the amount on hand, and, additional funds not being available, all bids were rejected. The balance of funds remaining on hand, $3,669.63, was deposited to the credit of the appropriation on June 7, 1901.

Money statement.

June 30, 1901, amount allotted during the fiscal year		$4,000.00
June 30, 1901, amount expended during fiscal year	$330.37	
June 30, 1901, balance unexpended, deposited during the fiscal year	3,669.63	
		4,000.00

Emplacements for two 15-pounder rapid-fire guns at Site No. 2.—For a summary of operations prior to July 1, 1900, see Annual Report of the Chief of Engineers for 1899, page 880, and page 921 of the same report for 1900.

No work was done during the fiscal year.

The guns and their mounts have not yet been furnished by the Ordnance Department.

The unexpended balance on hand of $82.27 was deposited to the credit of the appropriation on June 24, 1901.

Money statement.

July 1, 1900, balance unexpended	$82.27
June 30, 1901, amount returned to the Treasury during fiscal year	82.27

Preservation and repair of fortifications.—On March 18, 1901, an allotment of $200 was made for decreasing dampness in the mining casemate. Under this allotment the floor at the entrance was given a slope outwards and the casemate was given a wooden interior lining. On May 15, 1901, $200.00 were allotted for next fiscal year.

Condition June 30, 1901: The wharf and the road to the fort are in good condition. The moat is filled up. The sanitary condition is fairly good. There are two artesian wells, giving a good supply of water.

Armament: The torpedo casemate, cable tank, and the emplacements for two 15-pounder rapid-fire guns are in good condition, excepting that the latter needs some minor repairs, due to settlement. The 15-pounder guns and their mounts have not yet been furnished by the Ordnance Department.

Money statement.

July 1, 1900, balance unexpended	$29.84
June 30, 1901, amount allotted during fiscal year	400.00
	429.84
June 30, 1901, amount expended during fiscal year	187.10
July 1, 1901, balance unexpended	242.74
July 1, 1901, outstanding liabilities	42.50
July 1, 1901, balance available	200.24

Mining casemate.—On March 18, 1901, an allotment of $500 was made for fitting up the casemate with operating tables, electric wiring, etc. Work was begun May 19, 1901, and completed June 25, 1901. The existing single-room casemate was fitted up complete and everything put in good condition. An old shell-concrete magazine, directly opposite the door of the casemate, was fitted up for oil engine, given a wooden lining, and ventilated, the oil engine, dynamo, and their appurtenances installed, and connection made through an underground iron pipe with the storage battery in the casemate itself. At the close of the fiscal year the work was in good condition, ready to operate.

Money statement.

June 30, 1901, amount allotted during fiscal year	$500.00
June 30, 1901, amount expended during fiscal year	500.00

Preservation and repair of fortifications, Fort Clinch, Fla.—No funds were allotted for work at this post during the fiscal year. Of the amount on hand, $500 was transferred to allotment for preservation and repair of fortifications at Site No. 1.

No work was done during the fiscal year.

Condition June 30, 1901: The condition of the post is about the same as last year.

Armament: The 8-inch B. L. rifle and its converted 15-inch smooth-bore carriage were removed during the fiscal year and shipped elsewhere. Four 15-inch smooth-bore guns were condemned and sold, but have not yet been removed by the purchasers.

Money statement.

July 1, 1900, balance unexpended		$1,180.32
June 30, 1901, amount expended during fiscal year	$0.74	
June 30, 1901, amount transferred to other work during fiscal year	500.00	
		500.74
July 1, 1901, balance unexpended and available		679.58

Supplies for seacoast defenses.—On June 7, 1900, an allotment of $300 was made for filling such requisitions as might be made during the fiscal year ending June 30, 1901, by post commanders for electrical appliances and their preservation and repair. No requisitions were received from post commanders during the fiscal year, and requisition has not been made for any part of the funds.

Money statement.

July 30, 1901, amount allotted during fiscal year	$300.00
July 1, 1901, balance unexpended and available	300.00

3 N.

DEFENSES OF EAST COAST OF FLORIDA AND OF KEY WEST, FLORIDA.

Officers in charge, Capt. Thomas H. Rees, Corps of Engineers, until September 24, 1900, and since March 27, 1901, and Capt. Charles H. McKinstry, Corps of Engineers, from September 24, 1900, to March 27, 1901; assistants, Lieut. Edward M. Markham, Corps of Engineers, until September 11, 1900, and Lieut. Edmund M. Rhett, Corps of Engineers, since September 17, 1900; Division Engineer, Col. Peter C. Hains, Corps of Engineers.

DEFENSES OF EAST COAST OF FLORIDA.

Preservation and repair, Fort Marion, Fla.—For a brief historical sketch of this work, which was built during the Spanish possession of Florida and finished in 1756, attention is invited to the annual report of the officer in charge for 1889. It is not available for defense, but is worthy of preservation as an object of historical interest.

At the beginning of the fiscal year a balance remained of former allotment for preservation and repair. A portion of this amount was expended for locks for casemate doors.

Money statement.

July 1, 1900, balance unexpended	$129.00
June 30, 1901, amount expended during fiscal year	16.64
July 1, 1901, balance unexpended	112.36

Preservation and repair, St. Johns River, Florida.—On June 11, 1900, $1,100 was allotted for pay of watchman and care of torpedo and engineer property during the year ending June 30, 1901. A balance of $128.15 remained from a former allotment on June 30, 1900.

A watchman was employed the entire year. The torpedo material was overhauled, cleaned, and stored away, after the application of preservatives, in December, 1900, and in April, 1901. Unserviceable and obsolete mining material was shipped to Willets Point, N. Y., in April, 1901. A shipment of 60 boxes, packages, etc., of torpedo material was received from Willets Point and placed in storehouse. A harbor chart for the use of the artillery was made.

On May 18, 1901, $1,020 was allotted for pay of watchman and care of torpedo material during the fiscal year ending June 30, 1902.

Money statement.

July 1, 1900, balance unexpended	$1,228.15
May 18, 1901, amount allotted	1,020.00
	2,248.15
June 30, 1901, amount expended during fiscal year	958.91
July 1, 1901, balance unexpended	1,289.24
July 1, 1901, outstanding liabilities	60.00
July 1, 1901, balance available	1,229.24

Sites for fortifications.—At the close of the fiscal year proceedings were in progress for the acquisition of 117.7 acres of land, upon which it is proposed to erect permanent batteries.

DEFENSES OF KEY WEST, FLA.

Emplacements for four 10-inch and two 8-inch guns on disappearing carriages and for eight 12-inch mortars.—These emplacements are being built by contract under the provisions of the act of June 6, 1896. A contract was entered into with the Venable Construction Company, of Atlanta, Ga., on March 7, 1897, the work to be completed by January 1, 1898. Progress was slow and unsatisfactory, and a number of extensions of time were granted by the Secretary of War. The last extension of time expired July 23, 1900. On July 11, 1900, the contractor stated that he would make no further effort to complete the work. New bids for completing the batteries and building storehouses were opened November 30, 1900, and the contract was awarded to the lowest bidder, L. L. Leach & Sons, of Chicago, to be completed August 13, 1901.

At the close of the fiscal year these batteries remain practically in the same condition as on June 30, 1900. The new contractors have executed a small amount of sand fill in the roadway in rear of the 8-inch and 10-inch gun emplacements. They have installed necessary plant and secured dredging machinery and other appliances for executing the sand fill, and have received a quantity of material for use in storehouses.

On June 11, 1900, an allotment of $1,800 was made for providing communicating galleries between the gun emplacements.

The galleries were completed in December, 1900.

Road covering for batteries at Key West, Fla.—On May 4, 1899, an allotment of $3,000 was made from the appropriation for "Gun and Mortar Batteries," act of May 7, 1898. The work contemplated is the covering of the roadway from the six-gun battery to the mortar battery with 6 inches of crushed brick and concrete from the old fort and placing a curbing of concrete. About 1,000 cubic yards of brick have been crushed and 1,000 linear feet of curbing have been made. Further progress will await the completion of the sand fill of the roadway which is being executed by contract.

Money statements.

BATTERIES.

July 1, 1900, balance unexpended		$56,578.11
June 30, 1901, amount expended during fiscal year		5,370.84
July 1, 1901, balance unexpended		51,207.27
July 1, 1901, outstanding liabilities	$200.00	
July 1, 1901, covered by contracts	26,695.51	
		26,895.51
July 1, 1901, balance available		24,311.76

COMMUNICATING GALLERIES.

July 1, 1900, balance unexpended	1,800.00
June 30, 1901, amount expended during fiscal year	1,800.00

ROAD COVERING FOR BATTERIES.

July 1, 1900, balance unexpended	1,426.38
June 30, 1901, amount expended during fiscal year	284.76
July 1, 1901, balance unexpended and available	1,141.62

Four emplacements for 15-pounder rapid-fire guns.—These emplacements were practically completed, awaiting only the base castings for mounts, prior to June 30, 1900. The guns and mounts were received in October, 1900. These were mounted and the emplacements completed. They were turned over to the artillery command April 23, 1901.

Money statement.

July 1, 1900, balance unexpended	$1,880.75
June 30, 1901, amount expended during fiscal year	1,880.75

Emplacement for one additional 15-pounder rapid-fire gun.—On June 22, 1900, an allotment of $13,000 was made for two emplacements. On July 27 the project was modified to provide for one emplacement only, and $6,000 of the allotment were withdrawn. Work was begun in August, 1900. The gun and its mount were received in October, 1900. The emplacement was completed and gun mounted in February, 1901. It was turned over to the artillery command April 23, 1901.

Money statement.

July 1, 1900, balance unexpended		$13,000.00
July 27, 1900, amount withdrawn	$6,000.00	
June 30, 1901, amount expended during fiscal year	7,000.00	
		13,000.00

Emplacement for right-flank 15-pounder rapid-fire gun.—On April 7, 1901, the sum of $9,900 was allotted for this work from the appropriation for "Gun and Mortar Batteries," act of March 1, 1901. Work was begun in April, 1901, and was still in progress at the close of the fiscal year, the emplacement being nearly completed and ready for the base casting of the gun mount.

Money statement.

April 17, 1901, amount allotted	$9,900.00
June 30, 1901, amount expended during fiscal year	2,360.31
July 1, 1901, balance unexpended	7,539.69
July 1, 1901, outstanding liabilities	2,000.00
July 1, 1901, balance available	5,539.69

Battery commander's station.—On August 3, 1900, the sum of $9,850 was allotted from the appropriation for "Gun and Mortar Batteries," act of May 25, 1900, for this work. A contract was entered into with the American Bridge Company, November 26, 1900, approved December 26, 1900, to be completed June 28, 1901. No work was done by the contractors, and on the expiration of the contract time they were notified that their contract was voided.

Money statement.

August 3, 1900, amount allotted	$9,850.00
June 30, 1901, amount expended during fiscal year	716.22
July 1, 1901, balance unexpended	9,133.78

Preservation and repair of fortifications.—At the beginning of the past fiscal year a balance of $1.26 remained from former allotments. On June 11, 1900, the sum of $2,500 was allotted for the pay of fort keeper, care of torpedo material, and miscellaneous repairs during the fiscal year ending June 30, 1901.

On May 18, 1901, the sum of $2,305 was allotted for similar purposes for the fiscal year 1902.

All ironwork of ammunition hoists, cranes, beams, railings, trolley rails, galleries, etc., has been cleaned and painted. The buildings have received minor repairs and have been whitewashed and painted as necessary; ventilators have been set at the mortar battery; all mining material has twice been overhauled and cleaned, tested, painted, and stored; cistern of storeroom has been cleaned and repaired; broken sheave bracket of hoist has been repaired; face walls of 4.7-inch and 15-pounder (north) batteries have been coated with cement grout and alum wash; two switches were installed in trolley rails; obsolete and unserviceable mining material was shipped to Willets Point, N. Y.; and new mining material was received and cared for.

Money statement.

July 1, 1900, balance unexpended	$2,501.26
May 18, 1901; amount allotted	2,305.00
	4,806.26
June 30, 1901, amount expended during fiscal year	2,474.03
July 1, 1901, balance unexpended	2,332.23
July 1, 1901, outstanding liabilities	26.58
July 1, 1901, balance available	2,305.65

Supplies for artillery.—On May 10, 1900, the sum of $100 was allotted from the appropriation for "Preservation and Repair of Fortifications," act of March 3, 1899, for the purchase of supplies for electric-light plant at gun and mortar batteries, Key West, Fla.

Under this allotment all articles called for on approved requisitions have been purchased and turned over to the artillery.

Money statement.

July 1, 1900, amount unexpended	$34.25
June 30, 1901, amount expended during fiscal year	13.80
July 1, 1901, balance unexpended and available	20.45

Supplies for coast defenses.—On June 7, 1900, the sum of $600 was allotted from the appropriation for "Supplies for Sea Coast Defenses," act of May 25, 1900, for purchase of supplies for the defenses of Key West, Fla.

Three shelters for hygrometers and thermometers have been purchased and set up.

Articles called for on approved requisitions have been purchased and will be turned over to the acting engineer officer, Key West Barracks, Fla.

Money statement.

July 1, 1900, balance unexpended	$600.00
June 30, 1901, amount expended during fiscal year	46.62
July 1, 1901, balance unexpended and available	553.38

3 O.

DEFENSES OF TAMPA BAY, FLORIDA.

Officer in charge, Capt. Thomas H. Rees, Corps of Engineers; assistant, Lieut. Edmund M. Rhett, Corps of Engineers, since March 27, 1901; Division Engineer, Col. Peter C. Hains, Corps of Engineers.

Emplacements for eight 12-inch mortars.—These emplacements were completed and turned over to the artillery command on May 8, 1900.

830   REPORT OF THE CHIEF OF ENGINEERS, U. S. ARMY.

On March 7, 1901, an allotment of $1,100 was made for clearing up the ground around the site of the battery, storing plant, and removing and painting buildings. The traveling towers of the cable way, the bins used for storing rock, and a number of buildings no longer needed were torn down and their material stored. Several buildings were moved to make room for the new post buildings under construction by the Quartermaster's Department. The cement shed and the warehouse were painted. Railroad embankments no longer used were leveled off.

March 7, 1901, amount allotted	$1,100.00
June 30, 1901, amount expended during fiscal year	1,090.98
July 1, 1901, balance unexpended and available	9.02

Emplacements for three 15-pounder rapid-fire guns.—The project adopted was the conversion of a battery of two 8-inch rifles mounted on 15-inch smoothbore carriages into emplacements for three 15-pounder rapid-fire guns on balanced-pillar mounts.

Plans and estimates for this work were submitted July 3, 1900, and on August 3, 1900, an allotment of $15,000 was made from the appropriation for "Gun and Mortar Batteries," act of May 25, 1900.

The work of construction was begun in October, 1900, and continued until March, 1901. The emplacements were completed with the exception of the gun platforms, which can not be finished until the base castings for the mounts have been received.

There have been placed in the work 577¼ cubic yards of concrete and 72 cubic yards of facing mortar. Dampproof course, conduits, speaking tubes, ventilators, railings, and doors have been placed and the sand fill completed, sodded, and planted.

The following material was used:

693 barrels Portland cement.
387 cubic yards broken stone.
330 cubic yards sand.
193 cubic yards shell.

Money statement.

August 3, 1900, amount allotted	$15,000.00
June 30, 1901, amount expended during fiscal year	14,833.83
July 1, 1901, balance unexpended and available	166.17

Emplacement for one 15-pounder rapid-fire gun.—The plan and estimate of cost for this emplacement were submitted April 30, 1901. On May 6, 1901, the plans were approved and an allotment of $8,400 was made from the appropriation for "Gun and Mortar Batteries," act of March 1, 1901.

Up to the close of the fiscal year contracts had been let under circular proposals for the material necessary, and some of the material had been received. The line for the railway from the wharf to the site of the emplacement had been graded, and repairs to plant had been made, and preparations made to proceed with construction.

Money statement.

May 6, 1901, amount allotted	$8,400.00
June 30, 1901, amount expended during fiscal year	4.00
July 1, 1901, balance unexpended	8,396.00
July 1, 1901, outstanding liabilities	700.00
July 1, 1901, balance available	7,696.00

Emplacements for two 15-pounder rapid-fire guns.—Plans and estimates of cost of this work were submitted April 9, 1901.

On April 6, 1901, the plans were approved and the sum of $17,100 was allotted from the appropriation for "Gun and Mortar Batteries," act of March 1, 1901.

At the close of the fiscal year ending June 30, 1901, contracts had been let for the necessary material under circular proposals, and some of the material had been received, plant had been erected, and everything placed in readiness for active operations of construction.

Money statement.

April 6, 1901, amount allotted	$17,100.00
June 30, 1901, amount expended during fiscal year	1,192.06
July 1, 1901, balance unexpended	15,907.94
July 1, 1901, outstanding liabilities	900.00
July 1, 1901, balance available	15,007.94

Supplies for coast defenses.—On June 7, 1900, the sum of $500 was allotted from the appropriation for "Supplies for Sea Coast Defenses," act of May 25, 1900, to be applied to filling such requisitions as might be approved for the defenses of Tampa Bay.

Shelters for hygrometers and thermometers have been purchased and turned over to the post commander.

Upon requisition made by the acting engineer officer and approved by the Chief of Engineers, necessary supplies have been purchased and transferred to said officer.

Money statement.

July 1, 1900, balance unexpended	$500.00
June 30, 1901, amount expended during fiscal year	97.20
July 1, 1901, balance unexpended and available	402.80

Preservation and repair of fortifications.—In accordance with an estimate submitted April 26, 1900, the sum of $125 was allotted on June 7, 1900, from the appropriation for "Preservation and Repair of Fortifications," act of March 3, 1899, for the fiscal year of 1901.

Leaks in the ceiling of the dynamo room of the 8-inch disappearing gun battery were repaired and some gullies washed by rain in the sand slopes of the same battery were filled up and sodded.

In accordance with estimate submitted May 14, 1901, the sum of $375 was allotted on May 18, 1901, from the appropriation for "Preservation and Repair of Fortifications," act of March 1, 1901, for the fiscal year ending June 30, 1902.

Money statement.

July 1, 1900, balance unexpended	$125.00
May 14, 1901, amount allotted	375.00
	500.00
June 30, 1901, amount expended during fiscal year	58.30
July 1, 1901, balance unexpended and available	441.70

Care of mining material.—In compliance with General Orders, No. 1, Headquarters, Corps of Engineers, 1898, an estimate of funds required for this purpose was submitted June 1, 1900. On June 19, 1900, an allotment of $250 was made from the appropriation for "Preservation and Repair of Fortifications," act of May 25, 1900, for cleaning and protecting mining material for the six months ending November 30, 1900.

On November 16, 1900, an additional allotment of $15 was made for the purchase of air-tight boxes in which to store electrical instruments. This was from the appropriation under the act of June 6, 1896.

The mining material was thoroughly overhauled, and was cleaned, painted, classified, and stored on shelves and racks and in boxes, convenient for ready inspection or use. Galvanized iron boxes were purchased and used for storing electrical instruments.

Money statement.

July 1, 1900, balance unexpended	$250.00
November 16, 1900, amount allotted	15.00
	265.00
June 30, 1901, amount expended during fiscal year	258.19
July 1, 1901, balance unexpended	6.81

3 P.

DEFENSES OF PENSACOLA, FLORIDA.

Officers in charge, Capt. Clement A. F. Flagler, Corps of Engineers, until September 26, 1900, and Capt. William V. Judson, Corps of Engineers, since that date; assistants, Lieut. Lewis H. Rand, Corps of Engineers, until July 3, 1900, and Lieut. Gustave R. Lukesh, Corps of Engineers, from September 16, 1900, to March 14, 1901; Division Engineer, Col. Peter C. Hains, Corps of Engineers.

Extension of room for electric-light plant, 10-inch battery.—This work, mention of which was made in the last Annual Report, was completed with satisfactory results. Two new chambers were built; one for the generator and one for the storage battery, leaving the old room for the boiler.

Money statement.

July 1, 1900, balance unexpended		$2,300.00
May 3, 1901, deposited to credit of Treasurer United States	$10.34	
June 30, 1901, amount expended during fiscal year	2,289.66	
		2,300.00

Installation of searchlight.—This work consisted in erecting a small house some 1,500 feet from the dynamo room of the 8-inch battery, with which it was electrically connected; the construction of an inclined track, up which, mounted upon a car, the searchlight may be hauled to a service platform. A drum is provided for hauling up the searchlight. The thirty poles supporting the cable have been protected against rot with coal tar. The incline is 168 feet in length, and for incline and house 56 piers were provided.

Money statement.

Amount allotted during fiscal year	$1,500.00
June 30, 1901, amount expended during fiscal year	1,026.19
July 1, 1901, balance unexpended	473.81
July 1, 1901, outstanding liabilities	473.81

APPENDIX 3—FORTIFICATIONS. 833

Battery for four 15-pounder rapid-fire guns.—This battery was completed during the fiscal year, the work consisting of the installation of doors, hand railings, and latrine fixtures. The Engineer Department transported the guns and carriages to the emplacements. The battery was transferred to the artillery on April 30, 1901.

Money statement.

July 1, 1900, balance unexpended	$21.68
Amount allotted during fiscal year	360.00
	381.68
June 30, 1901, amount expended during fiscal year $378.50	
Deposited to credit of Treasurer United States............. 3.18	
	381.68

NOTE.—Out of the amount ($3.18) deposited to credit of Treasurer United States, $2.44 is outstanding for railroad transportation. Accounts have been forwarded for settlement.

The total cost of this battery completed is $20,603.84.

Communicating gallery, 10-inch battery.—The material is on hand and the work begun to connect the four loading platforms of this battery by means of a concrete-steel gallery.

Money statement.

Amount allotted during fiscal year	$1,600.00
June 30, 1901, amount expended during fiscal year	206.27
July 1, 1901, balance unexpended	1,393.73
July 1, 1901, outstanding liabilities	729.00
July 1, 1901, balance available	664.73

Communicating gallery, 8-inch battery.—The material is on hand and the work begun to connect the two loading platforms of this battery by means of a concrete-steel gallery.

Money statement.

Amount allotted during fiscal year	$700.00
June 30, 1901, amount expended during fiscal year	42.87
July 1, 1901, balance unexpended	657.13
July 1, 1901, outstanding liabilities	337.00
July 1, 1901, balance available	320.13

Mortar battery.—An allotment was received for gathering up and storing a part of the plant used in the construction of this battery and for the construction of a boathouse for the naphtha launch pertaining to fortification construction. This work was nearly completed during the month of June.

Money statement.

July 1, 1900, balance unexpended	$5.44
Amount allotted during fiscal year	500.00
	505.44
June 30, 1901, amount expended during fiscal year	442.35
July 1, 1901, balance unexpended	63.09
July 1, 1901, outstanding liabilities	55.16
July 1, 1901, balance available	7.93

ENG 1901——53

Shelter for position finder.—Principally for purposes of artillery drill and practice, a shelter was erected for a Type A position finder. This work was completed in December, 1900.

Money statement.

Amount allotted during fiscal year	$140.00
June 30, 1901, amount expended during fiscal year	140.00

Fire commander's station.—Drawings have been partially prepared for this construction, but the matter is now held in abeyance pending a decision as to change of size of house.

Money statement.

Amount allotted during fiscal year	$150.00
June 30, 1901, amounted expended during fiscal year	100.00
July 1, 1901, balance unexpended and available	50.00

Electric wiring.—Plans and specifications have been prepared and proposals solicited for the work of wiring for a system of exterior and interior lighting. The Engineer Department is installing the poles and the outside leads to and about the post from the 12-inch battery's electrical plant, while the Quartermaster's Department is furnishing the lamps and interior wiring.

Money statement.

Amount allotted during fiscal year	$2,300.00
July 1, 1901, balance unexpended and available	2,300.00

Remedying dampness in magazine No. 1, 12-inch battery.—This work consisted in raising the floor and building interior detached ceiling and walls of lead and brick, respectively. This particular magazine is being used in an experiment to determine the practicability of artificially drying the atmosphere contained, to which reference is made elsewhere.

Money statement.

Amount allotted during fiscal year		$600.00
May 27, 1901, amount deposited to credit of Treasurer United States	$0.25	
June 30, 1901, amount expended during the fiscal year	599.75	
		600.00

Doors for magazines, etc., 12-inch and 10-inch batteries.—Each magazine is to be provided with double doors and each shell room with a single door. Doors have been hung at magazine No. 1, 12-inch battery, and some of the ironwork for the other doors has been completed. In each case the doors are designed to be screwed up against stops faced with rubber so as to make the openings practically air-tight whenever desired.

Money statement.

Amount allotted during fiscal year	$625.00
June 30, 1901, amount expended during fiscal year	21.80
July 1, 1901, balance unexpended	603.20
July 1, 1901, outstanding liabilities	110.45
July 1, 1901, balance available	492.75

Doors for magazines, etc., 8-inch battery.—The work upon these doors has not yet been begun. The doors will be similar to those above described of the 10-inch and 12-inch batteries.

Money statement.

Amount allotted during fiscal year	$275.00
July 1, 1901, balance unexpended and available	275.00

Preservation and repair of fortifications.—Shore protection, 15-pounder battery: A change in the lagoon shore line permitted storm waves to attack the beach in the vicinity of the 15-pounder battery, which beach receded until the slopes proper were attacked. A small concrete sea wall, extended at either end by broken brick and mortar débris, in all 318 feet in length, was constructed with satisfactory results.

Repairs to slopes: From time to time the slopes have been injured by cattle and by heavy rains. All injuries have been repaired and the slopes are now in good condition.

Care of torpedo material: The torpedo plant and material received most careful attention in the way of repairs and application of preservatives. It was transferred to the artillery in excellent condition on May 27, 1901.

Care of and repairs to plant: All construction plant was maintained in good order so as to be serviceable when new work is begun. Instruments and electrical plant in the possession of the artillery were repaired as required. The rotary transformer, which had been damaged by an explosion in 1899, was repaired by its makers in St. Louis. Various and sundry repairs were made to windows and doors, drainage systems, fire boxes, boilers, stacks, etc. A ceiling was placed in the casemate occupied by the rotary transformer. The original ceiling had been destroyed in the fire following the explosion of 1899.

Remedying dampness in magazines: Under an allotment of $100 an experiment is under way to ascertain the practicability of artificially drying a magazine at reasonable cost. The work has not proceeded far enough to determine the results of this experiment, which involves the practical sealing of the magazine and the drying with calcium chloride.

Money statement.

July 1, 1900, balance unexpended	$4,430.23
Amount allotted during fiscal year	7,465.00
	11,895.23
June 30, 1901, amount expended during fiscal year	4,183.74
July 1, 1901, balance unexpended	7,711.49
July 1, 1901, outstanding liabilities	1,157.90
July 1, 1901, balance available	6,553.59

Supplies for seacoast defense.—From time to time electrical supplies were furnished on approved requisitions submitted by the acting engineer officer.

Money statement.

July 1, 1900, balance unexpended	$600.00
June 30, 1901, amount expended during fiscal year	117.00
July 1, 1901, balance unexpended	483.00
July 1, 1901, outstanding liabilities	141.73
July 1, 1901, balance available	$341.27

3 Q.

DEFENSES OF MOBILE AND MISSISSIPPI SOUND.

Officer in charge, Maj. William T. Rossell, Corps of Engineers; assistant, Lieut. Meriwether L. Walker, Corps of Engineers, from January 26 to April 6, 1901; Division Engineer, Col. Peter C. Hains, Corps of Engineers.

Mortar battery.—The approved project provides for the construction of a battery for eight 12-inch B. L. steel mortars, at an estimated cost of $140,000, subsequently increased by $15,000.

At the beginning of the fiscal year a small amount of concrete remained to be placed, and the sand parapet and a few minor details were incomplete.

During the fiscal year 5,355 cubic yards of sand were hauled from the sand pit by locomotive and placed in sand parapet by means of Lidgerwood cable way, completing the sand filling, the whole amounting to 45,993 cubic yards. Observation stations with stairways leading to them were constructed, containing 116.1 cubic yards of concrete, completing the concrete work, the whole amounting to 11,225.9 cubic yards, using 12,911 barrels of Portland cement, 5,744 cubic yards of sand, 8,970.5 cubic yards of gravel, and 509 cubic yards (net) of stone, including 4,804 square yards of granolithing. The sand parapet and slopes in rear of pavement, 9,367 square yards, were graded, covered with clay, and sodded; thickness of clay covering steep slopes, 1 foot; flat slopes, 6 inches, except in rear of battery, where it was very light. Clay was purchased for this work, 2,076.5 cubic yards; and Bermuda sod, 1,923.8 cubic yards. The refuse from the sod was used in part as a substitute for clay. The work of sodding, though recently completed, gives promise of very gratifying results. Clay was obtained from a distance of about 61 miles; sod, 125 miles; gravel for concrete, 130 miles; the gravel having to be washed and screened before loading on barges.

The installation of the electric plant was completed; mouthpieces and name plates placed on speaking tubes; doors and all ironwork repainted and locks placed on doors; copper hoods placed over all outside doors and over ventilators at entrance to air spaces; down spouts of copper, with iron guards at platform level, installed; perforated iron covers placed over drain openings; manholes for electric cable and wells for engine exhaust and boiler feed covered with movable cast-iron plates; system of trolleys completed. A barbed-wire fence 1,463 linear feet long was built round the battery, stiles placed at suitable intervals, and all painted. Plank walks aggregating 677 feet in length were built at the foot of slopes in rear.

The lower portions of the mortar carriages, assembled to the height of the loading platforms, were cleaned. Construction plant has been removed and stored, sodded slopes of the battery repaired, and weeds removed.

The work of the Engineer Department on this battery was practically completed at the end of February, 1901, and the battery was transferred to the artillery on May 20, 1901. The firing apparatus remains to be installed and the ground at the foot of the slopes protected against washouts.

Money statement.

July 1, 1900, balance unexpended	$11,230.89
Amount allotted during fiscal year	15,000.00
Amount transferred from 6-inch battery	1,250.00
	27,480.89
June 30, 1901, amount expended during fiscal year... $22,748.09	
Amount withdrawn from allotment of $15,000... 2,000.00	
	24,748.09
July 1, 1901, balance unexpended	2,732.80
July 1, 1901, outstanding liabilities	219.39
July 1, 1901, balance available	2,513.41

Battery for two 12-inch rifles.—The approved project provides for the construction of two emplacements for 12-inch B. L. rifles, mounted on disappearing carriages, at an estimated cost of $160,000.

At the beginning of the fiscal year the battery was completed and had been transferred to the artillery. During the fiscal year the base circle in west emplacement was raised to enable ordnance mechanics to make repairs and reset, the railroad trestle leading to wharf removed, rubber gaskets placed on junction and switch boxes of electric plant to render them impervious to moisture, the electric plant was cared for and storage battery charged until October, 1900, after which it was cared for and operated by the artillery.

Money statement.

July 1, 1900, balance unexpended	$506.21
June 30, 1901, amount expended during fiscal year... $452.85	
Unexpended balance turned back into the Treasury... 53.36	
	506.21

Battery commander's station.—An allotment was made by indorsement of the Chief of Engineers, dated September 27, 1900, of $6,000 from appropriation for "Gun and Mortar Batteries," act of May 25, 1900, to be applied to the construction of battery commander's station for 12-inch battery. Plans and specifications for the construction of this station were prepared by this office and submitted to the Chief of Engineers, but owing to the artillery bringing up the question as to the size of the instrument room, location of the tower, etc., action has been suspended pending a decision by the artillery board. At the end of the fiscal year the matter is still in abeyance.

Emplacements for 6-inch guns.—The approved project provides for the construction of emplacements for two 6-inch quick-fire guns, mounted on disappearing carriages, at an estimated cost of $55,000, subsequently increased by $15,000.

At the beginning of the fiscal year most of the materials required for construction had been received, the concrete work was about completed, and the greater part of the concrete framing removed.

During the fiscal year concrete stairways with cast-iron treads were constructed on flanks and in passageways leading from platforms into the interior. Pavements in rear were finished and granolithed, completing concrete work, the total amount in battery being 4,379 cubic yards, using 5,264 barrels of Portland cement, 2,203 cubic yards of sand, 3,148 cubic yards of gravel, and 85 cubic yards (net) of broken stone. Sand for the parapet was hauled from sandpit by an 8-ton locomotive and cars, 5,611 cubic yards being filled in the parapet, which was then sodded with 285 cubic yards of Bermuda grass, covering an area of 2,012 square yards. The grass was fertilized with cotton-seed meal. Split-tile drains were laid in sodded slopes. Ammunition cranes, trolleys, and trolley beams, with triplex blocks and all fixtures complete, were installed. The electric plant was also installed, consisting of a General Electric Company 20-kilowatt generator direct coupled to an automatic 9 by 7 inch engine of marine type, a vertical boiler jacketed with asbestos cover, a 60-cell lead chloride storage battery with a normal discharge of 40 amperes, a combination switchboard, three ventilating fans for magazines and dynamo room, iron-armored conduit concealed in concrete ceiling, junction boxes, wire, lamp fixtures, etc. All wiring is in iron-armored conduit and all lamp fixtures are moisture proof with steam-tight globe and guard fixtures, and brass-enameled shades in magazines, shot rooms, and galleries. Cables were laid in 12-inch conduit from switchboard in dynamo room to a manhole directly in rear and thence in smaller conduit to 8-inch and 15-pounder batteries, which are supplied with electric power from this battery. Chain ammunition hoists are provided with electric driving machinery, but are so arranged that hand power can be substituted if desired. A steel platform with stairway was erected, forming a means of communication between the loading platforms, and chain railing was placed along rear of platforms and at stairways. Steel doors were hung in passageways leading from platforms. Copper hoods were placed over exterior doors and ventilator caps at all openings leading into the air spaces. Mouthpieces and name plates were placed on speaking-tube system, completing same. Drains in the interior were covered with perforated covers. Bastions of the old work interfering with line of fire were leveled off. All wood and iron work was painted, using cork paint for ceiling beams. Very thin grout was applied to all the walls to diminish their porosity, producing a more uniform color and also improving the surface of walls.

Work on these emplacements was practically completed at the end of February, 1901, and they were turned over to the artillery May 20, 1901. The plant used in their construction was then taken down and stored.

Money statement.

July 1, 1900, balance unexpended		$14,929.91
June 30, 1901, amount expended during fiscal year	$11,172.27	
Amount transferred to mortar battery	1,250.00	
Amount turned back into Treasury	2,000.00	
		14,422.27
July 1, 1901, balance unexpended		507.64
July 1, 1901, outstanding liabilities		33.75
July 1, 1901, balance available		473.89

Mounting carriages on emplacements for two 6-inch guns.—By indorsement of the Chief of Engineers, dated June 19, 1901, an allotment of $750 was made from appropriation for "Gun and Mortar Batteries," act of March 1, 1901, for mounting carriages on two emplacements for 6-inch guns.

Emplacements for two 15-pounder rapid-fire guns.—The approved project provides for the construction of emplacements for two 15-

pounder rapid-fire guns on balanced-pillar mounts, at an estimated cost of $10,000.

Work on this battery was commenced in the early part of September, 1900, the Chief of Engineers having made an allotment of $10,000 from appropriation for "Gun and Mortar Batteries," act of May 25, 1900, for the purpose. The plant used in the construction of the 6-inch battery was also used on this battery. It was necessary to extend the railroad track but a short distance, by means of which concrete and all other materials were transported to the battery site. On this account and because there was a small surplus of material purchased for the 6-inch battery, the cost of the 15-pounder emplacements was considerably less than it would otherwise have been. There was 788 cubic yards of material excavated for foundations, which was placed in the sand parapet. The total amount of concrete placed was 733.4 cubic yards, using 1,005 barrels of Portland cement, 399 cubic yards of sand, and 554 cubic yards of gravel. In the sand parapet was placed 1,376 cubic yards of sand, 588 cubic yards of which was hauled from the sandpit about one-fourth mile distant, and the whole parapet was then covered with 892 square yards of Bermuda sod procured in the vicinity.

The magazines are lighted by electricity, current being supplied from the 6-inch battery through a lead-covered cable 515 feet long laid in a 6-inch conduit. All wiring is in conduit buried in concrete walls. All parts of the battery have sufficient slopes for draining. The magazines and counterweight wells drain into the areaways, which in turn are drained by 8-inch conduit to the front of the battery, where their ends are built into a block of concrete. A similar drain on each flank conveys the water from the pavement in rear. Air spaces extending above the level of ceilings were built in all thick walls adjacent to magazines. A waterproof course, consisting of three thicknesses of tarred felt laid separately in hot asphalt and draining into the air spaces, was put in the concrete above ceiling. All wood and iron work was painted, cork paint being used on ceiling beams. A gravel walk was built in rear of battery and the ground in the immediate vicinity graded. The site of battery was inclosed in a barbed-wire fence 480 feet long, with stiles at convenient intervals, the whole being painted.

Work of the Engineer Department on these emplacements was practically completed in the latter part of February, 1901, and they were transferred to the artillery on May 20, 1901.

Money statement.

Amount allotted during fiscal year		$10,000.00
June 30, 1901, amount expended during fiscal year	$6,025.82	
Amount turned back into Treasury	3,500.00	
		9,525.82
July 1, 1901, balance unexpended		474.18
July 1, 1901, outstanding liabilities		12.50
July 1, 1901, balance available		461.68

Preservation and repair of fortifications.—At the beginning of the fiscal year there was a balance unexpended of allotments previously made amounting to $2,518.61. By letter of the Chief of Engineers dated March 16, 1901, an allotment of $100 was made from the appropriation for "Preservation and Repair of Fortifications," act of May 25, 1900, for care of torpedo material. By indorsement of the Chief of Engineers, dated May 17, 1901, allotment was made from appropriation for "Preservation and Repair of Fortifications," act March 1, 1901, as follows:

For necessary miscellaneous repairs at one site	$2,275.00
For necessary miscellaneous repairs at another site	525.00

During the fiscal year permanent bench marks were established at all the batteries, the elevations being cut in the concrete. At the 8-inch battery 1,098 linear feet of barbed-wire fence were built along the front and flanks to protect the sodded slopes from cattle. Stiles were placed at suitable intervals and painted. The interior of this battery was painted with white asbestine and the superior slopes with green asbestine paint. Gutter drains were cut along the front edge of the concrete parapet and connected with drains of split terra cotta sewer pipe leading to the foot of the sodded slopes. The 4.7-inch and 15-pounder batteries at this place were also inclosed by 863 linear feet of barbed-wire fence. All wood and iron work of these two batteries and of the 8-inch and 12-inch batteries was repainted, sodded slopes repaired, and weeds removed therefrom.

In November, 1900, and again in May, 1901, all submarine-mine material on hand was inspected and measures taken to insure its preservation. The delicate instruments were removed from their airtight, copper-lined boxes, cleaned, dried, and repacked, and the boxes resealed. A mixture of white lead, tallow, and beeswax was applied to a part of the material, and paint to other parts. Rope and articles of like character were thoroughly aired and dried. Cable tank was drained, cables tested, the ends of cable reinsulated, and the tank refilled. The lock on door of casemate where this material was stored having been broken by some unknown person, a night watchman was employed there and remained on duty from March 20 to May 31, 1901, his services being paid for from funds allotted for care of torpedo material. Also additional daily visits were made to the torpedo casemate. All submarine-mine material at this post was transferred to the artillery garrison on June 15, 1901.

The sea slope of shore protection along northern beach was repaired, using 592 tons of rock and 80 barrels of rejected cement, distributed where needed with small lighters.

At another site: Latrine vault of old fort was filled with sand; débris removed from dry ditch and the drain for same cleaned; windmill and pump repaired; rubbish removed from parade, and some grading done. At the 8-inch battery weeds were removed from sodded slopes, an additional drain constructed, and slopes in rear repaired. Riprap of sea wall was repaired and slopes restored.

Money statement.

July 1, 1900, balance unexpended	$2,518.61
Amount allotted during fiscal year	2,900.00
	5,418.61
June 30, 1901, amount expended during fiscal year	1,853.41
July 1, 1901, balance unexpended	3,565.20
July 1, 1901, outstanding liabilities	41.09
July 1, 1901, balance available	3,524.11

Shore protection.—Under a contract dated November 1, 1899, with W. Chase Spotswood, of Mobile, Ala., for the construction of from 800 to 1,000 linear feet of shore protection, to be completed June 30, 1900, 370 linear feet of this shore protection had been completed and the mattress sunk for an additional distance of 155 linear feet at the beginning of the fiscal year, the contract not being completed on account of excessive high waters prevailing in the rivers of Alabama, from whence the material for construction was secured. An extension of the contract for thirty days was granted by the Chief of Engineers, by indorsement dated June 16, 1900, and under this extension 556 linear feet of shore protection and 83 linear feet of riprap ending was constructed, containing 901¾ cubic yards of stone and 1,075⅜ square yards of mattress, completing the work on the north beach and making a continuous sea wall from the old Engineer wharf eastward to the Quarantine wharf, the entire length being 3,704 linear feet, including the riprap ending.

There being a balance of $3,294.27 from allotment made by letter of the Chief of Engineers dated August 8, 1898, for construction of shore protection at one of the sites after completion of the work at that place as above, authority was requested and was granted by indorsement of the Chief of Engineers dated October 9, 1900, to apply these funds to the construction of about 200 linear feet of shore protection at another site in the neighborhood of site of the 15-pounder battery there, where the shore had suffered somewhat from erosion during the heavy storms prevailing in the summer of 1900. Proposals for this work, to be opened November 11, 1900, were invited, but no bids were received, due to the fact that the water was too cold at that time for laborers to work in it. Proposals were again invited, and two were received and opened in this office on June 13, 1901. Contract was awarded to W. Chase Spotswood, of Mobile, Ala., and has been prepared and forwarded to the Chief of Engineers for approval.

Money statement.

July 1, 1900, balance unexpended	$7,583.60
June 30, 1901, amount expended during fiscal year	4,638.62
July 1, 1901, balance unexpended	2,944.98
July 1, 1901, outstanding liabilities	3.60
July 1, 1901, balance available	2,941.38

Supplies for coast defenses.—By letter of the Chief of Engineers dated June 7, 1900, $600 was allotted from appropriation for "Supplies for Sea Coast Defenses," act of May 25, 1900, for the purchase of material to be supplied by the Engineer Department for the service of the coast artillery during the fiscal year 1901.

One hundred dollars of this money was drawn from the Treasury, of which $86.29 was expended in repairing boiler and replacing positive groups with new ones in electric plant of 12-inch battery.

3 R.

DEFENSES OF NEW ORLEANS, LOUISIANA, AND OF SABINE PASS, TEXAS.

Officers in charge, Lieut. Col. Henry M. Adams, Corps of Engineers, until June 8, 1901, after which date Lieut. Edward M. Adams, Corps of Engineers, was in temporary charge; assistant, Lieut. Edward M. Adams, Corps of Engineers, from September 17, 1900, to June 8, 1901; Division Engineer, Col. Henry M. Robert, Corps of Engineers (now brigadier-general, Chief of Engineers, United States Army, retired), until April 30, 1901.

NEW ORLEANS, LA.

Emplacements for two 15-pounder rapid-fire guns, first battery, Site No. 1.—Work on these emplacements was commenced on December 28, 1898, with funds allotted from the appropriation for "Gun and Mortar Batteries," act of July 7, 1898. At the beginning of the fiscal year the emplacements were practically completed, with the exception of the gun platforms, which awaited the arrival of the mounts.

The guns were delivered at the battery on September 19, 1900, and during October the outer base castings were placed and platforms completed. The guns were mounted by the troops. Report of the completion of the battery was made on November 2, 1900, and, under orders of the Secretary of War, dated December 24, 1900, it was transferred to the care of the garrison on January 17, 1901. The sum of $24,500 was expended on these emplacements.

Money statement.

July 1, 1900, balance unexpended	$788.08
June 30, 1901, amount expended during fiscal year	788.08

Emplacements for two 15-pounder rapid-fire guns, second battery.—An allotment of $10,000 for the construction of this battery was made June 16, 1900, from appropriation for "Gun and Mortar Batteries," act of May 25, 1900. The site selected was occupied by old concrete platforms originally constructed for 15-inch smooth-bore guns. The greater part of this concrete was allowed to remain in place as a foundation. Work was commenced on June 25, 1900, and in September, 1900, the emplacements were completed with the exception of the gun platforms, which can not be finished until the bottom castings of the mounts are received. The guns and carriages have not been received. The sum of $9,708.28 has been expended on these emplacements, and $291.72 remains available for finishing the platforms.

Money statement.

June 16, 1901, amount allotted	$10,000.00
June 30, 1901, amount expended during fiscal year	9,708.28
July 1, 1901, balance unexpended and available	291.72

Emplacements for four 6-inch rapid-fire guns.—On November 9, 1900, a provisional allotment of $30,000 was made from the appropriation for "Gun and Mortar Batteries," act of May 25, 1900, for constructing two emplacements for 6-inch rapid-fire guns on Ordnance Department pedestal mounts, in accordance with type drawings to be furnished later. This amount was withdrawn on April 23, 1901, and instructions were received to submit plans and estimates for four emplacements in accordance with the type plans received at about the same time. Preliminary to the preparation of plans an allotment of $340 was made April 27, 1901, from the appropriation for "Gun and Mortar Batteries," act of March 1, 1901, for making borings at the site proposed.

Plans and estimates were submitted on May 10, and were approved on May 17, 1901. The sum of $80,000 was allotted on the latter date from the appropriation for "Gun and Mortar Batteries," act of March 1, 1901.

Preparations for the construction of two of the emplacements, which will be located on land now owned by the United States, have been made. Materials have been ordered, and work was commenced on June 10, 1901. The site has been cleared, pile driver and railroad partially constructed, a water supply arranged, and part of the construction plant moved to the site.

The construction of the other two emplacements will be deferred until title is acquired to the proposed site.

Money statement.

April 27, 1901, amount allotted	$340.00
May 17, 1901, amount allotted	80,000.00
	80,340.00
June 30, 1901, amount expended during fiscal year	673.30
July 1, 1901, balance unexpended	79,666.70
July 1, 1901, outstanding liabilities	1,507.44
July 1, 1901, balance available	78,159.26

Range and position finders.—With an allotment of $8 made December 1, 1900, from the appropriation for "Gun and Mortar Batteries," act of July 7, 1898, iron hand rails were placed upon the platforms of the base-end stations in December, 1900.

Money statement.

December 1, 1900, amount allotted	$8.00
June 30, 1901, amount expended during fiscal year	8.00

Sites for fortifications.—On December 8, 1900, $250 was allotted from the appropriation for "Sites for Fortifications and Seacoast Defenses," acts of June 6, 1896, May 7, 1898, and March 3, 1899, for the purchase of a tract of land adjoining the present reservation, to be used as a site for emplacements for 6-inch rapid-fire guns.

The title papers to the tract were examined by the United States district attorney for the eastern district of Louisiana. Upon his report the Attorney-General stated that the owner could not convey an acceptable title, and he advised acquisition of the property by condemnation. This has not yet been accomplished.

A report was submitted March 26, 1901, stating what additional land should be acquired for all defensive purposes at this locality.

Money statement.

December 8, 1900, amount allotted	$250.00
July 30, 1901, balance unexpended	250.00

Sea walls and embankments.—On April 24, 1901, an allotment of $2,400 was made from the appropriation made by act of March 1, 1901, to be applied to repairing and raising the front levee on the river side of the reservation.

Preparations for executing the work when the stage of water in the river permits have been made. The land outside of the levee has been cleared of a large amount of drift wood and drained preparatory to excavation for material.

Money statement.

April 24, 1901, amount allotted	$2,400.00
June 30, 1901, amount expended during fiscal year	75.00
July 1, 1901, balance unexpended	2,325.00
July 1, 1901, outstanding liabilities	175.00
July 1, 1901, balance available	2,150.00

Preservation and repair of fortifications.—On June 9, 1900, $4,500 was allotted from this appropriation, act of May 25, 1900, to be applied to the fortifications at this locality during the fiscal year ending June 30, 1901.

To repair leaks in the 10-inch gun battery, 7,594 square feet of the superior slope were removed and replaced with a layer of concrete varying from 6 inches to 32 inches in thickness. The magazines have since been dry. The ironwork, doors, and superior and interior slopes of this battery were painted and magazines were whitewashed.

The superior slope of the 8-inch gun battery was repaired in places, the ironwork, doors, and superior and interior slopes were painted, magazines whitewashed, the floor at the entrance was sloped for drainage, and a tile drain was laid leading from the entrance to the moat.

The doors and superior slope of the first 15-pounder gun battery were painted, and the grass was cut at intervals.

The office building was weatherboarded, shingled, and painted, minor repairs were made to the dynamo plant, the wharf was repaired, a survey was made of the reservation, and the engineer property was cared for.

On May 20, 1901, an allotment of $1,500 was made from the appropriation of March 1, 1901, to be applied to repairing superior slope of the 8-inch gun battery, earth slopes of 15-pounder battery, painting ironwork of batteries, whitewashing magazines, caring for plant, and miscellaneous repairs during fiscal year ending June 30, 1902.

Money statement.

June 9, 1900, amount allotted	$4,500.00
May 20, 1901, amount allotted	1,500.00
	6,000.00
June 30, 1901, amount expended during fiscal year	4,500.00
July 1, 1901, balance unexpended and available	1,500.00

Changing location of electric-light wires and poles.—On September 6, 1900, an allotment of $115 was made from the appropriation for

"Preservation and Repair of Fortifications," act of May 7, 1898, for changing the location of the poles and restringing the electric-light wires rendered necessary by the construction of new buildings for the Quartermaster's Department. This work was completed during the month of September, 1900, at a cost of the amount allotted.

Money statement.

September 6, 1900, amount allotted	$115.00
June 30, 1901, amount expended during fiscal year	115.00

Supplies for coast defenses.—On June 7, 1900, an allotment of $500 was made from this appropriation, act of May 25, 1900, to be applied to the purchase of supplies for the artillery on requisitions duly approved by the Chief of Engineers. Five requisitions for electrical supplies were filled during the year, and a hood and collar for smokestack of dynamo house were purchased and installed.

Money statement.

June 7, 1900, amount allotted	$500.00
June 30, 1901, amount expended during fiscal year	369.68
July 1, 1901, balance unexpended and available	130.32

Emplacements for two 15-pounder rapid-fire guns, Site No. 2.—Work on these emplacements was commenced December 28, 1898, with funds allotted from the appropriation for "Gun and Mortar Batteries," act of July 7, 1898. At the beginning of the fiscal year the emplacements were practically completed with the exception of the gun platforms, which awaited the arrival of the mounts.

The guns and mounts were delivered at the battery on September 22 and 25, 1900, and during October the outer base castings were set and platforms completed. The guns were mounted by the troops. Report of the completion of the battery was made November 12, 1900, and under orders of the Secretary of War, dated December 14, 1900, it was transferred to the care of the garrison on January 17, 1901. The sum of $22,847.38 was expended on this battery.

Money statement.

July 1, 1900, balance unexpended		$1,652.62
November 17, 1900, amount restored to appropriation	$1,632.27	
June 30, 1901, amount expended during fiscal year	20.35	
		1,652.62

Preservation and repair of fortifications.—On June 9, 1900, $1,200 was allotted from this appropriation, act of May 25, 1900, to be applied to the fortifications at this locality during the fiscal year ending June 30, 1901.

The ironwork and superior slopes of the 8-inch and 15-pounder gun batteries were painted, a hood and collar were placed on smokestack, and other minor repairs were made to the dynamo plant.

Submarine-mining material was received and stored in the torpedo shed. All torpedo material was overhauled, inspected, and covered with preservatives twice during the year.

On January 12, 1901, an allotment of $350 was made from the act of May 25, 1900, for the hire of watchmen, and on June 5, 1901, $90 additional was allotted from the act of May 7, 1898, for the same purpose. Watchmen were employed to care for the torpedo material.

On May 20, 1901, $1,000 was allotted from the act of March 1, 1901, for repairing superior slope of 8-inch gun battery, painting ironwork of batteries, whitewashing magazines, caring for plant, and miscellaneous repairs during fiscal year 1902.

Money statements.

GENERAL REPAIRS.

July 1, 1900, balance unexpended	$44.88
June 9, 1900, amount allotted	1,200.00
May 20, 1901, amount allotted	1,000.00
	2,244.88
June 30, 1901, amount expended during fiscal year	1,244.88
July 1, 1901, balance unexpended and available	1,000.00

HIRE OF WATCHMEN.

July 1, 1900, balance unexpended	$90.00
January 12, 1901, amount allotted	350.00
June 5, 1901, amount allotted	90.00
	530.00
June 30, 1901, amount expended during fiscal year	440.00
July 1, 1901, balance unexpended	90.00
July 1, 1901, outstanding liabilities	45.00
July 1, 1901, balance available	45.00

SABINE PASS, TEXAS.

No fortification work was done at this locality during the fiscal year. No funds were available. The torpedo material purchased in 1898 was cared for until June, 1901, when it was transferred to Capt. C. S. Riché, Corps of Engineers, at Galveston, Tex.

---

3 S.

DEFENSES OF GALVESTON, TEX.

Officer in charge, Capt. Charles S. Riché, Corps of Engineers; assistant, Lieut. Meriwether L. Walker, Corps of Engineers, since April 7, 1901; Division Engineers, Col. Henry M. Robert, Corps of Engineers (now brigadier-general, Chief of Engineers, United States Army, retired), to April 30, 1901, and Col. Amos Stickney, Corps of Engineers, since May 9, 1901.

Mortar Battery No. 2.—This battery is designed for eight 12-inch mortars, and was being constructed by hired labor under an allotment from the appropriation for "Gun and Mortar Batteries," act of May 7, 1898. The estimated cost of this battery was $165,000.

Work was begun on this battery September 17, 1898, and the condition of the work at beginning of present fiscal year was as follows: Foundation and sheet piling all driven, concrete work complete except floor pavements, gun platforms, and observation stations, which were left until after the sand fill had been completed, outside plastering finished, and inside plastering finished to within 1 foot of floor line. Ventilating pipes, hand rails, and trolley rails in place; riprap revetment was being placed on outside of sheet piling; sand fill completed. Eight mortars and carriages on hand not mounted.

Up to September 8, 1900, the riprap revetment had been completed, and 1,367.32 cubic yards of soil had been placed on slopes, top, and rear of battery, and gun pits graded to elevation for concrete floors.

The hurricane of September 8, 1900, washed down nearly all of the sand and soil protection, also sand from under battery, leaving concrete portion of battery standing on piling with water underneath. Sheet piling and riprap revetment practically all carried away. Mortars and carriages on hand buried in sand.

No work has been done on this battery since the hurricane of September 8, 1900.

Future work on this battery will be conducted in connection with appropriation for "Reconstruction and Repair of Fortifications, Galveston, Tex."

Amount expended on this battery to June 30, 1901, $118,320.57.

Money statement.

July 1, 1900, balance unexpended	$18,878.21
June 30, 1901, amount expended during fiscal year	12,198.78
July 1, 1901, balance unexpended	6,679.43
July 1, 1901, outstanding liabilities	29.96
July 1, 1901, balance available	6,649.47

Two emplacements for 15-pounder rapid-fire guns, battery No. 2.— This battery is designed for two 15-pounder rapid-fire guns on pillar mounts, and was constructed by hired labor under an allotment from the appropriation for "Gun and Mortar Batteries," act of July 7, 1898. The estimated cost of the work was $15,000.

Work on this battery was begun January 9, 1899, and the condition of the work at the beginning of the present fiscal year was as follows: Battery complete, except concrete work for gun castings and blast surfaces; riprap protection partly placed. Riprap protection was completed during the month of August, 1900; also guns and equipment received.

The hurricane of September 8, 1900, washed away the sheet piling and riprap revetment, sand and earth protection, and sand from under battery, leaving concrete portion of battery standing on piling with water underneath.

No work has been done on this battery since the hurricane of September 8, 1900. Future work on this battery will be conducted in connection with appropriation for "Reconstruction and Repair of Fortifications, Galveston, Tex."

Amount expended on this battery to June 30, 1901, $13,116.69.

Money statement.

July 1, 1900, balance unexpended	$1,809.40
June 30, 1901, amount expended during fiscal year	1,426.09
July 1, 1901, balance unexpended	383.31

*Battery commander's station for 10-inch battery No. 1.—*An allotment of $2,000 was made on July 16, 1900, for the construction of this station. All material had been contracted for and part delivered up to September 7, 1900. The hurricane of September 8, 1900, washed away all the material and no further attempt was made to construct this station, and funds in hand were deposited to the credit of the appropriation.

Money statement.

Amount allotted July 16, 1900		$2,000.00
June 30, 1901, amount expended during fiscal year	233.85	
June 30, 1901, amount deposited with Treasurer of the United States	1,766.15	
		2,000.00

Preservation and repair of fortifications.—The balance on hand July 1, 1900 ($3,156.30), was expended in preserving and caring for engineer, ordnance, and torpedo property after the hurricane of September 8, 1900. As soon as possible after the hurricane a force was put to work clearing away wreckage and cleaning and oiling all parts of guns and equipment, so as to prevent this costly property from being ruined by the action of the salt water. Additional allotments amounting to $8,500 were also provided for preserving and caring for ordnance property, which was, by arrangement with the Ordnance Department, United States Army, when expended, to be refunded to the Engineer Department. Also allotments amounting to $9,000 have been made for this purpose by the Ordnance Department, United States Army.

Operations during the fiscal year were as follows:

At 10-inch gun battery No. 2: All parts of the guns and equipment have been kept clean, painted, and all bright work covered with petrolatum.

At 12-inch mortar battery No. 2: The ordnance pertaining to this battery had not been mounted and after hurricane of September 8, 1900, was buried in the sand. This ordnance was dug out of the sand, all parts cleaned, painted, and thoroughly oiled. A shed was erected over mortars and various loose parts to protect the same from the weather.

At 15-pounder rapid-fire battery No. 2, the guns and parts have been thoroughly cleaned, oiled, and placed under shed.

At 10-inch gun battery No. 1, both guns and carriages have been dismounted, placed in rear of battery, blocked up, oiled, and painted, and shed erected over same for protection from weather.

At 12-inch mortar battery No. 1, all mortars and parts cleaned, oiled, and painted, and shed erected over same for protection from weather. Oil engine pertaining to electric-light plant removed from power house, cleaned, and thoroughly oiled.

At 4.7-inch rapid-fire battery, guns and all equipment cleaned and oiled and put in good condition for use.

At 8-inch gun battery, east gun and carriage dismounted, cleaned, painted, and oiled. West gun and carriage cleaned, painted, and oiled.

At the close of the fiscal year all ordnance and engineer property is in good condition. Several minor parts of the ordnance property are missing.

Money statement.

July 1, 1900, balance unexpended		$3,156.30
June 30, 1901, amount expended during fiscal year		3,156.30
September 26, 1900, amount allotted		$5,000.00
January 23, 1900, amount allotted		3,500.00
		8,500.00
June 30, 1901, amount expended during fiscal year	$8,499.51	
June 30, 1901, amount deposited with Treasurer of the United States	.49	
		8,500.00

APPENDIX 3—FORTIFICATIONS.

Preservation of engineer work.—On January 3, 1901, an allotment of $5,000 was made for use in preserving the batteries standing on piling after the hurricane of September 8, 1900, from the action of the teredo, which were beginning to eat up the piling.

A sand-pump outfit was hired and a barge constructed and pump installed on same. At the close of the fiscal year sand had been filled under all of the batteries, and they are safe from further action of the teredo.

Money statement.

January 3, 1901, amount allotted	$5,000.00
June 30, 1901, amount expended during fiscal year	5,000.00

Reconstruction and repair of fortifications, Galveston, Tex.—Allotments amounting to $18,000 were made during the fiscal year for expenditure in preparation of plans and estimates, constructing field offices and quarters, overhauling and repairing plant, and preservation of engineer works.

At the close of the fiscal year plans and estimates had been submitted for approval, material had been received, and offices and storerooms were being constructed, pile driver and flat cars were being overhauled and repaired, and engineer works had been preserved from the action of the teredo.

Money statements.

April 9, 1901, amount allotted	$8,000.00
April 10, 1901, amount allotted	10,000.00
	18,000.00
June 30, 1901, amount expended during fiscal year	5,209.42
July 1, 1901, balance unexpended	12,790.58
July 1, 1901, outstanding liabilities	3,144.97
July 1, 1901, balance available	9,645.61

GUN AND MORTAR BATTERIES.

Two emplacements for 15-pounder rapid-fire guns, battery No. 1.

July 1, 1900, balance unexpended	$11.25
June 30, 1901, amount deposited with Treasurer of the United States	11.25

Three emplacements for 15-pounder rapid-fire guns.

July 1, 1900, balance unexpended	$212.36
June 30, 1901, amount expended during fiscal year	46.93
July 1, 1901, balance unexpended	165.43

TORPEDOES FOR HARBOR DEFENSE.

System of tracks, etc., for submarine-mining service.

June 30, 1900, balance unexpended	$76.49
June 30, 1901, amount deposited with Treasurer of the United States	76.49

REPORT OF BOARD OF ENGINEERS UPON THE DAMAGE TO THE FORTIFI-
CATIONS AT GALVESTON, TEX., BY HURRICANE OF SEPTEMBER 8, 1900.

OFFICE OF THE CHIEF OF ENGINEERS,
UNITED STATES ARMY,
Washington, November, 26, 1900.

SIR: I have the honor to submit herewith, in duplicate, the report of the Board of Engineers recently convened by my direction at Galveston, Tex., for the purpose of reporting upon the damage to the fortifications at Galveston Harbor by the hurricane of September 8, 1900.

Concurring in the views and recommendations of the Board, I recommend that this report be forwarded to Congress for such early action as the extraordinary conditions appear to demand.

It is reported by the Board that the estimate of $992,000 submitted for the reconstruction of the batteries will be increased by about $238,000, if work is delayed until the teredo has had time to destroy the foundation piles upon which some of the batteries are now supported.

Very respectfully, your obedient servant,
JOHN M. WILSON,
Brig. Gen., Chief of Engineers.
U. S. Army.

Hon. ELIHU ROOT,
Secretary of War.

ARMY BUILDING,
New York City, November 23, 1900.

GENERAL: The Board of Officers of the Corps of Engineers appointed to consider the damage done to the jetties and fortifications at Galveston, Tex., by the storm of September 8, 1900, has the honor to submit the following report:

The Board was constituted by the following orders:

Special Orders, }   HEADQUARTERS, CORPS OF ENGINEERS,
No. 43.   }   UNITED STATES ARMY,
                      Washington, September 15, 1900.

A Board of Officers of the Corps of Engineers, to consist of Col. Henry M. Robert, Maj. Henry M. Adams, Capt. Charles S. Riché, and Capt. Edgar Jadwin, will convene at Galveston, Tex., on or before October 20, 1900, upon the call of the senior member, to examine and report upon the condition of the jetties and the fortifications at that place, and to submit projects for such repairs and reconstruction as may be found necessary.

The junior member of the Board will act as recorder.

Upon the completion of the duty assigned them, the members of the Board will return to their proper stations.

The journeys required under this order are necessary for the public service.

By command of Brig. Gen. Wilson:
FREDERIC V. ABBOT,
Major, Corps of Engineers.

The instructions contained in the foregoing orders were supplemented by the following letter from the Chief of Engineers to the president of the Board:

OFFICE OF THE CHIEF OF ENGINEERS,
UNITED STATES ARMY,
Washington, September 17, 1900.

COLONEL: The press of the country has fully informed you of the terrible disaster at Galveston, Tex.

I have directed a Board to convene at Galveston, upon your call, not later than

October 20, for the purpose of making a careful and critical examination of the existing condition of the jetties and main ship channel and the fortifications constructed for the defense of the city and harbor.

The Board will consist of yourself, Major Adams, Captain Riché, and Captain Jadwin, and I have placed the date not later than October 20, in the hope that by that time Captain Riché may have been able to prepare full and detailed statements of existing conditions, as well as such other data as you may direct him to obtain for the use of the Board.

As you are aware, there are no funds now available for repair of the jetties or reconstruction of the fortifications, but I desire to submit a special report to Congress, covering the whole subject of the damage to works under our charge, not later than the first Monday in December, and I have to request that the report of your Board may be before me not later than November 24, if possible.

The report should show the condition of the jetties and main ship channel, with the estimated cost of repairs and such extension of jetties as you may deem absolutely necessary, and also the condition of each battery, whether it can be and should be renewed, and the approximate cost of such work, with such recommendations in each case as the Board deems best under the circumstances.

I suggest that you instruct Captain Riché to have prepared, as soon as practicable, the data your Board will need. I have notified him of the order convening it and the necessity of obtaining all possible information for its use.

Very respectfully,

JOHN M. WILSON,
Brig. Gen., Chief of Engineers, U. S. Army.

Col. H. M. ROBERT,
Corps of Engineers, U. S. A., New York City, N. Y.

By an indorsement of the Chief of Engineers, dated October 5, 1900, the Board was authorized to postpone its meeting at Galveston until October 22, 1900.

In accordance with the above instructions, the necessary steps were taken by Capt. C. S. Riché, Corps of Engineers, member of the Board, and also in charge of the Galveston district, to obtain full and accurate information on the existing condition of the works upon which the Board was ordered to report. He was hampered in this work by the fact that the storm had damaged his plant and had obliterated many of the stations used as points of reference for surveys. He succeeded, however, in having the desired information ready for the Board. This information was embodied in photographs, charts, and reports.

In general, the storm of September 8, 1900, was the most severe that is ever known to have visited the locality of Galveston. The tide rose in places to a height of 16 feet above mean low water; at the same time the wind is reported by the official of the United States Weather Bureau on duty at Galveston to have attained a velocity of 100 miles per hour and the barometer to have fallen to 28.53 inches. The high tide and the enormous force of the wind were assisted in their capacity for destruction by swift and powerful currents and waves. The next most destructive storm ever known in Galveston was that of September 15, 16, and 17, 1875. At that time the tide reached a height of 8.3 feet above mean low water. An idea of the far greater capacity for destruction of the recent storm can be obtained from the fact that while in the one of 1875 no lives were lost, in this one it is known that over 5,000 people perished; that the buildings in the city on the Gulf side were practically annihilated along the entire front of the city for a width of from two to six blocks, and that at the same time the Gulf shore was extensively eroded.

The Board convened in Galveston October 22, 1900, and after a general consideration of the information obtained for its use, made a careful and critical personal examination of the condition of the jetties and main ship channel, and of the fortifications constructed for the defense of the city and harbor of Galveston; also of the jetties at the mouth of the Brazos River.

The Board, during its daily sessions, from October 22 to October 27, 1900, inclusive, carefully considered the problems before it, and decided upon the general lines of the repairs necessary to be made. Drawings and computations required to complete the work of the Board were prepared under the direction of Captain Riché at Galveston. Under authority of Special Orders, No. 50, Headquarters, Corps of Engineers, November 15, 1900, the Board reconvened in New York City, November 20, 1900, for the final consideration of the various features of the subject and the preparation of the report, and continued its daily sessions in that city until November 23, 1900.

The defenses at Galveston include the following:

Fort San Jacinto.—Eight 12-inch mortars, two 10-inch breech-loading rifles, two 4.7-inch rapid-fire guns, two 15-pounder rapid-fire guns, one mining casemate, submarine-mining warehouses, cable tanks, and tracks for communication.

Fort Travis.—Two 8-inch breech-loading rifles, three 15-pounder rapid-fire guns.

Fort Crockett.—Two 10-inch breech-loading rifles, two 15-pounder rapid-fire guns, and eight 12-inch mortars.

The accompanying photographs[1] show the existing condition of the batteries clearly.

The mortar battery, the 10-inch battery, and the mining casemate at Fort San Jacinto were not constructed on piles, and are all so badly damaged that, in the opinion of the Board, it would be unwise to attempt to repair them. The Board recommends that the masonry of these structures be utilized for riprap. The Board is further of the opinion that these works should be replaced, and that the damage done to all the other batteries should be repaired. The other batteries were constructed on pile foundations 20 feet deep. All batteries were surrounded with sheet piling and with riprap of a size assumed as adequate to resist any storm heretofore experienced. The sand parapets were almost completely washed away by the recent storm. The greatest depth of scour existing at or near any of the batteries was 20 feet below mean low water.

The Board is of the opinion—

(1) That the concrete of all batteries should be extended down to the level of mean low water.

(2) That the concrete portions of the battery should be inclosed with a sand-tight pen of 12 by 12 inches piling, and extending from a little above mean low water to 30 feet below mean low water.

(3) That the front and exposed flanks of the batteries should be protected by a layer of 1 to 5 ton stone riprap, extending from the sand to 7½ feet above mean low tide, and from the concrete face of the parapet to the exterior slope, which should be capped with a mound extending to a level of 15 feet above mean low tide, having a width of 4 feet at top and side slopes of 2 on 3. The basin formed by this riprap and the concrete to be filled with sand of the usual cross section

---

[1] Not printed.

for parapet. The rear of battery and less exposed flank to be protected by a mound of riprap extending to a height of 9 feet above mean low water. In new construction the Board further recommends that the level of the magazine floors be held at an elevation of at least 10 feet above mean low water, and that the foundation piles extend to a depth of 30 feet below mean low water.

Following out the above general lines, the Board has the honor to submit the following estimate of the amount of money which should be appropriated to put each of the above-mentioned fortification works in proper condition. In this connection the Board desires to state that it deems that it will be wiser in restoring the mining casemate to construct it farther to the front, and adjacent to one of the gun batteries, preferably in the traverse of the 15-pounder battery at Fort San Jacinto.

Fort San Jacinto.

Battery for two 10-inch guns, reconstruction	$175,000
Battery for eight 12-inch mortars, reconstruction	290,000
Battery for two 4.7-inch R. F. guns, repairs	50,000
Battery for two 15-pounder R. F. guns, repairs	35,000
Mining casemate in traverse of 15-pounder battery, reconstruction	8,000
Submarine-mine warehouse, reconstruction	2,000
Cable tank, repairs	2,200
Tracks and wharf for submarine-mine service, reconstruction	5,800
Total	568,000

The above estimates are based upon the supposition that the railway track and trestle on the south jetty will be available. If this track and trestle should not be constructed in connection with the repairs to the jetty, then $55,000 should be added to the above total for the reconstruction of this track and trestle for use in the above fortification work.

Fort Crockett.

Battery for two 10-inch guns, repairs	$85,000
Battery for eight 12-inch mortars, repairs	180,000
Battery for two 15-pounder R. F. guns, repairs	30,000
Restoring railway approaches and fence around reservation	6,000
Total	301,000

Fort Travis.

Battery for two 8-inch guns, repairs	$85,000
Battery for three 15-pounder R. F. guns, repairs	35,000
Restoring railway approaches and fence around reservation	3,000
Total	123,000
Grand total	$992,000

The above estimates are based upon the existing condition of the batteries. It is impossible for the Board to foretell what the condition may be at the time such appropriation as Congress sees fit to make becomes available. It is within the range of possibility that all the batteries will become more damaged, and some of those now capable of repair, especially those at Fort Crockett, may become total wrecks.

In this case it will be necessary, in order to replace them, to provide for additional estimates of the following amounts:

Fort San Jacinto:
    Battery for two 4.7-inch R. F. guns.................................... $12,000
    Battery for two 15-pounder R. F. guns 8,000
Fort Crockett:
    Battery for two 10-inch guns 60,000
    Battery for eight 12-inch mortars...................................... 90,000
    Battery for two 15-pounder R. F. guns 8,000
Fort Travis:
    Battery for two 8-inch guns 50,000
    Battery for three 15-pounder R. F. guns............................... 10,000

    Total 238,000

The Board urges the importance of action for the protection from the teredo of the foundation piling under the concrete which is still standing. This protection can be obtained by filling sand around these piles, and is estimated to cost $15,000 for the seven batteries requiring this protection. Should sufficient funds for this work be not now available, there is serious danger of the weakening of these piles to such extent as will cause the concrete to fall, and in that case the estimates of the Board will be increased by about $238,000. The teredo has already gotten into these piles and prompt action is necessary.

The great cost of the repairs and reconstruction as compared with the original cost of the works is due to the additional storm protection now proposed.

The recent hurricane has demonstrated the necessity for this additional protection. During this hurricane the water level rose to heights of from 14 to 16 feet above mean low tide, the highest water previously known having been only 8.3 feet above this level.

In addition to the photographs referred to above, there is transmitted under separate cover a tracing[1] showing the characteristic cross section of battery proposed by the Board.

Respectfully submitted.

                        HENRY M. ROBERT,
                        Colonel, Corps of Engineers.
                        H. M. ADAMS,
                        Major, Corps of Engineers.
                        C. S. RICHÉ,
                        Captain, Corps of Engineers.
                        EDGAR JADWIN,
                        Captain, Corps of Engineers.

Brig. Gen. JOHN M. WILSON,
    Chief of Engineers, U. S. A.

---

3 T.

DEFENSES OF LAKE PORTS.

Officers in charge of defenses of the Detroit River, Lieut. Col. Garrett J. Lydecker, Corps of Engineers, until January 3, 1901, and Maj. Walter L. Fisk, Corps of Engineers, since that date; Division Engineers,

---

[1] Not printed.

APPENDIX 3—FORTIFICATIONS. 855

Col. John W. Barlow, Corps of Engineers (now brigadier-general, Chief of Engineers, United States Army, retired), until May 1, 1901, and Col. Samuel M. Mansfield, Corps of Engineers, since May 9, 1901. Officers in charge of defenses of Lake Champlain, Col. John W. Barlow, Corps of Engineers (now brigadier-general, Chief of Engineers, United States Army, retired), until May 1, 1901, and Capt. Harry Taylor, Corps of Engineers, since that date; assistant, Lieut. Robert R. Raymond, Corps of Engineers, since May 31, 1901; Division Engineer, Col. Charles R. Suter, Corps of Engineers, since May 9, 1901. Officers in charge of defenses of other lake ports in New York, Capt. Graham D. Fitch, Corps of Engineers, until April 24, 1901, and Maj. Thomas W. Symons, Corps of Engineers, since that date; Division Engineers, Col. George L. Gillespie, Corps of Engineers (now brigadier-general, Chief of Engineers, United States Army), until April 30, 1901, and Col. Charles R. Suter, Corps of Engineers, since May 9, 1901.

Fort Wayne, Michigan.—Nothing was done to this fortification during the year, nor were any expenditures made on account of it.

An allotment of $150, made June 9, 1899, was withdrawn June 1, 1901. The timber revetment on three sides of the rampart is now 40 years old, or more, is in a very bad state of decay, and altogether a most unsightly and unserviceable affair; for this reason it might be well to remove it so as to leave the whole rampart with interior earthen slopes, the condition in which the fourth side was placed several years ago. It would probably cost about $900 to make this change.

Fort Niagara, New York.—In May, 1901, a part of the river bank graded in 1897, which was injured by a heavy snow and sleet storm in April, was repaired. Sixty cubic yards of earth were hauled and placed on the injured bank, 260 linear feet of 4-inch tile drain laid, and about 200 square yards of sod placed.

The bank was watched during the fiscal year.

The amount expended during the fiscal year ending June 30, 1901, was $305.46.

Fort Ontario, New York.—No work of construction has been done since 1871.

The revetments at three places inside the fort, near the commanding officer's and lieutenants' quarters, have given way and will be repaired early in the coming fiscal year. An allotment of $450 has been made for this purpose.

Fort Montgomery, New York.—Under allotments for preservation and repair for this work a fort keeper was employed to care for the public property stored at the fort and repairs were made to the fences of the reservation.

Money statement.

July 1, 1900, balance unexpended	$719.35
May 10, 1901, amount allotted	540.00
	1,259.35
June 30, 1901, amount expended during fiscal year	523.28
July 1, 1901, balance unexpended	736.07
July 1, 1901, outstanding liabilities	45.00
July 1, 1901, balance available	691.07

3 U.

DEFENSES OF SAN DIEGO, CALIFORNIA.

Officer in charge, Capt. James J. Meyler, Corps of Engineers; Division Engineer, Col. Samuel M. Mansfield, Corps of Engineers, to November 23, 1900, and Col. Jared A. Smith, Corps of Engineers, since December 15, 1900.

Ten-inch gun battery.—The fourth emplacement, No. 1, of this battery was completed during the previous year. During the year just closed the roadway and outer portion of the terreplein in rear of the battery were regraded to a lower level in order to improve the surface drainage. The cement shed, concrete mixer, storage platforms, and tramway used in the construction of part of this battery had been allowed to remain on the parade for use in work on other batteries. They were removed, the material stored away, and the parade leveled off. Three of the emplacements of this battery had given much trouble because of dampness in rooms and passages. Ineffectual attempts to correct this trouble were reported in the last annual report. During the past year successful remedies were applied, which, with other minor work, is reported more fully under "Preservation and Repair of Fortifications," the appropriation from which the funds for the work were obtained.

Fifteen-pounder rapid-fire battery on west side of bay.—At the beginning of the fiscal year this battery was completed with the exception of one blast surface, a small amount of hand railing, and the two gun platforms, which had been for several months awaiting the arrival of the well linings for the gun mounts. During the year the blast surface was constructed and the greater portion of the platforms put in place, leaving wells for the base castings, which can be solidly embedded in the concrete when they arrive.

Five-inch rapid-fire battery.—At the beginning of the fiscal year this battery was completed with the exception of a few minor details, and the construction of the gun platforms which were then awaiting the arrival of the well linings. The gun carriages arrived in August and were hauled to the site of the battery, and the platforms were constructed with the base castings embedded in the concrete. Latrine fixtures were put in place and plumbing finished. The gun carriages were afterwards mounted by the troops. This battery was turned over to the artillery on November 17, 1900.

Battery commander's station.—At the beginning of the fiscal year this building was in progress of construction. During July the iron and steel roof, shutters, I-beams, etc., were put in place, fastened, and connected; the doors and windows and their casings were put in; and the necessary painting was done. The few small odd jobs remaining were finished up in September, and the station was turned over to the artillery on November 17, 1900, since which date a type A position finder has been installed.

Datum points for range finders.—An allotment of $450 was made by Department indorsement of July 27, 1900, for the construction of three datum marks in the harbor at points selected by a board of artillery officers. The marks were constructed in accordance with the board's specifications. Each consists of a 15-inch pine pile driven 15 feet or more, and covered by an 18-inch cast-iron pipe sunk 6 or 7 feet into the bottom and projecting 8 feet above mean lower low water. After allowing several months for the swelling of the wooden piles, the space inside the pipe, around and over the pile, was, in June, filled with concrete. The three marks are now completed and ready for transfer to the artillery.

Fifteen-pounder rapid-fire battery on east side of bay.—An allotment of $10,000 was made by Department indorsement of November 9, 1900, for the construction of these two emplacements, the district engineer to exercise his discretion as to whether the construction should begin at once or whether he had better wait until the question of the adjacent land proposed to be purchased is settled. Work on this battery will be commenced as soon as possible after the title to the above-mentioned land is approved by the Attorney-General.

Supplies for seacoast defenses.—An allotment of $300 was made by Department letter of June 7, 1900, for the purchase of material to be supplied by the Engineer Department under the provisions of General Orders, No. 66, Adjutant-General's Office, 1900, for the service of the coast artillery during the fiscal year 1901, upon a requisition of the commanding officer, duly approved by the Chief of Engineers. No supplies were requested by the artillery during the year.

Sites for fortifications and seacoast defenses.—An allotment of $20,500 was made by Department indorsement of January 30, 1901, for the purchase of additional land which was recommended for military purposes by the board of officers appointed in pursuance of the act of Congress of February 24, 1891. Negotiations for the purchase of this land from the owners have been in progress for several months and are now about completed, and the deeds to same have been placed in escrow in the Bank of Commerce in San Diego. Copies of the deeds, abstract of title, and other necessary papers have been submitted to the United States attorney for the southern district of California for examination and reference to the Attorney-General for his approval.

Preservation and repair of fortifications.—During the year the keeper was constantly employed caring for torpedo material and other engineer property. The torpedo storehouse and cable tank were looked after by him, and the materials stored therein kept in proper condition by cleaning, oiling, and painting. The torpedo casemate, cable tank, storehouse, and all torpedo material were transferred to the artillery on May 31, 1901, preparatory to which the switchboard, dynamo, electrical instruments, and other delicate appliances were unsealed from their air-tight tin-lined boxes and found well preserved. The oil engine, dynamo, cable, and instruments were tested sufficiently to determine their condition, and after a few minor repairs the buildings and materials were turned over in "good" condition.

The dynamite, which it was feared would become dangerous, was, by authority of the Department, sold at public auction and shipped away.

The keeper repaired old buildings, fences, and board walks; repainted the small boats; cared for the tools and other property, and assisted in various ways in construction work and in the surveys made during the year.

At the 10-inch battery, in Emplacements 2, 3, and 4, the cast-iron ratchet wheels on elevator windlasses, having proved too weak, were replaced by new ones of phosphor bronze. In Emplacements 3 and 4 the overhead trolleys running on Z-bar tracks, having been difficult to operate, were made to run satisfactorily by the addition of horizontal pilot wheels. Dampness due to seepage had caused much trouble during the previous year in Emplacements 2, 3, and 4, and all efforts to stop it had been unsuccessful. The assistant in local charge was directed to experiment with several possible remedies, and as a result a most successful one was adopted in the application of "P & B" paint, No. 3. The tops of Nos. 2, 3, and 4 were painted over and the cracks were filled in top of No. 1 and all four platforms. During the winter and spring the rains were the heaviest of several years, but throughout that period the rooms and passages remained perfectly dry.

During the month of June a survey was made of the north end of the military reservation, a portion of which is to be transferred to the Navy Department for use as a coaling station. In connection therewith a survey was made of the quarantine station grounds and of a small tract about the torpedo buildings to be reserved by the War Department. It was thought at the end of the month that the survey was completed, but complications have since arisen concerning the true boundaries of the quarantine station property which may necessitate further surveying before a map can be made.

Other work.—During the year considerable searching of records was done touching upon title to various portions of the military reservation and upon title to the quarantine station grounds.

All of the above work, with the exception of placing the datum marks, was done by hired labor. The work was in local charge of Assistant Engineer D. E. Hughes, and there is appended, from his report for the fiscal year, much interesting data on the matter of stopping leaks. (See Appendix 4 E.)

Money statement.

GUN AND MORTAR BATTERIES.

10-inch battery, Emplacement No. 2.

July 1, 1900, balance unexpended		$15.02
June 30, 1901, amount expended during fiscal year	$1.96	
July 25, 1900, amount restored to appropriation	13.06	
		15.02

10-inch battery, Emplacement No. 1.

July 1, 1900, balance unexpended	$106.95
June 30, 1901, amount expended during fiscal year	64.02
January 18, 1901, amount restored to appropriation	42.93

Emplacements for two 15-pounder rapid-fire guns, west side of bay.

July 1, 1900, balance unexpended	$979.89
June 30, 1901, amount expended during fiscal year	381.64
July 1, 1901, balance unexpended and available	598.25

Emplacements for two 5-inch rapid-fire guns.

July 1, 1900, balance unexpended	$338.77
June 30, 1901, amount expended during fiscal year	285.31
March 7, 1901, amount restored to appropriation	53.46

APPENDIX 3—FORTIFICATIONS. 859

Battery commander's station.

July 1, 1900, balance unexpended	$1,611.92
June 30, 1901, amount expended during fiscal year	1,611.92

Construction of datum points.

July 27, 1900, amount allotted	$450.00
June 30, 1901, amount expended during fiscal year	450.00

Two emplacements for 15-pounder rapid-fire guns, east side of bay.

November 9, 1900, amount allotted	$10,000.00
June 30, 1901, amount expended during fiscal year	1.05
July 1, 1901, balance unexpended and available	9,998.95

TORPEDOES FOR HARBOR DEFENSE.

Construction of torpedo storehouse.

July 1, 1900, balance unexpended	$18.66
June 30, 1901, amount expended during fiscal year	.52
July 25, 1900, amount restored to appropriation	18.14

SUPPLIES FOR SEACOAST DEFENSES.

July 1, 1900, balance unexpended	$300.00
July 1, 1901, balance unexpended and available	300.00

SITES FOR FORTIFICATIONS AND SEACOAST DEFENSES.

January 30, 1901, amount allotted	$20,500.00
July 1, 1901, balance unexpended and available	20,500.00

PRESERVATION AND REPAIR OF FORTIFICATIONS.

For fiscal year 1901.

July 1, 1900, balance unexpended		$1,200.60
June 30, 1901, amount expended during fiscal year	$1,140.60	
July 1, 1901, outstanding liability	60.00	
		1,200.60

For fiscal year 1902.[1]

May 10, 1901, amount allotted	$820.00
June 30, 1901, amount expended during fiscal year	3.70
July 1, 1901, balance unexpended	816.30
July 1, 1901, outstanding liabilities	162.00
July 1, 1901, balance available	654.30

Repairs to ammunition hoists and overhead trolleys, 10-inch battery.

January 3, 1901, amount allotted	$156.00
June 30, 1901, amount expended during fiscal year	156.00

[1] The expense of survey for coaling station is authorized to be paid from this allotment, an allotment to cover the sum so expended to be made on receipt of report of the amount required for the purpose.

3 V.

DEFENSES OF SAN FRANCISCO, CALIFORNIA.

Officer in charge of artillery defenses, Lieut. Col. Charles E. L. B. Davis, Corps of Engineers; assistant, Lieut. George B. Pillsbury, Corps of Engineers, from August 1, 1900, to June 22, 1901; Division Engineers, Col. Samuel M. Mansfield, Corps of Engineers, to November 23, 1901, and Col. Jared A. Smith, Corps of Engineers, from December 15, 1900, to May 3, 1901. Officer in charge of torpedo defenses, Lieut. Col. William H. Heuer, Corps of Engineers.

BATTERIES ON NORTH SIDE OF HARBOR.

At the close of the last fiscal year the condition of the work was as follows:

Two emplacements for 8-inch rifles on nondisappearing carriages.—The engineering work was completed, the guns mounted, and the battery was in charge of the artillery.

Emplacements for three 12-inch rifles on nondisappearing carriages.—The engineering work was completed, the guns were mounted, and the battery was in charge of the artillery.

Emplacements for two 5-inch guns on balanced-pillar mounts.—At the close of the last fiscal year the engineering work had been suspended awaiting the arrival of the metal work of pillar mounts. A road to site was built, excavation for concrete completed, concrete floor placed over ground area, and part of the quantity of gravel and sand required for concrete gathered and stored.

Emplacements for two 12-inch rifles on disappearing carriages.—The engineering work was completed. Guns not mounted.

WORK DONE DURING THE YEAR.

Two emplacements for 8-inch rifles on nondisappearing carriages.—No work was done.

Emplacements for three 12-inch rifles on nondisappearing carriages.—The only work done on this battery is accounted for under the allotment for preservation and repair of fortifications.

Emplacements for two 5-inch guns on balanced-pillar mounts.—Work having been suspended awaiting the ironwork, which was to be built in the concrete, it was resumed on the arrival of the same. The gun carriages, with pillar mounts, were delivered at the wharf by the Quartermaster's Department in December. The informal bid of James McMahon, the contractor who brought them across the bay, was accepted to deliver them at the battery site for the sum of $350.

The position of the battery, it being situated on a narrow ridge, made it impossible to place three guns here as first contemplated, and made it necessary to keep the width from flank to flank at a minimum figure. These conditions suggested a feature in the design, which was adopted, which placed the magazines under the loading platforms. Access to the manhole at the bottom of the gun cylinder is obtained through an opening 2 feet by 2 feet and about 2 feet above the magazine floor. The thickness of concrete between the cylinder and room is 2 feet 6 inches. The pillar mounts were placed on the gun centers and the engineering work resumed January 1.

The concrete of the floor, placed eighteen months before, was made of gravel and sand without broken stone, mixed in proportions 1 : 3 : 8. It was found to be very hard and satisfactory. Since the quantity of concrete required to complete the battery was small and crushed stone was not available at a reasonable price, it was deemed best to make the aggregate of the concrete of gravel alone, diminishing the proportions to 1 : 3 : 6. The concrete was made with a portable gravity mixer which had been used previously in the construction of emplacements for two 5-inch rapid-fire guns, and which is described in the Annual Report of the Chief of Engineers, 1900, page 1009. The conditions at the two places were quite similar, and the results obtained were about the same. The saving in labor by using the gravity mixer over the hand mixing amounted to about 20 cents per cubic yard of concrete placed.

The experience with wooden doors in the emplacements on the north side of the bay proved that, no matter how carefully they were made, warping, in time, would set in, which admitted the weather into the service rooms. Doors of sheet steel three-sixteenths inch thick, riveted to a 2-inch by 2-inch angle-iron frame, and stiffened with 1½-inch channels, were substituted at this battery, as they have proven very satisfactory in recent emplacements on the south side of the bay.

The latrine building was made of concrete and placed on the right flank of the battery, adjoining the main body of masonry, a cast-iron range closet, of three seats, being used in the plumbing fixtures instead of individual flushing closets.

In the original estimate for the battery an electric-light plant was provided. When the allotment was made it was directed to omit the plant, to keep the figures within the limit of $25,000. In the construction the battery was wired for lighting, lamps provided, and the system finished complete, so that at any time when power is provided it can be connected with but little expense. The interior conduit system of wiring was used, and it was made in every way to the standard for the best waterproof work.

The water service is connected with a concrete tank. The head of water is 250 feet, so to reduce the pressure on fixtures a small basin of 50 gallons capacity was built just above the emplacement and was provided with a ball cock to regulate the flow of water automatically.

All exterior walls, where back filled, were painted with paraffin paint, two-coat work, against which a foot of gravel was placed as the back filling progressed. The same was done on roofs where covered. The nature of the general excavation was rocky, and the slope of the ridge on which the battery is situated is more than 20 degrees; hence the back slope of roadway, on parade level, is very long. This was left bare because of the difficulty of placing loam upon it with any likelihood of its remaining permanently. All made banks and other slopes were sown with alfalfa. A rubble retaining wall of about 60 cubic yards contents was built along the cut where the side road leading into the battery adjoins the main road.

The engineering work of the battery was completed May 29. Whitewashing of the interior of the service rooms was done by the watchman and was finished in June. Authority having been given by the Chief of Engineers to mount the gun carriages, application was made to the commanding general, Department of California, to have the artillery troops do same. Assembling and cleaning of parts of the carriages by the troops are under way.

Appended is a detailed statement of the cost of the work:

Excavation		$3,260.58
Back fill		382.01
Concrete:		
Cement	$3,166.22	
Gravel	1,143.93	
Sand	698.40	
Stone, rubble	148.90	
Concrete labor	845.58	
Plant	360.52	
Frames	2,247.30	
		8,610.85
Ironwork:		
I-beams	$427.56	
Ring bolts	21.00	
		448.56
Drains and ventilation		346.77
Doors (5 steel, 2 wood)		385.62
Grading and sloping		347.48
Windows		146.84
Speaking tubes		75.33
Roads and road repairs		741.39
Water supply		322.25
Latrine		237.00
Cement finishing		701.75
Painting, including paraffin painting		203.09
Tools, and repairs of same		169.99
Blacksmithing		529.98
Hand railing, 80 linear feet		75.17
Electric-light wiring		339.71
Fireplaces		22.00
Steamer *Yosemite*		1,411.52
Concrete gutters		45.00
Rubble retaining wall		256.25
Superintendence and field-office expenses		1,894.78
Ordnance, transporting and setting		370.00
Stables		1,862.12
Contingency:		
City office expenses	$871.62	
Miscellaneous teaming	230.82	
Temporary buildings	44.63	
Holidays	166.67	
Maintenance of quarters	84.20	
Policing	273.56	
Storing old lumber	67.70	
		1,739.20
Total		24,925.24

Emplacements for two 12-inch rifles on disappearing carriages.—The guns were mounted in October, 1900, and the battery turned over to the artillery in August, 1900.

Installation of searchlight.—The plant for installing a trial searchlight on the north side of the bay was purchased in 1898 for the torpedo-defense service. It was transferred to this Department on November 9, 1900.

Contract was entered into with James McMahon on October 1, 1900, for the construction of a power house and a shelter for the projector; contract was approved by the Chief of Engineers October 24, 1900.

The building to receive the engine and the dynamo is of brick, 12-inch walls, built on a concrete foundation, with concrete floor, and finished with a slate roof. Its dimensions are 15 feet by 28 feet by 9 feet high. The shelter for the projector is of frame incased in galvanized sheet iron, with a galvanized iron roof. Its dimensions are 14 feet by 14 feet by 10 feet high. In front of and on the floor level is a platform 12 feet long, upon which the truck carrying the projector is run when the light is in service. The contractor began work on the buildings in December and finished them, after numerous delays, in February. The machinery was taken from storage at Goat Island, transported by contract to the wharf, whence it was delivered to site with teams by the Engineer Department, and erected.

The plant consists of a 16-horsepower Hornsby-Akroyd oil engine, belted to a 72-ampere 110-volt G. E. dynamo, and a 30-inch G. E. electrically-controlled projector. The distance between the power house and light is 1,300 feet, the current being carried by conductors of 60,000 cm. cross section, strung on a pole line. Several test runs were made after the plant was erected, the final being run on May 31, when the machinery had been satisfactorily adjusted and prepared to turn over to the artillery service. This plant forms no part of the searchlight system of the harbor, and was installed upon the request of the artillery service for practice purposes only.

The following statement shows the distribution of the cost of the work:

Preparing site and excavation	$135.25
Contract of James McMahon, for buildings	1,865.00
Electric wiring	50.23
Pole line, complete	80.07
Transportation of machinery	98.63
Erecting machinery and making tests	140.13
Painting	56.89
Superintendence	279.42
Sundries:	
Hardware $3.90	
Drains 6.50	
Water supply 7.96	
Printing 20.25	
Masons' work 16.00	
Miscellaneous teaming 12.25	
Policing 6.00	
	72.86
Total	2,778.48

Emplacements for two 12-inch guns on disappearing carriages and emplacements for eight 12-inch mortars.—Plans and estimates having been requested by the Department May 29, 1900, examinations were begun in June of the sites selected by The Board of Engineers, with a view of investigating the facilities for prosecuting the work.

The distance between the wharf and the site of the batteries being several miles over a mountainous road with an elevation of 640 feet at the highest point, the cost of transporting materials by this road would be almost prohibitory, so it was deemed best to make a hydrographic survey of a sheltered cove to determine whether a wharf could be built. The site of the wharf was selected, the depth of the outer end being 26 feet.

To connect the wharf approach with good grounds above by a road was found too expensive, hence a tramway, designed to carry loads up to 6 tons in weight, was decided upon and built, as will be described further on.

At the site of the mortar battery during the winter months the ground water rose to the surface. This condition suggested the probability of dampness in the service rooms and magazines at certain periods of the year, and it was therefore thought advisable to change its location. After careful examination the site selected in 1890 was found to be free from water and well adapted for a mortar battery. It is about an eighth of a mile to the southward and 40 feet higher in elevation, situated between two hills, which give excellent flank protection, some 80 feet higher than the levels selected for the mortar pits. The plans for the battery were not changed excepting in minor detail, but an additional allotment was made on April 20, 1901, to cover any possible contingency which might arise in completely finishing this type of defensive works. The carriages for the battery are being shipped from the East, and upon receipt will be delivered near the works by the Quartermaster's Department. An estimate was made for taking the carriages to the site by landing them at a beach near the wharf and then taking them overland to the works. This estimate was rejected by the Department as being too costly, with request to investigate other means for getting them to the emplacements. A small, narrow beach in the sheltered cove near the new wharf was examined and found suitable for landing a barge if the numerous rocks and boulders guarding the approach were blown out. After removing the rocks it is proposed to build ways, upon which the barge carrying the ordnance will be drawn and then unloaded. Owing to the hazardous nature of the work, due partly to the treacherous ocean swell which constantly washes the rocky shore and partly to the contracted area upon which the ways must be built, it was considered to be to the best interests of the Government to provide its own barge and to suit the dimensions to the conditions obtaining for the particular work. Negotiations are under way to purchase a barge 30 by 100 feet by 7 feet 6 inches deep, capable of transporting safely loads of 200 tons in weight. The barge is to be used also in the construction of the batteries for transporting supplies.

During March plans for the 12-inch emplacements were modified to suit a new site designated by The Board of Engineers, and an additional allotment was made April 20 to cover the changes. The active work of construction for the battery has consisted principally of providing the general plant for the construction of both emplacements. A start was made on the excavation during June, but with the very limited accommodations for workmen nothing effective can be done until the engineer buildings now under construction are completed, when a full force of men can be employed.

The question of the transportation of supplies having been determined upon—that is, that all supplies should be taken to the point direct—the subject of material for concrete was next considered. A porphyritic sandstone similar in character to the ledge found on one of the islands of the harbor, which has been operated as a quarry for thirty years, was found near the site for the 12-inch emplacement. The face of a cliff, running from the water's edge to an elevation of from 140 to 180 feet, proved, after careful prospecting, to be the most suitable place to make an opening for a quarry. A bench, at an elevation of 100 feet, was worked in for a distance of some 30 feet to provide a working floor. A stiff-leg derrick, lifting safely loads of 3 tons, will be placed near the edge of the cliff on its westerly or higher end to hoist the broken rubble to swing it around to the crusher platform. A new Gates rock crusher, No. 5, with smooth head, was purchased and is being erected. An elevator will store the crushed stone in a bin of 800 cubic yards capacity, whence it will be taken in mining cars to the concrete-mixing plant 500 feet away. It is expected to place the product, crushed to a maximum of 2-inch size, on the mixer platform at a cost not exceeding 90 cents per ton of crushed stone; the plant, when the quarry is fully opened, to have a capacity of 250 tons per day.

Sand running through every grade in size, in unlimited quantities, can be obtained from a beach within a third of a mile from the 12-inch emplacement. The sand will be collected with drag scrapers and teams and a bunker will be built on the beach to store it, whence it will be taken to the concrete-mixing plant in mining cars operated on a surface track. Water can be obtained in a gulch leading to the above beach. A wooden storage tank of 7,000 gallons capacity, or one day's supply when concreting, is to be erected at this point from which water will be elevated with a steam pump to a cement basin of 20,000 gallons capacity, this basin to be placed sufficiently high to afford a working pressure for a permanent water supply for the two batteries. For a temporary supply a windmill has been erected in the gulch and pumps to a 2,000-gallon tank placed at a sufficient elevation to give water to all points while preliminary work is going on.

The distance between the two emplacements being but 1,600 feet, with the 12-inch guns about 40 feet above the mortars, a concrete plant has been designed which will serve both batteries when connected by a simple tramway operated by gravity. A Lidgerwood cableway, capable of distributing loads of 3 tons over any point of the 12-inch emplacement, has been contracted for. Stones of a cubic yard and more in contents can be handled with the quarry plant, delivered to the cableway on the stone train, and with it placed in the concrete walls. By using large stones instead of small rubble in the concrete a decided saving is effected in addition to obtaining a concrete of superior value. An additional advantage in using the cableway is the economy of handling ironwork placed in the concrete as well as the lumber used in building the forms. It also does away with trestling used to support the false work of runways for cars.

Wharf and tramway.—By Department letter of July 25, 1900, it was directed that the sum of $2,000 from the allotment for the two emplacements for 12-inch guns on disappearing carriages be applied to making the necessary surveys for a dock, and to investigating the facilities for taking supplies from said dock to the battery sites above.

It was considered necessary to create landing facilities in connection with the work to be done, and after a preliminary investigation of the locality it was decided to erect a pile wharf from shore in the more sheltered part of the bight, under the lee of the projecting headland, carrying it into 26 feet of water at its extreme end. From the root of the wharf a tramway for a single car track was projected to reach the top of the bank at an elevation of 250 feet above the low-water plane.

The general design consists of a landing pier 50 feet by 100 feet, the axis of which is laid parallel to the direction of the ocean swell entering the cove. This pier abuts a section of wharf 24 feet wide by 80 feet long, and from the end of this section an approach 16 feet by 204 feet leads to the shore, built on a rise of 1 in 10. This was resorted to to lift the shore end high above the reach of the ocean surf, which is known to develop powerful destroying forces here. The landing and the middle section of the wharf have a floor height of 15 feet above the plane of mean lower low water, while the shore end of the approach reaches an elevation of 35.5 feet. The piles, all of which are creosoted, were placed 8 feet apart in a bent, while the bents are 10 feet distant in the landing pier and 12 feet in other sections of the wharf. The piles were capped by 12 by 12 inch timbers upon which the superstructure of stringers and floor rests. A system of iron tie rods, 1⅛-inch diameter, was adopted to brace the piles diagonally across from bent to bent.

The tramway, 578 feet long, begins at the root of the wharf and leads to the top of the bluff, rising in a horizontal distance of 522 feet to a height of 214.5 feet, its steepest grade being on a rise of 1 in 1.47, or at an angle of 34 degrees 13 minutes. A canyon, or depression in the cliff line, was chosen for the location of the tramway in order to make the ascent as advantageously as possible, and to do this properly it became necessary to make a cut or excavation at the beginning of the steeper grades 10 feet deep, from 10 to 15 feet wide, and about 60 feet long, containing about 400 cubic yards. The tramway consists of two longitudinal stringers 8 by 12 inches, 38 inches apart, center to center, so as to support a track of 36-inch gauge. These stringers are notched into 8 by 10 inch trestle caps, the trestles being timber structures of requisite height, varying from 22 feet to 5 feet, and spaced generally 12 feet from each other. The structure was calculated for a safe load of 6 tons, and will readily carry 10 tons without danger.

The general character of the sea bottom and of the cliffs in this locality is extremely rocky and precipitous. While it was feared that it might be very difficult to find a foothold for the piles, a careful hydrographic survey developed the fact that the rock existed in ledges only, and that it did not extend beyond a certain very well defined line, outside of which the bottom was found to be hard sand, offering no difficulty to the penetration of a pile. With this knowledge it was only a fair risk to undertake the construction of this work, being prepared beforehand that any emergency would have to be met by minor changes in driving and additional bracing, for which all due allowances were made. These preliminary investigations led to the final location of the structure, which was aligned as a tangent from the upper terminal of the tramway to the shore end of the landing pier; the latter was deflected 22 degrees to the westward to meet the force of the approaching swell and to afford a safe berth to vessels lying at its side. The eastern 100-foot face of this section was intended and designed to be the landing side of the wharf, where a vessel may pitch with the rolling swells, but where it may be least subjected to broadside thrusts against the structure. The details of construction of the plans were closely adhered to in the progress of this work.

In the driving of the piles the rocky ledge referred to was reached with section No. 2 and for several bents the piles could not be driven more than 1 foot, or practically nothing. A shoe proved of no utility and added nothing to the penetration; it would either turn or double up under the pile, or, if driving were persisted in, it would cause the pile to split at the bottom and destroy its usefulness altogether.

APPENDIX 3—FORTIFICATIONS. 867

These bents, resting on rock foundation, were tied and braced with every precaution to the adjoining bents by heavy iron straps and lateral braces from pile to pile in such a manner as to insure their stability. The penetration outside of the ledge was found satisfactory; piles were driven 15 feet into this bottom.

While the wharf stands in a very exposed locality, separated from the Pacific Ocean by a narrow neck of land not more than 400 feet wide, it is sheltered to such an extent that its safety is assured. All westerly weather, from the southwest or the northwest, is broken by the headland, or the projecting neck, which breaks the face of the swell and allows it to enter the cove only after its direction has been changed by curling around the southern extremity of the point. The severest winter weather is from the southeast. To this the wharf is fully exposed, but it is known to be a fact that a wind from this direction has no influence on the sea. It is a land wind and in sweeping across the bay it has no opportunity in that short space to make that violent and destructive sea that is created by the ocean winds from the westward. No imminent danger need therefore be apprehended from this source. The approaches to the pierhead are free from any dangers to navigation, so far as a very careful and extended series of soundings has been able to establish that fact.

The estimated cost of building the wharf and tramway, including 30-pound rail truck and derrick for lifting heavy loads, was $14,466. Bids were advertised for on October 8, and opened on November 8, when the contract was awarded to Richard McCann, San Francisco, who proved to be the lowest bidder. The contract was approved by the Chief of Engineers December 17, and one extension of time was granted, viz, sixty days. The contractor carried out the contract satisfactorily to final completion, May 25, 1901, under many adverse conditions of weather, state of sea, and difficulties of driving piles, together with the constant trouble of getting his material to this exposed locality, the roadways to which were frequently impassable during the heavy winter rains for weeks at a time.

Appended is a statement of the cost of the work:

CONTRACT OF RICHARD M'CANN.

510 cubic yards excavation, at 50 cents	$255.00	
10,876.5 linear feet piles, at $0.625	6,743.44	
91,283 feet B. M. lumber in wharf, at $23	2,099.51	
34,514 pounds iron in wharf, at $0.055	1,898.27	
30,886 feet B. M. lumber in tramway, at $27	833.92	
5,054.48 pounds iron in tramway, at $0.055	278.00	
1,164 feet railroad track, at $0.25	291.00	
1 iron shoe, at $2	2.00	
		$12,401.14
Pay of inspector	583.83	
Assistant to inspector	116.00	
Steamer *Yosemite*	232.00	
Superintendence	215.00	
Printing specifications	45.50	
Advertising for bids	32.38	
Excavation for terminal	110.21	
Sundries	21.99	
		1,356.91
Total		13,758.05

Engineer buildings.—The buildings which heretofore quartered the workmen and teams for the works on the north side of the bay were too far removed from the new emplacements to be of use; hence estimates were submitted on October 23 for new quarters, and were approved with the main battery plans. An allotment of $6,451 for these buildings was made October 31, 1900. The buildings are as follows: One mess house, seating 130 men; 2 bunk houses, each quartering 72 laborers and 16 mechanics; 1 stable, for 30 horses; 1 cement shed, for 3,800 barrels cement; 1 carpenter and blacksmith shop, an office, and a dwelling house for engineering assistants. The construction of these buildings is under way, one bunk house being about done, with the mess house under roof.

Electric-light and power plant.—In the original project for the 12-inch battery, submitted September 12, 1900, no dynamo room was provided, as it was understood the Department had under consideration the question of doing away with oil engines and having separate power houses for electric lighting and for running the motors of the ammunition hoists, and it was suggested that a power house could be built behind some of the hills in a safe place from which electric power could be distributed to all of the emplacements called for by the approved project. The Department instructions were to modify the rooms of Emplacement No. 2 to adapt them to the requirements of the new specifications about to be issued. In the revised estimate of October 23, 1900, these instructions were carried out and the necessary rooms for boiler, engine, and dynamo provided on the left flank of the battery for supplying electricity for the 12-inch emplacements and the mortar battery. This revised estimate was approved and an allotment of $23,595 made for the work.

A project having been approved for the installation of electric searchlights at the various harbors of the United States, an estimate of cost of installing those recommended for this district was called for and submitted. As this project requires the building of a power house not far from the 12-inch battery, the subject of a central power plant of sufficient capacity for supplying the power and light required for all the batteries to be built and for lighting the quarters for the garrison was recommended for consideration. This plan was approved and plans and estimates for the plant were requested by the Department. As a special Board of Engineer officers has the general subject of central plants for furnishing all electricity for battery and garrison purposes at seacoast fortifications, the preparation of plans and estimates has been deferred until the report of the Board is received.

Preservation and repair of fortifications.—Emplacements for three 12-inch guns on nondisappearing carriages: The protective coating of the top surfaces of the concrete was a 6-inch course of rock asphalt, laid by an expert, and was supposed to be waterproof as well as elastic, and proof against erosion from the gun blast. It did not prove elastic and developed large cracks, which permitted the rain to saturate it and then to soak on through the concrete to the rooms below. Had the surface received the constant kneading which a street under traffic is subjected to, it would doubtless have remained intact.

In the allotment for preservation and repair, year 1900–1901, sufficient funds were obtained to replace the asphalt covering with a concrete roof averaging 6 inches in thickness over an area of 1,500 square yards. Work was begun July 24, and finished September 22. The asphalt was removed principally with picks, and with hammers and wedges where it was sufficiently cohesive to come up in sheets. The asphalt removed, it was found that the concrete surface was pretty well saturated to the depth of an inch or more in places with the oils of the covering surface. This damaged concrete was entirely taken up, so that a thorough bond could be obtained between the new and the old work, at a cost of 33 cents per square yard. Over the cleaned surface a grouting of pure cement and water was swept with heavy stable brooms, a barrel of cement being used to about every 30 square yards of surface.

Sand and gravel for concrete were obtained from the beach and hauled to the battery with teams; the cement was taken from storage at the wharf. The concrete was made in proportions 1 : 2 : 5, with a finishing coat mixed 1 : 1¼. The cost of the 5-inch layer and 1-inch finish, complete, without superintendence was $1.368 per square yard, or $8.20 per cubic yard. The terreplein surface over the entrance gallery to magazines Nos. 4 and 5 leaked considerably, and this was taken up to a depth of 4 inches and restored with new concrete.

The past winter was one of normal rainfall, with one or two periods of protracted wet weather; every room and gallery in the three emplacements proved to be dry. Sufficient balance to paint the superior slopes of the restored surface was wanting at the end of the work, and this amount has been placed in the estimate for the next fiscal year. Appended is a detailed statement of the cost of the repairs:

Removing and storing old asphalt		$623.25
Concrete:		
Cement (all Portland)	$889.20	
Gravel	170.62	
Sand	169.92	
Forms	189.25	
Labor, concreting	211.43	
Labor, cement finishing	426.00	
		2,056.42
General blacksmithing		111.63
Miscellaneous teaming		118.79
Water supply		19.38
Maintenance of quarters		74.28
Steamer *Yosemite*		24.10
Tools		9.50
Superintendence		435.01
Policing		13.45
Total		3,485.81

Firing of ordnance.—During the year shots were fired from the batteries on the north side of the harbor as follows:

Two 8-inch rifles on nondisappearing carriages, 2 shots.
Three 12-inch rifles on nondisappearing carriages, 1 shot (middle gun).
Two 12-inch rifles on disappearing carriages, 5 shots (2 shots from gun No. 1 and 3 shots from gun No. 2).

Money statements.

GUN AND MORTAR BATTERIES.

Emplacements for two 5-inch rapid-fire guns.

July 1, 1900, balance unexpended	$14,993.25
July 1, 1900, amount received by value of cement transferred to other work	1,687.51
October 31, 1900, amount received by value of cement transferred to other work	1,068.60
	17,749.36
June 30, 1901, amount expended during fiscal year	17,549.59
July 1, 1901, balance unexpended	199.77
July 1, 1901, outstanding liabilities	125.00
July 1, 1901, balance available	74.77

Emplacements for two 12-inch rifles on disappearing carriages.

July 1, 1900, balance unexpended		$3,354.43
December 31, 1900, deposited to credit of Treasurer United States	$173.49	
June 30, 1901, amount expended during fiscal year	3,180.94	
		3,354.43

Installation of search light.

July 1, 1900, balance unexpended (allotted June 30, 1900)		$3,030.00
March 1, 1901, transferred to other work	$250.00	
June 30, 1901, amount expended during fiscal year	2,780.00	
		3,030.00

Emplacements for two 12-inch guns on disappearing carriages.

July 25, 1900, amount allotted	$1,000.00
October 31, 1900, amount allotted	114,710.00
April 20, 1901, amount allotted	6,500.00
	122,210.00
June 30, 1901, amount expended during fiscal year	6,606.23
July 1, 1901, balance unexpended	115,603.77
July 1, 1901, outstanding liabilities	2,881.77
July 1, 1901, balance available	112,722.00

Mortar battery for eight 12-inch mortars.

July 25, 1900, amount allotted	$1,000.00
October 31, 1900, amount allotted	89,362.00
May 11, 1901, amount allotted	16,505.00
	106,867.00
June 30, 1901, amount expended during fiscal year	3,241.98
July 1, 1901, balance unexpended	103,625.02
July 1, 1901, outstanding liabilities	578.16
July 1, 1901, balance available	103,046.86

Wharf and tramway.

October 31, 1900, amount allotted	$14,466.00
June 30, 1901, amount expended during fiscal year	13,310.55
July 1, 1901, balance unexpended	1,155.45
July 1, 1901, outstanding liabilities	447.00
July 1, 1901, balance available	708.45

APPENDIX 3—FORTIFICATIONS.

Engineer buildings.

October 31, 1900, amount allotted	$6,451.00
June 30, 1901, amount expended during fiscal year	432.00
July 1, 1901, balance unexpended	6,019.00
July 1, 1901, outstanding liabilities	3,222.65
July 1, 1901, balance available	2,796.35

Electric plant.

October 31, 1900, amount allotted	$23,595.00
July 1, 1901, balance available	23,595.00

PRESERVATION AND REPAIR OF FORTIFICATIONS.

July 1, 1900, balance unexpended		$4,623.67
May 22, 1901, amount allotted		2,734.00
		7,357.67
October 31, 1900, amount transferred to other work on account cement received	$889.20	
June 30, 1901, amount expended during fiscal year	3,629.27	
		4,518.47
July 1, 1901, balance unexpended		2,839.20
July 1, 1901, outstanding liabilities		95.80
July 1, 1901, balance available		2,743.40

BATTERIES ON ISLANDS IN HARBOR.

At the close of the last fiscal year the condition of the work was as follows:

Emplacement for one 8-inch rifle on nondisappearing carriage.—The emplacement was completed, the gun mounted, and the battery in charge of the artillery.

Emplacement for one 8-inch rifle on disappearing carriage.—The engineering work was completed, except setting base ring, which had not arrived. The gun was on hand.

Emplacements for two 5-inch rapid-fire guns on pedestal mounts.—Engineering work completed, except whitewashing interior of rooms and setting the pedestals, which had not been received.

WORK DONE DURING THE YEAR.

Emplacement for one 8-inch rifle on nondisappearing carriage.—No work was done on this emplacement.

Emplacement for one 8-inch rifle on disappearing carriage.—The base ring and carriage were delivered at the post dock by the Quartermaster's Department and were taken to the battery during the month by the artillery troops. The base ring was set by the Engineer Department in May, 1901, and all engineering work entirely completed. The battery was transferred to the artillery in August, 1900. Preparations were being made by the artillery for mounting the carriage.

Emplacements for two 5-inch rapid-fire guns on pedestal mounts.—The interior walls were whitewashed by the engineer watchman. The carriages for this battery have not arrived. The battery was transferred to the artillery in August, 1900.

Preservation and repair of fortifications.—A watchman was employed in the general care of engineer buildings and property and in painting interior walls of the 5-inch battery.

Money statements.

GUN AND MORTAR BATTERIES.

Emplacement for one 8-inch rifle on disappearing carriage.

July 1, 1900, balance unexpended	$1,235.33
June 30, 1901, amount expended during fiscal year	1,235.33

Emplacements for two 5-inch rapid-fire wire-wound guns.

July 1, 1900, balance unexpended		$2,034.88
July 1, 1900, amount transferred to other work on account cement received	$1,687.51	
June 30, 1901, amount expended during fiscal year	298.95	
		1,986.46
July 1, 1901, balance unexpended and available		48.42

PRESERVATION AND REPAIR OF FORTIFICATIONS.

July 1, 1900, balance unexpended	$1,000.00
May 22, 1901, amount allotted	1,022.00
	2,022.00
June 30, 1901, amount expended during fiscal year	720.00
July 1, 1901, balance unexpended	1,302.00
July 1, 1901, outstanding liabilities	50.00
July 1, 1901, balance available	1,252.00

BATTERIES ON SOUTH SIDE OF BAY.

At the close of the last fiscal year the condition of the work was as follows:

Emplacement for 8-inch rifle on disappearing carriage.—The emplacement was completed, except installing the ammunition hoist, setting the base ring, and mounting the gun.

Emplacements for three 8-inch rifles on disappearing carriages.—The engineering work was completed, the guns mounted, and the battery turned over to the artillery.

Emplacements for two 5-inch rapid-fire wire-wound guns.—The emplacements were completed, excepting the whitewashing of the interior rooms and setting of the base rings, which had not been received, and some minor details.

Emplacements for two 15-pounder rapid-fire guns.—Instructions had been received to select a site and to prepare plans and estimates for the construction of two emplacements for 15-pounder rapid-fire guns on balanced-pillar mounts, and this work was in progress.

Emplacements 6, 7, and 8 for 12-inch rifles on disappearing carriages.—The engineering work was completed, the guns mounted, and the battery turned over to the artillery.

Emplacements 9, 10, 11, 12, and 13 for 10-inch rifles on disappearing carriages.—The engineering work was completed, the guns mounted, and the battery turned over to the artillery.

APPENDIX 3—FORTIFICATIONS. 873

Emplacements 14, 15, 16, 18, and 19 for 12-inch rifles on nondisappearing carriages.—The engineering work was completed, the guns mounted, and the battery turned over to the artillery.

Emplacements B and C for 5-inch rapid-fire guns on pillar mounts.—These emplacements were begun in the spring of 1898, but, on account of the nonarrival of the cylinders for the pillars, the work was stopped after the excavation had been completed, the foundations laid, the relocator room erected, and some of the forms for the remaining work constructed. The I-beams and some rock and cement had been purchased and stored.

Emplacement D for 5-inch rapid-fire gun on pillar mount.—This battery was begun in May, 1900, but work was stopped after the completion of the excavation until the cylinder for the pillar should arrive.

Pneumatic dynamite gun battery.—The engineering work was completed and the battery turned over to the artillery.

Mortar battery No. 1.—Engineering work completed, the mortars mounted, and the battery turned over to the artillery.

Mortar battery No. 2.—Engineering work completed, the mortars mounted, and the battery turned over to the artillery.

Emplacements for two 6-inch guns on disappearing carriages.—The battery was entirely completed excepting the installation of some chain blocks, the carriages were mounted, and application for authority to transfer the battery to the artillery had been made.

Emplacements for two 12-inch guns on disappearing carriages.—At the beginning of the fiscal year the emplacements were completed except for installing the ammunition hoists and motors, laying the concrete aprons, painting and whitewashing the battery, and setting the base rings.

Emplacements for sixteen 12-inch mortars.—At the beginning of the fiscal year the excavation was completed, a concrete plant erected, the drainage system nearly completed, and about half the concrete foundations and mortar platforms laid. The construction of forms for the concrete work was well under way.

Land for fortification purposes.—The complaint in the condemnation suit had been filed and the answer of the owners made; the United States district attorney was preparing exceptions to the answer.

WORK DONE DURING THE YEAR.

Emplacement for one 8-inch gun on disappearing carriage.—The ammunition hoist was set in July. Upon the arrival of the carriage in January the base ring was set and the artillery mounted the gun. A tool room was erected in the reverse slope, racks were provided in the emplacement for the rammers, and several minor changes were made on the switchboard of the electric-lighting plant, and the emplacement entirely completed. The battery was transferred to the artillery in August, 1900.

Emplacements for three 8-inch guns on disappearing carriages.—A rammer rack and tool room were built for this battery. (See "Tool rooms and rammer racks," post.)

Emplacements for two 5-inch rapid-fire wire-wound guns.—The interior rooms were whitewashed, name plates for speaking tubes were purchased and put in place, and the battery transferred to the artillery in August. The base rings for this battery will be set as soon as received.

Emplacements for two 15-pounder rapid-fire guns.—Considerable delay was experienced in the selection of the site, three locations being thoroughly examined and abandoned on account of too expensive construction and other objections. A site was finally approved March 23, 1901, and the plans were approved April 11, 1901. A provisional allotment of $12,000 was made November 8, 1900. Of this $800 was withdrawn April 11, 1901, and $137.25 expended in the preliminary work, leaving $11,062.75 for the construction of the battery. The construction of the battery was begun immediately. During the latter part of April the site was cleared and the road to it put in good condition. In May a temporary tool and cement shed was put up, the excavation was made, forms erected, and about half the concrete put in. The excavation was in sand to a depth of from 7 feet in rear to 14 feet in front and in clay of moderate hardness below the sand. The excavation was carried on principally by four-horse scrapers, the clay being loosened by a plow. As the sand extended below the foundation on one corner of the emplacement, the excavation was here carried below grade to the clay and filled in to grade with concrete in the proportion of 1:5:11. The floors were made entirely separate from the walls and the space below them was filled in with sand to grade.

The concrete in the emplacement was in the proportion of 1:3:6, Portland cement of the "Hemmoor" and "Red Diamond" brands being used, and the mixing being by hand.

At the end of the fiscal year the work was completed except painting, whitewashing, top-dressing part of the rear slopes, wiring for electric lights, setting the doors, pointing the recesses for the doors, and policing and setting cylinders.

Emplacements 6, 7, 8, 9, 10, 11, 12, 13, 14, 15, 16, 18, and 19 for 10-inch and 12-inch rifles.—The only work done on these emplacements during the year is accounted for under the following headings or allotments which are given herein: Shelf lockers for dynamo rooms; observing station (6, 7, 8); electric-lighting plants; tool rooms and rammer racks; two battery commanders' stations (emplacements 18, 19).

Emplacements B and C for 5-inch rapid-fire guns on pillar mounts.—The cylinders for the pillars arrived in January, 1901, and the work of completing the battery immediately began. The forms were erected in February and concreting completed at the end of March. For the concrete Portland cement, coarse beach sand, and broken stone were used in the proportion of 1:3:6, measured loose, by volume, except in the retaining walls in rear of the emplacement, where the proportions were 1:3¼:8. The cement was of the "Cannon" and "Red Diamond" brands. The latter is an American Portland cement, manufactured in Utah. Although the quality of the cement used was good, the manufacturers supply it only in sacks, and, despite all reasonable care in storing, the cement in nearly 100 sacks out of the 2,810 sacks became more or less hardened by dampness. These sacks were transferred, with a portion of the rest of this cement, to the 15-pounder battery and were there used in subfoundation work.

The concrete was all mixed by hand and was of very good quality. Planes of weakness were left between portions of the emplacement that had unequal loads on the foundation, and lead flashings were inserted to prevent water from running down them and making its way laterally into the rooms.

All surfaces covered by earth were plastered and painted with paraffin paint, and a layer of cobblestone was placed next to them to secure the quick removal of water. The gun platforms over the magazines were given a slope of one-twentieth to insure prompt drainage. No other waterproofing was used. The refill, the grading and seeding, the cement finishing, and the carpentry work were completed in April. During May and June the battery was allowed to dry, and in the latter part of June the rooms were whitewashed and the electric wiring put in.

Emplacement D for 5-inch rapid-fire gun on pillar mount.—The cylinder arrived at the same time as the two for the other 5-inch guns for emplacements B and C, and the work on all three emplacements was carried on at the same time. The details of the work are the same as that for emplacements B and C.

Pneumatic dynamite gun battery.—Alterations were made to the switchboard of the electric plant.

Mortar Battery No. 1.—On May 11, 1901, $5,233 was allotted for changing azimuth circles and completing this battery. The old azimuth circles were removed, at a cost of about $4.49 per platform. A steam drill was purchased for the excavation of the concrete necessary to adapt the platforms to the new azimuth circles.

Mortar Battery No. 2.—Nothing was done during the year.

Emplacements for two 6-inch guns on disappearing carriages.—The battery was transferred to the artillery in August, 1900. The carriages are mounted, but the guns have not been received.

Emplacements for two 12-inch guns on disappearing carriages.—The ammunition hoists were installed in July, but the motors were not delivered until November, when they were installed. During the fall the battery was painted and the slopes were watered and cared for. After the winter rains began it was found that the shot galleries in both emplacements were leaking. The leak in Emplacement No. 1 was due to a crack across the platform, caused by unequal settlement from lack of uniformity in the foundations. The cause for the leak in Emplacement No. 2 was not evident. To discover whether it was due to a horizontal crack from the front face, the earth was excavated. No appreciable crack was found, however, and painting this surface and draining the earth in front of it had no appreciable result. The leaks are not so serious as to render the rooms unserviceable, and it is expected that after settlement has entirely ceased the leak through the cracks in Emplacement No. 1 can be stopped by a lead flashing.

Some difficulty was experienced from the washing of the exterior slopes by the rain. This was stopped, however, by cutting a gutter along the top of the slope and by draining the bottom.

In February and March the concrete aprons were put in and the rooms and passages were whitewashed. Although the fill had been in position for nearly a year there was a settlement of about one-half an inch in the aprons. As care had been taken to prevent the bounding of the apron with the parapet, this settlement was of no importance.

Nothing further remains to be done to this battery except to set the base rings, which have not yet arrived. A watchman is employed to keep off visitors and to care for the emplacement.

For the detailed statement of the cost of this battery see page 994, Annual Report Chief of Engineers, 1900.

Emplacement for one 12-inch gun on nondisappearing carriage.—
Plans and estimates were forwarded to the Department June 3, 1901, and were returned approved on June 14, 1901, an allottment of $60,000 being made for the work. Operations will be commenced during the next fiscal year.

Emplacements for sixteen 12-inch mortars.—Work on the floors and foundations, and on the forms, was prosecuted during July. To obtain as far as possible an equal settlement of the walls heavily weighted with earth, the foundations of the walls were constructed with offsets proportional to the load that they were to carry, and the floors were made separate from the walls, a sheet of tarred paper being inserted to prevent the bonding of the two together. The offsets caused a considerable increase in the amount of concrete used, but their construction was justified by the immunity of the battery from cracks.

The floors and foundations were completed in July, and concreting the rooms began about the 1st of August. The concrete was composed of Portland cement, principally "Scales," "Josson," "Cannon," and "Alsen," coarse beach sand, and crushed rock, in the proportion of 1 : 3¼ : 8, measured loose by volume. The rock was a blue metamorphic sandstone, quarried and crushed in the vicinity of San Francisco, and transported to the work in wagons. The sand was found on the ocean beach in the vicinity between high and low water marks. It was drawn above high water in scrapers at low tide and transported in wagons to the work.

To prevent the interruption of the work through slow delivery of stone, a storage bin with a capacity of 1,000 tons was constructed in rear of the center of the battery and filled before concreting began.

The description of the plant is given on page 1003 of the Report of the Chief of Engineers for 1900. The capacity of the storage bin is, however, there given erroneously at 2,000 tons instead of 1,000. The average day's run was about 250 cubic yards, and the cost $5.004 per yard, not including forms.

The erection of the forms and the concreting were carried first from the left flank, then from the right flank, toward the center, where the concrete mixer was situated. As soon as any part of the concrete had set for three or four days, the forms were taken down, and the cement finishers plastered the surfaces covered by earth. These surfaces were then painted. The backfilling followed as fast as possible after the cement finishing. The lumber of the forms and trestles was used over as many times as was practicable.

By the middle of September the concrete work was practically completed, but the wall and floor finishing was not completed until November. A large part of the mortar for cement finishing was mixed in the machine, which was not taken down until this work was practically completed. The saving in expense was not, however, very great.

Outside of the paraffin paint no waterproofing was used except around the north magazine, where the outside of the walls was covered by partition tile. Water had been met with at this point when the excavation was made.

The back filling was carried on chiefly by 4-horse scrapers, at a cost of 25.9 cents a cubic yard. It was completed in December.

The slopes of the 12-inch battery in the vicinity had been covered with soil from the reservation, consisting largely of sand. As soon as the winter rain set in, trouble was experienced from gullying. To avoid this in the mortar battery, loam was hauled from the Marine Hospital Reservation, at a cost of about 90 cents a cubic yard, and spread over the slopes. All the slopes were planted with oats, which soon sprang up and held the earth in place. In addition, the interior slopes were planted with cuttings of ice plant (*Mesembryanthemum crystallinum*), which has a very vigorous growth in this locality. The exterior slopes were, as far as could be without incurring too great expense, so shaped as to conform to the ground in the vicinity. To prevent the drifting sand, which is very troublesome in this locality, from blowing onto the slopes and into the pits, all the ground in the vicinity of the battery which had not previously been covered was planted with bunch grass (*Arundinario*), at a cost of about $75 per acre. This grass has proved very efficient in holding the sand in place.

The installation of the plumbing, the trolleys, and the electric-light plants occupied several months. An agreement was made with the firm to which the installation of the electric-light plant had been let to provide a switchboard in conformity with the specifications issued from the Office of the Chief of Engineers subsequent to the original agreement with this firm. A delay of several months was experienced before the installation was completed, the firm stating that some of the instruments could only be obtained in the East, and that some had to be made to order in order to fulfill the conditions imposed.

As the public water supply of San Francisco does not have at present sufficient pressure to supply the mortar battery, a well was sunk on the reservation and a windmill and a tank erected. The windmill gives an ample supply of water for the present needs of both the mortar battery and the 12-inch battery. There being at present no method of carrying away the drainage of the battery, a cesspool was constructed of sufficient size to hold the water from any ordinary rain until it can seep off into the soil. Both the windmill and the cesspool are to be regarded as merely temporary arrangements until either the Quartermaster's Department or the city build drainage and water-supply systems in the vicinity.

Two mortar carriages were received in November, two in December, and two in May. The base rings were set as soon as practicable after delivery. The mounting of the carriages is being carried on by the artillery.

A system of firing wires, with attachment plugs for connection to electric primers, was installed as far as was practicable before the mounting of the mortars. The system permits the firing of any pit either from a firing room or from the commanding officer's room. Current detectors are furnished in the commanding officer's room to indicate when the connections are ready for firing, and a safety switch is placed in each pit to prevent the firing of the mortars until the pit is clear.

Six mortar carriages were received and four of the base rings set.

The engineering work is completed except setting 10 base rings and the grates for the fireplaces, which have been shipped from the East, but which have not yet arrived. There are no leaks and no cracks except one or two unimportant ones in the retaining walls about the pit.

The following is a detailed statement of the cost of this battery:

Excavation:
Installation of hoisting engine and boiler, including repairs and refitting, material for running, and shelter for engine	$615.65	
Railroad track, laying and shifting	552.00	
Rent of steam shovel, cars, and track	3,052.94	
Oiling and repairing cars	839.96	
Pay of engineer and assistants	729.00	
Labor	13,698.80	
Teams	11,160.13	
Tools	123.62	
Explosives	815.27	
		$31,587.37

Forms:
Carpentry	$6,571.00	
Teams hauling lumber	279.82	
Material—		
Lumber	3,883.13	
Hardware	224.60	
Taking down forms—		
Labor	904.50	
Teams removing lumber	192.91	
		11,855.96

Concrete plant and tramway:
Excavation—		
Labor	$58.00	
Teams	83.56	
Road to concrete plant—		
Labor	177.75	
Red rock	428.04	
Installing machinery—		
Engineer	66.67	
Labor	107.50	
Elevators, bunker, and tramway—		
Carpenters' work	2,370.19	
Teams hauling lumber	105.30	
Material—		
Lumber	1,148.81	
Hardware	107.80	
Fittings of engine, packing, belting, and oils	250.99	
Rails, fishplates, and bolts	220.35	
Taking down plant—		
Engineer	70.83	
Labor	461.75	
Teams removing lumber	178.13	
Cleaning and boxing machinery—		
Engineer	17.00	
Helper	10.00	
		5,862.67

Cement:
1,000 barrels Scales, at $2.50	$2,500.00	
1,000 barrels Josson, at $2.50	2,500.00	
1,500 barrels Josson, at $2.60	3,900.00	
4,660 barrels Cannon, at $2.55	12,069.20	
1,092 barrels Alsen, at $2.05	2,238.60	
224 barrels Utah, at $2.33	521.92	
Storage in warehouses	355.90	
Storage at works	426.04	
Drayage	1,613.26	
		26,124.92
Average cost per barrel, $2.7568.		
Scraping sand		4,863.59

APPENDIX 3—FORTIFICATIONS.

Rock received, 22,969,457 pounds used:
- Rough concrete, 22,191,575 pounds $14,147.13
- Drains, sewers, and gutters, 153,312 pounds 97.74
- Dynamo bed, 41,688 pounds 26.57
- Floors, 308,707 pounds............................ 196.79
- Latrine, 224,150 pounds........................... 142.89
- Lookout, 50,025 pounds............................ 31.89

$14,643.01

Concrete work:
  Supplying mixer—
    Labor $353.60
    Teams..................................... 405.97
  Mixing, placing, and ramming—
    Engineer 255.00
    Labor 4,730.20
    Teams..................................... 252.42
  Incidentals—
    Repairing scales.......................... 35.75
    Weighing and receiving rock............... 291.00
    Tools..................................... 161.89

6,485.83

I-beams:
- 824 beams.. $5,339.34
- Storing and painting............................... 329.76
- Placing 235.07

5,904.17

Laying partition tile:
- Labor $96.00
- Teams... 11.46

107.46

    5 barrels cement...................... $13.75
    75 feet sand 2.45

    16.20

Top finish, mason and helpers 420.00
    318 barrels cement $878.58
    2,860 feet sand 93.52

    972.00

Plastering: Masons and helpers 766.00
    161 barrels cement.................... $444.36
    2,415 feet sand 78.97

    523.33

Pointing: Masons and helpers... 1,790.50
    79 barrels cement $218.04
    800 feet sand........................ 26.16

    244.20

Floor and sidewalks:
- Forms for masons $152.31
- Masons and helpers 1,312.00
- Getting and mixing material 160.75

1,625.06

    695 barrels cement $1,918.20
    308,707 pounds rock................. 196.79
    6,700 cubic feet sand 219.09

    2,334.08

Drains, sewers, and sumps:			
Labor		$1,825.75	
Teams		7.70	
Material—			
Sewer pipe and drain tile		641.11	
44 cesspools		41.80	
7 manhole covers		73.50	
66 barrels cement	$182.16		
153,312 pounds rock	97.74		
995 cubic feet sand	32.54		
	312.44		
Grates for sumps—			
Labor		113.67	
Material		38.09	
			$2,741.62
Ventilators:			
Carpenter (forms)		$161.00	
Masonry		104.00	
Sewer pipe		98.53	
Grates		25.67	
			389.20
Fireplaces: Four chimney tops and bases			11.60
Paraffin painting:			
Labor		$112.00	
Material		541.50	
			653.50
Backfill:			
Labor		$5,714.48	
Teams		5,693.49	
			11,407.97
Topdressing:			
Road to parapet		$195.37	
Loading and hauling loam—			
Labor		576.50	
Teams		3,534.07	
Topdressing		1,920.70	
			6,226.64
Grading:			
Labor		$152.50	
Teams		125.13	
Tools, 2 col. scrapers		15.00	
			292.63
Planting ice-plant cuttings:			
Labor		$101.00	
Teams		6.84	
			107.84
Planting grass:			
Labor		$516.75	
Teams		52.87	
100 pounds lupine seed		10.00	
Weeding slopes		54.00	
			633.62
Planting grass on reservation:			
Labor		$611.25	
500 pounds oats		9.80	
4,000 gum trees		72.00	
Gathering lupine seed		4.00	
			697.05
Gates and doors:			
Gates and hinges		$211.50	
Fitting doors, setting hinge blocks, carpentry, and masonry		202.56	
25 doors		814.17	
Hinge blocks		368.20	
Locks and steel rings		21.56	
Painting doors		65.00	
			1,682.99

APPENDIX 3—FORTIFICATIONS.

Windows:		
Carpentry	$33.50	
7 sets sash	49.00	
Hardware	17.85	
Lumber	7.30	
Window gratings	30.00	
		$137.65
Whitewashing:		
Labor	$198.00	
1 barrel lime	1.25	
		199.25
Equipment of battery:		
Speaking tubes	$207.67	
Material (pipe, fittings, mouthpieces, name plates, etc.)	1,211.38	
		1,419.05
9 barrels cement for pipe recesses........ $24.84		
Trolleys:		
Installation	$146.00	
Painting	90.72	
Trolleys	1,074.75	
		1,311.47
Tracks and turntables for powder trucks:		
Labor	$95.75	
Material—		
460 feet T-rail	48.30	
2 turntables	170.00	
4 push cars	222.00	
Lumber	8.05	
		544.10
Ringbolts		144.00
Bolts for mortars:		
Bolts	$2,644.80	
Paint for bolts	6.88	
		2,651.68
Electric-light plant:		
Dynamo bed, base for tank, and floors of rooms	$64.50	
Dynamo and electric supplies	4,579.54	
Doors for fan-motor recesses	10.07	
Electric-light strips—		
Carpentry	72.00	
Lumber	116.07	
Painting	72.00	
		4,914.18
Firing wires:		
Conduits	$37.00	
Laying wires	63.00	
175 feet 1-inch galvanized iron pipe and fittings	23.98	
		123.98
Firing boxes:		
Carpentry	$58.50	
Hardware	13.04	
		71.54
Mounting and setting 6 base rings and finishing pit No. 4:		
Moving rings into position	$40.00	
Setting	126.00	
Leading bolts	6.00	
Material (223 pounds pig lead)	13.38	
Drainage of pits	10.50	
		195.88
Finishing platforms in pit No. 4, labor		75.00
Material—		
29 barrels cement........ $80.04		
5,800 pounds sand........ 1.90		
	81.94	

ENG 1901——56

882   REPORT OF THE CHIEF OF ENGINEERS, U. S. ARMY.

Road leading to battery:
  Labor $668.90
  Teams 603.71
  Red rock 1,286.88
  Salt water for sprinkling 1.10
  Repair:
    Labor 32.00
    Teams 28.65
    Red rock 54.60
                      $2,675.84

Road in rear of pits:
  Labor $510.00
  Teams 250.60
                         760.60

Gutter:
  Excavation $71.98
  Carpentry 101.50
  Masonry 152.00
  Teams 16.77
                         342.25
  Material—
    50½ barrels cement $139.38
    750 cubic feet sand 24.52
                163.90

Water supply:
  Laying pipes and pumping water $553.15
  2 tanks 74.00
  Pipe and fittings 794.49
  Taking down tank 11.82
  Spring Valley Waterworks 246.64
                       1,680.10

Well:
  Prospecting for water $23.00
  Digging 128.00
  Concrete work 70.21
  Grading 6.00
  Windmill 110.00
Tank frame:
  Carpentry 58.25
  Teams, hauling lumber 5.73
  Painting tank 4.00
                         405.19
  Material—
    8 barrels cement $22.08
    120 cubic feet sand 3.92

Lookout:
  Excavation $69.75
  Carpentry 72.25
  Masonry 69.00
  Teams 17.65
  Material—
    1,965 feet lumber 33.48
    418 feet expanded metal 29.26
                         281.39

    27 barrels cement $74.52
    50,025 pounds rock 31.89
    405 cubic feet sand 13.24
                119.65

Stairs:
  Carpentry $92.50
  2,327 feet lumber 65.04
                         157.54

APPENDIX 3—FORTIFICATIONS.

Latrine:		
Excavation—		
Labor	$22.00	
Teams	27.34	
Forms—		
Carpentry	145.00	
Concreting and finishing	174.00	
Teams	46.42	
Material—		
504 feet expanded metal	35.28	
Sewer pipe and ventilators	1.14	
Fixtures	540.00	
Finishing interior—		
Carpentry	54.50	
Painting	16.00	
Lumber, doors, and hardware	65.03	$1,126.71
67 barrels cement............$184.92		
224,150 pounds rock..........142.89		
900 cubic feet sand............29.43		
357.24		
Cesspool:		
Labor	$79.75	
Teams	48.94	
Material	6.05	134.74
Stables:		
Hostler	$600.00	
Teamster	777.33	
Forage	891.29	
Harness repair, medicines, etc	16.54	2,285.16
Blacksmith shop:		
Labor	$1,404.08	
Material	422.75	1,826.83
Carpenter shop:		
Labor, jobbing	$286.61	
Tools, files, hammers, etc	25.32	
Screws, brads, nails	8.57	320.50
Wagonwork:		
Carpenter and blacksmith	$146.05	
Material—		
Single and double trees, yokes, felloes, oak, tires, etc	89.60	235.65
Buildings:		
Cement shed, office and tool shed, and repairs	$247.63	
Lumber	104.37	
Hardware	9.83	361.83
Policing:		
Labor	$861.45	
Teams	355.70	1,217.15
Cement testing:		
Trier of cement	$280.00	
Material and repairs	3.75	283.75
Watchman		872.00
Holidays		1,328.50
Paints, etc		102.50
Miscellaneous articles		66.87
Town office		5,165.00

884   REPORT OF THE CHIEF OF ENGINEERS, U. S. ARMY.

Field office	2,395.00
Racks for rammers, etc. (4 sets of 2 each)	53.70
	172,747.78

To which add estimated cost of work required to complete battery:

Grates for fire places, 4 at $16	$64.00	
Moving and setting base rings	660.00	
Firing wires	25.00	
		749.00

Total	173,496.78

COST OF CONCRETE.

Total quantities:

7,997 barrels cement, at $2.7568, at work	$22,046.13
11,095.79 tons rock, at $1.275, at work	14,147.13
4,400 cubic yards sand, at $0.883, at work	3,885.20
36,000 cubic feet water, at $6.50 per M, including pumping	234.00
Plant	5,862.67
Labor	5,997.19
Tools and incidentals	488.64
Forms	11,855.96
Total	64,516.92

Total quantity of concrete deposited, 10,500 yards.

Cost of concrete per cubic yard:

0.7616 barrels cement, at $2.7568	$2.099
1.0567 tons rock, at $1.275	1.347
0.419 cubic yards sand, at $0.883	.370
Water	.022
Proportional cost of plant	.558
Labor	.571
Tools and incidentals	.047
Forms	1.129
Total	6.143

Recapitulation, per cubic yard:

Material	$3.838
Mixing, placing, and tamping	1.176
Forms	1.129
Total	6.143

Installation of searchlight.—An allotment of $2,140 was made June 30, 1900, for the construction of a brick power house for a Hornsby-Akroyd oil engine and a corrugated-iron shelter for a 30-inch searchlight and for installing the engine and light. The plant was transferred from the torpedo-defense system, and was set up for practice purposes at the request of the artillery.

Bids for the construction of these buildings were advertised for and opened September 4, 1900. The acceptance of the lowest bid—that of James A. McMahon of $1,334 for the power house and $348 for the shelter—was authorized by the Chief of Engineers September 17, 1900, and the contract was approved October 24, 1900. The ground was cleared by hired labor, and work was begun by the contractor in November and finished January 31, 1901. The plant was transported in October and set up upon the completion of the buildings. The expense was $375 greater than was anticipated. As it was necessary to send East for some of the wire required for the pole line between the shelter and the light, the work was not completed and tested until April. The light had in the meantime been completed and tested. It was found that the engine was of such limited capacity that it was necessary to cut the fixed resistance out of the rheostat. It was once more necessary to send East for the fixtures required, so that it was not until June that a preliminary test was made. This test demonstrated that the pulley on the generator was of too small diameter and too narrow face. A new pulley has been ordered.

Shelf lockers for dynamo rooms.—Application having been made by the artillery for the construction of eight shelf lockers for tools and cleaning material in the dynamo rooms, the Chief of Engineers approved, October 8, 1900, the construction of these lockers from the funds allotted for two 12-inch gun emplacements. These lockers were completed in November, at a cost of $10.56 each.

Observing station (Nos. 6, 7, 8).—The artillery having reported that one of the observing stations for the type B Lewis depression range finder for emergency use did not embrace the field of view required, the construction of a supplementary station from the funds allotted from the two 12-inch gun emplacements was authorized by the Chief of Engineers November 10, 1900. This station was completed in January, at a cost of $245.69.

Electric-lighting plants.—In order to economize space in some of the dynamo rooms, the switch boards had been set against recesses in the walls and provided with hinges at the upper edge so that they could be turned up for inspection and alteration of the wires on the back. The artillery reported this arrangement as unsatisfactory, as there was condensation behind the boards, the boards were heavy, and in one case the movement of the board had caused a short circuit of the mains. A request was also made for additional instruments on the boards and for a switch-board at Mortar Battery No. 1, where none was provided. The wiring in Mortar Battery No. 1 was also in need of repair. An allotment of $1,050 was made for the alterations and additions requested. The work was completed in June, 1901, at a cost of $1,108.78, an additional allotment of $58.78 being made June 11, 1901.

Tool rooms and rammer racks.—The artillery having requested that tool rooms for the storage of tools and materials used in keeping the emplacements in order be constructed in those emplacements where no such rooms had been provided, and that racks be made for the sponges and rammers in each emplacement, an allotment of $700 was made by the Chief of Engineers December 11, 1900, for this work. The work was completed in April. The tool rooms were constructed of concrete and expanded metal, and were 9 feet by 13 feet and 7 feet high, with walls 6 inches thick. These rooms were constructed at an average cost of $274.03, one being built at the 8-inch battery and the other at Emplacements Nos. 18 and 19. The racks were constructed in the form of brackets, of oak, with iron braces. Sixteen sets were constructed, at an average cost in place of $9.50. Three were built for Emplacements Nos. 1, 2, and 3 of the 8-inch battery and one each for Emplacements Nos. 6 to 16 and 18 to 19, inclusive.

Two observing stations (at emplacements 18 and 19).—No stations for the type B emergency range finder having been supplied in two of the older 12-inch barbette batteries, an allotment of $800 for the construction of two stations was made February 26, 1901. Upon further consideration but one station was constructed, at a cost of $142.75, this fulfilling all the requirements. The work was completed in May.

Land for fortification purposes.—The exceptions to the answer of the owner were filed and disposed of in July. On November 24 an additional allotment of $502 was made for the employment of an expert witness on land values. The condemnation suit was begun in the United States circuit court on December 11 and concluded December 14. The jury found the value of the 44.95 acres of land needed for fortification purposes to be $39,555, which is at the rate of $900 per acre, and assessed the injury to the adjoining land at $3,900, which is at the rate of $300 an acre. This would make the total cost $43,555. The original allotment of $40,000 being thus insufficient, an additional allotment of $3,455 was made December 24, 1900.

An agreement was reached with the owner, with the consent of the court, to make some minor changes in the boundary lines. A resurvey was made for this purpose, and it was found that the acreage was reduced to 41.4.

An interlocutory decree was prepared and acted on by the judge of the United States circuit court in open court February 20, 1901. The decree was forwarded to the Attorney-General of the United States on that date by the United States attorney for the northern district of California. Authority from the Secretary of War for the payment of the award was received by telegram May 24, 1901, and on May 25, 1901, the sum of $42,162 was paid to the clerk of the United States circuit court, ninth circuit, Northern district of California, $37,260 being for 41.4 acres of land, and $4,902 being for the assessed injury to 16.34 acres, all in accordance with the final decree of the court.

Preservation and repair of fortifications.—A ball cock was purchased for the plumbing system at one of the forts. The fort keeper at another fort, assisted by such labor as was necessary, was employed in repairing roads and fences, cleaning drains, looking after the water supply, and painting wood and iron work in the new defenses. The firing carried on during the year proved very destructive to some light wooden latrines constructed in rear of these emplacements, and next year these buildings will be replaced by concrete ones. The emplacements are not in a particularly satisfactory condition with respect to leaking. During the summer no rain falls and there are no hot and sultry days. At this season, therefore, the emplacements are very dry. After the winter rains start water begins to show itself in quite a number of the rooms. The only possible solution seems to be to clean off the earth covering and apply a durable waterproofing, but this is an expensive process. Quite a liberal allotment has been made for this purpose for next year, and it is expected that some of the rooms will be rendered dry.

As the reservation for another of the forts is located near one of the principal pleasure resorts of the city, application was made for funds to construct a fence around it to keep off trespassers. An allotment of $1,500 was made for this purpose June 29, 1900, from the appropriation for "Preservation and Repair of Fortifications." To minimize the danger of destruction by a grass fire a barbed-wire fence was constructed in place of the picket fence contemplated, at a cost of $1,219.25. It was found necessary to plant bunch grass along it to prevent the wind from blowing the sand away from the posts. Shortly after the construction was completed a section of the north end of the reservation, about a hundred yards wide, slipped down hill for the

APPENDIX 3—FORTIFICATIONS.

distance of about a yard, throwing the fence out of line and breaking the wires.

Firing of Ordnance.—During the year guns were fired by the Ordnance Department as follows:

8-INCH B. L. RIFLE.

Emplacement No.	Gun No.	Shots fired.	Date.
1	2	2	Oct. 25, 1900.
2	3	1	Do.
3	8	2	Do.
3	8	3	Nov. 14, 1900.

10-INCH B. L. RIFLE.

Emplacement No.	Gun No.	Shots fired.	Date.
9	7	1	Oct. 30, 1900.
10	13	1	Do.
11	18	1	Do.
11	18	1	Nov. 15, 1900.
12	15	1	Nov. 5, 1900.
13	5	1	Do.
13	5	1	Nov. 6, 1900.
13	5	1	Nov. 15, 1900.

12-INCH B. L. RIFLE.

Emplacement No.	Gun No.	Shots fired.	Date.
14	9	1	Nov. 5, 1900.
15	6	1	Do.
18	19	1	Nov. 6, 1900.
6	5	4	Nov. 2, 1900.
6	5	2	Nov. 15, 1900.
7	8	2	Nov. 2, 1900.
7	8	1	Nov. 15, 1900.
8	40	1	Nov. 2, 1900.

It will be noted that in some cases more than one gun has the same number. This is due to the fact that these guns were made in different arsenals.

MORTAR BATTERY NO. 1.

Pit No.	Gun No.	Mortar No	Shots fired.	Date.
1	2	5	1	Oct. 26, 1900.
2	4	36	1	Do.
3	1	29	1	Do.
4	4	44	1	Do.

MORTAR BATTERY NO. 2.

Pit No.	Gun No.	Mortar No	Shots fired.	Date.
1	1	33	1	Oct. 29, 1900.
1	2	35	1	Do.
1	3	22	1	Do.
1	4	47	1	Do.
2	1	30	1	Do.
2	2	6	1	Do.
2	3	31	1	Do.
2	4	49	1	Do.
3	1	22	1	Do.
3	2	46	1	Do.
3	3	34	1	Do.
3	4	36	1	Do.
4	1	28	1	Do.
4	2	23	1	Do.
4	3	39	1	Do.
4	4	28	1	Do.

Money statements.

GUN AND MORTAR BATTERIES.

Emplacement for one 8-inch gun on disappearing carriage.

July 1, 1900, balance unexpended	$1,470.18
June 30, 1901, amount expended during fiscal year	1,470.18

Emplacements for two 5-inch rapid-fire wire-wound guns.

July 1, 1900, balance unexpended	$767.68
June 30, 1901, amount expended during fiscal year	724.90
July 1, 1901, balance unexpended and available	42.78

Emplacements for two 15-pounder rapid-fire guns.

November 8, 1900, amount allotted		$12,000.00
April 11, 1901, amount withdrawn	$800.00	
June 29, 1901, amount transferred to other works on account cement received	928.80	
June 30, 1901, amount expended during fiscal year	5,896.46	
		7,625.26
July 1, 1901, balance unexpended		4,374.74
July 1, 1901, outstanding liabilities		2,975.92
July 1, 1901, balance available		1,398.82

Emplacements for three 15-pounder rapid-fire guns.

June 13, 1901, amount allotted	$15,200.00
July 1, 1901, balance available	15,200.00

Two emplacements for 5-inch rapid-fire guns.

July 1, 1900, balance unexpended	$1,614.32
January 19, 1901, amount allotted	7,700.00
January 31, 1901, amount received by value of cement transferred to other work	54.00
June 29, 1901, amount received by value of cement transferred to other work	594.00
	9,962.32
June 30, 1901, amount expended during fiscal year	8,852.91
July 1, 1901, balance unexpended	1,109.41
July 1, 1901, outstanding liabilities	173.41
July 1, 1901, balance available	936.00

One emplacement for 5-inch rapid-fire gun.

July 1, 1900, balance unexpended	$5,096.84
January 31, 1901, amount received by value of cement transferred to other work	27.00
June 29, 1901, amount received by value of cement transferred to other work	334.80
	5,458.64
June 30, 1901, amount expended during fiscal year	5,093.40
July 1, 1901, balance unexpended	365.24
July 1, 1901, outstanding liabilities	6.84
July 1, 1901, balance available	358.40

APPENDIX 3—FORTIFICATIONS.

Pneumatic dynamite gun battery.

July 1, 1900, balance unexpended	$22,862.70
July 26, 1900, amount withdrawn	22,862.70

Mortar Battery No. 1.

May 11, 1901, amount allotted	$5,233.00
July 1, 1901, outstanding liabilities	90.75
July 1, 1901, balance available	5,142.25

Emplacements for two 6-inch guns on disappearing carriages.

July 1, 1900, balance unexpended	$1,055.74
June 30, 1901, amount expended during fiscal year	1,055.74

Emplacements for two 12-inch guns on disappearing carriages.

July 1, 1900, balance unexpended	$22,728.50
June 30, 1901, amount expended during fiscal year	14,859.96
July 1, 1901, balance unexpended	7,868.54
July 1, 1901, outstanding liabilities	60.00
July 1, 1901, balance available	7,808.54

NOTE.—Above expenditures during fiscal year include $84.48 for eight lockers for dynamo rooms of various batteries elsewhere, and $245.69 for observing station for Emplacements 6, 7, and 8.

Emplacement for one 12-inch gun on nondisappearing carriage.

June 14, 1901, amount allotted	$60,000.00
June 30, 1901, balance unexpended and available	60,000.00

Mortar Battery, sixteen 12-inch mortars.

July 1, 1900, balance unexpended	$99,515.65
June 30, 1901, amount expended during fiscal year	97,091.55
July 1, 1901, balance unexpended	2,424.10
July 1, 1901, outstanding liabilities	171.88
July 1, 1901, balance available	2,252.22

Installation of searchlight.

July 1, 1900, balance unexpended (allotment June 30, 1900)	$2,140.00
March 1, 1901, transferred from other work	250.00
March 20, 1901, amount allotted	125.00
	2,515.00
June 30, 1901, amount expended during fiscal year	2,512.64
July 1, 1901, balance unexpended and available	2.36

Electric-lighting plants.

July 1, 1900, balance unexpended	$1,300.96
July 26, 1900, amount withdrawn	300.96

Alterations, electric-lighting plants.

November 15, 1900, amount allotted	$1,050.00
June 30, 1901, amount expended during fiscal year	1,050.00

Tool rooms and rammer racks.

December 11, 1900, amount allotted		$700.00
January 31, 1901, amount transferred to other works on account cement received	$81.00	
June 30, 1901, amount expended during fiscal year	619.00	
		700.00

Two battery commanders' stations.

February 26, 1901, amount allotted		$800.00
May 16, 1901, deposited to credit of Treasurer United States	$657.25	
June 30, 1901, amount expended during fiscal year	142.75	
		800.00

NOTE.—Only one station built.

SITES FOR FORTIFICATIONS AND SEACOAST DEFENSES.

July 1, 1900, balance unexpended		$40,000.00
November 24, 1900, amount allotted		502.00
December 24, 1900, amount allotted		3,465.00
June 12, 1901, amount allotted		2.20
		43,969.20
May 28, 1901, deposited to credit of Treasurer United States	$1,352.90	
June 30, 1901, amount expended during fiscal year	42,616.30	
		43,969.20

PRESERVATION AND REPAIR OF FORTIFICATIONS.

July 1, 1900, balance unexpended	$2,145.14
May 22, 1901, amount allotted	8,244.00
	10,389.14
June 30, 1901, amount expended during fiscal year	1,943.74
July 1, 1901, balance unexpended	8,445.40
July 1, 1901, outstanding liabilities	118.05
July 1, 1901, balance available	8,327.35

Fence around reservation.

July 1, 1900, balance unexpended		$1,500.00
May 16, 1901, deposited to credit of Treasurer United States	$280.75	
June 30, 1901, amount expended during fiscal year	1,219.25	
		1,500.00

SUPPLIES FOR SEACOAST DEFENSES.

Alterations, electric-lighting plants.

June 11, 1901, amount allotted	$58.78
June 30, 1901, amount expended during year	58.78

MISCELLANEOUS.

Shelter for Lewis range finder.—The approved project of the Board of 1899 called for the construction of 16 range-finder shelters, type A. Under the project of the board of 1898 considerable work was done, but only 2 of the shelters were utilized in the project of the Board of 1899, viz, 1 on the north side and 1 on the south side of the bay. With the balance of funds on hand from the allotment made for work under the project of the Board of 1898, the construction of 6 new shelters was authorized, viz: On north side of harbor, 2; on islands in harbor, 1; on south side of harbor, 3.

At the close of the last fiscal year the condition of the work was as follows:

Five shelters were completed, viz, 1 on north side of harbor, 1 on island in harbor, and 3 on south side of harbor.

North side of harbor: Work was commenced on July 24, 1900, on the 2 remaining shelters authorized to be built, the operations being carried on in connection with the roof repairs, 3 12-inch emplacements. The work was completed September 22, 1900.

There were no special features in the construction of the shelters at either site, excepting that each was situated on a point difficult of access, which made the cost of handling the material somewhat above the normal for works on the north side of the bay. The concrete material, gravel, and sand was obtained from the beach, and the cement was taken from storage at the wharf. At the first site the character of the ridge, being steep and rocky, prevented building a road; the material, therefore, had to be let down a narrow trail with a windlass some 300 feet to the position. The difference in elevation between the two points was about 90 feet. At the second site it was deemed too expensive to construct a road for the comparatively small amount of material involved; it was taken up the face of the ridge with teams of 6 and 8 horses.

The roofs and the faces of the concrete where exposed to view from the bay were painted a dull brown. The roofs of the shelters built during the previous fiscal year have proven water-tight and the buildings are in good condition. Instruments were received, but not mounted for want of sufficient artillery troops at the respective posts. Appended is a statement showing details of cost. Leaving out the variable items of superintendence and boat expenses, it will be observed that the net cost per shelter is the same as for those built heretofore, i. e., about $1,200 per shelter.

Cost of two shelters:

Excavation, including grading	$264.75
Concrete, and cement finishing	546.94
Carpentry and hardware, with forms	543.58
Painting	66.40
Steel roofs	1,012.16
Superintendence	398.00
Boat expenses	215.18
Total	3,047.01
Each	1,523.51
Deducting last two items	306.59
Net cost per shelter without superintendence and boat	1,216.92

South side of harbor: Work was commenced on the fourth shelter in November, 1900, and was completed in February, 1901.

All of the eight range-finder shelters constructed have been turned over to the artillery.

Construction of steam vessel.—When the engineer operations were started at the 12-inch battery on the north side of the bay, it became manifest that the steam launch of this Department, the *Yosemite*, would be unable to do all the service required of a vessel tending the construction of the works. The *Yosemite* is of 10 tons displacement, is flat bottomed, and was built for upriver work. For the interior of the harbor, where no very heavy seas are met with, she has proven fairly satisfactory; for the heavy ocean swell and high cross seas to be encountered almost every day in the year in the Golden Gate Channel, it was found that she was not safe. Her capacity for carrying freight and workmen is limited, and she has no surplus power for towing.

The exposed position of the point where the works are being constructed makes the transportation of a large quantity of supplies a somewhat hazardous undertaking. It was therefore considered more economical for the Government to have a barge of its own, with a tug capable of towing it, for the transportation of heavy supplies. With this end in view a naval architect was engaged to prepare plans for a suitable vessel, the adopted dimensions of which are: Length over all, 77 feet 6 inches; breadth, 18 feet; load-draft depth, 7 feet, and of 102.5 tons displacement at this draft.

A contract was entered into on March 13, 1901, with Henry P. Christie, of San Francisco, Cal., for the construction of the vessel, the price being $20,000. This contract was approved by the Chief of Engineers on March 27, 1901. A supplementary contract was entered into on May 24, 1901, with Mr. Christie for changing the steam hoist of the vessel for the additional sum of $150.

The following work was done: Steaming and erecting of frames of hull and ceiling of same completed, deck frames erected, garboard and shear strakes put in complete, and frames for machinery set. The work on the hull was about 80 per cent completed. The engines were about 90 per cent done, but active work stopped on account of strike of machinists. The plates for the boiler arrived, but erection was not begun because of strike.

Datum beacons for range finders: An allotment of $725 was made February 13, 1901, for the construction of three datum beacons for use in connection with the Lewis depression range finder. Two of the beacons consist of a single pile of pine, 15 inches in diameter at the cut-off, driven from 10 to 15 feet into the bottom and cut off 7 feet above the plane of the mean lower low water. Around this is placed a cast-iron pipe 24 inches in diameter, penetrating 4 feet into the bottom and having its top 8 feet above the plane of the mean lower low water. An iron crosspiece is secured within the pipe, resting on the pile and fastened to it, to prevent the pipe from settling. The space within the pipe is filled with 1:2:5 concrete, rags being first shoved in to form a base for the concrete.

It was found impossible to drive a pile at the third location, and in this position four 1⅜-inch iron rods are set up in holes 5 feet deep on the top of a small rock, and the 24-inch pipe set over these. The tops of the rods are connected by crossbars and another rod passes under these bars and is secured to the pipe. The interior of the pipe is filled with concrete.

It is expected that these beacons will give a mark that will not settle and that will not be attacked by marine worms.

On account of the strong tides and heavy winds in the bay, there were few days when the work could be carried on in such exposed localities as those in which the piles are placed. In April the first pile was successfully placed, and an attempt made to place one in the third position. No penetration could be obtained and the pipe and pile fell over and were lost. In May the rock was prepared for this beacon and the work of setting it in position was completed on June 21. The beacon at the second position will be set during the early part of the next fiscal year.

Supplies for seacoast defenses.—A small amount of electrical supplies was purchased and some alterations were made to the switchboards of the electric plants.

Peace storage magazines.—In accordance with instructions from the Department, a report upon the subject of the necessity for the construction of peace storage magazines in this district, with estimates of cost, was submitted June 26, 1901. As it was not considered that the battery magazines now constructed are sufficiently dry for the safe storage of ammunition in large quantities for any protracted period of time, it was recommended that magazines of the type design be constructed at four points. The estimates were, respectively, $7,665.58, $6,511.16, $10,316.97, $7,554.43.

Installation of searchlights.—The Board of Engineers having prepared a project for the installation of searchlights at the various harbors of the United States, an estimate of the cost for the purchase and installation of the 25 lights approved for this district was called for and the report, accompanied by a chart showing the positions recommended for the lights, was submitted May 25, 1901.

The entire estimate was:

Power plants	$63,000.00
Searchlights	58,828.01
Underground wiring	5,377.60
Total	127,205.61

Two 6-inch rapid-fire guns on Ordnance Department mounts.—The sum of $30,000 was provisionally allotted for constructing emplacements for these guns. This allotment was subsequently withdrawn for application to other work. The preparation of plans for these emplacements was in progress at the close of the fiscal year.

Money statements.

GUN AND MORTAR BATTERIES.

Installation of range finders.

July 1, 1900, balance unexpended		$2,699.53
October 31, 1900, transferred to other work on account cement received	$179.40	
June 30, 1901, amount expended during fiscal year	2,520.13	
		2,699.53

Steam vessel.

November 28, 1900, amount allotted	$12,000.00
June 30, 1901, amount expended during fiscal year	5,076.69
July 1, 1901, balance unexpended	6,923.31
July 1, 1901, amount covered by contract	6,923.31

Datum beacons for range finders.

February 13, 1901, amount allotted	$725.00
June 30, 1901, amount expended during fiscal year	12.50
July 1, 1901, balance unexpended and available	712.50

Two emplacements for 6-inch rapid-fire guns.

November 9, 1900, amount allotted	$30,000.00
May 3, 1901, amount withdrawn	30,000.00

SUPPLIES FOR SEACOAST DEFENSES.

July 1, 1900, balance unexpended	$1,000.00
June 30, 1901, amount expended during fiscal year	92.25
July 1, 1901, balance unexpended and available	907.75

ABSTRACT OF CONTRACTS IN FORCE JUNE 30, 1901.

Contract for construction of steam vessel: Name of contractor, Henry P. Christie; price, $20,000; date of approval, March 27, 1901; date of commencement of work, April 11, 1901; date of completion, August 11, 1901.

Supplementary contract for construction of steam vessel (change in steam hoist): Name of contractor, Henry P. Christie; price, $150 additional to original contract price of $20,000; date of approval by Chief of Engineers, June 3, 1901; by Secretary of War, June 11, 1901.

TORPEDO DEFENSE.

During the year a large amount of torpedo material has been received from the depot at Willets Point and stored in the torpedo shed, and the obsolete material has been either condemned and sold or shipped back to the depot.

In January, 1901, a severe windstorm damaged the roof of the torpedo shed, which was repaired at a cost of $118.

On April 29, 1901, a landslide caused serious damage to the keeper's dwelling, necessitating its removal to a more secure site, a short distance from the old one, and considerable repairs. The work was completed in June, 1901, at a cost of $400.

Two searchlight outfits, complete with engines, were transferred to Lieut. Col. Charles E. L. B. Davis, Corps of Engineers, to be installed for the use of the artillery.

The usual policing and minor repairs have been done by the keeper, with such assistance as was necessary.

The cable tank house and torpedo shed are in good condition.

Money statement.

July 1, 1900, balance available at end of last fiscal year	$412.42
October 13, 1900, amount allotted	800.00
May 10, 1901, amount allotted	400.00
	1,612.42
June 30, 1901, amount expended during fiscal year	1,300.43
June 30, 1901, balance unexpended	311.99
June 30, 1901, outstanding liabilities	60.00
June 30, 1901, balance available at end of fiscal year	251.99

3 W.

DEFENSES OF MOUTH OF COLUMBIA RIVER, OREGON AND WASHINGTON.

Officer in charge, Capt. William W. Harts, Corps of Engineers, to August 18, 1900, and Capt. William C. Langfitt, Corps of Engineers, since that date; Division Engineer, Col. Samuel M. Mansfield, Corps of Engineers, to November 23, 1900, and Col. Jared A. Smith, Corps of Engineers, since December 15, 1901.

At the beginning of the present fiscal year the condition of the work was as follows:

Six emplacements for 10-inch rifles on disappearing carriages.—Emplacements 1–4 were entirely completed, and with their guns and carriages were turned over to the artillery in 1898.

Emplacements 5 and 6, A. R. F., had been completed and turned over to the artillery on June 28, 1900. The carriage and gun for Emplacement No. 5 had been mounted by the artillery. The gun for Emplacement No. 6 was on hand and the carriage shipped, but not received.

Emplacements for eight 12-inch mortars.—The mortar battery was fully completed, the carriages and mortars being mounted, and was turned over to the artillery on January 17, 1899.

Two emplacements for 6-inch rifles on disappearing carriages, model 1898, Site No. 1.—The construction of these emplacements had been completed and the battery turned over to the artillery on June 28, 1900. The carriages had been mounted by the artillery, the base rings being set by the Engineer Department. The guns had not been received.

Two emplacements for 15-pounder rapid-fire guns, Site No. 1.—The work on these was entirely completed and the emplacements turned over to the artillery on June 28, 1900. The base castings, mounts, and guns had not been delivered.

Two emplacements for 6-inch rapid-fire wire-wound guns, Site No. 1.—The provisional allotment of $15,000, made on December 2, 1899, for the construction of these emplacements was withdrawn for reasons stated in letter of the Chief of Engineers dated July 12, 1900. No work had been performed under this allotment.

One emplacement for 15-pounder rapid-fire gun, Site No. 1.—The plans for this had been approved and an allotment of $5,450 made for its construction. No work had been done at the close of the fiscal year, but material was being assembled looking to early commencement of work.

Electric-light station, Site No. 1.—This had been finished, and the plant, consisting of one 56¼-kilowatt Westinghouse dynamo, with switchboard and necessary instruments, belt driven by a 65-horsepower "Ideal" engine, to which steam is furnished by an 80-horsepower locomotive boiler, installed. Electric plants of this station and of the gun batteries were still in charge of the Engineer Department.

Mining casemate, Site No. 1.—This had been completed, with all shelves, tables, etc., in place.

Torpedo storehouse.—The storehouse was completed and all submarine material, except cables, stored in it.

Cable tanks.—Two cable tanks, with covering sheds, overhead traveler, and railroad connection, were fully completed and all submarine cables stored.

Battery commander's station, type A, Site No. 1.—This was completed and in use by the artillery, having been turned over to them under date of November 29, 1900.

Two emplacements for 8-inch rifles on disappearing carriages.—These were both completed and carriages and guns were mounted.

Emplacement for one 8-inch rifle on experimental disappearing carriage.—All construction work for it had been finished in May, 1898. The carriage had not yet been received. The rifle for this carriage was delivered on January 24, 1898.

These three 8-inch emplacements and the ordnance were turned over to the artillery on July 16, 1898.

Two emplacements for 6-inch rifles on disappearing carriages, model 1898, Site No. 2.—The construction work of these emplacements was completed and the battery turned over to the artillery on June 28, 1900. The carriages were mounted. The guns had not been delivered.

Two emplacements for 15-pounder rapid-fire guns, Site No. 2.—The construction work of these emplacements was completed and the battery turned over to the artillery on June 28, 1900. The base castings, mounts, and guns had not been received.

One emplacement for 15-pounder rapid-fire gun, Site No. 2.—The plans had been approved and the sum of $4,840 allotted for its construction. No work had been performed under the allotment, but the necessary material had been contracted for.

Electric-light station, Site No. 2.—Work on this had been completed and the following plant installed: One 16-brake horsepower Hornsby-Akroyd oil engine and an 11¼-kilowatt Westinghouse dynamo with switchboard and all necessary instruments, switches, etc. None of the electric-light plant of this station or that of any of the gun batteries had been turned over to the artillery.

Mining casemate, Site No. 2.—This had been completed by the addition of an oil engine and dynamo room to the original casemate.

Battery commander's station, type A, Site No. 2.—Completed and in use by the artillery.

Platform for 15-inch smoothbore gun.—The platform for this had been built and the gun and carriage mounted in 1898.

OPERATIONS DURING THE FISCAL YEAR.

Ten-inch gun battery, six emplacements.—The gun and carriage of emplacement No. 6 were mounted by the artillery in August. In accordance with approved plans, the storage battery which had been installed in Emplacement No. 3 was taken down and moved to a more suitable room in Emplacement No. 5.

Underground lead-covered cables were laid from the electric-light station to Emplacement No. 1 of the 10-inch battery, and from there the mains are carried under loading platforms and platforms in rear of traverses to Emplacement No. 5, doing away with all outside and overhead wires. The parapet surfaces of Emplacements 5 and 6 were given two coats of asphalt to stop leaks.

The large mixer building, the stone and sand bins, trestles, and ground tracks which were originally built for the construction of this battery, and later utilized in the building of all other fortification works, located between the parados and the battery, were all torn down, the grounds cleared of all débris, surfaced, and sodded.

Emplacements for eight 12-inch mortars.—The only work done here was the application of a thin coat of asphalt to the two pit aprons.

Two emplacements for 6-inch rifles on disappearing carriages, model 1898, Site No. 1.—The construction work on these had been practically completed last year. The ground around the battery was cleared of débris and graded, and a macadam road made. The emplacements were wired and the storage battery installed. The guns have not yet been received.

Water supply.—The water supply of the above three batteries was made independent of the post supply by the construction of a bricked well and installation of a Worthington steam pump at the electric-light station and rearrangement of the pipe lines for the 10-inch and 6-inch gun batteries; at the mortar battery a bricked well and an electric pump were provided.

Drainage system.—The work of changing the drainage system of the 10-inch and mortar batteries was completed in accordance with plans approved February 23, 1900, by connecting the sewers of the two batteries with a main 12-inch sewer emptying into the Columbia River.

Two emplacements for 15-pounder rapid-fire guns, Site No. 1.—The base castings, mounts, and guns for this battery were received December 20. The base castings were at once set by the Engineer Department. The guns were mounted by the artillery.

One emplacement for 15-pounder rapid-fire gun, Site No. 1.—The allotment for its construction was made on June 16, 1900. Work on it began in July and was completed in October, and the emplacement was turned over to the artillery on November 12, 1900. The base casting, mount, and gun have not yet been received.

Battery commander's station, type A, Site No. 1.—This was turned over to the artillery on November 29, 1900.

Two emplacements for 6-inch rapid-fire guns on pedestal mounts, Site No. 1.—The provisional allotment of $30,000 made in 1900 for two 6-inch rapid-fire wire-wound guns, formerly projected, was withdrawn and an allotment of $29,000 was made in its stead from act of March 1, 1901, for the construction of two emplacements for 6-inch rapid-fire guns, Ordnance Department pedestal mounts.

Upon receipt of the type design of emplacements for this mount, detailed drawings and estimates were prepared and submitted under date of May 23. These plans and estimates were approved June 3, 1901, and allotment made as above noted.

The work of excavation has been commenced, and the 15-inch smoothbore gun was moved from its platform to the banquette tread entirely clear of the emplacements to be built. The necessary material is being assembled.

Platform for 15-inch smoothbore gun.—The dismounting and removal of this gun were authorized by the Chief of Engineers, under date of June 3, 1901, to permit of the construction of the two 6-inch emplacements, pedestal mount.

Two emplacements for 8-inch rifles on disappearing carriages.—The storage battery, to serve the three 8-inch emplacements, was installed in Emplacement No. 2, but was not put into commission.

Emplacement for one 8-inch rifle on experimental disappearing carriage.—This carriage was received on October 1. Owing to some difference in spacing of the holes in the traversing circle and the anchor bolts as set, from platform plan furnished by the Ordnance Department, the setting of the circle had to be deferred until caliper template could be received from the East. The holes in the traversing circle were slightly out of their true position, and it was necessary to cut the concrete out from about one-half of the anchor bolts and spring them over to fit holes in casting. The carriage and gun were mounted by the artillery, the latter in June, 1901.

Two emplacements for 6-inch rifles on disappearing carriages, model 1898, Site No. 2.—The electric-light plant was installed, and consists of a duplicate oil engine and dynamo plant, the oil engines being Hornsby-Akroyd 7-brake horsepower, and the dynamos General Electric Company's 4½-kilowatt. This plant may be run singly or in parallel, and also serves the three 15-pounder emplacements on the left flank of this battery. The guns have not yet been delivered.

Two emplacements for 15-pounder rapid-fire guns, Site No. 2.—Nothing was done, as the base castings, mounts, and guns for these have not yet been received.

One emplacement for 15-pounder rapid-fire gun, Site No. 2.—The sum of $4,840 was allotted for its construction on June 16, 1900. The excavation of the site was very heavy and amounted to 3,200 cubic yards, while the concrete laid was only 295 cubic yards. This emplacement was completed early in October and was turned over to the artillery on October 28, 1900.

Battery commander's station, type A, Site No. 2.—This was turned over to the artillery on November 29, 1900.

Mining casemate, Site No. 2.—The oil engine for this casemate was taken to the site, the anchor bolts set, and all pipe connections made between the cooling tank, the engine, and the exhaust. A concrete base for the transformer was also put in. All shelves, tables, etc., were also erected as prescribed in the torpedo manual. The torpedo materials for this casemate are stored, the engine having been taken back and stored after fittings were all prepared.

Electric-light plants.—The completion of the remaining electric-light plants at both forts was subjected to many vexatious delays, due to nonarrival of the necessary supplies from the East. Both plants were finally completed and turned over to the artillery on October 29, 1900, and on January 19, 1901, respectively. All electric-light plants at both places have been in charge of and operated by the Engineer Department since the first part of the plant was installed early in 1898 until their final transfer to the artillery as above.

Preservation and repair of fortifications.—Electric-light plants: From allotments made June 9, 1900, from the appropriation for "Preservation and Repair of Fortifications," act of May 25, 1900, $600 and $150, the storage batteries were regularly charged about once every week, and the plants, wiring, etc., cared for during the fiscal year until the plants were turned over to the artillery. An additional allotment of $480 has been made for fiscal year 1902, from act of March 1, 1901, to be applied to stopping leaks in emplacements.

Storing and caring for torpedo material: All torpedo material has been kept in good order and condition in the storehouse, which is always dry and free from moisture. The semiannual inspection was made by the officer in charge on December 7, when everything was

APPENDIX 3—FORTIFICATIONS. 899

found to be in excellent condition. Preparatory to turning this new branch over to the artillery, everything was again checked up and obsolete material returned to the Engineer Depot.

In accordance with act approved February 2, 1901, providing for the transfer of submarine-mine defenses to the artillery, and in obedience to instructions received from the Chief of Engineers, detailed drawings of mining casemates, mine fields, complete list of materials, etc., were prepared, and with the materials, casemates, storehouse and cable tanks, turned over on April 30, 1901.

Supplies for coast defenses.—In order to enable the Engineer Department to supply the artillery with certain articles, as required by General Orders, No. 66, Adjutant-General's Office, 1900, the sum of $800 was allotted from the appropriation for "Supplies for Sea Coast Defenses," act of May 25, 1900. Under this allotment various electrical supplies have been furnished the commanding officer, their cost amounting to $335.16.

General remarks.—A full description of plant used, methods of construction, and other detailed information pertaining to the defenses of the mouth of the Columbia River may be found in Parts I of reports of the Chief of Engineers as follows: 1897, pages 756–763; 1898, pages 797–803; 1899, pages 993–1004, and 1900, pages 1018–1026.

The materials used were, as previously, obtained under sealed proposals and the work done by the United States by hired labor.

In the unloading and mounting of guns and carriages every possible assistance has been given the artillery in their work.

Upon completion of works of defense at one of the sites all engineer property was removed to the other, and the quarters, buildings, and wharf turned over to the Quartermaster Department November 21, 1900, these to be returned to the Engineer Department in like condition at some future date when again needed for construction work.

With all the gun emplacements turned over, the Engineer Department has prepared and furnished to the artillery complete detailed drawings, as follows:

Drainage drawings, giving regulations for care of gun batteries.
Drawings showing ventilating systems of emplacements.
Drawings of water supply and emplacement pipes.
Drawings of details of wiring of emplacements and switchboards and general plans of plants.

These works have been in the efficient charge of Assistant Engineer G. B. Hegardt, and there is submitted herewith a separate appendix which is an extract from his annual report, and which treats on matters of a technical nature of interest from an engineering point of view. (See Appendix 4 F.)

Money statements.

GUN AND MORTAR BATTERIES.

Emplacements for four 10-inch rifles, three 8-inch rifles, and eight 12-inch rifled mortars.

July 1, 1900, balance unexpended		$166.41
Deposited account difference sheet No. 42		.58
		166.99
June 30, 1901, amount expended during fiscal year	$155.57	
June 29, 1901, balance unexpended and deposited to the credit of the Treasurer United States	11.42	
		166.99

Ten-inch battery, two emplacements.

July 1, 1900, balance unexpended		$7,692.14
Deposited account difference sheet No. 21		.67
		7,692.81
June 30, 1901, amount expended during fiscal year		5,960.42
July 1, 1901, balance available		1,732.39

Emplacements for two 6-inch rifles, Site No. 1.

July 1, 1900, balance unexpended		$3,996.91
Deposited account difference sheet No. 42		3.12
		4,000.03
June 30, 1901, expended during fiscal year	$3,962.56	
June 29, 1901, balance unexpended and deposited to the credit of the Treasurer United States	37.47	
		4,000.03

Emplacements for two 6-inch rapid-fire guns, Ordnance Department, pedestal mounts, Site No. 1.

June 3, 1901, amount allotted	$29,000.00
July 1, 1901, outstanding liabilities	5,280.16
July 1, 1901, balance available	23,719.84

Emplacements for two 15-pounders, Site No. 1.

July 1, 1900, balance unexpended		$410.98
June 30, 1901, amount expended during fiscal year	$338.33	
June 29, 1901, unexpended balance deposited to the credit of the Treasurer, United States	72.65	
		410.98

Emplacement for one 15-pounder, Site No. 1.

June 16, 1900, amount allotted	$5,450.00
June 30, 1901, amount expended during fiscal year	5,348.05
July 1, 1901, balance unexpended and available	101.95

Emplacements for two 6-inch rifles, Site No. 2.

July 1, 1900, balance unexpended		$5,137.55
June 30, 1901, amount expended during fiscal year	$5,085.48	
June 29, 1901, unexpended balance deposited to the credit of the Treasurer United States	52.07	
		5,137.55

Fifteen-pounder battery, three emplacements, Site No. 2.

July 1, 1900, balance unexpended	$270.07
June 16, 1900, amount allotted for third emplacement	4,840.00
	5,110.07
June 30, 1901, amount expended during fiscal year	4,816.57
July 1, 1901, balance unexpended and available	293.50

Battery commander's station.

July 1, 1900, balance unexpended	$156.40
June 30, 1901, amount expended during fiscal year	156.40

APPENDIX 3—FORTIFICATIONS. 901

TORPEDOES FOR HARBOR DEFENSE.

Mining casemate, Site No. 1.

July 1, 1900, balance unexpended	$119.16
June 30, 1901, amount expended during fiscal year	119.16

PRESERVATION AND REPAIR OF FORTIFICATIONS.

Storing and caring for submarine-mining materials, prevention of dampness in magazines, and for care of electric-light plants.

July 1, 1900, balance unexpended		$1,120.76
May 10, 1901, allotted for fiscal year 1902		480.00
Deposited account of difference sheet No. 42		3.12
		1,603.88
June 30, 1901, amount expended during fiscal year	$792.98	
June 29, 1901, unexpended balance deposited to the credit of the Treasurer United States	74.20	
		867.18
July 1, 1901, balance unexpended		736.70
July 1, 1901, outstanding liabilities		10.00
July 1, 1901, balance unexpended and available		726.70

SUPPLIES FOR SEACOAST DEFENSES.

June 7, 1900, amount allotted	$800.00
June 30, 1901, amount expended during fiscal year	335.16
July 1, 1901, balance unexpended and available	464.84

3 X.

DEFENSES OF PUGET SOUND, WASHINGTON.

Officers in charge, Capt. Harry Taylor, Corps of Engineers, until November 30, 1900, and Maj. John Millis, Corps of Engineers, since that date; assistant, Lieut. Meriwether L. Walker, Corps of Engineers, till January 19, 1901; Division Engineers, Col. Samuel M. Mansfield, Corps of Engineers, until November 30, 1900, and Col. Jared A. Smith, Corps of Engineers, since December 15, 1901.

Emplacements for five 10-inch and two 12-inch guns on nondisappearing carriages.—At the beginning of the year these emplacements were practically completed, except the electric-light plant and the final grading and seeding of the superior slope.

During the year the superior slope was graded and seeded, and roads and paths in the rear of the battery were nearly completed. The mounting of all guns and carriages except one 12-inch gun and carriage was completed, and the guns and carriages were cleaned and painted. The carriage for one 12-inch gun has not been received. The gun is on hand. Three special ammunition trucks were constructed.

Emplacements for four 10-inch guns on disappearing carriages.—At the beginning of the year these emplacements had been practically completed, except the electric-light plant, and the guns had been mounted. During the year the superior slope was filled out with excavated material taken from the neighboring emplacements and seeded. All the guns were fired with service charges. No defects were developed.

Emplacements for three 10-inch guns on disappearing carriages.— These had not been commenced at the beginning of the year. During the year excavation for foundation of these emplacements was completed. Drains were laid, preparations for constructing concrete forms completed, and concrete plant was prepared for construction work.

*Emplacements for two 12-inch and four 10-inch guns on nondisappearing carriages.—*At the beginning of the year these emplacements had been practically completed, except the traverses in rear and the electric-light plant. All the guns had been mounted except one 10-inch.

During the year the traverses were nearly completed, the superior slope was trimmed and seeded, fixtures were placed in several of the battery rooms, and fitting up latrines was partly completed. The remaining 10-inch gun was mounted, and all the 10-inch guns were fired with service charges. No defects were developed. The 12-inch guns had previously been tested in the same manner.

*Mortar Battery No. 1.—*At the beginning of the year this battery was practically completed, except lighting plant, and the mortars had been mounted. During the year the slopes were regraded and seeded, road in front of the battery completed, and some minor repairs were made. One mortar in each pit was fired with service charge. No defects were developed.

*Mortar Battery No. 2.—*At the beginning of the year this battery had been practically completed, except the electric-light plant. During the year 16 mortars and carriages were mounted and partly cleaned and painted. The slopes are to be filled in places, trimmed, and seeded.

*Mortar Battery No. 3.—*At the beginning of the year this battery had not been commenced. It is to have two pits for four mortars each.

During the year the site was cleared and grubbed and excavation done by contract. Construction work is in progress by hired labor. Drains have been placed, concrete floors laid and ready for placing concrete forms. Plant for concrete work is nearly ready.

Mortar carriages for this battery have been received.

*Emplacements for three 8-inch guns on disappearing carriages.—*At the beginning of the year the site for this battery had been cleared, excavation partly made, and the construction plant partly prepared.

During the year the battery was constructed and nearly finished. Three guns were received; the carriages have not yet arrived.

*Emplacements for two 6-inch rapid-fire guns.—*Plans and estimates for these emplacements are in course of preparation.

Emplacements for 5-inch rapid-fire guns on balanced-pillar mounts.— There are two emplacements at each of Sites 1, 2, and 4. At the beginning of the year the emplacements at two of the sites had been practically completed. During the year the emplacements at the third site were finished. The cylinders have been set at all the sites and the top carriages are in place at three of the emplacements. The lighting plant is yet to be installed at each site.

*Emplacements for three 5-inch rapid-fire guns, mounts not determined.—*At the beginning of the year some material was on hand, but no work had been done. During the year emplacements for two of the guns, the only ones for which allotment has yet been made, were completed as far as they can be till questions as to type of gun and design of mount are settled.

Emplacements for two 15-pounder rapid-fire guns.—At the beginning of the year some material had been procured, but no construction work had been done. During the year the battery was partly constructed, something over half the concrete being in place.

Emplacements for four 15-pounder rapid-fire guns.—At the beginning of the year nothing had been done on this battery. During the year excavation was made, drainage system was laid, plant prepared, and the work is now ready for laying concrete as soon as rails and ties are procured for completing the railroad.

Emplacements for two 15-pounder rapid-fire guns.—At the beginning of the year some material had been procured, but no construction work had been done. During the year excavation was completed, the drainage system was laid, and plant was prepared, and the work is now ready for laying concrete.

Storehouse for torpedo material.—The building was practically completed, except heating and lighting plant, and the material on hand was moved into it.

Money statements.

GUN AND MORTAR BATTERIES.

Emplacements for five 10-inch and two 12-inch guns on nondisappearing carriages.

July 1, 1900, balance unexpended		$11,433.27
June 30, 1901, amount expended during fiscal year	$10,682.85	
Deposited to credit Treasurer, United States	3.23	
		10,686.08
July 1, 1901, balance unexpended		747.19
July 1, 1901, outstanding liabilities		716.42
July 1, 1901, balance available		30.77

Emplacements for three 10-inch guns on disappearing carriages.

June 30, 1901, amount allotted during year	$102,700.00
June 30, 1901, amount expended during fiscal year	31,519.77
July 1, 1901, balance unexpended	71,180.23
July 1, 1901, outstanding liabilities	6,961.32
July 1, 1901, balance available	64,218.91

NOTE.—Allotment made for two emplacements only.

Mortar Battery No. 1.

June 30, 1901, amount allotted during year	$6,000.00
July 1, 1901, balance unexpended and available	6,000.00

Mortar Battery No. 2.

July 1, 1900, balance unexpended	$2,959.13
Allotted since	6,300.00
	9,259.13
June 30, 1901, amount expended during fiscal year	2,959.88
July 1, 1901, balance unexpended and available	6,299.25

Mortar Battery No. 3.

June 30, 1901, amount allotted during year	$91,000.00
June 30, 1901, amount expended during fiscal year	38,585.85
July 1, 1901, balance unexpended	52,414.15
July 1, 1901, outstanding liabilities	11,530.75
July 1, 1901, balance available	40,883.40

Emplacements for three 8-inch guns on disappearing carriages.

July 1, 1900, balance unexpended	$59,700.73
Allotted since	15,000.00
	74,700.73
June 30, 1901, amount expended during fiscal year	72,572.31
July 1, 1901, balance unexpended	2,128.42
July 1, 1901, outstanding liabilities	1,783.24
July 1, 1901, balance available	345.18

Emplacements for two 6-inch rapid-fire guns.

June 30, 1901, amount allotted during year	$30,000.00
July 1, 1901, balance unexpended and available	30,000.00

Emplacements for 5-inch rapid-fire guns on balanced-pillar mounts.

Site 1:

July 1, 1900, balance unexpended	$3,929.10
June 30, 1901, amount expended during fiscal year	3,929.10

Site 3:

July 1, 1900, balance unexpended	3,849.18
June 30, 1901, amount expended during fiscal year	2,572.94
July 1, 1901, balance unexpended	1,276.24
July 1, 1901, outstanding liabilities	133.49
July 1, 1901, balance available	1,142.75

Site 4:

July 1, 1900, balance unexpended	483.93
June 30, 1901, amount expended during fiscal year	483.93

Emplacements for three 5-inch rapid-fire guns (mounts not determined).

July 1, 1900, balance unexpended	$15,372.44
Allotted since	3,200.00
	18,572.44
June 30, 1901, amount expended during fiscal year	9,147.00
July 1, 1901, balance unexpended	9,425.44
July 1, 1901, outstanding liabilities	2,286.45
July 1, 1901, balance available	7,138.99

NOTE.—Allotment made for two emplacements only.

Emplacements for two 15-pounder rapid-fire guns.

July 1, 1900, balance unexpended	$8,312.16
Allotted since	1,700.00
	10,012.16
June 30, 1901, amount expended during fiscal year	6,803.16
July 1, 1901, balance unexpended	3,209.00
July 1, 1901, outstanding liabilities	1,010.71
July 1, 1901, balance available	2,198.29

June 30, 1901, amount expended during fiscal year.....................	9,515.45
July 1, 1901, balance unexpended...	11,184.55
July 1, 1901, outstanding liabilities.......................................	2,522.84
July 1, 1901, balance available..	8,661.71

Emplacements for two 15-pounder rapid-fire guns.

July 1, 1900, balance unexpended...	$8,312.16
June 30, 1901, amount expended during fiscal year.....................	5,288.52
July 1, 1901, balance unexpended...	3,023.64
July 1, 1901, outstanding liabilities.......................................	1,077.38
July 1, 1901, balance available..	1,946.26

TORPEDOES FOR HARBOR DEFENSE.

Storehouse for torpedo material.

July 1, 1900, balance unexpended...	$6,423.1'
June 30, 1901, amount expended during fiscal year.....................	6,423.'

Fire and battery commanders' stations.—Contract was made for t construction and erection of two fire commanders' stations and ‹ battery commander's station. The erection of these at the site has yet been commenced.

Plans were prepared for one fire commander's station and on‹ tery commander's station in addition.

Money statements.

FIRE COMMANDER'S STATION, SITE 1.

July 1, 1900, balance unexpended..
June 30, 1901, amount expended during fiscal year.....................

July 1, 1901, balance unexpended..
July 1, 1901, amount covered by uncompleted contracts..............

July 1, 1901, balance available..

FIRE COMMANDER'S STATION, SITES 2 AND 3.

July 1, 1900, balance unexpended.................................
July 1, 1901, balance unexpended and available................

FIRE COMMANDER'S STATION, SITE 4.

July 1, 1900, balance unexpended.............................
June 30, 1901, amount expended during fiscal year..........

July 1, 1901, balance unexpended..........................
July 1, 1901, outstanding liabilities........................
July 1, 1901, amount covered by uncompleted contracts..

July 1, 1901, balance available..........................

BATTERY COMMANDER'S STATION, S

June 30, 1901, amount allotted during year.........
July 1, 1901, balance unexpended and available....

906 REPORT OF THE CHIEF OF ENGINEERS, U. S. ARMY.

BATTERY COMMANDERS' STATIONS, SITE 4.

June 30, 1901, amount allotted during year		$10,200.00
June 30, 1901, amount expended during fiscal year		87.45
July 1, 1901, balance unexpended		10,112.55
July 1, 1901, outstanding liabilities	$3.50	
July 1, 1901, amount covered by uncompleted contracts	5,150.00	
		5,153.50
July 1, 1901, balance available		4,959.05

Special allotments for auxiliary work.—Work under several special allotments has been in progress during the year. In each case the work has either been completed or well advanced. The allotments required to aid the purposes for which they were made, with money statements, are as follows:

Road betterment at Site No. 4.—Allotment of June 11, 1900, act of July 7, 1898, for road betterment, for retrimming and regrading slopes, and for planting a windbreak at batteries, $5,000.

Money statement.

July 1, 1900, balance unexpended	$5,000.00
June 30, 1901, amount expended during fiscal year	4,782.36
July 1, 1901, balance unexpended	217.64
July 1, 1901, outstanding liabilities	143.75
July 1, 1901, balance available	73.89

Improvements near Site No. 4.—Allotment of June 18, 1900, act of July 7, 1898, for clearing, grubbing, grading, and seeding, $2,934.

Money statement.

July 1, 1900, balance unexpended	$2,934.00
June 30, 1901, amount expended during fiscal year	2,934.00

Latrines and water-supply system at Site No. 4.—Allotment of March 20, 1901, act of March 1, 1901, for latrines and water-supply system, $3,200.

Money statement.

June 30, 1901, amount allotted during year	$3,200.00
June 30, 1901, amount expended during fiscal year	1,440.73
July 1, 1901, balance unexpended	1,759.27
July 1, 1901, outstanding liabilities	604.52
July 1, 1901, balance available	1,154.75

Grading and road construction at Site No. 1.—Allotment of January 9, 1901, act of May 25, 1900, for grading and road construction, $6,350.

Money statement.

June 30, 1901, amount allotted during year	$6,350.00
June 30, 1901, amount expended during fiscal year	5,129.45
July 1, 1901, balance unexpended	1,220.55
July 1, 1901, outstanding liabilities	965.35
July 1, 1901, balance available	255.20

Road construction at Mortar Battery No. 2.—Allotment of June 11, 1900, act of July 7, 1898, for road construction and for retrimming and regrading slopes, $3,700.

Money statement.

July 1, 1900, balance unexpended	$3,700.00
June 30, 1901, amount expended during fiscal year	2,477.55
July 1, 1901, balance unexpended	1,222.45
July 1, 1901, outstanding liabilities	20.00
July 1, 1901, balance available	1,202.45

Preservation and repair of fortifications.—Allotment of June 9, 1900, act of May 25, 1900, for preservation and repair at Site No. 4, $2,200.

Money statement.

July 1, 1900, balance unexpended	$2,200.00
June 30, 1901, amount expended during fiscal year	1,719.43
July 1, 1901, balance unexpended	480.57
July 1, 1901, outstanding liabilities	116.23
July 1, 1901, balance available	364.34

Allotment of June 9, 1900, act of May 25, 1900, for preservation and repair at Site No. 2, $1,300.

Money statement.

July 1, 1900, balance unexpended	$1,300.00
June 30, 1901, amount expended during fiscal year	876.90
July 1, 1901, balance unexpended and available	423.10

Allotment of June 9, 1900, act of May 25, 1900, for care of torpedo material, $1,000.

Money statement.

July 1, 1900, balance unexpended	$1,000.00
June 30, 1901, amount expended during fiscal year	1,000.00

New light-house station at Admiralty Head, Washington.—The act of March 3, 1899, making appropriation for fortifications, authorized an expenditure of not to exceed $8,000 from the funds appropriated by that act for moving or reconstructing the light-house station at Admiralty Head, Washington. The old light-house being unfit for moving, plans and specifications for a new station were prepared by the Light-House Department. These plans and specifications were turned over to the Engineer Department and the work was advertised. The lowest bid received was in excess of the appropriation. Nothing further has been done in the matter by this office.

Money statement.

July 1, 1900, balance unexpended	$8,000.00
June 30, 1901, amount expended during fiscal year	73.08
July, 1, 1901, balance unexpended and available	7,926.92

Supplies for seacoast defenses.—Under authority of the act of May 25, 1900, an allotment was made for the purchase of approved supplies for the artillery garrisons. No requisitions were received before the end of the year.

Money statement.

July 1, 1900, balance unexpended	$500.00
July 1, 1901, balance unexpended and available	500.00

Transporting, mounting, and painting ordnance at Site No. 1.—At the beginning of the fiscal year four 10-inch gun carriages, one 12-inch altered gun-lift carriage, and eight 12-inch mortar carriages were mounted. One 10-inch B. L. rifle, sixteen 12-inch B. L. mortars, and four 12-inch mortar carriages were on the beach.

During the fiscal year four 10-inch and two 12-inch B. L. rifles, one 10-inch gun carriage, four 12-inch mortar carriages, and two 5-inch rapid-fire gun carriages were received. One 10-inch gun carriage, four 12-inch mortar carriages, two 5-inch rapid-fire gun carriages, four 10-inch and two 12-inch B. L. rifles, and sixteen 12-inch B. L. mortars were moved from the beach to their emplacements.

One 10-inch gun carriage, twelve 12-inch mortar carriages, two 5-inch rapid-fire gun carriages, five 10-inch and one 12-inch B. L. rifle, and sixteen 12-inch B. L. mortars were mounted.

Five 10-inch rifles and carriages, one 12-inch rifle and carriage, sixteen 12-inch mortars, and eight 12-inch mortar carriages were cleaned, scraped, and painted.

Money statement.

July 1, 1900, balance unexpended	$3,746.01
Allotted since	2,725.00
	6,471.01
June 30, 1901, amount expended during fiscal year	5,964.41
July 1, 1901, balance unexpended	506.60
July 1, 1901, outstanding liabilities	391.55
July 1, 1901, balance available	115.05

Contracts in force during fiscal year.

SAND AND GRAVEL.

Name of contractor: Pacific Bridge Company.
Date of contract: October 31, 1899.
Date of approval: November 16, 1899.
Date of commencement: November 1, 1899.
Contract completed: December 31, 1900.

CONSTRUCTION OF TORPEDO STOREHOUSE.

Name of contractor: M. J. Carkeek.
Date of contract: March 19, 1900.
Date of approval: March 31, 1900.
Date of commencement: April 19, 1900.
Date of completion: August 19, 1900.
Time for completion extended to October 19, 1900.
Contract completed: October 16, 1900.

APPENDIX 3—FORTIFICATIONS.

CLEARING AND EXCAVATING FOR THREE 8-INCH GUNS ON DISAPPEARING CARRIAGES.

Name of contractor: W. F. Nelson.
Date of contract: April 9, 1900.
Date of approval: April 19, 1900.
Date of commencement: May 3, 1900.
Date of completion: August 3, 1900.
Time for completion extended to September 3, 1900.
Contract completed August 29, 1900.

CLEARING AND EXCAVATING FOR MORTAR BATTERY NO. 3.

Name of contractor: Hale & Smith.
Date of contract: January 3, 1901.
Date of approval: January 23, 1901.
Date of commencement: February 6, 1901.
Contract completed April 30, 1901.

OBSERVATION TOWERS FOR FIRE AND BATTERY COMMANDERS' STATIONS AT SITES NOS. 1 AND 4.

Name of contractor: New Jersey Foundry and Machine Company.
Date of contract: February 14, 1901.
Date of approval: March 19, 1901.
Date of commencement: June 25, 1901.
Date of completion: October 25, 1901.

3 Y.

DEFENSES OF SAN JUAN, PORTO RICO.

Officers in charge, Capt. William V. Judson, Corps of Engineers, until August 6, 1900, and Capt. Clement A. F. Flagler, Corps of Engineers, since October 19, 1900.

Range-finder station.—Owing to the desire of the artillery garrison of the defenses of San Juan, plans were prepared for the conversion of an existent semaphore tower on El Morro into a practice station for a type A range finder. Plans and estimates were prepared for the work, and $1,000 was allotted by the Chief of Engineers therefor. No work has as yet been done thereon.

Money statement.

GUN AND MORTAR BATTERIES.

June 30, 1901, amount allotted during fiscal year	$1,000.00
July 1, 1901, balance unexpended and available	1,000.00

Preservation and repair of fortifications.—This work was not begun until June 16, 1901, and during the remainder of the month slight repairs were made on the masonry work of El Morro.

Money statement.

June 30, 1901, amount allotted during the fiscal year	$1,600.00
July 1, 1901, outstanding liabilities	135.80
July 1, 1901, balance available	1,464.20

Road construction and miscellaneous work.—As Engineer officer of the Department of the East and of Porto Rico, the officer in charge superintended the construction of an extensive amount of road work in the island of Porto Rico, which is reported in full to the commanding general, Department of the East. Other department work consisted in the supervision of route sketches on practice marches and issuance of instruments and materials therefor, investigation of land titles, preparation of reports on defenses, furnishing of maps, etc. Money statements of operations relating to the above are as follows:

Money statements.

CIVILIAN ASSISTANTS TO ENGINEER OFFICERS, 1901.

June 30, 1901, allotted during fiscal year		$3,500.00
June 30, 1901, amount expended during fiscal year	$2,922.16	
July 1, 1901, reverted to United States Treasury	577.84	
		3,500.00

EQUIPMENT OF ENGINEER TROOPS, 1901.

June 30, 1901, amount allotted during the fiscal year	$500.00
July 1, 1901, balance unexpended	[1]500.00

[1] To be returned to the Treasury of the United States.

APPENDIX No. 4.

TECHNICAL DETAILS OF FORTIFICATION WORK.

4 A.

DEFENSES OF THE COAST OF MAINE.

[Officer in charge, Maj. S. W. Roessler, Corps of Engineers.]

Reference will here be made to certain engineering features that have characterized the fortification work in this district during the year. The methods outlined apply generally to all work now in progress.

Concrete.—Owing to the present low cost of domestic Portland cement ($1.58 per barrel delivered in Portland) it is being used exclusively, no natural cement having been purchased this season. Outside of the question of cost, however, the use of Portland cement, except in the heart of large masses, is advisable in this climate, owing to the wide range of temperature.

Concrete is being made wetter than formerly. It is conveyed from mixer to its position in the work in water-tight buckets or skips, so that none of the cement is wasted. Wet concrete is believed to possess advantages over dry concrete. It can be compacted at greatly reduced cost for ramming, it makes a more impervious mass, and one batch blends into the preceding one, thereby avoiding the horizontal seams that characterize work that is put in dry.

The proportions of the different ingredients used vary in accordance with the strength and density desired.

For all walls and masses not exposed to direct fire 1:4:8 concrete is used.

For walls and masses exposed to fire 1:3:6 concrete is used.

For the mass lying immediately over rooms and passages and below the moisture-proof course, where density or its equivalent imperviousness is desired, 1:3:5 concrete is used.

Where inequalities in the ledge make it necessary to carry parts of the foundations to considerable depths, the lower portions are made of 1:5:10 concrete.

Waterproofing.—The means used to prevent the infiltration of moisture into the rooms are practically in duplicate.

By the use of soap and alum in the mortar facing of both vertical and horizontal surfaces that are exposed to the weather, the building of positive slopes and generous gutters on all nearly horizontal surfaces, and the use of P. and B. paint or tar paper and pitch on the vertical surfaces abutting against the sand fill, the attempt is made to exclude all moisture from the concrete. To intercept, however, any water that may penetrate the concrete, a waterproof layer is placed in the concrete mass over all rooms and passages. This layer is crowned at one or more points, and the slopes lead to the surrounding air spaces.

In preparing the soap and alum mixture, 1 pound of soap is used to 100 pounds of water and 1 pound of alum to 100 pounds of cement.

The P. and B. paint is a commercial article, and as applied here costs in place 20 cents per square yard.

The tar paper and coal-tar pitch referred to are applied in alternate layers, and form a cheap and apparently durable waterproofing for vertical masonry surfaces abutting earth or sand fill.

The main waterproof layer immediately above rooms and passages has heretofore consisted of asphalt mastic one-half and three-fourths of an inch thick. When the latter thickness was used it was placed in two layers, each three-eighths of an inch thick.

It was mixed in the following proportions:

12 blocks crude asphalt (Seyssel or Newchatel.)
50 pounds refined asphalt.
4 to 6 pails coarse, clean sand.
5 pounds maltha or mineral tar.

Its cost, three-fourths of an inch thick, varied from $1.50 to $1.60 per square yard.

In future it is proposed to substitute for this a coating made up of three or more layers of asbestus felt, laid shingle fashion and united to each other and to the concrete by asphaltic cement.

This will be cheaper, less liable to crack, and, it is thought, equally durable in other respects.

Air spaces.—All the large emplacements (6-inch or greater) now under construction are being built with wide air spaces, 18 inches to 24 inches, separating the rooms from the parapet and gun platforms. The use of an air space limits the area of the waterproof layer in the concrete and reduces condensation. The wide air space costs but little more than the narrow one and possesses the following advantages over the latter:

(1) It is accessible.
(2) It facilitates ventilation. Rooms can be connected with the air space and the air space readily ventilated by flues without danger to the magazines.
(3) It facilitates drainage. This is more or less a local advantage. Rocky sites make underground drainage very expensive, and surface drainage to the roadway in rear is objectionable, owing to the length and severity of the winters. The bottom of the air space forms a gutter and receives the drainage of all the rooms. At suitable points the collected water is led away in pipes.

Floor drains.—All floors are drained to the sides of the rooms or passages. Gutters are constructed along the walls, and the low points are so placed that any water collected will pass to the air space by the most direct route.

Condensation.—The large air space around the rooms reduces the condensation materially, but does not entirely free the rooms at all seasons of the year. To further remedy this evil, all interior walls are being lined with porous hollow terra-cotta tiling 2 inches thick, placed at the time the concrete is placed. The tiling is placed loosely against the forms and the concrete rammed against the tiling. This tiling will subsequently be plastered with a lime-and-cement plaster to give it a neat finish. The ceilings are being formed by the use of arched corrugated iron between the flanges of the beams and a layer of plastered metal lath attached to the lower flanges.

Stairways.—Stairways with steel stringers and oak treads are being constructed, as cheaper than concrete steps and more serviceable in winter weather than all-steel stairways.

4 B.

DEFENSES OF BOSTON HARBOR, MASSACHUSETTS.

[Officers in charge, Col. Charles R. Suter, Corps of Engineers, and Capt. Harry Taylor, Corps of Engineers.]

SITE NO. 1.

Ammunition cranes.—The parade wall, which forms the rear of the battery of 12-inch rifles, is of cut granite and about 24 feet in height. An extra stiff crane was required to avoid the springing always found in the davit form of crane when the cross section of the mast is circular. It consists of a steel davit of I-beam section with a cast-iron gudgeon and bushing, resting in a cast-iron step and a wrought-iron collar securely bolted to the face of the parade wall. The weight of this crane is less than that of the ordinary form, while the strength and rigidity are greater and the cost is less than one-half.

SITE NO. 5.

Quicksand.—Quicksand was found in the eastern end of the excavation for the mortar battery, forming a very unstable foundation. Ordinary drains were found to permit the sand to escape with the water. A large well was therefore dug near at hand which drained the surrounding ground. When drained the sand became firm and hard.

The water thus secured is the best obtainable at present for the use in the power-plant boiler soon to be installed, and for this reason the drains have been kept separate from the main drainage system, and the well above referred to will be made permanent and provided with an overflow to prevent the rise of the water to a troublesome level.

Concrete.—Stone dust from the crusher is being used in the concrete instead of sand. This dust contains a smaller percentage of voids than sand, and a mixture of 1 part cement to 5 parts dust forms a much stronger mortar than 1 part cement to 3 parts sand. A series of tests is now being made, but will not be completed in time to accompany this report. The stone used in the concrete is crushed granite taken just as it comes from the crusher after passing over a ¼-inch sieve and through a 1½-inch sieve. The concrete is mixed as wet as it can be handled, and the proportion of stone to mortar is regulated so that the upper surface of the stone stands an inch or two above the surface of the nearly liquid mortar when the concrete is placed. The upper surface of the work appears to be of very poor concrete, but the successive batches of concrete supply mortar to the voids below and a perfect bond is secured. Constant care is necessary to keep the relative levels of stone and mortar correct, the amount of stone being varied as required. Concrete so laid has been found, by cutting, to be solid, and all the recent works so constructed have proved waterproof.

Horizontal cracks between successive layers of concrete have not developed in any work of this character, but are extremely common and well marked in work where a greater proportion of mortar was used.

Statement of cost of constructing two 5-inch rapid-fire gun emplacements.

Excavation and fill (2,500 cubic yards excavation; 2,200 cubic yards fill; trenching for walls, drains, conduit, and water supply included):			
Labor		$2,273.14	
Engine supplies		40.00	
			$2,313.14
Concrete (1,000 cubic yards):			
Mixing and placing (by hand)—			
Labor	$2,463.83		
Materials	3,817.03		
Engine supplies	88.00		
		$6,368.86	
Finishing surfaces (500 square yards)—			
Labor	$288.54		
Materials (for joints only)	13.80		
		302.34	
Waterproofing (350 square yards; 2 coats P. and B. paint)—			
Labor	$14.20		
Materials	93.60		
		107.80	
Whitewashing (475 square yards; 2 coats)—			
Labor	$23.30		
Materials	1.90		
		25.20	
Forms:			
Labor	$1,780.77		
Materials (much old lumber used)	260.15		
		2,040.92	
			8,845.12
Beams and columns:			
Labor		$145.16	
Transportation (hire)		33.25	
Materials (old railroad iron used to great extent)		130.90	
			309.31
Anchor bolts:			
Labor		$24.93	
Materials		190.00	
			214.93
Ring bolts:			
Material			11.50
Doors (6 single and 2 double doors):			
Labor		$311.56	
Materials		151.71	
Fittings		189.64	
			652.91
Two fireplaces and grates:			
Labor		$21.00	
Materials and grates		46.96	
			67.96

APPENDIX 4—TECHNICAL DETAILS, FORTIFICATION WORK.

Electric lighting and speaking tubes (including 120 feet 2-duct conduit and manhole):		
Labor	$379.81	
Materials, speaking tubes	23.50	
Materials, electric lighting	116.84	
		$520.15
Railings (90 feet 1¼-inch iron pipe):		
Labor	$68.79	
Materials	43.52	
		112.31
Two lifts:		
Labor	$92.10	
Lifts	670.00	
		762.10
Drainage (240 feet main drainage, 220 feet tile drains, 90 cubic yards of dry walls):		
Labor	$646.51	
Materials	144.20	
		790.71
Ventilation (about 70 feet 8-inch drain pipe, 8 iron plates, perforated):		
Labor	$13.15	
Materials	17.20	
		30.35
Permanent water supply (140 feet 2-inch iron pipe, 30 feet 1-inch iron pipe, 2 hydrants):		
Labor	$12.79	
Materials	92.09	
		104.88
Sodding and seeding (550 square yards sodding, about 600 square yards seeding):		
Labor	$260.82	
Material	2.55	
		263.37
Building road (1,300 feet, 16 feet wide):		
Grading, hauling gravel, and rolling—		
Labor	$2,657.28	
Materials (beach gravel used)	0.00	
	$2,657.28	
Gutters (2,500 feet, 2 feet wide, 9 inches deep, 10 manholes, and about 275 feet 10-inch drains)—		
Labor	$413.15	
Materials (beach stone used)	0.00	
	413.15	
		3,070.43
Plant:		
Transfer from other works, purchase, erection, and repair—		
Labor	$2,183.68	
Purchases:		
New plant	$63.25	
Replacements	263.58	
Repair	62.25	
Erection	20.00	
	409.08	
Transportation, hire of	339.50	
		2,932.26
Transportation (men, materials, and plant):		
Services	$823.67	
Repairs	76.00	
Supplies	145.47	
		1,045.14
Superintendence (services)		696.38
Office expenses and contingencies:		
Services	$859.30	
Rents and supplies	197.75	
		1,057.05
Total		23,800.00

SITE NO. 7.

Concrete.—The character of the concrete work was similar to that described above for Site No. 5, except that sand from the neighborhood of the works was generally used instead of crusher dust.

Fifteen-pounder emplacements.—These emplacements are designed to obviate the use of lifts, the ammunition being passed by hand to the gun platform. The guns are separated by an earth traverse which also affords overhead cover to the magazine. The guardrooms are provided with open fireplaces, as are all the living rooms of the batteries now being constructed in this district.

Traverses.—Traverses have been provided for in all recently designed batteries, except where an all-around fire is required. It has been observed that those batteries which are constructed with traverses are less conspicuous than those without them, except when the background against which the battery is seen is the sky.

The use of traverses has made it possible in the emplacements for 6-inch and 10-inch rifles on disappearing carriages to raise the magazine floors nearly or quite to the level of the loading platforms, thus permitting the ammunition to be handled by trolleys and trucks without the use of lifts.

Statement of cost of constructing two 15-pounder rapid-fire gun emplacements.

Concrete, 660 cubic yards (sand obtained on island)	$2,892.90
Forms	999.36
Excavation, 100 cubic yards	32.00
Fill, 1,555 cubic yards	1,277.77
Doors	435.00
Drainage	292.06
Steel beams	100.00
Railroad	62.40
Installing plant	300.00
Superintendence, office, and engineering expenses	3,498.91
Coal	375.57
Transportation (hire of)	273.00
Contingencies	1,461.03
Total	12,000.00

Statement of cost of partial construction of one 15-pounder rapid-fire gun emplacement to June 30, 1901.

Excavation, 50 cubic yards	$15.00
Drains	61.68
Concrete, 400 cubic yards	1,632.21
Forms	591.74
Installing plant	200.00
Beams	50.00
Contingencies	228.13
Total	2,778.76

VENTILATION AND CONDENSATION.

Ventilators are provided for each room in the batteries. Electric fans or blowers are in use in some works, but it is believed that natural ventilation is far preferable. Air should be exhausted from rooms and not forced in. In the latter case condensation is apt to take place.

Natural ventilation is secured by two ventilators placed as far apart as possible. The external openings should face in different directions if practicable. The movements of the external atmosphere will then affect the pressure in the ventilator flues differently and a gentle circulation will be set up. This result has been obtained to a highly satisfactory degree in recent works.

Careful observation of the action of different rooms in all kinds of weather indicate that the problem of condensation is not at all complex. If air be admitted to a room the temperature of whose walls is below the dew-point of the external air, condensation will take place. If the temperature of the walls is above this dew-point evaporation is to be expected. It is therefore apparent that ventilation should be controlled, and in hot, humid weather should be entirely prevented. The following observations have been made:

1. Rooms without ventilation: Damp and moldy at all times.
2. Rooms with free ventilation: Dry in cool weather and extremely wet in hot, humid weather.
3. Open passages: Dry in cool weather; temporarily wet at beginning of hot spells; dry after walls have become warm.
4. Rooms ordinarily ventilated, but closed during hot spells: Dry. In such rooms, thrown wide open on a hot day, beads of moisture may be seen to form upon the ceiling.
5. Rooms left open: Same as No. 2 above, only to a greater degree.

Air spaces in the walls of rooms appear to have no effect whatever upon the condensation.

It is believed that condensation can be entirely prevented by an intelligent use of ventilation. But the use of batteries requires them to be thrown wide open at times in hot, damp weather. Under such conditions condensation will be rapid. To lessen the effects of this, two provisions are now being made in this district. A narrow gutter is placed around each room at the foot of the wall and the highest point of the floor is at the center of the room. Thus all moisture on the wall is prevented from crossing the floor to the drain. Walls are also being faced with an absorbent brick which is not to be painted. Observation shows that in all cases where concrete, stone, metal, painted wood, or painted brick condense moisture freely and retain beads of water on their surfaces to drop at intervals on the floor, unpainted brick remains apparently dry, owing to the fact that it absorbs the condensed moisture. Such a wall will readily absorb more than a pint to each square foot of surface. A room so lined will therefore remain dry during any ordinary period of use.

4 C.

DEFENSES OF NEW YORK HARBOR.

[Officer in charge, Maj. W. L. Marshall, Corps of Engineers.]

In the construction of the fortifications at the eastern and southern entrances to New York Harbor, the methods employed in waterproofing of magazines and other rooms at emplacements, in whitening of interior walls, and in preventing the drifting of sand, are, perhaps, worthy of notice.

Waterproofing.—Various means were used in the endeavor to stop leaks in older constructions. Cracks were filled with grout; with linseed oil; with linseed oil, soap, alum, and cement; with melted sulphur; with asphaltic cement; and washes of soft soap and water followed by alum solutions were applied to surfaces of mortar and concrete—all with but limited and temporary success. The old emplacements are nearly incurable by such means.

In the construction of new batteries and emplacements great care has been taken in waterproofing, and the success attained seems so far nearly perfect. Leaks certainly may be prevented by care. The problem of preventing condensation of moisture in the air at surfaces of rooms is more costly to solve, but much simpler—a question of heat and cold.

The waterproofing of one of the new 12-inch emplacements may be taken as typical of the method of waterproofing more or less followed in all such works in this district.

The materials used were:

Asbestus roofing felt, Neptune brand, in rolls of 108 square feet, covering, when laid with overlaps and joints, 100 square feet, costing in New York, 82 cents per roll.

Asphaltic roof coating, costing in New York 32 cents per gallon, 1 gallon of which covers about 3 square yards of waterproofing (5 coats of paint).

Roofing cement, costing 5 cents per pound.

Soft soap, costing 1⅜ cents per pound, and pulverized alum, costing 3¼ cents per pound.

Roofing felt, roof coating, and roofing cement were obtained from the H. W. Johns Manufacturing Company.

The roofing felt was used on horizontal or slightly inclined surfaces. The soap-and-alum (Sylvester) process was used in "waterproof mortar" and applied to both horizontal and exposed vertical surfaces.

This mortar was made by taking one part cement and two and one-half parts sand and adding thereto three-fourths of a pound of pulverized alum (dry) to each cubic foot of sand, all of which was first mixed dry, then the proper amount of water—in which had been dissolved about three-fourths of a pound of soft soap to the gallon of water—was added and the mixing thoroughly completed.

The mixture is little inferior in strength to ordinary mortar of the same proportions and is impervious to water, and is also useful in preventing efflorescence. The alum is in excess for the reason that it coagulates other things than soap that may come to it.

The waterproofing scheme includes—

1. Porous tile facing between the concrete walls and earth parapets and embankments, with drains.

2. Air spaces 6 inches wide about all the interior of rooms of emplacements, with drains.

3. A system of intercepting surface drains, and drain pipes connected therewith, all as shown on typical plans.

4. Waterproofed surfaces as herein explained. These consist of—

(a) A composite waterproof course immediately above the roofs of all rooms of the emplacements.

(b) A second composite waterproof course immediately beneath the pavements of the superior slopes of the emplacements and 2 feet below the surfaces.

(c) Simple waterproof facing of all vertical surfaces exposed directly to rain, to guard against capillary action and percolation of moisture.

No waterproofing of floors of this battery nor of side walls of rooms not directly exposed to rain was placed.

The battery is on a moderately high location and is thoroughly sub-drained. Nevertheless some dampness of floors and bases of side walls by capillary action indicate that damp proofing of floors and walls would have had some justification. No water appears, but dampness is shown by slight discoloration of the walls and floor of at least one of the rooms for about 2 feet from the angle between them after heavy rains.

All rooms are absolutely free from leaks except the lobby, which, due to an error in not extending the waterproof course to the rear face of the gun platform, shows some leaks on the inside angle of rear wall of no material importance.

Instructions for laying felt waterproofing.—After laying ceiling beams, cover air spaces with brick, leaving one-fourth inch openings; fill in with concrete until the concrete is well above the beams; then form the surfaces so as to slope always toward the air spaces, carrying them over and beyond the air spaces or to drains and to the level of the top of air spaces or drains; finish all the surfaces as carefully as for sidewalks. The surfaces themselves should be well troweled or smoothed, and for one-half inch below them be made of waterproof "mortar" in a continuous sheet.

Begin at the lowest levels of the proposed surfaces to lay the asbestus felting, first well painting with roofing paint the surface to be covered with the first layer of roofing felt; then again paint with roofing paint the surface to be covered by the second course of roofing felt, including the overlap on the top of the first layer; then lay the second course of felt, exposing one-fourth the width of the lower layer along its lower edge. Continue in this manner, embedding each course in roofing paint and shingling the layers until the entire area is covered; then paint over the entire surface with roofing paint and let it dry. Then cover the area with a lean mortar, not less than 1 inch nor more than 1¼ inches thick, consisting of one part cement and 6 parts of coarse or "torpedo" sand, to form a porous protection to the felt, that will allow the passage of water stopped by it, while at the same time it will protect the felt against injury by projecting stones in the concrete above it. The concrete mass or pavement may then be laid over this porous layer. Under the pavements of the superior slopes and about 2 feet below the surface should be laid a similar waterproofing consisting in—

1. A layer of waterproof mortar with finished surface.
2. A waterproofing consisting in four courses of asbestus felt, shingled, each layer laid on and covered with a coat of roofing paint.
3. A layer of porous mortar to allow escape of water and to protect the felt.

At the 12-inch emplacement mentioned, in carrying up the concrete masses, all vertical walls exposed to rain or water were faced with an inch of waterproof mortar placed and rammed in position at the same time with the concrete backing, and the horizontal surfaces of all pavements and slopes were finished with a waterproof mortar.

All magazines and shell and shot rooms of batteries waterproofed as described are absolutely without leaks, and it is believed that the nature of the waterproofing will prevent the transmission or extension of all cracks to the rooms that are not accompanied by dislocation in level between the sides of the crack sufficient to shear or tear apart the waterproofing.

The cost of each complete course of felt waterproofing four layers thick, including all labor and materials, was 51 cents per square yard of surface covered.

One gallon of roofing paint completed 3 square yards of waterproofing.

Whitening of walls.—It is needless to say that walls painted white allow rooms to be more cheaply lighted than if painted with colors absorbent of light, but ordinary paints of linseed oil and white pigments are too costly, and therefore various cheap white paints have been tried. Various mixtures of whitewash, asbestus, cold-water paint, etc., have been tried, all of which either contain organic matter subject to decomposition, or in damp places mildew and spot. Ordinary whitewash rubs or scales off.

A mason employed on the work suggested for the purpose the use of lime and what he termed "painters' blue."

The mixture was experimented with, among other paints and washes, by Mr. John A. Yates, superintendent, and found to produce a white surface, adherent, and free from discoloration by fermentation, rot, or mildew, at a very low price.

Formula: Take 12 pounds unslaked lime, 1¼ to 2 ounces ultramarine blue in powder, slake the lime to the consistency of cream, mix in the paint powder, and apply to walls with a small brush, working well into the pores of the facing.

One coat of this mixture is generally sufficient.

Drifting sand.—The plans for constructing parapets for the protection of the dynamite-gun battery contemplated retaining walls to be a certain height, surcharged with the only material available, clean sand. In seeking a covering for preventing the shifting of this material under the influence of wind and rain, Capt. J. F. McIndoe, Corps of Engineers, suggested to me the employment of cinders, which is a waste product usually carried to sea and dumped.

A bargeload of the material was purchased at practically the cost of towing; some of the slopes and certain areas in the vicinity were covered with a layer of the material about four inches thick, the cinders being applied to the slopes wet, and afterwards compacted slightly by striking with a plank. After a year's exposure the slopes and angles are practically intact and the areas covered are clean.

The Ordnance Department has subsequently covered the sand surfaces near the proving grounds with cinders. This area presents a very clean and neat appearance.

The Long Island Railroad Company has also purchased large quantities of the material, which they find well adapted to the purposes of ballast, and to prevent shifting of sand near their tracks.

The material delivered at the fort costs from 25 cents unscreened to 45 cents screened per cubic yard. We used the unscreened material—gas-works cinders.

A cubic yard covers 9 square yards at an expense from $45 to $81 per acre for material, to which must be added the cost of grading, hauling, and distributing. The ashes and cinders, even of coal, furnish important elements of plant food, and, therefore, the use of the material ultimately assists in reclaiming sandy acres through a growth of vegetation.

Section Fort

Scale

along site of wall.

Brush

...al report, June 30, 1901.

...in, Corps of Engineers, U.S.A.

Eng 57 1

APPENDIX 4—TECHNICAL DETAILS, FORTIFICATION WORK. 921

4 D.

DEFENSES OF THE COAST OF NORTH CAROLINA.

[Officer in charge, Capt. Eugene W. Van C. Lucas, Corps of Engineers.]

Sea wall at Fort Caswell, N. C.—At this post the tidal range is 4.5 feet, and the adopted building level for fortification work is 12 feet. The storm of October 30-31, 1899, caused an extreme high tide of 10.7 feet, which overflowed a large part of the post and completely crippled means of communication between batteries, both wagon and rail roads having been destroyed in several places.

It was decided to insure against a repetition of such overflow and probable greater damage in the event of a similar storm by inclosing the post with a concrete sea wall, the top to be at a level of 12 feet above mean low water, and filling the interior of the post to the same level.

The accompanying sketch shows a section of sea wall, with mattress and stone protection on the exposed side. The wall, 6,612 feet in length, has been constructed as shown by the sketch, at a cost a little less than $10 per lineal foot. Several severe storms occurred during its construction, but only one did any damage, and that at a part of the sea wall, 114 feet long, where the mattress had not been ballasted with stone. The sea, breaking at the foot of the wall, speedily washed away the unballasted mattress, leaving the sand at the foot of the wall exposed to scour. The wall was quickly undermined, and, the concrete being of recent make and quite green, the wall pitched forward and had to be blown out and replaced by new wall. Wherever the mattress was in place and properly weighted with stone it served as an absolute protection to the wall, and showed a general tendency to accumulate sand. At one particularly exposed point it has been deemed advisable to increase the amount of stone on the mattress.

The interior will be filled in to the level of the top of the wall, after which no further trouble from overflow is anticipated.

In the event of an unusually severe storm, a break in this wall, while decidedly improbable, is not considered beyond the bounds of possibility. Should such a break occur, however, the resulting damage will be localized and confined to the immediate area, and repairs can be made at a very much less cost than would be entailed by a heavier cross section throughout.

Experience may indicate the desirability of increasing the width of mattress protection, but thus far the width of 12 feet adopted is apparently ample.

As fast as the sea wall was completed, sand backing, 10 to 15 feet wide, was filled in behind it. An ingenious and economical device, arranged for this purpose by Supt. Charles Schuster, in local charge, consisted of a half-yard Lancaster dredge bucket, with a Lidgerwood hoisting engine and 35-foot boom, the whole mounted on a platform, supported by four old railroad trucks and running on a double portable railroad track 12 feet between outside rails. The leading blocks for wire hoisting ropes were set 5 feet from the foot of the boom, making it swing automatically. The double track on which this dredge moved was placed on the outside of the sea wall and the sand was dug from the beach between high and low water lines, the resulting borrow pit being filled at the next high tide. The cost of placing sand behind the sea wall with this machine was less than 2 cents per cubic yard.

Emplacements for two 15-pounder and one 5-inch rapid-fire guns.—Magazines will have tile-lined and plastered walls and ceilings, with asphalt protection above the ceiling beams and between the double floors. Tile lining will also be used on the outside of the walls where in contact with sand. Stone lintels will be used over all doorways and pressed-brick facings at all corners and doorways.

The doors are double, each made of a solid steel sheet five-sixteenths inch thick, with heavy bronzed hinges and specially designed bronzed latch. They are hung to a solid cast-iron frame built into the wall, and when open will fold against the wall without occupying any of the limited floor space.

In an effort to avoid unequal settlement the sand for the parapet is being placed on the side while the concrete structures are being built.

Fire commander's station.—The structure is being built according to plans designed by The Board of Engineers for the Lewis range finder at low sites.

The ground at the site not affording sufficiently solid foundation, piles have been driven to support the concrete mass. In driving these piles the guide for the pile-driver hammer was suspended from the end of the derrick boom with entirely satisfactory results. With the boom the guide could be quickly adjusted, and the radius of the boom covered the entire area within which the piles were driven.

Telephone boxes were constructed for use on the gun platforms at two batteries—for one, of sheet steel on angle-iron frames, and for the other, of wood, the object being to test the relative merits of the two materials for resonance. They have not yet been sufficiently used to determine this point.

---

4 E.

DEFENSES OF SAN DIEGO, CALIFORNIA.

[Officer in charge, Capt. James J. Meyler, Corps of Engineers.]

EXTRACT FROM REPORT OF ASSISTANT ENGINEER D. E. HUGHES.

Stopping leaks.—Efforts in this direction the year before, and described in last year's report, were not successful. In 10-inch emplacements Nos. 2, 3, and 4 there was hardly a square without a leak, and several leaks had developed in No. 1, especially through the loading platform. Much experimenting on a small scale was done. Various proportions of glue, linseed oil, and litharge were tried, but long-continued wetting caused swelling and unsightly projection from the crack. Repeated wetting and drying, or swelling and shrinking, broke it loose from the concrete, except it got deep into cracks where swelling at the top protected the rest. Some experiments with brimstone were interesting. Briquettes, mostly of 1 cement to 3 sand, broken the year before, were mended. Mated pieces were returned to the molds after first cutting off the ends so they could be pulled apart to leave joints of varying widths, and molten sulphur of various temperatures was poured in. The briquettes were not heated. Sulphur heated just short of the viscous state, say 280°, gave the best practical results. When heated past the viscous state to the second liquefaction and to the burning temperature it would penetrate about as deep into a crack of given width, but it did not so promptly acquire the same strength. Though it was tough on the start and better able to stand shock, in a few days it became as brittle as the other. Four mended briquettes had their ends ground flat and were subjected to compression. They all failed under from 1,400 to 1,600 pounds by chipping at one end, and in no case was the failure at the 1-inch square mended section. Several

25"

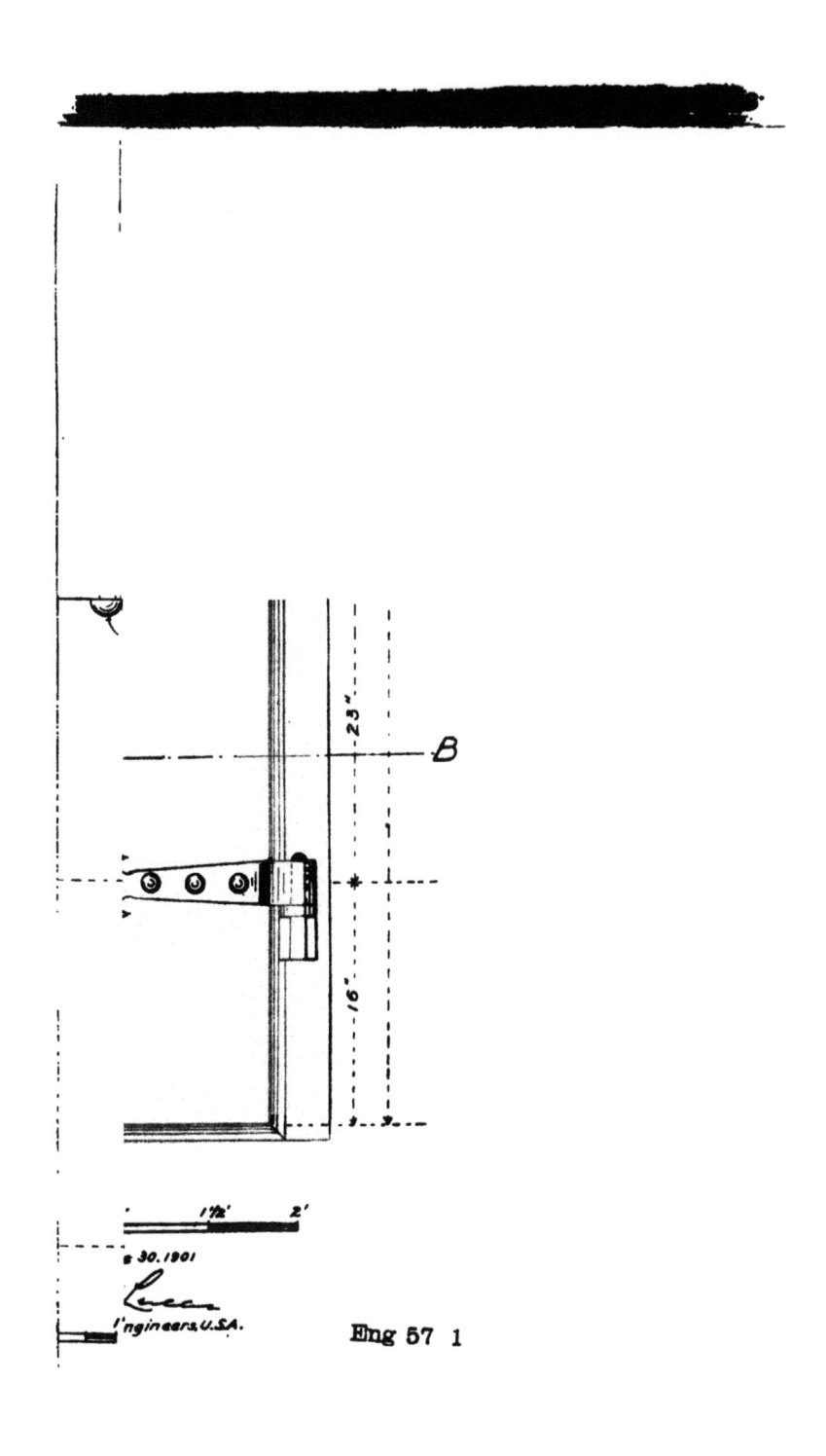

B

16"

9"

1½' 2'

30.1901

l'ngineers, U.S.A.

Eng 57 1

were subjected to tension, some within the hour, the last to-day after 11 months. As a rule and with joints three sixty-fourths to five sixty-fourths inch wide the strength ranged from 100 to 140 pounds per square inch. Wider joints seemed weaker, but there were not enough experiments to warrant exact conclusions. Whether the briquettes were of neat cement or of cement and sand, the failure was generally that of cohesion and not of adhesion. One briquette, of a weak kind, broke at 120 pounds one-fourth inch away from the joint. What more could one want? Well, the trouble was that in unheated concrete a crack narrower than three sixty-fourths inch would not fill an inch deep and in practice out in the wind temperature at pouring would probably be allowed to run down from 280° to the point of congealing, about 239°, giving still poorer results. While sulphur, if poured when cracks are widest, would often be satisfactory in openings an eighth of an inch or more wide, the shallow filling in narrower cracks, which are the most common, would probably cause chipping of concrete when a warmer day and expansion came. One wide crack clear through and across loading platform No. 3, due to settlement, was cut out V-shaped an inch wide and 1½ to 2 inches deep and filled with molten asphalt. It behaved perfectly all winter. It will be interesting to observe whether expansion and contraction will give it sufficient kneading to prevent its becoming friable.

Asphalt dissolved in naphtha seemed to do very well, but it had no apparent advantage over P. and B. No. 3 paint, and was not so convenient to apply. This paint was poured either from an oil can or through a petcock into all cracks. Some cracks required refilling at half-day intervals from 10 to 40 times. Tops of Nos. 2, 3, and 4 were painted all over. No. 1 and all four platforms had only the cracks treated. Some cracks at edge of platforms were an inch or so under the walls. These were shut off by 2-inch strips of cloth stuck L-shaped to floor and wall with paint and then painted over. The work has been successful so far. All rooms remained perfectly dry through the heaviest rains that this locality has had in years. It is expected that some cracks will need repouring in the fall, but the work is simple and cheap.

There has not at any time been any trace of moisture from condensation except in outside corridors where moisture-laden air swept through.

Settlement had reversed some floor slopes. Narrow trenches were cut in floors inside of some rooms to intercept water and lead it away.

There were a few damp spots on some walls of the 15-pounder battery. The casemate and engine room were always perfectly dry. So was the 5-inch battery except a spot in wall of latrine. This wall was made of time-honored "dry concrete," heavily tamped. The storeroom with similar 2-inch walls backed with earth but made of wetter concrete was dry. Its exposed 18-inch roof without interior "waterproof course" was also dry.

The experiences here are: (1) That with all the brands of cement that have been used shrinkage checks occur on exposed tops. (2) That a covering of earth, though but a foot thick, prevents such checking. No room here thus covered has ever leaked. (3) That the wet-mortar trowel-finished tops never leak except through cracks that lead to the more pervious interior and that such cracks are cheaply filled and made watertight by "P. and B." No. 3 paint. (4) That to make the hardest and the least permeable concrete it should be made quite wet—too wet for tamping with flat tampers. (5) That walls and roofs can be made cheaper and stronger and perfectly dry without any special roofing material within the mass, and without any air spaces or hollows in the walls. (6) That in this climate and in rooms that do not leak, circulation of air should be provided against rather than for, except in rooms for habitation.

4 F.

DEFENSES OF THE MOUTH OF COLUMBIA RIVER, OREGON AND WASHINGTON.

[Officers in charge, Capt. William C. Langfitt, Corps of Engineers, and Capt. William W. Harts, Corps of Engineers.]

EXTRACT FROM REPORT OF ASSISTANT ENGINEER G. B. HEGARDT.

Construction of gun emplacements, etc.—In the earlier works no asphalt was used in construction. Some of the emplacements were provided with ventilators and others not. The loading platforms had but little slope for drainage, and the joints of the stones of the granolithic finish were cut with the trowel with a view to prevent checking of top finish. Later works have asphalt cover over the magazines and shell rooms, with air spaces surrounding the most important rooms. No attempt has, so far, been made to use asphalt waterproof course over rooms under loading platforms, but these were constructed with the view of shedding the storm water freely. Hollow tile has not entered into the construction of any of the works, but in most instances blind drains of crushed rock were used wherever there was a fill against a room wall. A 3-inch thick layer of crushed rock was spread over the foundation before the laying of concrete to give greater elasticity to the foundation. Old rails were incorporated in the concrete foundation in nearly all of the works, where there was an apparent plane of weakness, and in other places where it was deemed important to better bind the concrete mass together.

Ample drainage and sewer facilities were provided for all works constructed.

Condition of emplacements as to dryness.—In the older works considerable trouble was experienced from leaky magazines and other rooms from water coming through the parapets, the rooms under loading platforms being very wet. Where ventilators were provided no condensation appeared, but rooms without them were at times very wet. In works recently constructed there has been little or no trouble from leaks, and none from condensation.

Methods used in stopping leaks and condensation.—To stop leaks through parapets and loading platforms, the checks and small cracks were at first cut out and filled with neat cement mortar, but proved to be of no value. The next experiment tried was to fill such checks, cracks, or joints with boiled linseed oil slightly heated, a small quantity of cement being incorporated with the oil, if the cracks were sufficiently large to admit of the cement. This treatment for a time proved very successful and prevented water percolating through the concrete surfaces until the changes in temperature became so great as to open the joints or cracks, but, in the main, the idea proved very useful. All surfaces against which there was a fill, and the tops of parapets, were at first the only surfaces coated with the alum-and-lye waterproof preparation mentioned in Annual Report of the Chief of Engineers, 1899, Part I, page 1002. From the beginning this wash was found to be strictly waterproof; at no time has there been the slightest trace of leaks through a surface so treated, provided no parting appeared in the concrete. At Site No. 1, where nearly all of the fills were sluiced in place, the water standing for days next to the concrete walls, no water ever seeped through the waterproof wash. The parapet surfaces of two emplacements at Site No. 1, and two at Site No. 2, were coated with asphalt to stop leaks.

The manner of application will later be referred to in these remarks.

Methods which have proved successful in stopping leaks and condensation.—The alum-and-lye preparation was used on all exterior concrete surfaces, on gun emplacements, cable tanks, torpedo storehouses, etc., and continues to give complete satisfaction. In addition to its waterproofing properties, this wash prevents fungus growth or discoloration on surfaces coated with it. In works constructed during this and the previous fiscal year the top surfaces of parapets and loading platforms were divided into stones 3 to 4 feet square, with a joint three-eighths of an inch wide and 2½ inches deep between them, which was afterwards filled with hot asphalt. These top surfaces were later given two coats of oil, darkened with lampblack to a color resembling asphalt. This was done both to further waterproof the concrete, as well as to make these surfaces more invisible, and as a protection to the eyes from the glare. Dividing the surfaces into stones, asphalting, and oiling proved entirely successful, and there has been no trouble from leaks in these emplacements. In the older works, where the application of oil alone failed to prevent leaks, the proper remedy was found by the following method: All checks and joints, whether regular or cross, were cut out to a depth of about three-fourths of an inch and about three-eighths of an inch in width, these grooves being then filled with hot asphalt and the top surfaces thoroughly coated with oil darkened with lampblack. It is of the greatest importance that the cut grooves be entirely cleaned of all dust and matter loosened by the cutting. Water under pressure gave the best satisfaction. Without first getting the grooves perfectly clean and dry the asphalt will not stick. The cutting out of surface cracks and joints, pouring the grooves full of asphalt, and oiling have been entirely successful in stopping leaks. Should new checks appear in a concrete surface, and they are easily detected, the remedy is simple and inexpensive. It requires no particular skill and can be done by ordinary laborers.

Some of the emplacement parapets were covered with two coats of asphalt. The method employed was as follows: The surface was first covered with as thin a course as possible of asphalt cement, heated to about 275° to 290°, the application being made on a warm, dry day. A second coat of asphalt cement with an admixture of 25 per cent of pure asphalt, to get a greater degree of hardness, was then applied and this last coat of asphalt sprinkled with a thin layer of cement. Wherever there is a joint in the top finish or a check or crack it must be cut out to a groove

APPENDIX 4—TECHNICAL DETAILS, FORTIFICATION WORK. 925

of the dimensions previously given for similar work, and the grooves must be clean and dry before pouring the asphalt. The joints and checks must be grooved to furnish sufficient plastic material at such places to allow for expansion and contraction. Asphalt will adhere perfectly to a surface which has previously been treated with linseed oil; in fact, the asphalt had the appearance of taking a better hold on the oiled surface than on the bare concrete. This application of asphalt to parapets has given good satisfaction, no leaks having since been discovered. The oiling of concrete surfaces after joints and checks were cut out and filled with asphalt has also been satisfactory. It is less expensive than asphalting and is not affected by the blast of the guns. It is well worth trying as an experiment, and if not entirely satisfactory asphalt cover can be applied on top of it. It seems probable that the constant yearly application of oil to a concrete surface will make it more and more impervious to water and its waterproofing conditions steadily improve.

Where rails have been used in concrete foundation—the soil being sand or clay—at planes of weakness, etc., there has been no parting of the concrete mass, and consequently the checks and cracks which had to be taken care of to stop leaks were, as a rule, only surface cracks. In the mortar battery, where no rails were used in the concrete, there are a number of cracks extending through the entire work.

Ventilation.—Where rooms were provided with ventilators there has been no condensation. Without them, they were nearly always wet and damp. This has been remedied by the installation of ventilators in all cases. They consist of sewer pipe, leading from the rooms to the surface of the concrete or earth parapet, and have, in every instance, given immediate relief, and all gun emplacements, casemates, etc., are entirely free from condensation. The ventilation of all rooms is wholly natural, no artificial means being employed. This is greatly aided by keeping the emplacement doors closed as much as possible at all seasons of the year, and particularly those of the magazines. In this way the natural ventilation is constant, all the air necessary for circulating purposes being admitted through crevices at doors, windows, etc., and the variation in temperature is kept at a minimum, and will vary in the magazines but a few degrees, summer or winter.

The remarks as to leaks, condensation, etc., are from conditions applicable to works at the mouth of the Columbia River, and may have to be varied to suit different localities. It may be stated, however, that the average annual rainfall is nearly 77 inches.

APPENDIX No. 5.

POST OF FORT TOTTEN, NEW YORK—UNITED STATES ENGINEER SCHOOL—ENGINEER TROOPS—ENGINEER DEPOT.

REPORT OF MAJ. W. M. BLACK, CORPS OF ENGINEERS, FOR THE FISCAL YEAR ENDING JUNE 30, 1901.

UNITED STATES ENGINEER SCHOOL,
Fort Totten, Willets Point, N. Y., August 6, 1901.

GENERAL: I have the honor to forward herewith, in duplicate, annual report on the post of Fort Totten, N. Y., the United States Engineer School, Engineer Troops, and the Engineer Depot, for the fiscal year ending June 30, 1901.

Very respectfully, your obedient servant,

W. M. BLACK,
Major, Corps of Engineers, Commanding.

Brig. Gen. G. L. GILLESPIE,
Chief of Engineers, U. S. A.

I.—POST OF FORT TOTTEN, NEW YORK.

The post-office and the telegraph office for this post are on the reservation and are known by the reservation name of Willets Point, N. Y.

The Bell Telephone Company has an office on the post connected with a central office at Flushing, N. Y.

The nearest railroad stations are Whitestone and Bayside, on different branches of the Long Island Railroad and about 2 miles distant.

Two mails are sent out and received daily, except Sundays, when there is but one, carried by post transportation to and from Whitestone.

The telegraph office is in the charge of a sergeant of the Signal Corps, who also acts as instructor in telegraphy for the enlisted men of the garrison.

Allotments and expenditures for repairs to buildings, etc., were as follows:

Appropriation.	Allotted.	Expended.	Purpose.
Military posts	$31,116.00	$31,116.00	Construction and plumbing, new artillery barracks.
Regular supplies	3,142.00	3,142.00	Heating and gas-piping new artillery barracks.
Barracks and quarters	7,150.00	6,909.00	Construction of new ordnance storehouse.
Do	775.00	775.00	Construction of new boathouse.
Do	2,396.50	2,396.50	Purchase of material for repairs to barracks and quarters.
Do	498.95	380.68	Purchase of material for repairs to plumbing.
Hospitals	645.84	503.28	Repairs to hospital.
Hospital steward's quarters	79.16	60.47	Repairs to hospital steward's quarters.
Army transportation	1,165.00	1,074.89	Repairs to roads.
Regular supplies	2,181.00	1,962.52	Purchase of material for repairs to structural heating.
Total	49,144.45	48,320.29	

The artillery barracks mentioned in the last annual report as under construction was completed and in May was occupied by the Eighty-second Company of Coast Artillery. After its occupation a report on the barracks was submitted by Capt. J. R. Williams, commanding the company. Captain Williams states:

The arrangement of the barracks is radically defective. The regulations contemplate that the men of each company shall be divided into four squads, and it is evident that the squads should be kept together under the noncommissioned officers. The arrangement of the barracks does not permit this. It is called a barrack for 120 men. There are 5 squad rooms, and 5 rooms for noncommissioned officers. With the present size of artillery companies, each squad should have accommodation for about 28 men, with a communicating or adjacent room for noncommissioned officers.

The squad rooms in the main building of the barracks are intended for only 20 men, and the noncommissioned officer's room adjoining is for a single occupant. There is a fifth large squad room on the second floor over the dining room and kitchen. This squad room is intended for 36 men, but the men in this room would belong, necessarily, to different squads—an unsatisfactory arrangement.

The ground plan as arranged requires three rows of bunks to be placed in each squad room, except in large squad room over the dining room, where there are only two rows. This crowds the squad room unduly, giving little or no space for chairs, arm racks, and other necessary articles of furniture. The space allowed for each bunk is 2¾ feet, with only 6 inches interval between some pair of bunks. As a matter of fact, most of the bunks in use measure over 33 inches with the mattresses. The free floor space is further reduced.

The rooms for noncommissioned officers are taken from the squad-room space, when the whole parallelogram should be devoted to the squad room itself. Further, noncommissioned officers' rooms are too small to hold comfortably both the sergeants of the squads. One sergeant of each squad must therefore room with the privates.

There should be an entrance to the basement from the exterior of the building, giving access to the closets and wash rooms without passing through the building itself. There is but a single stairway from the second story to the first story. There is no provision for exterior stairways, nor is there any veranda or exterior gallery except one in front on the first floor. There should be a second-story veranda at least in front, and it would be desirable to have a two-story veranda at each end of the main building also, having stairways from one floor to the other. The veranda in front should have a width of 12 feet, so as to give room for formation in bad weather. Ten feet, the present width, is hardly sufficient for this purpose.

The building has no third floor, and the loft is of little value for storage purposes on account of the way in which it is cut up by the roof trusses. Partitions should be made in one or more of the divisions of the basement, so as to give two or more additional lockup places for stores and workrooms. As the basement is arranged there are but two lockup rooms, one for the tailor and one for the barber.

There should be lockup places in the company office for such small articles as must be necessarily kept there. The building should be wired for electric lighting; it is piped for gas instead. There is not the slightest chance that the building will ever be lighted by gas, while it might be lighted by electricity from the existing plant for the fortifications. In case an additional barrack for artillery should be authorized at this station, which I hear is not improbable, it is to be hoped that a modification of the plan of the engineer barracks at this post may be followed rather than the plan of the present artillery barracks.

The plan of the engineer barracks is, in many respects, more satisfactory than the plan of the new artillery barracks. If the central building of the engineer barracks were arcaded between the front piazzas on the first floor, it would give a continuous covered gallery in front, where the whole organization could parade in bad weather. The width of this piazza should be increased from 8 feet to 11 or 12 feet.

The messing arrangements for the engineer companies are contained in a separate building, divided into three, each with mess hall and kitchen complete, for the three engineer companies that had been usually stationed here. This is not so convenient as having the mess in the building itself.

There is plenty of room in the basement of these barracks for a mess room and kitchen, or else a one-story "T," containing mess room and kitchen, could be added to the central building of the barracks. If the mess was placed in the basement, the height of the ceiling should be increased a foot or two.

Another objectionable feature in this and the other barracks of the post is the use of lath and plaster for interior finish. With the best washboards and wainscoting become receptacles for vermin, with which with the best of care a barrack is liable in time to become infested. An interior finish of hollow tile, enameled or painted, or even a hollow brick wall lined with painted or enameled brick would be more economical in the end, could be kept in neater condition, and would be cooler in summer and warmer in winter. With this interior finish, sound-deadened mill-floor construction for floors, and expanded metal plaster partitions, the building would be practically fireproof, as well as measureably vermin proof. Partitions in the attics and storeroom partitions in the basement should be of wire net, to permit better lighting and ventilation.

The practice of placing the closets and urinals in the basement is also objectionable from a sanitary standpoint. It would be better to place a fully appointed toilet room on each floor, one directly above the other, cut off from the remainder of the building by solid walls with door openings, as is the practice in office buildings of the present day. A large room for a gymnasium and handball is desirable. This could also be used for drills, inspections, etc., in inclement weather.

The garrison of the post during the year has consisted of engineer and artillery troops.

The reorganization of the Army with the much-needed increase of the engineer and artillery troops and the return of peace make necessary provision at this post to meet the new conditions.

Fort Totten is now the home of the Engineer School and the Engineer Depot, is the home station of the Battalion of Engineers, and the station of one company of coast artillery.

The United States Engineer School is intended to supplement the course of study at the United States Military Academy by providing instruction by reading, lectures, and examples in the more advanced parts of engineering practice, both military and civil, so as to better fit the graduate engineer officers for the active duties of their profession, concerning which they have learned but the rudiments at the Military Academy. An engineer without experience is worth but little. Mere theoretical training is not sufficient. A young man must obtain a knowledge of the experience of others while gaining his own.

The subjects to be learned at the school may be divided as follows in the order of importance:

1. Instruction in works of permanent and semipermanent fortification.
2. Instruction in the engineer duties with troops in campaign.
3. Instruction in civil and electrical engineering.

If this rating be correct, the station for the school should meet the following requirements:

For instruction in the theory and practice of fortification, the station should be so located as to permit frequent inspections of fortified places by the student officers, in order to familiarize them with the methods adopted for adapting the type works to the site; with the arrangement and quality of the armament adopted in accordance with the principles and considerations laid down in the approved project as governing for the particular position to be defended; with the construction methods employed and their advantages and faults, and, finally, to enable the student officers to have actual practice with the guns in the regular target seasons, in order to learn from actual contact what each type of gun may be expected to do, its requirements in service, and how well the facilities afforded by the emplacements and the adopted means for fire control meet these requirements.

For instruction in the engineer duties with troops in campaign, it is essential that the station be such as will afford facilities for training the officers and men in these duties. It should have a sufficient area with a diversified terrain, with ravines, level ground, and water in large and small bodies. It should have standing timber and brushwood. It should contain sufficient rock for blasting practice. The bodies of water should be such as will permit bridge drills of all kinds, pier construction, exercise with row, sail, and steam boats. There should be tide water with sufficient occasional wave action to familiarize the men with the handling of boats and material under conditions similar to those to be met in landing on coasts, and to permit the design and test of engineer plant to meet these conditions. Soil of a character to permit easy trenching and mining is desirable. If practicable, there should be area sufficient for the instruction of the troops in reconnaissance and scouting in the presence of an opposing body, and for combined operations with troops of other arms of the service. The last is not deemed an indispensable requisite, inasmuch as this instruction can be given in a summer camp such as to-day is held for the State troops and such as the General Government is sure to have in the future for the instruction of its troops. Were a large post, such as Fort Leavenworth, made the home station of a battalion of engineers other than that required at the school, this practice could be had in service with it.

For instruction in civil and electrical engineering the station should be near engineering works of magnitude of all kinds. The frequent inspection and study of such works are regarded as essential for the student officers, who, after leaving the school, rarely have time and opportunity for that practical training in very subordinate positions which is found so valuable in civil practice. Without the knowledge of plant, materials, and methods of construction so acquired the study of text-books is uninteresting and comparatively profitless. It should also be near a point where civil engineers can be met from time to time in an informal manner, near libraries of engineering literature and bookstores, where the latest publications can be found and examined as they appear.

After careful consideration it is the opinion of the staff of the school that the post of Fort Totten fulfills the requisites more fully than any existing reservation, and that the principal deficit is in area. This post forms an important part of the defenses of New York and must therefore be provided with an artillery garrison. The present artillery garrison (one company) is too small. At least two companies are required. The complement of engineer troops at the school should be sufficient to perform the regular garrison duties, to afford details for bridge, intrenching and other drills, for the practical instruction of the officers and men, to permit experimental work with engineer tools and materials to be carried on, and to give the officers at the school the experience in the handling and control of troops, for which they have so little opportunity in much of their duty. Three companies, the number which has always been stationed at the school, will be sufficient. In turn the troops at this post can receive instruction in many duties for which equal facilities could not be had at other home stations.

their varied duties in war and peace can be had by stationing one battalion at the Engineer School and one battalion at the Fort Leavenworth Infantry and Cavalry School, leaving the remaining battalion either for foreign service or for station at some other home station, such as the Presidio.

The Fort Totten reservation has a total area of 136.35 acres. Of this 18¼ acres are occupied by the fortifications, and about 14 acres on the west and south are marsh. There is sufficient acreage available for the buildings required for the garrison (three companies of engineers, the engineer band, and two or three companies of artillery, all with full complement of officers), for the Engineer School, and for the Engineer Depot. There is not sufficient area for a proper drill ground, and there is practically no woodland. The 14 acres of salt marsh can be reclaimed and made available by diking and filling with materials dredged from the adjacent shoal water of Little Neck Bay. An additional area of 64 acres should be bought on the west of the reservation. This land is to-day unimproved woodland and meadow, with about 8 acres of marsh adjoining the marsh of the reservation. This piece of marsh should be bought, if for no other purpose than to reclaim the entire marsh area adjoining the reservation, which has always been a source of disease and a breeding place for innumerable mosquitoes. The loss to the United States in the time of enlisted men alone, apart from the other and not easily computable loss due to the deterioration of the health of the entire command, arising from malarial sickness at this post, in one year, can be seen from the following extract from the report of the post surgeon:

FORT TOTTEN, WILLETS POINT, N. Y., *July 27, 1901.*

Copy of extract from the sanitary report for the month of March, respectfully furnished for the information of the commanding officer.

[Extract.]

* * * * * * *

During the year 1900, 131 cases of malarial fevers were taken upon the sick report at this post, involving a loss of 1,113 days to the Government. Estimating the cost of a man in actual pay and feeding, say about 57 cents in pay (averaging the pay of noncommissioned officers, first-class and second-class privates), and 17 cents as the cost of subsistence, we see a loss to the Government in money of some $813.62 on account of malaria alone during the year. We say nothing of other expenses, nor of the losses in drills and special instruction.

* * * * * * *

The above-mentioned 131 cases of malarial fevers represent 28.35 per cent of the total number of cases (462) admitted during the year.

Very respectfully,
W. F. CARTER,
Major and Surgeon, United States Army, Surgeon.

The reclamation of the marsh would go far toward removing the source of the malarial troubles.

The estimated cost of the improvements recommended is as follows:

For diking and reclaiming the marsh of the present reservation:
    Dredging and filling $18,000
    Riprap sea wall 17,000
For diking and reclaiming the entire marsh area:
    Dredging and filling...
    Riprap sea wall ....
For the purchase of land (about 64 acres).............................

The expenditure of the maximum sum recommended above, $114,000, would make the Fort Totten Reservation sanitary and of a size suitable for the important work for which its location on deep tide water, near the most important commercial center of the country, so well fits it. The usefulness of the school can then be further increased, if so desired, by imparting instruction in field military engineering to selected members of the National Guard.

Buildings.—This post, like others of the older posts of the service, was built up piecemeal, and only as absolute necessity required, from the hospital sheds which were placed here during the civil war. Of the 79 buildings now occupied on the post not more than 38 can be said to be adequate or in proper condition for the use to which they has to be put. The following list of the buildings, with a brief statement of their condition, was prepared by the quartermaster.

The buildings on the post may be divided into four classes, viz:

I. Buildings belonging to the Engineer Department, known as "fort buildings."
II. Depot buildings.
III. School buildings.
IV. Quartermaster's buildings.

I. Under the head of fort buildings are Nos. 57 and 58, engineers' cottages (these are old buildings, bad beyond repair, and while they answer their purpose for the engineer department they should be moved away, as they occupy desirable space in the garrison). No. 69, machine shop, occupied jointly with the school and depot. No. 79, stone shed. No. 88, blacksmith shop, occupied jointly with depot and school.

The fort buildings are under the supervision of Maj. W. L. Marshall, Corps of Engineers. If the new buildings are authorized as recommended, No. 57 and No. 58 would have to be moved. These are old buildings, in bad repair, not now in use, and occupy space required for the garrison. A suitable location near the battery can be given buildings to replace them should they be required.

II. Under the head of the depot buildings are C, wooden ponton shed; D, depot storehouse; E, depot machine shop; Nos. 67 and 67*a*, depot stables; No. 56, fireproof depot buildings; Nos. 73, 74, 75, 77, and 97, depot storehouses; 84, depot carpenter shop; 105, depot fireproof building.

These buildings, while some are not in good condition, answer their purposes for the present.

III. Under the head of school buildings are No. 59, electrical laboratory for officers; No. 60, tank house for No. 59; No. 61, enlisted men's electrical laboratory; No. 82, engine house for No. 61; No. 90, library and museum; No. 51, photographic laboratory (frame, one story; built 1882–83; cost, $5,668.69; condition fair); No. 63, astronomical observatory.

These buildings answer their purposes for the present time (considering the already approved addition to No. 90).

IV. Under the head of the quartermaster's buildings are the remaining buildings on the post. In general terms these buildings are in such a state that they are not fit to answer the purposes for which required, and in view of the changes necessary at present, due to the increased garrison, it would seem wise to consider the improvements absolutely necessary to make the post buildings answer for a garrison of this size.

cases unfit for use from a sanitary point of view. It would not be economical to replace the plumbing in such old buildings.

These buildings may be divided into four classes: (1) Offices and storehouses; (2) barracks; (3) officers' quarters; (4) enlisted men's quarters.

Under class 1, "Offices and storehouses," are—

No. 20. Administration building (frame building, two stories, built in 1868; cost, $11,523.75). Condition bad. Recommendation: Should be replaced by a new building. This building was once condemned as a hospital and has since been used for administration purposes.

No. 9. Quartermaster and commissary storehouse (brick building, one story and loft; built in 1896–97; cost, $9,216). Condition excellent. Recommendation: Present storage capacity is entirely inadequate. Should either be extended or an L built.

No. 21. Post bakery (brick building, one story). Condition excellent.

No. 23. Oil house (new brick building, one story). Condition excellent.

No. 24. Old mess hall (frame building, one story; built in 1870–71; cost, $5,685). Condition very bad; beyond repair. Should be torn down, site to be used for a new building.

No. 25. Old quartermaster storehouse (frame building, one story; built in 1869–70; cost, $650). Condition very bad; beyond repair. Recommendation: Should be replaced by a new storehouse.

No. 26. Old commissary storehouse (frame building, one story; built in 1869–70; cost, $650). Condition very bad; beyond repair. Recommendation: New storehouse to replace No. 25 should be made large enough to cover present use of this building.

These last three buildings are now used as storehouses by the Quartermaster and Subsistence departments and answer this purpose only in the absence of proper accommodations. There is no security of property against thieves or fire, and in the interest of the Government they should be replaced as recommended.

No. 28. Old bakery (frame buiding, one story; built in 1867; cost, $2,175). Condition very bad; beyond repair. Recommendation: New building not needed.

No. 29. Carpenter and paint shop (frame building, two stories; time built and cost unknown). Condition very bad. Recommendation: Should be replaced by a new building. The remarks on Nos. 24, 25, and 26 also apply to this building.

No. 30. Blacksmith shop (frame building, one story; time built unknown; cost, $260). Condition very bad. Recommendation: Should be replaced by a new building.

No. 30a. Old oil house. Condition very bad; beyond repair. Recommendation: Should be torn down.

No. 31. Quartermaster stables (frame building, one story and attic. Built in 1867; cost, $2,175, including old bakery). Condition very bad. Recommendation: Should be replaced by a new building.

No. 32. Stable, barrack, and wagon shed (frame building, one story; built in 1867); cost, unknown; built from old material). Condition fair. Recommendation: Barrack should be rebuilt.

No. 38. Post exchange (frame building, one story; time built and cost unknown). Condition bad. Recommendation: Should be replaced by a new building. This was one of the Grant Hospital buildings (1864).

No. 35. Ice house (frame building, one story; time built, unknown; cost, $882.) Condition bad, but answers the purpose.
No. 49. Quartermaster wagon shed. Condition poor.
No. 50. Ordnance storehouse (brick building, one story and attic). Condition excellent.
No. 92. Ambulance shed. Condition fair.
No. 104. Quartermaster coal shed. Condition fair.
No. 106. Guardhouse. Condition excellent.
No. 109. Fire-engine house. Condition good.
Under class 2, "Barracks," are—
No. 22. New mess hall (brick building, one story). Condition excellent.
No. 27. Artillery barracks (brick building, two stories and attic). Condition excellent.
Nos. 107, 108, and 110. Engineer barracks. Condition good.
No. 34. Band barracks (frame building, one story; built in 1871-72; cost, $276). Condition miserable. Recommendation: Should be replaced by a new barrack.
No. 37. Chapel (frame building, one story; built in 1873; cost, $6,051.56). Condition fair.
No. 68. School building (frame building, one story; time of building and cost unknown). Condition very bad. Recommendation: Could be replaced by some other building. This building was used as engineer office on the original fort work at this point and is in no condition to use for any purpose.
No. 52. Hospital (frame building, two stories; built in 1887-88; cost, $13,250). Condition fair.

Under class 3 are the following buildings, with notes and recommendations:

No. 1. Commanding officer's quarters (frame building, two stories and attic; built in 1867; cost, $12,242). Condition fair. Recommendation: Should be replaced by a new building; if replaced, could be moved and used for bachelor officers. With some repairs can be used for a few years more.

Nos. 2 and 3. Double set officers' quarters (frame building, two stories and attic; built in 1872; cost, $10,088.53). Condition fair. Recommendation: Should be replaced by a new building; if replaced, could be moved and used by noncommissioned staff officers.

Nos. 4 and 5. Double set officers' quarters (frame building, two stories and attic; built in 1867; cost, $12,500). Condition very bad. Recommendation: Should be replaced by a new building; if replaced, could be moved and used by noncommissioned staff officers.

Nos. 6 and 7. Double set officers' quarters (frame building, two stories and attic; built in 1867; cost, $12,500). Condition bad. Recommendation: Should be replaced by a new building; if replaced, could be moved and used by noncommissioned staff officers.

No. 10. Bachelor officers' quarters (frame building, two stories and attic; built in 1871; cost, $6,489.72). Condition very bad. Recommendation: Should be replaced by a new building.

Nos. 11 and 12. Double set officers' quarters (frame building, two stories and attic; built in 1879; cost, $9,774.56). Condition fair.

No. 13. Bachelor officers' quarters (frame building, two stories and attic; built in 1871; cost, $4,200). Condition very bad. Recommendation: Should be replaced by a new building. This building has been once condemned as an administration building, and has since then been moved, repaired, and used as bachelor officers' quarters.

No. 53. Officers' mess (frame building, two stories and attic). Condition good. This is also used as a school building, but the rooms are needed and a new school building should be provided.

Nos. 54 and 55. Double set officers' quarters (frame building, two stories and attic; built in 1887; cost, $18,560. Condition good.

Nos. 47 and 48. Double set officers' quarters (frame, two stories and attic; built in 1885–86; cost, $13,350). Condition good.

Under class 4 comes the following buildings:

No. 14. Noncommissioned staff quarters (frame building, one story and attic; built in 1872; cost, $962.36). Condition fair. Recommendation: Could be used by married soldiers in the event of Nos. 2 and 3 being replaced.

No. 15. Hospital steward's quarters (frame building, one story and attic; built in 1876; cost, $1,000. Condition fair.

No. 16. Noncommissioned officers' quarters (frame building, one story and attic; built in 1872; cost, $962.36). Condition fair.

No. 17. Noncommissioned officers' quarters (frame building, one story and attic; built in 1872; cost, $962.36). Condition fair.

No. 18. Noncommissioned staff officers' quarters (frame building, one story and attic; built in 1881; cost, $720). Condition fair. Recommendation: Could be used by married soldiers in the event of Nos. 2 and 3 being replaced.

No. 19. Noncommissioned staff officers' quarters (frame building, one story and attic; built in 1881; cost, $720). Condition very bad. Recommendation: Can be replaced by one of the sets of officers' quarters moved.

No. 36. Noncommissioned officers' quarters (frame building, one story; converted from old guardhouse; cost, $382). Condition fair.

Nos. 38 to 44, inclusive. Married soldiers' quarters (frame building, one story; built in 1871–72; cost, $484 each). Condition very bad; beyond repair. Recommendation: Could be replaced by buildings vacated by noncommissioned staff officers.

No. 45. Noncommissioned staff officers' quarters (frame building, one story and attic; built in 1884; cost, $1,200). Condition fair. Recommendation: If removed, could be used by married soldiers.

No. 46. Married soldiers' quarters (frame buildings, one story; built in 1871–72; cost, $484 each). Condition very bad; beyond repair. Recommendation: Could be replaced by buildings vacated by noncommissioned staff officers.

No. 70. Mechanics' quarters (frame building, one story and attic; built in 1862–63; cost unknown). Condition very bad; beyond repair.

No. 86. Noncommissioned officers' quarters (frame building, one story and attic; purchased from post trader in 1886; cost, $900). Condition fair. Recommendation: If replaced, could be used by married soldiers.

The buildings occupied by the families of married enlisted men are very old and in such condition as to be hardly fit for habitation. Their use by these families is permitted for the good of the service in permitting a limited number of women to live on the post to do laundry work for the garrison and for the benefit of the married men in assisting in the support of their families. Many of the houses are occupied by the families of men on foreign service and are of material aid to them. It is my opinion that the marriage of a limited portion of men serving in a second or subsequent enlistment should be officially authorized and provision made for their families on the post. In all branches of the service, and particularly in those which require much technical instruction, long service should be encouraged, since the value of the services of an efficient man increases with his experience, and the presence of such trained, experienced, and efficient men in a command is an invaluable aid to discipline and efficiency. It is impossible to make a thoroughly trained noncommissioned officer of engineers in one enlistment. It is equally impossible to retain this class of men in the service, unless provision is made for the marriage of some of them.

To determine the buildings required here under the new conditions for the school and garrison, the probable strength of the command is assumed as follows: One commanding officer; 2 medical officers; 3 companies of engineers and the engineer band with the full complement of officers, comprising 3 captains and 8 lieutenants; 2 companies of artillery with 1 major, 2 captains, and 4 lieutenants; 5 instructors of the Engineer School—a total of 24 officers. In addition there may be a number of officers at the school for instruction.

There are now at the post good barracks for the 3 companies of engineers and for 1 company of artillery. One band barracks and one artillery barracks are required. Provision is recommended below for the quarters for the noncommissioned staff and for married enlisted men.

The existing quarters provide for 13 married and 8 unmarried officers. Four of the married sets (4, 5, 6, and 7, two buildings) should be removed and transformed into quarters for noncommissioned staff. Two (2 and 3, one building) should be moved, as it now occupies one of the best sites, which should be used for a new building.

It is recommended that provision be made for 18 married officers and 12 unmarried officers (an allowance for 6 officers under instruction at the school). This would require the immediate construction of 9 sets of quarters for married officers and a building for bachelors.

Of buildings for the general use, an administration building is the only one which should be built at once. The building used for this purpose is a condemned hospital. It occupies a site which should be cleared so as to permit the new quarters to be disposed to the best permanent advantage. It is doubtful whether it would bear removal, but if it could it could be used for school purposes. There is no building on the post which is now available for the school for enlisted men or for the children. A new wing should be added to the commissary and quartermaster storehouse (No. 9). This building is too small for the present garrison. The administration building should be large enough to accommodate the headquarters and offices attached thereto, an office for the engineer depot, the telegraph office, the post-office, and 4 offices and a lecture room for the school.

Estimating the cost of the quarters required at 18 cents per cubic foot of contents below the eaves, and the administration building, barracks, and storehouse addition at $15\frac{1}{2}$ cents, making the size authorized in recent constructions of such character, and having the married sets in separate buildings, the estimated cost of the buildings recommended is as follows:

Nine sets of married officers' quarters.. $72,000
One building for unmarried officers.. 14,000
One administration building 12,000

One band barracks	$11,000
One artillery barracks for 120 men	34,000
One addition to commissary and quartermaster storehouse	10,000
Moving and refitting five buildings	10,000
Total	163,000

Officers of the Corps of Engineers on duty during the year are reported later; other officers have been on duty as follows:

Maj. W. F. Carter, surgeon, since July 1, 1900.
Capt. John R. Williams, Artillery Corps, commanding Eighty-second Company, Coast Artillery, since March 15, 1901.
Capt. G. W. Van Deusen, Artillery Corps, commanding Battery N, Seventh Artillery, later Eighty-second Company, Coast Artillery, July 1, 1900, to February 16, 1901.
First Lieut. H. L. Newbold, Artillery Corps, on duty with Battery N, Seventh Artillery, July 1, 1900, to August 4, 1900.
First Lieut. Frederick L. Buck, Artillery Corps, on duty with Battery N, Seventh Artillery, now Eighty-second Company, Coast Artillery, since August 3, 1900.
Acting Asst. Surg. Roy A. Wilson, since July 1, 1900.

II. UNITED STATES ENGINEER SCHOOL.

COMMANDANT.

Maj. John G. D. Knight, Corps of Engineers, United States Army, till April 29, 1901; since that date Maj. W. M. Black, Corps of Engineers, United States Army.

The regulations of this school are to be found in General Orders No. 63, Headquarters of the Army, series of 1897, and on pages 565–567, Annual Report of the Chief of Engineers United States Army, 1898.

The period of instruction of officers is two years, beginning October 1, the first month being devoted to reconnaissance work.

November 1, the time for beginning theoretical instruction found here two instructors, five officers of the first winter's class, and three officers of the second winter's class. November 24, one officer of the first winter's class joined by assignment. The operations of the school are reported below in the order of departments of instruction given in school regulations.

A tabulated statement follows showing officers under instruction and the parts of the course of instruction taken by them.

A.—DEPARTMENT OF MILITARY ENGINEERING.

Instructors: Capt. Francis R. Shunk, Corps of Engineers, until May 3, 1901; Capt. James F. McIndoe, Corps of Engineers, from that date.

The fourteen weeks' course of instruction began January 28, 1901, and continued until April 30, 1901.

Details of the course of instruction ordered, upon the recommendation of the academic staff, are as follows:

First week.—War ships: Classification, construction, armor, armament, speed, maneuvering power, draft, vulnerability, methods of attack on works, strength of navies of nations.

Second, third, and fourth weeks.—Seacoast guns and mortars: Kinds, construction, power, penetration, range, accuracy, mounts, rapid-fire guns.

Projectiles: Kinds and uses, effects, high explosives in shells, weights, storage, and handling.

Powder and other explosives: Kinds, uses, charges, storage, and handling.

Seacoast batteries: Types for different sites, location, design, estimates, construction, plant, stability of gun platforms, dampness in magazines, care, ammunition, service.

Fifth week.—Operations of defense: Preparation, control of batteries, range-finding, communications, relocating, service of guns, targets.
Protection against land attack.
Examples of engagements between ships and forts: Crimea, civil war, Egypt, Cuba.
Sixth, seventh, and eighth weeks.—Project for defense of designated harbor, with memoir and estimate of cost.
Field engineering: Works and trenches, object, location, design, construction, tasks and time, obstacles, construction and destruction, preparation of position for defense, attack and defense. Examples.
Demolitions.
Ninth, tenth, and eleventh weeks.—Military roads and telegraph lines, military bridges.
Reconnaissance of roads and positions, military topography, maps, manifolding.
The service of security and information.
Organization and tactics.
Twelfth week.—Transportation and care of troops, duties of engineer officers as staff officers.
Thirteenth and fourteenth weeks.—Study of campaigns, marches, and battles, with a view to illustrating the principles of strategy, logistics, and grand tactics.

As part of the examination in military engineering, officers were required to prepare projects for the defense of certain harbors.

B.—DEPARTMENT OF ELECTRICAL ENGINEERING.

Instructor: Capt. Francis R. Shunk, Corps of Engineers.

The sixteen weeks' course of instruction began November 1, 1900, and continued until February 26, 1901.

Details of the course of instruction ordered, upon the recommendation of the academic staff, were as follows:

First week.—Arc lamps.
Second week.—Incandescent lamps.
Third and fourth weeks.—Continuous-current motors and generators.
Fifth and sixth weeks.—Alternating-current motors, transformers, and polyphase apparatus.
Seventh week.—Conductors and insulators.
Eighth and ninth weeks.—Initial-power apparatus.
Tenth week.—Telegraph, telephone, and signaling apparatus and lightning protection.
Eleventh week.—Electro-thermal and electro-chemical applications and "X" rays.
Twelfth week.—Measuring and testing apparatus and miscellaneous.
Thirteenth and fourteenth weeks.—Submarine-mining material and applications.
Fifteenth and sixteenth weeks.—Specifications, tests, and general practical applications.

Practical work in planting and raising mines continued during the summer of 1900 with details of men from the engineer companies present under the supervision of officers who had taken the theoretical course during the previous winter.

C.—DEPARTMENT OF CIVIL ENGINEERING.

Instructors: Capt. Henry Jervey, Corps of Engineers, until March 11, 1901; Capt. James F. McIndoe, Corps of Engineers, from March 11 till May 3, 1901; Capt. Charles H. McKinstry, Corps of Engineers, since the latter date.

The first winter's course of nine weeks began March 1, 1901, and ended April 30, 1901.

Details of this course ordered, upon the recommendation of the academic staff, were as follows:

Surveying (three weeks).
(1) Preliminary surveys and examinations: Preliminary survey for engineering constructions, as roads, railroads, and canals. Preliminary examinations of navigable waterways as practiced by the Corps of Engineers, United States Army. Study of compass, chain, tape, and hand instruments.

(2) Topographical surveying: Object and method of survey. Instruments and cost of work. Detailed study of transit and stadia and plane table.

(3) Surveys of location: Organization of party for survey of canal route from the Illinois to the Mississippi River. Instruments and methods used. Estimate of cost. Information to be gathered as to right of way, rainfall, watersheds, drainage lines, public highways, sites of bridges, aqueducts, and culverts. Detailed study of wye level and rod.

(4) Hydrographic surveys: Objects and methods. Location of soundings; gauging of streams and tidal flow. Formulæ for measuring discharge over weirs. Survey of a river, of a bay or lake, of an exposed bar. Detailed study of precise levels and current meters.

(5) *Foundations (one week).*—Foundations on land and under water. Study of supporting soil, borings, test pits, etc. Use of piles, grillages of timber or I-beams, riprap, concrete. Use of caissons and cofferdams. Drainage of foundations.

(6) *Strength of materials (two weeks).*—Stresses of different kinds. Cordage, including rope, iron, and steel-wire rope and chain. Stone and masonry. Timber, including study of joints and fastenings and timber trestles. Steel and iron, including study of manufacture and shop work of material for metal bridges. Distribution of stresses in frames and trusses; study of simple bridge truss, timber roof truss, jib crane, boom derrick, crane derrick, noting also methods of joining parts.

(7) *Hydraulic cement and concrete (three weeks).*—Composition, manufacture, and characteristics of different kinds of hydraulic cement. Methods of testing. Specifications for Portland and natural hydraulic cements. Ingredients of concrete and determination of proportions. Proportions used for different purposes and with different cements. Methods of mixing and depositing; amount of water to be used; forms for concrete work—details to be observed in construction of same. Preparation of bill of materials and working drawings for the plant for mixing and depositing concrete and for handling material in the construction of a modern gun battery so far as to include the railway from wharf to site, material bins, structure for supporting mixer and mixer platform.

The second winter's course of eleven weeks began November 1, 1900, and ended January 24, 1901.

Details of the course ordered, upon the recommendation of the academic staff, were as follows:

(1) *Concrete (one week).*—Uses in civil and military works; use on land and under water. Durability under different conditions. Use in fireproof construction and in combination with iron. Ransome's patent methods; Melan arch construction. Waterproofing of concrete. Cost of concrete; methods of estimating and controlling same. Study of actual work and criticism of cost.

(2) *Regulation of rivers (one week).*—Object and methods. Detailed study of James River regulation. General study of Missouri River and others.

(3) *Canalization of rivers (two weeks).*—Use and description of fixed and movable dams. Study of improvement of the Great Kanawha River.

(4) *Canals; locks and lifts (one week).*—Study of methods of construction on the Illinois and Mississippi Canal. Description of systems connecting the Great Lakes and the Atlantic Ocean.

(5) *Dredging (one week).*—Objects in various localities. Methods and classification and description of dredges. Rate of work and cost. Measurement and supervision of work.

(6) *Improvement of harbors and estuaries on sandy coasts (one week).*—Use of jetties and breakwaters.

(7) *Breakwaters and light-houses—Location of bridges (one week).*—Construction and location of light-houses. Construction of breakwaters. Location of bridges across navigable waters.

(8) *Engineering plant and methods of construction (two weeks).*—Organization of working forces. Arrangement of plant relatively to site of work. Applications especially to frame and brick buildings, wharves, river and harbor works, and modern fortifications.

(9) *Preparation of estimates (one week).*—Timber trestle. Frame warehouse. Pile wharf in waters inhabited by the teredo. Steel bridge, including foundations and piers or abutments. Concrete lock. Two emplacements for 8-inch disappearing B. L. R.

The season for practical instruction extends from May 1 to November 1.

During the season 1900 hydrographic surveys were conducted by Lieutenants Brown, Fries, Smith, and Boggs, and astronomical work by Lieutenants Boggs, Smith, Wooten, Brown, and Fries.

During the present season of 1901 astronomical work has been carried on by Lieutenants Boggs, Smith, Jackson, Poole, and Jewett.

The following is the ordinary routine of observations with the several astronomical instruments after reasonable proficiency has been attained by preliminary practice:

Theodolite.—Determination of azimuth.

Sextant.—After becoming skillful in the use of this instrument upon the sun observers will deduce at least one satisfactory latitude by observing a north and a south star, using the time deduced from an east and west star, each based on ten altitudes taken on the same night. These observations for latitude and time must be made at the observatory. The observer may get "time" from an assistant, using a portable chronometer, and will determine by comparison the error of the standard chronometer at the observatory.

Chronograph.—Daily determination by time signal from Washington, D. C., of error and rate of astronomical clock.

Transit.—A satisfactory set of time observations will be taken by each officer on two nights, successive if possible, determining satisfactorily the error of the sidereal clock. The eye and ear method will be employed.

Zenith telescope.—Observers will first determine the level correction by daylight, using a distant terrestrial object, or at night, using a slow circumpolar star. They will then find the value of a turn of the micrometer by observing Polaris at elongation. Lastly, they will observe for latitude until they have obtained a satisfactory determination. Longitude by telegraph.

Lieutenants Brown and Fries, having been relieved from duty with the school March 11, 1901, to accompany the Second Battalion of Engineers to Manila, were granted certificates of proficiency on all subjects except practical astronomy, which had not been completed.

[c, completed; n. c., not completed.]

	Theoretical instruction.				Practical instruction.	Remarks.
	Electrical engineering.	Civil engineering.		Military engineering.		
			Winter's course.			
	First.	First.	Second.	Second.		
First lieutenants.						
Connor, Wm. D	c.	c.			n. c.	Joined Nov. 24, 1900; relieved from duty with the school June 17, 1901.
Boggs, F. C	c.	c.			n. c.	Joined July 2, 1901.
Smith, C. S	c.	c.	c.	c.	n. c.	
Wooten, Wm. P	c.	c.			n. c.	Joined Aug. 5, 1900; relieved from duty with the school June 25, 1901.
Brown, Earl I	c.	c.	c.		n. c.	Relieved Mar. 11, 1901.
Fries, Amos A	c.	c.	c.		n. c.	Do.
Woodruff, J. A	c.					Joined Sept. 20, 1900; relieved Mar. 11, 1901.
Markham, E. M	c.					Do.
Jackson, T. H	c.	c.			n. c.	Joined Sept. 20, 1900.
Second lieutenants.						
Poole, John H					n. c.	Joined May 21, 1901.
Jewett, Henry C					n. c.	Do.

The expansion of the two companies of engineers stationed at this post into four companies of the Second Battalion of Engineers, Company M of the Third Battalion, and a nucleus for Companies I, K, and L of the Third Battalion, as required under the Army reorganization act approved February 2, 1901, with the preparation of the Second Battalion for foreign service, and after its departure for Manila, P. I., June 17, the organization of the Third Battalion, required, on March 11, the relief of four student officers from duty at the school and practically all the time of the officers after April 30, so that, with the exception of some astronomical work, the school duties were suspended after the close of the winter's course.

A draft of regulations for the school, designed to place it in position for increased usefulness, was prepared by the academic staff, by direction of the Chief of Engineers, and submitted May 30, 1901.

NEW ENGINEERING FIELD MANUAL.

The work of compiling a field manual adapted to the requirements of our military system was begun by Capt. Thomas H. Rees, Corps of Engineers, and continued by Capt. Henry Jervey, Corps of Engineers, who, on being relieved from duty at this school, was succeeded by Capt. James F. McIndoe, Corps of Engineers.

The progress made to date is briefly as follows:

Chapters I, II, and III, on "Military Reconnaissance," "Bridges," and "Roads," respectively, have been compiled, criticised by selected officers of the Corps of Engineers, and returned to Willets Point for revision.

Chapter I, "Military Reconnaissance," has been revised in accordance with the criticisms, and the plates have been completed. Since the chapter was submitted for criticism additional paragraphs have been added on "Compilation and duplication of maps in the field," including lists of instruments and materials required for these purposes at the headquarters of an engineer company and battalion and of the chief engineer of an army or smaller command. Instructions for making field sketches are also to be inserted, and when this is done it is thought that these paragraphs should be subjected to criticism by experienced officers of the Corps of Engineers before they are incorporated in the Manual. With these exceptions Chapter I is ready for the printer.

Chapter II, "Military Bridges," has been partially revised in accordance with the criticisms and the plates have been completed. A number of omissions in the original manuscript have been supplied, but the chapter needs further careful revision before it will be ready for printing.

Chapter III, "Military Roads," has been partially revised in accordance with the criticisms and the plates have been nearly completed.

Chapter IV, "Military Railroads," has been commenced; a number of notes and sketches have been made, but the chapter is not ready for submission to the Chief of Engineers for criticism.

For the preparation of the plates a draftsman was employed from February 4, 1901, to June 30, 1901.

A portable searchlight apparatus was sent to the school for test under instructions contained in letter of the Assistant Adjutant-General dated January 2, 1901.

The transportation facilities on the post were too limited to admit of a test of portability, and all that could be done was to test the apparatus in place. The tests were made by Capt. Francis R. Shunk, Corps of Engineers, who reports as follows:

All parts were examined and the outfit tested by actual use.

The outfit comprises four trucks, carrying, respectively, the boiler, the engine and dynamo, the light, and an auxiliary hoisting outfit.

The boiler needs paint, but is otherwise in good condition. It was tested up to 150 pounds pressure, cold, and never gets beyond 100 pounds working pressure. Its capacity is nowhere given, but from an approximate calculation I should say it was 15 horsepower.

As the usefulness of a portable searchlight outfit depends largely upon the possibility of using wood as fuel, special attention was given to determining this point. It was found that wood was quite as satisfactory as coal.

The engine and dynamo are in excellent condition, need little attention, and do everything that is required of them. The total output is 10 kilowatts, or 13.4 horsepower.

The searchlight mechanism was found in good condition, needing only a little cleaning, tightening of nuts, etc. The obturator is so nearly at the principal focus that when a parallel beam was used the obturator was burned out. It can readily be moved, and I have directed that this be done.

As to the light itself, it is perhaps a truism to say that it works well when everything is going smoothly. To keep everything going smoothly requires the constant attention of an experienced man. The things that happen are easily corrected when one knows how, and to know how requires no special electrical or mechanical expertness, but does require considerable familiarity with the machine.

The hoisting apparatus is in good condition. As to the necessity of the hoist there is some difference of opinion. I believe it would be a useful but not an indispensable thing to have.

The body of the hoist truck clears the ground by 16 inches, not considering a pipe which projects below this, but could easily be put elsewhere. The boiler truck has a clearance of 18 inches, the dynamo truck of 21 inches, and the light truck of 24 inches.

The beams supporting the truck bodies are suspended below the rear axles, and could readily be put above them if deemed necessary. This would increase the clearance by about 6 inches; but I believe that a clearance of 16 inches is enough. I would recommend that the pipe referred to below the hoist be changed.

On the whole the plant is in excellent working order. As to its portability, each truck can easily be drawn by four mules and can go anywhere that a loaded wagon can go. I see no reason to question its utility in service.

These searchlights are intended, I believe, to accompany siege trains, and it has been suggested that the parts of the carriage be made uniform and interchangeable with corresponding parts of siege carriages. The running gear of the present carriages is quite different from that of the siege carriages, the wheels, for example, being 58 inches instead of 60 inches in diameter, and the axles, etc., of different size and pattern.

I am of opinion that the change is desirable, but do not feel competent to make detailed recommendations.

I concur in Captain Shunk's report, and would add that in preparing future outfits of this character changes should be made in the mount of the searchlight which would permit it to be readily dismounted and packed for transportation by rail or sea. In its present shape transportation by sea would be especially hazardous.

The statement of funds appropriated and expended for school purposes and the estimate of funds for the same are to be found in the following pages.

III. ENGINEER TROOPS.

Two companies of the Battalion of Engineers were stationed here during the year till March 2, 1901, the date of the receipt of the general order from the Adjutant-General's Office announcing the act of Congress approved February 2, 1901, concerning the reorganization of the Army.

The course of instruction was as follows:

| | Companies. ||
	C.	D.
Ponton and rope bridges; special instruction in rowing	June	August.
Field and siege works, hasty cover and deflading against infantry fire	July	June.
Submarine mines; special instruction of officers and selected noncommissioned officers in mining casemate duty, including firing of simulated triple groups on shore; swimming	August	July.
Trestle and spar bridges	September	October.
Target practice; reconnaissance; signaling for noncommissioned officers and selected privates	October	September.
Company and infantry battalion drills	November	

During the months from December to March, inclusive, the noncommissioned officers of each company were instructed daily in: (1) reconnaissance; (2) ponton manual; (3) field fortifications; (4) attack of fortified places.

Once a week each company was instructed in the manual of arms, firing, and bayonet exercise. Special instruction in the duties of litter bearers and the methods of rendering first aid to the sick and wounded was given weekly. Selected noncommissioned officers were instructed in photography.

A detachment of 50 men from Companies C and D was on duty at West Point, N. Y., after the departure of Company E. Their duties were to assist in the instruction of cadets in practical military engineering, to furnish details for guard, and teachers for the post school.

The detachment sent in February, 1900, to Alaska for duty in connection with road making is still absent on that duty.

One sergeant was sent April 27, 1901, to Fort Rodman, Mass., for duty in connection with the transfer of the submarine mining material to the commanding officer of that post. On June 30 he had not returned from that duty.

During September and October, 1900, with the permission of the governor of the State of New York, Companies C and D each encamped for a week on the grounds of the Creedmoor target range and engaged in target practice.

Companies A and B were on duty in the Philippine Islands the entire year, Company A having left this post May 24, 1898, and Company B July 5, 1899. Company E, which had been on duty at West Point, N. Y., left that post July 24, 1900, under orders to proceed to China to take part in the relief expedition to Pekin. Upon arriving at Nagasaki, Japan, its orders were changed to Manila, P. I., where it arrived September 3.

The duties of the engineer companies in the Philippine Islands were varied, including repairs to public buildings, roads, railroads, bridges, and ferries; construction of roads and bridges; reconnaissance, map making, and photography; duties in the office of chief engineers of departments; accompanying expeditions and making reconnaissance maps of roads thereon.

A detachment of 2 sergeants, 1 corporal, and 17 privates from Company B, under Lieutenant Ferguson, accompanied the first expedition to China, taking part in the capture of Tientsin and the march to Pekin and its capture. In addition to its presence in the firing line at Tientsin and Pekin, its duties comprised reconnaissance around Tientsin, on the march to Pekin, and on expeditions from Pekin; map making and photography; preparation of bridge material, construction and navigation of rafts from Tientsin to the neighborhood of Pekin with the relief expedition; keeping the road from Tung Chow to Pekin in repair for the wagon train.

Maj. John G. D. Knight was in command of the Battalion of Engineers, with the following staff: First Lieut. George P. Howell, adjutant; First Lieut. William B. Ladue, quartermaster.

Under the requirements of section 11 of the act of Congress approved February 2, 1901, fixing the enlisted force of the Corps of Engineers at one band and three battalions of four companies each, General Orders No. 22, Headquarters of the Army, Adjutant-General's Office, February 26, 1901, prescribed the following organization:

The First Battalion, to consist of Companies A, B, C, and D, at Manila, P. I.

The band and the Second Battalion, to consist of Companies E, F, G, and H, at Fort Totten, Willets Point, N. Y.

The Third Battalion, to consist of Companies I, K, L, and M, at Fort Totten, Willets Point, N. Y., except Company M, which was ordered to be formed at West Point, N. Y., from the detachment there. The remaining companies of this battalion were not to be formed until the organization of the Second Battalion was effected.

The designation of the existing Companies E, C, and D, of the Battalion of Engineers, was changed as follows:

Company E to Company C.
Company C to Company E.
Company D to Company F.

Telegraphic orders from the Office of the Adjutant-General of the Army were received March 7, 1901, directing that the Second Battalion be prepared for service in the Philippine Islands; and Special Orders No. 55, Headquarters of the Army, Adjutant-General's Office, March 8, 1901, assigned officers to the battalions and companies of engineers being organized.

Maj. John G. D. Knight was placed in command of the Third Battalion, with First Lieut. George P. Howell as adjutant and First Lieut. William B. Ladue as quartermaster. April 29, Maj. W. M. Black relieved Major Knight; June 17, First Lieut. W. D. Connor relieved Lieutenant Ladue, and June 25, First Lieut. W. P. Wooten relieved Lieutenant Howell.

In April, May, and June the Second Battalion was instructed in infantry drills, pontoniering, trestle and pile bridge and pier construction, hasty intrenching, foot reconnaissance, use of surveying instruments, cordage, camping, road building, and railway track laying; and special details in carpentry, masonry, plumbing, and blacksmith work.

The Second Battalion left this post for the Philippine Islands June 17, 1901, with a strength of 13 officers and 357 men.

After June 17 the work of recruiting, organizing, and instructing Companies I, K, and L, of the Third Battalion, was carried on. On account of the small garrison, available details for routine duties were reduced to a minimum, and to this end all the men (45 in number, of whom 7 were on detached service and 4 absent on furlough) were provisionally formed into I Company, with the intention of dividing into the three companies as soon as the enlisted strength should exceed 90 men.

To fulfill its duties properly under the form of organization of the United States Army, the battalions of engineers should be prepared to undertake and carry on engineer work of all kinds, including even work of municipal sanitation. With the class of men available this can be done, provided that facilities for instruction be provided in time of peace. Classes have been established on the post for instruction of selected men in carpentry, plumbing, mason work, blacksmith and machine-shop work, and the management of steam plant, floating and fixed.

It is very important that facilities be afforded for instruction in railroad construction and in the handling of locomotive engines, a branch of instruction to which great attention is paid in foreign services. The instruction should be given and the experience had with plant of standard size. One mile of track, one locomotive, and two small freight cars would be sufficient. The estimated cost of the necessary materials and plant is $10,000. It is earnestly hoped that an appropriation will be made for its purchase.

Officers of the Corps of Engineers were on duty with engineer companies as follows:

Battalion of Engineers—July 1, 1900, till February 28, 1901.

COMPANY A.

First Lieut. James B. Cavanaugh, joined October 1, 1900.
First Lieut. William P. Wooten, relieved June 27, 1900.
First Lieut. Horton W. Stickle.
First Lieut. Lewis H. Rand, joined August 24, 1900.

COMPANY B.

First Lieut. John C. Oakes.
First Lieut. Sherwood A. Cheney, joined July 20, 1900.
First Lieut. Harley B. Ferguson.
First Lieut. William Kelly, joined September 3, 1900.

COMPANY C.

Capt. Henry Jervey.
First Lieut. William D. Connor, joined November 27, 1900.
First Lieut. Louis C. Wolf, absent on sick leave.
First Lieut. Clarke S. Smith.
First Lieut. Earl I. Brown.
First Lieut. James A. Woodruff, joined September 20, 1900.
First Lieut. Thomas H. Jackson, joined September 22, 1900.
First Lieut. Edward M. Adams, joined August 1, 1900; relieved September 15, 1900.
First Lieut. Edmund M. Rhett, joined August 1, 1900; relieved September 15, 1900.

COMPANY D.

Capt. Francis R. Shunk.
First Lieut. Frank C. Boggs, joined July 5, 1900.
First Lieut. W. P. Wooten, joined August 6, 1900.
First Lieut. Amos A. Fries.
First Lieut. Edward M. Markham, joined September 22, 1900.
First Lieut. Gustave R. Lukesh, joined August 1, 1900; relieved September 15, 1900.

COMPANY E.

Capt. George A. Zinn, joined July 29, 1900; relieved September 6, 1900.
First Lieut. James B. Cavanaugh, joined July 24, 1900; relieved October 19, 1900.
First Lieut. James P. Jervey, relieved July 17, 1900.
First Lieut. Harry Burgess, joined July 29, 1900.
First Lieut. Frederick W. Altstaetter, joined January 23, 1901.
First Lieut. John R. Slattery, joined July 24, 1901.

Second Battalion of Engineers—since March 11, 1901.

First Lieut. James A. Woodruff, adjutant.
First Lieut. Edward M. Markham, quartermaster.

COMPANY E.

Capt. Henry Jervey.
First Lieut. Thomas H. Jackson, relieved May 29, 1901.
Second Lieut. Edward N. Johnston.

COMPANY F.

Capt. Robert McGregor, joined March 16, 1901.
First Lieut. W. P. Wooten, relieved May 29, 1901.
First Lieut. Earl I. Brown.
Second Lieut. Arthur Williams.

COMPANY G.

Capt. Jay J. Morrow, joined March 18, 1901.
First Lieut. Amos A. Fries.
First Lieut. Ernest D. Peek.

COMPANY H.

Capt. William W. Harts, joined March 31, 1901.
First Lieut. Gustave R. Lukesh, joined March 16, 1901.
Second Lieut. Elliott J. Dent.

Third Battalion of Engineers—Since March 11, 1901.

COMPANIES I, K, AND L.

Capt. Francis R. Shunk.
Capt. Charles H. McKinstry, joined March 30, 1901.
Capt. James F. McIndoe, joined March 9, 1901.
First Lieut. George P. Howell, joined June 25, 1901.
First Lieut. William D. Connor, relieved June 17, 1901.
First Lieut. Frank C. Boggs.
First Lieut. Clarke S. Smith.
First Lieut. William P. Wooten, joined May 29, 1901; relieved June 25, 1901.
First Lieut. Thomas H. Jackson, joined May 29, 1901.
Second Lieut. John H. Poole.
Second Lieut. Henry C. Jewett.

COMPANY M.

Capt. Joseph E. Kuhn.
Capt. James P. Jervey, relieved May 29, 1901.
First Lieut. William B. Ladue, joined June 17, 1901.

IV. ENGINEER DEPOT.

1. PUBLIC BUILDINGS, BOATS, CONSTRUCTIONS, ETC.

The property in the depot, consisting of the bridge and ponton equipage, stores for bridge and ponton trains, engineer, field, and torpedo service; astronomical, surveying, drawing, and electrical instruments; photographic supplies; materials for current repairs to buildings, boats, and machinery, has been cared for.

During the fiscal year no new constructions or additions to any of the depot buildings have been made. Minor repairs and painting were made as needed.

The depot stables were repaired by replacing the old flooring by a new one, whitewashing the entire interior of the building, and cleaning up the grounds surrounding the same.

A new flooring has been placed in the carpenter shop and shelves provided for in the mining casemate.

Brick piers have been substituted for wooden posts under floor beams of the two small storage sheds.

2. WORK OF THE DEPOT.

The usual routine care of property has continued, the incidental labor having been performed by enlisted men of the Engineer Battalion detailed on extra duty during the first ten months, when most of these men were relieved, and, on authority given by the Chief of Engineers, civilians employed.

Purchases under proposals were continued during the year of various materials, such as submarine mining supplies, surveying instruments, drawing materials, photographic outfits, bridge and ponton equipage, intrenching and other field-engineering supplies.

Delivery of professional periodicals for library of United States Engineer School has continued. Subscriptions for these have been renewed from January 1, 1901, for the current year. Various professional books, mostly of recent date, treating on various engineering subjects, have been added to the library during the year.

Six wooden ponton boats ordered during previous fiscal year have been delivered.

From the 18,000 feet, board measure, Oregon pine timber procured, 186 long balks, 187 short balks, and 15 trestle balks have been fitted up in the depot.

Four battery and forge wagons, fitted out with necessary tools and materials, were received from the United States Ordnance Department in May. They are for use in ponton trains.

A number of engineering models, loaned in 1900 to the United States Commission to the Paris Exposition, were received back in February.

The engineering models authorized by the Chief of Engineers, United States Army, to be sent to the Pan-American Exposition, Buffalo, N. Y., for the Engineer Department exhibit, were thoroughly overhauled and repaired, and left this post April 19, 1901.

Several models of forts and other curiosities captured in the Chinese forts were received here April, 1900, having been sent by First Lieut. H. B. Ferguson, Corps of Engineers. They are now on exhibition in the Museum of the United States Engineer School.

Materials for instruction of engineer troops in their special duties were procured from time to time as needed. Among the articles bought may be mentioned the following:

One electrical switch board (power board), similar to those used in the torpedo service; three portable testing sets; one Batson sketching case; twelve 20-foot long poles for ponton and trestle bridge instruction, and a supply of steel rails, ties, switches, etc. There was also received by transfer from other localities, for test and report, one searchlight outfit, portable, consisting of a generator truck, searchlight truck, boiler truck, and hoist truck.

Special attention was given the matter of procuring materials for the instruction of the enlisted men of the Second Battalion of Engineers, and all that could be done with the limited funds and short time available was accomplished before their departure for the Philippine Islands.

The work of checking up the great bulk of property in the Engineer Depot and the professional works of the library of the United States Engineer School was commenced early in May, but, owing to the magnitude and importance of this work and the other important duties at the close of the fiscal year, it was impracticable to complete this work. The work will be continued in the new fiscal year and carried on to completion.

Considerable drafting and clerical work was required in connection with the preparation of the new Engineering Field Manual. Extracts and copies of specifications and of blue prints relating to construction of public roads in the island of Porto Rico, submitted by Captain Judson, have been made and will form a part of the Field Manual.

In connection with the work of the depot, various reports were rendered to the Chief of Engineers, United States Army, as to condidition of the ponton and bridge equipage in the depot. Additions to ponton materials, issues of ponton materials and instruments, were made from time to time. Work of assorting, assembling, and repairing old ponton wagons was commenced. A detailed report of this work appears under the special heading of "Equipment of engineer troops."

3. DEPOT INSTRUMENTS.

Miscellaneous surveying instruments, reconnaissance and drawing materials have been procured from time to time under proposals opened July 18, 1900. Quantity and kinds were not specified, but specifications required bidders to be prepared to supply such number of each class as may be called for during the year at the prices bid. A special list of instruments and drawing materials was prepared on which bids were obtained, and, in addition to these lists, bidders furnished their catalogues with prices and discounts noted therein, which formed a part of their bids.

Under the appropriation of $3,000 for Engineer Depot, instruments, 1901, the following were purchased during the year:

5 engineer's transits.	1 3-arm metal protractor.
1 sextant.	3 triangles, German silver.
8 engineer's levels.	26 boxwood scales, 12-inch, triangular.
10 level rods.	2 aneroid barometers.
100 cavalry sketching cases.	1 clinometer.
2 prismatic compasses.	26 compasses, pocket.
1 odometer.	1 hand level.
1 set drawing instruments.	1 drawing board.
1 metallic tape, 50 feet.	2 vernier glasses.
1 T-square, steel.	5 small pieces of drawing instruments.

APPENDIX 5—POST OF FORT TOTTEN, N. Y., ETC.   949

All the above articles were bought at a total cost of $2,977.12. The sum of $22.75 was expended for repairing 1 transit and 1 level, leaving a balance of 13 cents from the $3,000 appropriated, which was returned to the Treasury.

Repairing and overhauling instruments on hand in the depot was continued in the depot repair shop as required for issue.

The following is a list of instruments that have been subject to more or less repairs during the year:

Four engineer transits, 3 engineer levels, 18 cavalry sketching cases, 3 Bradley's galvanometers, 2 Siemen's galvanometers, 42 circuit detectors, 12 prismatic compasses, 20 pocket compasses, 1 astronomical transit, 1 sextant, 1 astronomical clock, 1,500 circuit-regulator plugs.

Issues of instruments and reconnaissance materials were made to officers engaged on public works and surveys during the year, upon requisitions duly authorized by the Chief of Engineers, United States Army, as follows:

1 theodolite.
2 engineer transits.
3 engineer levels.
6 sextants.
4 level rods.
11 binocular field glasses.
1 3-arm protractor.
5 steel tapes, 100 feet.
1 steel tape, 50 feet.
1 standard steel bar.
8 prismatic compasses.
10 cavalry sketching cases.
7 pocket compasses.
1 aneroid barometer.
6 sets drawing instruments.

12 Abbot's protractors.
6 boxwood scales, 12 inch.
2 vernier glasses.
2 drawing boards.
1 steel T-square.
2 magneto machines, exploders; also a miscellaneous lot of small instruments and drawing materials, including numerous rolls of paper for use on cavalry and Batson sketching cases, and several rolls of paper 13 inches wide for use on self-registering tide gauges, in use by officers of the Corps of Engineers in charge of public works.

A number of surveying instruments and miscellaneous reconnaissance and drawing materials were issued from time to time during the year to details of the Engineer Battalion engaged in reconnaissance and hydrographic work for instruction purposes. On completion of this duty all articles so issued were returned to the depot.

During the year the following instruments were turned into the depot by officers in charge of public works and surveys and acting engineer officers, viz:

1 engineer's transit.
2 engineer's levels.
1 current meter.
2 theodolites.
2 sextants.
1 artificial horizon.
1 chronometer.
1 chronograph.
1 break-circuit key.
2 aneroid barometers.

2 watches.
1 astronomical transit and zenith telescope combined.
7 cavalry sketching cases.
4 pocket compasses.
5 sets drawing instruments.
1 pocket sextant.
21 odometers.
12 prismatic compasses.
1 binocular field glass.

As a rule, most of these instruments when received back are unserviceable. Those which were fit have been repaired when needed; others were set aside with the property intended for inspection and condemnation. A portion of the larger instruments received back were in use on surveys of the Yellowstone National Park. All these were received in very fair condition and require but slight repairs and overhauling to be fit for reissue.

A number of unserviceable instruments and drawing materials have accumulated in the depot on which the action of an inspector will be requested when practicable.

Issues of hygrometers and thermometers, for use in magazines of fortifications, was continued during the year, on duly approved requisitions, to the number of 47 hygrometers and 136 thermometers.

Purchases, issues, and receipts of instruments, drawing materials, etc., required for equipment of engineer troops for use in the field, and to chief engineer officers with army corps, etc., are referred to hereafter under the heading "Equipment of Engineer Troops."

4. EQUIPMENT OF ENGINEER TROOPS.

Allotments amounting to $19,250 have been made by the Chief of Engineers, United States Army, from time to time during the fiscal year from appropriation for "Equipment of Engineer Troops," act approved May 26, 1900, for "pontoon trains, intrenching tools, instruments, and drawing materials."

Materials of all descriptions required for field service of engineer organizations, such as surveying instruments, reconnaissance, and drawing materials, blue-print paper and cloth, field photographic materials, intrenching tools, sappers' and miners' tools, blacksmiths' and carpenters' tools, railroad supplies, and ponton and bridge materials, are all embraced under the term "Equipment of Engineer Troops."

The operations carried on during the year are reported on in two classes: *a, Instruments, intrenching tools, etc.*, and *b, Completing ponton trains.*

a. *Instruments, intrenching tools, etc.*

The principal articles purchased during the year were those covered by various requisitions received from engineer officers serving in the new foreign possessions, and from officers in charge of Alaska exploring expeditions, and referred to this office by the Chief of Engineers, United States Army, with authority to make shipments. Of the total sum allotted for class *a*, $11,000, only 83 cents remained unexpended at the close of the fiscal year.

During the year 12 requisitions were referred to this office. They have been filled with as little delay as possible, as follows:

	Requisitions.
Chief engineer, Division of the Philippines, Manila, P. I	5
Officer in charge of engineer troops at West Point, N. Y	3
Acting engineer officer, Washington Barracks, D. C	1
Engineer officer, Department of Alaska	1
Second Battalion of Engineers, before their departure for the Philippine Islands	1
Third Battalion of Engineers	1
Total	12

These were filled from supply in the engineer depot and by purchase under proposals. Instruments, drawing materials, and blue-print paper and cloth were obtained under standing proposals holding for the fiscal year. Implements, tools, materials, and photographic supplies were obtained under circular notices of from three to ten days, according to the time available for filling the requisition.

All materials shipped have been carefully prepared for export shipment. Those subject to atmospheric influences were specially pre-

APPENDIX 5—POST OF FORT TOTTEN, N. Y., ETC.   951

pared for the climate for which they were destined. Blue-print papers and blue-print cloth were put up in tin foil and, as a rule, 50 rolls put in a tin-lined case. Photographic materials were ordered to be freshly made and were put up in sealed tin cases; photographic chemicals in sealed bottles with glass stoppers.

From the various reports received from engineer officers serving in the Philippines it is gratifying to mention that all materials shipped from this depot have arrived there in good condition, as shown by the following extract from the annual report of Capt. John Biddle, Corps of Engineers, chief engineer of the Division of the Philippines, upon operations under the Engineer Department for the fiscal year 1900:

> The climate here is very hard on all materials, particularly that used in photography and map printing. Everything should be packed in small sealed packages so as not to be opened until needed. The blue-print paper sent from Willets Point in sealed cases has proved perfectly satisfactory and has kept well. It is, as far as I can learn, the only blue-print paper ever sent to this part of the world that has kept well. Both here and in Hongkong it has been considered impossible to preserve it, and what I have been obliged to buy here has been very poor.

The following tables, divided into the different classes of materials, give shipments during the year from the engineer depot upon the twelve requisitions received:

I. *Surveying instruments, reconnaissance, drawing, and blue-print materials.*

Item	Qty	Item	Qty
Artificial horizons....number..	2	Ink, india:	
Batson sketching cases...do....	21	Sticks ....number..	1
Barometers, aneroid.....do....	5	Bottles ....dozen..	6
Barometers, mercury cistern, number......................	1	Ink: Black, drawing, ½-pint bottles............number..	8
Books:		Assorted, drawing, ½-pint bottles........number..	131
Field............number..	213	Levels, engineers' ....do....	4
Level..............do....	132	Level rods:	
Reconnaissance .....do....	6	N. Y ....do....	6
Transit ....do....	132	Philadelphia........do....	1
Brushes, camel's hair, assorted, number......................	12	Odometers ....do....	6
Cavalry sketching cases, number......................	47	Paper: Blue-print, 36-inch (10-yard rolls) ....rolls..	400
Clinometers..........number..	9	Blue-print, 42-inch (10-yard rolls) ....rolls..	281
Compasses: Pocket ....do....	114	Brown-print, medium, 36-inch ....rolls..	10
Prismatic ....do....	26	Brown-print, thin, 36-inch, rolls	5
Cloth: Blue-print, 36-inch ..rolls..	75	Drawing, 19 by 24 inches, sheets...........dozen..	1
Blue-print, 42-inch ..do....	25	Drawing, mounted, 36-inch (10-yard rolls) ....rolls..	18
Tracing, 36-inch.....do....	13	Drawing, unmounted, 42-inch (10-yard rolls), yards	56
Tracing, 42-inch.....do....	12		
Chronograph, complete, number	1	500-foot rolls . ...rolls..	21
Chronometers: Break-circuit.....number..	1	100-foot rolls, for sketching cases ....rolls..	1
Mean solar...........do....	1	Pedometers..........number..	1
Portable............do....	3	Pencils:	
Drawing boards, 31 by 42 inches, number......................	1	Drawing, assorted..dozen..	216½
Drawing instruments .....sets..	5	Drawing, colored....do....	11
Erasers: Rubber.........number..	158	Pens: Crow quill..........do....	2
Steel ....do....	24		
Field glasses, binocular..do....	7		
Hygrometers ....do....	2		
Hand levels, reflecting...do....	9		

I. Surveying instruments, reconnaissance, drawing, and blue-print materials—Continued.

Pens—Continued.	
Gillot's No. 291 .....gross..	6
Gillot's No. 170 .....do....	6
Mapping ....do....	3
Plate glass, for blue printing:	
20 by 24 inches ....sheets..	1
29¾ by 41¾ inches....do....	6
39¾ by 59¾ inches....do....	2
Printing frames:	
20 by 24 inches...number..	1
30 by 42 inches, complete, with glass .....number..	2
40 by 60 inches, complete, with glass .....number..	1
Protractors, Abbot's .....do....	13
Rulers:	
Rubber, assorted ....do....	8
Steel, 36-inch ....do....	6
Steel, 30-inch ....do....	1
Saucers, cabinet, 4 in nest.nest..	1
Scales, triangular, boxwood, 12-inch..............number..	29
Sextants..............do....	2
Stop watches..........do....	1
Tapes:	
Metallic, 100-foot....do....	68
Steel, 50-foot........do....	13
Tapes—Continued.	
Steel, 100-foot....number..	1
Telescopes, zenith.......do....	1
Theodolites, medium, 10-inch, number.....................	1
Thermometers ......number..	4
Thumb tacks ....dozen..	156
Transits:	
Astronomical ....number..	1
Engineers',complete.do....	4
Triangles:	
Rubber, assorted ....do....	10
Wood, 6-inch, 45-degree, number.....................	36
Celluloid,10-inch,45-degree, number.....................	1
Celluloid, 10-inch, 60-degree, number.....................	1
Tubes, preserving ....number..	24
Vernier lamps ....do....	2
Water colors............boxes..	1
Water colors, assorted ..cakes..	28
Water-color brushes, 12 in set, sets........................	1
Scale guards ....number..	1
Trestles, folding, hard-wood, number.....................	2

II. Field photographic materials.

Acid:	
Acetic, glacial ....pounds..	12
Pyrogallic, c. p ......do....	3
Sulphuric, c. p ......do....	2
Alum, powdered ....do....	18
Amidol...................	½
American Annual of Photography and Photographic Times Almanac ....copies..	1
Aristo gold solution...bottles..	25
Aristo platino solution...do....	25
Borax................pounds..	1½
Bromide potassium......do....	2
Brushes:	
Camel's hair .....number..	1
Bristle ....do....	1
Camera:	
Premo A, 5 by 7 inches, number..................	2
Leather carrying case for same ....number..	2
Tripods for same...do....	2
Plate holders for same, number..................	12
Card mounts:	
5 by 7 inches ....number..	500
7 by 9 inches ....do....	200
10½ by 12½ inches....do....	200
Chloride of gold in 15-gr. bottles.................dozens..	2
Dry plates, Seed's:	
5 by 7 inches .....dozens..	65
8 by 10 inches ....do....	25
6½ by 8½ inches......do....	20
Duster, camel's hair..number..	1
Eikonogen............bottles..	6
Envelopes:	
Negative ....number..	220
Photomailing ....do....	500
Films for Eastman's No. 4 Panoram Kodak ....rolls..	10
Flashlight powder, "Illumino," ounces...................	2
Graduated glasses, assorted, number.....................	6
Filter paper ....sheets..	100
Funnels, glass........number..	2
Hydrochinon..........pounds..	1 1/16
Do ....bottles..	8
International Annual of Anthony's Photographic bulletin, copies	1
Lamps, ruby..........number..	1
Lanterns, dark room.....do....	1
Manual of Photographic Chemistry, Hardwich .....copies..	1
Masks:	
For 5 by 7 inch plates, number...................	4
For 8 by 10 inch plates, number...................	4
Metol:	
Hauff's ....ounces..	3
Do ....bottles..	8
Quinol developer, in tubes, gross	1
Negative racks ....number..	1
Nitrate of silver.......pounds..	2½
Paper, printing:	
Aristo platino, 5 by 7 inch sheets ....gross..	12

APPENDIX 5—POST OF FORT TOTTEN, N. Y., ETC.

II. *Field photographic materials*—Continued.

Item	Qty
Paper, printing—Continued.	
Aristo platino, 6½ by 8½ inch sheets...........gross..	3
Aristo platino, 8 by 10 inch sheets............gross..	10
Aristo platino, 17 by 20 inch sheets............gross..	1
Velox carbon, 5 by 7 inch sheets............gross..	12
Velox glossy, 5 by 7 inch sheets............gross..	2
Velox carbon, 8 by 10 inch sheets............gross..	5
Velox carbon, 20-inch sheets............rolls..	2
Solio, 5 by 7 inch sheets, gross...................	4
Paper, litmus..........sheets..	2
Photo paste............jars..	1
Printing frames, 5 by 7 inches, number................	12
Scales, standard, with weights in case............number..	1
Soda:	
Carbonate........pounds..	6
Hyposulphate ......do....	475
Sulphite............do....	17
Solio hardener..........do....	1
Do ....bottles..	2
Tubing, rubber............feet..	3
Trays:	
Agate, 11 by 14 inches, number................	2
Japanned..........do....	5
Rubber, 6 by 8 inches, number................	2
Rubber, 6½ by 8 inches, number................	3
Rubber, 8 by 10 inches, number................	3
Rubber, 14 by 16 inches, number................	2

III. *Intrenching tools, implements, etc.*

Item	Qty
Adzes:	
Assorted.........number..	84
Handles for.........do....	118
Anvils, assorted ....do....	35
Aprons, leather ....do....	2
Axes:	
Chopping............do....	4,124
Chopping, handles for......	
Broad ....number..	37
Broad, handles for...do....	45
Hand, with handles..do....	160
Augers, assorted, with handles, number...............	50
Bags, canvas, horseshoers', small, number...............	2
Bag strings..........pounds..	200
Balk, long, 5 by 5 by 27 inches, number...............	28
Bars, digging, double-ended, number...............	20
Beeswax ....pounds..	8
Billhooks...........number..	1,000
Blacksmiths' tools (field outfits) sets....................	4
Black tape ....packages..	10
Blocks:	
Single, assorted...number..	48
Double, assorted.....do....	68
Triple, assorted......do....	14
Snatch, assorted ....do....	14
Boxes, horseshoers'......do....	1
Candles, lantern ....gross..	1
Cant hooks ....number..	61
Carpenters' tools (field outfits), sets.....................	4
Chalk:	
White ....dozen..	6
Red ....do....	6
Chalk lines ....balls..	82
Chess, 13 feet ....number..	80
Chisels:	
Cold ....number..	163
Firmer ....do....	200
Framing ....do....	90
Hot ....do....	1
Masons' ....do....	4
Mortise............do....	300
Mortise, handles for..do....	250
Climbing irons..........pairs..	12
Climbing irons, straps.number..	12
Clinching irons..........do....	1
Come-alongs ....do....	16
Cotton duck:	
15-ounce............yards..	112
8-ounce.............do....	108
4-ounce.............do....	97
Crowbars............number..	400
Cutters:	
Bolt, large ....do....	4
Wire, assorted.......do....	208
Dolly, carpenters' ....do....	1
Files:	
Assorted............do....	352
Handles for.........do....	2
Forges, portable........do....	5
Fore-shoe punch and greaser, number................	1
Fuzes:	
F. F..............feet....	4,000
4-foot............number..	500
Electrical..........do....	500
Gimlets, assorted ....do....	50
Grindstones, assorted ....do....	24
Hammers:	
Ball pene............do....	20
Brick..............do....	4
Carpenters', assorted.do....	100
Carpenters', assorted, handles for........number..	100
Claw ....do....	76

III. *Intrenching tools, implements, etc.*—Continued.

Hammers—Continued.	
Hand ....number..	5
Chipping ....do....	56
Sledge ....do....	54
Sledge, handles for ..do....	62
Spiking, R. R ....do....	24
Stone................do....	43
Stone, handles for ...do....	35
Riveting ....do....	1
Shoeing ....do....	1
Hatchets:	
Assorted............do....	724
Handles for.........do....	1,298
Hardies ....do....	1
Iron, calking ....do....	8
Jackscrews:	
6-ton ....do....	10
10-ton ....do....	5
Assorted............do....	15
Knives:	
Drawing ....do....	75
Shoeing ....do....	2
Toe ....do....	1
Lamps:	
Rochester ....do....	12
Rochester chimneys.do....	12
Rochester wicks.....do....	12
Lanterns, complete......do....	224
Lantern:	
Wicks..............gross..	4
Globes, extra ....number..	24
Square glass ....dozen..	1
Levels, carpenters'....number..	50
Machetes ....do....	2,684
Machete sheaths ....do....	2,684
Mallets, calking ....do....	4
Mattocks ....do....	150
Handles for.........do....	150
Magneto machines, No. 3 (exploders)...........number..	27
Marline spikes ....do....	12
Mauls, heavy ....do....	4
Nails, cut, in 100-lb. kegs..kegs..	6
Nail punches........number..	1
Nippers, cutting, assorted, number	156
Oilers, brass..........number..	1
Oilstones ....do....	20
Palms, sailors'........do....	12
Pencils, black........dozen..	1
Pincers, shoeing......number..	1
Picks ....do....	8,024
Pick handles..........do....	9,048
Picks, miners'........do....	136
Pliers:	
Cutting, assorted ....do....	1,350
Telegraph, side cutting, number.................	14
Plumb and level sticks, masons', number............................	4
Ponton boats, wooden, number..	4
Post-hole diggers........do....	11
Post-hole scoops.........do....	3
Pritchels ....do....	1
Punches, round ....do....	1
Rack-a-rock, complete, with dipping outfit..........pounds..	200
Rasps, shoeing, 16 inches, number	1
Rakes, fire ....number..	1
Reels, chalk-line ....do....	20
Rope, manila:	
$\frac{3}{4}$-inch circumference, coils..	1
$1\frac{3}{4}$ inches circumference, coils	
$2\frac{1}{4}$ inches circumference, coils	4
Rules, 2-foot ....number..	83
Safety belts and straps...do....	4
Samson battery for chronograph, cells	8
Sand bags............number.	35,800
Sail needles, assorted ....do....	48
Sail twine.............balls..	24
Saws:	
Hand, cross-cut, assorted, number..................	208
Rip............. number..	2
Cross-cut (2 men)...do....	158
Cross-cut (2 men), handles for, pairs.................	182
Hack............number..	1
Hack, blades for....dozen..	3
Scythes:	
Grass............number..	20
Bush ....do....	100
Shovels:	
Short-handle.........do....	8,074
Long-handle.........do....	500
Miners'.............do....	50
Fire ....do....	1
Sickles ....do....	26
Sledges, assorted..........do....	302
Handles for.........do....	700
Spades ....do....	6,074
Squares:	
Steel ....do....	26
Try ....do....	25
Tacks, galvanized-iron, pounds..	6
Tapes:	
Metallic, 100-foot, number..	1
Steel, 100-foot ....do....	1
Tools, blacksmiths'.......sets..	21
Tool chests:	
Blacksmiths'.....number..	14
Carpenters', with tools, number	6
Tongs:	
$\frac{1}{2}$-inch and $\frac{3}{4}$-inch, number..	2
Smith's..............do....	1
Trowels ....do....	12
Masons' ....do....	4
Tracing tape ....feet..	1,152
Vises:	
Telegraph ....number..	18
4-inch jaw ....do....	1
Wheelbarrows, iron .....do....	5
Wire, leading, insulated...feet..	16,500
Wire, connecting......pounds..	3
Wrenches:	
Monkey, assorted, number..	66
Screw, 8-inch ....do....	1
Screw, 12-inch ......do....	1

APPENDIX 5—POST OF FORT TOTTEN, N. Y., ETC.   955

In preparing the Second Battalion of Engineers for service in the Philippines care was taken to fit out the battalion with the best and most suitable articles for service in the field. Lists for the various classes of supplies were prepared after considerable study by myself and the captains commanding the four companies of that battalion.

As a supply of the heavier tools was known to be in the Philippines, the equipment was limited to the special articles which it was believed should form a part of the equipment of the battalion headquarters and of each company.

The equipment for the battalion headquarters included—

One library of technical books, 1 field photographic outfit, 1 field astronomical outfit, and surveying instruments.

The equipment of each company included—

One surveying and drafting outfit, blacksmiths' tools, carpenters' tools, plumbers' tools, and intrenching tools and materials.

Instruments on hand in the depot selected for this battalion were sent to a reliable instrument maker for repairs, and were returned when completed.

All new instruments to complete the outfit were ordered under standing proposals.

Intrenching tools, materials, etc., with a few exceptions, were supplied from the depot, and the excepted articles were purchased under proposals.

For the necessary outfits of carpenters' and plumbers' tools, lists were prepared under my supervision by the captains of the Second Battalion, naming the carpenters' tools and plumbers' tools required. The articles needed in these sets were selected after consultation with officers who have had experience in the use of these tools in the field.

The necessary tool chests were constructed here from purchased materials, as the ordinary commercial tool chests are unsuitable for field use.

Experiments are being continued with a view to adopting a standard chest for each class of tools, suitable for wagon or pack transportation.

The following detailed lists show the materials furnished for equipment of the battalion headquarters:

1. Library of technical books, as follows (purchased by special authority of the Secretary of War):

1 copy Public Water Supplies, Turneaure & Russell.
1 copy Hazlehurst's Towers and Tanks.
4 copies Fieberger's Text-book on Field Forts.
1 copy Water Supply Engineering, Folwell.
1 copy Sewerage, Folwell.
1 copy Street Pavements, Tillson.
1 copy Railroad Construction, Webb.
1 copy Johnson's Surveying.
1 copy Topographic Surveying, Wilson.
1 copy Handbook for Architects (in two vols.), Kidder.
1 copy Engineer's Pocket Book, Trautwine.
1 copy Materials for Construction, Johnson.
1 copy Specifications and Contracts, Johnson.
1 copy Electric Lighting (in two vols.), Crocker.
1 copy Standard Wiring, Cushing.
1 copy Plumbing, Lawler.
1 copy Railroad Curves and Earthwork, Allen.
1 copy Railroad Curves, Shunk.
1 copy Masonry Construction, Baker.
1 copy Highway Construction, Byrne.
4 copies Inspection of Materials, Byrne.
1 copy Heating and Ventilation, Billings.
1 copy Sewer Design, Ogden.
1 copy Sewage, Rideal.
1 copy Land and Marine Engines, Roper.
1 copy Engineer's Handy Book, Roper.

1 copy Mechanical Engineer's Pocket Book, Kent.
1 copy Wooden Trestle Bridges, Foster.
1 copy American House Carpenter, Hatfield.
1 copy Thurston's Manual, I and II.
1 copy Military Hygiene, Woodhull.
1 copy Elements of Law, Davis.
1 copy Modern Method Sewage Disposal, Waring.
1 copy First Aid in Illness, Pilcher.
1 copy Railway Track, Tratman.
1 copy Elements of Railroading, Paine.
1 copy New Roadmaster's Assistant, Paine.
1 copy Bowditch's Navigator.

The above were packed in 1 box and weighed 129 pounds.

2. One field photographic outfit, as follows:

1 camera, 5 by 7 inches, Premo A.
1 tripod for the above.
1 leather carrying case for the above.
2 gross solio paper, 5 by 7 inches.
1 gross Aristo platino paper, 5 by 7 inches.
6 plate holders, 5 by 7 inches.
3 trays, hard rubber, 6½ by 8 inches.
3 trays, hard rubber, 8 by 10 inches.
6 frames, printing, 5 by 7 inches.
16 dozen dry plates, Seed's, 5 by 7 inches.
12 bottles Aristo gold solution.
12 bottles Aristo platino solution.
2 bottles solio hardener.
12 15-grain bottles chloride of gold.
2 graduated glasses.
1 ruby lamp.
1 glass funnel.
1 pocket scale.
1 negative rack.
1 brush, bristle.
1 brush, camel's hair.
500 card mounts, 5 by 7 inches.
200 envelopes, negative.
1 sheet litmus paper.
1 jar photo paste.
½ pound nitrate of silver.
1 pound alum, powdered.
1 pound acetic acid.
1 pound borax.
1 pound carbonate soda.
1 pound sulphite soda.
1 pound bromide potassium.
25 pounds hypo soda.
8 bottles hydrochinon.
8 bottles eikonogen.
8 bottles metol, Hauff's.

The above were packed in one box and weighed 354 pounds.

3. One field astronomical outfit, as follows:

1 astronomical transit.
1 zenith telescope.
1 chronograph, complete.
1 chronometer, break circuit.
3 chronometers, portable.
1 chronometer, mean solar.
1 theodolite, medium.
2 sextants.
2 artificial horizons.
1 barometer, mercury cistern.
4 thermometers.
2 hygrometers.
4 Vernier lamps.
2 Rochester lamps, complete with green shades.
12 extra lamp chimneys and 12 wicks for above lamps.
10 pounds mercury for artificial horizons.
8 cells of Sampson battery for chronograph.
500 feet of paper for use on chronograph.
1 complete set of blank forms for astronomical computations.
4 copies of the American Ephemeris and Nautical Almanac, 1901 to 1904.

4. Surveying instruments:

2 transits, engineers', complete.
2 levels, engineers', complete.
4 level rods, N. Y.
2 field glasses, binocular.

The following detailed lists show the materials furnished for the equipment of each company:

1. Surveying and drafting outfit, as follows:

1 Batson sketching case.
3 cavalry sketching cases.
2 clinometers.
3 protractors, Abbot's.
3 compasses, pocket.
1 field glass, binocular.
1 set drawing instruments.
2 rubber triangles.
2 rubber rulers.
1 barometer, aneroid.
1 scale, 12-inch boxwood, triangular.
1 preserving tube.
1 odometer.
1 hand level.
2 rolls drawing paper, 36-inch (10-yard rolls), mounted.
12 yards tracing cloth, 36-inch.
2 dozen thumb tacks.
30 colored pencils, assorted.
30 black pencils, assorted.
2 ½-pint bottles black drawing ink.
8 ¼-pint bottles colored drawing ink.
3 rubber erasers.
1 roll of 500 feet paper for use on sketching cases.

2. One set of blacksmiths' tools (one chest, weight 135 pounds), as follows:

1 cold chisel.
1 hot chisel.
1 flater, large.
1 flater, small.
1 set hammer.
2 punches, round.
2 punches, square.
5 swedges, bottom, assorted.
5 swedges, top, assorted.
5 fullers, assorted.
5 fullers, bottom, assorted.
1 hardie.

Blacksmiths' tools packed separately:

1 anvil, 85 pounds.
1 sledge.
3 handles for sledges.
1 portable forge.

3. One set carpenters' tools (one chest, weight 224 pounds), as follows:

2 hammers, claw, adze eye, 1 pound, with handles.
2 nail sets, ¼-inch and $\frac{1}{16}$-inch.
1 mallet, ringed, 6-inch head, 4-inch diameter, No. 14.
1 hatchet, shingling, No. 3, 4⅝-inch cut.
1 broad hatchet, No. 7, 7-inch cut.
1 scratch awl, handled, No. 0.
1 tool handle and tools, heavy, best grade.
4 handsaws, No. 9, Disston's best, 26-inch blade.
1 ripsaw, No. 12, Disston's best, 26-inch blade.
1 backsaw, 16-inch blade, best grade.
1 compass saw handle and 3 assorted blades, of best grade.
2 saw sets, No. 1.
1 bench hook.
1 set firmer chisels, 12 in set, ⅛-inch to 2-inch, socket-handled.
1 set framing chisels, 12 in set, ¼-inch to 2-inch, socket-handled.
1 drawknife, 10-inch blade.
1 iron-block plane, 7-inch.
1 jack plane, 15-inch, Stanley, wood bottom.
1 smooth plane, 9-inch, Stanley, wood bottom.
1 jointer plane, 22-inch, Stanley, wood bottom.
1 marking gauge, wood, square bar and head.
1 plumb and level, 24-inch, patent adjustable, brass bound.
1 T-bevel, sliding, 8-inch, brass screw and tip.
1 try square, rosewood handle, brass faced, 8-inch blade, graduated.
1 steel square, 2 feet 2 inches wide, $\frac{1}{16}$, $\frac{1}{12}$, ⅛, with measure 8 square and $\frac{1}{100}$ scale, with new board measure, giving feet and inches in full.
2 2-foot rules, fourfold, arch joint, boxwood, full brass bound.
1 metallic tape, Chestermans', 50 feet, feet and inches.
1 steel pocket tape, 12 feet, graduated sixteenths and metric system.
1 pliers, flat nose, 5-inch, cast steel.
1 cutting nippers, 7-inch, patent compound lever, nickel plated.
1 wing dividers, 8-inch, best grade.
1 steel rule, standard French measure, ½-meter.
1 plumb bob, 6-ounce, and cord, cast brass, steel pointed, screw top.
1 dozen chalk lines, braided, No. 2.
1 pound red chalk.
1 oil stove, 2 inches by 8 inches, mounted with cover, best grade.
1 oiler, brass, ½-pint.
1 glazier's diamond, plain ebony handle.
1 bench screw, wrought iron, wood handle, 1¼-inch screw, 15 inches long under collar.
1 pair hand clamps, carpenters', wood, 8-inch jaws.
1 belt punch, ⅛-inch diameter, for driving.
1 ratchet brace, New Haven pattern, 10-inch sweep, nickel plated, rosewood handle, lignum vitae head.
1 set auger bits, 13 in box, $\frac{4}{16}$ to $\frac{16}{16}$, best grade.
12 screw-driver bits, assorted sizes, to fit above brace.
16 ship augers, 4 of each, $\frac{12}{16}$, $\frac{14}{16}$, $\frac{17}{16}$, and $\frac{18}{16}$.
24 auger handles, to fit the above augers.
3 dozen saw files, assorted.
1 dozen flat files, assorted.
1 dozen file handles, wood.
1 dozen carpenters' pencils, best.
1 wrench, monkey, 10-inch, Coe's, black.
1 cold chisel, ¾-inch bit, best cast steel.
2 screw-drivers, best cast-steel blades, 6-inch and 12-inch, 1 of each.
1 glue pot, solid, 2 pints, with good brush and 1 pound glue each.
1 set steel stamps, $\frac{3}{16}$-inch letters, 26 letters in set.
1 burning brand, 1-inch letter, viz, "U. S. Engrs.," in frame.

4. One set plumbers' tools (two chests, weight 180 pounds each), as follows:

1 set adjustable pipe stocks and dies, size ¼ inch to 2 inches.
1 3-wheel pipe cutter, ¼ inch to 2 inches.
1 Stillson's pipe wrench, 14-inch.
1 Stillson's pipe wrench, 18-inch.
1 gas pliers, 6-inch.
1 gas pliers, 12-inch.
2 bending pins.
1 tape bore, New York pattern.
1 dresser, boxwood.
1 chipping knife, 5-inch.
1 shave hook, triangle.
1 shave hook, oval.
1 set of three-turn pins, boxwood.

1 bossing stick, boxwood.
1 grease, resin, and flour box, medium size.
1 copper soldering bolt, 1-pound.
1 copper soldering bolt, 3-pound.
2 cold chisels, 8 inches.
1 ladle, 3-inch.
1 melting pot, 5-inch.
1 Primus heater, No. 25, kerosene, with iron stand and melting pot.
1 soil pot and brush.
1 ball peen hammer.
1 straight peen hammer.

1 screw-driver, 10-inch.
1 asbestos joint runner.
1 compasses, 8-inch.
1 plumber's saw.
2 rasps, regular size.
2 flat files.
1 pipe vise, hinged, weight 28 pounds, to hold pipe $\frac{1}{8}$ inch to 3 inches.
100 pounds solder, half and half.
3 pounds resin.
5 pounds tallow.
25 pounds oakum.
5 pounds prepared soil.

5. Intrenching tools and materials, as follows:

1 hammer, brick.
1 masons' plumb and level stick.
1 masons' chisel.
3 wrenches, monkey, assorted.
2 post-hole diggers.
12 machetes.
12 sheathes for the above.
2 axes, broad.
4 handles, for broad axes.
3 trowels.
2 crosscut saws, two men.
8 handles, for crosscut saws.
6 hammers, railroad spiking, handled.
1 hammer, hand, stone.
2 hammers, stone.
25 axes, chopping.
75 handles for axes.
2 blocks, single, iron.
2 blocks, double, iron.
1 mason's trowel.
1 block, snatch, wood.
2 blocks, single, wood.
2 blocks, double, wood.
66 yards assorted canvas and cotton duck.
6 adzes.
12 handles for adzes.
1 grindstone, in frame.
3 come-alongs.
3 vises, telegraph.
2 spikes, marline.
2 pairs climbing irons.

2 sets climbing straps.
2 pliers, side cutting.
2 wire cutters, 14-inch.
1 mallet, calking.
2 irons, calking.
3 palms, sailors'.
12 sail needles.
2 hammers, ball peen.
2 hammers, chipping.
8 rules, 2-foot.
6 lanterns, complete.
6 extra globes for lanterns.
1 bolt cutter.
2 cant hooks.
6 shovels, long handle.
6 spades.
6 picks.
12 handles for picks.
6 hatchets.
12 handles for hatchets.
1 maul, heavy.
3 padlocks, with keys.
1,000 feet manila rope, 2$\frac{1}{4}$ inches circumference.
6 chalk lines.
18 shite chalks.
18 red chalks.
36 lantern wicks.
2 pounds beeswax.
6 balls sail twine.
385 feet tracing tape, 1-inch.

THIRD BATTALION OF ENGINEERS.

In purchases made for the equipment of the companies of the Third Battalion of Engineers, the lists prepared for the Second Battalion were followed, with the following modifications in the sets of carpenters' tools—

1 mallet, ringed, 6 inches by 4 inches, changed to 1 mallet, not ringed, 5$\frac{1}{2}$ inches by 3$\frac{1}{4}$ inches.
1 hatchet, shingling, changed to 1 hatchet, carpenters'.
1 broad hatchet, 7-inch cut, changed to 1 broad hatchet, 6-inch cut.
1 backsaw, 16-inch blade, to be omitted.
1 iron-block plane, 7-inch, to be omitted.
1 steel rule, standard, 1-inch, $\frac{1}{2}$-meter, to be omitted.
1 oiler, brass, $\frac{1}{2}$-pint, changed to 1 oiler, malleable iron, $\frac{1}{2}$-pint.
1 pair band clamps, carpenters', to be omitted.

16 ship augers, changed to 8 ship augers, 4 each of $\frac{1}{4}$ and $\frac{1}{8}$.
24 auger handles for the above, changed to 12 auger handles.
1 monkey wrench, 10-inch, changed to 1 monkey wrench, 12-inch.
1 cold chisel, changed to 2 cold chisels.
1 glue pot, solid, 2 pints, with brush and glue, changed to 1 pound Lepaige's prepared glue.
1 burning brand, 1-inch letters, changed to 1 burning brand, $\frac{1}{2}$-inch letters.
1 set steel stamps, 26 letters, $\frac{1}{4}$-inch, changed to 1 set steel letters and figures, $\frac{1}{4}$-inch.

These tools were packed in two chests, each 37 inches by 9 inches by 17¼ inches, weighing 107 pounds each.

No changes were made in the sets of plumbers' tools.

Three sets of each class were bought for Companies I, K, and L. Another set of each will be procured and furnished to Company M at West Point, N. Y.

Four sets of surveying, reconnaissance, and drawing instruments were bought for the four companies, each set consisting of the following articles, viz:

1 transit, engineers' complete, No. 5060 X, Keuffel & Esser catalogue, 1901.
1 level, engineer's complete, 18-inch telescope No. 5010, Keuffel & Esser catalogue, 1901.
1 level rod, New York.
1 level rod, Philadelphia.
1 tape, steel, 50-foot, decimal and duodecimal scales.
1 tape, steel, 100-foot, decimal and duodecimal scales.
1 field glass, binocular (made by Bausch & Lomb), 8 power.
1 barometer, aneroid, 6,000 feet altitude.
1 hand level, Lock's.
1 clinometer, Abney's.
1 triangle, celluloid, 45°, 10-inch.
1 triangle, celluloid, 60°, 10-inch.
1 steel ruler, 30-inch.

1 scale, 12-inch, paragon, triangular, divided in 10, 20, 30, 40, 50, 60 parts to the inch.
1 scale guard, german silver.
2 odometers, brass, in leather case.
8 compasses, prismatic, 3-inch, in leather sling case.
8 compasses, pocket, square, 3-inches by 3-inches.
2 folding trestles with drawing boards, hard-wood (No. 2553, Keuffel & Esser catalogue, 1901).
1 set drawing instruments with german silver protractor and 5-inch celluloid triangle.
1 protractor, draughtsman's, in morocco case (No. 1253, Keuffel & Esser catalogue, 1901).

The total aggregate weight of shipments made under the heading of "Equipment of engineer troops" exceeded 300,000 pounds.

During the year receipts in depot of tools and implements used in the field were as follows:

On October 9, 1900, a large lot of miscellaneous engineer equipment materials was received from the chief engineer of the division of Cuba, Havana, Cuba, consisting of intrenching tools, carpenters' and blacksmiths' tools, linemen's tools and materials, field photographic supplies, and miscellaneous materials. They were delivered here in 200 packages, weighing in all 16,001 pounds.

This was the only shipment of tools and implements of this class received in the depot during the year.

b. *Completing ponton trains.*

Six wooden ponton boats and timber for 186 long, 187 short, and 15 trestle balks, ordered during previous fiscal year, have been delivered. Under the allotments, amounting to $8,250, purchases of necessary materials to complete three divisions of advance-guard equipage and three divisions of reserve ponton train have been made during the year, as follows:

24 adzes, carpenters'.
24 axes, broad.
27 brushes, paint.
96 buckets, canvas.
500 handles for axes.
400 hatchets.
96 mallets, heavy.
1,665 pounds marline, tarred.
60 100-pound kegs nails, assorted.
200 needles, sailmakers'.
75 pounds paint, mixed.
24 palms, sailmakers'.
200 rack sticks.

9 coils rope, manila, 3 inches circumference.
10 coils rope, manila, 1½ inches circumference.
5 coils rope, manila, 1 inch circumference.
24 saws, hand crosscut.
192 scoops, grocers'.
96 shovels, scoop.
72 gross screws, iron, assorted.
20 200-pound kegs spikes, boat.
60 pounds twine, sail.
24 tool chests, with tools.
48 pickets.

The aggregate cost of the above supplies was $2,056.60. Four combined battery and forge wagons, complete, with tools, materials, etc., were furnished by the Ordnance Department and paid for by transfer of funds from the above allotment; the total cost of these was $4,916.70. Miscellaneous materials, such as paints, oils, pine, spruce, and oak timber, bar iron, iron rods, and hardware, needed during the year for repairing the old ponton wagons, were purchased at the aggregate cost of $497.65. The amount paid during the year for services of mechanics and laborers engaged in repairing the old ponton wagons was $772.59. Amount returned to the Treasury as unexpended balance, $6.46. Total as shown for the allotment referred to above, $8,250.

Issue of ponton and bridge materials during the year was limited to filling one requisition from the commanding officer Company M, Third Battalion of Engineers, at West Point, N. Y., for the following articles, which were sent there on June 15, 1901, viz:

Four wooden ponton boats, 80 chess, 13 feet, and 28 long balks.

A statement was prepared and forwarded to the Chief of Engineers, United States Army, on February 15, 1901, showing in detail the amount of ponton and bridge material on hand in good condition for immediate service; also an estimate of cost for one division of each advance and reserve ponton train equipage. In order to determine the condition of the various ponton, chess, tool, and forge wagons, details of the Battalion of Engineers were engaged during part of February and March in overhauling these wagons. On account of the very inclement weather during these months the work was suspended. It was then ascertained that of the wagons in storage but enough wagons for one division of each of advance and reserve train were in a serviceable condition.

With the exception of the ponton and chess carriages, three divisions of each of advance guard and reserve ponton trains were completed during the year by purchase of the materials and tools referred to on the preceding page. Of all the materials required for ponton divisions, a small supply over that required for the three divisions of each is now on hand in the depot.

The matter of fitting up the number of ponton and chess carriages required for these three divisions of each was taken up in the latter part of May, and at the close of the fiscal year more than the required number of carriages was available for immediate service.

Operations on ponton wagons.

The overhauling of the large number of ponton carriages stored in the large frame shed was undertaken in May. The work was commenced by engineer troops in the early part of May. The wagons were taken out of storage, overhauled, and those which could not be repaired set aside for condemnation. The preparation of the engineer command at the post for service in the Philippines again stopped the work. An attempt was made to obtain bids for sorting out, assembling the serviceable parts, and making the necessary repairs by contract. To this end informal proposals were asked of four reputable wagon builders in New York City. Only one bid was received, in which the price named was $90 per wagon. As this was regarded too high, it was concluded to have the work done by hired labor.

Authority for doing this was obtained from the Chief of Engineers, United States Army, May 23, 1901, together with an allotment sufficient to complete the wagons necessary for three divisions of each advance and reserve train. Arrangements were immediately commenced for the hire of mechanics and laborers, and work was begun here in earnest on May 31, 1901, and by June 30 the wagons required for the above divisions were completed and assembled, at an average cost of $12.83 per wagon.

In the progress of this work it was found that a large number of wagons can be repaired and made serviceable at small expense. The work was continued with the funds available until the end of the fiscal year, and the following is a statement of the number of wagons on hand, their condition, etc., on June 30, viz:

Wagons.	On hand as per return.	Repaired up to June 30.	Not repaired.
Ponton, balk, and trestle wagons	403	43	360
Canvas ponton or chess wagons	245	48	197
Tool wagons	11	8	3
Total	659	99	560

When the repairs are completed it is estimated that there will be ponton and chess wagons sufficient for 14 divisions of reserve train and 8 divisions of advance-guard train, with 103 extra ponton wagons (reserve train).

Further authority was given by the Chief of Engineers, United States Army, June 23, 1901, for continuing this work in the new fiscal year, and with the funds allotted from the appropriation for fiscal year 1902 the work will be systematically prosecuted and carried on to completion within the funds allotted and the time authorized, viz, September 30, 1901.

5. SUBMARINE-MINING MATERIALS.

Purchases of submarine-mining materials under the various allotments from appropriation for torpedoes for harbor defense have been made as authorized by the Chief of Engineers, United States Army, to supply deficiencies at the various localities where submarine mining materials are stored.

Specifications for materials so needed have been prepared and proposals invited, some under public notice and others under advertisements and formal contracts.

The following tabulated statement gives the total purchases of submarine-mining materials during the year, including deliveries of the articles so ordered and deliveries of articles ordered during the previous fiscal year:

159 torpedo anchors, 3,000 pounds each.
800 junction boxes, single, large.
275 junction boxes, single, small.
375 junction boxes, triple.
110 junction boxes, grand.
4,000 bolts and nuts for junction boxes.
900 multiple jointing boxes.
1,500 single jointing boxes.
293 compound plugs for mines.
900 extra glands for plugs.
50 megaphones.
1 ream emory paper.
36 blowpipes.
24 2-ring stands.
250 insulating cleats.
45 binocular field glasses.
8 reading microscopes.
144 marking crayons.

34 circuit detectors.
200 anchors, boat service, 500 pounds each.
400 cut-out boxes.
450 cut-out plugs.
1,700 mine shackles.
2,600 anchor shackles.
3,950 mooring sockets.
7,500 split pins for shackles.
1,147 split keys for mines.
150 feet lead pipe for cable tags.
268 pounds sheet copper for earth plates.
700 cans rubber cement.
11,000 feet rubber tubing, soft.
200 pounds brass jointers.
24 axles for cable-drum frames.

8 brakes for cable-drum frames.
1,200 pounds pig lead.
200 pounds antimony.
96 metallic tapes, 100 feet each.
3 testing sets, portable.
5 switch boards, complete.
5 storage batteries, each 40 cells.
180 solder pots.
4 transits, R. R., complete.
50 measuring drums and frames.
15,000 feet 3-inch lowering rope, hemp.
1,500 metal cups of composite metal, ball seats for new pattern circuit closers.
10 pounds fine magnet wire for rewinding circuit-regulator plugs.

Since the revision of the torpedo system, 1897-1898, and even in the old system, the service tool boxes, which form an important item of the system, have never been fully equipped according to the manuals. After the close of the Spanish-American war, of the 458 tool boxes in the depot but few were fully equipped. The total number of tool boxes called for by the approved lists for the various harbors was as follows:

Eighteen tool boxes A, 43 tool boxes B, 15 tool boxes C, and 61 tool boxes D; in all, 137 tool boxes. In addition to the equipment of these, a large number of tools to complete the equipment of tool boxes on hand at the various localities was called for, and not being on hand, were taken out of the depot tool boxes. Proposals were invited, and all of the tools required for the 137 boxes were ordered and delivered here during the year.

The tools so ordered and delivered number 3,568, including a great variety.

Under date of July 9, 1900, a statement of the approximate aggregate cost of accessory torpedo materials required to complete the torpedo outfits of the various harbors, as shown by the approved lists of district officers, and for which no provision has yet been made, was prepared and forwarded to the Chief of Engineers, United States Army, amounting to $156,500. Under the same date another statement of materials immediately required was forwarded. The estimated cost of these was $16,500, and this sum was allotted. These materials were purchased during the year, excepting certain articles in the purchase of which a delay was advisable for commercial reasons, approved by the Chief of Engineers.

Unserviceable torpedo material is now being returned to the depot. This will be replaced and deficiencies supplied during the coming fiscal year.

The mining materials shipped from this depot in July, 1900, to Galveston, Tex., according to approved project, were nearly all lost in the great storm, September, 1900. Only a few minor articles are available for issue from the depot to replace those lost. The estimated cost of the articles required to replace the lost ones will be about $18,500, including multiple cable.

Issues and shipments of submarine-mining materials.

In July, 1899, the Chief of Engineers, United States Army, furnished all officers of the Corps of Engineers in charge of submarine-mining stations with mimeograph lists of submarine-mining materials, corresponding to the lists of materials as given in the new torpedo manual for mining casemates, loading rooms, and for boat-service parties, requesting these officers to submit a detailed statement of the quantities of mining materials required, according to the project for the harbor, the quantities on hand, the number of articles to be supplied from the depot, and the number of articles that can be bought in local markets.

As already stated in last report, 29 of these lists, covering localities where torpedo materials are stored, have been referred to this office for consideration, revision, and correction when required. Copies of these lists were returned to this office after approval by the Chief of Engineers, United States Army, with instructions to issue materials called for by these lists and enumerated in these lists under the heading of "Number to be supplied from the depot," so far as available materials will permit. These lists have been consolidated in a book specially prepared for this purpose, in order to determine the proper distribution of the material available for issue from the depot, and the first issue was made on April 19, 1900, and continued since without interruption until April, 1901, when, owing to other important duties, the preparation of large shipments of submarine-mining materials became impracticable. Only a few small shipments of minor articles required to complete torpedo outfits in the process of transfer to the Artillery Corps have been made since that time. Shipments made during the year, according to approved lists, were as follows:

Number.	Date.	Quantity.	Number.	Date.	Quantity.
		Pounds.			*Pounds.*
1	July 3, 1900	87,630	11	Dec. 22, 1900	6,745
2	Aug. 2, 1900	22,994	12	Dec. 12, 1900	4,919
3	Aug. 17, 1900	20,611	13	Jan. 27, 1901	28,013
4	Sept. 4, 1900	24,688	14	Jan. 21, 1901	85,583
5	Sept. 14, 1900	16,597	15	Jan. 24, 1901	1,905
6	Oct. 16, 1900	34,357	16	Jan. 29, 1901	2,035
7	Dec. 12, 1900	46,199	17	Feb. 19, 1901	36,803
8	...do......	19,466	18	Feb. 28, 1901	16,900
9	Dec. 17, 1900	42,567	19	Apr. 5, 1901	7,883
10	Dec. 22, 1900	60,374	20	...do......	47,698

During the month of May, 1901, twelve small shipments of submarine mining materials, not furnished heretofore, to the various localities were made, aggregating 5,165 pounds.

All these shipments were made up of materials on hand in the engineer depot.

In addition to the above shipments the following materials were shipped direct from the works of the manufacturers to points where needed, the Quartermaster's Department receiving the same for transportation, viz:

1. Five electric storage batteries, each of 40 chloride accumulator elements, type D-5, and complete with all accessories, one to each of five points. Each complete battery, packed for shipment, weighed 2,372 pounds.
2. One hundred and fifty-nine torpedo anchors, each of 3,000 pounds, contracted for at Chattanooga, Tenn., were turned over to the Quartermaster's Department December, 1900, for transportation to four points.

The handling, packing, and shipping of these materials entailed considerable work during the year, both in the depot and in this office.

The total aggregate weight of the shipments exceeded 1,000,000 pounds.

The following statement gives the total of issues of submarine mining materials during the year:

Articles.	Quantity.
Acid, hydrochloric ....gallons..	4½
Sulphuric ....do....	4
Pots ....number..	27
Anchors, boat, 500 pounds........do....	155
Torpedo, 3,000 pounds........do....	159
Antimony ....pounds..	612
Anvils, 50 pounds..............number..	15
Balances, with weights, in case..do....	10
Balance weights for above ....do....	8
Batteries, bell ....do....	6
Signal, complete ....cells..	89
Signal, coppers for........number..	6
Signal, glass jars for ....do....	4
Signal, porous cups, large, for, number	12
Signal, porous cups, small, for, number	12
Testing, in case...........number..	9
Electric, storage..............do....	5
Battery zinc rods, extra..........do....	48
Beeswax ....pounds..	147½
Binding posts..................number..	23
Blocks, double, 6-inch............do....	45
Single, 6-inch.................do....	45
Books, note, 5 by 8 inches ....do....	386
Blowpipes, brass ....do....	17
Books, note, daily test ....do....	154
Brushes, battery ....do....	53
Dusting ....do....	45
Red lead ....do....	209
Buckets, iron.......................do....	18
Cable drum frames..................do....	68
Cable drum frame axles...........do....	77
Cable drum frame brakes ....do....	78
Cable tags, casemate ....do....	564
Canvas, cotton duck (1-yard pieces), pieces	20
Charcoal furnaces, 12-inch....number..	26
Solder pots for................do....	123
Chamois skins......................do....	10
Circuit closers, model 1897 ....do....	1,723
Extra steel balls for ....do....	18
Circuit regulator plugs, 1897......do....	997
Cleats, insulating....................do....	698
Connectors, double.................do....	401
Compound plugs, buoyant, 1897 ..do....	163
Ground, old pattern..........do....	60
Ground, mine, new pattern ..do....	101
Cotton waste ....pounds..	2,275
Crowbars ....number..	40
Cut-outs, unprimed ....do....	4,142
Crayons, marking ....do....	67
Cups, drinking ....do....	26
Cut-out boxes, new..................do....	894
Cut-out plugs, new ....do....	894
Dishes, evaporating, enameled ...do....	50
Amalgamating, 8-inch, iron ..do....	12
Melting, 12-inch...............do....	11
Earth plates, boat ....do....	170
Emery paper, assorted.........sheets...	233
Extension pieces, aluminum, for 39-inch and 40-inch mines .number..	405
Aluminum, for 43-inch and 46-inch mines.....................number..	375
Aluminum, for 48-inch mines, number	81
Flax twine ....pounds..	153 11/16
Flags, signal, with poles......number..	91
Flag poles for above, extra.......do....	9
Field glass, binocular.............do....	61
Funnels:	
Glass, assorted.................do....	82
Copper—	
Large.......................do....	1
Small.......................do....	1
Furnaces, "Primus heater"......do....	59
Fuzes, platinum, service..........do....	5,804
Galvanometers:	
Bradley ....do....	10
Bradley, cases for ....do....	2
Siemens-Halske, cases ....do....	2
Gaskets, usudurian, assorted..number..	5,827
Grappling irons...................do....	30
Glands:	
Iron, for compound plugs ...do....	644
Brass, for compound plugs ..do....	254
Insulating compound "Ozite," gallons	860
Junction boxes:	
Grand ....number..	94
Triple........................do....	924
Single, large ....do....	508
Single, small ....do....	586
Jointing boxes:	
Multiple ....do....	696
Single.........................do....	2,587
Jointers, brass ....pounds..	89
Ladles, steel, 4-inch ....number..	140
Lead, pig.......................pounds..	3,428
Lightning arresters ....number..	49
Mallets, heavy, 4 by 6 inches.....do....	12
Marine glue ....pounds..	100
Marline ....do....	1,431
Measuring drums and frames.number..	23
Megaphones, No. 2 ....do	106
Mercury, commercial ....pounds..	461
Mine numbers ....number..	555
Navy knives ....do....	910
Notes on electricity..............do....	11
Oil:	
Cylinder ....gallons..	5
Dynamo ....do....	0½
Lubricating...................do....	19
Operating boxes, new ....number..	77
Paraffin ....pounds..	530
Pencils ....number..	312
Plates, loading connections, VIII and X ....sets..	124
Plug switches ....number..	3
Red lead.......................pounds..	100
Resin ....do....	199
Riggers' screws...............number..	52
Reading microscopes ....do....	26
Resistance boxes ....do....	1
Rope:	
Buoy, cotton, 1½ inches circumference ....feet..	9,472
Manila, 2 and 2½ inches circumference (1,000 feet in coil)....coils..	28⅞
Hemp, lowering, 3 inches (1,000 feet in coil) ....coils..	7
Steel wire, ⅞ inch diameter...feet..	84,000
Rubber:	
Cement (½ pound boxes)..pounds..	185
Tubing, soft ....feet..	7,144
Rings, gland packing .....pounds..	248¾
Strips, india rubber, ⅛-inch...do....	76
Sal-ammoniac ....do....	360
Shackles:	
Large, anchor ....number..	2,738
Small, mine....................do....	2,987
Split pins for shackles...........do....	3,658
Graduated glasses ....do....	31
Split keys for mine cases ....do....	722
Shellac, dry....................pounds..	13
Soap, coal-oil.....................do....	110
Sockets, mooring, for ⅞-inch steel rope, number	3,694
Solder, special ....pounds..	40
Common.......................do....	228
Sounding lines, 3/16-inch, 100 feet each, number	50
Service detectors (circuit detectors), number	96
Sister hooks for anchors .....number..	68
Spirit, wood....................gallons..	78
Spirit lamp....................number..	13
Stands, two-ring, for above ......do....	20
Spoons, mercury ....do....	9
Staples:	
Wire, small ....pounds..	19½
Iron, large ....do....	170

APPENDIX 5—POST OF FORT TOTTEN, N. Y., ETC.

Articles.	Quantity.	Articles.	Quantity.
Stirrers, glass ....number..	26	Varnish:	
Sulphate of copper ....pounds..	680	Asphaltum................gallons..	15
Switch boards, new ....number..	16	French ....do....	3¼
Stud bolts:		Voltmeters..................do....	1
For ground mines............do....	11	Vermilion paint ....pounds..	15
For ground-mine buoys......do....	2	Vises, bench, large.........number..	14
Syringes, battery ....do....	25	Wash basins, agate ....do....	27
Tallow, mutton ....pounds..	290	Washers:	
Telephones:		Brass gland, new pattern .pounds..	390,₁₀
Boat service, complete....number..	44	Brass gland, old pattern .....do....	29¼
Wall, casemate ....do....	88	Lead, for torpedoes, assorted	
Testing sets, portable...............do....	9	number	4,951
Tool boxes:		White lead in oil ....number..	500
A, complete, with tools ......do....	10	Wire:	
B, complete, with tools ......do....	26	Kerite, No, 12 loading wire .feet..	21,490
C, complete, with tools ......do....	10	Kerite, No, 16, loading wire ..do....	74,000
D, complete, with tools ......do....	88	No. 19, cotton braided ....pounds..	42¼
Torpedo Manuals, 1898 ......copies..	110	Wrenches:	
Transits ....number..	4	Socket ....number..	73
Trucks, steamboat................do....	30	Socket, levers for..............do....	151
Turks-head collars:			
Large ....do....	1,026		
Small ....do....	8,310		

Tools for fitting out and completing tool boxes.

Articles	Quantity	Articles	Quantity
Backsaws ....number..	3	Pincers, carpenter's, 10-inch, number	40
Brushes, button ....do....	58	Pliers—	
Chisels—		Small, assorted ....number..	12
Cold ....do....	85	Cutting, 8-inch button ....do....	119
½-inch ....do....	8	Round nose.................do....	22
Dusters, camel's hair..............do....	7	Rules, boxwood, 1-foot ....do....	8
Earth plates....................do....	180	Round drive punches..........do....	180
Files—		Scissors, 8-inch...................do....	120
6-inch (small) assorted ......do....	13	Screw-drivers, 6-inch, flat........do....	8
14-inch, flat, bastard ....do....	16	Screw-drivers, small ....do....	9
6-inch, flat, bastard ....do....	127	Shears, 10-inch..................do....	8
Glue pots, small..................do....	1	Soldering coppers:	
Hammers—		Large ....do....	10
Riveting, 7-ounce ....do....	3	Small ....do....	8
Smith's, 3½ pounds ....do....	16	Tapes, metallic, 100 feet ....do....	49
Ball pene, 8-ounce ....do....	44	Tool handles, with tools ....do....	7
Hatchets ....do....	20	Vises, hand, 6-inch ....do....	13
Marline spikes ....do....	18	Vises, Stephens', 2-inch flat.....do....	4
Mallets, small..................number..	4	Wrenches:	
Nippers, small....................do....	10	S.........................do....	41
Oilers—		T.........................do....	132
Steel, small..................do....	19	Monkey, 15-inch.............do....	28
large..................do....	5	Monkey, 6-inch, combination.do....	9
Oilstones, 4 by 1½ inches..........do....	6	Stillson's 18-inch ....do....	70
Pencils, camel's hair.................	58		

Of the total number of stations to be fitted out, all but four have now been supplied according to the approved lists.

During the year various submarine mining materials were repaired at the depot repair shop by enlisted men of the Engineer Battalion, principally electrical instruments and a large number of circuit regulator plugs received here from the various localities.

Four hundred and three extension pieces and 5,200 lead washers were also made.

Eight thousand feet B. M. of boards were used in making packing boxes for the various shipments.

Under the instructions contained in General Orders No. 1, headquarters Corps of Engineers, United States Army, February 14, 1898, officers of the Corps of Engineers in charge of submarine mining materials at the various fortifications rendered reports of their semi-annual inspections of submarine mining materials under their charge to the Chief of Engineers United States Army. These reports have been referred to this office for recommendations and remarks. The **reports** on being received are reviewed and recorded and returned to the Chief of Engineers United States Army. During the fiscal year 35 were received and acted on as above.

Torpedo manuals.

Under the instructions from the Chief of Engineers United States Army, March 9, 1901, sent to all officers of the Corps of Engineers, torpedo manuals of the various editions were turned into the depot from officers of the Corps of Engineers and others to whom they were originally issued by this office for personal or professional use. Soon after date of these instructions manuals were received at this office daily, and at the close of the present fiscal year only a very limited number remained outstanding. Considerable work was entailed in attending to the correspondence with officers and others, and the number of communications exchanged in the calling in of these manuals exceeded 400. On June 3, 1901, a detailed report was submitted to the Chief of Engineers United States Army, showing numbers of copies received and numbers of copies still outstanding. June 4, 1901, 100 copies of the torpedo manual, edition of 1898, were expressed to the Chief of Engineers United States Army.

Torpedo experiments.

A barrel of red vaseline was purchased under proposals, and was used for experimental purposes with a view of adopting it as a substitute for insulating compound, now in use in the present torpedo system.

Several models of new types of circuit regulator plugs were made, and some of them have been experimented with.

Drawings of a new pattern cut-off box and new pattern single and multiple jointing boxes were prepared by the officer in charge of torpedoes for harbor defense and experiments with the same. Two of each of these boxes were ordered from three prominent manufacturers having facilities to turn out this class of work and delivered here in March, 1900. All these samples are now before the Board on the existing torpedo system.

Minor repairs have been made to the engineer wharf, used for torpedo experiments, and four dock piles were replaced during the year.

The two steamers, *Bushnell* and the *Dyne*, also the naphtha launch, have been repaired from time to time during the year. The *Dyne* was painted.

6. ROAD-MAKING MACHINERY FOR PHILIPPINE ISLANDS.

November 8, 1900, instructions were received from the Chief of Engineers United States Army to purchase materials, in open market if necessary, as promptly as possible, as called for by a requisition from Capt. John Biddle, Corps of Engineers, United States Army, chief engineer Division of the Philippines, at Manila, P. I.

This requisition was based upon materials required for road and bridge building in the Philippines, such as steam and hand pile drivers, pile-driver scows, road rollers, road scrapers, road plows, dump wagons, dump carts, and an assortment of working tools and implements, blacksmiths and machinists' tools.

For the purchase of these materials an allotment of $100,000 was made by the Philippine Commission from public civil funds, and deposited to the credit of the officer in charge of the engineer depot, with the assistant treasurer, New York City. As disbursements were made accounts for these funds were rendered to the Auditor for the Philippine Archipelago and island of Guam.

The matter of procuring the supplies was taken into hand immediately on receipt of the above instructions. The depot quartermaster, New York City, was consulted about the receipt and transportation of the materials as delivered to him by the various manufacturers and dealers.

Competition of from three to ten days was secured on very nearly all the articles purchased.

The first deliveries of articles ordered were made as early as November 14, 1900, six days after receipt of instructions. By December 2, 1900, nearly three-fourths of the articles called for were on board the steamship *Richmond Castle*, which sailed the same day from New York Harbor.

Pile-driver scows and steam and hand pile drivers not being in the market, they were ordered from reputable makers, and delivery of these was accomplished in three weeks from receipt of order. Scows and pile drivers were delivered knocked down, in order to take up as little space as possible. Pile drivers were fitted out with all necessary appliances and tools. The gross weight of pile drivers, with their outfits, was 110 tons.

Early in January, 1901, the delivery of the remaining articles was completed and taken on board the steamship *Lowther Castle*. Among this last instalment there were 100 3-ton road rollers.

Under instructions from the Chief of Engineers United States Army, of January 11, 1901, a detailed report of all materials purchased from the allotment mentioned was prepared and forwarded for the information of the honorable Secretary of War. This report contained a complete list of all the materials ordered and that have been actually shipped. The following is a copy of this detailed report:

Detailed report of the shipment of road-making machinery to the Philippine Islands in relation to compliance with instructions of November 7, 1900, received November 8, 1900, to purchase in open market if necessary, as promptly as possible, and to turn over to the Quartermaster's Department for shipment to Capt. John Biddle, Corps of Engineers, chief engineer Division of the Philippines, at Manila, P. I., certain engineering supplies. These supplies were as follows, and were delivered to steamers and on dates as indicated:

List of articles shipped.	Designations.	By S. S. Richmond Castle, sailed Dec. 2, 1900.	By S. S. Glenesk, sailed Dec. 28, 1900.	By S. S. Lowther Castle, sailed Jan. 26, 1901.	Date of delivery to steamers.
Machinery oil, in 5-gallon cans *a*	Gallons	100			1900. Nov. 14
Transits:					
Light mountain	Number	7			Nov. 16
Do	do	3			Nov. 21
Levels:					
Engineers, "Y"	do	15			Nov. 16
Do	do	5			Nov. 21
Steel chains, measuring 100 feet	do	20			Nov. 16
Level rods, N. Y.	do	20			Nov. 21
Shovels, D. H. No. 2, round point	do	3,600			Nov. 17
Do	do	5,976			Nov. 24
Do	do		5,928		Dec. 14

a No competition secured.

968   REPORT OF THE CHIEF OF ENGINEERS, U. S. ARMY.

List of articles shipped.	Designation.	By S. S. Richmond Castle, sailed Dec. 2, 1900.	By S. S. Glencok, sailed Dec. 23, 1900.	By S. S. Lowther Castle, sailed Jan. 26, 1901.	Dates of delivery to steamers.
					1900.
Files, assorted (Kearney & Foot)	Dozen	410			Nov. 17
File handles, for above files	...do...	84			Do.
Handles for picks	Number	11,000			Do.
Cut nails, 12-pennyweight (100-pound kegs)	Kegs	250			Nov. 19
Blacksmiths' tools (20 pieces to set)	Sets	100			Nov. 20
Machine bolts, ½-inch by 16-inch, with nuts	Number	3,000			Do.
Screw plates, ¼-inch to ⅟₁₆-inch, complete, with taps and dies, and extra sets of taps and dies, and box for each set.	Sets	10			Dec. 1
Do	...do...		40		Dec. 15
Platinum fuses, 10-foot wire, D. S.	Number	19,500			Nov. 23
Cotton safety fuses	Feet	10,000			Do.
Swage blocks, No. 1, 12½ by 4½ inches	Number	100			Nov. 24
Stands for the above swage blocks	...do...	100			Do.
Ship augers, with handles, assorted	...do...	100			Nov. 23
Hammers, carpenters', assorted	...do...	325			Do.
Plows, right hand, No. 106, complete	...do...	100			Nov. 26
Do	...do...		100		Dec. 22
Wheelbarrows, wooden, complete	...do...	2,000			Nov. 28
Dump carts, contractors', light	...do...	78			Do.
Do	...do...	10			Nov. 22
Do	...do...		12		Dec. 12
Wagons, dump, 4-wheeled, complete	...do...	15			Nov. 22
Do	...do...		35		Dec. 12
Scrapers, with steel bowls and 2 runners	...do...	25			Nov. 26
Scrapers, with steel bowls and without runners.	...do...	75			Do.
Wheel scrapers, No. 2, complete	...do...	100			Do.
Scows, for pile drivers, knocked down, complete with all materials needed for assembling.	...do...		2		Dec. 18
Steam pile drivers, complete with 7 tool boxes with tools, and 7 outfits of supplies to operate these pile drivers, and extra parts for engines and boilers.	...do...		7		Dec. 26
Wooden tackle blocks:					
8-inch (sets of 3)	Sets	90			Nov. 22
10-inch (sets of 3)	...do...	20			Do.
12-inch (sets of 3)	...do...	10			Do.
6-inch (sets of 3)	...do...	70			Nov. 24
14-inch (sets of 3)	...do...	10			Do.
Crowbars, pinch-point, light	Number	100			Nov. 22
Do	...do...	300			Nov. 24
Do	...do...	400			Nov. 20
Crowbars, wedge-point, light	...do...	800			Nov. 24
Grindstones, complete with frames	...do...	80			Nov. 22
Augers, carpenters', assorted	...do...	400			Do.
Handles for above augers	...do...	400			Do.
Drawing knives, carpenters', 8-inch	...do...	225			Do.
Crosscut saws, 26-inch	...do...	100			Do.
Ripsaws, 28-inch	...do...	50			Do.
Framing squares, steel, 2 inches wide	...do...	100			Do.
Oilstones:					
Arkansas	...do...	25			Do.
Washita	...do...	25			Do.
Lily white	...do...	30			Do.
Wrenches, monkey, assorted	...do...	50			Do.
Handles for quarry hammers	...do...	900			Nov. 23
Harness, single, for dump carts a	Sets	2			Do.
Do	...do...	10			Nov. 22
Do	...do...		88		Dec. 20
Quarry hammers, assorted	Number	100			Nov. 23
Do	...do...	550			Nov. 28
Machine bolts, ⅝ inch by 13 inches, with nuts	...do...	2,850			Nov. 20
Do	...do...	900			Dec. 1
Scow pile drivers, complete, with 2 outfits of supplies to operate these pile drivers.	...do...		2		Dec. 26
Hand pile drivers, complete, with 6 outfits of supplies to operate these pile drivers.	...do...		6		Do.
Road rollers (3-ton rollers), reversible, complete.	...do...			40	Dec. 27
					1901.
Road rollers, same as above	...do...			25	Jan. 18
Do	...do...			35	Jan. 19
Whiffletrees	Sets			312	Jan. 12
Yokes	Number			200	Jan. 2
Clevises	...do...			250	Do.

a No competition secured.

All the materials shipped were properly selected and ordered within ten days from receipt of instructions, and all of them were turned over to the Quartermaster's Department in less than two months' time thereafter.

APPENDIX 5—POST OF FORT TOTTEN, N. Y., ETC.   969

The receipt of this report was acknowledged in a letter from the War Department, of which the following is a copy:

WAR DEPARTMENT, OFFICE OF THE SECRETARY,
DIVISION OF INSULAR AFFAIRS,
Washington, D. C., February 7, 1901.

GENERAL: I have the honor to acknowledge the receipt of the detailed report of the shipment of road machinery for the Philippine Islands, submitted to the Secretary of War by your indorsement of January 29, 1901.

The report was read at length, with much interest, by the Secretary, who directs me to inform you of his appreciation of the prompt and workmanlike completion of the duty intrusted to your department, which reflects credit upon yourself and subordinates, Major Knight and First Lieutenant Howell.

Very respectfully,
CLARENCE R. EDWARDS,
*Lieut. Col. 47th Infty., U. S. V.,
Acting Asst. Adjutant-General.*

To Brig. Gen. JOHN M. WILSON,
Chief of Engineers, U. S. Army.

From the allotment of $100,000 made for these purchases the sum of $87,982.70 was actually expended, the balance of funds, $12,017.30, in hand after payments have been made for all materials shipped, was transferred June 17, 1901, to Mr. James G. Jester, disbursing agent, Philippine revenues, Washington, D. C.

Statement of funds.

I. ENGINEER DEPOT AT WILLETS POINT, N. Y.

Fiscal year 1899.

July 1, 1900, balance unexpended	$1,350.00
June 30, 1901, amount expended during fiscal year	1,350.00

II. ENGINEER DEPOT AT WILLETS POINT, N. Y.

Fiscal year 1900.

July 1, 1900, balance unexpended		$753.09
August 6, 1900, turned into the Treasury	$333.17	
June 30, 1901, amount expended during fiscal year	419.92	
		753.09

III. ENGINEER DEPOT AT WILLETS POINT, N. Y.

Congress appropriated for the fiscal year ending June 30, 1901—

1. For incidental expenses of depot (incidentals)	$5,000.00
2. For purchase of materials for use of United States Engineer School and instruction of engineer troops (materials)	1,500.00
3. For purchase and repair of instruments (instruments)	3,000.00
4. For library of the United States Engineer School, for purchase and binding of professional works of recent date treating of military and civil engineering (library)	500.00
Total	10,000.00

Of this there has been expended and pledged—

	Expended.	Pledged.	Total.
1. For incidental expenses of depot (incidentals)	$4,666.60	$331.48	$4,998.08
2. For purchase of materials for use of United States Engineer School and instruction of engineer troops (materials)	1,500.00		1,500.00
3. For purchase and repair of instruments (instruments)	2,071.12	928.75	2,999.87
4. For library of the United States Engineer School, for purchase and binding of professional works of recent date treating of military and civil engineering (library)	135.69	351.95	487.64
Total	8,373.41	1,612.18	9,985.59
Balance unexpended, to be turned into the Treasury			14.41

IV. Torpedoes for Harbor Defense.

The following allotments from the above appropriation were made from time to time and are available until expended:

1. Act March 3, 1899, for torpedo experiments:
   July 1, 1900, balance unexpended $2,715.76
   June 30, 1901, amount expended during fiscal year 822.04

   July 1, 1901, balance unexpended 1,893.72
   July 1, 1901, outstanding liabilities 85.00

   July 1, 1901, balance available 1,808.72

2. Act March 3, 1899, for purchase of designated classes of torpedo material:
   July 1, 1900, balance unexpended 22,522.45
   June 30, 1901, amount expended during fiscal year 22,522.45

3. Act May 25, 1900, for purchase of submarine mining materials, etc.:
   July 13, 1900, amount allotted 16,500.00
   June 30, 1901, amount expended during fiscal year 13,352.97

   July 1, 1901, balance unexpended 3,147.03
   July 1, 1901, outstanding liabilities 224.75

   July 1, 1901, balance available 2,922.28

4. Act March 1, 1901, for purchase of submarine mining materials, etc.:
   April 19, 1901, amount allotted 17,000.00
   June 1, 1901, amount withdrawn 700.00

   July 1, 1901, balance available 16,300.00

V. Equipment of Engineer Troops.

Fiscal year 1900.

1. Act March 3, 1899, for "Instruments, etc.:"
   July 1, 1900, balance unexpended $811.70
   June 30, 1901, amount expended during fiscal year $782.10
   June 30, 1901, amount withdrawn during fiscal year 29.60
                                                                                    ————
                                                                                    811.70

2. Act March 3, 1899, for "Fitting out poonton trains:"
   July 1, 1900, balance unexpended 906.91
   June 30, 1901, amount expended during fiscal year $904.09
   June 30, 1901, amount withdrawn during fiscal year 2.82
                                                                                    ————
                                                                                    906.91

Fiscal year 1901.

3. Act May 26, 1900, for "Instruments, intrenching tools, etc.:"
   From the above appropriation the following allotments have been made from time to time during the fiscal year to fill requisitions for instrument, drawing materials, photographic supplies, intrenching tools, etc., for use of engineer troops serving in our island possessions and for the use of exploring expeditions in Alaska, viz:
   August 2, 1900, amount allotted $2,000.00
   September 17, 1900, amount allotted 1,000.00
   April 2, 1901, amount allotted 2,000.00
   May 10, 1901, amount allotted 500.00
   June 5, 1901, amount allotted 2,600.00

APPENDIX 5—POST OF FORT TOTTEN, N. Y., ETC. 971

3. Act May 26, 1900, for "Instruments, intrenching tools, etc."—Cont'd.
June 12, 1901, amount allotted	$300.00
June 13, 1901, amount allotted	2,600.00

June 30, 1901, total of allotments	$11,000.00
June 30, 1901, amount expended during fiscal year	5,311.13

July 1, 1901, balance unexpended	5,688.87
July 1, 1901, outstanding liabilities	5,688.04

July 1, 1901, balance available to be turned into the Treasury	.83

4. Act May 26, 1900, for "Completing ponton trains:"
Under date of March 1, 1901, the following allotments were made for the purchase of four forge and battery wagons from the Ordnance Department, and for tools, etc., to complete in all respects three divisions of advance train and three divisions of reserve train equipage:
March 1, 1901, amount allotted	$6,750.00
May 23, 1901, amount allotted	1,500.00

June 30, 1901, total of allotments		8,250.00
May 20, 1901, amount withdrawn to make transfer of funds to the Ordnance Department in payment for four forge and battery wagons	4,916.70	
June 30, 1901, amount expended during fiscal year	1,707.29	
		6,623.99

July 1, 1901, balance unexpended	1,626.01
July 1, 1901, outstanding liabilities	1,619.55

July 1, 1901, balance available to be turned into the Treasury	6.46

VI. PRESERVATION AND REPAIR OF FORTIFICATIONS.

Under date of April 24, 1900, the sum of $1,000 was allotted for the purchase of hygrometers and thermometers for use at artillery posts.

July 1, 1900, balance unexpended		$424.16
June 30, 1901, amount expended during fiscal year	$9.10	
June 30, 1901, amount withdrawn during fiscal year	415.06	
		424.16

VII. APPROPRIATION "PHILIPPINE COMMISSION," ACT 1.

Under date of November 17, 1900, the following funds were deposited with the assistant treasurer United States, New York, N. Y., to the credit of the officer in charge of the engineer depot, for purchase of materials for road construction in the Philippines, viz:

Public civil funds United States military government of the Philippines.

November 17, 1900, amount assigned	$100,000.00
June 30, 1901, amount expended to end of fiscal year	87,982.70

June 17, 1901, balance unexpended	12,017.30
June 17, 1901, amount transferred to disbursing agent Philippine revenues, Washington, D. C	12,017.30

NEW APPROPRIATIONS.

I. The following items have been appropriated for the engineer depot at Willets Point, N. Y., for the fiscal year ending June 30,

1902, except item 5, which is available until expended, by the act approved March 2, 1901, and assigned to me for disbursement:

1. For incidental expenses of depot (incidentals).................... $5,000.00
2. For purchase of materials for use of United States Engineer School, and for instruction of engineer troops and for travel expenses of officers (materials) 1,500.00
3. For purchase and repair of instruments (instruments)............... 3,000.00
4. For library of United States Engineer School; for purchase and binding of professional works of recent date treating of military and civil engineering (library).. 500.00
5. For an addition to the building containing the collection of engineering models used for illustration, and the library of the United States Engineer School, *to be available until expended*.................... 12,000.00

Total... 22,000.00

II. The following allotments from the appropriation for equipment of engineer troops, 1902, act of March 2, 1901, have been assigned to me for disbursement by the Chief of Engineers, United States Army, viz:

1. For instruments, intrenching tools, drawing materials, etc., for fiscal year 1902 .... $3,000.00
2. For completing ponton trains; assorting, repairing, and assembling wagons of old ponton equipage 6,000.00

Total... 9,000.00

ESTIMATES.[1]

I. There will be required for the fiscal year ending June 30, 1903, the following for the engineer depot at Willets Point, N. Y.:

1. For incidental expenses of the depot, including fuel, lights, chemicals, stationery, hardware, extra-duty pay to soldiers necessarily employed for periods not less than ten days as artificers on work in addition to and not strictly in the line of their military duties, such as carpenters, blacksmiths, draftsmen, printers, lithographers, photographers, engine drivers, telegraph operators, teamsters, wheelwrights, masons, machinists, painters, overseers, laborers; repairs of and for materials to repair public buildings; machinery, and unforeseen expenses $5,000
2. For the purchase of materials for use of United States Engineer School and for instruction of engineer troops at Fort Totten, Willetts Point, in their special duties as sappers and miners; for land and submarine mines, pontoniers, torpedo drill, and signaling, and for travel expenses of officers on journeys approved by the Chief of Engineers and made for the purpose of instruction; provided, that the traveling expenses herein provided for shall be in lieu of mileage or other allowances................ 3,500
3. For purchase and repair of instruments, to be issued to the Corps of Engineers and to officers detailed and on duty as acting engineer officers, for use on public works and surveys.. 3,000
4. For purchase and binding of professional works of recent date, treating of military and civil engineering and kindred scientific subjects, for library of United States Engineer School 500
5. For one railroad outfit, consisting of 1 mile of track, one locomotive, and two small freight cars of standard size, for instruction of engineer troops in railroad construction and in the handling of locomotive engines, and accessories necessary to install and to operate this plant 10,000

Total... 22,000

[1] For estimates for the fiscal year 1902-1903 submitted by the Chief of Engineers, as revised to meet the new conditions resulting from the removal of the United States Engineer troops and school from Willets Point, N. Y., see pages 42-43.

The following explanation is submitted as to the increase made under Paragraph I, item 2, over the amount appropriated in the last act of Congress making appropriations for the engineer depot at Willets Point, N. Y., and as to item 5, asking $10,000 for a railroad outfit, viz:

Item 2. Instruction of the troops is required in mechanical trades in the care and management of steam plants, floating and fixed, and in bridge and railroad work, using materials of standard size to habituate the men in the handling of heavy materials and in road work. This instruction has not been given fully in the past, and to permit it the appropriation for this item should be increased to the figure given.

Item 5. It is very important that facilities be afforded for instruction in railroad construction and in the handling of locomotive engines, a branch of instruction to which great attention is paid in foreign services. A railroad outfit, as specified above under item 5, is desired to fulfill properly the duties outlined, and it is earnestly hoped that an appropriation will be made for its purchase.

II. There will be required for the investigation of points still unsettled in the submarine mining service, for the purchase of materials as are necessary therefor, and for incidental labor connected with the carrying on of experiments, the following:

1. For continuing torpedo experiments at Willets Point, N. Y., $5,000. This appropriation to be available until expended.

Remark under Paragraph II, item 1: At the end of the fiscal year $1,808.72 remain available of the allotment of $5,000 made by the Chief of Engineers, United States Army, April 5, 1899, and it is probable that this balance will be expended before the end of the fiscal year ending June 30, 1902.

It is recommended that the need of an additional allotment be considered when another appropriation for "Torpedoes for harbor defense" is asked for.

W. M. BLACK,
Major, Corps of Engineers, U. S. A.

List of contracts in force during the year.

1. For cut-out boxes:
    Name of contractor: The Roberts Machine Company, Collegeville, Pa.
    Date of contract: May 22, 1900.
    Date of approval: June 4, 1900.
    Time of commencement: June 15, 1900.
    Contract completed: August 25, 1900.
2. For four kinds of junction boxes and extra bolts and clamps:
    Name of contractor: Charles E. Ellicott, Canton, Md.
    Date of contract: May 25, 1900.
    Date of approval: June 11, 1900.
    Time of commencement: June 23, 1900.
    Contract completed: January 5, 1901.
3. For four kinds of jointing boxes and extra binding screws:
    Name of contractor: Western Electric Company, Chicago, Ill.
    Date of contract: May 31, 1900.
    Date of approval: July 2, 1900.
    Date of commencement: July 14, 1900.
    Contract completed: August 27, 1900.
4. For 159 cast-iron torpedo anchors, each weighing 3,000 pounds:
    Name of contractor: Chattanooga Car and Foundry Company, H. Clay Evans, proprietor.
    Date of contract: October 15, 1900.
    Date of approval: November 1, 1900.
    Date of commencement: November 12, 1900.
    Contract completed: December 27, 1900.

APPENDIX No. 6.

OPERATIONS OF THE ENGINEER DEPARTMENT IN THE PHILIPPINES.

REPORT OF MAJ. CLINTON B. SEARS, CORPS OF ENGINEERS, FOR THE FISCAL YEAR ENDING JUNE 30, 1901.

HEADQUARTERS DIVISION OF THE PHILIPPINES,
OFFICE CHIEF ENGINEER OF THE DIVISION,
Manila, P. I., August 17, 1901.

GENERAL: I have the honor to submit the following report on the operations of the Engineer Department in the Philippines for the fiscal year ending June 30, 1901.

The officers in charge of the Engineer Department, Division of the Philippines, have been Capt. (now Major) John Biddle, Corps of Engineers, to April 28, 1901. From that date until the end of the fiscal year I have been in charge.

There have been on duty in this office the following officers:

First Lieut. Frederick W. Altstaetter, Corps of Engineers, to January 22, 1901.
Capt. C. F. O'Keefe, Thirty-sixth Infantry, U. S. V., all the year as photographer.
First Lieut. Alvin R. Baskette, Thirty-seventh Infantry, U. S. V. (now first lieutenant, Third Infantry, U. S. A.), on duty since January 9, 1901, in charge of the filling of requisitions and shipment of engineer supplies.
Second Lieut. George E. Stewart, Nineteenth Infantry (now first lieutenant, Fifteenth Infantry), in charge of the map department since July 20, 1900.

At the headquarters of the department of northern Luzon, Capt. George A. Zinn, Corps of Engineers, has been on duty as engineer officer since September 6, 1900.

At the headquarters of the department of southern Luzon, First Lieut. John C. Oakes, Corps of Engineers, acted as engineer officer to May 28, 1901, and since that date First Lieut. Sherwood A. Cheney has so acted.

Capt. C. W. Meade, Thirty-sixth Infantry, U. S. V., has been in charge of the department of public works and of the water supply of the city of Manila to September 5, 1900, since which date First Lieut. Lytle Brown, Corps of Engineers (second lieutenant to February 2, 1901), has been in charge.

1. FIRST BATTALION OF ENGINEERS.

The organization of this battalion was effected under authority contained in the following order:

GENERAL ORDERS, }   HEADQUARTERS OF THE ARMY,
No. 22.   }   ADJUTANT-GENERAL'S OFFICE,
                      Washington, February 26, 1901.

The following orders of the Secretary of War are published for the information and government of all concerned:

Under the requirements of section 1 of the act approved February 2, 1901, "to increase the efficiency of the permanent military establishment of the United States," which provides that the enlisted force of the Corps of Engineers shall consist of one band and three battalions of four companies each, etc., the following organization is prescribed and will be effected without unnecessary delay:

The First Battalion, to consist of Companies A, B, C, and D, will be organized at Manila, Philippine Islands, under the command and direction of such officer of the Corps of Engineers on duty in the Division of the Philippines as the commanding general of the division may designate.

* * * * * * *

The designations of the present Companies E, C, and D of the Battalion of Engineers will be changed as follows:
Company E to Company C.

* * * * * * *

Recruiting will be at once commenced for the new companies to be organized, and battalion commanders are authorized to transfer to them enlisted men of the old companies when in their opinion such transfers would be in the interests of the service. All such transfers will be promptly reported to the Adjutant-General of the Army.

The companies composing the first and second battalions will, by authority of the President, consist of the maximum strength authorized by the act, namely: One first sergeant, 1 quartermaster-sergeant, 2 musicians, 2 cooks, 12 sergeants, 18 corporals, 64 first-class privates, and 64 second-class privates each. The new companies composing the Third Battalion will be organized with the minimum strength authorized, viz: One first sergeant, 1 quartermaster sergeant, 2 musicians, 2 cooks, 8 sergeants, 10 corporals, 38 first-class privates, and 38 second-class privates.

Officers will be assigned to the battalion in orders hereafter.
By command of Lieutenant-General Miles:

H. C. CORBIN, *Adjutant-General.*

Under the provisions of this order Maj. Clinton B. Sears, Corps of Engineers, was designated to command the battalion by the following order:

GENERAL ORDERS, } HEADQUARTERS DIVISION OF THE PHILIPPINES,
No. 79. *Manila, P. I., April 26, 1901.*

Under the provisions of General Orders, No. 22, current series, Headquarters of the Army, Maj. Clinton B. Sears, Corps of Engineers, United States Army, is designated to command the First Battalion, Corps of Engineers, and to direct the organization of the same as contemplated therein. He will submit to these headquarters a general scheme for effecting the organization, taking into consideration the present condition, distribution of duties, and needs of the service.

By command of Major-General MacArthur:

THOMAS H. BARRY,
Brig. Gen., U. S. V., Chief of Staff.

Previous to the submission of the general scheme called for in this order the following order and letter were received:

SPECIAL ORDERS, } HEADQUARTERS OF THE ARMY,
ADJUTANT-GENERAL'S OFFICE,
No. 55. *Washington, March 8, 1901.*

[Extract.]

* * * * * * *

10. By direction of the Secretary of War the following-named officers of the Corps of Engineers are assigned to the battalions and companies of engineers hereinafter designated, now being organized under the requirements of General Orders, No. 22, February 26, 1901, from this office:

Company A.—Capt. John Biddle, First Lieut. John C. Oakes, Second Lieut. Clarence O. Sherrill.

Company B.—Capt. George A. Zinn, First Lieut. William Kelly, Second Lieut. Walter H. Lee.

Company C.—Capt. William E. Craighill, First Lieut. Horton W. Stickle, Second Lieut. George R. Spalding.

Company D.—First Lieut. James B. Cavanaugh, First Lieut. Harry Burgess, Second Lieut. William G. Caples.

* * * * * * *

The commanding general, Division of the Philippines, will issue such further orders as may be necessary respecting officers assigned to the First Battalion.

* * * * * * *

By command of Lieutenant-General Miles:

H. C. CORBIN, *Adjutant-General.*

WAR DEPARTMENT,
ADJUTANT-GENERAL'S OFFICE,
Washington, March 9, 1901.

The COMMANDING OFFICER,
First Battalion of Engineers.
(Through Headquarters Division of the Philippines, Manila, P. I.)

SIR: Referring to the inclosed order assigning officers to the battalions and companies of engineers as organized under the act of February 2, 1901, you are authorized by the Secretary of War to select two lieutenants of the Engineer Corps from the following named:

First Lieuts. Sherwood A. Cheney, Frederick W. Altstaetter, Harley B. Ferguson, Lytle Brown, Lewis H. Rand, John R. Slattery, who are reported by the Chief of Engineers as probably available for the duty, to serve as adjutant, and quartermaster and commissary, respectively, of the battalion under your command, and to request the commanding general of the division to issue such orders as may be necessary to place the officers so selected on duty with the battalion.

You are further authorized by the Secretary to assign any one or two of the first lieutenants assigned to companies of the First Battalion to staff duty, filling their place or places by one or both of the officers selected by you from among those named, if you deem it advisable to do so.

Very respectfully,

W. H. CARTER,
Assistant Adjutant-General.

1 inclosure, par. 10, S. O., 55, A. G. O.

In compliance with the division order given above, the following scheme was submitted:

HEADQUARTERS FIRST BATTALION, CORPS OF ENGINEERS, U. S. ARMY,
Manila, P. I., May 4, 1901.

To the ADJUTANT-GENERAL, DIVISION OF THE PHILIPPINES,
Manila, P. I.

COLONEL: In compliance with S. O., No. 79, c. s., from headquarters of the division, I have the honor to submit the following general scheme for effecting the organization of the First Battalion, Corps of Engineers, taking into consideration the present condition, distribution of duties, and needs of the service.

The present conditions, etc., are as follows:

First. There are now organized three companies of engineer troops, Companies A, B, and E (the new C), officered by 10 first lieutenants and 4 second lieutenants of engineers.

Second. The headquarters of these companies are at Dagupan, Malate, and Caloocan, respectively.

Third. The officers and enlisted men of these companies are scattered over the island of Luzon in small detachments, engaged in the building and repair of military roads and bridges.

Fourth. The needs of the service are that this work be prosecuted as vigorously as possible, and be continued until the funds are exhausted, or until the rainy season stops the work, or until the charge of roads and bridges be turned over to the local civil governments.

Fifth. To undertake any organization of the battalion other than a skeleton one will seriously interfere with the present needs of the service.

PROPOSED ORGANIZATION.

Sixth. To appoint an adjutant and a quartermaster and commissary, a sergeant-major and a quartermaster sergeant, the quartermaster and quartermaster sergeant to remain on their present duties until their services can be spared, the adjutant to act as quartermaster and commissary, and the sergeant-major as quartermaster sergeant ad interim. The adjutant to be the recruiting officer of the battalion.

Seventh. The headquarters of the battalion to be established temporarily at this office, where there is convenient room, and where it will be near the commanding officer of the battalion.

Eighth. Company D to be skeletonized by the appointment of the legal quota of sergeants and corporals, viz, 1 first sergeant, 1 quartermaster sergeant, 12 sergeants, and 18 corporals. These noncommissioned officers, however, to continue on their present duties until their services are needed to officer the company as men may be assigned, when they will be called in, one or more at a time, as required. The company to be commanded by the adjutant ad interim.

Ninth. To leave the various officers and enlisted men at their present duties and stations, except as hereinbefore provided.

Tenth. As the present enforcement of the terms of General Orders, No. 55, Adjutant-General's Office, Washington, D. C., March 8, 1901, will create great confusion and necessitate the changing about of officers to place them in touch with their new companies, it is proposed to make these assignments on paper only, the anomalous position of any officer to be accounted for on the morning reports and pay and muster rolls as being on detached duty from the companies, or as belonging to Company X, but on temporary duty with Company Z, etc., as the case may be.

Eleventh. As soon as the rainy season stops work, concentrate the three companies now in the field at their respective headquarters and establish the headquarters of Company D at Caloocan with Company E (new C) or elsewhere in or near Manila where barracks can be obtained, and proceed with the permanent organization of the company by promoting second-class privates from the other companies to first-class privates in the new company, their old places in the old companies to be filled by recruits as fast as they can be obtained.

Twelfth. In case the roads and bridges be turned over to the civil authorities, assemble the whole battalion in comfortable barracks in or near Manila for instructions, drill, and discipline, the care of engineer equipage, the study and development of a more effective engineer field train, and the preparation of a manual of field engineering.

Thirteenth. That the battalion adjutant, as recruiting officer, be authorized to secure as many recruits as possible for the present companies, they being short many men under the increased allowance.

Fourteenth. That the battalion commander be authorized to apply to the Secretary of War through military channels for the transfer to Manila of the engineer band for assignment to the First Battalion for the following reasons:

(1) This is the senior battalion in its number, its length of service as individual companies, and the rank of its commanding officer.

(2) As a matter of public military policy it is thought that everything reasonably possible should be done to add to the comfort and encouragement of the enlisted men serving in the Philippines, and the three companies now here have certainly earned the privilege by their long, arduous, and effective work on the roads and bridges and other field duties, which work has been as exacting under the later conditions of peace as under those incident to hostilities.

Fifteenth. As the present companies are under the orders of the department commander, that the battalion commander be authorized to give directly to the company commanders all orders that relate to organization and returns and which do not interfere with or conflict with their orders under the department commanders, or that he be authorized to issue such orders in the name of the major-general commanding the division for transmission through the department commander, copies of orders so issued to be filed with the adjutant-general of the division for the information of the major-general commanding the division.

I remain, Colonel, very respectfully,

CLINTON B. SEARS,
Major, Corps of Engineers, U. S. A.,
Commanding First Battalion, Corps of Engineers.

This letter was received back on May 15, 1901, with the following indorsement:

[First indorsement.]

HEADQUARTERS DIVISION OF THE PHILIPPINES,
Manila, P. I., May 11, 1901.

Respectfully returned to the commanding officer, First Battalion of Engineers, Manila.

The scheme outlined herein for effecting the organization of the First Battalion of Engineers is approved, with the remark that it is of course understood that in calling in the noncommissioned officers for Company D, such action will be taken through these headquarters, the companies now being under the department commander.

The battalion commander is authorized to make any application for the engineer band that he desires.

By command of Major-General MacArthur:

S. D. STURGIS,
Assistant Adjutant-General.

APPENDIX 6—OPERATIONS IN THE PHILIPPINES. 979

Under this authority Major Sears assumed command of the First Battalion on May 16, 1901, and appointed the following staff: Adjutant, First Lieut. Harry Burgess, Corps of Engineers; quartermaster and commissary, First Lieut. Sherwood A. Cheney, Corps of Engineers; sergeant-major, Truman Organ; quartermaster-sergeant, William Harer.

The adjutant and the sergeant-major reported to these headquarters on May 30, the quartermaster-sergeant on June 15.

The quartermaster and commissary, Lieutenant Cheney, is still on duty with Company B.

On May 31 the designation of Company E, Battalion of Engineers, was changed to Company C, First Battalion of Engineers.

On June 7 Company D was partially organized by the transfer to it of 11 men from Company A, 12 from Company B, and 11 from Company C. From the men so transferred were appointed 1 first sergeant, 1 quartermaster-sergeant, 12 sergeants, 18 corporals, and 2 cooks (corporals). These men were left on duty with their old companies. The adjutant was designated to take charge of the company records and headquarters until such time as orders were issued for assembling the company. This is the present status of Company D.

On June 30, 1901, the strength of the battalion was as follows:

	Officers.	Enlisted men.
Field and staff	2	2
Company A	3	96
Company B	4	183
Company C	3	181
Company D		34
Total	12	896

During the year the following officers have been on duty with the battalion:

Maj. Clinton B. Sears, Corps of Engineers, commanding battalion since May 16, 1901.

First Lieut. Harry Burgess, Corps of Engineers, adjutant and acting quartermaster and commissary since May 30, 1901.

COMPANY A.

Capt. James B. Cavanaugh, Corps of Engineers, since October 1, 1901. (First lieutenant to April 30, 1901.)
First Lieut. Horton W. Stickle, Corps of Engineers, to May 10, 1901. (Second lieutenant to February 2, 1901.)
First Lieut. Lewis H. Rand, Corps of Engineers, since September 1, 1900. (Second lieutenant to February 2, 1901.)
Second Lieut. Clarence O. Sherrill, Corps of Engineers, since April 27, 1901.

COMPANY B.

First Lieut. John C. Oakes, Corps of Engineers, to May 23, 1901.
First Lieut. Sherwood A. Cheney, Corps of Engineers, since July 17, 1900.
First Lieut. Harley B. Ferguson, Corps of Engineers.
First Lieut. William Kelly, Corps of Engineers, since September 3, 1900. (Second lieutenant to February 2, 1901.)
Second Lieut. Walter H. Lee, Corps of Engineers, from April 24, 1901, to June 10, 1901.
Second Lieut. William G. Caples, Corps of Engineers, since April 24, 1901.

COMPANY C.

Capt. George A. Zinn, Corps of Engineers, from July 29, 1900, to September 6, 1900.
First Lieut. James B. Cavanaugh, Corps of Engineers, from July 17, to September 30, 1900.
First Lieut. James P. Jervey, Corps of Engineers, to July 19, 1900.
First Lieut. Harry Burgess, Corps of Engineers, from July 29, 1900, to May 30, 1901.
First Lieut. Frederick W. Altstaetter, Corps of Engineers, since January 23, 1901.
First Lieut. John R. Slattery, Corps of Engineers, since July 17, 1900. (Second lieutenant to February 2, 1901.)
Second Lieut. George R. Spalding, Corps of Engineers, since April 22, 1901.

COMPANY D.

The adjutant temporarily attached since June 7, 1901.

On June 10, 1901, Lieut. Walter H. Lee, who was accompanying as a volunteer a detachment of the Twenty-first Infantry under Capt. William H. Wilhelm, Twenty-first Infantry, was killed in an attack on the insurgent intrenchments near Lipa, province of Batangas.

Duties:
During the year the duties performed by the companies of the battalion have been, with a few exceptions, connected with road and bridge work in the island of Luzon. On September 12, 1900, the United States Philippine Commission appropriated $1,000,000 (United States currency) to be expended in the immediate construction and repair of highways and bridges in the Philippine Islands.

In anticipation of the passage of this act, and subsequent to the passage, officers of the battalion with detachments of enlisted men were sent out on mounted reconnaissances over certain lines of road in Luzon selected by the military governor. These reconnaissances were for the purpose of obtaining data for reports on the condition of the roads and for estimates for their repair. These reports were completed before the end of the rainy season.

Based upon the estimate thus made, allotments were made by the military governor for the different roads; but on account of the great extent of the roads requiring repairs the allotment made for any road was, as a rule, insufficient to do the work properly.

The different roads for which money was allotted were put in the charge of officers of the battalion as far as possible, but, as the number of engineer officers was entirely inadequate, a number of officers of infantry were assigned to this duty. In all cases detachments of enlisted men from the battalion were furnished to act as overseers. This work has been in progress since the latter part of the last rainy season and is not yet completed.

The officers and enlisted men have quickly adapted themselves to the conditions encountered in this work, and have carried it on with great success in spite of the scarcity of suitable road and bridge materials, and in the almost total absence of practicable transportation.

Lieut. Harley B. Ferguson, Corps of Engineers, with 15 to 20 men from Company B, was on duty with the expeditionary force in China until June 5, 1901. This detachment was too small to have undertaken any serious field engineering operations; but fortunately little of this work was required. Lieutenant Ferguson and his detachment were employed in the preparation and distribution of maps and collection of other information in the laying out of camps and other work, and in examining and reporting on the personnel and equipment of the engineer troops of the several foreign armies in China.

A detail of four noncommissioned officers and three privates from Companies B and E (now C) accompanied General Hare's expedition to Marinduque in October, 1900, and made sketches of the roads and trails traversed.

Details from the companies have also been furnished to the division and department engineer officers for map, photographic, and clerical work, and for duty at the engineer storehouse.

While on a road reconnaissance Lieut. F. W. Altstaetter, with a detachment of 3 engineers and 11 cavalry soldiers, was attacked on August 1, 1900, by a large party of insurgents (300 to 500 men) under Lacuna, at a small village 6 to 8 miles north of San Miguel de Mayuma. After a gallant fight, in which 4 of his men were wounded (one fatally), and after his ammunition was exhausted, Lieutenant Altstaetter was forced to surrender himself and detachment to the insurgents. The enlisted men were released by the insurgents within a few days, but Lieutenant Altstaetter remained a prisoner until exchanged on November 23, 1900, by Lacuna, for a major in the insurgent army.

Recommendations:

The necessity for training engineer troops in time of peace is much more apparent than in the case of any other of the troops of the line. For this reason it is recommended that an effort be made to have the engineer companies restored to a strength in time of peace very nearly what it is to be in time of war. Even if this can not be done, it will be of great advantage to allow the companies the full complement of noncommissioned officers. In the service in the Philippines it has been found that the work requires numerous small detachments, remote from a company officer, all of which detachments should be in the charge of a noncommissioned officer. This can not be done under the strength authorized in General Orders, No. 66, Headquarters of the Army, Adjutant-General's Office, Washington, D. C., May 13, 1901. Men suitable in the matter of education and training for noncommissioned officers of engineers can not be retained in the service as privates, since they can nearly always do better in civil life.

It is also recommended that the pay of a corporal of engineers be raised from $20 to $25 per month, for the purpose of inducing desirable corporals to remain in the service.

The enlisted men of the engineer battalions should be armed with the carbine and revolver instead of the infantry rifle, the carbine to be provided with a sling. The duties of engineers in the field frequently require them to be mounted, in which case the infantry arm becomes very inconvenient. The revolver is necessary for the protection of the men in those cases where the nature of the work requires the rifle to be laid aside. By authority of the division commander, practically all the enlisted men of this battalion have been supplied with revolvers, and in a few cases the carbine also has been supplied.

II. OFFICE WORK AND SUPPLY DEPARTMENT.

The office work has consisted in the keeping of records for the office of the division engineer and for the road and bridge work, and in the preparation of reports, returns, etc.

The operations of the supply department have been the collection of tools and materials for the construction of roads and bridges and the distribution of same to the various points where this work has been in progress.

The larger part of the tools and iron supplies was purchased by Maj. John G. D. Knight, Corps of Engineers, in charge of the Engineer Depot, Willets Point, N. Y., and shipped to Manila from New York. The cost of the articles sent in the two shipments by Major Knight was $87,866.60.

The list of articles included in shipments is as follows:

Steam pile drivers	7
Scows for steam pile drivers	2
Hand pile drivers, complete	6
Hand pile drivers, complete on scows	2
Road rollers, 3 ton, reversible, complete	100
Wheel dump wagons, complete	54
Light dump carts, complete	100
Wheel scrapers, steel bowl	100
Drag scrapers, steel bowl	100
Road plows, right hand, No. 106	200
Wooden wheelbarrows, "Jacobs, R. It."	2,000
Picks, and 9,000 extra handles	2,000
Shovels	15,500
Mattocks	1,850
Transits, complete	10
Y-levels, complete	20
100-foot steel chains	20
N. Y. level rods	20
Blacksmiths' forges	100
Blacksmiths' anvils	100
Blacksmiths' tools ...sets	100
Screw plates, complete, with dies, taps, etc ...do	50
Grindstones	80
Saws, assorted	450
Adzes	240
Ships' augers, assorted	500
Hammers, assorted	975
Small tools (various kinds of carpenters' and blacksmiths' tools)	5,700
Crowbars	1,500
Wooden tackle blocks, assorted sizes ...sets	200
Bar iron (round, square, and octagon) ...pounds	41,600
Nails and spikes, assorted sizes ...do	250,000
⅝-inch machine bolts, 12 and 16 inch, with nuts	6,750

In addition, the following is a partial list of tools and supplies purchased in Manila:

Rock crushers, steam, complete	4
Hoes and rakes	1,000
Gravel baskets	2,000
Buckets, G. I	360
Level rods	7
Metallic tapes	38
Saws, assorted	162
Hammers, assorted	500
Augers, assorted	400
Small tools (various kinds of carpenters', blacksmiths', and masons' tools)	1,300
Rope, manila ...pounds	32,400
Coils rope, wire	17
Iron, including castings, bar iron, etc ...pounds	182,000
Nails, assorted sizes ...do	48,000
Nuts and washers ...do	7,000
Bolts, assorted sizes	1,400
Dynamite ...pounds	11,500
Lime ...do	62,600
Cement ...barrels	3,100
Lumber ...feet, B. M.	820,000
Lumber, assorted, small ...linear feet	44,500
Piles	700

APPENDIX 6—OPERATIONS IN THE PHILIPPINES. 983

In addition to the above a large amount of miscellaneous supplies was purchased in Manila. Lumber and piling were also purchased by the officers in local charge of bridge work in the vicinity of the work. The above list represents what was purchased by the division engineer.

From the property listed above the requisitions made by the different officers in charge of work were promptly filled.

III. MAP WORK.

The compilation of the maps and reconnaissances received has been steadily progressing. One American and six Filipino draftsmen are at present engaged in this work. One soldier is detailed from the Engineer Battalion to do the blue printing, and has a Filipino assistant.

The provinces of Zambales, Pangasinan, Tarlac, Pampanga, Bulacan, Manila, Morong, Cavite, Batangas, and Laguna, Luzon Island, have been well traversed and plotted at a scale of 1 inch to the mile. The provinces of Nueva Ecija, Bataan, and Tayabas, and parts of Ilocos Sur and Ilocos Norte have also been mapped, but to a lesser extent, and are included in this inch map.

The island of Marinduque has been partially mapped, the important roads and trails being traversed and plotted in a very satisfactory manner.

The island of Panay, Fourth district Department of the Visayas, has been more thoroughly mapped than any other island of the archipelago. With but little exception every road and trail has been traversed and plotted at a scale of 1 inch to the mile.

Excepting the particular portion of the archipelago mentioned, the Spanish maps have been almost entirely relied upon. Many of these have been corrected and improved by officers and soldiers in the field, and give a good general knowledge of the country. All this general information has been included in the district maps which cover the entire archipelago, and are corrected to date as information is received.

All of the available reliable data have been included in the inch map, and this in turn is being reduced to a scale of 2 miles to the inch and prepared in accordance with the pamphlet entitled "Instructions for the Preparation of Military Maps," dated War Department, Adjutant-General's Office, Military Information Division, Washington, D. C., April, 1900.

Through the courtesy of the suboffice of the Coast and Geodetic Survey, Manila, P. I., in supplying their information and data of the correct geographical positions of various points, it will be practicable to correctly orient this map and in fact prepare it generally with very great accuracy. The correct geographical positions, together with the exact locations of the following Coast and Geodetic Survey astronomical stations have been furnished this office: Manila Cathedral, Cavite Church, Corregidor Island Light; Subig, Zambales province; Sual, and Dagupan Light, Pangasinan province; Balayan and Batangas, Batangas province.

North of Manila the Manila and Dagupan Railroad from the original Spanish survey carefully reduced to the desired scale and correctly oriented has been taken as a base line.

In preparing the skeleton sheets the coordinates were first carefully delineated according to the Smithsonian geographical tables and the data mentioned plotted. The various pueblos were then located from the best available information and the road sketches fitted in. Sometimes they had to be enlarged a trifle, but more often slightly reduced. The correct air-line measurement from Sual to Subig is 82.5 miles. The road sketches between these two stations, at a scale of 2 inches to the mile, traversed by Capt. Smith K. Fitzhugh, Thirty-sixth Infantry, U. S. V., and party after being carefully oriented scaled to 79.96 miles, thus being 2.54 miles short. This work was projected to the correct scale, distributing the error throughout the entire distance.

The accompanying summary of data will give an excellent idea of the compiling of this map south of Manila to Batangas and Balayan, this territory being reduced almost entirely from Spanish itineraries.

During the year upward of 8,800 maps have been distributed throughout the division, principally blue prints.

A very large assortment of instruments of various kinds has been issued to officers in the division on memorandum receipt, for the purpose of obtaining data for the compilation of maps.

Summary of air-line distances obtained for comparison in compiling the "half-inch map" south of Manila to Batangas and Balayan, Batangas province.

	Inch map.	Two of best charts.	Spanish survey.	"Half-inch" map.
	Miles.	Miles.	Miles.	Miles.
Taal to Tanauan			21.65	21.75
Taal to Maragondon			30.81	30.28
Maragondon to Tanauan			31.19	31.20
Manila to Muntinlupa	14.50	15.20 / 16.00	15.61	14.70
Manila to Maragondon	25.73	25.80 / 26.20	26.50	26.20
Maragondon to Muntinlupa	21.55	22.20 / 21.65	22.23	22.28
Corregidor to Maragondon		12.75 / 13.12		12.93
Muntinlupa to Corregidor		32.30		32.10
Corregidor to Balayan		31.66		32.08
Corregidor light to Batangas (astronomical station)				a 53.50
Balayan to Batangas (astronomical station)				a 24.97
Corregidor light to Manila Cathedral				a 30.32
Manila Cathedral to Cavite Church				a 8.53
Manila Cathedral to Balayan				a 47.78
Manila Cathedral to Batangas (astronomical station)				a 57.69

a These distances were calculated from United States Coast and Geodetic information.

IV. ROADS AND BRIDGES.

This work has been carried on under the $1,000,000 appropriation mentioned above.

Up to June 30, 1901, of this sum $780,500 had been transferred by the treasurer of the Philippines to the division engineer; $746,947.57 of this amount has been expended or transferred to officers in charge of work.

For the expenditure of this appropriation a general plan was submitted by the division engineer, including certain important lines of roads in the island of Luzon. This having been approved by the military governor, Officers of the Engineer Battalion were sent out to examine these roads and make estimates for their repair. The instructions given these officers were to submit a detailed report on the condition of the roads at the time examined and to make estimates for their repair, as follows:

1. For a first-class road with permanent bridges throughout.

2. A good wagon road to last at least through the next rainy season, with bridges or ferries, as were most suitable.

3. For the minimum repairs necessary for making the road passable through next rainy season for pack animals only.

4. For repairs for a dry-season road only.

The total of the estimates made for the selected roads for repairs according to the (2) plan above was more than twice the appropriation. For this reason certain of the selected roads were omitted, and the allotments, while following the (2) type, were considerably less than the estimates—often not more than one-quarter or one-half.

The greatest difficulty encountered in carrying out the road work has been the lack of suitable transportation. The native transportation, the carabao cart, can not be depended on for hauling road metal. The Quartermaster's Department supplied transportation to the extent of 587 mules and 148 wagons, the larger part of which was not supplied until near the end of the working season. However, the transportation has made it possible to do at least twice the work which could have been done if the native transportation had had to be depended upon.

Road metal is available at a comparatively few places, and on account of the lack of transportation it has been very difficult to obtain at the points where required. Gravel has been used almost throughout.

Lumber has been obtained principally from the United States and from Singapore. There are large forests of fine timber in Luzon, but it has been possible to obtain this only in small quantities, both on account of lack of transportation and on account of the difficulty of having the logs sawed up.

Native labor has, as a rule, been easy to obtain, at from 15 to 30 cents per day. When properly managed by good overseers the native unskilled labor is quite satisfactory, but it has been difficult to obtain good carpenters and masons.

In the island of Luzon about 700 miles of road have been worked over, the extent of repairs done varying from the repair of bridges, washouts, etc., to the complete rebuilding of a substantial road. Where new road was built the method has been to throw up a heavy embankment, with large ditches, covering with as thick a layer of gravel (in a few cases broken stone) as the allotment would permit.

The bridges built have varied according to circumstances. The larger number have been truss, pile, or trestle bridges. In a few cases the piers and the abutments or the entire bridge have been built of stone when this could be readily obtained.

V. EXPENDITURES.

(a) Funds allotted by Chief of Engineers:

"Civilian Assistants to Engineer Officers, 1901:"
Received $7,000.00
Expenditures $4,774.57
Turned into subtreasury at San Francisco, Cal............ 2,225.43
——————— 7,000.00

"Equipment of Engineer Troops, 1901:"
Received 3,000.00
Expenditures $586.94
Turned into subtreasury at San Francisco, Cal............ 2,413.06
——————— 3,000.00

The funds for "Civilian Assistants to Engineer Officers" have been expended for hire of employees in the office and field.

The funds for "Equipment of Engineer Troops" have been expended for instruments and supplies for drafting, map reproduction, and photography.

(b) *Public civil funds.*

Allotments from appropriation for construction of highways and bridges:

Amount received		$780,500.00
Expenditures:		
For tools and supplies and office expenses	$196,961.85	
For construction	549,985.72	
Balance on hand	33,552.43	
		780,500.00

In accordance with terms of the act of appropriation, these funds have been expended on the construction and repair of roads and bridges.

VI. GENERAL REMARKS.

The military operations for the year have been of such nature that the services of engineer troops have not been needed to accompany the small detachments operating against the insurgents. For this reason the engineer troops have had practically no work in the field during the year. The services, however, of the engineer officers and men in the repairing and construction of roads, bridges, and ferries have been of the greatest importance and equally arduous with service in the field. The lack of a sufficient number of engineer troops has been a serious handicap in carrying on this work, and the services of the entire battalion (as organized previous to February 2, 1901) could have been used to great advantage. The small number of engineer officers in the Philippines has rendered it necessary to secure the services of officers detailed from the cavalry, artillery, or infantry. The departments of the Visayas and of Mindanao and Jolo have never had as engineer officer an Officer of the Corps of Engineers. The department of northern Luzon was until quite recently divided into six districts, each having a district staff. The other three departments each have had four districts. Only one of these eighteen districts has had an Officer of the Corps of Engineers as engineer officer. A large part of the road and bridge work has been done by officers of other branches of the service.

This report has been prepared under my direction by First Lieut. Harry Burgess, Corps of Engineers, adjutant of the First Battalion of Engineers.

Very respectfully, CLINTON B. SEARS,
Major, Corps of Engineers, U. S. A.,
Chief Engineer Officer of the Division.

Brig. Gen. G. L. GILLESPIE,
Chief of Engineers, U. S. A.

INDEX.

[The references in roman are to part (or volume) and those in arabic to page. The letter "S" indicates the supplement.]

A.

Abrams Creek, Tenn., examination and survey .... I, 469; III, 2491, 2496
Absecon Inlet, N. J., removal of wreck at entrance .... I, 262; II, 1351
Acts of Fifty-sixth Congress, second session, affecting Corps of Engineers... V, 3837
Acushnet River, Mass.:
    Bridge between New Bedford and Fish Island .... I, 665
    Improvement of New Bedford Harbor .... I, 163; II, 1119
Agate Bay Harbor, Minn., improvement of .... I, 506; IV, 2824
Ahnapee Harbor, Wis., improvement of .... I, 519; IV, 2923
Alabama River, Ala.:
    Bridge at Selma .... I, 665
    Improvement of .... I, 361; III, 1786
Alafia River, Fla., bridge at Riverview .... I, 664
Alameda, Cal. *See* Oakland.
Albemarle and Chesapeake Canal, N. C., improvement of waterway via. I, 297; II, 1457
Albemarle Sound, N. C.:
    Examination and survey of waterway via .... I, 299, 309; II, 1511
    Improvement of waterway to Norfolk, Va., via Currituck Sound. I, 297; II, 1457
    Improvement of waterway to Norfolk, Va., via Pasquotank River. I, 296; II, 1455
Alexandria, La., bridge across Red River between Pineville and .... I, 659
Alexandria and Pineville Bridge Company, bridge of .... I, 659
Alice (barge), removal of wreck of .... I, 411; III, 1959
Allegheny, Pa.:
    Bridge across Allegheny River to Pittsburg (Fort Wayne Bridge) ...... I, 662
    Harbor lines in Ohio River at .... I, 119; IV, 2709
    Improvement of Pittsburg Harbor .... I, 480; IV, 2697
Allegheny River, Pa.:
    Bridge at Franklin .... I, 663
    Bridge between Oil City and Franklin .... I, 663
    Bridge between Pittsburg and Allegheny (Fort Wayne Bridge) .... I, 662
    Construction of locks and dams .... I, 482; IV, 2701
    Improvement by open-channel work .... I, 483; IV, 2707
    Improvement of Pittsburg Harbor .... I, 480; IV, 2697
Allouez Bay, Wis. (*see* Duluth Harbor) .... I, 507; IV, 2828
Alloway Creek, N. J., improvement of .... I, 244; II, 1332
Alpena Harbor, Mich., improvement of .... I, 555; IV, 3137
Altamaha River, Ga., improvement of .... I, 329; II, 1642
Alviso Harbor, Cal., improvement of .... I, 603; IV, 3410
Ambrose Channel, New York Harbor, N. Y., improvement of .... I, 224; II, 1285
Amite River, La., improvement of .... I, 381; III, 1875
Amphlet Slough, San Joaquin River, Cal., examination for closure of. I, 613; IV, 3454
Anchor, disk, use of the .... III, 2221
Anclote River, Fla., improvement of .... I, 348; III, 1760
Andura (Nandua) Creek, Va., improvement of .... I, 295; II, 1454
Annapolis Harbor, Md., harbor lines .... I, 119; II, 1396
Ann, Cape, Mass., construction of harbor of refuge in Sandy Bay .... I, 141; II, 1048
Antioch, Cal., examination and survey of waterway to Suisun
    Point .... I, 613; IV, 3449, 3452
Apalachicola Bay and River, Fla.:
    Improvement of bay .... I, 351; III, 1767
    Improvement of river, including the Cut-off .... I, 352; III, 1769
Applegate, Samuel (schooner), removal of wreck of .... I, 263; II, 1352
Appleton, Wis., bridge across Fox River Canal at .... I, 664

Appomattox River, Va.:
Examination and survey for deflection of, at Petersburg ... I, 299; II, 1467, 1471
Improvement of .... I, 294; II, 1452
Appoquinimink River, Del.:
Improvement of .... I, 250; II, 1339
Removal of wreck below Odessa Landing .... I, 263; II, 1352
Appropriations. *See* Fortifications *and* Rivers and harbors.
Aqueduct Bridge, Washington, D. C., repair of .... I, 669; V, 3637
Aqueduct, Washington, D. C. *See* Washington.
Aransas Pass, Tex., improvement of .... I, 409; III, 1952
Arcata, Cal. (*see* Humboldt Harbor) .... I, 611; IV, 3431
Arch Rock, San Francisco Harbor, Cal., removal of .... I, 604; IV, 3411
Ardanhu (steamer), removal of wreck of .... I, 174; II, 1147
Arkansas River:
Examination and survey for permanent improvement .... I, 433; III, 2128
Gauging (*see* Mississippi River) .... I, 425; III, 2072; S., 8, 45, 126
General improvement .... I, 426; III, 2098
Removal of obstructions .... I, 425; III, 2095
Arlington, Wash., bridge across Stilaguamish River .... I, 667
Armament. *See* Fortifications.
Arthur Kill, N. Y. and N. J.:
Harbor lines .... I, 118; II, 1279
Improvement of Staten Island-New Jersey channel .... I, 215; II, 1233
Arthur Lake, La. (*see* Mermentau River) .... I, 392; III, 1901
Artillery Corps:
Reservation at Willets Point, N. Y., transferred to the .... I, 42
Tugboat for transfer to the .... I, 38
Ashland, Ky., bridge across Ohio River between Ironton, Ohio, and ... I, 660
Ashland, Wis., improvement of harbor .... I, 509; IV, 2363
Ashland and Ironton Bridge Company, bridge of: .... I, 660
Ashley River, S. C., examination and survey .... I, 324; II, 1619, 1623
Ashtabula Harbor, Ohio:
Improvement of .... I, 581; IV, 3260
Water levels .... I, 681; V, 3776
Assawaman Bay, Del., improvement of waterway via .... I, 260; II, 1348
Assistants:
Civilian, to engineer officers .... I, 37, 38
On duty in Office of the Chief of Engineers .... I, 688
Astoria, N. Y., bridge across East River at Hell Gate, near .... I, 664
Astoria, Oreg. (*see* Columbia River, below Tongue Point) .... I, 634; V, 3565
Atchafalaya River, La., rectification of mouth by Mississippi River Commission .... I, 657; S., 3, 32
Atlanta, Knoxville and Northern Railway Company, bridge of ...... I, 668
Atlantic City, N. J.:
Bridge across Inside Thoroughfare at .... I, 664
Examination and survey of Beach Thoroughfare .... I, 263; II, 1353, 1355
Removal of wreck at entrance to Absecon Inlet .... I, 262; II, 1351
Removal of wreck in Atlantic Ocean, off .... I, 263; II, 1353
Atlantic County, N. J., bridge of .... I, 664
Atlantic Ocean:
Disbursements for examinations and surveys of waterways between Great Lakes and .... I, 118
Removal of wreck off Atlantic City, N. J .... I, 263; II, 1353
Removal of wreck off Seabright, N. J .... I, 223; II, 1247
Atlantic (South) States, removal of water hyacinths from Florida waters .... I, 341; II, 1746
Augusta, Ga.:
Improvement of Savannah River above .... I, 327; II, 1636
Improvement of Savannah River between Savannah and .... I, 326; II, 1634
Aux Becs Scies Lake, Mich. (*see* Frankfort Harbor) .... I, 550; IV, 3122

B.

Back Bay, Biloxi, Miss., bridge across .... I, 659
Back Cove, Portland, Me.:
Bridge (Tukeys) obstructing .... I, 668
Harbor lines .... I, 118; II, 1027
Improvement of .... I, 131; II, 1006

INDEX. 3

Back Creek, Md., removal of sunken logs .... I, 272; II, 1390
Bagaduce River, Me., improvement of .... I, 125; II, 996
Bailey, Electa (schooner), removal of wreck of .... I, 174; II, 1147
Baltimore and Ohio Railroad Company, bridge of .... I, 664
Baltimore and Potomac Railroad Company, contract with, for highway bridge
 at Washington, D. C .... I, 119
Baltimore Harbor, Md.:
 Defenses of .... I, 6, 22, 784
 Estimate of cost of deepening and widening channel of Curtis Bay, and
  of main ship channel of Patapsco River and .... I, 273; II, 1394
 Improvement at Spring Garden .... I, 266; II, 1379
 Improvement of channel to .... I, 264; II, 1374
 Improvement of channel to Curtis Bay .... I, 265; II, 1379
 Removal of wreck in Fort McHenry Channel .... I, 272; II, 1391
 Removal of wreck in North Point Creek .... I, 272; II, 1390
Bangor Harbor, Me.:
 Harbor lines .... I, 118; II, 1022
 Improvement of Penobscot River .... I, 126; II, 997
Bank protection, subaqueous, use of lumber mattress for .... III, 2212
Barbette gun carriages .... I, 8, 9
Bar Harbor, Me.:
 Construction of breakwater .... I, 122; II, 991
 Defenses of .... I, 13, 697, 911
Barren River, Ky., operating and care of lock and dam .... I, 503; IV, 2806
Bartholomew Bayou, La. and Ark.:
 Bridge across .... I, 660
 Improvement of .... I, 417; III, 2042
Bath, Me., bridge across New Meadows River .... I, 669
Battalion of Engineers .... I, 39, 43, 943, 975
Batteries:
 Dynamite .... I, 10
 Gun and mortar .... I, 5, 7, 37
 Sand, emergency .... I, 8
Baxter, Mary (schooner), removal of wreck of .... I, 263; II, 1352
Bay Ridge Channel, New York Harbor, N. Y., improvement of .... I, 226; II, 1291
Bayside Channel, New York Harbor, N. Y., improvement of .... I, 224; II, 1285
Beach Thoroughfare, N. J., examination and survey .... I, 263; II, 1353, 1355
Beattys Bridge, N. C., bridge across Black River, near .... I, 664
Beaufort Harbor and Inlet, N. C.:
 Examination and survey of waterway from South Mills to and including
  inlet .... I, 299, 309; II, 1511
 Improvement of harbor .... I, 304; II, 1495
 Improvement of waterway to Newbern .... I, 303; II, 1493
 Improvement of waterway to New River .... I, 304; II, 1496
Beaufort Harbor and River, S. C.:
 Defenses of Port Royal Sound .... I, 6, 25, 816
 Improvement of river .... I, 323; II, 1604
 Improvement of waterway to Savannah (*see* Savannah) .... I, 324; II, 1628
 Removal of sunken logs in waterway to Charleston .... I, 324; II, 1607
Beechridge, Ill., prevention of break in Mississippi River at .... I, 438; III, 2198
Bellaire, Benwood and Wheeling Bridge Company, bridge of .... I, 660
Bellaire, Ohio, bridge across Ohio River to Benwood, W. Va .... I, 660
Belle Isle, Detroit River, Mich., removal of wreck .... I, 570; IV, 3198
Belle River, Mich.:
 Bridge in St. Clair County .... I, 666
 Improvement of .... I, 560; IV, 3152
Bellingham Bay, Wash., log boom (*see* Puget Sound) .... I, 645; V, 3581
Benson (schooner), removal of wreck of .... I, 584; IV, 3269
Benton, Fort, Mont., improvement of Missouri River at ...... I, 452, 453; III, 2373
Benton Harbor and Benton Harbor Canal, Mich.:
 Bridges (5) obstructing Pawpaw River .... I, 668
 Improvements at (*see* St. Joseph Harbor) .... I, 537; IV, 3079
Benton Township, Mich., bridges (5) obstructing Pawpaw River at .... I, 668
Benwood, W. Va., bridge across Ohio River between Bellaire, Ohio, and .. I, 660
Benz, Rudolph, bridge of .... I, 665
Bergen County, N. J., bridge of .... I, 665
Beverly Harbor, Mass., examination and survey .... I, 150; II, 1065, 1068
Big Assawaman Bay, Del., improvement of waterway via .... I, 260; II, 1348

INDEX.

Big Barren River, Ky., operating and care of lock and dam .... I, 503; IV, 2806
Big Sandy River, W. Va. and Ky.:
    Final report on survey for locks and dams, including Levisa and Tug
        forks .... I, 496; IV, 2750
    Improvement of .... I, 490; IV, 2735
    Improvement of Levisa Fork .... I, 493; IV, 2742
    Improvement of Tug Fork .... I, 493; IV, 2742
    Operating and care of lock and dam .... I, 492; IV, 2741
Big Sarasota Bay, Fla. (*see* Sarasota Bay) .... I, 344; III, 1753
Big Sioux River, S. Dak.:
    Construction of ice harbor at Sioux City .... I, 456; III, 2373, 2377
    Examination for reservoir dam .... I, 458; III, 2395
Big Stone Lake, Minn. and S. Dak., survey for reservoir dam .... I, 450; III, 2342
Big Sunflower River, Miss., improvement of .... I, 424; III, 2070
Big Timber Creek, N. J., bridge below Gloucester .... I, 666
Billingsport, N. J., removal of wreck in Delaware River .... I, 263; II, 1352
Biloxi, Miss., bridge of city of .... I, 659
Biloxi Bay, Miss., bridge across Back Bay .... I, 659
Bismarck, N. Dak., improvement of Missouri River at ..... I, 452, 453; III, 2373, 2374
Black Lake, Mich., improvement of Holland Harbor .... I, 541; IV, 3092
Black River, Ark. and Mo., improvement of .... I, 431; III, 2121
Black River, La., improvement of .... I, 415; III, 2034
Black River, Mich.:
    Improvement at mouth .... I, 558; IV, 3147
    Improvement at Port Huron .... I, 559; IV, 3148
Black River, N. C.:
    Bridge at Still Bluff .... I, 661
    Bridge near Beattys Bridge .... I, 664
    Improvement of .... I, 306; II, 1499
Black River, Ohio, improvement of Lorain Harbor .... I, 577; IV, 3241
Black Rock Harbor, Conn. (*see* Bridgeport) .... I, 186; II, 1177
Black Rock Harbor, N. Y.:
    Examination and survey of Lake Erie entrance to .... I, 592; IV, 3342, 3345
    Harbor lines .... I, 119; IV, 3349
    Improvement of Buffalo entrance to .... I, 589; IV, 3324
Black Warrior River, Ala.:
    Examination and survey for Locks and Dams 1, 2, and 3, below Tusca-
        loosa .... I, 378; III, 1858, 1861
    Improvement above Tuscaloosa .... I, 365; III, 1816
    Improvement below Tuscaloosa .... I, 366; III, 1824
    Operating and care of locks and dams .... I, 366; III, 1819
Blackwater River, Fla. and Ala., improvement of .... I, 359; III, 1784
Blackwells Island, East River, N. Y., bridge at .... I, 665
Bladen County, N. C., bridge of .... I, 664
Block Island, R. I.:
    Construction of harbor of refuge .... I, 172; II, 1141
    Improvement of Great Salt Pond .... I, 174; II, 1144
Blood River, La. (*see* Tickfaw) .... I, 380; III, 1873
Bloomers, N. J., harbor lines in Hudson River from Pleasant Valley Land-
    ing to .... I, 118; II, 1270
Boards:
    For highway bridge at Washington, D. C .... I, 119
    Of Ordnance and Fortification .... I, 5
    On Fortifications and other Defenses (Endicott Board) .... I, 5
    On Torpedo System .... I, 5, 695
    The Board of Engineers .... I, 5, 691
Boat railway, Columbia River, Oreg. and Wash .... I, 625; V, 3491
Boats. *See* Dredge, Snag, *and* Tug boats, *and* Wrecks.
Bœuf River, La., improvement of .... I, 418; III, 2044
Bogue Chitto, La., improvement of .... I, 377; III, 1852
Bogue Falia, La., improvement of .... I, 379; III, 1872
Bogue Inlet and Sound, N. C., improvement of waterway via ...... I, 304; II, 1496
Boom Island, Mississippi River, Minn., bridge at .... I, 667
Boothbay Harbor, Me., bridge at .... I, 666
Boston and Albany Railroad Company, bridge of .... I, 662
Boston and Maine Railroad Company, bridge of .... I, 668

Boston Harbor, Mass.:
  Bridge across Chelsea Creek between Boston and Chelsea............... I, 662
  Bridge across Fort Point Channel at Cove street....................... I, 661
  Defenses of... I, 6, 15, 717, 913
  Examination and survey... I, 159; II, 1096, 1098
  Improvement of... I, 152; II, 1078
Bowlders. *See* Rock.
Brandts Ferry, San Joaquin River, Cal., bridge at......................... I, 661
Branford Harbor, Conn., examination and survey............... I, 198; II, 1188, 1191
Brazos River, Tex.:
  Effects of storm of September, 1900, on jetties...................... I, 412; III, 2022
  Examination and survey from the mouth to Waco ... I, 411; III, 1974, 2004, 2009
  Improvement between Velasco and Richmond......... I, 408, 409; III, 1950, 1951
  Improvement of mouth.. I, 407; III, 1940
Brazos Santiago Harbor, Tex., improvement of............................. I, 410; III, 1958
Brenneckes Shoals, Osage River, Mo., estimate of cost of completing Lock
    and Dam No. 1, at... I, 452; III, 2369
Bridgeboro, N. J., removal of wreck in Rancocas River above........ I, 262; II, 1351
Bridge Creek Landing, Va., wharf at.................................. I, 676; V, 3689
Bridgeport Harbor, Conn., improvement of............................ I, 186; II, 1177
Bridges:
  Alteration of, obstructing navigation................................. I, 667
  Aqueduct Bridge, Washington, D. C., repair of.................... I, 669; V, 3637
  Construction of... I, 659, 661
  Highway bridge, Washington, D. C.................................... I, 119
  Long Bridge, Washington, D. C., rebuilding of.................... I, 275; II, 1399
  Memorial Bridge, Washington, D. C.................................. I, 670; V, 3648
  Stone Bridge, Sakonnet River, R. I., alteration of................ I, 165; II, 1124
  Yellowstone National Park, construction, etc., of................ I, 682; V, 3777
Broad Creek River, Del.:
  Bridge at Laurel.. I, 666
  Improvement of... I, 270; II, 1386
Broadkill Creek, Del., improvement of................................. I, 260; II, 1347
Broad Sound, Boston, Mass. *See* Boston.
Bronx Kills, New York Harbor, N. Y., bridge across...................... I, 665
Bronx River, N. Y.:
  Bridge at Westchester avenue... I, 664
  Harbor lines... I, 118; II, 1266
  Improvement of... I, 201; II, 1203
Brooklyn, Cal. *See* Oakland Harbor.
Brooklyn, N. Y. *See* New York Harbor.
Brooklyn and Jamaica Bay Turnpike Company, bridge of...... .... I, 663
Brown County, Wis., bridge of... I, 662
Brown, Dick (steamboat), removal of wreck of............... I, 473; IV, 2646
Browning road, near Camden, N. J., bridge across Cooper Creek at........ I, 662
Browns Creek, N. Y., improvement of................................. I, 209; II, 1219
Brunswick, Ga.:
  Improvement of inner harbor... I, 331; II, 1649
  Survey of outer bar.. I, 334; II, 1663, 1665
Brunswick River, N. C., estimate of cost of removing obstructions at
    mouth.. I, 310; II, 1569
Buffalo Bayou, Tex., improvement of waterway via.................. I, 404; III, 1933
Buffalo Fork, Snake River, Wyo., road to Fort Washakie............. I, 686; V, 3823
Buffalo Fork, White River, Ark., improvement of................... I, 429; III, 2119
Buffalo Harbor, N. Y.:
  Examination and survey of Lake Erie entrance to Erie Basin and Black
    Rock Harbor.. I, 592; IV, 3342, 3345
  Harbor lines at Erie Basin and Black Rock Harbor............... I, 119; IV, 3349
  Improvement of... I, 587; IV, 3305
  Improvement of Buffalo entrance to Erie Basin and Black Rock
    Harbor... I, 589; IV, 3324
  Improvement of channels in waters connecting Great Lakes .... I, 563; IV, 3157
Buffalo, Wis., bridge across Fox River at.............................. I, 664
Buildings and grounds, public, District of Columbia.................. I, 675; V, 3689
Bull Rock Bridge, Bath, Me., obstructing New Meadows River............ I, 669
Burlington Bay, Minn., examination and survey............... I, 514; IV, 2889, 2897

Burlington Harbor, Vt.:
    Estimate of cost of repair and completion of breakwater .... I, 150; II, 1072
    Improvement of .... I, 146; II, 1052
Burns Cut-off, San Joaquin River, Cal., bridge across .... I, 664
Buttermilk Channel, New York Harbor, N. Y.:
    Examination and survey .... I, 229; II, 1299, 1303
    Improvement of .... I, 226; II, 1291
    Removal of wreck .... I, 229; II, 1299
Byram River, N. Y.:
    Harbor lines .... I, 118; II, 1261
    Improvement of Port Chester Harbor .... I, 198; II, 1198

C.

Cable galleries .... I, 38
Cache River, Ark., improvement of .... I, 430; III, 2120
Cache River, Ill., prevention of Mississippi River from breaking into. I, 438; III, 2198
Caddo (Fairy) Lake, Tex. and La. (*see* Cypress Bayou) .... I, 414; III, 2033
Cairo, Ill., prevention of break in Mississippi River near .... I, 438; III, 2198
Calais, Me., repair of piers in St. Croix River below .... I, 120
Calcasieu River, La., improvement of mouth and passes .... I, 394; III, 1903
California Débris Commission .... I, 656; V, 3625
California, department of, reconnaissances and explorations .... I, 683; V, 3800
Caloosahatchee River, Fla.:
    Examination and survey of Kissimmee River to the Gulf, via .... I, 350
    Improvement of .... I, 343; III, 1751
Calumet Harbor and River, Ill. and Ind.:
    Improvement of harbor .... I, 529; IV, 2995
    Improvement of river .... I, 530; IV, 3001
    Survey for waterway via .... I, 534; IV, 3048, 3058
Cambridge Harbor, Md., removal of wrecks .... I, 272; II, 1390, 1391
Camden, Ark., examination of Ouachita River at .... I, 425; III, 2090
Camden County, N. J., bridge of .... I, 662
Camden, Gloucester and Woodbury Railway Company, bridge of .... I, 666
Camden, N. J.:
    Bridge across Cooper Creek at Browning road .... I, 662
    Defenses of Delaware River .... I, 6, 21, 37, 770
    Improvement of Cooper Creek .... I, 239; II, 1329
    Improvement of Delaware River at .... I, 230; II, 1310
Canadian canal, St. Marys River, Ontario, commerce through .... I, 565; IV, 3173
Canals, etc. (*see also* Waterways):
    Albemarle and Chesapeake Canal, N. C., waterway via .... I, 297; II, 1457
    Allegheny River, Pa., locks and dams .... I, 482; IV, 2701
    Appropriation for operation, care, and maintenance .... I, 117, 118
    Arkansas River, locks and dams .... I, 433; III, 2128
    Atlantic Ocean to Great Lakes, waterways .... I, 118
    Barren River, Ky., lock and dam .... I, 503; IV, 2806
    Benton Harbor Canal, Mich. (*see* St. Joseph Harbor) .... I, 537; IV, 3079
    Big Barren River, Ky., lock and dam .... I, 503; IV, 2806
    Big Sandy River, locks and dams .... I, 490, 492, 496; IV, 2735, 2741, 2750
    Big Sioux River, S. Dak., examination for reservoir dam .... I, 458; III, 2395
    Big Stone Lake, Minn. and S. Dak., reservoir dam .... I, 450; III, 2342
    Black Warrior River, locks and dams .. I, 365, 366, 378; III, 1816, 1819, 1824, 1858
    Brazos River, Tex., locks and dams .... I, 411; III, 1974, 2004, 2009
    Canadian canal, St. Marys River, Ontario, commerce .... I, 565; IV, 3173
    Care, maintenance, etc., appropriation for .... I, 117, 118
    Cascades Canal, Columbia River, Oreg .... I, 626, 627; V, 3492, 3495
    Chicago Drainage Canal, connection of Chicago River with ...... I, 119; IV, 2992
    Chicago Drainage Canal, waterway via (act of 1899) .... I, 534; IV, 3048
    Chicago Drainage Canal, waterway via (act of 1900) .... I, 534; IV, 3058
    Chicago River, bridge across North Branch Canal at Division street,
        Chicago, construction of .... I, 666
    Chicago River, bridge across North Branch Canal at Division street,
        Chicago, reconstruction of .... I, 662
    Chicago River, bridge across North Branch Canal at Goose Island, Chi-
        cago .... I, 665
    Clubfoot and Harlowe Canal, N. C., waterway via .... I, 303; II, 1493

INDEX. 7

Canals, etc.—Continued.
Columbia River, Cascades Canal .... I, 626, 627; V, 3492, 3495
Columbia River, Celilo Falls to The Dalles Rapids, canals and
    locks.. I, 629; V, 3501, 3505
Congaree River, S. C., lock and dam........................ I, 319; II, 1594
Coosa River, Ga. and Ala., locks and dams...... I, 361, 363; III, 1788, 1790, 1792
Courtableau Bayou, La., lock and dam........................ I, 389; III, 1898
Cumberland River, Tenn. and Ky., locks and dams.... I, 461, 462; III, 2407, 2411
Davis Island dam, Ohio River, Pa............................ I, 473; IV, 2657
Delaware and Chesapeake Canal, Md., sunken logs .... I, 272; II, 1390
Des Moines Rapids Canal and dry dock, Mississippi River...... I, 441; III, 2284
Dismal Swamp Canal, examination and survey from South Mills to and
    including Ocracoke and Beaufort inlets .... I, 299, 309; II, 1511
Dismal Swamp Canal, improvement of waterway via............. I, 296; II, 1455
Duluth Canal, Wis., improvement of........................ I, 507; IV, 2828
Estherville-Minim Creek Canal, S. C. (see Santee River) .... I, 316; II, 1587
Fox River, bridge across canal at Appleton .... I, 664
Fox River, bridge across canal at Depere........................... I, 668
Fox River, bridge across canal at Lock 2, Kaukauna, reconstruction of. I, 662
Fox River, bridges obstructing canal at Lawe street and Wisconsin ave-
    nue, Kaukauna, alteration of.................................... I, 668
Fox River, bridges across canal at Menasha............................. I, 668
Fox River, locks and dams .... I, 525, 527; IV, 2953, 2958
Galena River, Ill., lock and dam................................ I, 442; III, 2293
Grand Rapids lock and dam, Wabash River .... I, 500, 501; IV, 2800, 2802
Great Kanawha River, W. Va., locks and dams........ I, 487, 488; IV, 2726, 2727
Great Lakes to Atlantic Ocean, waterways .... I, 118
Green River, Ky., locks and dams .... I, 502, 503; IV, 2805, 2806
Gowanus Canal, N. Y. (see Gowanus Bay) .... I, 226; II, 1291
Herr Island lock and dam, Allegheny River .... I, 482; IV, 2701
Illinois and Michigan Canal, waterway via (act of 1899) .... I, 534; IV, 3048
Illinois and Michigan Canal, waterway via (act of 1900) .... I, 534; IV, 3058
Illinois and Mississippi Canal, construction of .... I, 532; IV, 3014
Illinois and Mississippi Canal, lock and dam in Rock River at feeder. I, 534; IV, 3066
Illinois and Mississippi Canal, operating and care .... I, 442; III, 2291
Illinois River, Ill., locks and dams .... I, 531; IV, 3006, 3010
Kampeska Lake, S. Dak., reservoir dam in Sioux River .... I, 458; III, 2395
Kampsville lock and dam, Illinois River, Ill .... I, 531; IV, 3006, 3010
Kanawha River, W. Va., locks and dams............... I, 487, 488; IV, 2726, 2727
Kentucky River, Ky., locks and dams................. I, 494, 495; IV, 2744, 2746
Keweenaw Bay to Lake Superior, waterway............... I, 511, 512; IV, 2867
Lagrange lock and dam, Illinois River, Ill................ I, 531; IV, 3006, 3010
Levisa Fork, Big Sandy River, locks and dams .... I, 496; IV, 2750
Little Kanawha River, W. Va., lock and dam........... I, 486, 487; IV, 2723, 2724
Long Prairie River, Minn., and its sources, examination for reservoir
    dams .... I, 451; III, 2361
Louisville and Portland Canal, improvement and care.. I, 496, 499; IV, 2783, 2791
Louisville and Portland Canal, wreck............................ I, 505; IV, 2816
Maintenance, care, etc., appropriation for...................... I, 117, 118
Massena Canal, N. Y. (see Grass and St. Lawrence rivers).. I, 599; IV, 3377, 3389
Michigan Lake to Sturgeon Bay, examination and survey.. I, 527; IV, 2970, 2973
Michigan Lake to Sturgeon Bay, harbor of refuge................ I, 518; IV, 2922
Michigan Lake to Sturgeon Bay, improvement of................ I, 517; IV, 2914
Michigan Lake to Sturgeon Bay, operating and care............ I, 518; IV, 2919
Michigan Lake to Sturgeon Bay, wreck......................... I, 527; IV, 2970
Minim Creek-Estherville Canal, S. C. (see Santee River) .... I, 316; II, 1587
Mississippi River, Des Moines Rapids Canal and dry dock........ I, 441; III, 2284
Mississippi River, reservoirs, construction of .... I, 444; III, 2309
Mississippi River, reservoirs, examination of Long Prairie River and its
    sources.. I, 451; III, 2361
Mississippi River, reservoirs, operating and care................. I, 445; III, 2322
Mississippi River, reservoirs, survey of flowage lines .... I, 451
Mississippi River, St. Paul to Minneapolis, locks and dams .... I, 443; III, 2298
Mississippi River to Illinois River, construction of............... I, 532; IV, 3014
Mississippi River to Illinois River, lock and dam in Rock River at
    feeder.. I, 534; IV, 3066
Mississippi River to Illinois River, operating and care.......... I, 442; III, 2291

Canals, etc.—Continued.

Monongahela River, locks and dams	1, 477, 478, 479; IV, 2679, 2683, 2686
Morgan Canal, Tex., improvement of (see Galveston ship channel)	1, 404; III, 1933
Morgan Canal, Tex., operating and care	1, 405; III, 1937
Mosquito Creek Canal, S. C. (see Santee River)	1, 316; II, 1587
Muscle Shoals Canal, Ala	1, 465, 466; III, 2423, 2440
Muskingum River, bridge across canal, above Lowell	1, 660
Muskingum River, bridge across canal, at Zanesville	1, 667
Muskingum River, locks and dams	1, 485; IV, 2714
New York Harbor, N. Y., Gowanus Canal (see Gowanus Bay)	1, 226; II, 1291
North Branch Canal, Chicago River, bridge at Division street, Chicago, construction of	1, 666
North Branch Canal, Chicago River, bridge at Division street, Chicago, reconstruction of	1, 662
North Branch Canal, Chicago River, bridge at Goose Island, Chicago	1, 665
North Carolina Cut, N. C., waterway via	1, 297; II, 1457
Northern and Northwestern Lakes to Atlantic Ocean, waterways	1, 118
Ohio River, Davis Island dam, Pa	1, 473; IV, 2657
Ohio River, Louisville and Portland Canal, improvement and care	1, 496, 499; IV, 2783, 2791
Ohio River, Louisville and Portland Canal, wreck	1, 505; IV, 2816
Ohio River, movable dams	1, 474; IV, 2661
Operation, care, and maintenance, appropriation for	1, 117, 118
Osage River, lock and dam, construction of (see Missouri River Commission)	1, 658; S., 365, 382
Osage River, lock and dam, cost of completion	1, 452; III, 2369
Otter Tail Lake and River, Minn., reservoir dam	1, 450; III, 2341
Plaquemine Bayou, La., lock construction	1, 387; III, 1890
Poinsett Lake, S. Dak., reservoir dam in Sioux River	1, 458; III, 2395
Portage Lake and Lake Superior canals (see Keweenaw Point)	1, 511, 512; IV, 2867
Puget Sound to lakes Union and Washington	1, 646; V, 3583
Red Lake and Red Lake River, Minn., reservoir dam	1, 450; III, 2340
Rock River, Ill., canal around, construction of	1, 532; IV, 3014
Rock River, Ill., canal around, operating and care	1, 442; III, 2291
Rock River, Ill., lock and dam at feeder	1, 534; IV, 3066
Rough River, Ky., lock and dam	1, 504; IV, 2814, 2815
St. Clair Flats Canal, examination and survey	1, 571; IV, 3203, 3206
St. Clair Flats Canal, improvement and care	1, 568; IV, 3188, 3189
St. Lawrence Power Company's canal (see Grass and St. Lawrence rivers)	1, 599; IV, 3377, 3389
St. Marys Falls Canal, Mich	1, 564, 565; IV, 3161, 3173
Salmon Bay, Wash., waterway via	1, 646; V, 3583
Shilshole Bay, Wash., waterway via	1, 646; V, 3583
Sioux River, S. Dak., examination for reservoir dam	1, 458; III, 2395
Six-mile Island, Allegheny River, lock and dam	1, 482; IV, 2701
Springdale, Pa., lock and dam in Allegheny River	1, 482; IV, 2701
Sturgeon Bay and Lake Michigan Canal, examination and survey	1, 527; IV, 2970, 2973
Sturgeon Bay and Lake Michigan Canal, harbor of refuge	1, 518; IV, 2922
Sturgeon Bay and Lake Michigan Canal, improvement of	1, 517; IV, 2914
Sturgeon Bay and Lake Michigan Canal, operating and care	1, 518; IV, 2919
Sturgeon Bay and Lake Michigan Canal, wreck	1, 527; IV, 2970
Superior Lake to Keweenaw Bay, waterway	1, 511, 512; IV, 2867
Tennessee River below Chattanooga, canals, etc	1, 465, 466; III, 2423, 2440
Tennessee River, Muscle Shoals Canal, Ala	1, 465, 466; III, 2423, 2440
Tombigbee River, Ala., locks and dams	1, 366, 378; III, 1824, 1835, 1858
Traverse Lake, Minn. and S. Dak., reservoir dam	1, 450; III, 2342
Tug Fork, Big Sandy River, locks and dams	1, 496; IV, 2750
Turners Cut, N. C., examination and survey of waterway from South Mills to and including Ocracoke and Beaufort inlets, via	1, 299, 309; II, 1511
Turners Cut, N. C., improvement of waterway via	1, 296; II, 1455
Union Lake, Wash., waterway via	1, 646; V, 3583
Wabash River, Grand Rapids lock and dam	1, 500, 501; IV, 2800, 2802
Warrior River locks and dams	1, 365, 366, 378; III, 1816, 1819, 1824, 1858
Washington Lake to Puget Sound, Wash	1, 646; V, 3583
White River, Ark., locks and dams	1, 428; III, 2108
Yamhill River, Oreg., lock and dam	1, 631, 632; V, 3550, 3555

Canarsie Bay, N. Y., improvement of .... 1, 208; II, 1218

INDEX. 9

Cape Ann, Mass., construction of harbor of refuge in Sandy Bay..... I, 141; II, 1048
Cape Charles City Harbor, Va., improvement of................. I, 294; II, 1453
Cape Elizabeth, Me., bridge of town of.. I, 668
Cape Fear River, N. C.:
    Defenses of Wilmington... I, 6, 24, 812, 921
    Examination and survey at Wilmington, and thence to Fayetteville.. I, 310; II, 1552, 1557
    Harbor lines at Southport... I, 119; II, 1572
    Improvement above Wilmington.................................... I, 307; II, 1502
    Improvement at and below Wilmington............................ I, 307; II, 1504
    Improvement of Northeast Branch................................. I, 306; II, 1500
Cape Henry, Va., defenses at... I, 6
Cape Porpoise Harbor, Me., improvement of............................. I, 135; II, 1037
Cape Vincent Harbor, N. Y., improvement of........................... I, 597; IV, 3370
Capitol, Washington, D. C., telegraph line.............................. I, 676; V, 3689
Carlos Lake, Minn. (*see* Long Prairie River)............................. I, 451; III, 2361
Carrabelle Bar and Harbor, Fla.:
    Examination and survey of harbor.......................... I, 364; III, 1800, 1803
    Improvement of... I, 350; III, 1766
Carriages, gun:
    Barbette... I, 8, 9
    Disappearing.. I, 6, 8
Carrollton, Ky., bridge across Kentucky River at............................. I, 662
Carrollton and Prestonville Bridge Company, bridge of...................... I, 662
Carrollton Electric Railway and Bridge Company (*see* Carrollton and Prestonville Bridge Company).. I, 662
Caruthersville Harbor, Mo. (*see* Mississippi River Commission)....... I, 657; S., 3, 32
Carvers Harbor, Me., improvement of................................... I, 129; II, 1008
Cascades Canal, Columbia River, Oreg.:
    Construction of... I, 626; V, 3492
    Operating and care... I, 627; V, 3495
Casemates... I, 7, 12, 38
Cedar Creek, N. J., removal of wreck............................... I, 263; II, 1352
Centennial Lake, Miss. (*see* Yazoo River)........................... I, 421; III, 2052
Champlain Lake, N. Y. and Vt.:
    Burlington Harbor, Vt., estimate of cost of repair and completion of breakwater... I, 150; II, 1072
    Burlington Harbor, Vt., improvement of............................ I, 146; II, 1052
    Defenses of.. I, 6, 32, 854
    Narrows, improvement of.. I, 148; II, 1055
    North and South Hero islands, improvement of channel between...... I, 146
Charles River, Mass. *See* Boston Harbor.
Charleston Harbor, S. C.:
    Defenses of... I, 6, 25, 816
    Improvement of.. I, 320; II, 1598
    Removal of sunken logs in waterway to Beaufort, S. C............ I, 324; II, 1607
Charlevoix Harbor, Mich.:
    Bridge across Pine River... I, 665
    Bridge across South Arm of Pine Lake................................. I, 666
    Improvement of.. I, 552; IV, 3126
Charlotte Harbor, Fla., improvement of............................. I, 343; III, 1752
Charlotte Harbor, N. Y.:
    Improvement of.. I, 593; IV, 3355
    Water levels.. I, 681; V, 3776
Charts:
    Military and other.. I, 683, 685; V, 3799
    Northern and Northwestern Lakes........................... I, 677, 681; V, 3761
Chatham Harbor, Mass.:
    Improvement of.. I, 158; II, 1090
    Removal of wreck on Hardings Beach.............................. I, 174; II, 1147
Chattahoochee River, Ga. and Ala.:
    Improvement below Columbus, Ga................................ I, 355; III, 1775
    Improvement between Westpoint and Franklin, Ga............. I, 356; III, 1777
    Preliminary report on survey between Westpoint and Franklin, Ga.. I, 363; III, 1793
Cheboygan Harbor, Mich., improvement of.......................... I, 554; IV, 3135
Chefuncte River, La., improvement of.............................. I, 379; III, 1872
Chehalis River, Wash., improvement of............................. I, 644; V, 3580

Chelsea Creek and Harbor, Mass.:
  Bridge to Boston .... I, 662
  Improvement of creek (*see* Boston Harbor) .... I, 152; II, 1078
Chequamegon Bay, Wis. (*see* Ashland Harbor)............... I, 509; IV, 2863
Chesapeake Bay, Md. and Va.:
  Bridge across Kent Island Narrows, at Kent Island .... I, 665
  Cape Charles City Harbor, Va., improvement of .... I, 294; II, 1453
  Defenses of entrance, at Cape Henry, Va................................. I, 6
  Defenses of Hampton Roads, Va..................................... I, 6, 23, 802
  Milford Haven Harbor, Va., improvement of .... I, 284; II, 1415
  Waterway from Norfolk, Va., to Albemarle Sound, N. C., via Currituck
    Sound, improvement of .... I, 297; II, 1457
  Waterway from Norfolk, Va., to sounds of North Carolina, via Pasquo-
    tank River, improvement of.................................... I, 296; II, 1455
  Wreck near Craighill Channel light, Md., removal of .... I, 272; II, 1391
  Wreck near Old Plantation light-house, Va., removal of......... I, 298; II, 1462
  Wreck off Fort Monroe, Va., removal of .... I, 298; II, 1462
Chesapeake Transit Company, bridge of .... I, 665
Chesconnessex Creek, Va., examination and survey............ I, 299; II, 1478, 1481
Chester Creek, Pa., removal of wreck............................ I, 262; II, 1350
Chester River, Md., improvement of.............................. I, 267; II, 1381
Chicago and Northwestern Railway Company, bridge of .... I, 662
Chicago Drainage Canal, Ill.:
  Connection of Chicago River with.............................. I, 119; IV, 2992
  Waterway from Mississippi River to Lake Michigan, via, examination
    for, with plan and estimate (act of 1900)................... I, 534; IV, 3058
  Waterway from Mississippi River to Lake Michigan, via, survey for (act
    of 1899) .... I, 534; IV, 3048
Chicago Harbor and River, Ill.:
  Bridge across Little Calumet River at Riverdale .... I, 664
  Bridge across North Branch at Clybourn place .... I, 663
  Bridge across North Branch Canal at Division street, construction of... I, 666
  Bridge across North Branch Canal at Division street, reconstruction of. I, 662
  Bridge across North Branch Canal at Goose Island....................... I, 665
  Bridge across West Fork of South Branch at Mud Lake................... I, 663
  Bridges of Sanitary District at Harrison and Throop streets and Ashland
    avenue .... I, 662
  Improvement of Calumet (South Chicago) Harbor................ I, 529; IV, 2995
  Improvement of channels in waters connecting Great Lakes .... I, 563; IV, 3157
  Improvement of outer harbor................................... I, 528; IV, 2987
  Improvement of river .... I, 529; IV, 2992
  Waterway from Mississippi River to Lake Michigan at, examination for,
    with plan and estimate (act of 1900) .... I, 534; IV, 3058
  Waterway from Mississippi River to Lake Michigan at, survey for (act
    of 1899) .... I, 534; IV, 3048
Chicago, Milwaukee and St. Paul Railway Company:
  Bridge of, across Mississippi River, near Minneapolis, Minn .... I, 662
  Bridge of, across North Branch Canal, Chicago, Ill .... I, 665
Chickasahay River, Miss., improvement of .... I, 372; III, 1844
Chief of Engineers, officers on duty in Office of the................... I, 688
Chincoteague Bay, Va., improvement of waterway to Delaware Bay.. I, 260; II, 1348
Chipola River, Fla.:
  Improvement of lower river .... I, 352; III, 1769
  Improvement of upper river.................................... I, 353; III, 1771
Chippewa River, Wis., improvement of .... I, 445; III, 2327
Chitto, Bogue, La., improvement of.............................. I, 377; III, 1852
Choctawhatchee River, Fla. and Ala., improvement of .... I, 357; III, 1778
Choptank River, Md.:
  Improvement of.. I, 267; II, 1381
  Removal of wrecks in Cambridge Harbor .... I, 272; II, 1390, 1391
Christiana River, Del. (*see* Wilmington Harbor)................ I, 246; II, 1335
City of New Orleans (steamboat), removal of wreck of........... I, 473; IV, 2646
City Waterway, Tacoma, Wash. (*see* Tacoma).................. I, 655; V, 3593, 3595
Civilian assistants to engineer officers................................. I, 37, 38
Clark Fork, Columbia River, Wash. (*see* Pend Oreille River) .... I, 653; V, 3591
Clarke County, Wash., bridge of .... I, 661
Clatskanie River, Oreg.:
  Dredging plant for use on (*see* Columbia River)................. I, 640; V, 3575
  Improvement of .... I, 637; V, 3571

Clearwater River, Idaho, improvement of .... I, 628; v, 3501
Cleveland, Cincinnati, Chicago and St. Louis Railway Company:
    Bridge of, across Cuyahoga River at Cleveland, Ohio.................... I, 663
    Bridge of, across Pawpaw River, Mich................................. I, 668
Cleveland, Grover (schooner), removal of wreck of...................... I, 229; II, 1299
Cleveland Harbor Ohio:
    Bridge across Cuyahoga River at.. I, 663
    Engineering methods used in improvement of.......................... IV, 3213
    Examination and survey .... I, 585; IV, 3277, 3285
    Improvement of.. I, 578; IV, 3244
    Removal of wrecks... I, 584; IV, 3269, 3270
    Water levels.. I, 681; v, 3776
Cleveland, Ohio, engineer district, engineering methods used in the .... IV, 3213
Clinch River, Tenn.:
    Bridge at Kingston .... I, 660
    Final report on survey... I, 469; III, 2542
    Improvement of... I, 468; III, 2455
Clinton River, Mich., improvement of................................ I, 561; IV, 3153
Clubfoot and Harlowe Canal, N. C., waterway via.................... I, 303; II, 1498
Clubfoot Creek, N. C., improvement of waterway via .... I, 303; II, 1498
Coanjock Bay, N. C., improvement of waterway via .... I, 297; II, 1457
Cocheco River, N. H., improvement of .... I, 135; II, 1039
Coleman, A. T. (schooner), removal of wreck of .... I, 262; II, 1351
College Point, East River, N. Y., harbor lines....................... I, 119; II, 1305
Colon, Cristobal (steamboat), removal of wreck of .... I, 657; v, 3635
Colorado River, Nev., examination between El Dorado Canyon and Rioville .... I, 603; IV, 3402
Columbia (bugeye), removal of wreck of .... I, 272; II, 1390
Columbia, department of the, reconnaissances and explorations....... I, 683; v, 3799
Columbia River, Oreg. and Wash.:
    Dredging plant for use on tributaries below Willamette River.... I, 640; v, 3575
    Cascades Canal, construction of .... I, 626; v, 3492
    Cascades Canal, operating and care............................ I, 627; v, 3495
    Celilo, Oreg., improvement above.............................. I, 623; v, 3489
    Celilo Falls to The Dalles Rapids, boat railway .... I, 625; v, 3491
    Celilo Falls to The Dalles Rapids, examination and survey.. I, 629; v, 3501, 3505
    Clark Fork (*see* Pend Oreille River)............................. I, 653; v, 3591
    Gauging .... I, 640; v, 3576
    Mouth of, defenses at... I, 6, 34, 895, 923
    Mouth of, improvement at .... I, 635; v, 3567
    Mouth of, to Willamette River, improvement from................ I, 633; v, 3557
    Three-mile Rapids, improvement at............................. I, 625; v, 3491
    Tongue Point, Oreg., improvement below .... I, 634; v, 3565
    Vancouver, Wash., to Willamette River, improvement from...... I, 627; v, 3499
Comer B. (steamboat), removal of wreck of .... I, 473; v, 2646
Commencement Bay, Wash. (*see* Tacoma Harbor)........... I, 655; v, 3593, 3595
Commercial statistics, Sault Ste. Marie canals, Mich .... I, 565; IV, 3173
Communipaw Channel, N. J., removal of wreck in .... I, 223; II, 1247
Compton Creek, N. J., improvement of .... I, 220; II, 1242
Conecuh River, Ala., improvement of.............................. I, 360; III, 1784
Congaree River, S. C.:
    Improvement of... I, 318; II, 1592
    Improvement between Columbia and Granby .... I, 319; II, 1594
Congress, Fifty-sixth, second session, acts of, affecting Corps of Engineers.. I, 856
Conneaut Harbor, Ohio, improvement of........................... I, 582; IV, 3264
Connecticut, defenses of coast of .... I, 6, 17, 747
Connecticut River, Conn., improvement of, below Hartford .... I, 180; II, 1166
Contentnia Creek, N. C., improvement of .... I, 301; II, 1488
Contingencies of rivers and harbors, estimate of appropriation for .... I, 856
Continuing contracts .... I, 118
    Albemarle Sound, N. C., waterway via......................... I, 296; II, 1455
    Allegheny River, Pa., locks and dams.......................... I, 482; IV, 2701
    Ambrose Channel, New York Harbor, N. Y...................... I, 224; II, 1285
    Ashtabula Harbor, Ohio.. I, 581; IV, 3260
    Back Cove, Portland, Me .... I, 131; II, 1006
    Baltimore Harbor, Md.. I, 264; II, 1374
    Bay Ridge Channel, New York Harbor, N. Y.................... I, 226; II, 1291
    Big Sandy River, Ky. and W. Va............................... I, 490; IV, 2735
    Black River (Lorain) Harbor, Ohio.............................. I, 577; IV, 3241

12 INDEX.

Continuing contracts—Continued.
Black Rock Harbor, Buffalo, N. Y	1, 589; IV, 3324
Black Warrior River, Ala., below Tuscaloosa	1, 366; III, 1825
Black Warrior River, Ala., from Tuscaloosa to Daniels Creek	1, 365; III, 1816
Boston Harbor, Mass	1, 152; II, 1078
Bridgeport Harbor, Conn	1, 186; II, 1177
Buffalo entrance to Erie Basin and Black Rock Harbor, N. Y	1, 589; IV, 3324
Buffalo Harbor, N. Y	1, 587; IV, 3305
Calumet Harbor, Ill	1, 529; IV, 2995
Cape Porpoise Harbor, Me	1, 135; II, 1037
Charleston Harbor, S. C	1, 320; II, 1598
Chicago River, Ill	1, 529; IV, 2992
Christiana River, Del	1, 246; II, 1335
Cleveland Harbor, Ohio	1, 578; IV, 3244
Congaree River, S. C	1, 319; II, 1594
Croatan Sound, N. C., waterway via	1, 296; II, 1455
Cumberland River above Nashville, Tenn	1, 462; III, 2411
Cumberland Sound, Ga. and Fla	1, 333; II, 1655
Deep Creek, Va., and waters connecting with Pamlico Sound	1, 296; II, 1455
Delaware Bay, Del., harbor of refuge	1, 237; II, 1325
Delaware River, N. J., Pa., and Del	1, 230; II, 1310
Detroit River, Mich	1, 569; IV, 3190
Duluth and Superior Harbor, Minn. and Wis	1, 507; IV, 2828
East (Ambrose) Channel, New York Harbor, N. Y	1, 224; II, 1285
Elizabeth River, Va. to Pamlico Sound, N. C., waterway	1, 296; II, 1455
Erie Basin, Buffalo, N. Y	1, 589; IV, 3324
Everett Harbor, Wash	1, 648; V, 3587
Falls of Ohio River at Louisville, Ky	1, 496; IV, 2783
Galveston Harbor, Tex	1, 402; III, 1921
Gowanus Bay channels, New York Harbor, N. Y	1, 226; II, 1291
Grays Harbor, Wash	1, 642; V, 3578
Great Lakes, channels in connecting waters of	1, 563; IV, 3157
Gulfport, Miss., channel to Ship Island Harbor	1, 374; III, 1846
Hay Lake Channel, St. Marys River, Mich	1, 567; IV, 3185
Horn Island Harbor, Miss	1, 371; III, 1842
Hudson River, N. Y	1, 210; II, 1222
Illinois and Mississippi Canal, Ill	1, 532; IV, 3014
Indiana Chute, Falls of Ohio River, Louisville, Ky	1, 496; IV, 2783
Kenosha Harbor, Wis	1, 524; IV, 2945
Kentucky River, Ky	1, 494; IV, 2744
Keweenaw Bay to Lake Superior, Mich., waterway	1, 511; IV, 2867
Lorain Harbor, Ohio	1, 577; IV, 3241
Loutre, Pass a, Mississippi River	1, 383; III, 1878
Michigan City outer harbor, Ind	1, 535; IV, 3075
Milwaukee Bay, Wis., harbor of refuge	1, 522; IV, 2936
Mississippi River, at Pass a Loutre	1, 383; III, 1878
Mississippi River, Head of Passes to Ohio River	1, 657; S, 3, 32
Mississippi River, between Missouri and Ohio rivers	1, 435; III, 2169
Mississippi River, between Missouri River and St. Paul	1, 440; III, 2238
Mississippi River, between St. Paul and Minneapolis	1, 443; III, 2298
Mississippi River, Vicksburg Harbor, Miss	1, 421; III, 2052
Missouri River, below Sioux City, Iowa	1, 658, S., 365, 382
Mobile Harbor, Ala	1, 304; III, 1810
Monongahela River, W. Va. and Pa	1, 477, 478; IV, 2679, 2683
Narragansett Bay, R. I	1, 187; II, 1129
New Haven Harbor, Conn	1, 182; II, 1170
New York Harbor, N. Y., Ambrose Channel	1, 224; II, 1285
New York Harbor, N. Y., Gowanus Bay channels	1, 226; II, 1291
Norfolk Harbor, Va., to Pamlico Sound, N. C., waterway	1, 296; II, 1455
Northern and Northwestern Lakes, channels connecting	1, 563; IV, 3157
Oakland Harbor, Cal	1, 605; IV, 3413
Ocmulgee River, Ga	1, 330; II, 1646
Ohio River, Falls of, at Louisville, Ky	1, 496; IV, 2783
Ohio River, movable dams	1, 474; IV, 2661
Osage River, Mo	1, 658, S., 365, 382
Pamlico Sound, N. C., waterway to Norfolk Harbor, Va	1, 296; II, 1455
Pascagoula River, Miss	1, 371; III, 1842
Pasquotank River, N. C., waterway via	1, 296; II, 1455
Pass a Loutre, Mississippi River	1, 383; III, 1878

Continuing contracts—Continued.
Patapsco River, Md. ... I, 264; II, 1374
Plaquemine Bayou, La. ... I, 337; III, 1890
Portage Lake harbor of refuge, Mich ... I, 550; IV, 3119
Portland Harbor, Me., including Back Cove ... I, 131; II, 1006
Potomac River, below Washington, D. C ... I, 276; II, 1405
Providence River, R. I ... I, 167; II, 1129
Racine Harbor, Wis ... I, 523; IV, 2942
Red Hook Channel, New York Harbor, N. Y ... I, 226; II, 1291
Rockland Harbor, Me ... I, 128; II, 1000
Sabine Pass, Tex ... I, 398; III, 1910
Sacramento River, Cal ... I, 608; IV, 3420, 3423
St. Joseph Harbor, Mich. ... I, 537; IV, 3079
St. Marys River, Mich., at the falls. ... I, 564; IV, 3161
St. Marys River, Mich., Hay Lake Channel ... I, 567; IV, 3185
Sandbeach harbor of refuge, Mich ... I, 557; IV, 3144
San Francisco Harbor, Cal. ... I, 604; IV, 3411
San Pedro Bay, Cal ... I, 600; IV, 3397
Savannah Harbor, Ga ... I, 324; II, 1628
Savannah River, Ga., between Augusta and Savannah ... I, 326; II, 1634
Sheboygan Harbor, Wis ... I, 521; IV, 2931
Ship channel connecting waters of the Great Lakes ... I, 563; IV, 3157
Ship Island Harbor, Miss., channel to Gulfport. ... I, 374; III, 1846
South Chicago Harbor, Ill. (see Calumet Harbor) ... I, 529; IV, 2995
Superior Harbor, Wis ... I, 507; IV, 2828
Superior Lake to Keweenaw Bay, Mich., waterway ... I, 511; IV, 2867
Tampa Bay, Fla ... I, 345; III, 1756
Toledo Harbor, Ohio ... I, 572; IV, 3218
Tombigbee and Warrior rivers, below Tuscaloosa, Ala. ... I, 366; III, 1825
Turners Cut, N. C., waterway via ... I, 296; II, 1455
Union River, Me ... I, 124; II, 993
Vicksburg Harbor, Miss ... I, 421; III, 2052
Warrior River, Ala., below Tuscaloosa ... I, 366; III, 1825
Warrior River, Ala., from Tuscaloosa to Daniels Creek ... I, 365; III, 1816
White River (upper), Ark ... I, 428; III, 2108
Willamette River, above Portland, Oreg ... I, 631; V, 3550
Wilmington Harbor, Del ... I, 246; II, 1335
Winyah Bay, S. C. ... I, 314; II, 1582
Yamhill River, Oreg ... I, 631; V, 3550
Yazoo River, Miss., at the mouth ... I, 421; III, 2052
Contracts, continuing. See Continuing contracts.
Cook, W. S. (steamer), removal of wreck of ... I, 334; II, 1660
Cooper Creek, N. J.:
  Bridge at Browning road, near Camden ... I, 662
  Improvement of ... I, 239; II, 1329
Coos Bay, Harbor, and River, Oreg.:
  Dredging harbor ... I, 618; V, 3476
  Harbor lines in bay ... I, 119; V, 3544
  Improvement of entrance to bay and harbor ... I, 616; V, 3471
  Improvement of river ... I, 618; V, 3476
Coosa River, Ga. and Ala.:
  Improvement above East Tenn., Va. and Ga. R. R. bridge ... I, 361; III, 1788
  Improvement below East Tenn., Va. and Ga. R. R. bridge ... I, 363; III, 1790
  Operating and care of locks and dams ... I, 363; III, 1792
Coquille River, Oreg.:
  General improvement ... I, 614; V, 3464
  Improvement between Coquille and Myrtle Point ... I, 615; V, 3468
Core Sound, N. C., examination and survey of waterway via ... I, 299, 309; II, 1511
Corner Stake light, off Staten Island, N. Y., removal of wreck near ... I, 223; II, 1247
Corps of Artillery:
  Reservation at Willets Point, N. Y., transferred to the ... I, 42
  Tugboat for transfer to the ... I, 38
Corps of Engineers:
  Changes in personnel ... I, 3
  Laws of Fifty-sixth Congress, second session, affecting the ... V, 3837
  Number and distribution of officers ... I, 3, 4
  Officers on duty in Office of the Chief of Engineers ... I, 688
  Service of officers in the field, with troops, and as officers of United States volunteers, since April, 1898 ... I, 45

14
INDEX.

Coscob Harbor, Conn., improvement of .... I, 195; II, 1186
Courtableau Bayou, La., improvement of .... I, 389; III, 1898
Cowlitz River, Wash.:
    Dredging plant for use on (*see* Columbia River) .... I, 640; V, 3575
    Improvement of .... I, 639; V, 3573
Coytesville, N. J., harbor lines in Hudson River .... I, 118; II, 1270
Craft, sunken. *See* Wrecks.
Craig, Pete (steamer), removal of wreck of .... I, 334; II, 1660
Craighill Channel light, Chesapeake Bay, Md., removal of wreck near. I, 272; II, 1391
Cribs, Kenosha Harbor, Wis., moving of .... IV, 2948
Cristobal Colon (steamboat), removal of wreck of .... I, 657; V, 3635
Croatan Sound, N. C.:
    Examination and survey of waterway via .... I, 299, 309; II, 1511
    Improvement of waterway via .... I, 296; II, 1455
Crooked (Carrabelle) River, Fla. *See* Carrabelle Bar and Harbor.
Crum Creek, Pa., bridge in Delaware County .... I, 663
Cumberland River, Tenn. and Ky.:
    Gauging (*see* Mississippi River) .... I, 425; III, 2072; S., 8, 45, 126
    Improvement above Nashville, Tenn .... I, 462; III, 2411
    Improvement below Nashville, Tenn .... I, 461; III, 2407
    Removal of wreck at Dover Island, below Nashville, Tenn ..... I, 463; III, 2417
Cumberland Sound, Ga. and Fla.:
    Defenses of .... I, 6, 26, 821
    Engineering methods used in improvement of .... II, 1660
    Improvement of .... I, 333; II, 1655
Cumberland (steamer), removal of wreck of .... I, 411; III, 1959
Current River, Ark. and Mo., improvement of .... I, 431; III, 2124
Currituck Sound, N. C., improvement of waterway via .... I, 297; II, 1457
Curtis Bay, Baltimore, Md.:
    Estimate of cost of deepening and widening channel of .... I, 273; II, 1374
    Improvement of channel to .... I, 265; II, 1379
Cut-off, Apalachicola River, Fla., improvement of .... I, 352; III, 1769
Cuyahoga River, Ohio:
    Bridge at Cleveland .... I, 663
    Examination and survey of Cleveland Harbor .... I, 585; IV, 3277, 3285
    Improvement of Cleveland Harbor .... I, 578; IV, 3244
    Removal of wreck in Cleveland Harbor .... I, 584; IV, 3270
Cyclone of September, 1900. *See* Hurricane.
Cypress Bayou, Tex. and La., improvement of .... I, 414; III, 2033

D.

Daisy (canal boat), removal of wreck of .... I, 262; II, 1351
Dalecarlia Reservoir, Washington Aqueduct, D. C .... I, 671; V, 3651
Dams. *See* Canals *and* Waterways.
Darby Creek, Pa., bridge in Delaware County .... I, 663
Dardanelle, Ark. *See* Arkansas River.
Darien Harbor, Ga., improvement of .... I, 328; II, 1639
Darling Lake, Minn. (*see* Long Prairie River) .... I, 451; III, 2361
Davis Island dam, Ohio River, Pa., operating and care .... I, 473; IV, 2657
Dawson County, Mont., bridge of .... I, 659
Dayton, Fla., bridge across Halifax River .... I, 666
Deals Island, Tangier Sound, Md., removal of wreck .... I, 272; II, 1390
Débris, mining, in California .... I, 656; V, 3625
Decatur, Ala., bridge across Tennessee River at .... I, 662
Decatur County, Ga., bridge across Flint River in .... I, 660
Deep Creek Branch, Elizabeth River, Va., improvement of waterway
    via .... I, 296; II, 1455
Defender (steamer), removal of wreck of .... I, 505; IV, 2816
Defenses, seacoast. *See* Fortifications.
Delaware and Chesapeake Canal, Md., removal of sunken logs in Back
    Creek .... I, 272; II, 1390
Delaware and Hudson Company, bridge of .... I, 669
Delaware Bay and River, N. J., Pa., and Del.:
    Bridge at Trenton, N. J .... I, 661
    Defenses of .... I, 6, 21, 37, 770
    Delaware Breakwater, construction of .... I, 237; II, 1323
    Harbor of refuge in bay, construction of .... I, 237; II, 1325

INDEX. 15

Delaware Bay and River, N. J., Pa., and Del.—Continued.
  Improvement of river... I, 230; II, 1310
  Lewes, Del., construction of iron pier near .... I, 236; II, 1323
  Marcushook, Pa., improvement of ice harbor.................. I, 235; II, 1322
  Waterway to Chincoteague Bay, Va., improvement of........... I, 260; II, 1348
  Wrecks, removal of................................. I, 262, 263; II, 1350, 1351, 1352
Delaware Breakwater Harbor, Del.:
  Construction of breakwater .... I, 237; II, 1323
  Removal of wreck... I, 263; II, 1351
Delaware County, Pa., bridges across Darby and Crum creeks.............. I, 663
Delaware, Fort, Del., defenses at (see Delaware River) .... I, 6, 21, 37, 770
Delta Point, La. (see Mississippi River Commission).................. I, 657; 8., 3, 32
Dennis Creek, N. J., removal of wreck............................... I, 262; II, 1350
Department, Engineer, operations of, in the Philippines .... I, 43, 975
Departments, Executive, Washington, D. C., telegraph line .... I, 676; V, 3689
Departments, military:
  Operations of Engineer Department in the Philippines................ I, 43, 975
  Reconnaissances and explorations .... I, 683; V, 3799
Depere, Wis., bridge of city of... I, 668
Depot, Engineer, Willets Point, N. Y .... I, 40, 41, 42, 947
Derelicts. See Wrecks.
Derricks, floating, application of, to grading river banks to receive revetments .... III, 2225
Deschutes River, Wash. (see Olympia Harbor)...................... I, 645; V, 3582
Des Moines Rapids Canal and dry dock, Mississippi River, operation and care .... I, 441; III, 2284
Des Plaines River, Ill.:
  Waterway from Mississippi River to Lake Michigan via, examination for, with plan and estimate (act of 1900)................. I, 534; IV, 3058
  Waterway from Mississippi River to Lake Michigan via, survey for (act of 1899) .... I, 534; IV, 3048
Detroit, Mount Clemens and Marine City Railway, bridge of............... I, 666
Detroit River, Mich.:
  Examination of channel west of Grosse Isle..................... I, 571; IV, 3208
  Improvement of.. I, 569; IV, 3190
  Improvement of channels in waters connecting Great Lakes .... I, 563; IV, 3157
  Removal of wreck at Belle Isle.................................. I, 570; IV, 3198
Disappearing gun carriages.. I, 6, 8
Discharge measurements. See Gauging.
Disk anchor, use of the... III, 2221
Dismal Swamp Canal, Va. and N. C.:
  Examination and survey from South Mills to and including Ocracoke and Beaufort inlets .... I, 299, 309; II, 1511
  Improvement of waterway via................................ I, 296; II, 1455
District of Columbia. See Washington.
Dividing Creek (La Trappe River), Md., improvement of............ I, 268; II, 1382
Division engineers... I, 119
Divisions, engineer .... I, 119
Divisions, military:
  Operations of Engineer Department in the Philippines................ I, 43, 975
  Reconnaissances and explorations .... I, 683; V, 3799
Doboy Bar, Ga., improvement of..................................... I, 327; II, 1638
Dodson, Frank (canal boat), removal of wreck of .... I, 262; II, 1350
Dog Island anchorage, St. George Sound, Fla. See Carrabelle Bar and Harbor.
Dog River, Ala., bridge across... I, 665
Double Bayou, Tex., improvement of.............................. I, 408; III, 1950
Douglas, Wis., bridge of town of, across Fox River .... I, 664
Dover Island, Cumberland River, removal of wreck............... I, 463; III, 2417
Dredge boats:
  For Columbia River tributaries below Willamette River .... I, 640; V, 3575
  For Mississippi River and other waters........................ I, 383; III, 1878
  For works in Florida .... I, 342; II, 1749
  For works on Texas coast .... I, 408; III, 1950
Dubuque, Iowa, bridge across Mississippi River near Eagle Point .... I, 660
Dubuque and Wisconsin Bridge Company, bridge of...................... I, 660
Duck Creek (Smyrna River), Del.:
  Examination and survey.................................. I, 263; II, 1361, 1363
  Improvement of.. I, 252; II, 1340
  Removal of wreck .... I, 263; II, 1352

16   INDEX.

Duck Island Harbor, Conn., construction of harbor of refuge .... I, 181; II, 1169
Duluth Canal and Harbor, Minn.:
    Improvement of... I, 507; IV, 2828
    Improvement of channels in waters connecting Great Lakes..... I, 563; IV, 3157
    Notes on rock found in vicinity of .... IV, 2883
    Removal of wreck in harbor .... I, 514; IV, 2883
Dundee (schooner), removal of wreck of............................. I, 584; IV, 3269
Dunkirk Harbor, N. Y., improvement of............................. I, 586; IV, 3302
Durhams Ferry, San Joaquin River, Cal., bridge across .... I, 664
Duwamish River, Wash.:
    Bridge in King County .... I, 663
    Improvement of (*see* Puget Sound)............................. I, 645; V, 3581
Duxbury Harbor, Mass., improvement of............................. I, 156; II, 1086
Dyer County, Tenn., bridge of .... I, 667
Dynamite batteries .... I, 10

E.

Eads, James B., maintenance of South Pass Channel, Mississippi River, by
    representatives of .... I, 118, 379; III, 1865
Eagle Point, Dubuque, Iowa, bridge across Mississippi River near .... I, 660
East (Ambrose) Channel, New York Harbor, N. Y., improvement of.. I, 224; II, 1285
East Chester Creek, N. Y., improvement of .... I, 200; II, 1202
East, department of the, reconnaissances and explorations .... I, 683; V, 3799
Eastern Branch, Elizabeth River, Va. (*see* Norfolk Harbor) .... I, 292; II, 1447
East Haddam, Conn., bridge across Salmon River below Leesville .... I, 662
East River, Ga. (*see* Brunswick Harbor) .... I, 331; II, 1649
East River, N. Y.:
    Bridge at Blackwells Island, from Sixtieth street, New York City, to Long
        Island City .... I, 665
    Bridge at Hell Gate, near Astoria................................. I, 664
    Bridge at Little Hell Gate and Bronx Kills.............................. I, 665
    Harbor lines at College Point................................... I, 119; II, 1305
    Improvement of .... I, 205; II, 1211
    Improvement of Wallabout Channel................................ I, 208; II, 1218
    Removal of wreck off Greenpoint................................ I, 223; II, 1248
Ecorse, Mich. (*see* Detroit River) .... I, 571; IV, 3208
Ecorse Township, Mich., bridge of, across Rouge River .... I, 664
Edenton Bay, N. C., improvement of .... I, 297; II, 1460
Eldridge (schooner), removal of wreck of .... I, 272; II, 1391
Electrical connections, seacoast defenses................................. I, 13, 37
Elizabeth River, N. J., improvement of............................... I, 216; II, 1235
Elizabeth River, Va.:
    Bridge across Southern Branch................................... I, 665
    Examination and plan and estimate for improvement at Pinner Point,
        Norfolk Harbor .... I, 299; II, 1463, 1466
    Improvement of Norfolk Harbor and its approaches .... I, 292; II, 1447
    Improvement of waterway to Albemarle Sound, via Currituck
        Sound .... I, 297; II, 1457
    Improvement of waterway to sounds of North Carolina, via Pasquotank
        River... I, 296; II, 1455
    Improvement of Western Branch................................. I, 293; II, 1449
Elkpoint, S. Dak., improvement of Missouri River at .. I, 452, 454, 455; III, 2373, 2375
Elk River, Tenn. and Ala., improvement of.......................... I, 469; III, 2457
Elk River, W. Va., improvement of .... I, 489; IV, 2732
Ellis Island, New York Harbor, N. Y., removal of wrecks near........ I, 223; II, 1248
Elston Addition, Chicago, Ill., bridge across North Branch Canal, Chicago
    River, at Goose Island... I, 665
Embankments.. I, 11, 37
Emblem (schooner), removal of wreck of........................... I, 298; II, 1462
Emplacements .... I, 8, 9
Employees as civilian assistants to engineer officers .... I, 37, 38
Endicott Board... I, 5
Engineer Department, operations of, in the Philippines .... I, 43, 975
Engineer Depot, Willets Point, N. Y .... I, 40, 41, 42, 947
Engineer divisions.. I, 119
Engineer equipment of troops .... I, 37, 38, 943

INDEX. 17

Engineer officers, civilian assistants to................................. I, 37, 38
Engineer School... I, 38, 42, 937
Engineer troops:
    Distribution, duties, etc., of............................ I, 39, 41, 42, 943
    Equipment of... I, 37, 38, 943
Engineering methods:
    Defenses of Boston Harbor, Mass., technical details................. I, 913
    Defenses of mouth of Columbia River, technical details............. I, 923
    Defenses of coast of Maine, technical details...................... I, 911
    Defenses of New York Harbor, N. Y., technical details.............. I, 917
    Defenses of coast of North Carolina, technical details.............. I, 921
    Defenses of San Diego, Cal., technical details..................... I, 922
    Duluth, Minn., notes on rock found in vicinity of................. IV, 2883
    Erie Lake, west of Erie, Pa., harbors on......................... IV, 3213
    Kenosha Harbor, Wis., moving of cribs at........................ IV, 2948
    Mississippi River, between Missouri and Ohio rivers, use of the disk
        anchor.. III, 2221
    Mississippi River, between Missouri and Ohio rivers, use of lumber mat-
        tress for subaqueous bank protection........................ III, 2212
    Mississippi River, St. Louis Harbor, Mo., measurement of discharge at,
        by method of full-depth rod floats.......................... III, 2199
    Savannah, Ga., engineer district............................... II, 1660
    Road scraper and floating derrick, application of the, to grading river
        banks to receive revetments............................... III, 2225
Engineers, Battalion of................................... I, 39, 43, 943, 975
Engineers, Chief of, officers on duty in Office of the...................... I, 688
Engineers, Corps of:
    Changes in personnel.. I, 3
    Laws of Fifty-sixth Congress, second session, affecting the............ V, 3837
    Number and distribution of officers........................... I, 3, 4
    Officers on duty in Office of the Chief of Engineers................... I, 688
    Service of officers in the field, with troops, and as officers of U. S. vol-
        unteers, since April, 1898................................... I, 45
Engineers, division.. I, 119
Engineers, The Board of.. I, 5, 691
Equipment, engineer, of troops............................... I, 37, 38, 943
Erie Basin, Buffalo, N. Y.:
    Examination and survey of Lake Erie entrance to.......... I, 592; IV, 3342, 3345
    Harbor lines....................................... I, 119; IV, 3349
    Improvement of Buffalo entrance to.................... I, 589; IV, 3324
Erie Harbor, Pa.:
    Improvement of.................................... I, 585; IV, 3295
    Water levels....................................... I, 681; V, 3776
Erie, Lake:
    See also Northern and Northwestern Lakes.
    Engineering methods used at harbors on, west of Erie, Pa............ IV, 3213
    Removal of wreck off Cleveland, Ohio..................... I, 584; IV, 3269
    Removal of wreck off Sandusky, Ohio..................... I, 584; IV, 3269
    Water levels....................................... I, 681; V, 3776
Escambia River, Fla., improvement of...................... I, 360; III, 1784
Escanaba, Mich., water levels............................. I, 681; V, 3776
Esopus Creek, N. Y. (*see* Saugerties Harbor)................. I, 211; II, 1227
Essex River, Mass., improvement of........................ I, 141; II, 1047
Estherville-Minim Creek Canal, S. C. (*see* Santee River)........ I, 316; II, 1587
Estimates of appropriations required:
    Fortifications... I, 37, 38
    River and harbor examinations, surveys, etc.......................... I, 656
    River and harbor improvements.................................. I, 118
Eureka, Cal. (*see* Humboldt Harbor)....................... I, 611; IV, 3431
Eureka and Klamath River Railroad Company, bridge of................. I, 665
Eureka Slough, Cal., bridge across................................ I, 665
Everett Harbor, Wash., improvement of..................... I, 648; V, 3587
Examinations:
    Disbursements for surveys and, of waterways between Great Lakes and
        Atlantic Ocean... I, 118
    Of rivers and harbors, estimate of appropriation for................. I, 656
Executive Departments, Washington, D. C., telegraph line......... I, 676; V, 3689

ENG 1901——2

18   INDEX.

Executive Mansion, Washington, D. C .... I, 675; V, 3689
Exeter River, N. H.:
    Bridge between Stratham and Newmarket .... I, 668
    Improvement of.. I, 136; II, 1040
Explorations and reconnaissances, military..................... I, 683; V, 3799

                                      F.

Fairhaven Harbor, Mass. (*see* New Bedford)................... I, 163; II, 1119
Fairport Harbor, Ohio, improvement of .... I, 580; IV, 3255
Fairy Lake, Tex. and La. (*see* Cypress Bayou) .... I, 414; III, 2033
Falia, Bogue, La., improvement of............................. I, 379; III, 1872
Fall River Harbor, Mass., improvement of .... I, 169; II, 1134
Falls of Ohio River, Louisville, Ky.:
    Improvement of .... I, 496; IV, 2783
    Operating and care of Louisville and Portland Canal....... I, 499; IV, 2791
Fayetteville, N. C., examination and survey of Cape Fear River between
    Wilmington and... I, 310; II, 1552, 1557
Feather River, Cal.:
    Improvement of, including report of Board .... I, 608; IV, 3420, 3423
    Improvement of, by California Débris Commission .... I, 656; V, 3625
Ferd R. (steamer), wreck of (*see* Yazoo River)............. I, 420; III, 2048
Fernandina, Fla.:
    Improvement of Cumberland Sound........................... I, 333; II, 1655
    Improvement of waterway to Savannah, Ga................... I, 332; II, 1653
Ferry, E. P. (tug), removal of wreck of..................... I, 514; IV, 2883
Ferry (Fairy) Lake, Tex. and La. (*see* Cypress Bayou) .... I, 414; III, 2033
Field:
    Reconnaissances, explorations, etc., in the .... I, 683; V, 3799
    Service of engineer officers in the, since April, 1898.... I, 45
Filtration plant, Washington Aqueduct, D. C................... I, 674; V, 3680
Finders, range and position .... I, 10, 37
Finegan Slough, San Joaquin River, Cal., examination for closure of. I, 613; IV, 3454
Fire Island Inlet, N. Y., examination and survey.............. I, 223; II, 1249, 1255
Fish Island, Acushnet River, Mass., bridge between New Bedford and..... I, 665
Fishing Creek, N. C., improvement of .... I, 300; II, 1485
Five-mile River Harbor, Conn., improvement of................. I, 192; II, 1183
Flathead River, Mont., improvement of......................... I, 655; V, 3592
Flat Lake, La. (*see* Plaquemine Bayou) .... I, 387; III, 1890
Fleet Wing (schooner), removal of wreck of, in Mobile River, Ala .. I, 378; III, 1853
Fleetwing (tug), removal of wreck of, in Schuylkill River, Pa ...... I, 263; II, 1350
Flint, May (ship), removal of wreck of .... I, 613; IV, 3434
Flint River, Ga.:
    Bridge in Decatur County.................................. I, 660
    Improvement of .... I, 354; III, 1773
    Removal of wreck .... I, 363; III, 1798
Float, rod, full depth, method of discharge measurement ...... III, 2199
Floating derricks, application of, to grading river banks to receive revetments .... III, 2225
Florida:
    Defenses of east coast and of Key West .... I, 6, 26, 825
    Defenses of Pensacola..................................... I, 6, 27, 832
    Defenses of Tampa Bay..................................... I, 6, 27, 829
    Dredge and snag boat for works in......................... I, 342; II, 1749
    Removal of water hyacinths from waters in .... I, 341; II, 1746
Florida East Coast Railway Company, bridge of .... I, 667
Floyd, Sergt. Charles, monument to .... I, 687; V, 3827
Flushing Bay, N. Y., improvement of .... I, 204; II, 1210
Fontana (schooner), removal of wreck of.................... I, 570; IV, 3198
Fore River, Portland, Me.:
    City (Vaughan) bridge obstructing .... I, 668
    Harbor lines... I, 118; II, 1027
    Railroad bridge obstructing .... I, 668
Forked Deer River, Tenn., improvement of .... I, 459; III, 2405
Fort Bayou, Miss., bridge across .... I, 666
Fort Benton, Mont., improvement of Missouri River at.......... I, 452, 453; III, 2373

INDEX. 19

Fort Delaware, Del., defenses at (*see* Delaware River) .... I, 6, 21, 37, 770
Fortifications:
    Appropriations made by Congress .... I, 5, 6, 7, 41
    Appropriations required for 1902-1903, estimates of .... I, 37, 38
    Board of Engineers, The .... I, 5, 691
    Board of Ordnance and Fortification .... I, 5
    Board on Fortifications and other Defenses (Endicott Board) ...... I, 5
    Board on Torpedo System .... I, 5, 695
    Dynamite batteries .... I, 10
    Emergency sand batteries .... I, 8
    General statement, and progress of work .... I, 5
    Gun and mortar batteries .... I, 5, 7, 37
    Preservation and repair of .... I, 11, 37
    Projects .... I, 6, 37
    Range and position finders .... I, 10, 37
    Searchlights and electrical connections .... I, 13, 37
    Sea walls and embankments .... I, 11, 37
    Sites .... I, 12, 37
    Submarine mines .... I, 12, 38, 695
    Supplies for seacoast defenses .... I, 11, 37
    Technical details, defenses of Boston Harbor, Mass .... I, 913
    Technical details, defenses of mouth of Columbia River .... I, 923
    Technical details, defenses of coast of Maine .... I, 911
    Technical details, defenses of New York Harbor, N. Y .... I, 917
    Technical details, defenses of coast of North Carolina .... I, 921
    Technical details, defenses of San Diego, Cal .... I, 922
Fort McHenry Channel, Baltimore Harbor, Md.:
    Improvement of .... I, 264; II, 1374
    Removal of wreck .... I, 272; II, 1391
Fort Monroe, Va.:
    Defenses of Hampton Roads .... I, 6, 23, 802
    Removal of wreck off .... I, 298; II, 1462
Fort Morgan, Mobile Harbor, Ala., examination and survey of bar
    below .... I, 378; III, 1854, 1856
Fort Pierre, S. Dak., improvement of Missouri River at ..... I, 452, 454; III, 2373, 2374
Fort Point Channel, Boston Harbor, Mass.:
    Bridge at Cove street .... I, 661
    Improvement of .... I, 152; II, 1078
Fort Preble, Portland Harbor, Me.:
    Defenses at .... I, 6, 697, 911
    Tests of results of firing mortars at .... I, 7
Fort Smith, Ark. *See* Arkansas River.
Fort Totten, N. Y., post of .... I, 38, 927
Fort Washakie, Wyo., road to Buffalo Fork, Snake River .... I, 686; V, 3823
Fort Wayne Bridge, across Allegheny River, between Pittsburg and Allegheny, Pa .... I, 662
Fowler, John (steamboat), removal of wreck of .... I, 473; IV, 2646
Fox River, Wis.:
    Bridge at Appleton .... I, 664
    Bridge across canal at Depere .... I, 668
    Bridge across canal at Lock No. 2, Kaukauna, reconstruction of .... I, 662
    Bridges obstructing canal at Lawe street and Wisconsin avenue, Kaukauna, alteration of .... I, 668
    Bridge in Marquette County .... I, 664
    Bridges across canal at Menasha .... I, 668
    Bridge at Princeton .... I, 663
    Bridge at Wrightstown .... I, 662
    Improvement of .... I, 525; IV, 2958
    Improvement of Green Bay Harbor .... I, 516; IV, 2912
    Operating and care of locks and dams .... I, 527; IV, 2958
Foys Flats, Trent River, N. C., examination and survey through . I, 310; II, 1545, 1550
Franco Ferry, Fort Bayou, Miss., bridge at .... I, 666
Frankfort Harbor, Mich., improvement of .... I, 550; IV, 3122
Franklin, Pa., bridges across Allegheny River at and near .... I, 663
French Broad River, Tenn., improvement of .... I, 467; III, 2452
Friend, Lottie K. (schooner), removal of wreck of .... I, 263; II, 1350
Full-depth rod-float method of discharge measurement, illustration of ..... III, 2199

G.

Galena River, Ill., operating and care of lock and dam	I, 442; III, 2293
Galleries, cable	I, 38

Galveston Bay and Harbor, Tex.:
Defenses of	I, 6, 30, 846
Effects of storm of September, 1900, on fortifications	I, 32, 850
Effects of storm of September, 1900, on jetties and main ship channel	I, 412; III, 2018
Examination and survey of harbor from outer end of inner bar to Fifty-first street	I, 411; III, 1959, 1967
Examination and survey of inner harbor	I, 412
Improvement of Galveston-Texas City channel	I, 403; III, 1930
Improvement of harbor	I, 402; III, 1921
Improvement of waterway to Houston	I, 404; III, 1933
Improvement of West Bay	I, 406, 408; III, 1939, 1950
Removal of wrecks	I, 411; III, 1959
Gasconade River, Mo., improvement by Missouri River Commission	I, 658; S., 365, 382

Gauging:
Columbia River, Oreg. and Wash	I, 640; V, 3576
Mississippi River and principal tributaries	I, 425; III, 2072; S., 8, 45, 126
Mississippi River, at St. Louis, Mo., illustration of full-depth rod-float method of discharge measurement	III, 2199
Mississippi River, at St. Paul, Minn	I, 449; III, 2340
Northern and Northwestern Lakes	I, 681; V, 3776

Gauley River, W. Va., improvement of	I, 489; IV, 2733
Gedney Channel, New York Harbor, N. Y., improvement of	I, 224; II, 1285
Genesee River, N. Y. (see Charlotte Harbor)	I, 593; IV, 3355
Geneva Lake, Minn. (see Long Prairie River)	I, 451; III, 2361
George Lake, St. Johns River, Fla. (see Volusia Bar)	I, 337; II, 1739
Georges River, Me., improvement of	I, 130; II, 1004
Georgetown Harbor, S. C., improvement of (see also Winyah Bay)	I, 314; II, 1581, 1582
Georgia, defenses of coast of	I, 6, 26, 821
Georgia, Florida and Alabama Railway Company, bridge of	I, 660
Glassport Bridge Company, bridge of	I, 661
Glencove Harbor, N. Y., improvement of	I, 204; II, 1209
Glendive, Mont., bridge across Yellowstone River at	I, 659
Gloucester, Mass., improvement of harbor	I, 143; II, 1049

Gloucester, N. J.:
Bridge across Big Timber Creek	I, 666
Removal of wreck in Delaware River	I, 262; II, 1351

Goose Island, North Branch Canal, Chicago River, Ill., bridge at	I, 665
Goshen Creek, N. J., improvement of	I, 245; II, 1384

Government Printing Office, Washington, D. C.:
Construction of building for use of	I, 685; V, 3801
Telegraph line	I, 676; V, 3689

Governors Island, New York Harbor, N. Y., enlargement of	I, 228; II, 1298

Gowanus Bay, Canal, and Creek, N. Y.:
Bay Ridge, Red Hook, and Buttermilk channels, improvement of	I, 226; II, 1291
Gowanus Canal (see Gowanus Bay)	I, 226; II, 1291
Gowanus Creek Channel, improvement of	I, 227; II, 1296

Grading river banks to receive revetments, application of the road scraper and floating derrick to	III, 2225
Grand Haven Harbor, Mich., improvement of	I, 542; IV, 3095
Grand Lake, La. (see Mermentau River)	I, 392; III, 1901
Grand Marais, Mich., improvement of harbor of refuge	I, 513; IV, 2880
Grand Marais, Minn., improvement of harbor	I, 505; IV, 2821
Grand Rapids lock and dam, Wabash River, operating and care	I, 501; IV, 2802
Grand River, La., improvement of	I, 387; III, 1890

Grand River, Mich.:
Improvement of	I, 544; IV, 3098
Improvement of Grand Haven Harbor	I, 542; IV, 3095

Grand River, Ohio (see Fairport Harbor)	I, 580; IV, 3255
Granite State Land Company, bridge of	I, 666
Grass River, N. Y., examination and survey	I, 599; IV, 3377, 3384

INDEX. 21

Grays Ferry, Schuylkill River, Philadelphia, Pa., bridge at .... I, 665
Grays Harbor, Wash., improvement of, including bar entrance ...... I, 642; V, 3578
Great Kanawha River, W. Va.:
    Improvement of... I, 487; IV, 2726
    Operating and care of locks and dams................................. I, 488; IV, 2727
Great Lakes:
    Commercial statistics, Sault Ste. Marie canals, Mich............. I, 565; IV, 3173
    Defenses of... I, 32, 854
    Engineering methods used at harbors on Lake Erie west of Erie, Pa..... IV, 3213
    Improvement of channels in waters connecting................... I, 563; IV, 3157
    Notes on rock found in vicinity of Duluth, Minn...................... IV, 2883
    Surveys and charts .... I, 677, 681; V, 3761
    Water levels .... I, 681; V, 3776
    Waterways to Atlantic Ocean, disbursements for examinations and surveys... I, 118
Great Pedee River, S. C.:
    Examination and survey between Cheraw and the Wilmington, Columbia and Augusta Railroad bridge .... I, 324; II, 1607, 1614
    Improvement of... I, 312; II, 1578
Great Salt Pond, Block Island, R. I., improvement of............... I, 174; II, 1144
Great Sodus Bay, N. Y., improvement of harbor.................... I, 594; IV, 3360
Great South Bay, N. Y., examination and survey............... I, 223; II, 1249, 1255
Green Bay, Mich., water levels at Escanaba.......................... I, 681; V, 3776
Green Bay Harbor, Fox River, Wis., improvement of................ I, 516; IV, 2912
Green Jacket Shoal, Providence River, R. I., removal of............ I, 168; II, 1132
Greenleaf Bend, Mississippi River, Ill., prevention of break into Cache
    River .... I, 438; III, 2198
Greenpoint, N. Y., removal of wreck in East River off............... I, 223; II, 1248
Green River, Ky.:
    Improvement above mouth of Big Barren River.................... I, 502; IV, 2805
    Operating and care of locks and dams............................... I, 503; IV, 2806
    Reconstruction of Lock No. 2, at Rumsey............................ I, 502; IV, 2805
Greenville Harbor, Miss. (*see* Mississippi River Commission)......... I, 657; S., 3, 32
Greenwich Harbor, Conn., improvement of............................. I, 197; II, 1187
Greenwood, Miss., removal of wreck in Yazoo River.................. I, 420; III, 2048
Grenada County, Miss., bridge of....................................... I, 660
Grosse Isle, Detroit River, Mich., examination of channel west of... I, 571; IV, 3208
Grounds, public buildings and, District of Columbia .... I, 675; V, 3689
Gulfport, Miss., improvement of channel to Ship Island Harbor .... I, 374; III, 1846
Gulf States:
    Removal of water hyacinths from Florida waters .... I, 341; II, 1746
    Removal of water hyacinths from Louisiana waters.............. I, 395; III, 1906
Gun batteries .... I, 5, 7, 37
Guttenberg, N. J., harbor lines in Hudson River at.................. I, 118; II, 1273
Guyandot River, W. Va., improvement of............................. I, 489; IV, 2734

H.

Hackensack River, N. J., bridge across .... I, 665
Halifax River, Fla., bridge across .... I, 666
Hall, Richard (schooner), removal of wreck of .... I, 223; II, 1246
Hampton Beach, Me., bridge across Hampton River........................ I, 666
Hampton River, Me., bridge across.. I, 666
Hampton Roads, Va.:
    Defenses of.. I, 6, 23, 802
    Improvement of approaches to Norfolk Harbor.................... I, 292; II, 1447
    Removal of wreck off Fort Monroe................................... I, 298; II, 1462
Hancock, Mich., bridge across Portage Lake between Houghton and....... I, 664
Harbor lines, establishment of .... I, 118
    Allegheny City, Pa .... I, 119; IV, 2709
    Annapolis Harbor, Md .... I, 119; II, 1396
    Arthur Kill, N. J... I, 118; II, 1279
    Back Cove, Portland, Me .... I, 118; II, 1027
    Bangor Harbor, Me.. I, 118; II, 1022
    Black Rock Harbor, N. Y .... I, 119; IV, 3349
    Bloomers to Pleasant Valley Landing, Hudson River, N. J ...... I, 118; II, 1270
    Bronx River, N. Y .... I, 118; II, 1266

INDEX.

Harbor lines, establishment of—Continued.
　Buffalo, N. Y., at Erie Basin and Black Rock Harbor .... I, 119; IV, 3349
　Byram River, N. Y .... I, 118; II, 1261
　Cape Fear River, N. C... I, 119; II, 1572
　College Point, East River, N. Y .... I, 119; II, 1305
　Coos Bay, Oreg.. I, 119; V, 3544
　East River, at College Point, N. Y.................................. I, 119; II, 1305
　Erie Basin, Buffalo, N. Y... I, 119; IV, 3349
　Fore River, Portland, Me .... I, 118; II, 1027
　Guttenberg, N. J .... I, 118; II, 1273
　Hillsboro River, Fla .... I, 119; III, 1763
　Hudson River, at Guttenberg, N. J .... I, 118; II, 1273
　Hudson River, at Troy, N. Y... I, 118; II, 1268
　Hudson River, from Pleasant Valley Landing to Bloomers, N. J.. I, 118; II, 1270
　Lubec Harbor, Me.. I, 118; II, 1018
　Newark Bay, N. J .... I, 118; II, 1276
　New Jersey-Staten Island channel (see Arthur Kill)............. I, 118; II, 1279
　New York Harbor, N. Y., Arthur Kill................................. I, 118; II, 1279
　New York Harbor, N. Y., Bronx River .... I, 118; II, 1266
　New York Harbor, N. Y., at College Point, East River .... I, 119; II, 1305
　New York Harbor, N. Y., at Guttenberg, N. J .... I, 118; II, 1273
　Niagara River, N. Y., at Erie Basin and Black Rock Harbor .... I, 119; IV, 3349
　Ohio River, at Allegheny City, Pa .... I, 119; IV, 2709
　Pamlico River, N. C... I, 119; II, 1570
　Penobscot River, Me .... I, 118; II, 1022
　Pensacola Harbor, Fla .... I, 119; III, 1806
　Pittsburg Harbor, Pa., at Allegheny City .... I, 119; IV, 2709
　Pleasant Valley Landing to Bloomers, Hudson River, N. J .... I, 118; II, 1270
　Port Chester Harbor, N. Y .... I, 118; II, 1261
　Portland Harbor, Me... I, 118; II, 1027
　San Francisco Harbor, Cal... I, 119; IV, 3460
　Savannah Harbor, Ga .... I, 119; II, 1730
　Seabright, N. J... I, 118; II, 1282
　Severn River, Annapolis, Md .... I, 119; II, 1396
　Shrewsbury River, N. J.. I, 118; II, 1282
　Southport, N. C .... I, 119; II, 1572
　Staten Island-New Jersey channel (see Arthur Kill) .... I, 118; II, 1279
　Staten Island Sound (Arthur Kill), N. J .... I, 118; II, 1279
　Tampa, Fla.. I, 119; III, 1763
　Troy, N. Y .... I, 118; II, 1268
　Washington, N. C .... I, 119; II, 1570
Harbors and rivers. See Engineering methods and Rivers and harbors.
Hardings Beach, Chatham, Mass., removal of wreck on.............. I, 174; II, 1147
Harlem River, N. Y.:
　Bridge between One hundred and forty-fifth and One hundred and forty-
　　ninth streets, New York .... I, 663
　Improvement of .... I, 206; II, 1214
Harlowe Creek, N. C., improvement of waterway via.................. I, 303; II, 1493
Harrisonville Harbor, Mississippi River, Ill., examination of .... I, 439; III, 2226
Hartford, Conn., improvement of Connecticut River below .... I, 180; II, 1166
Hatch, A. S. (canal boat), removal of wreck of .... I, 223; II, 1247
Hat Slough, Wash. (see Puget Sound) .... I, 645; V, 3581
Haverstraw, N. Y., removal of wreck in Hudson River off............. I, 223; II, 1248
Havre de Grace, Md.:
　Examination and survey of rocks near harbor entrance...... I, 273; II, 1392, 1393
　Improvement of Susquehanna River above and below............ I, 264; II, 1374
Hawaiian Islands:
　Defenses of... I, 6
　Improvement of Pearl Harbor .... I, 612; IV, 3433
Hay Lake Channel, St. Marys River, Mich.:
　Improvement of .... I, 567; IV, 3185
　Improvement of channels in waters connecting Great Lakes .... I, 563; IV, 3157
　Preliminary report on survey .... I, 570; IV, 3200
Helena Harbor, Ark. (see Mississippi River Commission)............. I, 657; S., 3, 32
Hell Gate, East River, N. Y.:
　Bridge at, near Astoria... I, 664
　Improvement of.. I, 205; II, 1211
Hempstead Harbor, N. Y. (see Glencove) .... I, 204; II, 1209

INDEX. 23

Hendersons Point, Portsmouth Harbor, N H., examination and survey.. I, 149; II, 1057, 1062
Henry, Cape, Va., defenses at... I, 6
Herr Island lock and dam, Allegheny River, Pa., construction of.... I, 482; IV, 2701
Hillsboro Bay and River, Fla.:
    Harbor lines at Tampa... I, 119; III, 1763
    Improvement of... I, 347; III, 1758
Hillsboro County, Fla., bridge of... I, 664
Hills Ferry, San Joaquin River, Cal., bridge at... I, 666
Hiwassee River, Tenn., final report on survey up to the Ocoee........ I, 469; III, 2458
Holland Harbor, Mich., improvement of... I, 541; IV, 3092
Holmes River, Fla., improvement of... I, 358; III, 1780
Holston River, Tenn., final report on survey up to Kingsport......... I, 469; III, 2518
Homer B. (steamboat), removal of wreck of... I, 473; IV, 2646
Homme Dieu, Le, Lake, Minn. (*see* Long Prairie River)............... I, 451; III, 2361
Homochitto River, Miss., improvement of... I, 401; III, 1914
Honolulu, Hawaiian Islands, defenses of... I, 6
Hookton, Cal. (*see* Humboldt Harbor)... I, 611; IV, 3431
Hooper (schooner), removal of wreck of... I, 309; II, 1511
Hopefield Bend, Mississippi River (*see* Mississippi River Commission). I, 657; S., 3, 32
Horn Island Harbor, Miss., improvement of... I, 371; III, 1842
Houghton Mich., bridge across Portage Lake between Hancock and....... I, 664
Houghton County, Mich., bridge of... I, 664
Housatonic River, Conn., improvement of... I, 184; II, 1175
Houston, Tex., improvement of waterway to Galveston............... I, 404; III, 1933
Howard University Reservoir, Washington, D. C., construction of.... I, 673; V, 3666
Hudson County, N. J., bridge of... I, 665
Hudson River, N. Y. and N. J.:
    Bridge across, between Fifty-ninth and Sixtieth streets, New York City. I, 659
    Bridge at Troy, N. Y... I, 669
    Guttenberg, N. J., harbor lines... I, 118; II, 1278
    Haverstraw, N. Y., removal of wreck off... I, 223; II, 1248
    Improvement between Coxsackie and Troy, N. Y................. I, 210; II, 1222
    Peekskill Harbor, N. Y., improvement of... I, 213; II, 1230
    Pleasant Valley Landing to Bloomers, N. J., harbor lines.......... I, 118; II, 1270
    Rondout Harbor, N. Y., improvement of... I, 213; II, 1228
    Saugerties Harbor, N. Y., improvement of... I, 211; II, 1227
    Troy, N. Y., harbor lines... I, 118; II, 1268
Humboldt Harbor and Bay, Cal., improvement of................. I, 611; IV, 3431
Huntington Harbor, N. Y., improvement of... I, 203; II, 1208
Huron Harbor, Ohio, improvement of... I, 576; IV, 3236
Huron Lake:
    See also Northern and Northwestern Lakes.
    Improvement of harbor of refuge at Sandbeach, Mich.......... I, 557; IV, 3144
    Preliminary report on survey of waters connecting Lake Superior and .... I, 570; IV, 3200
    Water levels... I, 681; V, 3776
Hurricane of September, 1900:
    Brazos River, Tex., damage to jetties... I, 412; III, 2022
    Galveston, Tex., damage to fortifications... I, 32, 850
    Galveston, Tex., damage to jetties and main ship channel ...... I, 412; III, 2018
    Sabine Pass, Tex., damage at... I, 402; III, 1919
Hyacinths, water:
    Removal of, from Florida waters... I, 341; II, 1746
    Removal of, from Louisiana waters... I, 395; III, 1906
Hyannis, Mass., improvement of harbor of refuge............ I, 160; II, 1110
Hydraulic mining in California... I, 656; V, 3625
Hydraulics. *See* Engineering methods.

I.

Iberville Parish, La., bridge of... I, 668
Ida Lake, Minn. (*see* Long Prairie River)... I, 451; III, 2361
Illinois and Michigan Canal, Ill.:
    Examination, with plan and estimate, for waterway via (act of 1900) I, 534; IV, 3058
    Survey for waterway via (act of 1899) .... I, 534; IV, 3048

Illinois and Mississippi Canal, Ill.:
Construction of .... I, 532; IV, 3014
Examination for lock and dam in Rock River at feeder.......... I, 534; IV, 3066
Operating and care... I, 442; III, 2291
Illinois Central Railroad Company, bridge of....................... I, 664
Illinois River, Ill.:
Improvement of .... I, 531; IV, 3006
Operating and care of locks and dams .... I, 531; IV, 3010
Waterway from Mississippi River to Lake Michigan via, examination for, with plan and estimate (act of 1900)................... I, 534; IV, 3058
Waterway from Mississippi River to Lake Michigan via, survey for (act of 1899)... I, 534; IV, 3048
Indian River Bay, Del., improvement of waterway via.................. I, 260; II, 1348
Indian River, Fla., improvement of................................. I, 339; II, 1742
Indian River Inlet, Fla. (see Indian River)......................... I, 339; II, 1742
Indiana Chute, Falls of Ohio River, improvement of .... I, 496; IV, 2783
Indiana, Illinois and Iowa Railroad Company, bridge of .... I, 660
Inland routes. See Canals and Waterways.
Inside Thoroughfare, Atlantic City, N. J., bridge across............. I, 664
Irene Lake, Minn. (see Long Prairie River) .... I, 451; III, 2361
Iron State (barge), removal of wreck of.......................... I, 262; II, 1351
Ironton, Ohio, bridge across Ohio River between Ashland, Ky., and....... I, 660
Island Beach, N. J., removal of wreck in Shrewsbury River opposite. I, 223; II, 1247
Isle of Wight Bay, Md., improvement of waterway via................ I, 260; II, 1348

J.

Jackson County, Miss., bridge of..................................... I, 666
Jackson Creek, Md., removal of wreck............................... I, 272; II, 1391
Jamaica Bay, N. Y., bridge across.................................... I, 663
James River, Va.:
Improvement of... I, 289; II, 1423
Protection of Jamestown Island .... I, 291; II, 1437
Jamestown Island, James River, Va., protection of.................. I, 291; II, 1437
Jefferson, Pa., bridge across Monongahela River between Port Vue and.... I, 661
Jefferson, Tex., waterway to Shreveport, La. (see Cypress Bayou) ... I, 414; III, 2033
Jekyl Creek, Ga., improvement of waterway via..................... I, 332; II, 1653
Jersey City, N. J. See New York Harbor.
Johnsons Bayou, La., improvement of............................... I, 395; III, 1905
Johnsons Creek, Conn. (see Bridgeport Harbor) .... I, 186; II, 1177
Judith, Mont., improvement of Missouri River at .... I, 452, 453; III, 2373, 2374
Judith, Point, R. I.:
Construction of harbor of refuge............................... I, 171; II, 1138
Improvement of pond entrance.................................. I, 172; II, 1140
Jules (barge), removal of wreck of .... I, 411; III, 1959
Jupiter Inlet, Fla. (see Indian River).............................. I, 340; II, 1743

K.

Kalamazoo River, Mich., improvement at Saugatuck ..... I, 540, 541; IV, 3087, 3090
Kampeska Lake, S. Dak. (see Sioux River) .... I, 458; III, 2395
Kampsville lock and dam, Illinois River, Ill., operating and care.... I, 531; IV, 3010
Kanawha River, W. Va.:
Improvement of .... I, 487; IV, 2726
Operating and care of locks and dams .... I, 488; IV, 2727
Kansas City Southern Railway Company, bridge of.................. I, 660
Karquines Strait, Cal., examination and survey of San Joaquin River from Antioch, through Suisun Bay, to......................... I, 613; IV, 3449, 3452
Kaskaskia River, Ill., bridge across................................ I, 667
Kate (tug), removal of wreck of .... I, 411; III, 1959
Kaukauna, Wis.:
Bridge across Fox River Canal at Lock No. 2, reconstruction of........ I, 662
Bridges obstructing Fox River Canal at Lawe street and Wisconsin avenue, alteration of..................................... I, 668
Kelsy, Percy (steamboat), removal of wreck of .... I, 473; IV, 2646

INDEX. 25

Kennebec River, Me.:
    Defenses of... I, 6, 14, 697, 698, 911
    Improvement of... I, 130; II, 1005
Kenosha Harbor, Wis.:
    Bridge across Pike Creek.................................... I, 667
    Improvement of... I, 524; IV, 2945
    Moving of cribs at.. IV, 2948
Kent Island, Chesapeake Bay, Md., bridge across Kent Island Narrows.... I, 665
Kent Island Narrows, Chesapeake Bay, Md., bridge at Kent Island........ I, 665
Kentucky River, Ky.:
    Bridge at Carrollton.. I, 662
    Improvement of... I, 494; IV, 2744
    Operating and care of locks and dams........................ I, 495; IV, 2746
Kewaunee Harbor, Wis., improvement of............................ I, 519; IV, 2925
Keweenaw Bay and Point, Mich., improvement and operating and care of
    waterway to Lake Superior................................ I, 511, 512; IV, 2867
Keyport Harbor, N. J., improvement of............................ I, 220; II, 1241
Key West Harbor, Fla.:
    Defenses of... I, 6, 26, 825
    Improvement of... I, 340; II, 1744
Kill van Kull, N. Y. and N. J. (*see* Staten Island-New Jersey channel).. I, 215; II, 1233
King County, Wash., bridge of.................................... I, 663
Kingston, R. I.:
    Construction of Point Judith harbor of refuge............... I, 171; II, 1138
    Improvement of entrance to Point Judith Pond................ I, 172; II, 1140
Kingston, Tenn., bridge across Clinch River at................... I, 660
Kingston Bay, Mass. (*see* Duxbury Harbor)....................... I, 156; II, 1086
Kingston Bridge and Terminal Railway Company, bridge of.......... I, 660
Kinnickinnic River, Wis., examination of Milwaukee Harbor....... I, 527; IV, 2981
Kissimmee River, Fla., examination and survey to Gulf of Mexico.......... I, 350
Kittery, Me., bridge between Portsmouth Navy-Yard, N. H., and.......... I, 664
Kootenai River, Idaho and Mont.:
    Examination from Jennings to international boundary......... I, 655; V, 3603
    Improvement from Bonners Ferry to international boundary.... I, 654; V, 3591

L.

Lacenter, Wash., bridge across Lewis River at...................... I, 661
La Crosse Harbor, Wis., improvement of............................ I, 442; III, 2295
Lafourche Bayou, La., improvement of.............................. I, 386; III, 1887
Lagrange Bayou, Fla., improvement of.............................. I, 358; III, 1780
Lagrange lock and dam, Illinois River, Ill., operating and care....... I, 531; IV, 3010
Lanes Ferry, Obion River, Tenn., bridge at........................ I, 667
Larchmont Harbor, N. Y., improvement of........................... I, 199; II, 1201
La Trappe River, Md., improvement of.............................. I, 268; II, 1382
Laura Wilhelmina (sloop), removal of wreck of................... I, 272; II, 1390
Laurel, Del., bridge across Broad Creek River at.................. I, 666
Laws of Fifty-sixth Congress, second session, affecting Corps of Engineers.. V, 3837
Leader (schooner), removal of wreck of.......................... I, 570; IV, 3198
Leaf River, Miss., improvement of................................. I, 373; III, 1845
League Island Navy-Yard, Pa., removal of wreck in Schuylkill River.. I, 263; II, 1352
Leech Lake, Minn.:
    Construction of reservoir dam............................... I, 444; III, 2309
    Operating and care of reservoir dam......................... I, 445; III, 2322
    Survey of flowage lines of reservoir........................ I, 451
Lee, Drusilla B. (schooner), removal of wreck of................ I, 262; II, 1350
Lee Slough, Fla. (*see* Apalachicola River)....................... I, 352; III, 1769
Leesville, East Haddam, Conn., bridge across Salmon River below....... I, 662
Legislation of Fifty-sixth Congress, second session, affecting Corps of Engineers. V, 3837
Le Homme Dieu Lake, Minn. (*see* Long Prairie River)............. I, 451; III, 2361
Lemon Creek, N. Y. (*see* Staten Island-New Jersey channel)...... I, 215; II, 1233
Leonard, Jemima (barge), removal of wreck of................... I, 223; II, 1247
Levisa Fork, Big Sandy River, Ky.:
    Final report on survey for locks and dams................... I, 496; IV, 2750
    Improvement of.. I, 493; IV, 2742

Lewes, Del.:
    Construction of iron pier in Delaware Bay near .... I, 236; II, 1323
    Improvement of waterway to Chincoteague Bay, Va .... I, 260; II, 1348
Lewes River, Del. (*see* Broadkill Creek) .... I, 260; II, 1347
Lewes River Improvement Company (*see* Broadkill Creek).......... I, 260; II, 1347
Lewis River, Wash.:
    Bridge at Lacenter... I, 661
    Dredging plant for use on (*see* Columbia River) .... I, 640; V, 3575
    Improvement of .... I, 638; V, 3572
Licking River, Ky., survey of .... I, 476; IV, 2670
Little Assawaman Bay, Del., improvement of waterway via .... I, 260; II, 1348
Little Calumet River, Ill.:
    Bridge at Riverdale.. I, 664
    Survey for waterway via .... I, 534; IV, 3048, 3058
Little Harbor, N. H., improvement of harbor of refuge .... I, 137; II, 1041
Little Hell Gate, New York Harbor, N. Y., bridge across............ I, 665
Little Kanawha River, W. Va.:
    Improvement of... I, 486; IV, 2723
    Operating and care of lock and dam .... I, 487; IV, 2724
Little Mud River, Ga., improvement of waterway via................ I, 332; II, 1653
Little Narragansett Bay, R. I. and Conn. (*see* Pawcatuck River)..... I, 175; II, 1159
Little Pedee River, S. C., improvement of......................... I, 311; II, 1576
Little Pigeon River, Tenn., improvement of .... I, 467; III, 2454
Little River, La. (*see* Red River) .... I, 412; III, 2025
Little Rock, Ark. *See* Arkansas River.
Little Sarasota Bay, Fla. (*see* Sarasota Bay) .... I, 344; III, 1753
Little Sodus Bay, N. Y., improvement of harbor.................... I, 595; IV, 3363
Little Tallahatchie River, Miss. (*see* Tallahatchie) .... I, 422; III, 2067
Little Tennessee River, Tenn.:
    Bridge near Niles Ferry.. I, 668
    Examination and survey up to and including Abrams Creek. I, 469; III, 2491, 2496
Little Traverse Bay, Mich. (*see* Petoskey Harbor).................. I, 553; IV, 3129
Locks. *See* Canals *and* Waterways.
Logan, General, statue of .... I, 676; V, 3689
Long Bridge, Potomac River, D. C., rebuilding of .... I, 275; II, 1399
Long Island City, N. Y., bridge across East River to Sixtieth street, New
    York City .... I, 665
Long Island Sound, N. Y.:
    Defenses of eastern entrance .... I, 6, 17, 747
    Removal of wreck off Port Chester .... I, 223; II, 1246
Long Prairie River, Minn., examination of, and its sources .... I, 451; III, 2361
Long Sault Island, St. Lawrence River, N. Y., examination and survey
    at... I, 599; IV, 3389, 3391
Long Tom River, Oreg., improvement of .... I, 630; V, 3549
Lorain Harbor, Ohio, improvement of............................... I, 577; IV, 3241
Louise Lake, Minn. (*see* Long Prairie River) .... I, 451; III, 2361
Louisiana, removal of water hyacinths from waters in .... I, 395; III, 1906
Louisville, Ky.:
    Improvement of Ohio River at................................... I, 496; IV, 2783
    Operating and care of Louisville and Portland Canal............ I, 499; IV, 2791
    Removal of wreck in Louisville and Portland Canal.............. I, 505; IV, 2816
Louisville and Nashville Railroad Company, bridge of .... I, 665
Louisville and Portland Canal, Ky.:
    Enlargement of .... I, 496; IV, 2783
    Operating and care... I, 499; IV, 2791
    Removal of wreck... I, 505; IV, 2816
Loutre, Pass a, Mississippi River, La.:
    Closing crevasse in.. I, 382; III, 1877
    Constructing sill across .... I, 383; III, 1878
Lowell, Ohio, bridge across Muskingum River Canal, above.......... I, 660
Lower Machodoc Creek, Va., improvement of........................ I, 281; II, 1410
Lubec Channel and Harbor, Me.:
    Harbor lines .... I, 118; II, 1018
    Improvement of channel... I, 120; II, 968
Ludington Harbor, Mich., improvement of .... I, 548; IV, 3112
Lumber mattress, use of, for subaqueous bank protection .... III, 2212
Lumberton Branch, Rancocas River, N. J., improvement of........... I, 238; II, 1327

INDEX. 27

Lynn Harbor, Mass.:
Examination and survey... I, 159; II, 1092, 1093
Improvement of .... I, 150; II, 1075
Lynn Haven Inlet, Va., bridge across .... I, 665
Lyttes, Ephriam (sloop), removal of wreck of .... I, 272; II, 1391

M.

McConnelsville, Ohio, bridge across Muskingum River...................... I, 666
• *McDonald, Charley* (steamboat), removal of wreck of .... I, 473; IV, 2646
Macedonia (steamship), removal of wreck of .... I, 223; II, 1247
Maçon Bayou, La., improvement of..................................... I, 419; III, 2046
Maggie (schooner), removal of wreck of, in North Point Creek, Patapsco River, Md .... I, 272; II, 1390
Maggie (sloop), removal of wreck of, in Cambridge Harbor, Md ...... I, 272; II, 1391
Mahon (Harbor) River, Del., examination of .... I, 263; II, 1358
Main Ship Channel, New York Harbor, N. Y., improvement of ..... I, 224; II, 1285
Maine, defenses on coast of... I, 6, 7, 13, 697, 911
Malden River, Mass., improvement of .... I, 151; II, 1077
Mall, the, Washington, D. C., improvement of, including its connection with Potomac and Zoological parks .... I, 676; V, 3689
Malta, Ohio, bridge across Muskingum River .... I, 666
Mamaroneck Harbor, N. Y., improvement of .... I, 199; II, 1200
Manasquan River, N. J., improvement of .... I, 222; II, 1245
Manatee River, Fla., improvement of .... I, 345; III, 1755
Manchac Bayou, La., improvement of................................. I, 381; III, 1875
Manchester Harbor, Mass., improvement of........................... I, 144; II, 1051
Mandan, N. Dak., ice harbor in Missouri River near ...... I, 452, 456; III, 2378, 2377
Manhattan Borough, New York City, N. Y. *See* New York Harbor.
Manila, Philippine Islands, report upon work of department of city public works and water supply................................... I, 683, 684
Manistee Harbor, Mich., improvement of............................. I, 549; IV, 3116
Manitowoc Harbor and River, Wis.:
Bridge to connect State and Center streets .... I, 662
Examination for harbor of refuge .... I, 527; IV, 2978
Improvement of .... I, 520; IV, 2928
Manokin River, Md.:
Improvement of.. I, 270; II, 1387
Removal of wreck .... I, 272; II, 1390
Mantua Creek, N. J., improvement of .... I, 241; II, 1330
Maps:
Military and other... I, 683, 685; V, 3799
Northern and Northwestern Lakes............................... I, 677, 681; V, 3761
Marblehead Harbor, Mass., repair of sea wall .... I, 145; II, 1052
Marcushook, Pa., improvement of ice harbor in Delaware River...... I, 235; II, 1322
Marietta, Ohio:
Bridge of Ohio River Bridge and Ferry Company across Ohio River between Williamstown, W. Va., and .... I, 660
Bridge of Williamstown and Marietta Bridge and Transportation Company between Williamstown, W. Va., and .... I, 661
Marinette, Wis. (*see* Menominee Harbor *and* River)............ I, 515; IV, 2908, 2909
Marion, Mass., bridge across Weweanititt River .... I, 667
Marquette Bay and Harbor, Mich.:
Construction of harbor of refuge in bay........................... I, 513; IV, 2879
Improvement of harbor .... I, 512; IV, 2877
Water levels .... I, 681; V, 3776
Marquette County, Wis., bridge across Fox River in................... I, 664
Marthas Vineyard, Mass improvement of Vineyard Haven Harbor.. I, 162; II, 1115
Martin (schooner), removal of wreck of .... I, 570; IV, 3198
Martins Creek, Miss., bridge across Yalobusha River at mouth of........... I, 660
Mary Lake, Minn. (*see* Long Prairie River) .... I, 451; II, 2361
Mascot (steamer), removal of wreck of .... I, 363; III, 1793
Massachusetts, State of:
Bridges of, across Weweanititt River .... I, 667
Defenses of southeast coast of .... I, 6, 16, 735
Massena, N. Y., examination and survey of Grass River up to... I, 599; IV, 3377, 3384
Massena Canal, N. Y. (*see* Grass *and* St. Lawrence rivers) ..... I, 599; IV, 3389, 3391
Matanzas River, Fla. (*see* St. Augustine Harbor) .... I, 338; II, 1741

28 INDEX.

Matawan Creek, N. J., improvement of .... I, 219; II, 1240
Mattaponi River, Va., improvement of .... I, 287; II, 1419
Mattituck Harbor, N. Y., improvement of .... I, 201; II, 1205
Mattress, lumber, use of, for subaqueous bank protection .... III, 2212
Maumee Bay and River, Ohio:
   Bridges across river, near Toledo .... I, 667
   Engineering methods used in improvement of .... IV, 3213
   Improvement of Toledo Harbor .... I, 572; IV, 3218
Maumee Railway Bridge Company, bridges of .... I, 667
Maysville, Ky., examination and survey of Ohio River for harbor of refuge
   (ice harbor) at .... I, 477; IV, 2670, 2675
Meadowbrook (canal boat), removal of wreck of .... I, 263; II, 1352
Memorial Bridge, across Potomac River at Washington, D. C .... I, 670; V, 3648
Memphis Harbor, Tenn. (*see* Mississippi River Commission) .... I, 657; S., 3, 32
Menasha, Wis., bridges of city of .... I, 668
Menekaunee, Wis. (*see* Menominee Harbor *and* River) .... I, 515; IV, 2908, 2909
Menominee Harbor and River, Mich. and Wis.:
   Improvement of harbor .... I, 515; IV, 2908
   Improvement of river .... I, 515; IV, 2909
Merced County, Cal., bridge of .... I, 666
Mermentau River, La., improvement of, including tributaries .... I, 392; III, 1901
Merrimac River, Mass.:
   Improvement of .... I, 139; II, 1044
   Improvement of Newburyport Harbor .... I, 138; II, 1043
Methods, engineering. *See* Engineering methods.
Mexico, Gulf of:
   Removal of water hyacinths from Florida tributaries .... I, 341; II, 1746
   Removal of water hyacinths from Louisiana tributaries .... I, 395; III, 1906
Meyers, Edward L. (canal boat), removal of wreck of .... I, 262; II, 1352
Mianus River, Conn., improvement of .... I, 195; II, 1186
Michigan City Harbor, Ind.:
   Improvement of inner harbor .... I, 534; IV, 3074
   Improvement of outer harbor .... I, 534, 535; IV, 3075
Michigan, Lake:
   See also Northern and Northwestern Lakes.
   Canal to Sturgeon Bay, construction of harbor of refuge .... I, 518; IV, 2922
   Canal to Sturgeon Bay, examination and survey .... I, 527; IV, 2970, 2973
   Canal to Sturgeon Bay, improvement of .... I, 517; IV, 2914
   Canal to Sturgeon Bay, operating and care .... I, 518; IV, 2919
   Canal to Sturgeon Bay, removal of wreck .... I, 527; IV, 2970
   Water levels .... I, 681; V, 3776
   Waterway to Mississippi River, examination for, with plan and estimate
     (act of 1900) .... I, 534; IV, 3058
   Waterway to Mississippi River, survey for (act of 1899) .... I, 534; IV, 3048
Milan, Ill.:
   Construction of canal around Rock River at .... I, 532; IV, 3014
   Operating and care of canal around Rock River at .... I, 442; III, 2291
Milford Haven Harbor, Va., improvement of .... I, 284; II, 1415
Military divisions and departments:
   Operations of Engineer Department in the Philippines .... I, 43, 975
   Reconnaissances and explorations .... I, 683; V, 3799
Mill River, New Haven, Conn. (*see* New Haven) .... I, 182; II, 1170
Mill River, Stamford, Conn. (*see* Stamford) .... I, 194; II, 1184
Miltona Lake, Minn. (*see* Long Prairie River) .... I, 451; III, 2361
Milwaukee Bay, Harbor, and River, Wis.:
   Bridge across river at Chestnut street .... I, 661
   Construction of harbor of refuge in bay .... I, 522; IV, 2936
   Examination of harbor .... I, 527; IV, 2981
   Improvement of harbor .... I, 523; IV, 2939
   Water levels .... I, 681; V, 3776
Mina Lake, Minn. (*see* Long Prairie River) .... I, 451; III, 2361
Mines, submarine .... I, 12, 38, 695
Minim Creek-Estherville Canal, S. C. (*see* Santee River) .... I, 316; II, 1587
Mining, hydraulic, in California .... I, 656; V, 3625
Minneapolis, Minn.:
   Bridge of Chicago, Milwaukee and St. Paul Railway Company across
     Mississippi River near .... I, 662
   Bridges of Wisconsin Central Railway Company at Nicollet and Boom
     islands near .... I, 667

INDEX. 29

Minnesota River, Minn.:
 Improvement of.'... I, 447; III, 2334
 Survey of Big Stone and Traverse lakes for reservoir dams to improve
  navigation on.. I, 450; III, 2342
Mispillion River, Del.:
 Examination and survey.. I, 264; II, 1365, 1368
 Improvement of... I, 257; II, 1345
Mississippi River:
 Beechridge, Ill., prevention of break at......................... I, 438; III, 2198
 Boom Island, Minn., bridge at................................... I, 667
 Brainerd, Minn., to Sandy Lake dam, survey from............... I, 451; III, 2343
 Caruthersville, Mo. (see Mississippi River Commission).......... I, 657; S., 3, 32
 Delta Point, La. (see Mississippi River Commission)............. I, 657; S., 3, 32
 Des Moines Rapids Canal and dry dock, operation and care..... I, 441; III, 2284
 Dredge and snag boats above Missouri River, operation of....... I, 440; III, 2231
 Dredge and snag boats below Missouri River, operation of....... I, 434; III, 2166
 Dredge boats for passes of....................................... I, 383; III, 1878
 Dubuque, Iowa, bridge near Eagle Point......................... I, 660
 Eagle Point, Dubuque, Iowa, bridge near........................ I, 660
 Gauging at St. Louis, Mo.. III, 2199
 Gauging at St. Paul, Minn....................................... I, 449; III, 2340
 Gauging, including principal tributaries.......... I, 425; III, 2072; S., 8, 45, 126
 Greenleaf Bend, Ill., prevention of break into Cache River...... I, 438; III, 2198
 Greenville, Miss. (see Mississippi River Commission)............ I, 657; S., 3, 32
 Harrisonville Harbor, Ill., examination of....................... I, 439; III, 2226
 Head of Passes to headwaters, surveys from..................... I, 657; S., 3, 32
 Head of Passes to Ohio River, improvement, surveys, etc........ I, 657; S., 3, 32
 Helena, Ark. (see Mississippi River Commission)................ I, 657; S., 3, 32
 Hickman, Ky., to Slough Landing, Tenn., examination and survey.. I, 434; III, 2155, 2158
 Hopefield Bend (see Mississippi River Commission)............. I, 657; S., 3, 32
 La Crosse Harbor, Wis., improvement of......................... I, 442; III, 2295
 Loutre, Pass a, closing crevasse in.............................. I, 382; III, 1877
 Loutre, Pass a, constructing sill across.......................... I, 383; III, 1878
 Memphis, Tenn. (see Mississippi River Commission)............ I, 657; S., 3, 32
 Minneapolis, Minn., bridges near................................ I, 662, 667
 Minneapolis, Minn., to St. Paul, improvement from............. I, 443; III, 2298
 Missouri River, above, operation of snag and dredge boats...... I, 440; III, 2231
 Missouri River, below, removal of snags and wrecks............ I, 434; III, 2166
 Missouri River to Ohio River, discharge measurements at St. Louis, Mo. III, 2199
 Missouri River to Ohio River, disk anchor, use of............... III, 2221
 Missouri River to Ohio River, improvement from................ I, 435; III, 2169
 Missouri River to Ohio River, lumber mattress for subaqueous bank protection.. III, 2212
 Missouri River to St. Paul, Minn., improvement from........... I, 440; III, 2238
 Natchez, Miss. (see Mississippi River Commission).............. I, 657; S., 3, 32
 New Orleans, La., defenses of................................... I, 6, 30, 842
 New Orleans, La., improvement at, by Mississippi River Commission.. I, 657; S., 3, 32
 Nicollet Island, Minn., bridges at................................ I, 667
 Ohio River to Head of Passes, improvement, surveys, etc........ I, 657; S., 3, 32
 Ohio River to Missouri River, discharge measurements at St. Louis, Mo. III, 2199
 Ohio River to Missouri River, disk anchor, use of............... III, 2221
 Ohio River to Missouri River, improvement from................ I, 435; III, 2169
 Ohio River to Missouri River, lumber mattress for subaqueous bank protection.. III, 2212
 Outlet, improvement of.. I, 383; III, 1878
 Pass a Loutre, closing crevasse in............................... I, 382; III, 1877
 Pass a Loutre, constructing sill across........................... I, 383; III, 1878
 Passes of, dredge boats for...................................... I, 383; III, 1878
 Plaquemine Bayou, La., construction of lock................... I, 387; III, 1890
 Pokegama Falls, Minn., construction of reservoir dam.......... I, 444; III, 2309
 Pokegama Falls, Minn., operating and care of reservoir dam.... I, 445; III, 2322
 Pokegama Falls, Minn., survey of flowage lines of reservoir..... I, 451
 Reelfoot levee district (Hickman, Ky., to Slough Landing, Tenn.), examination and survey.. I, 434; III, 2155, 2158
 Reservoir dams at headwaters, construction of.................. I, 444; III, 2309
 Reservoir dams at headwaters, examination of Long Prairie River, Minn., and its sources.. I, 451; III, 2361

Mississippi River—Continued.
Reservoir dams at headwaters, operating and care.............. I, 445; III, 2322
Reservoir dams at headwaters, survey of flowage lines.............. I, 451
St. Louis Harbor, Mo., discharge measurements........................ III, 2199
St. Louis Harbor, Mo., improvement of........................ I, 438; III, 2196
St. Paul, Minn., gauging at.. I, 449; III, 2340
St. Paul, Minn., to Minneapolis, improvement from............ I, 448; III, 2298
St. Paul, Minn., to Missouri River, improvement from.......... I, 440; III, 2238
Sandy Lake dam to Brainerd, Minn., survey from................ I, 451; III, 2343
Slough Landing, Tenn., to Hickman, Ky., examination and survey.. I, 434; III, 2155, 2158
Snag and dredge boats above Missouri River, operation of....... I, 440; III, 2231
Snags and wrecks below Missouri River, removal of.............. I, 434; III, 2166
South Pass, maintenance of channel by representatives of James B. Eads.. I, 118, 379; III, 1865
South Pass, maintenance of channel by United States........... I, 385; III, 1881
Southwest Pass, project for improvement of.................. I, 383, 384; III, 1878
Vicksburg Harbor, Miss., improvement of...................... I, 421; III, 2052
Vidalia, La. (see Mississippi River Commission)................ I, 657; S., 3, 32
Water-level observations at St. Louis, Mo............................. III, 2199
Water-level observations at St. Paul, Minn.................... I, 449; III, 2340
Water-level observations on, including tributaries. I, 425; III, 2072; S., 8, 45, 126
Waterway to Lake Michigan, examination for, with plan and estimate (act of 1900).. I, 534; IV, 3058
Waterway to Lake Michigan, survey for (act of 1899)............ I, 534; IV, 3048
Wrecks, etc., above Missouri River, removal of................. I, 440; III, 2231
Wrecks, etc., below Missouri River, removal of................. I, 434; III, 2166
Mississippi River Commission.. I, 657; S., 3, 32
Mississippi Sound, Miss.:
Defenses of.. I, 6, 28, 836
Improvement of channel from Gulfport to Ship Island Harbor.. I, 374; III, 1846
Improvement of Horn Island Harbor............................ I, 371; III, 1842
Improvement of Ship Island Pass............................... I, 374; III, 1848
Missouri Junction, Ill., bridge across Kaskaskia River....................... I, 667
Missouri River:
Examination of Sioux River, S. Dak., for reservoir dam......... I, 458; III, 2395
Improvement from Stubbs Ferry, Mont., to Sioux City, Iowa.... I, 452; III, 2373
Improvement, surveys, etc., below Sioux City, Iowa .... I, 658; S., 365, 382
Plan and estimate for rectification of, at St. Joseph, Mo .... I, 452; III, 2367
Snagging upper river.. I, 457; III, 2391
Missouri River Commission.. I, 658; S., 365, 382
Mobile County, Ala., bridge across Dog River in........................... I, 665
Mobile Harbor and River, Ala.:
Defenses of.. I, 6, 28, 836
Examination and survey of bar below Fort Morgan........ I, 378; III, 1854, 1856
Improvement of harbor.. I, 364; III, 1810
Removal of wreck in river..................................... I, 378; III, 1853
Moccasin River (Contentnia Creek), N. C., improvement of.......... I, 301; II, 1488
Mokelumne River, Cal., improvement of.............................. I, 607; IV, 3419
Monmouth County, N. J., bridge of.. I, 663
Monongahela River, W. Va. and Pa.:
Bridge at South Tenth street, Pittsburg, Pa.............................. I, 662
Bridge between Port Vue and Jefferson, Pa............................. I, 661
Construction of locks and dams between Morgantown and Fairmont, W. Va.. I, 477; IV, 2679
Improvement at Locks Nos. 3 and 6.............................. I, 478; IV, 2683
Improvement of Pittsburg Harbor............................... I, 480; IV, 2697
Operating and care of locks and dams........................... I, 479; IV, 2686
Monroe, Fort, Va.:
Defenses of Hampton Roads................................... I, 6, 23, 802
Removal of wreck off... I, 298; II, 1462
Monroe Harbor, Mich., improvement of............................. I, 571; IV, 3215
Monuments:
To Sergt. Charles Floyd...................................... I, 687; V, 3827
Washington Monument, District of Columbia.................... I, 675; V, 3689
Moodus and East Hampton Railway Company, bridge of.................. I, 662
Moore, Harry (scow), removal of wreck of........................... I, 272; II, 1391

Morgan Canal, Tex.:
    Improvement of (*see* Galveston ship channel).................... I, 404; III, 1933
    Operating and care.. I, 405; III, 1937
Morgan County, Ohio, bridge of.. I, 666
Morgan, Fort, Mobile Harbor, Ala., examination and survey of bar below... I, 378; III, 1854, 1856
Mortar batteries... I, 5, 7, 37
Mosquito Creek Canal, S. C. (*see* Santee River)...................... I, 316; II, 1587
Mound City, Ill., prevention of Mississippi River from breaking into Cache River at.. I, 438; III, 2198
Moundsville, Wis., bridge across Fox River at......................... I, 664
Mount Desert, Bar Harbor, Me., construction of breakwater........... I, 122; II, 991
Mount Hope Bay, Mass., improvement of Fall River Harbor.......... I, 169; II, 1134
Mount Pleasant shore, Charleston, S. C., improvement at............ I, 320; II, 1598
Mud Lake, Chicago, Ill., bridge across West Fork of South Branch, Chicago River, at... I, 663
Mud Lake, La. (*see* Mermentau River)............................... I, 392; III, 1901
Mud River, Ga., improvement of waterway via....................... I, 332; II, 1653
Mud River, S. C. (*see* Savannah-Beaufort channel).................. I, 324; II, 1628
Murderkill River, Del., improvement of.............................. I, 254; II, 1342
Muscle Shoals Canal, Tennessee River, Ala., operating and care..... I, 466; III, 2440
Muskegon Harbor and River, Mich.:
    Examination of, with plan and estimate......................... I, 553; IV, 3131
    Improvement of.. I, 545; IV, 3103
Muskingum County, Ohio:
    Bridge of, across Muskingum River, at Zanesville ("Y" Bridge)...... I, 659
    Bridge of, across Muskingum River Canal, at Zanesville........... I, 667
Muskingum River, Ohio:
    Bridge above Lowell.. I, 660
    Bridge at McConnelsville and Malta............................. I, 666
    Bridge at Zanesville, across canal.............................. I, 667
    Bridge at Zanesville ("Y" Bridge)............................... I, 659
    Improvement of.. I, 485; IV, 2714
    Operating and care of locks and dams........................... I, 485; IV, 2714
Mystic River, Conn., improvement of.................................. I, 178; II, 1162
Mystic River, Mass.:
    Improvement of.. I, 151; II, 1077
    Improvement of, below mouth of Island End River............... I, 152; II, 1078

N.

Nandua Creek, Va., improvement of................................. I, 295; II, 1454
Nansemond River, Va., improvement of.............................. I, 293; II, 1450
Nanticoke River, Del. and Md., improvement of..................... I, 269; II, 1384
Nantucket, Mass., construction of harbor of refuge................... I, 161; II, 1112
Napa River, Cal., improvement of.................................. I, 609; IV, 3428
Narragansett Bay, R. I.:
    Defenses of... I, 6, 16, 735
    Examination and survey of Ohio Reef (Ledge)............ I, 175; II, 1154, 1156
    Improvement of.. I, 167; II, 1129
Narraguagus River, Me., improvement of............................. I, 121; II, 989
Nashville, Tenn.:
    Improvement of Cumberland River above...................... I, 462; III, 2411
    Improvement of Cumberland River below...................... I, 461; III, 2407
Natalbany River, La. (*see* Tickfaw)................................ I, 380; III, 1873
Natchez Harbor, Miss. (*see* Mississippi River Commission).......... I, 657; 8., 3, 32
Nauset Harbor, Mass., removal of wreck............................. I, 159; II, 1091
Navesink River, N. J. (*see* Shrewsbury)............................ I, 221; II, 1243
Navigable waters. *See* Bridges, Rivers and harbors, *and* Wrecks.
Navy Department, bridge of, between Portsmouth Navy-Yard, N. H., and Kittery, Me.. I, 664
Neches River, Tex., improvement of mouth......................... I, 396; III, 1907
Negro Cut, Indian River Inlet, Fla., improvement of................ I, 339; II, 1742
Neuse River, N. C.:
    Improvement of.. I, 302; II, 1492
    Improvement of waterway between Newbern and Beaufort....... I, 303; II, 1493
Neville Island, Ohio River, Pa., bridge across back channel at...... I, 661

Newark Bay, N. J.:
  Harbor lines .... I, 118; II, 1276
  Improvement of Staten Island-New Jersey channel .... I, 215; II, 1233
  Removal of wreck near Corner Stake light .... I, 223; II, 1247
Newark Plank Road Company, bridge of .... I, 666
New Bedford Harbor, Mass.:
  Bridge across Acushnet River to Fish Island .... I, 665
  Defenses of .... I, 6, 16, 735
  Improvement of .... I, 163; II, 1119
Newbern, N. C.:
  Examination and survey of Trent River at and above .... I, 310; II, 1545, 1550
  Improvement of Neuse River .... I, 302; II, 1492
  Improvement of Trent River .... I, 302; II, 1490
  Improvement of waterway to Beaufort, N. C .... I, 303; II, 1493
Newburyport Harbor, Mass., improvement of .... I, 138; II, 1043
Newfields, N. H., bridge of town of .... I, 668
New Haven Harbor, Conn.:
  Construction of breakwaters .... I, 183; II, 1173
  Improvement of, by dredging .... I, 182; II, 1170
New Jersey, bridge across Hudson River between Fifty-ninth and Sixtieth
  streets, New York City, and .... I, 659
New Jersey-Staten Island channel:
  Harbor lines in Arthur Kill .... I, 118; II, 1279
  Improvement of .... I, 215; II, 1233
  Removal of wreck near Corner Stake light .... I, 223; II, 1247
New London Harbor, Conn:
  Defenses of .... I, 17, 747
  Improvement of (*see* Thames River) .... I, 178; II, 1163
Newmarket, N. H., bridge across Exeter River .... I, 668
New Meadows River, Me., bridge across .... I, 669
New Orleans and Northwestern Railway Company, bridge of .... I, 660
New Orleans Harbor, La.:
  Defenses of .... I, 6, 30, 842
  Improvement of (*see* Mississippi River Commission) .... I, 657; S., 3, 32
Newport Harbor, R. I.:
  Defenses of .... I, 16, 735
  Improvement of .... I, 170; II, 1136
Newport River, N. C.:
  Improvement of Beaufort Harbor .... I, 304; II, 1495
  Improvement of waterway between Beaufort and New River .... I, 304; II, 1496
  Improvement of waterway between Newbern and Beaufort .... I, 303; II, 1493
New River, N. C.:
  Improvement of .... I, 305; II, 1497
  Improvement of waterway to Beaufort, N. C .... I, 304; II, 1496
New Shoreham, Block Island, R. I.:
  Construction of harbor of refuge .... I, 172; II, 1141
  Improvement of Great Salt Pond .... I, 174; II, 1144
Newtown Creek, N. Y.:
  Bridge between Vernon and Manhattan avenues, New York City ... I, 667
  Improvement of .... I, 207; II, 1216
New Whatcom, Wash., bridge across Whatcom Creek Waterway at .... I, 663
New York and New Jersey Bridge Company, bridge of .... I, 659
New York Connecting Railroad Company:
  Bridge of, across East River at Hell Gate, near Astoria .... I, 664
  Bridge of, across Little Hell Gate and Bronx Kills .... I, 665
New York Harbor, N. Y.:
  Ambrose Channel, improvement of .... I, 224; II, 1285
  Arthur Kill, harbor lines .... I, 118; II, 1279
  Arthur Kill, improvement of (*see* Staten Island-New Jersey channel) .... I, 215; II, 1233
  Astoria, bridge across East River at Hell Gate, near .... I, 664
  Bay Ridge Channel, improvement of .... I, 226; II, 1291
  Bayside Channel, improvement of .... I, 224; II, 1285
  Blackwells Island, bridge across East River at .... I, 665
  Bronx Kills, bridge across .... I, 665
  Bronx River, bridge at Westchester avenue .... I, 664
  Bronx River, harbor lines .... I, 118; II, 1266

INDEX. 33

New York Harbor, N. Y.—Continued.
Bronx River, improvement of .... I, 201; II, 1203
Buttermilk Channel, examination and survey............... I, 229; II, 1299, 1303
Buttermilk Channel, improvement of........................... I, 226; II, 1291
Buttermilk Channel, removal of wreck......................... I, 229; II, 1299
College Point, East River, harbor lines .... I, 119; II, 1305
Communipaw Channel, removal of wreck in................... I, 223; II, 1247
Corner Stake light, Newark Bay, removal of wreck near........ I, 223; II, 1247
Defenses of .... I, 6, 19, 757, 917
East (Ambrose) Channel, improvement of .... I, 224; II, 1285
East River, bridge at Blackwells Island, from 60th street to Long Island
  City... I, 665
East River, bridge at Hell Gate, near Astoria .... I, 664
East River, bridge at Little Hell Gate and Bronx Kills.......... I, 665
East River, harbor lines at College Point...................... I, 119; II, 1305
East River, improvement of..................................... I, 205; II, 1211
East River, improvement of Wallabout Channel................ I, 208; II, 1218
East River, removal of wreck off Greenpoint.................... I, 223; II, 248
Ellis Island, removal of wrecks near............................. I, 223; II, 1248
Flushing Bay, improvement of................................... I, 204; II, 1210
Fort Totten, post of .... I, 38, 927
Gedney Channel, improvement of.............................. I, 224; II, 1285
Governors Island, enlargement of .... I, 228; II, 1298
Gowanus Bay and Canal, improvement of...................... I, 226; II, 1291
Gowanus Creek Channel, improvement of .... I, 227; II, 1296
Greenpoint, N. Y., removal of wreck off .... I, 223; II, 1248
Guttenberg, N. J., harbor lines.................................. I, 118; II, 1273
Harlem River, bridge between 145th and 149th streets.......... I, 663
Harlem River, improvement of.................................. I, 206; II, 1214
Hell Gate, East River, bridge at, near Astoria .... I, 664
Hell Gate, East River, improvement of .... I, 205; II, 1211
Hudson River, bridge across, between 59th and 60th streets..... I, 659
Hudson River, harbor lines at Guttenberg, N. J................. I, 118; II, 1273
Improvement of.. I, 224; II, 1285
Kill van Kull (see Staten Island-New Jersey channel) .... I, 215; II, 1233
Lemon Creek (see Staten Island-New Jersey channel) .... I, 215; II, 1233
Little Hell Gate, bridge across .... I, 665
Long Island City, bridge across East River to 60th street........ I, 665
Main Ship Channel, improvement of............................ I, 224; II, 1285
Narrows to the sea, improvement from.......................... I, 224; II, 1285
Newark Bay, improvement of Staten Island-New Jersey channel I, 215; II, 1233
Newark Bay, removal of wreck near Corner Stake light......... I, 223; II, 1247
New Jersey-Staten Island channel, harbor lines in Arthur Kill... I, 118; II, 1279
New Jersey-Staten Island channel, improvement of .... I, 215; II, 1233
New Jersey-Staten Island channel, removal of wreck............ I, 223; II, 1247
Newtown Creek, bridge across................................... I, 667
Newtown Creek, improvement of................................ I, 207; II, 1216
Red Hook Channel, improvement of .... I, 226; II, 1291
Sandy Hook, N. J., removal of wreck at......................... I, 229; II, 1299
Spuyten Duyvil Creek (see Harlem River) .... I, 206; II, 1214
Staten Island-New Jersey channel, harbor lines in Arthur Kill... I, 118; II, 1279
Staten Island-New Jersey channel, improvement of............. I, 215; II, 1233
Staten Island-New Jersey channel, removal of wreck .... I, 223; II, 1247
Staten Island Sound (Arthur Kill), harbor lines .... I, 118; II, 1279
Staten Island Sound (Arthur Kill), improvement of (see Staten Island-
  New Jersey channel) .... I, 215; II, 1233
Supervision of... I, 656; V, 3607
Totten, Fort, post of... I, 38, 927
Wallabout Channel, improvement of............................ I, 208; II, 1218
Willets Point... I, 38, 41, 42, 927
Niagara River, N. Y.:
Buffalo Harbor, improvement of................................ I, 587; IV, 3305
Erie Basin and Black Rock Harbor, examination and survey of Lake
  Erie entrance... I, 592; IV, 3342, 3345
Erie Basin and Black Rock Harbor, harbor lines................ I, 119; IV, 3349
Erie Basin and Black Rock Harbor, improvement of Buffalo
  entrance..I, 589; IV, 3324

ENG 1901——3

Niagara River, N. Y.—Continued.
    North Tonawanda to Lake Erie, including Tonawanda Harbor, improvement from.. I, 590; IV, 3335
    Surveys (*see* Northern and Northwestern Lakes)................. I, 677; V, 3761
    Tonawanda to Port Day, improvement from...................... I, 591; IV, 3340
Nicollet Island, Mississippi River, Minn., bridges at...................... I, 667
Niles Ferry, Little Tennessee River, Tenn., bridge near.................... I, 668
Nisbet, W. F. (steamboat), removal of wreck of...................... I, 473; IV, 2646
Nomini Creek, Va., improvement of................................. I, 279; II, 1409
Nooksak River, Wash. (*see* Puget Sound) .... I, 645; V, 3581
Norfolk Harbor, Va.:
    Defenses of Hampton Roads....................................... I, 6, 23, 802
    Examination and plan and estimate for improvement at Pinner Point... I, 299; II, 1463, 1466
    Improvement of, and its approaches............................... I, 292; II, 1447
    Improvement of waterway to Albemarle Sound, via Currituck Sound... I, 297; II, 1457
    Improvement of waterway to sounds of North Carolina, via Pasquotank River.. I, 296; II, 1455
    Improvement of Western Branch, Elizabeth River............... I, 293; II, 1449
Norris, I. W. (schooner), removal of wreck of........................ I, 263; II, 1352
North Branch, Chicago River, Ill.:
    Bridge across, at Clybourn place, Chicago........................... I, 663
    Bridge across canal at Division street, Chicago, construction of........ I, 666
    Bridge across canal at Division street, Chicago, reconstruction of...... I, 662
    Bridge across canal at Goose Island, Cherry street, Chicago........... I, 665
    Improvement of... I, 529; IV, 2992
North Carolina, defenses of coast of............................ I, 6, 24, 812, 921
North Carolina Cut, N. C., improvement of waterway via............. I, 297; II, 1457
Northeast Branch, Cape Fear River, N. C., improvement of.......... I, 306; II, 1500
Northern and Northwestern Lakes:
    Commercial statistics, Sault Ste. Marie canals, Mich............. I, 565; IV, 3173
    Defenses of... I, 32, 854
    Engineering methods used at harbors on Lake Erie west of Erie, Pa.... IV, 3213
    Improvement of channels in waters connecting.................. I, 563; IV, 3157
    Notes on rock found in vicinity of Duluth, Minn .... IV, 2883
    Surveys and charts.. I, 677, 681; V, 3761
    Water levels .... I, 681; V, 3776
    Waterways to Atlantic Ocean, disbursements for examinations and surveys... I, 118
North Fork, Skagit River, Wash. (*see* Puget Sound) .... I, 645; V, 3581
North Hero Island, Lake Champlain, Vt., improvement of channel between South Hero Island and................................. I, 146
North Landing River, Va. and N. C., improvement of waterway via.. I, 297; II, 1457
North Point Creek, Patapsco River, Md., removal of wreck........... I, 272; II, 1390
North (Tolomato) River, Fla. (*see* St. Augustine Harbor).......... I, 338; II, 1741
North River, N. Y. *See* Hudson River *and* New York Harbor.
North River, N. C., improvement of waterway via.................. I, 297; II, 1457
North River, Wash. (*see* Willapa River)........................... I, 641; V, 3577
North Tonawanda, N. Y. (*see* Tonawanda).......................... I, 590; IV, 3335
Norwalk Harbor, Conn., improvement of........................... I, 191; II, 1181
Norwich Harbor, Conn. (*see* Thames River)........................ I, 178; II, 1163
Noxubee River, Miss., improvement of.............................. I, 370; III, 1840

O.

Oak Creek, Wis. (*see* South Milwaukee Harbor) .... I, 523; IV, 2942
Oakland Harbor, Cal.:
    Defenses of San Francisco....................................... I, 6, 33, 860
    Examination and survey .... I, 613; IV, 3434, 3445
    Improvement of .... I, 605; IV, 3413
Obion River, Tenn.:
    Bridge near Lanes Ferry... I, 667
    Improvement of .... I, 458; III, 2403
Occoquan Creek, Va., improvement of............................ I, 278; II, 1407
Ocmulgee River, Ga., improvement of............................. I, 330; II, 1646
Oconee River, Ga., improvement of............................... I, 329; II, 1644

INDEX. 85

Oconto Harbor, Wis., improvement of.................................. 1, 516; IV, 2910
Ocracoke Inlet, N. C.:
    Examination and survey of waterway from South Mills to and including .... 1, 299, 309; II, 1511
    Improvement of.. 1, 299; II, 1484
Odessa Landing, Appoquinimink River, Del., removal of wreck...... 1, 263; II, 1352
Office of the Chief of Engineers, officers on duty in 1, 688
Ogdensburg Harbor, N. Y., improvement of .... 1, 598; IV, 3374
Ohio Reef (Ledge), Narragansett Bay, R. I., examination and survey.. 1, 175; II, 1154, 1156
Ohio River:
    Allegheny City, Pa., harbor lines................................ 1, 119; IV, 2709
    Bridge at Bellaire, Ohio, and Benwood, W. Va..................... 1, 660
    Bridge at Ironton, Ohio, and Ashland, Ky......................... 1, 660
    Bridge at Neville Island, Pa., across back channel 1, 661
    Bridge at Parkersburg, W. Va..................................... 1, 664
    Bridge of Ohio River Bridge and Ferry Company between Williamstown, W. Va., and Marietta, Ohio.............................. 1, 660
    Bridge of Williamstown and Marietta Bridge and Transportation Company between Williamstown, W. Va., and Marietta, Ohio........... 1, 661
    Davis Island dam, Pa., operating and care .... 1, 473; IV, 2657
    Falls at Louisville, Ky., improvement of........................ 1, 496; IV, 2783
    Gauging (see Mississippi River).................... 1, 425; III, 2072; S., 8, 45, 126
    Improvement by open-channel work............................. 1, 470; IV, 2597
    Indiana Chute, Louisville, Ky., improvement of................. 1, 496; IV, 2783
    Louisville and Portland Canal, enlargement of .... 1, 496; IV, 2783
    Louisville and Portland Canal, operating and care............... 1, 499; IV, 2791
    Louisville and Portland Canal, removal of wreck................ 1, 505; IV, 2816
    Marietta, Ohio, to the Big Miami, survey from................. 1, 472; IV, 2608
    Maysville, Ky., examination and survey for harbor of refuge (ice harbor) at .... 1, 477; IV, 2670, 2675
    Movable dams, construction of................................. 1, 474; IV, 2661
    Pittsburg Harbor, harbor lines at Allegheny City................ 1, 119; IV, 2709
    Pittsburg Harbor, improvement of .... 1, 480; IV, 2697
    Sand Island, Ky., examination relative to purchase of .... 1, 505; IV, 2817
    Snag boat, operation of....................................... 1, 473; IV, 2646
    Wreck in Louisville and Portland Canal, removal of............ 1, 505; IV, 2816
    Wrecks, removal of certain .... 1, 473; IV, 2646
Ohio River Bridge and Ferry Company, bridge of 1, 660
Oil City, Pa., bridge across Allegheny River between Franklin and........ 1, 663
Oil City, Rouseville and Franklin Railroad Company, bridge of 1, 663
Oil City Station Railway Company, bridge of.......................... 1, 663
Okanogan River, Wash., improvement of .... 1, 652; V, 3590
Okaw (Kaskaskia) River, Ill., bridge across............................ 1, 667
Okechobee Lake, Fla., examination and survey of waterway via........... 1, 350
Oklawaha River, Fla., improvement of .... 1, 338; II, 1740
Old Orchard Shoal light, Raritan Bay, N. J., removal of wreck near . 1, 223; II, 1247
Old Plantation light-house, Chesapeake Bay, Va., removal of wreck near .... 1, 298; II, 1462
Old Tampa Bay, Fla. (see Tampa Bay) .... 1, 345; III, 1756
Olympia Harbor, Wash., improvement of .... 1, 645; V, 3582
Ontario Lake:
    See also Northern and Northwestern Lakes.
    Water levels... 1, 681; V, 3776
Ontonagon Harbor, Mich., improvement of......................... 1, 510; IV, 2865
Orange Mills Flats, St. Johns River, Fla., improvement at .... 1, 336; II, 1737
Ordnance. See Fortifications.
Osage River, Mo.:
    Estimate of cost of completing Lock and Dam No. 1, at Brenneckes Shoals .... 1, 452; III, 2369
    Improvement by Missouri River Commission................. 1, 658; S., 365, 382
Oswegatchie River, N. Y. (see Ogdensburg Harbor) .... 1, 598; IV, 3374
Oswego Harbor, N. Y.:
    Improvement of.. 1, 595; IV, 3365
    Water levels... 1, 681; V, 3776
Otter Creek, Vt., improvement of .... 1, 148; II, 1054
Otter Tail Lake and River, Minn., survey for reservoir dam .... 1, 450; III, 2341

Ouachita River, Ark. and La.:
  Examination of Camden Harbor, Ark .... I, 425; III, 2090
  Improvement of .... I, 415; III, 2034

P.

Pagan River, Va., examination and survey .... I, 299; II, 1474, 1477
Palmbeach, Fla., bridge across Lake Worth .... I, 667
Pamlico River, N. C.:
  Harbor lines at Washington .... I, 119; II, 1570
  Improvement of .... I, 301; II, 1487
Pamlico Sound, N. C.:
  Examination and survey of waterway via .... I, 299, 309; II, 1511
  Improvement of waterway to Norfolk, Va .... I, 296; II, 1455
Pamunkey River, Va., improvement of .... I, 288; II, 1421
Parkersburg, W. Va., bridge across Ohio River at .... I, 664
Parks, public, District of Columbia .... I, 675; V, 3689
Pascagoula River, Miss.:
  Improvement above mouth of Dog River .... I, 371; III, 1840
  Improvement below mouth of Dog River .... I, 371; III, 1842
Pasquotank River, N. C.:
  Examination and survey of waterway via .... I, 299, 309; II, 1511
  Improvement of waterway via .... I, 296; II, 1455
Passaic River, N. J.:
  Bridge across .... I, 666
  Improvement of .... I, 214; II, 1231
Pass a Loutre, Mississippi River, La.:
  Closing crevasse in .... I, 382; III, 1877
  Constructing sill across .... I, 383; III, 1878
Patapsco River, Md.:
  Defenses of Baltimore .... I, 6, 22, 784
  Estimate of cost of deepening and widening channel of Curtis Bay, and of
    main ship channel of Baltimore Harbor and .... I, 273; II, 1394
  Improvement of, and channel to Baltimore .... I, 264; II, 1374
  Improvement of channel to Curtis Bay .... I, 265; II, 1379
  Improvement of harbor at southwest Baltimore (Spring Garden) I, 266; II, 1379
  Removal of wreck in Fort McHenry Channel .... I, 272; II, 1391
  Removal of wreck in North Point Creek .... I, 272; II, 1390
Patchogue River, N. Y.:
  Examination and survey .... I, 223; II, 1249, 1255
  Improvement of .... I, 210; II, 1220
Pawcatuck River, R. I. and Conn., improvement of .... I, 175; II, 1159
Pawpaw River, Mich.:
  Bridges (5) obstructing, near Benton Harbor .... I, 668
  Improvement of (see St. Joseph Harbor) .... I, 537; IV, 3079
Pawtucket Harbor and River, R. I.:
  Examination of .... I, 175; II, 1152
  Improvement of .... I, 166; II, 1127
Peace Creek, Fla., improvement of .... I, 343; III, 1752
Pearl Harbor, Hawaiian Islands:
  Defenses of .... I, 6
  Improvement of .... I, 612; IV, 3433
Pearl River, Miss.:
  Carthage to Jackson, improvement from .... I, 376; III, 1850
  Edinburg to Carthage, improvement from .... I, 377; III, 1851
  Mouth, improvement of .... I, 375; III, 1848
  Rockport, improvement below .... I, 375; III, 1849
Pedee rivers, S. C.:
  Examination and survey of Great Pedee between Cheraw and the Wilmington, Columbia and Augusta Railroad bridge .... I, 324; II, 1607, 1614
  Improvement of Great Pedee .... I, 312; II, 1578
  Improvement of Little Pedee .... I, 311; II, 1576
Peekskill Harbor, N. Y., improvement of .... I, 213; II, 1230
Pender County, N. C., bridge of .... I, 661
Pend Oreille River, Wash., improvement of .... I, 653; V, 3591
Pennsylvania Railroad Company, bridge of .... I, 661

INDEX. 87

Penobscot River, Me.:
   Defenses of.. I, 6, 14, 697, 911
   Harbor lines at Bangor.. I, 118; II, 1022
   Improvement of... I, 126; II, 997
Pensacola Harbor, Fla.:
   Defenses of.. I, 6, 27, 832
   Harbor lines... I, 119; III, 1806
   Improvement of... I, 358; III, 1781
Pentwater Habor, Mich., improvement of............................ I, 547; IV, 3110
Pequonnock River, Conn. (*see* Bridgeport Harbor).................. I, 186; II, 1177
Pere Marquette Lake, Mich. (*see* Ludington Harbor)................ I, 548; IV, 3112
Pere Marquette Railroad Company, bridges of....................... I, 668
Petaluma Creek, Cal., improvement of............................... I, 610; IV, 3429
Petersburg, Va.:
   Examination and survey for deflection of Appomattox River
     at... I, 299; II, 1467, 1471
   Improvement of Appomattox River at.......................... I, 294; II, 1452
Petoskey Harbor, Mich., improvement of............................. I, 553; IV, 3129
Philadelphia, Pa.:
   Bridge across Schuylkill River at Grays Ferry................. I, 665
   Defenses of Delaware River................................... I, 6, 21, 37, 770
   Improvement of Delaware River at............................ I, 230; II, 1310
   Improvement of Schuylkill River at........................... I, 233; II, 1319
   Removal of wrecks in Schuylkill River................ I, 262, 263; II, 1350, 1352
Philadelphia and Chester Railway Company, bridges of............... I, 663
Philadelphia, Wilmington and Baltimore Railroad Company:
   Bridge of, across Broad Creek River, Del...................... I, 666
   Bridge of, across Schuylkill River, Pa........................ I, 665
Philippines:
   Operations of Engineer Department in the..................... I, 43, 975
   Report upon work of department of city public works and water supply,
     Manila.. I, 683, 684
Phillips, W. K. (steamer), removal of wreck of.................... I, 463; III, 2417
Pierre, S. Dak., improvement of Missouri River at........ I, 452, 454; III, 2373, 2374
Pierre, Fort, S. Dak., improvement of Missouri River at... I, 452, 454; III, 2373, 2374
Pigeon Bayous, La., improvement of................................ I, 387; III, 1890
Pike, Albert, statue of... I, 676; V, 3689
Pike Creek, Wis.:
   Bridge at Kenosha.. I, 667
   Improvement of Kenosha Harbor................................ I, 524; IV, 2945
Pinebluff, Ark. *See* Arkansas River.
Pine Lake and River (Charlevoix County), Mich.:
   Bridge across river at Charlevoix............................ I, 665
   Bridge across South Arm of lake.............................. I, 666
   Improvement of (*see* Charlevoix Harbor)..................... I, 552; IV, 3126
Pine River (St. Clair County), Mich., improvement of.............. I, 560; IV, 3150
Pine River, Minn.:
   Construction of reservoir dam................................ I, 444; III, 2309
   Operating and care of reservoir dam.......................... I, 445; III, 2322
   Survey of flowage lines of reservoir......................... I, 451
Pineville, La., bridge across Red River between Alexandria and..... I, 659
Pinner Point, Norfolk Harbor, Va.:
   Examination and plan and estimate for improvement at.... I, 299; II, 1463, 1466
   Improvement at... I, 292; II, 1447
Piscataqua River, Me. and N. H.:
   Bridge between Portsmouth Navy-Yard, N. H., and Kittery, Me..... I, 664
   Defenses of Portsmouth, N. H................................. I, 6, 15, 713
   Examination and survey of Hendersons Point, Portsmouth Harbor
     .... I, 149; II, 1057, 1062
Pittsburgh and Lake Erie Railroad Company, bridge of............... I, 661
Pittsburg Harbor, Pa.:
   Bridge across Allegheny River to Allegheny (Fort Wayne Bridge)..... I, 662
   Bridge across Monongahela River at South Tenth street........ I, 662
   Construction of Herr Island lock and dam, Allegheny River.... I, 482; IV, 2701
   Harbor lines at Allegheny City............................... I, 119; IV, 2709
   Improvement of.. I, 480; IV, 2697
   Operating and care of Davis Island dam, Ohio River........... I, 473; IV, 2657

Pittsburgh, Cincinnati, Chicago and St. Louis Railway Company, bridge of.	I, 663
Pittsburgh, Fort Wayne and Chicago Railway, bridge of	I, 662
Plaquemine Bayou, La.:	
Bridge across	I, 668
Improvement of	I, 387; III, 1890
Removal of water hyacinths	I, 395; III, 1906
Pleasant Valley Landing, Hudson River, N. J., harbor lines from Bloomers to	I, 118; II, 1270
Plymouth Harbor, Mass., improvement of	I, 157; II, 1087
Pneumatic dynamite batteries	I, 10
Pocomoke River, Md., improvement of	I, 271; II, 1388
Poinsett Lake, S. Dak. (see Sioux River)	I, 458; III, 2395
Point Judith Harbor and Pond, R. I.:	
Construction of harbor of refuge	I, 171; II, 1138
Improvement of pond entrance	I, 172; II, 1140
Pokegama Falls, Mississippi River, Minn.:	
Construction of reservoir dam	I, 444; III, 2309
Operating and care of reservoir dam	I, 445; III, 2322
Survey of flowage lines of reservoir	I, 451
Pollock Rip light-ship, Mass., removal of wrecks near	I, 174; II, 1147
Pollocksville, N. C., examination and survey of Trent River above and below	I, 310; II, 1545, 1550
Ponchatoula River, La. (see Tickfaw)	I, 380; III, 1873
Ponsett (Poinsett) Lake, S. Dak. (see Sioux River)	I, 458; III, 2395
Porcupine Island, Bar Harbor, Me., construction of breakwater	I, 122; II, 991
Portage Lake and River, Houghton County, Mich.:	
Bridge between Houghton and Hancock	I, 664
Waterway via	I, 511, 512; IV, 2867
Portage Lake, Manistee County, Mich., improvement of harbor of refuge	I, 550; IV, 3119
Portage River, Ohio (see Port Clinton Harbor)	I, 573; IV, 3227
Port Chester Harbor, N. Y.:	
Harbor lines	I, 118; II, 1261
Improvement of	I, 198; II, 1198
Removal of wreck off	I, 223; II, 1246
Port Clinton Harbor, Ohio, improvement of	I, 573; IV, 3227
Port Day, N. Y. (see Niagara River)	I, 591; IV, 3340
Port Harford, Cal. (see San Luis Obispo)	I, 602; IV, 3401
Port Huron, Mich., improvement of Black River at	I, 559; IV, 3148
Port Jefferson Harbor, N. Y., improvement of	I, 202; II, 1206
Portland, Ky.:	
Enlargement of Louisville and Portland Canal	I, 496; IV, 2783
Operating and care of Louisville and Portland Canal	I, 499; IV, 2791
Removal of wreck in Louisville and Portland Canal	I, 505; IV, 2816
Portland, Me.:	
Bridge of Boston and Maine Railroad Company obstructing Fore River.	I, 668
Bridge (Tukeys) obstructing Back Cove	I, 668
Bridge (Vaughan) obstructing Fore River	I, 668
Defenses of	I, 6, 7, 14, 697, 698, 911
Examination and survey for removal of Witch Rock	I, 133; II, 1009, 1015
Harbor lines	I, 118; II, 1027
Improvement of harbor	I, 131; II, 1006
Portland, Oreg.:	
Improvement of Willamette River above	I, 631; V, 3550
Improvement of Willamette River below	I, 633; V, 3557
Porto Rico:	
Defenses of	I, 6, 36, 909
Reconnaissances and explorations in	I, 683, 684; V, 3799
Removal of wreck in San Juan Harbor	I, 657; V, 3635
Port Royal (Beaufort) River, S. C.:	
Defenses of Port Royal Sound	I, 6, 25, 816
Improvement of	I, 323; II, 1604
Improvement of waterway between Beaufort, S. C., and Savannah (see Savannah)	I, 324; II, 1628
Removal of sunken logs in waterway between Beaufort, S. C., and Charleston	I, 324; II, 1628
Port Royal Sound, S. C., defenses of	I, 6, 25, 816

INDEX. 39

Portsmouth Harbor, N. H.:
    Bridge between Kittery, Me., and the navy-yard........................ 1, 664
    Defenses of.. 1, 6, 15, 713
    Examination and survey of Hendersons Point............ 1, 149; II, 1057, 1062
Port Tampa, Fla. (*see* Tampa Bay).................................. 1, 345; III, 1756
Port Vue, Pa., bridge across Monongahela River between Jefferson and.... 1, 661
Port Washington Harbor, Wis., improvement of.................... 1, 521; IV, 2934
Position finders, range and.. 1, 10, 37
Post of Fort Totten, N. Y... 1, 38, 927
Potomac (dredge), removal of wreck of, in Delaware Breakwater Harbor, Del... 1, 263; II, 1351
Potomac (steamboat), removal of wreck of, in Ohio River............ 1, 473; IV, 2646
Potomac Park, Washington, D. C.. 1, 676; V, 3689
Potomac River:
    See also Washington, D. C.
    Aqueduct Bridge, Washington, D. C., repair of.................... 1, 669; V, 3637
    Defenses of Washington, D. C.................................. 1, 6, 23, 791
    Highway bridge at Washington, D. C., plans, etc., for................. 1, 119
    Improvement at Washington, D. C............................. 1, 273; II, 1399
    Improvement below Washington, D. C........................ 1, 276; II, 1405
    Long Bridge, at Washington, D. C., rebuilding of............... 1, 275; II, 1399
    Memorial Bridge, Washington, D. C............................ 1, 670; V, 3618
Powow River, Mass., improvement of............................... 1, 140; II, 1046
Preble, Fort, Portland Harbor, Me.:
    Defenses at.. 1, 6, 697, 911
    Tests of results of firing mortars at.................................... 1, 7
Preliminary examinations of rivers and harbors, estimate of appropriation
    for.. 1, 656
President Roads, Boston, Mass. *See* Boston.
Princeton, Wis., bridge across Fox River at............................... 1, 663
Princeton and Northwestern Railway Company, bridge of................. 1, 663
Printing Office, Government, Washington, D. C.:
    Construction of building for use of............................ 1, 685; V, 3801
    Telegraph line.. 1, 676; V, 3689
Providence Harbor and River, R. I.:
    Improvement of.. 1, 167; II, 1129
    Removal of Green Jacket Shoal............................... 1, 168; II, 1132
Provincetown Harbor, Mass., improvement of...................... 1, 157; II, 1089
Public buildings and grounds, District of Columbia................. 1, 675; V, 3689
Puget Sound, Wash.:
    Defenses of.. 1, 6, 35, 901
    Improvement of, and tributaries.............................. 1, 645; V, 3581
    Improvement of waterway to lakes Union and Washington..... 1, 646; V, 3583
Pultneyville Harbor, N. Y., improvement of....................... 1, 594; IV, 3359
Punta Gorda, Fla. (*see* Charlotte Harbor)......................... 1, 343; III, 1752
Purification of water supply of Washington, D. C................... 1, 674; V, 3680
Puyallup River, Wash.:
    Bridge at Tacoma... 1, 666
    Examination and survey of Tacoma Harbor............... 1, 655; V, 3593, 3595
    Improvement of (*see* Puget Sound)............................ 1, 645; V, 3581

Q.

Quantico Creek, Va., examination of............................. 1, 292; II, 1440
Queen Anne's Railroad Company, bridge of................................ 1, 665
Queenstown Harbor, Md., improvement of....................... 1, 266; II, 1380
Quinnipiac River, Conn. (*see* New Haven Harbor)................ 1, 182; II, 1170

R.

Racine Harbor, Wis., improvement of............................ 1, 523; IV, 2942
Railway, boat, Columbia River, Oreg. and Wash.................... 1, 625; V, 3491
Raisin River, Mich. (*see* Monroe Harbor)........................ 1, 571; IV, 3215
Ranald (steamship), removal of wreck of......................... 1, 263; II, 1353
Rancocas River, N. J.:
    Improvement of.. 1, 238; II, 1327
    Removal of wreck above Bridgeboro........................... 1, 262; II, 1351

INDEX.

Range and position finders	I, 10, 37
Ransom, B. P. (canal boat), removal of wreck of	I, 223; II, 1248
Rappahannock River, Va., improvement of	I, 282; II, 1411
Raritan Bay and River, N. J.:	
Improvement of bay	I, 218; II, 1238
Improvement of Keyport Harbor	I, 220; II, 1241
Improvement of river	I, 217; II, 1236
Improvement of Shoal Harbor	I, 220; II, 1242
Removal of wreck near Old Orchard Shoal light	I, 223; II, 1247
Reconnaissances and explorations, military	I, 683; V, 3799
Red Hook Channel, New York Harbor, N. Y., improvement of	I, 226; II, 1291
Red Lake, Minn.:	
Improvement of (*see* Red River of the North)	I, 447; III, 2335
Survey for reservoir dam	I, 450; III, 2340
Red Lake River, Minn.:	
Improvement of (*see* Red River of the North)	I, 447; III, 2335
Survey for reservoir dam at outlet of Red Lake	I, 450; III, 2340
Red River, La., Ark., Tex., and Ind. T.:	
Bridge between Alexandria and Pineville, La.	I, 659
Examination from Shreveport, La., to Denison, Tex	I, 425; III, 2073
Gauging (*see* Mississippi River)	I, 425; III, 2072; S., 8, 45, 126
Improvement of	I, 412; III, 2025
Rectification of mouth by Mississippi River Commission	I, 657; S., 3, 32
Red River of the North, Minn. and N. Dak.:	
Improvement of	I, 447; III, 2335
Survey of Otter Tail Lake and River for reservoir dam to improve navigation on	I, 450; III, 2341
Survey of Red Lake and Red Lake River for reservoir dam to improve navigation on	I, 450; III, 2340
Reelfoot levee district, Mississippi River (Hickman, Ky., to Slough Landing, Tenn.), examination and survey	I, 434; III, 2155, 2158
Rensselaer and Saratoga Railroad, bridge of	I, 669
Reservations, public, District of Columbia	I, 675; V, 3689
Reservoirs:	
Big Sioux River, S. Dak., examination for	I, 458; III, 2395
Big Stone Lake, Minn. and S. Dak., survey for	I, 450; III, 2342
Kampeska Lake, S. Dak., examination for (*see* Sioux River)	I, 4, 8; III, 2395
Long Prairie River, Minn., and its sources, examination for	I, 451; III, 2361
Mississippi River, headwaters of, construction of	I, 444; III, 2309
Mississippi River, headwaters of, operating and care	I, 445; III, 2322
Mississippi River, headwaters of, survey of flowage lines	I, 451
Otter Tail Lake and River, Minn., survey for	I, 450; III, 2341
Poinsett Lake, S. Dak., examination for (*see* Sioux River)	I, 458; III, 2395
Red Lake and Red Lake River, Minn., survey for	I, 450; III, 2340
Sioux River, S. Dak., examination for	I, 458; III, 2395
Traverse Lake, Minn. and S. Dak., survey for	I, 450; III, 2342
Washington Aqueduct, D. C	I, 671, 673, 674; V, 3651, 3666, 3680
Revetments, application of the road scraper and floating derrick to grading river banks to receive	III, 2225
Rhode Island, defenses of southeast coast of	I, 6, 16, 735
Riverdale, Ill., bridge across Little Calumet River at	I, 664
Rivers and harbors:	
See also Engineering methods.	
Appropriation for examinations, surveys, etc., for 1902-3, estimate of	I, 656
Appropriations for improvements for 1902-3, estimates of	I, 118
Appropriations for operations during the past year	I, 117
Bridges	I, 659, 661, 667
Expenditures during the past year	I, 118
Harbor lines, establishment of	I, 118
Status of works	I, 118
Riverton, N. J., removal of wrecks in Delaware River below	I, 262; II, 1351
Riverview, Fla., bridge across Alafia River at	I, 664
Roach, Wm. H. (schooner), removal of wreck of	I, 272; II, 1390
Roads:	
Fort Washakie, Wyo., to Buffalo Fork, Snake River	I, 686; V, 3823
Scrapers, application of, to grading river banks to receive revetments	III, 2225
Yellowstone National Park	I, 682; V, 3777

INDEX.   41

Roanoke River, N. C., improvement of................................ I, 298; II, 1461
Robinson, Laura (schooner), removal of wreck of..................... I, 174; II, 1147
Robinsons Hole, Vineyard Sound, Mass., removal of wreck near..... I, 174; II, 1147
Rock found in vicinity of Duluth, Minn., notes on......................... IV, 2883
Rockhaven, N. Dak., ice harbor in Missouri River at....... I, 452, 456; III, 2373, 2377
Rockland Harbor, Me., improvement of .... I, 128; II, 1000
Rockport, Mass., construction of harbor of refuge in Sandy Bay ..... I, 141; II, 1048
Rock River, Ill.:
    Construction of canal around..................................... I, 532; IV, 3014
    Examination for lock and dam at feeder........................... I, 534; IV, 3066
    Operating and care of canal around .... I, 442; III, 2291
Rod float, full depth, method of discharge measurement, illustration of the.. III, 2199
Romerly Marsh, Ga., improvement of waterway via .... I, 332; II, 1653
Rondout Harbor, N. Y., improvement of.............................. I, 213; II, 1228
Root River, Wis. (*see* Racine Harbor) .... I, 523; IV, 2942
Rouge River, Mich.:
    Bridge at Dix avenue... I, 664
    Improvement of... I, 562; IV, 3155
Rough River, Ky.:
    Improvement of... I, 504; IV, 2814
    Operating and care of lock and dam .... I, 504; IV, 2815
Round Lake, Mich. (*see* Charlevoix Harbor)........................... I, 552; IV, 3126
Rover (steamer), wreck of (*see* Yazoo River)........................... I, 420; III, 2048
Rumsey, Ky., Lock No. 2, Green River..................... I, 502, 503; IV, 2805, 2806

S.

Sabine Lake, Pass, and River, Tex.:
    Defenses of.. I, 6, 30, 842
    Effects of storm of September, 1900, at Sabine Pass.............. I, 402; III, 1919
    Examination and plan and estimate for improvement of pass. I, 401; III, 1915, 1918
    Improvement of mouth of river and of channel through lake.... I, 396; III, 1907
    Improvement of river .... I, 397; III, 1908
    Improvement of Sabine Pass Harbor .... I, 398; III, 1910
Saco River, Me., improvement of .... I, 133; II, 1036
Sacramento River, Cal.:
    Bridge at Tehama.. I, 666
    Improvement of, including report of Board .... I, 608; IV, 3420, 3423
    Improvement of, by California Débris Commission .... I, 656; V, 3625
Sag Bay, N. Y., bridge across inlet connecting Sag Harbor Cove and....... I, 662
Sag Harbor Cove, N. Y., bridge across inlet connecting Sag Bay and ...... I, 662
Saginaw River, Mich., improvement of .... I, 555; IV, 3139
St. Augustine Harbor, Fla.:
    Defenses of... I, 26, 825
    Improvement of... I, 338; II, 1741
St. Clair County, Mich., bridge across Belle River in .... I, 666
St. Clair River and St. Clair Flats Canal, Mich.:
    Examination and survey of canal........................... I, 571; IV, 3203, 3206
    Improvement of... I, 568; IV, 3188
    Improvement of channels in waters connecting Great Lakes..... I, 563; IV, 3157
    Operating and care of canal .... I, 568; IV, 3189
    Removal of wreck in the rapids .... I, 570; IV, 3198
    Surveys (*see* Northern and Northwestern Lakes)................. I, 677; III, 3761
St. Croix Lake and River, Wis. and Minn., improvement of .... I, 446; II, 2329
St. Croix River, Me., repair of piers below Calais........................... I, 120
St. Francis River, Ark., improvement of.............................. I, 432; III, 2126
St. George Sound, Fla. *See* Carrabelle Bar and Harbor.
St. Johns River, Fla.:
    Defenses of.. I, 6, 26, 825
    Improvement between Jacksonville and the ocean.............. I, 335; II, 1733
    Improvement between Jacksonville and Palatka, including Orange Mills
        Flats... I, 336; II, 1737
    Improvement of Volusia Bar .... I, 337; II, 1739
    Removal of water hyacinths...................................... I, 341; II, 1746
St. Jones River, Del., improvement of .... I, 256; II, 1843
St. Joseph Harbor, Mich.:
    Bridge across St. Joseph River .... I, 660
    Improvement of... I, 537; IV, 3079

St. Joseph Harbor, Mo.:
  Improvement by Missouri River Commission.................. I, 658; S., 365, 382
  Plan and estimate for rectification of Missouri River at .... I, 452; III, 2367
St. Joseph River, Mich.:
  Bridge at St. Joseph... I, 660
  Improvement of.. I, 538; IV, 3083
St. Lawrence Power Company's canal (see Grass and St. Lawrence rivers)..I, 599; IV, 3377, 3389
St. Lawrence River, N. Y.:
  Cape Vincent Harbor, improvement of .... I, 597; IV, 3370
  Examination and survey at Long Sault Island............... I, 599; IV, 3389, 3391
  Ogdensburg Harbor, improvement of.............................. I, 598; IV, 3374
  Ogdensburg to foot of Lake Ontario, removal of shoals........... I, 597; IV, 3373
  Surveys (see Northern and Northwestern Lakes) .... I, 677; V, 3761
St. Louis and Southern Illinois Railway Company, bridge of .... I, 667
St. Louis Bay and River, Minn. and Wis. (see Duluth Harbor)....... I, 507; IV, 2828
St. Louis Harbor, Mo.:
  Discharge measurements... III, 2199
  Improvement of... I, 438; III, 2198
St. Marys River and St. Marys Falls Canal, Mich.:
  Commercial statistics.. I, 565; IV, 3173
  Improvement of channels in waters connecting Great Lakes...... I, 563; IV, 3157
  Improvement of Hay Lake Channel.............................. I, 567; IV, 3185
  Improvement of river at the falls.................................. I, 564; IV, 3161
  Operating and care of canal... I, 565; IV, 3173
  Preliminary report on survey, including Hay Lake Channel .... I, 570; IV, 3200
  Surveys (see Northern and Northwestern Lakes) .... I, 677; V, 3761
St. Paul, Minn., gauging Mississippi River at .... I, 449; III, 2340
St. Peters (Minnesota) River, Minn.:
  Improvement of .... I, 447; III, 2334
  Survey of Big Stone and Traverse lakes for reservoir dams to improve navigation on.. I, 450; III, 2342
Sakonnet Habor, Point, and River, R. I.:
  Examination and survey of rocks in harbor .... I, 175; II, 1148, 1150
  Increasing width and depth of draw opening in Stone Bridge.... I, 165; II, 1124
  Rebuilding and extending breakwater at Sakonnet Point......... I, 166; II, 1126
Salmon Bay, Wash., improvement of waterway via.................... I, 646; IV, 3583
Salmon Creek, N. Y. (see Pultneyville Harbor) .... I, 594; IV, 3359
Salmon River, Conn., bridge below Leesville, East Haddam............... I, 662
Sampit River, S. C. (see Georgetown Harbor) .... I, 314; II, 1581
San Antonio Estuary, Cal. See Oakland Harbor.
Sand batteries, emergency... I, 8
Sandbeach, Mich.:
  Improvement of harbor of refuge................................. I, 557; IV, 3144
  Water levels... I, 681; V, 3776
San Diego Harbor, Cal.:
  Defenses of... I, 6, 33, 856, 922
  Improvement of .... I, 599; IV, 3395
Sand Island, Ohio River, Ky., examination relative to purchase of.... I, 505; IV, 2817
Sandusky Harbor, Ohio:
  Engineering methods used in improvement of..................... IV, 3213
  Examination and survey .... I, 585; IV, 3270, 3275
  Improvement of .... I, 574; IV, 3230
  Removal of wreck... I, 584; IV, 3269
Sandy Bay, Mass., construction of harbor of refuge................... I, 141; II, 1048
Sandy Hook, N. J., removal of wreck at .... I, 229; II, 1299
Sandy Lake, Minn.:
  Construction of reservoir dam .... I, 444; III, 2309
  Operating and care of reservoir dam............................. I, 445; III, 2322
San Francisco Bay and Harbor, Cal.:
  Defenses of... I, 6, 33, 860
  Examination and survey of Oakland Harbor............... I, 613; IV, 3434, 3445
  Harbor lines... I, 119; IV, 3460
  Improvement of Oakland Harbor .... I, 605; IV, 3413
  Removal of Arch and Shag rocks .... I, 604; IV, 3411
  Removal of wreck in bay... I, 613; IV, 3434
Sanitary District of Chicago, Ill.:
  See also Chicago Drainage Canal.
  Bridges of, across Chicago River.. I, 662

INDEX. 43

San Jacinto River, Tex.:
  Improvement of (*see* Galveston ship channel).................. I, 404; III, 1933
  Removal of wreck of tug *Kate* .... I, 411; III, 1959
San Joaquin County, Cal.:
  Bridge of, across Burns Cut-off, San Joaquin River................. I, 664
  Bridge of, across San Joaquin River at Brandts Ferry............... I, 661
  Bridge of, across San Joaquin River at Durhams Ferry............... I, 664
San Joaquin River, Cal.:
  Bridge at Brandts Ferry .... I, 661
  Bridge across Burns Cut-off .... I, 664
  Bridge at Durhams Ferry .... I, 664
  Bridge at Hills Ferry .... I, 666
  Examination above mouth of Stanislaus River for closure of certain
    sloughs... I, 613; IV, 3454
  Examination and survey from Antioch, through Suisun Bay, to Karquines
    Strait .... I, 613; IV, 3449, 3452
  Improvement of .... I, 606; IV, 3416
  Improvement of, by California Débris Commission .... I, 656; V, 3625
San Juan Harbor, Porto Rico:
  Defenses of.. I, 6, 36, 909
  Removal of wreck .... I, 657; V, 3635
San Leandro Bay, Cal. *See* Oakland Harbor.
San Luis Obispo Harbor, Cal., improvement of.................... I, 602; IV, 3401
San Pedro Bay and Harbor, Cal.:
  Construction of deep-water harbor............................. I, 600; IV, 3397
  Improvement of Wilmington inner harbor .... I, 601; IV, 3399
Santee River, S. C., improvement of............................. I, 316; II, 1587
Sarasota Bay, Fla., improvement of.............................. I, 344; III, 1753
Sitanella (barge), removal of wreck of .... I, 223; II, 1247
Saugatuck Harbor, Mich., improvement of Kalamazoo River
  at... I, 540, 541; IV, 3087, 3090
Saugatuck River, Conn., improvement of.......................... I, 189; II, 1180
Saugerties Harbor, N. Y., improvement of .... I, 211; II, 1227
Saugus River, Mass.:
  Examination and survey of Lynn Harbor .... I, 159; II, 1092, 1093
  Improvement of Lynn Harbor................................... I, 150; II, 1075
Sauk River, Wis. (*see* Port Washington Harbor)................. I, 521; IV, 2934
Sault Ste. Marie, Mich.:
  See also St. Marys River.
  Commerce passing canals at .... I, 565; IV, 3173
  Water levels... I, 681; V, 3776
Sausal Creek, Cal. *See* Oakland Harbor.
Savannah, Ga., engineer district, engineering methods used in the......... II, 1660
Savannah Harbor and River, Ga.:
  Defenses of.. I, 6, 26, 821
  Engineering methods used in improvement of......................... II, 1660
  Examination and plan and estimate for improvement of har-
    bor.. I, 334; II, 1719, 1723
  Harbor lines at Savannah..................................... I, 119; II, 1730
  Improvement of harbor.. I, 324; II, 1628
  Improvement of river above Augusta .... I, 327; II, 1636
  Improvement of river between Augusta and Savannah .... I, 326; II, 1634
  Improvement of waterway to Beaufort, S. C.................... I, 324; II, 1628
  Improvement of waterway to Fernandina, Fla................... I, 332; II, 1653
  Removal of wrecks .... I, 334; II, 1660
Sayville, N. Y., improvement of Browns Creek.................... I, 209; II, 1219
Schuylkill River, Pa.:
  Bridge at Grays Ferry, Philadelphia.................................. I, 665
  Improvement of... I, 233; II, 1319
  Removal of wrecks .... I, 262, 263; II, 1350, 1352
Scituate Harbor, Mass., improvement of .... I, 156; II, 1085
Scrapers, road, application of, to grading river banks to receive revetments.. III, 2225
Scuppernong River, N. C., examination and survey............. I, 309; II, 1541, 1543
Seabright, N. J.:
  Bridge across Shrewsbury River at .... I, 663
  Harbor lines in Shrewsbury River at .... I, 118; II, 1282
  Removal of wreck in Atlantic Ocean off .... I, 223; II, 1247
Seabrook Beach, Me., bridge across Hampton River .... I, 666
Seacoast defenses. *See* Fortifications.

Searchlights .... I, 13, 37
Seattle, Wash., waterway from Puget Sound to Lake Washington ..... I, 646; v, 3583
Seattle and International Railway Company, bridge of .... I, 667
Seattle and Montana Railroad Company, bridge of .... I, 663
Sea walls .... I, 11, 37
Sebewaing River, Mich., improvement of .... I, 557; IV, 3142
Secretary Creek (Warwick River), Md., improvement of .... I, 268; II, 1383
Seekonk (Pawtucket) River, R. I.:
 Examination of .... I, 175; II, 1152
 Improvement of .... I, 166; II, 1127
Selma, Ala., bridge across Alabama River at .... I, 665
Service of officers of the Corps of Engineers in the field, with troops, and as
 officers of U. S. volunteers, since April, 1898 .... I, 45
Severn River, Md., harbor lines at Annapolis .... I, 119; II, 1396
Sewells Bridge, across York River, Me .... I, 667
Shag Rocks, San Francisco Harbor, Cal., removal of .... I, 604; IV, 3411
Shaws Cove, New London, Conn. (see Thames River) .... I, 178; II, 1163
Sheboygan Harbor, Wis., improvement of .... I, 521; IV, 2931
Sherman, General, statue of .... I, 676; v, 3689
Shilshole Bay, Wash., improvement of waterway via .... I, 646; v, 3583
Ship Island Harbor and Pass, Miss.:
 Improvement of channel to Gulfport .... I, 374; III, 1846
 Improvement of pass .... I, 374; III, 1848
Ship John light, Delaware Bay, removal of wreck .... I, 263; II, 1350
Shoal Harbor, N. J., improvement of .... I, 220; II, 1242
Shoalwater Bay (Willapa Harbor), Wash., improvement of .... I, 641; v, 3577
Shovelful light-ship, Mass., removal of wreck near .... I, 174; II, 1147
Shreveport, La.:
 Examination of Red River to Denison, Tex .... I, 425; III, 2073
 Improvement of waterway to Jefferson, Tex. (see Cypress Bayou). I, 414; III, 2033
Shrewsbury River, N. J.:
 Bridge at Seabright .... I, 663
 Harbor lines at Seabright .... I, 118; II, 1282
 Improvement of .... I, 221; II, 1243
 Removal of wreck opposite Island Beach .... I, 223; II, 1247
Sinepuxent Bay, Md., improvement of waterway via .... I, 260; II, 1348
Siner, David (schooner), removal of wreck of .... I, 174; II, 1147
Sioux City, Iowa:
 Construction of ice harbor in Big Sioux River .... I, 456; III, 2373, 2377
 Examination of Big Sioux River for reservoir dam .... I, 458; III, 2395
 Improvement of Missouri River at and above .... I, 452, 455; III, 2373, 2376
 Monument to Sergt. Charles Floyd near .... I, 687; v, 3827
 Snagging Upper Missouri River .... I, 457; III, 2391
Sioux River, S. Dak.:
 Construction of ice harbor at Sioux City .... I, 456; III, 2373, 2377
 Examination for reservoir dam .... I, 458; III, 2395
Sites for fortifications .... I, 12, 37
Siuslaw River, Oreg., improvement of mouth .... I, 619; v, 3478
Six-mile Island, Allegheny River, Pa., construction of lock and dam. I, 482; IV, 2701
Skagit River, Wash. (see Puget Sound) .... I, 645; v, 3581
Skiddaway Narrows, Ga., examination of .... I, 335; II, 1728
Slack-water systems. *See* Canals *and* Waterways.
Smyrna River, Del.:
 Examination and survey .... I, 263; II, 1361, 1363
 Improvement of .... I, 252, II, 1340
 Removal of wreck .... I, 263; II, 1352
Snag boats:
 For works in Florida .... I, 342; II, 1749
 For works on Texas coast .... I, 408; III, 1950
Snake River, Idaho, Oreg., and Wash.:
 Examination and survey from head of navigation to mouth. I, 629; v, 3525, 3529
 Improvement up to Asotin, Wash .... I, 623; v, 3489
 Road from Buffalo Fork to Fort Washakie, Wyo .... I, 686; v, 3823
Snohomish River, Wash.:
 Improvement of Everett Harbor .... I, 648; v, 3587
 Improvement of (see Puget Sound) .... I, 645; v, 3581
Snoqualmie River, Wash. (see Puget Sound) .... I, 645; v, 3581
Soda Lakes, La. (see Cypress Bayou) .... I, 414; III, 2033

INDEX. 45

South Arm, Mich., bridge of town of.. 1,666
South Arm of Pine Lake, Mich., bridge across............................ 1,666
South Atlantic States, removal of water hyacinths from Florida waters. 1,341; II,1746
South Branch, Chicago River, Ill.:
  Bridge across West Fork at Mud Lake, Chicago........................ 1,663
  Improvement of....................................... 1,529; IV, 2992
  Waterway from Mississippi River to Lake Michigan, via, examination
    for, with plan and estimate (act of 1900)................ 1,534; IV, 3058
  Waterway from Mississippi River to Lake Michigan, via, survey for (act
    of 1899) .... 1,534; IV, 3048
South Carolina, defenses of coast of..................................... 1, 6, 25, 816
South Chicago, Ill. (*see* Calumet Harbor) .... 1,529; IV, 2995
Southern Branch Drawbridge Company, bridge of......................... 1,665
Southern Branch, Elizabeth River, Va.:
  Bridge across.. 1,665
  Improvement of Norfolk Harbor and its approaches 1,292; II,1447
  Improvement of waterway to Albemarle Sound, via Currituck
    Sound 1,297; II,1457
  Improvement of waterway to sounds of North Carolina, via Pasquo-
    tank River 1,296; II,1455
Southern Pacific Company, bridge of 1,666
Southern Railway Company:
  Bridge of 1,662
  Examination and plan and estimate for improvement of Norfolk Harbor
    at pier of... 1, 299; II, 1463, 1466
South Fork of South Branch, Chicago River, Ill., improvement of... 1,529; IV, 2992
South Haven Harbor, Mich., improvement of...................... 1,538; IV, 3084
South Hero Island, Lake Champlain, Vt., improvement of channel between
  North Hero Island and 1,146
South Mills, N. C.:
  Examination and survey of waterway to and including Ocracoke and
    Beaufort inlets .... 1, 299, 309; II, 1511
  Improvement of waterway via.................................. 1, 296; II, 1455
South Milwaukee Harbor, Wis., improvement of .... 1,523; IV, 2942
South Norwalk, Conn. (*see* Norwalk) .... 1,191; II, 1181
South Pass, Mississippi River, La.:
  Maintenance of channel by representatives of James B. Eads. 1, 118, 379; III, 1865
  Maintenance of channel by United States..................... 1, 385; III, 1881
Southport, N. C., harbor lines in Cape Fear River at.............. 1,119; II, 1572
South River, N. J., improvement of .... 1,217; II, 1237
Southwest Pass, Mississippi River, La., project for improvement of. 1, 383, 384; III, 1878
Springdale, Pa., construction of lock and dam in Allegheny River... 1,482; IV, 2701
Spring Garden, Baltimore, Md., improvement of harbor at........... 1,266; II, 1379
Springwells Township, Mich., bridge of, across Rouge River 1,664
Spuyten Duyvil Creek, N. Y. (*see* Harlem River) .... 1, 206; II, 1214
Squan (Manasquan) River, N. J., improvement of................. 1, 222; II, 1245
Stage Harbor, Mass.:
  Improvement of Chatham Harbor .... 1,158; II, 1090
  Removal of wreck on Hardings Beach .... 1,174; II, 1147
Stamford Harbor, Conn., improvement of........................... 1,194; II, 1184
Stanislaus County, Cal., bridge of 1,666
Staten Island-New Jersey channel:
  Harbor lines in Arthur Kill....................................... 1, 118; II, 1279
  Improvement of .... 1, 215; II, 1233
  Removal of wreck near Corner Stake light .... 1, 223; II, 1247
Staten Island Sound (Arthur Kill), N. Y. and N. J.:
  Harbor lines .... 1, 118; II, 1279
  Improvement of Staten Island-New Jersey channel .... 1, 215; II, 1233
Statistics of commerce, Sault Ste. Marie canals, Mich .... 1, 565; IV, 3173
Statues, Washington, D. C .... 1, 676; V, 3689
Statutes of Fifty-sixth Congress, second session, affecting Corps of Engi-
  neers .... V, 3837
Steamboats. *See* Dredge, Snag, *and* Tug boats, *and* Wrecks.
Stilaguamish River, Wash.:
  Bridge near Arlington.. 1,667
  Improvement of (*see* Puget Sound)........................... 1, 645; V, 3581
Still Bluff, N. C., bridge across Black River at 1,661
Stillwater Harbor, Minn. (*see* St. Croix River)................. 1, 446; III, 2329

46   INDEX.

Stockbridge Landing, Lake Winnebago, Wis. (*see* Fox River)....... r 525; IV, 2953
Stone Bridge, Sakonnet River, R. I., increasing width and depth of draw
    opening... I, 165; II, 1124
Stonington, Conn., construction of harbor of refuge................. I, 177; II, 1161
Storm of September, 1900:
    Brazos River, Tex., damage to jetties .... I, 412; III, 2022
    Galveston, Tex., damage to fortifications........................ I, 32, 850
    Galveston, Tex., damage to jetties and main ship channel ...... I, 412; III, 2018
    Sabine Pass, Tex., damage at.................................. I, 402; III, 1919
Storm (steamboat), removal of wreck of............................. I, 473; IV, 2646
Stratham, N. H., bridge across Exeter River at...................... I, 668
Sturgeon Bay and Lake Michigan Canal, Wis.:
    Construction of harbor of refuge............................... I, 518; IV, 2922
    Examination and survey....................................... I, 527; IV, 2970, 2973
    Improvement of... I, 517; IV, 2914
    Operating and care... I, 518; IV, 2919
    Removal of wreck... I, 527; IV, 2970
Subaqueous bank protection, use of lumber mattress for.............. III, 2212
Submarine mines .... I, 5, 12, 38, 695
Success (sloop), removal of wreck of .... I, 223; II, 1247
Suffolk County, N. Y., bridge of.................................... I, 662
Suisun Bay, Cal., examination and survey of San Joaquin River from
    Antioch to Karquines Strait, through....................... I, 613; IV, 3449, 3452
Sullivan Falls Harbor, Me., improvement of......................... I, 123; II, 992
Sullivan Island shore, Charleston, S. C., improvement at............ I, 320; II, 1598
Sullivan River, Me., improvement of Sullivan Falls Harbor .... I, 123; II, 992
Sulphur River, Ark. and Tex.:
    Bridge across .... I, 660
    Improvement of (*see* Red River) .... I, 412; III, 2025
unken craft. *See* Wrecks.
Superior Bay and Harbor, Wis.:
    Improvement of .... I, 507; IV, 2828
    Notes on rock found in vicinity of Duluth, Minn .... IV, 2883
    Removal of wreck in Duluth Harbor .... I, 514; IV, 2883
Superior Lake:
    See also Northern and Northwestern Lakes.
    Commercial statistics, Sault Ste. Marie canals, Mich............. I, 565; IV, 3173
    Improvement and operating and care of waterway to Keweenaw
        Bay.. I, 511, 512; IV, 2867
    Notes on rock found in vicinity of Duluth, Minn .... IV, 2883
    Preliminary report on survey of waters connecting Lake Huron
        and .... I, 570; IV, 3200
    Water levels.. I, 681; V, 3776
Surveys:
    In military divisions and departments........................... I, 683; V, 3799
    Northern and Northwestern Lakes............................. I, 677, 681; V, 3761
    Of rivers and harbors, estimate of appropriation for............. I, 656
    Of waterways between Great Lakes and Atlantic Ocean, disbursements
        for .... I, 118
Susquehanna River, Md.:
    Examination and survey of rocks near entrance to Havre de Grace
        Harbor .... I, 273; II, 1392, 1393
    Improvement above and below Havre de Grace................. I, 264; II, 1374
Suwanee River, Fla., improvement of .... I, 349; III, 1762
Swinomish Slough, Wash., improvement of......................... I, 651; V, 3589
Synepuxent Bay, Md., improvement of waterway via................ I, 260; II, 1348

T.

Tacoma Harbor, Wash.:
    Bridge across Puyallup River..................................... I, 666
    Examination and survey .... I, 655; V, 3593, 3595
Tallahatchie River, Miss., improvement of .... I, 422; III, 2067
Tampa Bay and Harbor, Fla.:
    Defenses of... I, 6, 27, 829
    Harbor lines in Hillsboro River at Tampa .... I, 119; III, 1763
    Improvement of bay .... I, 345; III, 1756
    Improvement of Hillsboro Bay and River .... I, 347; III, 1758
Tangier Sound, Md., removal of wreck at Deals Island.............. I, 272; II, 1390

INDEX. 47

Tar River, N. C., improvement of.................................... I, 301; II, 1487
Taunton River, Mass.:
    Improvement of... I, 164; II, 1122
    Improvement of Fall River Harbor............................ I, 169; II, 1134
Tchefuncte River, La., improvement of .... I, 379; III, 1872
Teche Bayou, La.:
    Improvement of .... I, 391; III, 1899
    Removal of water hyacinths................................. I, 395; III, 1906
Technical methods. *See* Engineering methods.
Tehama, Cal., bridge across Sacramento River...................... I, 666
Telegraph line, Executive Departments, Washington, D. C.......... I, 676; V, 3689
Tennessee River:
    Chattanooga, Tenn., improvement above .... I, 464; III, 2419, 2421
    Chattanooga, Tenn., to Riverton, Ala., improvement.. I, 464,465; III, 2419, 2423
    Chattanooga, Tenn., to Riverton, Ala., survey from................. I, 470
    Decatur, Ala., bridge at... I, 662
    Gauging (*see* Mississippi River) .... I, 425; III, 2072; S., 8, 45, 126
    Muscle Shoals Canal, Ala., operating and care................. I, 466; III, 2440
    Riverton, Ala., improvement below................... I, 464, 466; III, 2419, 2428
Tensas River, La., improvement of................................ I, 419; III, 2046
Terraceia Cut-off, Fla. (*see* Manatee River) .... I, 345; III, 1755
Texas, dredge and snag boat for works on coast of................ I, 408; III, 1950
Texas City, Tex., deepening channel to Galveston .... I, 403; III, 1930
Thames River, Conn., improvement of.............................. I, 178; II, 1163
The Board of Engineers .... I, 5, 691
Thompson, Frank (barge), removal of wreck of .... I, 272; II, 1391
Thoroughfare, Inside, Atlantic City, N. J., bridge across................ I, 664
Three-mile Rapids, Columbia River, Oreg. and Wash., improvement at. I, 625; V, 3491
Thunder Bay River, Mich. (*see* Alpena Harbor) .... I, 555; IV, 3137
Tickfaw River, La., improvement of, including tributaries......... I, 380; III, 1873
Tillamook Bay and Bar, Oreg. improvement of .... I, 622; V, 3485
Tiverton, R. I., alteration of Stone Bridge across Sakonnet River .... I, 165; II, 1124
Toledo Harbor, Ohio:
    Bridges across Maumee River.. I, 667
    Engineering methods used in improvement of........................ IV, 3213
    Improvement of .... I, 572; IV, 3218
Tolomato River, Fla. (*see* St. Augustine Harbor).................. I, 338; II, 1741
Tombigbee River, Ala. and Miss.:
    Columbus to Fulton, Miss., improvement from .... I, 369; III, 1824, 1837
    Demopolis, Ala., below, improvement of................ I, 367; III, 1824, 1835
    Demopolis, Ala., to Columbus, Miss., improvement from .. I, 368; III, 1824, 1836
    Fulton to Walkers Bridge, Miss., improvement from ...... I, 370; III, 1824, 1839
    Mouth of Warrior River, just below, examination and survey for lock
      and dam .... I, 378; III, 1858, 1861
Tonawanda Harbor, N. Y., improvement of......................... I, 590; IV, 3335
Tongue Point, Columbia River, Oreg., improvement below .... I, 634; V, 3565
Tonnage, Sault Ste. Marie canals, Mich............................ I, 565; IV, 3173
Torpedoes... I, 5, 12, 38, 695
Totten, Fort, N. Y., post of..................................... I, 38, 927
Town Creek, Brunswick County, N. C., improvement of............ I, 308; II, 1509
Town River, Mass., improvement of................................ I, 154; II, 1083
Trail Creek, Ind. (*see* Michigan City Harbor)..................... I, 534; IV, 3074
Traverse Lake, Minn. and S. Dak., survey for reservoir dam....... I, 450; III, 2342
Trent River, N. C.:
    Examination and survey between Newbern and Trenton ... I, 310; II, 1545, 1550
    Improvement of... I, 302; II, 1490
Trenton, Mich. (*see* Detroit River).............................. I, 571; IV, 3208
Trenton, N. J., bridge across Delaware River at .... I, 661
Trenton, N. C., examination and survey of Trent River between Newbern
    and.. I, 310; II, 1545, 1550
Trinity River, Tex.:
    Examination from Dallas to Fort Worth...................... I, 411; III, 1970
    Improvement of (*see also* Brazos River)............... I, 405, 408; III, 1938, 1950
Troops:
    Engineer, distribution, duties, etc., of......................... I, 39, 41, 42, 943
    Engineer equipment of.. I, 87, 88, 943
    Service of engineer officers with, since April, 1898 .... I, 45

INDEX.

Troy, N. Y.:
Bridge across Hudson River at .... I, 669
Harbor lines in Hudson River at .... I, 118; II, 1268
Tugboats:
See also Wrecks.
For transfer to the artillery .... I, 38
Tug Fork, Big Sandy River, W. Va. and Ky.:
Final report on survey for locks and dams .... I, 496; IV, 2750
Improvement of .... I, 493; IV, 2742
Tukeys Bridge, Portland, Me., obstructing Back Cove .... I, 668
Tunnel, Washington Aqueduct, D. C., construction of .... I, 673; V, 3666
Turners Cut, N. C.:
Examination and survey of waterway from South Mills to and including Ocracoke and Beaufort inlets, via .... I, 299, 309; II, 1511
Improvement of waterway via .... I, 296; II, 1455
Turrets .... I, 7
Turtle River, Ga. (*see* Brunswick Harbor) .... I, 331; II, 1649
Twelve-mile Creek, N. Y. (*see* Wilson Harbor) .... I, 592; IV, 3353
Twin Rivers, Wis. (*see* Two Rivers Harbor) .... I, 520; IV, 2927
Two Harbors, Minn.:
Examination and survey of Burlington Bay .... I, 514; IV, 2889, 2897
Improvement of Agate Bay .... I, 506; IV, 2824
Two Rivers Harbor, Wis., improvement of .... I, 520; IV, 2927

U.

Union Bridge Company, bridge of .... I, 665
Union Lake, Wash., improvement of waterway via .... I, 646; V, 3583
Union (lighter), removal of wreck of .... I, 223; II, 1248
Union River, Me., improvement of .... I, 124; II, 993
United States Engineer School .... I, 38, 42, 937
United States Navy Department, bridge of, between Portsmouth Navy-Yard, N. H., and Kittery, Me .... I, 664
United States volunteers, service of officers of the Corps of Engineers as officers of, since April, 1898 .... I, 45
Urbana Creek, Va., improvement of .... I, 283; II, 1414

V.

Vanland Landing, Yazoo River, Miss., removal of wreck .... I, 420; III, 2048
Vaughan Bridge, Portland, Me., obstructing Fore River .... I, 668
Vermilion Bayou, La., improvement of channel, bay, and passes .... I, 391; III, 1900
Vermilion Harbor, Ohio, improvement of .... I, 577; IV, 3239
Vessels. *See* Dredge, Snag, *and* Tug boats, *and* Wrecks.
Vetra, Sarah E. (schooner), removal of wreck of .... I, 272; II, 1391
Vicksburg Harbor, Miss., improvement of .... I, 421; III, 2052
Vidalia Harbor, La. (*see* Mississippi River Commission) .... I, 657; S., 3, 32
Vinalhaven, Me., improvement of Carvers Harbor .... I, 129; II, 1003
Vineyard Haven, Mass., improvement of harbor at .... I, 162; II, 1115
Vineyard Sound, Mass., removal of wreck near Robinsons Hole ...... I, 174; II, 1147
Vining, J. P., et al., bridge of .... I, 666
Volunteers, U. S., service of officers of the Corps of Engineers as officers of, since April, 1898 .... I, 45
Volusia Bar, St. Johns River, Fla., improvement of .... I, 337; II, 1739

W.

Wabash River, Ind. and Ill.:
Improvement above Vincennes, Ind .... I, 499, 501; IV, 2801
Improvement below Vincennes, Ind .... I, 499, 500; IV, 2800
Operating and care of Grand Rapids lock and dam .... I, 501; IV, 2802
Waccamaw River, N. C. and S. C., improvement of .... I, 310; II, 1573
Wakefield, Va., wharf at Bridge Creek Landing, near .... I, 676; V, 3689
Walden Slough, San Joaquin River, Cal., examination for closure of . I, 613; IV, 3454
Wallabout Channel, N. Y., improvement of .... I, 208; II, 1218
Wappoo Cut, S. C., improvement of .... I, 322; II, 1603
Wareham Harbor, Mass., bridge across Weweanititt River .... I, 667
War maps .... I, 683, 685; V, 3799

INDEX. 49

Warrior River, Ala.:
    Examination and survey for Locks and Dams 1, 2, and 3, below Tuscaloosa... I, 378; III, 1858, 1861
    Improvement above Tuscaloosa.............................. I, 365; III, 1816
    Improvement below Tuscaloosa.............................. I, 366; III, 1824
    Operating and care of locks and dams above Tuscaloosa......... I, 366; III, 1819
Warroad Harbor and River, Minn.:
    Examination of.. I, 451; III, 2356
    Improvement of bar at mouth of river........................ I, 449; III, 2339
Warwick River, Md., improvement of.............................. I, 268; II, 1383
Washakie, Fort, Wyo., road to Buffalo Fork, Snake River........... I, 686; V, 3823
Washington, D. C.:
    Aqueduct Bridge, repair of................................. I, 669; V, 3637
    Aqueduct, Dalecarlia Reservoir............................. I, 671; V, 3651
    Aqueduct, filtration plant................................. I, 674; V, 3680
    Aqueduct, increasing water supply........................... I, 673; V, 3666
    Aqueduct, maintenance and repair........................... I, 671; V, 3651
    Aqueduct Tunnel and Howard University Reservoir............ I, 673; V, 3666
    Barracks, removal of engineer troops and school to........... I, 42
    Defenses of... I, 6, 23, 791
    Government Printing Office, building for use of.............. I, 685; V, 3801
    Highway bridge across Potomac River, plans, etc., for........ I, 119
    Improvement of Potomac River at............................. I, 273; II, 1399
    Improvement of Potomac River below......................... I, 276; II, 1405
    Long Bridge, across Potomac River, rebuilding of............. I, 275; II, 1399
    Mall, the, and Potomac and Zoological parks.................. I, 676; V, 3689
    Memorial Bridge... I, 670; V, 3648
    Public buildings and grounds, and Washington Monument....... I, 675; V, 3689
    Telegraph line connecting Executive Departments, etc......... I, 676; V, 3689
Washington, N. C.:
    Harbor lines in Pamlico River at............................. I, 119; II, 1570
    Improvement of Pamlico River............................... I, 301; II, 1487
Washington Barracks, D. C., removal of engineer troops and school to...... I, 42
Washington County, Ohio, bridge of............................... I, 660
Washington Lake, Wash., improvement of waterway to Puget Sound. I, 646; V, 3583
Washington Monument, D. C....................................... I, 675; V, 3689
Washita (Ouachita) River, Ark. and La.:
    Examination of Camden Harbor, Ark......................... I, 425; III, 2090
    Improvement of... I, 415; III, 2034
Wateree River, S. C., improvement of............................ I, 317; II, 1590
Water hyacinths:
    Removal of, from Florida waters............................ I, 341; II, 1746
    Removal of, from Louisiana waters.......................... I, 395; III, 1906
Water-level observations:
    Columbia River, Oreg. and Wash............................. I, 640; V, 3576
    Mississippi River and principal tributaries......... I, 425; III, 2072; S., 8, 45, 126
    Mississippi River, at St. Louis, Mo., illustration of full-depth rod-float method of discharge measurement............................... III, 2199
    Mississippi River, at St. Paul, Minn......................... I, 449; III, 2340
    Northern and Northwestern Lakes........................... I, 681; V, 3776
Waters, navigable. *See* Bridges, Rivers and harbors, *and* Wrecks.
Waterways (*see also* Canals):
    Beaufort, N. C., to Newbern................................. I, ; II, 1493
    Beaufort, N. C., to New River............................... I, ; II, 1496
    Charleston to Beaufort, S. C., sunken logs................... I, ; II, 1607
    Chincoteague Bay, Va., to Delaware Bay, Del.................. I, 303; II, 1348
    Delaware and Chesapeake Canal, Md., sunken logs............. I, 299; II, 1390
    Galveston to Houston, Tex.................................. I, 404; III, 1933
    Great Lakes to Atlantic Ocean.............................. I, 118
    Keweenaw Bay to Lake Superior, Mich....................... I, 511, 512; IV, 2867
    Kissimmee River, Fla., to Gulf of Mexico.................... I, 350
    Mississippi River to Lake Michigan (act of 1899).............. I, 534; IV, 3048
    Mississippi River to Lake Michigan (act of 1900).............. I, 534; IV, 3058
    Norfolk, Va., to Albemarle Sound, N. C., via Currituck Sound... I, 297; II, 1457
    Norfolk, Va., to sounds of North Carolina, via Pasquotank River. I, 296; II, 1455
    Portage Lake and Lake Superior canals (*see* Keweenaw Point). I, 511, 512; IV, 2867
    Puget Sound to lakes Union and Washington, Wash............. I, 646; V, 3583

ENG 1901——4

Waterways, etc.—Continued.
    San Joaquin River, Cal., to Karquines Strait................ 1, 613; IV, 3449, 3452
    Savannah, Ga., to Beaufort, S. C .... 1, 324; II, 1628
    Savannah, Ga., to Fernandina, Fla .... 1, 332; II, 1653
    Shreveport, La., to Jefferson, Tex. (see Cypress Bayou)......... 1, 414; III, 2033
    South Mills, N. C., to and including Ocracoke and Beaufort
        inlets.. I, 299, 309; II, 1511
    Superior Lake to Lake Huron, including Hay Lake Channel, St. Marys
        River... 1, 570; IV, 3200
Waukegan Harbor, Ill., improvement of............................... 1, 524; IV, 2951
Western Branch, Elizabeth River, Va., improvement of................ 1, 293; II, 1449
West Fork of South Branch, Chicago River, Ill.:
    Bridge across Mud Lake, Chicago 1, 663
    Improvement of .... 1, 529; IV, 2992
West Galveston Bay, Tex., improvement of .... 1, 406, 408; III, 1939, 1950
West Palmbeach, Fla., bridge across Lake Worth 1, 667
Westport Harbor, Conn., improvement of.............................. 1, 189; II, 1180
Weweanititt River, Mass., bridges across............................ 1, 667
Weymouth River, Mass., improvement of............................... 1, 155; II, 1084
Whatcom Creek Waterway, Wash., bridge at New Whatcom 1, 663
Whitehall Harbor, N. Y. (see Champlain Lake)........................ 1, 148; II, 1055
White House, Washington, D. C .... 1, 675; V, 3689
White Lake Harbor, Mich., improvement of............................ 1, 546; IV, 3107
White River, Ark.:
    Gauging (see Mississippi River) .... 1, 425; III, 2072; S., 8, 45, 126
    Improvement by open-channel work................................. 1, 427; III, 2105
    Improvement of Buffalo Fork .... 1, 429; III, 2119
    Improvement of upper river by locks and dams..................... 1, 428; III, 2106
White River, Ind., improvement of .... 1, 501; IV, 2804
Wicomico River, eastern shore of Maryland, improvement of........... 1, 270; II, 1386
Wilhelmina, Laura (sloop), removal of wreck of...................... 1, 272; II, 1390
Willamette River, Oreg.:
    Improvement above Portland .... 1, 631; V, 3550
    Improvement below Portland....................................... 1, 633; V, 3557
Willapa River and Harbor, Wash., improvement of .... 1, 641; V, 3577
Willets Point, N. Y.:
    Battalion of Engineers 1, 39, 43, 943, 975
    Engineer Depot 1, 40, 41, 42, 947
    Engineer School.. 1, 38, 42, 937
    Engineer troops 1, 39, 41, 42, 943
    Fort Totten, post of... 1, 38, 927
Williamstown, W. Va.:
    Bridge of Ohio River Bridge and Ferry Company across Ohio River
        between Marietta, Ohio, and................................... 1, 660
    Bridge of Williamstown and Marietta Bridge and Transportation Com-
        pany between Marietta, Ohio, and.............................. 1, 661
Williamstown and Marietta Bridge and Transportation Company, bridge of.. 1, 661
Wilmington, Cal.:
    Construction of deep-water harbor in San Pedro Bay .... 1, 600; IV, 3397
    Improvement of inner harbor...................................... 1, 601; IV, 3399
Wilmington, Del., improvement of harbor .... 1, 246; II, 1335
Wilmington, N. C.:
    Defenses of.. 1, 6, 24, 812, 921
    Examination and survey of Cape Fear River at and above.. 1, 310; II, 1552, 1557
    Improvement of Cape Fear River above............................. 1, 307; II, 1502
    Improvement of Cape Fear River at and below .... 1, 307; II, 1504
Wilson Harbor, N. Y., improvement of................................ 1, 592; IV, 3353
Winnebago Lake, Wis. (see Fox River)................................ 1, 525; IV, 2953
Winnibigoshish Lake, Minn.:
    Construction of reservoir dam .... 1, 444; III, 2309
    Operation and care of reservoir dam .... 1, 445; III, 2322
    Survey of flowage lines of reservoir............................. 1, 451
Winyah Bay, S. C., improvement of .... 1, 314; II, 1582
Wisconsin Central Railway Company, bridges of....................... 1, 667
Wisconsin Entrance, Duluth Harbor, Minn., improvement of........ 1, 507; IV, 2828
Wisconsin River, Wis.:
    Bridge across 1, 665
    Improvement of (see Fox River)................................... 1, 525; IV, 2953

INDEX. 51

Witch Rock, Portland Harbor, Me., examination and survey for removal of .... I, 133; II, 1009, 1015
Withlacoochee River, Fla., improvement of .... I, 348; III, 1761
Wolf River, Memphis, Tenn. (*see* Mississippi River Commission).... I, 657; S., 3, 32
Wolf River, Wis. (*see* Ahnapee Harbor).............................. I, 519; IV, 2923
Wolf River, Wis., tributary of the Fox (*see* Fox River)............. I, 525; IV, 2953
Woods Hole Channel, Mass., improvement of .... I, 162; II, 1117
Worth Lake, Fla., bridge across... I, 667
Wrecks, etc., removal of .... I, 117, 118
   Absecon Inlet, N. J., entrance..................................... I, 262; II, 1351
   Appoquinimink River, Del... I, 263; II, 1352
   Atlantic City, N. J., entrance to Absecon Inlet.................. I, 262; II, 1351
   Atlantic City, N. J., in Atlantic Ocean .... I, 263; II, 1353
   Atlantic Ocean, off Atlantic City, N. J .... I, 263; II, 1353
   Atlantic Ocean, off Seabright, N. J............................... I, 223; II, 1247
   Back Creek, Md.. I, 272; II, 1390
   Baltimore Harbor, Md., Fort McHenry Channel.................. I, 272; II, 1391
   Baltimore Harbor, Md., North Point Creek .... I, 272; II, 1390
   Beaufort to Charleston, S. C., inland passage.................... I, 324; II, 1607
   Belle Isle, Detroit River, Mich.................................... I, 570; IV, 3198
   Billingsport, N. J., below.. I, 263; II, 1352
   Bridgeboro, N. J., above.. I, 262; II, 1351
   Buttermilk Channel, New York Harbor, N. Y .... I, 229; II, 1299
   Cambridge Harbor, Md... I, 272; II, 1390, 1391
   Cedar Creek, N. J .... I, 263; II, 1352
   Charleston to Beaufort, S. C., inland passage.................... I, 324; II, 1607
   Chatham Harbor, Mass.. I, 174; II, 1147
   Chesapeake Bay, near Craighill Channel light, Md .... I, 272; II, 1391
   Chesapeake Bay, near Fort Monroe, Va.......................... I, 298; II, 1462
   Chesapeake Bay, near Old Plantation light-house, Va........... I, 298; II, 1462
   Chester Creek, Pa... I, 262; II, 1350
   Choptank River, Md., Cambridge Harbor.................. I, 272; II, 1390, 1391
   Cleveland Harbor, Ohio .... I, 584; IV, 3269, 3270
   Communipaw Channel, N. J .... I, 223; II, 1247
   Corner Stake light, off Staten Island, N. Y .... I, 223; II, 1247
   Craighill Channel light, Chesapeake Bay, Md .... I, 272; II, 1391
   Cumberland River... I, 463; III, 2417
   Cuyahoga River (Cleveland Harbor), Ohio .... I, 584; IV, 3270
   Deals Island, Md.. I, 272; II, 1390
   Delaware and Chesapeake Canal, Md., sunken logs .... I, 272; II, 1390
   Delaware Bay and River................................... I, 262, 263; II, 1350, 1351, 1352
   Delaware Breakwater Harbor, Del................................ I, 263; II, 1351
   Dennis Creek, N. J .... I, 262; II, 1350
   Detroit River, Mich... I, 570; IV, 3198
   Dover Island, Cumberland River .... I, 463; III, 2417
   Duck Creek (Smyrna River), Del.................................. I, 263; II, 1352
   Duluth Harbor, Minn... I, 514; IV, 2883
   East River, N. Y .... I, 223; II, 1248
   Ellis Island, New York Harbor, N. Y., near .... I, 223; II, 1248
   Erie Lake, off Cleveland, Ohio.................................... I, 584; IV, 3269
   Erie Lake, off Sandusky, Ohio .... I, 584; IV, 3269
   Flint River, Ga.. I, 363; III, 1793
   Fort McHenry Channel, Patapsco River, Md .... I, 272; II, 1391
   Fort Monroe, Va., off... I, 298; II, 1462
   Galveston Bay, Tex.. I, 411; III, 1959
   Gloucester, N. J., off .... I, 262; II, 1351
   Greenpoint, N. Y., off .... I, 223; II, 1248
   Greenwood, Miss., Yazoo River .... I, 420; III, 2048
   Hampton Roads, Va., off Fort Monroe........................... I, 298; II, 1462
   Hardings Beach, Chatham, Mass................................... I, 174; II, 1147
   Haverstraw, N. Y., off.. I, 223; II, 1248
   Hudson River, N. Y... I, 223; II, 1248
   Island Beach, N. J., opposite .... I, 223; II, 1247
   Jackson Creek, Md.. I, 272; II, 1391
   League Island Navy-Yard, Schuylkill River, Pa................ I, 263; II, 1352
   Long Island Sound, N. Y .... I, 223; II, 1246
   Louisville and Portland Canal, Ky .... I, 505; IV, 2816
   Manokin River, Md .... I, 272; II, 1390

52　　　　　　　　　　　　INDEX.

Wrecks, etc., removal of—Continued.
 Michigan Lake-Sturgeon Bay Canal, Wis........................ I, 527; IV, 2970
 Mississippi River, above Missouri River .... I, 440; III, 2231
 Mississippi River, below Missouri River .... I, 434; III, 2166
 Mobile River, Ala .... I, 378; III, 1853
 Monroe, Fort, Va., off .... I, 298; II, 1462
 Nauset Harbor, Mass .... I, 159; II, 1091
 Newark Bay, off Corner Stake light............................... I, 223; II, 1247
 New Jersey-Staten Island channel .... I, 223; II, 1247
 New York Harbor, N. Y., Buttermilk Channel..................... I, 229; II, 1299
 New York Harbor, N. Y., Communipaw Channel .... I, 223; II, 1247
 New York Harbor, N. Y., near Corner Stake light .... I, 223; II, 1247
 New York Harbor, N. Y., near Ellis Island .... I, 223; II, 1248
 New York Harbor, N. Y., off Greenpoint .... I, 223; II, 1248
 New York Harbor, N. Y., Sandy Hook .... I, 229; II, 1299
 North Point Creek, Patapsco River, Md........................... I, 272; II, 1390
 Odessa Landing, Appoquinimink River, Del....................... I, 263; II, 1352
 Ohio River .... I, 473; IV, 2646
 Ohio River, Louisville and Portland Canal, Ky.................... I, 505; IV, 2816
 Old Orchard Shoal light, Raritan Bay, N. J., near .... I, 223; II, 1247
 Old Plantation light-house, Chesapeake Bay, Va., near............ I, 298; II, 1462
 Patapsco River, Md., Fort McHenry Channel .... I, 272; II, 1391
 Patapsco River, Md., North Point Creek.......................... I, 272; II, 1390
 Philadelphia, Pa., Schuylkill River...................... I, 262, 263; II, 1350, 1352
 Pollock Rip light-ship, Mass., near................................ I, 174; II, 1147
 Port Chester Harbor, N. Y., off .... I, 223; II, 1246
 Porto Rico, San Juan Harbor .... I, 657; V, 3635
 Rancocas River, N. J .... I, 262; II, 1351
 Raritan Bay, N. J .... I, 223; II, 1247
 Riverton, N. J., below .... I, 262; II, 1351
 Robinsons Hole, Vineyard Sound, Mass .... I, 174; II, 1147
 St. Clair River, Mich... I, 570; IV, 3198
 Sandusky Harbor, Ohio... I, 584; IV, 3269
 Sandy Hook, N. J .... I, 229; II, 1299
 San Francisco Bay, Cal .... I, 613; IV, 3434
 San Jacinto River, Tex... I, 411; III, 1959
 San Juan Harbor, Porto Rico .... I, 657; V, 3635
 Savannah Harbor and River, Ga.................................. I, 334; II, 1660
 Schuylkill River, Pa .... I, 262, 263; II, 1350, 1352
 Seabright, N. J., off .... I, 223; II, 1247
 Ship John light, Delaware Bay .... I, 263; II, 1350
 Shovelful light-ship, Mass., near .... I, 174; II, 1147
 Shrewsbury River, N. J .... I, 223; II, 1247
 Smyrna River, Del.. I, 263; II, 1352
 Stage Harbor, Mass., on Hardings Beach.......................... I, 174; II, 1147
 Staten Island-New Jersey channel .... I, 223; II, 1247
 Sturgeon Bay and Lake Michigan Canal, Wis..................... I, 527; IV, 2970
 Superior Bay, Duluth Harbor, Minn .... I, 514; IV, 2883
 Tangier Sound, Md., Deals Island .... I, 272; II, 1390
 Vanland Landing, Yazoo River, Miss.............................. I, 420; III, 2048
 Vineyard Sound, Mass., near Robinsons Hole .... I, 174; II, 1147
 Wysocking Bay, N. C... I, 309; II, 1511
 Yazoo River, Miss .... I, 420; III, 2048
Wrightstown, Wis., bridge of town of, across Fox River .... I, 662
Wyandotte, Mich. (see Detroit River) .... I, 571; IV, 3208
Wysocking Bay, N. C., removal of wreck .... I, 309; II, 1511

Y.

Yalobusha River, Miss., bridge at mouth of Martins Creek................. I, 660
Yamhill River, Oreg.:
 Improvement of .... I, 631; V, 3550
 Operating and care of lock and dam............................... I, 632; V, 3555
Yankton, S. Dak., improvement of Missouri River at........ I, 452, 454; III, 2373, 2375
Yaquina Bay, Oreg.:
 Examination of.. I, 622; V, 3485
 Improvement of .... I, 620; V, 3482

Yazoo River, Miss.:
    Improvement above mouth... I, 420; III, 2048
    Improvement of mouth, including Vicksburg Harbor............ I, 421; III, 2052
    Removal of wrecks... I, 420; III, 2048
"Y" Bridge, across Muskingum River at Zanesville, Ohio.................. I, 659
Yellow Mill Pond, Bridgeport, Conn. (*see* Bridgeport) .... I, 186; II, 1177
Yellowstone National Park, improvement of.......................... I, 682; V, 3777
Yellowstone River, Mont., bridge at Glendive .... I, 659
York Harbor and River, Me., bridge (Sewells) obstructing navigation...... I, 667
York River, Va., improvement of .... I, 286; II, 1417
Yuba River, Cal. (*see* Sacramento River *and* California Débris Commission)... I, 608, 656; IV, 3420; V, 3625

Z.

Zanesville, Ohio:
    Bridge across Muskingum River at ("Y" Bridge)...................... I, 659
    Bridge across Muskingum River Canal at .... I, 667
Zeus (canal boat), removal of wreck of............................. I, 263; II, 1352
Zoological Park, Washington, D. C .... I, 676; V, 3689

O